Published by the American Automobile
Association, 1000 AAA Drive, Heathrow,
Florida, FL 32746-5063

This book has been prepared by AA
Publishing, Basingstoke, England exclusively for the American Automobile Association

Printed in the United States of America at
Quebecor Printing Kingsport, Kingsport,
Tennessee (on recyclable paper)

The following photographers and libraries
assisted in the preparation of this book:
James Davies Travel Photography 195,
529b; Nature Photographers Ltd 233 (E. A
James), 537b (C. K Mylne); Pictures Colour
Library 49, 71, 206, 207, 303b, 461a, 554;
Spectrum Colour Library 40, 48, 162, 163,
232, 529a; Zefa Pictures Ltd 41, 70, 194, 302,
460, 514, 515, 528, 536, 627

The remaining photographs are held in the
Automobile Association's own photo library
(AA PHOTO LIBRARY) and were taken by:
A. Baker 24, 303a; J. Blandford 378; M.
Birkitt 483a; J. Carnie 77b; J. Edmanson
482, 483b, 569b; P. Enticknap 452, 453a,
453b; D. Forss 498, 499; T. Harris 352;
S. Hill 379b; J. Holmes 403a; P. Kenward
241a, 630, 631a; A. Kouprianoff 56, 57,
62; K. Naylor 537a, 555; D. Noble 25; K.
Paterson 184, 185a, 185b, 216, 217b,
461b; D. Robertson 569a; C. Sawyer 174,
175, 240, 402, 403b; M. Short 379a; B. Smith
102; A. Souter 631b; R. Strange 77a, 241b;
W. Voysey 217a; P. Wilson 353, 568

Front cover photographs:
Paris, France – Steve Vidler/Leo de Wys;
Nusfjord Harbor, Lofoten Islands, Norway –
Fridmar Damm/Leo de Wys; *Copenhagen,
Denmark* – Tony Craddock/ Tony Stone
Images; *Château de Chenonceau, Amboise,
France* – Tony Craddock/Tony Stone Images

CONTENTS

AAA EUROPE TravelBook™

COUNTRIES AND PRINCIPALITIES

USING THE TRAVELBOOK

The purpose of the AAA Europe TravelBook
is to make your trip as smooth and enjoyable as possible.
Whether you are an explorer, a sports enthusiast, history buff or just plain
curious, you'll find many appealing things to see and do. The wealth of
facts, statistics and descriptions in this publication provide detailed
knowledge about places of interest throughout 45 countries of Europe.
The information in this guide is based on data supplied by the Automobile
Association of Britain. All copy is accurate at press time; however, since
material is necessarily prepared in advance of the publication date, there is
always the possibility that changes will occur after the guide is printed. If
you become aware of material that is inaccurate, please write to us at AAA
Member Comments, Box 61, 1000 AAA Dr., Heathrow, FL 32746-5063.
Each country is separated into two sections: first an introductory section
followed by an A-Z listing of the major sights for the country.

INTRODUCTION

Each country chapter begins with a two-page pictorial introduction that provides a broad image of the nation.

This is followed by the *Things to Know* box, which gives helpful information and addresses at a glance. Next is a more detailed introduction, which includes such specific topics as history, food, sports, travel, lodging and tipping.

For the larger destinations there is also a *Principal Touring Areas* section, which describes the various geographical regions of the country.

MAPS

There is a country map for each main country which pinpoints listed towns, and there are also city plans for the major cities and capital cities.

A-Z LISTING SECTION

This section begins with the capital city of each country and then lists cities
or sights alphabetically from A-Z according to the proper local spelling.
Should that spelling differ from a better known English variation, the English
version is listed as a cross reference.

	map reference page number for country and city maps	
symbol to denote AAA-affiliated automobile club branch		grid reference for country and city maps
	place name	
		star rating denoting must-see sight

▲ MAASTRICHT (463 B1) ★
LIMBURG *pop. 118,000*
Wedged between Belgium and Germany....

geographical sub-division

population figure

INTRODUCTION TO EUROPE

Istanbul or Vienna? Paris, London or Helsinki? Rome or Reykjavik? Draw any line through a map of Europe and you will see the extremes that it covers: from the eternal night of an Icelandic winter, to the endless summers of sultry Greece; from Portugal, starting point for explorers to the New World, to the emerging countries of Eastern Europe; from the former Communist Albania to the carefree lifestyle of the Republic of Ireland. At the very boundary of Europe, Turkey shares borders with Bulgaria as well as the Middle Eastern countries of Syria, Iran and Iraq.

In an area less than half the size of North America, Europe encompasses an infinite variety of cultures that are constantly changing. On January 1, 1993, Czechoslovakia became two new countries, the Czech Republic and the Slovak Republic. The former Yugoslavia broke into its component parts, whose final boundaries have yet to be determined. The ex-Soviet Republics of Estonia, Latvia and Lithuania regained their independence and turned towards the prosperity of western Europe. Russia is changing, too, but at a slower pace.

CULTURAL DIFFERENCES

The sense of cultural identity in Europe is strong, to the extent that, within some nations, different groups seek separation. The Basques of northern Spain and the Corsicans of France are just two examples of peoples with strong separatist movements. Corsican culture – reflected in both its language and cuisine – is part-French, part-Italian. The island of Corsica belongs to France, yet lies closer to Italy. Its southern tip almost touches the Italian island of Sardinia, which itself is geographically closer to North Africa than to Italy.

Sicily too is Italian, the largest island in the Mediterranean, marking Europe's southern boundary. Further east, in the island of Crete, visitors will quickly see the sense of quiet pride that distinguishes a Cretan from a Greek.

In the cooler climate of Alpine Switzerland, divisions work well. Three official languages – French, German and Italian – happily co-exist, and by 1999 the Swiss will be celebrating 500 years as an independent nation.

It seems appropriate that the political heart of Europe should be in Brussels, Belgium, another country of cultural differences. A third are French-speaking Walloons, while just over half are Flemings, speaking Flemish (a dialect of Dutch). The headquarters of the European Union are situated here.

THE EUROPEAN UNION

The seeds of today's European Union, which links the economic and, to some extent, legal systems of the member states, were sown in France in 1950 when it was suggested that the steel and coal resources of the Western European nations should be pooled. On March 25, 1957, the Treaty of Rome brought together France, (West) Germany, Italy, Belgium, The Netherlands and Luxembourg as the European Economic Community (E.E.C.), otherwise known as the Common Market. The intent of the E.E.C. was to remove trading and duty barriers, thereby improving the economic strength of the member nations in order to compete with the United States and Britain. In 1961 Britain applied to join the E.E.C., only to have its request vetoed in 1963 by President de Gaulle of France.

In 1972 the E.E.C. voted to accept Britain, Ireland, Denmark and Norway, though the citizens of Norway subsequently voted in a referendum to remain outside the E.E.C. Membership was increased to 10 nations in 1981 when Greece was admitted, to 12 members in 1986 with the admittance of Spain and Portugal, and to 15 in 1995 with Finland, Austria and Sweden. Other former Iron

EUROPE TRAVEL BOOK

REYKJAVIK
Akureyri
ICELAND

Tromsø
Kiruna
Mo I Rana

Norwegian Sea

SWEDEN

Trondheim
Umeå
Östersund   Sundsvall

NORWAY

Bergen
OSLO

STOCKHOLM

ATLANTIC OCEAN

Inverness

Kristiansand
Ålborg   Göteborg
Karlskrona
Baltic Sea

NORTHERN IRELAND
Glasgow   Aberdeen
Londonderry
Edinburgh
Galway   Belfast
Killarney   Newcastle upon Tyne

North Sea

Esbjerg   DENMARK
Odense   KØBENHAVN
Malmö   KALININGRAD
Gdansk

DUBLIN
REPUBLIC OF IRELAND   Liverpool   Manchester
Cork   Birmingham   GREAT
Bristol   BRITAIN
LONDON
NETHERLANDS
AMSTERDAM
Hamburg

Plymouth   Southampton   Dover
English Channel   Le   Calais   BRUSSEL
Havre   BELGIUM
BERLIN
Poznań
Köln   GERMANY
Wrocław   POL

Brest
Nantes
PARIS
LUXEMBOURG
Frankfurt-am-Main   PRAHA
CZECH REPUBLIC   Kraków

Bay of Biscay

La Coruña
Santander
FRANCE
Stuttgart
München
WIEN
BRATISLAVA
SLOVAK
Bordeaux
BERN
SWITZERLAND
Innsbruck   AUSTRIA   BUDAPEST
Clermont-Ferrand   Lyon
HUNGARY

Porto
Biarritz
Toulouse
Milano
Trieste   SLOVENIA   ZAGREB
PORTUGAL
ANDORRA
Génova
Venézia   CROATIA
Zaragoza   Marseille   Nice
Bologna
BOSNIA & HERCEGOVINA
LISBOA   MADRID
Barcelona
Split   SARAJEVO
SPAIN
Corse
ITALY
Pescara
Adriatic Sea
Ajaccio
Pescara   Fóggia
Sevilla   Valencia
Olbia   ROMA
TIRANE
Cádiz   Murcia
Islas Baleares   Sardegna
Nápoli   Brindisi
Málaga
Algeciras   Cagliari   *Tyrrhenian Sea*
Messina   ALBANIA
Palermo   Réggio de Calábria

MOROCCO   ALGERIA
TUNISIA   *Sicilia*
MALTA

Mediterranean

Curtain countries such as the Slovak and Czech Republics have shown a desire to join in the future.

Among the sweeping changes introduced by the E.U. was the lifting of restrictions at the end of 1992 on the movement of goods, services, capital, and workers and tourists between member states. Some countries have been quicker to implement changes than others, although it does mean that tourists – even non-E.U. citizens – will be able to cross between E.U. countries without showing their passport, while at airports, separate channels will exist for E.U. and non-E.U. citizens.

Proposed changes go much deeper than this. The Maastricht Treaty of 1991 suggested that there should be a single common European currency for at least some of its members by 1999. Britain and Denmark both later opted out of this scheme, indicating that true European union is as yet some way off. However, they agreed that there should be common E.U. foreign and defence policies. It also created the European Union (E.U.) out of the European Community (E.C.).

In addition to the E.U., the European Free Trade Association (E.F.T.A.) came into being on May 3, 1960, pursuing the idea of free trade between its member states: Austria, Switzerland, Norway, Sweden, Finland, Iceland and Liechtenstein. With some E.F.T.A. members such as Austria, Finland and Sweden later electing to join the E.U., this confirmed its status as the single most important European body.

THE WORKINGS OF THE EUROPEAN UNION

The workings of a body whose purpose is to impose some kind of unity on everyone, from Scandinavian fishermen to Greek olive growers, is obviously going to be complicated.

To most people, the concept of Europe now means the idea of the European Union. The organization centers on four main institutions.

The **Council of Ministers** contains government representatives from all member states, though its composition changes according to the subjects under discussion. This is the most powerful organization, where political and legislative decisions are made.

The **European Commission** is responsible for initiating proposals which are put to the Council of Ministers, and for implementing those proposals that are put into force. It has 17 members, one from each country, and in addition one extra member from France, Germany, Italy, Britain and Spain.

The **European Parliament** is based in Strasbourg and consists of elected representatives. There are 567 M.E.P.s (Members of the European Parliament), divided roughly on a proportional basis, so that Britain, Italy, France and Germany have 81, while Luxembourg has six. The European Parliament's main role is to provide some kind of democratic control over the other bodies, though this has not yet been fully realized. It has certain powers over the European Commission, and must be consulted over some legislative matters by the Council of Ministers.

Finally, the **Court of Justice**, based in Luxembourg, is responsible for seeing that the law is applied throughout the E.U., not just as regards the E.U.'s own treaties, but also as a final Court of Appeal on matters referred to it by national courts within member states. It also gives opinions on international agreements entered into by the E.U. The Court comprises 13 judges, with one judge from each state chosen by the Council of Ministers, and an extra judge taken from one of the larger members.

HARMONY AND DISCORD

In theory the ideas of harmony, equality and democracy throughout the Union are ideal, but in practice many of the agreements fail to be implemented. Although the intention is to have free movement of E.U. citizens between member states, traveling from, say,

France to Britain will entail a passport check as if the new regulations had not been implemented. The Court of Justice gave rulings in 1979 and 1980 that any item legally sold in one member state cannot be prohibited in another, except on grounds of public health risks. However, pornography, for example, is legally sold in Denmark or Germany, while it is illegal in Britain.

KALEIDOSCOPE OF CULTURES

It is, of course, these very differences that make Europe what it is. Many of its citizens fear this diversity will be lost if, for example, monetary union is imposed and, instead of the *franc, Mark, lira, krone, drachma, guilder, escudo, pound* or *peseta*, the E.C.U. (European Currency Unit) becomes the common currency. A great deal would be lost, certainly, but nothing could ever homogenize the strikingly divergent cultures that exist within Europe's 9.8 million square kilometers (3.8 million square miles), home to 502 million very different people.

The people of the Mediterranean countries are generally extrovert, dramatic and passionate. Political arguments rage in squares and cafés, where the men gather – these are also still predominantly patriarchal societies. Lives are lived outdoors in the hot summer months, except during early afternoon hours when stores close.

Similar in many ways – a Portuguese fisherman would have much in common with a Greek fisherman – the inhabitants of this vast land mass are still very different in their national characteristics. All are easy-going and friendly, yet the Portuguese have a distant, aloof air. They ask what else they could be, a small country sharing a peninsula with a much larger neighbor, Spain. They turn their back on Spain, and look away from Europe. It is not by chance that Portugal is a nation of navigators and explorers, of whom da Gama is only the best known.

As a nation the Spanish are as hospitable as any on the Mediterranean shores, yet they are much more relaxed than the excitable Italians, or the Greeks, who gave the world drama as well as democracy. An attempt to board a bus or ferry in Greece will confirm that the sense of drama has survived far more than any sense of democracy.

Italians see themselves as infinitely more sophisticated than their southern counterparts, with a sharper dress sense, and living much nearer to the heart of European fashion and culture. They would more likely look north to Paris than to Athens or Madrid, though temperamentally they are more at home in the south. The difference between the Italians and the French will be discovered should you try to speak a little of their respective languages. Italians invariably want to converse, and prefer communication to correct pronunciation. The French are more likely to correct the speaker, or to reply in flawless English. Renowned for a certain cultural snobbishness, only the French would have an Academy to keep their language pure, to guard against foreign imports such as *le weekend*.

The British, on the other hand, will be harder to befriend than the Italians or Spanish. Their characteristic coolness is a result of both climate and geography, as it was not until 1994 that the 31-mile Channel Tunnel united Britain with Europe. Whether this will help break down British reserve, and reservations towards Europe, remains to be seen.

Just a few miles across the Irish Sea in the Republic of Ireland, no one could be more open-hearted than the Irish. If temperature affects temperament, then the Irish confound the theory. The heavy rainfall that produces the Green Isle seems also to produce a sunny disposition in its people.

A more typical, and maybe even stereotypical, example of the theory are the people in the sometimes sun-starved Scandinavian countries of north-east Europe – Sweden, Denmark, Finland, Norway and Iceland – who do have a reputation for, if not coldness, at least a certain aloofness.

Between the Arctic Circle and the Mediterranean lie some of the most interesting countries in Europe, those that emerged in the late 1980s and early 1990s from behind the Iron Curtain, and are now starting to reveal their secrets to the rest of the world. Prague now rivals Paris for popularity, with more people wanting to visit than there are hotel beds available. The uncertainty about tourist facilities is just one of the adventures of traveling in this region, but this is more than compensated for the rewards available: the Black Sea resorts of Bulgaria, the Transylvanian Mountains of Romania, the architectural beauties of Budapest, and the châteaux of the Czech Republic are but a few of the jewels in what were, a mere ten years ago, seen as bleak and gray lands.

The visitor to this part of Europe must expect the unexpected; not merely in the culture and the countryside, but in the people. Most welcome visitors with a warmth suppressed for years, but among the older people are those who cannot shake off the decades when there was no free speech, and for them a mask remains. In this part of Europe travel becomes a much deeper experience, as in the Russian Federation, Moldavia, Ukraine and Belarus, where certainty has become uncertainty, and the countries have yet fully to define themselves.

Europe's kaleidoscope also contains some barely visible specks of color: tiny countries dwarfed by their big brothers. Surrounded by Rome is the independent state of the Vatican City, home to less than a thousand. San Marino is the world's smallest republic, founded in the 4th century AD in the Italian Apennine Mountains. Between Switzerland and Austria is Liechtenstein, founded 1719, and on the French Riviera is the principality of Monaco, ruled by the same Grimaldi family since the 13th century. Andorra is tucked into the Pyrénées between France and Spain, an autonomous republic since 1278. Small, it seems, is not only beautiful, but stable in the changing face of Europe.

FROM MOUNTAINS TO MEDITERRANEAN

As well as this diversity of cultures, Europe offers a contrast of climates and geography. Rivers run through its lands, inspiring music, poetry and legend: the Thames, the Danube, the Rhine, the Loire. It is home to famous peaks like Mount Olympus, the legendary home of the Greek Gods, the Biblical Mount Ararat, and the peaks of the Alps: Mont Blanc, the Matterhorn and the Jungfrau.

Many beautiful mountains are in Scandinavia, a dramatic region with fjords and lakes. In Norway the Sognafjord runs for over 161 kilometers (100 miles), to a depth of 1,219 meters (4,000 feet). Head south to eastern and central Europe and you get forests, wolves, wooden huts and the last European bison in the Bialowieza Forest between Poland and Russia. To the west is Germany, land of the Rhine, and of the Black Forest, its pines and mountain peaks. Beyond Germany lie the low countries, the flat Dutch and Belgian landscapes, with much of the land reclaimed from the sea, and the promise of wonderful flowers and good beers.

Across the water stand the Republic of Ireland and Britain's historical landscapes: Welsh castles and hills, Scottish lochs and remote mountain ranges, green Irish pastures and plunging cliffs, rolling English countryside and quiet villages. The Channel Tunnel connects Britain with the rest of Europe, speeding visitors to northern France and its fertile farmland, and beyond to its Mediterranean beaches and the mountainous borders of the Pyrénées and the Alps. Over the Pyrénées is the hot, high Iberian peninsula, the land of the Spanish mañana, and golden beaches that sweep around the Mediterranean's shores through the French and Italian rivieras, past Roman remains and the canals of Venice, to the Balkans, home of those Greek Gods, and on to Turkey, where Europe ends at Istanbul, on the Golden Horn, and Asia beckons across the Galata Bridge.

PRACTICAL INFORMATION

There is almost an infinity of ways in which to explore Europe, and the greatest difficulty will lie in the choice: of country or countries, travel methods, where to stay, and whether to go independently or on a program organized by a tour operator. Some escorted tours have very tightly packed schedules that cover a different city or even country each day. Traveling independently will allow you more time to soak up local atmosphere, but will necessitate meticulous forward planning and perhaps an intrepid spirit. Whichever method you favor, it's well worth visiting a AAA travel agent well in advance, to inquire about the various options.

BEFORE YOU GO

CLIMATE AND WHEN TO GO

The warm summer months are perennial favorites with vacationers; they go hand-in-hand with enjoyable European festivities. However, off-season rates, hotel availability and fewer tourists make winter a worthwhile alternative.

Weather

Generally, the weather of Eastern and Central Europe resembles that of the New England states: freezing temperatures in winter, rising to the mid-70s in summer. Naturally, there are exceptions: northern Poland, Russia and the Baltic States (Estonia, Latvia and Lithuania) have colder winters and cooler, but still pleasant, summers. Areas bordering the Mediterranean and the Black Sea tend to be warmer throughout the year.

Most southern European countries have warmer weather than the latitude would indicate. Summers are hot and dry; winters mild and rainy. Snow-covered mountains are never far away.

Despite its reputation, the weather in Britain is more pleasant than in other countries of similar latitude. Trends are hard to predict (there can be snow in June!), as a rule fog and rain are evident in early winter; summer is the driest season, and England's sunny "Indian summer" can extend into early November. Temperatures do not often rise above 26°C (80°F) or fall below –6°C (20°F).

TRAVEL ADVISORIES

The U.S. Department of State issues Consular Information Sheets and Travel Warnings concerning serious health or security conditions that might affect U.S. citizens. They can be obtained at U.S. embassies and consulates abroad, regional passport agencies in the United States and from the Citizens Emergency Center, 2201 C Street N.W., Room 4811, Department of State, Washington, DC 20520; tel: (202) 647-5225.

Consular Information Sheets provide information about entry requirements, currency regulations, health conditions, security, political disturbances, areas of instability and drug penalties. A "Travel Warning" is issued when the situation in a country is dangerous enough for the Department of State to recommend that Americans not travel there.

U.S. CUSTOMS INFORMATION

The helpful booklet *Know Before You Go* lists and explains all U.S. Customs regulations for travelers going abroad and returning. It is available from the U.S. Customs Service, P.O. Box 7404, Washington, DC 20044.

As might be expected, temperatures drop as the elevation of an area increases; see the temperature charts for each country for more information.

Public Holidays

From the religious pageants of Easter and Christmas to the folkloric festivals celebrating sunshine and harvest, public holidays reveal a country's character. Try to see as many special events as time permits. Public holidays are listed in each *Things To Know* box at the beginning of each country, and major festivals are described in the appropriate city listings. Banks and stores are often closed on public holidays, so don't count on these as your shopping days.

TEMPERATURE

To convert Fahrenheit to Celsius, subtract 32 from the Fahrenheit temperature, multipy by 5 and divide by 9; to convert Celsius to Fahrenheit, multiply by 9, divide by 5 and add 32.

CELSIUS	FAHRENHEIT
100	BOILING	212

37	100
35	95
32	90
29	85
27	80
24	75
21	70
18	65
16	60
13	55
10	50
7	45
4	40
2	35
0	FREEZING	32

-18	0
-21	-5
-24	-10
-27	-15

CUSTOMS IN EUROPE

Customs regulations are relatively few when it comes to what you may take into a country. See the *Things To Know* box in each country introduction for more detailed information.

ELECTRICITY

The electricity supply in most European countries is incompatible with U.S. electrical appliances, which will be damaged. Some U.S. stores sell electrical items for use overseas, but check the voltage requirements before you buy. Ask for a transformer, which converts high-voltage current into lower voltage for use with U.S. appliances.

HEALTH MATTERS

Health facilities in Europe generally range from good to excellent, and physicians, surgeons and specialists are available in all major cities and large towns. Make sure that you have quick access to cash and that your insurance policy is valid outside the United States.

The Centers for Disease Control and Prevention in Atlanta have a hot line offering international health requirements – including inoculation requirements and recommendations – and general advice for travelers. A touch-tone phone is needed for the service, which is available daily 24 hours; tel: (404) 332-4559. In addition, a booklet called *Health Information for International Travelers* can be obtained by sending $5 to the Superintendent of Documents, U.S. Government Printing Office, Washington, DC 20402.

INSURANCE

Automobile

An International Motor Insurance Certificate (green card) is advised for motorists taking their own vehicle overseas; a AAA travel agent can arrange this. In certain eastern European countries (Bulgaria, Estonia, Poland), as well as Andorra, it is compulsory to have one. The green card is not accepted in Belorussia,

When You Really Need to Speak Their Language...

Let the IDP Speak for You

When traveling overseas, carry an International Driving Permit...even if you're not planning to drive. Should you need to communicate with foreign authorities, this recognizable form of identification can help you get on your way more quickly. Valid in 168 countries, the permit contains your name, photo, and driver information translated into ten languages.

Before you travel the world, travel to any AAA office for your International Driving Permit. Bring your valid U.S. driver's license, $10, and two passport-size photos (also available at AAA offices).

Travel With Someone You Trust℠

the Baltic States, Moldavia, the Russian Federation and the Ukraine.

In most of Europe, public liability and property damage insurance is required for all vehicles. The cost of this insurance is included in the charge for vehicles that are rented or leased in Europe. U.S. residents wishing to purchase a vehicle while abroad can obtain through AAA clubs a short-term European automobile tourist insurance policy that is valid throughout Europe.

Coverage available to those using their own vehicles includes liability, medical payments and comprehensive and collision loss. Each policy includes a green card, proving that the policy conforms with all local insurance laws. For additional information contact your AAA club or phone AAA Foreign Motoring Insurance at (800) 222-4599.

Personal Accident and Sickness

Personal accident insurance is sold by many AAA travel agencies. While policy provisions may vary, typically they provide accidental death and dismemberment benefits when you travel by scheduled airline or another common carrier, including cruises, trains and motorcoaches when tickets are purchased through your AAA travel agency. Coverage of up to $500,000 is available.

TripAssist policies, available from AAA, are designed to provide help for travel-related problems almost anywhere in the world. They offer a broad range of services, including a 24-hour toll-free hot line staffed by multilingual coordinators, medical insurance, document and ticket replacement, legal help, emergency cash transfer, trip cancellation and interruption insurance, baggage insurance and travel accident insurance.

Baggage and Belongings

Baggage and personal effects insurance is available no matter how you travel. Many AAA travel agencies can issue a policy to afford coverage for up to 180 days. Included in most plans is coverage for clothing, jewelry and sports gear.

PASSPORTS AND VISAS

Passports

The primary document for U.S. citizens who travel abroad is the U.S. passport. Some countries require as much as six months' validity. Your spouse and young children cannot be included on your passport; each individual must have one. The U.S. Department of State has an inquiries line that provides information regarding passports; tel: (202) 647-0518.

Lost passports should be reported to Passport Services, U.S. Department of State, 1425 K Street N.W., Washington, DC 20504, or to the nearest passport agency, or, to the consular officer in any American embassy or consulate (see *Things To Know* box for each country).

Visas

A visa is a stamp affixed in your passport by an official of the country you plan to visit, indicating that your travel to that country has been approved.

Visa requirements are specified in each *Things To Know* box. A AAA travel agency can give you detailed information for each country you plan to visit.

WHAT TO TAKE

Clothing

The golden rule is to travel light. The widely differing temperatures (and rainfall) you are likely to encounter on a European vacation point to the need for layers and a light raincoat.

Dress codes in Mediterranean countries and eastern Europe are more formal than in other parts of Europe, or the U.S. In more expensive restaurants, people tend to dress well rather than casually. The code on beaches varies, even within the same locality, depending on the concentration of tourists in a particular place. On some beaches the custom will be to go topless, on others one-piece swimwear will be considered appropriate. When visiting churches or monasteries, modest attire is expected, and shoulders should be covered.

CLOTHING CONVERSION CHART

Men's suits

Britain	36	38	40	42	44	46	48
Europe	46	48	50	52	54	56	58
U.S.	36	38	40	42	44	46	48

Dress sizes

Britain	8	10	12	14	16	18
France	36	38	40	42	44	46
Italy	38	40	42	44	46	48
Europe	34	36	38	40	42	44
U.S.	6	8	10	12	14	16

Men's shirts

Britain	14	14½	15	15½	16	16½	17
Europe	36	37	38	39/40	41	42	43
U.S.	same as Britain						

Men's shoes

Britain	7	7½	8½	9½	10½	11
Europe	41	42	43	44	45	46
U.S.	8	8½	9½	10½	11½	12

Women's shoes

Britain	4½	5	5½	6	6½	7
Europe	38	38	39	39	40	41
U.S.	6	6½	7	7½	8	8½

DUTY-FREE SHOPS

High-quality merchandise from all over the world is featured in most duty-free shops.

Prices are generally about the same as you would expect to pay in the country of origin.

Don't be misled, however, by the word "duty-free." It simply means that the local merchant has been exempted from import taxes. All duty-free goods that return with you to the U.S. are still subject to U.S. import duties if you exceed your $400 limit.

Luggage

International airlines limit baggage by weight or by size. The requirements can vary from carrier to carrier. There is usually a charge for baggage that exceeds the maximum weight or size.

GETTING THERE

BY AIR

Air travel falls into three basic classes – first, business and economy – and rates vary according to season, one-way or round-trip passage, duration of trip and stopovers. Consult a AAA travel agent for reservations, special-value fares and the most direct air routes.

BY SEA

The *Queen Elizabeth II* cruise ship crosses the Atlantic regularly. Costs vary according to the class, type of accommodations, season and itinerary. Numerous air-sea combinations can be arranged. For additional information contact a AAA travel agency.

GETTING AROUND

CAMPING

Camping in Europe has become increasingly popular with North Americans. Thousands of camping areas maintain both primitive and modern sites; some have bungalows or ready-erected tents for rent. Fully equipped RVs are also available for delivery and collection.

International camping *carnets*, or permits, are available by writing the Family Campers and RVers, 4804 Transit Road, Building 2, Depew, N.Y. 14043; tel: (716) 668-6242.

CAR RENTAL

Most car rental companies in Europe will not rent to anyone under 21, even though such persons may have a valid U.S. license and an International Driving Permit (I.D.P.).

European cars are generally small, with manual transmission. Air-conditioning is only rarely available. Costs vary according to make, model, place and period of rental; a AAA travel agent can give you an estimate.

Be sure to inquire about local taxes; in France, for example, taxes increase rental rates by one-third. Make certain that you know exactly what insurance is included, and check whether you need a collision damage waiver (C.D.W.) – you might already be covered through your personal insurance policy or credit card company. Sometimes C.D.W. may not cover certain types of damage – e.g., in Greece damage to the underside of a car on a rough road may not be covered.

In some cases, a AAA travel agent can reserve a car for you before you leave, or can arrange for cars to be waiting for you on specified dates in major cities. Be sure to make your arrangements well in advance. If you plan to travel through several countries, ensure that the rental company has been informed and that you have the necessary documents. British rental agencies may require several days' notice to supply a car equipped for travel on the Continent.

DRIVING

While driving in most western European countries presents no particular hazards other than the peculiarities of language, signs, customs and local temperament, driving in some east European countries may present hazards of a different order. Seek the latest travel advice for these areas (see Travel Advisories on p.11).

Driving Documents

Although a valid U.S. driver's license is honored in most European countries, several (including Austria and Spain) require you to carry a translation of it in the local language. You should obtain an International Driving Permit (I.D.P.), which serves as an official, internationally recognized translation of your license. The I.D.P. is written in nine languages: Arabic, Chinese, English, French, German, Swedish, Italian, Spanish and Russian. A AAA office can issue an I.D.P., valid for a year. You must be at least 18, fill out an application form, present a valid U.S. driver's license, submit two passport-size photographs and pay a fee.

Currently I.D.P.s are needed in about 60 countries around the world, including eastern Europe. You must carry both your U.S. driver's license and your I.D.P.

If traveling to Spain, it is highly advisable to obtain a bail bond, which is available from your car insurers or as a component of a motoring travel insurance policy. An accident in Spain may result in the impounding of your car and property and the detention of the driver pending trial. A bail bond often facilitates their release.

Vehicle Equipment

The display of a warning triangle at the time of breakdown or accident is compulsory in the following countries: Austria, Baltic States, Belgium, Belorussia, Bulgaria, Czech Republic, Slovak Republic, Denmark, Germany, Greece, Hungary, Republic of Ireland (for vehicles exceeding 1,524kg/3,360lb), Italy, Luxembourg, Moldavia, Poland, Portugal, Russian Federation, Switzerland and the Ukraine. Indeed, it is recommended in all European countries.

The carrying of a first-aid kit is compulsory in Austria, Baltic States, Belorussia, Bulgaria, Czech Republic, Slovak Republic, Russian Federation, Greece, Moldavia, and the Ukraine. The same countries (except Austria, Czech Republic, Slovak Republic) also require the carrying of a fire extinguisher.

A spare set of light-bulbs is recommended throughout Europe, but they are compulsory in the Czech Republic, the Slovak Republic and Spain.

Accidents and Breakdowns

The procedure to be followed after an accident varies in each country, and you should consult the documentation that accompanies any insurance policy. In most countries, the police will need to be informed if an accident results in injury or substantial damage, and a report will have to be filed. The vehicle should not be moved before this is completed. In some countries in eastern Europe, even minor damage to a vehicle will necessitate a police report; and it may also be necessary to report to the State Insurance Authority (this is the case in Finland). Drivers should always exchange particulars with the other party; if one of the parties is uninsured, the police should be notified, however slight the damage.

In eastern Europe, any visible existing damage to a vehicle entering the country must be certified by the authorities at the time of entry. Damaged vehicles may only be taken out of these countries on production of such evidence.

We list below the European motoring organizations with which AAA is affiliated through the A.I.T., the international association of motoring clubs. If no breakdown service is offered by the motoring organization, we give phone numbers that can be used for assistance.

If you are in a rented car, the rental company will have made arrangements with a breakdown service; details of emergency telephone numbers will be given when you receive the car.

Emergency telephone numbers for Fire, Police and Ambulance services are listed in the *Things to Know* boxes.

Austria
Österreichischer Automobil-, Motorrad- und Touring Club (ÖA.M.T.C.), Universitätsstrasse 8, A1090 Vienna; tel: (0222) 402 7067. ÖA.M.T.C. has a 24-hour roadside assistance service (Pannenhilfe) and a tow service (Abschleppdienst); tel: 120.

Baltic States
(Estonia, Latvia, Lithuania)
No affiliated motoring organization. In case of breakdown, call the police for assistance; tel: 02.

Belgium
Touring Club Royal de Belgique (T.C.B.), 44 rue de la Loi, 1040 Brussels; tel: (02) 2332211. T.C.B. has a 24-hour breakdown service: Touring Secours/ Touring Wegenhulp. Tel: (070) 344777.

Britain
The Automobile Association (A.A.), Norfolk House, Priestley Road, Basingstoke, Hampshire RG24 9NY; tel: (01256) 20123. Royal Automobile Club

(R.A.C.), P.O. Box 700, Spectrum, Bond Street, Bristol BS99 1RB; tel: (0117) 9232444. Both clubs operate a 24-hour breakdown service for members.

Bulgaria
Union of Bulgarian Motorists (U.A.B.), 3 Place Positano, Sofia 1090; tel: (02) 86151. UAB patrols main roads daily in summer, until 19:00. In emergencies, tel: 1286, or 883978.

LIQUID MEASURE

CUSTOMARY
1 fluid ounce = 29.57 milliliters
1 pint = 0.47 liters
1 quart = 0.95 liters
1 gallon = 3.79 liters

METRIC
10 milliliters = 0.34 fluid ounces
1 liter = 2,11 pints
1 liter = 1.06 quarts
1 liter = 0.26 gallons
1 liter = 2.11 pints

U.S. LIQUID MEASURE
1 U.S. gallon = 3.79 liters
1 U.S. quart = .95 liter
6 U.S. gallons = 5 imperial gallons
The imperial measure is 20% larger than the U.S. measure

CONVERSION TABLE

GALLONS/LITERS		LITERS/GALLONS	
1	3.79	1	0.26
2	7.57	2	0.53
3	11.36	3	0.79
4	15.14	4	1.06
5	18.93	5	1.32
6	22.71	6	1.59
7	26.50	7	1.85
8	30.28	8	2.11
9	34.07	9	2.38
10	37.85	10	2.64
15	56.78	15	3.96
20	75.71	20	5.28
25	94.64	25	6.60
30	113.56	30	7.93

Czech Republic and Slovak Republic

Ustredni Automotoklub C.S.F.R. (U.A.M.K.), Na Strzi 9, 140 00 Prague 4. For breakdown, tel: (02) 123, or 0123.

Denmark

Forenede Danske Motorejere (F.D.M.), Firskovvej 32, P.O. Box 500, 2800 Lyngby, Copenhagen; tel: 45 93 08 00. In case of breakdown, contact the Falcks Redningskorps A.S. organization (see local directories for numbers) or Dansk Autohjaelp (tel: 31 31 21 44), which both maintain a 24-hour breakdown service.

Finland

Autoliitto Automobile and Touring-Club of Finland (A.T.C.F.), Hameentie 105, P.O. Box 35, 00551 Helsinki; tel: (90) 774 761. The A.T.C.F. has a 24-hour patrol service; tel: (90) 774 76400 (Monday to Friday), or 970 08080 (weekends).

France

Automobile Club National (A.C.N.), 5 rue Auber, 75009 Paris; tel: 44 51 53 99. French motoring clubs do not provide a roadside breakdown service. It's worth taking out a breakdown insurance policy (available through the A.A. in the United Kingdom); policyholders can get 24-hour assistance by calling 05 30 22 22 (freephone), or 72 17 12 00. On freeways, the police should be contacted; tel: 17.

Germany

Allgemeiner Deutscher Automobil-Club (A.D.A.C.), Am Westpark 8, 81373 Munich; tel: (089) 76766322. Deutscher Touring Automobil-Club (D.T.C.), Amalienburgstrasse 23, 81247 Munich; tel: (089) 8111212. A.D.A.C. has a breakdown service (Strassenwacht) and the D.T.C. has a patrol service; call the main A.D.A.C. or D.T.C. numbers for help.

Greece

The Automobile and Touring Club of Greece (E.L.P.A.), 2 Messogion Street, 11527 Athens; tel: (01) 779 1615. E.L.P.A. provides a 24-hour breakdown service in most big cities and on main roads, as well as on the islands of Crete and Corfu. Call 104 for assistance..

Hungary

Magyar Autoklub (M.A.K.), Romer Floris utca 4/a, 1024 Budapest; tel: (1) 2122821. M.A.K. has a patrol service on main roads, and can be summoned from gas stations, restaurants and so on, displaying the yellow sign Segelyszolgalat.

Ireland

Republic of Ireland: The Automobile Association (A.A.), 23 Rock Hill, Blackrock, Co. Dublin; tel: (01) 2833555. **Northern Ireland:** The Automobile Association (A.A.), 108-10 Great Victoria Street, Belfast; tel: (01232) 328924. The A.A.'s Breakdown Service is available to members on the same terms as in the U.K. Call 1-800 667788 (freephone) for advice in cases of breakdown.

Italy

Touring Club Italiano (T.C.I.), 10 Corso Italia, 20122, Milan; tel: (02) 85261. Automobile Club d'Italia (A.C.I.), 8 Via Marsala, 00185 Rome; tel: (06) 49981. The A.C.I. provides free towage from a breakdown to the nearest affiliated garage. Call 116 for assistance.

Luxembourg

Automobile Club du Grand-Duché de Luxembourg (A.C.L.), 54 route de Longwy, 8007 Bertrange, Luxembourg; tel: 450045. A.C.L. has a 24-hour service.

The Netherlands

Koninklijke Nederlandse Toeristenbond (A.N.W.B.), Wassenaarseweg 220, 2596 The Hague; tel: (070) 3141414. A.N.W.B. has a 24-hour patrol service (Wegenwacht) throughout the country. Tel: 06-0888 in case of breakdown.

Norway

Norges Automobil-Forbund (N.A.F.), Storgaten 2, 0155 Oslo 1; tel: 22341400. N.A.F. operates a limited road patrol service in summer. Tel: 22341600.

Poland
Polski Zwiazek Motorowy (P.Z.M.), ul. Sniadeckich 17A, 00-950 Warsaw; tel: (022) 259734. P.Z.M. operates a road patrol service in and around main towns.

Portugal
Automovel Club de Portugal (A.C.P.), rua Rosa Araujo 24, Lisbon 1200; tel: (01) 356 39 31. A.C.P. operates a 24-hour breakdown service. To call assistance, tel: (01) 942 50 95 (south of Pombal); and (02) 830 11 27 (north of Pombal).

Russian Federation, Belorussia, Moldavia and the Ukraine
There is no affiliated motoring organization, and motorists must seek help, in the event of an accident or breakdown, from the police; tel: 02. An accident report will be needed.

Spain
Real Automovil Club de España (R.A.C.E.), Calle Jose Abascal 10, 28003 Madrid; tel: (91) 4473200. R.A.C.E. runs a 24-hour breakdown service; tel: (91) 5933333.

Sweden
Motormannens Riksforbund (M), Sturegatan 32, 10240 Stockholm; tel: (08) 6903800. M operates a very limited road service on main roads during the summer. In cases of breakdown, you can call the Larmtjanst organization (telephone numbers are listed in local directories), or in an emergency tel: (020) 911111 (freephone) for assistance.

Switzerland
Touring Club Suisse (T.C.S.), rue Pierre Fatio 9, 1211 Geneva 3; tel: (022) 737 1212. T.C.S. has a patrol service and 24-hour breakdown service. Call 140 for help, or ask an operator for Autohilfe.

Highways
European highways (motorways) vary considerably, including signposting, conditions and maximum speeds. In general, the countries of north-west Europe (Britain, France, Germany, the Netherlands, Denmark, Belgium, Luxembourg, Sweden, Switzerland) have excellent, extensive highway systems.

There are no standard highways in Belorussia, Moldavia, the Russian Federation and the Ukraine. You should seek advice before planning a motoring trip in this area. The Baltic States have only one major hard-surfaced highway, the M12, linking Tallinn with Riga and Vilnius. Other countries in east Europe (including Czech Republic, the Slovak Republic, Hungary and Poland) have limited systems of varying standards.

Toll roads
In France, Spain, Greece and Italy, most highways are toll roads. In Italy, an automatic toll card (*Viacard*) can be bought in advance from toll booths and gas stations. In Austria, tolls are paid on the Brenner, Tauern, Pyhrn and Karawanken stretches. In Switzerland, a disk (*vignette*) is bought in advance at the border. Bulgaria's are paid at the border.

Route name systems
Many main European routes form part of the European International Network, most of which are identified by green and white signs and have the prefix "E." In Austria, Belgium, France, Germany, Italy and the Netherlands, most highways are in the "E" Route system. These routes may also be labeled with their national number, usually prefixed with "A" (e.g. in France, the E9, labeled green and white, is also the A71, labeled red and white). Britain and Hungary use the prefix "M" for their highways.

Facilities on the road
In some countries, there are no gas or service stations along highways, though they may be signposted off them. There are emergency telephones at intervals (usually 2 kilometers/1½ miles) along most European highways, although in Scandinavia they are infrequent as a result of the increasing use of mobile phones. If you break down on a high-

way, you may have to pay a fee for towing, unless you have a motor-breakdown insurance policy offered by one of the national motoring associations.

Gas

Gas (petrol) costs considerably more in Europe than in the U.S. As in the U.S, gas at highway stations costs more, and self-service pumps offer lower prices.

Octane levels in gas vary from country to country. Gas is usually graded as "normal" and "super," with "super" having the higher octane level.

The availability of unleaded gas is now widespread, and in some countries leaded "normal" gas is not sold. In Britain leaded gas is 90-octane, 2-star; 93-octane, 3-star; and 97-octane, 4-star. Unleaded gas is available in a single grade, i.e. 90-octane "premium."

Rules of the Road

Drinking and Driving

Driving under the influence of alcohol is punishable by law in all European countries. In most, you exceed the permitted level if you have a jigger of whisky or two cans of beer. Several countries require a zero level of blood alcohol.

LINEAR MEASURE

CUSTOMARY

1 inch = 2.54 centimeters
1 foot = 30.48 centimeters
1 yard = 0.91 meters
1 mile = 1.61 kilometers
1 acre = 0.4 hectare

METRIC

1 centimeter = 0.39 inches
1 meter = 3.28 feet
1 meter = 1.09 yards
1 kilometer = 62 miles
1 hectare = 2.5 acres

To convert kilometers into miles multiply by 0.6.

On-the-Spot-Fines

Fines for traffic violations must generally be paid on the spot, usually in local currency. See *Getting Around* under the appropriate country.

Parking

Designated "blue zones" in major cities are for short-term (usually 1 to 1½ hours) parking. Use of the blue zone requires you to post your arrival time at a conspicuous place on the automobile. Failure to indicate arrival time may result in a fine. "Red zones" in cities indicate longer-term parking; "green zones" usually designate areas where parking is prohibited.

In cities, watch for the "no parking" sign, usually a circle bisected by a diagonal line. A circle divided by an "X" indicates no stopping.

Pedestrian Crossings

In many cities, bold white diagonal lines known as "zebra stripes" mark the roadway. These areas always give the pedestrian the right of way and cars must stop. There also are a number of crossings controlled by lights for pedestrian use.

Right of Way

Drive on the right and pass on the left. In Britain and Ireland, however, drive on the left and pass on the right. In either case, passing laws are strictly enforced. Be sure to watch for road markings and do not cross a solid white or yellow line marking the center of the road.

Road Signs

Most countries use the International Road Signs, designed to be easily understood. Triangular signs, except the yield sign, warn of danger, and circular signs prohibit certain actions or tell of restrictions. Rectangular signs are informative.

In Continental Europe, it is customary to yield to traffic approaching from the right. However, when you see a yellow diamond-shaped sign with a white border, you have the right of way and may keep driving without yielding to traffic from the right. When the sign reappears with a diagonal line through it, then it is again necessary to give right of way to traffic coming along from the right.

Speed Limits
It is important to observe speed limits. Offenders may be fined and have their driver's license confiscated on the spot. It is often illegal to travel at a speed so slow that it obstructs normal traffic flow.

TRAIN TRAVEL

Train travel in Europe can prove an excellent way to get around, and can be very good value. It's worth doing some homework in advance, investigating the many special offers or passes available. They fall broadly into three types: unlimited travel within a fixed period (usually 15 or 21 days, or 1, 2 or 3 months); travel on a certain number of days within a longer period (typically 5 days within 15, or 15 within 30), often known as a "Flexipass"; and a very large variety of regional or local discounts or deals (for families, students, senior citizens; combining rail and bus, rail and car, or rail and boat; off-peak travel within a defined area, and so on).

Many of the fixed-period and "Flexi" passes cover several countries. For example, the EurailPass covers 17 countries; the EuroPass covers five. Others cover eastern Europe; Benelux, Britain, France and Scandinavia. There are several youth passes, applicable to people aged 26 or under. Almost all are available only to non-residents of participating countries, and can be purchased only outside the country – that is, before you leave the U.S. However, local "Rover" tickets and some other passes are available on the spot.

In most countries, children under four get to travel free of charge, and children aged four to 11 travel for half price. There are variations, however – for example, in Austria, children under seven travel free. Family passes may prove very good value.

For further information, refer to a AAA travel agent.

WEIGHT AND PRESSURE		
If you know:	*Multiply by:*	*To Find:*
ounces	28	grams
pounds	0.45	kilograms
grams	0.035	ounces
kilograms	2.2	pounds

Air pressure in automobile tires is expressed in kilopascals. Multiply pound-force per square inch (psi) by 6.89 to find kilopascals (kPa).
24 psi = 165 kPa
26 psi = 179 kPa
28 psi = 193 kPa
30 psi = 207 kPa

OTHER PUBLIC TRANSPORTATION
For details of public transportation other than train, see country entries.

EMERGENCIES

EMBASSIES AND CONSULATES
Embassies and consulates give advice and render assistance to their citizens in case of accident, serious illness or death. Consular agents may also be able to help in such matters as lost passports.

In the capitals and larger cities of Europe, U.S. tourists can register at American embassies; in certain other cities, at American consulates.

It is particularly wise to register with the nearest American embassy or consulate if you are traveling to eastern Europe or staying in any country for longer than one month. The addresses and phone numbers of American embassies and consulates are listed in the *Things To Know* box for each country.

VALUABLES

Money
If you are visiting several countries, it is best to buy traveler's checks in U.S.$ since few currencies are as easily exchanged and you will save yourself the cost of repeated currency exchanges.

If you will be spending most of your time in one country or if the U.S. dollar is declining in value and you want to lock in at the current rate, it might be a good idea to buy traveler's checks in foreign currency.

When exchanging money, it is always advisable to shop around. Banks (other than those at international borders) usually offer the best rates, but they generally charge a commission. Traveler's checks usually get a better rate of exchange than cash.

You can exchange foreign bills when you leave a country, but not coins. Save your exchange transaction receipts; some countries will not let you exchange local currency back to your own unless you can prove that your foreign holdings were originally in your own currency.

The currency of an eastern European country is worthless outside that country, and it is frequently illegal to export (see the *Things to Know* box for each country for further details).

Credit Cards

It is wise to have a backup source of funds in case your money is stolen or an emergency occurs. Take internationally recognized credit cards that will let you draw cash up to your credit limit. You can also use them to pay for purchases at thousands of locations across Europe.

Note that MasterCard is called Access in Britain and Eurocard in other parts of Europe. VISA is Barclaycard in Britain and Carte Bleue in France.

Theft

Travel lightly and do not leave luggage unattended in public places. Be sure not to travel with all of your money, credit cards and traveler's checks in one place. Consider leaving valuables in your hotel safe or a safe deposit box.

If possible, take advantage of indoor parking; don't leave your car on the street overnight.

AAA members should consider purchasing AAA baggage insurance at their local clubs.

RETURNING TO THE U.S.

U.S. CUSTOMS REGULATIONS

Declaration of Imports

Hints for returning U.S. residents are in the *Know Before You Go* booklet (see Travel Advisories on p.11). Customs Declarations Forms (CF 6059B) are distributed on ships and planes for you to complete for presentation to customs inspectors upon your arrival in the U.S. You can also obtain one in advance from customs offices. All articles acquired while abroad that accompany you on your return must be declared to Customs. This requirement includes any repairs to articles you have taken abroad and any gifts received while abroad.

To avoid paying duty on foreign-made items you owned before you went abroad, such as cameras, jewelry or watches, register them at a customs office before leaving the United States.

Duties

Returning residents of the U.S. are allowed a $400 duty-free exemption on articles for personal use or gifts if they have been out of the country a minimum of 48 hours and have not used this exemption within the preceding 30-day period. A flat-rate duty of 10 percent will be applied to the next $1,000 worth of merchandise; above this, various rates apply, depending on the article. Assessment is based on the retail value; remember to keep sales slips, and don't be tempted by a shopkeeper's offer to understate the cost of purchase. Genuine antiques (anything more than 100 years old) are duty-free; you'll need written proof of the article's age.

Items bought abroad and sent home by a U.S. resident or by the store will be subject to duty and taxes.

Gifts

Packages containing gifts whose total fair retail value does not exceed $50 in the country where you purchased them, may be sent duty-free to persons in the

U.S., provided that only one such package is received by the same person in one day. Gifts for more than one person may be mailed in the same package, provided each gift is individually wrapped and labeled with the name of the recipient. Duty on gifts exceeding $50 cannot be prepaid; it is collected by the U.S. Postal Service in the form of postage-due stamps. The gift allowance does not include alcohol-containing perfume valued at more than $5, alcoholic beverages or tobacco products. While traveling in Europe you may not send a gift to yourself, nor can persons traveling together send gifts to one other.

Restricted or Prohibited Articles

To prevent the introduction of plant and animal pests and diseases into the U.S., an agricultural quarantine bans the importation of certain fruits, vegetables, plants, livestock, poultry and meats. For details, request the leaflet *Travelers' Tips* from APHIS, Department of Agriculture, 6505 Belcrest Road, Room 628, Hyattsville, MD 20782.

Certain articles considered injurious or detrimental to the U.S. are prohibited, such as *absinthe*, liquor-filled confections, fireworks, lottery tickets and narcotics. Endangered animal or plant species and products made from them are prohibited, and import restrictions are placed on firearms and ammunition.

If you require medicines with habit-forming drugs or narcotics, ensure they are in their original containers, and carry a prescription authorizing their use to avoid customs problems on your return.

Alcoholic Beverages and Tobacco

A returning resident 21 years or older who is entitled to the $400 duty-free exemption may include one liter of alcoholic beverages for personal use or as a gift. Persons of any age may bring in 100 cigars and 200 cigarettes. Laws concerning the importation of cigarettes and alcohol vary from state to state.

AUTOMOBILE CLUBS IN EUROPE

For the benefit of members traveling abroad, the American Automobile Association maintains reciprocal agreements with many foreign motor clubs, a number of which are in Europe. Presentation of your valid AAA membership card at these participating clubs makes you eligible to receive all the services they give to their own members. This does not mean you'll receive the same services as those provided by AAA at home – operating philosophies differ around the world.

This reciprocal service for AAA members is for short-term visitors only. If you are going abroad for an extended period, you will have to become a member of the local club. Addresses of main offices are provided near the beginning of each country with an automobile club or association.

AAA's *Offices to Serve You Abroad* pamphlet, available from your local AAA club, lists auto club offices to serve you overseas and explains in detail the services you can expect from those clubs with which AAA has a full reciprocal agreement. As a member of both the AIT (Alliance Internationale de Tourisme) and the FIA (Fédération Internationale de l'Automobile), AAA also has additional but more limited sources of worldwide service available through AIT/FIA member clubs. They too are listed. A copy of this booklet should be taken along with your AAA membership card.

The symbol ▲ before the city or town name in the alphabetical listings denotes the presence of a main or branch office of an automobile club.

AUSTRIA

AUSTRIA IS A RICH COUNTRY: PROSPEROUS ECONOMI-
CALLY, BUT RICH ALSO IN SCENERY AND CULTURE, AND
WITH A PEOPLE WHOSE LOVE OF LIFE AND EASY-GOING
NATURE MAKES THEM RICH IN SPIRIT, TOO. WHOSE
SPIRITS WOULD NOT RISE, THOUGH, WITH SUCH A
SPLENDID CAPITAL CITY AS VIENNA?

ONE OF THE
WORLD'S GREAT
CITIES, VIENNA
IS THE CITY OF
SCHUBERT AND

STRAUSS, OF HAYDN, MOZART, BEETHOVEN, THE
VIENNA WOODS, THE BLUE DANUBE, OF FREUD, THE
SPANISH RIDING SCHOOL, OF CAFÉS AND CHOCOLATE
CAKE, AND THE MYSTERIES OF THE THIRD MAN.
BEYOND VIENNA LIES BEAUTIFUL COUNTRYSIDE, FROM
LUSH VINE-FILLED VALLEYS, WHERE EXCELLENT WINES
HAVE BEEN KEPT SOMETHING OF A SECRET, TO THE
MOUNTAIN LAKES AND HIGH PEAKS OF THE ALPS.

Left THE PICTURESQUE MARKET TOWN OF HALLSTATT, OVERLOOKING LAKE
HALLSTATT, DATES BACK TO PREHISTORIC TIMES
Above THE PALLAS ATHENE FOUNTAIN OUTSIDE THE PARLAMENT, VIENNA

THINGS TO KNOW

- **AREA:** 83,849 square kilometers (32,374 square miles)
- **POPULATION:** 7,586,400
- **CAPITAL:** Wien (Vienna)
- **LANGUAGE:** German
- **RELIGION:** Mainly Catholic but some Protestants also.
- **ECONOMY:** Industry, agriculture, tourism. Chief exports are machinery, iron and steel, and textiles.
- **PASSPORT REQUIREMENTS:** Required for U.S. and British citizens.
- **VISA REQUIREMENTS:** Not required for stays up to three months.
- **DUTY-FREE ITEMS:** 400 cigarettes or 100 cigars or 500 grams of tobacco; two liters of wine and one liter of distilled liquor; .25 liters of toilet water and 50 grams of perfume; two still cameras with one roll of 24-exposure film for each; one small movie camera with 10 rolls of film; one video camera.
  Note: If on the way to Austria, a stopover of more than 24 hours is made in any European country, the duty-free allowance of cigarettes, tobacco and distilled liquor is reduced.
- **CURRENCY:** The currency unit is the Austrian *schilling* (AS), divided into 100 *groschen*. Due to currency fluctuations, the exchange rate is subject to frequent change. No limit on Austrian and foreign currency brought into the country.
  Note: No limit on the exportation of foreign currency, but only 100,000 schillings may be taken out of the country.
- **BANK OPENING HOURS:** 8am–12:30pm and 1:30–3pm Monday–Wednesday and Friday, 8am–12:30pm and 1:30–5:30pm Thursday.
- **STORE OPENING HOURS:** Generally 8:30am–6pm Monday–Friday, 8:30am–1pm Saturday. In downtown Vienna shops do not close for lunch. Vienna's Dorotheum, a large pawn and loan house, publishes regular auction announcements.
- **BEST BUYS:** Leather goods, wooden crafts, porcelain, knitwear, ski

HISTORY

Because many principal trade routes, including the strategic Danube River (Donau), traverse this small nation, Austria has played an important part in European history. Following centuries of invasions by Romans, Goths, Huns and various barbaric tribes, Charlemagne brought a degree of stability to the country when he made it his eastern frontier (Ost Mark) in 799 AD.

In 962 AD Austria became a part of the Holy Roman Empire of the German Nation. Leopold of Babenberg was made Margrave of Austria in 976 AD and established his capital at Melk. His successors ruled the margravate, a duchy after 1156, until the death of the last

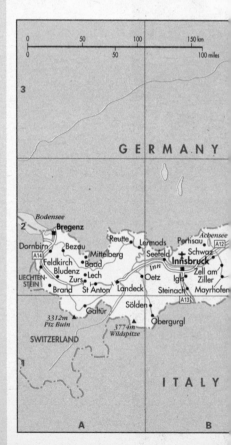

male heir in 1246. During the next 27 years a struggle for the throne ensued until Rudolph of Habsburg, the elected Holy Roman Emperor, was crowned Duke of Austria, beginning 645 years of that family's rule.

The Emperor Maximilian I, who ruled 1493–1519, increased the size of the Habsburg lands. His grandson Charles V ruled one of the world's greatest empires: Austria, the Netherlands, Belgium, Spain, Latin America (except Brazil), Naples, Sardinia, Sicily and a few provinces in eastern France. Charles divided his empire, and his brother Ferdinand got the Austrian lands in 1521, becoming King of Bohemia and Hungary in 1526. With the acquisition of the latter came

the responsibility of defending Christian Europe from Moslem Ottoman Turks, who were at the walls of Vienna by 1529.

During the turmoil of the Napoleonic era, the Holy Roman Empire passed away and was replaced by the Empire of Austria in 1806. The Congress of Vienna convened in 1815 to redraw the maps of Europe. As a result, the Habsburgs ruled an empire that included Germans, Romanians, Czechs, Slovaks, Hungarians, Poles, Italians, Croats, Slovenes and Serbs. A revolution, riots and war brought about the exclusion of the Habsburgs from the established Kingdom of Italy and the German Empire and resulted in the creation of the Dual Monarchy of Austria-Hungary in 1867.

clothing and equipment, local costumes, copper and iron work.

- **PUBLIC HOLIDAYS:** January 1; Epiphany, January 6; Easter Monday; Labor Day, May 1; Ascension Day; Whitmonday; Corpus Christi; Assumption Day, August 15; Austrian National Flag Day, October 26; All Saints' Day, November 1; Immaculate Conception, December 8; December 25–26.
- **USEFUL TELEPHONE NUMBERS:**
  Police: 133
  Fire: 122
  Ambulance: 144
- **NATIONAL TOURIST OFFICES:**
  Austrian National Tourist Office
  500 Fifth Avenue
  Suite 2009-2022
  New York
  N.Y. 10110
  USA
  Tel: 212/944-6880
  Fax: 212/73-04 568
  Wiener Fremdenverkehrsverband
  Obere Augartenstrasse 40
  A-1025 Wien
  Austria
  Tel: 1 211 140
  Fax: 1 216 84 92
  Salzburger Land –
  Tourismus Ges.m.b.H.
  Alpenstrasse 96
  A-5033 Salzburg
  Austria
  Postfach 8
  Tel: 662 20 506-0
  Telex: 633076
  Fax: 662 23070
  Tirol Werbung
  Bozner Platz 6
  A-6010 Innsbruck
  Austria
  Tel: 512 53 20/170, 171
  TTX: 3522229
  Fax: 512 53 20 150
- **AMERICAN EMBASSY:**
  Boltzmanngasse-16
  1090 Vienna
  Austria
  Tel: 0222 315511 (02221 from outside Austria

On June 28, 1914, the assassination of the Archduke Francis Ferdinand, heir to the Austrian throne, by a Serbian nationalist released global tensions that escalated into World War I. After the war, the non-German peoples of the empire established their own nations. The German members of the Reichstag, the Imperial Parliament, proclaimed the Republic of German-Austria in November 1918.

Confusion reigned between the World Wars while considerable agitation for union with the German Republic was thwarted by the Allied Powers. In 1938, Hitler annexed Austria to his Third Reich. Seven years later the armies of France, Great Britain, the Soviet Union and the United States occupied the land. After a decade of occupation, the Austrian Republic was restored.

FOOD AND DRINK

To request a menu in Austria, ask for a *Speisekarte*; if you ask for a menu, you might be brought the daily special. The fatted calf, in a variety of guises, appears on nearly every Austrian table. You can enjoy it as *Wienerschnitzel* (Viennese fillet of veal), or the memorable *Schnitzel cordon bleu* (veal, ham and cheese dipped in egg and breadcrumbs and fried). Pork makes its entrance as *Spanferkel* (roast suckling pig) and *Wildschweinbraten* (roast boar). *Heisse Würstel mit Senf* is simply a tasty frankfurter, served with mustard and a roll.

Noodle dishes are plentiful, but better remembered are the delightfully rich desserts. Among them are *Sachertorte*, Viennese chocolate cake with or without cream, and *Strudel*, made with apples, cherries or pot cheese. Viennese coffee or several varieties of beer and wine make fine dinner endings.

As delightful as the Austrian wines are the *Heurigen* (country wine taverns). The *Nobel-Heuriger* is the city version, sometimes more simply called *Weinstube*.

Local coffeehouses and *Konditoreien*, or pastry shops, serve light snacks.

SPORTS AND RECREATION

Skiing tops the list of sports in mountainous Austria. The ski season lasts from December to late spring. Mountain climbing also is popular.

For anglers, fly fishing is best in the mountain streams. Apply in advance to the local authorities for permission to fish. Golf and horseback riding can be enjoyed at many resorts. Swimming, water skiing, rowing and sailing are popular as well. While no special license is required for sailing boats under 9.75 meters (32 feet) long, official regulations require you to prove your ability to operate a sailing craft or to be accompanied by a qualified sailor.

GETTING AROUND

Austria's six major train lines, mostly electrified, range from slower trains serving smaller towns to expresses between Vienna and other large cities. Reduced rates offered by the Austrian Federal Railway system include discounts for travel in any one Austrian province and half fare for children under 15. The "Austria Ticket" gives special rates for travel on trains and buses for those under 26, as well as certain discounts on Danube steamboat cruises, aerial trams and chairlifts. Postal and local buses

serve areas off the railroad routes. River and lake cruises provide another enjoyable way to see the country.

Austria has an excellent system of roads and *Autobahnen*, or highways. Local conditions sometimes necessitate the use of tire chains; these can be rented from the Österreichischer Automobile Motorrad- und Touring Club (ÖAMTC).

Road identification signs use white letters and numbers on a green background for a European highway and white numbers on a blue background for an Austrian federal highway type I; the latter gives the right of way over all intersecting traffic. A yellow circular sign with black numbers is an Austrian federal highway type II, allowing no special right of way.

Seat belts are mandatory for driver and passengers, if the vehicle is so equipped; a child under 12 or under 1.50m cannot travel unless using a suitable restraint system. Speed limits are 50 k.p.h. (30 m.p.h.) in town, 100 k.p.h. (60 m.p.h.) on all out-of-town roads and 130 k.p.h. (80 m.p.h.) on expressways, unless otherwise posted. Visiting motorists are required to pay fines for motoring violations on the spot with Austrian schillings.

ACCOMMODATIONS

Gasthöfe, or small inns, are common in the small towns throughout Austria. Many lodgings include a Continental breakfast in their room rates and some serve *durchgehend warme Küche*, hot meals, between noon and 2pm and between 6pm and 9pm. *Jause*, or afternoon coffee, is normally served between 4 and 5pm.

If you prefer luxury, Austria has some 90 spas and resorts. About 100 youth hostels accommodate travelers as well, giving preference to those under 30. Austria also maintains about 400 campgrounds. Some might give a reduced rate if you have an international camping carnet, or permit. While the carnet is not required, some sites might ask for it.

AUTOMOBILE CLUB
The **Österreichischer Automobile Motorrad- und Touring Club** (ÖAMTC, Austrian Automobile Motoring and Touring Club), Schubertring 1–3, 1010, Vienna, has branch offices in various cities throughout Austria. The symbol ▲ beside a city name indicates the presence of a AAA-affiliated automobile club branch. Not all auto clubs offer full travel services to AAA members.

AUSTRIA

TIPPING

Restaurants in Austria usually include a service charge in the bill, but a tip of about 10 percent on top is expected, rounding off to the nearest 10 schillings. Tip taxi drivers 10 to 15 percent of the fare; tip bartenders about 10 percent of your beverage bill. Porters and bellhops normally receive about 20 schillings per bag and doormen about 15 schillings.

PRINCIPAL TOURING AREAS

Note: For descriptions of cities in **bold type**, see individual city listings.

KÄRNTEN

Kärnten, or Carinthia, is an Alpine province descending to the Klagenfurt Plain, with several scenic extremes. The mountains protect lakes in the area, resulting in a long, warm season ideal for swimming, water skiing or sunbathing. Mountain climbers have a choice of peaks, the most formidable being Grossglockner, which at 3,797 meters (12,457 feet) is the highest of the Austrian Alps.

NIEDERÖSTERREICH AND BURGENLAND

Niederösterreich, or Lower Austria, is the largest province and encompasses beauti-ful parts of the Danube country, with vineyards, castles, museums, palaces, villages and mountains. The Vienna Woods are a hiker's paradise. **Wien,** or **Vienna,** is a cosmopolitan city with a rich musical and architectural heritage.

Lower Austria's tiny eastern neighbor, Burgenland, adjoins the Slovak Republic, Hungary and Slovenia.

Numerous castles and fortified churches recall a less peaceful past. **Eisenstadt,** the capital, was the home of Franz Joseph Haydn.

SALZBURG AND OBERÖSTERREICH

Oberösterreich, or Upper Austria, and the federal province of **Salzburg** with its capital of the same name, are situated further west.

The presence of salt in the springs makes this a good spa center. The surrounding area, the Salzkammergut, is popular in summer and winter.

STEIERMARK

In the mountainous part of central and southeastern Austria are forests for walking, climbing and riding. Steiermark, or Styria, has several mountain and lowland resorts. **Graz,** an Old World university town, is known for its October Festival of Music and Drama.

TIROL

In the heart of Europe, the Tirol offers rugged, snow-capped peaks and green valleys. Rich with woods and meadows, it is known for its beautiful old villages and for the university town of **Innsbruck.** Many resorts are tucked away in its hills.

VORARLBERG

The subtly changing landscape in western Austria extends from the shores of Lake Constance (Bodensee) up to the glaciers of the Silvretta range. Mountain villages and lakes, meadows and deep valleys are surrounded by snow-capped gray mountains. **Bregenz,** the capital of this small province, holds an open-air music festival from July through August.

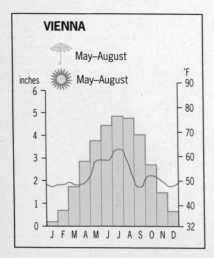

PLACES OF INTEREST

▲ WIEN ★

WIEN pop. 1,600,000

At the crossroads of Europe, Wien, or Vienna, was for a thousand years the capital of the far-flung Holy Roman and Habsburg empires. Today it is the capital of the Austrian Republic and serves as an international congress city. Though its people and ways have changed, Vienna has retained its imperial monuments, not as reminders of past glories, but as symbols of its present freedom.

UNDERGROUND VIENNA

The catacombs of St. Stephen's Cathedral offer a fascinating glimpse into the city's past. For less spiritual refreshment, the 12 Apostelkeller wine cellar at nearby Schönlaterngasse is a good introduction to city life.

Vienna's charm consists of many elements. This metropolis on the Danube river has lush parks and fine shops, hotels and restaurants. It also has some of the most beautiful Renaissance, baroque and rococo buildings in the world, as well as many buildings that embody *Jugendstil*, the Austrian version of art-nouveau architecture.

The Ringstrasse, or Ring, is the well-known boulevard which, with the Danube Canal (Donaukanal), encloses the Inner City, or First District of Vienna. The array of buildings on the broad, 4 kilometer (2½ mile) street includes the Parliament (Parlament), the State museums, the Opera House (Staatsoper), and the Imperial Palace (Hofburg), all interspersed with historic gardens. Kärntnerstrasse, Graben, Kohlmarkt and Mariahilferstrasse are the city's best known shopping streets.

If you visit Vienna in winter, you have a special advantage: it is the high season for cultural events. As the home of Franz Joseph Haydn, Wolfgang Amadeus Mozart, Ludwig van Beethoven, Anton Bruckner, Gustav Mahler, Franz Schubert, Johannes Brahms and Johann and Richard Strauss, the city almost breathes music. From September through June the Vienna State Opera performs, and there are operettas, ballets and chamber music. (Opera tickets, however, can be expensive and hard to get, so make sure you plan ahead.)

Vienna's musical offerings extend into summer as well, with such events as the Vienna Festival from mid-May to mid-June and a program of operettas and open-air and palace concerts taking place in July and August.

The Vienna Boys' Choir performs at the 9:15am mass in the Hofburg Palace Chapel on any Sunday or Holy Day from the first Sunday after September 15 to the last Sunday in June (except January 6, Corpus Christi and December 26). Written requests for tickets must be made at least eight weeks in advance to Verwaltung der Hofmusikkapelle, Hofburg, 1010 Vienna, Austria.

No matter what time of year you visit, you can buy a three-day "Rover Ticket", which is valid for the subway, the *Stadtbahn* (city train), *Schnellbahn* (fast city train), trams and buses. You can get the ticket for a small fee from the tourist information offices at Wien West, Wien Süd, the airport, Westbahnhof and Südbahnhof, as well as at all transport authority ticket offices.

AUSTRIA

BELVEDERE (32 D1), on Prince-Eugen-Str 27, with entrances on Karolinengasse and Ramweg, consists of two palaces built for Prince Eugene of Savoy. Lower, or Unteres, Belvedere is the former summer residence; it houses the Museum of Medieval Austrian Art and the Museum of Austrian Baroque. Upper, or Oberes, Belvedere was built several years later and used for festivities; it now contains the Austrian Gallery, which displays collections of 19th- and 20th-century paintings. The two palaces are linked by elegant terraced gardens.

HOFBURG (Imperial Palace) (32 C2), at 2 Michaelerplatz, dates from the 16th to 20th centuries and was the residence of Emperor Franz Josef and Empress Elisabeth. The chapel, which is the only part of the original castle that still stands, dates from the 13th century. The Habsburgs' gold table service is on display. The imperial apartments and staterooms also are open for viewing.

A fire swept through one wing of the palace in 1992, destroying the historical 18th-century Redoutensaal ballroom, among others. The adjacent National Library and the Schatzkammer, the treasure room, were spared. Restoration of this part of the palace is to continue through 1995.

Albertina Collection of Graphic Arts contains the Dürer Collection, which includes the well-known *Praying Hands*, as well as works by Michelangelo, Titian, Raphael and Rembrandt, among others.

Kapuzinerkirche (Capuchin Church) houses the crypt where the imperial family is buried. The church is entered from 2 Tegetthoffstrasse.

Spanische Reitschule (Spanish Riding School), Josefsplatz, is one of Vienna's most popular attractions. Reservations for Sunday performances of the Lippizaner horses must be made by written application to the school.

HOHER MARKT (32 D3), the oldest part of Vienna, was the center of the medieval town. Beneath the bustling square lie the ruins of a Roman settlement. Ruins can be entered at 3 Hoher Markt.

KUNSTHISTORISCHES MUSEUM (Museum of Fine Arts) (32 C2), Maria-Theresien Platz, contains one of Europe's finest collections of paintings, including works by Pieter Bruegel, Diego Velázquez,

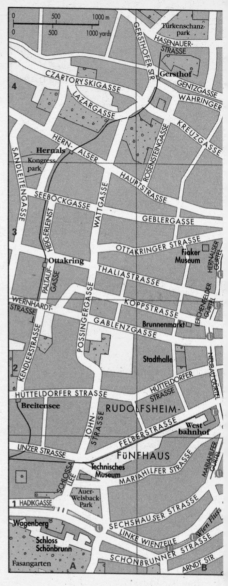

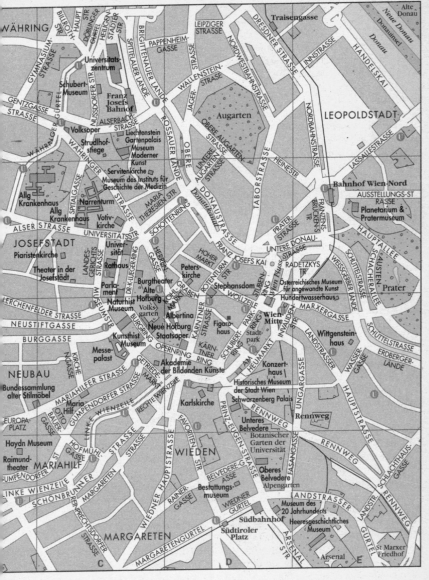

Titian, Rembrandt and Correggio. Egyptian and Oriental art is also represented in the museums' collection.

PARLAMENT (Parliament) (32 C3), 3 Dr. Karl-Renner-Ring, is housed in a neoclassical building that was opened to the public in 1883.

PRATER (32 E3), Hauptallee, was once a hunting reserve of the aristocracy, opened by Emperor Josef II; today it has a sports arena and amusement park with the *Riesenrad* (giant wheel), a landmark.

SCHLOSS SCHÖNBRUNN (32 A1), 13 Schönbrunner Schloss Strasse in the suburbs, is a lavish 1,200-room summer palace that has changed little since the time of Maria Theresa. The furnishings of the 45 rooms on view, as well as the fountains, parks and formal terraces, create a picture of unsurpassed elegance.

STAATSOPER (State Opera House) (32 D2), 2 Opernring, was built in the 1860s and carefully reconstructed following its destruction in World War II. The opera season extends from September to June, with daily performances.

STEPHANSDOM (St. Stephen's Cathedral) (32 D3), Stephansplatz, is an impressive Gothic structure that was consecrated in the mid-12th century. It has a 136-meter (450-foot) spire and many art treasures. The bell tower affords an excellent view of the city and houses the huge brass bell called Pummerin – "the boomer."

ACHENSEE (26 B2)
TIROL *elev. 853m. (2,815ft.)*
The Achensee lies between the Karwendel and Rofan mountains and is Tirol's largest and most attractive lake. The villages of Pertisau and Maurach provide leisure facilities for both summer and winter vacations.

ADMONT (26 D2)
STEIERMARK *pop. 3,100*
A market town in the Enns Valley, Admont has become a popular winter and summer resort.

ALTAUSSEE (26 C2)
STEIERMARK *pop. 1,900*
The little spa town of Altaussee is a summer and winter resort area on pretty Altausseer, in the Styrian section of the mountainous Salzkammergut region.

ATTERSEE (26 C2)
OBERÖSTERREICH *pop. 1,400*
Attersee, bordering the Alpine lake of the same name, dates from Roman times. The Attersee is the largest mountain lake in Austria, extending from the limestone cliffs of the Höllengebirge on the far southeastern bank to the low hills in the north.

Its west bank is an area of rolling hills and flourishing orchards. A road encircles the lake, passing Schörfling and other picturesque towns.

BADGASTEIN (26 C2) ★
SALZBURG *pop. 5,600, elev. 1,007m. (3,324ft.)*
Built on evergreen-covered slopes overlooking a rushing mountain torrent, Badgastein is revered for its spectacular setting and radioactive thermal springs.

BAD HOFGASTEIN (26 C2)
SALZBURG *pop. 5,960, elev. 795m. (2,623ft.)*
About 1 million litres (265,000 gallons) of thermal water comes daily from nearby Badgastein and fills three indoor pools linked via channels to outdoor pools, enabling visitors to swim inside or out. The water temperature stays between 32 and 34°C (90 and 93°F), providing cures and relaxation in summer and winter.

BAD ISCHL (26 C2)
OBERÖSTERREICH *pop. 13,100*
Once the site of Emperor Franz Josef's summer court, Bad Ischl is among the best equipped spas in Austria.

BAD KLEINKIRCHHEIM (26 C1)
KÄRNTEN *pop. 1,900, elev. 1,094m. (3,609ft.)*
Bad Kleinkirchheim is a popular resort and spa in the Nock Mountains of Kärnten, offering both summer and winter recreational facilities.

BREGENZ (26 A2)
VORARLBERG *pop. 27,000*
The capital of Vorarlberg Province, Bregenz is in the Alpine foothills on the shores of Lake Constance, the largest lake in Europe. It is an ideal starting point for trips by boat, bus, car or train to nearby Switzerland, Germany and Liechtenstein. A cable car trip to the top of Pfänder Mountain affords a fine view of the Austrian, Swiss and Bavarian Alps.

DÜRNSTEIN (26 D3) ★
NIEDERÖSTERREICH *pop. 2,000*
Dürnstein is on the Danube River between Melk and Krems in the beautiful Wachau region.

It has a ruined castle, where Richard the Lionheart was imprisoned in the 12th century. Surrounding vineyards produce fine wines.

EISENSTADT (26 E2)
BURGENLAND *pop. 10,100*
The capital of Austria's eastern province, Eisenstadt was once the home of Franz Joseph Haydn.

The Haydn home is now a museum, and his tomb is in a local church. The city makes a good starting point for motor trips in eastern Austria.

SCHLOSS ESTERHÁZY is the lavish palace where Franz Joseph Haydn composed and was conductor of a private orchestra at the court of the Esterházy princes.

FELDKIRCH (26 E1)
VORARLBERG *pop. 25,000*
Surounded by mountains, Feldkirch's well-preserved attractions include the remains of battlements and a small Gothic church.

In June one of the world's best known music festivals is held in Feldkirch. The "Schubertiade" focuses mainly on the works of Franz Schubert.

GMUNDEN (26 C2)
OBERÖSTERREICH *pop. 13,100*
Built on the north banks of the Traunsee, east of Salzburg, Gmunden is the principal town of the Salzkammergut region. A popular spa, Gmunden's past is reflected in its 17th-century parish church and the part-Gothic Ort Castle.

GOSAUSEE
OBERÖSTERREICH *elev. 867m. (2,846ft.)*
A stunning Alpine landscape unfolds at the Vorderer Gosausee, easily reached by car or bus. A 90-minute walk leads to Hinterer Gosausee, from where there are spectacular views.

▲ GRAZ (26 D2)
STEIERMARK *pop. 242,000*
Capital of the province of Styria and the second largest city in Austria, Graz is in the southeastern part of the country on the banks of the River Mur. It stages a popular Festival of Music and Drama in October. West at Piber is the stud farm where the Lippizaner stallions are bred for use at the Spanish Riding School in Vienna (see p.32).

DOM (Cathedral) was built in the 15th century by Emperor Frederick III. The exterior fresco depicts the *Divine Torments* – plague, locusts and war.

SCHLOSS EGGENBERG, 3.5 kilometers (2 miles) west, is a magnificent baroque castle built in the early 17th century, now housing a hunting museum. The grounds are maintained as a game preserve.

GURK (26 D1)
CARINTHIA *pop. 1,400*
Gurk, a small market town in a valley to the north of Carinthia, is known for its splendid Romanesque cathedral, built between 1140 and 1200, with baroque domes mounted on twin towers.

HALLEIN (26 C2)
SALZBURG *pop. 17,300*
DÜRRNBERG MINE, a 4-kilometer (2½-mile) long salt mine first used in 700 BC by the Celts, was opened to the public before World War I. Visitors use hardwood slides to reach a museum and salt lake near the bottom. A cathedral-like cavern containing marble statues and tablets can be seen from a boat on an illuminated lake.

HALLSTATT (26 C2) ★
OBERÖSTERREICH *pop. 1,200*
Largely untouched by the modern world, the ancient salt-mining town of Hallstatt is built on terraces that climb the steep mountain slopes above Lake Hallstatt. The town is noted for its relics of the pre-Christian Celtic period and also for its exquisite woodcarvings.

DACHSTEIN HÖHLEN (Dachstein Ice Caves) form one of Europe's largest underground complexes. They can be reached via cable car from Obertraun, a few miles to the east.

HEILIGENBLUT (26 C1) ★

KÄRNTEN *pop. 1,300, elev. 1,300m. (4,265ft.)*

Picturesque Heiligenblut, the highest town in Carinthia, is a winter resort and southern terminus of the Grossglockner Highway. The Gothic church is famous as a place of pilgrimage. There is also a well-known mountain-climbing school in the town. Heiligenblut is a touring center for Hohe Tauern, the second largest national park in Europe, which includes nearly 275 kilometers (170 miles) of marked trails and Alpine wildlife.

A 13-kilometer (8-mile) excursion over the High Alpine Highway leads to 3,797-meter (12,457-foot) Grossglockner, Austria's highest peak. Traffic is heavy in summer, so get an early start.

IGLS (26 B2)

TIROL *pop. 1,600, elev. 900m. (2,953ft.)*

South of Innsbruck, the hillside resort of Igls provides fine hotels and many recreational facilities – golf, tennis, swimming and riding, as well as a cable car to Patscherkofel.

▲ INNSBRUCK (26 B2) ★

TIROL *pop. 117,000*

In a valley of the mountainous border area, Innsbruck is the capital of the Tirol and within easy reach of the Tirolean Alps. Outside the city, there are beautiful glacier views from the Stubai Valley, which can be reached by way of Fulpmes. A drive along the Brenner Road to the 1,374-meter (4,508-foot) Brenner Plateau and the Italian frontier at Brenner Lake abounds in scenic contrasts. The Alpine Expressway to the south crosses the Europabrücke, a 0.3 kilometer (½ mile) bridge high above the Sill River Valley.

DOM ZU ST. JAKOB (St. Jacob's Cathedral) is a baroque cathedral of the early 18th century. A magnificent painting by Lucas Cranach the Elder, who lived for a short while in Vienna, adorns the space above the high altar.

GOLDENES DACHL (Golden Roof), Herzog-Friedrich-Str, is a small three-story late-Gothic balcony of a former palace in Stadtplatz, known for its gilded copper roof. The former royal residence was built by Maximilian I in 1500 as a royal box for watching spectacles in the square below.

HOFBURG (Imperial Palace), Rennweg 1, was built 1754-73 during the reign of Empress Maria Theresa. It contains splendid ornamentation, ceiling frescoes, pictures and tapestries.

HOFKIRCHE (Court Church) contains the magnificent marble tomb of Maximilian I, which is covered by 24 carved scenes depicting the emperor's deeds.

KITZBÜHEL (26 B2) ★

TIROL *pop. 8,100*

With its picturesque old houses and ancient archway, Kitzbühel is one of Austria's most fashionable winter sports and health resorts. The summits of the 1,655-meter (5,430-foot) Hahnenkamm and the 1,998-meter (6,555-foot) Kitzbüheler Horn are reached by cable car.

Such summer sports as golf, swimming, tennis and riding also are popular. An annual tennis tournament in early August draws top international talent.

SUMMERTIME REVELRY

Many visitors to Kitzbühel come for the *Kirtag*, a local festival that takes place on the first Saturday in August. Stalls are set up along the main streets, refreshments are served, and there's plenty of good-humored fun.

KREMS (26 D3)

NIEDERÖSTERREICH *pop. 22,700*

Krems is the principal city of the Wachau, an expanse of splendid scenery that stretches east along the Danube River from Melk to Krems. The area is renowned for its wine, and Krems is the center of the wine trade. Founded during the late 10th century, the city has Renaissance, baroque and rococo buildings.

KREMSMÜNSTER (26 D2)
OBERÖSTERREICH *pop. 6,000*
Ancient Kremsmünster is the site of a historic Benedictine abbey. Founded in 777 AD, it has ceiling frescoes, plaster moldings and a collection of paintings.

LECH (26 A2)
VORARLBERG *pop. 2,900, elev. 1,450m. (4,757ft.)*
A fashionable winter sports center, Lech lies in the superb skiing country of the Arlberg region. Summer visitors also enjoy this scenic spot, reached by the Flexen Pass Road from the Arlberg.

LIENZ (26 C1)
TIROL *pop. 12,000*
The capital of East Tirol, Lienz is an attractive riverside town that draws winter sports enthusiasts, mountain climbers and sun lovers. Lienz is an excellent starting point for trips over the magnificent Grossglockner Road and equally stunning valleys of East Tirol.

▲ LINZ (26 D3)
OBERÖSTERREICH *pop. 204,000*
The Danube River bisects Linz, capital of Upper Austria, and creates a major thoroughfare for rail, highway and river routes. The town has a number of old buildings and makes an ideal stopover for travelers from Salzburg to Vienna.

Among the city's places of interest is the Old Cathedral, where Anton Bruckner, the great Austrian composer of church music, was an organist.

STIFT ST. FLORIAN ABBEY, 18 kilometers (11 miles) east, is an excellent example of baroque architecture.

Said to be the largest abbey in Austria, it contains valuable paintings and the tomb of Anton Bruckner.

MARIA WÖRTH (26 D1)
KÄRNTEN *pop. 1,050*
One of the oldest Christian settlements in the area, Maria Wörth lies on the south shores of the warm Wörthersee, and is a flourishing resort away from the bustling tourist routes.

MARIAZELL (26 D2)
STEIERMARK *pop. 2,200, elev. 870m. (2,854ft.)*
Mariazell is a resort much favored by the Austrians. The town has a ski school, chairlift and facilities for winter sports.

MELK (26 D3) ★
NIEDERÖSTERREICH *pop. 6,000*
Ancient Melk, on the Danube River, marks the beginning of the Wachau, a beautiful stretch of winding river and vine-covered hillsides in Lower Austria.

Between 976 and 1110 AD, Melk was the seat of the Babenberg dukes, who ruled Austria. The town was later immortalized in the great German medieval epic poem *Nibelungenlied*.

STIFT MELK (Abbey of Melk), founded in 1089 on a cliff high above the river, was rebuilt between 1702 and 1726 in splendid high baroque style.

It is reputed to be the largest monastic building in Lower Austria – the south façade alone is 262 meters (860 feet) long. The library, which contains somewhere in the region of 100,000 volumes and other treasures, can be viewed.

ROBBER BARONS
In a romantic spot about 13 kilometers (8 miles) north of Melk, the ruined medieval castle of Aggstein has a grisly past. The knights who owned the castle were little more than highwaymen, robbing everyone who passed and incarcerating their victims in a narrow cell, called the *Rosengärtlein* (rose garden), until the ransom was paid.

AUSTRIA

MONDSEE (26 C2)
OBERÖSTERREICH *pop. 2,200*

Mondsee is a scenic summer resort town north west of the lake of the same name. The 11-kilometer (7-mile) long lake is one of the warmest north of the Alps, making it suitable for watersports.

OBERGURGL (26 B1)
TIROL *pop. 300, elev. 1,930m. (6,332ft.)*

The highest ski village in Austria, Obergurgl teems with skiers until late spring, when summer visitors begin to arrive. Reached by a mountain road that branches off the main Landeck-Innsbruck road, it is a starting point for glacier tours.

RADSTADT (26 C2)
SALZBURG *pop. 4,100, elev. 862m. (2,828ft.)*

A well-known winter sports resort, quaint Radstadt is an ideal starting point for mountain walks and climbs.

SAALBACH (26 C2)
SALZBURG *pop. 2,700, elev. 1,003m. (3,291ft.)*

Saalbach, in the Glemm Valley, is one of the most prestigious ski resorts in the Alps. The town includes nearly 204 kilometers (125 miles) of ski runs of all grades, and numerous skiing facilities. Other sporting activities, including climbing, hiking and golf, are also available.

ST. ANTON (26 A2)
TIROL *pop. 2,200, elev. 1,287m. (4,222ft.)*

St. Anton is the site of what is said to be the oldest ski school in Europe. The nearby valley station of a cable railroad provides easy access to 2,811-meter (9,222-foot) Valluga, which has a marvelous view as well as some unsurpassed ski terrain.

ST. GILGEN
SALZBURG *pop. 3,000*

St. Gilgen is a popular summer resort on Wolfgangsee, a well-known lake south east of Salzburg in the lake district. Surrounded by mountains, Wolfgangsee is 10 kilometers (6 miles) long and 114

meters (375ft) deep, and is a scenic summer resort.

ST. WOLFGANG (26 C2)
OBERÖSTERREICH *pop. 2,700*

Motorboat tours of the lovely Wolfgangsee depart from St. Wolfgang, a well-known resort. The town also is the starting point for the cogwheel railroad that ascends the 1,783-meter (5,850-foot) Schafberg from May to October.

▲ SALZBURG (26 C2) ★
SALZBURG *pop. 140,000*

Enchanting Salzburg, capital of the province of the same name, is almost in the center of Austria.

Flanking the Salzach River on the northern edge of the Eastern Alps, it is considered one of the most beautiful European cities because of its mountainous countryside and splendid architecture. Hikers head for the 1,853-meter (6,079-foot) Untersberg peak, accessible by cable car, and smaller Gaisberg. Also nearby are several lakes.

The birthplace of Wolfgang Amadeus Mozart, it is host to the Salzburg Festival from late July through August. Palace Concerts are held almost daily between Easter and October and less frequently during the rest of the year. Salzburg also celebrates an Easter Festival and Mozart Memorial Week, which takes place the last week in January.

DOM (Cathedral) is considered a fine baroque building north of the Alps.

ERZABTEI ST. PETER (Benedictine Abbey of St. Peter), 1 St. Peter Bezirk, was established during the late 7th century and is noted for its catacombs.

LUSTSCHLOSS HELLBRUNN (Hellbrunn Pleasure Castle) was built in the early 17th century for Bishop Marcus Sitticus. Watch out for the trick fountains – some operate mechanical figures, others balance balls on water jets. Wear casual clothes when visiting: hidden spouts can drench sightseers.

MARIONETTENTHEATER, Schwarzstrasse 24 near Mirabell Palace, has a repertory puppet company that performs from mid-April through September and tours the world in other months. The operas of Mozart are a specialty.

SEEFELD (26 B2) ★
TIROL *pop. 2,300, elev. 1,200m. (3,937ft.)*
Seefeld, one of Tirol's most popular and elegant winter resorts, boasts some fine cross-country skiing. The Gothic Parish Church has elaborate vaulting as well as mural paintings.

Beyond Seefeld, neighboring Bavaria is a pleasant summertime excursion area.

TAKING AIM
In August a special shooting competition is staged on the Prebersee, 8 kilometers (5 miles) north east of Tamsweg. Participants have to aim at the mirror image of the target on the lake. The bullets are then deflected off the surface and directed onto the target.

TAMSWEG (26 C2)
SALZBURG *pop. 5,260, elev. 949m. (3,114ft.)*
Nestling between mountains is the main town of the area called Lungau. Formerly an important medieval trading center, it is now a particularly favorite place in which to go hiking.

VELDEN AM WÖRTHERSEE
KÄRNTEN *pop. 7,700*
The largest summer resort in the Carinthian lake district, fashionable Velden stretches along the western bay of the Wörthersee.

Watersports are the great attraction by day, while a casino draws crowds at night. Dellach, west of the town, has an excellent golf course.

VIENNA – *see Wien on p.31.*

WAGRAIN
SALZBURG *pop. 2,900*
Wagrain is a small resort town in a spectacular mountain setting. Its recreational opportunities include swimming, tennis, skeet shooting, fishing, hiking on mountain paths and skiing on the resort's runs.

ZELL AM SEE (26 C2)
SALZBURG *pop. 7,960*
One of Austria's best known vacation resorts, this charming town derives its popularity from its idyllic position on the shores of an Alpine lake, surrounded by high mountains.

There are extensive facilities for skiers, and the lake is also perfect for many kinds of watersports in summer.

WONDERFUL WATERFALLS
A narrow-gauge railway line connects Zell am See with Krimml, where you can see some of the most impressive waterfalls in Europe. A steam engine makes the journey on certain days (contact the local tourist information office for details).

ZELL AM ZILLER (26 B2)
TIROL *pop. 1,870, elev. 535m. (1,754ft.)*
Surrounded by forests, Zell am Ziller is a busy summer and winter resort.

FESTIVE FROLICS
In May the village of Zell am Ziller celebrates the *Gauderfest*, a folklore festival that features competitions and potent *Gauderbier*, brewed specially for the occasion.

ZÜRS (26 A2)
VORARLBERG *elev. 1,596m. (5,237ft.)*
Zürs is one of Austria's smallest but most exclusive winter sports resorts. It is also one of the oldest, as skiing instruction began here in 1906. Zürs has only a few luxury hotels, but the surrounding terrain and the facilities on offer are superb.

THE BALKANS

The Balkans have always been a crossroads in Europe. In the one ostensibly communist country of Yugoslavia, there were Catholic Croats, Orthodox Serbs, Bosnian Muslims and other ethnic groups, now fighting over territories. Some areas that are currently unsafe for travel have not been covered in detail here. However, the on-going disputes hide the fact that there are Balkan countries, such as Slovenia and Albania, which are perfectly safe to visit. Slovenia shares a border and some breathtaking Alpine scenery with Austria, and an Adriatic coastline with Italy, while farther south ex-communist Albania offers archeological remains and unspoilt mountain scenery that reflect its Albanian name of *Shqiperi*: Eagle's country.

Left Stunning Lake Bled in Slovenia, once a popular tourist spot
Above Colorful designs adorn houses in the attractive city of Lubljana, Slovenia

Things to Know

- **Area**: Albania: 28,748 square kilometers (11,100 square miles); Slovenia: 20,256 square kilometers (7,821 square miles); Croatia: 56,539 square kilometers (21, 820 square miles); Bosnia: 51,129 square kilometers (19,740 square miles); Federal Republic of Yugoslavia: 102,170 square kilometers (39,450 square miles)
- **Population**: Albania: 3,250,000; Slovenia: 2,020,000; Croatia: 5 million; Bosnia (no reliable population information); Federal Republic of Yugoslavia: 11 million
- **Capital**: **Albania**: Tiranë
  Slovenia: Ljubljana
  Croatia: Zagreb
  Bosnia-Herzegovina: Sarajevo
  Federal Republic of Yugoslavia: Belgrade
- **Languages**: Albanian; Slovene; Croatian; Serbo-Croatian; Serbian
- **Economy**: **Albania**: major exports: mining products, eg. chromite, copper ore; tobacco, wool, fruit; **Slovenia**: industry, agriculture, forestry, tourism.
  Major exports: machines, transport equipment, industrial products
- **Passport Requirements**: Albania/Slovenia: required for U.S. citizens.
- **Visa Requirements**: Albania: no visa required. $10 airport fee payable on departure.
  Slovenia: no reliable information available
- **Currency**: Albania: the *lek* (Lk).
  Slovenia: the *tolar* (SIT), divided into 100 *stotins*. Due to currency fluctuations, the exchange rate is subject to change.
- **Bank Opening Hours**: Albania: 8:30am–1pm Monday–Friday; Slovenia: 8am–6pm Monday–Friday; 8am–12pm Saturday.
- **Store Opening Hours**: Albania: 9am–6pm Monday–Saturday; Slovenia: 7:30am–7pm Monday–

ALBANIA – History

Albania's historic towns bear witness to its long history of foreign invasions. The ancient Greeks and Romans left their marks on **Apollonia** and **Butrinti**, which are among the most important archeological sites in the Balkans. The port of **Durrës** also boasts significant classical remains. The museum towns of **Berat** and **Gjirokastër**, with their hilltop citadels, preserve the influence of the Ottoman Turks.

Tiranë, the capital, much affected by the unrest that accompanied the fall of communism, is slowly emerging from its long, self-imposed isolation from the rest of the world.

Food and Drink

Albanian cuisine bears signs of Greek and Turkish influence. Some typical dishes are *byrek* (minced meat, vegetables, eggs and cheese in flaky pastry); *fergese* (made with meat, eggs, white cheese and garlic); *koran* (succulent pink fresh-water fish from Lake Ohrid); and *fasule* (a thick soup of white, dry beans and onions).

The quality of locally produced wines is variable but some of the red wines are worth drinking.

Getting Around

Albania's transport systems are limited and unreliable. Albania's railways suffered considerable damage during the

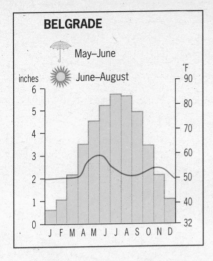

BELGRADE

May–June

inches
June–August
°F

revolution in 1992, and long-distance buses are cheap but extremely crowded. It is inadvisable to bring private cars into Albania.

ACCOMMODATIONS
Standards of comfort and service do not yet measure up to those found in Western Europe and the U.S. Albtourist runs hotels and holiday villages throughout the country, including the Llogara Tourist Village, situated in the high pine forest of a National Park, 37 kilometers (23 miles) from the city of Vlorë.

SLOVENIA – HISTORY
Slovenia lays claim to considerable geographical and cultural diversity.
Ljubljana, the capital, lies on a broad plain in the centre of Slovenia. The city's old quarter, situated between a thousand-year-old hilltop castle and the Ljubljana River, bears many Austro-Hungarian and Italian influences and boasts several splendid churches, palaces and monuments.

North-west Slovenia is a region of alpine valleys, mountains, wooded hills and beautiful glacial lakes, while eastern Slovenia has spring waters and thermal spas. Towards the north east lie the fertile plains and forests of Pannonia.

West of Ljubljana is the Karst region, a windswept limestone plateau famous for spectacular underground cave systems. Further west, Lipica, near the Italian border, is home to the famous Lippizaner white horses.

Along the Adriatic Coast are a string of attractive seaports and coastal resorts. The ancient ports of **Koper**, Izola and Piran were each subject to Venetian rule for five centuries and retain a distinctly Italian character.

FOOD AND DRINK
Slovenia's cuisine draws upon Alpine, Mediterranean and Central European influences.
There is a distinct Austrian flavor to the sausages, dumplings, Strudel and cakes of Slovenia's Alpine region, while the excellent seafood and pasta dishes found along the Adriatic coast have more than a taste of Italy.

Slovenia is best known abroad for its white wines, particularly such Rizlings as *Laski* and *Rienski* from the north east. Among the reds are the ruby-colored *Teran*. Slovenes also distil strong liquors from apples, pears, honey, plums, bilberries, and cherries.

GETTING AROUND

BY ROAD
Slovenia has over 241 kilometers (150 miles) of highway, over half of which have four lanes.
A small toll is charged on some highway sections: for example Razdrto–Ljubljana, Ljubljana–Kranj, Arjavas–Maribor/ Hoce.
Speed limits are 60 k.p.h. (37 m.p.h.) in towns, 80 k.p.h. (50 m.p.h.) on B roads, 100 k.p.h. (62 m.p.h.) on A roads and 120 k.p.h. (75 m.p.h.) on highways.

Emergency roadside help is available 24 hours a day from the Slovene Automobile Association (A.M.Z.) – dial 987 (see p.17 for other clubs).

Friday; 7:30am–1pm Saturday.
- **BEST BUYS:** Albania: handicrafts, briar pipes, filigree jewelry, rugs, copperware.
  Slovenia: ceramics, glass, wood carvings, leather goods
- **PUBLIC HOLIDAYS:** No information available for Albania.
  Slovenia: January 1, 2; February 8; Easter Sunday; Easter Monday; April 27; May 1, 2; June 25; August 15; October 31; November 1; December 25, 26
- **NATIONAL TOURIST OFFICES:**
  Albania: All tourist enquiries should be directed to Albania's embassies abroad.
  Albanian Mission
  320 East 79th Street
  New York
  NY 10021
  U.S.A.
  Albanian Embassy
  6 Wilton Court
  59 Ecclestone Square
  London
  SW1V 1PH
  England
  Tel: 0171 976 5295
  Slovenian Tourist Office
  122 East and 42nd Street
  Suite 3006,
  New York
  NY 10168 0072
  U.S.A.
  Tel: 212/682 58 96
  Slovenian Tourist Office
  57 Grosvenor Street
  London
  W1X 9DA
  England
  Tel: 0171 499 7488
- **AMERICAN EMBASSY:**
  Rruga E Elbasanit 103
  Tiranë
  Albania
  Tel: 355 42 32875
  4 Prazakova
  61000 Ljubljana
  Slovenia
  Tel: 301 485

BY RAIL

The Slovenian railway is well connected to the European rail network. Direct trains link Slovenia with Italy, Austria, Hungary and Croatia.

Notable is the EuroCity Mimara train that connects Ljubljana with Munich and Leipzig.

ACCOMMODATIONS

Hotels in Slovenia are divided into the following categories: L (deluxe), A (first class), B (superior tourist class with private bath), and C (rooms have hot and cold water but not usually their own bathroom). Private rooms can be rented in tourist regions through tourist offices or agencies. Campgrounds are plentiful.

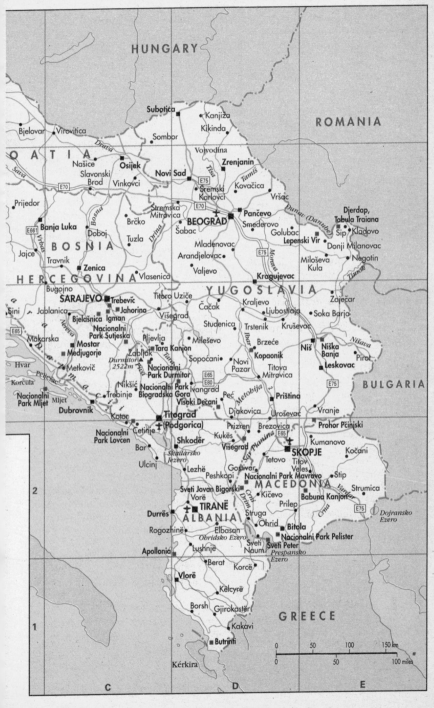

PLACES OF INTEREST

★ HIGHLIGHTS ★	
Berat, Albania	(see p.46)
Bled, Slovenia	(see p.47)
Bohinjsko, Slovenia	(see p.47)
Gjirokastër, Albania	(see p.46)
Ljubljana, Slovenia	(see p.47)
Postojnska Jama, Slovenia	(see p.47)

APOLLONIA (45 D2)
ALBANIA

The ancient Greek colonial settlement of Apollonia was founded in 588 BC near the Vjoses River and named after the god Apollo. In Roman times it was a center for Greek learning. Cicero described it as *"urbs gravis et nobilis"* – "a dignified and noble city." The site of the ancient city includes the remains of shops and houses, the theater, acropolis, and a nympheum, the Fountain of Cephisus, from the 3rd century BC.

BERAT (45 D1) ★
ALBANIA

A hilltop citadel above the banks of the Osumit River, Berat's origins lie in an ancient Illyrian settlement founded in the 4th to 5th centuries BC. It has been declared a U.N.E.S.C.O. World Heritage City in recognition of the importance of its treasures. The citadel has 14 churches, including the Church of Shen Todri (St. Theodore), with excellent 16th-century frescoes as well as some fine icons.

BUTRINTI (45 D1)
ALBANIA

Known to the ancient world as Buthrotum, Butrint is one of the most important archeological sites in Albania. Founded, according to legend, by refugees from Troy, Butrint was settled in turn by Illyrians, Greeks and Romans.

Among the remains are Illyrian walls (5th–4th century BC), the Temple of Aesculapius (3rd–2nd century BC), the amphitheater and the gymnasium.

DURRËS (45 C2)
ALBANIA

In ancient times the Adriatic port of Durrës was an important Greek colonial settlement, founded during the 7th century BC. In 1990 and 1991 Durrës was the scene for the attempted mass exodus of Albanians trying to escape desperate economic conditions. Today it is the center of Operation Pelican, the European Union food-aid operation. Among the town's ancient remains is the largest Roman amphitheater in the Balkans.

Other sites of interest include the Archeological Museum and the Summer Palace of King Zog, built in a grand Italianate style in the 1930s.

GJIROKASTËR (45 D1) ★
ALBANIA

A U.N.E.S.C.O. World Heritage City, Gjirokastër lies on the slopes of Mali i Gjere beneath a hilltop citadel. Many of the houses in the narrow and winding streets of the town have the character of little fortresses. The citadel itself was originally built in the 13th century, rebuilt by Ali Pasha of Tepelena in 1811 to 1812.

TIRANË (45 D2)
ALBANIA

In the Middle Ages Tiranë was a small village, but grew into a moderately sized town under Ottoman rule. It was chosen as Albania's capital after the First World War. Tourist facilities are undeveloped, but the adventurous will find much of interest, especially the Mosque of Etem Bey, constructed from 1794 and 1821. Also noteworthy are the Popular Cultural Museum, the Martyrs Cemetery and the Archeological Museum.

SKANDERBERG SQUARE, named for Albania's national hero, stands in the heart of the city. A bronze equestrian statue of Skanderberg was erected in 1968 on the 500th anniversary of his death. The Palace of Culture houses a concert hall, movie theaters and the National Library.

BLED (45 A5) ★
SLOVENIA

A fashionable resort in the 19th century and between the wars, Bled remains Slovenia's most popular holiday destination. Surrounded by forests and mountains, Bled is a center for such outdoor pursuits as skiing, walking, horse riding, angling and even parachuting. Its beautiful lake is the site for an international rowing regatta.

Bled Castle, perched on a 100-meter (328-foot) cliff, overlooks the lake.

The tiny island in the center of the lake is reached by gondola-like boats, and is home to the baroque church of Sveta Marjka Božja.

BOHINJSKO JEREZO (45 A5) ★
SLOVENIA

The 5-kilometer (3-mile) Bohinjsko Jerezo (Lake Bohinj) is situated 32 kilometers (20 miles) west of Bled in the Triglav Alpine National Park. Visitors can enjoy alpine and cross-country skiing in winter and a variety of other outdoor pursuits throughout the year.

MOUNT TRIGLAV, which soars to 2,863 meters (9,395 feet), is Slovenia's highest mountain. Experienced hikers wishing to ascend the mountain are advised to climb with an official guide recommended by the tourist office in Bled.

BOVEC (45 A5)
SLOVENIA

Bovec is a popular alpine resort in the upper Soča Valley. In winter, skiers come to tackle the pistes of 2,585-meter (8,480-feet) Mount Kanin, which rises above the town. Slovenia's only high mountain ski resort, Mount Kanin, normally has snow from November to May.

KOPER (45 A4)
SLOVENIA

This Adriatic coastal town, known as Capodistria in Italian, was ruled by Venice from 1279 to 1797. The town's old quarter retains a particularly strong Venetian character.

KRANJSKA GORA (45 A5)
SLOVENIA

Situated near the borders of Austria and Italy, 808 meters (2,650 feet) above sea level, Kranjska Gora has grown from a tiny Alpine village to the largest winter sports center in Slovenia. In summer, it is a base for hiking and mountaineering.

LJUBLJANA (45 A5) ★
SLOVENIA
pop. 340,000

The capital of Slovenia, Ljubljana is an attractive city whose character owes much to its long connection with the Austro-Hungarian empire. The city's old quarter is situated between Castle Hill and the Ljubljana River. You will find examples of Renaissance and baroque architecture, and of art nouveau. The celebrated 20th-century architect Jože Plečnik (1872–1957) also left his mark, notably in the two outer bridges of the Tromostovje (Triple Bridge), which connects the city's old and new quarters.

LJUBLJANA CASTLE stands on top of a hill in the center of the old town. Superb views from the tower over the old city and the Kamnik, Julian and Karawanken Alps to the north and north west.

PORTOROŽ (45 A4)
SLOVENIA

"Port of Roses" is Slovenia's biggest coastal resort. Its popularity dates to the mid-19th century when well-heeled visitors came to enjoy the properties of local mud and salt baths. Today stroll along the seafront, lie on sandy beaches, and gamble in the casino. Venice is only two hours away by hydrofoil.

POSTOJNSKA JAMA (POSTOJNA CAVES) (45 A5) ★
SLOVENIA

A labyrinth of underground caves, lakes and streams lies beneath the plateau of Slovenia's Karst region.

Over millions of years, the action of rainwater on stone has created spectacular rock formations.

BALTIC STATES

THE PEOPLE OF ESTONIA, LATVIA AND LITHUANIA HAVE LIVED THROUGH DRAMATIC EVENTS, AND ARE HAPPY TO SHARE THEIR EXPERIENCES WITH THE VISITORS THEIR COUNTRIES ARE NOW STARTING TO ATTRACT. GUIDES WILL TELL YOU WHERE THEY WERE WHEN REVOLUTION CAME, DELIGHTED THAT THEY ARE NO LONGER UNDER SOVIET DOMINATION. NOW THEY TALK FREELY OF THEIR OWN CULTURES, THRIVING AGAIN IN THEIR DIFFERENT WAYS.

ESTONIA AND ITS CAPITAL, TALLINN, ARE THE MOST WESTERNIZED, USED TO RECEIVING VISITORS FROM FINLAND. ABOVE THE CENTER OF MEDIEVAL TALLINN STANDS THE 14TH-CENTURY TOWER OF PIKK HERMANN ("TALL HERMANN"), FROM WHERE, IN 1989, A TWO-MILLION-STRONG HUMAN CHAIN BEGAN, TRAILING TO THE LITHUANIAN CAPITAL VILNIUS, DEMANDING INDEPENDENCE FROM MOSCOW.

Left LATVIA'S MEDIEVAL CAPITAL, RIGA, ON THE BANKS OF THE DAUGAVA RIVER
Above THE SPLENDID DOMES OF THE ALEXANDER NEVSKY CATHEDRAL IN TALLINN, ESTONIA

THINGS TO KNOW

- **AREA:** Estonia: 45,216 square kilometers (17,458 square miles);. Latvia: 64,589 square kilometers (24,938 square miles);. Lithuania: 65,300 square kilometers (25,174 square miles)
- **POPULATION:** Estonia: 1,574,000; Latvia: 2,686,200; Lithuania: 3,737,000
- **CAPITAL:** Estonia: Tallinn; Latvia: Riga; Lithuania: Vilnius
- **LANGUAGES:** Estonia: Estonian; Latvia: Latvian; Lithuania: Lithuanian and Polish.
  Russian is understood by the majority of people in these countries, but not willingly spoken.
- **ELECTRICITY:** 220v/50Hz AC; two round pin plugs.
- **PASSPORT REQUIREMENTS:** Required for U.S. citizens.
- **VISA REQUIREMENTS:** Required for U.S. citizens to Latvia only, valid for 30 days.
  For information about obtaining a visa in advance, telephone the Embassy of Estonia on 202 789 0320, the Embassy of Latvia on 202 726 8213 or the Embassy of Lithuania on: 202 234-5860.
- **DUTY FREE ITEMS:** Lithuania: 200 cigarettes, 20 cigars or 250 grams of tobacco; 2 liters of table wine; 1 liter of fortified wine; 1 liter of spirits; 10 liters of beer. No limit on personal items. In Latvia,: 1 liter alcohol and 200 cigarettes. Estonia has a lower alcohol allowance of 2 liters of ordinary wine or 1 liter of strong and 1 liter of ordinary wine.
- **CURRENCIES:** The currency unit in Estonia is the *Kroon*, divided into 100 *senti*; in Latvia it is the *Lat*, and in Lithuania it is the *Lita*, divided into 100 *cento*. Travelers cheques cannot be exchanged at many places; Amex is most widely accepted. U.S. $ and German Deutsch Marks are the most useful currencies, but the amount exported must not exceed the amount imported. Money can be changed at banks, hotels, airports, railroad stations and currency

HISTORY

The histories of Estonia and Latvia are essentially the same; Lithuania's also would be if not for their entry into an alliance with Poland that was to last for nearly four centuries. Distinct differences in culture and language remain, however.

The Latvians (or Letts) and Lithuanians descend from Indo-European stock; the Estonians belong to the Finno-Ugric group. Estonia and Latvia became considerably Germanized from the 13th to mid-16th centuries, so Lutheranism is the predominant religion. Most Lithuanians are Roman Catholic, due to long associations with Poland.

All three republics were forcibly Sovietized following World War II.

The Baltic region was known in ancient times as a source of fine amber. Trade with the Roman Empire and Germanic tribes continued throughout the whole of the 6th century.

With the decline of the Roman Empire, however, came less businesslike encounters. Vikings made their way into the Baltics in about 850 AD, followed by the Danes and Swedes in the 11th and 12th centuries. At the same time the Balts were experiencing their first hostile encounters with the Russians. But it was the Germans who were to gain the first real foothold into the region.

The German bishop Albert of Buxhoevdén began to establish his presence along the Daugava River in about 1200, and within 30 years his Knights of the Sword controled all of present-day Latvia and southern Estonia – a land known then as Livonia.

In 1237, the Teutonic Order absorbed the Knights of the Sword and over the next century extended their holdings to include the land of northern Estonia and all of Prussia to the south. The next 200 years saw great cultural development, agricultural improvements and commercial prosperity made possible by the Hanseatic League.

The German influence was not all-pervasive, however. The native Estonians, Latvians and Livs, though relegated to mere serfdom, managed to maintain their age-old traditions through folklore and craft work.

Meanwhile, various Lithuanian tribes were desperately trying to resist the

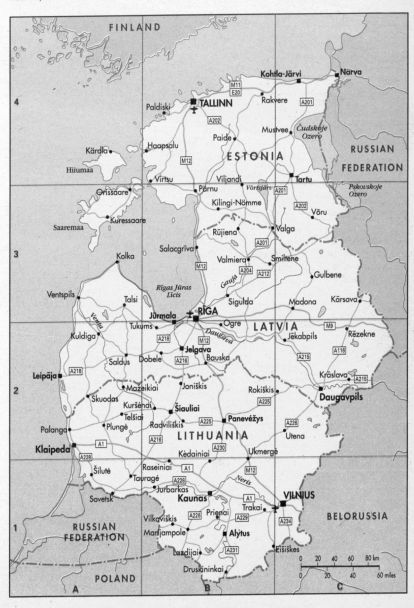

exchange points. Few places accept credit cards apart from car rental companies and larger hotels in Latvia. However the situation is improving.

- **BANK OPENING HOURS:** 9am–12:30pm Monday–Friday. Some open afternoons.
- **STORE OPENING HOURS:** Large stores stay open for nine hours, but may open at 8, 9 or 10am and close at 6, 7 or 8pm. They shut for an hour at lunchtime – sometimes 2–3pm. On Saturday they close at 5pm if open in the afternoon.
- **PUBLIC HOLIDAYS:** January 1; Lithuanian Independence Day, February 16; Estonian Independence Day, February 24; Good Friday; Easter Monday (Estonia); May Day, (Estonia and Latvia), May 1; Victory Day (Estonia) and Ligo Holiday (Latvia), June 23; St. John's Day (Estonia and Latvia) June 24; King Mindaugas' Crowning Day (Lithuania), July 6; All Saints' Day (Lith- uania), November 1; Rebirth Day (Estonia) November 16; Latvian Independence Day, November 18; December 25/26, New Year's Eve.
- **NATIONAL TOURIST OFFICES:**
  Pikk 71
  EE-0001 Tallinn
  Estonia
  Tel: 3722 601700
  Pils Square 4
  LV-1050 Riga
  Latvia
  Tel: 3712 229945
  Gedimino 30/1
  2695 Vilnius
  Lithuania
  Tel: 3702 226706
- **AMERICAN EMBASSIES:**
  Kentmanni 20
  Tallinn, Estonia
  Tel: 312 021
  Raina Boulevard 7
  Riga, Latvia
  Tel: 210 005 or 6
  6 Akmenu Street
  Vilnius
  Lithuania
  Tel: 223 031

German threat in a land which was then called Samogitia.

United under Grand Duke Mindaugas in 1236, the Lithuanians enjoyed a succession of powerful leaders who by 1430 had extended their territory as far east as Moscow and south as the Black Sea.

In 1385, to counter the encroaching Teutonic Order, Grand Duke Jogaila made a union with Poland and in turn became its king.

In 1410, Polish-Lithuanian forces broke the German stranglehold on the Baltics with a decisive victory at Tannenberg, hastening the decline of the Teutonic Order.

But the union with the more culturally advanced Poland served to diminish a Lithuanian identity.

Its citizens fell into serfdom and, like their northern neighbours, resorted to cultural self-preservation.

With the dissolution of the Teutonic Order in 1561, Estonia and Latvia again became a battleground. Sweden advanced from the north, Poland-Lithuania from the south; and, led by Ivan the Terrible, Russia from the east.

The era of devastation culminated in the Great Northern War of 1700 to 1721, by which Peter the Great finally claimed the Baltics for Russia. The conquest became complete in 1795 with the annexation of Lithuania from Poland.

The 19th century saw implemented a precarious balance of social reforms on the one hand and policies of Russification on the other.

Advances in education and human rights were countered with strict controls on language, religion and judicial and political participation.

Consequently, national identities were reawakened, but had to await the opportunity for realization.

The time came with the Bolshevik Revolution of 1917. Each of the Baltic States declared its independence and managed to maintain it through the First World War and a world-wide economic depression, until 1940.

The rise of Nazi Germany put an end to independence in the Baltic States. The alliance between Germany and the Soviet Union left them in the hands of Stalin, who dismantled their governments and subjected nearly 150,000 people to deportation or execution.

When the German-Soviet alliance ended in 1941, German forces moved in and the atrocities continued. Nearly 250,000, mostly Jews, were executed. At the war's end, another 200,000 fled advancing Soviet troops, and by 1949 about 500,000 had been deported to northern Russia and Siberia as the region was forcibly repopulated.

Over the next several decades farms were collectivised and an industrial economy began.

With the advent in 1987 of new Soviet leader Mikhail Gorbachev and his campaign of *perestroika* (restructuring) came increases in nationalist sentiment. Non-Communist political parties in each of the republics succeeded in legitimizing the native language and establishing freedoms of speech and the press as well as religion.

In March 1990, Lithuania became the first republic to declare its independence. Estonia and Latvia followed in August 1991 after the failed Soviet coup.

Formal recognitions of independence were given by both the US and the Soviet Union in September 1991.

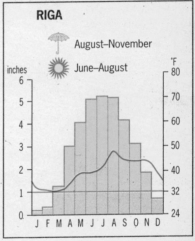

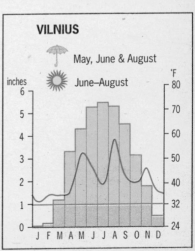

BALTIC STATES • ESTONIA, LATVIA, LITHUANIA

FOOD AND DRINK

The Baltic States offer widely varying cuisines – meat and dairy products feature widely.

Other common dishes to all three are pancakes (filled with fruit, jam or cheese) and sour cream. Surprisingly, there is little fresh fish. Most is smoked and salted.

In Estonia some traditional favorites are *seaspraad*, pork with sauerkraut, and *hapukapsa*, sauerkraut soup. *Sult*, or jellied veal, and *taidetud basikarind*, a roasted, stuffed veal, are just two of many good meat dishes.

Many Latvians wake up to a *zamieku brokastis*, or "peasant's breakfast," consisting of a huge omelette. Other traditional meals are *maizes zupa ar putukrejumu*, corn soup with cream, and *biezpiens ar kartupeliem*, *krejumi*, cottage cheese with potato, cream and butter.

Common fare in Lithuania are *virtinukai*, or ravioli-like dishes. Also popular are *bulviniai blynai*, potato pancakes; *cepelinai*, dumplings; and *šaltibarščiai*, cold soup. Unique to Lithuania is a strong local spirit called Black Balsam.

SPORTS AND RECREATION

Summer activities along the Baltic coast include sailing and windsurfing, while inland, canoeing (in Latvia and Lithuania) and fishing are popular on the many rivers.

In national parks, horse riding and walking have great appeal. Spectator sports include basketball, for which Lithuania has won Olympic golds.

GETTING AROUND

Since independence, each country has set up its own airline, mostly routed to Germany, Scandinavia and The Netherlands. Many north European carriers fly to the Baltic States, making it easily accessible from the U.S. via Amsterdam, Frankfurt or Scandinavia. America

TransAir operates twice-weekly flights from New York to Riga and summer charter flights operate from Chicago to Kaunas. Check with your travel agent.

Ferries take passengers from Helsinki and Stockholm to Tallinn. Riga is served by ferries from Kiel and Travemunde in Germany, from Copenhagen in Denmark and Stockholm in Sweden.

Public transportation in the Baltic States is cheap and slow. Cities are linked by trains (soft class, the highest, is only available on inter-city routes) and buses; towns are served by trolley buses, trams, local trains as well as taxis.

Car rental is available from international rental companies – take your driver's license and credit card with you and enough cash for a deposit.

Comprehensive insurance is advisable and cars should always be locked when they are parked.

The main roads are good; speed limits in built-up areas are 50 k.p.h. (30 m.p.h.) in Estonia, 60 k.p.h. (37 m.p.h.) in Latvia and Lithuania. Seat belts must be worn, and Estonian drivers keep their lights on in daytime. Gas stations are not in short supply, but sometimes gas is; it is the custom to pay for it before the pump is turned on. Only in Latvia can drivers drink alcohol before driving, with a limit of 0.05%.

ACCOMMODATIONS

Hotels are not classified and cover a wide range of prices, standards and architecture. Most hotels are at the cheaper end of the market, though things are slowly changing for the better, and some new hotels of luxury standard have now been built as joint ventures with western partners. Demand for rooms in these and upgraded hotels exceeds supply, and it is advisable to reserve well in advance. Lodging in private houses can be arranged; there are also campsites and youth hostels.

PLACES OF INTEREST

TALLINN (51 B4)
ESTONIA *pop. 481,500*
Tallinn, the capital of Estonia, is a beautifully preserved medieval town with city walls, church spires and buildings with steeply tiled roofs.

The old port sits on a hill, Toompea, dominated by Toompea Castle, built in the early 13th century. Only two walls and three towers from the original structure remain. The 13th-century Toomkirk was destroyed by fire in 1684 and has been restored; it has a baroque-style altar and several carved tombs of Swedish commanders.

The 15th-century bastion Kiek-in-die-Kök, whose name translates as "look in the kitchen," got its name from the local saying that from the castle heights a person could see through all the chimneys and into the kitchens. It is now a museum with weapons, maps and models of early Tallinn.

The onion-domed Alexander Nevsky Cathedral is nearby.

KUNSTIMUUSEUM (Fine Arts Museum), in Kadriorg Park at 37 Weizenbergi Street, is housed in the baroque Kadriorg Palace and contains over 17,000 modern Estonian, Russian and European works of art.

RIGA (51 B3)
LATVIA *pop. 916,500*
Riga is the capital of Latvia, on the banks of the Daugava River. A Hanseatic port, it can trace its history back to about 1200 AD.

Relics abound in the section between the right bank of the river and the city's canal, and include old fortifications as well as the 14th-century Gunpowder Tower, occupied by the Latvian War Museum.

Riga Castle, from the same era, houses three different museums, including the Museum of Latvian History.

Several well-preserved examples of distinctly medieval architecture survive; among these are the 17th-century Dannenstern Mansion, the Mansion of Peter I and 13th-century St. Jacob's Church. Formerly a walled city, the only surviving remnant is the Swedish Gate, with nine cannon balls embedded in its wall.

A great port and industrial center, Riga also is a city of parks, gardens and theaters. Most notable among these are Mežparks, the Opera and Ballet and the Latvia Philharmonia Orchestra.

VILNIUS (51 C1)
LITHUANIA *pop. 697,000*
The cultural and industrial heart of Lithuania, as well as its capital, Vilnius, at the confluence of the Neris and Vilnia rivers, was important as early as 1323, when it was chosen as the seat of the powerful grand dukes of Lithuania.

As the city grew, magnificent buildings appeared; those surviving include the Aušros Vartai (Gates of Dawn) and the Church of Saints Peter and Paul.

Most places of interest are near Gediminas Square in the center of the city; the reconsecrated St. Stanislaus Cathedral, the 16th-century Gothic St. Anne's Church and 14th-century Gediminas Castle are outstanding.

Excursions can be made to the nearby lake country, site of Trakai, Lithuania's 14th-century fortress-capital 30 kilometers (20 miles) west complete with a ruined castle.

KAUNAS (51 B1)
LITHUANIA *pop. 429,900*
Lithuania's second largest city, Kaunas is at the confluence of the Nemunas and Neris rivers.

This important industrial center was the capital of Lithuania between World Wars I and II. Though the architecture is predominantly modern, several historical sites remain.

The 15th-century Gothic Church of Saints Peter and Paul at Aleksotas Street is the city's oldest, while nearby the ruins of 14th-century Kaunas Castle can also be visited.

BALTIC STATES • ESTONIA, LATVIA, LITHUANIA

BELGIUM

Belgium is rather a neglected country on the travel map, the butt of jokes elsewhere in Europe about "boring Belgium." Anyone who has been there, though, knows the truth: it offers beaches, the best beer and chocolate in Europe, artists like Bruegel and Rubens, spa towns, the beautiful town of Bruges, and the mountains of the Ardennes. Belgium illustrates the rainbow nature of Europe. South are the Walloons, who speak French, while in the North the Flemings speak Flemish (Dutch). Yet the Walloons are not French, nor the Flemings Dutch. The capital, Brussels, is an historic and attractive city — no surprise that members of the European Union chose it for their main base.

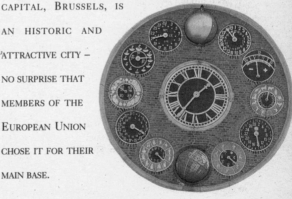

Left One of the more colorful parades which Belgium has to offer
Above The astronomical clock on the Zimmer Tower in Lier tells universal time

THINGS TO KNOW

- **AREA:** 30,519 square kilometers (11,799 square miles)
- **POPULATION:** 9,998,000
- **CAPITAL:** Brussel/Bruxelles (Brussels)
- **LANGUAGES:** Dutch, French and German
- **PASSPORT REQUIREMENTS:** Required for U.S. citizens.
- **VISA REQUIREMENTS:** Not required for stays up to three months.
- **DUTY-FREE ITEMS:** 200 cigarettes or 50 cigars or 100 cigarillos or 250 grams of tobacco; 2 liters of wine, 1 liter of liquor, 50 grams of perfume, one large bottle of toilet water, one still camera with 12 rolls of film, one movie camera with six rolls of film; one video camera. See also *The European Union*, page.xx
- **CURRENCY:** The currency unit is the Belgian *franc* (BF), divided into 100 *centimes*. Due to currency fluctuations, the exchange rate is subject to change.
- **BANK OPENING HOURS:** 9:30am–3:30 or 4pm Monday–Friday; many banks close for lunch.
- **STORE OPENING HOURS:** Major stores 9am–8pm Monday–Saturday, 9am–9pm Friday, others 9am–6pm Monday–Saturday.
- **PUBLIC HOLIDAYS:** January 1; Easter Monday; Labor Day, May 1; Ascension Day; Whitmonday; National Day, July 21; Assumption Day, August 15; All Saints' Day, November 1; Armistice Day, November 11; King's Birthday, November 15; December 25.
- **NATIONAL TOURIST OFFICES:** Belgian National Tourist Office 745 Fifth Avenue., Suite 714 New York, NY 10151 Tel: 212/ 758 8130 Fax: 212/ 355 7675 Commissariat-General De Tourisme: Grasmarkt 61/63 rue Marché-aux-Herbes B-1000 Brussel/Bruxelles Tel: (02) 504-03-90
- **AMERICAN EMBASSY:** 27 Boulevard du Régent B-1000 Brussel/Bruxelles Belgium Tel: (02) 513-38-30

HISTORY

Excellent ports and few natural defences have long made Frankish Belgium a natural battleground. Following Roman and Frankish occupations, the nation began to take shape under 14th-century Philip the Good, who annexed the Low Countries. Extending from the North Sea to the Rhône Valley, the duchy assumed commercial leadership in Europe, while the arts flourished. But with the death of Charles the Bold in 1477, control passed to the Habsburg rulers of Austria.

The Low Countries were allied with the Spanish Empire when the Austrian Charles I became King of Spain in the 16th century. With his abdication, internal tensions divided the area into the United Provinces (Holland) and the Spanish Netherlands (Belgium). France annexed Belgium and the principality of Liège in 1795, but Belgians were dissatisfied with French rule and the subsequent Napoleonic regime. With

Napoleon's defeat at Waterloo in 1815, the Congress of Vienna united Belgium with the United Provinces to form the Kingdom of the Netherlands. William of Orange, the first king, had to contend with a north that was Protestant and a south that was Catholic. On October 4, 1830, the southern provinces declared their independence, and the major European powers soon recognized the Kingdom of Belgium as a neutral nation.

Although Belgium was the scene of fierce battles in both World Wars, its recovery was swift and prosperous. The country's government is now a constitutional monarchy; local affairs are handled by nine provincial governments.

Belgium's King Baudouin was succeeded in 1993 by his brother, who became King Albert II. His wife is Queen Paola.

Internal cultural differences between the northern Flemish provinces and the southern French-speaking Walloon provinces have resulted in an unusual language situation. In the 19th century, French was the dominant language in business, government and education, though more than half of Belgium's population was Flemish-speaking. To diffuse tensions between the two groups, Flemish was made an equally official language in 1898. Today, Dutch (of which Flemish is a dialect) is the official language in the north, French in the south and German in the east. In Brussels, the capital, both Dutch and French are officially recognized.

FOOD AND DRINK

Surrounded by other countries known for their *haute cuisine*, Belgium has managed to create a cuisine that is unmistakably its own.

Tomates aux crevettes, tomatoes stuffed with shrimp, is a gustatory delight. *Witloof*, or chicory, garnishes a number of main dishes. The sandy Mechelen region produces wonderful asparagus; ham comes from the Ardennes. Mussels are especially good in Brussels and on the coast; in Namur fried eel is a local treat. Many varieties of *boudin*, or sausage, are always available. Seafood specialties such as lobster and *waterzooi* – fish or chicken stew – are invariably delicious. *Frites*, or fried potatoes, are a national favorite. Those with a sweet tooth can enjoy a variety of cakes, chocolates, waffles and typical biscuits, such as *speculoos*. Belgium also offers about 400 varieties of beer and nearly 200 types of *genièvre*, or gin.

SPORTS AND RECREATION

Belgian coastal resorts, particularly at Oostende, offer excellent swimming and watersports facilities. Deep sea, surf and trout fishing are available, but permits are required. Horse racing takes place in Brussels, Oostende, Waregem and Spa. Boaters can enjoy their sport at Oostende, Zeebrugge, Blankenberge

and Nieuwpoort. Golf, tennis and horseback riding facilities also are available. Other activities include canoeing on several rivers and along the coastline and skiing in the highlands.

GETTING AROUND

Belgium's excellent and varied transportation system includes electric rail lines throughout the country. Tourist season tickets, available for either five or eight days, can be obtained from most major railroad stations. Bicycles can be rented at many railroad stations as well. Cabs in the large cities are expensive, but trams and buses offer 1-day tickets that allow unlimited travel on both services.

Drivers in Belgium usually travel on a comprehensive system of toll-free highways. There are two highway numbering systems. A national network uses black and white signs with the prefix A; an international network uses green and white signs with the prefix E. Some "E" roads have a new numbering system that was introduced in 1986, so some signs may show two different numbers, an old and a new, for the same road. Road signs are in two languages: In the northern part of the country, signs are in Dutch (Flemish); in the south, they are in French. Brussels is the only area where signs are found in both languages.

AUTOMOBILE CLUB

The Touring Club Royal de Belgique (TCB, Royal Touring Club of Belgium), 44 rue de la Loi, Brussels, and the **Royal Automobile Club de Belgique** (RACB, Royal Automobile Club of Belgium), 53 rue d'Arlon, Brussels, have branch offices in various cities throughout Belgium. The symbol ▲ beside a city name indicates the presence of an AAA-affiliated automobile club branch. Not all auto clubs offer full travel services to AAA members.

The wearing of seat belts (if the car is so equipped) is mandatory for the driver and passengers. A child under 12 cannot occupy a front seat unless using a suitable restraint device or unless rear seats are not available or are already occupied by children. Speed limits are 50 k.p.h. (30 m.p.h.) in town, 90 k.p.h. (55 m.p.h.) on out-of-town roads and 120 k.p.h. (75 m.p.h.) on highways. Minimum speed on highways is 70 k.p.h. (45 m.p.h.). Non-residents of Belgium are required to pay fines for motoring violations on the spot in Belgian currency or U.S. dollars.

ACCOMMODATIONS

Belgium rates its hotels with from one to five stars – five stars being the best rating. The Belgian Tourist Authority publishes a list of lodgings; those approved by the authority post a special sign. The list can be obtained from Belgian tourist offices abroad as well as local tourist offices throughout Belgium. Breakfast is almost always included in the price of a room.

More than 800 campgrounds throughout Belgium provide inexpensive accommodations; some campgrounds offer a price reduction if you have an international camping carnet.

LANGUAGE

Dutch (Flemish), French and German are the three official languages in Belgium. Brussels is essentially bilingual (Dutch and French), due partly to its cultural and political importance and partly to its central location.

Flemish is spoken north of Brussels; French is spoken in the south and German in the east. (For useful expressions in French see p.249, for German see p.311, and for Dutch see p.467).

TIPPING

Generally, tipping is not practiced in Belgium because a 6 percent gratuity is usually included in the bill. If you do leave a tip of 10 percent, however, it will be readily accepted.

PRINCIPAL TOURING AREAS

Note: For descriptions of cities in **bold** type, see individual city listings.

Although French is widely spoken in Belgium, Flemish is the official language for the northern region of the country and is usually the *only* language spoken in that area.

Because of strong Flemish sentiments, all French place names have now been eliminated. Towns that were once known by their French spellings are now only referred to by their original Flemish names.

Among the towns whose names have been changed are the following: Bruges is now known as Brugge; Courtrai is Kortrijk; Louvain is Leuven; Malines is Mechelen; Ostend is Oostende; and Ypres is Ieper.

All road signs and European maps carry the Flemish designations. Brussels is still bilingual and is known as either Brussel (Flemish) or Bruxelles (French).

BRABANT

Belgium's only province not to be bordered by another country, Brabant is the heart of the nation and a centuries-old crossroads of the Continent.

It was a logical site for metropolitan growth: **Brussel/Bruxelles**, or **Brussels**, has a population of nearly 1 million. It also seemed to be an unfortunate choice for over six major European wars. **Waterloo**, the site of Napoléon's defeat, is the region's best-known battlefield.

EASTERN WALLOON PROVINCES

Belgium's land begins to rise in the south east, reaching the provinces of Liège, Luxembourg and Namur. The first region to be settled, this part of the country is an area of traditional Walloon sentiments. The picturesque Meuse River stretches between limestone cliffs, passing such economically important

BELGIUM

Sunlight reflecting the gabled houses on the River Leie at Korenlei (Corn Quay), in Ghent.

towns as **Dinant**, **Namur** and **Liège**. But summer visitors flock to the Ardennes region, which includes the best of the scenic Semois and Meuse valleys.

HAINAUT
Hainaut, a part of Walloon Belgium, has long shared economic and historical ties with neighboring France. The French architectural influence is most evident in **Tournai**, which boasts extensive art collections and the largest Gothic cathedral in Belgium. Not to be overlooked are the castle of Beloeil and ancient **Mons**, the provincial capital.

THE KEMPEN
The sandy, pine-strewn plain that supports much of industrialized Belgium is known unofficially as the Kempen; officially, it takes in the province of Antwerpen and Limburg. The port of **Antwerpen**, or **Antwerp**, on the River Schelde is the center of a large industrial and commercial area. Museum enthusiasts will enjoy the national art treasures to be found in the city. Outside the metropolitan area, **Mechelen** has its lovely 13th-century St. Rombaut's Cathedral.

WEST FLEMISH PROVINCES
East and West Flanders occupy the northern Flemish plain, which is criss-crossed by rivers and canals. In the north west, such delightful resorts as Zeebrugge and Het Zoute line the North Sea. Farther east, memorials pay tribute to past heroism, particularly in **Ieper**, rebuilt since its devastation in World War I. **Brugge** and **Gent**, once rival city-states, now vie for tourist attention with their splendid architecture.

BRUSSELS

☂ July–August

☀ May–September

inches | °F

6 — 90

5 — 80

4 — 70

3 — 60

2 — 50

1 — 40

0 — 32

J F M A M J J A S O N D

PLACES OF INTEREST

BELGIUM

▲ BRUSSEL/BRUXELLES ★

BRABANT *pop. 950,000*

Known as Brussel in Flemish, Bruxelles in French and Brussels in English, the capital of Belgium is an important banking, trade and transportation center, as well as the headquarters for the North Atlantic Treaty Organization (N.A.T.O.) and the European Union. The most influential leaders of Europe regularly convene in Brussels.

HOME OF THE EUROCRATS

Officially, there is no capital of Europe, but Brussels is the home of the European Commission, who often appear to be the driving force of the European ideal. As one of the centers of political power, Brussels has a cosmopolitan ambience, with cafés, pubs and restaurants creating a Euro-neighborhood in which the city's civil servants can be at their ease.

Skyscrapers and hotels have modernized the skyline of this French- and Flemish-speaking city. Old Brussels, with its narrow streets, brick shops and houses decorated with ornamental ironwork, recalls the city's medieval past. The *petit ceinture*, a series of boulevards where the city walls once stood, encircles the lower city, which contains the site of the Gothic Cathedral St. Michel, 13th-century Church of la Chappelle and the Gothic Church of Sablon. The upper city, with wide, tree-lined avenues, has large public squares and magnificent 18th- and 19th-century palaces.

Formerly home of the Renaissance scholar Erasmus, Brussels remains a cultural and educational center. The opera season runs from September to April, and the city has several excellent museums and art galleries.

One of Brussels' most prominent annual events is the Ommegang, a colorful pageant dating from 1549 and held at Grand Place in July. Titled Belgians don the costumes of their ancestors and join a procession led by a figure of Charles V.

Trips into the surrounding countryside can take in the castles and chateaux at Beersel, Gaasbeek, Groot-Bijgaarden, Horst and Rixensart. Near by are the grape-growing areas of Overijse, Hoeilaart and the Forest of Soignes, and the Abbaye de Villers ruins near Villers-la-Ville. Waterloo and its battlefield are about 16 kilometers (10 miles) south.

More information on the city and its attractions is available from the Tourist Office, 61 rue Marché-aux-Herbes (Grasmarkt), or Tourist Information Brussels (T.I.B.), City Hall, Grand-Place (Grote Markt).

BRUPARCK is a family leisure park containing a "Mini-Europe" exhibit, which has scale models of famous European buildings. Just outside the park is the Atomium, a spectacular monument composed of nine giant metal spheres that represent the atoms of an iron molecule. Designed for the 1958 World Expo, it is one of the city's best known symbols. An observation deck inside the topmost sphere affords superb panoramic views.

GRAND-PLACE (64 B2), dominated by the Gothic spire of the Hôtel de Ville (Town Hall) and the gabled Guild Houses, with their ornate Flemish baroque façades, is one of Europe's most beautiful public squares. The buildings are illuminated nightly from June to September.

BELGIUM

MANNEKEN-PIS (64 B2), rue de l'Etive, is an early 17th-century bronze statue of a boy using nature's own sprinkling system. A wardrobe of over 500 costumes presented to the statue is in the Musée Communal (Museum of the City of Brussels).

MUSÉE D'ART ANCIEN (Museum of Ancient Art) (64 B2), 3 rue de la Régence, offers a superb selection of paintings from the Flemish School from the 14th to the early 19th centuries. The museum connects to the Musée d'Art Moderne (*see below*).

MUSÉE D'ART MODERNE (Museum of Modern Art) (64 B2), place Royale 1, traces Belgian painting since the late 19th century.

PALAIS ROYAL (64 C2), Place des Palais, the 18th-century palace of the dukes of

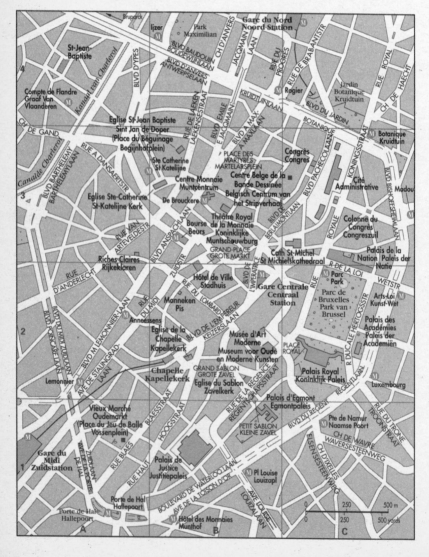

Brabant, was rebuilt at the beginning of the century for King Leopold II.

PLACE ROYALE (64 C2) is an elegant 18th-century square which is dominated by the equestrian statue of Godefroy de Bouillon, leader of the First Crusade.

▲ ANTWERPEN (58 C4) ★
ANTWERPEN *pop. 465,000*

Antwerpen (Antwerp), on the Scheldt River, is one of the world's largest commercial ports and an international business center with a lively nightlife.

During the Renaissance the city flourished as a center of Flemish culture. Rubens, Van Dyck and other well-known painters lived in Antwerp, and several of the city's museums display their works. The city is still culturally important. Theaters and nightclubs provide year-round entertainment, and opera runs from September to May. Diamond-cutting exhibitions can be seen at the Provincial Diamantsmuseum (Diamond Center) at Lange Herentalsestraat 31.

KONINKLIJK MUSEUM VOOR SCHONE KUNSTEN (Royal Museum of Fine Arts), Leopold de Waelplaats 1–9, is in a 19th-century neo-classical building. Its 2,500 paintings span five centuries.

MAYER VAN DEN BERGH MUSEUM, Lange Gasthuisstraat 19, is a reconstruction of a 16th-century townhouse. The highlight is probably Bruegel's *Dulle Griet* (*Mad Meg*), which shows a woman in an apron and armor charging the gates of Hell.

ONZE LIEVE-VROUWE KATHEDRAAL (Cathedral of Our Lady), Groenplaats 21, was completed in the 16th century after over 200 years. The largest cathedral in the Lowlands, it is known for its Gothic architecture and contains several masterpieces by Rubens, including three outstanding altarpieces. The 123-meter (404-foot) spire dominates the skyline.

PLANTIN-MORETUS MUSEUM, Vrijdagmarkt 23, is housed in the mansion of French-born printer Christophe Plantin. Among the exhibits are priceless manuscripts and a Librarium Prohibitorum, a list of "dangerous" books once banned by the Church.

RUBENSHUIS (Rubens' House), Wapper 9, the former home and studio of the great Flemish artist Peter Paul Rubens, who lived here from 1608 until his death in 1640, contains mementoes, a self-portrait and paintings from his school.

SINT-PAULUSKERK (St. Paul's Church), in the Veemarkt, is a 16th-century Gothic-style church with a baroque tower. In addition to fine woodcarvings and over 200 sculptures, the church has paintings by Rubens, van Dyck and Jordaens.

VLEESHUIS (Butchers' Guild House), Vleeshouwersstraat 38–40, is a Gothic palace whose hall was once used as a meat market. It now houses an archeological and craft industries museum, and has a noteworthy collection of 17th- and 18th-century musical instruments.

BOKRIJK (58 D3) ★
LIMBURG

Some 10 kilometers (6 miles) north east of Hasselt is an estate with a park, arboretum, rose garden and several lakes. The Open-Air Museum in the grounds recreates a medieval Flemish town and a typical Kempen village.

▲ BRUGGE (58 A4) ★
WEST-VLAANDEREN *pop. 116,700*

The medieval aura surrounding Brugge, or Bruges, dates from the city's beginnings during the 9th century and its 13th to 15th-century rise to importance as an inland trading port. The old buildings, gabled houses, splendid churches, picturesque streets, bridged canals and art treasures attest to this period of prosperity, which reached its peak during the 15th century.

Walking down the cobbled streets, riding in a horse-drawn carriage, boating down a canal or renting a bicycle are all satisfying ways to see Brugge. Markt, the city's main square, offers interesting old buildings. The Burg square near by offers such varied structures as the Basilica of the Holy Blood, the 14th-century Gothic Town Hall and the Renaissance-era Old Recorder's House.

Several other well-preserved buildings and numerous museums and art galleries, including the Brangwyn, Groeninge, Gruuthuse and Memling museums, are within walking distance.

Special events include Ascension Day, when the Procession of the Holy Blood makes its way through the city streets, bringing to life biblical characters and scenes.

BELFORT EN HALLE (Belfry and Halls), Markt, dates from the 13th to 15th centuries. Reached by a winding staircase of 366 steps, the 83-meter (272-foot) belfry commands an excellent view of the city and has a 47-bell carillon.

GROENINGE MUSEUM, on the Dijver Canal, contains works by such Flemish Primitive painters as van Eyck, van der Goes and Memling, as well as art from more recent periods.

GRUUTHUSE MUSEUM, on the Dijver Canal, was the palace of the Lords of Gruuthuse who owned the monopoly on the sale of *gruut*, a mixture of herbs and spices used in brewing beer. The 15th-century palace now exhibits Flemish pottery, furniture, weapons and goldsmiths' works.

HEILIG BLOEDBASILIEK (Basilica of the Holy Blood) was built between 1139 and 1149 in Romanesque style, evident in the crypt chapel. The upper chapel was remodeled in Gothic style in the 15th century, with later alterations. This chapel contains the Relic of the Holy Blood. The relic is carried around in a colorful procession on Ascension Day.

ONZE LIEVE VROUWEKERK (Church of Our Lady), Mariastraat, is primarily Gothic,

although it combines several different styles. Among its art treasures is a marble *Madonna and Child* by Michelangelo. The church includes the mausoleums of Mary of Burgundy and Charles the Bold.

SINT-JANSHOSPITAAL (St. John's Hospital), Mariastraat 38, was founded in the

---

GUILDS AND SOCIETIES

Guild houses were once a powerful force in Belgian society, and inscriptions such as *brasseurs* (brewers) and *bakkers* (bakers) can still be seen on buildings. Most existing guilds have strict membership and dress codes, and each honors a particular cause, however bizarre – the Confrérie de la Tarte, for example, is dedicated to a special kind of cheesecake!

12th century, and now houses the Memling Museum, a small collection of work by the 15th-century painter, Memling.

CHARLEROI (58 C2)
HAINAUT *pop. 207,000*
Named for Charles II of Spain, Charleroi was once an important fortified town. Sightseeing highlights include the Museum of Fine Arts, with works by Pierre Paulus and Magritte, and, 18 kilometers (11 miles) south west, the medieval village of Thuin.

DINANT (58 C2) ★
NAMUR *pop. 12,300*
Dinant is a popular tourist center on the Meuse River, and is crowned with an impressive citadel. Famous for its copperware and *couques* (ginger cookies), Dinant has an amusement park and bathing facilities, and is the starting point for river trips to Namur.

▲ EUPEN (58 E3)
LIÈGE *pop. 17,300*
Eupen is a thriving textile center at the confluence of the Vesdre and Hill rivers.

In addition to picturesque scenery, Eupen is renowned for its annual pre-Lenten carnival, an 18th-century baroque church and the unique Euro Space Center, housed in a futuristic building.

▲ GENT (58 B3) ★
OOST-VLAANDEREN *pop. 230,000*
Gent or Gand, the city of flowers and the capital of East Flanders, is on a series of islands at the confluence of the Leie and Schelde Rivers. In medieval times the city was a major commercial center and the seat of the Counts of Flanders. By the end of the 13th century, its flourishing textile industry had transformed it into one of Europe's largest cities. During the Renaissance, Gent became home to several Flemish artists, including the van Eyck brothers.

The narrow streets and medieval houses lend a picturesque quality to this city, which also is noted for its Gothic town hall, 7th-century Abbey of St. Bavo, attractive Citadel Park, Floralia Palace and nearby Castle of Laarne.

BELFORT EN LAKENHALLE (Belfry and Cloth Hall), on St. Baafsplein, are Gothic structures built between 1321 and 1426. Remodeled in 1913, the building is a symbol of freedom and has a 52-bell carillon.

GILDEHUIZEN (Guild Houses), on the Graslei, date from the 12th to 17th centuries and were built in the Romanesque, Gothic and Renaissance styles.

GRAVENSTEEN (Castle of the Counts of Flanders), St. Veerleplein, was built in 1180 by Philip of Alsace. It resembles the Crusader fortresses built in Syria. The dungeons and a gruesome torture room are still intact.

MUSEUM VOOR SCHONE KUNSTEN (Museum of Fine Arts), Nicolaas de Liemaeckereplein 3, contains paintings by old masters and is particularly noted for Flemish works, including Hieronymus Bosch's *The Carrying of the Cross*.

MUSEUM VOOR VOLKSKUNDE (Folklore Museum), Kraanlei 65, is housed in an attractive courtyard complex of restored almshouses from the mid-14th century.

ST.-BAAFSKATHEDRAAL (St. Bavon's Cathedral), St. Baafsplein, houses many art treasures, including the *Adoration of the Mystic Lamb* altarpiece by Jan and Hubert van Eyck. Completed in 1432, it is one of the most celebrated and enigmatic works in Western art.

DEVILISH CHOCOLATES
Don't leave Belgium without visiting a *chocolatier* (chocolate store), where delectable handmade pralines can be bought either in a presentation box, or selected according to your tastes. Remember, real cream doesn't keep, though this is unlikely to be a problem as Belgian chocolates are highly addictive!

STADHUIS (Town Hall), Botermarkt, is an intriguing architectural blend of Gothic and Renaissance styles. The Pacification of Gent, a peace treaty between Catholics and Protestants, was signed in 1576 in the Pacificatiezaal, one of a series of halls open to the public. Access by tour.

▲ HASSELT (58 D3)
LIMBURG *pop. 66,900*
Hasselt is a market town on the Demer River and famous for its Cathedral of St. Quintin, constructed on Romanesque foundations and built mainly in the 13th and 14th centuries.

IEPER (58 A3)
WEST-VLAANDEREN *pop. 35,000*
After Ieper, or Ypres, was reduced to rubble in World War I, its residents took care in reconstructing the town, especially the 13th-century Gothic Cloth Hall, with its lofty belfry, and the Cathedral of St. Martin. Several museums have art and history displays, and war memorials and cemeteries are near by.

About 500,000 fallen soldiers lie in 170 military cemeteries in the vicinity. The Lille Gate stands as a reminder of past glory, and the Menin Gate, the place where many thousands advanced toward the front, is an imposing British memorial to World War I dead.

LAKENHALLE (Cloth Hall), Grote Markt, is a magnificent Gothic hall, painstakingly rebuilt in 1933 after destruction in 1914. The 70-meter (230-foot) belfry is reached by 264 steps, and has a carillon of 40 bells. It now houses the Salient Museum, exhibiting artifacts from World War I.

KNOKKE-HEIST (58 A4)
WEST-VLAANDEREN *pop. 32,000*

The resort area of Knokke-Heist consists of five North Sea resort towns: Heist, Duinbergen, Knokke, Albertstrand, and Het Zoute. All are on an expanse of beach near the Dutch border, with Het Zoute regarded as the most sophisticated. The casino, golf course, tennis courts, stores, restaurants and nightspots make it a favorite resort.

▲ LEUVEN (58 C3)
BRABANT *pop. 85,000*

Leuven was a flourishing city in the Middle Ages. The seat of the dukes of Brabant for centuries, it is now known for the University of Leuven. Churches include the 15th-century Gothic St. Pieterskerk and baroque St. Michielskerk. The cobbled Oude Markt (Old Market) is the city's liveliest square and a popular student haunt, while the Stadhuis (Town Hall), in mid-15th-century Flamboyant Gothic style, is one of the most attractive buildings in Belgium.

GROOT BEGIJNHOF, founded in 1234, is the nation's largest community of lay nuns, and has over 70 magnificently restored 17th-century houses.

▲ LIÈGE (58 D3)
LIÈGE *pop. 196,300*

Once ruled by prince-bishops, Liège (Luik in Flemish) is at the confluence of the Meuse and Ourthe Rivers and gateway to the Ardennes. In an attractive region of rivers and forests, Liège is the largest French-speaking city in Belgium and a popular tourist destination.

CATHÉDRALE ST-PAUL, rue Bonne-Fortune 6, is a 13th-century Gothic construction with noteworthy statuary, stained glass and a fine interior.

CHÂTEAU DE JEHAY is a 16th-century castle on an islet 25 kilometers (16 miles) southwest of Liège containing a museum of Gothic to 18th-century furniture.

MONTAGNE DE BUEREN (Bueren Hill) off rue Hors-Château, is a steep passageway of some 400 steps leading to the ancient citadel. An impressive view rewards those able to make the climb.

PALAIS DES PRINCES EVÊQUES (Palace of the Prince-Bishops), palace Saint-Lambert, is a vast Gothic palace begun in the 9th century and rebuilt in the 16th and 18th centuries. Now the Palais de Justice, it has magnificent interior decor.

▲ MECHELEN (58 C3)
ANTWERPEN *pop. 75,000*

Mechelen, on the Dijle River, was once the capital of the Netherlands and for centuries the religious center of Belgium. Many of its buildings and much of its medieval atmosphere have survived. Mechelen was the center of Flemish cloth weaving, and is now known for its lace. A bellringing school in St. Rombaut's Cathedral attracts *carillonneurs* from all over the world.

Mechelen is home to two great paintings by Rubens: the *Adoration of the Magi* in the St. Janskerk and the *Miraculous Draft of Fishes* in Onze Lieve Vrouw over de Dijle.

SINT-ROMBOUTS KATHEDRAAL (St. Rombaut's Cathedral) dates from the 13th century and is considered one of the most beautiful in Belgium. Its 97-meter (318-foot) tower has a 49-bell carillon.

Inside the cathedral are some priceless paintings, including works by Van Dyck.

▲ MONS (58 B2)
HAINAUT *pop. 92,400*
A settlement that dates from the 7th century, Mons has quaint buildings, winding streets and old mansions. Its 15th-century Gothic town hall has some fine tapestries. A 17th-century baroque belfry stands on the site of the Castle of the Counts of Hainaut. The 87-meter (285-foot) tower contains a 47-bell carillon and affords splendid views.

▲ NAMUR (58 C2)
NAMUR *pop. 104,000*
Namur is the capital of the province of the same name. The old citadel on a promontory overlooking the city can be reached by road or cable car, and many of its fortifications can be visited.

MAISON DES SOEURS DE NOTRE DAME (House of the Sisters of Notre Dame), 17 rue Julie Billiart, houses the treasure of Oignies Priory, including silverwork from the 13th century.

▲ OOSTENDE (58 A4)
WEST-VLAANDEREN *pop. 69,000*
The most important and one of the oldest Belgian communities, Oostende is a port of embarkation for cross-channel trips to Dover in England. From May to October it is a popular seaside resort, with a racetrack, casino, golf course and beach.

▲ SPA (58 E2)
LIÈGE *pop. 10,300*
Spa has given its name to health resorts throughout the world. It was popular in the 18th and 19th centuries, when Europe's elite used its waters. Today it has a casino, racetrack and 18-hole golf course. Spa is the site of the Battle of Flowers parade on the second Sunday in August.

TONGEREN (58 D3)
LIMBURG *pop. 30,000*
As the oldest town in Belgium (founded in the 1st century) and the first in the country to adopt Christianity, Tongeren has a rich heritage. Its many Roman ruins include remnants of the city wall, while its Gallo-Roman museum has over 18,000 artifacts.

▲ TOURNAI (58 B3)
HAINAUT *pop. 67,800*
Divided by the Scheldt River, Tournai (Doornik in Flemish) was founded by Romans in the 3rd century; only Tongeren is older. It is famous not only for the architects, sculptors, goldsmiths and painters who were born or lived in the town, but also for tapestries, china and earthenware. The Museum of Fine Arts displays works by such old and modern masters as Rubens, Bruegel, Manet, Ensor and Van der Weyden.

The 13th-century belfry is the oldest in Belgium. A tourist office is opposite the belfry at 14 rue du Vieux Marché-aux-Poteries.

CATHÉDRALE DE NOTRE DAME (Cathedral of Our Lady), place de l'Évêché, is a Romanesque structure, completed in the 12th century. The sculptures on the west face of the cathedral date from the 14th to the 17th centuries and represent Adam and Eve, the apostles and the saints; 12th-century murals as well as paintings by Metsys, Rubens and Jordaens adorn the interior walls.

WATERLOO (58 C3) ★
BRABANT *pop. 27,900*
Napoleon met defeat at Waterloo in 1815; today the famous battlefield has monuments and memorials to those who died during the waning hours of the Napoleonic Empire. A sweeping view of the battlefield is available at the Butte du Lion (Lion Mound), a 40-meter (130-foot) mound which marks the spot where Prince William of Orange was wounded.

The nearby Panorama de la Bataille contains a lifelike panoramic painting of a French cavalry charge, which gives the visitor the frightening illusion of being involved in the action.

LUXEMBOURG

THE ARDENNES OF FRANCE AND BELGIUM SPREAD THROUGH LUXEMBOURG INTO GERMANY. IN THE PAST THESE LARGER COUNTRIES HAVE SPREAD THROUGH LUXEMBOURG TOO, TAKING ITS 2,590 SQUARE KILOMETERS (1,000 SQUARE MILES), THE SMALLEST MEMBER OF THE EUROPEAN UNION. IT IS, OFFICIALLY, A GRAND DUCHY, SMALL, BUT NOT INSIGNIFICANT AND DOES NOT RELY ON POSTAGE-STAMP REVENUE AS LUXEMBOURG CITY IS HOME NOT ONLY TO THE EUROPEAN COURT OF JUSTICE, BUT ALSO TO MANY INTERNATIONAL BANKS, WHICH STORE THEIR WEALTH HERE. THERE ARE MANY REMINDERS OF ITS 1,000 YEARS OF HISTORY, SUCH AS THE 16TH-CENTURY GRAND DUCAL PALACE AND THE 17TH-CENTURY NÔTRE DAME CATHEDRAL.

Left A TYPICAL LUXEMBOURG VILLAGE IS PRETTY BLICK AUF CLERVAUX
Above THE RIOT OF COLOR IN THE STAINED GLASS AT THE BASILICA IN ECHTERNACH IS OUTSTANDING

THINGS TO KNOW

- **AREA:** 2,585 square kilometers (998 square miles)
- **POPULATION:** 400,000
- **CAPITAL:** Luxembourg
- **LANGUAGES:** French, German and Luxembourgeois. English in main towns.
- **PASSPORT REQUIREMENTS:** Required for U.S. citizens.
- **VISA REQUIREMENTS:** Not required for stays up to three months.
- **DUTY-FREE ITEMS:** 200 cigarettes or 50 cigars or 100 cigarillos or 250 grams of tobacco; two liters of wine, one liter of spirits (or two liters of alcohol not exceeding 22 proof), 25 grams of eau de cologne, 50 grams of perfume, two movie cameras with a reasonable amount of film, two still cameras with a reasonable amount of film, one video camera and personal goods to the value of 2,000 FLUX.
- **CURRENCY:** The currency unit is the Luxembourg *franc* (FLUX), divided into 100 *centimes*. Belgian currency also is legal tender. There is no limit on the import or export of any currency.
- **BANK OPENING HOURS:** 8:30 or 9am–noon and 1:30pm or 2–4:30 or 5pm Monday–Friday.
- **STORE OPENING HOURS:** 8 or 8:30am–noon and 2–6 or 6:30pm Monday–Saturday; most large department stores are closed Monday morning.
- **PUBLIC HOLIDAYS:** January 1; Easter Monday; Labor Day, May 1; Ascension Day; Whitmonday; National Day, June 23; Assumption Day, August 15; All Saints' Day, November 1; December 25 and 26.
- **NATIONAL TOURIST OFFICE:** Luxembourg National Tourist Office 801 Second Avenue New York, NY 10017 Tel: 212/370 9850 Fax: 212/986 1188
- **AMERICAN EMBASSY:** 22 Boulevard Emmanuel Servais L-2535 Luxembourg Tel: 460123 Fax: 461401

HISTORY

In 963 AD, young Count Siegfried of the Ardennes acquired the ruins of a Roman fort built high on a cliff over the Alzette river. He rebuilt it into a mighty fortress, becoming the overlord of an independent fief of the Holy Roman Empire: Lucilinburhuc, after his "little fortress." Successive rulers extended their domains, and by the 13th century Luxembourg had become a significant power. The next century brought John the Blind, the most prominent warrior of his day and best remembered figure in the House of Luxembourg. His son, Charles IV, was king of Bohemia and Holy Roman Emperor, and through these positions continued his father's policy of expansion.

In the mid-15th century, the nation lost its independence to Philip the Good of Burgundy. For the next 400 years, Luxembourg's fortunes were closely linked with those of Belgium and Holland, as the Low Countries were alternately united and partitioned under the control of Spain, Austria and France.

In 1815 the Congress of Vienna pulled the Netherlandic region together under William I as the Kingdom of the Netherlands and a supposedly independent Grand Duchy of Luxembourg; an eastern section of Luxembourg was given to the duchy of Prussia. However, in 1830 the southern provinces split from the Netherlands to form the Kingdom of Belgium, taking with them a large section of Luxembourg that is today a Belgian province, also called Luxembourg. Nine years later, the Netherlands officially recognized the independence of Belgium and the remaining Grand Duchy. But it was not until 1867 that Prussian occupation of Luxembourg ended and true independence, autonomy and neutrality began.

In 1940 the German armies poured over the frontiers, just as they had in 1914. The country was occupied for four years, but if you drive through the peaceful countryside today, it is difficult to imagine this small domain as a battlefield. It has recovered remarkably from the ravages of war, becoming a prosperous modern nation.

As a Grand Duchy, Luxembourg is a constitutional monarchy governed under the Constitution of 1868.

FOOD AND DRINK

Smoked pork, broad beans and sauerkraut are specialties. The jellied suckling pig and ham of the Ardennes are popular dishes, as is black pudding (*treipen*). Trout, crawfish and pike are choices on summer menus; wild game is an autumn and winter favorite. Moselle wines are light and dry. Brewing is a very old industry, and local beer is excellent. Small plum tarts (*quetsch*) are a specialty during September.

SPORTS AND RECREATION

Visitors will find diversion in a jaunt through the countryside. The extensive network of marked pathways in Luxembourg is very dense, and walking tours are organized most weekends and holidays. There also are marked cycling trails. Fishing rights are often held by hotel owners. The Luxembourg Golf Course, near the capital, is one of the most spectacular in Europe.

GETTING AROUND

Luxembourg is easily reached by air, rail and bus and via good highways from Belgium, Germany, Switzerland and France. Once inside the country, every corner is accessible by road, rail or bus.

AUTOMOBILE CLUB
The Automobile Club du Grande-Duché de Luxembourg
(ACL, Automobile Club of the Grand Duchy of Luxembourg) is at Route de Longwy 54, Bertrange. Not all auto clubs offer full travel services to AAA members.

Excursion buses, leaving from the railroad station in Luxembourg City, make trips of varying durations into the countryside. Motorists can enjoy a leisurely drive through the Moselle Valley, with its verdant vineyards and rock-hewn wine cellars, reached by Route 1 from Luxembourg City.

Other scenic destinations are the flower gardens at the thermal springs spa and resort of Mondorf-les-Bains, the rugged hills and rock formations of Müllerthal and the artificial lake region of Esch-sur-Sûre and Vianden, both of which offer impressive castles.

The wearing of seat belts, if the car is so equipped, is mandatory for the driver and passengers. A child under 12 cannot occupy a front seat if rear seating is available and must use a special seat if sitting in the front.

Speed limits are 50 k.p.h. (30 m.p.h.) in town, 90 k.p.h. (55 m.p.h.) on out-of-town roads and 120 k.p.h. (75 m.p.h.) on highways. Visiting motorists are required to pay fines for motoring violations on the spot in Luxembourg francs.

ACCOMMODATIONS

Hotels are classified using from one to five stars, with five stars being the highest rating. There are official campgrounds throughout the country, but camping is permitted everywhere with the landowner's approval.

A list of hotels, inns and campgrounds and accompanying maps can be obtained from the Luxembourg National Tourist Office. An international camping carnet is recommended.

TIPPING

A 15 percent service fee is usually included in hotel and restaurant bills. If you see none listed, ask if it has been included. Tip taxi drivers 15 percent of the fare, and tip bellhops and porters about 20 francs.

PLACES OF INTEREST

LUXEMBOURG

LUXEMBOURG
pop. 75,400

More than 1,000 years old, the capital city of Luxembourg was once one of Europe's most important fortresses, with strategic advantages that were the envy of neighboring countries. Through the years the city's controlling powers encircled it with three protective walls and dug an underground labyrinth of connecting passages and shelters. Visitors can explore a section of this maze.

In the Middle Ages, Luxembourg was ringed by three walls and 18 forts, which were linked by 21 kilometers (13 miles) of tunnels and casemates carved from solid rock. A model of the old citadel can be seen on Place d'Armes.

The city of Luxembourg also has a modern side; along with Brussels, it serves as co-capital of the European Union (E.U.), which was created in Luxembourg.

A busy city, Luxembourg usually offers some kind of special event each month. The biggest is Schobermesse, a fair that started as the "Shepherd's Market" in 1340. It is held in late August and early September.

CASEMATES, Pont du Château and Place de la Corniche, are the network of underground fortifications – 21 kilometers (13 miles) in length – built to defend Luxembourg in the Middle Ages.

CATHÉDRALE NOTRE-DAME DE LUXEMBOURG, boulevard Franklin.D. Roosevelt, is an imposing Gothic-style structure built in the early 17th century.

MUSÉE NATIONAL (National Museum), Marché aux Poissons, includes some priceless works of art as well as impressive exhibits illustrating the region's Roman past.

PALAIS GRAND-DUCAL was renovated in the late 19th century, although some portions date back to 1572. There is a Changing of the Guard ceremony every Saturday morning.

ROCHER DU BOCK, the remains of the mighty fortress founded by Count Siegfried in 963, stand on the projecting outcrop of the Bock rocks.

BEAUFORT
pop. 1,200

At the heart of the area known as La Petite Suisse ("Little Switzerland"), the ruined castle of Beaufort occupies a striking position on a plateau surrounded by wooden slopes. Built on the site of a Roman camp, the castle dates from the 12th to 15th centuries.

CLERVAUX (59 E2)
pop. 1,600

Clervaux lies in a deep, narrow valley in the middle of the Ardennes, next to the Clerve River. On a small hill stands the feudal castle of Clervaux. Partially destroyed in World War II, it was once the seat of the Counts of Clervaux, from whom Franklin D. Roosevelt was descended. Clervaux's many historic structures, including the castle, chapel, abbey, parish church and monument of the Peasants' War, are illuminated from Easter through October. Nearby Munshausen and Weicherdange contain ancient churches with fine frescoes.

DIEKIRCH (59 E1)
pop. 5,600

Diekirch, surrounded by forests and orchards, is a resort in the Sûre Valley. Concerts, tennis, fishing and canoeing are favorite diversions. Also of interest is the parish church, which dates from the 5th and 6th centuries.

ECHTERNACH (59 E1)
pop. 4,200

Echternach is a vacation center on the Sûre River, which forms the border between Germany and Luxembourg. Echternach was popular as a vacation spot with the Romans, who built their villas on the town's seven hills. The Benedictine Abbey was founded by the Northumbrian monk St. Willibrord in the late 7th century. The town still has a strong medieval atmosphere, with old patrician houses and pointed gables, narrow streets and ancient ramparts. The Dancing Procession, held annually on Whittuesday, lures thousands of pilgrims and spectators.

The surrounding area is known as La Petite Suisse, Luxembourg's "Little Switzerland." The woods here are criss-crossed by hundreds of footpaths, where visitors can find good views and quiet spots among the rocks and waterfalls.

BASILIQUE DE ST. WILLIBRORD, within the Benedictine Abbey, dates from the 11th century and is one of the country's most important religious buildings. The vaults contain frescoes dating back to 1100. In the crypt is the marble sarcophagus of St. Willibrord, who is honored in the Dancing Procession.

EHNEN (59 E1)
pop. 2,100
East of the capital city and close to the German border, Ehnen is a small village of medieval character with narrow streets and a wine museum. The only circular church in Luxembourg is in Ehnen.

ESCH-SUR-SÛRE (59 E1)
pop. 200
The Ardennes market town of Esch-sur-Sûre is bordered on three sides by the Sûre River. Nearby Upper Sûre Lake is particularly conducive to recreation.

GREVENMACHER (59 E1)
pop. 3,000
Attractive Grevenmacher is a wine center in the Moselle Valley. The popular local sparkling wine can be tasted at the Caves Bernard-Massard and the Caves Cooperatives, which are open to visitors from April through October. Grevenmacher also boasts an exotic butterfly garden.

LAROCHETTE (59 E1)
pop. 1,300
The remains of medieval castles overlook Larochette, a picturesque old town in the valley of the Ernz Blanche. This popular tourist destination also is a starting point for walks through the beautiful surrounding woodlands.

MONDORF-LES-BAINS (59 E1)
pop. 2,900
Mondorf-les-Bains is in the serene valley of the Gander, which forms the Franco-Luxembourg border. Its modern thermal establishments have excellent facilities. Mondorf also is known for its casino, park and sports facilities. Summer, when the flower parks are in bloom, is the loveliest time to visit.

REMICH (59 E1)
pop. 2,600
This picturesque village on the banks of the Moselle River is an important wine center, the headquarters of the State Viticulture Institute. Visitors can sample the local *méthode champenoise* sparkling wine at the Caves St. Martin.

VIANDEN (59 E1)
pop. 1,500
Ancient ramparts, watchtowers and gates still stand guard over medieval Vianden, rising formidably out of the wild and hilly region of the Our River. Its reconstructed castle is an enormous fortress that dates from the late 4th century.

WILTZ (59 E1)
pop. 4,000
A scenic Ardennes town, Wiltz straddles a series of cliffs overlooking the Wiltz River. The town features a 17th-century château built on the foundations of a 12th-century castle that now houses the tourist office as well as two museums: the Museum of the Battle of the Bulge and the Musée Arts et Métiers, a museum of arts and handicrafts. An open-air festival of music and theater is held annually in the château gardens during July and August.

BRITAIN

Britain includes the three separate mainland nations of England, Scotland and Wales, as well as islands such as the Channel Islands. (If you add Northern Ireland it is the United Kingdom of Great Britain and Northern Ireland, or U.K.). Don't worry if you can't remember, most of the citizens can't either, but never refer to the Welsh, Scots or Irish as English – they are not, and many resent being ruled from London when they see themselves as separate. You will certainly see separate cultures, all steeped in history, as well as distinct landscapes: England's rolling green fields and country villages; Wales's hills and castles; Scotland's mountains and lakes; and Northern Ireland's cliffs and glens.

Left Shakespeare's wife, Anne Hathaway, lived here in Stratford upon Avon, England, before she married
Above left One of the famous landmarks of London – Big Ben
Above right Bagpipes produce the traditional music of Scotland

THINGS TO KNOW

- **AREA**: 130,378 square kilometers (50,339 square miles)
- **POPULATION**: 47,536,000
- **CAPITAL**: London
- **LANGUAGE**: English
- **ECONOMY**: Agriculture, industry, mining, tourism. Major crops barley, wheat, potatoes; extensive livestock and dairy production. Chief exports machinery, cars, chemicals, textiles. Large deposits of oil, natural gas, coal, iron ore; tin, copper, lead and clay also are important.
- **PASSPORT**: Required for U.S. citizens.
- **VISA**: Not required for stays up to six months.
- **DUTY-FREE ITEMS**: 200 cigarettes or 100 cigarillos or 50 cigars or 250 grams of tobacco; 4 liters of still wine, or 2 liters of still wine plus 1 liter of spirits or 2 liters of sparkling wine; 60 milliliters of perfume; 250 milliliters (¼ litre) of toilet water; and up to £36 value in other goods. Tobacco and alcohol products cannot be imported by persons under 17. Also see *The European Union on p.5.*
- **VALUE ADDED TAX**: Britain levies a Value Added Tax (V.A.T.) on goods purchased in the UK. You can be reimbursed for the taxes you pay, however, after you leave.
- **CURRENCY**: The currency unit is the British *pound sterling* (£) divided into 100 *pence* (p). Due to currency fluctuations, the exchange rate is subject to frequent change. There is no limit on the import or export of British currency or US traveler's checks. Banks will convert larger amounts into traveler's checks before departure.
- **BANK OPENING HOURS**: 9:30am–3:30pm (or 4:30pm) Monday–Friday. Some banks are now open on Saturday mornings.
- **STORE OPENING HOURS**: In London 9:30am–5:30pm Monday–Saturday (to 7 or 8pm also on Wednesday or Thursday. In suburbs and provinces 9am–5:30pm (to 1pm on Wednesday in some rural towns). Some stores are open 10am–5pm

HISTORY

The Romans occupied most of what is modern England until AD 412. When they withdrew, control reverted to tribal kingdoms. The Norman conquest in 1066 once again united England, under William the Conqueror, and territory expanded to include what is now Scotland, Wales and Ireland. The Magna Carta, granted by King John in 1215, guaranteed human rights against excessive use of royal power, and created the formula upon which the modern parliamentary system of government is based.

The late Middle Ages brought further changes and the legal system developed then is the basis of the current English and American legal systems. The development of universities and new religious orders contributed to cultural evolution.

The Elizabethan Age brought England into competition with Spain for territory in the New World, and the 19th-century British Empire, spurred by wealth from the Industrial Revolution, continued to expand into the 20th century.

A national system of primary education was begun in 1870, and in the early 20th century was expanded to include secondary education. Before World War I, Britain instituted pensions as well as health and unemployment insurance. After World War II, this was expanded to include today's National Health Service. Under the Labour Party, the Bank of England, the steel and coal industries, the railroads, and communications facilities were nationalized, although many reverted to private control during the next decades under the Conservatives.

The range of the British Empire diminished as almost all of Britain's colonies achieved independence in the 1950s and 60s. Ties to many of the former colonies, such as Australia and New Zealand, continue to be maintained, to a greater or lesser extent, through the Commonwealth.

FOOD AND DRINK

Many typical English dishes center on roast meat – beef, pork, lamb, poultry and game. Roast beef is accompanied by roast potatoes and Yorkshire pudding. Mint sauce is usually served with lamb, and currant jelly with poultry; pork is normally complemented by apple sauce. A treat is salmon, also available smoked, as are haddock and mackerel. Regional sea specialties include oysters. Stews and pies are particular favorites, with Lancashire hot pot a celebrated stew. Melton Mowbray in Leicestershire produces pork pies, and Cornwall Cornish pasties. Cheeses include Cheddar, Cheshire, Stilton, Double Gloucester, Red Leicester, Derbyshire, Lancashire and Wensleydale.

Tea is the national drink. Coffee enjoys almost equal popularity. Beer might be one of several distinct brews: mild, bitter (draft and keg), stout or lager. Lager resembles the cold, highly carbonated beer of the U.S. Pubs serve a wide range of non-alcoholic and alcoholic beverages, including gin, vodka, sherry and whisky. Permitted drinking hours are generally 11am to 11pm Monday to Saturday; noon to 3pm and 7pm to 10:30pm on Sunday, Good Friday and December 25.

SPORTS AND RECREATION

The national sports are cricket, rugby and football (soccer). The best place to watch cricket (watch out for those confusing rules!) in London is at Lord's or the Oval. The soccer season runs from August to May. Rugby is akin to North American football – try Twickenham for an international between two of the five nations: England, France, Wales, Scotland and Ireland. Flat (horse) racing enjoys a wide following. Steeplechase has a longer season with the Grand National in Liverpool in April. The Lawn Tennis Championships at Wimbledon are in the last week of June and first week of July, and Henley-on-Thames is the setting for the Royal Regatta in the first week in July.

GETTING AROUND

Three auto tape tours for a circle trip from London are available. Each 90-minute tape offers information on history, folklore and attractions. The tapes cover London–Glastonbury, Glastonbury–Stratford, and Stratford–London. Each can be purchased directly from CCInc. Auto Tape Tours, P.O. Box 227, Allendale, NJ 07401; tel: 201/236 1666.

AUTOMOBILE CLUB
The Automobile Association (AA), Fanum House, Basingstoke, Hampshire RG21 4EA, **has branch** offices in various cities throughout Britain. The symbol ▲ beside the city name indicates the presence of a AAA-affiliated automobile club branch. Not all auto clubs offer full travel services to AAA members.

National Trust Properties and other sights can be visited at no additional charge by purchasing a Great British Heritage Pass, available for 15 days or one month. The pass also allows entry to many museums at a discounted price. It can be obtained from your AAA travel agent and British Airways offices in the U.S. and Canada or from the British Travel Centre in London.

ACCOMMODATIONS

Bed and breakfast is a specialty. They are generally inexpensive and well run. Hotels in England are not government rated, but the AA publishes a list of them rated from one to five stars. Youth hostels usually give priority to hikers and cyclists. There are thousands of campgrounds – many are listed in the AA's *Guide to Camping and Caravanning in Britain and Ireland*.

TIPPING

Hotels include a 10 to 15 percent service fee, but tip chambermaids up to £1 a day and bellmen 50p to 75p per bag. Taxi drivers and waiters 10 to 15 percent.

Sunday. At Christmas many stores open on Sunday. Supermarkets are generally open 7 days.

- **BEST BUYS:** Porcelain from Worcester and Stoke-on-Trent; pewterware and sterling silver; Sheffield cutlery; antiques; tweeds and woolens, rainwear and leatherware. **Note:** if the purchase is an antique valued at more than £35,000, an export license is required to take it out of the country.
- **PUBLIC HOLIDAYS:** January 1, or closest weekday; Good Friday; Easter Monday; May Day, first Monday in May; Spring Bank Holiday, last Monday in May; Late Summer Holiday, last Monday in August; December 25, or closest weekday; Boxing Day, December 26 or closest weekday.
- **USEFUL TELEPHONE NUMBERS:** Police, Fire, Ambulance – 999
- **NATIONAL TOURIST OFFICE:** British Tourist Authority (BTA) Suite 701, 551 Fifth Avenue New York NY 10176-0799 Tel: 212/986 2200 or 1-800-462 2748
- **AMERICAN EMBASSY:** 24 Grosvenor Square London W1A 1AE England Tel: 0171 499 9000 (telephone enquiries only)

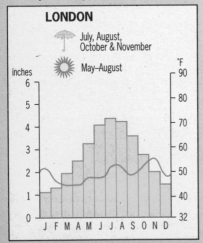

LONDON

July, August, October & November

May–August

PRINCIPAL TOURING AREAS

EAST ANGLIA

The varied seaside and sturdy rural interior of Essex is a favorite playground for Londoners. About 2,428 hectares (6,000 acres) of the county belong to London. This is the Epping Forest, a remnant of a former royal hunting ground. **Suffolk** has cornfields and marshlands, moated manor houses and reed-roofed cottages. **Norfolk**'s bow-shaped coast stretches from south of Great Yarmouth to the north-west inlet, the Wash. Popular among sailing and boating enthusiasts are **Norfolk's Broads**, 30 open lagoons linked by rivers, lakes and manmade channels to form more than 322 kilometers (200 miles) of navigable waterways. **Cambridgeshire** has no coast, but long, straight dikes. **Cambridge** has a university – spires, cloisters, chapels and bridges in a setting of gardens and a river.

HOME COUNTIES

Hertfordshire is traversed by roads that have been major thoroughfares since Roman times; Ridgeway Path is Britain's oldest road. Within commuting distance north of London, it has lost much of its former rural character. **Bedfordshire** is where the broad Ouse River enters from Buckinghamshire and meanders across this grassy county. Bedfordshire's south is hillier, with the Chiltern Hills and a lower sandstone ridge farther south. Ruling **Buckinghamshire**'s south is the low chalk ridge of the Chiltern Hills. Dense forests of beech blanket much of the ridge, and there is a network of footpaths. The Thames River forms the northern boundary of **Berkshire,** while the Lambourn Downs govern the west. In the north the Vale of the White Horse takes its name from an old attraction: a white horse carved into a chalky hillside. Across the Thames from Berkshire is **Oxfordshire**. Ancient **Oxford**, the most famous of the towns along the Thames, is characterized by the dignified lawns and soaring spires of its university.

MIDLANDS

Gloucestershire has a landscape of rivers, woods, old towns and mellow hills. The **Forest of Dean** dominates the south west, split from the rest of the county by the Severn River. The rest of Gloucestershire offers the hilly **Cotswolds** and their wool market towns: Chipping Campden, North Leach, Stow-on-the-Wold and Cirencester.

North of Gloucestershire are the lands of two formerly separate counties, now merged into **Hereford and Worcester**. The western section, formerly called Herefordshire, is characterized by peaceful meadows with red-and-white cattle, and several old market towns. Hereford, a cathedral city with a long history, is the political and geographical center of the area. The eastern part of Hereford and Worcester, formerly Worcestershire, has a small corner of the Cotswolds in the south. The fruit-growing Vale of Evesham and the Malvern Hills, with a holiday spa in their lee, share this part of the county. Worcester, an old cathedral town on a great plain, is the largest city. **Warwickshire** is best known as William Shakespeare's England, for there are many sites associated with the poet, notably at Stratford-upon-Avon. Other facets of this densely populated region include the old county town of Warwick, with its famous castle. West Midlands to the north west offer Coventry and Britain's second largest city, Birmingham.

Northamptonshire is a county with rural and urban sections. Open fields and pasturelands constitute the northern section, while Northampton, the county town, makes up the southern section. Adjacent **Leicestershire** is associated with manufacturing; this county also is known for its fine grazing lands.

On the border with Wales to the west is **Shropshire**, cut into two contrasting regions by the Severn River. The northern portion is a well-watered plain broken here and there by a solitary hill.

The county town of Shrewsbury is in a loop of the river between the halves of the county. The southern half of Shropshire is a hilly region that includes a 16-kilometer (10-mile) ridge of heathlands called the Long Mynd. **Staffordshire**, between Shropshire and Derbyshire, is familiar as Arnold Bennett country. In the north are the "Five Towns" of his novels; Stoke-on-Trent is the best known. Collectively called the Potteries, these towns still produce fine porcelain and china. The steep-sided valley of the Dove is a pleasant introduction to **Derbyshire**. Competing for popularity are several other valleys – Wolfscote, Beresford and Monsal Dales – and the rocky crags and peatlands of the Peak District. The very name **Nottinghamshire** is inseparable from legends of the outlaw hero Robin Hood. However, scholars now believe that the real Robin Hood was not from Nottingham at all. Real historic inhabitants of this county were Lord Byron and D.H. Lawrence. **Lincolnshire** is the most eastern part of the Midlands. Rolling green hills of the chalk Wolds, busy North Sea fishing ports and seaside resorts are found in the northernmost section. Lincoln, with an immense medieval cathedral and ruins dating from the Roman occupation, is part of the western region. The county's southern lands are reminiscent of The Netherlands, with flat, drained fens and Dutch-gabled houses.

NORTH EAST

Northumberland, the most northern county in England, is a scenic region full of history. The Pennine Hills run the length of the county and merge in the north with the Cheviot Hills. Higher hills, moorlands and manmade woods lie south of the Cheviots. An older feature of this part of Northumberland is what remains of Hadrian's Wall, which once marked the northern boundary of Britain under Roman rule. **County Durham** is easily divided into east and west. The densely populated east has been a region of coal mining and shipbuilding since

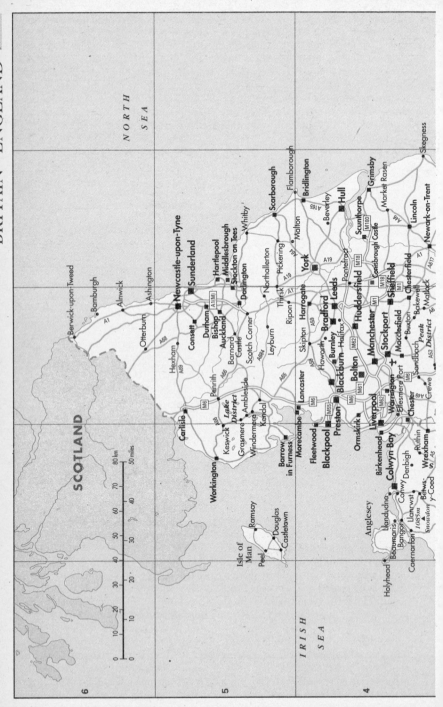

the beginning of the Industrial Revolution. Prominent in this mass of factories, ports and new towns is Durham, a medieval city on the winding Wear River. The west of the county is higher tableland; frequent rainfall and flat terrain have formed poorly drained moors. A few small mining towns and villages still dot the landscape. **North Yorkshire**'s seacoast is decorated with such holiday towns as the fishing port of Whitby, closely associated with Captain Cook. North Yorkshire also is known for its moorlands, now a national park. The **Yorkshire Dales** are equally scenic with woods, meadows, streams and waterfalls forming one of the grandest landscapes in England. York is the oldest of North Yorkshire's cities. Ancient streets and walls, twisting lanes, medieval market squares and timbered houses reflect 1,900 years of history; towering above the city is York Minster. South Yorkshire's center is Sheffield, the county's steel metropolis. South east of North Yorkshire, **Humberside** contains the chalky Yorkshire Wolds, which form a hilly arc from Hull to the Flamborough Peninsula, where they meet the sea as white cliffs. **West Yorkshire** contains great wool cities, including Leeds.

NORTH WEST

On England's northern border is **Cumbria**. The northernmost section of the county is not on the usual tourist itinerary, but therein lies its attraction. In the south west are the austere and boulderstrewn Cumbrian Mountains, among them Scafell Pike, the highest point in England. Perhaps most pleasing in terms of scenery is Cumbria's southern region, with green vales, lofty fells and mountain streams. Here, too, are the largest waters of the **Lake District** – Windermere and Ullswater – and the peaks of Helvellyn.

Greater Manchester covers a region devoted to manufacturing. Manchester, for centuries a center of British textile production, is a cultural leader and university city. Just north of the Greater

Manchester region are **Lancashire**'s moorlands, wooded dales and beaches. **Merseyside** contains the outlet for the Mersey River, which meets the sea at Liverpool. **Cheshire** has a share of industry in its textile factories in Macclesfield, grain and oil processing centers at Ellesmere Port and railroad center at Crewe. Even so, the dominant impression of this county is one of woods, meres and "magpie" houses of darkened timbers and white-painted plaster.

SOUTH AND SOUTH EAST

Wiltshire, in southern England, has grasslands and grainfields, chalky downs and clear streams. Among the fields and hills are the region's stone-built towns and villages. Historic houses include haunted Littlecote and Elizabethan Longleat. However, Wiltshire's best-known sight is a spired medieval city rising out of a meadow: **Salisbury**. Equally well known is the 4,000-year-old assembly of monoliths near Amesbury called **Stonehenge** – a mysterious place associated with Druids both ancient and modern.

Between Wiltshire and West Sussex is **Hampshire**. Representing the county's older aspect are villages of thatched and timbered cottages; several old seaside

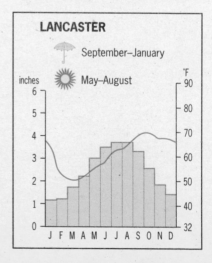

LANCASTER

September–January

May–August

towns and the capital of Saxon England, **Winchester**. Oddly, among the old is the New Forest, a hunting preserve of Norman kings. **East and West Sussex**, with their fine coast, served as an entrance for invading Romans, Saxons, Danes and Normans. Paralleling West Sussex's coast are the chalky **South Downs**. Just inland of these hills is the Vale of Sussex, a region of quiet hamlets, old market towns and great estates. The northern part of the Sussex counties is a landscape of heaths and woodlands. In the Wealden hills of west **Kent** is **Tunbridge Wells (Royal)**, among the most elegant of English spas. Pilgrim's Way is an ancient route that runs along a high ridge of Kent's North Downs. Though historians today doubt that this was indeed the path of medieval pilgrims, it is nonetheless an enjoyable method of approaching **Canterbury**, the fine cathedral city that was the objective of these travelers. **Surrey,** in the south contains lakes and rivers, open heaths and dense woods, and many admirable old towns. The dominant feature of this region is a stretch of the North Downs, which form a long wall across the whole county from east to west.

SOUTH WEST
Westernmost is the ancient Celtic land of **Cornwall**, steeped in stories of the sea and older Arthurian legend. At the tip of Cornwall, a mass of granite cliffs called **Land's End** falls away into the sea. East of Cornwall is **Devon**, a county with coasts on both the English and Bristol Channels. The emptiest and perhaps loveliest feature of Devon is its interior, encompassing the timeless and sometimes desolate **Dartmoor National Park**, as well as attractive villages and lush, green farmlands. **Dorset**, facing the English Channel east of Devon, is a county of stone and thatch villages, rich pastures and contrasting stretches of bracken and briars. Along its coast are sandy beaches and chalk or sandstone heights. North west of Dorset is **Somerset**, known both for its Bristol Channel coast and hilly interior. To the east, where the coast is gentler, are Somerset's resorts. Inland are more hills, the peaceful green Quantocks and the gaunt yellow Mendips, pocked with caverns and gorges. Excursions to the north, in the county of **Avon**, lead to **Bath**, prestigious since Roman times, west to Queen Charlton and Chew Magna and on even further west to **Bristol**.

TWO GREAT NATIONS DIVIDED BY A COMMON LANGUAGE
Some of the following may help you with the linguistic gulf that separates the United States from Britain:

American	British
elevator	lift
collect call	reverse-charge call
one-way ticket	single ticket
round-trip ticket	return ticket
pants	trousers
underwear	pants
nylons	tights
restroom	toilet
trunk/hood	boot/bonnet
gas	petrol
traffic circle	roundabout
underground pedestrian passage	subway
subway	tube/underground
liquor store	off-licence
check (in restaurant)	bill

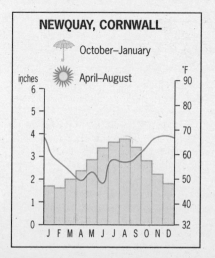

NEWQUAY, CORNWALL

October–January

April–August

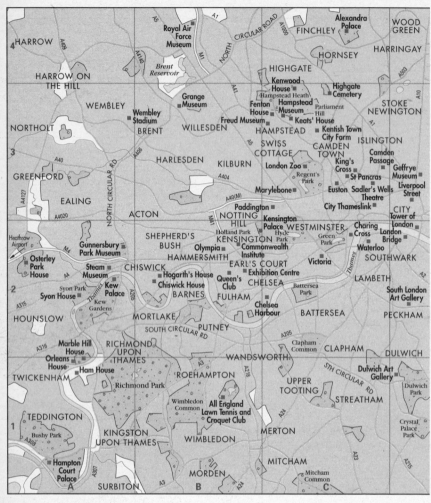

LONDON
pop. 6,800,000

HISTORY

Encompassing 1,580 square kilometers (610 square miles) and nearly eight million people, London offers tremendous variety. From humble beginnings as a small port on the Thames River, it has spread to incorporate suburban towns and villages.

Despite the creation of a Green Belt in 1938, and the government's earnest attempts to encourage industries to locate in other cities, London continues to expand to such a degree that it is sometimes difficult to determine where the city stops and the country begins. The Greater London conurbation is defined as a collection of 32 metropolitan boroughs, each with some form of local self-government.

The founding of the city is usually attributed to 1st-century Romans, who likely chose their site on the north bank near the estuary for its easy defense from invasion and ready access to the

LONDON

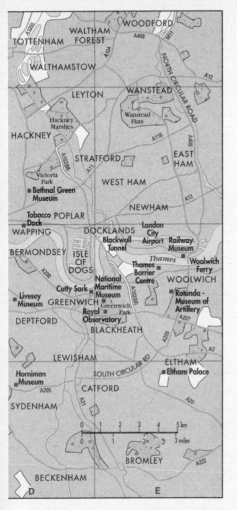

Londoners demanded – and got – a charter assuring them of special liberties.

Medieval London grew at a phenomenal pace. Preoccupied with commerce, the city had more than 100 craft guilds by the 13th century. Its wharves were piled high with the goods of trade, and its waterways teemed with vessels from throughout Europe.

By the mid-16th century, London controlled more than three-quarters of the country's trade. Its size contributed to the ascendancy of Britain, for in this city were collected the capital and imagination necessary to initiate the nation's great maritime adventures.

With an estimated 500,000 inhabitants, London was likely the most populous city in Europe by the mid-17th century. It also was among the first cities to experience big-city problems: widespread poverty, filth, crime and overcrowding. Not the least of its troubles was the threat of epidemics; in 1665 the city experienced its last and worst bout with the Bubonic plague. By the end of the year, at least 75,000 had perished and thousands had fled.

Following the Great Plague was yet another, more devastating calamity – the Great Fire. Originating in Pudding Lane on September 2, 1666, the blaze consumed most of the city in four days, destroying the cathedral, 80 churches, thousands of dwellings and virtually all civic buildings. By September 5, hardly a fifth of London remained.

The London that emerged from the ashes was a more durable city. The streets were wider and straighter; houses were built of brick; markets were enlarged; quays were raised; and the Fleet River, long a filthy sewer, was covered over. Though Sir Christopher Wren's sweeping architectural plan was never realized, he did give the city St. Paul's Cathedral as well as dozens of churches.

sea. Archeological evidence indicates that *Londinium* was a center of land and water trade routes. Though not the principal city of Roman Britain, London was sufficiently important to deserve protective walls and a fortress. By the 3rd century, the trading community had its own mint.

London was a city of some consequence by the time of the Norman conquest and became a political capital as well with the arrival of William the Conqueror. From the outset of royal occupancy,

London quickly resumed its dominant position, controlling the economic and political power of Britain and boasting some of the finest literary and philosophical minds in the kingdom. The metropolis continued to grow; at the time of the first census in 1801, the city and immediate surroundings counted more than a million residents.

Technological innovations in the 19th century further altered the community. Established as the commercial, political and intellectual capital of the British Empire, London assumed the additional role of industrial giant and became the dreary city described by Dickens.

During World War I, London was attacked, and though many were killed and much destroyed, the damage of World War I was only a fraction of the destruction the city was to endure in the next World War.

The death toll from German air raids in World War II was more than 30,000 and the value of property lost immeasurable. Nevertheless, by the 1950s, London had revived and begun to prosper as it never had before.

London today wears its 2,000 years of history with dignity. Though constantly undergoing renewal of some sort, reminders of the past are carefully guarded. Alongside modern skyscrapers are the crumbling remnants of the city's Roman wall.

The only drawback to exploring London is that there is perhaps too much to see and do!

GETTING THERE
BY PLANE AND TRAIN
Most visitors to London arrive via Heathrow Airport. From its four terminals, buses run to downtown London every 20 or 30 minutes; taxis are readily available. The Underground connects Heathrow with central London.

Many charter flights also arrive at Gatwick Airport. There is a direct rail link to Victoria Station and the Gatwick Express fast train service runs frequently. Stansted Airport is approximately 50 kilometers (30 miles) north east of London; British Rail links the airport to central London via Liverpool Street Station, a 45-minute train ride.

GETTING AROUND
Visitors unaccustomed to driving on the left and unfamiliar with London's street plan should avoid driving, particularly during morning (8am–9:30am) and evening (4:30 to 6:30pm) rush-hour traffic.

PARKING
Parking meters operate in the greater part of central London, usually during work hours. At other times, meter spaces can be used without payment. Meters, when they must be used, are operable for periods of 15 minutes to 2 hours; it is illegal to restart a meter for the same vehicle. In addition to the coin-operated meters, there are ticket parking meters.

There also are numerous parking lots above and below ground. Clamping of illegally parked vehicles is common and fines are costly. "Red routes," with a complete ban on parking, are marked with red lines at the side of the road.

CAR RENTAL
Renting a car in London is relatively easy but should be arranged prior to arrival, particularly during tourist or holi-

GREEN SPACES
Despite the number of manmade structures ancient and modern in central London, there also are acres of well-tended parks. Londoners are quick to point out that you can walk for over 3 kilometers (2 miles) from Kensington Palace to Waterloo Bridge and be nearly always surrounded by grass and trees.

day seasons. In London, hotels, travel services, major airports and railroads can arrange rental. Most cars have manual gear change but automatics are available. Chauffeured rentals also are an option.

PUBLIC TRANSPORTATION

London's cabs are typically black, and cab drivers are regularly tested on their knowledge of the city. Fares are determined on an initial charge plus mileage, with extra fees for large parcels, luggage or pets. A table of fares, extra charges and conditions must be posted in each cab. For longer trips, you and the driver should agree a fare in advance. A tip of 10 to 20 percent is usual. You can hail a cab virtually anywhere, though the best procedure is to wait at a cab rank.

The Tube, or Underground, is generally the fastest method of traveling, with an extensive network of trains. Where the Underground does not reach, it affords connections with suburban trains or buses. Many stations have elevators; all major stations have escalators.

Fares are determined by distance traveled. Purchase tickets either from staff at a window or a coin-operated machine.

Slower but perhaps more enjoyable are the double-decker buses. From the upper level of one of these red buses you will be treated to some exceptional views of London.

Note: Attraction listings in this guide usually include the nearest Tube stop, denoted by a (U) for Underground.

WHAT TO DO
SIGHTSEEING

For additional tourist information, contact the London Tourist Board and Convention Bureau, Victoria Station Forecourt, London SW1, or the British Travel Centre, 12 Regent Street, London SW1Y 4PQ. To order a list of Visitorcall information telephone numbers, tel: 0171 971 0026.

BUS, TRAIN, LIMOUSINE OR CARRIAGE TOURS

Original London Transport Sightseeing Tours offer tours of the city's landmarks, tel: 0181 877 1722. Other bus touring options are London Hop On Hop Off, tel: 0171 357 0594.

The Travel Card entitles you to one-day unlimited travel on British Rail, the Underground or city buses around London and surrounding areas. A Photocard is required if you wish to purchase a week, month or longer season ticket. Photocards are free, but you must supply a passport-type photograph. Both the Travel Card and the Season Ticket can be purchased at British Rail offices, the British Travel Centre, Underground stations or any London Regional Transport Travel Information Centre.

BOAT TOURS

A leisurely way to see much of riverside London is by boat. A popular two-hour tour originates at Westminster Pier just below Westminster Bridge. Other departure points include Tower, Charing Cross and Greenwich piers. Trips on London's Regents Canal begin from Camden Lock and Little Venice.

PAGEANTS AND CEREMONIES

No other city in the world is characterized by such pomp and pageantry. There are literally hundreds of ceremonies in tradition-conscious London. Listed below are some of the most popular ones, but there are many more to choose from.

CHANGING OF THE GUARD occurs daily (every other day mid-August to March 31) in front of Buckingham Palace. At 11:30am, a band leads the new guard, in full dress, from Chelsea or Wellington barracks to the palace and, after the replacement of the old with the new, leads the old guard back to the barracks. **Changing of the Queen's Life Guard** takes place at 11am (10am Sunday) at the Horse Guard's Arch in Whitehall. The new guard rides daily from Knightsbridge Barracks. Arrive early.

LORD MAYOR'S SHOW is held on the second Saturday of November, and has been for the last 50 years of its existence. The newly elected mayor rides in a great gilded coach from the Guildhall to the Royal Courts of Justice to take the oath of office before the Lord Chief Justice. Pikemen in armor accompany the mayor to the Courts and then back to the Guildhall.

MOUNTING THE GUARD is the cavalry version of the Changing of the Guard. It occurs daily at 11am (10am Sunday) at Horse Guard's Parade, the great square facing Whitehall. Units of the Household Cavalry form the guard. When the Queen is in London, additional troopers and a trumpeter also participate.

STATE OPENING OF PARLIAMENT, in late October or early November, is one of the most colorful events of the ceremonial year. The Queen, arriving at the Houses of Parliament in the Irish State Coach, is met by the robed and wigged Law Lords and other Officers of State. In the House of Lords, she presents a prepared speech outlining the government's activities for the coming session.

TROOPING THE COLOUR is such a spectacle that crowds attend the rehearsals. The actual ceremony, marking the official birthday of the Queen, takes place on Horse Guard's Parade on a selected Saturday in June. The color, or flag, of one of the five regiments of Foot Guards is displayed to the music of bands. The Foot Guards line up to await the arrival of the Queen and the Household Cavalry. The sovereign inspects the parade while riding in a carriage, and the color is trooped before her. The last part of the ceremony is the great marching display.

It is a matter of pure luck whether you will be able to get a ticket for the ceremony itself (around 50,000 people apply for 4,000 seats). To try, write requesting tickets (maximum two) to the Brigade Major, Trooping the Colour, Household Division, Horse Guards, Whitehall, between January 1 and March 1. Include a stamped addressed envelope. If you don't succeed, however, you can apply for tickets to the dress rehearsals on the two preceding Saturdays.

SPORTS AND RECREATION

Although not generally regarded as a recreational center, London does offer a wide variety of sporting activities. Outdoor and indoor pools provide opportunities for **swimming** throughout the year. **Ice-skating** rinks and **tennis** courts are scattered throughout the metropolis. **Horseback riding** is available on the trails of Hyde Park. More than 200 courses provide **golf**; the courses usually welcome visitors but are often crowded, especially at weekends. Current golf course information appears in the publication *Golf Monthly*.

By far the most popular spectator sport is **soccer** (football), while **hockey**, **boxing**, **wrestling**, **ice hockey** and **greyhound**, **cycle** and **auto racing** excite countless fans. **Cricket** can be watched at Lords and the Oval, **rugby** at Twickenham and, of course, **lawn tennis** at Wimbledon in June and July. Epsom, site of the Derby and Oaks, and Ascot, home of the Royal Ascot, are the best **horse racing** tracks.

WHERE TO SHOP

Bond Street has jewelers and art galleries; Savile Row is known for fine tailoring; Charing Cross Road has old books; and King's Road showcases contemporary fashions. St. James's is for "the discerning gentleman," and Oxford Street and Kensington High Street boast some of the best-known stores. Shops specializing in elegant menswear can be found in the Burlington Arcade.

Harrod's is Britain's largest department store; its five floors incorporate everything from baked pheasant to fine crystal. Be sure to dress appropriately as visitors without shirts are turned away. Shoppers with less to spend might prefer Selfridges on Oxford Street, with excellent take-home gifts, or nearby Marks and Spencer, noted for value.

A vast selection of delicacies can be found in the food halls of Fortnum and Mason, on Piccadilly. Liberty, on Regent Street, is well known for its selection of fabrics.

For something old as well as new, London is the world's largest dealer in antiques and artworks. Christie's and Sotheby's are the most reputable names in the trade, and King's Row one of the best sources. The time-honored Chelsea Antique Market, King's Row and the Portobello Market on Portobello Road are best visited early to avoid crowds.

Covent Garden (WC2) was the old fruit and vegetable market renovated in the 1970s to contain a variety of specialty shops, art galleries and restaurants. Shoppers can easily spend an entire day browsing in the area and watching the street entertainment, which continues into the evening.

WHERE TO STAY – WHERE TO EAT

Although there are thousands of hotels in London, from April to August the city is overrun with visitors, and adequate accommodation for impromptu travelers is hard to find. Reservations are essential for the centrally located establishments.

London's finest and most expensive hotels are in the loosely defined West End, which includes Westminster, St. James's and Mayfair. Since the 19th century, the West End has been the stylish place to dine and shop. If luxury or location are not so important, the choice is greater. There are excellent hotels with lower rates outside the West End.

Visitors with special interests can choose hotels convenient to what they wish to do or see. Museum devotees might prefer Bloomsbury or Kensington; visitors intent on eating and drinking might seek lodgings in Soho. Those interested in history might want a place in the City.

Many London hotels offer complete meal service. Some serve only breakfast and are not usually licensed to serve alcohol. Most of these establishments, which often have "house" or "court" in their names, are comfortable and well maintained.

In some hotels, services and facilities are at a minimum, but are inexpensive, and you may prefer these more homey places. For a small fee the London Tourist Board, in Victoria Station next to the British Rail ticket office, gives advice on budget hotels and hostels for visitors without reservations.

Along with the city's great hotels, some of the best restaurants are in the West End. Mayfair and adjacent St. James's contain several of the finest eating establishments in London. By far the greatest concentration of London's foreign restaurants is in the brash, neon quarter of Soho.

The oldest chophouses, simple taverns serving hearty fare, are in the City. Historically interesting as the favorites of Dickens and William Makepeace Thackeray, these old places are still popular luncheon spots among the City's business people.

Reservations are usually necessary for the chic or particularly popular restaurants. It is usual to tip around 10 percent. Before leaving a tip, check to see if a service fee has been added to the bill; if it has, tips should be about 5 percent.

ENTERTAINMENT
NIGHTLIFE
Once the pubs close around 11pm, many clubs, late-night restaurants, theaters and cinemas take over. Nightlife lives in Mayfair, scene of hotels and restaurants

BRITAIN • ENGLAND

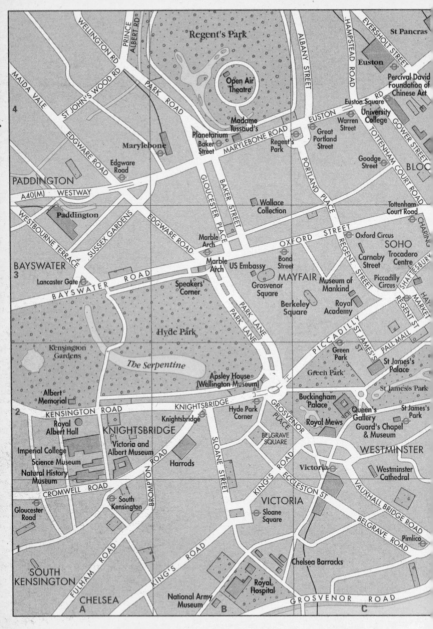

that offer dinner and dancing very late, and the nightclubs, which are actually private clubs invented to circumvent the liquor laws. In the first category are the great hotels-cum-clubs, including The Dorchester, Grosvenor House, Mayfair Intercontinental and Hilton.

Among those places offering dinner, dancing and floor shows are The Savoy and Quaglino's.

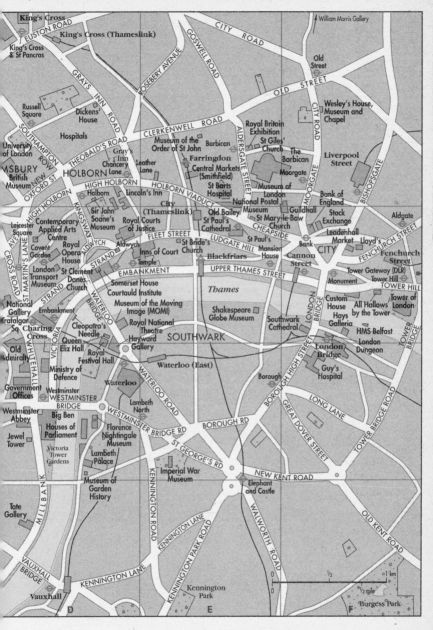

Wine bars are a fashionable alternative to pubs and discos. At Brahms & Liszt in Covent Garden, visitors can buy wine by the glass or bottle and listen to live jazz and blues music. Another popular night spot and restaurant also known for its rock 'n' roll memorabilia is the Hard Rock Café on Piccadilly. Nightclubs, in the British sense, have membership fees that vary depending on the establishment. Legally there is a 48-hour wait between application and membership, but this technicality is not always regarded. Application must be made in person on the club premises. A passport is an introduction into many clubs where membership is normally restricted. Clubs are subject to the whims of those who patronize them and often appear and disappear almost overnight. The Hippodrome, on the corner of Leicester Square, and Stringfellows, 16 Upper St. Martin's Lane, are two of the most famous at the time of going to press.

Ordering beverages often poses a dilemma for visiting Americans: When asking for a beer, specify the type desired – lager, bitter, ale, etc. If you're fond of ice in mixed drinks or sodas, ask for extra if you want more than a couple of cubes.

London's Underground trains stop running around 1am; be sure to make alternative plans for transportation or save sufficient money for the cab fare if you plan to stay out later. For complete listings of events and venues, consult *Time Out*, London's weekly guide to what's happening around town.

Note: The mention of any area or establishment in the preceding sections is for information only and does **not** imply endorsement by AAA.

THEATER AND CONCERTS

Most of London's legitimate theaters are in or near Shaftesbury Avenue, the Haymarket or St. Martin's Lane in the West End. Notable exceptions are the Aldwych Theatre in WC2, the Royal Theatre on the South Bank in SE1, and the Barbican in EC2, the London home of the Royal Shakespeare Company.

London newspapers advertise plays, and the weekly entertainment guide *What's on in London* describes each very briefly. The selection is excellent – everything from old works being revived to exciting new plays. Tickets are available from the box office or through agencies that charge nominal fees.

Though plays are in English, a language lesson is still in order! The orchestra to Americans is known as the stalls; the balcony is the dress circle; and the second balcony is the balcony. During intervals (intermissions), drinks and ice creams are available. Curtain time varies but is often at 7:30pm. Some theaters have twice-nightly shows, with the first show at 6 or 6:15pm and the second between 10:30 and 11pm.

London's principal concert halls are the Royal Festival Hall on the South Bank and the Royal Albert Hall in Kensington. Covent Garden is the home of both the Royal Opera and the Royal Ballet. The Coliseum has the English National Opera. Major newspapers and magazines such as *Time Out* and *What's on in London* furnish details for concerts, recitals, operas and ballets at these places and elsewhere.

ESPECIALLY FOR CHILDREN

For children, London is a feast of color and sound, from the clattering red double-decker buses to the multihued Crown Jewels in the famed Tower of London; from Buckingham Palace's heel clicking, scarlet- and gold-clad Queen's Guard to the blue-helmeted "Bobbies."

In Regent's Park is London Zoo, where children under 12 can pet or ride certain animals. Youngsters enjoy the comic antics of the pelicans that inhabit St. James's Park, and for the strong at heart, there are the Chamber of Horrors at Madame Tussaud's and the London Dungeon south of the river. A variety of theaters cater exclusively to children. Many have Saturday matinées as well as morning and afternoon performances throughout the week. These include the Little Angel Marionette Theatre and the Young Vic. Several legitimate theaters and cinema houses have special shows for children on Saturday mornings.

PLACES OF INTEREST

★ HIGHLIGHTS ★	
British Museum	(see p.95)
Buckingham Palace	(see p.95)
Hampton Court Palace	(see p.96)
Houses of Parliament	(see p.96)
National Gallery	(see p.99)
St. Paul's Cathedral	(see p.100)
Tate Gallery	(see p.100)
Tower of London	(see p.101)
Westminster Abbey	(see p.101)
Whitehall	(see p.102)

BANK OF ENGLAND (92 F3), EC2 (U: Bank), stands on the north side of an open space called simply "Bank." It also borders on Threadneedle Street, which gives the bank its nickname: "The Old Lady of Threadneedle Street." Founded in 1694, it was built mostly by Sir John Soane in the late 18th century. Its interesting old architecture, however, is overwhelmed by the fortresslike enlargements of the 20th century.

BRITISH MUSEUM (92 D4) ★, Great Russell Street WC1 (U: Russell Square, Tottenham Court Road), dates from 1753, when the British Government purchased the private collection of Sir Hans Sloane and the Harleian Manuscripts. The museum first opened at Montagu House in Bloomsbury in 1759; the present building was begun behind the site in 1823. Later additions extend well beyond the original location, and the museum has become one of the world's largest.

Its treasures include prints, drawings and manuscripts; coins and medals; ethnographic articles; and an unrivaled collection of antiquities. In addition to relics of ancient Britain, there are valuable treasures from Assyria, Babylonia, Egypt, Greece and Rome.

The museum is far too large to be seen in one visit, but entry is free so trips can be made. Those who have limited time but who wish to see samples of all the collections can do so by visiting the Edward VII Gallery.

British Museum Library, containing more than six million volumes, is the country's largest. Historically interesting is the large Reading Room, where many scholars have labored, including Karl Marx.

BUCKINGHAM PALACE (92 C2) ★, SW1 (U: Green Park, St. James's Park), was built in 1703 by the Duke of Buckingham. It became the official residence of British sovereigns in 1837 during the reign of Queen Victoria. Today Queen Elizabeth II lives in the palace; when she is in residence, the Royal Standard (flag) flies above it. The palace is open to the public for a limited period during the summer up to and including 1997 to help pay for repairs to the fire-damaged Windsor Castle.

Buckingham Palace is familiar to most visitors as is the scene of the Changing of the Guard. The palace is at the western end of The Mall, a broad thoroughfare that serves as the impressive setting for state processions. Along The Mall are other sites, including Clarence House, where the Queen Mother lives; St. James's Palace; Marlborough House; and Carlton House. Opposite these palaces is St. James's Park. The Mall entrance is guarded by the enormous, stately Admiralty Arch.

CENOTAPH, in Whitehall SW1 (U: Westminster), was designed by Sir Edwin Lutyens and commemorates those who died in both world wars.

CENTRAL CRIMINAL COURT (92 E3), EC4 (U: St. Paul's), or more familiarly, Old Bailey, stands on Newgate Street at the site of the Newgate Prison, which was demolished in 1902. The street was widened long ago to accommodate the crowds who came to view executions. The public today enjoys watching the more peaceful option of courts in session.

CHELSEA ROYAL HOSPITAL (92 B1), Royal Hospital Road SW3 (U: Sloane Square), was founded in 1682 by Charles II for veteran and invalid soldiers, and built by Sir Christopher Wren that same year. In the central quadrangle of the great Wren building is a bronze statue of the king by Grinling Gibbons. The hospital is the home of the Chelsea Pensioners, known for their tricorne hats and scarlet coats (navy blue in winter).

CLEOPATRA'S NEEDLE (92 D3), Embankment Gardens (U: Embankment), dates from about 1475 BC, which makes it the oldest of the city's structures. Its name is a misnomer, for the obelisk, though Egyptian, never belonged to Cleopatra. Victorian relics are sealed in its base.

COURTAULD INSTITUTE GALLERIES (92 D3), at Somerset House, Strand WC2 (U: Embankment, Temple) houses the art galleries of the University of London. In addition to the Courtauld Collection of French Impressionist and Post-Impressionist paintings, it includes the Lee Collection of Old Masters; the Roger Fry Collection; the unusual Gambier-Parry Collection of Old Masters; sculptures; majolica; ivory and metalwork.

CUTTY SARK AND GIPSY MOTH IV (86 E3), Greenwich Pier SE10, are two very different ships. The *Cutty Sark* is the last survivor of the tea clippers, made obsolete by steam. Reconditioned and permanently berthed at Greenwich, the ship now serves as a museum of figureheads and paintings. The *Gipsy Moth IV* is the well-known yacht in which Sir Francis Chichester made his epic solo voyage around the world in 1966.

DULWICH ART GALLERY (86 D1), on College Road SE21, is the oldest public picture gallery in England and has an outstanding collection of old masters.

GREEN PARK (92 C2) (U: Green Park). This delightful 53-acre green triangle bounded by Piccadilly, Constitution Hill and Queen's Walk seems miles removed from the busy streets that surround it.

HAMPSTEAD HEATH (86 C3) (U: Hampstead) encompasses some 800 acres of grassy hills and wooded dells in London's north.

HAMPTON COURT PALACE (86 A1) ★, 10½ miles south west at Hampton Court, was begun by Cardinal Wolsey in 1514 but functioned as a royal residence from 1525 to 1760. In the late 17th century, Sir Christopher Wren was commissioned to enlarge the house, and the principal façades seen now date from that time. The palace was the favorite country residence of King Henry VIII, who played tennis and jousted in its gardens. Five of his six wives lived in the palace with him, and the ghosts of two of them, Jane Seymour and Catherine Howard, are said to inhabit the house.

BLUE PLAQUES

The idea of placing plaques on the houses or sites where distinguished people once lived was devised in 1866 by William Ewart. The first was placed on the birthplace of Lord Byron in Holles Street, and there are now over 400 blue plaques. To qualify you have to have been dead for over 20 years, born more than 100 years ago, and to have made "some important contribution to human welfare or happiness."

HMS *BELFAST* (92 F3), Morgan's Lane, (near London Bridge) SE1 (U: London Bridge). This well-preserved World War II battle cruiser served her country until the 1960s and now houses an exhibition of military history.

HOUSES OF PARLIAMENT (92 D2) ★, Parliament Square SW1, (U: Westminster) are known officially as the Palace of Westminster, but little remains of the original structure, and no sovereign has lived in the building since Henry VIII. Most of the early buildings were lost in a fire in 1834, and the present buildings were designed by Sir Charles Barry and constructed between 1837 and 1847. The House of Commons was destroyed by bombs in World War II and has since been rebuilt. The most familiar symbol of the Victorian Gothic buildings is the 320ft Clock Tower with its 13½-ton timepiece, Big Ben, whose resonant chimes can be heard throughout London.

Parliament traditionally opens with the Queen's Speech from the Throne in the House of Lords; no sovereign has entered the House of Commons since Charles I in 1642 (see below). A flag on top of Victoria Tower by day and a light in the Clock Tower by night indicate that Parliament is in session. Parliament normally sits from mid-October to the end of July, except for the weeks after Christmas and Easter.

THE GUNPOWDER PLOT

On November 5, 1605, Guy Fawkes and a number of other Roman Catholic conspirators attempted to blow up the Houses of Parliament, along with James I and his ministers. To this day, effigies of Guy Fawkes are burned on bonfires and fireworks are set off on November 5 every year throughout England. Furthermore, before the ceremonial State Opening of Parliament each year, the cellars of the Houses of Parliament are still checked by the Yeomen of the Guard and the Queen presides over the State Opening from the House of Lords, as no monarch has been admitted to the Commons since 1642, when Charles I forced entry and tried to arrest five MPs.

HYDE PARK (92 B3) (U: Hyde Park Corner, Marble Arch) and adjacent Kensington Gardens make up the largest public park in central London. The 620 acres once belonged to the Abbey of Westminster, but with the Dissolution of the Monasteries in 1536, the land became the private hunting ground of Henry VIII. In the 18th century, the park was opened to the public, and its large artificial lake immediately became popular among boating and sailing enthusiasts.

The lake separates the parklands into two unequal sections, with Hyde Park on the east and Kensington Gardens on the west. Kensington Gardens includes the great Kensington Palace, as well as the Round Pond, favored by model yachting enthusiasts, and the delightful statue of Peter Pan. Scenic Hyde Park has a well-known corner dedicated to free speech, Speakers' Corner, where anyone can stand and hold forth on a soap box on Sunday mornings.

Albert Memorial, in the park opposite Royal Albert Hall, depicts Queen Victoria's prince consort examining the catalogue of the Great Exhibition of 1851. In the process of being restored, the memorial will be under scaffolding until the year 2000.

IMPERIAL WAR MUSEUM (92 E2), Lambeth Road SE1 (U: Lambeth North), is dedicated to all aspects of the two world wars and campaigns in which British and Commonwealth forces have been involved since 1914.

INNS OF COURT (92 E3) (U: Holborn) are corporate legal societies that have the sole right to prepare barristers and grant permission to establish a barristers' practice in England. The four Inns of Court are the Inner and Middle temples, Gray's Inn and Lincoln's Inn; each is interesting historically and architecturally.

The Temple between Fleet Street and the Embankment houses the first two; its name comes from the Knights' Templar and their connection with the law. Of architectural note is the restored 12th-century church.

Gray's Inn, reached by way of a 17th-century gateway from High Holborn, has long been associated with the teaching of law; a law school existed as early as the 14th century. The society's beautiful gardens are open to the public, but are subject to close at short notice. Lincoln's Inn is set around the tree-shaded Lincoln's Inn Fields off Chancery Lane. Reached through the magnificent Henry VIII Gateway, its rose-colored brick buildings include a hall, chapel, offices and chambers, mostly Tudor and Georgian in style.

KENSINGTON GARDENS — *see Hyde Park on p.97.*

KENSINGTON PALACE, STATE APARTMENTS AND ROYAL CEREMONIAL DRESS COLLECTION (86 B2), west end of Kensington Gardens W8 (U: High Street Kensington). Kensington Palace was rebuilt by Sir Christopher Wren for William III in the late 17th century. William Kent further remodeled and enlarged the palace for George I. The site served as the royal residence until 1760.

The State Apartments, with many sections by Sir Christopher Wren and William Kent, contain paintings, art objects, costumes and furniture that once belonged to royal residents. The Royal Ceremonial Dress Collection displays costumes worn at court from 1750 to the 1930s.

KENWOOD HOUSE – THE IVEAGH BEQUEST (86 C3), 4 miles north at Hampstead Lane NW3 (U: Hampstead), is a remarkable mansion with grounds adjoining London's unspoiled Hampstead Heath. The architect Robert Adam rebuilt the mansion in its current Georgian style for the first Earl of Mansfield. In 1927 its owner, the first Earl of Iveagh, bequeathed the house and its excellent art collection to the nation; the Rembrandts and Jan Vermeers are especially famous.

KEW GARDENS (86 A2), 9 miles west on Kew Road (U: Kew Gardens), were landscaped in the 18th century as private botanic gardens in the grounds of Kew Palace. Today the 300 acres form the Royal Botanic Gardens, with thousands of species of trees, shrubs and herbaceous plants. Though mainly dedicated to the study of horticulture and botany, the gardens also are interesting to non-botanists; notable are the Succulent, Orchid and Palm houses. Many of the plants and trees here suffered from the storms of 1987.

MADAME TUSSAUD'S (92 B4), Marylebone Road NW1 (U: Baker Street), contains life-size wax models of many internationally famous – and infamous – people such as Margaret Thatcher, Luciano Pavarotti and Michael Jackson. Some of the wax figures date from the 18th century, when Madame Tussaud first established herself in Paris; almost 60 years later she settled in London.

MARBLE ARCH (92 BE3), W1 (U: Marble Arch), at the west end of Oxford Street on the corner of Hyde Park, was designed by John Nash in 1827 as an entrance to Buckingham Palace. However, it was too small for state coaches and was moved to this site in 1851. Marooned in the middle of a huge roundabout, only members of the royal family are allowed to pass through it.

MONUMENT (92 F3), Monument Street EC3 (U: Monument), was designed by Sir Christopher Wren to commemorate the Great Fire of 1666. The winding 311-step staircase leads to a gallery 160 feet up. Climbers who make it are rewarded with a magnificent view of the City.

MUSEUM OF LONDON (92 E4), The Barbican, London Wall EC2 (U: St. Paul's, Barbican), traces the city's history from prehistoric to modern times. The museum combines the collections of the Guildhall and Kensington Palace.

MUSEUM OF THE MOVING IMAGE (MOMI) (92 D3), South Bank, Waterloo SE1 (U: Waterloo), traces the history of the cinema from early experimentation to modern animation. The museum features a replica of a 1950s British cinema including hands-on exhibits and films that visitors can watch. You can also take part and watch yourself giving interviews with the famous, or reading the news.

NATIONAL GALLERY (92 D3) ★, Trafalgar Square WC2 (U: Charing Cross), houses a representative collection of European schools of painting. Especially prominent are the works of Leonardo da Vinci, Raphael, John Constable, Jan Vermeer and Rembrandt.

National Portrait Gallery, behind the National Gallery in St. Martin's Place, has paintings and sculptures of well-known British men and women from all walks of life from the Tudor period to the present day, including controversial portraits of the Princess of Wales and the Queen Mother.

NATIONAL MARITIME MUSEUM (86 E2), 5 miles south east at Romney Road, Greenwich, SE10, has more than a mile of galleries showing models, paintings, instruments and relics that collectively depict the maritime history of Britain.

Old Royal Observatory, founded in 1675 by King Charles II, is the site of the prime meridian, or longitude zero, and the place where Greenwich Mean Time is determined. You can stand with one foot in the western hemisphere and one foot in the eastern. Some 16 galleries chronicle mankind's efforts to map space and measure time. Highlights include interactive displays, the Time Gallery, and the Octagon Room.

NATURAL HISTORY MUSEUM (92 A2), Cromwell Road SW7 (U: South Kensington), contains sizeable collections of animals, insects and plants, extant and extinct, as well as rocks and minerals. Noteworthy are the dinosaurs exhibition, the evolution illustration, the Whale Hall, the insect and fossil mammal galleries, and the Meteorite Pavilion.

NELSON'S COLUMN , WC2 (U: Charing Cross), rises 185 feet above Trafalgar Square. Built to commemorate Admiral Horatio Nelson's 1805 victory, the column is topped by a statue of the admiral and flanked by four bronze lions.

OLD BAILEY – *see Central Criminal Court on p.95.*

PLANETARIUM (92 B4), next to Madame Tussaud's on Marylebone Road NW1 (U: Baker Street), has a huge dome on which is projected a spectacular representation of space. Simulated journeys through the heavens last about 40 minutes.

REGENT'S PARK (D92 B4) (U: Regent's Park) was laid out by John Nash in the early 19th century. Intended originally as an elegant residential suburb, it became a public park in 1838. Its 472 acres contain playing fields, tennis courts, tree-shaded walks, a rose garden, a pretty lake for boating and sailing, a pond on which children sail their toy boats and a fine open-air theater.

London Zoo, is one of the most comprehensive and best housed collections of animals in the world. Particularly outstanding are the children's zoo, the "Moonlight Hall" of nocturnal animals, the Monkey House and the giant walk-through aviary designed by Lord Snowdon and inhabited by exotic birds.

SAVILE ROW

Parallel with New Bond Street, three blocks east, is Savile Row, a byword for gentlemen's tailoring. Tommy Nutter (at No.19) designs Elton John's clothes, and his impeccably tailored suits are worn by many women. Savile Row was where the Beatles made their last public appearance, an impromptu performance on the roof of the Apple Building in 1969.

ST. JAMES'S PALACE (92 C2), SW1 (U: Green Park), at the corner of St. James's Street and Pall Mall, is a great brick mansion built in 1532 for Henry VIII. From 1698 to 1861 it was the sovereign's official London residence. Sentries of the Brigade of Guards parade in front of its picturesque gatehouse daily. The palace is not open to the public, but you may visit the Chapel Royal, to which visitors are admitted for Sunday services from the first Sunday in October to Good Friday. Just west of the palace is Clarence House, residence of the Queen Mother.

ST. JAMES'S PARK (92 C2) (U: St. James's Park) was a virtual swamp until drained by Henry VIII as a nursery for the royal deer. In the 17th century, Charles II introduced ducks and other birds to its long lake. Much later, in 1825, John Nash laid out the 93 acres alongside the Mall as a park. The lake and its island are preserved as a refuge for waterfowl and comical pelicans that are London's favorite pets.

ST. MARTIN-IN-THE-FIELDS CHURCH, Trafalgar Square WC2 (U: Charing Cross), was designed by James Gibbs, a pupil of Sir Christopher Wren. The classical church, which was rebuilt from 1722 to 1724, stands on one of the busiest squares in the world. Its richly decorated interior is particularly notable. A café is housed in the crypt below.

ST. MARY-LE-BOW CHURCH (92 E3), Cheapside EC2 (U: St. Paul's), is a Wren-designed church much damaged in World War II but since fully restored. Surviving the war intact was the Renaissance campanile, one of the finest examples of Sir Christopher Wren's work.

The church's bells have been cast from the metal of the original ones. Each bears a passage from the Psalms, with the first letter of each inscription spelling out D Whittington. According to tradition, it was the Great Bell of Bow that called Dick Whittington, the well-known mayor, back to London.

ST. PAUL'S CATHEDRAL (92 E3) ★, Ludgate Hill EC4 (U: St. Paul's), was built from 1675 to 1710 to replace a Gothic church destroyed in the Great Fire of 1666. The magnificent baroque structure is the crowning achievement of English architect Sir Christopher Wren. Notable features are the classic proportions of the church and the great dome, an engineering feat in its time. High above is the Whispering Gallery, a spot at which whispers on one side of the dome are audible from the other. From the Stone Gallery there are views of the City, but the finest panoramas are from the Golden Gallery on top of the dome.

The enormous crypt is almost a cathedral in itself, with the massive tombs of Lord Nelson, the Duke of Wellington and other notable figures. This, too, is the burial place of Sir Christopher Wren. An inscription above the architect's tomb reads: *Si monumentum requiris, circumspice* – "If you seek a monument, look around you."

SCIENCE MUSEUM (92 A2), Exhibition Road SW7 (U: South Kensington), presents the history of science and industry with displays of machinery, apparatus and instruments. There are working exhibits and lots of interactive possibilities, which are popular with children.

SHAKESPEARE'S GLOBE MUSEUM, New Globe Walk SE1, is built on the site of Shakespeare's original Globe theater. This reproduction playhouse will eventually stage the Bard's plays.

SYON HOUSE (86 A2), near Isleworth, dates from the early 15th century. In the 18th century, Robert Adam redesigned parts of the great Tudor house, and landscape architect Capability Brown laid out its grounds, which now include a display of British horticulture. Catherine Howard, the fifth unfortunate wife of Henry VIII, was imprisoned in the house before her execution in 1542.

TATE GALLERY (92 D1) ★, Millbank SW1 (U: Pimlico), has an unrivaled collection of British paintings, including works by William Blake and the Clore Gallery, dedicated to works by J. M. W. Turner.

There also are modern British and foreign paintings and sculptures, notably French Impressionist works.

THE THAMES FLOOD BARRIER (86 E2), downstream from Greenwich Pier SE10. Each of the Thames Flood Barrier's gates weighs 3,000 tons and is 45 feet high. Together they constitute the world's biggest moveable flood barrier. A visitor center on the Unity Way explains the barrier's workings and you can tour around the structure by boat.

TOWER OF LONDON (92 F3) ★, Tower Hill EC3 (U: Tower Hill), is among the oldest of London's historic places. Built as a fortress by William the Conqueror, it served first as a royal residence and later as a prison with a long and savage history. The principal keep of the medieval complex is the White Tower, dating from 1078; this and later keeps were prisons of such notables as Sir Walter Raleigh and Princess Elizabeth. A paved square marks the site where many of England's greatest, such as Thomas More, and Henry VIII's wives, were beheaded.

Of architectural note in the tower is St. John's Chapel in the central keep, the oldest church in London and a fine example of Norman style. Also worth seeing is the armor collection, which includes the gargantuan suit of Henry VIII. Most prominent among collections, however, are the Crown Jewels, displayed under maximum security in the Jewel House. Among these royal riches are a 226,800-gram (8,000-ounce) punchbowl, enormous serving dishes and gold flagons, jewel-studded coronation robes and the font used in royal christenings since 1841. The tower's history gallery, near the "Bloody Tower," where the young princes were murdered, offers models, pictures and text relating to the history of the tower.

TROCADERO CENTRE (92 C3), 13 Coventry Street W1 (U: Piccadilly Circus), houses the Guinness World of Records, the Wax Works, Alien War and Quasar laser games and the Emaginator technically advanced cinema that really makes you feel you are flying through space.

VICTORIA AND ALBERT MUSEUM (92 A2), Cromwell Road SW7 (U: South Kensington), displays fine and applied arts from all countries and periods. The Raphael cartoons, post-Classical sculpture, period dress collection, British miniatures, watercolors and Oriental art are of particular interest. One gallery is devoted to the work of American architect Frank Lloyd Wright. This is a huge museum, and it is not advisable to attempt to see it all in one visit.

WESTMINSTER ABBEY (92 D2) ★, Parliament Square SW1 (U: Westminster), is London's greatest Gothic church. Founded by Edward the Confessor in the 11th century, the abbey was enlarged and embellished by later monarchs. What appears today is mostly the product of the 13th-century reign of Henry III; important additions since that time have been the Tudor chapel of Henry VII as well as the Wren towers at the western entrance.

Since the 11th century, the church has been the coronation site of English kings and queens. The Coronation Chair in Edward the Confessor's Chapel is a 13th-century oak throne; in a recess beneath it is the Stone of Scone. Most sovereigns from Henry III to George II have been interred in the abbey, along with the country's greatest statesmen, scientists and poets.

One of the most visited spots in the abbey is Poets' Corner, which contains the graves of Edmund Spenser, Geoffrey Chaucer, John Dryden, Samuel Johnson, Robert Browning, Charles Dickens, Thomas Hardy, Rudyard Kipling and Alfred, Lord Tennyson. The Tomb of the Unknown Warrior is a representative of servicemen killed in World War I.

The museum in the abbey's crypt contains surviving pieces of the original abbey and wax effigies of many who lie buried in the church. These images were customarily displayed at the funerals of their subjects.

WESTMINSTER CATHEDRAL (92 C2), Ashley Place SW1 (U: Victoria), is the seat of England's only cardinal and thus the most important Roman Catholic church in the country. The neo-Byzantine structure was completed in 1903; the inlaid stone piazza is the result of recent redevelopment. Of note in the interior are the Eric Gill bas-reliefs depicting the Stations of the Cross. The gallery of the 284-foot tower affords views over the whole of London.

WESTMINSTER HALL, Houses of Parliament, New Palace Yard SW1 (U: Westminster), was built between 1097 and 1099, although the great oak roof was added 300 years later.

The hall served as the chief law court until 1883; Charles I was tried and condemned to death at this site in 1649. All visits must be arranged with a member of Parliament.

WHITEHALL (92 D2) ★ SW1, is the short thoroughfare extending south from Trafalgar Square towards Palace of Westminster (Houses of Parliament). Along the wide street are Britain's chief government offices, including the Treasury, the Foreign Office, the Admiralty and the Horse Guards, which houses some of the departments of the War Office. No. 10 Downing Street, an unimposing side street, is the residence of the Prime Minister, and No. 11 that of the Chancellor of the Exchequer; the street is closed to the public due to threats of bombings. Nearby are the offices of the original New Scotland Yard – the police headquarters in London. **Banqueting House** is all that survived the 18th-century fire that destroyed Whitehall Palace, after which the street is named. Designed in 1619 by Inigo Jones, it is among the most beautiful of London's buildings. Charles I was beheaded in front of the hall, and today a glorious equestrian statue of the king – with his head on – graces a spot nearby.

The Houses of Parliament (or Palace of Westminster) sit splendidly on the Thames River

PLACES OF INTEREST

```
★ HIGHLIGHTS ★

Bath                    (see p.104)
Cambridge               (see p.107)
Canterbury              (see p.108)
Dartmoor                (see p.111)
   National Park
Lake District           (see p.117)
   National Park
Oxford                  (see p.121)
Peak District           (see p.122)
   National Park
Stratford-upon-Avon     (see p.125)
Windsor                 (see p.127)
York                    (see p.129)
```

ALDERNEY (82 E1) – *see Channel Islands on p.109.*

ALNWICK (82 C6)
NORTHUMBERLAND *pop. 7,200*
Alnwick lies in Northumberland's eerie border country, where medieval barons built grim castles during the centuries of Scottish-English wars. Many of these strongholds still stand; among them are the castles of Alnwick, Dunstanburgh and Warkworth. Alnwick Castle was the Norman stronghold of the Percy family.

AMBLESIDE (82 C5)
CUMBRIA *pop. 3,400*
Ambleside, with its old stone houses and rushing stream, is a popular walking and rock-climbing center as well as a good point from which to journey into the English Lakeland. Lake Windermere is popular with boaters and water-skiers.

AMESBURY (82 C2)
WILTSHIRE *pop. 6,500*
On the edge of Salisbury Plain is Amesbury, which took its name from 19th-century Amesbury Abbey. The abbey grounds are a park including a Palladian bridge and Gay's Cave, the site where John Gay composed *The Beggar's Opera.* (See also Stonehenge on p.125.)

ARUNDEL (82 D1)
WEST SUSSEX *pop. 3,200*
ARUNDEL CASTLE, which dominates this south coast town, has been the seat of the Dukes of Norfolk, Earl Marshals of England, and their ancestors for more than 700 years. The building contains rare 16th-century furnishings.

ASCOT – *see Windsor on p.127.*

BAKEWELL (82 C4)
DERBYSHIRE *pop. 4,000*
CHATSWORTH, 3 miles east, in a park beside the Derwent River, is a stately house known for its gardens and fountains. The house is filled with pictures, antique furniture and rare books.

BAMBURGH (82 C6)
NORTHUMBERLAND *pop. 400*
The ramparts of Bamburgh Castle dominate the peaceful resort of Bamburgh. Off the coast are the tiny Farne Isles, the site of a noted bird sanctuary. To the north west and linked to the shore by a causeway is Lindisfarne, or Holy Island.

BAMBURGH CASTLE was once the seat of Northumbrian kings. The armory of the restored Norman fortress contains a large weapons collection.

BANBURY (82 C3)
OXFORDSHIRE *pop. 39,700*
A sizeable marketing and manufacturing center, Banbury is best known for its cross of nursery rhyme renown (now a 19th–century replica). Nearby are several noteworthy old houses: 6 miles north of Banbury is Farnborough Hall, a National Trust Property that is a mostly 18th-century house with extensive grounds; Upton House, 7 miles north west, also is a National Trust Property; known for its fine furnishings, porcelain, tapestries and paintings.

SULGRAVE MANOR, 7 miles north east, off B4525 in Sulgrave, is a compact 16th-century manor house that was the home of Lawrence Washington, an ancestor of George Washington.

BATH (82 C2) ★
AVON *pop. 80,000*
Roman colonists suffering from the damp northern climate built large pools to take advantage of the curative hot springs they found around Bath. Today visitors flock to see the baths, which are remarkably complete in layout and are among the finest Roman remains in Britain. The Roman baths were first discovered in the late 19th century, lying 20 feet below street level.

Bath enjoyed its greatest fame in the 18th century, when wealthy Britons vacationed in the town. Spacious houses, public buildings, arches, terraces and colonnades of cream-colored stone recall that era. Recent additions to the well-planned town do not detract from the prevailing Georgian style of architecture, which is preserved in such streets as Royal Crescent, The Circus, Queen's Square and Great Pulteney Street.

Plaques mark the elegant dwellings of Bath's celebrated past residents. Also retaining the history of the city are the 18th-century Pump Room, Assembly Rooms with their Museum of Costume, abbey church, guildhall and Victoria Art Gallery. For additional information, contact the Tourist Information Centre, Abbey Chambers, Abbey Church Yard, Bath, Avon BA1 1LY, tel: 01225 462831.

AMERICAN MUSEUM, 2½ miles from town, is housed in Claverton Manor and contains American decorative arts.

NO. 1 ROYAL CRESCENT is a completely restored 18th-century stone townhouse, now partially converted to a museum.

ROMAN BATHS and PUMP ROOM, next to Britain's only hot spring, were built in the 1st century AD and served pilgrims visiting the Temple of Sulis Minerva. The Roman Temple Precinct beneath the Pump Room also can be examined.

BATTLE (82 E2)
EAST SUSSEX *pop. 6,300*
The small market town of Battle lies a few miles inland from Hastings. Its name is appropriate; the town marks the site of the 1066 Battle of Hastings.

BATTLE and DISTRICT HISTORICAL SOCIETY MUSEUM, Memorial Hall, contains many items connected with the battle, including a half-scale reproduction of the Bayeux tapestry.

BODIAM CASTLE, 6½ miles north east, is a 14th-century fortress-castle surrounded by a picturesque lily-covered moat.

BEACONSFIELD (82 D2)
BUCKINGHAMSHIRE *pop. 11,100*
Beaconsfield is an elegant old town of inns and 17th-century houses that has not always been so placid: Highwaymen once haunted the thick woods nearby.

A historic moment to more peaceful times is the 17th-century Quaker meeting house in the nearby village of Jordans. The structure has been little altered since it was built. The grave of William Penn, founder of Pennsylvania and Philadelphia, is in the churchyard.

BEAULIEU (82 C1)
HAMPSHIRE *pop. 800*
THE NATIONAL MOTOR MUSEUM, in the grounds of Beaulieu (pronounced BEW-ly) Abbey, founded by Lord Montagu in 1952, commemorates his father, who was a pioneer in motoring. Over 200 vehicles on display detail the history of motoring since 1895.

▲ BEDFORD (82 D3)
BEDFORDSHIRE *pop. 77,000*
WOBURN ABBEY AND DEER PARK, 12½ miles south west at Woburn, is the ancestral home of the Dukes of Bedford. This palatial 18th-century mansion contains a fine collection of paintings and furnishings.

The well-stocked Wild Animal Kingdom and Leisure Park in the grounds has many rare animals.

BEVERLEY (82 D4)
HUMBERSIDE *pop. 23,200*

A market town, Beverley was once walled. The ramparts are gone, but one of the five admission gates, the 15th-century North Bar, remains. Also reminiscent of the town's early cloth-trading days are the 18th-century guildhall and market cross, and Lairgate Hall, an attractive mansion now used as council offices.

BEVERLEY MINSTER, destroyed and rebuilt several times in the course of its long history, is one of the most notable Gothic churches in the country. Significant features of the interior are the 14th-century Percy Tomb, a monument to that family; the glass in the great east window; and Early English choir stalls and misericords.

BIBURY (82 C2)
GLOUCESTERSHIRE *pop. 500*

ARLINGTON ROW is a collection of early 17th-century stone cottages along the Coln River. The Row is a favorite with photographers. Nearby is Arlington Mill, housing the Cotswold Museum.

BIDEFORD (82 B2)
DEVON *pop. 12,200*

CLOVELLY is a small village on the Torridge River, 8¹/₂ miles west of Bideford. The houses and cottages lean together on steep streets that descend to the harbor, and the village is considered one of the most picturesque in England.

BIRMINGHAM (82 C3)
WEST MIDLANDS *pop. 1,024,100*

In William the Conqueror's 11th-century survey of lands, the *Domesday Book*, Birmingham is described as "worth 20 shillings and having nine tenants living under the lord of the manor." Some ten centuries later, Birmingham is the metropolis of the Midlands, the second largest city in Britain, and a sizeable manufacturing center.

Not an ancient city, Birmingham developed much of its current appearance at the end of the 19th century, a time of extensive urban renewal. Victoria Square, the principal plaza, is surrounded by governmental and commercial buildings, including the city's neo-classical town hall. The Symphony Hall, one of the finest concert halls in Europe, is nearby, inside the International Convention Centre.

West of Victoria Square is the Central Library and beyond it the Hall of Memory, commemorating citizens killed in both world wars. The old market area of the Bull Ring has been redeveloped as a modern shopping center.

Birmingham is most productive in the arts. The City of Birmingham Symphony Orchestra, the Birmingham Royal Ballet and the D'Oyley Carte Opera Company are all resident in the city.

In addition to its three universities, Birmingham also has an institute for the fine arts.

Inland water cruises of the region are available. For additional tourist information, contact the Visitor Information Centre at 2 City Arcade, Birmingham, West Midlands B2 4TX; tel: 0121-643 2514 and at 130 Colmore Row, Birmingham B2 5TJ; tel: 0121-693 6300.

CATHEDRAL CHURCH OF ST. PHILIP, was initially designed by Thomas Archer and consecrated in 1715. The large baroque structure has several later additions, notably the Burne-Jones stained-glass windows depicting scenes from the life of Christ.

CITY OF BIRMINGHAM MUSEUM AND ART GALLERY, Chamberlain Square, is noted for its pre-Raphaelite works.

BLACKPOOL (82 B4)
LANCASHIRE *pop. 143,800*

Originally a fishing village, Blackpool has mushroomed into Britain's largest holiday resort, known to Britons as the "Playground of the North," the chief attractions are the beach, Blackpool Sea Life Centre and the Blackpool Tower, a 520-foot imitation of the Eiffel Tower that dominates the seafront. The city has three piers, the Winter Gardens and Opera House, and the famous Blackpool Pleasure Beach.

BODMIN (82 A1)
CORNWALL *pop. 14,500*

Bodmin is a sombre-looking granite town on the southwestern edge of Bodmin Moor. On the main Land's End road, Bodmin is a good point from which to explore the tip of Cornwall and the north and south coasts.

LANHYDROCK, 2½ miles south east, is a restored 17th-century mansion with a gatehouse, Victorian servants' quarters and a picture gallery containing 17th- to 20th-century family portraits.

BOSTON (82 D3)
LINCOLNSHIRE *pop. 36,600*

Ancient Boston on the Witham River enjoyed its heyday as a 13th-century Hanseatic wine- and wool-trading town. It is better known to U.S. visitors for associations with the Massachusetts city founded by religious malcontents from the English Boston. Links with the American city are maintained in several different ways.

On Scotia Creek south east of Boston is a granite memorial to the first pilgrims, who in 1607 attempted to flee to religious freedom in the New World.

▲ BOURNEMOUTH (82 C1)
DORSET *pop. 154,000*

The south coast's largest resort, Bournemouth came of age in the Victorian era and retains the atmosphere of that time. The town is midway along the southern English coast, making it convenient for visits to historic sites in nearby Hampshire and Wiltshire.

COMPTON ACRES GARDEN, 3 miles west on Canford Cliffs Road, is one of the finest gardens of its kind in Europe. It contains exotic plants and priceless statuary; also of note are the Japanese, Italian, Roman and English gardens.

▲ BRADFORD (82 C4)
WEST YORKSHIRE *pop. 295,000*

A primary wool-manufacturing center, Bradford dates from Norman times. The National Museum of Photography, Film and Television, has studios, galleries and displays presenting various forms of photography and film-making.

BRONTË PARSONAGE MUSEUM, 8 miles north west at Haworth, is the home of the Brontë sisters, 19th-century novelists. The house contains mementoes of their lives.

▲ BRIGHTON & HOVE (82 D1)
EAST SUSSEX *pop. 233,400*

Brighton became a fashionable health and bathing resort with the patronage of King George IV in the late 18th century. Three miles of seafront, shopping in The Lanes (charming little back streets), and Europe's largest marina add to its charms. It is one of England's most fashionable resorts.

Hove, the adjoining town, is distinguished by imposing, Regency-style buildings with spacious lawns.

> ### PIERS OF THE REALM
> The pier, that familiar feature of the seaside, is descended from the much earlier quay, built to land cargo and passengers on an open shore. In 1823 Brighton constructed its famous Chain Pier, like a suspension bridge tiptoeing gracefully into the English Channel (which destroyed it in a storm in 1896). Sadly, piers are now an endangered species, being costly to repair and maintain.

ROYAL PAVILION, Old Steine, was built in 1787 for the Prince Regent, later King George IV. The architect John Nash redesigned the pavilion into a whimsical-looking structure of Indo-Chinese-Moorish style. Extensive structural restoration has taken place.

▲ BRISTOL (82 C2)
AVON *pop. 372,600*

At the outlet of the Avon River is Bristol, hailed as the port where many historic voyages began. In 1497 John Cabot sailed from Bristol on a journey that led to the discovery of the northern half of the New World.

Though severely damaged by air attacks in World War II, Bristol retains a number of architectural treasures.

The city's grandest ecclesiastical structure is the 13th-century Church of St. Mary Redcliffe, resembling a cathedral in its floor plan. Bristol's Theatre Royal is the oldest theater in England still in use.

CLIFTON SUSPENSION BRIDGE, over the Avon Gorge, was considered a daring feat of engineering when it was built in the 19th century. It still offers excellent views. A toll is charged for automobiles.

MATTHEW VISITORS' CENTRE, Redcliffe Quay, is the site of a reconstruction of the ship John Cabot sailed to the New World. The *Matthew* will actually sail across the Atlantic in 1997.

BROADWAY (82 C3)
HEREFORD AND WORCESTER
pop. 2,100

A pretty village of honey-colored houses and tidy gardens, Broadway was known as the "Painted Lady of the Cotswolds" during the 19th century.

BROADWAY TOWER COUNTRY PARK, 1 mile south east, is a park surrounding a tower built in 1799 by the sixth Earl of Coventry. Three floors of the tower contain exhibits; an observation room and telescope provide splendid views of the 12 nearby counties.

BUXTON (82 C4)
DERBYSHIRE *pop. 20,800*

One of the highest towns in England, Buxton is a mountain spa. Visitors enjoy the invigorating climate, thermal springs, golf courses and sports events; the Easter steeplechase is a yearly contest.

▲ CAMBRIDGE (82 D3) ★
CAMBRIDGESHIRE *pop. 101,200*

The early prosperity of old Cambridge was due in great part to its namesake – a bridge across the Cam River that was the only crossing on a major trade route between eastern and central England. Cambridge began to emerge as a seat of learning early in the 13th century with the town-and-gown troubles at Oxford, although the first college, Peterhouse, was not established until 1284.

In the course of a few centuries, Cambridge gained 22 more colleges and became significant in the shaping of English life. Just a few of the many eminent names associated with the university include William Pitt the Younger; diarist Samuel Pepys; scientists Sir Isaac Newton and Charles Darwin; and several poets, writers and politicians.

The university and college buildings – courts, halls, gates and chapels – form a rich sampling of styles from Norman to modern. Most prominent among them is imposing King's College Chapel. Not far away is Queens' College, founded in the 15th century by queens Margaret of Anjou and Elizabeth Woodville.

Other structures worth noting are the old court of Corpus Christi, the 17th-century hall of Clare and the entrance gateway to St. John's.

The city's manmade enchantment is enhanced by gardens and commons with such curious names as Jesus Green, Midsummer Common, Sheep's Green and Christ's Pieces. Most favored are the Backs, landscaped lawns extending for half a mile behind the main row of colleges. The Cam River, winding its way through the Backs, is spanned here and there by a bridge – the graceful stone bridge at Clare, the Bridge of Sighs at St. John's and the Mathematical Bridge at Queens' College. The University Botanic Garden at Cory Lodge comprises 40 acres of excellent botanical collections.

Punting (a type of boating) along the Backs is a favorite Cambridge pastime, and there are facilities for many other kinds of sport as well. For additional tourist information contact Tourist Information Centre, Wheeler Street, Cambridge, Cambridgeshire CB2 3QB; tel: 01223 322640.

CAMBRIDGE CEMETERY is 3 miles west on the A45; here is the final resting place for more than 3,800 American soldiers who lost their lives during World War II.

FITZWILLIAM MUSEUM, Trumpington Street, was founded in 1816. The art collection is now one of the best in Britain.

KING'S COLLEGE CHAPEL, built from 1445 to 1515, is one of the finest examples of the English Perpendicular style. Visitors come not only to view this impressive building, but also to hear the choral and organ music. The chapel's memorable Festival of Nine Lessons and Carols is broadcast throughout the world every Christmas Eve.

CANTERBURY (82 E2) ★
KENT *pop. 35,000*

A settlement even before the Roman era, Canterbury is one of England's oldest and most historic cities. It was here that Augustine, on a mission from Rome in the 6th century, initiated the English people's conversion to Christianity. With the establishment of an abbey and later a cathedral, Canterbury became the prime "See of England" and functioned as a principal religious and cultural center throughout the Saxon period.

Rich in medieval historical associations, Canterbury is often remembered as the scene of Archbishop Thomas à Becket's murder by four knights of King Henry II in 1170. Becket was canonized in 1173.

By the 14th century, Canterbury had become a tourist town, its industry based on the pilgrimages to the shrine of St. Thomas. This aspect of the city's history is captured in Geoffrey Chaucer's *Canterbury Tales*, which recounts the journey of a group of fictional pilgrims from London about 1390.

The city's greatest monument is the cathedral, which bears the stamp of many people and events.

Many old almshouses also still stand, among them 11th-century St. John's and 12th-century St. Thomas' of Eastbridge, where pilgrims stopped to rest and eat. For further tourist information contact the Tourist Information Centre 34 St Margaret's Street, Canterbury, Kent CT1 2TG; tel: 01227 766567.

CATHEDRAL, founded by Augustine, has been reconstructed and enlarged several times during its long history. The structure today is largely Perpendicular in style, with Norman and Early English sections. A vast and imposing building, it is visible from all parts of Canterbury and beyond. Its most remarkable feature is the 235-foot bell tower, known both as Bell Harry and Angel Steeple, after the gilded angel that once graced its top. Two bulkier towers with tiered buttresses rise from the west front; one is the original structure from 1465, the other a 19th-century copy.

With a long nave and an unusually long choir, the building is more than 300 feet long. At the eastern end is a circular tower known as the Corona, or Becket's Crown. On the northern side of the cathedral are the remains of the once great monastic buildings, which include the 15th-century Great Cloister, the Norman dormitory, the library and the Chapter House.

Chapels extend from the double aisles of the choir, and the choir walls and arcades curve inward. The Trinity Chapel, occupying the eastern end of the church, contained the tomb of St. Thomas until 1538, when Henry VIII ordered the shrine destroyed and the remains of the saint scattered. The 13th-century stained-glass windows, which illustrate the miracles wrought by St. Thomas, were mostly spared.

Near the site of the shrine is the tomb and effigy of Edward the Black Prince, who died in 1376. Henry IV and Joan of Navarre also are interred in this section.

CHILHAM CASTLE GARDENS, 5 miles south west on A252 at Chilham, is a 17th-century mansion (not open to the public) reputedly created by architect Inigo Jones and landscaped by the redoubtable Capability Brown.

CARLISLE (82 C5)
CUMBRIA *pop. 73,200*
Lying very near Scotland, Carlisle figured in the bloody era of border warfare. Its castle was erected in the 11th century and rebuilt many times, and has carved messages on its walls from Scottish prisoners captured in the 1745 rebellion.

HADRIAN'S WALL stretches almost 74 miles from Wallsend to Bowness. Built 122–26 AD, it was designed to defend the frontier of the Roman province from ancient northern tribes. At Vindolanda Fort near Hexham, 30 miles east of Carlisle, a section of the wall is reconstructed to its original form.

CERNE ABBAS (82 C1)
DORSET
Secluded Cerne Abbas is known for its row of overhung Tudor cottages and for the remains of a 10th-century abbey. On nearby Giant Hill is the so-called Cerne Giant, a 180-foot fertility figure carved in chalk, thought to have been created during the Roman occupation.

▲ CHANNEL ISLANDS (82 E1)
pop. 142,200
The Channel Islands – Jersey, Guernsey, Alderney, Sark and Herm – are favorite vacation spots in Britain. Visitors are attracted by the mild channel climate and tax-free shopping.

Jersey, the largest of the islands, is only 14 miles from the French coast and, even after centuries of British domination, bears a medieval French air. St. Helier, Jersey's capital, is a small but lively town; shops, restaurants and nightspots line its narrow streets.

Although flat sandy beaches flank St. Helier, much of Jersey's coastline consists of tumbling cliffs and heathery slopes dotted by picturesque harbor towns. On the rugged east coast is Gorey, whose tidy cottages are dwarfed by the battlements of Mont Orgueil Castle. The 12th- and 13th-century structure is one of the best preserved medieval concentric castles in Britain.

Guernsey is well liked for its placid holiday beaches. Sandy coves and bays are protected by the granite headlands of the indented coast. St. Peter Port, the island's capital, is a pleasant town of stone houses and streets. Granite stairs and cobbled lanes climb the hill and provide views of the harbor and medieval castle below. Colorful markets are stocked with the region's produce.

Alderney, reached by sea from Guernsey, is an unspoiled island of silvery sand dunes, pools and hidden bays.

On the tiny, rocky island of Sark, motor vehicles are strictly prohibited and travel is limited to bicycles or horse-drawn carriages.

The tiny island of Herm lies between Guernsey and Sark. A single hotel, a few cottages, dunes, woods and an old manor house are the entertainment; Shell Beach is a favorite place for swimming.

Jersey and Guernsey are served by daily flights from many locations in Britain, and by ferry from several ports in Britain and St. Malo in France.

CHELTENHAM (82 C2)
GLOUCESTERSHIRE *pop. 90,500*
The Cotswold town of Cheltenham has been a favorite holiday resort since the 18th century, when its three saline springs were discovered. Much of that era lives on in the Regency buildings, wide tree-lined streets and pleasant parks. Drinking water can still be obtained at the town hall and the Pittville Pump Room, a masterpiece of Greek Revival style.

Popular as a sports center, the spa is the site of the biggest steeplechase in Britain. The National Hunt Festival (Gold Cup) takes place in March. The town hall, opera house and civic playhouse offer other entertainment. Every

July fans of avant-garde music flock to Cheltenham for the International Festival of Music.

CHEDWORTH ROMAN VILLA, 8½ miles south east, dates from 180 to 350 AD. Rediscovered in 1864, it is probably the best-preserved Roman villa in Britain.

▲ CHESTER (82 C4)
CHESHIRE *pop. 122,000*

Like most English towns with "caster," "cester" or "chester" in their names, Chester dates from the Roman times. These names are derived from the Latin word *castra*, meaning camp.

Much of medieval Chester was built on top of the Roman city and survives today. The walls surrounding the town follow the line of the Roman walls; even the four main streets were laid along their ancient predecessors.

Chester also is noted for 16th- and 17th-century timber-framed houses. The Rows, a line of "gingerbread" buildings with shops on the first and second stories, are of particular interest. The upper-floor shops have their own arcaded walkways.

The visitor center presents Roman and later local history through a film show, a life-size exhibit of Victorian Chester and maps and prints. For additional tourist information, write to the Visitor Centre, Vicars Lane, Chester, Cheshire CH1 1QX; tel: 01244 351609.

CHICHESTER (82 D1)
WEST SUSSEX *pop. 25,300*

Though now a quiet country town, Chichester was important during the Roman era when it functioned as a *regnum*, or reigning area. Reminders of that time are the city walls, built about 200 AD, and the nearby Roman palace and museum.

GOODWOOD HOUSE, 3 miles north east, is the unusual, but stately home of the dukes of Richmond. The three-sided house, designed by James Wyatt in 1780, is representative of Sussex stonework. It contains collections of paintings and valuable Sèvres porcelain. On the property is Goodwood Racecourse, the site of a prestigious annual meet (horseracing) in late July and early August.

ROMAN PALACE, 1 mile west at Fishbourne, was discovered in 1960 under a few feet of soil. A large structure with four colonnaded wings enclosing a formal garden, it is the largest Roman palace in Britain and famous for its mosaics. The opulent structure was probably built about 75 AD for Cogidubnus, a Briton king.

WEALD AND DOWNLAND OPEN-AIR MUSEUM, 6 miles on A286 at Singleton, is an assemblage of historic buildings depicting regional life from the Middle Ages to the 19th century.

CHIPPING CAMPDEN (82 C3)
GLOUCESTERSHIRE *pop. 2,000*

The market town of Chipping Campden lies near the northern edge of the Cotswolds; the lovely old houses lining its main street are made of the stone from the well-known hills.

HIDCOTE MANOR GARDEN, 3 miles north east, is a series of formal gardens separated by unusual varieties of hedges.

CIRENCESTER (82 C2)
GLOUCESTERSHIRE *pop. 17,000*

The unofficial capital of the Cotswold region, Cirencester (pronounced SIGHren-sester) is an excellent center for touring this land of gentle hills and stone-built villages. In the town itself are many gray stone inns and houses built by medieval merchants.

▲ COLCHESTER (82 E2)
ESSEX *pop. 151,900*

Established as a Roman colony, Colchester is England's oldest town on record. Ruins include a long stretch of ancient wall, recovered buildings and dikes, many sculptures and inscribed stone tablets. A fine collection of Romano-British antiquities is housed in the dungeon of Colchester's remarkable 11th-century castle.

▲ COVENTRY (82 C3)
WEST MIDLANDS *pop. 304,400*

Coventry rose to fame in the Middle Ages as a producer of woolen cloth. During the Industrial Revolution the town became a manufacturing city. Its heavy industry made it a prime target for German bombers in World War II, and much of the central city, including the cathedral church, was destroyed.

A new traffic-free shopping center is one feature of the rebuilt city. Standing in this modern sector is a statue of medieval resident Lady Godiva, who according to legend rode naked through town on market day to protest her husband's unfair taxation of the citizens.

Nearby Warwick Castle (see Warwick on p.126) is an excursion.

CATHEDRAL, designed by Sir Basil Spence, was begun in 1954 and incorporates the ruins of its 14th-century predecessor. The Sutherland tapestry behind the high altar and *God's Revelations*, a bronze group by Sir Jacob Epstein depicting St. Michael and the Devil, are features.

DARTMOOR NATIONAL PARK
(82 B1) ★
DEVON

Long before it became a national park, the desolate Dartmoor plateau was a favorite setting for English detective stories. The bleak uplands, unfenced and uninhabited remains of ancient mountains, are pocked with peat bogs and dotted with heather. Weirdly shaped, isolated granite headlands, the tors, soar to more than 2,000 feet above sea level.

Not many people live on Dartmoor today, but this land was inhabited as early as 2000 BC. Evidence exists in the forms of stone circles, enclosures and monoliths, silent memorials to Britain's Bronze Age denizens.

The best way to explore the park is on foot or by horseback. Hikers should take sturdy boots, a compass and a competent guide who can circumnavigate the dangerous peat bogs. Small towns on the moor's edge, including Yelverton, Ashburton and Bovey Tracey, are popular as touring centers.

DARTMOUTH (82 B1)
DEVON *pop. 5,600*

Dartmouth, a seaport on the Dart estuary, has figured often in naval history. From Dartmouth Richard I's crusaders set off in 1190 for the Holy Land. A memorial commemorates a more recent event. In 1944, U.S. troops left from Dartmouth to participate in the World War II invasion of Normandy.

Though damaged by World War II bombs, many old buildings have been preserved. Especially worth noting are a row of 17th-century houses on the waterfront at Bayard's Cove.

▲ DERBY (82 C3)
DERBYSHIRE *pop. 220,700*

A market town since the Middle Ages, Derby gained an industrial aspect in the 19th century. Manufacturing a great assortment of goods from engines to underwear, it is best known for the making of fine porcelain, an industry created by William Duesbury in 1756.

ALL SAINT'S CATHEDRAL CHURCH dominates the town with its graceful 178-foot tower. Inside, the stained glass is superb.

DERBY MUSEUM AND ART GALLERY, on The Strand, contains items of archeological and historical interest. Exhibits include a reconstructed public house.

KEDLESTON HALL, about 4 miles north west, was built in neo-classical style by English architect Robert Adam. Some 50 acres of carefully tended grounds surround the country house.

ROYAL CROWN DERBY WORKS rose to fame after their founding by William Duesbury and Andrew Planche in 1750. The identifying crown trademark and the "crown" in the name was permitted by George III, who was favorably impressed when he visited the porcelain company in 1783. In the next century, Queen Victoria appointed the company manufacturers to the Crown and added the "royal" to the name.

The company maintains its standards of excellence and is world renowned. Reservations for tours must be made well in advance. Contact Tours Operator, Royal Crown Derby Porcelain Co, Osmaston Road, Derby DE3 8JZ; tel: 01332 7128000.

DORCHESTER (82 C1)
DORSET *pop. 14,200*
Founded by the Romans, Dorchester has evidence of an even earlier settlement. It was the home of Judge George Jeffreys, who with four other judges tried and executed hundreds of rebels in the Bloody Assize of 1685.

HARDY'S COTTAGE is 3 miles north east at Higher Bockhampton. The writer, Thomas Hardy, was born in this little thatched house in 1840; it contains a small collection of items associated with him. The cottage can be visited only by appointment; contact the custodian or the local National Trust office.

MAIDEN CASTLE, 1½ miles south west, is England's greatest prehistoric fort. Quadruple walls and complicated double entrances served as the fortifications of the early Celts.

▲ DOVER (82 E2)
KENT *pop. 34,300*
Dover has long been a cross-channel port. The Romans, who called it *Dubris*, built a lighthouse here to guide their troops across the Channel. In the Middle Ages, it was chief among the Cinque Ports, and during World War II it withstood heavy German shellfire from Calais. Surviving reminders of earlier times include a 12th-century castle. The road north west to Canterbury follows the route of Roman Watling Street.

ROMAN PAINTED HOUSE, New Street, is part of an exceptionally well-preserved Roman town house containing 1,800-year-old wall paintings.

DUNSTER (82 B2)
SOMERSET *pop. 800*
Dunster's 17th-century house and old castle (a National Trust Property) make it one of the prettiest villages on Exmoor. The oldest structure is the castle, owned by only two families, the Mohuns and the Luttrells, in the course of its 1,000 years.

DUNSTER CASTLE AND MILL, 3 miles south east of Minehead, was built on the site of a mill mentioned in the Domesday Survey of 1086. The present mill, built in the 18th century, was restored to working order in 1979.

DURHAM (82 C5)
COUNTY DURHAM *pop. 41,200*
The city of Durham, on the Wear River, is dominated by a staid Norman castle and cathedral. The castle is now part of the University of Durham. The cathedral is considered the finest example of Norman architecture in Europe – it is best visited with a guide.

ELY (82 D3)
CAMBRIDGESHIRE *pop. 12,000*
The name Ely means Eel Island, a reference to the dietary staple of its early Saxon dwellers. Ely was an island when Hereward the Wake and his followers held out against William the Conqueror. Not until the 17th and 18th centuries were the flat, low-lying fens drained for farming. A few isolated patches remain, protected by the National Trust.

ELY CATHEDRAL has overlooked the town and surrounding countryside since the Middle Ages. "The Monarch of the Fens," as it is known, was begun about 1080 on the site of the 7th-century monastery.

It is a harmonious mix of several architectural styles. It is mainly Norman, but major sections represent Early English, Perpendicular and Decorated Gothic. Alan de Walsingham, who designed the exterior, also contributed the designs for the Lady Chapel and choir stalls.

Beneath the lantern tower is an octagon that separates the great choir from the 208-foot nave. The massive western tower, rising 270 feet, was added in the 15th century as a complement to the lantern.

EPSOM (82 D2)
SURREY *pop. 68,400*
Epsom is primarily known for Epsom Downs Racecourse, where the horse race, the Derby, occurs during the first week of June. Epsom Salts take their name from the mineral springs responsible for the town's origin as a spa.

ETON – *see Windsor on p.127.*

▲ EXETER (82 B1)
DEVON *pop. 103,000*
The county town of Exeter sits on a hill sloping to the Exe River. Its great variety of architectural styles range from medieval to modern. Medieval walls partly surround the city, and passages built in the Middle Ages run under the main streets (guided tours available). There are pubs claiming to be the regular haunt of people like Sir Francis Drake.

EXETER CATHEDRAL, situated in the town center, was completed in 1369. Of note are the 60-foot bishop's throne and medieval tombs. Two Norman towers were built in 1133.

FOLKESTONE (82 E2)
KENT *pop. 45,300*
Once an important channel port and terminus of regular boat services to the Continent, Folkestone is now the boarding point for the Hoverspeed Seacat, with crossings to Boulogne four times a day. It is also a summer resort and fishing center. The new 32-mile Channel

---

THE CHANNEL TUNNEL

The project to build a link from England to France has had a long germination; diggings were made as far back as Napoleonic times. The Anglo-French venture that has finally come to fruition, a railroad tunnel from Folkestone in Kent to Sangatte near Calais, in France, has created a mountain of complications. British Rail made errors over a high-speed rail link to London, houses were bought up for demolition, but then the route was changed and the houses remained empty. Recession hit and time and financial estimates were way off. Despite all these setbacks, the first trains to cross beneath the Channel finally made their journey in September 1994.

Tunnel, opened in 1994, connects Folkestone with Calais in France.

GLASTONBURY (82 C2)
SOMERSET *pop. 7,500*
Historic Glastonbury has many literary associations. Joseph of Arimathea is said to have brought the Chalice of the Last Supper to this town, supposed by some to be the Avalon of King Arthur and his knights. The town has numerous monuments and relics.

ABBEY, in ruins, is where King Arthur and his wife, Queen Guinevere, are said to be buried. In the grounds is the Glastonbury Thorn, which allegedly sprang from St Joseph's staff and which blossoms each Christmas.

GLOUCESTER (82 C2)
GLOUCESTERSHIRE *pop. 97,000*
Gloucester is an old strategic city that once guarded the lowest crossing on the Severn River and the routes into Wales. Fortified first by the Romans, the city was later walled by the Normans. Its most important medieval monument is

the cathedral; other historic sites are the City East Gate, with its Roman and medieval gate towers and moat in an underground chamber; the St. Mary de Crypt Church; the ruins of St. Oswald's Priory; and The New Inn, a medieval hostelry. Bishop Hooper's Lodging is now a folk museum.

CATHEDRAL, was founded in the 12th century as a monastic church and re-founded by Henry VIII as a cathedral. The east window, dating from the 14th-century, is the largest stained-glass window in England.

THE PROTECTION OF BIRDLIFE

The Wildfowl and Wetlands Trust at Slimbridge in Gloucestershire is dedicated to the protection of wetland sites and has wildfowl collections at eight centers in Britain. The Royal Society for the Protection of Birds (R.S.P.B.) is the principal body concerned with wild birds and their environment, and has 120 reserves in Britain.

GLYNDEBOURNE (82 D1)
EAST SUSSEX *pop. 300*
Tiny Glyndebourne, near Lewes, is noted chiefly for its Opera House, which is in the middle of an English garden. The Glyndebourne Festival Opera performs from April to August. Dinner is served during intermission or visitors can bring their own meals; reservations must be made well in advance.

BENTLEY WILDFOWL AND MOTOR MUSEUM is 5 miles north east at Halland. Wildfowl from around the world can be seen on the grounds, including black swans, mandarin duck and flamingo.

GRASMERE (82 C5)
CUMBRIA *pop. 1,600*
Grasmere is a good point from which to hike to the surrounding mountains and lakes of the Lake District. Poet William

Wordsworth lived in this town for nine years; his grave and those of his family are in the village churchyard.

DOVE COTTAGE AND THE WORDSWORTH MUSEUM are south of the village at Town End. Dove Cottage was the residence of William Wordsworth. The Wordsworth Museum, opposite the cottage, houses manuscripts, paintings and various items associated with the poet.

RYDAL MOUNT, 2 miles south east at Rydal, was the Wordsworth family home from 1813 until the poet's death in 1850.

GREAT MALVERN (82 C3)
HEREFORD AND WORCESTER
pop. 30,800
Most vacationers have yet to fully discover this charming sheltered town. Modern attractions include a spa, an outdoor swimming pool, a golf course, winter gardens and theater long associated with performances of George Bernard Shaw and J.M. Barrie.

GUERNSEY (82 E1) – *see Channel Islands on p.109.*

▲ GUILDFORD (82 D2)
SURREY *pop. 61,600*
Guildford, the county town of Surrey, is set on the Wey River where it has cut through the North Downs. Its steep High Street is lined with old buildings; the half-timbered guildhall dates from the 17th century, as does Abbot's Hospital, a group of almshouses. Modern buildings include the Yvonne Arnaud Theatre and the law courts. Near the cathedral is the University of Surrey. Well-tended parks and gardens recall the town's ancient name, derived from the Saxon phrase meaning "ford of the golden flowers."

CATHEDRAL, on Stag Hill, is the town's most conspicuous landmark. The simplified Gothic structure was designed by Sir Edward Maufe. Begun in 1936, it was completed in 1962.

CLANDON PARK, 3 miles east, at West Clandon, is a Palladian house built about 1735, probably by Giacomo Leoni.

WISLEY GARDEN, 5 miles north east off the A3 at Wisley, is a 250-acre display of experimental flowers, fruit and vegetables. Walks wind through rock gardens containing heather and alpine plants.

THE BATTLE OF HASTINGS

Every British schoolchild knows the date 1066, when the Battle of Hastings between William of Normandy and King Harold took place at Battle (as it is now called). Strangely, the great turning point in English history was a haphazard affair. The English (Saxons) should have trounced the French, who were vastly outnumbered and fighting uphill. However, they made a strategic blunder in storming downhill when they thought some of the Normans were retreating; this left a hole in the Saxon defenses on the top of the slope, which the Normans promptly filled.

HARROGATE (82 C4)
NORTH YORKSHIRE *pop. 69,300*
Harrogate is a well-known, fashionable spa and convention center; wide streets and spa gardens are typical. At the edge of the town gardens is the Royal Pump Room, an 1804 octagonal structure built over a sulphur spring. The Pump Room is now a museum of local history, and the sulphur spring can be tasted.

HAREWOOD HOUSE and BIRD GARDEN, 6 miles south, is the home of the Earl and Countess of Harewood, designed in 1759 by John Carr and Robert Adam. The bird garden has exotic species.

KNARESBOROUGH CASTLE is 3 miles north east at Knaresborough. This ruin of a 14th-century stronghold above the Nidd River includes two baileys, a keep, and gatehouses.

HASTINGS & ST. LEONARDS-ON-SEA (82 E1)
EAST SUSSEX *pop. 81,900*
Despite its popularity, the coastal resort of Hastings retains much of the character of its fishing port past. In the eastern part of town, narrow streets lined with tiled cottages lead down to the old harbor area. The remains of a Norman castle are on a cliff overlooking the beach.

West is St. Leonards-on-Sea, principally a residential area with family hotels and boarding houses. Along the 3 miles of seafront stretches a continuous promenade, with many vacation amenities .

There are fine views over the Channel and the countryside from East Hill, Ecclesbourne Glen and the Fire Hills.

HATFIELD (82 D2)
HERTFORDSHIRE *pop. 29,000*
HATFIELD HOUSE was built by the first Earl of Salisbury from 1607 to 1611 and has been the home of the Cecil family since then. In the garden are the remains of the Old Palace, where Queen Elizabeth I was imprisoned by her half sister Mary I from 1555 to 1558. The house contains some of Elizabeth's personal items, as well as notable works of art.

HEREFORD (82 C3)
HEREFORD AND WORCESTER
pop. 48,400
Hereford is a flourishing agricultural town. Its 12th-century sandstone cathedral contains a collection of rare books and the Mappa Mundi, a 13th-century world map. Of additional interest are the 15th-century Booth Hall. Not far from the Welsh border, Hereford is a good base for excursions into Wales.

HERM – *see Channel Islands on p.109.*

HERTFORD (82 D2)
HERTFORDSHIRE *pop. 22,400*
Hertford is an ancient county town at the convergence of the Lea, Beane and

Rib rivers. Elizabeth I spent much of her childhood in the town's castle, of which only a gatehouse remains today. Wings were added in the 18th and 20th centuries. The castle grounds, often the site of band concerts, are open to the public.

▲ HULL (82 D4)
HUMBERSIDE *pop. 245,100*
Hull, or more properly Kingston-upon-Hull, is an important seaport 20 miles from the eastern coast at the confluence of the Hull and Humber rivers. Places to visit include Ferens Art Gallery, the Transport and Archaeological Museum, the Town Docks Museum, and the Holy Trinity Church, with its notable brickwork. Significant among Hull's old houses is the Wilberforce House, 17th-century home of William Wilberforce, who instigated the abolition of slavery.

▲ IPSWICH (82 E3)
SUFFOLK *pop. 119,600*
The port of Ipswich lies at the head of the Orwell estuary. An industrial town, Ipswich is not without historic interest. The painter Thomas Gainsborough was a resident for a long time; many of his works, along with those of John Constable, are on display at the museum and art gallery of Christchurch Mansion. Also in Ipswich are the beautiful Sparrowe's House, a 16th-century dwelling that now serves as a bookshop.

IRONBRIDGE (82 C3)
SHROPSHIRE *pop. 1,500*
Ironmaster Abraham Darby first smelted iron using coke as a fuel in Ironbridge in the early 18th century. The process contributed significantly to Britain's leadership in the Industrial Revolution. Locally, it was responsible for the creation of the world's first iron bridge. His 196-foot bridge still spans the town.

IRONBRIDGE GORGE MUSEUM is a series of seven museums preserving major sites of the iron industry along a 4-mile section of the Severn River.

JERSEY (82 E1) – *see Channel Islands on p.109.*

KENDAL (82 C5)
CUMBRIA *pop. 23,600*
The very old market town of Kendal, in the lush Kent Valley, is a good starting point for exploring the English Lakeland. Kendal also is interesting in itself, with cobbled streets and quaint archways.

ABBOT HALL, in Kirkland, houses both an art gallery and a museum of Lakeland life and industry.

LEVENS HALL, 5 miles south west, is a well-preserved Elizabethan mansion with a topiary garden.

SIZERGH CASTLE, 3½ miles south west, has been the home of the Stricklands for more than 700 years. The oldest section of the current structure is the pele tower, built about 1340. Notable interior features are the fine paneling and ceilings, antique furniture, works of art and Stuart and Jacobite relics.

LAKELAND TERMS
Small lakes are called tarns, mountains are fells, streams are known as becks, spotted black-faced sheep are Herdwicks, white-faced ones are Swaledales. Force means waterfall.

KESWICK (82 B5)
CUMBRIA *pop. 5,600*
Keswick on Derwent Water is an excellent base for touring the northern part of the Lake District. Most of the attractions in this part of the country are purely scenic. Castle Head, a half mile south, offers splendid views of Derwent Water and Bassenthwaite Lake; Latrigg, to the north east, affords a higher vantage point and more extensive vistas. John Ruskin praised Friar's Crag, which overlooks the northeastern end of Derwent Water, for its panoramas. The area is also known for its associations with the English

Romantics. Wordsworth was born in Cockermouth, and Sir Walter Scott and Samuel Coleridge Taylor visited him in Grasmere.

MIREHOUSE, 3 miles north west, is a 17th-century manor house with well-preserved rooms and original furniture.

LAKE DISTRICT NATIONAL PARK (82 C5) ★
CUMBRIA

In north-west England, the Lake District National Park, just 40 miles across, is an area of rugged windswept mountains, interspersed by tranquil lakes. Spring and autumn are the best times to visit, when the area is less crowded. The western district is more remote, with England's highest peak, Scafell Pike (3,025 feet). Walking, climbing and sailing are popular, while there are strong literary connections with the 18th-century poets Wordsworth and Coleridge.

VISITOR CENTER, on A591 at Brockhole, is set in 32 acres of woodland on the eastern shore of Lake Windermere and has exhibits relating to Lakeland.

▲ LEEDS (82 C4)
WEST YORKSHIRE *pop. 454,700*

Leeds has a diversified industrial base. One of the prices of obvious success has been a coat of grime on its fine Victorian buildings, including the Corn Hall, the Infirmary and the town hall. More utilitarian complexes of glass and reinforced concrete have risen nearby.

Leeds has three fine theaters, a leading British university and an excellent art gallery, as well as Britain's only remaning music hall, the City Varieties.

TEMPLE NEWSAM HOUSE AND PARK is 3 miles east. The house is Jacobean with 18th-century additions, and the prominent 18th-century landscape architect Capability Brown redesigned the more than 900-acre grounds as a park. The Knights Templar once had a prosperous farm on these extensive grounds.

LEEDS CASTLE (82 E2)
MAIDSTONE, KENT

Some 4 miles south east of Maidstone on the B2163, Leeds Castle has its origins in Anglo-Saxon England and was a gift from William the Conqueror to a cousin who fought with him in the Battle of Hastings. The grounds incorporate parkland, aviaries, wildlife and a golf course. The most spectacular views of the castle are from the air.

LEWES (82 D1)
EAST SUSSEX *pop. 15,000*

The old market town of Lewes bears the stamp of hundreds of years of history. Oldest among its extant monuments is a Norman castle, largely in ruins. Barbican House, on the castle grounds, contains archeological finds. Along the town's narrow medieval streets are many old buildings, including tile-hung houses of the 17th century, Georgian buildings of local stone and several old inns. The town is renowned for its fires and torchlight processions on November 5, Guy Fawkes' night (see p.97).

BLUEBELL RAILWAY, 7 miles north off the A275, is a renovated steam train on which passengers can take a 5-mile trip through the Bluebell Woodland. The train departs from Sheffield Park station.

▲ LINCOLN (82 D4)
LINCOLNSHIRE *pop. 80,400*

On a high plateau above the Witham River, Lincoln dominates much of Lincolnshire and is itself commanded by its magnificent cathedral. Medieval Lincoln is more than 1,000 years old. Close by the cathedral are the ruins of an 11th-century castle built by William the Conqueror. Steep cobbled streets go down to the lower, newer town.

CATHEDRAL CHURCH OF ST. MARY was begun late in the 12th century and completed in the 14th century. It remains one of the best examples of the Early English and Decorated styles of English Gothic architecture.

The cathedral's 365-foot spire is visible for miles. Like much of medieval Lincoln, it is built of local limestone.

LINCOLN CASTLE, Castle Hill, was begun in the 11th century by William the Conqueror. A Norman bailey and two motte mounds survived the period; a Victorian prison chapel also is intact.

MUSEUM OF LINCOLNSHIRE LIFE, Burton Road, paints a picture of local life since the late 18th century.

▲ LIVERPOOL (82 C4)
MERSEYSIDE *pop. 457,500*
King John granted a charter to the fishing village of Liverpool on the north bank of the Mersey River in 1207. By the 18th century, the village had become a sizeable port, participating actively in England's West Indies trade. All of this contributed to the teeming city of today.

Though a great seaport with miles of docks, Liverpool also is known for its generous patronage of the fine arts and education. The city also contributed several bands to the "British Invasion" of music in the 1960s, foremost among them the Beatles.

Two tunnels connect Liverpool to Birkenhead across the Mersey, but the finest views of the city's docks and landing platforms are from the ferries. The Royal Liver Building dominates the waterfront. On top of its 295-foot towers are statues of the mythical Liver Bird, which according to local tradition gave Liverpool its name. Once a functioning dock, Albert Dock has been restored to include shops, restaurants and museums.

For further tourist information, contact the Merseyside Welcome Centre, Clayton Square Shopping Centre, Liverpool, Merseyside L1 1QR; tel: 0151-709 3631; or the Tourist Information Centre, Atlantic Pavilion, Albert Dock, Liverpool, Merseyside L3 4AA; tel: 0151-708 8854.

ANGLICAN CATHEDRAL, occupies a commanding position at the summit of St. James Mount. Designed by Sir Giles Gilbert Scott, the red sandstone building is a modern version of the Gothic style. With an interior height of 119 feet and a length of 619 feet, it is the largest ecclesiastical structure in England and the largest Anglican cathedral in the world.

BEATLES STORY, Britannia Pavilion at Albert Dock, has exhibits featuring recreations of Liverpool's Cavern Club, Hamburg's Star Club, Brian Epstein's record shop and London's Abbey Road Studios.

PORT SUNLIGHT HERITAGE CENTRE, situated 4½ miles south at 95 Greendale Road, is a 130-acre garden village which was built by the soap baron Lord Leverhulme in the late 1800s.

ROMAN CATHOLIC CATHEDRAL OF CHRIST THE KING is a vast modern structure on Mount Pleasant designed by award-winning architect Frederick Gibberd.

TATE GALLERY, Albert Dock, houses works from the National Collection of 20th-century art.

WALKER ART GALLERY, William Brown Street, houses a collection of paintings, sculptures and drawings dating from the 1300s to the present day.

LUTON (82 D2)
BEDFORDSHIRE *pop. 169,000*
Luton is an industrial and manufacturing town, easily reached via the M1 motorway from London.

KNEBWORTH HOUSE, GARDENS AND CONTRY PARK, 8½ miles east at Stevenage, includes a 250-acre park and the home of the Lytton family. The house contains a Jacobean banquet hall and a Gothic state drawing room. The park includes a deer park.

LUTON HOO, 2 miles south east on B653, was designed and built by Robert Adam in the 18th century. The gardens were designed by Capability Brown. The house contains a fine collection of paintings, porcelain and jewels.

WHIPSNADE WILD ANIMAL PARK, 6 miles south west, encloses 600 acres on the edge of the Chiltern Hills. Over 3,000 animals can be seen in mostly natural surroundings.

LYME REGIS (82 B1)
DORSET *pop. 3,500*

The Georgian fishing village of Lyme Regis also is a seaside resort with charming houses and fossil-studded cliffs.

THE FOWLES CONNECTION

The Cobb at Lyme Regis is a windswept wall curving out to sea which gained inter–national fame through the film The *French Lieutenant's Woman*, based on the novel by John Fowles.
The Cobb is medieval in origin, and the undercliff, riddled with landslips, is designated a National Nature Reserve.

MALMESBURY (82 C2)
WILTSHIRE *pop. 4,200*

WESTONBIRT ARBORETUM, 5½ miles north west, was laid out in 1829 by the squire of Westonbirt. The 600-acre tree reserve is especially colorful in autumn.

▲ MANCHESTER (82 C4)
GREATER MANCHESTER *pop. 450,100*

Manchester is the capital of England's cotton manufacturing industry and one of the country's busiest cities. It dates from Roman times, but gained prominence in the 18th and 19th centuries after construction of the Manchester Ship Canal provided access to the flourishing port of Liverpool. Growth accelerated as trade was established with the New World.

Although most of the Victorian architecture of old Manchester has been destroyed, a few areas survive. For further information, contact Manchester Visitor Centre, Town Hall Extension, Lloyd Street, Greater Manchester M60 2LA; tel: 0161-234 3157.

CITY ART GALLERIES, Mosley Street, has paintings by the old masters, George Stubbs, Thomas Gainsborough, J. M. W. Turner and the Pre-Raphaelites.

WHITWORTH ART GALLERY, University of Manchester, Whitworth Park, was founded in 1889 by royal charter. Principal collections include watercolors by Blake, Turner and the Pre- Raphaelites as well as Cézanne, Van Gogh and Picasso; and the Whitworth Tapestry, designed by Paolozzi in 1968.

MAN, ISLE OF (82 B5)
pop. 50,500

In the Irish Sea between Northern Ireland and the north-west coast of England lies the colorful Isle of Man, 31 miles long and 13 miles wide. One of the smallest independent countries under the British Crown, the island retains its own parliament, the Tynwald, and makes its own laws and controls taxation. The official language is a form of Celtic Manx similar to Gaelic.

Douglas, the capital and main port, also is the largest city and leading resort. On Prospect Hill is the House of Keys, home of Manx parliament. Annual events include the Manx Grand Prix in September and the International Tourist Trophy races in June.

Castletown, south of Douglas, is the island's former capital. Its leading attraction is Castle Rushen, a beautifully preserved medieval stronghold that guards the harbor's entrance.

Ramsey is the principal northern resort and boasts a fine golf course.

Port Erin is a quiet resort town from which side trips to the uninhabited island, the Calf of Man, can be arranged.

Peel is an old fishing port on the west coast noted for its kippers. Also in Peel are the ruins of 15th-century Peel Castle and the Cathedral of St. German. On its outskirts rises tiered Tynwald Hill, from where new laws are proclaimed.

MARLBOROUGH (82 C2)
WILTSHIRE *pop. 7,000*
The small downland town of Marlborough is known for its wide High Street, lined with excellent Georgian buildings, coaching inns and shops.

Ancient remains on the chalk downlands near Marlborough include the Iron-Age hill fortress of Barbury Castle, 4 miles north west. The White Horse, carved into the chalk in 1804, is 1 mile south west beside A4.

MIDHURST (82 D2)
WEST SUSSEX *pop. 4,660*
PETWORTH HOUSE, about 5½ miles east, was rebuilt in the late 17th century.

The house is famous for its fabulous art collection, on loan to the National Trust from the Treasury, with works by Turner, Gainsborough, Holbein, Frans Hals and Rembrandt. A deer park, designed by Capability Brown, surrounds the house.

▲ NEWCASTLE-UPON-TYNE (82 C5)
TYNE AND WEAR *pop. 203,600*
Though very old, Newcastle-upon-Tyne has the face of a modern industrial town. As early as the 1830s urban renewal began; congested areas were cleared, and streets became broad thoroughfares. Rebuilding continues with the civic center, the modern library, the Laing Art Gallery and a modern shopping district. With so much building and rebuilding, the city still boasts 1,400 acres of open spaces, including the vast Town Moor.

BEDE'S WORLD, Jarrow, 9 miles east, is a museum and working farm commemorating Venerable Bede, the Anglo-Saxon monk who wrote one of the first ever history books in 731 AD.

▲ NORTHAMPTON (82 D3)
NORTHAMPTONSHIRE *pop. 186,000*
On the banks of the Nene River, this is an industrial center famous for boots and shoes. Charles II destroyed part of the town during the Civil War because shoes were made for Cromwell's army.

ALTHORP HALL, 5 miles north east on A428, has been the Spencer family home since 1508. It was the childhood home of the Princess of Wales and is now lived in by her brother, Charles, who inherited the title recently. The collection of pictures, furniture and china is impressive.

▲ NORWICH (82 E3)
NORFOLK *pop. 173,300*
Ancient Norwich spreads comfortably over the Norfolk hills, the spire of its prominent landmark – the Cathedral of the Holy Trinity – easily notable. A thriving settlement at the time of the Norman Conquest, Norwich has prospered since the 10th century as the see of East Anglican bishops.

Probably the most picturesque area is Elm Hill, with old houses and cobbled streets. Other places include the 12th-century Music House, the oldest house in the city; and Strangers' Hall, a museum of 16th–19th-century domestic life.

Near to the Norfolk Broads and the coast, Norwich is a good center for touring these areas.

CATHEDRAL OF THE HOLY TRINITY was begun in the 12th century, but has many later additions. The nave and tower are typically Norman, but the magnificent spire above the tower is from the 15th century. The tower soars at 315 feet; the varied tracery of the cloister arches required 130 years to complete.

NORWICH CASTLE, occupying the city's highest hill, retains its Norman keep; gardens fill the ancient moat.

▲ NOTTINGHAM (82 D3)
NOTTINGHAMSHIRE *pop. 279,700*
Nottingham gained fame as the home of Robin Hood, the medieval outlaw whose lair was in Sherwood Forest. The city has long been noted as the center of the English lace trade.

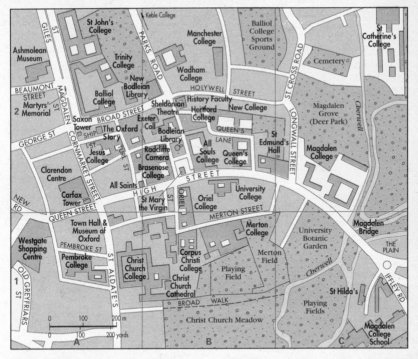

The Goose Fair, a three-day event, is held on the first Thursday of October in the Forest Recreation Ground, a surviving fragment of Sherwood Forest.

D. H. LAWRENCE BIRTHPLACE MUSEUM, 8a Victoria Street, Eastwood, is the birthplace of the English novelist. The house has been restored and furnished in typical Victorian working-class style.

NEWSTEAD ABBEY, 11 miles north, is the former home of Lord Byron. The house contains relics of his life and works.

NOTTINGHAM CASTLE MUSEUM, once the home of Robin Hood's arch-enemy, the Sheriff of Nottingham, is now a museum and art gallery.

▲ OXFORD (82 C2) ★
OXFORDSHIRE *pop. 115,800*
The venerable university and cathedral city of Oxford originated as a religious settlement in the Saxon period. Though

tradition has it that Alfred the Great founded the university, it was probably not until the 12th century that students flocked to Oxford to study in the monastic establishments. In the 13th century several colleges – University, Balliol and Merton – emerged; each considers itself the oldest.

Since the 13th century, the history of Oxford has been the history of the university, with its far-reaching academic and religious activities and its influential lecturers and scholars. From the few colleges in the 13th century, the university has grown to include some 35 colleges, as well as important scientific research facilities, museums and several excellent libraries, including the Bodleian.

Though factories and houses now stretch across the suburbs, this City of Dreaming Spires remains largely unchanged. Old Oxford's showpiece is the High Street, simply called the "High," an ancient street lined with the imposing stone buildings of the university's

BRITAIN · ENGLAND

schools. Dating mainly from the 15th to 17th centuries, the colleges are built around traditional quadrangles; each has its own chapel, hall, library and gardens.

In addition to the popular and traditional pastimes of college life, rowing, punting, swimming and fishing, or simply strolling along the riverbank, are favorite leisure activities. For additional tourist information contact Tourist Information Centre, The Old School, Gloucester Green, Oxford, Oxfordshire OX1 2DA; tel: 01865 726871.

ASHMOLEAN MUSEUM (121 A2), Beaumont Street, is England's oldest museum.It contains European, Egyptian and Near Eastern antiquities and world art.

BODLEIAN LIBRARY (121 B2), in four buildings on Parks Road and Broad Street, was founded in 1602 by Sir Thomas Bodley. It has over 3 million volumes, none of which may leave the library.

COLLEGES OF THE UNIVERSITY are clustered in the central part of the city; most are on or within a short walk of the High. The following is by no means a complete list of Oxford's colleges. Access to some colleges is restricted. Details from the tourist information center.
All Souls (121 A2), High Street, was established in 1438 by Archbishop Chichele of Canterbury. The gateway and front quadrangle date from the period.
Brasenose (121 B2), Radcliffe Square, dates from 1509. The present buildings were constructed on top of the sites of several older halls; the gate tower and hall date from the founding.
Christ Church (121 A1), St. Aldates, known as The House, was founded in 1546 as Cardinal College by Thomas Wolsey. When Wolsey fell into disfavor, it was renamed King Henry VIII College. After its chapel became the cathedral of the diocese in 1546, the college gained its present name. A local landmark is Wren's Tom Tower, wherein hangs the 7½-ton bell Great Tom, dedicated to St. Thomas of Canterbury.

Magdalen (121 C2), High Street, has changed little in appearance since the 15th century. The college is at the end of the High, on the Cherwell River; the Magdalen Walks follow the river and there is a deer park on the grounds.
Merton (121 B1), Merton Street, was founded in Malden in 1264, and transferred here in 1274.
Trinity (121 A2), Broad Street, founded in 1555, is the traditional rival of adjacent Balliol. Trinity incorporates parts of the 14th-century Durham College.
University (121 B2), High Street, is one of the oldest residential colleges, though the existing buildings only date 300 years.

SAINT MARY THE VIRGIN (121 B2), next to All Souls College, is the university church and is mentioned in William the Conqueror's 11th-century *Domesday Book*.

SHELDONIAN THEATRE (121 B2), Broad Street, was designed by Sir Christopher Wren and built in 1669. Once the university printing shop, the theater is now the scene of the Encaenia every June in which honorary degrees are conferred.

PEAK DISTRICT NATIONAL PARK (82 C4) ★

If the image of pastoral Britain is manifest anywhere, it is in the Peak District National Park, 452 sq miles of heather and peat-laden moorland hills, striking wooded dales, tunnels and caverns.

The park extends to Oldham in the north, Ashbourne in the south, and Sheffield and Chesterfield in the east; in the west it nearly surrounds Buxton.

For more information, contact the Peak District National Park, Aldern House, Baslow Road, Bakewell, Derbyshire DE45 1AE, or visit the tourist information center at The Crescent in Buxton, or Old Market Hall on Bridge Street in Bakewell.

PENZANCE (82 A1)
CORNWALL *pop. 19,600*
As a port for the Cornish tin trade and a haven for smugglers, Penzance prospered long before its development as a

seaside resort. The most westerly town in England, it has a particularly mild climate. Enjoy the 4 miles of sandy beach.

LAND'S END, 9 miles south west, is the 200-acre western tip of English mainland, perhaps best known as one of two points that mark the farthest distance one can travel in Britain. The other point is John O'Groats in Scotland.

MINACK THEATRE, 8 miles south west, at Porthcurno, is a Greek-style open-air theater built on rugged cliffs.

ST. MICHAEL'S MOUNT, across the bay, is linked to the mainland at low tide by a causeway; a ferry runs in summer.

▲ PLYMOUTH (82 B1)
DEVON *pop. 242,600*
Plymouth has been the starting point for several pivotal historical events. From here Sir Francis Drake sailed to engage the Spanish Armada, and it was from this port that the Pilgrim Fathers sailed in the *Mayflower* to found a colony in the New World – an event marked by a memorial stone. The town suffered considerable damage during World War II, but a few historic areas remain; inside the Barbican area is the Old Quarter, with narrow streets, old houses and a busy harbor.

▲ PORTSMOUTH & SOUTHSEA (82 D1)
HAMPSHIRE *pop. 181,100*
Portsmouth, an important naval dockyard noted for its shipbuilding, is linked with the busy seaside resort of Southsea, on the small peninsula of Portsea Island across from the Isle of Wight. These two settlements form the city of Portsmouth. The city lies between two natural harbors: Portsmouth and Langstone.

PORTSMOUTH HISTORIC SHIPS, The Hard. Three famous ships are on display here: **HMS** *Victory* was Nelson's flagship during the Battle of Trafalgar in 1805. The nearby Royal Naval Museum depicts the military hero and his exploits.

HMS *Warrior* was launched in 1860 as the world's first iron-hulled armored warship. Now restored, it portrays life aboard a 19th-century warship.
Mary Rose **Shiphall and Exhibition** features Henry VIII's flagship that sank off Portsmouth during a battle in July 1545. The ship was raised in 1982 after lying for four centuries in the mud and is remarkably well preserved.

RIPON (82 C5)
NORTH YORKSHIRE *pop. 14,600*
CATHEDRAL is a small structure embodying a variety of architectural styles from the 12th to 15th centuries. Saint Wilfred's Needle is a narrow opening through which supposedly only the virtuous can squeeze.

FOUNTAINS ABBEY AND STUDLEY ROYAL, 4 miles south west off B6265, is the largest monastic ruin in Britain and surrounded by a vast park. The abbey was founded by Cistercian monks in 1132 and the park and landscape garden were laid out from 1720 to 1740.

NORTON CONYERS, 3 miles north, is a Jacobean house believed to have figured in Charlotte Brontë's *Jane Eyre*. A display of Brontë family relics includes a collection of furniture.

ST. ALBANS (82 D2)
HERTFORDSHIRE *pop. 77,200*
Founded before the time of Christ, St. Albans is a market town built on the site of the Roman city of *Verulamium*. Among the ancient ruins are a large theater dating from the 2nd century and a hypocaust (Roman heating system).

ST. ALBANS CATHEDRAL, an 11th-century church named for the first British saint, stands on the site of his martyrdom. The 550-foot abbey has one of the longest naves in Britain.

SHAW'S CORNER, 6 ½ miles north at Ayot St. Lawrence, was G. Bernard Shaw's home for 44 years and the place of his death in 1950. The contents of several rooms remain as they were during his residence.

▲ SALISBURY (82 C2)

WILTSHIRE *pop. 37,000*

Salisbury, known for its cathedral, is a charming town surrounded by hills and four rivers. It was laid out on a grid plan by Bishop Poore in the 13th century. For tourist information contact the Tourist Information Centre, Fish Row, Salisbury, Wilts SP1 1EJ; tel: 01722 334956.

CATHEDRAL, built from 1220 to 1280, with some later additions, is a masterpiece of early Gothic architecture. The spire, added in the 14th century, is the tallest in England.

OLD SARUM, 2 miles north, on A345, was probably an Iron Age camp; later it was the site of a Norman castle and cathedral town. Its foundations can still be seen; there is a small museum.

SANDRINGHAM (82 E3)

NORFOLK

SANDRINGHAM ESTATE is the royal family's country home and the place George V loved "better than anywhere in the world." The house is closed to the public when the royal family are in residence. The house contains paintings of the royal family that date from 1845.

SANDWICH (82 E2)

KENT *pop. 4,600*

For hundreds of years Sandwich was an important port on England's east coast. During the past centuries the sea has withdrawn, leaving the town center more than 2 miles from the shore. Many ancient buildings survive, lending their medieval charm. The exclusive Royal St. George's golf course is nearby.

SARK – *see Channel Islands on p.109.*

SCILLY ISLES (82 A2)

The Isles of Scilly, a group of about 140 islands about 30 miles off the south-west tip of England, are part of an almost submerged granite mass that has been broken up by the sea. They can be reached from Penzance by boat (summer only), by helicopter and from Land's End by fixed-wing aircraft.

Five of the islands are inhabited: St. Mary's, Tresco, St. Martin's, St. Agnes and Bryher. St. Mary's, the largest, is really three islands joined by a sandbar, and boasts Hugh Town, the only city. Tresco is the home of the islands' governor and offers gardens, the ruins of an abbey and two crumbling fortifications.

▲ SHEFFIELD (82 C4)

SOUTH YORKSHIRE *pop. 528,300*

Sheffield, an industrial city on the Don River, is noted for the manufacture of steel and cutlery.

Of note are the City Museum and the 15th-century cruciform church of St. Peter and St. Paul. The church bishop's house is a 15th-century, half-timbered structure preserved as a museum of domestic life. In Sheffield Castle, Mary, Queen of Scots was held captive by the Earl of Shrewsbury for 14 years.

SHREWSBURY (82 C3)

SHROPSHIRE *pop. 63,900*

Shrewsbury is an old town on a neck of land formed by the Severn River. The town is thought to have been founded by Britons who abandoned the Roman city of *Viroconium*, 5 miles south east. Shrewsbury Castle is an old landmark, having been built soon after the Norman Conquest. The structure seen now dates mostly from the 14th century.

▲ SOUTHAMPTON (82 C2)

HAMPSHIRE *pop. 196,500*

Southampton has distinguished itself as a modern commercial port for more than 1,000 years. The city offers shopping centers, a university, and sports facilities.

Tudor House is a half-timbered house now used as a museum containing antiques and historical exhibits. The Bargate is a medieval gateway, now the focal point of the city center.

▲ STOKE-ON-TRENT (82 C4)
STAFFORDSHIRE *pop. 247,000*

Fine pottery and porcelain have been made in Stoke-on-Trent since before the Romans. Josiah Wedgwood set up a pottery business in 1759 and developed his famous blue and cream china, stamped with John Flaxman's classical design. The Wedgwood Visitor Centre is 5 miles south at Baralston. Josiah Spode and his son, specialists in bone china and pottery, were contemporaries. There are tours of their factory on Church Street.

At the beginning of the 19th century, Thomas Minton developed his fine transfer-printed earthenware; his work can be seen at the Minton Museum.

A few of the old bottle-shaped brick ovens remain; Gladstone Pottery Museum at Longton is a restored Victorian pottery that contains examples.

ALTON TOWERS, 12 miles east, is considered Europe's finest theme park, with over 125 rides, shows and attractions.

STONEHENGE (82 C2)
AMESBURY (see p.103)

A World Heritage site, 2½ miles west off the A303, this is an imposing collection of prehistoric stone monuments and one of history's most baffling mysteries. Experts believe the monoliths, which can only be viewed from behind a perimeter fence, were set in place about 5,000 years ago as a religious and cultural center for early herding clans.

STOW-ON-THE-WOLD (82 C2)
GLOUCESTERSHIRE *pop. 2,100*

At the junction of eight roads, Stow-on-the-Wold, a busy market town and site of an annual fair, is a favorite as one of the prettiest Cotswold villages.

STRATFORD-UPON-AVON (82 C3) ★
WARWICKSHIRE *pop. 20,900*

Had it lacked one 16th-century poet, this medieval market town would never have become known to so many. But William Shakespeare is believed to have been born, married and buried here, and

visitors come to trace his life. Many sites associated with him remain; most belong to the Shakespeare Birthplace Trust, which has restored the buildings to their original appearance. An admission ticket to all trust properties is available at any of the five houses.

Although actor David Garrick established something in the way of a Shakespearean festival as early as 1769, a permanent theater was not built until 1879. Today's Royal Shakespeare Theatre was built in 1932 to replace an older building destroyed by fire. Shakespearean dramas take place from April to January.

Many shops and hotels have been renovated in half-timbered, 16th-century style, so the town seems similar to how it must have looked in Shakespeare's day. The town is best investigated on foot.

A typical exploration might begin with the house on Henley Street where he was born. From this point, it is just a short walk to Chapel Street, site of the town hall and the Shakespeare Hotel, supposedly the original great house of Hugh Clopton, a 15th-century mayor of London. Where Chapel Street meets Chapel Lane is Thomas Nash's House, now a museum, next to the foundations of the house in which Shakespeare died. Also on Chapel Lane is the 15th-century Guild Chapel of the Holy Cross.

On nearby Church Street is the grammar school that Shakespeare probably attended and the Guildhall where he might have seen plays by traveling companies. Church Street continues to Old Town, site of two noteworthy old houses, Hall's Croft and Avoncroft. At the end of Old Town on Trinity Street is the 15th-century church in which the Bard and some of his family are buried.

For additional tourist information contact the Tourist Information Centre, Bridgefoot, Stratford-upon-Avon, Warwickshire CV37 6GW; tel: 01789 293127.

ANNE HATHAWAY'S COTTAGE, at Shottery, a mile's walk from Stratford, has been well preserved and is probably the most photographed farmhouse in England.

HALL'S CROFT, Old Town, is a fine Tudor house that was the home of William Shakespeare's daughter Susanna and her husband, Dr. John Hall.

NEW PLACE, Chapel Street, adjoining the foundations of the house where William Shakespeare spent his last five years, has an Elizabethan Knot garden. Entry is through the adjoining Nash's House.

SHAKESPEARE'S BIRTHPLACE, Henley Street, is where Shakespeare's father worked as a glover and wool dealer and where the poet was born.

TINTAGEL (82 A1)
CORNWALL *pop. 1,800*
Legend names picturesque Tintagel as the birthplace of King Arthur. The town faces the Atlantic on the rugged coast of Cornwall, which has been designated an area of outstanding natural beauty.

TINTAGEL CASTLE, on a rocky headland above the sea, is a ruined, mainly 13th-century fortress. Excavations have revealed remains from the 5th century.

TORQUAY (82 B1)
DEVON *pop. 58,700*
Torquay is on a promontory above Tor Bay. The exceptionally mild climate has promoted the cultivation of subtropical vegetation. With its palm trees, unusual plants and Italianate style of architecture, Torquay has a Mediterranean appearance and is the focus of the "English Riviera."

TUNBRIDGE WELLS (ROYAL) (82 D2)
KENT *pop. 45,300*
Since the early 17th century, Tunbridge Wells has been a resort. During the reign of Queen Anne and the Georges, the spa rivaled Bath, and today it remains a popular retreat.

CHIDDINGSTONE CASTLE, 6½ miles north west in a well-preserved village, Chiddingstone, is a 19th-century building restored from a 17th-century house.

HEVER CASTLE AND GARDENS, about 7 miles north west toward Edenbridge, is remarkable for its age – it dates from the 13th century – but is best known as the childhood home of Anne Boleyn, second wife of Henry VIII.

KNOLE, 9½ miles north in Sevenoaks, is one of the largest and finest private houses in England. Begun in the 15th century, it was greatly expanded in the 17th century.

PENSHURST PLACE AND GARDENS, about 5 miles north west off B2176 amid beautiful parklands, was the birthplace of Elizabethan poet Sir Philip Sidney; it has been the home of his descendants since the 16th century.

WARMINSTER (82 C2)
WILTSHIRE *pop. 16,500*
LONGLEAT HOUSE, 4 miles south west, is home to the Marquess of Bath. An Italian Renaissance structure in a parklike setting, Longleat is considered one of the finest Elizabethan houses in the country. The 200-acre Safari Park contains freely roaming African animals.

WARWICK (82 C3)
WARWICKSHIRE *pop. 22,800*
WARWICK CASTLE, parts of which date from Norman times, is an imposing, well-preserved medieval fortress that is still inhabited. The state apartments display furniture and armor collections; the parkland was designed by Capability Brown and contains peacocks.

WELLS (82 C2)
SOMERSET *pop. 9,400*
Wells is an ancient settlement in a valley between the Mendip Hills to the north and the plains to the south. The narrow, twisting streets and the aged buildings create a medieval atmosphere.
Make an excursion to the great caves of Wookey Hole, 2 miles north east.

CATHEDRAL OF ST. ANDREW, from 12th to 14th century, is the third church to be erected on the site. The church is noted for its carvings of angels, prophets and saints, which are considered some of the best work of their kind in England.

WESTERHAM (82 D2)
KENT *pop. 3,400*
CHARTWELL, 2 miles south east off the B2026, is the home in which Winston Churchill spent the happiest years of his private life. Many of his mementoes and paintings have been preserved.

WESTON-SUPER-MARE (82 B2)
AVON *pop. 66,600*
CHEDDAR GORGE, 10 miles south east, is a ravine enclosed by 450-foot limestone outcrops. A series of caverns includes stalagmites, stalactites and deep lakes.

WIGHT, ISLE OF (82 C1)
pop. 125,000
The Isle of Wight, 23 miles long and 13 miles wide, lies a mile off the southern coast of England. Its 147 square miles encompass towns, lush vegetation, rolling farmlands and craggy cliffs.

Newport is the capital and chief town. Cowes is a principal port and center for sailing and yachting. Osborne House at East Cowes was Queen Victoria's residence at the time of her death in 1901.

Carisbrooke, the old island capital, has a 12th-century castle built on the site of a Roman fort. Freshwater Peninsula, on the western end of the island, is marked by "The Needles," three huge chalk rocks rising from the water.

Other resorts are Ryde, Sandown, Ventnor and Yarmouth.

WINCHCOMBE (82 C3)
GLOUCESTERSHIRE *pop. 4,100*
SUDELEY CASTLE AND GARDENS, ½ mile south east off A46, date from the 12th and 15th centuries. The castle is the former home of Catherine Parr and Charles I.

WINCHESTER (82 C2)
HAMPSHIRE *pop. 35,600*
Winchester was the capital and regional seat of government under the Romans,

Saxons, Danes and Normans until William the Conqueror moved his court to London. Kings and princes, including Alfred the Great, Edward the Confessor and William the Conqueror, were crowned or buried in Winchester.

WINCHESTER CASTLE preserves the 13th-century Great Hall containing a table said to be King Arthur's Round Table.

WINCHESTER CATHEDRAL is surpassed only by Westminster Abbey as the shrine of royalty. The present cathedral was built sometime after the Norman Conquest, but investigation has revealed evidence of earlier cathedrals. Writer Jane Austen is buried at this site.

WINCHESTER COLLEGE, College Street, is one of the oldest public schools in England and has been largely unaltered since its founding in 1382.

WILLIAM WORDSWORTH
The famous poet was born in Cockermouth in 1770. His childhood here influenced his poetry in later life. He lived from 1799 to 1808 at Dove Cottage in Grasmere, following a life of plain living and high thinking, with his wife Mary and sister Dorothy. He is appropriately buried in Grasmere churchyard.

WINDERMERE (82 C5)
CUMBRIA *pop. 8,000*
Windermere lies at the foot of Orrest Head beside the largest lake in England, Lake Windermere.

A region of extremes and contrasts, the surrounding area has some of the best scenery in the English Lakeland, immortalized by William Wordsworth.

WINDSOR (82 D2) ★
BERKSHIRE *pop. 31,500*
The Victorian riverside town of Windsor owes its fame to the great royal castle. The history of the immediate region,

however, is traceable for centuries prior to King William I's establishment of the royal dwelling. Saxon kings maintained a palace in Windsor, and the Romans built a fortress.

ASCOT, located south of Windsor Great Park, is the site of the famous racecourse. The Royal Ascot meeting, initiated by Queen Anne in 1711, is held in late June.

ETON SCHOOL, at the end of High Street, is a prestigious public school, founded in 1440 by Henry VI. Many politicians and statesmen attended this school. Much of the original atmosphere is maintained; the Early English chapel retains rare Flemish-style murals, and the cloisters date from the 16th century.

THORPE PARK, 7 miles south west, combines fun with history in a lake and parkland setting. The theme park has over 70 attractions, and there are exhibits on the achievements of Britons from the Stone Age to the Norman invasion. Lessons in water skiing and sailboarding are also available.

WINDSOR CASTLE, the royal residence, is set in the 4,800-acre Great Park and represents every major stage in the history of English architecture. Aside from its historic and architectural importance, it is a veritable museum of fine furnishings and artwork. In November 1992 a fire caused extensive damage, and some areas are closed for renovation.

WOODSTOCK (82 C2)
OXFORDSHIRE *pop. 2,800*
BLENHEIM PALACE, off A44, is the estate given by the nation to John Churchill, 1st Duke of Marlborough, in gratitude for his victory at Blenheim in 1704. Sir John Vanbrugh designed the stately palace, which is surrounded by a beautiful 2,000-acre park. Displays include the iron bed in which Churchill was born. His burial place is in the village churchyard of Bladon, south of the park.

WORCESTER (82 C3)
HEREFORD AND WORCESTER
pop. 80,000
An old city on the Severn River, Worcester is an industrial center noted for glovemaking and porcelain. The town might be best known for the sauce that takes its name.

CATHEDRAL, dating from the 11th to 14th centuries, was begun by Bishop Wulfstan on a much older site and built in the shape of a double cross. The sandstone structure contains a number of chapels and the tombs of King John.

SIR EDWARD ELGAR
(1857–1934)
Elgar's musical education was derived mainly from his experience as a violin player, as a singer at the church where his father was an organist, and from browsing the scores in his father's music shop in Worcester. Elgar's early works were recognized only locally, but his international reputation was assured when Richard Strauss acclaimed the ever-popular Enigma Variations (1899). Then the Pomp and Circumstances Marches (1901–30) won widespread popularity. His music epitomizes Edwardian England in its nostalgic qualities.

ELGAR'S BIRTHPLACE MUSEUM, 3 miles west off A44 at Crown East Lane, Lower Broadheath, is the cottage where British composer Sir Edward Elgar was born in 1857. Inside are scores, photographs, letters and other memorabilia.

YEOVIL (82 C2)
SOMERSET *pop. 38,000*
MONTACUTE HOUSE, 4 miles west, is an Elizabethan mansion completed in 1601. It includes collections of china, old glass, Jacobean and Tudor portraits, tapestries and paneling, a Jacobean garden and a landscaped park.

▲ YORK (82 D4) ★

NORTH YORKSHIRE *pop. 100,00*

York, on the Ouse River, remains remarkably complete as a fort town of the Middle Ages; The Shambles and Stonegate are among the best-preserved medieval streets in Europe. Four medieval bars, or gates, lead through walls that stretch for 3 miles around the city. A walk on the rampart walls evokes the time when Constantine the Great was proclaimed emperor in York; the town was then a Roman fortress known as *Eboracum.*

In the 8th century, York became the northern ecclesiastical capital and gained world acclaim as a learning center under Alcuin, an English scholar. With its outstanding cathedral and other churches, the city ranks second only to Canterbury in ecclesiastical importance. The curfew bell of St. Michael's has tolled nightly, with few exceptions, since 1066.

In addition to its medieval and half-timbered houses and fine churches, York possesses the Georgian mansions Micklegate House and Bootham School. Young's Hotel, a charming old inn near the cathedral, is the birthplace of Guy Fawkes, who created a stir in 1605 by trying to blow up Parliament.

For additional tourist information contact the Tourist Information Centre, De Grey Rooms, Exhibition Square, York, North Yorkshire YO1 2HB; tel: 01904 621756.

BENINGBROUGH HALL, 6½ miles north west off A19, is an early 18th-century house that features a fine hall, staircase, friezes and paneling.

CASTLE HOWARD, lying 14 miles north east was built between 1699 and 1726. The great domed mansion contains exhibits of china, furniture and paintings, as well as an extensive collection of 18th- to 20th-century clothing. The Temple of the Four Winds, by architect John Vanbrugh, and a mausoleum are also on the grounds.

CASTLE MUSEUM, housed in an old prison on Tower Street, next to Clifford's Tower, has reconstructions of period streets, parks, interiors and costumes. Of special note is the extensive display devoted to past Yorkshire Regiments; exhibited are uniforms, swords, rifles, medals and ceremonial artifacts. There is also a collection of toys, domestic items and a corn mill to be viewed.

JORVIK VIKING CENTRE, Coppergate, is a former Viking settlement site uncovered by archeologists. Visitors board "time cars" at a platform and watch the 20th century recede as they descend to a Viking city recreated beneath modern York. The authentic 10th-century buildings have been reconstructed on the sites where they were found.

MINSTER, whose three towers dominate the entire city, is the largest medieval cathedral in England. Built over a period of 250 years and completed in the 15th century, it is an intriguing jumble of architectural styles. The present church is the third on the site since the early 7th century. Exhibits show models of the Roman, Anglo-Saxon and Norman structures once present.

Also displayed in the minster are the gold, silver and jewelry of the Minster treasury. The Great East Window and 128 other stained-glass windows are outstanding, with the *Five Sisters* considered the loveliest.

YORKSHIRE MUSEUM AND GARDENS, Museum Gardens, displays some of the finest Roman, Anglo-Saxon, Viking and medieval treasures found in Britain. It is set in 10 acres of botanical gardens containing a section of the Roman city wall, observatory and the ruins of a medieval abbey and its guesthouse.

THE YORK STORY, at the Heritage Centre at Castlegate, is devoted to the social and architectural aspects of York. Exhibits, artwork, filmstrips and craft demonstrations are offered.

THINGS TO KNOW

- **AREA:** 5,463 square miles
- **POPULATION:** 1,578,000
- **CAPITAL:** Belfast
- **LANGUAGE:** English
- **ECONOMY:** Agriculture, industry and tourism.
- **PASSPORT REQUIREMENTS:** *See England*
- **VISA REQUIREMENTS:** *See England*
- **DUTY-FREE ITEMS:** *See England*
- **CURRENCY:** *See England*
- **BANK OPENING HOURS:** 9:30am–4:30pm Monday–Friday.
- **STORE OPENING HOURS:** 9am–5:30pm Monday–Saturday (to 9pm Thursday in Belfast). In some areas shops close on Wednesday afternoon.
- **BEST BUYS:** Linen, damask, lace, Belleek porcelain, Irish whiskey. Note: An export license is required to export any antique valued at more than £35,000.
- **PUBLIC HOLIDAYS:** January 1 or closest weekday; St Patrick's Day March 17; Good Friday; Easter Monday and Tuesday; May Day; Spring Bank Holiday last Monday in May; Orangeman's Day July 12; Summer Holiday August (last Monday); December 25 or closest weekday; December 26 or closest weekday
- **NATIONAL TOURIST OFFICES:**
  Northern Ireland Tourist Board
  Suite 701, 551 Fifth Avenue
  New York
  NY 10176-0799
  Tel: 212/922 0101
  Fax: 212/922 0099
  Northern Ireland Tourist Board
  St Anne's Court
  59 North Street
  Belfast
  BT1 1NB
  Tel: (01232) 246609
  Fax: (01232) 240960
- **AMERICAN CONSULATE:**
  Queen's House
  14 Queen Street
  Belfast BT1 6EQ
  Tel: (01232) 328239 or 242520
  Fax: (01232) 248482

NORTHERN IRELAND

HISTORY

After more than 25 years of troubles, Northern Ireland is, at time of writing, experiencing its longest ever period of peace. The Irish Republican Army (I.R.A.) and its political wing Sinn Fein both agreed to a permanent ceasefire towards the end of 1994, and since then a gradual process of demilitarization has been taking place.

Historically political and social turmoil has always been a feature of life in the six counties commonly known as Ulster. The political division of Ireland by act of British Parliament in 1920 was not an altogether surprising move. Colonies of English and Scottish settlers were "planted" in the fertile areas around the ancient province of Ulster beginning in the 12th century. But the confiscation and subsequent redistribution of some 750,000 acres of Catholic land by Oliver Cromwell in 1650 laid the foundation for strife in centuries to come.

With a population more than two-thirds Protestant, resistance to any form of Irish Catholic control prompted the six counties of Northern Ireland to choose self-government within the United Kingdom when Ireland became independent in 1922. Protestants controled the government; Catholics had virtually no political or economic power. Ulster became the home of vast shipyards and engineering concerns – resulting in a larger, more diverse economic base than that enjoyed by citizens of the agrarian-based republic.

The Catholic minority of Ulster, however, gained little from this good fortune. Over time, such economic disparity led to a shift in attitude within the Catholic community, with a growing emphasis on full and equal rights as British citizens rather than the previous insistence on a united Ireland.

Violent clashes between civil rights marchers and Unionist extremists in 1968, however, set the stage for more militant postures from the I.R.A. who were defending the Catholic minority, and the Ulster Volunteer Force and Ulster Defence Association, who were in support of the Protestant majority. The situation grew even more volatile with the decision by the Unionist government to institute internment of I.R.A. members without trial.

Terrorism increased, fierce rioting took place in Belfast and Londonderry, and the Catholic population (both in Northern Ireland and the Irish Republic) joined in their rejection of parliament and the demand for a united Ireland. In 1969, the British army was dispatched to Northern Ireland in order to act as a peacekeeping force.

A significant blow to self-government came in 1972. Increased tension and vio-lence from all the various factions culmi-nated in the killing of 13 civil rights protesters in what became known as "Bloody Sunday." Within a few weeks, Britain suspended Northern Ireland's parliament and imposed direct rule.

On August 31, 1994, the I.R.A. announc-ed a ceasefire in its violent campaign; in January 1995, British troops stopped patroling the streets in daylight hours. At the time of going to press, it is impossi-ble to say whether this will hold, but whatever the immediate political devel-opments, the army barracks and R.U.C. (Royal Ulster Constabulary) stations will still be heavily fortified. Checkpoints will still have to be passed, and not adhering to parking restrictions may still cause security alerts.

SPORTS AND RECREATION

Golfers find some 80 courses to tempt them, including championship links at Newcastle and Portrush. Anglers and

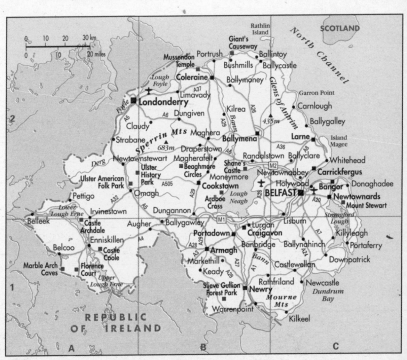

boating enthusiasts flock to the lakes and rivers, while pony trekking through the largely unspoiled countryside has become a favourite pastime.

Belfast and Londonderry boast museums, theaters, stores and monuments. The countryside, dotted with castles and legend-haunted sites, is equally enticing. Forests, lakes and unspoiled stretches of coast delight nature lovers.

TIPPING

A gratuity charge is usually included in the restaurant bill, otherwise a tip of 10 percent is customary.

PRINCIPAL TOURING AREAS

Note: For descriptions of cities in **bold type**, see individual city listings.

Conveniently, a coast road provides an easy means of visiting most of County Antrim's attractions. The scenic drive starts in **Belfast** and skirts Belfast Lough to the coast proper. The Coast Road itself originates at **Larne**, a seaside resort and terminus of ferry crossings from Scotland.

Continuing north, the road passes headlands, bays and coastal towns. Some of these small resorts are good bases for

---

> ### AUTOMOBILE CLUBS
> **The Automobile Association** (AA) has an office at Fanum House, 108–10 Great Victoria Street, Belfast. **The Royal Automobile Club** (RAC) has an office at RAC House, 79 Chichester Street, Belfast. Not all auto clubs offer full travel services to AAA members.

traveling inland to the Glens of Antrim – sheltered valleys of woods and waterfalls. Farther north is Ballycastle, and not far away is the **Giant's Causeway**. One of the country's best known tourist sites is not even near the coast; Lough Neagh is a 153-square-mile lake that County Antrim shares with four other counties.

West is County Londonderry, with an expansive coast. Its principal town, **Londonderry,** is the second largest in the province and a tourist destination.

South of County Londonderry is County Tyrone, the largest but least populous of the six counties. Dominating the region, otherwise, are the wild moorland summits of the Sperrins. The road leading from Newtonstewart to Draperstown is a good way to see these lonely heights.

In the far south west lies pretty County Fermanagh, best known for its lakeland. The historic county town of **Enniskillen** is the starting point of a 57-mile circuit around Lough Erne, the largest of County Fermanagh's lakes.

Smallest of the six counties is County Armagh, noted for its fruit orchards, roses and fine, old towns. The chief magnet in County Armagh is the town of **Armagh**, with an ecclesiastical history stretching far back into the Irish past.

County Down is known for its scenery, particularly for its Mountains of Mourne, which in the words of a well-known song "sweep down to the sea."

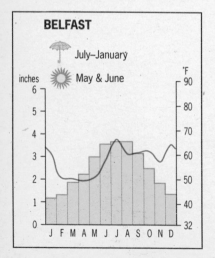

BELFAST

☂ July–January

☀ May & June

inches / °F

PLACES OF INTEREST

▲ BELFAST ★

BELFAST *pop. 416,700*

The capital of Northern Ireland, Belfast is a modern city situated in a district of mountains, loughs and rivers.

For additional tourist information, contact Tourist Information Center, St. Anne's Court, 59 North Street, Belfast, Co. Antrim BT1 1NB; tel: 01232 246609.

BELFAST CASTLE, Antrim Road, is a handsome edifice built in 1870 by the third Marquis of Donegal in the Scottish fortified-house style.

BOTANIC GARDENS (133 A1), Stranmills Road, on the south side of the city, is a 38-acre park with a Tropical Ravine, Palm House and Ulster Museum.

CITY HALL (133 B3), in Donegal Square, is marked by a copper dome and sculptured pediment. Inside is a fresco depicting the city's history.

BRITAIN • NORTHERN IRELAND

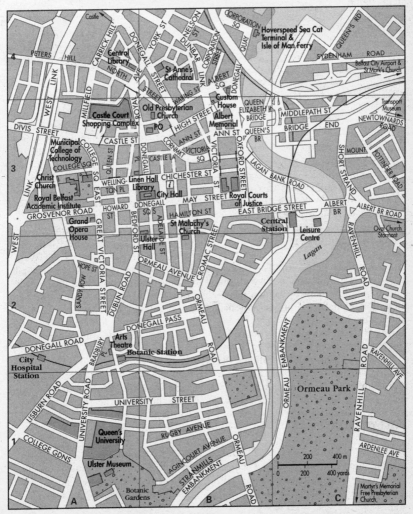

BRITAIN · NORTHERN IRELAND

★ HIGHLIGHTS ★

Belfast	(see p.133)
Giant's Causeway	(see p.135)
Larne	(see p.135)
Ulster-American Folk Park	(see p.135)

ARMAGH (131 B1)
CO. ARMAGH *pop. 12,700*
Capital of the county, Armagh has been the ecclesiastical center of Ireland since the 5th century. Today it is the seat of both Protestant and Roman Catholic archbishoprics and has two cathedrals. Navan Fort, 2 miles west, is an important prehistoric site, with a center nearby that portrays its history.

ST. PATRICK'S CATHEDRALS crown hills on opposite sides of the city. Sections of the Protestant cathedral date from the 8th century. The Roman Catholic cathedral was completed in 1873.

BALLINTOY (131 B2)
CO. ANTRIM *pop. 200*
The striking white tower of Ballintoy parish church dominates this village, which lies between Knocksaughey and the sea. A winding road leaving the harbor takes drivers past a house of cubes built by a Belfast artist.

CARRICK-A-REDE ROPE BRIDGE, spanning a 60-feet wide chasm, is a swinging bridge originally built by salmon fishermen. Traditionally the bridge only had one handrail, but even with the second rail, crossing the bridge 80 feet above sea level requires courage and care.

To satisfy a 300-year-old tradition, the bridge is erected every year at Easter and dismantled in the fall. It is a National Trust Property.

BALLYGALLEY (131 C2)
CO. ANTRIM *pop. 400*
Ballygalley, a little seaside town, is in a good location for exploring the Glens of Antrim. It offers opportunities for golf, tennis, yachting, swimming and fishing.

BANGOR (131 C2)
CO. DOWN *pop. 46,600*
Once the site of one of Europe's great monastic schools, Bangor is one of the most popular seaside resorts in Ireland and is noted for its fine beaches.

Ward Park offers waterfowl ponds, a nature trail, a children's zoo and facilities for tennis, bowling and putting. Castle Park features an arboretum.

BUSHMILLS (131 B2)
CO. ANTRIM *pop. 1,400*
The two mills that give the town its name can be seen on the River Bush.

OLD BUSHMILLS DISTILLERY, said to be the world's first licensed distillery, was founded in 1608. Tours of the distillery and its visitor center are available.

DOWNPATRICK (131 C1)
CO. DOWN *pop. 8,200*
St. Patrick is reputed to have been buried at Downpatrick in the grounds of the cathedral. The site where St. Patrick built his first church in Ireland, in 432 AD, is in nearby Saul.

ENNISKILLEN (131 A1)
CO. FERMANAGH *pop. 10,400*
Enniskillen is an island town between two channels of the Erne River. Enniskillen Castle embraces the Water Gate, a 17th-century, turreted fairy-tale building on the Erne River; the barracks, a square of massive 18th- and 19th-century buildings; and Maguire's Castle, a three-storey keep. The keep houses the Fermanagh County Museum and Regimental Museum.

FLORENCE COURT, 8 miles south west, is a fine Georgian house built by John Coles, father of the first Earl of Enniskillen. The house is noted for its rococo plasterwork.

MARBLE ARCH CAVES, 12 miles south west on A4A32 off Enniskillen–Sligo Road, is one of Europe's most prominent historic limestone cave systems.

LARNE (131 C2) ★
CO. ANTRIM *pop. 18,200*

Larne is an ideal base for touring the magnificent Antrim Coast Road and the Glens of Antrim. The Mountains of Mourne and the Ulster Lakeland District are both less than a 2-hour drive from Larne.

LONDONDERRY (131 A2)
CO. LONDONDERRY *pop. 62,700*

Derry, the widely accepted, older name of Londonderry, comes from the Irish *doire*, a place of oaks. The area has been the site of repeated conflicts since an abbey was built by St. Columba in 546 AD. Derry was renamed by the city of London, at whose expense the town was rebuilt and its protective walls erected in the early 15th century.

CITY WALLS were built in 1617. Averaging 20 feet in height and thickness, they have survived three attacks and nearly four centuries. Their protection has given Derry the title of "Maiden City." Platforms, monuments and cannon surmount the walls.

NEWCASTLE (131 C1)
CO. DOWN *pop. 6,200*

Newcastle is a small seaside resort on the west end of Dundrum Bay, where the Mountains of Mourne sweep down to the sea. The Royal County Down Golf Course, one of the best in Britain, stretches along the seafront at the northern end of town.

DUNDRUM CASTLE, 4 miles north, is a 12th-century fortification built by John de Courcy. Noted for its round keep, the castle is very well preserved.

NEWTOWNARDS (131 C2)
CO. DOWN *pop. 20,500*

MOUNT STEWART HOUSE AND GARDEN, 5 miles south east, was the home of the Marquesses of Londonderry, of whom Lord Castlereagh is best known.

The house is filled with a stunning collection of family treasures, including *Hambletonian*, one of George Stubbs' most celebrated paintings.

OMAGH (131 A2)
CO. TYRONE *pop. 14,600*

OMAGH MELLON HOUSE AND ULSTER AMERICAN FOLK PARK ★, 5 miles north west, is an outdoor museum that tells the story of Ulster's link with the United States. The park is centered on the ancestral home of the Mellon family, who were founders of the Mellon Bank of Pittsburgh. Costumed guides demonstrate traditional crafts, including horseshoeing in a reconstructed forge.

PORTRUSH (131 B2)
CO. ANTRIM *pop. 5,100*

Portrush is a popular seaside town above basalt cliffs. Its golf course and coastal rock formations are world renowned.

GIANT'S CAUSEWAY ★, 7 miles east, consists of more than 40,000 basalt columns formed millions of years ago from cooling lava. The pillars are to be found in peculiar groupings often resembling such objects as an organ and a cannon.

PRESIDENTIAL LINKS

A dozen Americans of Ulster stock have made it to the White House, 11 as presidents. Some of the more memorable are Andrew Jackson; Ulysses S. Grant; Woodrow Wilson, whose ancestral home is at Dergalt near Strabane; and Theodore Roosevelt, who came from Antrim.

STRABANE (131 A2)
CO. TYRONE *pop. 9,300*

The second largest town in Co. Tyrone, below the Mourne River, Strabane is of considerable historic interest. Gray's Print Shop, where John Dunlap, printer of the American Declaration of Independence, was apprenticed, is on the main street. President Woodrow Wilson's ancestral home is a few miles away.

THINGS TO KNOW

- **AREA:** 30,405 square miles
- **POPULATION:** 5,094,000
- **CAPITAL:** Edinburgh
- **LANGUAGES:** English and Gaelic
- **ECONOMY:** Agriculture, mining, whisky distilling.
- **PASSPORT REQUIREMENTS:** *See England*
- **VISA REQUIREMENTS:** *See England*
- **DUTY-FREE ITEMS:** *See England*
- **CURRENCY:** The currency unit is the Scottish pound (£), equal in value to the English pound. Currencies of the two countries are generally interchangeable, although many stores in England do not accept Scottish pounds (banks will). *See England*.
- **BANK OPENING HOURS:** 9am–4pm Monday–Friday. Hours may vary; some banks may be open Saturday morning.
- **STORE OPENING HOURS:** 9am–6pm Monday–Saturday (to 7:30 or 8:30pm Thursday in some larger towns); some shops close one afternoon at 1pm.
- **BEST BUYS:** Tweeds, woolens, silks from Paisley and Glasgow; Scotch whisky. Note: If the purchase is an antique valued at over £35,000, an export license is required to take it out of the country.
- **PUBLIC HOLIDAYS:** January 1 or closest weekday day after New Year's celebration; Good Friday; May Day, first Monday in May; Spring Holiday, last Monday in May; Late Summer Holiday, first Monday in August; December 25 or closest weekday; Boxing Day, December 26 or closest weekday.
- **NATIONAL TOURIST OFFICES:**
  British Tourist Authority (BTA)
  Suite 701, 51 Fifth Avenue
  New York, NY 10176-0799
  Tel: 212 /986 2200 or 1-800-462 2748 (toll-free); Fax: 1-212-986 1188
  Scottish Tourist Board
  23 Ravelston Terrace
  Edinburgh EH4 3EU
  Tel: (0131) 332 2433
- **AMERICAN CONSULATE:**
  3 Regent Terrace
  Edinburgh EH7 5BW
  Tel: 0131 556 8315

SCOTLAND

HISTORY

By the 4th century, the Picts, Celtic Scots, Britons and Angles had formed distinct kingdoms in the northern part of the island that today contains England, Scotland and Wales. United as the Kingdom of Scotland early in the 11th century, the country soon became a feudal state to England. The death of the last legitimate Scottish heir 250 years later left the country struggling to maintain a separate identity. Robert Bruce – crowned king in 1306 – was ultimately successful: Independence was recognized by the Treaty of Northampton in 1328. Scottish autonomy was doomed, however; in 1567 Mary, Queen of Scots, was forced to abdicate her throne. Upon the death of Elizabeth I, Mary's son James ascended to the English throne, bringing the two countries together under one crown.

THE LOVER OF MARY QUEEN OF SCOTS

James Hepburn, Earl of Bothwell, was the lover of Mary, Queen of Scots, the possible father of James VI, and the murderer of Darnley, the queen's second husband, whose body was found strangled. He then divorced his wife and secretly married the queen at Dunbar Castle in 1567. The lovers were forced to part later after continued pressure from enemies, and Bothwell was imprisoned in the Danish Castle of Dragsholm, where he died insane.

The 1707 Act of Union formally united England and Scotland as Great Britain. The Scots gained representation in Parliament and control of their church and legal system, but sacrificed their autonomy in every other respect. The peace did not last long. In 1714 Queen Anne of Great Britain died, ending the Scottish-supported Stuart line.

Scotland's desire to restore the Stuarts to power resulted in failed rebellions in 1715 and 1745. England retaliated with the Act of Proscription, which outlawed many aspects of the dominant Highland culture. Although it was subsequently repealed in 1782, the face of Scotland was changed permanently.

Scotland's Industrial Revolution began in the early 19th century, shifting the majority of the population to the Central Lowlands and introducing an industrial economy. This initiated the labor movement as a political force in the 1880s. The country played an important industrial role in World War I, but swift and uncontroled growth resulted in a severe depression at the war's end. The crisis encouraged the rise of liberalism and the organization of the Scottish National Party in 1934, but the conservatives regained control and under their leadership the country's administration was returned to Edinburgh in 1939.

A strong nationalistic pride has emerged in Scotland but has been slow to gain momentum in the political arena. In 1979 a referendum calling for the establishment of a nationally elected Scottish assembly failed to pass, although the Scottish National Party continues to press for an independent state.

FOOD AND DRINK
Scottish fare is another tradition that survives today, although British dishes are found throughout Scotland. *Finnan haddie* and *Arbroath smokie*, smothered in butter or cream, head the fish menu; they are most properly enjoyed at breakfast, along with the traditional porridge. Haggis is not an elusive three-legged animal, as canny Highlanders would have you believe, but a spicy mixture of chopped meat and oatmeal cooked in a sheep's stomach. A specialty of the Isle of Skye is the *partan*, or crab, which is made into pies. Equally intriguing is late afternoon high tea, in which the beverage is accompanied by assortments of baps, bannocks, scones, shortbreads and other pastry surprises. Best remembered by many visitors, however, is a product born of the thrifty tradition of mashing surplus barley – Scotch whisky. A visit to any of the distilleries is one of the best ways to appreciate the local nectar. As cafés can be few and far between on the road, it is common practice to ask your hotel to pack a lunch for traveling.

SPORTS AND RECREATION
Geographically, Scotland can boast that it has something for everyone. The mountains, lochs and rivers attract mountain climbers, anglers, hikers and walkers. Classic salmon streams include the Tweed, Tay, Dee and Spey. The sport of golf as we know it today originated in Scotland. As a result, some of the oldest and most prestigious courses in the world are in this country – among them St. Andrews, Turnberry, Troon, Gleneagles and Carnoustie.

Other sports have a home in Scotland, also – pony trekking around Callander and Aberfoyle and mountain climbing in the Highlands, which are challenging to even experienced climbers. A network of hiking trails and hostels allows the hardy to penetrate Scotland's more remote countryside. Skiing is popular at Glencoe, Braemar and Aviemore. Aviemore also offers swimming, skating, racket ball, movie theaters and discos.

GETTING AROUND
Travelers with an interest in history enjoy Edinburgh, with its ancient castle and great palace, monuments and museums. Sites throughout the country recall battles, births, burials, religious movements and romantic legends. Those with a liking for literature head for places associated with Robert Louis Stevenson, Robert Burns and Sir Walter Scott.

Shoppers and souvenir hunters will find the best selection of Scottish goods in such centers as Edinburgh, Glasgow, Dundee and St. Andrews.

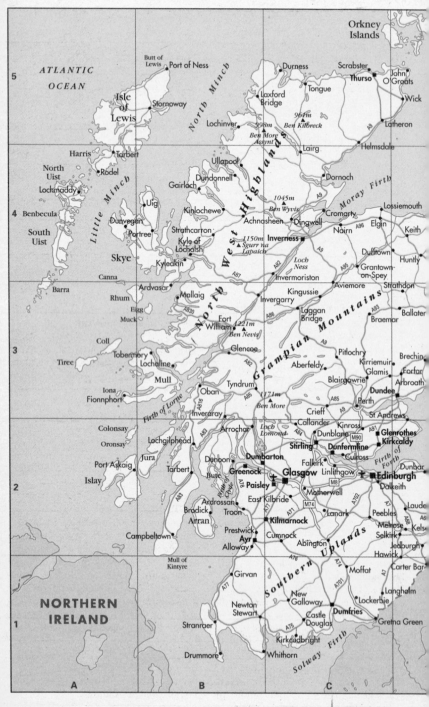

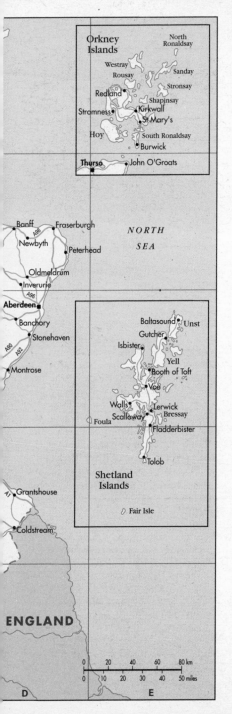

PRINCIPAL TOURING AREAS

Note: For descriptions of cities in **bold type**, see individual city listings.

HIGHLANDS AND ISLANDS

Scotland's Highlands are minuscule alongside the world's great mountains, but the peaks are nevertheless impressive, for they share the landscape with a wild sea, tumbling streams and peaceful inland lochs. It is a lonely land, where members of the animal kingdom thrive: Golden eagles and sea birds soar, wildcats and red deer roam the fields and forests, and salmon and trout abound in the streams.

Bordering the Lowlands north of Glasgow is Upper Strathclyde, a region of peaks, lochs and moors, best known for its history. To the north west across the Firth of Lorne lies **Mull,** a large island among the Inner Hebrides; to the north east is Central, with imposing **Stirling** Castle. The Trossachs, a collection of lakes, streams and high hills, resound with tales of Rob Roy, a Scottish Robin Hood; the origin of Sir Walter Scott's lovely Lady of the Lake adds to the enchantment of this region. Golfers find **Perth,** in Tayside, attractive for the nearby Gleneagles courses.

North east, from **Dundee** to **Aberdeen,** Grampian is a fertile land of farms, forests, rugged shores and little fishing ports. Farther inland, the majestic Grampian Mountains form a long wall across Scotland; farther north are the lofty Cairngorms and the Monadhliaths. The Highland Wildlife Park at Kincraig, 7 miles south west of **Aviemore,** features many species of Highland wildlife.

The north-east coast along Moray Firth is often referred to as the Scottish Riviera, an indication of this region's vacation atmosphere. A principal magnet of the central Highlands is neither coast nor mountain, but a lake – long Loch Ness, part of the Great Glen across Scotland. According to folklore, a sea monster makes its home in the loch.

North and west of historic **Inverness** rise the loneliest and wildest lands in Britain, forming the tip of the Highland region. Scotland's north also includes its far-flung islands. Off the west coast are the Hebrides, where Gaelic is still the first language of most of the islanders. The more distant **Orkneys** and **Shetlands** off the north-east coast bear a Nordic stamp, once part of a vast Viking kingdom.

LOWLANDS

Tradition dictates that the southern half of Scotland be called the Lowlands, although this region is low only in a relative sense. Composed of grassy hills and dales, the Lowlands are devoted largely to grain farming and sheep raising. Yet this portion of Scotland holds two-thirds of the population and virtually all of Scottish industry.

The southernmost region on Solway Firth is known as Dumfries and Galloway. This area of few towns is the hilly home of red deer, curly-horned sheep and hardy Galloway cattle. Farther north, in Strathclyde, the Firth of Clyde's shoreline is dotted with such seaside and golf resorts as **Ayr,** Ardrossan, Troon and Girvan. In the firth rises **Arran,** an island of glens, streams and lochs.

West of Arran and **Bute** island is the long Kintyre Peninsula. Close by are the islands of Islay and Jura.

Though the Firth of Clyde is edged by quiet towns and uncrowded beaches, it reaches inland to one of the largest and busiest cities in Britain – **Glasgow.** Loch Lomond and the Trossachs lie to the north, the Southern Uplands to the south. The Uplands, where both the Tweed and Clyde rivers originate, are the green, hilly home of sheep. The Uplands have many great old houses and castles. On the Tweed River, **Peebles** is a small textile town specializing in, not surprisingly, the manufacture of tweeds and knits.

North east of Peebles is Lothian; manufacturing and market towns are typical of this region, but so are castle ruins and resorts. Here, too, is Scotland's capital, **Edinburgh.** Across the Firth of Forth lies the former Kingdom of Fife, with its fine old city of **St. Andrews,** where golf was invented. The Royal and Ancient Golf Club remains.

South east of Peebles are the Borders, where ruined abbeys, impressive houses and grim castles recall centuries of Scottish-English warfare.

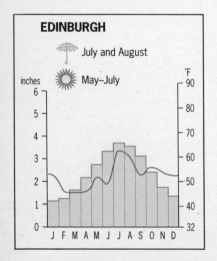

EDINBURGH

July and August

May–July

PLACES OF INTEREST

★ HIGHLIGHTS ★	
Aberdeen	(see p.144)
Aviemore	(see p.145)
Callander	(see p.146)
Edinburgh	(see p.141)
Glasgow	(see p.147)
Glencoe	(see p.148)
Inverness	(see p.149)
St. Andrews	(see p.152)
Shetland Islands	(see p.153)
Skye	(see p.153)

▲ EDINBURGH ★

LOTHIAN *pop. 438,700 See map pp.142–3*
From among the Lowland hills along the Firth of Forth rises Edinburgh, the administrative and cultural capital of Scotland. Though evidence suggests habitation as early as the Iron Age, the present city dates from the 11th-century reign of Malcolm II and Queen Margaret. The Middle Ages were times of continual fluctuation as the citizens fought invasion and poverty. As a result, Edinburgh's early development was greatly impeded.

Two walls were erected around the city, inhibiting expansion. The last, Flodden Wall, was built in a fearful reaction to the English victory at Flodden in 1513 and contained the city for almost 250 years. Crowded and confined as they were, 17th- and 18th-century residents built upward. Some structures reached 14 stories.

Not until the Act of Union in 1707 joined Scotland to its traditional enemy did the city begin to spread beyond its old boundaries. Edinburgh began to emerge as an intellectual capital of Europe. The golden age of the late 18th and early 19th centuries included such literary figures as James Boswell, Robert Burns and Sir Walter Scott, as well as philosopher David Hume and political economist Adam Smith.

Although today's Edinburgh has land-scaped gardens and squares and busy thoroughfares, it still bears the stamp of its long and often grim history. This is particularly true of Old Town. Here, dominating the city from atop Castle Rock, is Edinburgh's oldest and most prominent survivor – the castle-fortress.

Between the castle and the gates of Holyroodhouse, the 16th-century palace associated with the ill-fated Stuarts, stretches the aptly named Royal Mile, the center of oldest Edinburgh. A walk down these ancient streets – Lawn-market, High Street and Canongate – is like a promenade through the past.

Near St. Giles' Cathedral, two relics mark historic sites: the Old Tolbooth and the Mercat Cross. A heart-shaped pattern in the street is all that remains of the Old Tolbooth, an ancient prison. At the Mercat Cross, townspeople gathered in 1513 to hear about the death of James IV and 10,000 Scots at Flodden.

Closer to the palace, in what was formerly the separate burgh of Canongate, many 17th-century buildings have been restored. Beyond the Palace of Holy-roodhouse, Edinburgh evolves into a vast park, out of which rises the 823-foot summit of Arthur's Seat, an extinct volcano that can be easily climbed for a panorama of the city and surrounding countryside. In the southern quarter of Old Town are Edinburgh University and the Royal Museum of Scotland.

Though Old Town is of more historic interest, it is in New Town, characterised by Georgian architecture, that the heart of the city lies. Princes Street marks the division between the old and new and is the main thoroughfare. Stores, hotels, clubs and restaurants line its northern side, while its opposite side is formed by Princes Street Gardens.

A particularly enjoyable time to visit the city is during the Edinburgh International Festival, which takes place the last two weeks in August. The official program includes opera, ballet, symphony concerts, plays, movies and art exhibitions. On the unofficial Fringe Programme are numerous theatrical, musical and comedy events. The Military Tattoo, staged by Scottish regiments each evening (except Sundays) on the floodlit castle esplanade, ranks among Edinburgh's most spectacular events.

For further tourist information on Edinburgh, contact the Tourist Information Centre, Waverley Market, 3 Princes Street, Edinburgh EH2 2QP; tel: 0131-557 1700.

THE CASTLE (143 B1), Royal Mile, has been occupied by both Scottish and English rulers over the centuries. Although it stands on a strategic rock used as a fortress since the 7th century, reliable records date the castle from the 11th century. The 1076 St. Margaret's Chapel is considered the oldest building.

Inside are the Crown Room with the Honours of Scotland, older than the Crown Jewels in the Tower of London, and the Royal Apartments, where in 1566 Mary, Queen of Scots, gave birth to James VI. Though haunted from birth by the question of his legitimacy, the young prince first became the King of Scotland, then James I, King of England.

On one side of the Castle Yard, the 16th-century Great Hall with its former banquet rooms now is an armory; below the Hall are the Casemates, large vaulted rooms with ancient doors bearing the carved pictures and signatures of prisoners held during the Napoleonic Wars.

On the opposite side of the Yard is the Scottish National War Memorial, commemorating some 100,000 Scots who died in World War II.

CITY ART CENTRE (143 C2), 2 Market Street, is the home of Edinburgh's permanent fine arts collection of 3,000 paintings, drawings, prints and sculptures, most of them by Scottish artists.

EDINBURGH ZOO, at the Scottish National Zoological Park, Corstorphine Road, is considered one of the finest zoos in Europe. Birds, reptiles and mammals are displayed on 80 acres of grounds, which offer panoramic views.

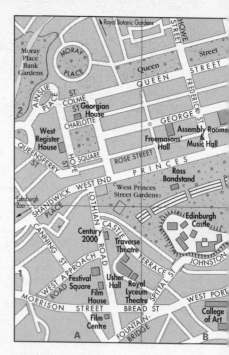

JOHN KNOX HOUSE, 43–5 High Street, is a 15th- to 16th-century house built by a goldsmith to Mary, Queen of Scots.

The house is traditionally associated with John Knox, the preacher and reformer. Displays document the building and development of the house from the 15th century to the present.

MUSEUM OF ANTIQUITIES (143 C2), Queen Street, illustrates the history of Scotland from the Stone Age to the present.

NATIONAL GALLERY OF SCOTLAND (143 B2), The Mound, contains paintings by Scottish and European masters from the 14th to 19th centuries.

PALACE OF HOLYROODHOUSE (143 E2), surrounded by the Queen's Park, is the official residence of the Queen when she is in Scotland.

Begun during the 16th century by James IV, the palace was expanded and redecorated by succeeding royalty. Among its occupants were Bonnie

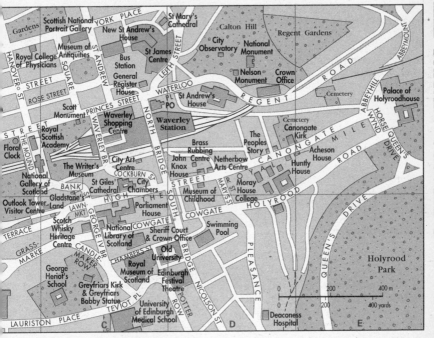

Prince Charlie, a resident in 1745 during his unsuccessful attempt to win the Crown, and Mary, Queen of Scots, who lived in the palace 1561–7.

The palace also was the scene of two historic events. In 1566, Queen Mary saw her secretary and alleged lover, David Rizzio, murdered by a group of nobles that included her consort Lord Darnley. In 1603 James VI learned of his succession to the English throne.

The old Royal Apartments, the Throne Room and the present State Apartments, with their rich tapestries and period furnishings, are of particular interest.

Holyrood Abbey, next to the palace, was founded in 1128 by David I, who, according to legend, built it as a penance for hunting on a holy day.

On that day, on the site of the abbey, a miracle is said to have occurred as the king was about to be attacked by a stag. As he grabbed the animal by the antlers, it disappeared and was replaced by a Holy Cross – or Rood.

ROYAL BOTANIC GARDENS, Inverleith Row, originated in 1670 as a medicinal garden at Holyrood and was moved to its present site in 1823. The 70 acres of gardens include an arboretum.

ROYAL MUSEUM OF SCOTLAND (143 C1), Chambers Street, is ranked among the finest of Britain's museums. Its exhibits encompass decorative arts of the world, archeology, ethnography, natural history and other sciences.

ST. GILES CATHEDRAL (143 C2), Royal Mile, is the site where John Knox, leader of the Protestant Reformation, preached his fiery sermons from 1559 to his death in 1572. Built in the 14th and 15th centuries, the church was greatly altered during the 16th-century Reformation and restored in the 19th century. A feature is the 15th-century spire.

SCOTT MONUMENT (143 C2), in East Princes Street Gardens, has a marble statue of the author at its base. Towering above is a 200-foot Gothic spire adorned by statuettes of characters from Sir Walter Scott's novels and poems.

SCOTTISH NATIONAL PORTRAIT GALLERY (143 C2), Queen Street, displays portraits of individuals who have contributed to Scottish history. These figures, which include royals, rebels, soldiers, and writers, are portrayed in various media.

THE WRITERS' MUSEUM (143 C2), off Lawnmarket, is a 17th-century dwelling containing manuscripts and relics of literary greats Robert Burns, Sir Walter Scott and Robert Louis Stevenson.

ABERDEEN (139 D3) ★
GRAMPIAN *pop. 211,100*

The noble northern city of Aberdeen fairly bristles with history; its motto "Bon Accord" was the rallying cry of the ruling Bruce family.

A number of buildings in Aberdeen are of historical interest. The Church of St. Nicholas is largely a product of the Middle Ages, as is the castlelike St. Machar's Cathedral. The Mercat Cross in Castle Street and, Provost Skene's House date from the 17th century; Provost Ross's House in Shiprow is a century older and houses the Aberdeen Maritime Museum.

A grim relic now incorporated into municipal buildings is the Old Tolbooth, the scene of public executions until 1857. A part of the tolbooth that remains is the "Maid of Aberdeen," said to have been the prototype of the guillotine. A statue of Lord Byron in front of Aberdeen Grammar School recalls that this poet attended the school 1794–8.

The Granite City, as Aberdeen is known, is on the coast and has three major industries – fishing, tourism and oil-based business.

Aberdeen lies near the most "castled" part of Scotland. Between the Grampians and the coast, in the valleys of the Don, Dee and Ythan, are castles remarkable for their their variety. *Bouchmorale* is the Gaelic word meaning "majestic

dwelling," and Balmoral is just that in its role of summer residence for the British Royal Family. They have come to Balmoral each summer traditionally since 1853.

ABERDEEN MARITIME MUSEUM, Provost Ross's House, Shiprow, depicts the highlights of Aberdeen's maritime history through drama and pictures. The museum is housed in the third oldest building in Aberdeen.

CRAIGIEVAR CASTLE, 24 miles west, remains virtually unchanged since its construction in the 17th century. Its solid lower walls rise to a riot of turrets, gables and conical roofs. Inside are magnificent plaster ceilings.

CRATHES CASTLE AND GARDEN, 14 miles west, was finished in 1596 on land given to the Burnett family by Robert the Bruce. Inside are painted ceilings; outside are gardens with yew hedges planted in 1702.

PITMEDDEN GARDEN, 14 miles north, near the village of Udny, is a fine example of a 17th-century Great Garden. Its elaborate floral designs, fountains, pavilions and sundials are carefully arranged on four spacious parterres, three of which are based on designs once used at Holyrood Palace.

ARBROATH (139 D3)
TAYSIDE *pop. 24,500*

The pleasant odor of woodchip fires pervades Arbroath; this fishing port is the home of Scotland's "smokies," North Sea haddock smoked over oak fires. Arbroath is also a holiday destination, with a beach, seaside walks and a golf course; a world-renowned course is 8 miles south at Carnoustie.

ARBROATH ABBEY, now in ruins, dates from the 12th century. It was the temporary hideaway of the Stone of Scone after the Coronation Stone's removal from Westminster in 1950.

ARRAN (139 B2)

STRATHCLYDE *pop. 3,600*

Called "Scotland in Miniature," the island of Arran has sandy bays, glens and lochs, rolling hills and lofty ridges. Its caves have sheltered fugitive kings. Vacation resorts are Brodick, Machrie and Blackwaterfoot.

BRODICK CASTLE, GARDEN AND COUNTRY PARK, at Brodick, was built in 1456 as a residence for the Dukes of Hamilton. The 60-acre grounds enclose two gardens, one formal, dating from 1710, and the other a woodland with a notable display of rhododendrons.

AVIEMORE (139 C3) ★

HIGHLAND *pop. 2,400*

The Speyside village of Aviemore is a year-round vacation spot. At the foot of the Cairngorm Mountains, Aviemore is a winter sports center. In warmer months, it is a favourite base for hikers and mountain climbers. Anglers fish for salmon and trout in the Spey River; boating enthusiasts take to nearby Loch Morlich.

The Aviemore Centre includes stores, restaurants, hotels, a theater, a concert hall, a swimming pool, an artificial ski slope and rinks for skating and curling. Scotland's Whisky Festival takes place in Aviemore in late November.

AYR (139 B2)

STRATHCLYDE *pop. 56,000*

Ayr is principal among the vacation towns and steamer ports that dot the coast along the Firth of Clyde. It also has connections with the poet Robert Burns. The Brig o' Doon of *Tam o' Shanter* fame still spans the river, as does the Auld Brig o' Ayr. Here also is Kirk Alloway, where the poet's father is buried.

Of non-literary interest in this Burnsian landscape are the granite cliffs, sand and shingle beaches and barren moorlands. Within a 20-mile radius of Ayr are several standing castles and houses, as well as the ruins of many others – among them Blair House, Dunure, Dundonald and Seagate.

ALLOWAY is perhaps best known as the birthplace of Scotland's national poet, Robert Burns.

Burn's Cottage is the thatched house where Robert Burns was born in 1759; it is now a museum. On the grounds is Burns' Monument, built in 1823.

CULZEAN CASTLE, 12 miles south on A719, is an enormous mock-Gothic mansion set in a 563-acre park overlooking the Firth of Clyde. It was designed by Robert Adam in 1777.

BRAEMAR (139 C3)

GRAMPIAN *pop. 400*

Braemar, a village in the typical Highland country of Lower Grampian, is especially popular with summer visitors. The Royal Highland Gathering, an exhibition of Scottish sports held in September, is usually attended by the Royal Family. Balmoral Castle is 6 miles east from Braemar.

BUTE (139 B2)

STRATHCLYDE *pop. 14,400*

The hilly Cowal Peninsula partly encircles Bute, an island separated from the mainland peninsula by a curve of water called the Kyles of Bute. Boats of every kind cruise this sheltered stretch. Settled in prehistoric times, the island abounds in barrows, cairns, cists and other stone monuments. The scenery, mild climate and proximity to the most populous part of Scotland have made Bute a favorite vacation site. The coastal

---

CURLING

For at least 350 years this team game, similar to bowls, but played on ice, has been played all over Scotland. The curling stones are made from granite and have handles let into the top. The object is to slide the stones along the ice into a tee. The team with the most stones at the center is the winner.

---

town of Rothesay is its chief resort and steamer port.

CALLANDER (139 C2) ★
CENTRAL *pop. 2,500*

Callander is on an ancient route to the Highlands and perhaps represents Scotland at its romantic best. During the early 18th century, the outlaw Rob Roy roamed the surrounding countryside. A century later, Sir Walter Scott immortalized the benevolent bandit in his well-known novel. Scott also wrote of a *Lady of the Lake*, the lady being Ellen Douglas and her lake, Lock Katrine.

West of Callander are three lochs – Venachar, Katrine and Ard – and south of these lakes are the birch-covered hills and sweeping moorland known collectively as the Trossachs.

CAMPBELTOWN (139 B2)
STRATHCLYDE *pop. 6,100*

Campbeltown is the main settlement of the long Kintyre Peninsula, the first Kingdom of Scotland. The town was originally Dalruadhain, seat of the Dalriadan kings. Today visitors fish from the rocky seashore and golf at Machrihanish, 5 miles west.

CULLODEN – see Inverness on p.149.

CULROSS (139 C2)
FIFE

Picturesque Culross, with its cobbled streets and 16th-century houses, is a well-preserved period town. Culross Abbey is a Cistercian monastery that contributes substantially to the town's medieval aura. Founded by Malcolm, the Earl of Fife, in 1217, the abbey is still used. The choir functions as a parish church; parts of the nave remain, and the central tower is still intact.

DUFFTOWN (139 D4)
GRAMPIAN *pop. 1,600*

The "Capital of Scottish Malt Distilling," ancient Dufftown is also noted for its medieval buildings. The Mortlach parish church, just south of Dufftown,

reputedly dates from the 11th century. Balvenie, on a hill above the Fiddich River, is one of Scotland's earliest and largest stone castles, dating from the 15th and 16th centuries.

GLENFIDDICH DISTILLERY, near Balvenie Castle, was founded in 1887. The visitor center has a whisky museum and a bar.

DUMFRIES (139 C1)
DUMFRIES AND GALLOWAY
pop. 31,600

Dumfries straddles the Nith River, its halves joined by five bridges. Close to the English border, the town suffered from frequent raids.

Dumfries is best known as the home of Robert Burns from 1791 to his death in 1796. Here, while working as an excise officer, he wrote some of his finest songs, including *Auld Lang Syne*. His statue graces High Street. Additional reminders of the poet are in the municipal museum, the Globe Inn and the Hole in the Wa' Tavern.

BURNS HOUSE, on Burns Street, is where Robert Burns died in 1796. Memorials and personal relics are on display.

BURNS MAUSOLEUM, St. Michael's Churchyard, is a Grecian temple that is the burial site of the poet, his wife Jean Armour and their five sons. For access contact the attendant at Burns House.

▲ DUNDEE (139 D3)
TAYSIDE *pop. 174,300*

Despite attempts by the English to destroy it, medieval trappings survive in centuries-old Dundee. The cross on the City Churches grounds dates from 1586.

Places of interest include the Barrack Street Natural History Museum, featuring natural history and wildlife exhibits, and the McManus Galleries Museum, which focuses on shipping and industry. Dundee's 1,300 acres of parks include Camperdown, the site of Camperdown House, a 19th-century mansion that contains a tea room; east on the Firth is

Broughty Ferry, a resort and residential suburb that stems from a fishing village.

▲ DUNFERMLINE (139 C2)
FIFE *pop. 52,100*

Now devoted to the production of textiles, Dunfermline was once capital of Scotland. Examples of its past history are the 11th-century abbey and the crumbling royal palace, birthplace of the unfortunate Charles I, the British king whose authoritarian rule in the first half of the 17th century provoked a civil war that resulted in his execution.

Another major figure born in Dunfermline was Andrew Carnegie, who made his fortune in the United States and gained renown as an industrialist and philanthropist. Remembering his roots, Carnegie gave the town its park that surrounds the 17th-century Pittencrieff House.

ELGIN (139 C4)
GRAMPIAN *pop. 20,300*

Elgin, on the Lossie River, is a principal market for a large garden area. It is a convenient center for visiting this region of salmon rivers and medieval castles.

Lossiemouth, 5 miles north on the Firth, is a seaside resort. The town of Forres, 12 miles west, is mentioned in William Shakespeare's *Macbeth*.

FORT WILLIAM (139 B3)
HIGHLAND *pop. 11,100*

In "Scotland's Great Glen," Fort William began as an earth and wattle fort; today it is a point of departure for touring the Western Highlands. The history of the region is kept alive in the West Highland Museum, and local folk traditions are revived in the Highland Games each August.

BEN NEVIS (4,406ft.) is the tallest mountain in Britain. It also may be one of the oldest; its age is estimated to be 500 million years. Only experienced climbers should attempt to scale the dangerous northern flanks. The less seasoned can conquer the mountain via the stony

---

HIGHLAND GAMES
Athletes compete at these traditional Highland gatherings, held all over Scotland during the summer. Events include "putting the stone" and "tossing the caber." They say that the games started with martial contests held by King Malcolm Canmore in the 11th century to find the strongest men to fight the Normans.

5-mile trail that originates near Fort William on the bank of the Nevis River. Wear sturdy footwear and warm, waterproof clothing.

GLAMIS (139 D3)
TAYSIDE *pop. 240*

GLAMIS CASTLE is the celebrated home of the Earls of Strathmore. The present Queen Mother is the daughter of the 14th earl. According to William Shakespeare's *Macbeth*, Duncan was murdered at this site. Architecturally as well as historically interesting, the castle's 13th-century nucleus is enhanced by corbels, wings and turrets in the 17th-century French château style.

▲ GLASGOW (139 C2) ★
STRATHCLYDE *pop. 697,000*

Founded by the missionary St. Mungo about 550 AD, Glasgow on the Clyde spent its first few centuries as an obscure religious center.

The 19th century ushered in the Industrial Revolution; with a nearby source of coal and a substantial labor pool, Glasgow competed with other industrial giants. Foundries and factories of many varieties appeared, and with the Clyde River widened and dredged, shipbuilding grew.

Obviously a city of industry and commerce, Glasgow has other faces as well. Acres of green space can be found in Linn Park, on the banks of a small lake in Botanic Gardens, and in Glasgow Green in the city center. Such scenic spots as the Trossachs, Loch Lomond and the Kilpatrick Hills are all within a few hours of the city.

Glasgow is architecturally a product of the early and mid-19th century, and a few Victorian confections survive. Just as interesting are examples of Charles Rennie Mackintosh's early modern style. A handful of pre-19th-century structures remain, such as the cathedral, the Trades' Hall, Provand's Lordship, and Provan Hall, a delightful restored 15th-century house.

For additional tourist information, contact the Tourist Information Centre, 35 St. Vincent Place, Glasgow G1 2ER; tel: 0141-204 4400.

BOTANIC GARDENS, Queen Margaret Drive, off Great Western Road, was established in 1817. In addition to the 42 acres of flowers, herbs and shrubs are greenhouses sheltering such exotic flora as orchids and tree ferns.

BURRELL COLLECTION, Pollok Country Park, was opened in 1983 by Queen Elizabeth II. Among over 8,000 items on display are Chinese bronzes; Turkish pottery; Near Eastern rugs and carpets; and artifacts from Iraq, Egypt, Greece and Italy.

GLASGOW ART GALLERY AND MUSEUM, in Kelvingrove Park, was financed by profits from Glasgow's 1888 International Exhibition. The neo-Gothic buildings house important collections of works by both old and new artists.

GLASGOW CATHEDRAL stands on a hill in the oldest part of the city and dates mostly from the 13th century. There has been a church on the site since St. Mungo founded one in the 6th century.

PROVAND'S LORDSHIP, 3 Castle Street, was built in 1471 and is the oldest domestic building in Glasgow. It now contains a museum of Flemish tapestries and *petit point*, period furniture and historical paintings.

TENEMENT HOUSE, 145 Buccleuch Street, Garnethill, is a carefully restored 1892 first-floor apartment whose parlor, bedroom, kitchen and bath contain their original fixtures. The apartment and its contents, preserved by The National Trust for Scotland, paint a picture of life in Glasgow in the early 1900s.

UNIVERSITY OF GLASGOW was established by papal order in the mid-15th century. The institution has occupied its impressive neo-Gothic quarters on Gilmorehill since 1870.

Hunterian Art Gallery, maintains a major collection of works by James McNeill Whistler and Charles Rennie Mackintosh, as well as reconstructed interiors from Mackintosh's Glasgow home, collections of Dutch, Flemish, Italian and British 17th- and 18th-century paintings, and a collection of 19th- and early 20th-century Scottish paintings.

GLENCOE (139 B3) ★
HIGHLAND *pop. 200*

Stretching from Rannoch Moor to Loch Leven, mountainous Glencoe has been described as the most scenic glen in Scotland. Tradition claims Ossian's Cave as the birthplace of the 3rd-century poet. Signal Rock, north of the Coe River, has a more infamous history: It was here in 1692 that the signal was given for the treacherous massacre of the MacDonald Clan by Robert Campbell and his troops, who had been guests of the MacDonalds for 12 days. A monument honoring those slain stands near the road to Invercoe.

GLENCOE VISITOR CENTRE, Ballachulish, is surrounded by more than 14,000 acres of Highland country which are very popular for walking and hiking.

GRANTOWN-ON-SPEY (139 C4)
GRAMPIAN *pop. 1,500*

In summer Grantown-on-Spey, on the winding Spey River, is a favorite resort of salmon fishermen; in winter, skiers flock to its ski school and Cairngorm slopes. The town itself is an attractive collection of 18th-century Georgian buildings; walks thread through nearby Beachan Wood and Glen Beg.

INVERARAY (139 B3)
STRATHCLYDE *pop. 500*
Inveraray is relatively new by Scottish standards, having been rebuilt in the 18th century after its destruction by Royalists in the 17th. The cottages and parish church of the white-walled town have changed little since then. The church has an unusual dividing wall, which makes possible simultaneous services in English and Gaelic.

AUCHINDRAIN TOWNSHIP – OPEN-AIR MUSEUM, 6 miles south west at Auchindrain, re-creates 18th- and 19th-century folklife in restored period buildings on farmland. Traditional crops and livestock are displayed.

▲ INVERNESS (139 C4) ★
HIGHLAND *pop. 42,600*
A county town steeped in British history, Inverness has reminders of such historical figures as St. Columba; Mary, Queen of Scots; and Oliver Cromwell. Its monuments include the remains of a Pictish fort, a 17th-century clock tower, part of a fort erected by Cromwell's army and a 19th-century cathedral.

CULLODEN, a few miles south east at Drummossie Muir, was the scene of a 1746 battle that was the last Scottish bid for independence and began the breakdown of the traditional clan system.

Here Bonnie Prince Charlie, the last hope of the Scottish Stuarts, was defeated by the English Duke of Cumberland.

Old Leanach Cottage, around which the battle raged, contains the Battlefield Museum with its collections of historical maps, relics and a battle plan.

URQUHART CASTLE, 17 miles south west, was once Scotland's largest castle. On the banks of Loch Ness, the ruins date from the 14th century when the castle was built on the site of an earlier fort.

THE LOCH NESS MONSTER
Mystery has always surrounded the Loch Ness monster, or "Nessie" as she is familiarly called. She is supposedly a dinosaur-like beast whose alleged appearances on the surface of the water (photographic evidence seems to exist) make even the most cynical of visitors stop a little longer – just in case. The Official Loch Ness Monster Exhibition at Drumnadrochit, 14 miles south west of Inverness, tells the legend of the monster from 565 AD to the present, and demonstrates the latest technology employed to "solve" the mystery.

ISLAY ISLAND – *see Mull on p.150.*

JEDBURGH (139 D2)
BORDERS *pop. 4,500*
One might never guess that peaceful Jedburgh and its hilly, green surroundings have had a stormy past. Jedburgh's castle changed hands often during the Border Wars and was destroyed in 1409. Historically interesting are Queen Mary's House, where she lived in 1566 and the remains of medieval Jedburgh Abbey.

JURA ISLAND – *see Mull on p.150.*

KELSO (139 D2)
BORDERS *pop. 5,500*
On the Tweed River and just north of the Cheviot Hills, Kelso is a salmon-fishing center and point from which to explore the gentle countryside. The medieval abbey, mostly in ruins, was once among the wealthiest in Britain.

▲ KILMARNOCK (139 C2)
STRATHCLYDE *pop. 47,200*
Kilmarnock's fame as the site of the world's largest whisky-bottling concern began in 1820, when grocer Johnny Walker began blending his well-known product in the town. Robert Burns pub-

lished his first book of poems in Kilmarnock, a success that reversed his decision to emigrate to Jamaica. The town's museum, within a monument to Burns, contains a copy of that book.

KINLOCHEWE (139 B4)
HIGHLAND pop. 100
At the head of Loch Maree, Kinlochewe is a good point of embarkation for exploring the remote Highlands.

BEINN EIGHE NATIONAL NATURE RESERVE, west of Kinlochewe, was founded in 1951 as the first nature reserve in Britain. Its 10,000 acres include remnants of the Caledonian pine forests, part of Loch Maree and the Coire Mhie Fhearchair, an impressive hollow in the shadow of Beinn Eighe.

KINROSS (139 C2)
TAYSIDE pop. 4,000
The country town of Kinross lies in the scenic countryside between the Ochil Hills and the Firth of Forth.

LOCH LEVEN CASTLE, on an island in the lake, is an impressive reminder of a once-forbidding fortress. Though mostly 15th century in design, it incorporates masonry from a besieged predecessor. Mary, Queen of Scots, was a guest in the castle – much against her will – in 1567. Inaccessible during winter, the castle is reached by ferry when it is open.

▲ KIRKCALDY (139 C2)
FIFE pop. 49,600
FALKLAND PALACE AND GARDEN, 11 miles north, was built in 1542 for James V and was a favorite hunting lodge of Scottish kings for a century thereafter. Of note are its state apartments and tennis court, one of the oldest in existence.

LAIRG (139 C4)
HIGHLAND pop. 700
At the foot of Loch Shin, where five roads converge, Lairg is a good starting point for touring the country's northern areas. There are lochs and mountains to

the west, moorlands to the north, and beaches and golf courses to the east.

LINLITHGOW (139 C2)
LOTHIAN pop. 11,100
Old, if not old looking, Linlithgow preserves its 17th-century town hall, medieval parish church and the ruins of a royal palace. The church was first consecrated in 1242 and largely rebuilt after a fire in 1424. Its spire of gilded aluminium was added in 1964.

HOPETOUN HOUSE, 6 miles east, was begun in the late 1600s by Sir William Bruce of Kinross. Most of the mansion is the creation of 18th-century architect William Adam and his sons. Among its valuable contents are original Chippendale furniture.

LINLITHGOW PALACE occupies a knoll overlooking the town's lake. Built between the 15th and 17th centuries, the palace was a favorite residence of Scotland's royalty.

LOCH NESS – see Inverness on p.149.

LOCH NESS – see Inverness on p.149.

MELROSE (139 D2)
BORDERS pop. 2,100
Called Kennaquhair in two of Sir Walter Scott's novels, Melrose is in the center of the region associated with this great Romantic. Scott is interred 5 miles south east at Dryburgh, another ruined abbey.

ABBOTSFORD HOUSE, 2 miles west, was Sir Walter Scott's home from 1817 until his death in 1832. It contains mementoes of the writer, as well as collections of rare books, armor and weapons.

MULL (139 B3)
STRATHCLYDE pop. 2,700
Cliffs and beaches, lakes, forests and moors characterize Mull, the second largest island of the Inner Hebrides archipelago off Scotland's west coast.
   Overlooking the Sound of Mull and the Firth of Lorne, the small port of Craignure is the ancestral home of the

Clan MacLean. Nearby is 13th-century Duart Castle; another castle, in ruins, is on the edge of Loch Buie. Mull's chief town and fishing port is Tobermory.

From Fionnphort on the island's southwestern coast, it is possible to take a trip to tiny Iona, where St. Columba initiated his missionary work in the 6th century, or to tinier Staffa, an uninhabited island remarkable for its basaltic caves and columns. Fingal's Cave, whose Gaelic name *An Uamh Ehinn* means "musical cave," inspired the *Hebrides* Overture of Felix Mendelssohn. The nearby Treshnish Isles are the domain of sea birds.

Farther south over the Firth of Lorne lie rugged Jura, a large island with few people and many beautiful beaches, and Colonsay. A narrow strait separates Colonsay from Oronsay, site of a ruined medieval priory. Southernmost of the principal islands in the Hebrides is Islay (*EYE-la*), with its beaches and bays and reminders of much earlier denizens.

OBAN (139 B3)

STRATHCLYDE *pop. 8,100*

Oban's harbor is always busy with fishing boats, yachts and steamers that carry travellers to Scotland's western islands. Yachts are most plentiful during the West Highland Yachting Week, held from late July to early August.

In addition to Oban's tiny granite cathedral, there are several interesting castles nearby. Thirteenth-century Dunollie was once the seat of the Lords of Lorn; Gylen, on the nearby island of

---

FINGAL'S CAVE

The cathedral-like cave which inspired Mendelssohn's Hebrides Overture is one of several on the tiny uninhabited island of Staffa north of Iona. Boat trips leave from Oban in summer to see the black columns of smooth basalt rising up out of the sea, the results of volcanic action.

Kerrera, is still the home of the MacDougalls. Dunstaffnage, 3 miles north, is an impressive and formidable castle with 10-feet-thick walls.

ORKNEY ISLANDS (139 E5)

ORKNEY *pop. 17,000*

Settled by Vikings in the 9th century, the Orkney Islands were ruled from Norway and Denmark until 1468, when a Norwegian king gave them to Scotland in lieu of a dowry for his daughter, who married James III.

Though politically part of Britain, the islands seem different – Norse crafts and traditions are obvious everywhere. In the summer the days are long, and even in this northern archipelago, in the same latitude as southern Greenland, the Gulf Stream tempers the climate.

About half the 60-odd islands are inhabited; the rest belong to seals and sea birds. Most of the islanders, who draw their livelihoods from the fertile hills rather than the sea, live on Mainland, largest of the islands.

Here is the harbor town-capital of Kirkwall, its steep-roofed, stone houses set on streets that wind around a medieval cathedral. St. Mary's on Holm Sound is a favorite among yacht enthusiasts, and Stromness in the west is known for its lobster and crab exports.

Ferries cross to Stromness from Aberdeen twice daily and from Scrabster twice a week. In summer a ferry runs from John O'Groats to Burwick.

EARL PATRICK'S PALACE, Kirkwall, was built about 1607 by Patrick Stewart, Earl of Orkney. Although now roofless, the Renaissance palace is one of the finest buildings of its kind in Scotland.

MAES HOWE CHAMBERED CAIRN, 9 miles west of Kirkwall at Finstown, is Britain's best-preserved megalithic tomb; it dates from 1800 BC. Viking carvings and runes are visible.

SKARA BRAE, 17 miles north west of Kirkwall, is a Stone Age village that, because it was covered with sand for most of its existence, is very well preserved. Stone furniture and fireplaces can be seen as their owners left them.

PEEBLES (139 C2)
BORDERS *pop. 6,700*
An unhurried town on the Tweed River, Peebles was once frequented by Scottish royalty, who hunted in Ettrick Forest.

Now devoted to the manufacture of tweeds and knits, the town keeps some of its past intact: the Mercat Cross, the ruins of 13th-century Cross Kirk, portions of the town walls, a 15th-century bridge and several old houses.

Anglers fish for trout and salmon during their respective seasons.

TRAQUAIR HOUSE, 6 miles south east, was built largely in the 17th century but dates from the 10th century. This gray stone house of small-paned windows and miniature turrets has been an occasional home to 27 British monarchs.

There are many reminders of Mary, Queen of Scots, as well as valuable silver and glass, books and manuscripts, tapestries and 13th-century embroideries.

▲ PERTH (139 C3)
TAYSIDE *pop. 42,100*
One would never know by looking at Perth that this city on the Tay River is centuries old and was once the capital of Scotland. Several invasions and later demolitions in the name of progress or religion have taken their toll.

Significant among what remains of the old is St. John's Kirk, a mostly 15th-century structure on the site of an early medieval church. In 1559, reformer John Knox preached a sermon denouncing the "idolatry" of the Roman Catholic Church; his congregation set about destroying monasteries and all art arbitrarily deemed "idolatrous."

Just north of the city is Scone, where Scottish kings were once crowned. The Stone of Scone, traditionally regarded as Jacob's Pillow, is said to have been brought from the Holy Land in the 9th century. In 1296, the English Edward I took this Stone of Destiny to its present and permanent home in London.

SCONE PALACE, 1 mile north, is a castle-like house built on the site of the 12th-century abbey destroyed by zealous followers of John Knox. A religious center until the Reformation, it was for several centuries the scene of Scottish coronations. The present 19th-century palace contains extensive collections of china, ivory, French furniture, Vernix Martin vases, and art objects.

PITLOCHRY (139 C3)
TAYSIDE *pop. 2,300*
Set on Tayside's splendid rivers and hills, Pitlochry is a fine inland vacation spot. Chief among its attractions are local streams where the salmon run. The town has an excellent golf course and the modern Festival Theater, scene of almost continuous concerts and plays during the warmer months.

BLAIR CASTLE, 7 miles north west at the village of Blair Atholl, first built in 1269 for the Duke of Atholl, is now owned by the present duke. Altered over the years it was restored to its present castlelike appearance by David Bryce, a 19th-century architect. Visitors can see tapestries, portraits, furniture and porcelain, as well as Jacobite relics.

PORTREE – *see Skye on p.153.*

ST. ANDREWS (139 D3) ★
FIFE *pop. 14,000*
Originating in the 6th century as a Celtic religious settlement, St. Andrews quickly became a cultural center in Scotland.

Augustinians erected the yellow stone cathedral in the 12th century, and additional holy orders established communities. Bishops and archbishops inhabited the castle set on a rocky promontory above St. Andrews Bay.

A society of scholars formed the very first university in Scotland in St. Andrews in 1412.

Still important as a university town, St. Andrews is best known as a vacation center and the home of golf. The Royal and Ancient Golf Club has been the world's principal rule maker for the sport since its founding in 1754. For a fee, visitors may play this or any of the city's other six courses.

CATHEDRAL is a 12th- and 13th-century ruin of the largest cathedral in Scotland. Many of the precinct walls have survived; a museum contains an important collection of Celtic and medieval sculpture, as well as several later gravestones.

SCONE – *see Perth on p.152.*

SHETLAND ISLANDS (139 E3) ★
SHETLAND *pop. 22,000*
It is difficult to imagine a part of Scotland in which Gaelic has never been the native tongue and where the kilt is a rarity, but Shetland is that part. Away from the mainstream of Scottish history, these far-flung islands have a unique past all their own.

Monuments from eons past prove the islands were settled by an anonymous neolithic people, but the settlers who left the distinct cultural stamp were the Norsemen, who arrived here in the 9th century and stayed. Their language, Norn, disappeared, but sea birds, places and parts of boats, among other things, still bear Viking names.

Officially known as Zetland, from the Nordic Hjaltland, this county is a collection of more than 100 rocky islands and skerries. Of the 24 that are inhabited, Mainland is the largest.

Slightly fewer than a third of the islanders live in the capital and fishing port of Lerwick. The small island of Bressay shelters the harbor, a haven to fleets fishing the northern seas. Every January the town revives its Viking past in the uproarious festival of Up-Helly-Aa, a pagan plea for the sun to return.

The nearby town of Scalloway preceded Lerwick as capital and is the seat of the judicial branch of the government.

North of Mainland is Yell, second largest of the islands, and beyond it, Unst. Unst's lighthouse at Muckle Flugga is the northernmost inhabited spot in Britain. Lying to the south midway between the Shetlands and the Orkneys is Fair Isle. Owned and protected by the National Trust for Scotland, the tiny island is a favorite of the region's feathered visitors and of the ornithologists who observe them. Fair Isle also is known for its knitwear of colorful Norse-inspired patterns.

JARLSHOF PREHISTORIC SITE, 25 miles south of Lerwick at Sumburgh, encompasses Bronze Age, Iron Age, Viking and medieval settlements.

SKYE (139 B4) ★
HIGHLAND *pop. 8,800*
The island of Skye remains much as Bonnie Prince Charlie must have seen it more than 200 years ago – its coastal hamlets still unhurried and attractive and its interior rocky and brooding. Portree is the capital. A new road bridge links Kyle of Lochalsh on the mainland to Kyleakin, while ferries run from Mallaig to Armadale on Skye or from Glenelg to Kylerhea. Broadford in the south of the island is a good touring base for the beautiful Cuillin hills.

▲ STIRLING (139 C2)
CENTRAL *pop. 29,200*
The royal burgh of Stirling lies between two of Scotland's most famous battlefields. North east is where Sir William Wallace rallied his countrymen to defeat an English army in 1297. A few miles south east is Bannockburn, where in 1314, Robert the Bruce led the Scots to victory against an English army three times their size. Bannockburn Centre has audiovisual progams on the battle.

STIRLING CASTLE, Upper Castle Hill, rises on a steep c rag above the town. Fortresses have occupied this site since early medieval times, and the present structure dates from the 16th century.

- **AREA:** 8,019 square miles
- **POPULATION:** 2,857,000
- **CAPITAL:** Cardiff
- **LANGUAGES:** English and Welsh
- **ECONOMY:** Agriculture, manufacturing, engineering. Beef and dairy cattle, sheep. Crude steel major export; coal, zinc, slate and wools.
- **DUTY-FREE ITEMS:** *See England*
- **CURRENCY:** *See England*
- **BANK OPENING HOURS:** 9:30am–4 or 5pm Monday–Friday.
- **STORE OPENING HOURS:** 9am–5:30pm Monday–Saturday. Outside Swansea and Cardiff stores can sometimes close at 1pm on Wednesday.
- **BEST BUYS:** Handicrafts, including ironwork, leatherwork, basketry, pottery, wooden spoons, dolls; woolens. Note: If purchase is an antique valued at over £35,000, an export licence is required to take it out of the country.
- **PUBLIC HOLIDAYS:** *See England*
- **USEFUL TELEPHONE NUMBERS:** Police 999; Fire 999; Ambulance 999
- **NATIONAL TOURIST OFFICES:** British Tourist Authority (BTA) Suite 701, 551 Fifth Avenue New York, NY 10176-0799 Tel: 212/986 2200 or 1-800-462 2748 (toll-free) Fax: 1-212-986 1188 British Tourist Authority (BTA) Thames Tower Black's Road Hammersmith London W6 9EL (written enquiries only) Wales Tourist Board Brunel House 2 Fitzalan Road Cardiff CF2 1UY Tel: 01222 499909 Fax: 01222 485031
- **AMERICAN EMBASSY:** 24 Grosvenor Square London W1A 1AE Tel: 0171 499 9000 (telephone enquiries only)

WALES

HISTORY

As a definite social entity Wales had its beginnings in the 6th and 7th centuries, when Saxon invasions forced some of Britain's inhabitants into the mountainous west. In the 8th century the Celtic Wealhs, as these people were called by the Anglo-Saxons, were confined to their hilly land by a great earthwork that stretched from the Dee River in the north to the Severn's mouth in the south. Wales, the region west of Offa's Dyke, remained largely independent until the 13th century, when England's Edward I overcame the last princes of this loosely united realm, built his grim castles to subdue the Welsh and gave his son to the nation as Prince of Wales.

The ascendance of the Welsh Tudor line to the English throne finally assured Welsh-English unity. The Act of Union in the reign of Henry VIII in the 16th century barred Welsh as the language of legal and administrative matters. Moreover, the principality was carved into English-style shires, and Welsh representatives were sent to the London Parliament. Since this time England and Wales have legally been one. Nonetheless, strong regional sentiments and an interest in the conservation of the Welsh heritage characterize this proud principality.

SPORTS AND RECREATION

With its rugged northern heights, Wales is naturally a favorite among climbers. More gentle than Snowdonia's mountains are the Brecon Beacons in the south. Pony trekking is popular – and a good way to travel the rolling green hills. The Welsh seacoast, with its sandy bays and quiet towns, attracts those seeking less strenuous activities. Golfers enjoy excellent courses – more than 100 – including two of championship caliber at Harlech. Freshwater fishing, however, is undoubtedly the most popular outdoor pastime. Angling associations and some riverside hotels own coveted stretches of water; ask local river authorities whom to approach for permission to fish.

Souvenir seekers will find a colorful assortment of handicrafts, from hand-painted pottery to copper lusterware. Many items are decorated with a leek – the vegetable that symbolizes Wales. An old and romantic art is the carving of wooden love spoons, traditionally given by young men to their sweethearts but today more sought after by tourists. Wales also is popular for its woolens, which combine ancient patterns with bright, new colors.

PRINCIPAL TOURING AREAS

Note: For descriptions of cities in **bold type**, see individual city listings.

NORTH

The northernmost part of Wales is Anglesey Island, a part of Gwynedd County. A long bridge across Menai Strait connects the island to the rest of the country. Geologically interesting – rock formations are the oldest in Wales – Anglesey is historically important as an ancient center of Celtic culture and as the ancestral home of the Tudors.

On the coast, alongside placid-looking villages, is formidable Beaumaris Castle; like most Welsh castles, it resulted from Edward I's intent to keep the Welsh subdued. Anglesey's greatest tourist attraction is the little town that has the distinction – perhaps dubious – of having the longest place name in Britain: Llanfairpwllgwyngyllgogerychwyrn-drobwllllantysiliogogogoch, known simply as Llanfair P G.

Just across the Menai Strait lie the northern lands of mainland Gwynedd County, a region of walled medieval towns, Norman castles, delightful woodland villages like **Betws-y-Coed** and Beddgelert, and such enjoyable sea-side resorts as **Llandudno** and **Conwy**.

The best attractions, however, are the natural ones of Snowdonia, the incomparable region named for the majestic central peak Snowdon, at 3,560 feet the highest mountain in Wales and England. Snowdonia National Park offers wild mountains, high passes, green valleys and wood-fringed lakes.

> **SNOWDON SAFETY**
>
> If you intend climbing Mount Snowdon, beware that, although it may not look like the Alps or the Rockies, it is full of dangers and has claimed many lives. Make sure you are properly clothed and equipped; check the weather forecast, take a good map, compass and provisions, and tackle only those walks well within your capabilities. Tell someone where you are going and when you expect to return – perhaps by leaving a note with your hotel.

Inhabitants throughout the ages have left a wealth of monuments – Iron Age, Roman and early Irish relics and Norman castles. The most notable of the last, **Harlech**, figured in the Wars of the Roses and is remembered in song. Convenient to the national park is Gwynedd County's rugged southwestern coast, with ports, sandy beaches and such pleasant resorts as Portmeirion, on Cardigan Bay.

Clwyd County in the north-east corner of Wales is well liked for its noisy coastal resorts and its quieter scenic vales. Among the former are **Colwyn Bay**, Rhyl and Prestatyn, each with safe sandy beaches and plenty of amusements. The towns also share the coast with castles and castle ruins, the remnants of medieval Britain.

SOUTH AND CENTRAL

The south of Wales, more densely populated and more industrialized than the north, contains landscapes foreigners

BRITAIN • WALES

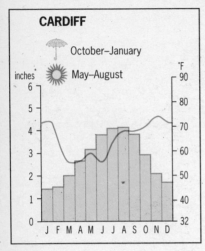

CARDIFF

☂ October–January
☀ May–August

inches
6
5
4
3
2
1
0

°F
90
80
70
60
50
40
32

J F M A M J J A S O N D

most often associate with Wales: mine-pocked, slag-covered hills; 19th-century coal towns with rows of look-alike houses; and busy port cities with docks and smokestacks. These images, however, are only a fraction of the real picture.

The southwestern peninsula, which forms Dyfed County, has a long and often rugged coastline, a large section of which is a national park. Seaside towns include **Tenby** and, at the end of St. Bride's Bay, **St. David's**, the smallest cathedral city in Britain. The southern Carmarthen Bay area is best known for its many castles and its wild and empty countryside. The city of **Carmarthen** is known as the birthplace (one of several) of the Arthurian wizard Merlin, while

the small seaside town of **Laugharne** is associated with writer Dylan Thomas.

One of the most colorful regions in the country is northern Dyfed County. Here traditional artisans are most numerous, and Welsh is the first language of the largely rural population. A prime vacation area, it is known for its splendid coast, peaceful seaside towns and the resort and university city of **Aberystwyth**.

South east of Dyfed County are the three Glamorgan counties. In West Glamorgan County lie the flourishing ports of **Swansea**, Port Talbot and Neath, as well as the scenic Gower Peninsula. In Mid Glamorgan County is the coal-mining region of the Rhondda Valley.

West of **Cardiff** in South Glamorgan County is the spacious Vale of Glamorgan, with impressive sea views and landscapes. To the east in Gwent County is the scenic Wye Valley and the town of **Monmouth**, with medieval fortifications and a castle setting immortalized by William Shakespeare.

Adjacent to the Glamorgan counties is the inland county of Powys, stretching along more than half the Welsh/English border. In its south is the 520-square-mile Brecon Beacons National Park. This great unpolluted area encompasses the peaks and the grass-clad hills of the Beacons, as well as the heathery slopes of the Black Mountains.

Radnor Forest, in eastern Powys County, has sheep-dotted hills and deep valleys. Since the 18th century, this part of Wales has been known for such spas as Llandrindod Wells and its nearby rivals, Builth Wells and Llanwrtyd Wells.

Northern Powys County is a quiet region of hills and moors, which seem in places to be inhabited only by badgers, otters, martens and kites. Set in the verdant Dovey Valley is **Machynlleth**, one of the oldest settlements in Wales.

AUTOMOBILE CLUBS
The Automobile Association
(AA) has an office at Fanum House, 140 Queen Street, Cardiff.
The **Royal Automobile Club** (RAC) has an office on Newport Road, Cardiff. The symbol ▲ indicates the presence of a AAA-affiliated automobile club branch. Not all auto clubs offer full travel services to AAA members.

PLACES OF INTEREST

▲ **CARDIFF** (82 B2)
SOUTH GLAMORGAN *pop. 279,500*
The busy city of Cardiff, in the most populous part of Wales, has been the country's capital only since 1955, although it has been a major coal-shipping port and manufacturing center for more than a century.

Visitors enjoy the broad tree-lined streets, National Museum of Wales, Civic Centre and City Hall, as well as arcaded shopping streets, the Cardiff Market and the New Theatre. Parks, gardens, restaurants, movie houses and facilities for a wide range of sports enhance the newer city.

Easily reached from Cardiff are Caerphilly, known for its castle and the crumbly cheese that bears its name, and Bridgend, with its 12th-century castle and fortified monastery. Penarth, with garden, esplanade and marina, is 4 miles from the capital.

For additional tourist information, contact the Tourist Information Centre, Central Railway Station, Central Square, Cardiff CF1 1QY; tel: 01222 227281.

CARDIFF CASTLE, dating from 1093, occupies the site of an earlier Roman fort. Though remodeled in the 19th century, it has its original well-preserved keep.

LLANDAFF CATHEDRAL is 2½ miles north west in Llandaff, a small town now incorporated into Cardiff. The first structure on this site was a 6th-century wooden church; its 12th-century stone successor was rebuilt after suffering serious damage in World War II. An obviously recent addition is Sir Jacob Epstein's aluminium sculpture of Christ in Majesty.

NATIONAL MUSEUM OF WALES, Cathays Park, has exhibits on archeology, botany, zoology, geology, industry and art.

ABERDOVEY (82 B3)
GWYNEDD *pop. 1,000*
The name Aberdovey (Aberdyfi) describes this port's position at the Dyfi's River mouth. The coastline was once more distant, evidenced by the sunken tree trunks visible at low tide. Local legend claims that a drowned city also lies in the bay; its bells ringing from the deep are said to portend trouble.

Known for its harbor and miles of sandy beach, the town also is popular as a center for exploring inland.

ABERGAVENNY (82 B2)
GWENT *pop. 14,900*
Set among wooded hills, Abergavenny is an excellent center from which to explore the Brecon Mountains region and the castles that lie along the Welsh border. Of interest in the town is St. Mary's Church and its monuments.

ABERGAVENNY MUSEUM AND CASTLE dates from the 12th to the 14th centuries; its walls, towers and gateway remain. A museum contains exhibits that document local history.

BIG PIT MINING MUSEUM, 4½ miles south west at Blaenavon, allows a close look at a mine that operated until 1980. Visitors are given mining helmets and lamps to descend the 300-foot shaft. Sturdy shoes and warm clothing are recommended.

ABERYSTWYTH (82 B3)
DYFED *pop. 11,200*
In addition to its beaches, resort facilities, harbor and promenades,

BRITAIN · WALES

Aberystwyth boasts an arts center in its university and the national library, which has a wealth of literary treasures. Gardens are near a ruined Norman castle on the seafront.

DEVIL'S BRIDGE, 12 miles east, is reached by a 1-hour steam railway ride up the wooded Rheidol Valley. Of the three bridges spanning the Mynach River as it plunges 300 feet to join the Rheidol, the Devil's Bridge is the oldest and lowermost.

NATIONAL LIBRARY OF WALES, Penglais Hill, is one of Britain's six copyright libraries and specializes in Welsh and Celtic literature.

BANGOR (82 B4)
GWYNEDD *pop. 16,000*
On the site of an early monastery, the northern town of Bangor took its name from the wattled fence, or *bangor*, that once surrounded the holy house. Though no longer a monastic settlement, Bangor is a cathedral city, its present church a 19th-century creation of Sir Gilbert Scott.

PENRHYN CASTLE, 3 miles east at Landegai off A5122, was built in neo-Norman style 1820–45. Thomas Hopper designed the "Norman" furniture, paneling and ceilings. An industrial railroad, a doll museum and a Victorian walled garden are of interest.

BEAUMARIS (82 B4) ★
GWYNEDD *pop. 1,500*
With its early Victorian terraces, half-timbered houses and old inns, Beaumaris on Anglesey Island is among the prettiest towns in Wales.

BEAUMARIS CASTLE was built in 1295 by Edward I to guard the strait separating Anglesey Island from the rest of Wales. The thick, turreted curtain, or outer walls, and the higher inner walls that protected the main part of the fortress still stand.

BETWS-Y-COED (82 B4) ★
GWYNEDD *pop. 800*
Tiny Betws-y-coed, whose name means Chapel in the Wood, is tucked away in the wooded hills of the Gwydir Forest. Recreational activities available include fishing, riding, skiing and golf. Long regarded as a good base for touring the Snowdonia region, the community is near several enchanting spots: 15th-century Pont-y-Pair, or Bridge of the Cauldron, near a wild reach of the Llugwy River; Swallow Falls on the same stream; and Fairy Glen and Conwy Falls on the Conwy River.

LOVE SPOONS
Throughout rural Wales during the 17th, 18th and 19th centuries, young men would spend many an evening carving wooden "love spoons." These would be presented to the ladies they courted. If accepted, it was a sign that courtship would lead to marriage.

BRECON (82 B3) ★
POWYS *pop. 7,500*
A center popular with tourists, Brecon has two museums, medieval castle ruins and a cathedral dating from the 13th century. Visitors can enjoy golf, canal cruising and trout fishing in the Usk and its tributaries.

The principal attraction of the region, however, is Brecon Beacons National Park, encompassing high hills and empty moorlands, peaceful lakes and tumbling streams, and occasional reminders of early human habitation. At Storey Arms Youth Hostel, 8 miles south west, is the beginning of a trail up the 2,906-foot Pen y Fan, the highest of the mountains called "beacons" and a vantage point for much of Wales.

CAERNARFON (82 B4) ★
GWYNEDD *pop. 9,400*
Dominating this otherwise peaceful-looking resort is the enormous bulk of 13th-century Caernarfon Castle. The

first English Prince of Wales, Edward II, was born in Caernarfon in 1284. His investiture at the castle in 1301 began the tradition that extends through the investiture of Prince Charles in 1969.

SNOWDON MOUNTAIN RAILWAY, 7 miles south at Llanberis, operates coal-fired steam locomotives, which climb the 4½ miles to the summit of Snowdon.

CARMARTHEN (82 B3)
DYFED pop. 14,500

The appearance of much of Carmarthen belies its ancient origins, but "Merlin's town" is very old, as proven by the ruin of a Roman fort, remaining medieval streets and the remnants of a Norman castle. A monument in Nott Square marks the martyrdom site of a bishop burned in Carmarthen in 1555.

Carmarthen lies at the center of a region notable both for its scenery and historic sites. Scattered over the green hills are the impressive remains of medieval castles and such reminders of Iron Age inhabitants as the great hill fort Carn Goch in the Vale of Tywi.

CHEPSTOW (82 C2)
GWENT pop. 10,400

Chepstow is a good center for excursions through the Wye River valley; 4 miles north is 13th-century Tintern Abbey, the Cistercian church that inspired William Wordsworth's poem.

COLWYN BAY (82 B4)
CLWYD pop. 27,700

A north coast resort long favored by families, Colwyn Bay has a 3-mile promenade and a safe, sandy beach.

WELSH MOUNTAIN ZOO overlooks Colwyn Bay. Elephants, deer, reptiles, tropical birds, bears and penguins are among the animals displayed in natural settings.

CONWY (82 B4) ★
GWYNEDD pop. 3,900

Guarding the mouth of the Conwy River is massive Conwy Castle, its walls

extended to encompass what was once the entire town. Though no longer needed, the town's defenses are in good condition; you can walk atop the 15-foot-thick ramparts of the turreted castle. Boating enthusiasts enjoy the river.

BODNANT GARDENS, 4 miles south on the opposite bank of the river, were laid out in 1875 by Henry Pochin and extended by several of his descendants. The 87 acres of gardens include collections of camellias, rhododendrons, magnolias, roses and azaleas. The hillside site offers views of nearby Snowdonia.

CONWY CASTLE, reigning over the town, was built in the 13th century for Edward I and figured in centuries of medieval warfare. An unusual feature is the castle's shape – the half-mile of walls form the outline of a Welsh harp.

DOLGELLAU (82 B3)
GWYNEDD pop. 2,300

Sombre, slate-built Dolgellau is a good center for walking or pony trekking. More challenging are several possible climbs up Cader Idris, the 3,000-foot mountain that dominates the skyline south of Dolgellau. Visitors are warned of the myth attached to the mountain: Whoever spends the night on Cader Idris risks waking the next day mad or a poet.

HARLECH (82 B3) ★
GWYNEDD pop. 1,100

HARLECH CASTLE, built by Edward I, is a vast stronghold dominating Tremadog Bay. Protected by the sea on one side and a moat on the other, it was the last Welsh castle to fall to the English. The three-story gatehouse and four towers are prominent features, offering views of the Snowdon Range and Lleyn Peninsula.

PORTMEIRION, 8 miles north at Porthmadog, is a re-creation of an Italian village on a wooded peninsula that juts into Cardigan Bay. The sandy beach here is about 1 mile long.

HOLYHEAD (82 A4)
GWYNEDD *pop. 13,300*

Holyhead is an ancient settlement on rocky Holy Island in northernmost Wales. The island, which bears the stamp of ages of human habitation, is reached by a causeway from Anglesey Island. As long ago as 2000 BC, Holyhead was a port for Welsh-Irish trade.

In addition to its many prehistoric sites, Holy Island has its natural attractions. Most obvious is Holyhead Mountain, the summit of which provides views of the Cumberland Mountains, Snowdonia, the Isle of Man and, on clear days, Ireland.

LAUGHARNE (82 A2)
DYFED *pop. 1,000*

Picturesque Laugharne, by the sea, has a harbor and castle but is best known as a home of writer Dylan Thomas, who lived by the Taf River. Many contend – though Thomas denied it – that the town and its residents served as models for *Under Milk Wood*.

DYLAN THOMAS' BOAT HOUSE was the riverside home of the poet for 16 years. Family furniture and photographs remain; an audiovisual presentation and information panels tell about the poet.

▲ LLANDUDNO (82 B4) ★
GWYNEDD *pop. 17,600*

The large resort of Llandudno is on a spit of land between two sandy beaches. From the quieter West Shore there are panoramas of Conwy Bay and more distant Snowdonia. A statue of Lewis Carroll recalls that the author often came to Llandudno to visit the Liddells and their daughter Alice, for whom he wrote his best known story.

Enclosing the principal beach, North Shore, are two rocky headlands; 676-foot Great Orme Head, the larger of the promontories, is a playground in itself. Of the several approaches, the most pleasant is on foot through the Happy Valley, a garden remarkable for its rare flowers and trees.

LLANGOLLEN (82 B3) ★
CLWYD *pop. 3,100*

Tiny Llangollen lies at the head of the Vale of Llangollen. In addition to its unspoiled surroundings, the town has several historic attractions: the 14th-century stone bridge across the Dee River, the remains of an 18th-century castle, the well-known old house Plas Newydd and the ruined abbey of Valle Crucis.

Llangollen is well known among music lovers as the site of the International Musical Eisteddfod, held since 1947. Early every July folk singers and dancers from around the world descend upon the town to compete with one another. In order to be certain of good seats, make reservations many months in advance; tel: 01978 860236 or write Llangollen International Musical Eisteddfod, Eisteddfod Office, Llangollen, Clwyd LL20 8NG.

CHIRK CASTLE stands about 6 miles south east near the village of Chirk. Built in 1310 by Roger Mortimer, it has been continuously occupied. The massive retangular castle includes some remarkable features – elaborately worked iron gates dating from the 18th century, interesting 16th-century decorative interior features and some excellent portraits of the Stuart kings. On the grounds are traces of Offa's Dyke, the extensive earthwork built by that 8th-century King of Mercia.

HORSE DRAWN BOATS AND CANAL EXHIBITION CENTRE, The Wharf, combine exhibits and 45-minute boat rides to enlighten visitors about Britain's canal era. The museum contains models, photographs, murals and slides pertaining to the canal commerce of the 18th century. Horsedrawn boats (schedule varies) travel the Vale of Llangollen.

PLAS NEWYDD is east of town on A5. From 1780 to 1831, this black-and-white half-timbered house was the home of two Irish aristocrats, Miss Sarah Ponsonby and Lady Eleanor Butler. Though locally regarded as eccentric, the "Ladies of Llangollen" were widely known for their wit and hospitality. Their many friends included such personages as William Wordsworth and the Duke of Wellington. Aside from its historical associations, the house is interesting for its furnishings and interior details, especially the stained glass.

MACHYNLLETH (82 B3)

POWYS *pop. 2,000*
The great champion of Welsh independence, Owain Glyndwr, made Machynlleth his capital in 1404. The town grew in succeeding centuries as a result of its position at the junction of a number of coach roads.

CENTRE FOR ALTERNATIVE TECHNOLOGY, Llwyngwern Quarry, promotes the development of natural energy sources. Solar collectors, windmills, water wheels and a conservation house demonstrate energy-saving techniques; organic gardening and fish cultures show self-sufficient ways of food production.

MONMOUTH (82 C2)

GWENT *pop. 9,000*
On the border at the junction of the Wye, Monnow and Trothy rivers, historic Monmouth provides a convenient center for touring the Wye Valley. The castle, now in ruins, was built by William FitzOsbern and was the birthplace of Henry V in 1387.

ST. DAVID'S (82 A3) ★

DYFED *pop. 1,500*
St. David's takes its name from the 16th-century patron saint of Wales. Though seemingly in the middle of nowhere, the town is at the junction of what were once well-traveled routes across the coastal region. The 12th-century cathedral was the object of pilgrimages during the Middle Ages.

Close to St. David's are many scenic bays, beaches, cliffs and islands. A half-mile from the coast lies Ramsey Island, a privately owned nature reserve accessible by way of a boat service offered by local fishermen.

▲ SWANSEA (82 B2)

WEST GLAMORGAN *pop. 282,600*
The seaport of Swansea has long been the metallurgical capital of Wales. Still mainly industrial, this second largest city in Wales also is the site of the University College of Swansea, the Glynn Vivian Art Gallery and the Royal Institution of South Wales. The last includes a museum devoted to the natural and cultural history of the district.

TENBY (82 A2) ★

DYFED *pop. 5,000*
A popular small resort on a rocky promontory overlooking two sandy bays, Tenby preserves several medieval monuments: St. Mary's Church, the Tudor Merchant's House and 13th-century walls. Caldy Island, 2½ miles out to sea, is the site of an old priory church and a modern monastery.

Pembroke Castle, 10 miles west, is an impressive 12th- to 13th-century fortress with a 80-foot round keep.

WELSHPOOL (82 B3)

POWYS *pop. 4,900*
POWIS CASTLE, on the south edge of Welshpool, was built by Owain ap Gruffyd in 1250. Though obviously a medieval castle, the structure has undergone some interior renovation. The plasterwork and paneling are late 16th century, and the ornate staircase is 17th century. The 18th-century gardens are the creation of Capability Brown.

▲ WREXHAM (82 B4)

CLWYD *pop. 41,700*
Wrexham is the industrial center of northern Wales. The pinnacled steeple of St. Giles' Church rises above the city; the church is known for its wrought-iron gates. In the churchyard lies the tomb of Elihu Yale, the 17th-century merchant who founded the American university that bears his name.

BULGARIA

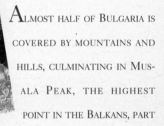

Almost half of Bulgaria is covered by mountains and hills, culminating in Musala Peak, the highest point in the Balkans, part of the Rila Mountains, with the remote Rila Monastery. In the thick forests on these slopes are bears, wolves, wild cats and elk. To the north is the capital, Sofia.

After many years behind the Iron Curtain, Bulgaria is trying to find its place on the economic map of Europe. It stands between Greece and Turkey to the south, and the Carpathian Mountains to the north. On its western edge its former Communist ally, Yugoslavia, has fragmented, and in the east it shares the Black Sea shores with Russia. Vacation resorts on the Golden Coast are becoming rapidly westernized. The north-east corner boasts Bulgaria's greatest river, the Danube (Dunav).

Left In the small village of Shipka, near Kazanlâk, the gold domes and brightly-colored façade of the Memorial Church attract the eye
Above During May and June, the scent of Damask roses fills the air

THINGS TO KNOW

- **AREA:** 111,000 square kilometers (42,857 square miles)
- **POPULATION:** 8,900,000
- **CAPITAL:** Sofia
- **LANGUAGE:** Bulgarian
- **RELIGION:** Bulgarian Orthodox, Moslem
- **ECONOMY:** Industry, agriculture, tourism. Products are machinery, chemicals, steel, textiles; wheat, corn, barley, seed oils, potatoes, tobacco.
- **ELECTRICITY:** 220 volts, continental two-round-pin plugs. Adaptor and/or transformer required for non-continental appliances.
- **PASSPORT REQUIREMENTS:** Required for U.S. citizens.
- **VISA REQUIREMENTS:** Not required for stays up to one month by U.S. citizens. Visas take about seven working days to be processed and cost $30/£20.
- **DUTY-FREE ITEMS:** Personal belongings; radio; one bicycle; 250 cigarettes; one liter of liquor; two liters of wine; one still and one movie camera; one video camera.
- **CURRENCY:** The currency unit is the *lev* (LEVA), divided into 100 *stotinka*. Due to currency fluctuations, the exchange rate is subject to frequent change. No limit on import or export of foreign currency, but all currency must be declared. However, visitors are not permitted to either import or export any Bulgarian currency at any time. Leva not spent in Bulgaria may be exchanged on presentation of a receipt of origin.
- **BANK OPENING HOURS:** 9am–4pm Monday–Friday. Money can also be exchanged outside banking hours at hotels and private exchange bureaux. Credit cards are not widely accepted.
- **STORE OPENING HOURS:** 8:30am–6pm Monday–Friday, 8:30am–2pm Saturday.
- **BEST BUYS:** Ceramics, embroidered clothing, linens, carpets, Valley of the Roses perfume, leather, coffee sets.
- **PUBLIC HOLIDAYS:** January 1; Liberation Day, March 1; Easter Sunday and Monday; Labor Day, May 1; Education Day, May 24; December 25.

HISTORY

Bulgaria, northern Greece and European Turkey were home to the Thracians, an Asiatic people, who were conquered by Philip II of Macedonia and his son Alexander the Great in the 4th century BC. After the defeat of Macedonia in 168 BC the Romans became the dominant power in the Balkans.

By the 1st century they had established the provinces of Moesia and Thrace. But Roman rule collapsed under the invasions of the Bulgars, who merged with the great migration of Slavic tribes in the 6th and 7th centuries. Not until the First Bulgarian Kingdom was established in 681 AD was the flowering of a national identity possible. St. Cyril and St. Methodius created the Slavonic alphabet in 863 AD; Christianity was declared the state religion two years later and the country became the center of Slav culture. Under King Simeon, who ruled from 893 to 927 AD, Bulgarian literature attained its golden age and the kingdom's land holdings expanded to their greatest limits. Internal friction weakened the country and led to the Byzantine occupation from 1018 to 1185.

Independence was regained during the Second Bulgarian Kingdom, which brought about a renaissance in architecture, painting and literature. In the late 14th century central authority was so weakened by opposition from over-powerful nobles, that little resistance was offered to the Turkish threat. The 15th-century occupation ended religious, cultural and political freedom, and brutally suppressed opposition. Only in secluded monastries such as Rila and Troyan was the Bulgarian spirit kept alive, until in the late 18th century national feelings and political expectations gradually grew.

A failed uprising in 1876 and the subsequent Turkish massacres roused international consciousness and enlisted Russian help in the successful Liberation

War of 1877–8, which inaugurated the Third Bulgarian Kingdom of 1879–1944.

Tempted by the offers of Macedonia, which many thought to be part of their country, Bulgaria sided with the Germans in both world wars.

When the former Soviet Union declared war on Bulgaria in 1944, the country subsequently signed an armistice with the Allies. The monarchy was overthrown and the People's Republic of Bulgaria was founded September 8, 1946, after a referendum.

Communist rule lasted for nearly 50 years, until on November 10, 1989, Todor Shivkov resigned. Parliament subsequently voted to revoke the constitutionally guaranteed dominance of the Communist Party.

Today Bulgaria is transforming its political and economic role in Europe. The leader of the opposition, Dr. Zhelyu Zhelev, was chosen as Bulgaria's first non-Communist president in August, 1990. The first non-Communist government came to power in November, 1991, after the Union of the Democratic Forces won the elections. In January, 1992, President Zhelev was re-elected in the first direct presidential elections.

FOOD AND DRINK

Bulgarian cuisine is mainly influenced by its neighbors, the Turks. Meals begin with salads, usually accompanied by a shot of *rakiya* (grape or plum brandy). Grilled meats are very popular, and there are excellent stews with meat and vegetables cooked slowly together. Bulgarian yoghurt is delicious and is served at breakfast and used in cooking.

Typical dishes include *tarator*, whipped yoghurt soup; *gyuvech*, a mixture of green beans, tomatoes, eggplant, peppers, potatoes and meat; *drob surma*, lamb liver baked with fried rice; *kebabches*, peppery meatballs; *shopska salata*, salad with grated white cheese, cucumber and tomatoes; and *pulmeni chushki*, pepper filled with cheese and fried in batter.

Melnik, Misket, Muscatel and Tamyanka are good local wines. Bulgarians like their food hearty, traditional and varied, and they take time to savor meals; service in restaurants is characteristically unhurried. The main meal is usually eaten in the middle of the day.

SPORTS AND RECREATION

Bulgaria offers many sporting activities for both spectators and participants alike, including the International Ski Competition at Aleko and bicycling's Tour of Bulgaria. Downhill skiing takes place at the resorts of Borovets, Vitosha and Pamporovo.

Soccer, volleyball and basketball are popular nationally, and the Black Sea beaches are excellent for watersports. Anglers find trout in the Rila Mountain lakes and pike and carp in the Black Sea and the Danube River. Hunters can contact a variety of new travel agents to arrange vacations in any of 15 game preserves. Quarry include deer, game birds and wild boar.

GETTING AROUND

The main Bulgarian railroad line runs from Belgrade (Beograd), Serbia, to Istanbul, Turkey, passing through Sofia and Plovdiv. Other important routes are the Trans–Balkan, which includes the Sofia–Burgas and Sofia–Varna lines, and

---

AUTOMOBILE CLUB
The Union des Automobilistes Bulgares
(UAB), Union of Bulgarian Automobilists) has offices at 3 Place Positano, Sofia. The symbol ▲ beside a city name indicates the presence of a AAA-affiliated automobile club branch. Not all auto clubs offer full travel services to AAA members.

- USEFUL TELEPHONE NUMBERS:
  Police 166
  Fire 160
  Ambulance 150
  Roadside Assistance 146
- NATIONAL TOURIST OFFICES:
  Balkan Holidays
  41E 42nd Street
  Suite 508
  New York
  NY 10017
  U.S.A.
  Tel: 212/573 5530
  Balkan Holidays
  Sofia House
  19 Conduit Street
  London
  W1R 9TD
  Tel: 0171 491 4499
  Fax: 0171 491 7068
  National Tourist Authority
  Committee for Tourism
  1 Sveta Nedelya Square
  1040 Sofia
  Tel: 02 87 08 98
  Fax: 02 88 20 66
- AMERICAN EMBASSY:
  1A Stamboliiski Boulevard
  25402 Sofia
  Bulgaria
  Tel: 02 88 48 05
  Fax: 02 80 18 77

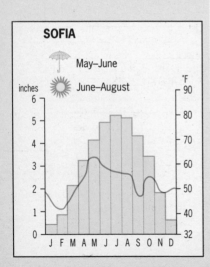

SOFIA

May–June

June–August

the Ruse–Varna route. There are three international airports, and a network of internal flights; regular passenger boats and hydrofoils serve Varna and Burgas on the Black Sea coast and ports along the Danube River. Several international bus routes pass through Sofia.

Highways and secondary roads are mostly well maintained. The main east–west approach runs from Serbia to Turkey and passes through Sofia. Other major highways connect Sofia to Burgas on the Black Sea Coast, and link the Black Sea resorts. Road signs are usually written in both Cyrillic script and Roman letters.

The wearing of seat belts (if the car is so equipped) is mandatory for the driver and front-seat passenger outside populated areas; a child under 12 cannot travel in the front seat. Speed limits are 60 k.p.h. (35 m.p.h.) in town, 80 k.p.h. (50 m.p.h.) out of town and 120 k.p.h. (75 m.p.h.) on highways. Visitors who have held a driver's license for less than two years must not exceed 50 k.p.h. (30 m.p.h.) in town, 70 k.p.h. (40 m.p.h.) on out-of-town roads and 100 k.p.h. (60 m.p.h.) on highways. Drivers are required to pay fines for motoring offences on the spot.

In rural areas gas stations are often far apart and sometimes run out of gas. So fill up often when traveling off the beaten track.

ACCOMMODATIONS
Hotels and private rooms for rent in Bulgaria are classified as deluxe, first class, second class and third class. The number of private hotels is growing.

Campers will find 130 campsites in the country, rated as special, first or second class. In summer many well-equipped campgrounds are open along the Black Sea, in the mountains and near cities and towns frequented by tourists. Most sites have chalets for rent. An international camping carnet is recommended. Bulgaria allows camping only at officially designated campgrounds.

TIPPING
Waiters will expect a *stotinki*, or small tip; usually about 10 percent.

SPECIAL EVENTS
The god of wine, Dionysus, is said to have taught viticulture to the ancient Thracians, and the February feast of Tryphon Zarezan honors him with singing, dancing and drinking. Other vacations include June fire-dancing rituals in the Stranja Mountains and Easter week celebrations featuring Bulgarian costumes. Sofia's National Folk Ensemble is internationally known for its song and dance programs.

PRINCIPAL TOURING AREAS

Note: For descriptions of cities in **bold type**, see individual city listings.

Sofia, Bulgaria's capital is set against a background of mountains. Trips by bus or car from Sofia to the spa Isker Lake (Yavovir Iskâr), **Rila** Monastery (Manastir), Bankya, Mount Vitosha, or the mountain resort of **Borovets** can be made in a day. Other possibilities are three- to 14-day tours of the country with trips to monasteries, museums and caves.

BLACK SEA COAST
The Black Sea washes Bulgaria's eastern coast. Furrowed by coves and headlands, the long stretches of fine sand attract visitors in spring, summer and fall.

North of **Varna**, itself a popular beach resort, there are three modern beach resorts, the tranquil Sts. Konstantin and Elena, Albena and Zlatni Pyasâtsi.

Burgas is a lively cultural, industrial and fishing center with its own beach. Just north of Burgas are the therapeutic mud baths of Pomorie. Pomorie also produces a choice wine, Pomorie Dimiat. **Nessebâr** has architecture recalling a long period of Byzantine rule. **Slânchev Bryag**, or Sunny Beach, is a leader among the Black Sea resorts.

South of Burgas, the slopes of the Strandja Mountains stretch to the sea. At the ancient port of Sozopol, rustic buildings and fishermen tending their nets contribute to a charming seascape. Beyond Sozopol there is little development, the beaches are often deserted. Towards the Turkish border, the coastline is rocky and there are attractive coves. One of the charms of Bulgaria's Black Sea coast is that, despite its popularity, it is always possible to get away from the crowds. Much of the coast is undeveloped; forests, villages, vineyards and farmland border empty beaches.

NORTHERN BULGARIA
The Danubian Plain and the Balkan Range make up northern Bulgaria. This richly forested region is crisscrossed by a network of rivers and roads. High above a bend in the Jantra River, the city of **Veliko Târnovo** is built on a slope of the Balkan Mountains.

In the western foothills is Belogradchik, a resort area known for its unusual geological formations. Nearby Magoura Cave (Magura Peshtera) contains guano paintings by Bronze Age inhabitants. On the Danube River is Vidin, which has a fortress and 15th-century monuments. Pleven, farther into the Danube Valley, has monuments and museums commemorating the Russo-Turkish War of 1876–78. Nearby Kailuka Park has accommodations and campgrounds. On the banks of the Danube River is **Ruse**, a sophisticated city with an opera house, theaters, museums and art galleries.

PLOVDIV AND THE VALLEY OF THE ROSES
Plovdiv, on the plain between **Sofia** and Istanbul, Turkey, is a convenient starting point for touring central Bulgaria.

Nearby are the Bachkovo Monastery, 13th-century Assen Fortress, Hissarya Spa and the Valley of the Roses.

About an hour's drive north of Plovdiv, the Valley of the Roses (Rosova Dolina) has acres of damask roses which provide the oil base for the world's perfumes. The best time to tour is in May and June, when the fragrance of roses fills the valley as workers harvest the blooms, and donkey carts carry the sacks to nearby distilleries. There are several attractive small towns in the valley, Sopot, Karlovo and Kalofer, and at the eastern end, the city of **Kazanlâk**; a short drive south east leads to Stara Zagora. Both of these cities have sites of ancient civilizations.

SOUTHERN MOUNTAIN REGION

Southern Bulgaria has the country's highest and most extensive mountain region. The Rila and the Pirin ranges (Rila Planina/Pirin Planina) have rocky peaks interspersed with lakes and brooks. The Rhodope Mountains (Rodopi Planina) to the east encompass rolling hills, pastureland and dense forests.

In the Rila range is the south's major tourist draw, the **Rila** Monastery. The chief ski resort is **Borovets,** lying about 70 kilometers (43 miles) south of **Sofia**; nearby 2,925-meter (9,596-foot) Mount Musala is the highest peak on the Balkan Peninsula. Melnik, in the southwestern region of the Pirin Mountains, is

noted for its architecture, its rich red wine, and the strange-shaped sandstone cliffs which surround it. The mountain resort of **Pamporovo**, 84 kilometers (52 miles) south of **Plovdiv** in the Rhodopes (Rodopi Planina), has ski areas and coniferous forests.

USEFUL EXPRESSIONS IN BULGARIAN

Bulgarian, the official language, is a South Slavonic tongue and is closely related to Russian. The Cyrillic alphabet is used, and it's important to remember that a sideways shake of the head means "yes," while a nod means "no." English is generally only understood in Sofia, Plovdiv and the main tourist resorts.

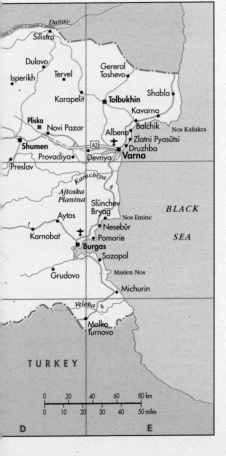

hello	zdraveí (singular/familiar) sdravéite (plural/polite)
good-bye	dovizhdane
good morning	dobró útro
please	mólya
thankyou	blagodaryá, mercí
yes/no	da/ne
excuse me	izvinéte
you're welcome	nyáma zashtó
Do you speak English?	govórite li anglíski?
I do not understand.	ne vi razbíram
What is the time?	kólko e chasút?
How much does it cost?	kolko struva tova?
I have broken down.	kolata me se povrédi
Where is the nearest service station?	kudé e naiblízkiya ávtoservíz?
Which is the road to Sofia?	koi e pútyat za Sófia?
Where is ...?	kudé se namira ...?
Where are the restrooms, please?	kudé e toalétnata, mólya?
museum	muzéi
art gallery	hudózhestvena galériya
restaurant	restoránt
open/closed	otvóreno/zatvóreno

NUMBERS

1	edin, edna, edno
2	dve, dva
3	tri
4	chetiri
5	pet
6	shest
7	sedem
8	osem
9	devet
10	deset
20	dvaiset
30	triiset
40	chetiriiset
50	petdeset
60	shestdeset
70	sedemdeset
80	osemdeset
90	devetdeset
100	sto

PLACES OF INTEREST

BULGARIA

▲ SOFIA (168 A2) ★

SOFIA *pop. 1,300,000*

The nation's capital since 1879, Sofia is fringed by the western mountains of Bulgaria. The city's history began in the 8th century BC, when it was known to the Thracians as *Serdica*.

It was occupied by the Romans, and during the Middle Ages, under the intermittent rule of Constantinople, it acquired its Byzantine architecture. Later, the Ottoman Empire left Sofia a heritage of Moslem architecture, and succeeding styles include those of the Bulgarian Renaissance.

Sofia's cultural calendar revolves around the Opera House, Concert Hall, National Art Gallery and National Theater, all in the heart of the city.

The History Museum has outstanding exhibits. The Borisov Park, has an open-air theater and sports facilities. There are several monasteries near the city.

Trips can be made to Bankya, a mineral spa; Pancharevo and Isker lakes; Borovets, a mountain resort and ski center; the rocks of Belogradchik and Magoura Cave; and Koprivshtitsa, a museum town near the capital.

BUJUK DJAMIJA (Great Mosque), 2 Alexander Stamboliiski Boulevard, dates from the 15th century. With its nine lead-covered domes, it is the finest surviving example of Moslem architecture in Bulgaria.

Archeologicheski Musei (Archeological Museum), in the mosque, has ceramic, silver and bronze finds from the prehistoric, Roman and medieval eras.

CERKVA ALEKSANDER NEVSKI ★ (Alexander Nevsky Memorial Church) dominates the impressive square of the same name. The church was begun in 1882 and consecrated in 1924. The great gold-domed structure is built in the style of a Byzantine basilica, with Renaissance, Russian and Oriental elements. Under the largest dome, which is 51 meters (167 feet) high, are the great bells, whose peals can be heard 32 kilometers (20 miles) away. Features are the carved marble iconostasis and thrones, alabaster and onyx columns and paintings by well-known Bulgarian and Russian artists.

CERKVA SVETA SOFIA (Church of St. Sofia), Alexander Nevsky Square, inspired the city's name. It was built in the 6th century as a Christian church under Byzantine rule. St. Sofia's architecture reflects strong Byzantine and Romanesque styles. Centuries later it served as a mosque while under Ottoman rule.

CERKVA SVETI GEORGI (Rotunda of St. George), off St. Nedelya Square, dates from the Roman occupation, when it was possibly a temple or public bath. Under the rule of Constantine the Great, the first Roman emperor to be converted to Christianity, it became a church. It was vandalized by nomads and rebuilt, but much of the original beauty remains, particularly in the medieval frescoes.

ETHNOGRAFSKI MUSEÎ (Ethnographic Museum), Alexander Battenberg Square, shares the former royal palace with the National Art Gallery. Regional costumes, tapestries and jewelry present a picture of Bulgarian culture.

NATIONAL HISTORY MUSEUM ★, in the Palace of Justice on Vitosha Boulevard, contains exhibits illustrating Bulgaria's role in world history and culture. The Rogozen silver and Panagyurishte gold treasures are spectacular.

VITOSHA, a 2,290-meter (7,513-foot) mountain in a recreational park, is 8 kilometers (5 miles) south. There are rivers, gorges and waterfalls, and hiking trails and excellent skiing facilities. Vitosha can be reached by road and ski lift.

Bojanska Cerkva (Church of Boyana) is an 11th-century church with 13th-century frescoes that have been compared to the greatest works of the Italian Renaissance. The anonymous paintings are remarkable for their realistic style and as predecessors to the early Italian masters.

ALBENA (168 E3)
VARNA

A resort on the Black Sea coast north of Varna, Albena has a modern skyline and spacious beach with watersports, tennis, cycling, volleyball and basketball. Entertainment includes movies, concerts, and folklore displays. The restaurants offer moderately priced family-style service and often have live music.

BOROVETS (168 B2)
SOFIA *pop. 500*

A popular winter and summer resort on the northern slopes of the Rila Mountains, Borovets is at the foot of Mount Mussala. The scenery, comfortable climate and winter sports facilities makes it a popular venue for international events.

▲ BURGAS (168 D2)
BURGAS *pop. 200,000*

Burgas is a cultural center, busy commercial town and popular resort on the southern Black Sea coast. An oil refinery makes the port one of the busiest on the Black Sea. There are cafés and shops, historic buildings, theaters and concerts.

▲ GABROVO (168 C2) ★
GABROVO *pop. 80,000*

ETURA ETHNOGRAPHIC MUSEUM is situated 8 kilometers (5 miles) to the south of Gabrovo and was established to preserve and teach the craft skills which originally made the town famous in the 19th century.

ROSES

Bulgaria's Rosova Dolina (Valley of the Rose) lies between Kazanlâk and Klisura. Here over 70 percent of the world's *attar*, or oil, of roses is produced. It is, literally, worth its weight in gold.

The rose was brought to Europe by Crusaders returning from the Holy Land, hence its name, the Rose of Damascus, or Damask Rose. The roses are harvested in late May/early June, and picked between 3 and 8am, before the sun is hot enough to evaporate the oil. Each acre yields about 3 million rosebuds, but it takes over 1.2 hectares (3 acres) of roses to produce just one liter of the precious attar. Rose oil is the basis of most modern perfumes. The residual products are used to make medicines, cosmetics, rose jam and liqueurs, as well as the seductive Turkish delight.

KAZANLÂK (168 C2)
STARA ZAGORA *pop. 58,000*

Kazanlâk is the chief town in the Valley of the Roses. A 3rd-century BC burial chamber built for a Thracian chief and his wife has been excavated nearby. Murals depict scenes from the life of a people admired even by the ancient Greeks for their wealth and culture.

Near the town is a fascinating Museum of the Rose Industry.

KOPRIVSHTITSA (168 B2) ★
SOFIA

In the Sredna Gora Mountains, houses lining the narrow, cobbled streets have intricately carved ceilings, bay windows and verandas. The whole town has been declared an architectural monument.

NESSEBÂR (168 E2) ★

BURGAS *pop. 7,000*

An exhibition – "Nessebâr Through the Ages" – is housed in the 10th-century St. John the Baptist Church, which also has 16th- and 17th-century frescoes.

PAMPOROVO (168 B1)

SMOLIJAN

A winter resort in the Rhodope Mountains, Pamporovo has excellent skiing. The coniferous forests are ideal for hiking. Smolyan, Oustovo and Raikovo are known for their colorful carpets, Rhodope blankets and goats' hair rugs.

▲ PLOVDIV (168 B1) ★

PLOVDIV *pop. 360,000*

Settled long before Philip II of Macedonia conquered it in the 4th century BC and named it *Philipopolis*, Plovdiv is one of the oldest cities in Europe. The well-preserved Hissar Kapiya (Gate of the Fortress) leads to the Old City, Plovdiv's major attraction, which has cobblestone alleys and quaintly decorated houses from the National Renaissance period.

Plovdiv is also a modern industrial center. Just south lie the forests and rocky peaks of the Rhodope Mountains, a favorite excursion and camping area.

ARCHEOLOGICESKI MUSEI (Archeological Museum), in the Old City, is known for its cache of gold and silver objects, dating from the Thracian period.

BACHKOVSKI MANASTIR (Bachkovo Monastery), founded in 1038, contains priceless icons and frescoes.

CHASOVNIKOVA KULA (Clock Tower), on Sahat Tepe, is probably the oldest clock in Eastern Europe. The hill affords panoramic views of the town.

DJUMAYA DJAMIYA, on Stambolijski Square, is a 15th-century mosque, built on the site of a Christian church.

GEORGIADI HOUSE, Starinna Street, was built 1846–48 by the master builder Georgi of Constantinople. A fine example of a graceful house, it contains a Museum of the Renaissance and an exhibition on the political history of Bulgaria.

HOUSE OF ARGYR KOUYUMDJIOGLOU, on Dr. Comakov Street, was designed by the builder Georgi in the mid-19th century. The symmetrical house has richly ornamented exteriors and interiors. An ethnological museum inside contains reproductions of craftsmen's workshops, old farming tools, spinning and weaving implements and national costumes.

RILA (168 A2) ★

SOFIA

RILA MANASTIR (Rila Monastery), had considerable religious influence in the Middle Ages and was a center of resistance against Ottoman domination. The monastery as it stands today is what remains of the 10th-century buildings of John of Rila, who fled the excesses of court life to found a hermitage. Over the centuries succeeding restorations were impressive, with the final form established in the mid-19th century during the Bulgarian Renaissance.

Hrelyu's Tower, 23 meters (75 feet) tall), and its valuable painting date from the 14th century. The commanding outer walls contrast with the striped arcades, columns, flights of stairs and flowing fountains of the inner courtyard. The church has vaults and walls covered with frescoes, heavily ornamented chandeliers and a carved wooden iconostasis. **Rila Museum**, on the ground floor, contains parchment manuscripts, icons, weapons, vestments and coins.

▲ RUSE (168 C3)

RUSE *pop. 151,500*

Ruse was a Roman fort built in the 1st century. Captured by the Ottomans in the 14th century, it became an important commercial town. Today it is a major port and industrial center. Interesting sights include fine baroque buildings, the Museum of Transportation and spacious Lipnik Park.

Ruse is linked with Romania by Friendship Bridge. About 25 kilometers (16 miles) south of Ruse is the medieval town of Cerven; 10 kilometers (6 miles) farther is the monastery of Ivanovo, cut from solid rock.

STREET NAMES

In Bulgaria many streets are named after political figures. This has resulted in recent changes as the communist heroes are replaced by former kings and figures from history. However, three old street names are certain to survive. Vassil Levski was a leading revolutionary against the Ottoman occupation, captured and executed by the Turks. Hristo Botev was an inspiring revolutionary and poet, who was killed in action during the April Uprising in 1876. Ivan Vazov was a contemporary of Levski and Botev. His poems and novels, especially the famous *Under the Yoke*, give a vivid picture of the brutality and corruption of life in the Ottoman Empire.

SLÂNCHEV BRYAG (168 E2)
BURGAS

White sand beaches have made Slânchev Bryag, or Sunny Beach, a modern resort popular with families.

Traditional Bulgarian food and music can be found at folk-style restaurants, and the streets are busy with pavement artists and musicians.

SOZOPOL (168 E2) ★
BURGAS *pop. 4,000*

The ancient fishing village of Sozopol, on the Black Sea coast, is a popular resort distinguished by winding, cobbled streets, old buildings and architecturally interesting churches.

▲ VARNA (168 E3)
VARNA *pop. 300,000*

Varna is a Black Sea resort, ancient port, important industrial, cultural and vacation center. One of the oldest inhabited places in the Balkans, Varna has monuments believed to have been built by prehistoric civilizations. The Archeological Museum contains fine examples of Thracian, Greek and Roman art.

▲ VELIKO TÂRNOVO (168 C2) ★
TÂRNOVO *pop. 90,000*

The town achieved its greatest prominence as the medieval capital of the Second Bulgarian Kingdom, 1187–1396. The Old Town lies on the western bank of the Yantra. Most of its churches and civic buildings were erected during the 19th-century National Renaissance. The town can be reached by rail or major road, including the route to the south west through the Valley of the Roses.

ARBANASSI, about 4 kilometers (2½ miles) north east of Târnovo, reached the height of its prosperity in the 17th and 18th centuries. From outside the houses look like small fortresses, but inside the carved wooden ceilings and comfortable furnishings are evidence of the wealth of the inhabitants. The prosperous merchants also endowed local churches, which have lavish and beautiful frescoes.

CHETIRIDESET MACHENITSI (Church of the 40 Martyrs), Assenova Quarter, is a 13th-century church and royal mausoleum that was later converted into a Turkish mosque. The independent Kingdom of Bulgaria was proclaimed here in 1908.

ZLATNI PYASÂTSI (168 E3)
VARNA

This resort (which translates as Golden Sands) is just north of Varna. Its fine beach is over 4 kilometers (2½ miles) long, and slopes gently into the sea, which has no dangerous currents.

The historic and interesting Aladza Monastery is 3 kilometers (2 miles) south west of the town.

CZECH REPUBLIC

PRAGUE (PRAHA) WAS ALWAYS THE GOLDEN CITY, ITS WEALTH OF BAROQUE BUILDINGS AND GOTHIC CHURCHES SCARCELY TOUCHED BY WARS, INSTEAD WATCHING OVER THE 1968 PRAGUE SPRING AND THE VELVET REVOLUTION OF 1989, WHEN A PLAYWRIGHT BECAME PRESIDENT. MUCH OF THIS HAPPENED IN WENCESLAS SQUARE, FIRST STOP ON ANY ITINERARY, CLOSELY FOLLOWED BY THE OLD TOWN SQUARE AND CHARLES BRIDGE, WHICH LEADS TO HRADČANY – PRAGUE CASTLE. PRAGUE IS ONE OF THREE U.N.E.S.C.O. WORLD HERITAGE SITES IN THE CZECH REPUBLIC, THE OTHERS BEING TELČ AND ČESKÝ KRUMLOV. ČESKÝ KRUMLOV STANDS, LIKE PRAGUE, ON THE VLTAVA RIVER; AN INCOMPARABLY BEAUTIFUL TOWN. TELČ IS AN ALMOST PERFECTLY-PRESERVED 16TH-CENTURY TOWN. WITH ITS MANY CHÂTEAUX AND SPA TOWNS, THE CZECH REPUBLIC MAY CENTER ON PRAGUE, BUT IT HAS MUCH ELSE BESIDES.

Left THE SMALL WINE PRODUCING TOWN OF KARLŠTEJN NESTLES IN THE VALLEY BELOW THE IMPRESSIVE BOHEMIAN KARLŠTEJN CASTLE
Above THE ASTRONOMICAL CLOCK IN STAROMĚSTSKÉ NÁMĚSTÍ

THINGS TO KNOW

- **AREA:** 78,864 square kilometers (30,442 square miles)
- **POPULATION:** 10,300,000
- **CAPITAL:** Praha (Prague)
- **LANGUAGE:** Czech
- **RELIGION:** Roman Catholic/Protestant
- **ECONOMY:** Engineering, vehicles, chemicals, textiles, brown coal, iron ore, mixed agriculture.
- **ELECTRICITY:** 220 volts, continental two round-pin plugs. (In some older parts 120 volts.) Adaptor and/or transformer required for non-continental appliances.
- **PASSPORT REQUIREMENTS:** Required for U.S. citizens.
- **VISA REQUIREMENTS:** Not required for stays under 30 days.
- **DUTY-FREE ITEMS:** 250 cigarettes or tobacco equivalent; 1 liter of liquor, 2 liters of wine; ¼ liter of cologne; gifts up to 3,000 Czech crowns in value.
- **CURRENCY:** The currency unit is the Czech *crown* (*česká koruna* – Kč), divided into 100 *hellers* (*halíř*). There are no restrictions on the import and export of foreign currency and traveler's checks up to the amounts declared on entry. Czech crowns may be imported/exported up to 5,000 Kč.
- **BANK OPENING HOURS:** 9am–5pm Monday–Friday, maybe closed during lunch.
- **STORE OPENING HOURS:** 9am–6pm Monday–Friday, 9am–1pm Saturday. Food stores open from 6am. Late night shopping Thursday. Increasing numbers of stores open Sunday.
- **BEST BUYS:** Bohemian glass and crystal, gems (especially garnets), costume jewelry, porcelain; toys, dolls, puppets; handicrafts, compact discs.
- **PUBLIC HOLIDAYS:** New Year's Day, January 1; Easter Monday; May Day, May 1; Liberation Day, May 8; Saints Cyril and Methodius, July 5; Master John Huss, July 6; Independence Day, October 28; Christmas, December 24–26.

HISTORY

Celts came first to Czechoslovakia, then Teutons, followed in the 6th century by Slav tribes, who formed the Great Moravian Empire. Under Charles IV of Luxembourg the capital, Prague, became the political and cultural center of 14th-century Europe. In later years, the country was riven with political and religious strife; preacher Jan Hus was burnt at the stake in 1415, while the Thirty Years War was heralded in 1618 by the defenestration of Catholic councillors from the windows of Prague Castle. After the Battle of the White Mountain in 1620 the Czechs were ruled from Vienna by the Habsburgs.

The collapse of the Habsburg Empire led to the creation of the new state of Czechoslovakia in 1918. In 1938 the Munich Conference left Czechoslovakia powerless in the face of Nazi Germany and in 1939 the country was dismembered, Bohemia and Moravia becoming a Nazi protectorate. In 1945, U.S. troops liberated western Bohemia, and the Red Army freed the rest of the country. Communists seized power in 1948, and an attempt in 1968 by reformists, led by Alexander Dubcek, to establish "Socialism with a human face" was crushed by Soviet-led troops.

With the collapse of communism throughout Eastern Europe in 1989 the Czechs brought about a "Velvet Revolution." Playwright Vaclav Havel was elected president. Differences between Czechs and Slovaks on how to form a new democratic state led to an agreement in 1992 to separate. The Czech Republic was proclaimed on January 1, 1993.

FOOD AND DRINK

Meals might begin with cold meats and pickles and end with a cream cake. Smoked foods and soups are Czech specialities. Meat, very often pork, is served well done and accompanied by gravy, dumplings and *sauerkraut* or red cabbage. Fresh vegetables and fruit are rare. The national drink is beer, rated by connoisseurs as the best in the world.

SPORTS AND RECREATION
The country has a high reputation in tennis, ice hockey and gymnastics. Soccer is popular both for fans and players. Outdoor activities like climbing, fishing and rambling are popular. Watersports take place on the many large reservoirs.

GETTING AROUND
International air services center on Prague's Ruzyně Airport and there is a network of internal services. The rail network is good and fares are low. The bus network serves every settlement in the country, and there are a number of international services, e.g. to London. Public transportation in cities, by Metro (in Prague), tram and bus is generally excellent. The highway system is good, though becoming increasingly crowded.

AUTOMOBILE CLUB
Ustredni Automotoklub
CSFR (UAMK, Central Automobile Club) has its headquarters at Na Rybníčku 16, 120 76 Praha 2. The symbol ▲ beside a city name indicates the presence of a AAA-affiliated automobile club branch. Not all auto clubs offer full travel services to AAA members.

Drivers and passengers must wear seat belts. Children under 12 may not travel in the front seat. Speed limits are 60 k.p.h. (35 m.p.h.) in urban areas, 90 k.p.h. (55 m.p.h.) in the country and 110 k.p.h. (65 m.p.h.) on highways. Motoring fines must be paid on the spot.

ACCOMMODATIONS
Hotels are classified by star ratings which range from one (basic) to five (de luxe). The hotel stock is growing and older hotels are being modernized. More and more private residents are providing bed and breakfast facilities, particularly in Prague, and there are numerous campgrounds, many with chalets.

TIPPING
It is customary at a restaurant to give a gratuity of 10 percent, likewise with taxis. Hotel porters should receive a few crowns, as should lavatory attendants.

PRINCIPAL TOURING AREAS

Note: For descriptions of cities in **bold type**, see individual listings.

PRAGUE AND SURROUNDING AREA
Prague is the largest historic city in Europe not to have been devastated by war. Its architectural heritage is incomparable, and since the fall of communism it has become one of Europe's liveliest and culturally most vibrant cities. It is at the heart of the province of Bohemia and many of the major tourist attractions are within reach of a day trip. These include romantic castles, as well as the richly wooded gorges of Vltava, Sázava and Berounka.

WESTERN BOHEMIA
The border with Bavaria is marked by the cool green uplands of the Sumava

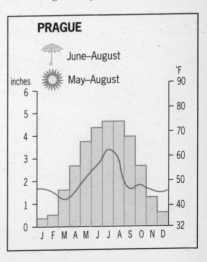

PRAGUE

June–August

May–August

- **USEFUL TELEPHONE NUMBERS:**
  Police 158, Fire 150; Ambulance 155
- **NATIONAL TOURIST OFFICES:**
  The Czech Center
  1009–1011 Madison Avenue
  New York NY 10028
  Tel: 212/535 8814/5
  Fax: 212/772 0586
  Administration of Czech Centres
  Hradčanské náměstí 5
  Praha 1
  Tel: 02 241 82880
  Fax: 02 245 510975
- **AMERICAN EMBASSY:**
  Třžiště 15, Unit 1330
  11801- Praha 1
  Czech Republic
  Tel: 02 242 19844;
  Fax: 02 531 200

(Bohemian Forest), wonderful walking country. Embedded in woodlands are the spa towns Karlovy Vary, Mariánske Lázně and Františkovy Lázně, and the medieval city of Cheb. Plzeň is home to Pilsener beer and heavy industries.

NORTHERN BOHEMIA

This is one of the most industrialized r ions, with many power plants. Acid rain has damaged some of the forest, but much remains. The Krkonoše (Giant Mountains) are popular with hikers in summer and skiers in winter.

SOUTHERN BOHEMIA

Delightful villages with high-gabled houses and baroque churches typify this area. Most of the towns date from the Middle Ages and nearly all of them, like

CZECH CASTLES

Richly endowed with castles and fine country houses, the countryside of the Czech Republic reflects an aristocratic past. Under communism there was no place for these splendid residences and they either became museums, were turned into schools and hostels, or simply mouldered away. After 1989, the process of restitution began, with many buildings returned to their owners and slowly restored to something resembling their former glory.

tiny Český Krumlov, and České Budějovice, with its huge Renaissance square, have been preserved intact.

MORAVIA

In the north, forested highlands provide a green background to the industrialized area around Ostrava. There are exquisite small towns, like Kroměříž and Telč, some of the finest castles and chateaux, and villages among the vineyards.

USEFUL EXPRESSIONS IN CZECH

hello	ahoj
good-bye	na shledanou
please	prosím
thankyou	děkuji
yes/no	ano/ne
good morning	dobrý den
good evening	dobrý večer
good night	dobrou noc
why?/when?	proč?/když?
where?/what?	kde?/co?
how much?	kolik?
Do you speak English?	mluvíte anglicky?
I don't speak Czech.	nemluvím česky
I don't understand.	nerozumím
sorry	promiňte
you're welcome	děkuji
quickly/slowly	rychle/pomalu
cold/hot	studený/horký
left/right	nalevo/napravo
open/closed	otevřenō/zavřeno
expensive/cheap	drahý/levný
near/far	blízko/daleko
day/week	den/týden
month/year	měsíc/rok
café/restaurant	kavárna/restaurace
church	kostel
cathedral	chrám
castle	hrad
town	město
bridge	most
tower	věž
palace	palác
garden	zahrada
monastery/convent	klášter
square	náměstí
market	trh
pharmacy	lekárna
city hall	radnice
station	nádraži
avenue	třída

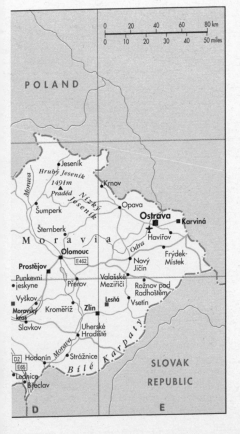

CZECH REPUBLIC

PLACES OF INTEREST

PRAHA ★

CENTRAL BOHEMIA *pop. 1,210,000*
Praha, or Prague, is an ancient metropolis which has preserved its rich heritage through centuries of war and discord.

Divided by the Vltava River, the city has four historic quarters: Hradčany, the castle district high above the river; Malá Strana, the Little Town, on the west bank, its streets lined with baroque palaces; Staré Město (Old Town) centered on Town Hall Square; and the Nové Město (New Town) centered on Václavské náměstí, Wenceslas Square.

In the 14th century, under Emperor Charles IV, the city became the capital of the Holy Roman Empire; the great Gothic cathedral and Charles Bridge (Karlův Most) were built and the New Town laid out. The 19th century left a legacy of great public buildings such as the National Theater and National Museum. Prague was at the forefront of art-nouveau and early modern building. However, stagnation under communism left its center untouched.

The city offers numerous theatre performances, several orchestras, chamber ensembles, organ concerts in churches, and puppet shows. The Prague Spring music festival in May attracts many visitors.

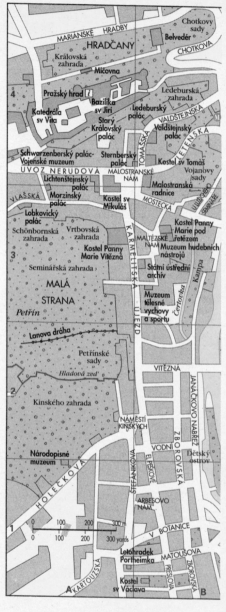

Prague pubs (*hospody*) are just as famous. There are wine bars (*vinárny*) and an increasing number of restaurants.

The city center is compact and best explored on foot with help from the superb public transportation system.

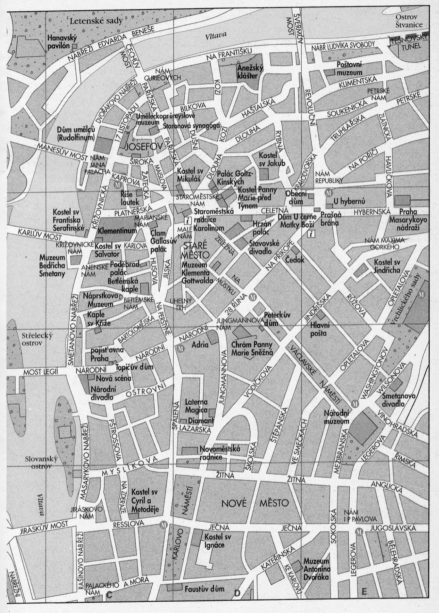

Tickets are available at tobacconists and hotel receptions; a fixed fare is charged regardless of the distance traveled.

Karlštejn Castle, 28 kilometers (17 miles) south west, was built by Charles IV as a holy shrine and repository for the crown jewels. Other castles include Křivoklát, 44 kilometers (27 miles) west, and Konopište, 40 kilometers (25 miles) south east, the home of Archduke Franz Ferdinand. His assassination at Sarajevo in 1914 led to the outbreak of World War I.

CZECH REPUBLIC

ANEŽSKÝ KLÁŠTER (St. Agnes' Convent) (180 D4), Staré Město, is a convent dating from 1233 and painstakingly restored to house the National Gallery's collection of 19th-century Czech art.

BERTRÁMKA (Mozart Museum), Mozartova 169, is the villa where Mozart completed his opera *Don Giovanni*, only hours before its first performance at the Estates Theater in the Old Town.

HRAD (180 A4) ★, Hradčany, Prague's Castle, has been a Slav fortress, a princely palace, a seat of empire, and now the residence of the president. As well as presidential offices, it contains churches, concert halls, museums, gardens and restaurants, and the views from its windows and terraces are the best in the city.
Bazilika Sv. Jiří (St. George's Basilica) has a baroque west front, but the twin towers and sober interior are Romanesque. Concerts are held here, while the adjoining monastery has been converted into a gallery of Czech art.
Katedrála Sv. Víta (St. Vitus Cathedral), has a distinctive outline of twin spires and a central tower capped by a Renaissance helmet. The interior has treasures from all periods of Bohemian art and includes the spectacularly decorated Gothic St. Wenceslas Chapel.

SVEJK TO THE RESCUE

One of the foremost characters of Czech literature is Jaroslav Hasek's Good Soldier Svejk, a seeming simpleton whose cheerful innocence reduces the oppressive Austrian army of World War I to chaos and confusion. Like most male Czechs, Svejk likes his beer, arranging to meet his mate Vodicka in his favorite pub, the Chalice, "at half-past six" when the war is over. The Chalice is still there in Prague's New Town, a mecca for lovers of beer and Hasek's subversive soldier.

Královská zahrada (Royal Garden). Among the fine old trees and formal gardens is the Renaissance belvedere, a graceful summer palace.
Starý Královský palác (Royal Palace). Above the 12th-century cellars is the Vladislavský sál (Vladislav Hall). It was from a window in the St. Louis Wing that the Catholic councillors were thrown in 1618, the incident which set off the Thirty Years War.
Zlatá ulička (Golden Lane) is lined with pretty but tiny houses, the dwellings of the alchemists employed to turn base metal into gold for Emperor Rudolph II.

JOSEFOV (Joseph's Town) (180 C4), Staré Město, is named after Emperor Joseph II who freed the Empire's Jews. Its principal monuments include the mysterious Old Jewish Cemetery, the Jewish Town Hall with its baroque clock tower, and the Gothic Old-New Synagogue.

KARLŮV MOST (Charles Bridge) (180 B3–C3) ★, built in 1357, is carried on 16 massive Gothic arches across the Vltava from the Old Town to Malá Strana.

MALOSTRANSKÉ NÁMĚSTÍ (Little Town Square) (180 A4–B4) ★ lined with palaces and fine town houses is dominated by the huge St. Nicholas' Church.

OBECNÍ DŮM (Municipal House) (180 E3), Staré Město. Of all the art-nouveau buildings in Prague, this is the most extravagant. It contains restaurants, bars, assembly halls and the Smetana Hall.

PETŘÍN HILL (180 A3) makes a wonderful green background to views of the city. There is a funicular railway to the top; a lookout tower modeled on the Eiffel Tower, and Strahov Monastery.

STAROMĚSTSKÉ NÁMĚSTÍ (Old Town Square) (180 D3) ★ has a memorial to Jan Hus. The square is especially crowded when the figures above the ancient astronomical clock appear. The towers of Tyn Church rise above the square.

ŠTERNBERSKÝ PALÁC (Sternberg Palace) (180 A4–B4), Hradčany, houses the National Gallery with many Old Master and French Impressionist pictures.

VÁCLAVSKÉ NÁMĚSTÍ (Wenceslas Square) (180 D2–E2) Shops, hotels, restaurants, movie theaters and nightspots line the square. In front of the National Museum is the famous statue of St. Wenceslas.

ZÁMEK TRÓJA (Troja chateau) was built as an out-of-town residence for Count Šternberg. It is now the home of the city's collection of Czech art.

BRNO (178 D1)
MORAVIA *pop. 390,000*
Brno has many historical buildings and interesting museums. To the east is the Napoleonic battlefield of Austerlitz (Slavkov) with its Memorial to Peace and baroque palace where the ceasefire was signed. The Moravian Karst district to the north has a deep chasm and over 400 caves. Lying 88.5 kilometers (55 miles) to the south west is Vranov castle.

DÓM NA PETROVĚ (St. Peter's Cathedral) stands on Petersburg (Petrov Hill), the highest point of Brno's Old Town.

ŠPILBERK is Brno's hilltop citadel. For many years it served as a prison; it is now the city museum.

ČESKÉ BUDĚJOVICE (178 B1)
SOUTHERN BOHEMIA *pop. 95,000*
Founded in the 13th century, the city is focused on a central square. Arcaded buildings line its long sides, with baroque façades concealing the medieval structure behind. The Radnice (City Hall) has towers and gargoyles. The square is overlooked by the Černá věž (Black Tower) which houses the bells of the cathedral. České Budějovice's name in German is Budweis, and it is famous for its beer, a rival to Plzeň's Pilsener.

HLUBOKÁ 10 kilometers (6 miles) north west is a 13th-century castle rebuilt in English Tudor style in the 19th century. It has fine furniture, tapestries and paintings, and the stables now house a collection of Czech art.

ČESKÝ KRUMLOV (178 B1) ★
SOUTHERN BOHEMIA *pop. 14,000*
The medieval town is laid out around a little square with a Renaissance town hall, while the 300-room castle is high above. It has courtyards, a tower with a Renaissance cap, and a moat. A ballroom is painted with *trompe l'oeil* figures and a baroque theater, still with the original stage machinery and equipment.

KARLOVY VARY (178 A3) ★
WESTERN BOHEMIA *pop. 58,000*
Guests have been coming here since the 16th century to sample the healing sulphurous springs. It reached the peak of its prestige at the turn of the century. Karlovy Vary also hosts an International Film Festival every second July and there is an annual Music Festival. The town is famous for its porcelain and herbal liqueur, *Becherovka.*

MARIÁNSKÉ LÁZNĚ (178 A2) ★
WESTERN BOHEMIA *pop. 15,000*
There are fine late 19th-century hotels built to serve the cosmopolitan guests who once flocked to the ultra-fashionable spa of Marienbad.

OLOMOUC (178 D2)
MORAVIA *pop. 106,000*
This north Moravian city has many protected historic buildings. Its focal point is the spacious Horní náměstí (Upper Square) with a huge baroque column and an astronomical clock. Every July it hosts the national garden festival, Flora Olomouc.

TELČ (178 C1) ★
MORAVIA *pop. 5,000*
Surrounded by fishponds, and entered through defensive gateways, this tiny medieval town in southern Moravia has a fine center: arcaded houses with fanciful gables line the cobbled square.

HUNGARY

IT IS SAID THAT A HUNGARIAN IS THE ONLY PERSON WHO CAN FOLLOW YOU INTO A REVOLVING DOOR AND COME OUT IN FRONT. WHETHER HUNGARY CAN COME OUT IN FRONT AS IT ENTERS MODERN EUROPE REMAINS TO BE SEEN. THE IRON CURTAIN CAME DOWN IN 1919 AND WAS NOT LIFTED FOR 70 YEARS, DESPITE BRAVE ATTEMPTS IN 1956. TWO MILLION OF THESE STRONG-WILLED PEOPLE LIVE IN THE CAPITAL CITY OF BUDAPEST; THE TWO CITIES, BUDA AND PEST, DIVIDED BY THE DANUBE RIVER (DUNA). IT IS ONE OF THE THREE GREAT CITIES OF CENTRAL AND EASTERN EUROPE, ALONGSIDE PRAGUE AND VIENNA; A CITY OF THE HABSBURG EMPIRE, MUSIC AND RICH, HEARTY FOOD. MUCH OF HUNGARY'S COUNTRYSIDE IS MADE UP OF RIVERS AND LAKES, THE LARGEST LAKE BEING BALATON IN THE WEST, ITS SHORES DOTTED WITH POPULAR RESORTS.

Left BUDAPEST'S MAGNIFICENT PARLIAMENT BUILDING ON THE DANUBE
Above left DETAIL ON THE MAIN DOOR OF ST. STEPHEN BASILICA IN BUDAPEST
Above right HUNGARIAN DOLL IN TRADITIONALLY EMBROIDERED COSTUME

THINGS TO KNOW

- **AREA:** 93,030 square kilometers (35,919 square miles)
- **POPULATION:** 10.4 million
- **CAPITAL:** Budapest
- **LANGUAGE:** Hungarian
- **RELIGION:** Roman Catholic.
- **ECONOMY:** Industry, construction, agriculture. Exports are machinery, fruit, bauxite, vegetables, textiles, footwear.
- **ELECTRICITY:** 220 volts.
- **PASSPORT:** Required for U.S. citizens.
- **VISA REQUIREMENTS:** Not required for stays up to three months.
- **DUTY-FREE ITEMS:** 250 cigarettes or 50 cigars or 250 grams tobacco; 1 liter of liquor, 2 liters wine; food for three days; gifts, once a year, up to 10,000 forints; personal belongings. Valuable personal effects must be declared on entry.
- **CURRENCY:** The currency unit is the *forint* (FT), divided into 100 *fillérs*. The exchange rate is subject to frequent change. No limits on import of foreign currency, but a declaration is required.
- **BANK OPENING HOURS:** 9am–5pm Monday–Friday.
- **STORE OPENING HOURS:** 10am–6pm Monday–Friday, 9am–1pm Saturday; most department stores open 10am–7/8pm weekdays.
- **BEST BUYS:** Herend porcelain, silverware, hand-made pottery, embroidery, lace, costumed dolls, shoes.
- **PUBLIC HOLIDAYS:** National Holiday, January 1; Easter Monday; Labor Day, May 1; St Stephen's Day, August 20; Proclamation of the Republic, October 23; December 25–26.
- **NATIONAL TOURIST OFFICES:** Hungarian Travel Bureau 1 Parker Plaza, Suite 1104 Fort Lee, NJ 07024 Tel: 201/592 8585 Tourinform Süto Utca 2, Budapest Tel: 117 9800; Fax: 117 9578
- **AMERICAN EMBASSY:** Szabadság Tér 12 Budapest 1054 Tel: 112 6450

HISTORY

The founders of the Hungarian nation-state, the Magyars, crossed the Carpathian Mountains in 896 AD. By 907 AD they had defeated the Slavs and Germans and were secure in their new homeland. In 1241–42 the Mongols stormed in from the east, leaving a trail of almost total destruction, but the country recovered, pushing its boundaries outwards in the 14th century and enjoying a Golden Age from 1458 to 1490.

In 1485 Hungary's king stormed Vienna and occupied Austria, Styria and Carinthia. All these lands were soon lost, and in 1526, Turks routed the Hungarian army in the disastrous battle at

Mohács. In 1541 Turkish forces occupied Buda, and virtually the whole of Hungary remained a part of the Ottoman Empire until the Habsburgs recaptured Buda in 1686. In 1848 Lajos Kossuth led a revolt that the Habsburgs only managed to put down with the help of the Russian tzar. In 1867, what became known as "The Compromise" allowed the Hungarian state a high degree of autonomy within the Habsburg Empire.

In 1919 a short-lived Soviet Republic was declared under the leadership of Bela Kun, but the Red Terror was soon followed by the far more savage White Terror of counter-revolutionary Admiral Miklos Horthy, who proclaimed himself regent. In 1920 Hungary was forced by the Allies to give up two-thirds of her territory to the neighboring states of Romania, Czechoslovakia and Yugoslavia. The bitter resentment this caused is still felt today, and during World War II led Hungary to side with Nazi Germany. Much destruction was caused as the Red Army invaded the country from 1944 to 1945.

After the war Hungary became part of the Soviet bloc. A heroic attempt to throw off foreign domination and one-party communist rule was made in 1956, but was crushed by Soviet tanks. In 1989 the government began dismantling the Iron Curtain along the border with

HUNGARY

Austria, helping to precipitate events that led to the downfall of communism across eastern Europe. Hungary is now a multi-party state, and although the reformed and renamed Communist Party now shares power, Hungary is firmly committed to democracy, a free-market economy and membership of the E.U.

FOOD AND DRINK
The red pepper gives Hungary its best known spice – paprika. It is combined with flour, onions and pork to create several Hungarian specialties. Potatoes and tomatoes added to the mixture produces *gulyás* (goulash). A similar dish is *pörkölt*, often made with vegetables, game or poultry; with sour cream, *pörkölt* become *paprikas*. *Rétes* is a thin, flaky pastry with apple, sour cherry or nuts. *Palacsinta* are thin pancakes. Around Eger are red wines, including the dry, dark Bull's Blood, *Egri Bikavér*. Part of the harvest of the orchards is distilled into fiery spirits like *barackpálinka* – apricot brandy.

SPORTS AND RECREATION
The lack of a seashore is made up for by Lake Balaton, excellent for swimming and sailing, though there are restrictions on power boating and water skiing. There are plenty of swimming pools and spas. Stables, studs and riding schools abound. Lakes and rivers are populated by pike, perch and carp. There's some skiing in the mountains in the north, as well as skating in Budapest's City Park.

GETTING AROUND
Ferihegy (Budapest Airport) is linked to most European capitals by direct flights and there is also a direct service to New York operated by Malev, the national airline. Most internal trips are made by rail using the network operated by MAV (Hungarian State Railway). There are rail connections with neighboring countries and Germany, as well as Paris and London. The network of internal bus services is well developed.

Public transportation in cities is efficient and cheap, though often overcrowded. Some cities have trams and trolley buses as well as ordinary buses, and Budapest has a subway. Boat trips on the Danube and on Balaton are a must, and there is a hydrofoil linking Budapest with Vienna.

AUTOMOBILE CLUB
Magyar Autoklub
(MAK, Hungarian Auto Club) is at Romer Floris Utca 4/A, Budapest. The symbol ▲ beside a city name indicates the presence of a AAA-affiliated automobile club branch. Not all auto clubs offer full travel services to AAA members.

The road system is well developed and maintained. The motorway between Budapest and Vienna was completed in December 1995. Traffic is heavy in Budapest and visitors are advised to leave their cars in car parks and travel by public transportation. Speed limits are 50 k.p.h. (30 m.p.h.) in urban areas, 80 k.p.h. (50 m.p.h.) on ordinary highways, 100 k.p.h. (60 m.p.h.) on limited access highways, and 120 k.p.h. (75 m.p.h.) on major highways. Seat belts must be worn and children under 12

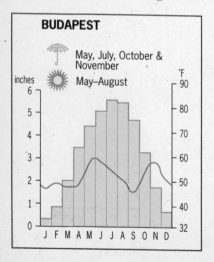

BUDAPEST

May, July, October & November
May–August

may not ride in the front seat. Motoring fines must be paid on the spot.

ACCOMMODATIONS

Hotels are graded from one (basic) to five (de luxe), the latter often being operated by one of the major chains like Hungarhotels, Pannonia and Danubius. Pensions and private rooms are often a good alternative to hotels. There are campgrounds in all holiday areas, often with chalets as well as tents.

ARTS AND ENTERTAINMENT

Concert halls are open all year; summer events feature Haydn at Fertöd's Esterházy Palace, Beethoven at Martonvásár and medieval court pieces in Budapest's Buda Castle. The Budapest Arts and Music weeks in early fall show off the opera houses, music halls and theaters, and Budapest's Spring Festival in mid-March includes symphonic concerts, opera, jazz and folklore nights, operetta and ballet.

TIPPING

Tipping is an accepted practice. Tip 10 to 15 percent of the bill in restaurants and about 25–50 forints to doormen, taxi drivers and bellhops.

PRINCIPAL TOURING AREAS

Note: For descriptions of cities in bold type, see individual city listings.

BUDAPEST AND THE DANUBE

The Danube River is often referred to as the main street of **Budapest** because it divides the capital into two. A fascinating holiday destination, Budapest is also a good place to start tours of the Danube Bend. The charming town of **Szentendre** is an artists' colony. The river runs through a gorge at the fortress of **Visegrád**, which dates from the reigns of Renaissance kings. The gorge extends west to **Esztergom**, headquarters of Hungarian Catholicism. Farther west are the regional centers of **Györ** and **Sopron**.

GREAT PLAIN (ALFÖLD)

The Great Plain begins on the outskirts of Pest and covers most of eastern Hungary. It is mostly farmland and home to cattle, sheep and the almost-extinct bustard. The region is especially popular for riding. Kecskemét is known for its apricot brandy and stunning art-nouveau architecture. Debrecen is the second largest city and a Protestant stronghold.

LAKE BALATON

Lake Balaton is a vacation favorite. The flat, southern shore has several resorts known as the Hungarian Riviera. Siófok is the largest, but Balantonföldvár, Balatonlelle and Fonyód are also popular, with sandy beaches, good accommodations and fine views. The north shore has vines, woods and volcanoes.

NORTHERN MOUNTAINS

Northern mountains contain the finest vineyards in Hungary. The Mátra Mountains are one of the major attractions of Hungary with the retreats of Mátrafüred and Mátraháza; the spa of Parád; and Kékestetö, at 1,014 meters (3,330 feet), Hungary's highest mountain. At the foot of the Mátra is Gyöngyös, capital of the country's wine industry. To the east are the Bükk, or Beech Mountains with wineries at Eger.

USEFUL EXPRESSIONS IN HUNGARIAN

hello	szia!/szervusz!
(can also mean goodbye!)	
good-bye	viszontlátásra
good morning	jó reggelt kivánok
good evening	jó estét
please/thankyou	kérem/köszönöm
yes/no	igen/nem
excuse me	bocsánat
you're welcome	szivesen
Do you speak English?	beszél angolul?
I don't understand.	nem értem.
What is the time?	hány óra van?
Where are the restrooms?	hol van a WC/ mosdó?

PLACES OF INTEREST

HUNGARY

┌─────────────────────────────────┐
│ ★ **HIGHLIGHTS** ★   │
│ Budapest   (see p.190)   │
│ Fertöd   (see p.191)   │
│ Lake Balaton   (see p.191)   │
└─────────────────────────────────┘

▲ BUDAPEST (191 C2) ★

BUDAPEST *pop. 1,992,000*

Originally three separate cities, Buda and Óbuda on the west bank and Pest on the east merged in the late 19th century to form Budapest. Each historic core has kept a distinctive identity.

The walled city of Pest was outgrown in the 19th century when grand boulevards were laid out, but the medieval Inner City is still the commercial, financial and governmental district.

Across the river on the hilly west bank is Buda. Medieval Buda grew on the narrow plateau of Castle Hill.

Even older is Óbuda, built on the site of the Roman town of Aquincum at the foot of the hill. The hot springs here were known to the Romans and the Turks. The waters of more than 100 thermal springs are enjoyed today in centuries-old baths and modern swimming pools.

Budapest has two opera houses, five concert halls, numerous theaters and a large sports stadium. The Budapest Ensemble of Folklore Dancers performs almost every day during summer, and the International Music Festival is held in the fall.

Excursions along the Duna (Danube) are an enjoyable way to view the city. A ride on Europe's oldest subway, which runs between Vörösmarty Tér (Vörösmarty Square) in the Inner City and City Park, and a scenic trip on the ski lift that climbs to the highest point of Buda's wooded hills should not be missed.

AQUINCUM, the Roman city, has left many traces in the modern face of Óbuda, including the Amfiteátrum, the Herkules-Villa and Military Baths. The Aquincum Museum has a Roman organ.

BELGRÁD RAKPART (Danube Promenade) (192 C2) was formerly called the Korzo. Elegant folk once came to see and be seen here. It offers a wonderful panorama of the Danube, its bridges, and Buda.

┌─────────────────────────────────┐
│ **TIME FOR A DIP?**   │
│ Springs and spas supply Hungary │
│ with mineral waters in profusion.│
│ Both Roman and Turkish rulers   │
│ exploited the thermal springs of│
│ Aquincum in Budapest. No visitor│
│ should miss a dip, perhaps   │
│ among the half-submerged chess │
│ players in the open-air Széchenyi│
│ Gyógyfürdö (Szechenyi baths), or│
│ in the mysterious vaulted pools │
│ deep beneath the wonderful   │
│ art-nouveau Gellert Hotel.   │
└─────────────────────────────────┘

BUDAI-HEGYSÉG (Buda Hills) rise 530 meters (1,735 feet) from the Buda bank of the Danube. A chair lift takes visitors to the top, or there is a cog-wheel railway which connects with the Pioneer Railway, a narrow-gauge line running 2.4 kilometers (1½ miles) through the hills and run by children.

GELLÉRT-HEGY (Gellert Hill) (192 B1). This limestone cliff rears up on the west bank of the Duna (Danube). It is named after a saint who toppled to his death from the summit, which is now largely occupied by the Citadella, built by the Habsburgs to control the Hungarians after the revolution of 1848. The Freedom Monument, dominated by the huge figure of a woman, commemorates the liberation of the city from German occupation in 1945.

HÖSÖK TERE (Heroes' Square) (192 D4) contains the Millenary Monument, erected in 1896 in celebration of the country's thousand-year existence.

MAGYAR NEMZETI GALÉRIA (National Gallery) (192 B2), in the Budavári Palace, displays Hungarian paintings and sculptures from the 11th century to the present day.

MAGYAR NEMZETI MÚZEUM (National Museum) (192 D2), Múzeum körút 14–16, has exhibits on the history of the Hungarian people from prehistoric times.

MARGIT-SZIGET (Margaret Island) (192 B4) lies between two arms of the Duna (Danube). It is an island of tranquility.

ORSÁGHAZ (Parliament Building), a neo-Gothic structure with pinnacles, gables, turrets and a great dome, was the largest building in the world on completion in 1902. Guided tours are available.

THE HUNGARIAN CROWN

The Hungarian crown is a powerful symbol of statehood. Over the years it has been hidden, stolen, spirited away, bought and sold. At the end of World War II it was taken to Vienna, to Fort Knox, and only returned to Hungary in 1978.

SZENT ISTVÁN BAZILIKA (St. Stephen Basilica) (191 C3) has a neo-Renaissance dome that is a landmark of the Inner City.

SZÉPMŰVÉSZETI MÚZEUM (Museum of Fine Arts) (192 D4), Hősök tere, has a superb collection of Italian, Spanish, Dutch and Flemish paintings.

VÁRHEGY (Castle Hill) (192 A3–D2) is the 1.6-kilometer (1-mile) ridge whose defenses were improved following the Mongol invasion of 1241. The defense of Castle Hill by the Germans toward the end of World War II left it in ruins, but meticulous rebuilding has restored it to its former charm.
Halászbástya (Fishermen's Bastion) is one of the best viewpoints in the city. It was completed in 1903 and is named in honor of the fishermen who defended this section of the ramparts.

Mátyás-Templom (Matthias Church). Dedicated to the Virgin Mary, this much-rebuilt Gothic church is named after King Matthias.

Founded in the 13th century, it was rebuilt in the 14th and turned into a mosque by the Turks.
Budavári Palota is the Royal Palace which contains the Nemzeti Galeria (National Gallery), the Országos Széchenyi Könyvtár (National Library) and the Budapesti Történeti Múzeum (Budapest History Museum).

▲ EGER (186 D3)
HEVES *pop. 63,000*
Eger takes pride in the products of its orchards and vineyards, and visits can be made to Eger's wine cellars. Also of interest are the ruins of Eger's old castle.

▲ ESZTERGOM (186 B3)
KOMÁRP *pop. 33,000*
Stephen, the first king, was born and crowned here. There are remains of Roman, medieval and Turkish construction on the citadel. Climb to the cathedral dome for a panorama over the town, the Danube, and the Slovak Republic.

▲ FERTÖD (186 A2) ★
GYÖR-SOPRON
Inspired by Louis XIVs Versailles, Prince Esterházy built the palace in 1766 and furnished it with mirrored salons, statues and fountains, Chinese decorations and luxurious rooms.

The Haydn Festival is held here in late summer.

▲ GYÖR (186 B2)
GYÖR-SOPRON *pop. 130,000*
Of Roman origin, Györ was once a border fortress. It has many 18th-century houses, stately squares and narrow streets.

KÁPTALAN HILL overlooks the Raba River just before it joins the Danube. This strategic point has remains of the old walls and bastions. The greatest treasure is a masterpiece of the goldsmith's art, the reliquary bust of St. Ladislas.

HUNGARY

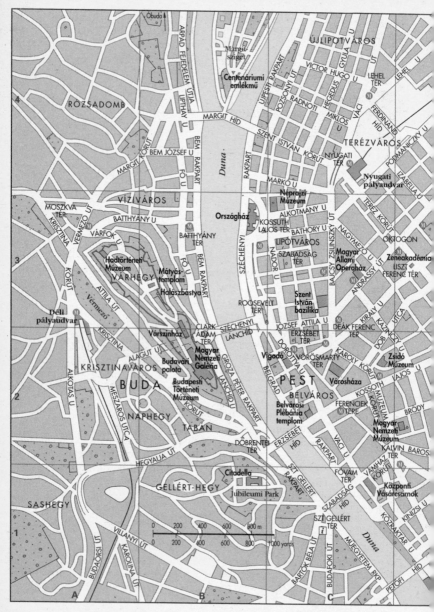

LAKE BALATON (186 B2) ★
SOMOGY AND VESZPREM

The lake is nearly 81 kilometers (50 miles) long, divided by the Tihany peninsula, where a car ferry connects with the south shore. Ferries connect all the larger resorts and are one of the best ways of exploring.

BADACSONY, an old volcano, rises steeply from the north shore to a 438-meter (1,437-foot) summit.

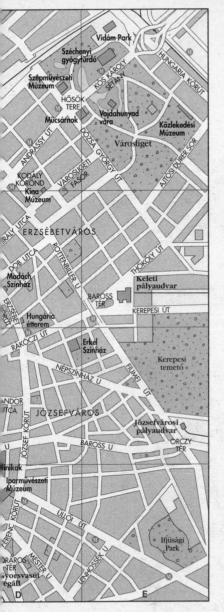

▲ PÉCS (186 B1)
PÉCS *pop. 170,000*

Pécs is at the confluence of the Danube and Drava rivers. There is a 4th-century Christian chapel and cemetery, and an 11th-century cathedral, where the first Hungarian university was built in 1367.

Pécs is a good center for exploring the wooded Mecsek Hills to the north. To the south east are the vineyards of the Villany area, and the medieval fortress at Siklós is 29 kilometers (18 miles) south.

▲ SOPRON (186 A2)
GYÖR-SOPRON *pop. 55,000*

Sopron has a large number of preserved buildings. Noteworthy are the Italianate Storno House, now an art gallery; the Renaissance Fabricius House; the 13th-century Goat Church of the Benedictines and the Gothic St. George Church; the Pharmacy Museum, and medieval Synagogue. Sopron is also a noted wine center.

SZENTENDRE (186 C3)
PEST *pop. 17,000*

Today Szentendre is popular with artists, and works by local painters hang in the Ferenczy and Czóbel museums.

TATA (186 B2)
KOMÁROM *pop. 23,000*

Its setting on Lake Tata and hot springs make Tata a natural resort. Historically, Tata was the residence of Hungarian kings. The Cifra Mill dates from 1587, and the Kisebb Kastely was a country estate of the Esterházy princes.

VISEGRÁD (186 C3)
PEST

In the 14th century, King Charles Robert of Anjou built a palace at Visegrád which was rebuilt in Renaissance style by King Matthias. In 1943 it was rediscovered; excavation and restoration have revealed a red marble fountain, a cloistered Gothic courtyard and sculpture. Nearby is the huge fortification Salamon Torony (Solomon's Tower), built in the 13th century. Fellegvár Citadel, a 13th-century fort, offers a memorable view.

BALATONFÜRED, built around a spa, retains its early 19th century atmosphere.

SIÓFOK has 16 kilometers (10 miles) of beach, and is generally regarded as the vacation capital of Balaton.

POLAND

Poland was reborn in December 1989 when the new political party, Solidarity, replaced the old Communist government. It is used to being reborn. In the 15th and 16th centuries it became a leading light before being swallowed up by neighbors. Born again after World War I, the invasion of Poland by Hitler led to World War II.

Polish people have a love of life, and seem to bounce back from anything. Warsaw (Warsawa) was all but destroyed during World War II, and reconstruction of the Old Town involved close examination of prints and paintings before rebuilding took place. The countryside is mostly farmland, with horse-ploughing, hoeing and haymaking. In the south are the High Tatra Mountains, shared with the Czech Republic. They have more than enough splendor for both countries.

Left The Old Town Market Square in Warsaw is surrounded by fine Renaissance and baroque architecture
Above Traditional dress is still worn in the Tatra Mountains

THINGS TO KNOW

- **AREA:** 312,683 square kilometers (120,727 square miles)
- **POPULATION:** 38,300,000
- **CAPITAL:** Warszawa (Warsaw)
- **LANGUAGE:** Polish. German also widely spoken.
- **RELIGION:** mostly Catholic
- **ECONOMY:** Coal, copper, steel production, engineering, chemicals and shipbuilding; fishing and forestry; much agricultural production in the hands of small farmers.
- **PASSPORT REQUIREMENTS:** Required by U.S. citizens.
- **VISA REQUIREMENTS:** Not required for stays up to three months.
- **DUTY-FREE ITEMS:** 250 cigarettes or tobacco equivalent; ¼ liter of liquor or ¾ liter of wine; gifts up to a value of U.S.$100; certain items for personal use e.g. cameras (still and movie), video recorder, sporting equipment.
- **CURRENCY:** The unit of currency is the *zloty* (ZL) divided into 100 *groszy*. From January 1, 1995, the zloty was divided by a factor of 10,000. However, it is likely that the exchange rate will continue to fluctuate. At the time of going to press, the zloty is not freely convertible and may not be taken into or out of the country.
- **BANK OPENING HOURS:** 7:30am–5pm Monday–Friday, 7:30am–2pm Saturday.
- **STORE OPENING HOURS:** Variable. Food stores 6 or 7am–6pm (earlier in country areas) Monday–Friday, supermarkets 7am–7pm, other shops 10am–6pm Monday–Friday. Many shops closed Saturday, others open 7am–1pm.
- **MUSEUM OPENING HOURS:** Variable, but most closed Monday and on days following a holiday.
- **BEST BUYS:** Dolls in folk costumes, handwoven rugs, handicrafts, woodcarvings, ceramics, leather goods, silverware, jewelry, amber, cut glass.

HISTORY

The Polish nation originated with the Polanian, Vistulan, Silesian, East Pomeranian and Mazovian tribes that shared a common culture and formed city-states with regional leaders, thus establishing the dynasties that were to rule Poland.

In 1320, after several centuries of invasion and internal chaos, King Wlayslaw Lokietek I unified Poland, and in 1333 the last of the Piast dynasty, Casimir the Great, came to power. During his reign he codified common law, established a university, protected minorities, fortified castles and built roads. The Polish victory over the Teutonic Order (Germany Crusaders) at the Battle of Tannenberg in 1410, marked the beginning of Poland's Golden Age. The economy flourished, and intellect and the arts were exemplified by the scientific contributions of Nicolaus Copernicus, the poetry of Jan Kochanowski and the political philosophy of Andrzej Frycz-Modrzewski.

Russia, Prussia and Austria took more than a quarter of Poland's territory in the First Partition of Poland in 1772. This sparked Polish patriotism and led to economic and political reforms. A new constitution in 1791 granted peasants and the middle class political rights, while the elective monarchy was abolished.

During this time education flourished, democracy dominated politically, and art and literature became important again. This was the beginning of the independent Polish state, but it all came to an abrupt end when Catherine II of Russia ordered an invasion in 1793, resulting in the Second Partition of Poland.

Polish nationalists battled but could not repel the powerful Russian, Prussian and Austrian troops. In 1795, the three powers divided the rest of Poland among themselves in the Third Partition of Poland, marking the disappearance of the country from the European map.

The 19th century was marked by patriotic uprisings that were quickly suppressed. Despite the unrest, this period was noted for great advances in literature, the arts and science.

In 1918, Poland gained its freedom after Germany and Austria fell in World War I and the Tsarist regime in Russia was overthrown. In 1920 soldier-politician Josef Pilsudski led the Polish legionnaires against the Russian Bolsheviks in the Polish-Soviet War, and the Treaty of Riga following the war granted Poland former Russian territories.

In 1939 the country was attacked by Nazi Germany and, despite heroic resistance, was swiftly defeated. A new part-

ition followed. Much of the country was absorbed into Germany, while an area centering on Krakow and Warsaw was contemptuously named the "General-gouvernement." The whole of the east part of Poland was then annexed by the Soviet Union.

The Polish intelligentsia (teachers, lawyers and priests) was systematically destroyed by the Nazis, as were nearly all of the Jews. The Soviets also exacted their toll: hundreds of thousands of Poles were deported to Siberia, and more than 10,000 Polish officers were massacred at Katyn, demonstrating Joseph Stalin's brutality. Poles in exile fought on several fronts against Germany: with the western Allies in the Middle East, Italy and

Specialist stores include Cepelia (folk products), Desa (handicrafts and works of art), Jubiler and Orno (jewelry). Pemex and Baltona shops sell a variety of imported goods.

- **PUBLIC HOLIDAYS:** January 1, Easter Monday; Labor Day, May 1; Constitution Day, May 3; Corpus Christi, May/June; Feast of the Assumption, August 15; All Saints' Day, November 1; Independence Day, November 11; December 25–26.
- **USEFUL TELEPHONE NUMBERS:**
  Police 997
  Fire 998
  Ambulance 999
- **NATIONAL TOURIST OFFICES:**
  Orbis
  342 Madison Avenue
  New York
  NY 10173
  Tel: 212/867 5011
  Polorbis Travel
  82, Mortimer Street
  London
  W1N 7DE
  Tel: 0171 637 4971
- **AMERICAN EMBASSY:**
  al. Ujazdowskie 29
  Warsaw
  Poland
  Tel: 02 6283 041/9

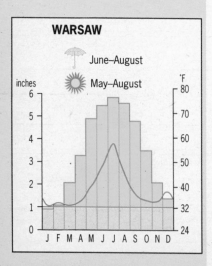

WARSAW

June–August

May–August

France, and, after the Nazi attack on the Soviets in 1941, with the Red Army.

Postwar Poland lay in a state of economic despair; losses exceeded 6 million people and the land was in ruin. At the Potsdam Conference in 1945, Poland's eastern territories went to the Soviet Union, but the country was compensated with former German lands to the west. Stalin's goal after the war was the Sovietization of Poland. The Communist Party of Poland was revived in Warsaw under the name of the Polish United Workers' Party, and created the kind of totalitarian regime acceptable to its Soviet masters.

When Wladyslaw Gomulka came to power in 1956, Poland's hopes for greater freedoms arose, but Gomulka soon abandoned the principles of shared leadership. His attacks on the Roman Catholic church and outdated economic policies led to yet more unrest. By 1970, the deteriorating economy led Polish shipyard workers to strike and riot. Gomulka was removed from the Politburo and replaced by Edward Gierek, who introduced economic reforms.

Despite Gierek's new program, the economy worsened and by 1980 Poland faced severe shortages of food and electricity. The people were frustrated with the government, and Gierek's overthrow was hastened by union-inspired strikes in the shipyards and coal mines.

The Politburo then began negotiations with Lech Walesa, the leader and cofounder of the independent trade union called Solidarity. An agreement was signed and concessions were made to the strikers, but unrest continued, and in 1981 Solidarity's increased demands for democratic reforms led Wojciech Jaruzelski, who had taken over as leader, to impose martial law and to outlaw Solidarity, a bitter decision which nonetheless saved the country from the dreadful possibility of a Soviet invasion.

Martial law was lifted in 1983, following a visit by Pope John Paul II. In 1985, when Mikhail Gorbachev was appointed as the Soviet leader, hopes for the future soared. Gorbachev's liberal theories, the determination of Walesa and Solidarity, the backing of Pope John Paul II and the persistence of Polish citizens all forced the communists to take part in talks in 1989. In April 1989 legal status was restored to Solidarity, and the Communist Party agreed to the formation of a new law including non-communist representation by freely elected candidates.

In the general elections held June 1989, Solidarity won the overwhelming support of the people, and although many parliamentary seats had been reserved for the communists, the movement was able to form a government. Tadeusz Mazowiecki became Prime Minister. He was the first non-communist to head the government of a Warsaw Pact nation. Jaruzelski was re-elected president.

In 1990 the first free presidential elections since World War II were held. Solidarity leader Lech Walesa became the new president. In 1993 the government, by then headed by the country's first woman prime minister Hanna Suchocka, suffered defeat on the issue of privatization. In subsequent elections the Communist Party, now reformed and renamed Social Democracy of the Republic of Poland, received a substantial number of votes, and, together with the Peasant Party, formed a government. The new coalition continues to implement the reforms helping Poland in its transition from communism to democracy and a market economy.

FOOD AND DRINK

Soups, fish and rich desserts are characteristic. Specialities include *karp po polsku*, carp cooked in raisin sauce; *barszcz*, beetroot soup; *chlodnik*, iced soup with beetroot and cream; *golabki*, meat, rice and cabbage leaves; *kolduny*, small mutton turnovers; *pierozki*, large dumplings with meat, plums or white cheese; *bigos*, a stew made with sour cabbage and a variety of meats; and *kuropatwa w smietanie*, young partridge in cream sauce.

Tea and Turkish coffee are popular. Polish beer is good, and imported wine is plentiful. The national drink is vodka, which is consumed in a variety of forms and flavors. Popular brands include *wisniowka*, sweet or dry cherry; *jarzebiak*, dry vodka flavored with rowan berries: and *zubrowka*, flavored with bison grass found only in one region of the country. Polish cognac is *viniak*. *Miod* (mead) is a delicious liqueur made from honey.

SPORTS AND RECREATION

Poland has numerous resorts with sports facilities on mountain slopes, at the seaside and lakeshore. The Masurian and Augustow lake district is a fishing and boating paradise. The love of horses is reflected in the country's reputation for outstanding breeds. You can take horseback vacations at resort or stud farms. The slopes of the Tatra are dotted with hikers and mountain climbers in summer; skiers from January to March. Winter sports facilities are widely available, particularly at Zakopane.

GETTING AROUND

There are direct scheduled flights linking Warsaw with New York and Chicago and with a number of European cities. LOT (Polish Airlines) connects Warsaw with major cities throughout Poland. Ferry services operate from the Baltic harbor towns of Świnoujście, Gydnia or Gdańsk to ports in Germany, Denmark, Sweden and Finland and there is also a

AUTOMOBILE CLUB
Polski Zwiazek Motorowy (PZM, Polish Motor Union), which has its offices at ul. Kazimierzowska 66, Warsaw, is the Polish club affiliated with AAA. Not all auto clubs offer full travel services to AAA members.

weekly service linking Gydnia with London (Tilbury) and Middlesborough in England. Local ferries and hydrofoils connect towns and resorts along the Baltic coast. PKP (Polish State Railway) operate a dense network of internal passenger services, though trains on some lines may be slow and crowded. Fast and comfortable Eurocity trains link Warsaw with Berlin and Vienna and other international trains run from Warsaw and other major cities to many other European cities, including London. There are express bus services to Warsaw and Cracow from London. Public transportation in cities is comprehensive and cheap, though often crowded.

The main roads in Poland usually have good asphalt or concrete surfaces, but other roads are often narrow and their quality varies greatly. The driver and all passengers must wear seat belts. Children under 10 are not permitted to travel in the front seat.

Speed limits are 60 k.p.h. (35 m.p.h.) in urban areas, 90 k.p.h. (55 m.p.h.) on country roads and 110 k.p.h. (65 m.p.h.) on highways. Motorists must pay fines for motoring violations on the spot.

ACCOMMODATIONS

Hotels range from a small number of deluxe hotels with western European prices to extremely basic unmodernized establishments at very economic rates. Good facilities are often found in private pensions and most cities have offices arranging accommodation in private houses and apartments. There are campsites throughout the country.

ARTS AND ENTERTAINMENT

The Polish arts, including sophisticated theater, are a source of national pride. Most cities have a theater and in the recent past experimental companies have won an international reputation for their boldness and innovation. Concerts and musical events are presented in Warsaw, Posnan and elsewhere.

PRINCIPAL TOURING AREAS

Note: For descriptions of cities in bold type, see individual city listings.

BALTIC COAST

Some 520 kilometers (325 miles) of sandy beaches along the Baltic Coast offer resorts, health spas and quiet fishing villages. The summer season lasts from June to September. During these months the weather averages between 18 and 27°C (65 and 80°F) and water temperatures are around 21°C (70°F).

In north-west Poland, Świnoujście is a good base for touring Wolin Island, a national park with lakes, spectacular sand dunes and the resort of Międzyzdroje. Kamien Pomorski and Kolobrzeg combine medieval monuments with modern resort attractions. Darlowo has preserved parts of its medieval past. East is the fishing village of Leba near two lakes which are part of a national park.

The Hel Peninsula is a pleasant combination of pine woods and beaches. The Amber Coast, the name given to the beaches around the Wisla (Vistula) Delta on the north-east Baltic Coast, was so named because of the yellowish tint of the sand and the amber discoveries. Forests alternate with resorts and fishing villages, while along the shore of Gdańsk Bay stretches the great conurbation known as the Tri-City, consisting of the modern port of Gdynia, the resort of Sopot, and historic Gdansk.

CENTRAL POLAND

Central Poland is the main food-producing region and a major touring area with forests, parks and the Odra, Wisla (Vistula), Warta and Bug rivers. On the banks of the Warta is Poznań, a busy marketplace and cultural center. Torún was the birthplace of Copernicus. Highway E30 leads to a cluster of cities surrounding Warszawa, or Warsaw, the capital. Zelazowa Wola, Chopins birth-place is 53 kilometers (33 miles) west, and Kampinos Forest, a national park is 20 kilometers (12 miles) north west.

Route 81 stretches south to **Lublin**, with its many academic and architectural achievements. On the border with Belorussia to the east is the great Bialowieza, the largest virgin forest in Central Europe, covering 582 square kilometers (225 square miles). Part of it is a reserve for European bison, extinct elsewhere and "backward" breeding techniques have reproduced the tarpan.

LAKE DISTRICTS

Inland from the Baltic Coast are literally thousands of lakes in secluded, wooded hills. West of the Vistula (Wisla) River is the Pomeranian lake district, and to the east, the Masurian lake district. About 20 kilometers (12 miles) west of **Gdańsk**, medieval Kartuzy is a center for touring the Kashubian region renowned for the beauty of its lakes, forests and hills.

This whole region is ideal for fishing (particularly pike), sailing, canoeing and swimming. Ostróda is the focal point for watersports on Lake Drweckie; Olsztyn, on the Lyna River, is the chief vacation center of the Masurian district. About 100 kilometers (100 miles) east of Olsztyn are Gizycko, popular for sports, and Ruciane-Nida, a lovely resort deep in the Piska Forest. The best time to visit the area is from May to September.

MOUNTAIN REGIONS

The mountainous region of southern Poland abounds with magnificent scenery and opportunities for winter and summer recreation. The Sudeten Mountains (Sudety), in the south west, have yet to be discovered by tourists. Spruce forests and clean lakes typify this sparsely inhabited land. The Jelenia Gora Basin has many villages and spas and is a good center for excursions into the Sudetes.

The Tatra Mountains (Tatry), in the south east, is the most beautiful of the Carpathian Mountains. Winter resorts and spas dot its hills. At Zakopane, an international ski center, the season lasts from December to April. Spring and summer are equally enjoyable here. From Zakopane excursions can be made east to the Pieniny range, crossed by the Dunajec River gorge. Tours can continue east along the border into the Beskidy, where scenic settings include Krynica resort.

SILESIA

Silesia is a major industrial zone. The area around Katowice, the region's capital and cultural center, is one of Poland's most densely populated areas. Factories are one aspect of Silesia, but there are also cool green forests and quiet streams. The Kingdom of the Frogs is an angler's paradise on the banks of the Vistula River (Wisla). It begins about 60 kilometers (37 miles) south of Katowice at the twin city of Bielsko-Biala. Wrockaw has been completely rebuilt after wartime devastation. To the east of Katowice is ancient Kraków or Cracow, for centuries the country's capital, which survived the war with most of its treasures intact.

USEFUL EXPRESSIONS IN POLISH

good morning	dzień dobry
good evening	dobry wieczór
good night	dobranoc
please/thankyou	proszę/dziękuję
yes/no	tak/nie
excuse me	przepraszam
you're welcome	witam
Do you speak English?	Czy ktoá mówi po angielsku?
I don't understand.	Nie rozumiem
What is the time?	Która godzina?
How much is that?	Ile płacę?
Where are the restrooms?	Gdzie są toalety?
I'd like ...	Chciałbym ...
Can you help me, please?	Proszę mi pomóc?
where/when/how	gdzie/kiedy/jak
palace/castle	palac
fortress	zamek

PLACES OF INTEREST

POLAND

▲ WARSZAWA (197 B2) ★

WARSZAWA pop. 1,650,000

Warszawa, or Warsaw, the capital, lies on the banks of the Wisla (Vistula) River. The city is believed to have been founded in the early 14th century and became the capital of the Polish-Lithuanian state in 1596 under King Sigismund III.

A long history of foreign rule includes 18th-century oppression by Russia and Prussia and it became capital of the Kingdom of Poland in the 19th century under Russian rule. Following World War I, Warsaw became the capital of the restored Polish State.

In 1939 the Germans humiliated Warsaw by making Cracow the capital of their *General-gouvernement*. In 1944, as the Red Army approached, the city rose against the Nazis, but in spite of incredible heroism the Warsaw Uprising was defeated. In an act of vengeance the city was razed to the ground and the population deported.

After the war, Warsaw, abandoned and ruined, made its reconstruction a national priority. The historic core has been rebuilt as it was and today it is a thriving, teeming metropolis.

Several monuments recall a heroic past: among them the *Heroes of the Warsaw Ghetto* – Jews who took up arms and fought against the Nazis.

In Ogrod Saski, the Tomb of the Unknown Soldier commemorates Polish soldiers who have lost their lives through centuries of battle.

Warsaw has numerous theaters and museums. The Filharmonia presents concert and opera performances, and folk dance groups often appear. The magnificent Grand Theater of Opera and Ballet houses the State Opera.

Music festivals play a prominent part in cultural life. The Autumn Festival of Modern Music in September is one of the best: the popular Jazz Jamboree is in October. The Sozynki Harvest Festival is in September.

About 50 kilometers (31 miles) west of Warsaw is Zelazowa Wola, whose most famous son was Chopin. Leading Polish pianists give concerts of his music every Sunday in May and September. Chopin memorabilia are exhibited in the beautifully restored and charming house where he was born.

At Lowicz, about 85 kilometers (53 miles) west of Warsaw, Polish customs are observed, particularly at Corpus Christi in late May or early June. Costumes are worn at church festivals all year.

LAZIENKI ★ is a park laid out in the 18th century. The Palace on the Water once housed King Stanislaw August, the last Polish monarch. The Theater on the Island offers summer musical productions. Pianists give recitals in summer at the foot of the Chopin memorial.

MUZEUM FRYDERYKA CHOPINA ★, Ostrogski Palace, 11 Okolnik, has displays relating to the 19th-century composer and pianist.

MUZEUM NARODOWE (National Museum) 3 Al Jerozolimskie, has a collection of Polish art dating from the 14th to 20th centuries. The frescoes, especially those of St. Ann, are particularly noteworthy.

PALAC KULTURY I NAUKI ★ (Palace of Culture), Plac Defilad, was a gift from Stalin to the Polish people. The 37-storey skyscraper is in the bizarre Stalinist Wedding-cake style. It houses theaters, cinemas, restaurants, museums, galleries, a swimming pool, and casino. The top floor has views of the city.

PUSZCZA KAMPINOSKA (Kampinos Forest) is a national park 20 kilometers (12 miles) north west, a rare example of wild countryside coming right to the edge of a major city. Wildlife includes wild boar, elk and beavers. The memorial Cemetery for the Heroes of Warsaw is here.

STARE MIASTO (Old Town) ★, on the left bank of the Vistula, is a vision of the past, a re-creation based on architectural plans and detailed paintings of Bernardo Bellotto. The Old Town Market Square is surrounded by 17th- and 18th-century Renaissance and baroque houses. Medieval fortifications still stand.

Katedra Sw. Jana (Cathedral of St. John), Swietojanska, a serene Gothic structure, is one of Poland's oldest churches. Henryk Sienkiewicz, author of the 19th- century novel *Quo Vadis* is buried here.

Muzeum Historyczne M. St. Warszawy (Warsaw Historical Museum), 48 Rynek Starego Miasta, inhabits reconstructed houses in the Old Town Market Square. Its collection traces the history of Warsaw. The documentary films telling the story of resistance are very moving.

WILANÓW, a baroque palace built by King Jan III Sobieski, is 10 kilometers (6 miles) away at the end of the Royal Way. A sound-and-light spectacle takes place in summer.

ZAMEK ★ is the royal castle, blown up by the Nazis in 1944 and restored using furnishings and fittings hidden away during the war. As well as the royal apartments, it contains the chambers where the Sejm – Poland's parliament – used to meet. In Castle Square is the King Sigismund Column, the symbol of Warsaw.

CZESTOCHOWA (197 B1)
KATOWICE *pop. 274,000*
This industrial city is best known for the 14th-century shrine at Jasna Gora

(Bright Mountain) whose greatest treasure is the icon – the *Black Madonna*, which became a key symbol of Poland in the 18th century.

CHOPIN
Chopin (1810–49) was born Fryderyk Szopen, and although his family lived in the house in Zelazowa Wola for only a year after his birth, he often returned to the area, where his talent found inspiration in the local vibrant music traditions. Echoes of Mazovian folk music can be heard in many of his compositions.

▲ GDAŃSK (197 B3) ★
GDAŃSK *pop. 462,000*
This ancient harbor city symbolises the centuries-old conflict between Poland and Germany.

Between the two world wars Gdańsk (Danzig in German) was nominally a free city, but the status of its predominantly German population was used by Hitler as one of his pretexts for attacking Poland in September 1939.

In the 1970s and 80s it was the cradle of popular discontent with Communism and it was here that *Solidarity* was born.

Almost totally destroyed in World War II, the old town has been restored.

Places of interest include the 14th-century town hall, medieval fortifications, several canals and the 14th-century Wielki Mlyn, or Great Mill.

The Gothic church of St. Mary accommodates 25,000 people. The quayside Gdańsk Crane dates from the 15th century and is the biggest of its kind in Europe. It houses part of the city's excellent maritime museum.

MALBORK CASTLE, 55 kilometers (34 miles) south east, is one of the best-preserved medieval structures throughout the whole of Europe.

Works of art include a huge painting of the Battle of Grunwald.

POLAND

▲ KRAKÓW (197 B1) ★
KRAKÓW *pop. 745,000*

Kraków, or Cracow, on the Vistula River to the north of the Tatra Mountains, was capital of Poland between the 11th and the 17th centuries. It was one of the few cities not devastated in World War II and is on the list of sites of significant cultural value compiled by UNESCO.

Here are superb examples of Gothic, baroque and Renaissance architecture in the Main Market Square as well as in the Wawel complex. Churches from different periods are scattered around; among them the Church of St. Felix and Adaukt, a Romanesque basilica.

The city's cultural life is well developed, with theater, cabaret, rock and jazz clubs, and classical concerts. In June there are several major arts festivals.

CZARTORYSKI, a branch of the National Museum at sw. Jana 19, houses fine art works including Leonardo da Vinci's *Lady with the Ermine.*

OJCÓWSKI PARK NARODOWY (Ojców National Park), 20 kilometers (12 miles) north west, is a deep gorge on the Pradnik River with hundreds of caverns, rock formations, rare bird species, and castle ruins that date from the 13th century.

OSWIECIM, 70 kilometers (43 miles) west, is the site of the Auschwitz-Birkenau concentration camp. Some 1½ to 2 million people died in Nazi gas chambers. The great majority were Jews, but many Gypsies died here too, as well as people from virtually every European nation.

RYNEK GLOWNY (Main Market Square) is the site of many fine, old residences. **Kosciol Mariacki** (St. Mary's Church) on Main Market Square, is one of the finest Gothic churches in Poland. Stained-glass windows enhance the gilding of the interior. On the hour, a trumpeter sounds his horn briefly from the taller of two towers, commemorating the Tartar siege of 1241 and the brave trumpeter who died trying to warn the town of the danger.

Sukiennice (Cloth Hall), on Main Market Square, was established by the Guild of the Textile Merchants as a place to display and sell their wares. The first floor houses the National Gallery of Polish Painting from the 18th to 20th century.

UNIWERSYTET JAGIELLONSKI (Jagiellonian University), South-west Anny Street, (1364) was where Copernicus studied. **Collegium Maius** (Museum of the University) contains the Golden Globe of Copernicus, one of the first globes to show the American continent.

THE FALL OF GDANSK
Some of the first shots of World War II were fired in Gdansk, then nominally a free city under League of Nations protection, but whose German population were converted to Nazism. Stormtroopers attacked the defended Poczta Polska, an event described with great gusto in the novel *The Tin Drum,* by Gunter Grass.

WZGORZE WAWELSKIE (Wawel Hill), with its castle and cathedral towering over the city centre, is a reminder of the centuries when Cracow was the capital of Poland. **Katedra na Wawelu** (Wawel Cathedral) was built in the 14th century. It is the mausoleum of no fewer than 41 of the country's 45 monarchs. The great Zygmunt bell in the tower was cast in 1520 in honor of King Sigismund I. There's a fine view over the city from the top of the tower.

Zamek na Wawelu (Wawel Castle) is Renaissance with an arcaded courtyard. Until the 16th century, it was the home of Polish kings. Collections include priceless Flemish tapestries, the crown treasury, the armory and oriental art.

▲ LUBLIN (197 C2)
LUBLIN *pop. 350,000*

Lublin is of great historical and cultural interest. An ancient settlement, it was one of the first cities to be liberated during World War II and became the capital of Poland in 1944.

The old town has houses in Renaissance and baroque style. The Market Square is a charming area leading to the 14th-century Church of the Dominicans.

Lublin Castle, a 14th-century structure, was used by the Nazis as a prison during the Second World War, and it now houses a museum.

POZNAŃ (197 A2)
POZNAŃ *pop. 580,000*
Poznań has been a famed marketplace for a thousand years. Visitors will find a number of museums, theaters, churches and palaces. The town hall, Dzialynski Palace, and Przemyslaw Castle are both worth visiting.

Biskupin, 85 kilometers (53 miles) north east, offers an Iron Age village with an archeological museum and a reconstruction of 2,500-year-old buildings.

MUZEUM INSTRUMENTOW MUZYCZNYCH (Museum of Musical Instruments), Old Town Square, has a collection of stringed instruments from the 16th to the 20th centuries. A room devoted to Chopin contains his piano.

▲ SZCZECIN (197 A3)
pop. 415,000
Szczecin (Stettin in German) is a cultural and industrial center as well as home to famous shipyards. Rebuilt after World War II, it has many restored historic buildings and monuments.

Among the attractions are a cathedral and neo-Gothic Town Hall. A baroque palace, part of the National Museum, has medieval sculptures and Renaissance jewelry. The harbor is best experienced by boat.

ZAMEK KSLAZAT POMORSKICH (Castle of the Pomeranian Dukes), on Kusnierska Street near the Odra, houses a museum, art gallery and wine cellar.

The castle's impressive south wing has two Gothic towers, a prison and clock tower.

TORÚN (197 B3) ★
BYDGOSZCZ *pop. 202,000*
One of Poland's best-preserved medieval towns, Torún was the birthplace in 1475 of astronomer Copernicus, whose theory of the Earth's role in the solar system revolutionized man's concept of the universe. Among sites remaining are the house where he was born and a church where he studied. Facing the Market Square is the Gothic town hall where Copernicus' father was councillor. The Copernican tradition continues at Torún's Copernicus University.

Torún's reputation for confectionery originated in the Middle Ages. Traditional specialities include honey-and-spice gingerbread.

★ WROCLAW (197 A2)
WROCLAW *pop. 640,000*
Wroclaw (Breslau in Germany) is the capital of Lower Silesia and one of Poland's oldest cities. Towards the end of World War II, the Nazis declared the city a fortress; the resulting 4-month siege left it in ruins. After the expulsion of its German inhabitants the city was repopulated by Poles, many of them from the old city of Lvov which had become part of the Soviet Union.

The old city is laid out around the Odra River. There is a wealth of restored historic buildings, among them the magnificent Gothic town hall. Houses near the Market Square were rebuilt in their original Renaissance and baroque styles. Other attractions include the Botanical and Zoological Gardens and museums.

ZAKOPANE (197 B1)
KRAKÓW *pop. 30,000*
The timber chalets of Zakopane lie at the foot of the spectacular peaks and crags of the Tatra Mountains which reach their highest point at the summit of Rysy (2,500 meters/8,199 feet). The largest mountaineering and winter sports center in Poland, the town also is a health resort. One thrilling winter sport is shooting the rapids of the Dunajec River in rafts made of hollowed logs.

ROMANIA

Known throughout the world as the land of Count Dracula (the Transylvanian Mountains run across the center), it is others who have sucked the blood from a once prosperous country.

The post-war Soviet system gave it one of the highest growth rates in Eastern Europe, until the arrival of the Ceauşescu family, who tore the heart from the country for their own ends.

Now it is starting over, and visitors should allow for the lack of services and expect some poverty. However, the people are welcoming, and you will find some of the most magnificent scenery in Europe.

The capital, Bucureşti (Bucharest), once called the "Paris of the Balkans" because of its gracious architecture and grand boulevards, happily has life once more coursing through its veins.

Left Bran Castle in Transylvania, home of the famous vampire, Dracula, is full of atmosphere
Above The Sibiu traditional costume is somber but impressive

Things to Know

- **Area:** 237,500 square kilometers (91,699 square miles)
- **Population:** 23,269,000
- **Capital:** Bucureşti (Bucharest)
- **Language:** Romanian
- **Religion:** Romanian Orthodox
- **Economy:** Agriculture, mining, industry: wheat and corn; petroleum, natural gas, minerals; machinery, metals, food processing, electronics, chemicals, oil.
- **Electricity:** 220 volts, continental two-round-pin plugs. Adaptor and/or transformer required.
- **Passport Requirements:** Required for U.S. citizens.
- **Visa Requirements:** Required for most visitors. Visas are obtainable from the Embassy of Romania, 1607 23rd Street, NW, Washington, DC 20008; (tel: 202/ 232 4747). Tourist visas are valid for 60 days and may be extended to 120 days: they may also be obtained at any border point of entry.
- **Duty-Free Items:** Within reasonable limits, tourists may import duty-free goods for personal use, and food and medicines necessary for their stay. All valuable goods must be declared on entering and leaving the country. It is forbidden to introduce radioactive substances, drugs, guns of any caliber ammunition. Pets require anti-rabies vaccination certificates.
- **Currency:** The currency unit is the *leu*. Due to currency fluctuations, the exchange rate is subject to frequent change. The import and export of Romanian lei is prohibited. Foreign currency can be exchanged into lei at any branch of the Romanian National Bank, at NTO (National Tourist Office) exchange offices or at other authorized organizations.
  Before departing Romania, unspent lei in any amount should be exchanged and the initial exchange slip should be presented.
- **Bank Opening Hours:** 9am–noon and 1–2pm Monday–Friday; 9am–12:30pm Saturday.

History

The inhabitants of what is now Romania were known as Dacians, and were conquered by Rome in 106 AD. The Romans withdrew in 275 AD under pressure from invading tribes. These incursions continued until the 9th century, when the dominant Bulgars were displaced by the Magyars.

The Dacians retreated to the security of Transylvanian mountains, eventually forming the Vlach peasantry under Magyar rulers. The Romanian language, unique among its Slavic neighbors, is believed to be a remnant of the Dacians' Latin preserved through the Vlach.

The Vlach formed the principalities of Walachia and Moldavia in the 13th

century, and in 1859 the assemblies of Walachia and Moldavia united under the name of Romania. The Middle Ages saw struggles among the Magyars, Turks, Austrians and Poles for supremacy. The Turks dominated during the 16th and 18th centuries; Russia held control during the first half of the 19th century. The Treaty of Paris ended the Russian protectorate, and in 1859 Walachia and Moldavia elected Alexandru Ioan Cuza as prince. Cuza abdicated in 1866 and Carol I was elected prince. Romania joined Russia during the Russo-Turkish War, and its independence was secured through the Treaty of Berlin, which settled the war in 1878.

Romania sided with the Allies in August 1916, and declared war on Austria-Hungary and sent forces into Transylvania. The Central Powers gained control of Bucharest and Hungary's old borders were restored in May 1918. Romania was governed by a pro-German ministry until November 1918, when Allied victory became certain. The following month a Romanian assembly announced a resolution incorporating Transylvania and again declared war on Austria-Hungary.

The Treaty of Trianon gave most of the region to Romania in 1920, but northern Transylvania was awarded to Hungary by Germany and Italy during World War II. In 1939 Romania allied with Germany until a coup in 1944, led by King Michael, overthrew the alliance. At Yalta Romania was effectively sold to Russia.

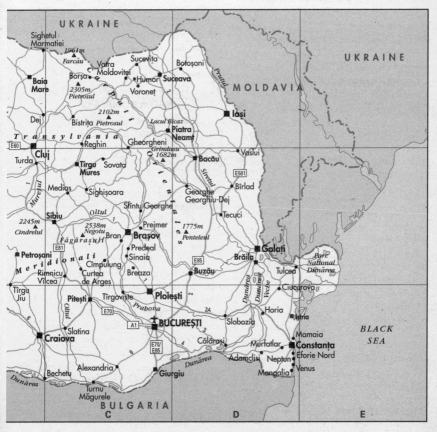

- **STORE OPENING HOURS:** 8am–8pm Monday–Friday; 8am–2pm Saturday; 8am–noon Sunday.
- **BEST BUYS:** Handwoven fabrics (including carpets and wall hangings); wood-carvings, embroideries and other handicrafts; food specialties; wines; records.
- **PUBLIC HOLIDAYS:** January 1 and 2; May Day, May 1 and 2; Romanian National Holiday, December 1.
- **USEFUL TELEPHONE NUMBERS:**
  Police: **955**
  Fire: **981**
  Ambulance: **961**
  Emergency Hospital (Bucharest): **679 4310.**
- **MEDICAL ASSISTANCE:** Tourists may obtain medical assistance at any state or private hospitals, clinics and dispensaries. First aid is free; other services are chargeable. No vaccines are needed to enter Romania.
- **EMERGENCY RADIO MESSAGES:** On the Black Sea Coast *Radio Vacances* transmits urgent messages in Romanian, French, English, German and Russian daily from mid-May to September 30.
- **NATIONAL TOURIST OFFICES:**
  Romanian National Tourist Office
  342 Madison Avenue
  Suite 210
  New York; NY 10173
  Tel: 212/697 6971
  Fax: 212/697 6972
  Romanian National Tourist Office
  17 Nottingham Street
  London
  W1M 3RD
  Tel: 0171 224 3692
  Fax: telephone the number above and ask for the fax tone
  Romanian State Travel Agency
  Carpaţi
  7 Magheru Blvd
  Sector 1, Bucharest
  Tel: 401 614 5160
  Fax: 401 312 2594
- **AMERICAN EMBASSY:**
  Strada Tudor Arghezi 7–9
  Bucharest
  Tel: 401 210 4042

A people's republic was proclaimed on December 30, 1947 under Soviet domination, which lasted until 1965 when the Soviets were ejected from all government posts. The country was renamed the Socialist Republic of Romania. Oppressive policies were established, aimed at total self-sufficiency, rapid industrialization and the abolition of a national debt. By 1989 Romania was without a national debt, and with reserves in the bank. This was wiped out by the coup in December 1989. Now the national debt stands at more than $4 billion. The KGB and other international agencies assisted in the overthrow of Nicolae Ceauşescu, and both he and his wife were executed on December 25, 1989.

The pro-Stalinist National Salvation Front took control. In June 1990 secret police clashed violently with anti-government protesters. President Ion Iliescu and his neo-communist party were elected in 1992, making little progress in promoting market reforms.

NADIA COMANECI
Nadia Comaneci, now a U.S. citizen, was the first Olympic gymnast to receive a perfect 10 all-round.

FOOD AND DRINK
Romanian food has some Turkish influence. Cabbage *a la Cluj* is finely minced with meat and cream; Moldavian *pirjoale* is meat croquettes.

Typical dishes are *mititei*, chopped, spiced sausage; *sarmale*, spiced meat and rice in vine leaves; *mamaliguta*, maize-flour pancakes; and *friptura* – grills. Fish is a specialty, and fresh vegetables are seasonal. Middle Eastern pastries like *baklava* and *cataif* are popular, as are *prejtura* (pastries).

Tzwica and *palinka* are fiery brandies. Vodka is liberally consumed. Notable wines are Dealul Mare, Riesling, Muscatel (Muscat-Otonel) and Pinot Negru.

Cotnari and Murfatlar are good dessert wines. Romanians drink a Turkish-type coffee and they like their tea served Russian style.

STEAUA

Steaua, Bucharest's leading soccer club, was managed by Valentin Ceauşescu, the late president's elder son. A frustrated player, not allowed to play by his parents, he helped lead Romania's international squad to victory in the European Cup in 1986, and to come second in 1989. He joined the World Cup squad in 1994 and watched Romania's near success in the United States.

SPORTS AND RECREATION

Romanians enjoy soccer, hardball, tennis, volleyball, gymnastics, boxing, motorcycle racing, mountaineering, winter sports and watersports. They have been world champions in handball, European cup winners at soccer, Olympic gold medallists in gymnastics and watersports. The national sport is *oina*, which resembles American baseball. Thermal spas are at Felix, Sovata, Herculane, Mangalia, and Neptun.

GETTING AROUND

Highways are generally uncrowded; motorists should strictly adhere to speed limits: 60 k.p.h. (35 m.p.h.) in town and 70 to 90 k.p.h. (40 to 55 m.p.h.) out of town. Seat belt use is not mandatory. A child under 12 may not ride in the front seat. All vehicles must be equipped with a first-aid kit and warning triangle. Visiting motorists must pay fines for motoring violations on the spot with Romanian lei. Accidents must be reported to the police before repairs are undertaken.

ACCOMMODATIONS

Hotels follow the international star system. To ensure suitable accommodations, contact ACR or Carpaţi-Bucureşti

for reservations, or any large hotel. Campers have their choice of more than 100 campgrounds throughout the country – some have chalets for rent.

TIPPING

Tip in dollars. Salaries are low and everyone expects to be tipped.

PRINCIPAL TOURING AREAS

Note: For descriptions of cities in **bold** type, see individual city listings.

BLACK SEA COAST

Romania's Black Sea riviera has miles of beaches and resorts. On the southern coast is the leading port of **Constanţa**. A few miles north is popular Mamaia, and on an inland waterway lies ancient Istria. The fortified city of Callatis was established by the Greeks in the 6th century BC. The twin resorts of Eforie Nord and Sud offer a lively nightlife. Eforie Nord, with its curative Tekirghiol mud treatments, is one of the largest and best-equipped spas in Europe. The Danube (Dunarea) Delta is a rich, ever-changing, scene, reached from ancient **Tulcea**.

BUCHAREST AND THE SOUTHERN PLAINS

Bucharest lies between the Danube River and the Carpathian foothills surrounded by the fertile Walachia plain. Baneasa Forest, 10 kilometers (6 miles) north of Bucharest, has exhibits of plant and animal life. Farther north is Breaza with traditional Romanian houses and folk costumes. Craiova, Curtea de Argeş Tirgovişte and Cimpulung Muscel have museums displaying the area's archeological riches.

CARPATHIANS

The Carpathian Mountains (Carpatii) dominate the countryside from the north to the south west.

The Făgăraşuli Range, with its waterfalls and glacial lakes, extends over 72 kilometers (45 miles). At the foot of the

Bucegi Range, the road through Romania traverses the Prahova Valley, featuring deep ravines and grottoes. The Rodnei Range has a lovely alpine lake, Lala, and a winter sports resort, Borsa.

The 1,904-meter (5,803-foot) Ceahlau Massif is characterized by strangely shaped peaks sculpted by wind and rain; in the calcified Giurgeului Massif the winding Bicaz River has created a number of dramatic gorges.

Also in this area are the spectacular Pietrele Doamnei rocks. Parallel to the eastern Carpathians, Lake St. Anne occupies the crater of an extinct volcano. Where the Oltul River meets the southern Carpathians is medieval Sibiu.

NORTHERN MOLDAVIA
Northern Moldavia, or Bukovina, has Romania's richest folk art legacy; monasteries, churches, and citadels all display frescoes. Notable examples are the Last Judgement scenes of Voronet Church; a poem in pictures at Humor Monastery; delightful, delicate wall portraits at Arbore Church; the *Siege of Constantinople* at Moldavia Monastery; and other works at Sucevita Church.

TRANSYLVANIA
In the north-west corner of Romania is Transylvania. Among the cities are Cluj, with its historic monuments, and Braşov, at the foot of Mount Timpa. Sinaia and Predeal offer winter sports facilities, and Prejmer is an intact feudal fortress town. Transylvania is best known for associations with Vlad Dracul, known as Vlad

The Impaler, a 15th-century Romanian prince with distinctive methods for dispatching his enemies.

Brooding Bran Castle, near Braşov, retains the influence of Count Dracula; serene Sighisoara was his birthplace.

USEFUL EXPRESSIONS IN ROMANIAN

Pronunciation Tip: read each letter individually, there are no diphthongs. Don't pronounce single "i" at the end of a word. Read: ce as che as in chair; ci as chi as in chip; ţ as tz; ş as sh as in shop; â as a in map.

good morning	bună dimineaţa
good evening	bună seara
good-bye	la revedere
yes/no	da/nu
please	vă rog
thank you	mulţumesc
excuse me	scuzaţi-mă
Do you speak English?	Vorbeşte cineva aici engleza?
I don't understand.	Nu inţeleg.
Where is?	Unde est?
How much is that?	Cât costă?
today	azi
tomorrow	mâine
month	lună
when?	când?

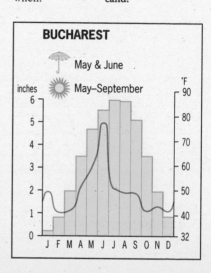

BUCHAREST

May & June

May–September

PLACES OF INTEREST

▲ **BUCUREŞTI (208 C1) ★**
BUCUREŞTI *pop. 2,000,000*
Bucureşti (Bucharest) has earned several nicknames in its 500-year history as Romania's capital: The Garden City and Little Paris of Eastern Europe are two, both justified.

Like Paris, there's an Arc de Triomph with five boulevards radiating outward. One leads from tree-lined Sos Kiseleff and the old President Hotel into Calea Victoriei, the busy heart of Bucharest. Another, Trandafirilor, skirts Herăstrău Park. Parks, such as Cismigiu and Tineretului, within and around the city, and lakes and woods, such as at Băneasa, make it a green city, rich in floral beauty.

Nestling between the huge apartment blocks are ancient palaces, churches and monuments. One sight not to be missed is the People's Palace.

International fairs and exhibitions are held annually in Bucharest, as well as both classical and rock music festivals. Bucharest has more than 24 theaters, many movie theaters and a beautiful opera house. It has a great nightlife.

CASA POPORULUI (People's Palace) ★, Europe's largest building, has marble floors and enormous chandeliers. There are many floors where no visitors are allowed, housing government offices.

LACUL SI PADUREA SNAGOV (Snagov Lake and Forest) ★ is 40 kilometers (25 miles) north. Its beach offers facilities for watersports, including fishing. On a tiny island in the lake stands the 15th-century Snagov Monastery.

MAGOŞOAIA PALACE, 14 kilometers (9 miles) north west, overlooks a lake. Built in 1702, the palace is now a museum with exhibits of medieval art.

MUZEUL COLECTILOR DE ARTA (Art Collections Museum), 111 Calea Grivitei and Calea Victoriei, exhibits works by Romanian classical painters, old masters and Oriental artists.

MUSEUL DE ARTA AL ROMÂNIEI (Art Museum of Romania), 1 Calea Victoriei, has galleries of medieval, modern and contemporary art with works by Romanian and European masters.

MUSEUL NATIONAL DE ISTORIE (National History Museum), 12 Calea Victoriei near B-dul Republicii, covers the history of Romania from the neolithic age.

PADUREA BĂNEASA (Băneasa Forest), 10 kilometers (6 miles) north, has botanical gardens, a zoo and a deer reserve.

PARCUL HERĂSTRĂU (Herastrau Park) ★ offers watersports, recreational facilities, an amusement park, an open-air theater and a library.
Museul Satului (Village Museum) boasts more than 300 authentic peasant houses and buildings from all parts of Romania.

▲ **BRAŞOV (208 C2) ★**
BRAŞOV *pop. 336,000*
Braşov dates back to the 12th century. Medieval landmarks chronicle a rich and varied history.

Poiana Braşov, an all-year-round sports resort, lies just above, and Predeal, with superb skiing, is 30 kilometers (19 miles) away. Bran Castle, the 14th-century fortress, is nearby. From Poina Braşov, there is a breathtaking view of the Bucegi Range from the

ROMANIA

ROMANIA

Cristianul Chalet, some 1,198 meters (3,930 feet) above sea level. Etched into the range is a magnificent sphinx. Also nearby is Sinaia and Peles Castle.

BISERICA NEAGRA (Black Church), a large Gothic cathedral begun in 1385 and completed 100 years later, derives its name from its blackened walls, the result of a fire in 1689. It has an enormous 1839 organ with over 4,000 pipes.

BISERICA SFINTU NICOLAE (St. Nicholas Church) is Romanian Orthodox. Built in the 15th century, it contains paintings by 19th-century artist Misu Pop. Paintings from the 16th century are in the chapel.

CASA SFATULUI (Council Hall) is a 15th-century construction with thick walls, vaulted halls and a Trumpeter's Tower. It houses the Regional Museum of History and the Art Museum.

▲ CLUJ (208 B3)
CLUJ *pop. 300,000*
Cluj is the capital of Transylvania. It has a university and several museums and theaters. Much of its charm stems from medieval architecture, displayed in the Tailor's Bastion, the Franciscan monastery and churches.

BISERICA REFORMATA, str Mihail Kogăniceanu, was built in the 15th century. It served as the church of the Franciscan monastery of Friars Minor.

BOTANICAL GARDENS AND MUSEUM is Romania's largest, with a 10-hectare (25-acre) collection of world plant life.

CASA NATALA A LUI MATEI CORVIN (Matthias Corvinus' Birthplace) is at Piata Muzeului. A 15th-century Hungarian king, Corvinus was the first European monarch to try to expel invading Turks.

MUZEUL ETNOGRAFIC AL TRANSILVANIEI (Transylvania Ethnography Museum), str 30 Decembrie 21, houses large collections of Romanian folk art.

▲ CONSTANŢA (208 D1) ★
CONSTANŢA *pop. 320,000*
More than 27 centuries ago the Greeks founded the city of Tomis on the Black Sea, near the legendary Mamaia. The ruins form the foundation of contemporary Constanţa, Romania's principal port. The seafaring tradition is evident in the Genovese lighthouse and in the aquarium, which contains more than 2,000 exhibits. The Museum of History and Archeology and the 3rd-century Roman mosaic in the square are of interest. Constanţa offers an opera house, a theater, a casino and a sports stadium.

Trips can be taken to the Black Sea resorts including nearby Mamaia and Murfatlar, the main wine-producing area.

MAMAIA, the Miami of Romania, is a narrow tongue of golden sand washed on the east by the Black Sea and on the west by the freshwater Lake Siutghiol. Hotels, shops, cafés and casinos have been neatly arranged amid rose gardens and lawns. The resort has an open-air theater and a 6.5-kilometer (4-mile) beach fully equipped for watersports. The National Folklore Festival is held in late July or early August.

IAŞI (208 D3)
IAŞI
A fine 14th-century city with a very mixed culture. The Yiddish Theater originated here and today Iaşi is the seat of Minority Group Studies, attached to a fine university. Many of Romania's great literary figures stemmed from the area.

▲ SIBIU (208 C2)
SIBIU *pop. 175,000*
The capital of Sibiu county and a major university city, Sibiu has preserved its walled old town. The baroque Brukenthal Palace, converted in 1817 into the Brukenthal Museum, features noted history and natural history sections. The art section has folk and fine art, and works by world masters. The personal library of Samuel Brukenthal, governor of Transylvania 1777–87, has rare volumes.

Modern Sibiu is a commercial city that provides wide cultural opportunities. Nearby at the commune of Simbata de Jos is a Lippizana stud farm where visitors can ride horseback in the foothills of the Fagaras Mountains.

▲ SUCEAVA (208 C3) ★
SUCEAVA *pop. 90,000*

Suceava, the medieval capital of the princes of Moldavia, has had a long and colorful history. This former market town is now a modern city, with industrial and residential districts beside medieval monuments and churches.

The surrounding hill country of northern Moldavia is known for beautiful painted churches and monasteries with unusual exterior frescoes. As well as the five main churches and monasteries around Suceava, in the area historically known as Bukovina, there are some impressive 12th- to 15th-century ruins and a 17th-century princely inn.

BISERICA SFINTU DUMITRU (St. Demetrius Church) was founded by Prince Petru Rareş in the 16th century. The exterior is decorated with glazed discs and bricks; the interior has fine frescoes.

CITADELA dates from 14th to 16th centuries; it is being excavated and restored.

MANASTIREA DRAGOMIRNA (Dragomirna Monastery) was founded by Metropolitan Atanasie Crimca in 1609. The tall church introduced elements that became characteristic of Moldavian architecture.

MANASTIREA PUTNA (Putna Monastery), founded in the 15th century by Stephen the Great, houses his tomb and a medieval museum inside.

MANASTIREA VORONET (Voronet Monastery), 12 kilometers (7 miles) south west, is sometimes called the "Sistine Chapel of the East" for its art and architecture. The exterior frescoes include *The Last Judgement*, which covers the entire western façade.

TIMIŞOARA (208 A2)
TIMIŞ

Capital of Timiş county on the Timiş River, and close to the Serbian border, this is a pleasant university town.

Timişsoara will be remembered as the starting point of the 1989 revolution. The square, dating back to the Austro-Hungarian Empire, mirrors those of Sibiu and Braşov.

Decebal's bridge depicts his crossing in Roman times, his elephants supporting the bridge on either side.

PELE'S CASTLE, SINAIA

After leading a coup to overthrow Hitler's ally, Marshal Ion Antonescu, King Michael of Romania was led away from the castle at gun-point and exiled. Antonescu was executed. King Michael, cousin to Queen Elizabeth of England, now resides in Geneva. He was allowed to return to his homeland only once, in 1992, but proved so popular that he has been escorted away from the airport twice, the last time in October 1994. In the meantime, statues are being erected martyring Antonescu.

▲ TULCEA (208 D2) ★
TULCEA

The Danube River ends its journey through Europe by splitting into three rivers and pouring its riches into the Danube Delta and later the Black Sea.

Founded by ancient Greeks and now a thriving fishing center, Tulcea is a picturesque town with a number of attractions. The imposing Azizir Mosque, the Delta Museum, and an aquarium with species of fish found along the Danube River's path through Europe should be included in a walking tour of the town.

Along the riverfront, pelicans, water-lilies and rustling reeds create a pleasant setting. The Danube Delta can be toured by organized boat trip.

RUSSIAN FEDERATION

THE WORLD'S LARGEST NATION STRETCHES FROM EASTERN EUROPE TO THE SHORES OF THE PACIFIC OCEAN AND FROM THE ARCTIC CIRCLE TO MONGOLIA. THE EUROPEAN CORNER CENTERS ON MOSCOW AND ST. PETERSBURG. TRAVEL IS NOT AS RESTRICTED AS IT WAS, BUT LIMITS ARE PLACED BY THE LACK OF GOOD FACILITIES. HOWEVER, THIS IS MORE THAN COMPENSATED FOR BY A LOOK AT ONE OF THE GREATEST AND MOST MYSTERIOUS OF COUNTRIES, HIDDEN FOR SO LONG BEHIND THE IRON CURTAIN. NOW WE CAN SEE RED SQUARE AND THE FAMILIAR ONION DOMES OF ST. BASIL'S CATHEDRAL IN MOSCOW, STROLL INSIDE THE KREMLIN, AND TRAVEL ON THE GLORIOUS METRO STYSTEM. THE MAIN ATTRACTION IN ST. PETERSBURG IS THE HERMITAGE MUSEUM. BEYOND THE UNKNOWN COUNTRY BECKONS CURIOUS TRAVELERS.

Left THE FAIRY-TALE ONION DOMES OF ST. BASIL'S CATHEDRAL IN MOSCOW
Above left MATRYOSHKA DOLLS MAKE DELIGHTFUL GIFTS TO TAKE HOME
Above right ROOF-TOP SPIRES ON THE TEREM PALACE IN MOSCOW'S KREMLIN

THINGS TO KNOW

- **AREA:** 22,027,421 square kilometers (8,504,796 square miles)
- **POPULATION:** 273,200,000
- **LANGUAGES:** Russian, plus more than 100 others.
- **ECONOMY:** Industry, agriculture. Chief exports include machinery, iron and steel, timber and petroleum products.
- **PASSPORT:** Required for U.S. citizens.
- **VISA:** Required for all visitors. The visa is granted by all four Russian consulates, 1825 Phelps Place. NW, Washington, DC 20008 or the Russian Consulate, 2790 Green Street., San Francisco, CA 94123, and is valid for the time and itinerary indicated when the booking was made. Tel: 202/939 8918 for the Russian Consulate or 415/202 9800 for the Russian Consulate General. For more information on visa requirements, contact your local AAA club.

  Persons wishing to visit relatives must apply directly to the Russian Consulate for a Visitor's Visa.
- **CUSTOMS RESTRICTIONS:** Items such as prescription drugs, computers and cassettes may be imported for your own personal use. Recorded video cassettes (i.e. commercial movies) are prohibited. Do not try to export icons or objects of historical value without consulting the Russian authorities (tel: 975 4460, in Moscow).
- **CURRENCY:** In Russia the currency unit is *rouble* (RUF), divided into 100 *kopecks*. Due to currency fluctuations, the exchange rate is subject to frequent and dramatic change. All currency and travelers' checks must be declared at customs. Roubles can be brought into and taken out of Russia and the republics, but you cannot take out more roubles than you imported. The limit is R500,000. There is no limit on the amount of U.S. currency that may be imported; however, the amount exported must not exceed the amount imported. The State Bank Certificate (F-377), which shows the amount of currency converted, is needed to exchange

HISTORY

Political instability has shaken this part of the world since the 9th century, when the Vikings were invited to govern the medieval principality of Novgorod. This led to the formation of the territory known as Kievan Rus', which became powerful with the growth of trade and the introduction of Christianity. In the 13th century the Tartars invaded Kiyev, bringing corruption and turmoil. During the 16th-century reign of Ivan the Terrible, the nation became centralized.

Grievances against subsequent tsars gave rise to demands for constitutional reform. Although the December 14, 1825 uprising was quelled, resistance continued. A revolution in 1905 provoked strikes and protests against Tsar Nicholas II. The

Bolshevik Revolution of 1917 opened the door for the Communist Party. Led by Vladimir Ilyich Lenin, the Bolsheviks overthrew tsarism, and the Union of Soviet Socialist Republics was formed. Lenin put into practice what political philosopher Karl Marx had envisioned when he wrote the Communist Manifesto in 1847: a one-class society working collectively for the good of the state.

In 1924 Lenin's successor, Joseph Stalin, initiated a reign of terror. The Soviet entity that emerged was severely battered during World War II.

The era after World War II was one of political upheaval. Successive leaders continued the ideological struggles with the West. The appointment of Mikhail Gorbachev as general secretary of the Communist Party in 1985 was an innovation. In 1987 he initiated a program of reforms aimed at democratization. In May 1989, Gorbachev was elected president of the Soviet Union, thus acquiring the nation's top leadership role in legislative and policy-making bodies.

In 1991, a failed coup resulted in the eventual breakup of the Communist Party. On August 18, Gorbachev was put under house arrest by a hardline communist rebel group. They demanded that power be turned over to them. Gorbachev refused. The Red Army and the people, led by Boris Yeltsin, the recently elected president of the Republic of Russia, denounced the coup and demanded that Gorbachev be released. On August 21, he was. As a result, Yeltsin emerged as the new hero of the people.

Yeltsin proclaimed that the U.S.S.R. was ceasing its existence amd announced the formation of the Commonwealth of Independent States (CIS). Gorbachev, unwilling to break up the Soviet Union, resigned on December 25, 1991.

Eleven sovereign republics joined the commonwealth: Russian Federation, Belorussia, Ukraine, Armenia, Azerbaijan, Kazakhstan, Kygyzstan, Moldavia, Tajikistan, Turkmenistan and Uzbekistan. Georgia and the three Baltic States of Estonia, Latvia and Lithuania were recognized as independent nations.

The commonwealth's transition to a stable market-based economy failed to materialize, and its citizens have fallen victim to inflation, criminal activity and disillusionment. The political fabric was loosely knit, and it was stretched by age-old ethnic conflicts and unanswered questions about military authority and foreign relations. By March 1993, Boris Yeltsin was fighting for his political life. Parliamentary leaders proclaimed Vice-President Alexander Rutskoi Russia's new president and holed up in the Russian parliament building. Yeltsin ordered troops to storm the building and some 200 soldiers and civilians died. Elections in December 1993 gave control of the lower house to the extreme right-winger, Vladimir Zhirinovsky.

FOOD AND DRINK

Many dishes have a distinct regional flavor: Ukrainian, Uzbek and Armenian cooking, for instance, differ from that of the rest of the country. Try chicken *Kiev* and Caucasian *shashlik* (lamb); *chakhokhbili*, fried chicken or fish; Armenian *piti*, vegetable soup; *cheburek*, meat patties in baked dough; *uzbek*, lamb en brochette; *zakuski*, hors d'oeuvres, and *okroshka*, cold vegetables. Caviar, yogurt and sour cream appear on most menus, as do many varieties of the local pancake (*blini*). Tea and fruit juices are popular, and the drink *kvas*, made from fermented black bread. Vodka is served very cold.

ARTS AND ENTERTAINMENT

Music and literature have a rich heritage. Moscow has more than 30 theaters and six concert halls. Choirs, orchestras, folk dance groups, puppet theaters and the circus draw many visitors. Internationally acclaimed ballet is performed by St. Petersburg's

unused roubles for foreign currency. Transactions in hard (Western) currencies are forbidden, although many people will ask to be paid in U.S. dollars, which is the most widely accepted currency. It is important that notes presented for exchange are in good condition. Beware of counterfeit notes. Credit cards are now accepted by major hotels and restaurants

- CURRENCIES: **Belarussia** – *Rouble*; **Moldova** – 1 *Lei* = 100 *Bani*; **Uzbekistan** – *Sum*; **Armenia** – *Dram* and *Lum*; **Kyrgyzstan** – *Som*; **Turkmenistan** – 1 *Manat* = 100 *Tenge*; **Tajikistan** – *Rouble*; **Azerbaijan** – 1 *Manat* = 100 *gyapik*; **Kazakhstan** – *Tenge*.
- BANK HOURS: 9am–5pm Monday–Friday.
- STORE HOURS: Large shops and stores 9am–7pm Monday–Saturday, small shops and stores 11am–7pm Monday–Saturday. All stores, except GUM and other department stores, are closed one hour for lunch.
- MUSEUM HOURS: Most museums are open 11am–7pm Tuesday–Saturday, 11am–5pm Sunday. Some close on the last day of the month.
- BEST BUYS: Chess sets, books, records, fur hats, wooden dolls, jewelry, embroidered blouses and hats, crystal, decorative objects and caviar.
- USEFUL TELEPHONE NUMBERS: Police: 02; Ambulance: 03; Fire: 01
- NATIONAL TOURIST OFFICES: Intourist 630 Fifth Avenue, Suite 868 New York, NY 10111 Tel: 212/757 3884 Intourist 219 Marsh Wall Isle of Dogs London E14 9PD, England Tel: 0171 5388600
- AMERICAN EMBASSIES: Novinskiy Bulvar 19/23 Moscow, Russia Tel: 252 2451/252 2459 Furshtadtskaya ul 15 St. Petersburg, Russia Tel: 812 274 8235

Mariinskiy (Kirov) Dance Company and Moscow's Bolshoi Ballet.

The best known festivals are St. Petersburg's White Nights in June, Kiyev's Ukrainian Arts Festival from late May to early June and Moscow's Russian Winter Festival in late December and early January.

SPORTS AND RECREATION
Popular spectator sports are soccer, basketball, gymnastics and wrestling. Skiing and mountain climbing are favored in the Elbrus and West Caucasus areas. Black Sea resorts have fine beaches.

GETTING AROUND
There are designated entry points, some for coaches only, and some for cars. Cars can be transported by sea to St. Petersburg. Direct flights to Moscow and St. Petersburg are operated from the U.S. and Canada by Delta and Aeroflot, and to the Russian Far East by Alaska Airlines. Many European carriers have connecting flights.

Aeroflot serves Moscow, Kiyev, St. Petersburg and other major cities. Train lines go from Moscow, St. Petersburg, Kharkov and Kiyev. Boat lines connect the Danube River with the Black, Caspian and Baltic seas. Cruise boats ply the Volga and Dnieper rivers. More than 400 cities throughout the republics may be visited. Arranged itineraries and prepayment for accommodation, *both of which are required*, can be made through a travel agent.

Regulations governing motoring by visitors are complex and frequently change. Full insurance documentation must be carried at all times, in addition to an International Driving Permit and and International Certificate for Motor Vehicles. Contact the New York office of Intourist (see left) for information.

ACCOMMODATIONS
Intourist makes reservations for visitors traveling to Russia and the republics.

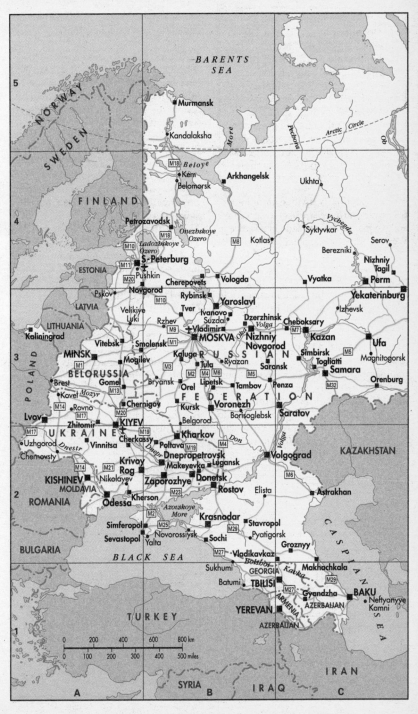

RUSSIAN FEDERATION

Accommodation is divided into deluxe, first class and tourist class. Reservations and payment must be made in advance in Western currency to obtain a visa.

Campgrounds are numerous and open from May to September. Campground reservations must be made in advance in Western currency through a travel agent approved by Intourist.

SPECIAL REGULATIONS
Although restrictions have eased, photographing sites of strategic importance is still forbidden; these may include military objects, factories, rail stations, shipyards or ports, bridges, radio facilities, airports or border crossings. Foreigners may not send exposed film out of Russia and the republics. It is unlawful to sell Western goods. The use of dollars is now prohibited.

TIPPING
Tips are much appreciated. Give waiters and taxi drivers 10 percent. Tip others several roubles.

PRINCIPAL TOURING AREAS

Note: For descriptions of cities in **bold type**, see individual city listings.

BLACK SEA COAST
Yalta, Pearl of the Black Sea, is one of many scenic cities in a popular vacation area with health centers, beach resorts and seaports. **Odessa**, Sochi, Batumi and Sukhumi have exotic gardens.

CAUCASUS
The Caucasus, mild and scenic, has several mineral spas. In Azerbaijan are 9th-century Baku and Neftyaniye Kamni, a town built on stilts over the Caspian Sea. Armenia, with older-than-Rome Yerevan as its capital, is a highland republic. The separate nation of Georgia, with its cultural center and capital **Tbilisi**, encompasses both beach resorts and snow-capped mountains. To the north, the Greater Caucasus Mountains offer skiing and climbing.
Note: earthquakes have severely damaged large areas of the Caucasus. Ethnic clashes and political uncertainties have made travel there difficult.

NORTH-WEST RUSSIA
Near the Gulf of Finland is a well-traveled touring area highlighted by **St. Petersburg**. The area known for the distinctive Karelian art and architecture, Kizhi, presents outstanding examples. **Minsk** is capital of Belarus. **Novogorod** lies on the road to historical Tver'. Farther south, **Moscow**, Russia's capital, is a cultural hub and center for excursions. Just east of Moscow are the twin cities of **Vladimir** and **Suzdal**.

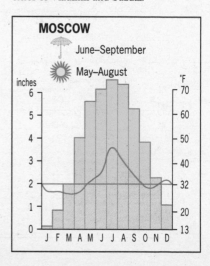

MOSCOW
June–September
May–August

SIBERIA (not covered by map)

Rich in natural resources, Siberia is a vast area of cedar forests and blue-gray mountains. The region's industrial nature is evidenced by Novosibirsk's enormous hydroelectric station. Further east across Siberia is the cultural center of Irkutsk; nearby is Lake Baikal, the world's deepest lake.

UKRAINE

The Republic of Ukraine is an industrial and agricultural center that preserves distinctive folklore and art. Kiyev is an ancient Russian territory. Lvov is a 13th-century town whose flourishing past under the tsars is reflected in a museum in a 16th-century house. Historical Rovno was founded in the 13th century with the coming of the Tartars and was ruled until the 17th century by Polish warlords. The road from Slovakia passes 10th-century Uzhgorod that has a medieval castle-museum, and continues through the Carpathians to join the route from Poland. There is also the cultural center of Odessa, on the Black Sea, picturesque Chernovtsy and 14th-century Vinnitsa.

VOLGA

The green steppes lining the Volga River south of Moscow has several sizeable cities. Kazan and Volgograd are major seaports and industrial centers. Rostov has a reputation as one of the most attractive cities in Russia, in spite of its industry.

WEST-CENTRAL ASIA

Fields of "white gold" a fine-staple cotton, cover the endless plains of west-central Asia. The cities of Bukhara, Tashkent and Samarkand are influenced by Moslem tradition. Ashgabat' is the capital of Turkmenistan, noted for its carpets. Almaty, capital of Kazakhstan, and Dushanbe, capital of Tajikistan, are also of interest; between them rise the Tien Shan, or Celestial Mountains.
Note: Ethnic clashes and political uncertainties in Tajikistan and Azerbaijan have made travel there difficult.

USEFUL EXPRESSIONS IN RUSSIAN

hello	zdrávstvuytye
good morning	dobroye utro
good afternoon	dobriy dyen'
good evening	dobriy vyechyer
good night	spokoynoy nochi
good-bye	dosvidaniya
please	pozhalusta
thankyou	spasibo
yes	da
no	nyet
good	khoroshiy
bad	plokhoy
how long	skol'ko
how far	kak dalyeko
big	bol'shoy
small	malyen'kiy
excuse me	izvinitye
cheap	dyeshoviy
expensive	dorogoy
left	lyeviy
right	praviy
you're welcome	pozhalusta
Do you speak English?	Zdyes' kto-nibud' govorit po-angliyski?
I don't understand.	Ya nye ponimayu.
What is the time?	Kotoriy chas?
Waiter!	Ofitsiant!
Waitress!	Ofitsiantka!
How much is that?	Skol'ko eto stoit?
Do you take credit cards?	Vi byeryote Kryeditniye Kartochki?
Where are the restrooms?	Gdye tualyety?
I'd like ...	Ya khotyel bi ...
Can you help me, please?	Pomogitye mnye, pozhalusta?
Please write it down.	Pozhalusta, napishitye.
where	gdye?
when	kogda?
how?	kak?
hot/cold	goryachiy/kholodniy
old/new	stariy/noviy
free (vacant)	svobodniy
occupied	zanyatiy
yesterday	vchyera
today	sevodnya
tomorrow	zavtra
just a minute	syechas

PLACES OF INTEREST

RUSSIAN FEDERATION

NOTE

Due to the changing political situation, it has not always been possible to provide up-to-date information on attractions.

▲ MOSKVA (221 B3) ★

RUSSIAN FEDERATION *pop. 8,500,000*

A major manufacturing center, Moskva (Moscow) is also a city of the arts and learning, with ballet and opera, drama and musical comedy, theaters, concert halls, museums and art galleries.

Take a boat trip along the river, which gives fine views of spires, gold domes, and wedding-cake-style buildings.

ANDRONIKOV MONASTYR (Andronikov Monastery) (226 E3), Ploshchad Pryamikova 10, is south east of Moscow by the river. It was rebuilt in stone in the 15th century. The buildings include the Cathedral of the Saviour and the Church of the Archangel Michael and St. Alexius. Icons from the 15th to 19th centuries are in the Museum of Ancient Russian Art.

ARBAT, the capital's main shopping street, has small stores, street artists, musicians and stall-holders.

DOM-MUZEY CHEKHOVA (Chekhov House Museum) (226 B4), Kudrinksaya Ulitsa 6, was the playwright's home from 1886 to 1890, where he wrote *Ivanov*.

GUM (Gosudarstvennyi Universalnyi Magazin – State Universal Store), was constructed 100 years ago. Wrought-iron work embellishes the galleries and a domed, glass roof covers it.

KRASNAYA PLOSHCHAD (Red Square) is familiar as Moscow's parade ground.
Lenin Mausoleum (Mauzoley Lenina) contains the sarcophagus of the former leader. There are plans to remove him to St. Petersburg for burial with other family members.
Vasilia Blazhennovo Sobor (St. Basil's Cathedral) was constructed in the 16th century by Ivan the Terrible. It has nine chapels, each with an intricate dome.

KREML (Kremlin) was originally a 12th-century wooden fortress. It now holds the Russian Federation government offices.
Arkhangelskiy Sobor (Archangel Cathedral) was begun in the 16th century. It includes the tomb of Ivan the Terrible.
Blagoveshchenskiy Sober (Annunciation Cathedral) dates from the 15th century, and contains some beautiful icons.
Dvorets Kongressov (Congress Palace) was built in 1961 and hosts conferences and cultural events.
Kolokolniya Ivan Velikiy, a bell tower, built by Ivan the Terrible, has 22 bells and more than 30 small chimes.
Oruzheinaya Palata (The Armory) has an outstanding collection of royal treasures.
Uspenskiy Sobor (Assumption Cathedral), with five gold domes, contains magnificent icons and decorations.

MOSKOVSKIY UNIVERSITET (Moscow University) was founded in 1755 by the Russian scientist Lomonosov.

MUSEY IZOBRAZITELNYKH ISKUSSTV (in Pushkin Fine Arts Museum) (226 B3), Ulitsa Volkhonka 12, has a large collection of French paintings of the Impressionist and Post-Impressionist schools.

MOSCOW METRO

Recognizable by the large, red letter M on the pavement, the entrance to Metro stations bring you to another world. The first line, from Sikolniki to Park Kultury, opened in the 1930s. Stations on this line are resplendent with marble, mosaics, and murals, and lit with chandeliers.

MONSTER CANNON

In the Kremlin grounds stands the beautifully decorated cast-iron King of Cannons. Weighing 40 tons, with a bore of 91 centimeters (36 inches), it was cast in 1586 for the feeble-minded son of Ivan the Terrible, but never fired.

NOVODEVICHY MONASTYR (226 A2), Pirogovskaya Bolshaya, is an early 16th-century convent with murals and icons.

SERGIEVO POSAD (ZAGORSK) ★, 72 kilometers (45 miles) north east of Moscow, is the site of the Trinity Monastery founded by St. Sergius in 1345. The Cathedral of the Assumption, with onion-shaped domes, has frescoes and the tomb of Boris Godunov. In the church of the Holy Trinity lies St. Sergius.

TRETYAKOVSKAYA GALERYA (Tretyakovsky Gallery) (226 C2), Lavrushinksy Pereulik 10, houses Russian art.

ALMATY

KAZAKHSTAN *pop. 625,000*

Almaty, capital of Kazakhstan, lies in the foothills of the Tien Shan Mountains. Apart from the Central State Museum, there are two concert halls, a circus, theater, the Arasan Baths, and tea houses.

GORKY PARK is on the right bank of the Malaya Alma-Atinka River. A miniature zoo, a children's railway and a large swimming pool are among its attractions.

ZENKOVSKII SOBOR, Panfilov Park, is a cathedral built without nails in 1904.

BUKHARA

UZBEKISTAN *pop. 200,000*

This city, over 2,000 years old, stands on the banks of the Zeravshan River, on the Silk Route. Part of the city walls remain, protecting the fortress, mosques and *medressehs* (Islamic theological colleges).

▲ DUSHANBE

TAJIKISTAN *pop. 519,000*

Capital of Tajikistan, Dushanbe makes textiles and foodstuffs. It offers a circus, several theaters, a movie studio, folk orchestras, and a philharmonic society.

IRKUTSK

RUSSIAN FEDERATION *pop. 582,000*

Irkutsk is the principal city of eastern Siberia, concentrating on heavy industry and the fur trade. It has a folk art museum, circus, and fine arts museum.

LAKE BAIKAL ★, about 64 kilometers (40 miles) north east of Irkutsk, is the deepest lake in the world, measuring about 1,737 meters (5,700 feet). There are 2,000 kinds of flora and fauna, including species found only here. Boat trips are available from May through the summer.

▲ KIYEV ★

UKRAINE *pop. 2,500,000*

Founded in 860 AD, Kiyev is home of the Shevchenko Opera/Ballet Theater.

BOTANICHESKY SAD (Botanical Gardens), Shevchenko Boulevard, displays thousands of species including an unusual collection of lilacs.

DVORETS KULTURY (Palace of Culture), 50 Vladimirskays Street, houses the Theater of Opera and Ballet and theaters for Russian and Ukrainian drama.

KIZHI, an island on Lake Onega, is a haven for 18th-century wooden buildings. Preobrazhenye Church is an 11-story masterpiece built without nails.

RUSSIAN FEDERATION

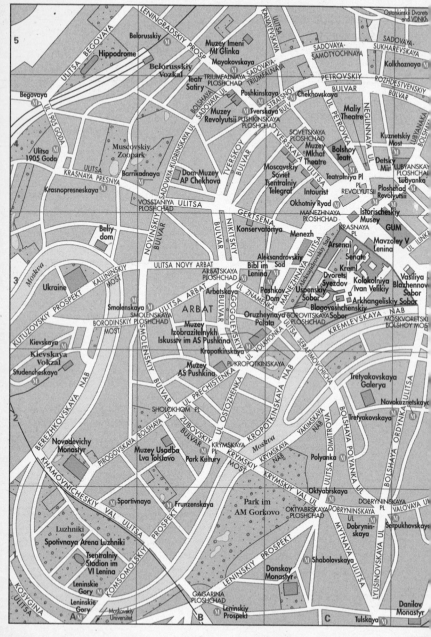

SOFISKY SOBOR (St. Sophia Cathedral), Bogdan Khmelnitsky Square, was founded in 1036 to celebrate victory over the Pechenegs, a tribe of nomadic invaders.

▲ **MINSK (221 A3)**
BELORUSSIA *pop. 1,500,000*
Minsk, the capital of Belorussia, was almost destroyed during World War II.

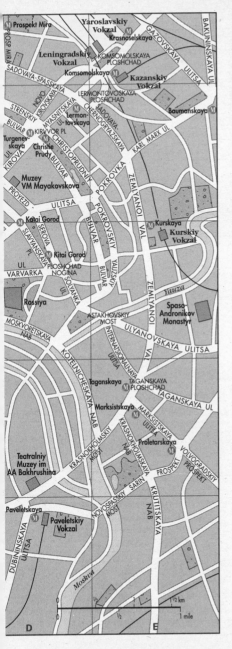

Map labels: Prospekt Mira, Yaroslavskiy Vokzal, Krasnoselskaya, GAZOVSKAYA ULITSA, BAKUNINSKAYA UL, PROSP MIRA UL, Leningradskiy Vokzal, KOMSOMOLSKAYA PLOSHCHAD, SADOVAYA-SPASSKAYA, Komsomolskaya, Kazanskiy Vokzal, STRENSKIY BULVAR, NOVO KIROVSKAYA, MYASNITSKAYA, LERMONTOVSKAYA PLOSHCHAD, CHKADOVAYA UL, CHERNOGRIAZSKAYA, Baumanskaya, Lermon-tovskaya, KARL MARX UL, Turgenev-skaya, KIRVVOR PL, CHRISTOPRUDNIY, Christie Prudy, BULVAR, UL KIROVA, Muzey VM Mayakovskova, POKROVKA, POKROVSKIY BULVAR, ZEMLYANOI VAL, ULITSA, Kitai Gorod, SEROVA, Kurskaya, SLAVANSKAYA PL, Kitai Gorod, Kurskiy Vokzal, UL VARVARKA, PLOSHCHAD NOGINA, SOLYANKA, YAUZSKY BULVAR, ZEMLYANOI VAL, Rossiya, Yauza, MOSKVORETSKAYA NAB, ASTAKHOVSKIY MOST, Spaso-Andronikov Monastyr, KOTELNICHESKAYA NAB, INTERNATSIONALNAYA ULITSA, ULYANOVSKAYA ULITSA, ZEMLYANOI VAL, Taganskaya, TAGANSKAYA PLOSHCHAD, TAGANSKAYA UL, Marksistskaya, MARKSISTSKAYA ULITSA, Teatralniy Muzey im AA Bakhrushina, KRASNOKHOLMSKIY MOST, KRASNOKHOLMSKAYA NAB, Proletarskaya, VOLGOGRADSKIY PROSPEKT, SARIN PROSPEKT, KRUTITSKAYA NAB, Paveletskaya, NOVOSPASSKIY MOST, Paveletskiy Vokzal, DUBININSKAYA ULITSA, Moskva, D, E, ½ km, ½, 1 mile

NOVGOROD (221 A4) ★

RUSSIAN FEDERATION *pop. 220,000*
Novgorod was known as Great Novgorod in the Middle Ages. It has a unique architectural ensemble of buildings and the Kremlin, surrounded by ramparts.

KREMLIN, or Detinets, on the west bank of the Volkhov, is from the 11th century. The walls extend more than 450 meters (1,475 feet) and have nine towers.
Granovitaya Palata, in the Kremlin, is a Gothic palace dating from 1433 with outstanding 11th- to 19th-century frescoes.
Sofisky Sobor (Cathedral of St. Sophia) was erected 1045–50 in the Novgorod Kremlin. Its huge, 12th-century Byzantine bronze doors open onto an array of spectacular frescoes and icons.

NOVGORODSKY ISTORICHESKY MUSEI (Novgorod History and Art Museum) contains medieval icons including tablets depicting the Ascension and the lives of various saints.

ODESSA (221 A2)

UKRAINE *pop. 1,000,000*
Odessa is a large port on the Black Sea. It is also a resort with beaches, saline baths and a mild climate. Of interest are the catacombs, where resistance workers lived during the last war. There are also museums on archeology and art.

Energies have now gone into rebuilding. Minsk has a variety of cultural institutions, and art and history museums show the colorful folk culture of Belorussia.

RUSSIAN FEDERATION

CAVEAT TOURIST

The internal situation of the Russian Federation and the former republics is unstable, and changes may affect tourists. The process of de-Leninization, for example, means that towns, streets and buildings named after Lenin and his comrades are being renamed, so be prepared for some changes.

A 200-kilometer (124-mile) tour can be made north east to historic Kherson on the Dnieper River. Near Kherson is the Askanija-Nova Nature Reserve.

OPERNY TEATR (Opera House) is a neo-classical building once host to musical events conducted by Tchaikovsky.

POTEMKINSKY STUPENY (Potemkin Steps), Primorsky Boulevard, was so named after 2,000 people were shot in 1905 when they gathered in support of mutinying sailors on the battleship *Potemkin*.

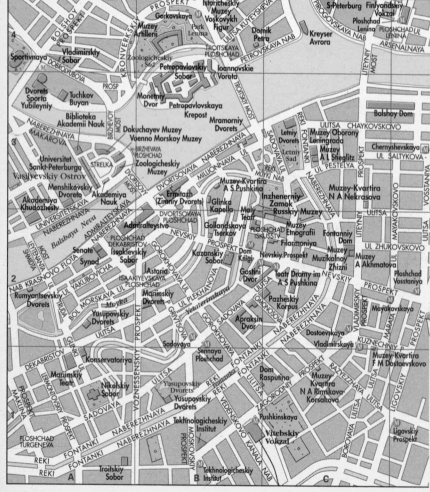

▲ **SANKT-PETERBURG** (221 A4) ★
RUSSIAN FEDERATION *pop. 5,000,000*
Sankt-Peterburg (St. Petersburg) traces
its history to the founding in 1703 of the
Fortress of Peter and Paul by Peter the
Great. Despite a tumultuous history, it
has maintained a graceful, cosmopolitan
atmosphere. In addition to being an
artistic and historical gem, the city is a
major industrial center and port.

First called St. Petersburg, then
Petrograd, the city was named Lenin-
grad in 1924 before reverting to St.
Petersburg in 1991. It was the cradle of
the Great October Revolution in 1917
which created the first Soviet state and
is also famed for its citizens' withstanding a 900-day siege in World War II.

There are over 50 museums, including the enormous Hermitage with 3 million exhibits, 19 kilometers (12 miles) of
galleries, and over 1,000 rooms! There
are 20 theaters and concert halls, with
the Mariinskiy (Kirov) and Maly Opera
and Ballet. Of special interest is the
White Nights Festival, held in late June.

ADMIRALTEYSTVO (Admiralty) (228 A2) is
where the first ships of the Russian navy
were built. Its tall, gold spire can be seen
from many of St. Petersburg's streets. It
is used today by the Russian navy.

ERMITAZH (Hermitage Museum) (228 B3)
is a former royal residence now housing
one of the world's greatest art collections. It stands on the south bank of the
Neva River and consists of three inter-
linked buildings; a fourth, the small
Hermitage Theater, is closed to visitors.

The largest building is the baroque
Winter Palace (Zimniy Dvorets), designed by Rastrelli for the Tsarina Elizabeth
in 1762 and boasting unforgettable
rooms with chandeliers, magnificent
throne rooms, and precious wood floors.

On the first floor is western European
art, with early works by Rembrandt and

PETER THE GREAT
Born in 1672, Peter became tsar
when he was 10 years old, and
that year traveled to Holland and
England incognito to learn about
shipbuilding. He returned with the
plan of westernizing Russia, built
up a large navy to dispatch the
Turks and extended northern
Russia by defeating the Swedes in
the 21-year Northern War. He
created St. Petersburg, his
"Window to the West," at great
cost to human life, drafting thousands of laborers to work on the
cold, marshy land.

Rubens, as well as furniture, silver, tapestry and porcelain. On the floor above are works by Cézanne, Degas and Monet.

Rooms in the eastern section of the ground floor have prehistoric cultures and art and culture from the East, which also continues on the second floor.

Adjoining the Winter Palace is the Small Hermitage, built in the 1760s as a retreat for Catherine the Great. Today it exhibits her collection of Flemish and Dutch pictures.

The third building is the Large Hermitage, by the Winter Canal. On the ground floor are Greek and Roman works – sculpture, mosaics and painting.

ISAAKIEVSKIY SOBOR (St. Isaac's Cathedral) (228 A2), Isaakievskaya Ploshchad, contains a museum tracing the history of its construction. The interior has paintings, sculptures and mosaics by Russian masters, and good views from the dome.

KAZANSKIY SOBOR (Kazan Cathedral) (228 B2), Kazanskaya Ploshchad (built 1801–11), was modelled on St. Peter's in Rome. The interior has the icon of Our Lady of Kazan as well as the tomb of Marshal Kutuzov.

LETNIY DVORETS (Summer Palace) (228 C3), on the Neva River, was designed by Trezzini (1710–14). Plainly furnished, it is notable for its lack of luxury. Peter the Great designed the Letniy Sad (Summer Gardens), now a public park.

MUZEY-KVARTIRA A. S. PUSHKINA (Pushkin House-Museum) (228 B3), Reki Moiki Naberezhnaya 12, is Pushkin's last home. A room contains the clock whose hands still point to the hour of his death.

NEVSKIY PROSPEKT (228 B2) is lined with the finest stores, restaurants and cafés. Canal trips are from Anchikov Bridge.

PAVLOSK, 30 kilometers (18 miles) south of St. Petersburg, covers 607 hectares (1,500 acres) and was once the estate of Catherine the Great's son, Paul I. There

is a distinct similarity between Pavlovsk and Jefferson's buildings Monticello and the University of Virginia in the U.S.

PETERHOF, 30 kilometers (19 miles) west, was Peter the Great's summer palace. Only Monplaisir, a small building with picture galleries, was completed before he died. The Great Palace was completed in the 1750s, in the reign of Peter's daughter Elizabeth.

PETROPAVLOVSKAYA KREPOST (Peter and Paul Fortress) (228 B3), Ploshchad Revolutsii, was built for the defense of St. Petersburg. Peter the Great laid the cornerstone in 1703. It is now part of the History Museum.

PLOSHCHAD DEKABRISTOV (Decembrist's Square) (228 A3), commemorates the Russian revolutionaries who rebelled against the tsar in 1825. A statue of Peter the Great tops a boulder in the square.

RUSSKIY MUZEY (Russian Museum) (228 C2), Mikhailovsky Palace, Inzhenernaya Ulitsa 4/2, contains works of Russian art, including painting and drawings.

TSARSKOE SELO (Tsar's Village) ★, is 25 kilometers (15 miles) from St. Petersburg. Peter the Great bought an estate here for his wife. Alexander Palace is closed to the public, and is surrounded by a park with a Chinese village.
Dacha A. S. Pushkina (Pushkin's Dacha) is the house which Pushkin and his wife rented in the summer of 1831.
Yekaterinskiy Dvorets (Catherine Palace), Komsomolskaya Ulitsa, was originally a stone house commissioned by Catherine I in 1717. Her daughter Elizabeth brought in the architect Rastrelli to extend it and create the baroque façade. In the park is a Turkish bath, a pavilion, and a cemetery where Catherine buried her pet dogs.

VASILYEVSKIY OSTROV (Vasilyevskiy Island) (228 A3), lies in a fork of the Neva River. The first government buildings

(Twelve Colleges) were built here and the Menshikovsky Dvorets (Palace) is now a museum of 18th-century life. At the east point of the island (Strelka) are two lighthouses.

SAMARKAND ★
UZBEKISTAN *pop. 470,000*

Samarkand dates from 329 BC, but it achieved its greatest recognition in the 14th and 15th centuries when it served as the capital of Turkish Timur's central Asian empire. Today it offers mosques, mausoleums and *medressehs*. Of interest are the ancient Observatory of Ulugbeg, the *medressehs* of Ulugbeg and Tillya-Kari, and ruins of Bibi-Khanum mosque.

GUR-EMIR MAVZOLEY (Mausoleum) is an outstanding monument with geometric patterns and topped with a blue dome. Timur's tomb lies under a slab of jade inside, marked with the epitaph "Were I alive today, mankind would tremble."

SUZDAL (221 B3) ★
RUSSIAN FEDERATION

The long history of Vladimir and Suzdal has given these twin cities many historic sites. During the reign of the Vladimir-Suzdal princes, the arts flourished, and a new school of painting developed.

KREMLIN is surrounded by ramparts and turrets. Inside stands the 13th-century Rozhdenstvenny Sobor (Cathedral of the Nativity) with five onion domes studded with stars. The interior has rich frescoes.

▲ TASHKENT
UZBEKISTAN *pop. 2,000,000*

Tashkent is the capital of Uzbekistan and the main city in the Ferghana Valley. Since a 1966 earthquake only a few monuments remain: the Alisher Navoi Opera House, the Berak-Khan Medresseh, and the Besh Agach Theater.

The Uzbek State Museum of Art has carvings and embroideries; the Museum of Applied Art has crafts and jewelry; and the Antique Jewelry Museum has a collection of Asian stones.

TBILISI (221 C1)
GEORGIA *pop. 1,279,000*

Ancient Tbilisi, capital of Georgia, was fortified in the 4th century BC. Reminders of its vibrant past still survive. Ruins of the Narikal Fortress date from the 4th century BC, while the Cathedral of the Assumption and the Zion Temple all are 6th-century structures.

A cable car climbs 600-meter (1,970-foot) Mount Mtatsminda, the highest point in Tbilisi.

VLADIMIR (221 B3)
RUSSIAN FEDERATION *pop. 300,000*

Vladimir (founded 1108) has Golden Gates (1164) copied from those in Kiyev.

DMITRIEVSKY SOBOR (St. Dimitri's Cathedral) was built in stone (1197) and its exterior has exceptional bas reliefs of birds, plants and animals.

USPENSKY SOBOR (Assumption Cathedral) has five golden domes and tombs of the Vladimir-Suzdal princes.

YALTA (221 B2)
UKRAINE *pop. 80,000*

Yalta is in a large, natural amphitheater facing the Black Sea and sheltered by mountains. It enjoys an exceptionally mild climate and has catered to health seekers for more than a century.

BOTANICHESKY SAD (Nikitsky Botanical Gardens) is about 8 kilometers (5 miles) east of Yalta. It has a collection of 8,000 species of ornamental plants.

CHEKHOV MEMORIALNY MUSEI (Chekhov Memorial Museum), Kirov Street 112, is where Chekhov wrote *The Three Sisters* and *The Cherry Orchard*.

LIVADIA, 3 kilometers (2 miles) west of Yalta, was built as the summer palace of the tsars in Italian Renaissance style. In February 1945 it was the site of the Yalta Conference, where plans were made for the Allied defeat of Germany, as well as guidelines for the founding of the U.N.

RUSSIAN FEDERATION

SLOVAK REPUBLIC

THE SLOVAKS SAW THEMSELVES AS THE NEGLECTED HALF OF CZECHOSLOVAKIA, AND THIS EVENTUALLY CAUSED THE COUNTRIES TO SPLIT ON JANUARY 1, 1993. ECONOMICALLY POOR THOUGH IT MAY BE, THE SLOVAK REPUBLIC IS RICH IN NATURAL BEAUTY, IN PARTICULAR THE IMPOSING TATRA MOUNTAINS. THIS IS AN AREA FOR WALKING IN SUMMER, SKIING IN WINTER, AND WATCHING FOR WILD BOAR AND BEARS THAT STILL LIVE IN THE FORESTS ON THE LOWER SLOPES OF THE TATRAS. NEARBY IS THE APTLY NAMED SLOVENSKY RAJ, THE SLOVAK PARADISE, A GENTLER REGION OF RIVERS AND GORGES, FORESTS AND FALLS, AND THE DOBSINA ICE CAVE, A HUGE UNDERGROUND FROZEN LAKE.

IF EMPHASIS IS PLACED ON THE COUNTRYSIDE, IT IS BECAUSE THE SLOVAK CAPITAL, BRATISLAVA, CANNOT HOPE YET TO COMPETE WITH ITS NEIGHBORS, PRAGUE, VIENNA AND BUDAPEST.

Left BEAUTIFUL STRBSKE PLESO IN THE HIGH TATRAS MOUNTAINS
Above THERE ARE STILL BROWN BEARS TO BE SPOTTED IN THE MOUNTAINS IN THE SLOVAK REPUBLIC

THINGS TO KNOW

- **AREA**: 49,000 square kilometers (18,919 square miles)
- **POPULATION**: 5,310,000
- **CAPITAL**: Bratislava
- **LANGUAGE**: Slovak
- **RELIGION**: Roman Catholic
- **ECONOMY**: Engineering and chemicals, textiles and electronics, livestock production, arable crops, fruit and wine, forestry.
- **ELECTRICITY**: 220 volts, continental two-round-pin plugs. Adaptor and/or transformer required for non-continental appliances.
- **PASSPORT REQUIREMENTS**: Required for U.S. citizens.
- **VISA REQUIREMENTS**: Not required for stays of under 30 days.
- **DUTY-FREE ITEMS**: 250 cigarettes or corresponding amounts of other tobacco products; 2 liters of wine; 1 liter of liquor; ½ liter of cologne; gifts of up to 1,000 crowns in value and personal items suitable to the length and purpose of visit (clothing, personal jewelry, tools, sports equipment, video cameras, still cameras, portable typewriters, radios, cassette players, etc). The import of pure alcohol or pornographic items is prohibited.
- **CURRENCY**: The currency unit is the Slovak *crown* (*Slovenská koruna: Sk*), divided into 100 *hellers* (*halier*). Visitors may not import or export any local currency; if currency is purchased prior to entering the country it may be confiscated. There is no limit to the import of foreign currency, but it must be declared on a written attachment to the visa. German *Marks* and U.S. dollars are easily exchanged and sometimes accepted in payment.
- **STORE OPENING HOURS**: 8am–6pm Monday–Friday, 8am–7 or 8pm Thursday, 8am–2pm Saturday.
- **BANK OPENING HOURS**: 8am–12 noon Monday–Friday and often 1:30–3:30pm.
- **BEST BUYS**: Carved wooden items (axes, kitchen articles, toys), ceramics from Modra and Stupava, leather, fur coats

HISTORY

Slav tribes occupied the area of the present-day Slovak Republic during the 5th century AD. The arrival of the Magyars in the 10th century spelled the end of the Great Moravian Empire of which the Slovak Republic had been a part.

For a thousand years the country was part of Hungary, ruled by Hungarian lord-bishops. When Budapest fell to the Turks in 1541, however, Bratislava became the capital of Hungary.

The situation whereby any Slovak with ambitions to rise from the peasantry had no choice but to become Magyarized became intolerable in the 19th century, the age of nationalism.

Slovak writers and clerics promoted their native language and culture, but independence from Hungary only came after World War I, when Slovaks joined with the Czechs to form the new Republic of Czechoslovakia.

With the occupation of Bohemia and Moravia by Nazi Germany in 1939 the nominally independent Slovak state was established.

The Slovak National Uprising of 1944 was put down by the German army after months of fierce fighting. Between 1948 and 1989 Slovaks shared the same dismal fate as Czechs in communist Czechoslovakia.

Nationalist grievances remained, and found expression after the fall of communism; in 1993 Slovak and Czech politicians agreed to separate their countries, and since January 1, 1993, the Slovak Republic has been truly independent for the first time in its history.

FOOD AND DRINK

A typically rather heavy Central European cuisine is made more exciting by Hungarian influences like the extensive use of paprika.

Mutton and goose make a change from pork and chicken, and fish such as trout and carp are bred in ponds.

Sheep's cheese is widely available, and a favorite dish with just about everyone is *halušky*, noodles with cheese sauce and diced bacon.

Patisseries accompany strong Turkish style coffee, while alcoholic drinks include excellent wines from the vineyards in the plains and along the southern fringe of the mountains as well as the gin-like *borovička* and the plum-based spirit, *slivovice*.

SPORTS AND RECREATION

Soccer and tennis enjoy an enthusiastic following in the Slovak Republic, but the country's rugged terrain makes it a leader in the provision and enjoyment of outdoor recreation of all kinds.

Every child learns how to ski, and ice hockey is a popular sport. There are endless opportunities for walking and climbing in the mountains.

Sailing and other watersports take place on a number of large artificial lakes and every town has a swimming pool.

Mountains and forests harbor an abundance of game for the hunter.

GETTING AROUND

Numerous border crossings link the Slovak Republic to the Czech Republic, Austria, Hungary, the Ukraine and Poland. Bratislava (Ivánka) Airport is served by an increasing number of international flights.

Internal flights are limited, but it is possible to fly from Bratislava to Poprad to get to the High Tatra Mountains.

The road system has been extensively modernized, though there are few freeways and mountain roads require drivers to observe special caution.

Public transportation by train and bus is cheap and every settlement is served. Local trains can be very slow.

Drivers and passengers must wear seat belts. Children under 12 may not travel in the front seat.

Speed limits are 65 k.p.h. (35 m.p.h.) in town (indicated by the place-name sign), 90 k.p.h. (55 m.p.h.) out of town and 110 k.p.h. (65 m.p.h.) on highways. Fines must be paid on the spot.

There is no lower limit for consuming alcohol before driving.

ARCHITECTURAL BEAUTY

Traditional rural architecture has been preserved in many Slovak villages. Timber farmhouses, set at right angles to the street, have steeply pitched roofs and are usually only one room wide. Perfectly conserved examples can be seen in a number of open-air museums or *skanzens*, like the one outside the town of Martin in Central Slovak Republic, but perhaps the most evocative buildings are those in the village of Vlkolinec, saved from change and progress by the village's remoteness – until recently it could only be reached on foot! Near the town of Ruzomberok, Vlkolinec has now been declared a World Heritage Site by U.N.E.S.C.O.

AUTOMOBILE CLUB
Slovensky Automotoklub
(Slovak Republic Automobile Club) has its headquarters at Martincikova 20, Bratislava. The symbol ▲ beside a city name indicates the presence of a AAA-affiliated automobile club branch. Not all auto clubs offer full travel services to AAA members.

and hats, sheepskins, traditional blouses and shirts, liquor (*slivovice* plum brandy, *borvicka* gin), glass.

- **PUBLIC HOLIDAYS:** New Year's Day and establishment of Slovak Republic, January 1; Easter Monday; May Day, May 1; Day of Liberation, May 8; Saints Cyril and Methodius, July 5; Anniversary of Slovak National Uprising, August 29; Christmas, December 24–26.
- **NATIONAL TOURIST OFFICES:** There is no tourist office in New York for the Slovak Republic, but try Slovakia Travel (no address available) Tel: 212/213 3865 Bratislava Tourist Office no address available Bratislava Slovak Republic Tel: 427 212205/5661575
- **AMERICAN EMBASSY:** no address available Bratislava Slovak Republic Tel: 427 333338 (changing to 5333338)

ACCOMMODATIONS

There are over 1,000 hotels in the country, classified by star ratings from one (basic) to five (deluxe). These are being added to and older hotels are undergoing modernization. More private residents are providing bed and breakfast facilities and there are numerous campgrounds.

TIPPING

It is customary to round up the bill at a restaurant or give a gratuity of 10 percent, likewise with taxis. Hotel porters should be given a tip of a few *crowns*, as should restroom attendants.

USEFUL EXPRESSIONS IN SLOVAK

good morning	dobré ráno
good afternoon	dobré odpoledne
good-bye	na shledanou
please	prosím
thankyou	dekuju
castle	hrad
château	zámok
church	skostol
square	námestie
city hall	radnica

PRINCIPAL TOURING AREAS

BRATISLAVA AND SURROUNDING AREA

In the south-west corner of the country, almost within sight of Vienna 64 kilometers (40 miles) upstream on the Danube, is the Slovak Republic's cosmopolitan capital, Bratislava, with a wealth of museums and architectural treasures.

Beginning in the suburbs, the forested heights and vine-clad lower slopes of the Little Carpathian Mountains stretch away to the north east.

The old town of Trnava, the Slovak Rome with many churches, is 48 kilometers (30 miles) away, while 32 kilometers (20 miles) further on is the most prestigious of the country's many spa towns, Piešťany, which became one of Europe's most fashionable resorts in the years before World War I.

CENTRAL SLOVAK REPUBLIC

This is the country's mountainous heartland, centered on industrial towns like Žilina and Martin, and ancient mining cities like Kremnica, Banská Bystrica and Banská Štiavnica. The Great and Little Fatra ranges are little known to outsiders, but immensely popular with local ramblers and skiers.

River gorges are guarded by romantically sited castles, like ruined Strečno on the Váh River or Oravský Zámok perched on a high crag above the Orava River.

THE TATRAS AND EASTERN SLOVAK REPUBLIC

The Low Tatra ranges attract locals for winter sports and summer fresh air, but the Slovak Republic's most spectacular mountains are the High Tatras, a series of jagged peaks rising abruptly from the plain. Here are old upland resorts like Štrbské Pleso, Starý Smokovec and Tatranská Lomnica, with ski runs and hiking trails aplenty, and some of Europe's last bears lurking in the forest.

The Spiš region is dominated by the huge ruined fortress of Spišský Hrad, and has several fine old towns like Kežmarok and Levoča, founded by German settlers who migrated here in the Middle Ages.

Košice is the metropolis of the Eastern Slovak Republic, a region where there is a minority ethnic Ukrainian population and villages with wonderful timber churches.

Ždiar is noted for its folk costumes, worn on Sundays and holidays.

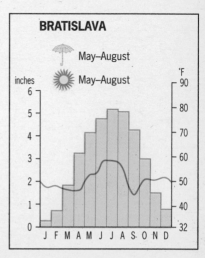

PLACES OF INTEREST

★ HIGHLIGHTS ★	
Bardejov	(see p.239)
Bratislava	
Dóm (Cathedral)	(see p 238)
Hrad (Castle)	(see p.238)
Námestie (Square)	(see p 238)
Levoča	(see p.239)
Vysoké Tatry	(see p.239)

BRATISLAVA ★
BRATISLAVA-VIDIEK *pop. 444,500*

One of the most fascinating cities along the Danube, Bratislava straddles the mighty river at the point where the Slovak, Hungarian and Austrian frontiers meet. Its formidable-looking castle perches on the last crag of the Carpathian Mountains, at its foot the intricate lanes and alleyways of the medieval city which grew up in the 12th and 13th centuries, but whose character has been ruined by insensitive building during the communist years.

BRATISLAVSKÝ HRAD (Castle) ★ With its four corner towers, the massive and much rebuilt castle has a very distinctive outline and is nicknamed "the upturned table" due to its towers.

Since independence it has become one of the symbols of Slovak statehood and is used for government and ceremonial purposes as well as housing the collections of the National Museum. The stiff climb up to the castle terrace is well worth it for the marvelous view over the Danube and the city.

DÓM SV. MARTINA ★ (St. Martin's Cathedral) was the setting for the coronation of no fewer than 11 Hungarian monarchs, crowned here during the Turkish occupation of Budapest.

An outstanding example of Gothic architecture, it has been joined as a prominent city landmark by the modern S.N.P. Bridge which carries an expressway over the Danube River.

HLAVNÉ NÁMESTIE ★ (Main Square) is at the heart of the Old Town. The statue of Roland on a Renaissance fountain looks towards the Radnica (Old Town Hall) housing collections of the City Museum.

MICHALSKÁ BRÁNA (Michael's Gate) is the only remaining gateway of several which formed a part of the city fortifications. Its lower parts are Gothic, its cap, 51 meters (167 feet) high, baroque. The streets running south from its archway are lined with splendid burghers' houses and aristocratic palaces. This is the university quarter, scene of the ferment that helped to bring down communism in late 1989, when students and citzens formed the movement called Public Against Violence, the Slovak equivalent of the Czech Civic Forum.

NÁRODNÁ GALÉRIA (National Gallery), an ultra-modern structure facing the Danube, is the best place in which to get acquainted with Slovak art, whose 20th century practitioners like Ludovit Fulla and Martin Benka painted many colorful scenes of traditional life.

SLAVÍN is the monument in the city center commemorating the many Soviet soldiers who fell while liberating the city in the last months of World War II.

BANSKÁ BYSTRICA
CENTRAL SLOVAK REPUBLIC
pop. 51,000

This medieval mining city above the lush valley of the Hron River was built on the profits from the silver and copper ores in the surrounding mountains. The long and sloping marketplace is lined with the fine 15th- and 16th-century houses. Banská Bystrica was at the center of the Slovak National Uprising (S.N.P.) of 1944, when the army joined partisans to redeem the country from the strain of collaboration with Nazi Germany. The revolt was crushed only after bitter fighting. These stirring events are commemorated in the futuristic SNP Memorial building. Other old mining towns in the area include Kremnica, with its ancient royal mint, and Banská Štiavnica, with a developing open-air museum of mining.

SOCIAL CONSCIENCE

Juraj Janosik (1688–1713) was Slovakia's Robin Hood, a genial brigand who is supposed to have robbed the rich to pay the poor. Janosik was born in the village of Terchova in the mountains of the Central Slovak Republic, and turned to brigandage when his father was punished by his feudal master for nursing his sick wife rather than working in the fields. Janosik's short life came to an end when he was betrayed and put to death in the marketplace of the little town of Liptovsky Mikulas.Terchova is now a mountain resort, dominated by a stunning metal sculpture of its local hero.

BARDEJOV ★
EASTERN SLOVAK REPUBLIC
pop. 30,000
This ancient town was at its most prosperous in the 15th and 16th centuries. Its well-preserved walls date from the 14th century. The marketplace is surrounded by colorful merchants' houses, while the town hall has a fine collection of icons. Bardejov has a substantial minority population of Ukrainians, and close to the town's spa (6 kilometers/4 miles north) is an open-air museum with timber buildings.

LEVOČA ★
EASTERN SLOVAK REPUBLIC
pop. 13,000
The most exquisite of the old towns of the Spiš district, Levoča has a broad main square lined with burghers' mansions. In the middle of the square stands

a fine example of Renaissance architecture, the town hall, while St. James's Church has one of the country's greatest art treasures, the wonderful altarpiece by the famous 14th-century woodcarver Master Paul. A nearby hilltop is crowned by a church which is the scene in July of a popular pilgrimage.

SPIŠSKÝ HRAD (SPIŠ CASTLE)
EASTERN SLOVAK REPUBLIC
Now a spectacular ruin, this was the largest castle in Central Europe, dominating the main east–west route through the Slovak Republic. The crag on which it is built was first inhabited in the 5th millennium BC. The castle withstood attack by Tartars in 1241, but was abandoned by its owners in the 18th century.

VYSOKÉ TATRY (HIGH TATRAS) ★
EASTERN SLOVAK REPUBLIC
The main range of the High Tatras is only a few miles long, but with its series of jagged peaks it is one of the most spectacular mountain chains in Europe. Tourism is exceptionally well developed, with a mountain railway linking the string of mountain resorts among the glorious conifer forests which clad the lower slopes of the mountains.

Štrbské Pleso is centered around a lake and is characterised by ultramodern hotels and excellent ski facilities, while the older resorts of Tatranská Lomnica and Starý Smokovec have a charming turn-of-the-century atmosphere.

The Tatras are as popular in summer as in winter, with many miles of hiking trails leading up from the forest towards the peaks. The highest summit is at Gerlachovský štít (2,655 meters/8,711 feet), while Lomnický štít (2,631 meters/8,635 feet) can be reached by cable car. The whole area is a national park, and is preserving the beauty and wildlife that includes animals like wolves and even bears, which are still rare in other parts of Europe. There is a good museum of the national park at Tatranská Lomnica.

FRANCE

FRANCE IS FOOD. IT IS ALSO ART AND HISTORY, ARCHITECTURE AND LANDSCAPE, PARIS AND PROVENCE; BUT ABOVE AND BEYOND ALL OF THESE, IT IS FOOD. INDEED THE MAP OF FRANCE READS LIKE A MENU: ARMAGNAC, CHAMPAGNE, BEAUJOLAIS, BORDEAUX, COGNAC, CAMEMBERT, ROQUEFORT, CHABLIS, BRIE. TOWNS AND VILLAGES ARE UNITED BY THEIR BUTCHER, BAKER, CAFÉS AND MARKETS. YOU'LL FIND BETTER FOOD IN FRANCE THAN ANYWHERE ELSE IN THE WORLD.

THIS IS A CULTURED COUNTRY, WHERE POLITICS AND ART ARE NOT JUST RESERVED FOR AN EDUCATED ELITE; THE WRITER IS RESPECTED AND THE ARTIST REVERED. FLAUBERT, ZOLA, SARTRE, MONET, DEGAS, MANET, TOULOUSE-LAUTREC AND CÉZANNE ARE JUST SOME OF THE NAMES OF FRENCH CULTURE, AS FAMILIAR AS THOSE OF FRENCH CUISINE.

Left THIS *BOULANGERIE* BOASTS "BREAD FOR EVERY OCCASION"
Above left SUNFLOWERS WERE AN INSPIRATION FOR VINCENT VAN GOGH
Above right BEAUJOLAIS GRAPES PRODUCE THE WORLD-FAMOUS WINES

Things to Know

- **Area:** 551,670square kilometers (220,668 square miles)
- **Population:** 56,184,000
- **Capital:** Paris
- **Language:** French
- **Religion:** Largely Roman Catholic.
- **Economy:** Industry. mining, agriculture. aircraft, autos, textiles, chemicals are chief products. Large coal, iron ore, bauxite deposits. Main crops: wheat, barley, dairy products; many small, diversified farms. Leading wine producer; tourist-related industries important..
- **Passport Requirements:** Required for U.S. citizens.
- **Visa Requirements:** Not required for stays up to three months.
- **Duty-Free Items:** Purchased duty-free or outside of the European Union – 200 cigarettes or 100 cigarillos or 50 cigars or 250 grams tobacco; 1 liter of spirits or 2 liters of fortified wine; 60ml of perfume; 250ml of toilet water; 500 grams of coffee; 100 grams of tea; 300 francs' of other goods, sports equipment; two still cameras of different sizes with 10 rolls of film for each; one movie camera with 10 rolls of film; video equipment; other personal belongings. Also see *The European Union*, p.5.
- **Value Added Tax:** France levies a Value Added Tax on goods purchased within its borders. You can avoid paying the V.A.T., however, by asking to have the tax deducted from the price of almost any object you buy to take home as part of your luggage. You also can be reimbursed by applying for a refund when you leave the country.
  To receive a V.A.T. refund, you must have purchased goods costing a minimum of 400 francs, including taxes. Present the pink copy of your sales invoice and a stamped envelope supplied by the vendor to the French customs official before you register your luggage. The customs official will mail the sales ticket back to the vendor from whom you made your purchases and he or she will mail you a refund.

History

Inhabited by the Celts and known as Gaul, southern France became a Roman province with Julius Caesar's conquest in 58–51 BC. Barbarian invasions ended Roman domination in the 5th century and resulted in the formation of a kingdom under the Franks. Clovis I was the first Christian king of France, but Charlemagne, who ruled from 768 to 814 AD, was historically more important, for he was the first of a succession of rulers of the Holy Roman Empire. Charlemagne's death resulted in partition of the empire into domains – Normandy, Aquitaine, Burgundy, Flanders and others.

From this period until the 17th century, successive French kings struggled to control the great vassalries and unite the country politically and territorially. These were the times of the Hundred Years' War, the Thirty Years' War and numerous struggles with English and Spanish kings, popes and barons. The land became a checkerboard, with pieces alternately lost and gained. Civil war further divided the populace over religious policies. Eventually a centralized monarchy emerged, only to perish with the capture of the Bastille in 1789. With the rise of Napoleon Bonaparte, France embarked upon a glorious era that lasted until the Little Corporal's defeat at Waterloo in 1815.

The Bourbons returned to power, and France was again a monarchy until the revolution of 1848 made the country a republic. Napoleon III established the Second Empire in 1852, but the country reverted to being a republic after the Franco-Prussian War in 1870. In the 20th century, France endured both world wars and following the second, the Fourth Republic was established. Numerous governments, political parties and a fight to retain Algeria as a French possession were some of the country's concerns during the 1950s. As France sought to solve these problems, General

Charles de Gaulle was recalled to power in 1958 as premier, and the people of France voted to establish the Fifth Republic, which continues today.

Socialist candidate François Mitterand was elected president in 1981, and France's banks and major industries were nationalized. In 1986 France began a privatization program in which some 80 state-owned companies were sold. Mitterand was elected to a second seven-year term in 1988. Since then the the right-wing parties gained increasing power, and in 1995, the neo-Gaullist leader, Jacques Chirac, was elected president.

FOOD AND DRINK

Whether selecting from the menus of tiny bistros on the Riviera or those of elegant Parisian restaurants, dining is always a pleasure. The French custom of eating the main meal at noon may seem sensible after a strenuous morning of sightseeing. To accompany a meal, inexpensive local wines in carafes rather than bottles are a wise selection. The *plat du jour* (dish of the day) is invariably delicious. Meals generally consist of *hors d'oeuvres*, an *entrée* of meat or fish with vegetables, cheese and fruit or dessert.

Each region of France has its own culinary specialties. Burgundy, noted in particular for fine food and wine, is known for *boeuf bourguignon*, a stew made from beef marinated in red wine, as well as for *quenelles* (pike dumplings) and artichoke hearts stuffed with *foie gras* (goose liver), sauerkraut, and Strasbourg apple tarts with cream. In Brittany the emphasis is on seafood, including oysters, crawfish and sardines. *Homard à l'américaine,* lobster with cream, is a specialty. The Provençal dishes of the Riviera are heady with garlic. Other acclaimed dishes are the *bouillabaisse* of Marseilles, a fish soup, and the *salade niçoise* of Nice, a combination of anchovies, celery, olives, peppers, tomatoes and tuna. The Île-de-France boasts *Châteaubriand aux pommes,*

steak with apples, and *crêpes suzette*; Rouen, in Normandy, is noted for duck; and Languedoc for its *cassoulet,* stew of goose, mutton, pork and beans. From the Champagne region come preparations of succulent ham, shrimp, trout and the celebrated Champagne wine. Salmon from the Loire, chicken dishes of Gascony and the fluffy omelettes of Mont-Saint-Michel are other fine examples of French gastronomy. France produces around 347 different cheeses, including Camembert, Brie, Roquefort, and many other blue cheeses.

SPORTS AND RECREATION

The French relish spectator sports like bicycle racing, soccer, boxing and horse racing. The national Tour de France bicycle race draws international attention for three weeks at the beginning of July. Boxing takes place in Paris at the Palais Omnisports de Paris-Bercy, which is also the main stadium for basketball, and at the Stade Pierre de Coubertin. Tennis, notably the French Open in late May/early June, takes place at the Stade Roland-Garros in Paris. Popular racetracks near Paris are Auteuil, Chantilly, Longchamp, Vincennes, and St. Cloud. The latter two also have golfing greens. Golf links and tennis courts are generally found in French resorts. Yachting, swimming, fishing, golf, tennis and horseback riding can be enjoyed at the Riviera resorts and at the Atlantic coastal resorts of Biarritz and Deauville. International yachting regattas at coastal resorts are held in summer. Ski resorts in the Alps and Pyrénées offer all winter sports.

GETTING AROUND

Driving through the French countryside is an experience no one should miss, but navigating a car through the large cities, especially Paris, should be avoided. Many country roads are tree-lined, clean, fast and well marked. Generally, road surfaces are in good repair. Rules of the road are similar to those in the United States. Driving is on the right and passing on the left. Priority is given to traffic

- **CURRENCY:** The currency unit is the French *franc* (FF), divided into 100 *centimes*. Due to currency fluctuations, the exchange rate is subject to frequent change. There is no import duty on the import or export of currency.
- **BANK OPENING HOURS:** 9am–noon and 2–4pm Monday–Friday; some banks are open Saturday and closed Monday.
- **STORE OPENING HOURS:** 9am or 10am to 6:30pm or 7:30pm Monday–Saturday; some food stores open Sunday morning; small stores are closed Monday; some department stores are closed Monday morning; stores in small towns often close noon to 2pm.
- **BEST BUYS:** Fashionable clothing, perfume, jewelry, gloves and antiques.
- **PUBLIC HOLIDAYS:** January 1; Easter Sunday and Monday; Labor Day, May 1; Anniversary 1945 Victory in Europe Day, May 8; Ascension Day; Whitsunday and Whitmonday; Bastille Day, July 14; Assumption Day, August 15; All Saints' Day, November 1; Armistice Day, November 11; December 25.
- **USEFUL TELEPHONE NUMBERS:**
  Police 17
  Fire 18
  Ambulance 18
- **NATIONAL TOURIST OFFICES:**
  French Government Tourist Office
  Suite 222, 610 Fifth Avenue
  New York
  NY 10020
  Tel: 900/990 0040 (50¢ per minute)
  Also Offices In:
  Chicago, Dallas and Beverly Hills
  French Government Tourist Office
  178 Piccadilly
  London
  W1V 0AL
  Tel: 0891 244123
  Fax: 0171 493 6594
- **AMERICAN EMBASSY**
  2 Avenue Gabriel
  75382 Paris 8
  France
  Tel: 1 43 12 22 22
  Fax: 1 42 66 97 83

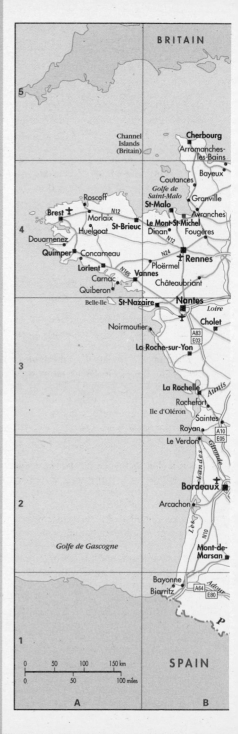

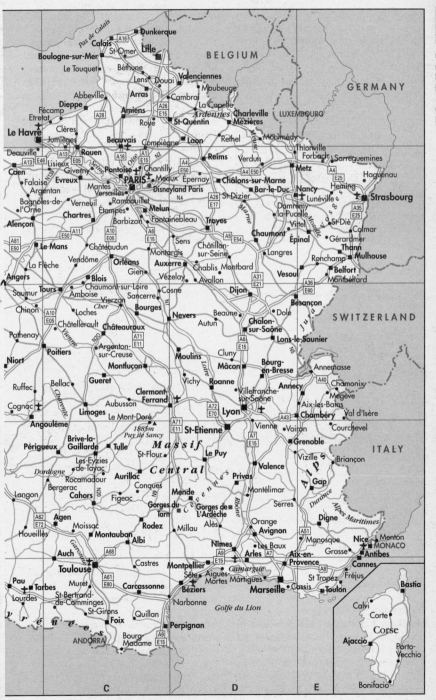

Dunkerque
Calais
Boulogne-sur-Mer
St-Omer
Lille
Le Touquet
Béthune
Lens
Douai
Valenciennes
BELGIUM
GERMANY
LUXEMBOURG
Maubeuge
Abbeville
Arras
Cambrai
La Capelle
Ardennes
Charleville-Mézières
Monmédy
Thionville
Forbach
Sarreguemines
Dieppe
Amiens
Roye
St-Quentin
Laon
Rethel
Verdun
Metz
Haguenau
Fécamp
Etretat
Le Havre
Clères
Jumièges
Beauvais
Compiègne
Reims
Châlons-sur-Marne
Nancy
Heming
Lunéville
Strasbourg
Deauville
Rouen
Pontoise
Chantilly
Meaux
Epernay
Bar-le-Duc
St-Dié
Colmar
Caen
Lisieux
Giverny
PARIS
Disneyland Paris
Versailles
St-Dizier
Domrémy-la-Pucelle
Vittel
Gérardmer
Thann
Mulhouse
Falaise
Argentan
Bagnoles-de-l'Orne
Evreux
Mantes
Verneuil
Rambouillet
Etampes
Melun
Fontainebleau
Troyes
Chaumont
Epinal
Ronchamp
Belfort
Montbéliard
Alençon
Chartres
Barbizon
Sens
Châtillon-sur-Seine
Langres
Vesoul
Le Mans
Châteaudun
Vendôme
Montargis
Auxerre
Chablis
Montbard
Dijon
Besançon
SWITZERLAND
La Flèche
Orléans
Gien
Vézelay
Avallon
Angers
Blois
Chaumont-sur-Loire
Cosne
Tours
Amboise
Vierzon
Sancerre
Bourges
Nevers
Beaune
Dole
Saumur
Chinon
Loches
Châteauroux
Autun
Chalon-sur-Saône
Lons-le-Saunier
Pathenay
Châtellerault
Argenton-sur-Creuse
Moulins
Mâcon
Bourg-en-Bresse
Annemasse
Chamonix
Niort
Poitiers
Vichy
Roanne
Villefranche-sur-Saône
Annecy
Megève
Ruffec
Bellac
Gueret
Clermont-Ferrand
Aix-les-Bains
Chambéry
Val d'Isère
Cognac
Limoges
Aubusson
Le Mont-Doré
Lyon
Vienne
Courchevel
Angoulême
1885m
Puy de Sancy
St-Etienne
Voiron
Grenoble
ITALY
Périgueux
Brive-la-Gaillarde
Tulle
St-Flour
Massif
Le Puy
Vizille
Gap
Briançon
Les-Eyzies-de-Tayac
Rocamadour
Aurillac
Central
Valence
Langon
Bergerac
Conques
Mende
Montélimar
Digne
Alpes Maritimes
Houeilles
Agen
Moissac
Cahors
Figeac
Gorges du Tarn
Gorges de l'Ardèche
Serres
Menton
MONACO
Auch
Montauban
Albi
Rodez
Millau
Alès
Orange
Avignon
Manosque
Nice
Antibes
Toulouse
Castres
Montpellier
Nîmes
Les Baux
Arles
Aix-en-Provence
Grasse
Cannes
Pau
Tarbes
Muret
Carcassonne
Sète
Aigues-Mortes
Martigues
Marseille
Cassis
St Tropez
Fréjus
Lourdes
St-Bertrand-de-Comminges
St-Girons
Foix
Narbonne
Béziers
Golfe du Lion
Toulon
Bastia
ANDORRA
Bourg-Madame
Perpignan
Calvi
Corte
Corse
Ajaccio
Porto-Vecchio
Bonifacio

emerging from the right, unless otherwise signposted. Low beams should be used in urban areas and the use of the horn kept to a minimum. In areas where there is no street lighting, parking lights should be left on wherever possible during evening hours.

> ### ACCOMMODATION BOOKING OFFICES
> Many French *départements* have accommodation booking offices under the name Loisirs d'Accueil. Usually charging no fee, they reserve hotels, gîtes and campgrounds. For a list of these offices send a stamped, addressed envelope to the French Government Tourist Office.

The wearing of front and back seat belts, if fitted, is mandatory for the driver and passengers. A child under 10 cannot occupy a front seat unless in an approved fitted seat facing backward. The speed limit is 50 k.p.h. (31 m.p.h.) in town. In good weather, out-of-town limits are between 90 k.p.h. (55 m.p.h.) and 110 k.p.h. (68 m.p.h.), depending on the type of road, but these are reduced to between 80 k.p.h. (49 m.p.h.) and 100 k.p.h. (62 m.p.h.) in wet weather. Limits on toll motorways are 130 k.p.h. (80 m.p.h.) during good weather and 110 k.p.h. (65 m.p.h.) during wet, and 50 k.p.h. (31 m.p.h.) in fog when visibility is less than 50 meters (55 yards). There is a minimum speed limit of 80 k.p.h. (49 m.p.h.) for the outside lane on motorways during daylight hours with good visibility, on level ground. Visiting motorists are required to pay fines for violations on the spot with French francs or travelers' checks.

ACCOMMODATIONS
Hotels in France are rated from one to four stars. In special circumstances, an "L" is used to designate a deluxe rating. Hotels in Paris usually include breakfast in the price of the room. Hotels in the provinces may not include breakfast.

Logis de France, a state-run concern, operates more than 4,000 small, family-run, mostly one- and two-star hotels around France, except Paris. They are often near major highways, reasonably priced, and offer a good way to experience rural French customs.

Relais Routier signs inform travelers of nearby restaurants that offer substantial meals and often lodging at reasonable prices. Local tourist offices (*Syndicates d'Initiative* or *Offices de Tourisme*) can help you with hotel selections and other forms of lodging.

Youth hostels in France give priority to traveling young people. There are about 10,000 campgrounds, including 35 on castle grounds. Local tourist offices have specific information. While not required, an international camping *carnet* may be requested at "*castels et camping-caravanning*" campgrounds or the "*forets domaniales*" sites in state forests.

TIPPING
Tipping is a way of life in France. Nearly everyone who serves you expects a tip. Hotels and restaurants include a hefty service fee (up to 15 percent) in their bills, but waiters look for an additional 5 to 7 percent. The cloakroom attendant should receive a tip per item; a washroom attendant 2 francs and a doorman 5 francs. Some cabs have an official scale of charges, but it is usual to give about 10 percent of the fare.

PRINCIPAL TOURING AREAS
Note: For descriptions of cities in **bold type**, see individual city listings.

ALPS
This mighty barrier of mountains in the south east of France has some of the most spectacular scenery in Europe. Vacationers flock to its winter and summer resorts: Courchevel, Gap, Tignes, Val d'Isère and many other winter

resorts beckon skiers; Annecy, Digne and Talloires attract summer sunbathers; and Aix-les-Bains, Briançon, Chamonix and Megève provide all-year enjoyment.

AUVERGNE
In the heart of the Massif Central, this spa center has watering places at Le Mont-Dore, Royat and Vichy. The terrain near Clermont-Ferrand and Le Puy is known for its volcanic rock formations.

BASQUE COUNTRY AND THE PYRÉNÉES
The Pyrénées is one of the most attractive parts of France, with Atlantic beach resorts such as Biarritz and Hendaye, and scenic mountains. The Basque people express themselves through dancing and carnivals, poetry, playing pelota and vigorous campaigning for status as an independent nation.

BRITTANY
The sea plays a dominant role in the lives of the Bretons, whose 1,200-kilometer (746-mile) western coast is a jagged line of rocky cliffs and sandy beaches. This is a colorful region of fishing hamlets, native customs, prehistoric megaliths and unusual churches and cottages. Among the coastal towns are La Baule, Bénodet, Concarneau, Dinan and Quiberon; cities are Nantes, Rennes, Brest, St-Malo.

BURGUNDY
The ancient province of Bourgogne is renowned for incomparable wines and wonderful food. September and October are grape harvesting months. From May to September Burgundy is alive with concerts, wine fairs, festivals, plays and art exhibitions. Dijon, ancient capital of the Burgundian dukes, holds an annual Gastronomic Fair in November. Autun is rich in museums and art. Mâcon produces many high-quality wines; Vézelay was one of the most important pilgrimage sites during the Middle Ages.

CHAMPAGNE AND ALSACE-LORRAINE
Lying between Alsace-Lorraine and Paris in north-east France, Champagne hardly needs an introduction for its well-known bubbling wine. A good time to visit is during the autumn grape harvest. Visit the cathedral at **Reims**, where the Kings of France were crowned. Alsace-Lorraine is French with a German accent. The region is best known for its beer, white wines and rich, distinctive cuisine. Strasbourg is here with its great rose-colored cathedral; Mulhouse is a major printing and textile center; and

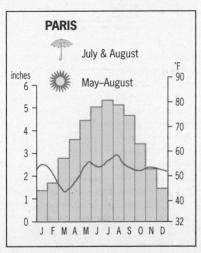

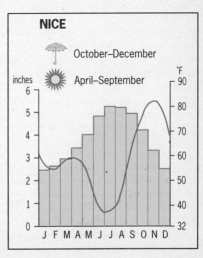

FRANCE

there are the resort towns of Gérardmer and Vittel. The Wine Road of the Vosges, vineyards and medieval villages and cities also are in this area.

DORDOGNE AND LES LANDES

One of the longest rivers in the country, the Dordogne is associated with wooded valleys, cliffs and the prehistoric caves around Les Eyzies-de-Tayac. Fortified towns, such as Domme and Monpazier, recall the medieval struggles between France and England. Here, between the Gironde River and almost to the Basque coast, lie Les Landes, a vast area of pine forests, lakes, sand dunes and beaches, noted for oysters, marinas and vineyards.

ÎLE-DE-FRANCE

Feudal castles, ancient forests, peaceful villages and scenes taken from the pages of French classics are everywhere. Check out the palaces of **Versailles**, Fontainebleau and Malmaison, the cathedral of Chartres and the village of Barbizon.

JURA MOUNTAINS

The Jura Mountains form a barrier some 230 kilometers (143 miles) long between France and Switzerland and make up a region of great natural beauty. The mountains are a challenge to those wanting to rough it and a haven to those seeking solitude and tranquility. The city of Bourg-en-Bresse, a striking combination of old and new, is at the foot of the Jura Mountains. Other important towns are the industrial centers of Champagnole and Dole, the home of Louis Pasteur.

LOIRE VALLEY

This magnificent château country attracts many visitors; the countryside is as beautiful as the fairy-tale castles that were built by French kings and nobles. Explore this enchanting area, preferably on a leisurely cruise ship that stops at the châteaux along the way. Blois, Cheverny, Amboise, Chinon, **Tours** and Saumur, as well as strikingly medieval Chaumont-sur-Loire and Montargis, are particularly worth visiting.

NORMANDY

Fertile farmlands, sandy beaches and resorts draw vacationers to the north-west province of Normandy in summer. Alençon is a former fortress noted for its lace making; Honfleur is the birthplace of Impressionist art; Louviers has its church of Notre-Dame; and Avranches boasts a view of Le Mont-St-Michel on its rocky island. Deauville, Trouville and Le Touquet are the resorts. The scene of Allied landings in World War II, many towns and buildings in this region were destroyed, but have been rebuilt.

RHÔNE VALLEY, LANGUEDOC AND PROVENCE

From **Lyon** to Marseille, the Rhône Valley is a treasure trove of Roman ruins. The vast arena and baths of **Nîmes**, the paved streets, mosaics and theater of Vaison-la-Romaine, and the great amphitheater and pagan burial grounds of Arles are found in this area. Orange, Avignon and Valence are a few of the cities steeped in centuries of history. Languedoc is another area for unusual historical excursions. Toulouse, foremost city in southern Gaul for many centuries, and the medieval city of Carcassonne merit a visit, as well as hilltop villages of Manosque, Méjanes and Meyragues. Les Stes Maries-de-la-Mer is in a marshy fen known as the Camargue that serves as a natural reserve.

RIVIERA AND CORSICA

From Marseille to Menton extends one of the world's most publicized play-grounds – the French Riviera, or Côte d'Azur. Along this strip of Mediterranean coast are colorful fishing ports and villages, luxury hotels, casinos, blue waters and the spectacular Corniche drive from Nice to Monaco. Visit La Napoule, Cassis, Èze, Le Lavandou, Miramar, Théoule-sur-Mer, Ste.-Maxime and St.-Tropez. For a change of pace, enjoy the mountainous beauty of Corsica. Ajaccio, the capital of Corsica (Corse), and Bastia, a medieval port, are accessible by either air or sea.

USEFUL EXPRESSIONS IN FRENCH

hello	bonjour
good morning	bonjour
good evening	bon soir
good night	bonne nuit
good bye	au revoir
please/thankyou	s'il vous plaît/merci
yes/no	oui/non
excuse me	excusez-moi
you're welcome	de rien/je vous en prie
Do you speak English?	parlez vous anglais?
I don't understand.	je ne comprends pas.
sorry	pardon
What is the time?	Quelle heure est-il?
How much is that?	Combien est-ce?
Where are the restrooms?	Où sont les toilettes?
I'd like ...	Je voudrais ...
Can you help me, please?	Pouvez-vous m'aider, s'il vous plaît?
Can you speak more slowly?	S'il vous plaît, parlez moins vite.
Do you take credit cards?	Acceptez-vous les cartes de crédit?
where/when/how	ou/quand/comment
hot/cold	chaud/froid
old/new	vieux/vieille (f) nouveau/nouvelle (f)
open/closed	ouvert/fermé
no smoking	défense de fumer
The check, please.	L'addition, s'il vous plaît
yesterday	hier
today	aujourd'hui
tomorrow	demain
breakfast	le petit déjeuner
lunch	le déjeuner
dinner	le dîner
entrance	entrée
exit	sortie
stores	les magasins
market	le marché
bakery	la boulangerie
butcher	la boucherie
food store	l'alimentation
pharmacy	la pharmacie
delicatessen	la charcuterie
fishmongers	la poissonnerie

railroad station	la gare
railroad platform	le quai
subway station	la station de métro
gas station	un poste à essence
parking lot	un parking
straight on	tout droit
right	à droite
left	à gauche
opposite	en face de
behind	derrière
in front of	devant
before	avant
near	près
here/there	ici/là

DAYS OF THE WEEK

Sunday	dimanche
Monday	lundi
Tuesday	mardi
Wednesday	mercredi
Thursday	jeudi
Friday	vendredi
Saturday	samedi

NUMBERS

1	un/une
2	deux
3	trois
4	quatre
5	cinq
6	six
7	sept
8	huit
9	neuf
10	dix
11	onze
20	vingt
21	vingt-et-un
22	vingt deux
30	trente
40	quarante
50	cinquante
60	soixante
70	soixante-dix
80	quatre-vingt
90	quatre-vingt-dix
100	cent
1,000	mille

FRANCE

PARIS

pop. 2,152,333
(Metropolitan area *pop.10, 651,000*)

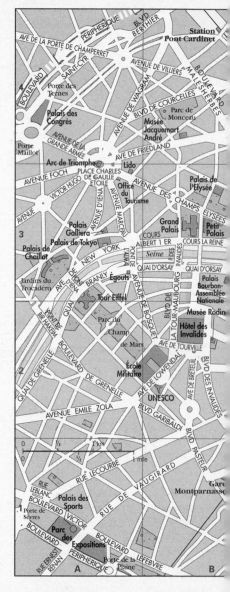

If it seems that everything has been said about Paris, then it is up to the visitor to discover the city for themselves, for it offers infinite variety. It is a city for late-nighters, early risers, strollers, culture-vultures, for high fashion, low-lifers, gourmands, ascetics, flower-givers, flesh-seekers, wine-drinkers, the *avant-garde*, the old hat, lovers of buildings, lovers of art, or just plain lovers.

Spend your time walking in parks, along leafy boulevards, looking in shop windows, sitting in cafés, or overdosing on art in the overwhelming Louvre or the Musée d'Orsay. Visit Versailles, Montmartre and Montparnasse. Paris is the sum of the great names that have lived, loved, painted, described and shaped her: Eiffel, Hemingway, Trotsky, Picasso, Piaf, Rodin, Scott Fitzgerald. It combines the great with the everyday: markets, *boulangeries*, unshaven men carrying *baguettes* through back streets, fur-clad women leading poodles in parks.

Images of the Eiffel Tower, of bookstalls along the Seine and the gardens surrounding the Louvre are all enhanced by the city's grand perspective.

Culturally, Paris easily lives up to expectations. The Louvre, Notre-Dame, the architecturally tradition-shattering Centre Pompidou, theaters and opera all delight the eye as well as the ear.

Paris is a contemporary collage of very different communities, with a backdrop of narrow streets, village-style shops, bars, bistros and markets, faded apartment buildings and striking new ones, parks and gardens, courtyards and shadowed alleys.

As a mecca for lovers, Paris casts a romantic net across café tables and along the banks of the Seine. High-fashion Paris centers in the *salons* of the great *couturiers* and at ultra-chic boutiques.

Gastronomically, Paris manages to continue to specialize in elaborate and calorific delicacies in an age of health consciousness and fast-food.

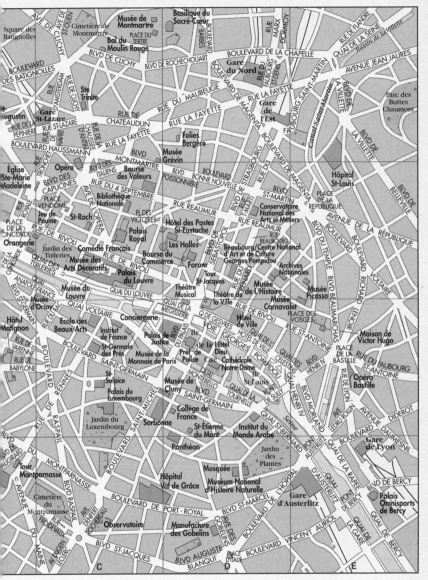

HISTORY

Paris' history stretches back over 2,000 years. A Gallic tribe, the Parisii, erected fortifications around their settlement on an island in the Seine. The Romans razed it and built their own city, *Lutetia*. A series of Hun invasions were later repelled under the leadership of Gen-eviève, who was to become the city's patron saint. The besieging Franks and their Christian king, Clovis I, made Paris their capital in 508.

It remained so until 584 when later Franks removed the crown and the set-tlement's political importance. The

FRANCE

Carolingians, under Charlemagne, moved the capital to Aix-la-Chapelle during the 8th century. The election of Hugh Capet to the throne in 987 AD gave power back to Paris.

The Capetian monarchy reigned for 350 years. To this period belong the Cathédrale de Notre-Dame and the Sorbonne College, founded by Robert de Sorbon for poverty-stricken students. The school was later to become the core of the University of Paris. Development in the 14th century was slowed not only by the Black Death, which plagued the city from 1348 to 1349, but by the Hundred Years' War, which was waged between 1337 and 1453.

Prosperity began to return to the city in the latter half of the 15th century. The influence of the Italian Renaissance gave new splendor to city architecture as Paris became the center of French royalty in the 1500s.

Paris entered a golden age in the 17th century. Blaise Pascal brought distinction to philosophy, and Jean-Baptiste Racine and Molière the same to the theater. The arts continued to flourish in the 18th century with the painters Antoine Watteau and Jean-Honoré Fragonard, the musician Christoph Willibald von Gluck (born in Germany but a Paris resident), and the writers Voltaire and Jean-Jacques Rousseau.

Streets were expanded and homes and public buildings constructed, including the École Militaire, the Panthéon and the Église-Ste.-Marie Madeleine. The French Revolution beginning with the storming of the Bastille on July 14, 1789, established Paris as the new capital of a centralized France.

Rapid industrialization followed; gas lighting was introduced, and Paris received its first railroad in 1837. The social consequences of this development, combined with overpopulation, brought squalor to older parts of the city and in part accounted for the revolutions of 1830 and 1848. City Prefect Baron Georges Eugène Haussmann was commissioned by Emperor Napoleon III to remedy the situation.

Haussmann designed a network of wide avenues and boulevards which are still in use today. He also inaugurated the city's modern sewer and water system and rebuilt the ancient market of Les Halles. The Eiffel Tower was constructed in 1889 and a World Exposition held alongside it. The first Métro line opened 10 years later.

In the 20th century, Paris weathered the battering of two world wars and emerged undaunted. Drastic redevelopment in the 1960s and 1970s not only accommodated a growing population but produced a string of startling new buildings. Recent rebuilding has been on a more intimate scale, and attention has been given to cleaning and renovating decaying quarters and providing housing.

Paris is a multi-faceted city, each face revealing its own distinctive features. One is the Place de l'Opéra, in the city's center, from which radiate streets filled with shops, elegant restaurants and cozy bistros and cafés.

Another is the Champs Élysées, one of the world's best known avenues. At one end of this tree-lined boulevard stands the focal point of the Place Charles de Gaulle, the massive Arc de Triomphe; at the other is the huge Place de la Concorde. In between are a children's fair and the Grand et Petit Palais, as well as parks, cafés and movie houses.

The Seine River and its two islands, a geographically and historically significant section of Paris, provide an easy escape from city noise and congestion. The Île de la Cité, Paris' oldest section, is the ancient setting for "La Grande Dame" of European Gothic architecture: the Cathédrale de Notre-Dame. Île Ste.-

Louis, once the home of such famous French citizens as Baudelaire and Theophile Gautier, retains its 17th-century charm along quiet, house-lined streets.

Prominent in both legend and geography is Montmartre, which to many constitutes the heart of Paris. The name is a distillation of "Mont des Martyres", the Mount of Martyrs, and recalls the martyrdom of Paris' first bishop, St.-Denis, who was beheaded on the slopes of this hill, at 130 meters (427 feet) the highest point in the city. The area attracted such artists as Toulouse-Lautrec, Pierre Auguste Renoir, Georges Seurat, Pablo Picasso and Georges Braque.

Today parts of Montmartre have become either shoddy or blatant tourist traps. There are still, however, numerous pretty back streets, churches and cemeteries, in addition to the only vineyard in Paris. The area is also a setting for nightclubs, cabarets and restaurants. You'll also quite likely have your portrait painted or caricature drawn in the main square at the top of Montmartre.

No overview of the city would be complete without a mention of the Rive Gauche, or Left Bank. Traditionally associated with romance and unconventionality, the area is a center for students from the nearby Sorbonne and the University of Paris. Artists congregate on the Left Bank; their work is frequently to be seen on display.

Artists and writers also inhabit Montparnasse, another well-known area. Le Dôme, at the intersection of boulevards Raspail and Montparnasse, was a favorite spot for Hemingway, Miller and other famous authors. From the Tour Montparnasse you can enjoy some of the best views of the city.

Farther west, in the Invalides district, rises the proud spire of the Eiffel Tower, perhaps the most widely recognized symbol of the city.

GETTING THERE
BY CAR, PLANE AND TRAIN
Paris is as accessible by car as any large European city, with highways leading in and out in every direction. Trans-Europe arteries are A1 north autoroute, A4 east autoroute, A6 south autoroute, A10 south-west autoroute and A13 west autoroute.

Two international airports service Paris: Orly, 14 kilometers (9 miles) south, and Charles de Gaulle, 23 kilometers (14 miles) north east at Roissy. Air France buses run every 12 minutes from Orly and between 15 and 20 minutes from Charles de Gaulle into the center of Paris. The Orlyval train line runs every 4 to 8 minutes from Orly to suburban Anjony station, where connections can be made into the city.

At Charles de Gaulle Airport, a unique hotel – Cocoon – accommodates weary travelers. The 6.5-square-metre (70-square-foot) soundproof rooms are air-conditioned and furnished with a bed, table, TV, telephone, clock, closet and tiny bathroom with a shower. For reservations telephone 48 62 06 16.

French trains, highly regarded throughout Europe, approach Paris from 12 routes into one of six main line stations.

GETTING AROUND
Driving in Paris is, at best, difficult and, at worst, hazardous. Traffic is heavy, and many areas are constantly beset with traffic jams. Most streets are one way, and it is possible to drive miles out of your intended way if you are ignorant of the city's intricate layout. The best advice may be to garage your car upon arrival and use public transportation. The use of front and back seat belts is mandatory and children under 10 years are not permitted to travel in the front seat.

PARKING
On-street parking is limited. Pay facilities can be found throughout the city.

CAR RENTAL

Paris has numerous car rental agencies. A comprehensive list of these, along with contract requirements, is available at the Paris Convention and Visitors' Bureau and national automobile dealers. To rent a car, you must be in possession of a valid driver's license for at least one year and be at least 18, though with most international companies it is 20 or 23, with an upper age limit (Avis excepted) of between 60 and 65.

TAXIS

Should you need to use a taxi, opt for a metered cab. There is a standard pickup charge and an extra charge for pickups at airports and railroad stations and for luggage weighing more than 5 kilos (11 pounds). You can usually hail a cab from the street, except during rush hours (8–9am and to 5–6:30pm). If you cannot flag a cab, check with the doorman at your hotel, or refer to the phone directory for assistance, but be warned: the time it takes a taxi to reach you is added to the pickup charge.

PUBLIC TRANSPORTATION

The quickest and most efficient transportation is the Paris Métro, one of the best subway systems in the world. Its passageways are well-marked and its color-coded maps easy to follow. Only one fare is charged, regardless of distance. This, coupled with the comfortable trains running on 13 lines every 2 to 10 minutes, makes the Métro the ideal way to get around.

The Métro operates from 5:30am to 12:30am. (The letter "M" throughout this guide denotes the nearest Métro station or stations to the relevant sight). Tickets – single, or books of ten (*carnet*) can be purchased at newsagent shops (*tabacs*) or subway stations. *Formule*, a card valid for one day for unlimited travel on the Métro and buses can be bought at the Paris Convention and Visitors' Bureau and subway stations. If you plan to use the Métro extensively, you can buy a *coupon jaune*, which allows unlimited travel on the subway or Parisian bus system for one week, or a *carte orange*, which is good for one month. You must supply a photograph of yourself to purchase these tickets.

Also available are special *Paris Visite* multi-mode tickets, designed for tourist travel in and around Paris. The tickets can be purchased from the Régie Autonome des Transports Parisians (RATP) for unlimited travel aboard the Métro or buses; discounts on several entrance fees also are included. *Paris Visite* tickets are available for 3- or 5-day consecutive periods. The *formule*, *coupon jaune*, *carte orange* and the *Paris Visite* also allow you to travel on the RER (Réseau Express Regional), suburban train service, plus some suburban services of the national SNCF rail network.

Buses operate daily from 6:30am to 8:30pm; some lines run until 12:30am and night buses also run. Tickets can be bought singly or in books of ten (*carnet*). Each route is divided into three sections, a ticket is valid for one or two sections.

WHAT TO DO

SIGHTSEEING

BOAT TOURS

The sightseeing boats that ply the Seine offer an exhilarating way to see some of the finest sights of Paris. *Bateaux-mouches*, perhaps the best known of the large tour boats, depart from Pont de l'Alma on the Right Bank. Other tour boat companies include Bateaux Parisiens, Vedettes du Pont-Neuf and Vedettes de Paris.

HELICOPTER TOURS

Sightseeing trips around Paris by helicopter are offered by Hélifrance, Héliport de Paris, tel: 1 45 54 95 11.

SPORTS AND RECREATION

Although typically characterized as a city of art and cuisine, Paris also offers

PARIS

varied recreational opportunities. Professional soccer takes place on Sundays at the Parc des Princes and Colombes Stadium; rugby also has a following. The French Open Tennis Tournament takes place at Stade Roland-Garros in late May/early June. Horse races take place daily at any one of eight city racetracks; the most important meeting is the Prix de l'Arc de Triomphe at Longchamp. Boxing, frequently held at the Palais des Sports, is also a favorite. The new Palais Omnisports, 2 kilometers (1.2 miles) south east of Notre Dame in the Bercy section, is the setting for a variety of top sporting events as well as musical events that draw large crowds.

If you'd rather play sports than watch them, there are all-year facilities for tennis, bowling and swimming. Aquatic sports are a frequent indulgence; a leisure complex including a swimming pool, sports hall, billiard room, photographic collections and a tropical greenhouse is in the vicinity of the Centre Pompidou. Facilities for golf, riding, hunting and fishing are all within reach of the city. Cycling enthusiasts can take advantage of rentals in or out of Paris.

Details in English regarding special events taking place in Paris are recorded on tape and available daily 24 hours; tel: 1 47 20 88 98.

WHERE TO SHOP
Whether you're seeking a pair of shoes or a first edition novel, you'll delight in what occupies the shelves and store windows of Paris. If your budget allows, you can purchase high-fashion originals by the demigods of design. Fortunately, most of the leading fashion houses, including Dior, Chanel, Givenchy, St.-Laurent and Cardin, have boutiques that sell lower-priced accessories and ready-to-wear clothing.

The dozens of shops on the principal shopping streets – rue Faubourg St.-Honoré, rue de Rivoli, avenue Montaigne and their neighbors – stock the perfumes, silk scarves, rainwear, leather goods, jewelry, antiques, crystal and ceramics for which the city is internationally known. The bastion of the "good life", the Ritz, shares place Vendôme with several perfumeries, excellent menswear stores and Wilmart, which sells lovely fabrics. Major department stores to search out are Printemps, Galeries Lafayette and Au Bon Marché.

There also are shopping malls. The Palais des Congrès de Paris Boutiques, at 2 place de la Porte-Maillot, features a Japanese department store, craft stores, restaurants and boutiques. Montparnasse Shopping Center, at the intersection of rue de l'Arrivée and rue du Départ, has a Chinese department store and swimming pool among its attractions. The Forum les Halles, 1–7 rue Pierre-Lescot, is a four-level shopping center with movie theaters, restaurants and a pool.

Generally, department stores are open 9:30–6:30pm Monday–Saturday; some are open until 9 or 10pm one night a week. Fashion boutiques, perfumeries and other smaller stores are open 9 or 10am–7pm Monday–Saturday (some close for lunch, noon–2pm). Hair salons are usually closed on Monday.

Several unusual stores deserve special mention. Trousselier, boulevard Haussmann, resembles a florist's shop, but all its bouquets are hand-crafted from silk. Au Nain Bleu, rue Faubourg St.-Honoré, has a selection of toys. For elegant edibles go to Fauchon, rue Tronchet.

A complex comprised of nearly 300 fashion and jewelry stores and eating establishments is close to the Centre Pompidou. On the small streets of Montparnasse and St.-Germain-des-Prés are tiny galleries showing and selling about-to-be-discovered artworks. On the quays of the Seine, the *bouquinistes*, or booksellers, dispense secondhand books, new and old postcards, old prints and maps.

FRANCE

FRANCE

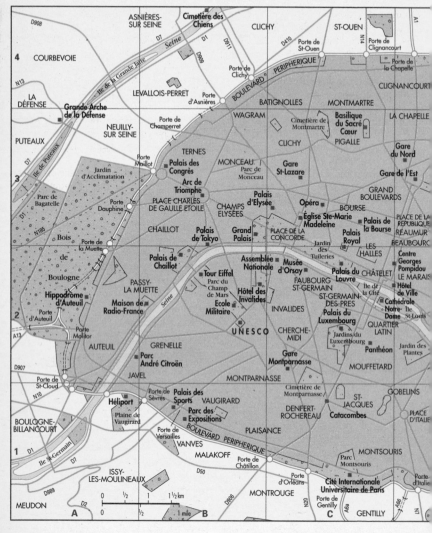

Nearby, on the Île de la Cité, is the multi-colored Marché aux Fleurs (flower market), its wares subject to wilting, but well worth photographing. The market is open 8am–7:30pm daily; on Sunday it becomes a bird market.

Somewhat out of the way, but worth the visit, is the Porte de Clignancourt's Marché aux Puces, the Flea Market, in St.-Ouen just past the northern boundary of Paris. It features fine antiques and de-

signer furniture along with traditional flea market bric-à-brac.

Other sections of the market include Marché Vernaison, at 99 rue de Rosiers and 136 avenue Michelet; Marché Paul-Bert, at 16 rue Paul-Bert; Marché Jules-Valles at 5 rue Jules-Valles; and Marché Mailik at 60 rue Jules-Valles.

The market is open from 7am to 7:30pm Saturday–Monday, though hours vary among stores.

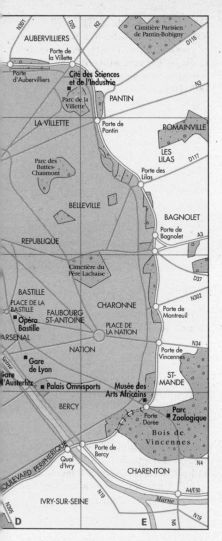

WHERE TO STAY AND WHERE TO EAT

Like many other Parisian endeavors, running a hotel has evolved into something of an art form; hoteliers have established a tradition of excellent service for their patrons. The large number of accommodations is rated by the government according to quality and price range and given a rating from one-star to four-star luxury. Moderately priced hotels, which usually have a bath in each room, are abundant on both the Left and Right banks.

Although the height of the tourist season in Paris, June and August, results in less of a squeeze than in some other cities, it is always advisable to make a reservation. September and October are particularly jammed with trade shows and conventions that flood the city with additional visitors, making reservations even more necessary.

Many hotels offer special deals for weekend breaks in winter. If you do not have reservations, check with the local tourist office, where you can reserve a room for a small fee. If you decide to look for a room on your own, your chances of finding something suitable are much better early in the day.

Parisian restaurants range from small, economical bistros to celebrated gastronomic shrines. The largest concentration of eating spots is to be found near the Champs-Élysées. Foreign and French cuisine abounds throughout the city. Most restaurants close one day per week, and many shut down entirely for the Parisian vacation period, in late July and August. It is always advisable to make reservations to dine at the most popular establishments well in advance.

The Vanves flea market on avenue Georges-Lafenstre has a wide variety of items for sale including books, secondhand clothes, old photographs, toys and table ware, and general bric-à-brac; it is open from 7am to 7:30pm from Saturday to Sunday.

The Aligre flea market, at place d'Aligre, specializes in secondhand clothing, old china and silver; it is open from 7:30am to 12:30pm Monday to Saturday.

ENTERTAINMENT
NIGHTLIFE

Whatever your tastes in evening entertainment, Paris can satisfy them all. From the sophisticated, bejeweled Paris

FRANCE

Opéra to the endless throngs of people on busy streets, the night breathes life into this age-old city.

There is no limit to the variety in entertainment and atmosphere offered by Parisian bars and music halls, so a tour of them, which can be arranged through your hotel, is a good way to begin. Many of the clubs emphasise jazz, burlesque or an international theme. Jazz clubs include New Morning, 7–9 rue des Petites-Écuries, and Le Petit Journal, 71 boulevard St.-Michel. Possibly the most popular show in town is the Folies Bergère at 32 rue Richer, but reserve your seat well in advance – the show is always sold out.

Other extravaganzas are offered at the Lido, 116 Champs-Élysées; the Moulin Rouge, place Blanche; and the Paradis Latin, 28 rue Cardinal Lemoine.

Discotheques include Les Bains, 7 rue du Bourg L'Abbé; Olivia Valère, 40 rue du Colisée; and Le Palace, 8 rue du Faubourg Montmartre. The City Rock Café, rue de Berri, is an American restaurant that contains the first rock 'n' roll museum in France. Mementoes of Bill Haley, Buddy Holly and the Beatles are displayed. Bands perform in the basement several times weekly.

Cafés and hotel cocktail bars can be amusing and entertaining, particularly if you speak French. Most movies are shown in the original version (advertized as "VO" – *version original*) with French subtitles, but some are dubbed – if you don't speak French, make sure you look out for the "VO" sign! Paris is a center for experimental art movies, and they feature regularly. Experimental movies are shown at the Palais de Chaillot Cinémathèque, place du Trocadéro.

Note: The mention of any area or establishment in the preceding sections is for information only and does **not** imply endorsement by the AAA.

THEATER AND CONCERTS

Parisian theaters offer a broad selection of presentations, but the majority are acted in French. Mysteries and light comedies have long been popular; operas and classics also have a following. You can see the works of Molière and others at the Comédie Française and at the Théâtre National de l'Odéon. The Théâtre National de Chaillot also has an interesting repertoire.

The Opéra Comique, which specializes in light ballet, and the Opéra Garnier, with traditional ballet, as well as the Opéra Bastille, which performs grand opera and ballet, have fine repertoires and artists.

On the lighter side of theater are the musicals and variety shows commonly held at the Théâtre Châtelet or Théâtre Mogador. Contemporary or experimental theaters include the Théâtre de la Ville, place du Châtelet, and the Théâtre du Soleil, in an old warehouse at Vincennes, avenue de la Pyramide. In addition to private theater, several state-operated stages offer a schedule of medium-priced performances.

Tickets can be purchased from several ticket agencies throughout Paris, including Allo Chèque Théâtre, telephone: 1 42 46 72 40, and American Express, telephone: 1 42 66 09 99, but service fees can run as high as 25 percent of the total ticket price.

Music runs the gamut from classical to rock. The Paris Orchestra performs regularly at the Théâtre des Champs-Élysées. Concerts and recitals of many kinds are given at the Palais de Chaillot, Salle Gaveau and Salle Pleyel. Check with local churches and cathedrals, which also sponsor recitals.

The Olympia, 28 boulevard des Capucines, and the Palais des Sports, Porte de Versailles, are concert centers for followers of new and contemporary music. The

Palais Omnisports de Paris-Bercy and Le Zenith at La Villette feature pop concerts and occasional opera.

ESPECIALLY FOR CHILDREN

To make the most of a Parisian vacation, if traveling with children, avoid August, when many of the shops they may find exciting and interesting are closed. Bastille Day (July 14), though crowded, offers a feast of sound and color. The chimeras and gargoyles of Notre Dame will delight the young sightseer, as will the view from Montmartre or a visit to the the Arc de Triomphe or the top of the Eiffel Tower.

Perhaps the best bet is the Disneyland Paris theme park at Marne-La-Vallee, 32 kilometers (20 miles) outside Paris (see p.284 for more details).

Museums with a special appeal for children are the Musée de la Marine, the Musée de l'Homme in the Palais de Chaillot, and the Musée Grevin (waxworks museum). Another alternative is the Aquarium de Trocadéro, in the Jardin du Palais de Chaillot. Discovery is the key word at the Inventorium of the Cité des Sciences et de l'Industrie.

Zoos are another remedy for restlessness. The Zoo de Vincennes, 53 avenue de St.-Maurice, is the city's largest. The Jardin des Plantes, on the Left Bank at 57 rue Cuvier, contains a zoo as well as plant and insect exhibits.

Parisian parks provide an excellent outlet for excess energy. Jardin d'Acclimatation, the Bois de Boulogne, near avenue Neuilly, and the Jardin du Luxembourg, rue de Vaugirard, have slides, swings, marionette shows, animal and go-kart rides and other amusements.

Punch and Judy shows, performed in easily followed French, take place at the Marionettes de Champs-de-Mars, the Marionettes de Vaugirard or the Marionettes du Luxembourg.

PLACES OF INTEREST

★ PARIS HIGHLIGHTS ★	
Arc de Triomphe	(see p.259)
Beaubourg (Centre Pompidou)	(see p.259)
Cité des sciences et de l'Industrie	(see p.260)
Hôtel des Invalides	(see p.261)
Louvre	(see p.261)
Musée d'Orsay	(see p.262)
Notre-Dame	(see p.262)
Opéra	(see p.263)
Sacré-Coeur	(see p.264)
Tour Eiffel	(see p.264)

ARC DE TRIOMPHE (251 A4) ★, place Charles-de-Gaulle (M: Charles-de-Gaulle Étoile), was built 1806–36 to commemorate the victories of Napoléon Bonaparte. Under the vault of the arch is the Eternal Flame and the Tomb of the Unknown Soldier of World War I. The roof provides a splendid view of the 12 broad, tree-lined streets that radiate from place Charles-de-Gaulle. Access is via the underpasses beneath the surrounding chaos of traffic.

BEAUBOURG (CENTRE GEORGES POMPIDOU) (251 D3) ★, rue Rambuteau at rue St.-Merri (M: Hôtel-de-Ville, Rambuteau, Châtelet), also is known simply as Beaubourg. Opened in 1977 to some controversy, the large structure is a steel and glass box suspended from beams supported by visible scaffolding. Escalators run through brightly painted tubes on the exterior of the building.

Inside is the National Museum of Modern Art; the Public Information Library, the city's first public library; the exhibition rooms of the Industrial Design Center, with extensive displays illustrating the impact of design on all facets of modern life; the Institute of Research and Co-ordination of Acoustic Music; a movie theater; rooms for temporary exhibitions; and a restaurant.

FRANCE

BIBLIOTHÈQUE NATIONALE (251 C3), rue de Richelieu (M: Bourse, Palais-Royal, Quatre-Septembre, Pyramides), is in the former palace of Cardinal Jules Mazarin. It contains one of the world's greatest collections of books, including the libraries of the kings of France (access for research only). Historical manuscripts, medals and antiquities are on display in the Cabinet des Médailles et Antiques, open for public access.

BOIS DE BOULOGNE (256 A2), in the western part of the city (M: Porte d'Auteuil, Porte Dauphine, Porte Maillot), open for public access, is a 845-hectare (2,088-acre) forest park. Once the hunting ground of kings, it was transformed by Haussmann into a delightful park with a variety of attractions from gardens, lakes and restaurants to the popular Auteuil and Longchamp racetracks.

BOIS DE VINCENNES (256 E1), in the eastern part of the city (M: Château-de-Vincennes), is a 995-hectare (2,459-acre) forest park that contains the city's largest zoo. Inside the park is the Château de Vincennes with its 14th-century tower, the keep, and Holy Chapel. The château was in turn a royal residence, a prison, a World War II headquarters and a torture house during the German occupation.

BOURSE DU COMMERCE (251 C3), in the business district south east of place de l'Opéra (M: Bourse), is the French Stock Exchange. Built on the site of a convent in 1826 and remodeled in 1888, it once served as a corn exchange. The domed hall is now a busy commodities market.

CATACOMBES (256 C1), place Denfert-Rochereau (M: Denfert-Rochereau), were built as limestone quarries in Gallo-Roman times. For many years they were used as a cemetery – bones and skulls are piled up along the walls of the twisting passages. During World War II, they were used as the H.Q. for the French Resistance. Bring a sweater and a flashlight. Guided tours are available.

CIMETIÈRE DES CHIENS (256 B4), Île d'Asnières, is a cemetery dedicated to animals. Two of the most well-known occupants are Rin-Tin-Tin and Barry, a lifesaving St. Bernard of the Swiss Alps.

CIMETIÈRE DU PÈRE LACHAISE (256 E2), east of the Marais district on avenue de la République (M: Père-Lachaise), is the oldest and best-known Parisian cemetery. The burial ground dates from the Middle Ages and is noted not only for its monuments and sculptures by well-known artists, but for the graves of such famous figures as Pierre Abélard and his lover Héloïse, Édith Piaf, Balzac, Sarah Bernhardt, Chopin, Molière and Oscar Wilde. American singer Jim Morrison of The Doors is also buried here.

CIMETIÈRE SURESNES, 8 kilometers (5 miles) west, contains the graves of over 1,500 Americans who died in the two world wars. A memorial chapel lists those lost and gives the location of all overseas cemeteries where Americans killed in action are buried.

CITÉ DES SCIENCES ET DE L'INDUSTRIE (256 D4) ★, 30 avenue Corentin-Cariou (M: Porte de la Villette), on the northeast perimeter, showcases modern science and technology through exhibits, shows, games and other experiences. Featured is a planetarium; La Médiathèque, a multi-media library; and a discovery area for children. In Parc La Villette is La Géode, a shiny steel globe housing a spherical movie theater, Le Cinaxe travel simulator, and a World War II submarine. (See La Villette on p.264).

CITÉ INTERNATIONALE UNIVERSITAIRE DE PARIS (256 C1), boulevard Jourdan (south part of the Left Bank) (M: Cité-Universitaire), was built to accommodate students during the 1918 housing shortage.

COLLÈGE DE FRANCE (251 D2), rue des Écoles (M: Maubert-Mutualité), was founded in 1530 by François I. The professors are appointed by government.

FRANCE

DÉFENSE, GRANDE ARCHE DE LA (256 A3), north west at Parvis de la Défense (M: Grande Arche de la Défense), is a cubic unit weighing 305,000 tons and measuring 109 meters (358 feet) on each side. It is encased in marble and has a vault that could hold Notre-Dame complete with spire. The belvedere offers an extensive view of the city.

DISNEYLAND PARIS – see p.284.

ÉCOLE MILITAIRE (251 A2) (M: École Militaire), is a magnificent 18th-century structure facing the Eiffel Tower across the broad Champs-de-Mars. Officers of the French military train here; Bonaparte is among its renowned graduates. Not accessible to the public.

ÉGLISE STE.-MARIE MADELEINE (251 B3), place de la Madeleine (M: Madeleine), is an exquisite marble structure built in the 18th and 19th centuries in the style of a Greek temple. The bronze doors are impressive; the murals on the inside façade depict the life of Mary Magdalene, for whom the church was named.

ÉGOUTS (251 A3), place de la Résistance (M: Alma-Marceau), is a massive network of sewers laid out by the engineer Belgrand in 1860. They have been popularized in several films, including *Phantom of the Opera*. Access is available.

ESPACE SALVADOR DALI, rue Poulbot, Montmartre, (M: Anvers, Blanche, Pigalle), is an exhibition displaying over 300 original works of Salvador Dali, the 20th-century Spanish Surrealist painter .

GRAND ET PETIT PALAIS (251 B3), avenue Winston Churchill (M: Champs-Élysées-Clemenceau), was built for the Universal Exhibition of 1900 and now displays artistic and technical exhibits. The Grand Palais houses the Palais de la Découverte, a center for scientific study with a planetarium. The Musée du Petit Palais has art exhibits which date from antiquity to the 20th century.

HÔTEL DES INVALIDES (251 B2) ★, Esplanade des Invalides (M: Invalides, Latour-Maubourg, École-Militaire, Varenne). The Hôtel des Invalides was designed by Libéral Bruant and completed by Jules Hardouin-Mansart who added the Église du Dôme. Napoléon Bonaparte's tomb rests under the apex of the gold dome. The 196-meter (643-foot) edifice of the Hôtel also houses the Musée de l'Armée, among others.

INSTITUT DE FRANCE (251 C2), 23 quai de Conti (M: Pont-Neuf, St.-Germain-des-Prés), houses five French academies, including the Académie Française. Its members, the "Forty Immortals", edit the French dictionary. Guided tours.

INSTITUT DU MONDE ARABE (Arab Cultural Exhibit Center) (251 D2), rue des Fossés St.-Bernard (M: Cardinal-Lemoine, Jussieu), houses a museum of Arab history, a library, an auditorium and a display area for exhibitions of Islamic and contemporary Arabic art.

JARDIN DES PLANTES (251 D1), 57 rue Cuvier (M: Jussieu, Monge, Gare d'Orléans-Austerlitz), contains 10,000 species of classified plants and some of the oldest trees in Paris, including a cedar of Lebanon, the Musée National d'Histoire Naturelle, and a small zoo.

JARDIN DES TUILERIES (251 C3), extending from the Louvre to the place de la Concorde (M: Concorde, Tuileries), contains 17th-century gardens by André Le Nôtre.

JARDINS DU TROCADÉRO (251 A3) (M: Trocadéro), facing the Eiffel Tower, is known for its fountains and lake. .

JEU DE PAUME (251 C3), place de la Concorde (M: Concorde), has been completely reconstructed. The gallery features modern art exhibitions, including plastic arts, movie and video.

LOUVRE (251 C3) ★, place Carrousel (M: Palais-Royal-Musée du Louvre). The

FRANCE

Palais du Louvre houses one of the world's great museums, the Musée du Louvre; an encyclopedic museum divided into seven departments, from ancient times to the mid-19th century. Works of art include the *Venus de Milo* and Da Vinci's enigmatic *Mona Lisa*.

Access to the museum from the courtyard is through I. M. Pei's glass pyramid, which stands in striking contrast to the historic palace.

MAISON VICTOR HUGO (251 E2), 6 place des Vosges (M: St.-Paul, Chemin-Vert, Bastille), contains drawings, furniture, paintings and documents relating to the life of the 19th-century French writer.

MALMAISON ET BOIS-PRÉAU, avenue du Château de Malmaison, 10 kilometers (6 miles) north west of Paris, was one of Bonaparte's homes. Malmaison was the favorite residence of Josephine, and where she lived after her divorce in 1809. Together with the neighboring Château de Bois-Préau, it forms two museums dedicated to Napoléon.

MANUFACTURE DES GOBELINS (251 D1), 42 avenue des Gobelins (M: Gobelins), is the site of a tapestry workshop founded in 1440. Visitors can view artisans at work. Guided tours.

MARCHÉ AUX FLEURS (251 D2), place Louis-Lépine and adjoining quays, on the Île de la Cité (M: Cité), is one of the largest and prettiest flower markets in the city. On Sunday it is transformed into a colorful – and noisy – bird market.

MUSÉE DES ARTS DÉCORATIFS (251 C3), 107 rue de Rivoli (M: Palais-Royal, Tuileries), houses interesting historical collections of interior furnishings from the Middle Ages to the present in addition to a fashion museum.

MUSÉE CARNAVALET (251 E3), 23 rue de Sévigné (M: St.-Paul, Chemin-Vert), depicts through a group of furnished rooms the history of Paris since the reign of Henry IV. The mansion was originally the home of Madame de Sévigné, noted chronicler of the 17th century.

MUSÉE DE CLUNY (251 D2), 6 place Paul-Painlevé (M: St.-Michel, Cluny, Odéon), is among the most attractive 15th-century edifices in Paris. It contains one of the richest medieval collections in the world, with tapestries, enamels, and ceramics. The remains of thermal baths are here.

MUSÉE GRÉVIN (251 C4), 10 boulevard Montmartre (M: Richelieu-Drouot, Rue Montmartre), is a wax museum similar to Madame Tussaud's in London.

MUSÉE DE LA MONNAIE DE PARIS (Museum of Coins and Medals) (251 C2), 11 quai de Conti, tells the story of the French people through coins and medals dating from 300 BC to the present.

MUSÉE D'ORSAY (251 C3) ★, 1 rue de Bellechasse (M: Solférino), is in a restored hotel and railroad station originally built for the Universal Exhibition of 1900. It specializes in 19th-century paintings and sculptures, with a particularly fine exhibit on architecture. Some rooms have a section devoted to decorative arts of the Third Republic.

A collection of Impressionist and Post-Impressionist art has works by Cézanne, Manet, Monet, Pissarro and Van Gogh.

MUSÉE PICASSO (251 E2), 5 rue de Thorigny in the Hôtel Salé Juigné (M: Chemin-Vert, St.-Paul), contains over 200 paintings, 158 sculptures, 16 collages, 29 relief paintings and 3,000 drawings by Picasso, the pioneer of Cubism.

MUSÉE RODIN (251 B2), 77 rue de Varenne (M: Varenne), in the Hôtel Biron, contains a priceless collection of the great sculptor's works, including *The Thinker*, *Gateway of Hell* and *Meditation*.

NOTRE-DAME, CATHÉDRALE (251 D2) ★, Île de la Cité (M: Cité), is considered one of the most beautiful cathedrals in the world and a masterpiece of medieval art. Begun in 1163 and completed in 1345, its flying buttresses make it an excellent example of Gothic architecture. Its size and three rose windows are awe-inspiring. Road distances in France are calculated from the "0km." point on the square on which it stands. (Note: some parts may be being renovated.)

OPÉRA (251 C3) ★, place de l'Opéra (M: Opéra), was designed by Garnier. Opened in 1875, the Opéra is one of the world's largest theaters, with a gold and red auditorium and an enormous stage, ornate sculptures, works of art and other lavish decorations.

The Grand Staircase is 10 meters (33 feet) wide at its base; the steps are white marble with balustrades of Algerian onyx. The Grand Foyer (open for viewing along with the auditorium when there are no rehearsals) has a vaulted mosaic ceiling, mirrors and columns.

PALAIS BOURBON-ASSEMBLÉE NATIONALE (251 B3), facing place de la Concorde (M: Assemblée Nationale Invalides), was the former residence of the Dowager Duchess of Bourbon and now home to the Assemblée Nationale. The library painting by Delacroix is impressive.

PALAIS DE CHAILLOT (251 A3), place du Trocadéro (M: Trocadéro), built for the Universal Exhibition of 1937, houses museums, a theater and a movie theater.
Musée de la Marine displays marine vessels and an interesting collection of marine paintings, designs and models covering the naval history of France since the 17th century.
Musée de l'Homme is an ethnological/anthropological museum with exhibits from every corner of the world.
Musée du Cinéma Henri Langlois follows the history of motion pictures with costumes, models, and technical apparatus.
Musée National des Monuments Français presents casts of major works of French architecture and sculpture from the 10th to 19th centuries.

PALAIS DE JUSTICE (251 D2), Île de la Cité (M: Cité), was the H.Q. of the Counts of Paris during the Norman invasions. Today it houses the Law Courts, Conciergerie and Sainte-Chapelle.
Conciergerie was the prison where thousands awaited their fate during the Revolution. The silent rooms and cells vividly evoke events of the Reign of Terror. Among the guests were Marie Antoinette, Robespierre and Danton.
Sainte-Chapelle is considered the finest specimen of Gothic architecture in Paris. Louis IX built the shrine to hold his most valued relics, notably the Crown of Thorns.

PALAIS DU LUXEMBOURG (251 C2), 15 rue de Vaugirard (M: Luxembourg), was built in the 17th century as a residence for Marie de Médicis. Today the palace is the seat of the French Senate and only accessible to the public by appointment. Sculptures and fountains adorn the extensive gardens. Food is available.

PALAIS ROYAL (251 C3), behind the Théatre Comédie Française (M: Palais-Royal), was a home of Cardinal de Richelieu. Today old houses and shops border the palace gardens on three sides. Visitors can see the well-known black and white striped Buren's Columns.

PANTHÉON (251 D1), place du Panthéon, (M: Cardinal-Lemoine, Jussieu), was originally designed to be a church but in 1791 became a burial place for prominent French citizens, including Victor Hugo, Jean-Jaurès, Rousseau, Voltaire and Zola.

PARC ANDRÉ-CITROËN (256 A2), between rue St.-Charles and the Seine (M: Balard, Javel), is a futuristic garden opened in 1992 on the site of a former Citroën factory. A huge lawn is graced by several gardens and over 2,000 trees. Guided tours of the park are available.

PARISTORIC (251 B4), 78 blvrd. des Batignolles (M: Villiers), depicts the 2,000-year history of Paris on a giant screen.

FRANCE

PLACE DE LA BASTILLE (251 E2) (M: Bastille) was once the site of the fortress prison. The liberation of prisoners by rioting crowds on July 14, 1789 marked the beginning of the French Revolution. Today it is a large square with a memorial column rising from its center and topped by the Spirit of Liberty.

It is also the home of the Opéra de la Bastille, designed by Canadian architect Carlos Ott and completed in 1989. It can seat up to 2,700 spectators. Guided tours are available – write to Opéra de la Bastille, Service des Visites, 120 rue de Lyon, 75102 Paris, France.

PLACE DE LA CONCORDE (251 B3), at the eastern end of the avenue des Champs-Élysées (M: Concorde), was the scene of bloody executions during the French Revolution. Today it is one of Paris' loveliest squares, with fountains and monuments representative of the cities of France. The obelisk, symbolizing harmony and peace, was given to Charles X by Mohammed Ali in 1829.

PLACE DU TERTRE (251 C4), Montmartre (M: Abbesses, Lamarck-Caulaincourt), was once the public square of the village. Today the square is crowded with artists displaying their works – you'll be amazed by the choice on offer. You can also get a caricature drawn here.

PLACE VENDÔME (251 C3), rue de la Paix (M: Tuileries), has harmonious buildings surrounding a column erected in 1810 by Bonaparte in honor of his German and Austrian campaigns. The column is covered with the bronze from 1,200 cannons captured at Austerlitz in 1805.

SACRÉ-COEUR (BASILIQUE DU) (251 D4) ★, Montmartre (M: Abbesses, Château-Rouge, Lamarck-Caulaincourt), was built to fulfil a vow after the Franco-Prussian War. The outside gallery of the 90-meter (259-foot) dome provides a magnificent view of Paris. The interior of the basilica is lavishly decorated with exquisite mosaic and enamel work.

ST.-GERMAIN-DES-PRÉS (251 C2), place St.-Germain-des-Prés (M: St.-Germain-des-Prés), is the oldest church in Paris, dating from the 10th century.

ST.-JULIEN-LE-PAUVRE, 17 rue du Petit-Pont (M: St.-Michel, Maubert-Mutualité), is a tiny church with an unusual feature: two nightclubs in its catacombs.

ST.-SÉVERIN, 1 rue des Prêtres-St.-Séverin (M: St.-Michel), is one of the oldest Gothic churches in Paris; construction began in the 13th century. It is noted for its fine stained-glass windows.

SORBONNE (251 D2), off boulevard-St.-Michel (M: Cluny-La Sorbonne, Maubert-Mutualité, Luxembourg), is one of the oldest universities in Europe. It was founded as a theological school for poor students in 1253 by Robert de Sorbon, a chaplain of St.-Louis. The school is now affiliated with the University of Paris. Particularly impressive is the Grand Amphitheater.

TOUR EIFFEL (251 A3) ★, Champs-de-Mars (M: Champs-de-Mars, Bir Hakeim), is perhaps the most recognizable Paris landmark. The 307-meter (1,007-foot) iron masterpiece was built 1887–90 for the Universal Exhibition of 1889. It recently underwent structural renovation and shed about 1,000 of its 7,300 tons.

The first level houses a restaurant and theatre/museum depicting its history. A mezzanine offers views of the interior and the Palais de Chaillot Gardens. The second level has another restaurant, and the third floor, at 276 meters (905 feet), offers spectacular views as far as 67 kilometers (42 miles) on a clear day.

LA VILLETTE (256 D4), in the north east of the city (M: Porte de la Villette), is a scientific, cultural and recreational facility. The Cité des Sciences et de l'Industrie is the main feature (see p.260). There is also the Cité de la Musique, and various other cultural facilities, as well as a park with leisure activities.

PLACES OF INTEREST

AIGUES-MORTES (245 D1)

GARD *pop. 5,000*

Rising out of the low-lying marshes of the Camargue, the Rhône delta area of southern France, Aigues-Mortes was founded in the 13th century by St. Louis as a port from which to launch the Seventh and Eighth Crusades. His son, Philip the Bold, completed fortifications whose ramparts and towers remain virtually intact.

AIX-EN-PROVENCE (245 D1) ★

BOUCHES-DU-RHÔNE *pop. 123,800*

Aix-en-Provence was founded as a thermal springs resort in 122 BC on the site of the first Roman settlement in Gaul. It has long been a cultural center, with museums, stately buildings, old churches and a university that was established in 1409. The city is still an important therapeutic spa with a variety of thermal treatment centres and many types of resort entertainment – casinos, theater and facilities for most sports. The International Music Festival is held in July and August.

ATELIER DE CÉZANNE, Paul Cézanne's studio, is a short distance north on the road to Entremont. Personal belongings and tools are on display.

CATHÉDRALE ST.-SAUVEUR, rue Gaston-de-Saporta, dates from the 5th to 15th centuries. The church is best known for its triptych *Les Buissons Ardents* ("The Burning Bushes"), painted during the 15th century. The cloisters, carved door panels, sculpture and tapestries also are distinctive.

MUSÉE GRANET, place St.-Jean-de-Malte, houses a collection of paintings including eight of Paul Cézanne's works, others by the Provençal artist Granet, and pre-Roman sculpture.

AIX-LES-BAINS (245 E3)

SAVOIE *pop. 24,700*

Aix-les-Bains, a fashionable spa dating from the Roman occupation of Gaul, is best known for its treatment of rheumatoid conditions. In addition to the casino, racetrack, pools and baths, the resort offers sailing and water skiing, as well as winter sports facilities at Mount Revard. Extensive Roman ruins include the Arch of Campanus, the Temple of Diana and the baths. The town also maintains a modern art collection with works by such artists as Corot, Degas and Rodin.

Side trips can be taken to the summit of Mount Revard, to the nearby Abbey of Hautecombe and around Lake Bourget, France's largest natural lake, on a boat that leaves from the Grand Port. The abbey was founded by St.-Bernard and was used as a burial place by the princes of the House of Savoy.

MUSÉE FESCH, 50 rue Fesch, exhibits over 1,000 paintings in a collection donated by Cardinal Fesch, Napoléon's uncle. Its Italian Primitive works are second to only those of the Louvre in Paris.

ALBI (245 C2)

TARN *pop. 46,600*

The Cathédrale de Ste.-Cécile here is a

FRANCE

monumental fortress built to protect the clergy during the Inquisition. Paintings, carvings and ornamentation richly enhance its interior.

MUSÉE TOULOUSE-LAUTREC in the Palais de la Berbie, has the world's largest collection of the painter's works.

AMBOISE (245 C3)
INDRE-ET-LOIRE *pop. 11,000*
The medieval church of St.-Denis, with its 16th-century works of art, the Hôtel de Ville, which houses a historical museum and the Musée de la Poste are all in the center of town.

CHÂTEAU D'AMBOISE is a late Gothic castle which served as a royal residence in the 15th and 16th centuries. Its huge round towers with wide spiral ramps accommodated kings and chariots and were the scene of merciless killings. Leonardo da Vinci is said to be buried in the Chapel of St. Hubert, once a part of the Queen's Apartments. Former residents include Catherine de Medici. Floodlit in summer, the château is the setting for sound-and-light shows.

CHÂTEAU DE CHENONCEAU, 12 kilometers (7 miles) south east, is a Renaissance château built on a bridge across the Cher River. Erected in the early 16th century, it belonged to six women in succession, including Diane de Poitiers and Catherine de Medici. Sound-and-light shows take place in summer.

CHÂTEAU DU CLOS-LUCÉ is the 15th-century manor house where the artist Leonardo da Vinci died. It contains machine models of da Vinci's inventions, including the first self-propelled vehicle, airplane, helicopter, parachute, and swing bridge. There is also a 55-minute film on his life.

AMIENS (245 C5)
SOMME *pop. 131,900*
Amiens, on the Somme River, is the capital of the Picardy region. It is where

Jules Verne, renowned author of fantasy, lived until his death; his former home is now the Jules Verne Information Center. The Musée de Picardie has archeological finds and paintings. Old Amiens, near the cathedral, has been restored recently and is lively with cafés and restaurants.

Nearby is the underground village of Naours. Constructed as a fort during the 3rd and 4th centuries, it was used during World War II as a secret hideaway from German invaders.

CATHÉDRALE DE NOTRE DAME, which dates from the 13th century, is remarkably beautiful and harmonious in its design. One of the largest Gothic cathedrals in France, it measures more than 145 meters (180 feet) long and 112 meters (370 feet) to the top of the spire.

LES ANDELYS
EURE *pop. 8,500*
The product of the merged twin settlements of Grand and Petit Andely, Les Andelys is a small town beside the Seine River. To the south of Petit Andely are the imposing remains of Château Gaillard, built by Richard the Lionheart in the late 12th century. Views of the Seine Valley from this clifftop site are spectacular.

ANGERS (245 B4)
MAINE-ET-LOIRE *pop. 141,400*
Angers is known for its horticultural exhibitions and superb public gardens. The regional wines (white, red and rosé d'Anjou) are world-renowned. There is a Museum of the Grape Vine and the Anjou Wine Fair is held in winter. The liqueur Cointreau is also produced in Angers; the distillery may be visited.

CATHÉDRALE ST.-MAURICE, which dates from the 12th century, dominates the town with its Gothic spires; the stained-glass windows, Romanesque doorway and nave are impressive.

CHÂTEAU, a 13th-century fortress, houses the 14th-century Apocalypse Tapestry, which is the largest surviving medieval tapestry in the world.

HÔPITAL SAINT-JEAN is a 12th-century hospital that features cloisters, cellars and a series of tapestries by Jean Lurçat.

HÔTEL PINCÉ, a fine example from the Renaissance period, houses the Pincé Museum with its collection of oriental art.

MUSÉE DE LA COMMUNICATION, Château de Pignerolle, covers all aspects of communication, including the human voice, printing, the telephone, radio and television, and satellites.

ANGOULÊME (245 B3)
CHARENTE *pop. 42,900*
The old fortified town of Angoulême overlooks the Charente River. The town walls have been converted into boulevards that afford views of the surrounding countryside. The ornate 12th-century Cathédrale St.-Pierre, restored during the 19th century, is a good example of Romanesque architecture; 75 figures depicting Judgement Day cover one side of the building. Also of interest are the Chapelle des Cordeliers, the Musée Archéologique and the Centre National de l'Image (National Cartoon Museum).

ANNECY (245 E3)
HAUTE-SAVOIE *pop. 49,600*
Annecy is a well-known health resort and vacation spot on the shore of beautiful Lake Annecy. The picturesque old quarter, with its medieval houses and winding canals, contains the château, an old castle with 13th- and 15th-century towers, and the Palais de l'Ile, a fortress and former prison built on an island in the Thiou canal. A trip around the lake, from moorings near the Hôtel de Ville, can be made by steamboat in 1½ hours.

ANTIBES (245 E2)
ALPES-MARITIMES *pop. 70,000*
Antibes has been a resort since the mid-19th century, but vestiges of Greek and Roman occupation indicate that the spot was popular much earlier. Offering the best in resort entertainment, Antibes is host to several international festivals. Picasso presented a number of his works to the city, and they are now in the Musée Picasso. A museum in nearby Biot contains paintings and mosaics by Fernand Léger, who with Picasso founded Cubism.

Cap d'Antibes, a 4-kilometer (2½-mile) long peninsula, is an exclusive playground covered with luxurious villas and gardens. The Cap, Antibes and Juan-les-Pins make up the whole of the Antibes community.

MUSÉE PICASSO, in the Château Grimaldi, the former residence of the Prince of Antibes and later the home and studio of Picasso, now houses one of the largest collections of his works.

ARCACHON (245 B2)
GIRONDE *pop. 11,800*
Arcachon is a well-known resort near the Bay of Biscay. A resort much frequented by European aristocracy in the 19th century, the slightly eccentric architecture of the villas of the Ville d'Hiver (Winter Town) dates from that period. Today visitors flock to the yacht marina, sports facilities and the local museum, with its aquarium and archeological and historical collections.

ARLES (245 D1) ★
BOUCHES-DU-RHÔNE *pop. 52,100*
Arles, on the Rhône River, has a prestigious past. Founded by Julius Caesar in 49 BC, it became the most important settlement in Roman Gaul.

In and near the city are many Roman ruins, including statuary, an amphitheater, aqueducts and baths. The paleo-Christian burial ground, Les Alyscamps, lies on the outskirts of town.

Vincent Van Gogh lived in Arles and made the city the subject of several paintings shortly before his death; the Office de Tourisme provides a map guiding you to the many sites he painted in the region.

LES ARÈNES ROMAINES is a spectacularly well-preserved amphitheater from the 1st century, once seating 25,000, now seating 12,000 for bullfights and concerts in summer.

CATHÉDRALE ST.-TROPHIME, which dates from the 12th century, is well-known for its sculptured portal and cloister behind the church.

THÉÂTRE ANTIQUE, begun by Caesar Augustus in the 1st century BC and finished 150 years later, provides the setting for various summer events.

ARROMANCHES-LES-BAINS (245 B4)
CALVADOS *pop. 400*

Arromanches-les-Bains is a seaside resort that attracted international attention during World War II when it was the site of "Mulberry B," one of two artificial harbors used for landing Allied troops and supplies after the D-Day invasion. The best view is from the viewpoint indicator at the top of the cliff.

ARROMANCHES 360° presents a 20-minute film depicting Arromanches' involvement in the Allied invasion.

MUSÉE DU DÉBARQUEMENT (Landings Museum) is on the beach. Films and exhibits depict the Allied invasion of June 6, 1944, and the construction of the artificial harbors.

AUXERRE (245 D4)
YONNE *pop. 38,800*

Ancient Auxerre, near the wine-producing district of Chablis, dates back to the Gallo-Roman era. A beautiful city, Auxerre borders the Yonne River and is surrounded on three sides by orchards. The Musée Leblanc-Duvernoy is one of several local museums; its 18th-century Beauvais tapestries and artifacts are of particular interest.

CATHÉDRALE ST.-ETIENNE was founded in 400 AD by St.-Amâtre. Most of the structure that stands today, however, was built much later. Of note are the 11th-century crypt with 12th- and 13th-century frescoes, the 16th-century stained-glass window, the choir and three portals with sculptures depicting the Last Judgement.

AVIGNON (245 D2) ★
VAUCLUSE *pop. 87,000*

One of the great art centers of France, Avignon was the residence of the Popes from 1309 to 1377. The city abounds in reminders of lavish 14th-century papal courts. Villeneuve-les-Avignon, across the Rhône River, contains a fort, a Carthusian monastery and a museum with *The Coronation of the Virgin*.

Remains of a Roman bridge and aqueduct, the Pont du Gard, are 20 kilometers (12 miles) west.

CATHÉDRALE-DE-VAUCLUSE, about 24 kilometers (16 miles) east of Avignon, was immortalized by the 14th-century love poet Petrarch, who spent 30 years at the site.

MUSÉE DU PETIT PALAIS, place du Palais, is a 14th-century structure converted into an art museum. Rooms display Italian and French paintings of the 14th to 16th centuries; two rooms contain sculptures from the 12th, 13th and 14th centuries. It was the residence of the Cardinal of Avignon and has been renovated to reflect its original appearance.

PALAIS DES PAPES, place du Palais, a grand example of medieval architecture, was built in the 14th century as a fortress and papal residence.

PONT ST.-BENÉZET, dating from the 12th century, is a bridge made popular by the folk song *Sur le Pont d'Avignon*.

AZAY-LE-RIDEAU – *see Tours on p.298.*

BAGNOLES-DE-L'ORNE (245 B4)
ORNE *pop. 900*

Together with neighboring Tessé-la-Madeleine, Bagnoles-de-l'Orne is the largest spa in western France. The area adjoins a wooded lake that is fed by the Vée River. Waters from the river, a therapeutic 25°C (77°F), are particularly attractive to persons with circulatory disorders. Bagnoles-de-l'Orne has a variety of entertainments, sporting facilities and a casino.

BARBIZON (245 C4)
SEINE-ET-MARNE *pop. 1,400*

Barbizon derives its name from the 19th-century landscape painters who worked in the city and founded the Barbizon school of painting. The studios of Jean-François Millet and Théodore Rousseau are open to the public; the Inn of Père Ganne, where artists once gathered, is now a muséum.

LES BAUX-DE-PROVENCE (245 D2)
BOUCHES-DU-RHÔNE *pop. 500*

Les Baux-de-Provence is a medieval village on top of a high hill overlooking rugged countryside. The settlement was once a stronghold of lords who claimed descent from Balthazar, one of the biblical three kings. Today Les Baux is a collection of white limestone buildings and huge rocks. The Cité Morte (Dead City) contains the ruined shells of the ancient town, including an imposing medieval fortress in a cliff-top setting. In accordance with the ancient rites of Provence, a midnight procession bearing candles makes its way to the old church in place Saint Vincent on Christmas Eve. The town's name is also claimed by the aluminum ore, bauxite. In a disused quarry just outside Les Baux, the Cathédrale d'Images presents a sound-and-light show of the town's history.

BAYEUX (245 B4)
CALVADOS *pop. 14,700*

Bayeux rose to importance in the 10th century as the principal town of the Duchy of Normandy. It also was the first French town to be liberated during World War II.

Famed for the Bayeux Tapestry, a medieval embroidery depicting the events that led to the Battle of Hastings,

Bayeux still has cobbled streets and timbered houses, escaping damage during World War II.

CATHÉDRALE DE NOTRE-DAME is a Norman Gothic church. Although originally completed in 1077, only two Romanesque towers and the crypt remain from that era. The interior contains frescoes, ironwork and woodcarvings.

CIMETIÈRE COLLEVILLE-ST. LAURENT, 15 kilometers (9 miles) north west, contains the graves of 9,000 Americans killed during World War II.

On a cliff overlooking Omaha Beach and the English Channel, the site has a garden and a memorial with maps and narratives describing the massive military operation that took place at the site. A bronze statue commemorates the young Americans who lost their lives.

MUSÉE MÉMORIAL DE LA BATAILLE DE NORMANDIE, boulevard Fabian Ware, chronicles the events of the Battle of Normandy, which occurred between June 6 and August 22, 1944, through models and dioramas.

TAPISERIE DE BAYEUX is in the Centre Guillaume le Conquérant. This 900-year-old band of linen, 70 meters (230 feet) long and 0.5 meters (20 inches) wide is a masterpiece of medieval craftsmanship. The 58 scenes, embroidered in worsteds of eight colors, depicted for an illiterate audience the historic event of the defeat of Harold II of England by William, Duke of Normandy, at the Battle of Hastings, which established the Normans as rulers of England, as well as showing many facets of Norman life. Wrongly credited to William's Queen Mathilde, the tapestry (it is actually an embroidery) is now believed to have been commissioned by the city's Bishop Odo, William's half brother, as well as being produced by an English workshop.

Protected by glass and special lighting, the tapestry is accompanied by a recorded commentary provided in

English, German and French. Viewing of the tapestry is preceded by a slide-show and an exhibition explaining the background to the events it depicts.

BAYONNE (245 B1)
PYRÉNÉES-ATLANTIQUES *pop. 40,100*
Capital of the French Basque country, Bayonne is tucked into the south-west corner of France.

The Musée Basque is dedicated to the region's folklore, and the Musée Bonnat features priceless paintings. The 13th-century Cathédrale de Ste.-Marie adds Gothic beauty to the town.

MUSÉE ÎLE-DE-FRANCE, at Cap-Ferrat, contains Baroness Ephrussi de Roths-child's rich art collection including Gothic and Italian Renaissance pieces, tapestries, porcelain and paintings and canvases by Fragonard, Boucher, Renoir and Sisley. Gardens surround the villa.

BEAUNE (245 D3)
CÔTE-D'OR *pop. 21,300*
Beaune is a wine center in the Burgundy region with several wine and grape festi-vals. The Museum of Burgundy Wine, housed in the Hôtel des Ducs de Bour-gogne, displays documents and tools pertaining to the history of the vineyards and wines from ancient times.

Beaune is also noted for its historical treasures. The 15th-century Hôtel-Dieu, built as a hospital for the poor, has a painting collection.

ARCHÉODROME, 6 kilometers (4 miles) south, depicts life in the Gallo-Roman era through buildings, fortifications, bur-ial chambers, a temple and a villa.

BESANÇON (245 D3)
DOUBS *pop. 113,800*
Besançon is the capital of the Franche-Comté region. It has been important since the Roman era and was once under the control of the Spanish. Medieval buildings are the 16th-century Palais Granvelle and the Cathedral of St. Jean, with its astronomical clock.

Besançon is the center of France's watchmaking industry; it is also the birth-place of Victor Hugo. The International Music Festival is held in September.

The many woods and public parks and gardens have earned Besançon the title of France's "Greenest City."

CITADELLE, rue des Fusillés-de-la-Ré-sistance, is on a hill overlooking Besan-çon. Built by the Spanish and the mili-tary engineer Vauban, the fort houses the Museum of the Resistance and Deportation, the Museum of Natural History, including a zoological park and a Folklore Museum.

MUSÉE DES BEAUX ARTS ET D'ARCHÉO-LOGIE, place de la Révolution, is one of the oldest and richest museums in France. It contains European paintings, drawings and sculpture from the Middle Ages to present day; also a collection of Egyptian, Greek and Roman antiquities.

FRANCE'S NATIONAL MUSEUMS

The 34 state-owned national museums hold some of France's richest treasures. They are closed on Tuesday, with the exception of Versailles (see p.299), the Trianon Palace (see p.299) and the Musée d'Orsay (see p.262) which are closed on Monday. Under 18s are admitted free; 18–25s and over 60s are half-price; and it is only half the normal admission fee to all on Sunday.

BÉZIERS (245 D1)
Béziers, on the Orb River near the Med-iterranean, is the wine-producing center of the Languedoc-Roussillon region.

An old city, Béziers has a somewhat macabre history: as many as 20,000 resi-dents were slain when the town was taken in the Albigensian Crusade of the 13th century.

A source of pride is the Cathédrale St.-Nazaire, built mainly in the 13th and 14th centuries. The Allées Paul-Riquet, named after the Béziers native who built the Canal du Midi, is a maze of attractive narrow streets dotted with art galleries and museums devoted to the history of wine and winemaking, leading to a garden – Plateau des Poètes – with busts of famous writers and a panoramic view.

BIARRITZ (245 B1)
PYRÉNÉES-ATLANTIQUES *pop. 28,700*
Biarritz is a fashionable summer and winter resort on the Atlantic coast at the foot of the Pyrénées. In addition to several beaches, it has casinos and sports facilities. Also of interest is the Musée de la Mer with an aquarium and seal pool, and the Musée de l'Automobile Miniature, housing 6,000 scale models of cars.

BLOIS (245 C4)
LOIR-ET-CHER *pop. 49,300*
Blois marks the center of the Loire Valley's great château region. Several of the Loire's mansions, including those at Chambord, Chaumont, Cheverny and Ménars, are near this old industrial town.

CHÂTEAU DE BEAUREGARD, 6 kilometers (4 miles) south east, has exceptional decoration which has remained unchanged since the 16th and 17th centuries. Its portrait gallery is the largest in Europe, and there is a rare 16th-century kitchen.

CHÂTEAU DE BLOIS is an excellent example of French architecture; it contains elements from the Middle Ages to the classical period.
Best known for its handsome 16th-century stairway, it also contains the Musée des Beaux-Arts consisting of frescoes, paintings and religious art.

CHÂTEAU DE CHAMBORD, 18 kilometers (11 miles) south east, is an enormous 16th-century structure of 440 rooms, the largest château in the Loire Valley. The palace has a double spiral staircase and rich ornamentation throughout.

CHÂTEAU DE CHEVERNY, 14 kilometers (9 miles) south east, is a 17th-century mansion with original classical furnishings. A hunter's museum features a collection of antlers and maintains a kennel.

BORDEAUX (245 B2)
GIRONDE *pop. 210,300*
A major port on France's Atlantic coast and one of the world's wine capitals, Bordeaux and the surrounding vineyards are dotted with châteaux that have given their names to many popular red and white wines.

CATHÉDRALE ST.-ANDRÉ, place Pey-Berland, dates from several periods and has interesting sculptures.

GRAND THÉÂTRE, place de la Comédie, is considered one of the most beautiful theaters in Europe.

MUSÉE DES BEAUX-ARTS, 20 cours d'Albret, houses a collection of impressive paintings from the Renaissance to the 20th century.

BOULOGNE-SUR-MER (245 C5)
PAS-DE-CALAIS *pop. 43,700*
Boulogne-sur-Mer is a leading commercial and passenger port with a hovercraft and catamaran service to Dover, England as well as a catamaran service to Folkestone, England. The upper portion of the town contains historic buildings including a 13th-century castle, the 19th-century Cathedral of Notre-Dame and remains of the medieval town walls.

NAUSICAÀ, built on the beach at the entrance to Boulogne harbor, has 15,000 square meters (161,450 square feet) of aquarium space. The center provides an insight into the sciences related to the sea and its natural resources.

BOURGES (245 C3)
CHER *pop. 75,600*
The town of Bourges is an important cultural focal point in central France. Despite modernization, medieval and

Renaissance history still lives in its buildings and streets.

Important structures include the 13th-century Cathedral of St.-Étienne, with its stained-glass windows; the Musée du Berry in the Hôtel Cujas, with an archeological collection and art objects; the Musée des Arts Decoratifs in the Hôtel Lallemant; and the Palais de Jacques Coeur, former home and trade center of the medieval financier.

BREST (245 A4)
FINISTÈRE *pop. 148,000*

One of the best natural harbors in France, Brest has a long history as a naval and commercial port. The city dates from before the 14th century, but bombings in both world wars destroyed almost all the historic buildings. As a result, Brest is a very modern city.

Places of interest are the Arsenal and the naval base, the Naval Museum and the Museum of Old Brest. The Pont de Recouvrance across the Penfeld River is said to be the biggest drawbridge in Europe, but opening its 87-meter (285-foot) span takes only a few seconds.

OCÉANOPOLIS, Port de Plaisance du Moulin Blanc, is a culture and science center dedicated to the sea that contains over 500,000 liters (132,100 gallons) of aquarium space.

CAEN (245 B4)
CALVADOS *pop. 112,800*

Caen, a rich industrial and commercial city in northern France, was almost entirely destroyed in the 1944 Normandy invasion. Excellent city planning, however, has brought about complete reconstruction and Caen's monuments have been restored and industries have been rebuilt.

Important at the time of the Norman Conquest, Caen has notable 11th- and 12th-century buildings. The massive Abbaye aux Hommes and the Abbaye aux Dames, built respectively by William the Conqueror and his queen, Mathilde, are well worth a visit.

CHÂTEAU FÉODAL, dating from the 11th century, is one of the oldest castles in France. It now contains the Musée des Beaux-Arts, particularly good for French and Italian works from the 17th and 18th centuries.

MÉMORIAL, avenue de Maréchal Montgomery, covers the history of the 20th century through exhibits, a film of D-Day and a modern film – *Espérance* (*Hope*) on the consequences of World War II and the dangers threatening the planet. It also houses a Nobel Peace Prize gallery.

CAGNES-SUR-MER
ALPES-MARITIMES *pop. 34,900*

Cagnes-sur-Mer, between Antibes and Nice, is a town that encompasses the old Provençal city of Haut-de-Cagnes, with its imposing castle, and the fishing village of Cros-de-Cagnes, with its fine beach. Haut-de-Cagnes was one of Renoir's favorite spots and is still an artists' colony.

CHÂTEAU-MUSÉE, originally built as a fortress, has a collection of paintings, 17th-century furnishings and superb coastal views. The Château-Musée served as the town's prison until the 17th century, when Baron Jean Henri Grimaldi made it into a palatial home. An ethnographic museum traces the making of olive oil through the ages.

MUSÉE RENOIR, in Les Collettes, the last home and studio of Renoir, houses some of the artist's best work.

CAHORS (245 C2)
LOT *pop. 19,700*

Ancient towers and belfries lend the town a medieval atmosphere. The 14th-century Pont Valentré is a particularly fine example of French military architecture; its three battlemented towers have guarded the western approaches since the 14th century.

St.-Cirq-Lapopie, on an escarpment overlooking the Lot River, 33 kilometers

(21 miles) east of Cahors, is a medieval settlement so well preserved that the entire village is classified a historic site.

CALAIS (245 C5)
PAS-DE-CALAIS *pop. 75,300*
Calais, an industrial center, is the cross-Channel port for ferry services from Dover, England. Situated 5 kilometers (3 miles) south, Coquelles is the French terminus of the new 50-kilometer (31-mile) cross-Channel link – Eurotunnel. The English terminal is at Cheriton, near Folkestone.

Travel through the Eurotunnel is via Le Shuttle, a train that accommodates passengers, vehicles, campers, RVs, motorcycles and buses. Le Shuttle operates daily 24 hours; it departs every 15 minutes during peak travel times and hourly at other times. Tickets can be purchased in advance or at a toll booth; reservations are not required. The trip takes about 35 minutes, whereas a conventional ferry ride can take between 1¼ and 1½ hours.

There is also a high-speed passenger service known as Eurostar, operating at speeds of up to 300 k.p.h. (185 m.p.h.), between London (Waterloo), England, and Paris and Lille; journey time is 2 and 3 hours respectively. There are 15 departures each way a day and tickets can be purchased from railway stations or travel agents.

CANNES (245 E1)
ALPES-MARITIMES *pop. 68,700*
Cannes, though not as large as Nice, is also an elegant year-round resort on the French Riviera. Between the beach and some of the city's most fashionable hotels is the palm-lined boulevard de la Croisette, with the Casino Municipal at the west end and the Palm Beach Casino (open summer only; currently under restoration) at the east. The Palais des Festivals is host to the famous International Cannes Film Festival in May.

West of the yacht harbor is the old town, with narrow streets that lead to the public market and up Mount Chevalier

to a section called Le Suquet. Here are the 17th-century Gothic church of Notre-Dame d'Espérance; and the 12th-century Tour du Suquet, a watchtower built by the Monks of Lérins containing the Musée de la Castre, which displays artifacts from ancient Mediterranean civilizations.

The Lérins Islands of Ste.-Marguerite and St.-Honorat are worth visiting (20 minutes by boat). Ste.-Marguerite is the site of the prison that held the well-known *Man in the Iron Mask*.

CARCASSONNE (245 C1)
AUDE *pop. 43,500*
Carcassonne has a long history as a frontier fortress. The Aude River divides it into two sections: the Ville Basse (Lower Town), founded in the 13th century and now forming the modern town, and the center of Carcassonne, the Cité, which dates from the Roman occupation in the 1st century. It developed into a thriving medieval town with formidable fortifications. These fell into disrepair after the Wars of Religion, but were comprehensively restored in the 19th century. The Cité's double-walled and turreted fortress, rising from a precipitous plateau and illuminated at night, now forms one of the most extravagant fortresses in Europe.

CARNAC (245 A4)
MORBIHAN *pop. 4,200*
This town is known for its prehistoric megaliths. Over 3,000 standing stones, erected between 5,500 and 1,000 BC, are set in rows that stretch across the surrounding countryside for several miles. Le Menec and the megaliths of Keriavel or Kermario are of particular interest.

CASSIS (245 D1)
BOUCHES-DU-RHÔNE *pop. 8,000*
Cassis is a picturesque fishing port and resort sunk between towering limestone cliffs. The old port, frequented by artists earlier this century, is lined with waterfront cafés, fish restaurants and small hotels. South west are three *calanques*,

dramatic deep-water inlets slashed into the cliffs, reached by boat or footpath; they are popular with scuba divers and rock climbers.

CHABLIS (245 D4)
YONNE *pop. 2,600*

On the Serein River, Chablis lends its name to the popular crisp, white wine produced in the town for centuries; a festival in late November celebrates the end of the winemaking season.

CHÂLONS-SUR-MARNE (245 D4)
MARNE *pop. 48,400*

Ancient Châlons-sur-Marne is the center of the surrounding area's wine trade. Among the 17th- and 18th-century buildings are the Louis XVI-style Préfecture and the Hôtel de Ville.

BASILIQUE NOTRE-DAME-EN-VAUX, 8 kilometers (5 miles) east, at L'Épine, is a striking example of Romanesque-Gothic architecture. The Basilique de Lumière, a laser light show, dramatically accents its beauty.

CATHÉDRALE St.-ÉTIENNE dates from the 12th century. Its renowned stained glass can be seen in the transept and the choir.

MUSÉE DU CLOÎTRE DE NOTRE-DAME-EN-VAUX is a 12th-century church housing a fine collection of religious sculpture.

MUSÉE GARINET is a reconstruction of a bourgeois house of the 19th century.

MUSÉE MUNICIPAL displays medieval sculpture and exhibits pertaining to archeology and folklore. A collection of paintings dates from the 16th century to the present.

CHALON-SUR-SAÔNE (245 D3)
SAÔNE-ET-LOIRE *pop. 54,600*

A bustling town in eastern Burgundy, Chalon-sur-Saône is the scene of one of the most joyous Mardi Gras carnivals in France. Of historical interest are the towers, the wooden houses, the Denon Museum with collections of local archeology, art and furniture, and the Cathedral of St.-Vincent, dating from the 11th century. Of more recent interest is the Photography Museum; Chalon is the birthplace of Joseph-Nicéphore Niepce, the inventor of photography.

CHAMONIX (245 E3)
HAUTE-SAVOIE *pop. 9,700*

The popular Alpine resort of Chamonix is near the French-Swiss border. Perpetually snowy, Europe's highest peak, 4,807-meter (15,771-foot) Mont Blanc towers above the scenic valley. In 1786, Michel-Gabriel Paccard became the first person to scale Mont Blanc. The Musée Alpine gives a history of Mont Blanc and its conquerors.

The Mont Blanc Tunnel enables motorists to drive from Chamonix to Courmayeur in Italy.

The site of the first Winter Olympic Games in 1924, Chamonix has facilities for all winter sports, as well as tennis, golf, swimming and mountain climbing.

CHANTILLY (245 C4)
OISE *pop. 11,300*

Elegant Chantilly has long been a great center of horse-racing, horseback riding and dressage, and is still a training center for thoroughbreds.

A popular attraction is the 16th-century castle of the Dukes of Condé, set among ornamental lakes and well-groomed flower beds.

> **FRANCE PAST AND PRESENT**
>
> "France is the most brilliant and dangerous nation in Europe, best suited to become in turn an object of admiration, hatred, pity, terror, but never of indifference."
> These are the words of Alexis de Toqueville in the 19th century, but the notion is just as relevant today.

CHÂTEAU, rebuilt in the 19th-century, is flanked by stone stables built in the 18th century to house 240 horses and 500 hunting dogs. The Musée Condé, displaying paintings, jewels, manuscripts and miniatures, is within the palace. **Musée Vivant Du Chevalet Du Poney**, in the large 18th-century stables, has horses and ponies of different breeds as well as wooden models representing various equestrian disciplines. Also depicted are trades and activities associated with horses and equestrian shows.

PARC ASTÉRIX, at Plailly, 14 kilometers (9 miles) south east, is a theme park based on the adventures of French comic strip hero Astérix. The park has more than 100 attractions, including reconstructions of the Astérix village and a Paris street. In the Roman Arena and Camp, actors portray Roman soldiers and gladiators. Rollercoasters, water rides and a dolphinarium also are featured.

CHARTRES (245 C4)
EURE-ET-LOIR *pop. 39,600*
Chartres is best known for its Cathedral of Notre-Dame, an architectural wonder that dominates the town's gabled houses and cobbled streets.

CATHÉDRALE NOTRE-DAME, which dates from the 13th-century, is a masterpiece of early Gothic architecture. Although parts of the cathedral have been restored, the stained-glass windows remain as they were seven centuries ago.

CHÂTEAU DE MAINTENON, 18 kilometers (11 miles) north east, is largely 16th and 17th century, but the square tower dates from the 12th century.

CHÂTILLON-SUR-SEINE (245 D4)
CÔTE-D'OR *pop. 6,900*
A city in a park, Châtillon-sur-Seine is dominated by its 11th-century Church of St. Vorles. The old church and many houses rise on a hillock above the Seine River, but the little town offers much more than a pleasant setting. At Vix, 7 kilometers (4 miles) north, in the Renaissance house of Philandrier, is the Treasure of Vix, one of the most sensational archeological discoveries of the 20th century. The collection includes relics dating from about the 6th century BC, as well as Celtic antiquities.

CHAUMONT-SUR-LOIRE (245 C4)
LOIR-ET-CHER *pop. 900*
Château de Chaumont, above the Loire River, is an imposing 15th-century Gothic structure. Inside are fine tapestries and furniture; a cedar tree park, gardens and stables with carriages are to be enjoyed in the grounds.

CHERBOURG (245 B5)
MANCHE *pop. 27,100*
A principal ferry port with connections to England and Ireland, commercial port, shipbuilding and naval center, Cherbourg is on the northern coast of the Contentin Peninsula.

It is at the western end of the coast that saw the Normandy invasion of 1944. The Museum of the War and Liberation above nearby Fort du Roule traces the invasion and subsequent course of war.

Rewarding side trips include the coastal drives around the Cap de la Hague, the wild, rocky coast north west of Cherbourg, and the Val de Saire region to the east.

CHINON (245 B3)
INDRE-ET LOIRE *pop. 8,600*
The riverside town of Chinon has retained much of its medieval appearance manifested in its three ancient, ruined fortresses. Fort St.-Georges was built by King Henry II and is reputedly where he died in 1189; the Château du Milieu is where Joan of Arc was received by the Dauphin in 1429; and the Fort du Coudray is where she slept during her stay. The Château du Milieu has displays on medieval royal architecture, Joan of Arc and historical scenes with waxworks.

Maison des États-Généraux, where Richard the Lionheart died in 1199, is now the Musée du Vieux Chinon.

CLERMONT-FERRAND (245 D3)
PUY-DE-DÔME *pop. 136,200*

Clermont-Ferrand is considered the capital of the Auvergne, with spectacular scenery and extinct volcanoes. The city overlooks a valley to the east and the Monts Dômes to the west. It has a number of old buildings built of black volcanic rock. The Musée du Bargoin contains Roman and prehistoric relics.

CLUNY (245 D3)
SAÔNE-ET-LOIRE *pop. 4,400*

Cluny's history revolves around the Benedictine abbey built in the 10th century. The abbey became a learning center in the Middle Ages, and its monks traveled across Europe founding brother orders. The original abbey church was 187 meters (613 feet) long; it was the biggest church in the Christian world until St. Peter's in Rome was built.

Although much of the structure was destroyed in the early 19th century, some sections remain, giving a good impression of what the whole edifice looked like. The best view of the abbey and of the many old houses in town is from the top of the Tour des Fromages.

COGNAC (245 B3)
CHARENTE *pop. 19,500*

The old city of Cognac is in the heart of brandy country; it is surrounded by vineyards that are the source of the well-known cognac brandies. In addition to its distilleries, which may be visited, the region is known for the 12th-century Church of St. Léger, Renaissance houses and towers, and the Château de Valois, birthplace of François I, in a lovely park.

MUSÉE DU COGNAC, within the Musée Municipal, 48 boulevard Denfert-Rochereau, has displays on the history, distillation and sale of cognac.

CONQUES (245 C2)
AVEYRON *pop. 400*

The old village of Conques is known for its church of Ste.-Foy, considered one of the best examples of Romanesque architecture in southern France. A carving of the *Last Judgement* is inside. There is also 9th- to 16th-century religious art, including a gilded wooden statue of Ste.-Foy, one of the oldest Christian statues.

CORSE (CORSICA) (245 E1)
pop. 249,700

The Mediterranean island of Corsica, 183 kilometers (133 miles) long and 83 kilometers (50 miles) wide, lies off the French and Italian coast in the Gulf of Genoa. It has been called a continent in miniature with mountains soaring to over 2,000 meters (6,000 feet), an abundance of rivers and streams, and a rich diversity of flora and fauna. The island has a history stretching back over 8,000 years with many monuments of great architectural value.

The island can be reached by scheduled flights from Paris, Lille, Lyon, Marseille, Nice and Toulon and by frequent ferry services from Marseille, Toulon and Nice to the two main ports of Ajaccio and Bastia.

AJACCIO *pop. 55,500*

The seaport and capital of Corsica was Napoléon Bonaparte's birthplace. Today Ajaccio is the principal town on the island with numerous monuments and museums commemorating Napoléon; including the house where he was born, and the church where he was baptized.

BASTIA *pop. 45,000*

Bastia, the ancient port of Corsica, was once a Genoese stronghold. The fishing settlement lies at the foot of vine-clad hills. Visit the old Governor's Palace housing the Ethnographic Museum, the citadel and several churches.

COURCHEVEL (245 E2)
SAVOIE

Regarded as one of the greatest skiing centers in Europe, Courchevel is the core of a complex of resorts. Along with nearby Albertville, Courchevel was the center for the 1992 Winter Olympics. This community in the Savoie region of the Alps consists of four towns ranging in elevation from 1,300 meters (4,265 feet) to 1,850 meters (6,070 feet). Courchevel also supports a lively cultural life.

DEAUVILLE (245 B4)
CALVADOS *pop. 4,300*

Deauville, in north-west France, is an extremely fashionable seaside resort and where the Parisian jet-set spend their holidays; in summer, its population swells to 40,000.

The height of the tourist season is in August, when the racetrack holds one of the most popular meets in France and the world polo championship takes place. Les Planches is a wooden promenade lined with gardens and nightclubs that runs the length of the beach.

Sports facilities abound, and there is a casino. Deauville is also the setting of the Festival of American Cinema each September.

DIEPPE (245 C5)
SEINE-MARITIME *pop. 35,900*

Dieppe is probably France's oldest seaside resort. Although the city is now a major commercial and passenger port with a ferry service to Newhaven in England, it has retained many of its old alleys and its castle, which contains a museum of the history of Dieppe and its coastline.

A plaque commemorates the August 1942 Canadian commando raid.

DIGNE (245 E2)
ALPES-DE-HAUTE-PROVENCE
pop. 16,400

A popular tourist center beside the Bléone River, Digne enjoys a warm, dry climate. The town is known for the production of lavender and fruit.

The southern Alps and the Bès Valley are within easy traveling distance.

MUSÉE MUNICIPAL has exhibits pertaining to prehistory, archeology, mineralogy and natural history. The paintings on display include works from the French, Flemish, Dutch and Italian schools.

NOTRE-DAME-DU-BORG is a Romanesque cathedral that dates from the 13th and 14th centuries.

DIJON (245 D3)
SEINE-MARITIME *pop. 46,700*

In its heyday, Dijon served as capital of the Burgundian dukes. These wealthy independent nobles contributed many of the city's artistic and architectural treasures. Their most conspicuous monument is the Palais des Ducs et des États de Bourgogne, now the Hôtel de Ville; another palace, the Palais de Justice, was the meeting place of the duchy's 16th-century parliament. Dijon's nobles built spectacular mansions, many of which stand in the city center.

Remarkable among the several churches are St.-Philibert, with its Romanesque nave, and Notre-Dame and St. Michel, with elaborately carved exteriors. The Cathédrale St. Bénigne, originally an abbey church, dates from the 14th century. Nearby in a monastery is an archeological museum with relics of Dijon's earliest residents, the Romans, who had a prominent military installation.

An art center since the Renaissance, Dijon also is an epicurean capital. The surrounding countryside produces some of the finest wines in the world. Dijon itself is recognized for *cassis* (blackcurrant liqueur), snails, spice bread and mustard. From the end of October to the beginning of November, gastronomes gather for the Foire Internationale et Gastronomique, a magnificent display of good food and drink.

HÔTEL DE VILLE, in the city center, incorporates the substantial remains of the 14th-century Palais des Ducs et des États de Bourgogne.
Musée des Beaux-Arts, one of the outstanding art museums in Europe, was founded in the 18th century and contains European paintings and sculptures.

MUSÉE GREVIN DE BOURGOGNE 13 avenue Albert I, displays waxwork scenes which portray Burgundy's history.

FRANCE

DINAN (245 B4)
COTES-D'AMOR *pop. 11,600*
Dinan is a wonderfully preserved medieval town enclosed within 600-year-old walls and guarded by an impressive fortress. Visitors stroll the narrow cobbled streets and admire the timber-front houses, little port, and craft shops. The Jardin Anglais offers fine panoramic views over the valley of the Rance River.

DINARD
ÎLE-ET-VILAINE *pop. 19,900*
A seaside resort, Dinard became popular with Britons and Americans in the 19th century. Today tourists visit the town for its sports facilities, beaches and casino, or just to stroll the beachfront Promenade Clair-de-Lune.

AQUARIUM ET MUSÉE DE LA MER shows visitors the marine life of the Brittany coast and details the expeditions of Commander Charcot, a local explorer.

DISNEYLAND PARIS – *see Marne-la-Vallée on p.284.*

DOLE (245 D3)
JURA *pop. 26,600*
Dole borders both the Doub River and the Rhine-Rhône Canal. This attractive industrial city is the birthplace of Louis Pasteur and contains an interesting museum illustrating his work.

DOMRÉMY-LA-PUCELLE (245 D4)
VOSGES *pop. 200*
Joan of Arc was born in tiny Domrémy beside the Meuse River in 1412. Her birthplace, Maison Natale de Jeanne d'Arc, has been preserved. A museum next to the house contains mementos of her life. Two kilometers (1 mile) south is the Basilique du Bois-Chenu, marking the spot where Joan first heard voices summoning her to fight for France.

DOUARNENEZ (245 A4)
FINISTÈRE *pop. 16,500*
Ancient Douarnenez gradually merged with the neighboring towns of Ploaré,
Pouldavid and Tréboul to form one of France's major fishing ports. Lobster and sardines are the town's chief commodities. Visitors are drawn to the beaches, watersports, old churches, Port-Musée laid out along the quays of the Port-Rhu, and the Musée du Bateau, with its extraordinary collection of traditional European boats.

DUNKERQUE (245 C5)
NORD *pop. 70,300*
Dunkerque, or Dunkirk, is noted as the embarkation point for the retreat of British troops in June 1940. During the war, more than 75 percent of the city was destroyed, but it has been almost entirely rebuilt. There are museums of fine art, contemporary art and of the port. A cross-Channel ferry service connects the city with Ramsgate, England.

ÉPERNAY (245 D4)
MARNE *pop. 26,700*
Surrounded by vine-covered hills, Épernay is known for its champagne. The town shares with nearby Reims its status as the core of this region's champagne trade. The avenue de Champagne is lined with sumptuous neo-Renaissance or classical-style buildings connected with the champagne trade. Beneath the avenue you can visit over 100 kilometers (60 miles) of tunnels storing millions of bottles of champagne. The town museum contains a section devoted to champagne production.

ÉTRETAT (245 C5)
SEINE-MARITIME *pop. 1,600*
The popular seaside resort of Étretat is distinguished by two imposing chalk cliffs that stand at either end of its beach. Falaise d'Amont (Downstream Cliff) is surmounted by a small chapel; Falaise d'Aval (Upstream Cliff) is cut in its center by a huge natural archway. The distinctive L'Aiguille (The Needle) stands slightly offshore.

A restored covered market in the place Maréchal Foch is of interest. A monument to the aviators Charles

Nungesser and François Coli, who attempted unsuccessfully to fly across the Atlantic in 1927, is on Falaise d'Amont near a museum dedicated to the pair.

ÉVREUX (245 C4)
EURE *pop. 49,100*

Évreux is the administrative and religious capital of the *département* of Eure. An important agricultural market town, it has achieved considerable industrial and economic growth in recent years.

CATHÉDRALE NOTRE-DAME dates from the 10th century. Although severely damaged in the French Revolution and World War II, the cathedral still retains 13th- to 16th-century stained-glass windows, fine woodwork and small chapels.

MUSÉE MUNICIPAL is in the Bishop's Palace, near the Cathédrale Notre-Dame. Inside are an archeological wing with artifacts from the Middle Ages, an exhibit on local history and a collection of 19th-century paintings.

LES EYZIES-DE-TAYAC (245 C2)
DORDOGNE *pop. 900*

Les Eyzies-de-Tayac is an archeologist's delight, for it was in this area that some of the first Cro-Magnon skeletons were discovered. Extensive caves near the town such as Grotte de Font-de-Gaume and Grotte des Combarelles contain prehistoric drawings and paintings. A 10th-century castle/fortress houses the Museum of Prehistory.

FALAISE (245 B4)
CALVADOS *pop. 8,100*

William the Conqueror was born in the huge castle in 1027; the ruins of the fortress can still be seen in this Ante Valley town.

The place Guillaume-le-Conquérant contains a statue of the illegitimate son of Robert, Duke of Normandy, and Arlette, a Falaise tanner's daughter; other statues commemorate the first six dukes of Normandy. There is also a fountain dedicated to Arlette.

MUSÉE AOÛT commemorates the Battle of the Falaise Gap with documents, models and photographs, and the ultimate end to the Battle of Normandy, with armored vehicles, uniformed soldiers and models demonstrating the arrival of Canadian soldiers in Falaise.

FÉCAMP (245 C5)
SEINE-MARITIME *pop. 20,800*

Fécamp was once France's most important cod port, with trawlers embarking as far away as Newfoundland in search of the fish. A museum devoted to the fishing industry remembers those days. The town also is the home of 19th-century novelist Guy de Maupassant, born at nearby Miromesnil Castle, and the place of origin of Bénédictine liqueur.

Fécamp's church of La Trinité contains the Precious Blood relic; pilgrimages are made on the Tuesday and Thursday following Trinity Sunday.

FIGEAC (245 C2)
LOT *pop. 9,500*

Figeac is best known for the Needles of Figeac, two 15-meter (50-foot), 12th-century obelisks on the outskirts of town that are believed to mark the original limits of the local abbey's jurisdiction. Several well-preserved buildings in the vicinity of rue Delzhens and rue Gambetta are of interest.

TEN FRENCH CITIES

Ten French cities have grouped together to form a package for tourists. Besançon, secret city; Dijon, tasteful city; Lille, eclectic city; Lyon, city of refinement; Metz, shimmering city; Nancy, city of surprises; Nîmes, city of passion; Orléans, faithful city; St.-Étienne, friendly city; Toulon, welcoming city. For an inclusive price visitors have access to the main cultural attractions of that city for a period of three days. Details from tourist offices in each city.

FRANCE

ÉGLISE ST.-SAUVEUR, the former abbey church, dates from the 12th century. Some of its additions are more recent.

HÔTEL DE LA MONNAIE is a restored Gothic building once the town mint and now a tourist information center.

MUSÉE CHAMPOLLION, rue des Frères Champollion, birthplace of Egyptologist Jean-François Champollion, one of the first scholars to decipher hieroglyphics, has three showrooms. One focuses on Champollion's life, another contains Egyptian items lent by the Louvre, and the third, the script room, holds a reproduction of the Rosetta stone.

FONTAINEBLEAU (245 C4) ★
SEINE-ET-MARNE *pop. 15,700*
Fontainebleau's palace, gardens and forest are thought by some to symbolize the spirit of France even more than Versailles. It was at Fontainebleau that Napoléon Bonaparte signed his abdication papers. Because of its outstanding natural beauty, the area was a favorite subject of the 19th-century Barbizon School painters, who included Millet and Rousseau.

Le Fôret de Fontainebleau is one of Europe's most magnificent forests, covering 20,000 hectares (49,420 acres). These woods were a favorite hunting preserve of the French nobility.

PALAIS DE FONTAINEBLEAU is the grandiose castle on which French kings once lavished their tastes and fortunes. Built in the 12th century, it reflects François I's taste for the Italian Renaissance style. Henri IV, Napoléon Bonaparte and Louis Philippe later made additions to the palace and gardens. Some of their apartments, as well as those of Marie Antoinette, are open to visitors.

Of special interest are the Red Room, scene of Napoléon's abdication, the Council Room and Throne Room. The Royal Apartments contain the Gobelin tapestries and a mantelpiece designed by Italian Francesco Primaticcio. Today

one wing of the palace houses a summer school with courses in music and arts.

FRÉJUS (245 E1)
VAR *pop. 41,500*
The port of Fréjus was founded by the Romans as a shipbuilding town. Here Octavius built the ships that defeated Mark Antony and Cleopatra at the Battle of Actium.

Now Fréjus is a resort known for its beach, extensive Roman ruins, including a theater, amphitheater and aqueduct, and vineyards and orchards. Also of interest is the 5th-century baptistry of the town's cathedral.

GIEN (245 C4)
LOIRET *pop. 16,500*
Gien's strategic location on the north bank of the Loire River made it a frequent target for bombings in World War II, but much of the town has been restored to its original charm. Gien is known for the manufacture of *faïence*, a high-glaze, decorative pottery.

MUSÉE INTERNATIONAL DE LA CHASSE, in a 15th-century château, contains displays of *faïence*, armor, trophies and paintings.

GIVERNY (245 C4) ★
EURE *pop. 500*
The small village of Giverny, 5 kilometers (3 miles) south east of Vernon, was where the leading French Impressionist painter Claude Monet lived from 1883 until his death in 1926.

Giverny is normally crowded with tourists, particularly from spring to autumn – the only time you can visit Monet-associated sights.

MAISON ET JARDIN DE CLAUDE MONET, the country home in which the famous artist lived and painted for more than 40 years, has been restored as a museum. It is surrounded by the gardens he designed and developed as his private painting environment.

The house displays furnishings Monet used, reproductions of some of the 'artist's masterpieces and his famed collection of Japanese prints.

Outside, the main gardens are a kaleidoscope of fruit tree blossoms and seasonal flowers. The water garden, with its Japanese bridge, weeping willows and lily pond, is itself an expression of Monet's art.

MUSÉE D'ART AMERICAIN, 99 rue Claude Monet, features works of 19th- and 20th-century American Impressionist painters who were influenced by their stay at Giverny, and whose works are now famous in their own right.

GORGES DE L'ARDÈCHE
ARDÈCHE
Here the Ardèche River has carved out 27 kilometers (17 miles) of extraordinary gorges. The best views are from the D290 from Vallon-Pont-d'Arc to Pont-St.-Esprit, a succession of roadside belvederes hundreds of feet above the river.

The main feature is the Pont d'Arc, a spectacular natural arch over the Ardèche River, 66 meters (217 feet) wide, which is a popular spot for canoeists. Canoes can be rented from Vallon.

At Suze-la-Rousse, 16 kilometers (10 miles) east of Pont-St.-Esprit, is the only wine university in Europe. Located in a 15th-century château, the university is open to all lovers of wine.

GORGES DU TARN (245 C2) ★
LOZÈRE
One of the natural wonders of Western Europe, the Gorges du Tarn are where the Tarn River has carved out a dramatic deep gorge, rising to a height of 600 meters (1,968 feet), in the limestone hills of the Cévennes. The canyon is at its most impressive between the villages of Le Rozier and Ste.-Énimie. The roads through the canyon and along the cliff offer scenic views at every turn.

The village of Ste.-Énimie is acknowledged as one of the most beautiful in the whole of France. Boat and canoe trips down the Tarn (spring to fall only) originate at La Malène.

At the northern end of the canyon the Tarn River leads to Florac, where a wide mountain road (the Corniche des Cévennes), with breathtaking views, runs to St.-Jean-du-Gard.

GRAND CANYON DU VERDON ★
ALPES-DE-HAUTE-PROVENCE ET VAR
Between Castellane and Moustiers-Ste.-Marie, where the Verdon River cuts through the mountainous Plateau de Valensole, is the most spectacular gorge in Europe. The Grand Canyon du Verdon, more than 21 kilometers (13 miles) long, comprises a series of deeply incised gorges with limestone cliffs plunging 700 meters (2,300 feet). The best way to see it is from the Corniche Sublime on its southern side or the route des Crêtes on its northern side; both offering breathtaking panoramas.

The main tourist center is Moustiers-Ste.-Marie, at the lower end of the canyon; an interesting old village famous for its distinctive pottery which is displayed in the local Musée de la Faïence.

GRASSE (245 E2)
ALPES-MARITIMES *pop. 42,400*
Grasse is a city of flowers and aromas in the Maritime Alps. It is the world capital of the perfume industry and three perfume distilleries can be toured for no charge: the Fragonard on boulevard Fragonard, the Galimard on the Cannes road and the Molinard on boulevard Victor Hugo. Each has a retail outlet. Alternatively you can visit the Musée de la Parfumerie.

The old town center has a tumble-down appeal. Places of interest are the Hôtel de Ville, which once served as a bishop's palace; the 12th-century cathedral; and the 18th-century Villa-Musée Fragonard with works by Fragonard, born in Grasse.

GRENOBLE (245 D2)
ISÈRE *pop. 150,800*
Surrounded entirely by the French Alps, Grenoble was a popular winter sports center long before it was selected

as the center for the 1968 Winter Olympics. Bolstered by the excellence of its industries and prestige of its university, Grenoble has a worldwide reputation.

Despite modern bustle, the city carefully conserves the treasures of its past, which include the 11th-century Cathedral of Notre Dame, the Renaissance Palais de Justice and the 15th-century Hôtel de Ville.

The Law courts, used as Parliament by the Dauphins, have noteworthy ceilings and woodwork. Grenoble has many museums; the Museum of Painting and Sculpture houses one of the finest collections outside of Paris.

LE HAVRE (245 B5)
SEINE-MARITIME *pop. 195,900*

King François I founded Le Havre, originally called Le Havre de Grace, in the 16th century. Today it is France's second port with ferries to England and Ireland, having been completely rebuilt from the ravages inflicted during World War II. The city's museums include the Old Havre Museum, which chronicles local history, and the Museum of Art, which houses a rich collection of Impressionist and modern paintings. Next to the city is the resort suburb of Ste.-Adresse, which has a fine beach.

HONFLEUR
CALVADOS *pop. 8,300*

Honfleur served as an important fishing and commercial port for several centuries and received such explorers as Samuel de Champlain, who founded Québec in 1608. The town grew until the 19th century, when Le Havre, across the Seine River, supplanted it in economic importance.

The Impressionist school was later founded by Boudin, Corot and other painters. The Boudin Museum exhibits some of their works. Ste.-Catherine, a wooden church built in the 15th century by shipwrights, is also of interest.

Honfleur is a living postcard of a town, with timber-framed houses overlooking winding streets. It has an old-world ambience, yet still possesses a thriving atmosphere.

The greatest pleasure is to be had simply wandering its streets, quays and squares. Art galleries and artists' shops line the Vieux Bassin, or Old Harbor, keeping artistic traditions.

HUELGOAT (245 A4)
FINISTÈRE *pop. 1,700*

Considered one of the most beautiful inland towns in Brittany, Huelgoat benefits from its picturesque setting. Anglers fish Huelgoat's lake and the Argent River; hikers and nature lovers walk the Allée Violette, a trail through the Arrée Mountains that passes streams, lush vegetation and mounds of granite rocks. Of particular interest is Roche Tremblante, or Trembling Rock, a massive slab of granite that trembles when gently pushed.

JUMIÈGES (245 C5)
SEINE-MARITIME *pop. 1,600*

Abbaye de Jumièges was founded in the 7th century and grew into a well-known education center during the Middle Ages. Now partly ruined, the abbey retains its nave, chancel and portions of the transept. The chapter house and the storeroom date from the 12th century.

KAYSERSBERG
HAUT-RHIN *pop. 2,800*

This tiny wine-producing town is the birthplace of Nobel Peace Prize winner Albert Schweitzer. The town still retains a number of 16th- and 17th-century half-timbered buildings and shops, as well as a centuries-old fortified bridge that spans the Weiss River.

CENTRE CULTUREL ALBERT SCHWEITZER, 126 rue du Général-de-Gaulle, is a monument to the theologian, philosopher, musician and mission doctor, who was awarded the Nobel Peace Prize in 1952. From 1913 until his death in 1965 he directed the hospital he founded in the jungles of Gabon. The center contains a museum dedicated to his life and work.

LILLE (245 C5)
NORD *pop. 172,100*

Lille, capital of Flanders, is the leading industrial and commercial city in northern France. It is known for textiles, metal products and various foodstuffs. Representative of Lille's historic character are several 16th- to 18th-century churches, a number of old houses and a 17th-century citadel.

MAISON NATALE DU GÉNÉRAL DE GAULLE, 9 rue Princesse, is General de Gaulle's birthplace and now a museum including personal mementos of the President and the black Citröen in which he narrowly avoided assassination in 1962.

MUSÉE D'ART MODERNE, 4 kilometers (2½ miles) east of Lille in Villeneuve d'Ascq, features a collection of works by Braque, Picasso, Léger, Miró and Modigliani.

MUSÉE DE BEAUX-ARTS, place de la République, is the second largest museum in France, after the Louvre. Among its many valuable works are paintings by Goya, Van Gogh, Rubens and van Dyck.

LIMOGES (245 C3)
HAUTE-VIENNE *pop. 133,500*

Artisans use the pure white clay of St.-Yrieix, a short distance south, to produce the namesake china famed for its delicacy and translucence. David Haviland, an American, built a factory in the town to produce china utilizing the same fine materials but with designs more suited to American tastes. The porcelain factories and enamel workshops can be visited; details are available at the Office de Tourisme, boulevard de Fleurus.

Other points of interest include the 1786 Bishop's Palace, which contains the Museum of Limousin History; and the Musée National Adrien-Drubouché, which offers a history of porcelain.

LISIEUX (245 C4)
CALVADOS *pop. 23,700*

Pilgrims from all over the world visit Lisieux to pay homage to Ste.-Thérèse.

As a child, Ste.-Thérèse lived in Les Buissonnets, now considered a shrine. The vast Basilique de Lisieux, consecrated in 1954, contains the tombs of the saint's parents; her own shrine is in the Carmelite Chapel. Also in the town is Cathédrale de St.-Pierre, one of the oldest Gothic churches in Normandy, and the Museum of Old Lisieux, inside one of the town's timber-framed houses.

LOURDES (245 C1)
HAUTES-PYRÉNÉES *pop. 16,300*

It was in Lourdes on February 11, 1858, that Bernadette Soubirous, a young peasant girl, witnessed an apparition of the Virgin Mary; near the site of the vision a curative spring miraculously appeared. Today Lourdes is visited by millions of people each year.

BASILIQUE, begun in 1871 at the site of Ste.-Bernadette's visions (18 in all), is filled with banners and tablets of gratitude for miraculous cures. In front of the basilica is the richly decorated Church of the Rosary; next to the basilica is the fountain from which pilgrims drink. Esplanade des Processions extends before the church, with a crucifix 12 meters (39 feet) high at one end and a colossal statue of the Virgin Mary at the other. Nearby is the Grotte de Massabielle, the site of the apparitions.

LYON (245 D3) ★
RHÔNE *pop. 415,500*

Lyon, one of France's major cities, at the confluence of the Rhône and Saône rivers, traces its history from Roman occupation. It was not until the introduction of the silk industry in the Middle Ages that Lyon gained international importance. Its textile industry expanded with the introduction of power looms, and today Lyon remains France's chief manufacturer of silk. The International Fair of Lyon is held every spring.

As well as museums and Roman monuments, Lyon has a university, theaters, concert halls, stadiums and a botanical garden. The restored old quarter on the

FRANCE

right bank of the Saône is now the focus of Lyonnais *chic*, with Renaissance palaces, designer shops and eating places. Lyon is considered the world capital for gastronomy, from exclusive restaurants to the typical Lyonnais, bistro-style *bouchon*. Lyon is also known for its Beaujolais and Côtes-du-Rhône wines.

Via highway N84 is the medieval village of Pérouges which has been scrupulously restored and old crafts revived, albeit for tourists.

MUSÉE DE L'AUTOMOBILE is 12 kilometers (7 miles) north at Rochetaillée, off highway D-433 on the Saône River. Restored automobiles, motorcycles, bicycles and public transport vehicles are housed in two buildings. Many historic cars are displayed, including Hitler's bullet-proof Mercedes, along with photographs, posters and automotive accessories.

MUSÉE DES ARTS DÉCORATIFS, 30 rue de la Charité, houses 17th- and 18th-century furniture, ceramics, silver and tapestries.

MUSÉE DES BEAUX-ARTS, 20 place des Terreaux, housed in a former 17th-century abbey, contains a fine selection of paintings and sculpture including works by Veronese, Tintoretto and Rubens.

MUSÉE DE LA CIVILISATION GALLO-ROMAIN 17 rue Cléberg, has architecture as exceptional as the collections it houses. On display are examples of Roman relics, including mosaics, sculptures, jewelry, ceramics, weapons, tools and coins.

MUSÉE HISTORIQUE DES TISSUS, 34 rue de la Charité, displays priceless examples of Lyon's rare and exquisite silks from the 17th to the 20th centuries, as well as European tapestries, and textiles.

MÂCON (245 D3)
SAÔNE-ET-LOIRE *pop. 37,300*
Mâcon is a peaceful, dignified city on the Saône River, surrounded by the Mâconnais wine-producing area. A Romanesque cathedral and a Louis XV

pharmacy are among its attractions. The poet Alphonse Marie Louis de Lamartine was born in Mâcon, and the town is a pilgrimage center for admirers of his works. The Musée Lamartine is housed in the Hôtel Sennecé.

LE MANS (245 B4)
SARTHE *pop. 145,500*
Le Mans is known for its 24-hour motor race, held each June. Of architectural interest is the primarily Romanesque Cathedral of St.-Julien, dating from the 12th, 13th and 14th centuries, while its medieval center was the setting for the film *Cyrano de Bergerac*. The city's several museums encompass archeology, automobiles, painting and sculpture.

MARNE-LA-VALLÉE
SEINE-ET-MARNE
Thirty-two kilometers (20 miles) east of Paris on autoroute A4, exit 14, or by RER railroad, line A, Chessy-Marne-La-Vallée station, or by shuttle bus gets you to Disneyland Paris. It is based on the Disney theme parks in the United States and comprises 2,000 hectares (4,940 acres). Visitors can walk along Main Street, U.S.A.; relive Disney classics and European culture in Fantasyland and Adventureland; ride a rollercoaster in Frontierland, travel through space in a flight simulator at Discoveryland's Star Tours or take a trip in a flying machine based on a design by Leonardo da Vinci. Disneyland Paris also offers seven hotels, a log-cabin and an 18-hole golf course.

MARSEILLE (245 D1)
BOUCHES DU RHÔNE *pop. 880,500*
Ancient Marseille, on the Mediterranean, began as the Greek settlement of Massalia in 600 BC. Its status as a port reached a commercial zenith in the 19th century with the rebuilding of the French colonial empire in Africa and Asia and the opening of the Suez Canal.

Today, the loss of the French colonies along with a worldwide shipping slump has brought about a relative decline. The city, however, has grown and modernized significantly since the Second World War.

Marseille, France's largest port and second largest city, is busy and cosmopolitan. The main street, La Canbière, was in the days of sea travel a mighty boulevard where sultans and princes met for business. Today it is lined with more modest stores and cafés.

Used primarily by fishing boats and small pleasure craft, the Vieux Port is still the heart of the city. There are boat trips from here to the rocky island of Château d'If, a forbidding 16th-century castle and former prison. Marseille's modern port lies to the north.

Among old treasures to be found are the Cathedral of the Major, an unusual combination of 12th- and 19th-century architectural styles, and the 12th-century Abbey of St.-Victor, with its 5th-century catacombs. There are also museums of history, fine art and the decorative arts.

The French national anthem, composed by Claude Joseph Rouget de Lisle in 1792 as *The War Song of the Army of the Rhine*, was renamed *The Marseillaise* by Marseille volunteers as they marched in support of the Revolution.

LAND OF CHEESE

"The French will only be united under the threat of danger. Nobody can simply bring together a country that has 265 kinds of cheese." (Charles de Gaulle).

MUSÉE DE LA VIEILLE CHARITÉ contains Egyptian and Mediterranean archeology and African art.

PALAIS LONGCHAMP, dating from 1860, houses the Fine Arts Museum and the Natural History Museum.

MENTON (245 E2)
ALPES-MARITIMES *pop. 29,100*
Menton, near the Italian border, consists of two districts: the old town, with typical Mediterranean buildings, narrow streets and Italian baroque churches, and the modern town, with broad avenues and contemporary buildings. The Musée des Beaux-Arts, in the 18th-century Palais Carnoles, houses a collection of paintings by 18th- to 20th-century artists, and the Hôtel de Ville has a marriage chamber that was decorated by French artist Jean Cocteau between 1957 and 1958.

METZ (245 D4)
MOSELLE *pop. 119,600*
Metz is an ancient city at the confluence of the Moselle and Seille rivers. First colonized by the Romans, Metz persevered through the Middle Ages, withstanding many sieges.

An early center of Christianity, it was the seat of great bishops. The Cathedral of St.-Étienne (13th to 16th century), rising impressively above the town, has magnificent stained glass. A smaller but older Christian landmark is the 4th-century Church of Pierre-aux-Nonnains, possibly the oldest church in France. Many buildings from the Middle Ages and the 18th century survive.

MUSÉE D'ART ET D'HISTOIRE, rue du Haut Poirier, is housed in structural remains ranging from the walls of Roman baths to the façade of a Renaissance convent and a 15th-century granary.

MOISSAC (245 C2)
TARN-ET-GARONNE *pop. 12,100*
On the Tarn River, Moissac was a religious center in the Middle Ages. Today it is known for dessert grapes.

ÉGLISE ST.-PIERRE, the former abbey church, was built in Gothic and Romanesque styles in the 11th century.

Additions include cloisters and the south doorway, carved with scenes pertaining to the Apocalypse.

MONTPELLIER (245 D1)
HÉRAULT *pop. 208,000*
Montpellier, capital of the Languedoc-Roussillon region, is a dynamic modern

city of high-tech industry and bold new architecture. It is also an intellectual center with a thriving university. Its many 17th- and 18th-century buildings and gardens around rue de l'Ancien Courrier in the Quartier Ste.-Anne preserve the elegance of another era.

Modern Montpellier is centered on Antigone, an ambitious neo-classical architectural project.

NEW ROME?

The most extraordinary city project is that of Montpellier in southern France where Catalan architect Ricardo Bofill has designed medium-rent social housing in neoclassical style that is, in the words of the local mayor, "the Rome of tomorrow."

MUSÉE FABRE, rue Montpellier, contains Old Master and 19th-century paintings including works by d'Angers, Delacroix and Courbet.

PROMENADE DU PEYROU, with views of the Mediterranean, Alps and Pyrénées, is noted for its 18th-century bathing pavilion, fountains and aqueduct. The 1593 botanical gardens, Jardin des Plantes, are said to be the oldest in France.

MONT-ST.-MICHEL (245 B4) ★
MANCHE pop. 72

Photographers have long been captivated by France's premier tourist attraction, Mont-St.-Michel, on a granite islet about 2 kilometers (1¼ miles) off the Normandy coast.

The small walled city rises majestically from the slopes of the mount, which is topped by a formidable monastery. Though the city is not entirely surrounded by water during low tide, the stretch of sand connecting it to the mainland is not safe for walking; use the permanent connecting causeway.

Mont-St.-Michel was established in the 10th century when St. Aubert, bishop of Avranches, was instructed by the Archangel Michael to build an oratory on the rock. The small chapel was replaced by a Benedictine monastery, which was a celebrated seat of learning. For centuries, Mont-St.-Michel resisted not only the ravages of water and weather but also the onslaught of the English in the Hundred Years' War and the attempted invasions of the Huguenots.

By 1800, the monastery had lost its monks, and the island became a state prison. Not until 1874 was the restoration of the monastery begun, and today Mont-St.-Michel is a national shrine.

Along the Grande Rue, the steep main thoroughfare leading up to the monastery, there are shops, restaurants and even hotels. There is also a waxwork museum with figures associated with Mont-St.-Michel's history, and a maritime museum.

The monastery is illuminated at night and during the summer evenings it is the setting for son-et-lumière shows.

MORLAIX (245 A4)
FINISTÈRE pop. 16,700

Morlaix, on a narrow estuary of the English Channel, was once a prominent port; today's marine commerce consists of pleasure craft and a small fishing fleet. The town's most visible and impressive landmark is the two-story, 280-meter (919-foot) viaduct. The best place to view the structure, built in 1864, is from the place des Otages near the station.

Other places of interest are rue Grand, a street filled with venerable houses and old-fashioned shops; and the 16th-century Duchess Anne's House, with its ornately carved staircase.

MULHOUSE (245 E4)
HAUT-RHIN pop. 108,400

Despite industrialisation, Mulhouse retains traces of the former medieval fortified town that once existed. These include Bollwerk Tower, dwarfed now by the modern European Tower. The town hall, with its painted façade, is a fine example of Renaissance architecture. However, it is for its array of outstanding museums that Mulhouse mainly attracts visitors.

A zoo south east of town offers views of the city, the Black Forest, the Jura Mountains and the Bernese Alps.

MUSÉE FRANÇAIS DU CHEMIN DE FER is the most important railway museum in continental Europe, with around 100 locomotives and carriages; railway memorabilia is displayed in a disused station.

MUSÉE DE L'IMPRESSION SUR ÉTOFFES, 3 rue des Bonnes Gens, displays printed fabrics from around the world produced since the mid-18th century. An information center contains 3 million samples of fabrics, designs and textile prints. Demonstrations of printing processes take place in summer.

MUSÉE NATIONAL DE L'AUTOMOBILE, 192 avenue de Colmar, has an extensive collection of automobiles dating from the late 19th century. More than 500 vehicles are displayed, including the highly acclaimed Royale limousine.

NANCY (245 D4)
MEURTHE-ET-MOSELLE *pop. 99,400*
The historic capital of Lorraine, Nancy is well known for place Stanislas, an 18th-century town architectural complex that has been listed by UNESCO as a World Heritage Site. The square is dominated by the ornate Hôtel de Ville, with exits from the square guarded by richly gilded ironwork grilles. The 16th-century town has been completely renovated and is the site of the Musée Lorraine, housed in the Ducal Palace.

NANTES (245 B3)
LOIRE-ATLANTIQUE *pop. 245,000*
Nantes is an Atlantic port on the Loire River, once France's most important port. The city boasts a fine Gothic cathedral, museums, a planetarium, theaters, concert halls, sports facilities and a university and is also known for its varied restaurants and pre-Lenten carnival. Jules Verne was born in Nantes in 1828.

CHÂTEAU DES DUCS DE BRETAGNE, place Marc Elder, is the former residence of the dukes of Brittany and where Gilles de Rais, Baron de Retz, the original Bluebeard, was imprisoned and subsequently condemned to death. It now houses three museums: of popular art, decorative art, and maritime history.

MUSÉE DES BEAUX-ARTS, 10 rue Georges Clémenceau, with paintings from the 13th century to the present day, is considered one of the best fine-art museums in France.

MUSÉE JULES-VERNE, 3 rue de l'Hermitage, depicts the life of the author of *Journey to the Centre of the Earth*, *Twenty Thousand Leagues Under the Sea* and *Around the World in Eighty Days*.

NEVERS (245 C3)
NIÈVRE *pop. 42,000*
Nevers, at the junction of the rivers Loire and Nièvre, has been called the Pointed Town because of its many gables, belfries and towers. Ste.-Bernadette of Lourdes is buried in the convent of St.-Gildard.

The first French china factory was established in Nevers in the 16th century; its Musée Municipal Frédéric Blandin has fine exhibits of china and glass. The church of St. Étienne is in the Romanesque style; the Cathedral of St.-Cyr and Ste.-Juliette, restored, blends Romanesque and Gothic architecture.

NICE (245 E2) ★
ALPES-MARITIMES *pop. 342,400*
The Greeks who colonised Nice in the 4th century BC probably did not visualize it as a playground with hotels, golf courses and promenades, but the city has been just that for the past two centuries. Its incomparable setting on the hill-framed curve of the Baie des Anges, and the region's benevolent climate, made this role almost inevitable.

Dominating the front is the château. A hill rather than a castle, it held the city's fortress until the 18th century. Shaded walks and lookout points accommodate today's invaders. On the eastern side of this hill is the harbor, which is always busy with yachts, merchant ships, fishing boats and the steamers that carry tourists and supplies to Corsica.

West of the château is the cramped and quaint Vieille Ville, where tall, shuttered houses crowd the crooked streets. The quarter also contains the Marché aux Fleurs and the 17th-century cathedral. The Paillon River forms the unofficial boundary that separates the Vieille Ville from the modern city. Along the 6-kilometer (4-mile) seafront is the flower-decked Promenade des Anglais, named after the English who underwrote its construction in the 19th century.

Lining the town side are the white-washed façades of hotels, private mansions and such public buildings as the Palais Masséna, now a museum of art and history. A shingle beach is on the sea side of the promenade; beyond it is the blue water that gave the Côte d'Azur its name.

Catering to sun-worshipers and fun-lovers the whole year, Nice is especially lively from January to April. Horse racing, regattas, theater, casinos, nightclubs and festivals vie for a share of the tourist's time and energy. The highlight of the season is the Carnival, which occurs during the two weeks preceding Lent. Carnival's elaborate processions, masked balls and fireworks exhaust even the hardiest celebrants by the time Ash Wednesday arrives.

Contrasting with Nice's coastal setting and winter warmth are the Alpine ski resorts which are less than 2 hours away by road. Only 12 kilometers (7 miles) away is Èze, with its feudal castle and gardens.

CIMIEZ is a fashionable suburb and the site of notable Roman ruins. Gladiatorial contests were once held in the arena, which seated 4,000. Statuary, sarcophagi and other objects from these sites are in the archeological museum. The Gallo-Roman amphitheater in the gardens is the site of a jazz festival in July.

MUSÉE D'ART ET D'HISTOIRE, 65 rue de France, in Palais Masséna, is an elegant villa decorated in First Empire style. Provençal pottery, arms, local archives, 15th- and 16th-century local primitive art, and Italian Renaissance and French Impressionist works can be seen.

MUSÉE DES BEAUX-ARTS, 33 avenue des Baumettes, houses more than 600 sculptures and paintings by the creator of the modern poster, Jules Chéret, and smaller collections by Rude, Rodin, Fragonard and Raoul Dufy.

MUSÉE NATIONAL MESSAGE BIBLIQUE MARC CHAGALL, avenue du Docteur Ménard, contains a superb collection of Chagall's paintings, including *Biblical Message*, which encompasses 17 canvases; sculptures, stained-glass windows, and tapestries are also on display.

NÎMES (245 D2) ★
GARD *pop. 128,500*

Nîmes was a Gaulish settlement before it fell to the Romans around 121 BC. Emperor Augustus looked favorably on the city and granted it many privileges, which paved the way for a new prosperity and a thriving metropolis.

Nîmes is also the birthplace of denim (de Nîmes), which was exported to the southern USA in the 19th century to clothe its slaves.

LES ARÈNES, dating from the 1st century, is the best-preserved Roman amphitheater in the Roman world. It seats more than 20,000 spectators. Bullfights and assorted programs are presented.

JARDINS DE LA FONTAINE, laid out in the 18th century, contain a magnificent display of both Roman and 18th-century architecture, including the Fountain of Nîmes, the Temple of Diana and the Magne Tower, built in 16 BC.

MAISON CARRÉE, a 1st-century Roman

temple, encloses the Museum of Archeology and its famed *Venus of Nîmes*.

NIORT (245 B3)
DEUX-SÈVRES *pop. 57,000*

Niort, the principal town of the province of Deux-Sèvres in western France, was once a Huguenot stronghold. Of interest are the Romanesque keep housing the Musée Ethnographique et Archéologique, the Musée des Beaux-Arts (temporarily closed) and the nearby Roman town of Sanxay, between Niort and Poitiers via highways, N11 and D5/A62.

West of Niort and extending to the ocean is the Marais Poitevin, a maze of arable and pasture fields sometimes called Green Venice.

Between the *conches* (large ditches) and channels lined by poplars, ashes, alders and willows are many forms of wildlife, including eel, pike, heron, snipe, duck and kingfishers. This half-aquatic, half-countryside landscape can be discovered by punt or pleasure boat.

FRENCH CUISINE

French cuisine epitomizes the complexities of the national character. Science, sensuality and creativity combine to produce, at its best, food fit for the gods. Every region has its specialties refined from generation to generation.

ORANGE (245 D2)
VAUCLUSE *pop. 27,000*

Orange, in the Rhône Valley, traces its history back to the Roman Empire. Its Roman buildings include the Arc de Triomphe, dedicated to Julius Caesar in the 1st century A.D., a theater and a Roman gymnasium. Dutch residents in the 17th century carried the name of their town to America, where they founded a city in New Jersey.

THÉÂTRE ANTIQUE, place des Mounets, which dates from the 1st century BC, is one of the best surviving examples of a theater from early Mediterranean civilisation with superb acoustics. It now offers dramatic performances in summer.

ORLÉANS (245 C4) ★
LOIRET *pop. 105,000*

Former royal city and capital of France during the 10th and 11th centuries, Orléans is above all remembered as the city liberated by the peasant heroine Joan of Arc. She drove the English from the city on May 8, 1429, ending a lengthy siege, and is honoured in annual events. World War II bombings destroyed many of the original structures associated with Joan of Arc. You can, however, retrace her steps in the 17th- to 19th-century Cathédrale de Ste.-Croix and the Maison de Jeanne d'Arc, a replica of the house (it was rebuilt in 1964) in which she stayed in 1429.

ST.-BENOÎT-SUR-LOIRE, 35 kilometers (22 miles) east, was one of the most celebrated intellectual centres of the Middle Ages. The Abbaye de Fleury is an 11th- to 13th-century Romanesque masterpiece, with a noteworthy chancel and a crypt containing the relics of St. Benoît.

SULLY-SUR-LOIRE, 42 kilometers (26 miles) east, includes an outstanding 14th-century château.

PAU (245 B1)
PYRÉNÉES-ATLANTIQUES *pop. 82,200*

On a steep hill overlooking the valley of the Gave de Pau, Pau is French King Henri IV's birthplace. The town is a popular year-round resort and a good base for excursions into the Pyrenees. The boulevard des Pyrénées offers a spectacular mountain panorama. In the town's château are the Béarnaise Museum and a fine collection of Flemish and Gobelin tapestries.

PÉRIGUEUX (245 C2)
DORDOGNE *pop. 30,300*

On the left bank of the Isie River, Périgueux, the centre of Périgord, is known for its prehistoric relics and art. Rich prehistoric collections can be found

FRANCE

in the Périgord Museum. Of architectural interest is the mostly Byzantine Cathedral of St.-Front.

About 40 kilometers (25 miles) south east is the village of Les Eyzies-de-Tayac, where some of the first Cro-Magnon skeletons were discovered.

PERPIGNAN (245 C1)
PYRÉNÉES–ORIENTALES *pop. 106.000*
Perpignan, near the Spanish border, is permeated with Spanish influence. Noteworthy buildings include the Castillet, a 14th-century brick fortress, now a museum, the Cathedral of St.-Jean, a majestic example of medieval architecture; and the Palace of the Kings of Majorca, a well-restored 13th- to 14th-century castle surrounded by ramparts.

South of Perpignan, from Argèles to the Spanish border, the Pyrénées come right to the shore, creating a magnificent rocky coastline known as the Côte Vermeille. Prettiest of the resorts along this stretch is Collioure, a haunt of artists from the beginning of the century.

MUSÉE CASA PAIRAL (Musée Catalan des Arts et Traditions Populaires), in Castillet, has exhibits relating to local history, agriculture and traditions.

PETIT TRAIN JAUNE, 49 kilometers (30 miles) east at Villefrance-de-Conflent, is the starting point of the open-air "Little Yellow Train" which trundles delightfully for 2½ hours through the Pyrénées to the border town La-Tour-de-Carol.

POITIERS (245 C3)
VIENNE *pop. 78,900*
Poitiers, regional capital and university center, is a charming city that contains many rich examples of Romanesque architecture.

Of note are the churches of Notre-Dame-La-Grande, St.-Hilaire and the St.-Jean Bapistry; built in the 4th century, the last is one of the oldest in France. The splendid stained-glass windows of the Gothic Cathedral of St.-Pierre also are worth seeing.

FUTURSCOPE, at Jaunay-Clan, 7 kilometers (4 miles) north, is a high-tech entertainment center featuring the Kinémax cinema, with a giant 600 square meter (2,153 square foot) screen; the Dynamic cinema, where the spectators' seats are dwarfed by the image; the 3-D cinema; the 180° cinema; the 360° cinema; the Omnimax 180° cinema; the Show-Scan 60-frame-a-second cinema; and the Gyrotour.

There are many specific attractions for children including an enchanted lake, magic carpet gardens of Europe and Aquascope.

LE PUY (245 D2)
HAUTE-LOIRE *pop. 21,800*
Le Puy occupies an extraordinary site on enormous volcanic peaks and plateaux that jut from the green plain of Velay. The city is celebrated for its delicate lace; the Crozatier Museum houses a fine collection.

CATHÉDRALE NOTRE-DAME-DU-PUY was built on a platform beneath the summit of Mont Amis.

Noted for its façade of multicolored lava and the Carolingian Bible of Theodulph, the 12th-century church is overshadowed by Notre-Dame-de-France, a statue that was cast in 1860 from melted-down Russian cannon captured in the Battle of Sebastopol.

CHAPELLE ST.-MICHEL D'AIGUILHE a 10th-century chapel, is perched on a 76-meter (250-foot) volcanic needle; and it's a 268-step climb.

QUIMPER (245 A4)
FINISTÈRE *pop. 59,400*
The thriving commercial community of Quimper, on the Odet River, is known for its decorative pottery, a twin-towered cathedral, festivals and museums. Musée de la Faïence has 2,500 examples of the pottery (*faïence*) for which the town is famous. Musée Breton, in the former Bishop's Palace, has exhibits concerning Breton history and traditions.

RAMBOUILLET (245 C4)
YVELINES *pop. 24,300*

Rambouillet is a charming town noted for its 14th- to 18th-century château, one of the official residences of the president. You can visit when the president is not in residence. Also of interest are the National Sheep Farm, founded by Louis XVI, and nearby Rambouillet Forest.

REIMS (245 D4)
MARNE *pop. 180,600*

Because the industrial city of Reims was heavily damaged during both world wars, it has a large number of contemporary buildings.

Reims, along with Épernay, is in champagne country. The viticulture zone, with its special chalky sub-soil, is officially protected by French law. The zone covers 33,994 hectares (84,000 acres); more than 24,281 hectares (60,00 acres) are planted with vines.

BASILIQUE DE St.-RÉMI IS an 11th-century abbey and now the city's museum of history and archeology, with collections from prehistoric to medieval times, including a large military history section.

CATHÉDRALE is illuminated inside and out in the evenings in summer. The cathedral's most well-known sculpture is the *Smiling Angel.*

CENTRE DE L'AUTOMOBILE FRANÇAISE, 84 avenue Georges Clemenceau, contains a collection of 150 old French automobiles, including some rarities, as well as over 2,000 toy automobiles.

MUSÉE DES BEAUX-ARTS, 8 rue Chanzy, is housed in an 18th-century former abbey and is one of the most highly acclaimed fine arts museums in France.

SALLE DE LA REDDITION, 12 rue Franklin Roosevelt, in Reims technical college, contains the room where the German surrender was signed on May 7, 1945. The walls are covered with the operational maps used by Eisenhower.

RENNES (245 B4)
ÎLLE-ET-VILAINE *pop. 197,500*

Rennes was once the capital of Brittany and was almost destroyed by fire in 1720. All that remained was a corner of the city known as Les Lices, containing the Palais de Justice, the city's sole surviving monument from that time. The city has been rebuilt in a handsome classical style. The Jardin du Thabor botanical gardens and the collections of Renaissance and Breton works in the Museum of Fine Arts and Archeology are of interest.

The Brittany Cemetery at St. James, 50 kilometers (31 miles) north east, is the resting place for Americans who lost their lives during the 1944 Normandy and Brittany campaigns.

ÉCOMUSÉE DE LA BINTINAIS, an ancient farm south of Rennes, is now an open-air museum of local farming implements and machinery.

PALAIS DE JUSTICE, which dates from the 17th century, is the former parliament building of Brittany. The landmark was heavily damaged by fire in February 1994 and is closed indefinitely.

ROCAMADOUR (245C2)
LOT *pop. 600*

Tiny Rocamadour lies near a narrow gorge of the Alzou River. Its single street is lined with houses built in the Middle Ages to shelter pilgrims coming to pay homage to St. Amadour. A chapel dedicated to the saint is in the cliff.

GOUFFRE DE PADIRAC, north west of Rocamadour, is a series of galleries carved by a subterranean river 103 meters (338 feet) below ground level.

LA ROCHELLE (245 B3)
CHARENTE-MARITIME *pop. 73,100*

An ancient fortified town with a rich history connected with the sea, it was from here that pioneer ships set sail for the New World.

La Rochelle has many works of art and features several museums, including

FRANCE

the Museum of the New World linking the town and the Americas. La Rochelle is also known for its yachting. To the south are the seaside resorts of Angoulins and Châtelaillon.

Just off the coast of La Rochelle, but connected to the mainland by a toll-bridge, is Île de Ré. This is an island of sandy beaches and flower-filled villages.

LA ROCHE-SUR-YON (245 B3)
VENDÉE pop. 45,200
The capital of the *département* of Vendée, La Roche-sur-Yon was laid out by Napoléon Bonaparte during the early 19th century.

In place Napoléon, neo-classical buildings surround an equestrian statue of the conqueror.

CHÂTEAU DE GILLE RAIS, 55 kilometers (34 miles) north east at Tiffauges is a medieval castle with secret corridors, dungeons and a whispering gallery.

ECOMUSÉE, 45 kilometers (28 miles) north east at Les Eppesses, features Vendéen period villages as well as several craft activities.

The complex has been created around the 15th- and 16th-century Château de Puy du Fou.

MEMORIAL DE VENDÉE, 24 kilometers (15 miles) north at St.-Sulpice-le-Verdon; a 16th- and 17th-century fortified manor house, La Chabotterie, contains relics of the Vendée Wars which took place from 1793 and ended here in 1796.

RONCHAMP (245 E4)
HAUTE-SAÔNE pop. 3,100
CHAPELLE NOTRE-DAME-DU-HAUT, built between 1951 and 1955 by Swiss architect and city planner Le Corbusier, is thought by many to be the most important religious structure built during the last several centuries.

Its massive sculptured walls, sweeping roof and unusual dimensions offer a dramatically modern contrast to the country's many medieval churches.

ROUEN (245 C4) ★
SEINE-MARITIME pop. 102,700
Settled by Celts, Ratumakos, as Rouen was first called, became Rotomagus to the Romans before evolving into Rouen in the Middle Ages. Its position in a natural amphitheater on the Seine rendered the town important as a commercial and cultural center, but also made it the target of sieges and sackings.

The most memorable invasion was that of the English in the Hundred Years' War. After subjecting the city to a six-month siege in 1418–19, Les Goddones, as these unwelcome guests were called, settled down and stayed until 1449. It was during their occupation that national heroine Jeanne d'Arc was brought to Rouen, interrogated and finally, in 1431, burned at the stake as a heretic.

The Wars of Religion in the following century brought additional woe, depressing economic activity and depopulating the city. Rouen's worst devastation, however, came during the 20th century when bombings in World War II reduced much of the commercial and industrial center to rubble.

Despite serious battering over the centuries, Rouen still earns its title of Ville Musée, or Museum City. This applies not only to the number and excellence of the city's museums, but also to the well-preserved quarters of medieval and Renaissance Rouen. The grandest monument is the cathedral. Several other churches are notable, including the Gothic St.-Maclou and 14th-century St.-Ouen. Ste.-Jeanne d'Arc contains a rare collection of 16th-century stained glass.

In the place du Vieux-Marché, now a busy, modern square, a stone marker indicates where the Maid of Orléans was burned at the stake. The Musée Jeanne d'Arc on the square and the Tour Jeanne d'Arc, where the French national heroine was briefly held, recall various episodes from her career as a leader. Nearby on rue de la Pie is another museum, the birthplace of 17th-century dramatist Pierre Corneille. Novelist Gustave Flaubert was born in Rouen; his house on rue de Lecat contains mementoes of his family and medical curiosities.

The Palais de Justice, a wedding cake of chiseled stone, is an unbridled expression of the grandeur of the French Renaissance. From the simpler 14th-century Beffroi the curfew is still rung nightly at 9pm. This belfry once housed the giant clock, Le Gros Horloge, which now occupies an adjacent arch. The belfry adjoining Gros Horloge can be entered by a staircase dating from 1447 housing a small museum of old clocks. From the top there is a view of the city.

In addition to its wealth of architectural treasures, Rouen has facilities for most conventional sports. Small passenger boats cruise the Seine, allowing a closer look at the city's large commercial port. If arriving by car, take time to drive around the Corniche de Rouen, a curved road that climbs the hills above the city to the south east and provides bird's-eye views of the vista below.

CATHÉDRALE NOTRE-DAME, place de la Cathédrale, received its library, staircase and other finishing touches in the 15th century from the hand of master stone-mason Guillaume Pontifs. Exterior features of the church are the two dissimilar towers of the west front, the richly decorated doorways and the great cast-iron spire which rises 151 meters (495 feet) above the city.

Worth viewing outside are the 14th-century sculptures in the transept gables; inside, the beautiful staircase leading to the library, and the 13th-century choir with its stained glass. A tomb containing the heart of Richard the Lionheart is in the ambulatory.

ARCHEVÊCHÉ PALAIS is separated from the cathedral by the picturesque Cour-des-Libraires. A part of the chapel where Jeanne d'Arc was tried still remains.

ÉGLISE ST.-MACLOU, in the shadow of the cathedral, was completed in 1517. Aside from its Flamboyant Gothic architectural design, the church is noteworthy for its Renaissance door panels and organ.

MUSÉE DES ANTIQUITÉS, rue Thiers, is the largest fine arts museum in Normandy, boasting notable collections of Impressionist paintings and other art objects from the 16th to the 20th century.

MUSÉE DES BEAUX-ARTS, 198 rue Beauvoisine, is a particularly noteworthy museum in the cloister galleries of a former convent. In addition to the Greek, Egyptian and Oriental collections, there are excellent exhibits that trace the history of Rouen from its occupation by the Romans to its architectural and commercial zenith during the Renaissance.

MUSÉE LE SECQ DES TOURNELLES, adjoining the Musée des Beaux-Arts, is housed in the former church of St. Laurent. The displays, 12,000 pieces in total including grilles, balconies, doorknockers and keys, form the largest collection of wrought iron in Europe.

ST.-BERTRAND-DE-COMMINGES
(245 C1)
HAUTE-GARONNE *pop. 200*

Tiny St.-Bertrand-de-Comminges dates from a tribal settlement between 350 and 250 BC. In the 1st century, the Romans discovered the town's thermal springs; today many Roman relics can be viewed, including the forum baths, amphitheater and basilica.

The present settlement was founded on a hill in the 12th century. Several old houses remain; of particular interest are the two beside the town gate, which itself is a remnant from the 1st century.

Work on the cathedral began about the time the second town was settled. Originally built in Romanesque style, the structure underwent alterations between the 14th and 16th centuries.

GROTTOES DE GARGAS, 7 kilometers (4 miles) north west, are caves that contain paintings of animals and stencils of human hands estimated to be around 30,000 years old.

St.-Étienne (245 D2)

LOIRE *pop. 199,400*

St.-Étienne was once an important industrial city in the center of a rich metallurgical basin. One of its several schools is devoted to the study of mining. Today, such diverse products as silk and chocolates are produced. St.-Étienne also has several museums, a chamber of commerce housing works of art and the fine Gardens of Rez. A church bearing the city's name dates from the 15th century.

MUSÉE D'ART ET D'INDUSTRIE is devoted to the past industry of St.-Étienne and includes a working mine and a collection of contemporary art.

MUSÉE D'ART MODERNE exhibits a wide variety of modern art, including works by Pablo Picasso and Henri Matisse.

St.-Germain-en-Laye

YVELINES *pop. 39,900*

St.-Germain-en-Laye is a popular vacation spot for Parisians. One of its main attractions is a Renaissance château built by François I, now housing the Musée des Antiquités Nationales, one of the world's premier archeological collections including the first known image of a woman's face from over 22,000 years ago. The long terrace and beautiful gardens were designed by André Le Nôtre. The terrace is known for its superb view of Paris, the valley of the Seine and the surrounding countryside. Mary Stuart, Queen of Scots, lived in this château until her marriage to the French Dauphin, and James II spent his last years of exile there.

MUSÉE DU PRIEURÉ, 2 rue Maurice-Denis, is devoted to late 19th-century French artists and their work. The house containing the museum has a varied history. In 1678, the Marchioness of Montespan had it built for deprived people; in 1681, the house was turned

into the Royal General Hospital by Louis XIV and retained this status until 1803, when it became a warehouse and painter's studio.

From 1875 to 1905 the house was a retirement home for Jesuit fathers; in 1910, the painter Maurice Denis came to live and work at the property, acquired it in 1914 and began the development of the art collection.

St.-Jean-de-Luz

PYRÉNÉES-ATLANTIQUES *pop. 13,000*

As well as being a picturesque Basque summer resort, St.-Jean-de-Luz is the chief tuna port of France. St.-Jean Baptiste Cathedral is where in 1660 Louis XIV married María Theresa of Spain; the Musée du Souvenir contains their marriage contract. Across the harbor, Ciboure is the birthplace of early 20th-century composer, Maurice Ravel.

St.-Malo (245 B4)

ÎLLE-ET-VILAINE *pop. 48,100*

Bordered by the sprawling modern city, the ancient citadel, or Ville Close, lies on a rocky island which is connected to the mainland by a causeway called the Sillon. It was from this site that mariner Jacques Cartier sailed to discover the St. Lawrence River. The island's location and fortifications made it an ideal pirate stronghold; the medieval Tour Quic-en-Groigne is a historical waxworks museum that contains souvenirs of the buccaneers who frequented the island.

Île du Grand Bé, where the desolate tomb of François René de Châteaubriand is located, can be reached at low tide. The tides of St.-Malo Bay have a range that ranks among the world's greatest, sometimes extending as far as 13 meters (43 feet).

St.-Omer (245 C5)

PAS-DE-CALAIS *pop. 14,400*

St.-Omer, an elegant town on the banks of the Aa River, is surrounded by marshland and is the market garden of the region. The town offers several interesting sights. The Grand Palace is flanked by 17th- and 18th-century merchants' houses; a market is held at the palace every Saturday. The Notre Dame Cathedral, built from the 13th to 16th centuries, contains many notable works of art. An 18th-century mansion houses the Sandelin Museum, which displays Flemish, Dutch and French paintings from the 15th century as well as tapestries and archeological finds. At Argues is the renowned glass and crystal works.

ST.-RÉMY-DE-PROVENCE
BOUCHES-DU-RHÔNE *pop. 9,300*
In St.-Rémy-de-Provence are the ruins of the ancient Greco-Roman town Glanum. Among the 1st-century structures still standing are the municipal arch and the mausoleum erected in honor of the grandsons of Emperor Augustus. The town's hospital was where Van Gogh went after cutting off his ear. The 16th-century astrologer and prophet Nostradamus was born here; his predictions are still studied.

ST.-TROPEZ (245 E1)
VAR *pop. 5,800*
An old Provençal town on the Riviera, St.-Tropez was first popular as an artists' colony and now attracts yachtsmen and tourists. "St. Trop," as it is known, became one of the world's top spots for displays of fashion and fashionable behavior in the 1950s and 1960s. Though losing some of its exclusivity, the heart of the resort, the Vieux Port, retains exorbitant restaurants, glitzy yachts and famous people. The 16th-century citadel has a fine view over the town. A festival of music, dancing and flowers is in mid-May.

MUSÉE DE L'ANNONCIADE, place Georges Grammont, exhibits a collection of early 20th-century works by such artists as Paul Signac, Georges Rouault, Henri Matisse and Raoul Dufy.

STE.-MÈRE-ÉGLISE (245 B5)
MANCHE *pop. 1,600*
The market town of Ste.-Mère-Église was the target of the U.S. 82nd Airborne

Division's parachute drop on June 5, 1944; it was the first French town to be liberated during the Battle of Normandy. The first milestone on Liberty Road, the road taken by the Americans as they moved inland, is outside the town hall.

MUSÉE DU DÉBARQUEMENT À UTAH BEACH, in Ste.-Marie-du-Mont to the south east, illustrates the plight of American troops in the fierce battle of Utah Beach. A glassed viewing gallery overlooks the battle site.

MUSÉE DE LA FERME DU COTENTIN depicts a turn-of-the century farm typical of the region through reconstructed scenes of daily life.

MUSÉE DES TROUPES AEROPORTÉES, in the center of the town, is in the form of a parachute and documents the story of the town's liberation by American troops on June 5, 1944.

LES STES.-MARIES-DE-LA-MER
BOUCHES-DU-RHÈNE *pop. 2,200*
Unofficial capital of the Camargue region, Stes.-Maries-de-la-Mer is known for its *course libre* and *abrivado*, variations on the bloodless bullfight popular in Pamplona, Spain.

On the feast days of May 24–25, gypsies from throughout Europe converge to worship their patron saint Sarah; legend claims her as servant to the Biblical Mary Salome and Mary Jacobaeus, for whom the town was named.

The gypsies carry the statue of Sarah to the sea where it is bathed. The 12th-century fortress/ church, center of the pilgrimage, contains relics of the French Revolution. Also worth seeing is the town hall's Musée Baroncelli, which presents a selection of unusual local crafts and customs.

SALINS-LES-BAINS
JURA *pop. 3,600*
Salins takes its name from the saltworks responsible for the town's prosperity.

FRANCE

Today thermal waters are its main attraction with lovely fountains playing between historic monuments.

SALINE ROYALE, in the village of Arc-et-Senans, 20 kilometers (12 miles) north west of Salins-les-Bains, is an exceptional piece of industrial architecture. Built in 1775, but not used for salt production since 1895, it is listed on U.N.E.S.C.O.'s Register of World Monuments.

SARLAT-LA-CANÉDA (245 C2)
DORDOGNE *pop. 9,900.*
Yellow ocher stone houses and quaint narrow streets have been carefully restored to preserve the old world charm of Sarlat-La-Canéda, a typical French country town. *Pâté de foie gras* and walnuts, the town's specialties, can be found in local restaurants.

Sarlat-La-Canéda offers a lively market every Saturday, a drama festival in July and August and regular concerts in the 16th-century cathedral. Year-round places of interest are the cathedral and the Lantern of the Dead, a 12th-century cylindrical tower that was probably built to commemorate the miracles performed in the town by St. Bernard. Of architectural note are the hôtels Maleville and Plamon, the latter a private home of local cloth merchants.

Near Montignac, 25 kilometers (16 miles) north west, the Grotte de Lascaux contains some of the best preserved prehistoric cave paintings ever discovered. A replica cave, Lascaux II, nearby, show the authentically copied drawings.

SAUMUR (245 B3)
MAINE-ET-LOIRE *pop. 30,100*
Saumur, in the château region of the Loire Valley, has been a notable town since the 11th century, when it was a fortress. Today it is renowned for its riding school and 14th-century château. Heavily damaged during World War II, Saumur has been rebuilt. Residents take an active part in the French wine industry. The sparkling wine caves, in suburban St.-Hilaire-St.-Florent, are of inter-

est. About 16 kilometers (10 miles) south west at Doué-La-Fontaine lies the highest concentration of troglodyte dwellings in France. The caves now house a zoo, where many endangered species reside.

CHÂTEAU, which dates from the 14th century, dominates the valley with its elaborate towers and walls. Two museums are in the grounds.
Musée Des Arts Décoratifs contains collections of porcelain and ceramics, Limoges enamel, tapestries and a variety of other furnishings.
Musée Du Cheval chronicles the history of horsemanship with antique saddles, stirrups, bits and engravings.

VILLAGE TROGLODYTIQUE, about 17 kilometers (10 miles) west at Rochemenier, is an underground troglodyte village. Many of the caves were occupied in the Middle Ages. Several underground houses were inhabited in the 19th century, and a few are still used.

STRASBOURG (245 E4) ★
BAS-RHIN *pop. 252,300*
Originally Celtic, briefly Roman and for much of its existence Germanic, old Strasbourg, on the Ill River, wears its centuries gracefully.

La Petite France is the name given to the well-preserved and pedestrianized medieval quarter in the south-west section of the city. Its high-gabled gingerbread houses on narrow streets and canals date from the 16th and 17th centuries, when millers, tanners and fishermen thronged the area.

The area is best viewed from the *ponts couverts* (covered bridges), which are no longer covered, and better still from the walkway on top of the Barrage Vauban.

Strasbourg's rose-colored cathedral recalls the city's early ecclesiastical importance and the several centuries of struggles between bishops and citizens. The river port, east of the city on the Rhine, points to Strasbourg's long-time role as inland port and trading center.

Known for its printing industry, Strasbourg was the site of Johann Gutenberg's early experiments with movable type. A statue of the 15th-century inventor stands in the square named after him. Seven centuries earlier, two nobles took the Strasbourg Oath; the text of this *Serment de Strasbourg* is considered the oldest written French document.

Also associated with the town is the French national anthem, composed in 1712 and later given its southern French name *La Marseillaise*. Important today as an industrial and administrative enclave, Strasbourg is the headquarters of both the multinational Council of Europe and European Parliament. Gourmets know the city for Alsatian cuisine in general and *pâté de foie gras* in particular.

The Parc de l'Orangerie contains a beautiful formal garden laid out in honor of Empress Josephine in 1804, plus facilities for bowling, canoeing and a zoo.

Boat trips are available along the Rhine and the Ill rivers. A mini-train makes daily tours of Strasbourg's old section in summer.

CATHÉDRALE NOTRE-DAME, with its 142-meter (464-foot) spire, dominates the city. Begun in the 11th century and finished in the 15th century, it is architecturally varied, with Romanesque as well as transitional and Gothic features. Noteworthy are its stained glass, statuary and the lacelike tracery of its windows. The 19th-century astronomical clock springs to life at 12:30pm. A figure representing Death strikes the hour; Christ appears and blesses his Apostles; and a cock crows in memory of Peter's denial. Arrive by 12:15pm for a good view.

CHÂTEAU DES ROHAN, the former palace of the bishops dating from the 18th century, now contains several museums. One has local archeological finds; another is devoted to decorative arts.

Best known is the Musée des Beaux-Arts, with works from the 14th to 19th centuries by Giotto, El Greco, Peter Paul Rubens and Rembrandt. Also displayed is the mechanism of the cathedral's original astronomical clock, which was replaced in 1842.

MUSÉE ALSACIEN, 23–25 quai Saint-Nicolas, is devoted to popular arts, with special displays relating to religious art, viticulture, and clog, rope and artificial flower making.

MUSÉE DE L'ŒUVRE NOTRE-DAME, 3 place du Château, houses much of the art assembled in the cathedral over the centuries, as well as exhibits tracing the evolution of distinctive Alsatian art from the 11th to 17th centuries.

TOULOUSE (245 C1)
HAUTE-GARONNE *pop. 358,700*
Known for its rose-red brick buildings, Toulouse's beginnings can be traced to the Roman period. It was capital of the Visigoths through much of the 5th century and was the chief town of the Carolingian kingdom of Aquitaine.

Toulouse contains many medieval churches, notable the St.-Étienne Cathedral and the Romanesque basilica of St.-Sernin. The church of Notre-Dame-du-Tour has an interesting gabled façade with ornamentation achieved entirely through the use of brick. There are also opulent Renaissance and 16th-century buildings. Many of them are houses built by merchants who prospered from the discovery of obtaining dye from the woad plant; today they operate as hotels.

Toulouse is rich in museums. The Augustins, in a former convent, contains sculptures and religious paintings by Peter Paul Rubens and Eugène Delacroix. The Musée Paul Dupuy displays works by artisans from the medieval period to the present; included are coins, clocks and a re-creation of an early 17th-century pharmacy. Toulouse also has more than 100 gardens, including the Royal Gardens, created in 1754.

Modern Toulouse has prospered from extraordinary development in aeronautics and the aerospace industry leading

FRANCE

to the development of the Hermes space shuttle. The city also serves as a trading center between the Mediterranean and the Aquitaine basin, whose farm products it markets.

TOURS (245 C3)
INDRE-ET-LOIRE *pop. 129,500*

An important center of learning and commerce since the Middle Ages, Tours, capital of Touraine, is a popular stopping place for travelers exploring the Loire Valley.

The well-restored 15th-and 16th-century half-timbered houses around the place Plumereau are of special interest, as is the beautiful Gothic Renaissance Cathedral of St.-Gatien, with a collection of fine stained glass.

The former residence of the Kings of France, the 13th- to 15th-century Château Royal de Tours now houses a waxworks museum, local history museum and tropical aquarium. Tours also has museums devoted to fine arts, history, archeology, natural history, local crafts, the military, costumes and wine.

AZAY-LE-RIDEAU, 28 kilometers (17 miles) south west, is well known for its 16th-century Renaissance château, which is surrounded by parkland and rests partly on the bank of the Indre River. Fine furnishings, tapestries and an impressive main staircase highlight the interior.

CHÂTEAU ET JARDIN DE VILLANDRY, about 15 kilometers (9 miles) south west, is a 16th-century castle overlooking magnificent Renaissance gardens laid out on three levels.

TROYES (245 D4)
AUBE *pop. 59,300*

A prosperous city on a tributary of the Seine, Troyes was once capital of the Champagne province.

Merchants traveled to Troyes in the Middle Ages to attend its trade fairs and in the 16th century to buy hosiery, which is still manufactured.

The houses built during Troyes' golden age can still be seen in La Ruelle aux Chats. Here are half-timbered Renaissance dwellings with turrets and porch roofs. Troyes also has many noteworthy churches. Of particular interest are the Cathedral of St.-Peter and St.-Paul, with its stained-glass windows and rich treasury, and the churches of Ste.-Madeleine and St.-Jean.

Floodlights illuminate the cathedral during the Cathédrale de Lumière spectacle from June to September.

MAISON DE L'OUTIL ET DE LA PENSÉ OUVRIÈR, 7 rue de la Trinité, exhibits a vast collection of tools and books used by French craftsmen through the ages.

MUSÉE D'ART MODERNE, Old Episcopal Palace, place St.-Pierre, features more than 2,000 works of French art dating 1850–1950.

Exhibits include paintings, drawings, sculptures, ceramic pieces, glassware and tapestries, as well as African and Oceanic art. The garden area displays pieces of sculpture amid pleasant surroundings.

MUSÉE DES BEAUX-ARTS, D'ARCHÉOLOGIE ET MUSÉE D'HISTOIRE NATURELLE is in the former Abbey of St.-Loup. Displays include weapons and gold jewelry from the tomb of a barbarian chief and a large archeological collection.

MUSÉE DE LA BONNETERIE chronicles the history of Troyes' hosiery industry with old looms, knitting machines and displays of stockings, gloves, bathing costumes and underwear.

VAL D'ISÈRE (245 E2)
SAVOIE *pop. 1,700*
elev. 1,840m (6037ft)

One of the best equipped European ski resorts in eastern France, Val d'Isère is the home of the Low Countries' ski championships.

The season usually continues through May on slopes that can sometimes rise as high as 12,300 feet.

VERDUN (245 D4)
MEUSE *pop. 20,500*

Verdun is often considered a "warrior town" both because of its location in northeastern France and its long history in military affairs. The most celebrated chapter in Verdun's past was written in 1916, when the town's gallant resistance to a long and cruel siege saved Paris in one of the bloodiest battles of World War I. Tributes to this resistance are *Défence*, a group of statuary by Auguste Rodin, and the *Monument to Victory and the Dead* by Jean Boucher. Excursions can be made to the battlefields.

The Meuse-Argonne Cemetery lies 35 kilometers (22 miles) north west at Romagne-sous-Montfaucon. Here rest the largest number of American military men killed in Europe, most of whom died in the Meuse–Argonne offensive of World War I.

About 44 kilometers (27 miles) south east is the St.-Mihiel Cemetery at Thiaucourt, where over 4,000 American soldiers who died 1914–18 are buried.

MUSÉE ALPHONSE-GEORGE POULAIN, 12 rue du Pont, in a mansion dating from the 15th century, houses collections of French and American Impressionist art. It is one of the few museums in France that specializes in animal art.

VERSAILLES (245 C4) ★
YVELINES *pop. 87,800*

CHÂTEAU DE VERSAILLES, which dates from the 17th century, is the magnificent hallmark of the former royal city of Versailles. Built by Le Van and Jules Hardouin-Mansart for Louis XIV, this sumptuous prototype of French classical architecture has been the setting for many dramatic and ironic events – the meeting of the Estates General in 1789, the proclamation of the German Empire in 1871, the direction of France's government 1871–9 and, finally the signing of the 1919 Treaty of Versailles.

The most interesting parts of the building are its historic first-floor apartments, which include the King's Grand Apartment, with six opulent drawing rooms; the Hall of Mirrors, a beautiful extravagance from the days when mirror glass was extremely expensive; the apartments of Louis XIV and Louis XV; and the Queen's Great and Small Apartments. All of these rooms are decorated with numerous works of art by the reigning masters of the period.

The Historical Museum in the palace has exhibits depicting French history from the 15th century; the 17th- and 18th-century rooms house portraits of the royal family and the court of Versailles. Parts of the château are now being restored, a project that will take place over 50 years.

The symmetry of the largest palace gardens in Europe is impressive. They contain statues, fountains and the Trianon, two more modest residences; Grand Trianon was built for Louis XIV, and Petit Trianon for Louis XV.

The palace can be reached from Paris by car (take Autoroute de l'Ouest) or an organised bus excursion, or train.

VICHY (245 D3)
ALLIER *pop. 27,700*

Vichy is a world-renowned spa that dates from Roman times;. it is vibrant with flowers and parks. Festivals, horse racing, sailing, golf, swimming, rowing, tennis and riding are available in season. The famed Vichy water is bottled in a state factory near the railroad station; also worth a visit are the Musée de Vichy and Maison du Missionnaire.

VIENNE (245 D2)
ISÈRE *pop. 29,500*

Vienne was the "Vienna Pulchra" of the Roman poet Martial, and there are numerous vestiges of the beautiful Vienna of Roman times. Among the substantial ruins are the Temple of Augustus and Livia, the Temple of Sybil, the Circus Pyramid, aqueducts and a Roman theater. This town also has interesting medieval monuments, including the 6th-century Church of St.-Peter and the 7th-century Tomb of St.-Léonien.

THINGS TO KNOW

- **AREA:** 1.8 square kilometers (7 square miles).
- **POPULATION:** 30,000
- **CAPITAL:** Monaco-Ville
- **LANGUAGE:** French
- **RELIGION:** Largely Roman Catholic
- **ECONOMY:** Tourism, light industry; stamp sales; cosmetics; chemicals.
- **PASSPORT:** Required for U.S. citizens.
- **VISA:** Not required for up to 3 months.
- **DUTY-FREE ITEMS:** 400 cigarettes, 50 cigars or 500 grams of tobacco; 1 liter of spirits (over 22 proof) or 2 liters (up to 22 proof) and 2 liters of wine; two still cameras with 10 rolls of film; one movie camera with 10 rolls of film; video equipment, which should be declared verbally to Customs on entry.
- **CURRENCY:** The unit of currency is the French *franc* (FF), 1FF=100 *centimes*. No limit on import or export of foreign currency, but for amounts exceeding 50,000 FF visitors should complete a currency declaration form upon arrival.
- **BANK OPENING HOURS:** 9am–noon and 2–4pm Monday–Friday.
- **STORE OPENING HOURS:** 9am–noon and 2:30–7pm Monday–Saturday; many stores are closed Monday morning.
- **BEST BUYS:** Cosmetics, costume jewelry, dolls, paintings, antiques.
- **PUBLIC HOLIDAYS:** January 1; Festival of St. Dévote, January 27; Good Friday; Easter Monday; Labor Day, May 1; Ascension Day; Whitmonday; Corpus Christi; National Day (Bastille), July 14; Assumption Day, August 15; All Saints Day, November 1; National Day, November 19; Immaculate Conception, December 8; December 25–26.
- **NATIONAL TOURIST OFFICE:**
  845 Third Ave, 19th Floor
  New York, NY 10022
  Tel: 800/753 9696
- **AMERICAN EMBASSY:**
  2 Avenue Gabriel
  75382 Paris 8
  France
  Tel: 1 43 12 22 22
  Fax: 1 42 66 97 83

MONACO
(244 E2)

HISTORY
The Phoenicians and Greeks were among the first settlers of Monaco, and the area passed from one ruler to another until 1297, when the Grimaldi family took control. The current ruler is Prince Rainier III, who was married to the movie star Grace Kelly – she was tragically killed in a car accident in 1982. Their children, Prince Albert and princesses Caroline and Stephanie, still make the headlines, most recently Princess Caroline, whose husband, Stefano Casiraghi, died in a speedboat accident.

SPORTS AND RECREATION
Once a popular wintering stop for aristocrats, Monte Carlo now has tourists year round, with visits from over 2 million. Attractions include the Grand Prix, a world-famous car race held through the streets of Monte Carlo in May, and the Fête du Prince, on November 19, with fireworks, pageants, golf tournaments, and yacht races. Dining, dancing and gambling are other diversions.

GETTING AROUND
Monaco is noted for a mild climate and magnificent scenery. At the foot of the Maritime Alps, it can be reached by air, land, sea or road, along the Route de la Moyenne Corniche, extending west to Nice, in France, and east to the Italian border. Insurance requirements and traffic regulations are the same as in France.

ACCOMMODATIONS
Monaco classifies hotels with one to four stars. Many of the most luxurious hotels are in Monte Carlo. Breakfast is not usually included in the price of a room. There are no campgrounds in Monaco.

TIPPING
Nearly every bill you are handed will include a gratuity charge, so unless the service is outstanding, leave no tip.

PLACES OF INTEREST

★ HIGHLIGHTS ★

Jardin Exotique	(see p.301)
Musée Océanographique	(see p.301)
Palais du Prince	(see p.301)
Casino	(see p.301)

MONACO
pop. 2,000

On a rocky peninsula jutting into the Mediterranean, Monaco-Ville is the old city and seat of Monaco's government. Guarded by ramparts, narrow streets climb the slope to the Prince's Palace high above the sea. The 19th-century Romanesque Cathedral of St-Nicholas contains works of art by Bréa. The Parliament Building and the Oceanographic Museum are also of interest.

JARDIN EXOTIQUE ★ contains thousands of species of cacti, flowering plants and palm trees. The Grotte de l'Observatoire, an underground prehistoric cave, and the Musée d'Anthropologie Préhistorique can be accessed.

MUSÉE OCÉANOGRAPHIQUE ET AQUARIUM ★, avenue St-Martin, is an architectural masterpiece dedicated to the marine sciences. The 90-tank aquarium is considered one of the best in Europe.

PALAIS DU PRINCE ★ can be visited when the Prince is not at home. Rooms on view are the gallery with 16th-century frescoes, the Louis XV and the Mazarin salons, the Throne Room, the main Courtyard of Honor, and the Ste.-Marie Tower. The changing of the guard takes place in the square daily at 11:55am.

LA CONDAMINE
pop. 11,000

La Condamine is Monaco's residential district and business center. Numerous exotic yachts are moored in the harbor.

The local church is dedicated to Ste.-Dévote, a 3rd-century martyr.

MONTE-CARLO
pop. 9,500

Monte-Carlo is synonymous with the jet set; every year the *crème de la crème* of the business and entertainment world gather to bask in the sun, gamble at the Casino and watch each other. There are many excellent hotels, restaurants, and several theaters. The Monte-Carlo Sporting-Club, with its dance clubs and gambling salons, contributes to an unsurpassed nightlife. The city's gardens, parks and beaches enhance its natural beauty.

CASINO ★, famed as the world's largest, is Monte-Carlo's main attraction. Established in the 19th century, the grandiose building is replete with marble, gilt mirrors and crystal chandeliers. There is an admission charge to both public and private rooms. Minimum age for admission is 21 and passports must be presented. The Casino also offers several bars, a cabaret and restaurant. The atrium leads into the Salle Garnier Opera House.

EXPOSITION DE LA COLLECTION DE VOITURES ANCIENNES DE S.A.S. LE PRINCE DE MONACO, Terrasses de Fontvieille, is a collection of vintage and classic cars.

MUSÉE DE POUPÉES ET AUTOMATES, 17 avenue Princesse Grace, is housed in the Sauber Villa, designed by the noted architect Charles Garnier. The doll collection dates from the 18th and 19th centuries. The miniature furnishings and rose garden also are well worth seeing.

AUTOMOBILE CLUB
L'Automobile club de Monaco is at 23 boulevard Albert 1er, Monte-Carlo. Not all auto clubs offer full travel services to AAA members.

GERMANY

ALTHOUGH UNITED, GERMANY IS STILL DIVIDED INTO THE PROSPEROUS WEST AND THE PENURIOUS EAST. THE SYMBOL OF THAT DIVISION, BERLIN, REMAINS ONE OF THE MOST EXCITING CITIES IN EUROPE.

THERE ARE PLENTY OF OTHER ATTRACTIVE, HISTORIC CITIES, TOO, FROM HAMBURG IN THE NORTH TO MUNICH (MÜNCHEN) IN THE SOUTH. MUNICH'S OCTOBER BEER FESTIVAL BELIES THE FACT THAT IT IS ONE OF EUROPE'S MOST CIVILIZED CITIES, WITH ENVIABLE MUSEUMS AND GALLERIES. NEARBY, ARE THE BAVARIAN LAKES AND SNOW-CAPPED ALPS, JUST ONE OF MANY BEAUTIFUL REGIONS. FARTHER WEST, AND THE SOURCE OF THE DANUBE (DONAU), IS THE MOUNTAINOUS BLACK FOREST (SCHWARZWALD), WHILE TO THE NORTH; THE RHINE (RHEIN) CUTS THROUGH THE RHINE GORGE AND CONTINUES PAST MAGNIFICENT CASTLES.

Left SPECTACULAR NEUSCHWANSTEIN, SET AGAINST A MOUNTAIN BACKDROP
Above left BRASS BANDS PLAY AT THE OKTOBERFEST IN MUNICH
Above right STEINS ARE POPULAR IN PASSAU

Things to Know

- **Area:** 357,000 square kilometers (137,838 square miles)
- **Population:** 80,300,000
- **Capital:** Berlin
- **Language:** German
- **Religion:** Some three-quarters of the population of Germany is Christian, half of these being Protestant and half Roman Catholic. Every town has a church, and religious festivals are an important part of the calendar (see *Public Holidays* p.306). Other religions are catered for in the cities; for addresses of local places of worship, ask at the tourist office.
- **Economy:** Industry and agriculture. Steel, machinery (Ruhr Valley, Berlin, etc.), vehicles, chemicals and textiles. Shipbuilding at North Sea ports; smaller skilled industries in the south west. Cattle, potatoes, grains, sugar beets, fruit and wine. Transportation, communications, tourism and energy production (coal, hydroelectric, oil-fired and nuclear).
- **Electricity:** The current in Germany is 220 volts, 50 cycles. Plugs are the round two-pin type.
- **Passport:** Required for U.S. citizens.
- **Visa:** Not required for stays up to 3 months.
- **Duty-Free Items:** 200 cigarettes or 100 cigarillos or 50 cigars or 250 grams of tobacco; 1 liter of spirits or 2 liters of spirits with less than 22 percent alcohol; 2 liters of wine; 500 grams of coffee or 200 grams of instant coffee; cameras and film in reasonable amounts for personal use; 50 grams of perfume; 0.25 liter of cologne.
- **Currency:** The currency unit, the German *Mark* (DM), is divided into 100 *pfennigs* (Pf). Coins come in 1, 2, 5, 10 and 50Pf and 1,2, 5DM; notes in 5, 10, 20, 50, 100, 200, 500 and 1,000DM denominations. Because of currency fluctuations, the exchange rate is subject to frequent change. There is no limit on either the import or the export of German or foreign currency.

History

Ancient Germany was settled by numerous tribes; the Franks controlled the area when Charlemagne was crowned emperor of the Holy Roman Empire in 800 AD. Feudalism hastened the empire's disintegration into regional duchies and kingdoms. In the early Middle Ages, merchants of several German towns, most notably Hamburg, Bremen and Lübeck, formed the Hanseatic League to promote mercantile interests. Their influence on commerce was widespread and is still reflected in the old quarters of these cities.

By the time Frederick II ascended the throne in 1740, the stage was set for the rise of the Kingdom of Prussia. The ruler had inherited a small but flourishing empire. Under his direction, the building of theaters, palaces and monuments transformed Berlin from a provincial city on the Spree River into a cultural center that attracted the world's aristocrats.

In the early 19th century Prussia and the other German states, as well as most of Europe, became part of Napoléon Bonaparte's French empire until 1813. Germany existed as a loose federation of states until 1848, when the popular desire for more unified rule led to widespread civil unrest. It was not until 1871, however, that Otto von Bismarck, the "Iron Chancellor," molded these small states into a great empire that assumed an increasing role in international affairs. The empire crashed with Germany's defeat in World War I.

The Nazi Party came to power for several reasons: lack of confidence in the Weimar Republic, Germany's first foray into democratic government; resentment over the severe terms of the Treaty of Versailles, which took German land and natural resources and demanded the payment of enormous reparations; and concern over the Depression. Named chancellor by President Paul von Hindenburg in 1933, Adolf Hitler took complete control of the government in 1934 and pursued an imperialistic policy that by 1939 had resulted in war.

At its defeat in 1945, Germany was divided into four zones of occupation: American, English, French and Russian. The American, English and French zones consolidated in 1949 to form the Bundesrepublik Deutschland (Federal Republic of Germany), with Bonn as its capital. The Soviet zone became the Deutsche Demokratische Republik (German Democratic Republic).

Under Konrad Adenauer, chancellor 1949–63, West Germany embarked on a full-scale economic recovery through a combination of U.S. aid and a modified version of free-enterprise capitalism. Meanwhile, East Germany's highly centralized and oppressive communist regime also experienced revivification but lagged behind the more successful West Germany. In 1961 the Berlin Wall was erected literally overnight and marked the end of free movement between East and West Germany.

The call for change was not heard until 1989, when the dramatic increase in economic defectors from East Germany, reforms in neighboring Poland and the former Soviet Union's *glasnost* policy

resulted in relaxed travel restrictions and emigration policies with Eastern Europe. The Berlin Wall began to tumble in late 1989; the unification of the two Germanys became official on October 3, 1990. The Federal Republic of Germany, with Berlin as its capital, continues to consolidate its status as one of Europe's most prosperous nations.

FOOD AND DRINK

The cities of Hamburg, Braunschweig and Frankfurt have given their names to familiar meat specialties, and much German food reflects regional modes of preparation. In eastern Germany the food is hearty and simple; pork, fish, potatoes, sausages and chicken are among the staples. Restaurants can be crowded at peak times.

Western Germany is known for its dark breads, and Bavarian beer is world-renowned. Many areas also produce good local beer that is drunk with *Schnapps*, another German favorite. Of the many white wines produced in Germany, perhaps the best known are those from the Rhine and Mosel regions.

SPORTS AND RECREATION

Germans are great sports enthusiasts. Nearly every town of substantial size has its own stadium and athletic field for soccer games and track meets. Soccer, called *Fussball*, is the national sport. Other popular athletic pursuits are swimming, tennis, sailing, boxing, hunting, mountain climbing and skiing. Automobile, motorcycle and bicycle races are also common. Germany has some excellent water- and winter-sports facilities and its many lakes and streams provide good fishing. Golf courses are open to tourists in almost a dozen cities.

GETTING AROUND

Hamburg can be reached by car ferry from Harwich, England and the ports of Kiel, Lübeck, Travemunde and Puttgarden can be reached likewise from Scandinavia.

AUTOMOBILE CLUBS
Allgemeiner Deutscher Automobil-Club (ADAC, National German Automobile Club), Am Westpark 8, 81365 München, and Automobilclub von Deutschland (AvD, Automobile Club of Germany), Lyoner Strasse 16, Frankfurt, have branches in various cities throughout Germany. The symbol ▲ beside a city name indicates the presence of an AAA-affiliated automobile club branch. Not all auto clubs offer full travel services to AAA members.

- **BANK OPENING HOURS**: 8:30am–1pm and 2:30–4pm Monday–Friday, to 5:30pm Thursday.
- **STORE OPENING HOURS**: 9am–6:30pm Monday–Friday (some to 8:30pm Thursday), 9am–2pm Saturday (to 6pm first Saturday of month).
- **BEST BUYS**: Hand-carved clocks, beer tankards, toys; peasant dresses and costumed dolls; fashions, including leather and woolens; porcelain figurines and dishes, including antiques; silver and steel tableware; luggage, cameras, binoculars.
- **PUBLIC HOLIDAYS**: January 1; Good Friday; Easter Sunday and Monday; May 1 – Labor Day; Ascension Day; Whitmonday; Corpus Christi; June 17 – Day of Unity; October 3 – Unification Day; Repentance Day; November 1 – All Saints Day; and December 25–26.
- **USEFUL TELEPHONE NUMBERS**:
  Police – 110
  Fire – 112
  Ambulance – 112
- **NATIONAL TOURIST OFFICE**:
  German National Tourist Office
  122 E. 42nd St.
  Chanin Building, 52nd Floor
  New York
  NY 10168-0072
  U.S.A.
  Tel: 212/661 7200
  German National Tourist Office
  444 South Flower Street
  Suite 2230
  Los Angeles
  CA 90071
  U.S.A.
  Tel: 213/688 7332
  German National Tourist Office
  65 Curzon Street
  London
  W1Y 7PE
  England
  Tel: 0171 495 3990
- **AMERICAN EMBASSY**:
  Delchmanns Avenue 29
  53170 Bonn
  Germany
  Tel: 0228 3391

An ultramodern, efficient, toll-free autobahn (highway) system, allied to a dense network of generally well-maintained major and minor roads awaits motoring tourists in Germany. Roads in eastern Germany are generally poor and in need of repair. If your vehicle has seat belts, wearing them is mandatory. A child under 12 may not travel unless using a suitable restraint system. Speed limits in built-up areas should not exceed 50 k.p.h. (30 m.p.h.). On all open roads the speed limit is 100 k.p.h. (60 m.p.h.); 130 k.p.h. (80 m.p.h.) is the maximum on autobahns except where signs indicate the limit. Visiting motorists are required to pay fines or deposits for motoring violations on the spot with Deutsch Marks or travelers' checks.

Rail travel is efficient and convenient. Special rail rates are available through Eurailpass, Europass, or with the German Rail Pass, available through German Rail, DER Tours, 11933 Wilshire Boulevard, Los Angeles, CA 90025. Major cities sell visitors a 24-hour public transportation ticket, available at local tourist offices, in train stations and airports or near the city hall. Trains in eastern Germany can be crowded; reservations made several hours in advance are recommended.

ACCOMMODATIONS

The German National Tourist Office (D.Z.T.) distributes a list of hotels and offers tourists a computer reservation system (see *Things to Know* opposite). Local tourist offices can usually help you find a room. Further information is available from Deutsches Jugendherbergswerk, Postfach 1455, D-32756 Detmold. More than 600 hostels are available to members of any association that is affiliated with the International Youth Hostel Federation. Campers will find thousands of campgrounds, nearly a quarter of which are open all year. Some campgrounds might give a discount if you have an international camping carnet; some campgrounds also require it.

TIPPING

Hotels and restaurants normally add a 10 to 12 percent gratuity charge to the bill, but satisfied customers often leave a small additional tip. Taxi-drivers and hairdressers expect a tip of 10 to 15 percent of the bill. Tip porters and doormen 1DM per bag; coatroom attendants expect ½ to 1DM. In addition, bartenders should be given a small tip.

PRINCIPAL TOURING AREAS

Note: for descriptions of cities in **bold** type, see individual city listings.

BAVARIA

Bavaria is Germany's most popular tourist destination as much for its spectacular mountain scenery as for its well-preserved old cities and numerous fairy-tale castles. Geographically, Bavaria comprises four regions. Franconia, in the north, has been part of Bavaria for nearly 200 years. Its capital is **Würzburg**, and it includes former imperial cities such as **Bamberg**, the medieval city of **Nürnberg** and **Bayreuth**, with its Wagner Festival. Upper Bavaria (confusingly in the south), includes **München**, the state capital, and the snow-capped Bavarian Alps in the south. In the south west is the region of Allgäu/Bavarian-Swabia, with the Allgäuer Alpen Mountains in the south and rolling countryside further north. **Augsburg** is its imposing capital, which can trace its origins back to Roman times. East Bavaria is less visited than the other areas, but has equally fine scenery. **Regensburg** is the capital of Lower Bavaria; **Passau** is famous for its Italianate baroque architecture.

BLACK FOREST

Cuckoo clocks, spectacular scenery, mountain lakes and health spas all are characteristic of the Black Forest, or Schwarzwald, region in southwestern Germany. A good way to see the Black Forest is by car. The High Route, or Hochstrasse, extends from **Baden-Baden** to Freudenstadt; the Valley Route, or Tälerstrasse, traverses the Murg and Kinzig valleys between Rastatt and Wolfach; and the Baden Wine Road, or Badische Weinstrasse, connects Baden-Baden with Basel, Switzerland, by traversing the Rhine Valley.

BRANDENBURG

Contained within the historic Brandenburg region are many of the roots of what is now Germany. Centers include **Potsdam**, the royal city of Frederick the Great, and **Berlin**, now capital of

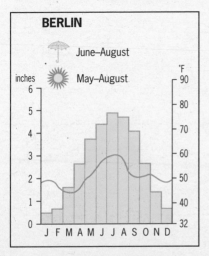

BERLIN

June–August

May–August

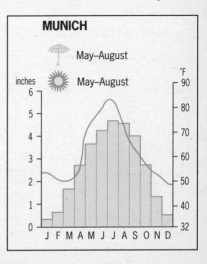

MUNICH

May–August

May–August

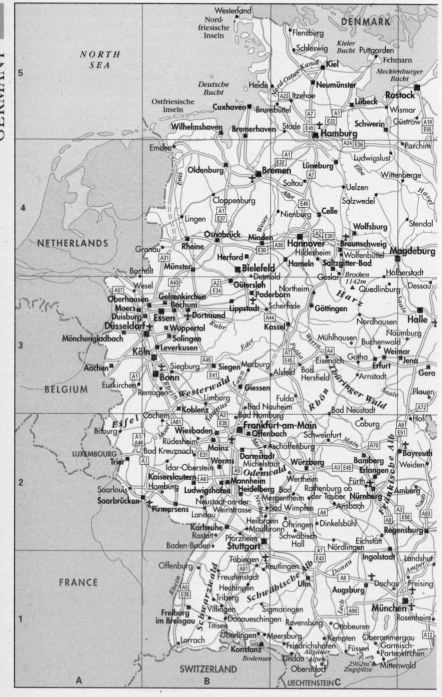

Germany and many of whose magnificent baroque buildings have been restored or rebuilt after their destruction in World War II. To the south east of Berlin is the Spreewald (Spree Forest), a peaceful conservation area criss-crossed by canals and rivers.

BREMEN AND EAST FRIESLAND
The old Hanseatic port of **Bremen** is a good starting point for exploring this region of northwestern Germany.

FRANKFURT AND HESSE
The cosmopolitan city of **Frankfurt-am-Main** is the center of a region known for its folklore. To the north west are the Taunus Mountains, a favorite vacation area for Frankfurt residents.

HANNOVER, WESERBERGLAND AND HARZ MOUNTAINS
Industrial **Hannover**, has many interesting museums and medieval buildings, while Weserbergland, a scenic area along the Weser River, has Renaissance houses and several spas. This region is another that is known for its folklore. Meanwhile, the Harz Mountains have several medieval cities with beautiful half-timbered buildings and a strong trend to continue traditional customs.

LAKE KONSTANZ AND SWABIAN JURA
Lake Konstanz, the Bodensee, is in the Alpine foothills where Germany, Switzerland and Austria meet. This popular resort center offers swimming, boating and fishing. Upper Swabia, bounded by the Donau (Danube) in the north, is noted for baroque architecture.

LÜNEBURGER HEIDE
Lüneburger Heide (Lüneburg Heath), is a vast region in northern Germany that is now a national park and wildlife reserve.

MECKLENBURG-LOWER POMERANIA
A former duchy and province of the German Reich, Mecklenburg-Lower

GERMANY

Pomerania occupies northeastern Germany. It is a land of geographic variety: grassy marshland and sandy soil characterize hilly central Mecklenburg. Along the coast, steep cliffs give way to sandy beaches and shifting dunes; and in the north, hard clay soils support a variety of vegetation. There is **Schwerin**, in the west of the province and built on the shores of Schwerin Lake; Wismar, a scenic harbor town on an inlet of the Baltic; **Rostock**, an important fishing center. Güstrow, a farming center on the Nebel River; and Waren, a resort town on Müritz See (Lake Müritz).

MOSEL VALLEY

This twisty river, with gentler scenery than the Rhine, joins it at **Koblenz**, and the Moselweinstrasse goes as far as **Trier**, a Roman town, now center of the Mosel wine trade. Some of the prettiest places along the river are Beilstein and Cochem with their castles (ruined and reconstructed respectively), and Bernkastel, totally devoted to the grape.

The Ahr River, with terraced vineyards (producing red wine) and ruined castles on its crags, flows through the Eifel area north of the Mosel to join the Rhine near Remagen. In the north is **Aachen**, Charlemagne's first capital.

NECKAR VALLEY

This beautiful region of vineyards and woodlands includes some of Germany's most acclaimed tourist destinations: **Mannheim**, with its Fasching celebration; the university town of **Heidelberg**; the wine city of **Heilbronn**; and the cultural center of **Stuttgart**.

Castles are plentiful in the Neckar Valley: the town of Neckarsteinach boasts four, and Zwingenberg and Neckarzimmern each have one. Also of interest is **Bad Wimpfen**

RHEINLAND

The Rhine is Germany's longest river, and while its northern part is wide and

sluggish, and flows through heavily populated cities such as **Düsseldorf** and **Köln**, certain stretches further south are very attractive. The most appealing section is the Rhine gorge, between **Koblenz** and **Bingen**. Just before **Rüdesheim**, the river swings east, and this section, with the wooded Taunus Mountains to the north, as far as **Mainz**, is called the Rheingau. A special Wine Route, the Deutsche Weinstrasse, has been created from Bockenheim, west of Worms, running south to Schweigen on the French border.

The small area to the west of the Rhine in the south of Germany is the Pfälzer Wald (the Palatinate Forest), encompassing Germany's smallest *Land*, Saarland, known for its coal fields, on the French border. Most of it is a national park, heavily wooded and dotted with castles and villages. North of the Palatinate runs the Nahe River, which flows into the Rhine just after Bingen. This area does not hold a great deal of interest for the tourist apart from Idar-Oberstein, where precious stones are cut and displayed, and two spa towns of Bad Münster and Bad Kreuznach.

The Lahn River cuts through the Westerwald and Taunus, flowing into the Rhine on its eastern side at Lahnstein, dominated by the restored castle of Burg Lahneck. Much of the riparine scenery is undramatic, apart from Kaiser Wilhelm's favorite resort of Bad Ems, medieval **Limburg**, and the picturesque town of **Marburg**, clustered around its hilltop castle.

SACHSEN

Sachsen, or Saxony, was the name of several overlapping territories in German history. Today known as the area that stretches north from Thüringen, or Thuringia, to Brandenburg and east to Lusatia, Saxony is a fertile, mountainous farming region that is almost wholly within the Elbe River basin. The region's major centers are: Zwickau, a manufacturing city; industrial Chemnitz; Freiberg; **Dresden**; **Bautzen**; **Meissen**, home of the famed porcelain factory; and **Leipzig**, in the heart of Saxony.

SCHLESWIG-HOLSTEIN

Schleswig-Holstein, a hilly region of forests and meadows, shares a peninsula with Denmark. On the western side it faces the North Sea, while offshore are several islands: strung along the north coast are the Dutch-looking Ostfriesische Inseln (East Frisian Islands); and off the west coast are the Nordfriesische Inseln (North Friesian Islands).

The region's two biggest towns are the Hanseatic ports of **Bremen** and **Hamburg**, both with plenty of sights. **Kiel**, the province's capital, has less to offer (it was badly bombed in the war), but is still a busy shipping center on account of its canal.

THÜRINGEN

Thüringen, or Thuringia, home of the ancient Thuringian Forest, is an area of rounded hills and gentle forests interspersed with towns and cities. It includes the small but thriving Nordhausen at the southern foot of the Harz Mountains, Mühlhausen, **Eisenach** with its Wartburg Castle, and **Weimar**, the stately town from which rose the short-lived republic of the same name.

USEFUL EXPRESSIONS IN GERMAN

hello	Guten Tag
good morning	Guten Morgen
good evening	Guten Abend
good night	Gute Nacht
good-bye	Auf Wiedersehen
please/thankyou	bitte/danke
yes/no	ja/nein
excuse me	Verzeihung
you're welcome	bitte
Do you speak English?	Sprechen Sie Englisch?
I don't understand.	Ich verstehe nicht.
What is the time?	Wie spät ist es?
How much is that?	Wieviel kostet das?
Where are the restrooms?	Wo sind die Toiletten?
I'd like ...	Ich würde ...
Can you help me, please?	Können Sie mir helfen, bitte?
where/when/how	wo/wann/wie
hot/cold	heiss/kalt
old/new	alt/neu
open/closed	offen/geschlossen
big/small	gross/klein
Do you take credit cards?	Akzeptieren Sie Kreditkarten?
yesterday/today/ tomorrow	gerstern/heute/ morgen
to the left	nach links
to the right	nach rechts
straight ahead	gerade aus
vacant/occupied	frei/besetzt

DAYS OF THE WEEK

Sunday	Sonntag
Monday	Montag
Tuesday	Dienstag
Wednesday	Mittwoch
Thursday	Donnerstag
Friday	Freitag
Saturday	Samstag/ Sonnabend

NUMBERS

1	ein	30	dreizig
2	zwei	40	vierzig
3	drei	50	fünfzig
4	vier	60	sechzig
5	fünf	70	siebzig
6	sechs	80	achtzig
7	sieben	90	neunzig
8	acht	100	hundert
9	neun	1,000	tausend
10	zehn		
20	zwanzig		
21	ein-und-zwanzig		
22	zwei-und-zwanzig		

GERMANY

PLACES OF INTEREST

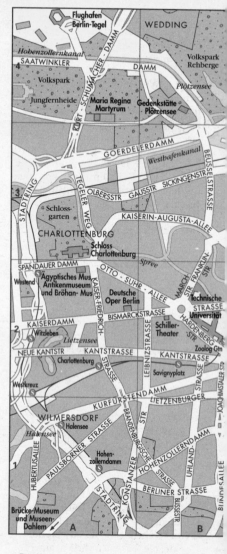

▲ BERLIN ★

BERLIN *pop. 3,200,000*

Berlin, a city once divided by the Berlin Wall, is now free of the imposing barrier of concrete and barbed wire erected in August 1961 by the German Democratic Republic (or G.D.R.).

The 1989 destruction of this symbol of the postwar division of Germany signaled the move toward the unification of the two Germanys.

Berlin first knew glory in the 15th century under the Hohenzollerns, who governed from the city on the Spree River initially as electors of Brandenburg, then as kings of Prussia and later as emperors of Imperial Germany.

Berlin gained further prominence as the cradle of the Second Reich, which was established by Otto von Bismarck in 1871 and served as the capital until 1914, with the outbreak of World War I. The Weimar Republic that rose five years later was short-lived, due to an ailing economy that produced a depression. The republic fell in 1933 when Hitler became chancellor, but Berlin remained the capital, this time of the Third Reich.

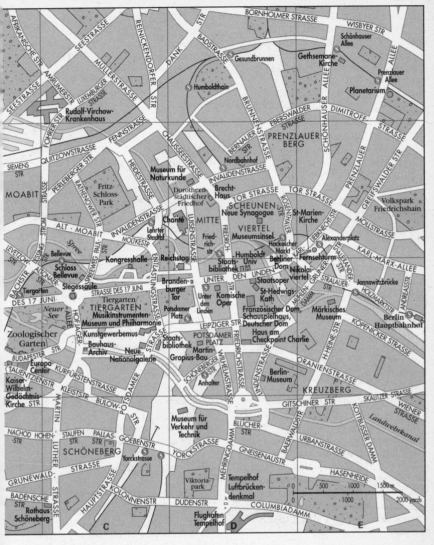

The bombings of World War II destroyed half of Berlin, leveling almost all of its baroque structures. During the Soviet battle for the city, Hitler took his life in a bunker near the Brandenburger Tor (Brandenburg Gate). The postwar governments, anxious to forget Hitler and recall Berlin's former luster, set about rebuilding and restoring.

Berlin is both a modern showpiece and a monument of Germany's rich – and chaotic – past. Restored baroque palaces and medieval churches adjoin high-rise apartment complexes and glass-walled buildings. The main avenue of the former eastern sector, Unter den Linden (Under the Lime Trees), dates from the Imperial Berlin of the Hohenzollerns, and sweeps gracefully through the core of the city before ending in front of the historic Brandenburger Tor.

GERMANY

In the former western sector, the Kurfürstendamm and the surrounding streets are the center of tourist activity; the majority of the city's theaters, opera houses, museums, nightclubs and restaurants are in this area.

As a result of being a divided city, Berlin has over 80 museums, several duplicated. It is possible that some will strive to stay separate, but others will want to unite. The same applies to the field of culture. There are three opera houses of international standing: the Deutsche Oper Berlin (west); Staatsoper Unter den Linden (east), next door to the Staatskapelle; and the Komische Oper Berlin (east), which performs comic operas.

Operettas and musicals are performed at the Theater des Westens.

The standard of music is also world-class. The Berlin Philharmonic performs in its own modern building (Philharmonie) near Kemperplatz, while the Berlin Symphony Orchestra, the city's other main orchestra, plays frequently at east Berlin's main concert venue, the Konzerthaus. Waldbühne is a huge open-air arena where concerts – classical and pop – are performed in summer. Jazz, rock and folk music are easily found in the city.

Theaters offer a full range of plays, while puppets, political satire, cabarets, revues and drag shows all have a place in Berlin. Nightlife is still livelier in the west, with bars, discos, nightclubs and café-restaurants. Cinemas are numerous, and the annual Film Festival (February) is always popular.

ÄGYPTISCHES MUSEUM – *see Schloss Charlottenburg on p.316.*

ALEXANDERPLATZ (312 E3) marks the end of the processional route from the Brandenburger Tor, via Unter den Linden.

It was named after Tsar Alexander I in 1805 and was first a marketplace.

The World Clock and Friendship Fountain now adorns it, but it is still surrounded by ugly postwar buildings.

ALTE NATIONALGALERIE, Bodestrasse, Museuminsel, contains drawings and paintings from the late 18th century, French 19th-century art, German Impressionist paintings, and modern paintings and sculpture.

ANTIKENSAMMLUNG – *see Schloss Charlottenburg on p.316.*

BODEMUSEUM ★, am Kupfergraben, Museuminsel, exhibits objects of art and culture from ancient Egypt, early medieval Italy and the early Christian era of the western Roman Empire. It also contains European paintings from the Gothic period to the 18th century. The Skulpturesamm-lung (Sculpture Collection) consists mainly of German works.

BRANDENBURGER TOR (Brandenburg Gate) (312 D2) ★, at the end of Unter den Linden, was built in 1788–91 as the imperial entrance to Berlin. Napoleon confiscated the Quadriga, the four-horse chariot of the Goddess of Victory which sits on top of the gate, when he captured Berlin in 1806; it was returned to the city after the emperor's defeat in 1814.

The gate was a stronghold for government troops in the 1919 communist uprising and was badly damaged in World War II. A replica of the Goddess of Victory, a gift from the former West Berlin, now decorates it.

FERNSEHTURM (312 E3), a slender television tower topped by a revolving globe with a protruding spike, is Berlin's tallest structure at 365 meters (1,198 feet). The globe at 207 meters (679 feet) includes a viewing gallery and a café.

HAUS AM CHECKPOINT CHARLIE (312 D2), Friedrichstrasse 44, near the former crossing point, describes by means of films and photos the escape attempts by East Berliners, many of which failed.

JAGDSCHLOSS GRÜNEWALD (Hunting Palace), Grünewaldsee, is a Renaissance mansion dating from 1542. It is now a museum housing art and hunting-trophy collections. Among its treasures are portraits of Roman emperors and works by Rubens and Cranach the Elder.

KAISER-WILHELM-GEDÄCHTNIS-KIRCHE (312 B2), Breitschieldtplatz, commemorates the first ruler of the Second Reich. The west tower remains from the original church, built 1891–5.

KUNSTGEWERBEMUSEUM (Museum of Applied Arts) (312 C2) is in the Köpenick Palace in the Köpenick district and at Tiergarten – Matthäiskirchplatz 10, Berlin 30. Both museums contain beautiful European items of gold, silver, glass, ceramics and furniture.

MÄRKISCHES MUSEUM (312 E2), am Köllnischen Park 5, focuses on Berliners' contributions to literature, art and science.

MARTIN-GROPIUS-BAU (312 D2), Stresemannstrasse 110, Kreuzberg. This Renaissance-style, 19th-century building with sculptures and paintings starting from that period, covers Expressionism to New Objectivity. It also has an exhibition on the role of the Jewish community in Berlin.

MUSEEN DAHLEM is a huge building containing several worthy collections, originally funded by the Henry Ford Foundation to vie with East Berlin's Pergamon collection.

MUSEUM FÜR NATURKUNDE (Natural History Museum) (312 D3), Invalidenstrasse 43, is one of the largest natural history museums in the world.

MUSEUM FÜR VÖLKERKUNDE (Ethnography Museum) is very extensive and well displayed, with bronzes from Africa, boats from the South Seas, and pottery and sculpture from South America. (Lansstrasse entrance.)

MUSIKINSTRUMENTEN MUSEUM (312 C2), Tiergartenstrasse 1, has a collection of musical instruments that spans five centuries.

NEUE NATIONALGALERIE (312 C2) ★, Potsdamer Strasse 50, Tiergarten, is a modern structure designed by Ludwig Mies van der Rohe. The building combines the National Gallery, with its 19th-century works, and the Gallery of the 20th Century. In the Art Library are period costumes and photographs.

PERGAMONMUSEUM ★, Bodestrasse 1–3, Museuminsel, is considered one of the finest museums of ancient art in the world. It includes Hellenic and Roman architecture from Asia Minor, the Pergamon Altar and the Market Gate of Miletus, Babylonian sculptures, the Ishtar Gate and the Processional Way.

RATHAUS SCHÖNEBERG (312 C1), John-F. Kennedy-Platz, was the seat of the West Berlin Government from 1948. It was here that John F. Kennedy made his 1963 speech *"Ich bin ein Berliner."* The Freiheitsglocke in the tower, a replica of the Liberty Bell, was donated by the people of the United States. In the room at the base of the tower is the Freedom Scroll, signed by 17 million Americans to express solidarity with West Berliners.

REICHSTAG (312 D2) ★, Platz der Republik, once housed the German Parliament, but was burnt by the Nazis in 1933. Rebuilt in the 1950s, it is again undergoing refurbishment, to become the seat of the Bundestag in 1998.

ST.-MARIEN-KIRCHE (312 E3), Karl-Liebknecht-Strasse 8. First built in Gothic style in the 13th century, the nave survives. The fresco entitled *Totentanz*, or *Dance of Death*, is believed to have been painted in 1484.

SCHLOSS BELLEVUE (312 C2), Tiergarten, was built in 1785. The palace, rebuilt since its destruction in World War II, has been the official Berlin residence of the president since 1959.

GERMANY

GERMANY

SCHLOSS CHARLOTTENBURG (312 A3) ★, Luisenplatz, was completed in 1695 as the summer palace for the future queen, Sophie Charlotte, and later enlarged to become the country home of Prussian kings. It was restored after World War II and is Berlin's most impressive example of baroque architecture. On the ground floor of the Knobelsdorff Wing are 19th-century paintings from the Nationalgalerie and above is the reconstructed gilt Golden Gallery built for Frederick the Great. The Royal Apartments are a series of ornate baroque rooms, the most sumptuous being the Ovale Saal and the Porzellankabinett (Porcelain Collection); the Chapel is also fine.

In the informal Palace Gardens are the Schinkel Pavilion, the domed Belvedere and the Royal Mausoleum.

Ägyptisches Museum (Egyptian Museum) Schloss Strasse 70. One of Berlin's split museums – other Egyptian exhibits are in the Bode Museum. The highlights are a bust of Queen Nefertiti and the 2,000-year-old Kalabasha Gate.

Antikensammlung (Antiquities Collection), Schloss Strasse 1. Minoan, Greek and Etruscan treasures from the former imperial collection. Fine Roman silver from Caesar Augustus' time.

Museum für Vor-Und Frühgeschichte (Museum of Pre- and Early History) in the west wing of Charlottenburg, contains material from early cultures, particularly the Bronze and Iron Ages.

SCHLOSS PFAUENINSEL (Peacock Island Palace) is on the west edge of Berlin on an island in the Havel River. The palace is built along the lines of a late 18th-century ruined castle.

SIEGESSÄULE (312 C2), Strasse des 17 Juni, a column nearly 60 meters (200 feet) tall, commemorates the successful German campaigns of the Franco-Prussian War. A climb to the top affords a panorama of Berlin.

SPANDAU, a 12th-century moated castle 10 kilometers (6 miles) north west,

served as the fortress, state prison and treasury of the German kaisers for several centuries.

TIERGARTEN (312 C2) ★, a former royal hunting ground, is now a large park replanted with trees, offering canal and lakeside walks. In the south-west corner is the Zoologischer Garten (zoo), while in the north-east corner is the Sowjetisches Ehrenmal (Soviet War Memorial, Strasse des 17 Juni).

ZEUGHAUS (Arsenal), Unter den Linden 2, was rebuilt after bombing to become the German Historical Museum (Deutsches Historisches Museum), displaying arms and weapons as well as masks of dying warriors.

AACHEN (306 A3)
NORDRHEIN-WESTFALEN *pop. 246,000*
Aachen is a noted spa with the hottest springs 76°C (168°F) in northwestern Europe. Once Charlemagne's capital, it is also known as Aix-la-Chapelle. The 9th-century octagonal chapel within the cathedral contains Charlemagne's tomb and a valuable treasury; a restored 14th-century town hall stands on the site of Charlemagne's palace.

COUVEN MUSEUM, Hühnermarkt 17, chronicles the history of Aachen. Exhibits include furniture, fireplaces, Italian stucco-work and household utensils.

INTERNATIONALES ZEITUNGSMUSEUM (International Press Museum), Ponstrasse 13, displays newspapers, magazines and journals from around the world, some dating from the 17th century.

ANSBACH (306 C2)
BAYERN *pop. 40,000*
The quiet Frankish town of Ansbach became the seat of the Margraves of Brandenburg-Ansbach, who endowed it with many fine buildings. Every two years a Bach Festival is held here. St.-Gumpert-Kirche is a Gothic church, with three towers and many family tombs.

MARKGRAFENSCHLOSS is an ornately furnished 18th-century rococo palace, with state rooms, a two-story frescoed Great Hall and the Margrave's Audience Room. It is surrounded by a fine park, the baroque Hofgarten.

ASCHAFFENBURG (306 B1)
BAYERN pop. 65,000
Aschaffenburg, overlooking the Main River, is famous for parks and imposing buildings, many decorated by the 16th-century painter Matthias Grünewald.

SCHLOSS JOHANNISBURG is a large Renaissance palace built 1605–14 as a residence for the bishops of Mainz. The state rooms are hung with pictures by German and Flemish masters.

SCHÖNBUSCH, 3 kilometers (2 miles) west, is a small summer residence built in 1780. It is surrounded by delightful formal gardens, with a lake, classical buildings and follies.

STIFTSKIRCHE is a Gothic church with a Romanesque cloister and a later tower. Inside are paintings by Matthias Grünewald and Lucas Cranach.

AUGSBURG (306 C1)
BAYERN pop. 250,000
Augsburg is Bavaria's oldest city. Its position at the confluence of two rivers made it an ideal trade route from southern Europe to northern Italy, a fact recognized by the Emperor Augustus who founded the city in 15 BC. It reached its economic peak as a financial center in the 16th century when it was ruled by two wealthy merchant families, the Fuggers and Welsers.

The town played an important role in the Reformation: the Peace of Augsburg finally recognized the right of Protestants to follow their own faith. Augsburg was also the birthplace of Leopold Mozart, father of Wolfgang Amadeus (the Mozarthaus has memorabilia), and the home and workplace of the painters Holbein the Elder and

Younger, and, more recently, of Rudolf Diesel and Wilhelm Messerschmidt.

DOM, on Hoher Weg, was built in 995 AD and rebuilt in the 14th century in Gothic style. Within are five stained-glass windows, said to be the oldest in Germany, and Romanesque bronze doors with panels depicting the story of Adam and Eve. Altar paintings are by Hans Holbein the Elder.

RATHAUS (town hall), with its two onion-domed towers, is regarded by some as the finest secular Renaissance building in Germany. It was designed by Elias Holl (1615–20) and its Golden Hall has a coffered ceiling and frescoes.

STS.-ULRICH-UND-AFRA, at the southern end of Maximilianstrasse, is a 15th-century Gothic basilica with the plain Romanesque tomb of St. Afra and the rococo one of St. Ulrich.

SCHAETZLERPALAIS, Maximilianstrasse, was built 1512–15 and includes the German baroque gallery and an ornate Festsaal (Banqueting Hall). The adjacent State Gallery displays works by Hans Holbein and Albrecht Dürer.

BADEN-BADEN (306 B2)
BADEN-WÜRTTEMBERG pop. 50,000
Baden-Baden has long been a popular German spa: the Roman Emperor Caracalla knew the virtues of its waters almost 2,000 years ago.

The town has a neo-classical spa building (Kurhaus) overlooking a well-kept park (Kurgarten).

NEUES SCHLOSS (New Palace), Römerplatz, dates from the 15th century. Held within is the Zähringer Museum's notable art collection.

RÖMISCHE BADRUINEN, beneath the Römerplatz, were the baths of the Emperor Caracalla. The ancient heating system and a small church (Spitalkirche) are of interest.

BAD HOMBURG (306 B2)
HESSEN *pop. 52,000*
This town is known for its springs, found in the Kurpark, laid out in English style during the mid-19th century when the spa was very fashionable.

SCHLOSS, 4 kilometers (2½ miles) north west on the south slope of the Taunus, was built for Prince Friedrich II von Homburg, the title figure in Heinrich Wilhelm von Kleist's drama *Prinz Friedrich von Hamburg*.

BAD MERGENTHEIM (306 C2)
BADEN-WÜRTTEMBERG *pop. 21,000*
A center for the Teutonic Knights, this spa town is on the Romantische Strasse.

DEUTSCHORDENS SCHLOSS was the Renaissance residence of the Teutonic Order from 1525 to 1809. The exterior of the building is highly ornate and inside is a fine staircase, the Knights' Museum and a baroque church.

KNIGHT'S TALE
The Grand Order of Teutonic Knights was founded in the Holy Land in 1128. After the Order adopted Lutheranism in 1525, those still loyal to Roman Catholicism established themselves and continued their charitable works until Napoléon dispossessed the order in 1809.

BAD WIMPFEN (306 B2)
BADEN-WÜRTTEMBERG *pop. 6,000*
The splendid old fortified town of Bad Wimpfen overlooks the Neckar River. Many of the winding cobbled streets are lined with half-timbered, gabled houses. The 13th- century church has a Gothic cloister, and the upper town is dominated by remains of the Hohenstaufens' former imperial palace.

BURG GUTTENBERG 20 kilometers (12 miles) north is one of the oldest and best-preserved castles in the Neckar Valley; the property has belonged to the same family for 18 generations.

BAMBERG (306 C2)
BAYERN *pop. 70,000*
Bamberg, set on seven hills above the Regnitz River, has been a religious center since the Emperor Heinrich II established a bishopric here in 1007. As a result, the city has a wealth of churches, abbeys and cloisters, as well as an ancient university. Other attractions are "Little Venice," a row of fishermen's houses along the riverfront, the baroque Church of St. Martin, built by the Dientzenhofer brothers around 1690, and the Gothic Obere Pfarrkirche.

ALTE HOFHALTUNG is the partly ruined former residence of Bamberg's prince-bishops, and now houses a museum.

ALTES RATHAUS, the Old Town Hall, is a half-timbered building standing on an island in the river. Originally Gothic, it was later decorated in rococo style.

DOM, on the Domplatz, is Bamberg's impressive Gothic cathedral. Inside, the 13th-century statue of the Knight of Bamberg, the tomb of Heinrich and the renowned Marienaltar (Nativity Altar) carved by Viet Stoss (1523) are outstanding among the statuary.

KLOSTERKIRCHE ST. MICHAEL, founded in 1015 as part of a Benedictine Abbey, is approached by a baroque flight of steps. Inside are bishops' tombs, Romanesque columns and a vault-ceiling painting of 600 herbs. Views from the terrace.

NEUE RESIDENZ (New Residence), 8 Domplatz, was built around 1700 as the official residence of the prince-bishops. Magnificently decorated rooms in baroque style include the State Library, the Chinese Room and the Emperor's Room. Outside is the Rose Garden.

POMMERSFELDEN, 21 kilometers (13 miles) south west, is famous for its imposing castle, Schloss Weissenstein, built 1711–18 for the local bishop by Johann Dientzenhofer. The double staircase was designed by the bishop and has a *trompe-l'oeil* ceiling. The Hall of Mirrors, the Banqueting Hall and the five-storeyed Marble Hall (summer concerts held here) are all sumptuous.

SCHLOSS ALTENBURG, once a bishop's castle, is 3 kilometers (2 miles) outside Bamberg on the highest hill. Inside is a neo-Gothic chapel; fine views.

BAUTZEN (306 E3)
SACHSEN *pop. 50,000*

Built on a granite promontory above the Spree River, Bautzen was known to be a Slavic settlement as early as the 11th century. Germans took the town in 1033 and made it a part of Bohemia; then it became a part of Saxony in the Middle Ages. Named the capital of the Federation of Lusatian Cities in 1346, Bautzen was and is a cultural and political center for the Lusatian Sorbs (Wends), a people of West Slavic descent who migrated here over 1,000 years ago.

The late-Gothic cathedral (Petridom) serves both Catholics and Protestants. Much of the old town wall and bastions survive, and from the leaning Reichenturm, once a defensive tower, good views are to be had. The Alte Wasserkunst (Water Tower; 1588) now houses a Technological Museum. Schloss Ortenburg, a 15th-century castle with later additions, dominates the town and houses a Sorb Museum.

BAYREUTH (306 D2)
BAYERN *pop. 73,300*

Bayreuth's cultural tradition began with the Margrave Christian of Hohenzollern, who established his capital here in the 17th century and who built many baroque and rococo buildings. A century later, Margravine Wilhelmina, sister of Frederick the Great, continued his policies. Her husband commissioned an Italian architect to build a baroque opera house (Markgräfliches Opernhaus);

each May the Fränkische-Festwoche (18th-century opera and music) takes place here. It was this building which attracted Richard Wagner when he was looking for a suitable venue for the production of his opera cycle, *The Ring*. Now his works are performed at the annual Bayreuth Festival (July and August) in the Festspielhaus.

ALTES SCHLOSS, Maximilianstrasse, dates from the early 14th century and was rebuilt in the 1750s. Damaged by fire in 1945, it has not been rebuilt.

EREMITAGE SCHLOSS, 5 kilometers (3 miles) east, was the second residence of the Margrave of Brandenburg-Bayreuth and his wife, Wilhelmina. The 18th-century Old Castle contains some bare cells, while the New Castle features an ornate Sun Temple. Fountains play in the landscaped English gardens.

MARKGRÄFLICHES OPERNHAUS (Margrave Opera House) is on the Opernstrasse and was erected between 1745 and 1748 by order of the Margravine Wilhelmina for use as a private theater. This rococo structure is host to the Franconian Festival Weeks of 18th-century concerts and ballets.

NEUES SCHLOSS, Ludwigstrasse, is the lavish rococo palace hastily constructed at the request of Wilhelmina (1753–4), with a series of lovely rooms, each decorated in a different style. Outstanding are the Japanese Room, the Mirror Room and the Ballroom. The Hofgarten, a 17th-century park, adjoins.

RICHARD WAGNER FESTSPIELHAUS, on the Nibelungenstrasse, is the Festival Theater Richard Wagner designed. Its inward and outward appearance of simplicity reflects his desire to create an ideal setting for his music-dramas.

RICHARD WAGNER MUSEUM, Haus Wahnfried, Richard-Wagner-Strasse, has a collection of Wagnerian mementoes.

GERMANY

BERCHTESGADEN (306 D1)
BAYERN *pop. 8,200*

Most important for skiing, Berchtes-gaden has also long been known for its talented woodcarvers. Nearby is the vil-lage of Au, where local costumes are dis-played. Natural attractions include the Gorge of the Wimbach (passable from May to mid-October) and the Eis Höhle, an ice cave at Schellenberg.

In a deep, quiet gorge 5 kilometers (3 miles) south lies one of the most popular Alpine lakes: Königssee. On either side rise tremendous jagged cliffs formed in part by the Watzmann, one of the highest Bavarian peaks. Boat trips can be made on the lake: at one of the stops, the Chapel of St. Bartholomä is framed in an Alpine setting.

HEIMAT MUSEUM (Folklore Museum), Schroffenbergallee 6, displays wood-carvings, Berchtesgaden wood-chip boxes, toys and folk crafts.

SALZBERGWERK (Salt Mines), Bergwerk-Strasse, has brought the city prosperity since it began operation in 1515. A guid-ed trip through the mines is available.

SCHLOSS, first a monk's priory and then a palace for the royal family of Bavaria, is now a museum of artistic treasures collected by Crown Prince Rupert.

STIFTSKIRCHE, Schlossplatz, is a twin-spired abbey church originally built in the 12th century in Romanesque style. After a fire, one portion was rebuilt in Gothic style.

BERLIN – *see p.312.*

▲ BIELEFELD (306 B4)
NORDRHEIN-WESTFALEN *pop. 316,000*
As the Linenweaver's Fountain with its pipe-smoking figure suggests, Bielefeld is an industrial town.

BURG SPARRENBURG affords an extra-ordinary view over the Ravensburg country and the Teutoburger Forest.

Built in the 13th century, the palace was restored in the 19th century. There are catacombs and a playing-card museum.

BONN (306 B3)
NORDRHEIN-WESTFALEN *pop. 296,000*
Bonn is the former capital of the Federal Republic of Germany. In December 1990 Berlin was reinstated as the German capital, but Bonn remains the center of government and administration until the move is completed. Although Bonn dates from Roman times, clusters of modern buildings have sprouted amid its ancient churches, quiet parks and elegant 18th-century homes. The German parliament meets in the Bundeshaus on Adenauerallee from October to July.

FESTIVE BONN

From May to October Bonn offers a free cultural events program on the market square. Known as "Bonner Sommer," the series fea-tures theater presentations, musi-cal productions and puppet shows. The historic town hall serves as the stage setting. A Beethoven Festival is held here every three years.

Bonn is surrounded by one of Europe's most striking landscapes. Seven kilo-meters (4 miles) south of Bonn is Bad Godesberg. Famous for its panoramic view of the Siebengebirge, this spa and summer resort is the site of the ruins of a castle that was erected by the Archbishops of Cologne in the 13th and 14th centuries.

BEETHOVEN'S GEBURTSHAUS, Bongasse 20, is where the composer was born in 1770. It now houses a museum, with musical works, portraits and instruments.

MÜNSTER, Münsterplatz, dates from the 12th century. This mainly Romanesque church contains some baroque furnish-ings and some fine cloisters.

POPPELSDORFER SCHLOSS (Prince Elector's Palace), 171 Meckenheimer Allee, is a striking 18th-century palace showing French and Italian influences. The building is now part of the university, while the grounds serve as the Botanical Gardens.

RHEINISCHES LANDESMUSEUM, at 14 Colmantstrasse, houses a collection of Roman and Frankish relics and a Neanderthal skull. Medieval paintings and other works of art are also displayed.

BRAUBACH
RHEINLAND-PFALZ pop. 3,800
MARKSBURG above the town is the only completely preserved 11th-century castle on the Rhine River. It is unusual in that it has been inhabited continuously since the 12th century.

BRAUNSCHWEIG (306 C4)
NIEDERSACHSEN pop. 260,000
Braunschweig reached its peak in the 12th century under Henry the Lion, who commissioned many works of art for his city. Braunschweig, or Brunswick, became an important trading center and later (1753–1918) the residence of the Dukes of Brunswick. Although much damaged in World War II, several pockets of old buildings remain, the most appealing being the Altstadtmarkt with half-timbered houses, the cathedral and some Gothic churches.

BURGPLATZ is the medieval center of the old town; it faces the Burg Dankwarderode, an early fortress Henry chose as his residence. The present edifice was built in the last century and houses a museum of medieval art and artifacts.

DOM, Burgplatz, is a Romanesque cathedral dedicated to St. Blasius. Interior features include the tomb of Henry the Lion, a seven-branch candelabrum and 13th-century wall paintings.

HERZOG (DUKE) ANTON ULRICH MUSEUM on Museumstrasse, built in the 1880s, was named after this duke as his own art collection forms the core. The pictures in this collection, including those by Cranach, Holbein and Van Dyck, went on display in 1754, making this Germany's first museum.

▲ BREMEN (306 B4)
BREMEN pop. 530,000
Although 65 kilometers (40 miles) from the North Sea, this Free Hanseatic city on the Weser River is the oldest seaport in Germany. Along the river is the old area of Schnoor, with narrow streets and small cottages, many of which have been restored.

BÖTTCHERSTRASSE, off Marktplatz, once a narrow lane of coopers' workshops, was transformed in the 1920s to a fashionable street. At No. 6 is Kunstsammlung Roseliushaus, a 15th-century merchant's mansion with collections of medieval furniture and paintings.

DOM ST.-PETRI, Marktplatz Sondstrasse 10–12, is an 11th-century cathedral with an interior of Romanesque and Gothic styles. The bronze font dates from the 13th century, and an 11th-century crypt lies beneath the organ loft. The Bleikeller (lead cellar) contains several mummies.

FOCKE-MUSEUM, Schwachhauser-Heerstrasse 240, the Bremen State Museum of Art and History, charts the town's history.

KUNSTHALLE (Bremen Art Gallery), am Wall 207, more than 150 years old, features works by many European artists.

MARKTPLATZ, surrounded by the city's finest old buildings, is considered the most architecturally significant main square in the country.

NEUES MUSEUM WESERBURG BREMEN (New Museum Weserburg), Teerhof 20, displays works by both German and American artists, on loan from several private collections.

LEGENDARY LOGO
The Bremen Town Musicians' motif (a donkey, dog, cat and rooster) appears on many buildings. According to the fairy-tale by Jakob and Wilhelm Grimm, these animals planned on becoming town musicians in Bremen because they were no longer desired as domestic animals, but they never arrived.

RATHAUS, opposite the cathedral, is a 15th-century town hall with a Renaissance façade. A bronze statue of the Bremen Town Musicians adorns its western side.

BRUNSWICK – *see Braunschweig on p.321.*

BURGHAUSEN (306 D1)
BAYERN *pop. 17,500*
The 1,000-year-old town of Burghausen maintains a medieval atmosphere in the ancient houses of its Altstadt.

BURG is a 13th-century fortress that overlooks the town and is the longest castle in Europe. It includes a Gothic chapel and houses an art gallery, photograph collection and local history museum.

CELLE (306 C4)
NIEDERSACHSEN *pop. 71,500*
Celle is an old ducal city that retains a medieval atmosphere through its wealth of 16th- and 17th-century timbered houses in the attractive Altstadt. In the fall, horses bred in the former ducal stables take part in the spectacular Parade of Stallions.

HERZOGSSCHLOSS (Palace of the Duke) was originally a fortress built in the late 13th century, where the Dukes of Braunschweig-Lüneburg resided for 300 years. Still surrounded by a moat, the castle was rebuilt in Renaissance style. The ornate rooms, the Gothic chapel "with Renaissance décor" and the 1674 theater are all worth seeing.

CHIEMSEE (306 D1)
BAYERN
In Bavaria's largest lake are two islands with 8th-century Benedictine abbeys, accessible by steamer from Prien. The smaller island, Frauensel (Women's Island), retains its nunnery. The larger island is Herreninsel (Men's Island), which had a monastery; all that remains today is a Gothic church and old palace. The island is also the site of King Ludwig's Schloss Herrenchiemsee, modeled on Versailles but unfinished.

COBLENCE – *see Koblenz on p.333.*

COBURG (306 C2)
BAYERN *pop. 44,000*
This 900-year-old town reflects both Renaissance and Gothic influences in its attractive buildings, but is best known for its massive castle-fortress, the "Crown of Franconia."

SCHLOSS EHRENBURG, in the city center, was the residence of the dukes of Coburg from 1547 to 1918 and the boyhood home of Prince Albert, consort to Queen Victoria of England. The Riesensaal (Giants' Room) has 28 huge figures supporting the ceiling.

VESTE COBURG, 2 kilometers (1 miles) east, is one of Germany's largest and strongest citadels. This 12th-century castle-fortress brought the city prominence during the Middle Ages. The structure was remodeled and strengthened in the 16th century by Duke Johann Casimir and completely restored about 1900. Of special note is the paneled Luther Room where Martin Luther took refuge during the Augsburg Diet in 1530. The castle houses significant collections of paintings, engravings, carriages, porcelain and weapons.

COLDITZ (306 D3)
SACHSEN
The village's main attraction is striking Colditz Castle, a top-security prisoner-of-war camp during World War II.

COLOGNE – *see Köln on p.333.*

CONSTANCE – *see Konstanz on p.334.*

DETMOLD (306 B4)
NORDRHEIN-WESTFALEN *pop. 68,000*
Detmold is the former capital of the Lippe Principality, and the Lippisches Landesmuseum has a collection of relics from the Stone, Bronze and Iron ages. The Residenzschloss still belongs to the family and has period rooms and fine Brussels tapestries.

Near Detmold are the medieval towns of Lemgo, Blomberg and Schwalenberg. Also nearby is Horn, known for its early Romanesque bas-relief of the *Descent from the Cross.*

DINKELSBÜHL (306 C2) ★
BAYERN *pop. 11,000*
Dinkelsbühl borders the Wörnitz River in Bavaria. The medieval town has been preserved, and its architecture is typical of southern Germany. Fifteenth-century St. George's Cathedral and the Deutsches Haus are of special interest.

Dinkelsbühl has particular appeal to children, not only for its gingerbread, but also for its Kinderzeche, a week-long children's festival (July).

DONAUESCHINGEN (306 B1)
BADEN-WÜRTTEMBERG *pop. 19,600*
Donaueschingen is a popular tourist center at the head of the Danube; a tremendous 19th-century fountain marks the actual river source. The Karlsbau displays the works of Swabian artists and the Furstenburg Castle has a fine collection of porcelain.

▲ DRESDEN ★
SACHSEN *pop. 500,000*
Ancient Dresden began as a Slav settlement on the north bank of the Elbe River sometime before the 13th century. Later, a second settlement was founded on the other river bank and in 1270 Margrave Henry the Illustrious chose the twin towns as the capital of Saxony. After Henry's death Dresden was trans-ferred from ruler to ruler until Duke Albrecht of the Wettin dynasty moved his residency here from Meissen in 1485.

In the late 17th and 18th centuries, electors Augustus I and Augustus II remodeled Dresden in fabulous rococo and baroque style, making it one of the showplaces of Europe. Many splendid buildings survived the Seven Years' War (1756–63) and the city prospered in the 19th century. Sadly, Dresden was bombed heavily in 1945.

Several of the baroque and rococo buildings that once clustered around the castle have since been rebuilt, among them the Semper Opera House, the Japanese Palace, the Zwinger complex and the Hofkirche. The ruins of the Frauenkirche, until recently preserved as a memorial in its ruined state, are currently being restored.

SAXON SWITZERLAND
In the 19th century, this area (south east of Dresden and now a national park) was a source of inspiration for many artists of the Romantic School. A "Painters Path" was created, leading through valleys and across mountains from Dresden, via Pillnitz, to the Czech border.

ALBERTINUM (1559) is one of Dresden's two museum complexes. Built in 1559, the glass-domed structure contains various forms of art.
Gemäldegalerie Neuer Meister (Picture Gallery of New Masters) displays paintings by 19th- and 20th-century masters, as well as works by German Impressionists, 20th-century socialist artists and 19th-century genre painters.
Grünes Gewölbe (Green Vault) contains one of Germany's largest royal collections of 15th- to 18th-century silver, gold and jewelry.

KREUZKIRCHE, by the Altmarkt, is one of Dresden's finest baroque structures, with a famous Boys' Choir (Kreuzchor).

MUSEUM FÜR GESCHICHTE DER STADT DRESDEN (Museum of the Town of Dresden) is in the Landhaus, an 18th-century palace. Exhibits include photographs that show Dresden before and after the bombings of World War II.

THE ZWINGER is the pride of Dresden. Designed by Pöppelmann and built 1711–32, the Zwinger was planned as part of a large palace. The square court with its U-shaped extensions is considered one of the most successful baroque designs ever conceived. The galleries and pavilions, some now used as museums, are linked to form a court that functions as an outdoor theater.

Gemäldegalerie Alter Meister (Picture Gallery of Old Masters), in the Semper Gallery, contains Raphael's *Sistine Madonna* and Giorgione's *Sleeping Venus* in addition to a dozen Rembrandts, five Tintorettos and works by Titian, Rubens and Van Dyck.

Historisches Museum (Historical Museum), in the Semper Gallery's east wing, displays costumes from the Saxon court, weapons and oriental items.

Porzellansammlung (Porcelain Collection) consists of early porcelain from the Han, Tang and Ming dynasties and from the Meissen factory.

Zoological Museum displays ancient hunting weapons and artifacts from the 17th and 18th centuries.

▲ DÜSSELDORF (306 B3)

NORDRHEIN-WESTFALEN *pop. 570,000*
Düsseldorf is an important Rhine River city that was founded in the 13th-century. It is one of the most important economic and cultural centers in Germany with many restored buildings, fine museums, art collections, private residences, theaters and concert halls.

Cafés, fashionable boutiques, jewelers, dress shops and art shops are found along Königsallee, Düsseldorf's main street. The town is proud of its open spaces: the L-shaped Hofgarten in the center; the Südpark to the south and Nordpark to the north.

ALTES RATHAUS (Old Town Hall), Marktplatz, is a 16th-century restored brick building with Renaissance gables.

KUNSTMUSEUM, Ehrenhof 5, contains European art from the Middle Ages to the present, with emphasis on German art of the 19th and 20th centuries.

DÜSSELDORF DIARY

Düsseldorf is host to theatrical productions and festivals throughout the year. Drama is performed at the Schauspielhaus, comedies and satires at Komödchen, and opera at the Opera House.

In July the Grand Marksmen's Contests and Local Fair are held on the Oberkassel bank of the Rhine River. More than 3,000 booths and numerous rides compete during the nine-day event. A grand parade and fireworks display compose the finale. The winter carnival season lasts from mid-November until mid-February.

KUNSTSTAMMLUNG NORDRHEIN-WESTFALEN (State Art Collection of North Rhine-Westphalia), Grabbepl 5, features 20th-century works, including Klee, Ernst, Mondrian, Miró and Chagall.

LAMBERTUSKIRCHE, Schlossufer, is a 14th-century church with a crooked spire. Inside look out for the Renaissance tomb of Duke William the Rich, and a Gothic tabernacle.

SCHLOSS BENRATH, 10 kilometers (6 miles) south east at Benrather Schossalle 104, is an 18th-century rococo castle housing a regional museum; baroque gardens extend to the Rhine.

SCHLOSS JÄGERHOF, at the east end of Jägerhofstrasse, is an 18th-century baroque-style hunting palace. It houses the Goethe Museum, and the Ernst Schneider Foundation, which contains Meissen porcelain and silverware.

▲ **EISENACH** (306 C3)
THÜRINGEN *pop. 45,000*
Eisenach was founded about 1150 by the Landgraves of Thuringia. It is most renowned as the site of the 11th-century Wartburg Castle, where Martin Luther began translating the New Testament into German in 1521. The town was also the birthplace of J.S. Bach in 1685.

BACHHAUS, am Frauenplan 21, was the Bach family home. A collection of musical instruments, 17th-century furniture and a display chronicling the lives and works of the family are inside.

LUTHERHAUS, where Martin Luther lived as a boy, has a collection of bibles and 16th-century religious books.

THÜRINGER MUSEUM, in the 18th-century former ducal palace, contains glassware, a picture gallery, wood sculpture, Thuringian porcelain and items from the Middle Ages.

MINSTRELS

In the Middle Ages, music and poetry competitions were held for wandering minstrels. The culture-loving descendants of Count Ludwig I promoted art and music at their court in Wartburg Castle in Eisenach and hosted the competition (*Sängerkrieg*) for the German troubadors (*Minnesänger*). One minstrel was Wolfram von Eschenbach, who wrote part of the epic *Parzifal* here; many years later Wagner used the theme in his opera *Tannhäuser*.

WARTBURG CASTLE was known to exist as early as 1067. Built by Landgraves on a hill above the village, it was where Luther sought refuge during the Reformation. Inside the castle are Gothic and baroque furniture, a Romanesque Knights' Hall, and a huge Festsaal (banqueting hall) decorated with frescoes by Moritz von Schwind.

▲ **ERFURT** (306 C3)
THÜRINGEN *pop. 220,000*
Many of Eurfurt's buildings date from the 16th century, when Martin Luther was a novice at the monastery; most notable are the half-timbered houses lining 600-year-old Krämer Bridge. The cathedral has fine stained-glass windows and a baroque high altar; next to it is the Church of St. Severus, an early Gothic hall church. The Angermuseum contains many medieval works of art.

ESSEN (306 B3)
NORDRHEIN-WESTFALEN *pop. 620,000*
Sightseeing highlights in this industrial city are the Gruga Park and the Münsterkirche, a 9th-century Romanesque basilica, with some valuable medieval works of art in its treasury (Schatzkammer). Of artistic importance is the Folkwang Museum, which houses a collection of prominent modern works.

FLENSBURG (306 C4)
SCHLESWIG-HOLSTEIN *pop. 87,000*
Flensburg's location on the fiord of the same name near Denmark has earned it the nickname "Gate to the North."
Sights include the Nordertor (a city gate), the Nordermarket, the fishing quarter of Jügenby, and the Städtisches Museum.

SCHLOSS GLÜCKSBURG, about 9 kilometers (6 miles) north east, is a Renaissance-style lake palace which was built around 1585.

▲ **FRANKFURT-AM-MAIN** (306 B2)
HESSEN *pop. 627,500*
Frankfurt, in the center of Germany, has experienced history from the Roman occupation to the time when early German kings were elected here and Holy Roman emperors were crowned in the cathedral.
Opposed to Prussianism but never radical, Frankfurt later became a stronghold of liberalism and a major trading center. Much of the city, including Germany's largest Altstadt (old town),

GERMANY

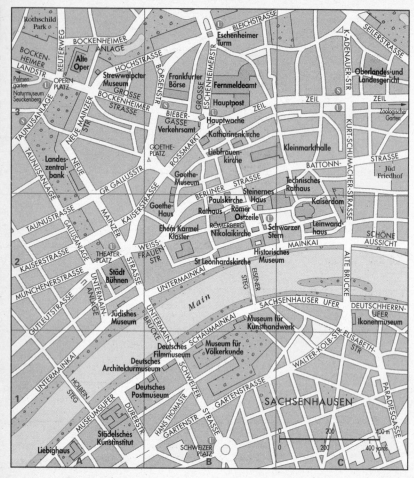

was devastated in 1944; some of the older buildings have since been sensitively restored.

In front of the cathedral, excavated remains from Roman and Carolingian times now constitute the Historical Gardens (Historischer Garten).

Today, Frankfurt is Germany's financial capital and commercial center. It is also the hub of the publishing industry and hosts international trade fairs, as well as supporting the arts.

The Alte Oper (Old Opera House) has been restored but is now used for conferences and concerts, while operas and plays are performed in the Städtische Bühnen complex. Many venues around town host concerts of all types, plus plays and and films. A string of museums lines the south bank of the river (Museumsufer) in Sachsenhausen, whose old quarter is full of inns offering local foods.

ESCHENHEIMER TURM (Eschenheimer Tower) (326 B3), a striking five-turreted tower built in 1428 and nearly 50 meters (155 feet) tall, is part of the old town walls.

GOETHEHAUS UND GOETHEMUSEUM, Grosser Hirschgraben 23 (326 B2/B3), is a reconstruction of the childhood home of Johann Wolfgang von Goethe, (1749–1832). The adjoining museum displays documents and paintings by artists of his day.

HISTORISCHES MUSEUM (326 B2) incorporates the medieval Rententurm (tower), the 12th-century castle founded by Emperor Frederick I (Barbarossa), and its Saalhof Kapelle (Romanesque Chapel), the city's oldest building. Inside are scale models of old Frankfurt, a Children's Museum and coins.

JÜDISCHES MUSEUM (326 A2) deals with the history of the town's former influential Jewish community. The displays include mementoes from the Nazi period.

KAISERDOM (326 C2), St. Bartholomew's red-sandstone cathedral, where emperors were crowned from 1562, rests on Carolingian foundations that date from 852 AD. Between the 13th and 15th centuries it was enlarged in the Gothic style. The 9-meter (310-foot) tower, choir stalls and treasury can be seen by guided tour.

LIEBIGHAUS MUSEUM (326 A1), on Museumsufer, exhibits early sculpture collected from Sumeria, Egypt and Greece, and also later pieces from Germany and Western Europe.

MUSEUM FÜR KUNSTHANDWERK (Museum of Applied Arts) (326 B2) has an outstanding collection of European glass, ceramics and furniture; Islamic carpets; oriental jade and lacquerwork; and a section which is devoted to books and manuscripts.

NATURMUSEUM SENCKENBERG, Senckenberganlage 25, displays large fossils, animals, plants and geological items in a self-teaching environment.

RÖMERBERG (326 B2), a cobbled square where royal ceremonies were once held, was rebuilt in the 1980s. Along the west side are some half-timbered houses (Römer), with stepped gables, which once formed the Rathaus (Town Hall), originally built 500 years ago. In the upper stories is the Kaisersaal (Imperial Hall), where coronation banquets of Holy Roman Emperors took place. On the east side, six more houses have been rebuilt in traditional style. On the south side is the Romanesque Nikolaikirche (St. Nicholas' Church) and opposite stands Paulskirche, built in the 18th century as a Lutheran preaching hall.

ST. LEONHARDSKIRCHE (326 C2), on Mainkai, west of Eiserner Steg, retains octagonal towers and doorways from a 13th-century Romanesque basilica. Gothic modifications were made in the 15th century.

STÄDELSCHES KUNSTINSTITUT (326 A1), Schaumainkai 63, is an art gallery boasting works by Dürer, Cranach, Grien, Botticelli, Rubens, Rembrandt, Renoir, Goya and others.

ZOOLOGISCHER GARTEN, on Alfred-Brehm-Platz, is a leader in zookeeping methods, where rare animals which are difficult to care for in captivity are bred.

▲ FREIBURG IM BREISGAU (306 B1)
BADEN-WÜRTTEMBERG *pop. 179,000*
The old university city of Freiburg im Breisgau is the entrance to the southern Black Forest. The cathedral, the university (founded in 1457), medieval gates, and Kaufhaus are sightseeing highlights. Schlossberg (Castle Hill), 460 meters (1,510 feet) high, gives a fine view. The Augustinermuseum houses Upper Rhenish art from the Middle Ages as well as baroque sculpture.

MÜNSTER, Münsterplatz, is a Gothic cathedral reflecting the architectural styles of the 13th, 14th and 15th centuries. The 116-meter (380-foot) spire is a latticework of stone; artwork adorns the tympanum, west porch and south side. The tower offers views over the 18th-century Münster platz (Market Square).

GERMANY

FULDA (306 C3)
HESSEN *pop. 56,500*
Ancient Fulda, on the Fulda River, originated with a once-celebrated abbey founded by Sturmius, a disciple of St. Boniface, in 744 AD. The present St. Boniface Cathedral exemplifies Italian baroque style. Also of interest are the 9th-century Michaelskirche, the oldest undamaged church in Germany.

SCHLOSS FASANERIE, 4 kilometers (2½ miles) north west, was the summer palace of the Archbishops of Fulda. The baroque structure was later developed into an entertainment center.

STADTSCHLOSS has evolved from a 14th-century medieval castle into a baroque residence. Of interest are the princes' and emperor's halls, mirror cabinet, orangery and local history museum.

FÜSSEN (306 C1) ★
BAYERN *pop. 16,500*
The old mountain town of Füssen on the Austrian border was originally a fortress guarding the pass through the Alps. Its strategic position is the starting point of the Romantic Road. The beauty of Füssen's mountain backdrop and lake-dotted countryside make it a popular resort and winter sports center. Two Königsschlösser (Royal Castles) connected with Ludwig II are close by, 3 kilometers (2 miles) from town.

HOHENSCHWANGAU was a medieval fortress of the Knights of the Swan, demolished by Napoleon and restored by King Maximilian II, who tried to re-create a medieval castle. Ludwig II lived here as a child.

HOHES SCHLOSS (late 15th century) is the former summer palace of the prince-bishops of Ausgsburg.

NEUSCHWANSTEIN is a turreted granite structure that served as the model for the castles at Disneyland and Walt Disney World. The extravagantly decorated castle, built in the 1870s but unfinished, was the inspiration of Ludwig II.

ST.-MANG-KIRCHE, Lechhalde, is a former Benedictine monastery founded in the 8th century. The present church was reconstructed in baroque style in the 18th century and is now a local museum. It incorporates the earlier Chapel of St. Anne, on the walls of which is painted the *Totentanz* (*Dance of Death*).

GARMISCH-PARTENKIRCHEN (306 C1) ★
BAYERN *pop. 26,500*
The relatively flat ground of Germany's foremost winter sports center (two towns joined together) is surrounded by mountains, including 2,963-meter (9,721-foot) Zugspitze, the country's highest point. Snow can be expected from mid-December through March; the peak tourist season is Christmas. From May to October it is a popular health resort.

GOSLAR (306 C4)
NIEDERSACHSEN *pop. 46,000*
Goslar is an old imperial town on the northern edge of the Harz mountains which can trace its beginnings back to the 11th century. The town prospered from silver mining until about 1350 and was a founder member of the Hanseatic League. The buildings reflect the town's former wealth, and also here are the impressive 19th-century murals in the German emperors' Romanesque palace. The Rathaus has a splendid Council Chamber (Huldigungssaal), covered with frescoes dating from 1500.

HALLE (306 D3)
SACHSEN-ANHOLT *pop. 230,000*
Salt deposits near Halle were discovered as early as 4000 BC and supported a flourishing salt trade on the Saale River. In 968 AD, Halle was chartered as a town of the Holy Roman Empire. During the Middle Ages, feuds between the salt-workers and the owners of the salt flats prompted the archbishop to build the Moritzburg fortress. Destroyed by fire in 1637 and

rebuilt after 1897, the fortress now contains an art gallery (Staathiche Galerie) with 19th- and 20th-century works.

In addition to its industrial history, Halle was the birthplace of Handel in 1685. Today Halle honors its most prominent resident with the annual Handel Festival, and his statue stands in the Marktplatz close to the Roter Turm (Red Tower), a late-Gothic belfry.

HALLE CATHEDRAL was built in the 13th century as a Dominican monastery and contains statues of several saints.

HALLOREN UND SALINENMUSEUM (Saltworks Museum) demonstrates how salt was extracted and portrays the lifestyle of the salt-workers.

HANDELHAUS is the baroque house where Handel was born. A collection of instruments and exhibits detailing his life and works are displayed.

MARKTKIRCHE UNSER LIEBEN FRAUEN (Market Church) is a late-Gothic hall church with four towers, each pair originating from two earlier Romanesque churches. Martin Luther preached here, Handel learned the organ and Johann Sebastian Bach's son, Friedmann, served as the church organist.

▲ HAMBURG (306 C4) ★
HAMBURG *pop. 1,650,000*
Almost completely destroyed in World War II, Hamburg on the Elbe River, one of Europe's major ports and Germany's second largest city, is today an outstanding example of urban modernity. The city owes much of its character to Lake Alster, which is separated by the Lombard Bridge into Aussen (Outer) and Binnenalster (Inner Alster). The banks of the Outer Alster are dotted with the city merchants' white villas; along the Inner Alster are hotels and commercial buildings. One row of attractive gabled warehouses from the 17th century still stands in Diechstrasse, near the Nikolai Fleet Canal.

In the lively St. Pauli entertainment quarter, the Reeperbahn and side streets are lined with restaurants, nightclubs, dance halls, shooting galleries and other amusement spots. Hamburg has three municipal theaters, over 30 private ones, and Germany's oldest opera house. The Hamburg Card, on sale at hotels and tourist information offices, entitles visitors to free travel and museum entry, and to discounts on sightseeing tours.

HAUPTKIRCHE ST. MICHAELIS, Krayenkamp and Ost-West-Strasse, is a baroque church built between 1751 and 1762. "Michel," the rotunda-topped tower, provides a panorama of the city.

KUNSTHALLE (City Art Museum), off Glockengiesserwall 1, specializes in German medieval, Romantic and primitive paintings, but also has 17th- and 18th-century European art.

MUSEUM FÜR HAMBURGISCHE GESCHICHTE, off Holstenwall, traces the development of the city from medieval times. Displays include models of Old Hamburg, railways and ships.

MUSEUM FÜR KUNST UND GEWERBE (Museum for Arts and Crafts) one block west of Steintorwall, contains exhibits from Europe and Asia arranged chronologically, beginning with the Middle Ages. There is also an art-nouveau (*Jugendstil*) section.

RATHAUS, Rathausmarkt, is a fine neo-Renaissance building with a vaulted ceiling where the city's parliament meets. The spire rises nearly 113 meters (370 feet).

HAMELN – *see Hameln below.*

HAMELN (306 C4)
NIEDERSACHSEN *pop. 58,000*
According to legend, Hameln's rats were driven out of town in 1284 by the Ratcatcher. When the townspeople refused to pay him, he charmed the

children away with his magic pipe. Hameln, or Hamelin, is also known for its stone Renaissance Weser houses with timbered façades and gables, decorated with coats of arms and carvings; fine examples are in Osterstrasse: the Stiftsherrnhaus, Rattenfängerhaus, Dempterhaus, Hochzeitshaus (House of Weddings) and Leisthaus.

LEISTHAUS, 9 Osterstrasse, is an old patrician building that now houses the Museum Hameln, with a religious art collection and several rooms furnished in styles of their period.

HANNOVER (306 C4)
NIEDERSACHSEN *pop. 510,000*
Lively, industrial Hannover is the capital of Niedersachsen, Lower Saxony. The royal House of Brunswick was based in Hannover from the late 17th century, and it subsequently inherited the British throne in 1714 through a marriage to the House of Stuart. This situation prevailed until 1837 when the House split. The city was bombed in World War II but has now been reconstructed.

The oldest part of the town is the charming Altstadt (Old Town), with many half-timbered gabled buildings including the 17th-century Ballhof, a former sports hall and now a theater, and the Altes Rathaus (Old Town Hall), built in 1455. The Roter Faden (Red Thread) is a walking tour painted in red on the ground leading to 36 places of interest. From late May to early September, the annual Herrenhausen Festival of concerts, plays, ballets and illuminations is held.

HERRENHÄUSER GARTEN, off Nienburgerstrasse, is an extensive, immaculately kept garden complex developed in the late 17th and early 18th centuries by the Brunswick family. These are Germany's only unspoiled baroque gardens.

HISTORISCHES MUSEUM, am Hohen Ufer, incorporates the Beginen Tower,

a remaining piece of the old city walls. Apart from telling the history of the city, the museum displays four state coaches still owned by the House of Hannover.

KESTNER MUSEUM, Trammplatz 3, was founded in 1889; in addition to its Egyptian collection, the museum has examples of ancient Mediterranean and medieval arts and crafts, china and porcelain, and miniature works of art.

LEIBNIZHAUS, in Old Town, was the home of philosopher and mathematician Gottfried Wilhelm von Leibniz. Once regarded as one of the finest houses in Germany, this Renaissance building was opened in 1983 as a meeting place for scientists from all over the world.

BIG DRINKER

In the Fassbau (Wine Vat Building) of the Schloss is the celebrated Great Vat, a symbol of the Bacchanalian spirit of the Palatine. Nearby is a figure of dwarf court jester Perkeo, who, according to legend, drank unaided the contents of the 2,500-liter (5,550-gallon) receptacle.

LEINESCHLOSS (Leine Palace) is at Heinrich-Wilhelm-Kopf-Platz 1. Built 1636–40 and reconstructed 1817–42, the palace is now a meeting place of the Lower Saxony parliament.

MARKTKIRCHE, just off Kamarshstrasse, is a 14th-century Gothic church with a fine altarpiece and stained glass.

NEUES RATHAUS (New Town Hall), Trammplatz 2, was built 1901–13 by Hermann Eggert and Gustav Halmhuber. Models of the city from 1689 to the present are displayed in the dome hall. An elevator ride up the dome tower affords a nice view of the area.

NIEDERSÄCHSISCHES LANDESMUSEUM (Museum of Lower Saxony), am

Maschpark 5, is devoted to archeology, natural history and ethnology. The art gallery exhibits European art.

OPERNHAUS, on Georgstrasse, is one of the finest opera houses in Germany; it was designed in the 19th century by architect Georg Laves.

HECHINGEN (306 B1)
BADEN-WÜRTTEMBERG *pop. 16,600*
Hechingen is an old town in the Swabian Jura usually visited by travelers heading for nearby castles.

HOHENZOLLERN BURG is 5 kilometers (3 miles) south on Zollern Mountain. Here the Hohenzollerns ruled their small Swabian fiefdom prior to becoming margraves of Brandenburg, kings of Prussia and emperors of Germany. The present castle, built 1850–67 on the site of earlier structures, employs the ground plan of the medieval fortress that preceded it. Inside are the tombs of several Prussian kings, a museum with art objects and documents depicting Prussian history, and two chapels.

HEIDELBERG (306 B2)
BADEN-WÜRTTEMBERG *pop. 132,000*
The tranquil riverside setting of Heidelberg was an inspiration to several 19th-century German writers, including Goethe. The 16th-century castle is the most prominent landmark, but the colorful Church of the Holy Spirit and Renaissance buildings associated with the university are also of interest. As a result of French attacks and a fire, much of the early town was destroyed at the end of the 17th century. However, many baroque buildings remain.

KURPFÄLZISCHES MUSEUM (Palatinate Museum), Hauptstrasse 97, exhibits prehistoric items, coins and porcelain. Displays include the Twelve Apostles Altar, carved in 1509 by Tilman Riemenschneider and discovered over two centuries later under many thick coatings of paint.

SCHLOSS, overlooking the slate-roofed old city and Neckar Valley, is majestic even in its half-ruined state. For five centuries, electors of the Palatinate Dynasty lived here until its virtual destruction in 1693.

Its fortifications include towers and gates, and now house noteworthy collections. The Friedrichsbau boasts an extensive gallery of German notables: a Charlemagne; Ruprecht III, founder of the university; and Friedrich II, creator of the Ottheinrichbau, in whose vaults is the German Apothecary Museum.

HEILBRONN (306 B2)
BADEN-WÜRTTEMBERG *pop. 111,000*
Heilbronn is a thriving industrial community. It was devastated in World War II, but is now rebuilt.

Two buildings date back to the 13th century: the House of the Order of the Teutonic Knights; and the Church of St. Peter and Paul. The city holds many festivals – a nine-day one for wine (Weinfest), and a boat pageant (Neckarfest) which alternates with the town festival (Stadtfest). A horse fair (Pferdmarkt) is held in February.

BURG GUTTENBERG, 20 kilometers (12 miles) north, is one of the oldest and best-preserved castles in the Neckar Valley. The interior is a good example of medieval craftsmanship, and has a wooden library; the defense structures are also of interest.

HILDESHEIM (306 C4)
NIEDERSACHSEN *pop. 105,000*
Hildesheim's places of interest include the cathedral, known for its bronze doors with biblical scenes; a purportedly 1,000-year-old rosebush; the Basilica of St. Godehard; St. Michael's Church; and the 15th-century Templarhaus.

The Roemer-Pelizaeus Museum contains Egyptian art.

SCHLOSS MARIENBURG, 20 kilometers (12 miles) north west near Nordstemmen, was begun between 1860 and 1868 by

George V, the last king of Hannover, but was never completed. The neo-Gothic structure offers some extensive views and a museum.

▲ KARLSRUHE (306 B2)
BADEN-WÜRTTEMBERG *pop. 270,000*
Shaped like a fan with majestic avenues radiating from its 18th-century Margrave's Palace, Karlsruhe so impressed Thomas Jefferson that he suggested it as a model for Washington, D.C. The city is an important inland harbor and one of Germany's major industrial centers.

SCHLOSS is a reconstruction of the mid 18th-century late-baroque residence of the Margraves of Baden. Surrounded by gardens, the palace is now the home of the Badisches Landesmuseum (Baden Museum of Local History), which has exhibits of antiques and arts and crafts of the region.

THE GRIMM BROTHERS
Jacob and Wilhelm Grimm were born in Hanau in 1785 and 1786, and came to live in Kassel to take up their posts as court librarians. They wrote down stories and fairy-tales which had been transmitted by word of mouth for centuries. Many tales, such as *Hansel and Gretel* and *Red Riding Hood*, originated from the area around Trendelburg (Hessen). A third brother illustrated the tales and the first collection was published in 1812. Kassel devotes a museum to them.

KASSEL (306 C3)
HESSEN *pop. 197,000*
In 1277, Landgrave Heinrich of Hessen chose Kassel, on the Fulda River, as his residence, and the family remained here for over 600 years. In the early part of the 18th century they created the grand park of Wilhelmshöhe and also encouraged industry. Much of the town was destroyed during World War II (arms were manufactured here) but it has now been rebuilt.

Kassel proudly preserves its parks and gardens, and every five years holds a multimedia avant-garde art festival called *Documenta*.

DEUTSCHES TAPETENMUSEUM, Brüder-Grimm-Platz 5, features wall coverings from the late Middle Ages to the present, including tapestries from the 16th to 19th centuries.

LANDESMUSEUM (Hessian Provincial Museum – same building as Tapeten Museum) contains applied art, astronomy and physics exhibits, prehistoric finds and amber.

SCHLOSS WILHELMSHÖHE is on a slope of the Häbichtswald forest area, about 14 kilometers (9 miles) west. The layout, in the form of an inverted "V," is unique in Europe. The ornately decorated Schloss houses the State Art Collection, first assembled by the Landgraves of Hesse. The Gallery of Old Masters contains over 600 paintings, with a large number of Rembrandts, as well as works by Van Dyck, Titian and Tintoretto.

The museum also has an excellent sculpture gallery.
Löwenburg in the southern section of the park, was built 1793–8 in the form of a Gothic-style English castle ruin. An armor collection is inside.

SCHLOSS WILHELMSTAL, about 15 kilometers (9 miles) north west, is a small rococo palace set deep in the forest. Built about 1760, it houses period furniture, porcelain and portraits by Johann Heinrich Tischbein.

▲ KIEL (306 C4)
SCHLESWIG-HOLSTEIN *pop. 245,000*
Kiel is the capital of Schleswig-Holstein, and is the site of the canal that connects the Baltic with the North Sea.

On land, visitors can enjoy parks and beaches; at sea, an annual regatta is held in June.

SCHLESWIG-HOLSTEIN FREILICHTMUSEUM is 6 kilometers (4 miles) south west at Molfsee. Farms and buildings dating from the 16th through 19th centuries have been reassembled here.

▲ KOBLENZ (306 B3)
RHEINLAND-PFALZ *pop. 107,000*
Patricians' houses and noblemen's mansions give evidence of the cultural past of Koblenz, now a thriving wine center. The Romans established a fort as early as 9 BC, making Koblenz one of the oldest towns in Germany. It was a royal seat of the Franks and later, after World War I, served as the headquarters of the Joint Allied Commission for the Rhineland. Because most of Koblenz was destroyed in World War II, the rebuilt city has a modern appearance.

Ninth-century St. Kastor's is said to be the oldest church; the more recent St. Florin's was built in the 12th century. The 18th-century Rathaus reflects elaborate baroque style.

FESTUNG EHRENBREITSTEIN, rising more than 117 meters (385 feet) above the Rhine, is a massive neo-classical fortress that commands a panoramic view of the river valley. An earlier defense built in the 11th century by Erembert was destroyed by the French in 1801. The present structure, built by Prussians 1817–28, is one of the strongest fortresses in Europe. Today, the fortress houses a memorial to the German army, a youth hostel and the Landesmuseum (Regional Museum).

▲ KÖLN (306 B3)
NORDRHEIN-WESTFALEN *pop. 992,000*
Köln (Cologne), founded by the Romans in 38 BC, is now traversed by entire streets of new buildings to replace the medieval ones destroyed during the war; luckily the twin-towered cathedral and a group of Romanesque churches have survived. Museums, a concert hall, small theaters and the Rhine Garden Recreation Area are all near the cathedral. The liveliest time of year is January and February, which is carnival season.

DOM (Köln Cathedral) is one of the largest Gothic structures in the world. Its foundation dates from 1248, but the edifice was not complete until 1880. The first monumental crucifix in Northern Europe, created before 1000, and the Golden Shrine of the Three Magi, are of special interest.
Schatzkammer (Cathedral Treasury) includes collections of medieval codices, sacred relics, and gold and ivory items.

RÖMISCH-GERMANISCHES MUSEUM, on the south side of the cathedral, portrays early Roman life along the Rhine. The extensive glassware and earthenware collections from the 1st to 5th centuries are augmented by the Tomb of Poblicius and the Dionysus Mosaic.

ST.-GEREON KIRCHE, Gereondriesch 2–4, is a ten-sided tower constructed in the late 4th century as a memorial chapel for martyrs. A later Romanesque church was built adjoining it.

SCHLOSS AUGUSTUSBURG at Brühl, 14 kilometers (9 miles) south west was the 18th-century residence of the Archbishop of Köln. The palace contains valuable furnishings, and the grand staircase by Balthasar Neumann is especially noteworthy. Formal gardens surround the palace. Brühl also has Germany's largest theme park, Phantasieland, run on the lines of Disneyland.

SCHNÜTGEN-MUSEUM, in Cäcilienkirche, just off Cäcilienstrasse 29, contains ecclesiastical art from the early Middle Ages to the baroque era. Collections include ivory carvings, goldsmiths' work, sculptures, textiles and paintings.

WALLRAF-RICHARTZ LUDWIG MUSEUMS at Bischofsgartenstrasse. The Ludwig Museum houses modern art from Impressionist works to the most recent trends. In the other museum are medieval paintings, 17th- and 18th-century Dutch masterpieces and 20th-century German and French works.

KONSTANZ (306 B1)
BADEN-WÜRTTEMBERG *pop. 75,000*

Surrounded by Switzerland except for its waterfront on Lake Constance (Bodensee), the town blends medieval and cosmopolitan atmospheres.

Remnants of its distinguished past recall the Council of Konstanz, which was invoked by Emperor Sigismund in 1414 to end the schism in the Christian world, during which three men claimed to be the rightful pope. During the council's four-year duration, the population increased as Konstanz became the residence of bishops and kings. By 1418, Martin V had been elected pope, and Jan Hus, one of the most noted precursors of Protestantism, had been condemned for heresy and burned at the stake.

Konstanz is a cultural and economic center, due primarily to its ideal location on shipping routes. The town has a Renaissance Rathaus and local museum (Rosgartenmuseum) with a collection of historic and cultural treasures. The city offers facilities for watersports, gambling and cruises.

MÜNSTER, Münsterplatz, is a Romanesque cathedral, begun in the 11th century and which now reflects the architectural styles of the 600 years during which construction continued. Of note are carved panels in the main façade's doorway, the rich treasury, the 9th-century crypt and the tombs.

LANDSHUT (306 D1)
BAYERN *pop. 60,000*

The seat of Bavarian dukes 1204–1503, Landshut retains much of the atmosphere of a medieval capital despite the growth of modern suburbs. The banks of the Isar River are lined with Gothic buildings, including 15th-century St. Martinskirche, with a 133-meter (435-foot) brick steeple said to be the highest in the world. The city's main event is the Landshuter Hochzeit, a triennial commemoration of a medieval duke's wedding.

Landshut's other points of interest include its Gothic churches – Dominikanerkirche, St.-Jodokskirche, Heilig-Geist-Kirche – and the baroque Kloster Seligenthal, a Cistercian convent (1259).

The Burg Trausnitz, a medieval fortress high above the city, and the Stadtresidenz, reputed to be the oldest Renaissance palace in Germany, once housed Landshut's dukes; the latter is now an art gallery.

LANGENBURG
BADEN-WÜRTTEMBERG *pop. 1,900*

SCHLOSSMUSEUM, in Schloss Langenburg, has a good collection of historic weapons, porcelain, portraits and hunting trophies, as well as displays pertaining to 12th-century fortifications. The Schloss is also home to the Deutsches Automuseum.

▲ LEIPZIG (306 D3)
SACHSEN *pop. 530,000*

Leipzig's position above the confluence of the Piesse, Parthe and West Elster rivers earned the town a mention in written history as early as 1015 AD, when it was called Urbs Libzi. A burgeoning foreign

---

RICHARD WAGNER

Richard Wagner was born in Leipzig in 1813 and studied musical composition at Leipzig University. His *Symphony in C Major* was performed at the Leipzig Gewandhouse in 1833, a dozen years before he earned public acclaim for *Rienzi*, a five-act grand opera first performed in Dresden.

---

trade in the Middle Ages helped to establish two annual fairs at Leipzig, and by 1700 it was Germany's most powerful commercial center.

Cultural stirrings began in Leipzig when Johann Sebastian Bach was appointed the city's musical director in 1728. The city entered military history during the Napoleonic Wars with the Battle of Leipzig in 1813.

Leipzig is important as an intellectual, cultural and industrial city. The ancient Leipzig Trade Fairs still take place in early March and September.

In spite of being severely damaged in World War II and neglected in the ensuing 40 years, Leipzig is gradually picking up the pieces and re-establishing itself. Historic buildings include the Altes Rathaus, the Old Stock Exchange, Auerbach's Cellar and the 13th-century Thomaskirche.

LIMBURG (306 B3)
HESSEN *pop. 31,100*
The 13th-century Cathedral of St. George stands on a rocky height, dominating Limburg an der Lahn. Murals in the early Gothic church date from the building's construction. The city itself contains many old half-timbered houses.

SCHLOSS WEILBURG, 20 kilometers (12 miles) north east on B49 at Weilburg, is a 16th-century Renaissance palace renovated in baroque style around 1700. Richly furnished rooms reflect the styles of the 16th to 19th centuries.

LINDAU (306 C1) ★
BAYERN *pop. 24,100*
Lindau am Bodensee is an island resort on Lake Constance (Bodensee) with Renaissance and baroque houses built by rich merchants in the Middle Ages. The local history museum (Haus zum Cavazzen) has an interesting collection.

LÜBECK (306 C4) ★
SCHLESWIG-HOLSTEIN *pop. 216,000*
Lübeck's docks, old streets and brick buildings testify to the prosperity the city enjoyed in the late Middle Ages, when it was the seat of the powerful Hanseatic League. Architectural monuments include the towered Holsten Gate, the cathedral with its carved triumphal cross, and the brick Rathaus.

Between the town's main streets is a maze of secluded interconnecting courts and passageways, which have been restored and are open to the public. The fashionable Baltic resort town of Travemünde is 15 kilometers (9 miles) north east, with ferry connections to Denmark, Finland and Sweden.

LÜNEBURG (306 C4)
NIEDERSACHSEN *pop. 60,000*
Lüneburg is an ancient spa town with many restored Gothic and Renaissance buildings, including the churches of St. John and St. Nicholas. The medieval Rathaus is the oldest in Germany and contains notable artworks.

▲ MAGDEBURG (306 D4)
SACHSEN-ANHALT *pop. 287,000*
Magdeburg was a tiny settlement on the Elbe River near Slavic territories when Otto I founded the Benedictine Abbey of Sts. Peter, Maurice and Innocent here around 937 AD. Until it was burned down in the 12th century, Magdeburg played an important role in the German colonization of the lands east of the Elbe.

Magdeburg rose from its ashes to become a thriving commercial center by the 13th century and went on to function as a leading member of the Hanseatic League. The town survived the attacks of imperial forces during the Thirty Years' War, but fell in 1631 to the Count of Tilly, who burned the city again and murdered 20,000 of its 30,000 inhabitants. Magdeburg became a secular duchy under the Peace of Westphalia in 1648, and was passed on to the electorate of Brandenburg in 1680. It became part of the Kingdom of Westphalia in 1806 after being defeated by Napoléon Bonaparte. The city gained new prominence in 1815, when it was chosen as the capital of the Prussian province of Saxony.

The town was badly damaged in World War II. Modern Magdeburg has, however, preserved or restored several of its historic buildings, including the cathedral. The town museum contains

GERMANY

the original 13th-century Magdeburg Rider, which is considered the oldest German equestrian statue in existence.

DOM ST. MAURITIUS UND KATHERINA (Cathedral of Sts. Maurice and Catherine), exemplifies Gothic and Romanesque styles. Its basilica has a polygonal choir aisle and Ernst Barlach's memorial to the Fallen of World War I.

KLOSTER UNSER LIEBEN FRAUEN (Monastery of Our Lady) illustrates the Romanesque style of the 11th and 12th centuries. The church, cloisters and refectory (now restored) are considered some of the best examples of monastic architecture of this period.

MAINZ (306 B2)
RHEINLAND-PFALZ *pop. 180,000*
Mainz is the capital of Rhineland-Palatinate. In medieval times the in- telligentsia and the church dignitaries of the Holy Roman Empire assembled here. Reflecting the city's past are the Romanesque cathedral; the Gutenberg Museum and the Central Romano-Germanic Museum in the south wing of the electoral palace. The windows in St. Stephanskirche were created by Chagall. The city holds a wine festival in August and September, and Fastnacht, a German version of Mardi Gras, is of particular interest.

ST.-MARTINS DOM (St. Martin's Cathedral) was begun in AD 975, but most of it was constructed from the 11th through 13th centuries. It is one of the best examples of Romanesque religious architecture on the upper Rhine River. **Dom und Diözesan Museum** (Cathedral and Diocesan Museum), in the cloister, displays medieval sculpture.

MANNHEIM (306 B2)
BADEN-WÜRTTEMBERG *pop. 310,000*
Mannheim is an important industrial crossroads at the junction of the Rhine and Neckar rivers. The castle, the Jesuit Church and the Rathaus are the city's most admired buildings.

THE MARBURG COLLOQUY
Held in the Schloss in 1529, the Marburg Colloquy had as its main participants Martin Luther and Ulrich Zwingli, who debated the question of the Eucharist. Although the question was not resolved, other points raised at the meeting had far-reaching effects on the development of the Reformation movement.

MARBURG (306 B3)
HESSEN *pop. 75,000*
Marburg has remained intact since medieval times, and is attractively - situated on the steep banks of the Lahn Valley. In the lower town, several buildings which once belonged to the Order of Teutonic Knights cluster around Elisabethkirche, the first Gothic building in Germany, elaborately decorated with statues, frescoes and winged altars. In the upper town, is the Marktplatz (with half-timbered houses) and the attractive late-Gothic Rathaus.

SCHLOSS, 1.5 kilometers (1 mile) west of town, is a massive 13th-century Gothic palace inhabited by the descendants of St. Elizabeth. It has a fine chapel and Knights Hall (Rittersaal).

MAULBRONN (306 B2)
BADEN-WÜRTTEMBERG *pop. 5,900*
MAULBRONN ABBEY is one of the oldest Cistercian abbeys in the country. The Romanesque abbey church dates from the mid-12th century and there is also a 14th-century chapter house, a 13th-century refectory and cloisters.

MEERSBURG (306 B1)
BADEN-WÜRTTEMBERG *pop. 5,000*
Meersburg means "sea castle." Its location on Lake Constance (Bodensee) makes it a popular place for people who enjoy rowing and sailing.

ALTES SCHLOSS was originally begun in the 7th century and was the residence of prince-bishops of Konstanz, who made several structural changes and additions. It later became the home of the Westphalian 19th-century poet Annette von Droste-Hülshoff. The four gables, dungeons and castle keep are noteworthy.

MEISSEN (306 D3)
SACHSEN *pop. 36,000*

Slaves founded Meissen, formerly Misni, on the Elbe River just north west of Dresden before the 10th century. King Henry I proclaimed the settlement a German town in 929 AD, and 39 years later the community became the seat of the Margrave of Meissen.

In 1205, having become one of the largest German settlements in the east, the town was chartered as Meissen. The town's golden age occurred in the 13th and 14th centuries, when the Albrechtsburg Castle and several Gothic cathedrals were built. The surviving 13th-century Dom is in the courtyard of the castle. Meissen is, however, best known for its fine hard-paste porcelain industry, which was moved from Dresden in the early 18th century.

MICHELSTADT (306 B2) ★
HESSEN *pop. 16,000*

The Odenwald mountain town of Michelstadt boasts architecture that dates almost exclusively from the 15th century. Among the buildings are the half-timbered 1484 town hall, the Stadtkirche, and the library. In the market square is St. Michael's Fountain. The Odenwald Museum displays local art and handicrafts.

MINDEN (306 B4)
NORDRHEIN-WESTFALEN *pop. 78,000*

Minden, an old Hanseatic city, has a cathedral and Renaissance houses.

SCHLOSS BÜCKEBURG, about 10 kilometers (6 miles) south east, is a lake castle with Renaissance and baroque additions. Inside are a baroque chapel and golden hall, and an art gallery.

MITTENWALD (306 C1)
BAYERN *pop. 8,300*

Mittenwald, in the valley of the 2,160-meter (7,087-foot) Karwendel Mountains, is noted for its ski facilities. It is also a health resort and offers good walking and climbing. The town itself is very attractive: many of the old houses lining the streets are decorated with murals.

▲ MÜNCHEN (306 D1) ★
BAYERN *pop. 1,300,000*

Munchen or Munich, once regarded as the "German Rome," is Germany's third largest city and is capital of Bavaria. Its early rulers were keen for Munich to become one of the cultural centers of Europe, and today its museums house some of the best collections in Germany.

Though the town dates from the 9th century, it did not begin to prosper until it was granted market rights in 1158. About a century later it became the home of the Wittelsbachs, a ducal family linked to the town for more than 700 years. These Bavarian rulers fortified their capital and decorated it with magnificent residences, elegant parks and gardens, regal streets and squares, churches, art galleries, theaters and concert halls. The Wittelsbachs were in great part responsible for Munich's ascendancy as a center of German music, literature and visual arts.

The last Bavarian king, Ludwig III, abdicated the throne in 1918, and Munich pursued its image as a city of industry and innovation. Politically significant as the headquarters of the Nazi Party, it was the scene of the 1923 *putsch* against Bavarian authorities and the setting for the conference of 1938.

Munich was heavily bombed during World War II, but reconstruction was rapid and dramatic. Today the architecture of the diverse city illustrates each era it has survived.

The traditional center of the old city is the Marienplatz, which marks the intersection of medieval trade routes. South of the square lies the medieval section of the city, a triangular area roughly delineated by Sendlinger Strasse and Zweibrücken.

The center of Munich is easily explored on foot as much of the old part is traffic-free. A good starting point is the Hauptbahnhof (Central Station); east of this is Karlsplatz, also called Stachus, and down Neuhauser Strasse, and Kaufingerstrasse is Marienplatz. South east of Marienplatz is the Heiliggeistkirche (Holy Trinity Church), founded in the 13th century. Close by is the Viktualienmarkt, a large open-air food market.

Further north is Max-Joseph Platz, dominated by the huge Nationaltheater and rococo Ehemaliger Postamt (former main post office). The Hofbräuhaus, Munich's best-known beer hall (founded in 1589), is nearby.

The most dignified of Munich's squares is the Odeonsplatz. From here you can see the baroque Theatinerkirche and, opposite it, the Feldernhalle (Generals' Hall), built in 1837. The nearby Hofgarten is a relaxing place to escape from the city bustle.

The Isar River runs on the east side of the city and along its banks, northward, extends the Englischer Garten. On the far side is the Maximilaneum, now the seat of the Bavarian Parliament. Also north is Schwabing, an area popular with Munich's youth.

There is no shortage of entertainment: the Nationaltheater hosts the Bayerische Staatsoper (Bavarian State Opera), as well as ballet and concerts. Maximilianstrasse is the theater area, and the Residenztheater and Kammerspiele are venues for both classical and modern drama.

Munich has its own resident orchestras (the Bayerisches-Rundfunk-Sinfonie and the Münchener Philharmonie), and the Kulturzentrum am Gasteig (Gasteig Arts Center) on Kellerstrasse is one of the city's main concert venues. Jazz is popular, mostly played in Schwabing, while discotheques and nightclubs thrive throughout the city.

Munich is famous for its 16-day Oktoberfest, which begins on the last or

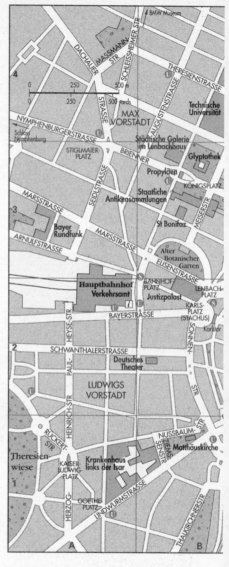

penultimate Saturday in September. It originates from the large fair held in 1810 to celebrate the marriage of Prince (later King) Ludwig I to Therese of Saxe-Hildburghausen. Fasching is the pre-Lenten carnival with colorful decorations and masquerades.

Modern Franz Josef Strauss Airport lies 29 kilometers (18 miles) north east of the city center. Trains and express buses

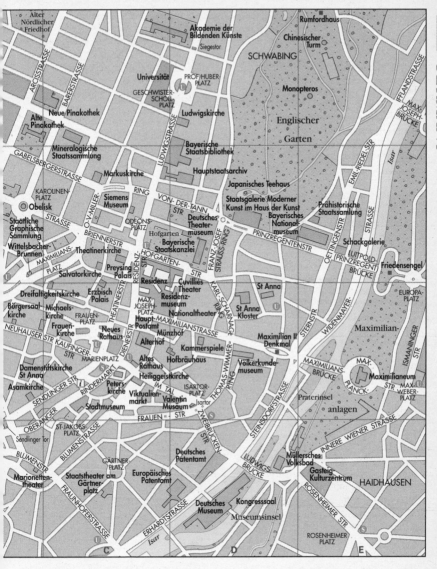

Map of München showing:

Alter Nördlicher Friedhof, Akademie der Bildenden Künste, Siegestor, Rumfordhaus, Chinesischer Turm, SCHWABING, ARCISSTRASSE, BARERSTRASSE, Universität, PROF.-HUBER-PLATZ, GESCHWISTER-SCHOLL-PLATZ, Neue Pinakothek, Ludwigskirche, Monopteros, Englischer Garten, Alte Pinakothek, LUDWIGSTRASSE, Bayerische Staatsbibliothek, Mineralogische Staatssammlung, GABELSBERGERSTRASSE, Markuskirche, Hauptstaatsarchiv, IFFLANDSTRASSE, MAX-JOSEPH-BRÜCKE, Isar, EMIL-RIEDEL-STR, KAROLINEN-PLATZ, Obelisk, RING, VON-DER-TANN-STR, Siemens Museum, Japanisches Teehaus, Staatsgalerie Moderner Kunst im Haus der Kunst, Prähistorische Staatssammlung, Staatliche Graphische Sammlung, STRASSE, O.-V.-MILLER, BRIENNERSTR, ODEONS-PLATZ, Deutsches Theater-museum, Bayerisches National-museum, OETTINGENSTR, STRASSE, Wittelsbacher Brunnen, Theatinerkirche, Hofgarten, Bayerische Staatskanzlei, PRINZREGENTENSTR, Schackgalerie, MAXIMILIANS PLATZ, Salvatorkirche, Preysing Palais, HOFGARTEN-STR, RESIDENZ-, FRANZ-JOSEF-STRAUSS-RING, LUITPOLD-(PRINZREGENT)-BRÜCKE, Friedensengel, Dreifaltigkeitskirche, Erzbisch Palais, Residenz, Cuvilliés Theater, Residenz-museum, St Anna, EUROPA-PLATZ, Bürgersaal-kirche, Michaels-kirche, THEATINERSTR, MAX-JOSEPH-PLATZ, Nationaltheater, St Anna Kloster, KARL-SCHARNAG-RING, STERNSTR, WIDENMAYERSTR, NEUHAUSER STR, FRAUEN-PLATZ, Frauen-kirche, Neues Rathaus, Haupt-Postamt, MAXIMILIANSTRASSE, Maximilian II Denkmal, Maximilian-, ISMANINGER STR, KAUFINGER-STR, DIENERSTR, Münzhof, Alterhof, Kammerspiele, Völkerkunde-museum, MAXIMILIANS BRÜCKE, MAX.-PLANCK-STR, Maximilianeum, MAX-WEBER-PLATZ, Damenstiftskirche St Anna, MARIENPLATZ, Altes Rathaus, Hofbräuhaus, Heiliggeistkirche, THOMAS-WIMMER-RING, Praterinsel, Asamkirche, RINDERMARKT, Peters-kirche, IM TAL, ISARTOR-PLATZ, anlagen, SENDLINGER STR, Viktualien-markt, Valentin Musaum, Isartor, STEINSDORFSTRASSE, OBERANGER, Stadtmuseum, FRAUEN-STR, ZWEIBRÜCKEN-STR, INNERE WIENER STRASSE, ST-JAKOBS-PLATZ, BLUMENSTRASSE, HAIDHAUSEN, Sendlinger Tor, BLUMENSTR, GÄRTNER-PLATZ, Deutsches Patentamt, LUDWIGS-BRÜCKE, Müllersches Volksbad, ROSENHEIMER STR, Marionetten-theater, Staatstheater am Gärtner-platz, Europäisches Patentamt, Gasteig-Kulturzentrum, FRAUNHOFERSTRASSE, ERHARDTSTRASSE, Deutsches Museum, Kongresssaal, ROSENHEIMER PLATZ, Isar, Museumsinsel

A B C D E

depart for the Hauptbahnhof every 20 minutes during the day; the trains run until the early hours. The city's public transport system is excellent: as well as the rapid transit rail system there is an underground railway, streetcars and buses. Tickets can be bought from machines, for a single journey or for several journeys. A day travel ticket may be more economical – always remember to cancel the ticket in a special machine once you have boarded the vehicle. Taxis from the airport are expensive.

ALTE PINAKOTHEK (339 B4), Barerstrasse 27, contains one of the most impressive art collections in the world. The gallery houses European masterpieces of the 14th through to the 18th centuries. Notable are works of Dürer, Rubens,

Van Dyck, Rembrandt, El Greco and Pieter Brueghel.

ASAMKIRCHE (339 B2), Sendlinger Strasse 61, is a masterpiece of rococo architecture built by the two Asam brothers (1733–46) originally as a private family church. Dedicated to St. Johann Nepomuk, (one bone and his wax effigy lie in a glass reliquary), the white and gold interior is statuary and decoration run riot; a ceiling fresco depicts the saint's life.

BAYERISCHES NATIONALMUSEUM (Bavarian National Museum) (339 D3), main building at Prinzregentenstrasse 3, houses Bavarian arts and crafts from the Middle Ages to the 18th century.

BMW MUSEUM, Petuelring 130, houses a collection of cars, motorcycles and airplane engines and traces the technological developments of our time.

DACHAU – see box opposite.

DEUTSCHES MUSEUM , on the Isarinsel (Isar Island), is one of the best science and technology museums in the world. Exhibits include the latest scientific and technological innovations.

ENGLISCHER GARTEN (339 D4) was the idea of an American soldier, Benjamin Thompson, who in 1789 persuaded the elector to drain some marshland and create a garden. The area is really a large city park and is a popular picnic spot. From the Monopteros (rotunda), built in 1837, is a good view of the city skyline.

FRAUENKIRCHE (339 C2), just west of Neues Rathaus, is a mammoth Gothic church with twin onion-shaped towers. The structure, badly damaged in World War II, has been restored and holds many works of Gothic art.

GLYPTOTHEK (339 B3), Königsplatz 3, is a classical building which contains Greek and Roman statues collected by Ludwig I. Do not miss the carved pediment from

---

CONCENTRATION CAMPS

Part of Germany's history which many wish had never happened are the concentration camps. The sites are now preserved as memorials, containing permanent exhibitions and showing films recording conditions. At Dachau, near Munich, the first such camp, the gas chambers and crematorium still stand. Sachsenhausen, in a Berlin suburb, has only recently been opened and the large site remains much as it was, with the addition today of photographs and information boards of the horrors. At Buchenwald, 10 kilometers (6 miles) north west of Weimar, over 50,000 people died.

---

the Aphaia Temple in Aegina. The adjacent Antikensammlungen (Antique Collection) holds Etruscan jewelry, Greek vases and small statues.

MICHAELSKIRCHE (St. Michael's Church) (339 C2), Neuhauser Strasse 52, was built at the end of the 16th century in Renaissance style, the baroque features being added later. The vaulted aisle is said to be the second largest in Europe, after St. Peter's in Rome. In the crypt is the tomb of "mad" Ludwig II.

NEUE PINAKOTHEK (New Picture Gallery) (339 C4), Barerstrasse, is the repository of 18th- and 19th-century paintings and sculpture, many by Bavarian artists such as Gustav Klimt and Carl Spitzweg. French Impressionists (Cézanne and Gauguin) are represented, and one of van Gogh's *Sunflowers* is exhibited, as is a small collection of art-nouveau works.

NEUES RATHAUS (339 C2), Munich's "new" town hall, was completed in the 19th century and dominates Marienplatz. Crowds gather in the square to watch the hall's glockenspiel (carillon), a mechanical timepiece with many dancing figures.

PETERSKIRCHE (St. Peter's Church) (339 C2), Rindermarkt, is the oldest of the city's parish churches, a mixture of ornate styles from Gothic to 17th and 18th centuries. Notable statues include a 15th-century representation of St. Peter, while the bones of St. Munditia, patron saint of single women, lie in a jeweled shroud inside a glass box.

RESIDENZ (339 C3), entered from Residenzstrasse 1, is a complex of buildings built by the Wittelsbach family between the 16th and 19th centuries as a royal residence. Though destroyed in World War II, the opulent palace has been painstakingly rebuilt. The Residenz Museum, entered from Max Joseph Platz 3, must be visited twice to see all the rooms, as they open at various times.

Highlights include the Ahnengalerie (Ancestors' Gallery) with over 100 family portraits, the Grotto Court, and the Antiquarium, a huge, vaulted chamber originally built to display the family's antiquities, and later decorated with frescoes. The eight Reiche Zimmer (Rich Rooms) are sumptuous, as are two 17th-century chapels.

The Schatzkammer (Treasury – entrance from Residenzstrasse) contains crowns, clocks, caskets and religious treasures. The charming rococo Cuvilliés-Theater (named after its designer, a former court dwarf) is decorated with gold and stucco; Mozart's opera *Idomeneo* was first performed here and the theater is still in use. From Hofgartenstrasse, entrance is made to the Ägyptischer Kunst (Egyptian Collection).

SCHLOSS NYMPHENBURG (Nymphenburg Palace), 11 kilometers (7 miles) north west, was built 1664–1758 as a summer residence for Bavarian rulers. The Schönheitsgallerie (Gallery of Beauties) contains portraits of the 36 ladies most admired by Ludwig I. In the two-story Grand Marble Hall are frescoes by Clemens von Zimmerman. The Marstall Museum displays royal coaches. As enjoyable as the palace is its glorious park, with woods, lakes and pavilions – miniature palaces in themselves.

SPIELZEUG MUSEUM (Toy Museum), the tower of Altes Rathaus (339 C2), Marienplatz, has a collection of toys, covering a 200-year period. The Festsaal (Dance Hall), in the other part of the building, can also be visited.

STÄDTISCHE GALERIE IM LENBACHHAUS (339 B3), Luisenstrsse 33, is an Italianate villa owned by Franz von Lenbach (a 19th-century Bavarian painter), with his furnishings and portraits, as well as those by 20th-century Expressionists such as Kandinsky, Klee, Maske and Marc.

STADTMUSEUM (City Museum) (339 C2), St. Jakobsplatz 1, is a museum devoted to Munich's past. Dancing puppets carved by Erasmus Grasser in 1480 are unusual examples of secular German Gothic art. There are also separate collections of weapons, musical instruments and a history of the brewing industry.

MUNICH – *see München on p.337.*

MÜNSTER (306 B4)
NORDRHEIN-WESTFALEN *pop.* 252,000
Münster is the capital of Westphalia and the site of Westphalian University. The arcaded market square (Prinzipalmarkt), regional museums and the Aasee (lake) area attract sightseers.

DOM, Hortsberg, is said to be the largest restored church in the province. Highlights of this 13th-century church are the transept's altarpiece of St. John and the silver tabernacle.
Domkammer (Cathedral Chamber) displays treasures that include an 11th-century gold reliquary of St. Paul.

RATHAUS (Town Hall), Prinzipalmarkt, is a high-gabled Gothic mansion dating from the 14th century. It was destroyed in World War II, then rebuilt to its original style. The Peace Hall contains precious Gothic wood furnishings.

GERMANY

GERMANY

NAUMBURG (306 D3)
SAXON-ANHALT *pop. 31,000*
Situated high above the Saale Valley, Naumburg was founded in the early 11th century as a fortress by the Margrave of Meissen. Many old buildings survive, including a 15th-century gate (Marientor) and late-Gothic Rathaus.

DOM is early Gothic/late Romanesque, with four towers, two choirs and a cloister. In the west choir stand famous life-size sculptures of the Twelve Founder Figures, carved in limestone around 1250.

▲ NEUSTADT AN DER WEIN-STRASSE (306 B2)
RHEINLAND-PFALZ *pop. 50,000*
Neustadt celebrates every October with the selection of the German Wine Queen and baptism of the new wine. The Festival Hall and busy Market Square testify to the town's involvement in the wine trade, and there are numerous wine inns along its street where you can taste the products. On the slopes of the Hardt Mountains you can see the 700-year-old ruins of Wittelsbach Castle.

NÖRDLINGEN (306 C2)
BAYERN
In the 14th century, Bavarian traders flocked here for the Whitsun Fair held by the Rathaus (outside stairway added later). The town's subsequent economic stagnation kept it intact, so today it is a complete medieval town with ramparts. From the tower of the late-Gothic St. George's Church (365 steps up) is a view of the town and the crater (Ries) formed by a meteorite.

NUREMBERG – *see Nürnberg below*.

★ NÜRNBERG (306 C2)
BAYERN *pop. 500,000*
Nürnberg, or Nuremberg, a former imperial center dating from the 11th century, is today the principal city of Franconia and one of the largest cities in Bavaria. The city was founded in 1040 as

a stronghold by Henry III, Duke of Bavaria and Emperor of Germany. It became a trading center devoted to building and patronage of the arts in the 12th and 13th centuries, reaching its economic and cultural peaks during the 15th and 16th centuries when it was the unofficial capital of Germany.

The Thirty Years' War brought devastation, but industrialization in the 19th century re-established the city's eminence. The city was badly bombed in World War II, and in 1945 the Allied trials of German war criminals were held here.

The Altstadt is the most charming part of the city: medieval walls guarded by 80 towers and pierced by four gateways still enclose it. Much of the charm stems from the high-roofed, half-timbered dwellings and gabled façades. Nuremberg was the home of Albrecht Dürer and Hans Sachs, immortalized in Wagner's opera *Die Meistersinger von Nürnberg*. The Toy Trade Fair (February) and the Christkindlmarkt (the month before Christmas) are Nuremberg's most celebrated events.

DÜRER-HAUS, in Altstadt, was where painter and engraver Albrecht Dürer (1471–1528) lived from 1509. Several of his drawings are displayed.

FRAUENKIRCHE (Church of Our Lady), Hauptmarkt, is a 14th-century church with a mechanical clock that presents its "Seven Electors" daily at noon, paying homage to the Holy Roman Emperor.

GERMANISCHES NATIONALMUSEUM (Germanic National Museum); Kornmarkt, on the site of a former Carthusian monastery, surveys German art and cultural history. It also contains works by Dürer and Cranach, woodcarvings by Tilman Riemenschneider, old apothecary shops and an antique toy collection.

KAISERBURG, overlooking the city from the north, was the home of emperors from the 11th to the 15th centuries. The castle was destroyed during World War II, but has since been restored. The Romanesque Imperial Chapel is impressive, as is the view of the town from the Sinwellturm (tower).

ST. LORENZKIRCHE, on Lorenzerstrasse, the largest church in Nuremberg and one of the few to have survived the bombing of World War II, is noted for its exquisite rose window. Other items of interest are an early 15th-century crucifix and the Annunciation, a woodcarving by Veit Stoss.

ST. MARTHAKIRCHE, between Königstormauer and Königstrasse, is where the Meistersingers held their classes 1578–1620. Glass paintings from the 14th and 15th centuries can be seen.

ST. SEBALDUSKIRCHE, facing the Altes Rathaus, is a 13th-century church with a bronze shrine of St. Sebald by Peter Vischer and his sons. Other noted works are the St. Peter altarpiece, the bronze font and fine stained-glass windows.

SCHÖNER BRUNNEN, Hauptmarkt, a 14th-century Gothic fountain, is ornamented at its base by figures of the Seven Electors, and heroes of the Old Testament and Middle Ages. A statue of Moses surrounded by the prophets tops the 18-meter (60-foot) spire-like structure.

OBERAMMERGAU (306 C1)
BAYERN *pop. 4,600*
When Germany's Black Plague of 1634 stopped short of tiny Oberammergau, the townspeople vowed to present a play honoring the Passion of Christ every 10 years. The continuing tradition has won world fame as evidenced by half a million visitors during the 100-day period.

The scenic Bavarian town (at 834 meters/2,736 feet) sustains interest in non-play years with its 18th-century rococo church covered with frescoes, including the dome. Many houses in the village are also decorated.

SCHLOSS LINDERHOF is 14 kilometers (9 miles) south west of town. Built by Ludwig II in Italian Renaissance and French rococo styles, this lavish palace includes a Hall of Mirrors and gilded furniture and ornamentation. It is sur- rounded by gardens dotted with several small buildings and the strange Venus Grotto, modeled on the set of *Tannhäuser*.

OBERSTDORF (306 C1)
BAYERN *pop. 11,000*
Oberstdorf, at 815 meters (2,674 feet), is among the best-known Bavarian wintersports centers. Its tennis, swimming and fishing facilities also make it a favorite summer resort. Oberstdorf leads to the peaceful Kleinwalsertal Valley, whose entrance from its own country, Austria, is blocked by the Alps.

ÖHRINGEN (306 C2) ★
BADEN-WÜRTTEMBERG *pop. 16,700*
Öhringen has a 17th-century castle and a Gothic church. Its museum has collections of pewter and pottery objects.

NEUENSTEIN SCHLOSS is 6 kilometers (4 miles) east. This 16th-century castle belonged to the ruling Hohenlohe family and its Renaissance furnishings give an impression of court life in centuries past.

OSNABRÜCK (306 B4)
NIEDERSACHSEN *pop. 150,000*
Charlemagne laid the foundation for modern Osnabrück, and the fortified city subsequently became an important commercial center and judicial seat. Its place in history was assured when negotiations for the Treaty of Westphalia were held in 1648, forging the way for the end of the Thirty Years' War. Modern Osnabrück is a manufacturing town, and as the seat of a bishopric is the largest diocese in northern Germany.

Much of the city was rebuilt after World War II, but the medieval town hall remains as Osnabrück's best-known tourist attraction. Also worth a visit are St. Mary's Church, St. Peter's Cathedral

GERMANY

and the Church of St. John, all Gothic buildings featuring unusual ornamentation and artwork.

RATHAUS (Town Hall), on Markt, features a statue of Charlemagne surrounded by eight emperors. The Treaty of Westphalia was proclaimed from its steps, and in the Peace Chamber, where the talks took place, are portraits of the negotiators as well as the original chandelier (1554).

OTTOBEUREN (306 C1)
BAYERN *pop. 7,300*
OTTOBEUREN KLOSTER was founded by the Benedictines in 764 AD and did well under Charlemagne's patronage. The church was rebuilt from 1737 onwards by Johann-Michael Fischer and is now Germany's largest baroque church, with an airy nave 90 meters (230 feet) long. In its richly decorated interior, full of statues and paintings, the stuccowork was carried out by J. M. Feuchtmayr and the frescoes by J. J. Zeiller. Its two fine organs were built by K. J. Kniepp. The abbey buildings include a museum with exquisite furniture, and a lavishly decorated baroque library with marble columns and painted ceilings.

PASSAU (306 D1)
BAYERN *pop. 50,000*
Passau reflects its past as the medieval town where, in 1552, the Holy Roman Emperor Charles V yielded to Protestant prince-bishops at the Treaty of Passau. The city reflects the influence of Italian architects and occupies the point where the Danube, Inn and smaller Ilz rivers converge. The streets are built on various levels, rising to the hill in the town's center, and quaint archways join the houses. The Residentsplatz, by the cathedral, is an attractive square lined with handsome merchants' houses and bishops' palaces.

DOM, a 15th-century Gothic cathedral, has an unusual octagonal dome. After the Great Fire of 1662, the building was

transformed into a masterpiece of Italian baroque architecture. It houses one of the world's largest church organs.

NEUE RESIDENZ was the 18th-century former palace of Passau's prince-bishops. The elaborate baroque interior contains lavish furnishings and houses the Diocesan Museum and Cathedral Treasury.

RATHAUS (Town Hall), built in the 14th century near the Danube, is decorated with murals representing scenes from the Niebelungen sagas.

VESTE OBERHAUS, on a hill across the Danube River, is a fortress begun in the 13th century by the prince-bishops and added to over the centuries. It is now a local and regional history museum.

▲ POTSDAM (306 D4) ★
BRANDENBURG *pop. 140,000*
Potsdam, at the confluence of the Nuthe and Havel rivers, is the former capital of Brandenburg province.

Founded by Slavs before the 11th century, Potsdam was an electoral residence of Frederick William, the Great Elector, in the mid-17th century. A century later Frederick the Great selected the town for a royal residence, and Potsdam became the intellectual and military center of Prussia. Frederick and the succeeding kings of Prussia built many of the baroque structures for which Potsdam is known.

In the 18th century, Dutch settlers added their own architectural accents to Potsdam, further enhancing the city's collection of ornate buildings. Although the city sustained heavy damage during the bombings of the Second World War, several of its most beautiful buildings have survived.

CECILIENHOF PALACE, built in the early 20th century, was the site of the Potsdam Conference, July to August 1945.

NEUES PALAIS was built 1763–9 as a summer residence for Prussia's royal family.

The walls of the 19th-century receiving room are embedded with semi-precious stones and seashells.

SANS SOUCI PALACE, built by Knobelsdorff (1745–53), is considered one of the finest examples of German rococo architecture in the world. The Picture Gallery displays works by artists such as Rubens and Tintoretto, and in the landscaped park is a Chinese tea-house and a grand fountain.

THE POTSDAM AGREEMENT

This agreement divided Berlin, Vienna and Austria into four zones, and set up procedures for the denazification, decentralization, demilitarization, deindustrialization and democratization of Germany and Austria in 1945.

QUEDLINBURG (306 C3)
SACHSEN-ANHALT *pop. 28,000*

Henry I established Quedlinburg in AD 922 as a fortress on the Bode River in the Lower Harz Mountains. Otto I added a new dimension to town life when he built an imperial abbey in 968 AD and designated his daughter as the abbess. As a member of the Hanseatic League in the 1400s, Quedlinburg flourished. It came under the rule of Saxony before becoming part of the Kingdom of Prussia in the 18th century.

Today Quedlinburg is an industrial and manufacturing city that has preserved a number of its half-timbered houses, medieval churches and battlements. The 16th-century castle stands on the site of the original fortress. The 11th- and 12th-century Church of St. Servatius includes the remains of the original abbey church.

RASTATT (306 B2)
LUSTCHLOSS FAVORITE, 8 kilometers (5 miles) south west, was the pleasure palace of Margravine Sibylla Augusta, wife of Ludwig the Turk. The interior decorations are opulent and unusual.

REGENSBURG (306 D2) ★
BAYERN *pop. 128,000*

"Regensburg's situation is enchanting," Johann Wolfgang von Goethe once said. As early as 179 AD, the Romans established a military encampment here and called it Castra Regina.

Regensburg claims to be Germany's largest medieval town, which fortunately escaped damage in World War II. In the Middle Ages, it was one of Europe's most prosperous cities and about 20 Italian-style tower houses survive. Its attractive features include the 12th-century Schottenkirche St. Jakob, the 12th-century Steinerne Brücke (stone bridge) that extends nearly across the Danube, and the Rathaus, the Gothic town hall. The Porta Praetoria, a ruined Roman gate, was once the northern watchtower on the Danube River.

DOM, Domplatz, is one of the finest examples of German Gothic architecture. Built between the 13th and 15th centuries, with its spires added in the 19th century, it contains some 14th-century stained-glass windows and medieval sculptures. Gothic cloisters include two chapels, one Romanesque with original frescoes. The Regensburger Domspatzen (Sparrows of Regensburg Cathedral) boys' choir is one of the best known in Germany.

SCHLOSS THURN UND TAXIS, incorporates the former Benedictine Monastery of St. Emmeram, founded in the 8th century, its baroque interior designed by the Asam brothers. Ornate royal tombs stand here, and three crypts lie below.

STADTMUSEUM, in a former monastery on Berthodstrasse, recounts the town's social and cultural history.

▲ ROSTOCK (306 D4)
MECKLENBURG-VORPOMMERN *pop. 252,000*

At the head of the Warnow River estuary 13 kilometers (8 miles) below its entry into the Baltic Sea, Rostock is a fishing and shipbuilding center that has preserved many of its medieval monuments. Formed by the union of three separate towns in 1265, Rostock was an influential member of the Hanseatic League in the 14th century. The city became part of the Mecklenburg province in 1314 and later passed to the Dukes of Mecklenburg-Schwerin, then to the Schwerin and Güstrow rulers before gaining independence. In 1419, one of Europe's first universities was founded here.

Significant medieval structures, many now restored, include the 1230 Gothic Church of St. Mary, the early 15th-century St. Peter's Church and the 15th-century town hall, which has a 17th-century baroque façade. Portions of the ruined town walls and gates can still be seen. The tower and roof space of Nikolaikirche, the town's oldest church, are now apartments and offices.

MARIENKIRCHE (St. Mary's Church), built in 1230, is a well-preserved example of Gothic architecture. Notable features include the late-Gothic altarpiece, an astronomical clock, a baroque high altar and the bronze font.

Rothenburg ob der Tauber
(306 D2) ★
BAYERN *pop. 11,000*
Set high above the Tauber Valley, Rothenburg is one of the most picturesque towns in Bavaria, with its well-preserved walls along which visitors can walk. Within, the crooked, cobbled streets are lined with half-timbered houses and dotted with fountains.

Two museums are the Reichsstadtmuseum (Imperial City Museum; Rothenburg became an imperial city in 1274), with a medieval workroom, and the Mittelälterliches Kriminalmuseum (Middle Ages Crime Museum), with instruments of torture and cells.

Other points of interest are the Double Bridge (14th century), and the Burggarten on the site of the former castle from where there is a good view of

the townscape. The best work of the master sculptor Tilman Riemenschneider, the Holy Blood Altar, is in the Gothic Church of St. Jakob.

On Whit Sunday, the Meistertrunk (Masterdraught) is celebrated to recall a turning point in the Thirty Years' War, when the mayor saved the town by quaffing 3 liters (5 pints) of wine.

Rothenburg's location on the Romantische Strasse and the Burgstrasse means it is always crowded.

RATHAUS (Town Hall) stands in the Marktplatz. Half is 13th-century Gothic and half is Renaissance (1572–8), with arches added later.

RÜDESHEIM (306 B2)
HESSEN *pop. 9,600*
The importance of Rüdesheim as a wine center is reflected in its unusual wine museum and in the wine festival held every September. This Rhine River town is known for its old houses with turrets and gables, and its busy tourist street, Drosselgasse. Ehrenfels Castle and St. Hildegard's Church are of interest, and the nearby Neiderwald Monument overlooks the Rhine River.

BRÖMSERBURG, on the banks of the Rhine River, was built during the 12th century and reconstructed seven centuries later. Here are the Rheingau Museum and a wine museum.

▲ SAARBRÜCKEN (306 A2)
SAARLAND *pop. 200,000*
Saarbrücken, on the Franco-German border, is a university and congress city as well as a major trade center for Europe. The Prince's Palace and the Ludwigskirche are excellent examples of 18th-century baroque architecture. There is also an industrial and natural history museum.

SCHLESWIG (306 C4)
SCHLESWIG-HOLSTEIN *pop. 26,000*
The old capital of the Dukes of Gottorf is situated at the head of the Schlei

GERMANY

River, an inlet on the Baltic. A Viking museum at Haithabu recalls the town's earliest history.

DOM is a Gothic cathedral dedicated to St. Peter. The chancel contains the 16th-century Bordesholm altarpiece.

NYDAM-BOOT is a 14th-century ship discovered in the marshes of Nydam during the 18th century.

SCHLOSS GOTTORF is a 16th-century castle. Inside are the Schleswig-Holstein Museum as well as the Prehistoric Museum.

SCHWÄBISCH HALL (306 C2) ★
BADEN-WÜRTTEMBERG *pop. 32,600*
Schwäbisch Hall is one of the most picturesque towns in the Swabian Forest, and lies on the banks of the Kocher River. The 15th-century parish church is atop a broad 18th-century staircase and contains tombs and unusual furnishings. The Rathaus (town hall) is baroque, and one of the town's most important buildings. The town contains medicinal springs, and the Hällisch Fränkisches Museum in a former mansion (the Keckenburg) chronicles the town's history.

An outdoor summer theater festival is held on the Marktplatz.

▲ SCHWERIN (306 C4)
MECKLENBURG-VORPOMMERN
pop. 130,000
Schwerin was settled by Sorbs before the 11th century. The town first gained official recognition when Henry the Lion chartered it in 1160. A bishopric was established here 10 years later and the town became the seat of a countship around the same time. During the Middle Ages, Schwerin was made the capital of the Mecklenburg-Schwerin region. In 1934 it was named capital of the Mecklenburg state.

The Gothic cathedral, begun in 1270 and completed in 1890, includes a library, museums and a conservatory.

The huge ducal palace, which served as the residence of the Mecklenburg dukes, was rebuilt in 1843 in the style of a French château and now houses the state parliament. In one wing is the palace church, dating from the 16th century. To the south is a large baroque garden, with an orangery, exotic trees and a canal. In another area of the garden is the state theater and the Staathisches Museum, which houses a famous collection of 17th-century Dutch paintings.

SCHWETZINGEN (306 B2)
BADEN-WÜRTTEMBERG *pop. 19,000*
Schwetzingen is known for its baroque palace park, the Schlossgarten, inspired by Versailles. A stage festival takes place in May and June in the town's 18th-century rococo theater.

SIGMARINGEN (306 B1)
BADEN-WÜRTTEMBERG *pop. 15,000*
Sigmaringen's strategic position by the upper Danube made it the minor capital of the Hohenzollern princes.

SIGMARINGEN SCHLOSS, a palace on a rock high above the upper Danube Valley, was for centuries the headquarters of the Swabian Catholic branch of the Hohenzollerns. The Renaissance palace was constructed on the site of an older castle in the 16th century. Restored in 1893, the castle contains exhibits of arms and a rococo chapel.

SOLINGEN (306 B3)
NORDRHEIN-WESTFALEN *pop. 163,000*
Solingen is one of Europe's oldest producers of cutlery. Berg, which is now incorporated into Solingen, was the capital of Bergische Land in the Middle Ages. It also was the seat of the Counts of Berg, residents of Berg Castle.

DEUTSCHES KLINGENMUSEUM (German Museum of Blades), Wuppertaler Strasse 160, commemorates Solingen's flatware industry and its 600-year-old sword-making tradition.

GERMANY

SCHLOSS BURG, an early medieval castle overlooking the Wupper River, houses the Bergisches Museum, providing a history of the castle and the region.

▲ STUTTGART (306 B2)
BADEN-WÜRTTEMBERG *pop. 559,000*
Stuttgart is set amid wooded hills, orchards and vineyards, and its modern buildings punctuate gardens and parks.

The largest city in southwestern Germany and capital of Baden-Württemberg, Stuttgart is an important railroad junction and prosperous industrial center. Its ballet and opera are worldfamous, and every three years it hosts an international Musikfest with leading world orchestras.

Nearby are the popular health resort of Bad Cannstatt, the rococo Schloss Solitude and Schwäbisch-Gmünd, a jewelry and silversmith center. Some of the best scenery of the Neckar Valley is just north of Stuttgart.

ALTES SCHLOSS (Old Palace) is in the center of town facing the Schillerplatz. The original moated castle, now the Karlsplatz wing, was erected in the 14th century, and the other Renaissance sections were added in the 16th century. It was reconstructed in 1948 after it was gutted by fire in 1944. The palace surrounds a Renaissance courtyard and houses a Protestant chapel.
Württembergisches Landesmuseum (Württemberg State Museum) displays prehistoric and religious relics and medieval art. A highlight is the Württemberg Crown Jewels.

FERNSEHTURM is a 483-meter (1,585-foot) TV tower on the Hoher Bopser; a spectacular view is had from its restaurant and observation platform at 150 meters (500 feet).

LUDWIGSBURG SCHLOSS, 14 kilometers (9 miles) north, is a huge baroque palace. Of its 450 rooms, 75 with ornate rococo and classical furnishings are open to the public. A formal park surrounds the

---

SOLINGEN STEEL

The swords that brought medieval fame to Solingen have been succeeded by Solingen steel knives, razor blades and scissors. Many of the city's foundries are relatively small and some are even quite picturesque.

---

palace and includes the Märchengarten, or Fairytale Garden, where the tales of the brothers Grimm are performed by mechanical figures.

MERCEDES-BENZ MUSEUM contains a collection of commercial and luxury cars, plus ship and airplane engines.

PLANETARIUM, Neckarstrasse 47, is one of the most modern in the world. Changing presentations, lectures, seminars and exhibits reflect the most current information in space technology.

PORSCHE MUSEUM is at Porschestrasse 42 in Zuffenhausen. Fifty vehicles illustrate the development of the Porsche car.

SCHILLER NATIONALMUSEUM, in Marbach am Neckar, exhibits fine artifacts pertaining to the poet Friedrich von Schiller and other Swabian writers.

SCHLOSS SOLITUDE (Solitude Palace), 10 kilometers (6 miles) south west, is a rococo castle perched on the edge of a plateau. It was built 1763–7 by the French architect La Guépière as a summer residence for the Württemberg court.

STAATSGALERIE, Konrad-Adenauer-Strasse 30–32, contains a collection of 14th- to 16th-century works by old German masters and members of the Dutch and Italian schools. There is also a display of modern art by French and German Expressionists.

STIFTSKIRCHE (Collegiate Church) was founded in the 12th century and rebuilt in the 15th century; although damaged in World War II, it has since been restored. An important piece of Renaissance sculpture in the choir is a series of 11 counts of Württemberg.

WILHELMA ZOO was built as a summer residence for Wilhelm I; it is now home to a harmonious combination of plants and animals.

TRAVEMÜNDE – *see Lübeck on p.335.*

TRIBERG (306 B1)
BADEN-WÜRTTEMBERG *pop. 6,000*
This Black Forest town, at 690–1,112 meters (2,261–3,668 feet) is best known for Gutach Falls, the highest in Germany at 162 meters (531 feet).

TRIER (306 A2)
RHEINLAND-PFALZ *pop. 99,000*
Remnants of Trier's past give an almost continuous account of European history. Among the traces of Roman civilization are a bridge across the Mosel River, three baths, the basilica, a 20,000-seat amphitheater and the Porta Nigra, a massive city gate. Medieval buildings include the Romanesque cathedral, the Basilica of St. Matthias and the baroque St. Paulinuskirche.

TÜBINGEN (306 B1)
BADEN-WÜRTTEMBERG *pop. 78,000*
Tübingen is an old university city on the banks of the Neckar River noted for its peaceful, medieval appearance. It has been a home to such poets and philosophers as Eduard Mörike, Hegel, Schelling and Friedrich Hölderlin, whose house has been converted to a museum. The Platanenallee is a popular promenade on an island in the Neckar. Sights include the castle and the 15th-century Church of St. George.

ÜBERLINGEN (306 B1)
BADEN-WÜRTTEMBERG *pop. 19,600*
Überlingen, on the shore of Lake Constance (Bodensee), has lakeside walks that cross the sites of former fortifications. The Town Hall, with its Gothic council

chamber, the Münster, and the Städtisches Museum, with 18th-century woodcarvings, are worthy of a visit. Gothic Salem Abbey and the castle of Heiligenburg lie 21 kilometers (13 miles) east.

ULM (306 C1)
BADEN-WÜRTTEMBERG *pop. 110,000*
Ulm, on the Danube River, is a major entrance to the Swabian and Algäu mountain districts. It is also the birthplace of Albert Einstein. The 14th- century Gothic cathedral is among the stateliest in Germany and is said to have the highest church steeple in the country – 161 meters (528 feet). Its highlights include detailed reliefs, numerous sculptures, colorful stained-glass windows and masterful stone filigree work.

Also of interest in Ulm is the Bread Museum and the Ulm Museum, which deals with art and culture from the Middle Ages. The Fishermen's Quarter, with its picturesque half-timbered houses, is also worth a visit.

WEIMAR (306 C3) ★
THÜRINGEN *pop. 62,000*
Weimar is noted in historical records as early as 975 AD, but the city earned a permanent place in history during the 18th and 19th centuries as the intellectual center of Germany. The home of such literary giants as Goethe and Schiller, Weimar attracted other intellectuals of the period, including Liszt and Nietzsche, who came to Weimar to live and work.

By 1919, Weimar's impressive history made it the ideal venue for leaders of the German National Assembly to draw up the constitution of the new German Republic. The Weimar Republic, as the government was known, lasted 1919–33, when Adolf Hitler secured the chancellorship of Germany. Although damaged in World War II, many of the city's most impressive structures have now been restored, including the 1767 Wittumspalais; the Schloss Weimar, built 1790–1803; Schloss Belvedere, built 1724–50; and Schloss Tiefurt.

Other places of interest are Sts. Peter and Paul Church, the Goethe National Museum and his Townhouse (his Garden House is across the Ilm River), the homes of Schiller and Liszt and the Goethe-Schiller Mausoleum. The Wittumspalais was built in the 1770s for Duchess Anna Amalia, who was a bastion of the town's cultural life.

WERTHEIM (306 C2)
BADEN-WÜRTTEMBERG *pop. 21,700*

A town of distinctly medieval appearance, Wertheim is at the confluence of the Main and Tauber rivers. Gabled, half-timbered houses line the streets; the view of the town from the left bank of the Tauber is particularly scenic. Sights include the 16th-century Renaissance Angel's Well monument, the church and the ruins of a castle.

WIESBADEN (306 B2)
HESSEN *pop. 260,000*

This pleasant city on the Rhine River, now the capital of Hessen, was created by the Romans around the thermal springs. Now a neo-classical building, the Kurhaus, set in a large park, houses the spa. Wiesbaden, with its theaters, orchestras and a ballet company, is host to the International Festival of Music and Drama in May.

WITTENBERGE (306 D4)
SACHSEN-ANHALT *pop. 51,000*

An old town on the Elbe River, Wittenberg is known as the place where Martin Luther posted his 95 Theses against the Roman Catholic Church of All Saints in 1517, starting the Reformation. The doors were burned in 1760 and much of the church was damaged, but the building has since been restored, and contains Luther's grave. His theses are engraved in Latin on the bronze doors that were installed in 1858.

A settlement as early as 1180, Wittenberg was an official residence for the electors of Saxony and the House of Wettin. Although the French, who occupied the town in 1806, improved

its fortifications, the Prussians successfully stormed Wittenberg in 1814 and officially possessed the city by 1815.

LUTHERHAUS is where Martin Luther lived and worked during his stay in Wittenberge. The Museum of History and Reformation inside contains an extensive collection of Luther's manuscripts, along with several portraits of the reformer, a number of bibles from before and after the Reformation, and many paintings by Lucas Cranach, Daniel Hopfer and others.

MELANCHTHONHAUS (1536), was the home of reformer Phillipp Melanchthon until his death in 1560. Displays chronicle the life and works of the theologian, who worked closely with Martin Luther.

STADTKIRCHE ST. MARIEN (CHURCH OF ST. MARY) is where Martin Luther preached. The altar, designed by Lucas Cranach, commemorates the Reformation with scenes of Martin Luther and Phillipp Melanchthon. The church's Gothic features are also of interest.

WOLFENBÜTTEL (306 C4)
NIEDERSACHSEN *pop. 50,000*

This small town of half-timbered houses has changed little since it was built as Germany's first planned town in the 15th century. The Dukes of Braunschweig and Lüneburg lived in the grand, white Schloss (1432–1754), the largest in Lower Saxony, of which only the original moat survives; the rest is a mixture of Renaissance and baroque styles, with a notable tower.

HERZOG-AUGUST-BIBLIOTHEK houses the books of Augustus the Younger, whose library was the largest in Europe in the 17th century. Early printed books and manuscripts are shown here and in the Zeughaus (Arsenal); the most famous is Henry the Lion's 12th-century Gospel.

LESSINGHAUS is a late-baroque building which housed the librarian. From 1770 to 1781 the incumbent was the playwright Lessing, who wrote *Nathan der Weise* here.

WORMS (306 B2)
RHEINLAND-PFALZ *pop. 76,000*
The old Rhine River town of Worms is very important in religious history. It was in this town in 1521 that the edict against Martin Luther was issued by the Diet of Worms; there is a monument in his honor.

Worms also has the oldest Jewish cemetery in Europe, dating from the 11th century. The Backfischfest in late August/early September is one of Rhineland's liveliest annual wine festivals.

DOM (Cathedral) was built in the 11th and 12th centuries and is said to be the purest example of Romanesque architecture in Germany. Five late-Gothic sandstone reliefs from the demolished Gothic cloisters adorn the north aisle.

WÜRZBURG (306 C2)
BAYERN *pop. 128,000*
St. Boniface established a bishopric in the 8th century, changing this Roman outpost on the Main River into an important ecclesiastical center. Over the centuries, Würzburg was host to several imperial diets, and in the 16th century it joined the ranks of Germany's university cities. Würzburg was badly destroyed in World War II, but today is a thriving commercial city. It still has strong links with the wine industry and is famous for its wine festivals; the September fair is the biggest. Würzburg also hosts music festivals – baroque in May, Mozart in June and Bach in September.

ALTE MAINBRUECKE, a bridge erected across the Main in the 15th century, is adorned with baroque statues of 12 saints.

DOM, Parade-Platz, dates from the 11th century. Destroyed during World War II, this predominantly Romanesque cathedral has been rebuilt. Opposite is Neumünster, a Romanesque basilica

TILMAN RIEMENSCHNEIDER
An abundance of trees and the importance of religion may go some way towards explaining the extraordinary skill of Bavarian woodcarvers. The most famous is Tilman Riemenschneider (1460–1531) who came to Würzburg in his early twenties and sculpted in sandstone, wood and marble with equal ease, capturing the folds of clothing and facial expressions. His greatest work is the Holy Blood Altar in the Church of St. Jakob in Rothenburg ob der Tauber. Other sculptures are to be found in Bamberg and Würzburg and smaller churches in Bavaria.

whose crypt contains the grave of Irish missionary St. Kilian.

FESTUNG MARIENBURG, high above the city, was first a Celtic hill fort and later a fortified castle which served as a residence of Würzburg's prince-bishops from the 12th until the 17th centuries.

It has Renaissance and baroque additions and now houses the Mainfränkisches Museum, with displays depicting local history including works by Bavaria's greatest sculptor, Tilman Riemenschneider. In the courtyard stands an 8th-century circular church.

RESIDENZ, Residenzplatz, is one of the largest baroque palaces in Germany; Balthasar Neumann had this structure built in 1744 to house the prince-bishops. Its huge rooms are sumptuously decorated. Tiepolo painted the ceiling above the grand staircase – said to be the biggest in the world – and also frescoes in the Kaisersaal (Emperor's Hall).

SCHLOSS VEITSHOECHHEIM, 7 kilometers (4 miles) north east, was the summer palace of the prince-bishops. Built in 1682, it was reconstructed in the 18th century, as was the exquisite rococo garden.

GREECE

The blue and white on the flag of Greece are the colors of the country: vivid blue summer skies and proudly whitewashed houses and churches that dazzle the eyes. Against this background the black-garbed Orthodox priests go by, while black-dressed widows show the loyalty of marriage and family ties. Greece is its people: among the most welcoming in the world, their language has the same word for both stranger and guest.

Greece is a landscape of mountains and islands, many only tiny specks where a handful of people live. It was in the capital, Athens (Athína), that democracy, theater, philosophy, and the Olympic Games were born. The Parthenon still dominates the modern city center, a reminder of a noble past.

Left Experience the tranquility of Sounion's Temple of Poseidon at sunset
Above A kilted guard outside the Parliament building in Athens

THINGS TO KNOW

- **AREA:** 238,536 square kilometers (92,099 square miles), including all groups of islands.
- **POPULATION:** 10,066,000
- **CAPITAL:** Athína (Athens)
- **LANGUAGE:** Greek
- **RELIGION:** Greek Orthodox
- **ECONOMY:** Tourism and shipping most important. Industry, mining, agriculture. Textiles (mostly cotton), chemicals, food processing; lead, zinc, iron ore, lignite; wheat, grain, olives, raisins, wine grapes, citrus fruit, tobacco.
- **PASSPORT REQUIREMENTS:** Required for U.S. citizens
- **VISA REQUIREMENTS:** Not required for stays up to three months
- **DUTY-FREE ITEMS:** Items for personal use, including camping equipment; 200 cigarettes, 50 cigars or 250 grams of tobacco; 1 liter of spirits and 2 liters of wine; 500 grams of coffee or 200 grams of coffee extract; 100 grams of tea or 40 grams of tea extract; 50 grams of perfume and ¼ liter of eau de cologne; 1 still and 1 movie or video camera (with reasonable amount of film or tape); portable radio; record player; tape recorder; typewriter; musical instrument; bicycle; sports equipment; camping equipment. Gifts and personal articles under 10,500 drachmas and not for resale also are duty free.
- **CURRENCY:** The currency unit is the Greek *drachma* (DR). Due to currency fluctuations, the exchange rate is subject to frequent change. There is no limit on foreign currency brought into the country. Visitors may import up to 100,000 drachmas; no more than 20,000 drachmas may be exported in bank notes of 500 drachmas. Up to $1,000 in foreign currency may be exported freely by short-term visitors. Declaration of imported currency must be made at time of entry into Greece.
  Some shops, particularly those selling gifts, will accept U.S. dollars as payment for purchases.

HISTORY

Greek culture originated in the 3rd millennium BC with the Minoan civilization, situated on the island of Kríti (Crete). A series of invasions from the north, initially by the Myceneans and later the Dorians, gradually shifted the center of culture to the mainland, and by the 8th century BC the city-state had become well established. The greatest of the city-states were Athína (Athens), a maritime power and cultural leader, and Spárti (Sparta), Athens' chief rival. An alliance between the two deflected the threat of Persian invasion, heralding the Golden Age of Greece in the 5th century BC. These 30 years of peace saw extraordinary achievements, most of which have served as models for Western civilization. Democracy flowered, the Parthenon and other temples were built, great strides were made in the arts, and the study/discipline of philosophy reached its zenith.

The re-emergence of Spartan hostility ended this golden era with the Peloponnesian Wars. During this period of severe instability the city-states became an irresistible target for Philip II of Macedon, the "barbarian" who overpowered and united them early in the 4th century BC. Philip's successor was his son – Alexander the Great. Alexander soon conquered the Persian Empire and set off to repeat his success in the Far East. Though he never achieved his goal, he did succeed in spreading Greek culture throughout the civilised world. His untimely death resulted in the gradual dissolution of the Macedonian Empire, paving the way for Roman occupation in the 2nd century BC.

The Romans may have conquered the land, but Greek culture remained intact. Christianity spread throughout the Roman Empire, mainly due to the prevalence of the Greek language. The empire was split in 395 AD, creating the Byzantine Empire in eastern Greece and Turkey. Constantinople – then the cen-

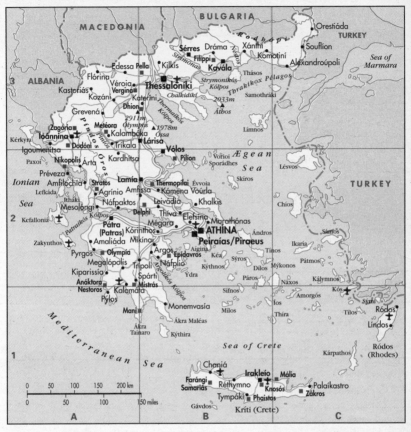

ter of Greek culture – became its capital, and though Greece was raided by invaders including the Goths, Slavs, Huns and Arabs, the new empire recovered quickly. It then entered a period of renaissance, shaken only by the iconoclastic movement which eventually resulted in the Great Schism between the Roman Catholic and Greek Orthodox churches.

The Fourth Crusade of 1204 proved too much for the Byzantine Empire, besieged because of its split with the Latin church. Greece was divided among the victors and again subjected to a series of conquests. Constantinople fell to the Ottoman Turks in 1453 and the Ottoman Empire was established. Centuries of

oppression followed, spurring a Greek revolt in 1770. The rebellion failed, but growing dissension and international pressure had significantly weakened the Turkish empire. Independence was won in 1829 and the Bavarian prince, Otto, was installed on the throne in 1833. He was replaced 30 years later by George I, and during the remainder of the 19th century Greece regained much of its former territory. It was not until 1913 that Kríti (Crete) became part of Greece.

Declared a republic in 1924, the monarchy was reinstated under George II in 1935. Italy invaded in October 1940, followed by the Germans in April 1941, bringing Greece into World War II. A civil war against Communist rebels

- **BANK OPENING HOURS:** 8am–2pm Monday–Friday; certain foreign exchange counters are open Saturday, Sunday and afternoons and evenings.
- **STORE OPENING HOURS:** 8am–3pm Monday, Wednesday and Saturday, 8am–2pm and 5.30–8.30pm Tuesday, Thursday and Friday. Shops catering for tourists can sometimes have longer opening hours.
- **BEST BUYS:** Pottery from the islands, silver and copper items, embroideries, handwoven textiles, rugs, costumed dolls, gold jewelry, shoes. Antiquities that have not been imported may not be exported.
- **PUBLIC HOLIDAYS:** January 1; Epiphany, January 6; Shrove Monday*; Independence Day, March 25; Good Friday*; Easter*; Pentecost Monday*; Labor Day, May 1; Whitmonday; Assumption Day, August 15; Greek National Day, October 28; December 25–26.
  *Movable holidays, Eastern Orthodox calendar
- **USEFUL TELEPHONE NUMBERS:**
  Police 100
  Fire 199
  Ambulance 199
- **NATIONAL TOURIST OFFICES:**
  Greek National Tourist Organisation
  645 Fifth Avenue, Olympic Tower
  New York
  NY 10022
  Tel: 212/421 5777
  Greek National Tourist Organisation
  4 Conduit Street
  London
  England
  Tel: 0171 734 5997
  Greek National Tourist Organisation
  2 Amerikis Street
  Athens 10564
  Tel: 01 322 3111
- **AMERICAN EMBASSY:**
  91 Vasillisis Sophias Boulevard
  10160 Athens
  Greece
  Tel: 01 721 2951 or 721 8401

began in 1946 and was concluded in 1949. Led by the conservative Centre Union Party, Greece joined NATO in 1952. In 1967, a coup started by Colonel George Papadopolous sent King Constantine into exile in Italy and placed the country under military rule. General Dimitríos Ioannides succeeded Papadopolous in 1973 and in 1974 tried to assassinate the president of Cyprus and unite the island with Greece. Turkish occupation of northern Cyprus (which they still occupy today) nearly resulted in war, but the Ioannides regime lost military backing, which enabled the New Democracy Party to win the elections. The monarchy was abolished in 1974 and a republic instituted instead.

Greece joined the European Community in 1981, the year that the Panhellenic Socialist Party (P.A.S.O.K.), under Andreas Papandreou, was elected. A vacuum occurred in 1989 when elections left no party with a decisive majority.

Stability returned in April 1990 when the New Democracy Party, led by Constantine Mitsotakis, won a majority. The populous rejected the government's economic reforms, however, and voted the Socialists back into power in October 1993. Papandreou returned as premier.

FOOD AND DRINK

Another form of Greek heritage is its cuisine. Try such favorites as *dolmades*, cabbage or vine leaves rolled around minced meat and rice; *souvlakia*, spit-roasted vegetables and meat; and *moussaka*, layers of eggplant, meat and white sauce. Seafood is superb, particularly sole, squid, red mullet, lobster and shrimp. Lamb and suckling pig are roasted over charcoal. Desserts like *baklava* and *kataifi* are sticky and very sweet.

The Greek palate gives water a high place among beverages, and coffee is served in varying degrees of strength and sweetness. A different taste has been given to wine by the addition of resin, or *retsina*. If this flavor does not please you, the word for "no resin" is *aretsinoto*. *Ouzo*, usually served as an aperitif, is a drink flavored with anise. Restaurant owners often encourage you to visit the kitchen, where you can point to your choice of dish.

SPORTS AND RECREATION

Track and field events have been among the most popular sports in Greece since the origin of the Olympic Games in 776 BC, but basketball, soccer and car racing now attract large followings. The coastline, indented by gulfs and inlets, has good beaches, harbors and excellent opportunities for fishing. The clear, deep waters off the islands of Ródos (Rhodes) and Kérkyra (Corfu) appeal to spear fishermen, and yachts cruise in and around Phaleron Bay. There are tennis clubs near Athens and fine golf courses near Athens, Corfu and Rhodes. Ski enthusiasts head for the northern slopes.

GETTING AROUND

A variety of tours around mainland and insular Greece can be made by combining land and sea transportation. One - or multi-day guided bus tours depart from Athens for mainland sites, and cruises, scheduled steamers and car ferries leave Athens' port of Peiraías (Piraeus) for all island groups. Ferry travel requires a reasonable amount of time and careful scheduling. You should make local reservations for steamer and ferry services.

Buses are available on many islands, as are rental cars. Visitors are advised to deal only with established car rental agencies. Motorbikes and scooters can also be rented, but many roads are poor and helmets should be worn. Direct air services link Athens with principal cities on the islands; highways and a well-developed road system provide access to the north and south mainland.

Road signs are in both Greek and English. Speed limits for cars are 50 k.p.h. (30 m.p.h.) in urban areas, 80 k.p.h.

(50 m.p.h.) on highways and 100 k.p.h. (60 m.p.h.) on highways. Seat belt use is mandatory for the driver and front-seat passenger, children under 10 must ride in the back. Visiting motorists must pay the fine for motoring violations in Greek drachmas at a public treasury office within 10 days.

A ferry route of roughly 200 kilometers (125 miles) leaves Piraeus for Sýros, Tínos and Mýkonos Islands to the east, and can continue to Náxos and Thíra (Thera). These are part of the Cyclades (*see Aegean Islands on p.363*). Steamer or ferry connections can be made from the Cyclades to Crete, which is situated 100 kilometers (62 miles) from Thíra.

A more ambitious tour begins with a drive north west from Athens to Elvsís (Eleusis), Thíva, Leivádia, Delphi, Amfissa and Náfpaktos. The route goes to the Peloponissos, near Pátra (Patras), the point of origin for steamer and ferry routes to the islands off the west coast (*see Ionian Islands on p.366*). The trip from Athens to Pátra also can be made on the highway that runs along the north coast of the Peloponissos.

Another tour of about 75 kilometers (50 miles) goes north from Athens, crosses the Evvoikós Gulf by bridge to Khalkis on Évvoia, and proceeds east and north for about 90 kilometers (55 miles) to Kimi, with its distant view of the island of Skýros. This tour might continue from

---

AUTOMOBILE CLUB
The Automobile and Touring Club of Greece (ELPA), 2-4 Messogion Street, Athens, has branch offices in various cities throughout Greece. The symbol ▲ beside a city name indicates the presence of a AAA-affiliated automobile club branch. Not all auto clubs offer full travel services to AAA members.

Kimi's port by steamer or ferry to Skýros and its sister islands of the northern Sporades. More extensive ferry tours or steamer cruises to the islands in the east leave from Piraeus, proceed around the Attiki Peninsula, and cross the Aegean Sea to the Island of Chíos. From Chíos, other connections are available north to the islands of Lésvos (Lesbos), Límnos, Samothráki (Samothrace) and Thásos or south to Sámos, Kálymnos, Kós and Ródos.

ACCOMMODATIONS

Hotels in Greece are rated either deluxe or a letter from A to E. "Xenia" hotels are government-operated offering good service at reasonable prices. The National Tourist Organization of Greece runs many of the 90 campgrounds. Some offer reduced rates with an international camping *carnet*, or permit.

ARTS AND ENTERTAINMENT

Innumerable scenic settings scattered over the mainland and islands offer the ruins of ancient Greek structures. These ancient wonders draw not only archeological interest, but also that of classics students.

The Athens Festival for the Dramatic Arts, held from June to September, is representative of the nation's preservation of its artistic heritage.

TIPPING

Restaurants and hotels usually add a service fee to their bills, but it is customary to tip an extra 5 to 10 percent. Chambermaids expect a tip, as do concierges and doormen. The minimum tip considered acceptable is 100 drachma.

USEFUL EXPRESSIONS IN GREEK

hello/good-bye	yássas
please/thank you	parakaló/efcharistó
yes/no	ne/óchi
good morning	kaliméra
good evening	kalispéra
good night	kaliníkta
How much is ...?	póso káni?
Do you speak English?	milate angliká?
I do not speak Greek.	then miló helliniká
you're welcome	parakaló
where is ...?	poo íne ...?
bank	trápeza
church	eklisía
doctor	iatrós
entrance/exit	isothos/éxothos
hotel	xenodochío
hospital	nosokomío
post office	tachithromío
police	astinomía
pharmacy	farmakío

DAYS OF THE WEEK

Sunday	Kiriakí
Monday	Deftéra
Tuesday	Trití
Wednesday	Tetárti
Thursday	Pémpti
Friday	Paraskeví
Saturday	Sávato

NUMBERS

1	éna	9	ennía
2	dío	10	déka
3	tria	20	ikosi
4	tésser	30	triánda
5	pénde	40	saránda
6	éxi	50	peнínda
7	eptá	100	ekató
8	októ	1,000	chília

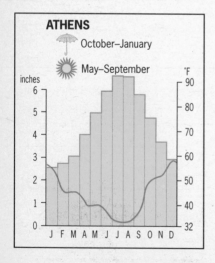

ATHENS

October–January

May–September

inches / °F

J F M A M J J A S O N D

PLACES OF INTEREST

ATHENS – *see Athína below.*

▲ **ATHÍNA**
CENTRAL GREECE *pop. 3,028,000*
See map on p.360.
Cosmopolitan Athína, or Athens, is a museum of antiquity. Every year countless vacationers come to the capital of Greece to see classical art and architecture, and to enjoy the exciting nightlife and varied cultural offerings.

Athens dates from about 3500 BC. It gained prominence in the 6th century BC when Solon encouraged the growth of agriculture and commerce by revising Draco's Code, which had punished both trivial and serious crimes with death. A few decades later Cleisthenes directed the city in the most outstanding accomplishment of the ancient era – the creation of democracy.

Following several remarkable victories over the Persians, Athens assumed military supremacy among the Greek city-states and constructed a far-flung empire that included most of the Aegean islands. Beautiful buildings sprang up, the arts flourished, and the city gained renown as the cultural capital of the world. Athens also gained a reputation as a city of letters as several fine schools opened.

During Roman times Athens maintained its position as a cultural capital, but it lapsed into relative obscurity under Byzantine and Turkish rule. When King Otto arrived in the capital of the new Kingdom of Greece in 1834, he found an impoverished village with 6,000 inhabitants. Today, Athens is a thriving modern metropolis, an important commercial headquarters and again a center of learning.

Most of the remains of ancient Athens lie near the Akropolis (Acropolis). From one of these, the Areopagus, home of the ancient court of justice, the Apostle Paul preached to the Athenians in the 1st century. A memorial on Filopapou also dates from the time of Paul. The Athenian assembly met on nearby Pnyx. Also of interest are Hadrian's Library and the Plaka, or old quarter.

The busy seaport of Peiraías, or Piraeus, 14 kilometers (9 miles) west, serves metropolitan Athens. The Ellinikó Airport is 12 kilometers (7 miles) south of the city. Most places of interest are within walking distance of downtown hotels.

In addition, Athens boasts parks, boulevards, outdoor cafés, and sports and entertainment facilities.

The carnival season is celebrated from late February to mid-March. The outstanding event of the summer season is the Festival of Music and Drama, from mid-June to September. Performances are given by the National Theater of Greece, State Orchestra, national folk dance groups, guest orchestras and ballet and opera companies.

Ancient dramas, though spoken in Greek, come through with force to international visitors because of the classical form and intensity of presentation. Authentic settings for the performances are the amphitheater on Likavitós and the Odeon Iródou Attiko.

GREECE

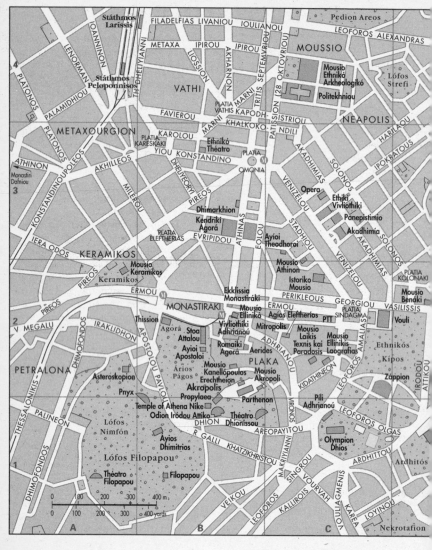

Connected to Athens in antiquity by the famed long walls of Themistocles, Peiraías is today linked to the capital by a series of residential and industrial suburbs. Attractions include one of the Mediterranean's busiest and most crowded harbors; the frequent folk dancing performances at the Hellenistic Theater of Zea; and classical fortifications that replaced the walls of Themistocles in the 4th century BC.

An archeological museum displays items from the classical, Hellenistic and Roman periods, and a maritime museum houses ship models, uniforms and paintings. Steamers depart daily from Peraías to the Greek islands.

Athens is also a convenient center for exploring the attractions of rural Attiki, and the sunny Apollo Coast south east of Athens is dotted with seaside resorts that boast fine seafood restaurants.

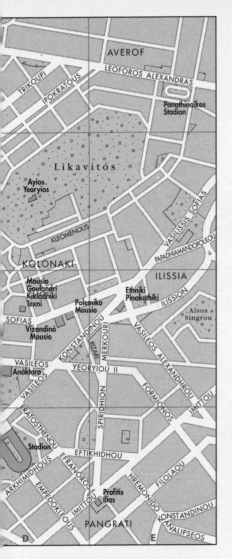

1953–6 of marble and has 134 Doric and Ionic columns. A fashionable shopping area during ancient times, it now houses archeological finds from the Agora.

Thission, the Temple of Hephaestus, god of the forge, dominates the Agora. Dating from the 5th century BC, this temple with Doric columns is one of the best preserved in Greece.

AKROPOLIS (Acropolis) (360 B2) ★, a limestone hill rising above the city, is the site of the most outstanding ancient Greek ruins. It was inhabited by the first Athenians about 3500 BC; by 1400 BC it had become the residence of the kings of Athens. In the 6th century BC, a temple honoring Athena was erected, and the hill was regarded as a holy shrine. More temples, including the Parthenon and Erechtheion, were built in ensuing centuries.

The Akropolis was a center of religious activity until the Christian Roman Emperor Theodosius banned pagan worship in 429 AD. During the Byzantine era it was converted to Christian use, and the Turks later established a garrison here.

The Akropolis is the principal tourist attraction of Greece. Automobiles must be parked at the base of the hill; it is about a 10-minute walk to the gate.

Erechtheion a temple dedicated to Athena and Poseidon, was finished shortly after the death of Pericles. The portico is supported by six *caryatids*, stone columns in the form of women, that represent the maidens who carried offerings to Athena during the Panatheniac procession.

Mousio Akropoli contains many of the archeological finds uncovered on the Akropolis since the mid-19th century. Highlights include front sections of the Parthenon, Erectheion and Temple of Athena Nike, and a collection of classical female statues.

Parthenon, the Virgin's Chamber, is regarded as a perfectly proportioned building and one of the world's greatest architectural treasures. Dedicated to Athena, it was erected between 447 and 432 BC by order of Pericles. The building was designed by Ictinus, and the

AERIDES (Tower of the Winds) (360 B2), an octagonal Roman structure, was designed as a hydraulic clock. It is inscribed with allegorical figures of the winds.

AGORÁ (360 B2), a wide and ancient market place, was the center of Athenian life in Hellenic times. It is the site of several outstanding classical buildings.

Stoa Attalou, a long open-air concourse, faces the Agora. It was reconstructed in

sculptures executed by Phidias. The interior has been roped off to visitors.

Propylaea, which means "gateway to the temple", is the entrance to the Akropolis. Five openings pierce a huge wall, which includes a portico with Doric columns facing the Akropolis temples.

Temple of Athena Nike has erroneously been called Nike Apteros or Winged Victory. An attractively proportioned structure with Ionic columns, the temple has been restored several times.

KENTRO LAIKIS TEXNIS KAI PARADOSIS (Museum for Greek Folk Art), 17 Kidathinaion, Plaka, displays traditional Greek art, including woven shrouds, priests' vestments and crosses.

KERAMIKÓS CEMETERY (360 A2) was a fashionable burial place in ancient times. It contains some beautiful sculptured memorials. The Mousío Keramikós displays artifacts from the cemetery.

LIKAVITÓS HILL is popular for its evening views across the floodlit Akropolis. Either take the funicular service, or walk through pine-scented woods to the 277-meter (909-feet) summit.

MONASTIRÁKI is a small square that gets its name from a monastery that once stood here. This is one of the focal points of the city, with a host of lively cafés and market stalls.

MONASTIRI DAFNIOU is 10 kilometers (6 miles) from Athens. Built in the 11th century, it is a fine example of Byzantine architecture. Particularly noteworthy are the mosaics within the church, including a figure of Christ. Between mid-July and mid-September the Daphni Wine Festival is held, offering an opportunity to sample more than 70 kinds of wines.

MOUSÍO BENÁKI (360 D2), Vasilissis Sofias and Koubari Street, houses the private collection and library of Antoníos Benakis. Greek relics and artworks from the prehistoric, classical, Byzantine and post-Byzantine periods are exhibited; of special note are the Chinese ceramics.

MOUSÍO ELLINIKON MOUSIKON ORGANON (Museum of Greek Musical Instruments), Dhioyenous 1–3, has three floors, each devoted to a different type of instrument. Headphones allow visitors to hear recorded examples while reading the explanations.

MOUSÍO ETHNIKÓ ARKHEOLOGIKÓ (National Archeological Museum) (360 C4) ★, 44 Patission, has a fine collection of classical statuary, pottery, stone carvings, jewelry and other works of art from excavations through Greece. The Mycenic Collection is one of the richest in the world. Frescoes are from a 3,000-year-old civilization on the island of Thíra.

MOUSÍO GOULANDRI KIKLÁDHIKI TEXNI (Goulandris Museum of Cycladic Art), Neofytou Douka 4, houses Nikolas Goulandris' private collection of ancient Greek art, spanning many centuries.

ODION IRÓDOU ATTIKO (Theater of Herod Atticus) (360 B1), a 5,000-seat theater, was erected by the Romans in 161 AD. The Festival of Music and Drama is held here from June to September.

OLYMPION DHIOS (Temple of Olympian Zeus) (360 C1) is the largest temple in Greece and adjoins the Arch of Hadrian. Although begun in 515 BC, it was not completed until the 2nd century AD.

PILI ADHRIANOÚ (Arch of Hadrian) (360 C1) was built in honor of the Roman emperor in the 2nd century AD. It separates the city of Theseus of Hellenic Athens from the Roman city of Hadrian.

STADION (360 D1) is a reconstruction of the 70,000-seat, 2,000-year-old structure. Site of the first modern Olympic games in 1896, it still stages athletic events.

THÉATRO DHIONISSOU (Theater of Dionysius) (360 B1) was built in 534 BC, about

GREECE

the time of the birth of drama in Athens. Athenians filled the theater's 17,000 seats to view works by Aeschylus, Sophocles, Euripides and Aristophanes.

VIZANDINÓ MOUSÍO (Byzantine Museum) (360 D2), 22 Vasilissis Sofias, presents works from the early Christian to the late Byzantine eras.

WAR MUSEUM OF GREECE (360 D2), Vasilissis Sofias, has exhibits pertaining to Greek military achievements.

AEGEAN ISLANDS

There are more than 1,000 islands in the Aegean Sea, and most are ideal for sunning, swimming, fishing and boating.

The southwestern group of Aegean islands, the Cyclades (Kiklades), received their name in antiquity because it was believed that they formed a circle around the sacred island of Dílos. Places of interest include the classical ruins on Dílos, Kéa and Kímolos; Byzantine churches on Kýthnos, Sífnos and Páros; and caves on Antíparos. A good time to visit is during the Feast of the Holy Virgin on August 15.

There are more islands in the Dodekanisos (Dodecanese) group than their name – which means 12 – indicates. The position of the Dodecanese in the southeastern Aegean made them vulnerable to invasions, Venetians and Turks. As a result, they are dotted with *kastra* (castle), ruins and Byzantine churches.

In the northern Aegean are two island groups. The eastern islands along the coast of Turkey offer ancient artifacts, Byzantine relics and Venetian garrisons. The northwestern group, the Sporades, are close to the Greek mainland and north of the large island of Évvoia; these green isles have interesting *kastra* and churches. Further north lie Thásos and Samothráki, accessible from the mainland ports of Kavála and Alexandroúpoli.

Islands of the Aegean listed under their own names are Dílos, Kálymnos, Kárpathos, Chíos (Khíos), Kós, Lésvos (Lesbos), Mýkonos (Mikonos), Mílos (Melos), Náxos, Pátmos, Samothráki (Samothrace), Ródos (Rhodes), Sámos, Thásos and Thíra (Thera).

ÁGHION OROS

From the 9th century, religious zealots came to Ághion Oros (Mount Oros – 1,905 meters/6,250 feet – but more commonly called Mount Áthos), to live as hermits. Before entering the Holy Mountain, visitors must obtain a permit from the Ministry of Foreign Affairs in Athens or the Office of the Governor-General in Thessaloníki.

Female visitors are forbidden and men under 21 must be accompanied by their fathers unless part of a student group and accompanied by an older supervisor. However, most people satisfy their curiosity from a beach nearby, or a boat trip round the peninsula.

AETOLIA AND EPIROS

Although visited less frequently than the rest of the country, western Greece has much to offer travelers. In antiquity, Epiros was ruled by King Pyrrhus, before the Aetolian League spread its influence throughout Greece. Octavian defeated Antony and Cleopatra at Actium in 31 BC, near modern Préveza.

Centuries later the English poet Lord Byron, a hero of the Greek War for Independence, established his headquarters at Mesolongi, where he died in 1824. Today, Hellenic ruins can be seen at Dodóni and Stratos; Roman remains are at Nikopolis; and a Venetian castle graces Náfpaktos. Individual towns listed separately are Árta and Ioánnina.

AÍGINA (355 B2)

CENTRAL GREECE pop. 10,000

Zeus abducted the nymph Aegina to this scenic island and it is from this legend that Aígina takes its name. In ancient times the island was a commercial power that even vied briefly with Athens for supremacy on the seas; today it is a popular tourist destination.

The island's capital and principal port is also named Aígina. The town's main attraction is the nearby Sanctuary of Aphaea, which contains a well-preserved temple erected in the 5th century BC.

ÁRGOS (355 B2)
PELOPONISSOS *pop. 19,000*

As one of the principal cities of classical Greece, Árgos ruled a state that controlled the northeastern Peloponnese. Over the centuries this city vied with Sparta for rule of the peninsula.

Today Árgos ranks as a major tourist destination and boasts a number of ancient ruins. At the foot of Mount Larissa are the Roman Baths, with marble fixtures, mosaics and statuary; a 20,000-seat theater dating from the 3rd or 4th century BC; and the Roman Odeon, which has several mosaics. The Sanctuary of the Pythian Apollo is on Mount Aspis. Also of interest are a museum housing a collection of local archeological finds and a 13th-century Frankish fortress.

Excursions can be made to the historic site of Mikínai (Mycenae) 17 kilometers (11 miles) north, and to Neméa, 30 kilometers (19 miles) north. The latter, where Hercules slew the Nemean Lion, has several outstanding temple ruins. Some 8 kilometers (5 miles) east of Árgos is Tirins. Legendary birthplace of Hercules, this deserted town is noted for its cyclopean walls and palace of the 14th century BC.

Also of interest is Lerni, 10 kilometers (6 miles) south, noteworthy for its remains of neolithic houses. Hercules is said to have battled the Hydra here.

ÁRTA (355 A2)
EPIROS *pop. 20,000*

King Pyrrhus' capital in ancient times, Árta became the seat of the Byzantine despotate of Epiros during the 13th and 14th centuries. There are many remnants of the later era, including several churches. The town is dominated by a medieval fortress and is noted for the Bridge of Árta.

CANDIA – *see Irakleío on p.366.*

CENTRAL GREECE
Ancient Athens, followed by Thíva (Thebes), established hegemony over most of Greece. Vestiges of this glorified time are pervasive and make Attiki (Attica), as Central Greece is known, the most important tourist region. Here are the historic monuments of Athens, the battlefield of Marathónas and the shrines of Elefsína (Eleusis) and Delphi.

The sunny Apollo Coast, the country's major seaside resort area, stretches from Peiraías to the Temple of Poseidon at Cape Sounion. Among the more notable resorts are Glyfáda, with its golf course; pine-edged Varkiza; photogenic Lagonisi; and Vouliagmeni, with its remains of the Temple of Apollo. Other places of interest are the classical ruins at Vravron and the spa of Loutraki.

Except for Delphi, the rest of central Greece is not frequently visited by tourists. Places of interest include medieval *kastra* at Amfissa, Lamía and Leivádia; the spas at Loutrá Ypátis and Kámena Voúrla; and the battlefield at Thermopílai (Thermopylae). The former glory of Thíva is displayed in the town's small museum.

Places in central Greece listed under their own names are Athína (Athens), Delphi, Aígina, Elefsína (Eleusis), Ýdra (Hydra) and Sounion.

CHANIÁ (355 B1)
KRÍTI *pop. 60,000*

Chaniá's port is at Soúda Bay, one of the greatest natural harbors in the Mediterranean, and a very important U.S. naval base. The town was first inhabited by the Minoans, when it was called Kydonia. The old part is found inside the 16th-century Venetian walls and along the old harbor waterfront, lined with tavernas.

Other sights in the old town include Minoan excavations, an archeological museum housed in the Venetian church of St. Francis, the nearby cathedral and the Firkas Naval Museum, housed in a bastion in the old port.

CHÍOS (355 C2)
AEGEAN ISLANDS *pop. 54,000*
In the 9th century BC, Homer taught on Chíos (also known as Khíos or Híos); the Dascalopetra is a mound near Vrontádos where the poet and a school of bards known as the Homeridae congregated.

The fame of Chíos stems primarily from its medieval monuments. There are *kastra*, or castles, at Volissos in the north west; at Chíos, the capital; and at Armólia in the south.

In the center of the island is 11th-century Nea Moni, an octagonal church with some beautiful and outstanding Byzantine mosaics.

Other places of interest include the classical temple at Fana, an 8th-century Byzantine church north of Vrontádos and the walls of medieval Pyrghi.

CORFU – *see Kérkyra on p.369.*

CORINTH – *see Kórinthos on p.369.*

CRETE – *see Kríti on p.370.*

DELPHI (355 C2) ★
CENTRAL GREECE *pop. 3,000*
Legend says that through the priestess Pythia, Apollo spoke to rulers, generals and commoners who came from throughout the classical world to consult the Oracle of Delphi.

It was also the site of the quadrennial Pythian games until the Christian Emperor Theodosius abolished both the games and the oracle in AD 393.

ARCHAIOLOGIKÓS CHOROS (Sacred Precincts), forming a square in the heart of Delphi, were considered the touchstone between gods and mortals.

Dominating the site are the ruins of the 4th-century BC Temple of Apollo, with its inscriptions still intact, and the original theater, altars and stadium.

Nearby is the remarkably preserved 5th-century Tholos building.

MOUSEION DELFON (Museum of Delphi) has an excellent collection. Best known of the artworks is the bronze *Charioteer*. Also notable are pediments from the Temple of Apollo, carved pieces from the Athenian Treasury and the inscrutable Sphinx of the Naxians.

PIGI KASTALIÁS (Castalian Spring), at the edge of the Sacred Precinct, gushes from two enormous cliffs. Its waters were used to cleanse the Temple of Apollo and to purify its priests and pilgrims.

DÍLOS (355 B2)
AEGEAN ISLANDS
The birthplace of Apollo, the sun god, and his sister Artemis, the huntress, ancient Dílos (Délos) was a holy shrine dedicated to Apollo. The Greeks built many temples honoring the handsome deity and decreed that no person could be born or die on the island. By the 4th century BC, as the ancient religion began to decline, Dílos became settled as a major commercial center.

Only day-trips are available as there are no accommodations for tourists and only limited eating facilities.

ARCHEOLOGICAL SITE includes the entire island. The three Temples of Apollo and the stone lions on the Sacred Way date from the island's holy days. The Minoa Fountain, Temple of Leto, Herion, theater and houses were built in Hellenistic times. Also of interest are the Roman Agora, sanctuary of the Egyptian gods, and the Archeological Museum.

ELEFSÍNA (355 B2)
CENTRAL GREECE *pop. 15,000*
When Pluto abducted Persephone to Hades, grieving Demeter journeyed to Elefsína (Eleusis), where, after securing the return of her daughter for six months of the year, the goddess of agriculture taught man to sow wheat. As a result, the grateful inhabitants erected a shrine

GREECE

GREECE

which became the headquarters of the most well-known of classical religious cults, the Eleusinian Mysteries.

The main attraction is the Telesterion, the hall of initiation. Unfortunately, only the floor plan of this 5th-century BC structure remains.

ELEUSIS – *see Elefsína on p.365.*

EPÍDAVROS (355 B2) ★
PELOPONISSOS
In ancient times, Epídavros (Epidauros) was a prominent health spa and religious center; today it is an area of villages and pine-clad hills. Classical Greek theater is highlighted during the Epídavros Festival, held from July to August.

ARHEA EPÍDAVROS (Ancient Epidauros) is 19 kilometers (12 miles) inland from Palaias Epídavros. It is the site of several outstanding classical buildings, including the Shrine of Asclepius, a gymnasium, a stadium and the Avaton, which provided lodging for pilgrims.
Museum displays archeological discoveries and models of Epidauros' temples, as well as several inscribed columns.
Theater is the best preserved in Greece. Erected in the 4th century BC, this 14,000-seat structure is the site of a Festival of Ancient Drama from July through September.

HERAKLION – *see Irakleío opposite.*

HYDRA/ÍDHRA – *see Ýdra on p.377.*

▲ IOÁNNINA (355 A1)
EPIROS *pop. 40,000*
Ioánnina has many Byzantine relics and a marked oriental character. Founded by the Emperor Justinian in the 6th century AD, it later became the capital of Epiros and a major trading center. An archeological museum is in the local park, which has a lake and an island holding several monasteries.

DODÓNI, 22 kilometers (14 miles) south west, was the site of the oldest oracle in Greece and is considered the birthplace of Hellenism. From 2000 BC to the 4th century AD, the ancients came to Dodóni to consult Zeus, king of the gods. There are several ancient ruins, including the Acropolis, priests' quarters and a Doric temple. The large theater, dating from the 3rd century BC, hosts a festival of ancient drama in August.

IONIAN ISLANDS
The mythical priestess Io, having incurred the jealousy of Zeus' queen Hera, was changed into a heifer that plunged into the sea in fearful flight. Since then, the sea and islands off the west coast of Greece have been known as Ionian.

In Homer's *Odyssey* the islands composed the kingdom of Odysseus, hero of the Trojan War. Several tombs and palaces date from that era (the Mycenaean). There are also numerous medieval fortifications from the Venetian occupation of the 14th to 18th centuries.

Kythira is far to the south and economically part of the Peloponnese, Kákinthos is known for its gardens, and Kefallonía is noted for its dense pine forests.

The 17th-century BC poetess Sappho is said to have met her death in a leap from Lefkáda's famed White Cape. Paxoí is the smallest and least crowded of the seven larger islands; Kérkyra (Corfu) rivals in beauty the loveliest islands throughout Greece; and Itháki is known worldwide from Homer's *Odyssey*.

Ionian Islands listed under their own names are Itháki (Ithaca), Kérkyra (Corfu) and Kakinthos (Zakynthos).

IRAKLEÍO (355 B1) ★
KRÍTI *pop. 102,400*
Irakleío (Heraklion), ancient Candia, is the largest city and principal port of entry on Crete. More than 1,100 years old, it has become a major archeological center for the eastern Mediterranean.

Heraklion's historic reminders include Venetian churches, the world-famous archeological museum and a 17th-century stone fountain. A Venetian fortress in the harbor has an iron gate embellished with the Lion of St. Mark.

ARCHEOLOGIKON MOUSEÍO (Archeology Museum), off Liberty Square, features neolithic and Minoan artifacts from Knosos and other sites, including frescoes, pottery and weapons. It is one of Greece's most important museums.

KNOSOS, 5 kilometers (3 miles) south east, was first inhabited 5,000 years ago. It was the capital of a powerful Minoan kingdom and is by far the largest of the Minoan palaces. It was here Theseus slew the Minotaur, and King Minos presided over his splendid court.

Little was known of the Minoan civilization until 1899, when Sir Arthur Evans made his important discoveries here. About 2 hectares (5 acres) have been excavated to date. Many buildings, including the royal apartments and the Throne of Minos, can be seen.

IRAKLION – *see Irakleío on p.366.*

ITHACA – *see Itháki below.*

ITHÁKI (355 A2)
IONIAN ISLANDS *pop. 5,000*

It was from Itháki that Odysseus set out for Troy, returning later to rescue Queen Penelope from evil suitors who desired the kingdom's riches. Vathy, the capital, is an attractive town and a good center for exploring the surrounding countryside made known by Homer's *Odyssey.*

Arethusa Fountain, described in the epic, is identified with a scenic wooded area at the foot of a sea cliff at the island's southeastern end. The Grotto of Nymphs, where Odysseus hid his treasure, and the Marathia highlands, where he was welcomed home by the loyal swineherd, Emaeus, are a few of the supposed counterparts from the epic.

KAKINTHOS (355 A2)
IONIAN ISLANDS *pop. 30,000*

A magical island of exceptional natural beauty, Kakinthos (Zákynthos) was once thought to be part of the kingdom of Odysseus. A powerful earthquake in 1953 destroyed most of its Venetian buildings, but the island still retains its attractiveness. Also known as Zante, it passed through periods of Roman, Byzantine, Frankish, Venetian, Napoleonic and finally British control (1809–64) before joining Greece along with the rest of the Ionian Islands in 1864. The island is the most important breeding area in the Mediterranean for the rare and endangered loggerhead turtle *Caretta caretta.*

In addition to Kakinthos town, places of interest include the northern tip of the island for its spectacular Kianoun or Blue Grotto caves; and the 15th-century monastery of Anafonitrias, with its frescoes, medieval tower and cell of Dionysos, patron saint of Kakinthos.

Kakinthos Town. The town is surprisingly attractive given the disastrous earthquake in 1953, but fortunately it was rebuilt following the original Venetian pattern. The few buildings to survive the earthquake include the Venetian castle and the 15th-century church of Aghíos Nikolaos, now also restored. Other sights include rebuilt Aghíos Dionyssíos church, at one end of the port; a Byzantine museum; and the Museum of Solomos.

KALÁMAI – *see Kalamáta below.*

▲ KALAMÁTA (355 A1)
PELOPONISSOS *pop. 44,000*

The attractive port of Kalamáta (Kalámai), capital of Messenia, is dominated by the Kastro, a 13th-century crusader castle. Places of interest include the local museum; Aghii Apostoli, a 14th-century Byzantine church; and a convent known for the silks its nuns weave.

ARHEA MESSÍNI, ancient Messenia, is 35 kilometers (22 miles) north west on Mount Ithomi and accessible by a 9-kilometer (6-mile) road. Founded in 396 BC, this city is today partially occupied by the village of Mavrommati.

Places of interest include the town walls, the theater, stadium and Agora.

KALAMBÁKA (355 A3) ★
THESSALIA *pop. 5,000*

Kalambáka is on a broad plain in north-western Thessalia. Its 13th-century church has interesting frescoes.

METÉORA is a huge rock mass 9 kilometers (6 miles) north of town. Centuries of erosion caused the formation of these pillars of stone that range from 26 to 90 meters (85 to 295 feet) high. In the 11th century hermits came to the area to live in caves, and 200 years later St. Athanasíos founded the first monastery, the Great Meteoron. By the 15th century there were thousands of monks and 24 monasteries.

Today only four monasteries are still inhabited. Great Meteoron, dedicated to the Metamorfossis (Transfiguration), has a 12-sided cupola and outstanding 16th-century frescoes; it is regarded as one of the best examples of Byzantine architecture in Greece. Aghíos Stefanos contains fine filigree work. Also worth a visit are the 14th-century Roussanou; Aghia Triada, with its arcaded façade; and Varlaam, with an interesting 15th-century chapel.

KÁLYMNOS (355 C2)
AEGEAN ISLANDS *pop. 13,000*

Kálymnos, one of the northern Dodecanese islands, is as varied and colorful as giant Ródos (Rhodes), which lies to the south. The contrasting terrain of Kálymnos ranges from barren mountaintops to fine beaches and fertile valleys with orange and olive groves.

The sponge industry is important to the island economy, and a solemn ceremony each Easter marks the sponge divers' departure for northern Africa. Five months later, a joyful festival honors their return.

KÁRPATHOS (355 C1)
AEGEAN ISLANDS *pop. 7,000*

The Carpathian Sea, a sparkling and beautiful waterway between Ródos (Rhodes) and Kríti (Crete), gets its name from the island of Kárpathos. Colorful costumes and distinctive, festive weddings are part of the folklore that has been preserved over the ages in this relatively remote spot.

▲ KAVÁLA (355 B3)
MAKEDONIA *pop. 57,000*

Kavála (Kaválla), the Neapolis of the Romans, was the port of ancient Philippi. Places of interest include the 15th-century Church of Our Lady, a prominent 16th-century aqueduct and a 14th-century Byzantine castle. The Kavála Archeological Museum exhibits items from local excavations.

OLIVES

Evident in Minoan art and described by Homer in both the *Iliad* and the *Odyssey*, cultivation of the olive began around 5,000 years ago. Olive oil was revered, and was awarded to the greatest athletes and used by the aristocracy as an oil to smooth on after bathing, before coming into more general culinary use.

Olives and their oil are still one of the basic staples of Greek life, as they have been for centuries. Produced in hundreds of different varieties, shapes, sizes and colors, the choice can be daunting to the tourist. Kalamata are the most famous Greek olives – elegant, glossy, black, meaty and firm.

FILIPPI, or Philippi, is 16 kilometers (10 miles) north west at the foot of Mount Pangeon. In this city fortified by Philip of Macedon in 356 BC, Thucidides was exiled and two of Julius Caesar's betrayers, Brutus and Cassius, met death following defeat by Octavian and Mark Antony in 42 BC. The Apostle Paul established his first European congregation in this city.

Extensive ruins of ancient Philippi remain. Remnants of the Agora include public buildings, sacred gates, baths and wrestling rings. During the summer, ancient tragedies are performed in the theater in conjunction with the Athens Festival of Music and Drama.

KÉRKYRA (355 A3)
IONIAN ISLANDS *pop. 115,000*
Kérkyra (Corfu) is the northernmost Ionian island. Its scenic attractions include sites associated with Homer's *Odyssey*; visitors now bathe where Odysseus was rescued by Nausicaa.

At the northern end of the island are many good beaches, pretty fishing villages and beautiful coves. Near Kassiópi are Byzantine ruins. For the more adventurous, there is Mount Pandokratoras and its monastery.

Palaiokastrítsa, to the west, is considered the island's most beautiful spot, having splendid views of the east and west coasts. Korissia Lagoon, to the south, is excellent for bathing and picnicking.

Kérkyra. Kérkyra was built during the Venetian occupation, and the citadel on the east is a reminder of Venetian power. The citadel is separated from the town by one of the largest and most beautiful squares in Greece, the Spianada.

Achilleion Palace, 9 kilometers (6 miles) south at Gastouri, was built as a retreat by Empress Elizabeth of Austria in 1891 and later used by Kaiser Wilhelm II. Today it is an elegant casino. A museum displays imperial souvenirs.

Aghíos Spyridon is a 16th-century church where St. Spyridon's bones are preserved in a gilded casket. There is a beautiful icon screen and a rich collection of gold and silver offerings.

Archeologikon Mouseion (Archeological Museum), 5 Vraila Street, houses several local finds.

Museum of Asiatic Art, housed in the Regency Royal Palace contains pieces of Chinese, Japanese and Indian art from the neolithic period to the 19th century.

Palati St. Mikolos and St. Geogiou is a Georgian mansion built in the early 19th century by the British. It once served as Government House.

KHÍOS – *see Chíos on p 365.*

KÓRINTHOS (355 B2) ★
PELOPONISSOS *pop. 21,000*
Strategic Kórinthos (Corinth) was settled by the Greeks about 1000 BC and developed as an important commercial and sea power, with ports on the Kórinthos and Saron gulfs. The Romans destroyed Corinth in 146 BC and 102 years later built a new city that rose to become the capital of the province. The Apostle Paul came to Corinth several times to build a Christian congregation and later wrote his "Epistles to the Corinthians." The city was razed by the Goths in 541 AD, and by earthquakes in 1858 and 1928. Today Kórinthos is a modern city located near the impressive Kórinthos Canal.

ACROCORINTH, on a hilltop high above ancient Corinth, was the site of the Temple of Aphrodite. The Byzantines later built a fortress, since modified by crusaders, Venetians and Turks.

ARHEA KÓRINTHOS is 7 kilometers (4 miles) from modern Kórinthos. Here are the remains of the Temple of Apollo, the Agora and the Pirene Fountain. There are also several Roman ruins, including the Odeum and the Rostra, where the Apostle Paul preached. A museum displays artifacts from the site.

KÓRINTHOS CANAL is a wonder of the modern world and an impressive engineering feat, over 6 kilometers (4 miles) long 27 kilometers (17 miles) wide with walls towering 90 meters (295 feet). Although Emperor Nero first ordered the works to begin, the Peloponnese was only finally separated from the rest of the Greek mainland in 1893.

KÓS (355 C1)
AEGEAN ISLANDS *pop. 20,000*
Hippocrates was born on Kós, or Cos, in 460 BC, and throughout antiquity this island, attracted the sick and infirm to its Shrine of Asclepius, god of healing. Today, visitors come to Kós to view

ancient ruins and medieval monuments, and to relax at seaside resorts.

Kós Town. The island's capital and chief port, is a popular resort town with lively tavernas and fine beaches. Its several noteworthy buildings include the 14th-century fortress of the Knights of St. John that guards the harbor. In the town's western section are remains of ancient Roman baths, a villa with interesting mosaics and a Greek theater.

Other places of interest include a Christian basilica from the 4th or 5th centuries, an 18th-century mosque and a Byzantine church. At the local museum is a huge statue of Hippocrates and a plane tree under which he is alleged to have taught.

Asclepeion, 6 kilometers (4 miles) west, is the Shrine of Asclepius. The remains of temples and baths date from the sanctuary's heyday as a major healing center.

TURTLES AND TOURISTS: AT LOGGERHEADS

On the beaches of Zakynthos, Crete and the Peloponnese the females of the endangered loggerhead turtle *Caretta caretta* emerge at night from the sea to lay their eggs in underground nests. The disturbance of tourist developments, pollution and motorboats all take their toll. Like tourists, the turtles make use of the beaches from June to August, but unlike tourists only one out of a thousand young will reach the reproductive age of 30 years.

▲ **KRÍTI** (355 B1) ★

Kríti (Crete) is the largest and most historically important Greek island. Prior to the development of classical civilization on the mainland, this beautiful island witnessed the rise of a culture that dominated the eastern Mediterranean from 2600 to 1100 BC. During this era, the Minoan, arose the legends of King Minos, the Minotaur and the Labyrinth.

Crete lapsed into relative obscurity until 395 AD, when the Byzantines gained control. They built churches and made Gortys the capital. After an interlude of Arab control from 823 to 961, the island was invaded in 1204 by the Venetians, who held it until the Turkish conquest 400 years later.

Sights include Venetian fortifications at Chaniá and Réthymno, and Byzantine churches at Gortys and Kristá.

There are Minoan sites at Phaistos, Knosos, Zákros and Mália.

Crete also has a number of excellent beaches, and the interior is renowned for its lovely scenery; of special note is Farángi Samariás (Samariás Gorge). Irakleío (Heraklion) is Crete's largest city.

RÉTHYMNO is dominated by an impressively massive 16th-century fortress which also looks down over the old Venetian and Turkish quarters.

FARÁNGI SAMARIÁS (Samariás Gorge) is the longest gorge in Europe, extending 18 kilometers (11 miles) into the White Mountain massif, and can only be traversed by foot.

Dramatic cliffs tower up 500 meters (1,640 feet); the narrowest part is only 3 meters (10 feet) wide and is called the "Iron Gates."

The gorge is only passable from spring to autumn as rain can make it not only impassable but dangerous.

LÉSVOS (355 C2) ★

AEGEAN ISLANDS *pop. 97,000*

In the 6th century BC, Lésvos (Lesbos) was the center of the literary activity that produced the early lyric poetry of Sappho and her contemporaries.

Lesbos is a rugged isle with outstandingly beautiful scenery. There are several beaches, including those at Plomári, Sígri, Vaterá and near the Gulf of Yera. In medieval times, the Byzantines, Genoese and Venetians occupied Lesbos and erected impressive fortresses at Ántissa, Ayasso, Eresós, Kalloní, Messagros, Míthymna, Mytilíni and Vigla.

Other places of interest include the early Christian basilicas at Ághia Paraskeví, Argala and Ariala; the ancient ruins at Eresós; and the spa of Thermís (Lourópoli).

MAKEDONIA AND THRAKI

In the 4th century BC, Alexander the Great set out from Makedonia (Macedonia) to conquer the world. He crossed Thraki (Thrace), the traditional bridge between Europe and Asia, and advanced as far as India.

Makedonia and Thraki were later occupied by the Romans, followed in turn by the Byzantines and Turks.

Thessaloníki, the second-largest city in Greece and Makedonia's capital, is a good center for exploring the region's attractions, which range from the ancient sites of Filippi, Pella and Vergina to the medieval and Byzantine monasteries of Aghion Oros, the Holy Mountain. The lakeside resort of Kastoriás and the mountain village of Flórina provide opportunities for sport and relaxation. Mount Ólympos, legendary abode of the gods, is south west of Kateríni,

Byzantine churches are scattered throughout Thraki and the towns of Xánthi and Komotiní, with their lovely mosques, minarets and open-air cafés, are characteristically oriental.

Places in Makedonia and Thraki that are listed under their own names are Aghion Oros, Kavála, Samothráki (Samothrace), Thásos and Thessaloníki.

MEGALÓPOLIS (355 A2)

PELOPONISSOS *pop. 3,000*

Founded in 369 BC as a bulwark against Spartan power, Megalópolis now sits on a major route in the Peloponnese.

ARTHEA MEGALOPOLIS, the ancient city, is 1 kilometer (½ mile) north. The 21,000-seat theater was reputed to be the largest in ancient Greece, and the Thersilion, the indoor meeting-place of The Ten Thousand, could accommodate 16,000. Other sights include the Temple of Zeus Soter and the Agora.

MIKÍNAI (355 B2)

PELOPONISSOS

"The town rich in gold" of Homeric legend, Mikínai, or ancient Mycenae, is one of the most well-known historic sites in Greece. According to the poets, it was founded by Perseus, who built the town walls with the aid of the Cyclops. The city soon became the capital of a great empire. Agamemnon set out from Mycenae to conquer Troy, only to return to die at the hands of Aegisthus, the seducer of his wife, Clytemnaestra.

With the archeological discoveries of Heinrich Schliemann in the late 19th century, Mycenae's legendary past entered the realm of historic fact. The town was actually founded centuries before the time of Perseus, probably in the 14th century BC during the early Bronze Age.

Following the fall of Knosos in about 1400 BC, the town's influence spread throughout the Aegean, culminating in the sacking of Troy sometime between 1250 and 1180 BC. Invading tribes destroyed Mycenae around 1100 BC, though it remained inhabited throughout most of the ancient period.

ARCHEOLOGICAL SITE includes all of ancient Mycenae. The Acropolis, surrounded by the Cyclopean Walls, is entered through the Lion Gate, a 14th-century BC structure topped with a bas-relief of two lions. Within the Acropolis are the Circle of Tombs, the foundations of the palace that might have been built by Perseus, a Hellenistic cistern and various dwellings.

Outside the Acropolis are the Tholos Tombs, including a grave circle dating from 1600 BC; the so-called Treasury of Atreus, one of Mycenae's best-preserved buildings; and the 13th-century BC domed Tomb of Clytemnaestra.

MÍLOS (355 B1)

AEGEAN ISLANDS *pop. 4,500*

Mílos (Melos) is one of the most colorful islands of the Cyclades (Kiklades). Its capital, Plaka, also known as Mílos, has a

Frankish fortress and two old churches. Near by is the site where French archeologists discovered the *Venus de Mílo*, now on display in the Louvre in Paris.

MONEMVASÍA (355 B1) ★
PELOPONISSOS

Lying 59 kilometers (37 miles) south east of Sparta, Monemvasía is a now largely uninhabited medieval town, but which once housed a population of some 60,000. Once part of the mainland until an earthquake separated it in 375 AD, it is now reached by a causeway from the new town (called Gefyra), a small, modern port on the mainland.

The strategically positioned 13th-century medieval town is an intricate network of alleys, with only a single tunneled entrance to the town, hence its name Moni Emvasia or Monemvasía.

It has several churches worth visiting, including a 13th-century cathedral and the church of Agíos Pavlos, built in 956 AD but converted into a mosque and now a small museum.

MOUNT ÁTHOS – *see Ághion Oros on p.363.*

MYCENAE – *see Mikínai on p.371.*

MÝKONOS (355 B2) ★
AEGEAN ISLANDS *pop. 5,000*

Bright, white houses, windmills and churches are the hallmarks of Mýkonos (Mikonos). The island is a fashionable resort, its many beaches offering excellent swimming.

Mýkonos. Mýkonos' chief town and port, sharing the same name as the island, has a cosmopolitan atmosphere. Its nearest beaches are Ornos, 3 kilometers (1.9 miles) south and Aghíos Stefanos, 3 kilometers (1.9 miles) north.

Places of interest include the busy harbor area and the local museum, which displays artifacts from Dílos.

The church of Paraportiani, with its stairstep chapels and arched bell-tower, is an outstandingly beautiful example of Cycladic architecture.

MYTILÍNI – *see Lésvos on p.370.*

NÁFPLIO (355 B2) ★
PELOPONISSOS *pop. 10,000*

The port of Árgos in antiquity, Náfplio (Naufplion) is today the chief city of the Argolis, a farming region. With its narrow streets and Venetian buildings, the city provides a charming setting overlooking the sea. The Venetian fortress affords Palamidi, a spectacular view.

Excursions can be made to the 12th-century Monastery of Zoodochos Pigi, 2 kilometers (1.2 miles) outside of town; to the Mycenaean ruins at Tirins, 4 kilometers (2½ miles) north; and to ancient Epídavros, 25 kilometers (16 miles) east.

NÁXOS (355 C2)
AEGEAN ISLANDS *pop. 20,000*

Scenic Náxos is the largest of the Kiklades (Cyclades). Famed in antiquity for its quarries, it is now noted for architectural remains. On Palatia, a small island facing Náxos harbor, is a temple gate from the 6th century BC. Dating from the Byzantine era are several churches and monasteries, all with frescoes, icons and other works of art.

Among the more notable are those at Apiranthos, Avlonitsa, Halki, Kirochori and Náxos.

In medieval times, Náxos was the seat of a Venetian duchy; most of the island's towns have fortresses dating from then, French crusaders built the castle at Filoti in the 13th century.

At Flerio, 12 kilometers (7 miles) south of the capital, are classical marble workshops and quarries where unfinished sculptures can be seen.

OLYMPÍA (355 A2) ★
PELOPONISSOS

Having defeated Augeas, King of Elis, Hercules, the son of Zeus, decreed that the men of Greece should assemble in Olympía every four years for a series of challenging athletic contests to commemorate his victory.

From 776 BC to 393 AD, the Olympic games, dedicated to Zeus, were the most

GREECE

important international events in the Hellenic world. Today the sacred flame is still kindled at Olympía and is borne by runners to the games.

HOLY ALTIS contains most of the ruins of ancient Olympía, including the temples of Zeus and Hera, Altar of the Gods, Exedra of Herod Atticus, hippodrome, gymnasium and stadium.

MOUSEION OLYMPÍAS has an outstanding collection of sculpture, helmets and weapons. Among the statues are Praxiteles' *Hermes* and Peoníos' *Victory*.

OROS ÓLYMPOS (355 A3)
MAKEDONIA
Situated 89 kilometers (55 miles) south west of Thessaloníki and north of Larisa, Oros Ólympos (Mount Olympos) is the legendary home of the Greek gods and was not scaled by man until 1913. The name is given to the whole limestone mountain range of which the highest peak – the highest in Greece – is Mount Olympos at 2,916 meters (9,568 feet).

PÁTMOS (355 C2) ★
AEGEAN ISLANDS *pop. 2,500*
St. John is thought to have composed the *Book of Revelation* during his exile on Pátmos in AD 95. A monastery dedicated to him was founded 93 years later, and pilgrims have journeyed to view the memorabilia connected with the apostle ever since. The grotto where he supposedly lived is 2 kilometers (1.2 miles) south of Skala.

PÁTMOS, the island's principal settlement, is an attractive village of whitewashed houses. It exhibits a markedly Byzantine character, with many buildings dating from the 10th century.
St. John Theologo's towers over the town. Founded in 1088 by St. Christodoulos, this black-stone monastery resembles a medieval fortress.

It contains outstanding frescoes, art objects and many manuscripts, including a collection of 33 pages of the *Gospel of St. Mark*, inscribed in the 5th century on purple vellum.

▲ PÁTRA (355 A2)
PELOPONISSOS *pop. 142,000*
Pátra (Patras), capital of the Peloponnese and one of Greece's largest cities, is a busy port. Among its places of interest are Aghíos Andreas, a church that contains the remains of St. Andrew; the Roman Odeon, a reconstructed 2nd-century theater; and the local museum.

Excursions can be made to Girokomion, a 9th-century monastery 3 kilometers (1.9 miles) south; to the Achaia Clauss Winery, 8 kilometers (5 miles) outside of town; and to the 15th-century castle at Rion, 11 kilometers (7 miles) east. The beach of Chrisi Akú, or Golden Sands, is 3 kilometers (1.9 miles) from Pátra.

A good time to visit the city is during the two-week pre-Lenten Carnival.

PATRAS – *see Pátra above.*

PEIRAÍAS – *see Athína on on p.359.*

PELOPONISSOS
The Peloponnese, the large land mass in southern Greece, was a cradle of civilization. In the 2nd millennium BC, it witnessed the rise of the highly developed Mycenaean culture, and by the 8th century BC it was a major center of enlightenment. The Romans occupied the region in the 2nd century BC and were followed by Byzantines, crusaders, Venetians and Turks.

Relics of times past are the main attractions of the Peloponnese. The Mycenaean tombs at Mikínai and the classical temples of Olympía and Vasses are only a few of the region's monuments of antiquity; the churches at Mistras are but a small portion of the peninsula's Byzantine heritage.

The Peloponnese also boasts magnificent scenery that varies from the vineyards and currant groves of Achaea in the north to the rugged mountains of the isolated Mani region in the south. From bustling Pátra to quiet Monemvasía, the entire coast is lined with excellent beaches and picturesque ports.

Places in the Peloponnese listed under their own names are Árgos, Epídavros (Epidauros), Kalamáta (Kalámai), Kórinthos (Corinth), Megalópolis, Mikínai (Mycenae), Náfplio (Naufplion), Olympía, Pátra (Patras), Pýlos, Spárti (Sparta) and Trípoli.

PÝLOS (355 A1)
PELOPONISSOS

Pýlos actually refers to three sites in the western Peloponnese. The modern town, sometimes called Navarino, is on the southern side of the Bay of Navarino. To the north is classical Pýlos (Pilos), which is also known as Koryfási. The Pilos (Pýlos) of Homeric fame, Epano Eglianos, is near the village of Chóra. Only modern Pýlos is inhabited.

Modern Pýlos is dominated by a crusader castle, the Neokastro. Koryfási was fortified by the Athenians in 425 BC, captured by the Spartans 16 years later and abandoned in medieval times. Places of interest include several ancient ruins and the old Venetian fortress, Paleaokastro. Excursions can be made to the 13th-century Venetian castle 15 kilometers (9 miles) south at Methóni.

EPANO EGLIANO lies 10 kilometers (6 miles) inland near the village of Chóra. It was at this site that Homer's hero Nestor ruled his powerful kingdom from what is today the largest and best-preserved Mycenaean palace in Greece. This structure, probably occupied before 1700 BC, was destroyed by fire in about 1200 BC.

RHODES – *see Ródos below.*

RÓDOS (355 C1)
DODECANESE ISLANDS *pop. 88,000*

The historic island of Ródos (Rhodes) has some of the most fascinating attractions in Greece. Here are ancient ruins and medieval monuments, picturesque mountain villages and fine beaches.

Rhodes was a commercial center dominated by the democratic city-states of Líndos, Ialissos and Kámeiros. In the 5th century BC the island's inhabitants founded the town of Ródos, whose citizens 200 years later celebrated a victory over the Persians by erecting the Colossus of Rhodes. The colossus was a 30 meters (98 feet) statue of the sun god Helios, who was later replaced in Greek mythology by Apollo. One of the seven wonders of the ancient world, it collapsed during an earthquake in 225 BC.

In the 14th century the Knights Hospitallers of St. John of Jerusalem converted Rhodes into a Christian bastion at the crossroads of the Levant, the eastern Mediterranean coastline. They built fortresses at Líndos and Ródos; both structures survive today.

Other places of interest include the wooded Valley of the Butterflies, fine beaches and the ruins of Ialissos, Kámeiros and Líndos. The ancient life of Líndos is recalled by its graceful Temple of Athena.

RÓDOS was home to the great stone colossus but the city's fame stems primarily from its association with the Knights Hospitallers, or Knights of Ródos. This order, founded in Jerusalem in the 11th century, resided in this city from 1309 until the Turkish conquest of 1522. Here the knights cared for the sick and poor, protected Christian pilgrims *en route* to the Holy Land, waged war against Islam and erected one of the most outstanding hospitals of the medieval era. The Italians, who gained control of Rhodes in 1912, restored much of the medieval city and built the modern town to the north.

Akropolis, south west of the medieval city, is the site of several ruins from the 2nd century BC, including a theater, stadium and three temples.

Medieval City looks much as it did in the times of the Knights of Ródos. Walls that vary in thickness from 2 to 12 meters (6½ to 40 feet) and extend more than 4 kilometers (2½ miles) surround the old inner city; they date from the 14th to 16th centuries. Guided tours depart from the Palati Ippoton Rodou.

The medieval city is divided into two areas. The Collachium, the City of the Knights, has the remains of the Temple of Aphrodite, which date from the 3rd century BC. The Bourg, or lower town, is the city's Turkish quarter. Attractions include the Mosque of Suliemann, the Archbishop's Palace, a Turkish fountain and a Byzantine church.

In the Collachium the knights built the Lodge of St. John and the fortified Cathedral. Bounded by the Liberty Gate, Marine Gate, Clock Tower and the Palace of the Grand Masters, this area encloses an early hospital and the Street of the Knights.

Odos Ippoton, the most well-known street in the city, faces most of the attractions of the Collachium, including the museum and the seven inns that served as the headquarters for the various nationalities that constitute the Knights Hospitallers.

Palati Ippoton Rodou (Palace of the Grand Masters), a 14th-century Gothic fortress, was the headquarters of the Knights Hospitallers in medieval times. Today this massive building houses ancient mosaics, statuary and ceramics.

Ródos Museum is the former Hospital of the Knights of Ródos. In times past, outstanding physicians cared for ailing pilgrims in this austere 15th-century structure. Today it contains Mycenaean funerary objects, ancient coins, vases from the 6th and 7th centuries BC, and classical sculptures, including the famed *Aphrodite of Ródos*.

SALONICA – *see Thessaloníki on p.376.*

SÁMOS (355 C2) ★
AEGEAN ISLANDS *pop. 45,000*
In ancient times the mountainous island of Sámos was regarded as the birthplace of Hera, and the Heraion on the south coast was one of the goddess's most important shrines from the 8th to 6th centuries BC. A column from one of the largest temples in ancient Greece remains, as well as other artifacts.

Near Tigani is the famed underground aqueduct of Eupalinos, which can still be explored. Other places of interest include the museum in Sámos, the island's capital, and the medieval fortress, ancient ruins and local museum in Pithagorion, home of Pythagoras.

SAMOTHRÁKI (355 C3)
THRAKI *pop. 4,000*
Homer claimed that Poseidon viewed the Greek attack on Troy from on top of 1,600-meter (5,249-feet) Mount Fengari on Samothráki (Samothrace).

The fame of this north Aegean island, however, stems from its association with the cult of the Cybele, a group of powerful deities whose mysteries attracted enormous numbers of initiates in the 3rd century BC.

PELEOPOLIS, 6 kilometers (4 miles) east of Kamariotissa, was the location of gatherings of the cult of the Cybele. Among the ruins, mostly from the 3rd century BC, are the Sanctuary of the Cybele; the Rotunda, or Arsinoeion; and Nike Fountain. A museum houses local finds.

SANTORINI – *see Thíra on p.377.*

SOUNION
CENTRAL GREECE
Cape Sounion was in ancient times a strategic location guarding the entrance to the Saronic Gulf. Now it is a major tourist spot along the Apollo Coast.

NAOS POSEIDONOS (Temple of Poseidon) overlooks the sea from its hilltop vantage. This marble structure, with 12 Doric columns bleached white by the sun, was erected in the 5th century BC.

SPARTA – *see Spárti below.*

SPÁRTI (355 A2)
PELOPONISSOS *pop. 12,000*
Spárti (Sparta) began its rise to power in the 8th century BC, when it conquered

neighboring Messínia and gained control of the southern Peloponnese. By the 6th century BC this city, where daily life was highly regulated in a militaristic fashion, was the strongest in Greece.

French crusaders came to Sparta in the 13th century and built a fortress on nearby Mount Taygetus. The Byzantines followed and established Mistrás on the same site as the capital of the Despotate of Morea (Peloponnese). This magnificent city became a center of art and learning. With the coming of the Turks in the 15th century, however, decline set in; the last families were evacuated in 1952. Today Mistrás is a museum city, while Sparta, rebuilt in the 19th century, is the capital of Laconia.

The ancient Spartans built few great monuments and erected no walls; of the ruins that remain, the most notable are the Temple of Athena, the Agora and the Sanctuary of Artemis Orthia.

MISTRÁS, 6 kilometers (4 miles) west, once housed 45,000 people, but only remnants of its mansions, churches and monasteries are still evident. Its Byzantine churches have outstanding frescoes. Aghii Theodoroi is the oldest; Perivleptos contains the most beautiful artwork. Aghíos Dimitríos, seat of the Orthodox archbishop in the 14th and 15th centuries and also the site of the coronation of the last Byzantine emperor, is the largest.

Other places of interest in Mistrás include the walls of the despot's palace, Aghia Pantanassa monastery and the ruins of a 13th-century crusader fortress.

THÁSOS (355 B3)
MAKEDONIA *pop. 16,000*
The fine beaches, wooded hillside and picturesque villages of Thásos attract visitors seeking quiet relaxation.

ARCHEOLOGICAL SITE, 3 kilometers (1.9 miles) south east near Limenária, has ancient Greek and Roman ruins. Among the more notable ruins are the theater, Agora, Temple of Athena and Sanctuary

of Pan. The town walls, in good condition, are interspersed with several impressive gates. A museum is on site.

THERA – *see Thíra on p.377.*

THESSALIA
Thessalia is centaur country, for these mythological creatures are said to have roamed in antiquity. The coast is lined with many fine beaches, and 1,575-meter (5,167-foot) Mount Pilion is topped by a number of quiet resorts. Of special note is the Vale of Tempi, one of the most scenic areas in Greece.

The only place in Thessalia listed under its own name is Kalambáka, near by is the famous rock mass of Meteora.

▲ THESSALONÍKI (355 B3) ★
MAKEDONIA *pop. 406,500*
Cassander of Macedonia founded a city at the foot of Mount Chortiatis in 315 BC and named it for his wife, Thessaloníki, the sister of Alexander the Great.

Thessaloníki (formerly known as Salonica) grew rapidly until it became the capital of Roman Macedonia.

During the Byzantine period Thessaloníki assumed an importance second only to Constantinople as the major metropolis of the empire. The city was occupied by the Turks in 1453 and remained an Ottoman possession until 1912. A fire in 1917 and repeated bombings in World War II destroyed many of the older buildings.

Despite this, Thessaloníki today has some of the best examples of Byzantine art and architecture. Numerous churches contain mosaics, frescoes and icons.

AGIA SOPHIA, Agia Sophia and Ermou streets, is an 8th-century Byzantine church. Prominent among the mosaics is the 11th-century Ascension in the dome.

AGÍOS DIMITRÍOS, Aghou Dimitrou Street, was built on the spot where Dimitríos, patron saint of the city, was martyred by Emperor Galerius. The restored 5th-century church, now the largest in Greece, has five adjoining naves and original marble pillars with carved capitals. The crypt and mosaics are noteworthy.

ARCHEOLOGICAL MUSEUM, off the road to the airport, boasts the celebrated finds of the Hellenistic Tombs at Derveni, which were discovered in 1961. Included are gold jewelry and a 4th-century gilt silver vase with intricate details.

LEVKÓS PIRGOS (White Tower), at the east end of King Constantine Avenue, is a 15th-century Venetian fortification.

PANAGIA ACHEIROPOEITOS (Our Lady Not Painted by Human Hands), Egnatia Street, is so named because the icon of the Virgin is said to have appeared miraculously centuries ago. Fine Byzantine mosaics decorate the walls.

PÉLLA is 38 kilometers (24 miles) north west of Thessaloníki. The capital of Macedonia in Hellenic times, it was the birthplace of Alexander the Great and the scene of his tutoring by Aristotle. Excavations begun in 1957 have uncovered ancient buildings and remarkable pebble mosaics.

PILI GALERIOU (Arch of Galerius), spanning the Via Egnatia, was constructed by the Romans in 303 AD. It has relief carvings portraying Emperor Galerius' victory over the Persians.

THÍRA (355 C1)
KIKLADES *pop. 10,000*

A highly developed civilization flourished on the island of Thíra (Thera), until a volcanic explosion in the 2nd millennium BC shattered the island.

Today Thíra, also known as Santorini, for the island's patron St. Irene, is a tourist favorite. The east coast is lined with black volcanic pebble beaches excellent for swimming.

Near Mesa Vouna to the south are the ruins of ancient Thíra, where classical monuments, temples and an Egyptian sanctuary can be seen. Ruins of the Minoan city destroyed by the volcano in 1500 BC have been found at Akrotíri.

THÍRA, the island's capital, is on a cliff some 270 meters (885 feet) high overlooking the harbor and volcanic crater. Of major interest are the local archeological finds displayed in the museum.

TRÍPOLI (355 A2)
PELOPONISSOS *pop. 22,000*

Trípoli is the capital of Arkadia, the land of Pan, nymphs and pine forests. Although it boasts no ancient monuments, it is a popular resort.

Some 8 kilometers (5 miles) to the south is Tegea, the site of a Temple of Athena from the 4th century BC. Also in Tegea is a restored Byzantine church containing interesting modern mosaics.

About 30 kilometers (19 miles) west, near Andrítsaina, is the Temple of Apollo Epikourious, one of the best-preserved temples in Greece and worth seeing in spite of its difficult mountainous location. With Doric columns set against the backdrop of the surrounding mountains, the temple presents a breathtaking view.

ÝDRA (355 B2)
CENTRAL GREECE *pop. 3,000*

A bohemian atmosphere permeates Ýdra (Hydra), for this rugged, island is a fashionable resort that has attracted a large colony of artists and writers.

In the 19th century Ýdra was the headquarters of a group of wealthy sea captains who played an important role in the Greek War. They built impressive mansions that, together with several monasteries and the absence of wheeled traffic, give the island its unique and quaint atmosphere.

Ironically, the island is so celebrated for its undisturbed atmosphere that up to 40,000 tourists flood the area daily in July and August; thus, an off-season visit is recommended.

ZAKYNTHOS – *see Kakinthos on p.367.*

REPUBLIC OF IRELAND

Conversation matters in Ireland, time does not. A journey from home to shop can take half a morning ... and why not? A stranger will not be strange for long, especially in the pub, where drink flows and music plays. The land is green, well-watered by the Atlantic rain, though even on the wettest day the Irish will merely remark that it is "a bit soft." Four seasons in one day, they claim, the more so in the west, the land of the towering Cliffs of Moher and the off-shore Aran Islands.

Dublin, the capital, has the feel of a village and can be enjoyed on foot. Here is the Liffey, whose waters are turned into the renowned Guinness. Time will only matter to the visitor in Ireland when it begins to run out.

Left Magnificent views can be had of Darrynane, in County Kerry
Above left A Tralee (traditional music) is often played in pubs
Above right The South Cross at Kells

THINGS TO KNOW

- **AREA:** 70,285 square kilometers (27,137 square miles)
- **POPULATION:** 3,548,000
- **CAPITAL:** Dublin
- **LANGUAGES:** English and Gaelic
- **RELIGION:** Ireland has many churches, both Church of Ireland (Protestant) and Roman Catholic; Dublin has a mosque and a synagogue.
- **ECONOMY:** Agriculture, industry. Livestock; barley, wheat and other grains; root and green crops. Food processing; metals and engineering; textiles, clothing and footwear; electronics; brewing and distilling.
- **ELECTRICITY:** 220 volts; adaptor required for non-continental appliances.
- **PASSPORT REQUIREMENTS:** Required for U.S. citizens.
- **VISA REQUIREMENTS:** Not required for stays up to three months.
- **DUTY-FREE ITEMS:** Up to 200 cigarettes or 100 cigarillos or 50 cigars or 250g of tobacco; 2 liters of wine and 1 liter of spirits; 50g of perfume; ¼ liter of toilet water; and gifts valued up to £34 IR (£17 IR for those under 15 years old). Also see *The European Union on p.5.*
- **CURRENCY:** The Irish *punt* (IR) is divided into 100 *pence.* Due to currency fluctuations, the exchange rate is subject to frequent change. There are no restrictions on the amount of foreign or Irish currency that may be imported, but large amounts to be re-exported should be declared on entry. Visitors and residents leaving Ireland may only export up to £100 IR in Irish currency and up to £500 IR in foreign currency in addition to the imported amount declared on entry.
- **BANK OPENING HOURS:** 10am–12:30pm and 1:30–3pm Monday–Friday. Also 10am–12:30pm and 1:30–5pm Thursday in Dublin; open one evening a week in most other towns.
- **STORE OPENING HOURS:** 9am–5:30pm Monday–Saturday. Stores outside the cities frequently close one day a week (usually Wednesday or Saturday).

HISTORY

Ireland, born of conflict, struggles to maintain and prosper in the wake of generations of invasion and the fight for self-determination. Two important characteristics distinguish the struggle for Irish independence: Ireland has remained staunchly Catholic, and to an extent is still in a state of political and cultural limbo, being neither completely free of British influence nor completely absorbed by English custom.

The Gaels of Western Europe, people of Celtic origin who invaded Ireland around 300 BC, formulated the blueprint for Irish society and culture. Druids maintained the social order and independent mini-kingdoms were generally grouped under an overlord whose position was more honorary than jurisdictional. This arrangement was preserved until the 5th century AD, when St. Patrick worked to convert the people to Christianity and replaced druid priests with monastic leaders. During the Dark Ages, the Irish enjoyed some of their most profound cultural, literary and artistic successes. One of these works, an elaborately decorated example of the Gospels called the *Book of Kells*, is on display at Trinity College in Dublin.

The 12th century saw a shift in the political foundation which launched more than 800 years of struggle between the English and Irish, and which continues to have a profound effect today. Henry II, with the support of popes Adrian IV (the only English pope) and Alexander III, invaded and declared himself Lord of Ireland in 1171. This marked the first time the Church was linked to a foreign administration, thereby terminating Gaelic Ireland's independence. The following years brought attempts by the English to replace papal loyalty with loyalty to the Crown. Oliver Cromwell's victory over Irish resistance in 1650 brought a ban on the practice of the Catholic faith; it also gave Cromwell the opportunity to seize Catholic lands, which were handed out to British subjects as rewards for Crown loyalty.

The Test Act of 1704 continued the anti-Catholic discrimination, tying the right to hold office to a willingness to receive communion in the official (Protestant Church) of Ireland. Irish resentment escalated until 1796, when Theobald Wolfe Tone and the United Irishmen rebelled. Two years later, Wolfe Tone and his followers were defeated and British Prime Minister

William Pitt began campaigning for a merger of the English and Irish parliaments. In order to secure this, promises were made regarding Catholics' rights to representation. The resultant United Kingdom, created under the 1800 Act of Union, established London as the seat of authority but denied Catholic access to parliament based on the same laws invoked under the Test Act.

Daniel O'Connell, a young Catholic lawyer, was elected in 1828 to the British

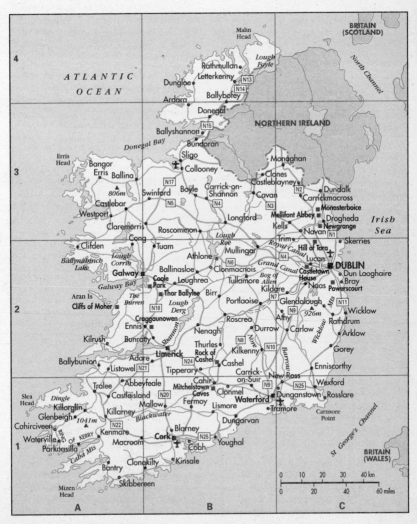

- **BEST BUYS:** Tweeds, linen, woolens, knits, lace, rugs, blankets, woodcarvings, smoking pipes, pottery, jewelry, Connemara marble and Waterford crystal.
- **PUBLIC HOLIDAYS:** January 1; St. Patrick's Day, March 17; Good Friday; Easter Monday; 1st Monday in June; August Monday, 1st Monday in August; last Monday in October; December 25; St. Stephen's Day, December 26.
- **USEFUL TELEPHONE NUMBERS:**
  Police 999
  Fire 999
  Ambulance 999
- **NATIONAL TOURIST OFFICES:**
  Irish National Tourist Office
  757 Third Avenue
  New York
  NY 10017
  Tel: 212/418 0800
  Fax: 212/371 9052
  Irish Tourist Board
  150 Bond Street
  London
  W1Y OAQ
  Tel: 0171 493 3201
  Fax: 0171 493 9065
  Irish Tourist Board
  14 O'Connell Street
  Dublin
  Tel: 01 874 7733
  Fax: 01 284 1751
- **AMERICAN EMBASSY**
  42 Elgin Road
  Ballsbridge
  Dublin 4, Ireland
  Tel: 01 668 7122
  Fax: 01 668 8274

AUTOMOBILE CLUB
The Automobile Association (AA) has offices at 23 Rock Hill, Blackrock, County Dublin. The symbol ▲ beside the city name indicates the availability of an AAA-affiliated automobile club branch. Not all auto clubs offer full travel services to AAA members.

Parliament; as a Catholic, however, he was barred from sitting in Parliament under the Act of Union. Fearing the backlash that might occur from the increasing agitation for Catholic emancipation, Parliament yielded to the pressure and revoked the required oath of allegiance to the Church of Ireland. A growing nationalism was emerging within the Catholic community, and talk of home rule escalated. But the potato famine in the mid-1840s forced the Irish to focus much of their energy on survival – not nationalism. In an agrarian-based society, potatoes were an economic and dietary staple; blight and overworked fields, however, led to massive crop failure. The population was decimated, with more than a million deaths and at least as many emigrants, mainly to the United States. Resentment over what the Catholic majority viewed as British indifference to their plight further inflamed home-rule sentiment.

Once the famine had subsided, nationalism regained momentum. After several unsuccessful attempts, a bill was passed in Parliament granting home rule to the Irish, but excluding six Ulster counties in the north where Protestants enjoyed a majority. World War I, however, interrupted implementation of the 1914 Home Rule Bill. Precipitated by frustration over the postponement, the 1916 Easter Rising was one of the first violent

---

IRISH WHISKEY
Uisce beatha, or "water of life," was supposedly invented by Irish missionary monks, who had gained the knowledge from a Middle Eastern method of making perfume from what they called an alembic, or still.
It is said that Queen Elizabeth I was partial to a drop of whiskey, a taste probably acquired from Sir Walter Ralegh, who had been presented a 145-liter (32-gallon) cask of it from the Earl of Cork.

displays by the Irish Republican Army – an organized army of Sinn Féin ("Ourselves Alone") party members who were determined to fight British rule through guerrilla warfare. Although not militarily successful, it proved to be the catalyst for uniting the Irish in their demand for nationhood.

In 1921 the Irish Free State was declared a self-governing area with its own parliament, although still within the British Commonwealth of Nations. A separate parliament was set up in the six Ulster counties now known as Northern Ireland; the Protestant majority was adamantly opposed to home rule, fearing the Catholic majority to the south. Tensions in the south erupted into civil war over this alliance with the British Commonwealth and the attendant oath to the Crown, planting the seeds of antagonism that brought about the drafting of a new constitution in 1937 (still under the auspices of the British Commonwealth) and, finally, the declaration in 1949 of the Republic of Ireland as an independent nation free of British control. Although the political situation in Northern Ireland remains unresolved, citizens of the Republic have moved forward in their quest for economic stability and greater world participation.

FOOD AND DRINK

Irish food is wholesome and plentiful. Favorites such as steak, roast beef, mutton and lamb are excellent and always available. The island is also particularly well known for its seafood – Dublin Bay prawns, lobsters, smoked salmon and oysters are delicacies of exceptional flavor. And to accompany your feast, how about a pint of Guinness stout, followed by a glass of Irish whiskey? Ireland's pubs are renowned, many offering live entertainment that includes traditional music.

SPORTS AND RECREATION

An enthusiasm for sports is an integral part of the Irish character, and the country is a vast preserve for golfers, anglers and hunters. Fine golf courses are numerous, and both freshwater and saltwater fishing are excellent. Horse racing, soccer and rugby are also extremely popular although hurling and Gaelic football are the national games.

GETTING AROUND

Car ferries link Ireland with Britain and France. Services from Britain run from Fishguard to Rosslare, Holyhead to Dun Laoghaire, Holyhead to Dublin, Pembroke to Rosslare and, during summer only, Swansea to Cork. From France, ferries operate from Le Havre and Cherbourg to Rosslare, and from Roscoff and Le Havre to Cork.

Roads are divided into three categories: national primary, national secondary and regional. Driving is on the left-hand side and roads are narrow. Cyclists, pedestrians and livestock constitute the main driving hazards. Road signs are in Gaelic and English. Front-seat occupants must wear seat belts; a child under 12 may not occupy a front seat unless using a suitable restraint system. Speed limits are 50 k.p.h. (30 m.p.h.) in developed areas and 90 k.p.h. (55 m.p.h.) outside these areas. There are no on-the-spot fines.

ACCOMMODATIONS

Many types of accommodations are available, from first-class luxury hotels to more modest but still comfortable second- and third-class establishments. Guest houses are also popular. More information can be obtained from the Automobile Association or the Irish National Tourist Office.

TIPPING

Restaurants and hotels generally include a 10 to 15 percent service, eliminating the need to tip further. Ask if this is done; if not, leave 10 to 15 percent. Tip taxi-drivers 10 percent of the fare, and doormen and porters about 40 pence. Bartenders and theater ushers do not expect a tip.

REPUBLIC OF IRELAND

PRINCIPAL TOURING AREAS

Note: for descriptions of cities in **bold type**, see individual city listings.

DONEGAL AND SLIGO

North-west Ireland is noted for its spectacular indented coast. The cliffs, deep glens and fishing villages of Donegal and the sandy beaches of **Sligo** are shadowed by mountains; castles and lakes also characterize the region.

DUBLIN AND THE EAST COAST

The long, gentle coastline of the Irish Sea attracts thousands of visitors to the beaches and resorts of the east coast, where many remains from the Bronze Age still exist. **Kildare**, with its lush green pastures and ancient bogland, is known as a sporting, racing and hunting region. Louth, Ireland's smallest county, figures in many folktales.

Meath is in the wooded Blackwater river region, and, of course, there is **Dublin**, the city of James Joyce.

THE MIDLANDS

Central Ireland, unlike the rest of the country, is relatively flat. Of special interest is **Clonmacnois**, Ireland's best-known monastic city. **Athlone** is an excellent departure point for exploring the islands of Lough Ree, several of which contain ruins of ancient churches.

THE SOUTH WEST

Bordered by rugged coastline and island-strewn bays, Ireland's south west boasts magnificent mountain scenery, best seen from the circular Ring of Kerry drive on the Iveragh Peninsula. County Tipperary has some interesting ancient buildings, the most notable being the Rock of Cashel, and the region also boasts the popular castle at **Blarney**.

Towns include **Adare**, **Killarney**, **Limerick** and **Waterford**, all of which have many fine old buildings, while Glenbeigh, **Kenmare** and **Lismore** serve as recreational centers.

THE WEST COAST

Historic **Galway** makes an ideal base for touring this lake-studded region on the shores of the Atlantic. The 200-meter (700-foot) **Cliffs of Moher**, the limestone-dominated Burren and mountainous Connemara, all make for rewarding excursions. And some 50 kilometers (30 miles) from Galway are the **Aran Islands**, the setting for some ancient ruins and whose residents still maintain a largely traditional way of life.

USEFUL EXPRESSIONS IN IRISH

Bord Fáilte (Irish Tourist Board) – pronounced *bord fawlcha*
Céad míle fáilte ("a hundred thousand welcomes") – *kay-d mille fawlcha*
céilídh (Irish dance night) – *kaylee*
Gaeltacht (Irish-speaking region) – pronounced *gale-tackt*
Garda Síochána (police) – *gawrda shee-kawnah*
poteen (alcohol distilled from potatoes, illegal and often dangerous) – *potcheen*
sláinte (cheers, good health) – *slawn-cha*
slán (good-bye) – *slawn*
Taoiseach (Prime Minister) – *teeshock*
uisce beatha (whiskey, literally "water of life") – *ishka baha*
Mná means women and **Fir** means men on public restrooms.

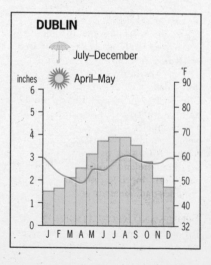

DUBLIN

🌂 July–December

inches   ☀ April–May   °F

PLACES OF INTEREST

▲ DUBLIN ★

COUNTY DUBLIN *pop. 1,025,300*

Dublin, the capital of the Republic of Ireland, has one of the loveliest settings in Europe. On Dublin Bay, the "Town of the Hurdle Ford" – *Baile Atha Cliath* in Gaelic – is sheltered on the north by the rocky mass of Howth Head. The Liffey River cuts through the city and is crossed by many picturesque bridges. The name Dublin is derived from the Gaelic word for black pool: *dubhlinn*.

First mentioned by the great map-maker Ptolemy in 140 AD, Dublin claims a long and turbulent history. Following centuries of invasions by Vikings, Normans and English, the city became a center of agitation for Irish independence, which culminated in the Easter Rising of 1916, when the Irish Volunteers seized the General Post Office. Although this rebellion was crushed, Dublin became the storm center for the violent struggles that followed. Today, an elected city council and the city manager make up Dublin Corporation, which administers the city.

Dublin has produced some of the world's greatest literary figures. Most notably, the city was the home of James Joyce, whose writings are mostly based in the city of his birth. Also born in Dublin were Oscar Wilde, who attended Trinity College, and Jonathan Swift, who served as Dean of St. Patrick's Cathedral. George Bernard Shaw was born at No. 33 Synge Street in 1856.

Compact Dublin combines age-old charm with modern advantages. With the exception of two cathedrals and a few ancient churches, most of the architecture dates from the 18th century, when the city enjoyed special prominence. Also of interest are the Georgian houses that line Merrion Square. American visitors are especially interested in Leinster House and Dublin Castle: the Irish-born architect of the White House, James Hoban, borroed many of its features from these buildings.

However, perhaps the most outstanding feature of Dublin is the pub, where visitors can relax over a mug of hearty Irish brew. Many pubs attract artists, writers, actors and students. Singing pubs are loud and friendly.

Dublin offers many recreational facilities. There are fine parks, including attractive St. Stephen's Green and Phoenix Park. The National Botanic Gardens are also of interest. Hunting, fishing, golfing, horse racing and greyhound racing are popular. There are several bowling greens. Many fine beaches are near by; Malahide, 14.5 kilometers (9 miles) north, and Killiney, 16 kilometers (10 miles) south, are popular with Dubliners. Powerscourt Estate, about 19 kilometers (12 miles) from Dublin in Enniskerry (see p.399), is also a popular excursion.

Annual events include the St. Patrick's Day Parade and related festivities on March 17; the world-renowned Dublin Horse Show in August; and the Theatre Festival in October.

ABBEY THEATRE (The National Theatre) (386 B3), Lower Abbey Street, presents plays by the giants of Irish literature.

REPUBLIC OF IRELAND

William Butler Yeats and Augusta Lady Gregory were instrumental in its founding in 1904, three years after the birth of the Irish literary theater. The Peacock Theatre annex offers lunchtime and evening performances.

BANK OF IRELAND (Old Parliament House) (386 B3), College Green, designed to house the Irish Parliament, it was made redundant by the 1800 Act of Union.

CHESTER BEATTY LIBRARY AND GALLERY OF ORIENTAL ART, 20 Shrewsbury Road, Ballsbridge, contains a rare collection of Islamic manuscripts and miniatures, oriental paintings, western prints, rare books and biblical papyri donated to the city by Irish-American mining engineer Sir Alfred Chester Beatty.

CHRIST CHURCH CATHEDRAL (386 A3), Lord Edward Street near Winetavern Street, was founded in 1038 by Sitric Silkenbeard, the first Viking Christian King of Dublin. Largely rebuilt since then, it retains its ancient crypt.

CUSTOM HOUSE (386 C3), near the junction of Gardiner Street Lower and

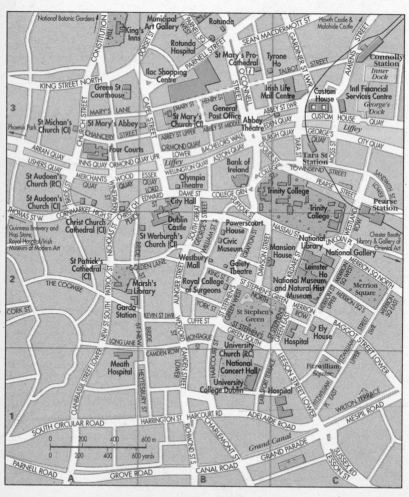

Amiens, was built in 1791 and is one of Dublin's finest buildings. Gutted by fire in 1921, it was restored and is still in use.

DUBLIN CASTLE (386 B2), with two towers and a partial wall, is the city's most outstanding legacy of the Middle Ages. Of interest are the Record Tower, state apartments, Church of the Most Holy Trinity, and remains of Norman and Viking defenses. The inauguration of the President of Ireland and related ceremonies are held in St. Patrick's Hall.

DUBLIN CIVIC MUSEUM (386 B2), 58 South William Street, has old maps, pictures, models and archeological finds which trace the city's history from Viking times.

DUBLIN NATURAL HISTORY MUSEUM, (386 C2) Upper Merrion Street, displays a comprehensive collection of native Irish species and exotic animals.

DUBLIN'S WRITERS MUSEUM, 18–19 Parnell Square North, in two restored 18th-century buildings, records Dublin's rich literary heritage from the 8th-century *Book of Kells* to the present.

FOUR COURTS (386 A3), Inns Quay beside the river, houses the Irish Law Courts. Built in 1785 and damaged in 1922 during the Civil War, it has been restored.

GENERAL POST OFFICE (386 B3), O'Connell Street, was the headquarters of the Irish Volunteers during the Easter Rising of 1916. The 1818 structure was partially destroyed by fire but later rebuilt. A plaque and statue commemorate the Easter Rising.

GUINNESS BREWERY, at St. James Gate, was founded in 1759. Its original 9,000-year lease will not require renewal for quite some time! One of the largest breweries in the world, it produces beer from the original yeast strains.

GUINNESS HOP STORE, Crane Street, was established in 1876 as a hop store and

---

BILLY-IN-THE-BOWL

The mid-18th century was a worrying time for residents of Stoneybatter in north-west Dublin. Billy-in-the-Bowl was born with no legs, but by sitting in an iron bowl and propelling himself with his arms, he was fully able to get around. Unfortunately, he used his well-developed upper body strength to seize sympathetic passers-by and strangle them for their purses. Once the long arm of the law finally caught up with him, he was sentenced to "as much hard labor as his condition would allow" for the rest of his days.

---

now houses "The World of Guinness" exhibition. The history of the well-known beer is depicted through an exhibition. The Cooperage displays cooper's tools and oak casks; visitors can also see the Transport Gallery or taste Guinness beer at the Sample Bar.

HOWTH CASTLE, is 14.5 kilometers (9 miles) north east, and is known for its attractive gardens and rhododendron walk, at its floral best in May and June.

HUGH LANE MUNICIPAL GALLERY, Parnell Square, occupies Charlemont House, a Georgian mansion. Inside are collections of Irish works and art from the modern French and British schools.

LEINSTER HOUSE (386 C2), Kildare Street, is a Georgian mansion built for the Duke of Leinster in 1745. The Dáil (lower house) and Seanad (senate) of the Irish Parliament now convene here.

MALAHIDE CASTLE, is 13 kilometers (8 miles) north east, and one of Ireland's oldest castles (12th century). Tours pass Irish period furniture and historical Irish portrait collections. Additional paintings from the National Gallery depict Irish life during the last few centuries.

MANSION HOUSE (386 C2), Dawson Street, residence of the lord mayors of Dublin since 1715, saw the signing of the 1919 Irish declaration of independence and the 1921 Anglo-Irish truce.

NATIONAL BOTANIC GARDENS, are located 4 kilometers (2½ miles) north at Glasnevin, encompassing 20 hectares (50 acres) of grounds planted with common and uncommon varieties of flowers, shrubs and trees.

NATIONAL GALLERY OF IRELAND (386 C2) ★, Merrion Square, contains the work of masters of most European schools, including Rembrandt, El Greco, Goya, Sir J. Reynolds and Degas. Portraits of Irish national figures line the staircase.

GUINNESS

Dublin in 1759 saw one Arthur Guinness establish a brewery where he began to experiment with a beverage from London. This brew was made with roasted barley and named "Porter" after its popularity with the Covent Garden porters. Forty years later all production efforts were concentrated on this distinctive drink, and in the early 1800s an even stronger, extra stout beer was produced. It was this rich, black liquid with a creamy head that soon gained world renown.

NATIONAL MUSEUM (386 C2) ★, Kildare. Street, houses the Treasury with masterpieces of Celtic and medieval metalwork, including the Tara Brooch and the Ardagh Chalice (both 8th century), and the 12th-century Cross of Cong. Other displays illustrate Viking and Norman times, the 1916 Easter Rising and the Civil War.

PHOENIX PARK ★ covers 690 hectares (1,700 acres) in the west of Dublin. Within it are the People's Gardens, the Zoological Gardens, the Magazine Fort, and the residences of the President of Ireland and the U.S. ambassador.

Zoological Gardens were founded in 1830 and today exhibit many species of birds and animals.

ROYAL HOSPITAL/IRISH MUSEUM OF MODERN ART, Military Road, Kilmainham, is one of the finest 17th-century buildings in Ireland. The museum includes international and Irish art of the 20th century.

ST. AUDOEN'S CHURCH (386 A3), High Street, is the oldest parish church in Dublin (12th century), with three of the oldest bells cast in 1423. Near by is the 1215 St. Audoen's Arch, the only surviving gate in the city's walls.

ST. MARY'S PRO-CATHEDRAL (386 B3), Marlborough Street, was designed by exiled patriot John Sweetman and built 1815–25. The famous Palestrina Choir sings Latin mass on Sundays at 11am.

ST. PATRICK'S CATHEDRAL (386 A2), Patrick Street, was founded in 1190 and restored in the 19th century. Its interior is impressive. Jonathan Swift, dean 1713–45 and author of *Gulliver's Travels*, is buried in this Protestant cathedral.

TRINITY COLLEGE (386 C3) ★, on College Green, has educated many prominent persons. Although Queen Elizabeth I granted a charter to a group of Dubliners in 1591, no structures from that period remain. Most of the present buildings were erected in the 18th century; the Palladian façade was added in 1759. The oldest building is the red-brick Rubrics.

College Library, completed in 1732, has an impressive collection of books and manuscripts. The brilliantly illuminated 8th-century *Book of Kells*, formerly kept at the Monastery of Kells in County Meath, is on display.

ADARE (381 B2)
COUNTY LIMERICK *pop. 800*
Adare is an enchanting little village with half-timbered houses, thatch-roofed

REPUBLIC OF IRELAND

cottages, good hunting and fishing and interesting ecclesiastical ruins.

BLACK ABBEY, north east of Adare, is a 14th-century Augustinian friary noted for its west window, cornice, Tudor rose, tower and 15th-century cloister.

WHITE MONASTERY of Trinitarian monks of the Order for the Redemption of Christian Captives is the only known house of this order in Ireland. The monastery was founded in 1230 and enlarged 42 years later.

ARAN ISLANDS (381 A2) ★
COUNTY GALWAY *pop. 1,500*
The three main islands that make up Aran lie 48 kilometers (30 miles) west of Galway, connected by ferry services and regular flights. The islanders are resourceful subsistence farmers, working "made" ground of sand and seaweed in a rugged and treeless land.

Some residents, especially those on the island of Inishmaan, continue to spin and weave their own clothing. Islanders still use the *currach*, a small boat of ancient design made of tarred canvas stretched over a wicker frame.

The three islands have ruins of ancient forts, monasteries and churches. Foremost among several prehistoric sites is Dun Aengus on Inishmore, a semicircular fort built at the edge of a 90-meter (300-foot) cliff. Another of Inishmore's prehistoric forts is well-preserved Dun Eochaill near the village of Oghil. Ninth-century Teampall Bheanain is said to be the world's smallest church: it measures less than 3.5 meters (11 feet) in length. On Inishmaan is Dun Conor, a well-preserved stone fort, and the cottage in which the writer J. M. Synge lived during his stay on the islands. Inisheer, the smallest of the islands, has a ruined castle inside a prehistoric fort.

ARKLOW (381 C2)
COUNTY WICKLOW *pop. 8,000*
Arklow is at the mouth of the Avoca River. In days past, the community was a busy shipping and fishing center; today it is one of the foremost seaside resorts on the eastern coast. It has sandy beaches and facilities for golf, tennis, boating, fishing and shooting. In town there is a memorial to Father Michael Murphy, who led a local rebellion that was crushed by the British in 1798.

ATHLONE (381 B2)
COUNTY WESTMEATH *pop. 9,500*
Athlone, on the Shannon River near Lough Ree, is a point of departure for river excursions. The great tenor John McCormack was born here in 1884, and the museum in the town's 13th-century Anglo-Norman castle documents his life.

BALLINA (381 A3)
COUNTY MAYO *pop. 6,900*
Ballina lies on the Moy River near loughs Conn and Cullin. The town is a golfing and angling center; it also offers boating, swimming, shooting, mountain climbing and trekking. The Ballina (Moy) Salmon Festival is held in July.

To the east rise the long ridges of the Ox Mountains, site of the country's peat bogs, one of the area's major fuel sources. Rosserk Abbey, 8 kilometers (5 miles) north of Ballina, is a well-preserved 15th-century Franciscan friary.

BALLINASLOE (381 B2)
COUNTY GALWAY *pop. 6,500*
Dating from before the 12th century, Ballinasloe is a thriving market town known for its livestock fairs. Ireland's "travellers" elect their "king" at the renowned Ballinasloe Horse Fair in October. Sights include ruined churches and castles, and the battlefield of Aughrim, where in 1691 Irish forces fought for the Stuarts against William of Orange. A museum has articles from the battle and archeological items.

BALLYNAHINCH LAKE (381 A2)
COUNTY GALWAY
Ballynahinch Lake, a well-known angling center in Connemara, offers pleasant mountain and lake scenery.

CLONFERT ABBEY, founded in the 6th century by St. Brendan "the Navigator," lies 10 kilometres (6 miles) south. The ruins and rebuilt edifices include an intact Irish Romanesque doorway.

BANTRY (381 A1)
COUNTY CORK *pop. 2,900*
Bantry is a quaint town on Bantry Bay, which was the site of French naval invasions in the 17th and 18th centuries. Bay fishing offers rewarding catches.

BANTRY HOUSE, south west, is a Georgian mansion set in terraced Italianate gardens overlooking the bay. The house is richly furnished with art and antiques, including a tapestry made for Marie Antoinette. The French Armada Exhibition Center, housed in a renovated courtyard, relates the history of the failed French invasion led by Irish rebel Wolfe Tone in 1796.

BLARNEY (381 B1)
COUNTY CORK *pop. 2,000*
BLARNEY CASTLE AND GARDENS is home to the Blarney Stone, famed for the eloquence it is said to impart to those who kiss it. The stone is in the upper tower of the castle, and the visitor, held by the feet, must lean backwards down a shaft to receive the gift of the gab.

BUNDORAN (381 B3)
COUNTY DONEGAL *pop. 1,600*
One of Ireland's principal coastal resorts, Bundoran is on the southern shore of Donegal Bay framed by the Sligo Leitrim Mountains. It is believed that the first recorded history of Ireland was compiled in Bundrowes, just west of town, by the Abbot of Donegal and three other scholar-friars, who labored 1630–6 to chronicle the 4,500 previous years. Their effort is called the *Annals of the Four Masters*.

THE FOUR MASTERS MEMORIAL, situated to the north in Donegal, is a 7.5-meter (25-foot) obelisk inscribed with the names of the four scholastic monks known as the Four Masters: Michael O'Clery, Peregrine O'Clery, Peregrine Duignan and Fearfeasa O'Mulconry.

BUNRATTY (381 B2)
COUNTY CLARE
The village of Bunratty is known for its castle and Bunratty Folk Park. The latter contains farmhouses and craft shops re-erected and furnished to reflect 19th-century rural Irish life.

BUNRATTY CASTLE, dating from the mid-15th century, is Ireland's most complete medieval castle. It houses the Lord Gort Collection of furniture, objects of art, and paintings and tapestries dating from before 1650. The castle hosts "medieval banquets," which come complete with serving wenches.

CAHIR (381 B1)
COUNTY TIPPERARY *pop. 2,100*
A hunting and fishing center, Cahir gets its name from the *caher*, or stone fort, that once was present. The town is a good starting point for touring the Galtee Mountains.

CAHIR CASTLE, on an island in the Suir River, is one of Ireland's best-preserved castles. It dates mainly from the 15th century, although its oldest parts were built in 1164. The fully restored structure has two courts, a massive square, a keep and a great hall.

CASHEL (381 B2) ★
COUNTY TIPPERARY *pop. 2,500*
ROCK OF CASHEL, a 60-meter (200-foot) hill, was the seat of the Munster kings from 370 to 1101 AD. Legend states that the devil took a bite from the Slieve Bloom Mountains (leaving a gap known as the Devil's Bit) and spat forth this limestone outcrop when surprised by St. Patrick. The Rock is crowned by a number of impressive medieval buildings, the oldest being the 27-meter (90-foot) Round Tower, dating from the 10th century. Cormac's Chapel, begun in 1127, is a fine example of Irish Romanesque

architecture. The roofless 13th-century cathedral is the largest building on the summit. A replica of a 12th-century high cross stands at the spot where St. Patrick baptized King Aengus, Ireland's first Christian king, in the 5th century. The original cross is in the museum in the 15th-century Hall of the Vicars.

CASTLETOWN HOUSE ★
COUNTY KILDARE

Situated at Celbridge, 6.5 kilometers (4 miles) west of Lucan, this is considered by many to be Ireland's finest Georgian country house. Designed in the Palladian style by Italian architect Alessandro Galilei in 1722, the now-restored house contains excellent plasterwork by the Francini brothers, Irish furniture and paintings of the period, the Pompeian Long Gallery with its Venetian chandeliers, and an 18th-century print room.

CAVAN (381 B3)
COUNTY CAVAN pop. 3,300

Cavan is the capital of its county. In ancient times it was the territory of the O'Reillys, rulers of East Breany; many historic sites are connected with them. A belfry tower from the 14th-century Franciscan friary still stands. Other places of interest include a crystal factory and a local folk museum.

CEANANNUS MÓR (KELLS) (381 C3)
COUNTY MEATH pop. 3,700

Originating as a 6th-century monastic settlement founded by St. Columcille, Ceanannus Mór (Gaelic for Kells) is today a market town. The Book of Kells, an 8th-century manuscript, is an heirloom of the town's monastery. It is now in the Trinity College Library in Dublin (see p.388), but a facsimile is in the town's St. Columba's Church.

The round tower in the Church of Ireland churchyard is a fine example of this type of structure, with its five windows pointing to the five ancient roads leading into town. South Cross, near the round tower, is the most interesting of Ceanannus Mór's five high crosses. Erected about the 9th century, it is ornately sculptured. Market Cross, used as a gallows in 1798, is in the town center.

CLIFDEN (381 A2)
COUNTY GALWAY pop. 800

Clifden, the main town of the Connemara region, overlooks Ardbear Bay and is an excellent departure point for excursions. Good bathing, riding, tennis and fishing can be enjoyed. The Connemara Pony Show is in mid-August.

CLIFFS OF MOHER (381 A2) ★
COUNTY CLARE

These awe-inspiring sheer cliffs, which stretch for 8 kilometers (5 miles) along the coast of Clare, are home to a variety of sea birds. At the north-east end, the cliffs' highest point, you will find O'Brien's Tower, a folly built by 19th-century M.P. Sir Cornelius O'Brien. The nearby visitor center offers displays on local history, legends, birdlife and geology. Not far away is Spanish Point, where the Spanish Armada foundered in 1588.

CLONMACNOIS (381 B2) ★
COUNTY OFFALY

Founded by St. Ciaran in 545 AD, the monastic city of Clonmacnois flourished as a religious and scholastic center until its destruction in the 16th century.

Many of the country's kings, saints and scholars are buried here, including St. Ciaran and the last High King of Ireland.

Standing by a bend of the Shannon River, the ruins of Clonmacnois include two round towers, eight churches and a cathedral; there are also many carved gravestones and several of Ireland's famed high crosses, decorated with biblical scenes interlaced with imaginary beasts. O'Rourke's Tower, dating from 964 AD, is 18 meters (60 feet) high.

CLONMEL (381 B1)
COUNTY TIPPERARY pop. 12,400

Walled Clonmel is on the Suir River, shadowed by the Comeragh Mountains.

REPUBLIC OF IRELAND

The birthplace of 18th-century novelist Laurence Sterne, author of *Tristram Shandy*, Clonmel has preserved several interesting Georgian buildings, including the classical courthouse. The town is the site of the National Breeders Stakes', which attract greyhound fanciers from March to April.

COBH (381 B1)
COUNTY CORK *pop. 8,400*

Cobh, a seaport on Great Island, was the point of departure for many Irish emigrants bound for the New World, who left the port in the dreaded "coffin ships." Many of the great transatlantic liners also berthed here, including the ill-fated *Titanic* and *Lusitania*. Cobh's past is vividly re-created in the Queenstown Project heritage center.

THE SINKING OF THE *LUSITANIA*

Sailing from New York to Liverpool during World War I, a civilian ship called the *Lusitania* was sunk off Cobh. Naturally, the Germans were blamed, but a recent allegation suggests the Allies contrived and carried out the attack to persuade the U.S. to enter the war. Suspicion and casualties were increased by the unusual absence of patroling British warships, and by the fact that the German government had placed advertisements in New York papers warning passengers not to take the sailing. Some passengers survived but nearly 1,200 died.

CATHEDRAL OF ST. COLMAN, a fine Victorian high-Gothic structure, stands on the hilltop dominating the town. Designed by Augustus Pugin in 1868, it is ornately decorated with blue granite. The cemetery contains the graves of writers John Tobin and the Rev. Charles Wolfe, as well as many victims of the 1915 *Lusitania* tragedy.

CONG (381 A2)
COUNTY MAYO *pop. 200*

Cong lies on a neck of land between Lough Mask and Lough Corrib. Cong Abbey, dating from the 12th century, was an important monastic center for over 700 years. Near by are numerous stone caves formed by a subterranean river connecting the two lakes.

COOLE PARK (381 B2)
COUNTY GALWAY

The dramatist Augusta Lady Gregory entertained William Butler Yeats and Edward Martyn in Gort at Coole House, where plans for Dublin's 1904 Abbey Theatre were formulated. Although the house was demolished during the 1930s, the grounds of the estate have survived, as has the "autograph tree," a copper beech carved with the initials of such famous visitors as Yeats, George Bernard Shaw and George Russell.

▲ CORK (381 B1)
COUNTY CORK *pop. 410,400*

Cork, Ireland's third largest city, lies on the Lee River at the landward end of a fine harbor. The city has main avenues lined with boutiques and department stores, as well as winding cobblestone streets, little shops and stalls. Cork is also a center from which to tour the south-west coast of Ireland.

CORK PUBLIC MUSEUM, the city's history is illustrated in this Georgian mansion in Fitzgerald Park, north of the University.

CRAWFORD MUNICIPAL ART GALLERY, Emmet Place, is housed in the former Georgian Custom House; its collections include 18th- and 19th-century paintings, sculpture, silver and stained glass.

ST. ANNE'S OF SHANDON, Church Street, was built 1722–6 and is famed for its bells, immortalized in the lines of the ballad: "...the bells of Shandon that sound so grand on the pleasant waters of the River Lee." Visitors can ring the carillon daily.

ST. FIN BARRE'S CATHEDRAL, Bishop Street, stands on a 1,300-year-old ecclesiastical site. Built in Gothic-revival style, the 1870 cathedral features a 75-meter (240-foot) tower, figures from the parable of the Wise and Foolish Virgins, mosaic work, and a wrought-iron baptismal font.

UNIVERSITY COLLEGE is one of the constituent colleges of the National University of Ireland, headquartered in Dublin. The college's predominately Tudor Gothic buildings were erected in the 19th century. The library has a collection of early printed books, stones inscribed with ogham (an early writing form), and geological and natural history exhibits. Honan Chapel is 12th-century Hiberno-Romanesque in style.

THE PAPER

The first edition of the *Cork Examiner* appeared in August, 1841, just before the Potato Famine. As most of the population of Cork were too poor to buy papers, and many were illiterate anyway, it seemed a crazy venture. However, through those harrowing times and others, "the paper" – as it is known locally – has never lost a single day's printing. As a distinguished and dignified piece of journalism, Cork's daily newspaper seems to epitomize the independent spirit of the city.

CRAGGAUNOWEN (381 B2) ★
COUNTY CLARE

The Craggaunowen Project, 10 kilometers (6 miles) south east of Ennis in County Clare, contains a full-scale reconstruction of a *crannóg*, a Bronze Age lake dwelling. The brainchild of art historian and archeologist John Hunt, the project includes a reconstructed ring fort and replicas of furniture and tools and utensils. Also displayed is the *Brendan*, a replica of the leather boat used, according to tradition, by St. Brendan "the Navigator" in the 6th century.

DROGHEDA (381 C3)
COUNTY LOUTH *pop. 23,600*

Drogheda, a picturesque port on the Irish Sea, has borne the impact of several invasions. It is a good point for exploring the Boyne Valley, where Protestant William of Orange defeated Catholic James Stuart in 1690. The well-marked battlefield can be toured.

Near Drogheda are several important prehistoric and monastic sites, including the famous Newgrange burial cairn and Mellifont Abbey.

ST. LAURENCE'S GATE is the only remaining portal in Drogheda's town walls. The 13th-century gate is considered to be one of the best preserved in the country.

DUNDALK (381 C3)
COUNTY LOUTH *pop. 29,100*

Dundalk, the capital of County Louth, has weathered the passing of Celtic, Norman, Jacobite and Williamite armies. Its early 19th-century courthouse and town hall are striking; an immense old windmill is an impressive landmark. South of Dundalk is the Proleek Dolmen megalithic tomb. Recreational pursuits include golf, tennis, fishing, hunting and horse racing.

DUNGANSTOWN (381 C1)
COUNTY WEXFORD

The village of Dunganstown is the ancestral home of the Kennedy family: John F. Kennedy's great-grandfather was born in a cottage here. Near by, at Slieve Coillte, is the John Fitzgerald Kennedy Memorial Park, financed by the Irish government and Irish-American societies. The 252-hectare (623-acre) park is a vast arboretum with around 5,000 varieties of trees and shrubs.

DUN LAOGHAIRE (381 C2)
COUNTY DUBLIN *pop. 54,500*

Dun Laoghaire (pronounced *dun-LEARy*), a landing point for ferries from

Britain, is a popular coastal resort 13 kilometers (8 miles) south east of the capital. The 100-hectare (250-acre) harbor, with its massive piers, took 50 years to build. James Joyce once lived south west of the city at Sandycove.

JAMES JOYCE TOWER, built by the British in 1804 as a defence against a possible invasion by Napoleon, has walls 2.5 meters (8 feet) thick and an original entrance 3 meters (10 feet) above the ground, formerly reached by rope ladder.

In 1904 the tower was the temporary home of James Joyce, who depicted this setting in the opening scene of *Ulysses*. The structure is now a museum devoted to the author.

PINK TROUT

You may see the odd roadside sign depicting a fish, and the legend "Save the Sea Trout." These are due to local concerns about fish-farming and effects on the wild species. One theory is that sea lice from the farmed fish are spreading into wild shoals and wiping them out. However, one thing you can be sure of is that the fish on your plate is more likely to have been fed pink-tinted food pellets than swum free.

ENNIS (381 B2)
CLARE *pop. 6,200*
Ennis, the chief town of County Clare, is an excellent center for excursions to nearby castles and abbeys. Ennis Abbey, founded in 1241, has some 14th-century sculptures. Quin Abbey, dating from 1402, lies 10 kilometers (6 miles) east.

GALWAY (381 A2)
GALWAY *pop. 37,800*
Galway, the capital of County Galway, was conquered by the Normans in the 13th century. The city is an excellent starting point for exploring the west coast, including the Connemara region, Lough Corrib and the Aran Islands.

There are fine resorts and beaches at nearby Salthill.

The Galway Races in July/August and the Galway Oyster Festival in September attract many visitors. The Blessing of the Sea ceremony in August signals the start of the herring season.

COLLEGIATE CHURCH OF ST. NICHOLAS was built by Norman settlers in 1320. Local legend has it that Christopher Columbus heard mass here before he set off on his voyage to the New World.

JOHN FITZGERALD KENNEDY MEMORIAL PARK, in the center of Eyre Square, commemorates the U.S. president and his visit to the city in 1963.

LYNCH'S CASTLE is a well-preserved example of a 16th-century merchant's house and has a mullioned façade.

SALMON WEIR BRIDGE is the place to watch shoals of salmon as they make their way upstream to spawn from mid-April to early July.

SPANISH ARCH CIVIC MUSEUM, in the south-west quarter, dates from the days when Spain and Ireland had trading ties. Galway City Museum at the arch is devoted to the city's history.

UNIVERSITY COLLEGE is one of the constituent colleges of the National University of Ireland. The library contains old city records and rare books.

GLENDALOUGH (381 C2)
COUNTY WICKLOW
In the 6th century, St. Kevin came to the wild, beautiful Vale of Glendalough to live the life of a hermit. After he built a monastery in Glendalough, the region became a prominent center of learning. Besides the sites connected with the saint, there are many places of interest dating from the 11th and 12th centuries.

SAINT KEVIN'S KITCHEN, dating from the 6th century, is a well-preserved ruin of an early Irish barrel-vaulted oratory. Many of the slabs bear interesting decorations and inscriptions.

HILL OF TARA (381 C2)
COUNTY MEATH

The Hill of Tara, 8 kilometers (5 miles) north east of Trim, is the site of what was once the religious and cultural capital of pre-Christian Ireland. Dating from 2000 BC, the hill was the seat of the High Kings until 1022. It supposedly witnessed St. Patrick's lighting of the Paschal fire on Easter, 433 AD. Among the remains are the Mound of Hostages, a passage grave in which the skeleton of a boy wearing a necklace of bronze, amber and jet was found, and a pillar stone thought to be the Coronation Stone of Kings.

KENMARE (381 A1)
COUNTY KERRY pop. 1,100

Kenmare, on the Ring of Kerry, is at the head of Kenmare Bay.

Excellent opportunities for ocean and freshwater fishing, swimming and boating are available, as are hiking, mountain climbing, pony-trekking, horseback riding, golf and tennis. Specialties for shoppers are the woolens produced by local weavers.

KILDARE (381 C2)
COUNTY KILDARE pop. 4,200

A center of the Irish horse breeding and training industry, Kildare dates from 470 AD, when St. Brigid founded a double monastery here.

IRISH NATIONAL STUD (Tully Estate), situated 1.6 kilometer (1 mile) east, was set up in 1902 by Colonel William Hall and has since produced many prominent racehorses. Visitors can see the horses being exercised and groomed
Irish Horse Museum traces the history of the horse in Ireland. Among the displays is the skeleton of steeplechaser Arkle.
Japanese Gardens, in the grounds, were created by the Japanese gardener Eida and his son Minoru between 1906 and 1910. Their design symbolically portrays man's progress from birth to eternity.

ST. BRIGID'S CATHEDRAL, a 19th-century restoration of the original 1223 structure, has interesting antiquities.

KILKENNY (381 B2) ★
COUNTY KILKENNY pop. 9,500

A pre-Norman town on the Nore River, Kilkenny combines a distinctive old-world atmosphere with modern features. Dominating the city from its highest point is St. Mary's Cathedral, an early Gothic-revival edifice dating from 1843.

DUNMORE CAVE, is 11 kilometers (7 miles) north, and one of the finest limestone caves in Ireland; its "Market Cross" stalagmite is more than 6 meters (20 feet) high. The bones of over 40 people were found here; they are thought to have died after seeking refuge from a Viking attack.

JERPOINT ABBEY, south east near Thomastown, is a ruined Gothic Cistercian abbey with a 12th-century Romanesque nave. The cloisters are decorated with human figures, and the church contains medieval tomb effigies.

KILKENNY CASTLE was the ancestral stronghold of the Butler family until this century. The castle was originally a 12th-century Norman fortress, but most of its present structure dates from the early 19th century. The hammer-beamed picture gallery, lined with portraits, is impressive. The castle stables house the Kilkenny Design Workshops, where local artists produce a range of high-quality craft items.

KILKENNY COLLEGE is the 200-year-old successor to St. John's College, where William Congreve, George Farquhar, Jonathan Swift, John Banim and George Berkeley studied.

KYTELER'S INN is the restored medieval home of Dame Alice Kyteler, who was

REPUBLIC OF IRELAND

condemned as a witch and charged with killing four husbands in 1324. She escaped to Scotland, leaving her poor maid to take her place at the stake.

ROTHE HOUSE, constructed in 1594, is an excellent example of Tudor architecture. It contains a costume gallery, a museum and a library.

ST. CANICE'S CATHEDRAL occupies the site of an earlier church whose round tower still stands. Inside the cathedral are 16th-century sepulchral monuments. St. Canice's Library contains 3,000 volumes from the 16th and 17th centuries.

SHEE ALMS HOUSE, Rose Inn Street, built in the late 16th century, now houses City Scope, a *son et lumière* show featuring a three-dimensional scale model of 17th-century Kilkenny, plus the tourist information office.

KILLARNEY (381 A1)
COUNTY KERRY *pop. 7,700*
The bustling market town of Killarney is one of Ireland's most popular tourist spots. The surrounding countryside is renowned for its scenery, including the three lakes of Killarney south of the town. The lakes' many islands, especially Innisfallen with its 7th-century abbey ruins, are favorite destinations by boat. Killarney is a good starting point for a drive along the Ring of Kerry, one of Europe's finest coastal drives.

The trip to the Gap of Dunloe, traditionally reached by pony, is equally rewarding. Here is some of the area's most beautiful scenery: Macgillycuddy's Reeks, Ireland's highest mountains; Tomies and Purple mountains; Cummeenduff, also called Black Valley; and Upper Lake, with its wooded crags of Eagle's Nest. The descent from the gap, 242 meters (795 feet) above sea-level, can also be accomplished by boat, leaving Upper Lake via the "Coleman's Eye" channel and "Long Range" strait, shooting the rapids at Old Weir Bridge and finishing at Ross Castle. Boatmen

demonstrate a bugle's echo against the great crag of Eagle's Nest.

CATHEDRAL OF ST. MARY, New Street, was built in 1846 under the direction of noted English architect Augustus Pugin. The limestone cruciform church has a massive stone tower.

KILLARNEY NATIONAL PARK, the former Muckross Estate, is 4 kilometers (2½ miles) south. Donated to the Irish government by its American owners, the 4,450-hectare (11,000-acre) park incorporates most of the county's lake district.
Muckross Abbey, on the eastern shore of Lough Leane, suffered the depredations of Cromwell's troops, who left it roofless in 1652. The 15th-century Franciscan abbey remains well preserved.
Muckross House, the 19th-century neo-Tudor mansion of this former private estate, has a separate entrance for motorists 5.5 kilometers (3½ miles) south of Killarney off N71. It now contains a museum of Kerry folklore; in the basement craft center, a weaver, blacksmith and potter demonstrate their trades. The grounds include rhododendrons, azaleas and a rock garden.

ROSS CASTLE is 2.5 kilometers (1½ miles) south west, overlooking Lough Leane. This 14th-century Irish fort figured prominently in the Cromwellian Wars. The castle is closed to the public, but boat rentals are available for lake trips.

KILLORGLIN (381 A1)
COUNTY KERRY *pop. 1,300*
The small fishing town of Killorglin is known for its annual three-day Puck Fair in August. The festivities include a goat named Puck being crowned "king" of the town in a colorful traditional ceremony.

KINSALE (381 B1) ★
COUNTY CORK *pop. 1,800*
Overlooking the winding estuary of the Bandon River, Kinsale has an old-world appearance with its narrow streets, ruins and Georgian houses. The local museum,

housed in the town's Dutch-style 17th-century courthouse, contains exhibits related to the sinking of the *Lusitania*. Also of interest are the 12th-century Norman St. Multose Church; remains of the 1314 Carmelite friary; Desmond Castle, which held French prisoners during the Napoleonic War; and star-shaped Charles Fort (1677).

The town, famed for its restaurants, hosts an international Gourmet Festival in the first week of October, attracting discerning diners from around the world.

Excursions can be made to the Old Head of Kinsale, site of the 1915 sinking of the *Lusitania* (see *Cobh* p.392), and to Ballinspittle, where excavations have indicated that the Ballycatten Ring Fort dates from about 600 AD.

LIMERICK (381 B2)
COUNTY LIMERICK *pop. 60,700*
Limerick is the gateway to the Shannon Valley and the excellent fishing area of Lough Derg. The city dates from the 9th century AD, when the Danes made it a base. As a seat of the kings of Munster, it suffered many attacks during the Middle Ages. The nickname "City of the Violated Treaty" stems from forgotten promises of religious tolerance following the Williamite victory over the Jacobites in Limerick in 1691. The Treaty Stone, on which the treaty is said to have been signed, is on a pedestal on the west side of Thomond Bridge.

Portions of original city walls and old gateways recall those turbulent days; Georgian buildings embellish the modern side of Limerick. St. John's Square, constructed about 1751, is noteworthy for its unusual layout and architecture.

The ruins of Mungret, a 7th-century monastery is 5 kilometers (3 miles) from Limerick on the coast road.

GOOD SHEPHERD CONVENT, Good Shepherd Lane, is where Limerick lace is made. Visitors can view the process.

HUNT MUSEUM is in the University of Limerick, 5 kilometers (3 miles) from Limerick. Among the treasures in its collection of Celtic and medieval antiquities are the Antrim Cross and a Bronze Age shield.

KING JOHN'S CASTLE, east side of Thomond Bridge, is a 13th-century Norman castle marked by an imposing twin-towered gatehouse and battle-scarred walls. The castle's history is explored in the visitor center, where archeological finds are also displayed.

ST. JOHN'S CATHEDRAL is a 19th-century Gothic structure with a spire that rises 85 meters (280 feet). Of interest are a Madonna by Benzoni and the statue of Patrick Sarsfield, who was a hero of the 1690–1 siege.

ST. MARY'S CATHEDRAL was originally built as a palace in the 12th century. Among its most interesting features are the high tower, Romanesque doorway, 15th-century choir stalls and ornately carved 15th-century misericords. In summer, the cathedral is the setting for a *son et lumière* show highlighting episodes from the city's history.

ST. SAVIOUR'S, a 19th-century Dominican church, houses many treasures, including a 17th-century statue of Our Lady thought to have been brought from Flanders by Patrick Sarsfield, the cross of a 17th-century bishop, the 1639 Kilmallock Dominican Chalice, the 1647 Sarsfield Chalice and a 1951 fresco by Father Aengus Buckley.

LISMORE (381 B1)
COUNTY WATERFORD *pop. 1,100*
Lismore, noted for its excellent fishing, dates from the 7th century AD when St. Carthage founded a monastery here that became one of the renowned universities of Europe. Chemist Robert Boyle and dramatist and poet William Congreve were born in Lismore. An audiovisual presentation in the award-winning heritage center relates the history of the town. Also of interest are two cathedrals:

Church of Ireland St. Carthage's, and the Roman Catholic Cathedral.

LISMORE CASTLE, the Irish seat of the Dukes of Devonshire, was once home to Sir Walter Raleigh. Built by Prince John in 1185, the castle was extensively remodeled in the 19th century. The gardens are open during the summer.

MELLIFONT ABBEY (381 C3)
COUNTY LOUTH
Situated 8 kilometres (5 miles) west of Drogheda, this is the 12th-century ruin of the first Cistercian house established in Ireland. Among the remains are a Romanesque cloister, a two-storey octagonal lavabo, or washing place, and a 13th-century chapter house.

ST. OLIVER PLUNKETT

St. Oliver Plunkett, Archbishop of Armagh and Primate of All Ireland, lived 1629–81 and was canonized in 1976. He lived in the troubled years when Catholicism was being suppressed by the English. In 1678, Plunkett was arrested after Titus Oates falsely alleged that he was plotting to bring French soldiers into Ireland. Although his achievements had brought him the friendship of Ulster's Protestant clergy, Plunkett was executed on July 1, 1681 in London for "treason," his offense being simply that he was an unrepentant Catholic. After the execution, Plunkett's severed head was rescued and taken back to Ireland, where it now resides in the Catholic Church of St. Peter, Drogheda.

MONASTERBOICE (381 C3)
COUNTY LOUTH
This celebrated monastic site, located 8 kilometers (5 miles) north west of Drogheda, includes three high crosses, a 30-meter (100-foot) round tower, two churches, a tombstone and a sundial.

The elaborately sculptured crosses vary in height from 5–6.5 meters (16–21 feet). Muirdeach's Cross, one of the finest high crosses in Ireland, is thought to have been made in the 10th century.

MULLINGAR (381 B2)
COUNTY WESTMEATH pop. 7,900
The angling center of Mullingar also has facilities for golf, tennis, racket ball, pitch and putt, horseback riding, hunting, swimming, sailing and dog racing.

CATHEDRAL OF CHRIST THE KING was built in 1936; its twin towers dominate the landscape. The mosaics of saints Patrick and Anne near the high altar were designed by the Russian Boris Anrep. An ecclesiastical museum houses the vestments of St. Oliver Plunkett, executed for "treason" in London in 1681.

NEWGRANGE (381 C3) ★
COUNTY MEATH
Newgrange is 11 kilometers (7 miles) south of Drogheda in the valley of the Boyne and is the site of a 5,000-year-old megalithic tomb. Around 11 meters (36 feet) high, the tomb covers 0.4 hectares (1 acre) of ground and is surrounded by an incomplete circle of stones. The front walls of the mound are faced with brilliant-white quartz stones. A burial chamber with a funnel-shaped roof is connected to the tomb by a long passageway. On the morning of the winter solstice, the rays of the sun penetrate a narrow slit in the stone and illuminate the chamber for about 15 minutes. This phenomenon is reproduced artificially for visitors at the end of guided tours. An information center is on the grounds.

Less well known than Newgrange are the burial cairns of Dowth and Knowth, both situated only a few miles away.

PARKNASILLA (381 A1)
COUNTY KERRY
On the Ring of Kerry, Parknasilla overlooks the island-studded Kenmare River, an ocean estuary. Because of the effects of the Gulf Stream and

Parknasilla's sheltered location, this exotic place has subtropical plants. Near by Sneem is a charming village with several interesting churches. The most notable, St. Michael's (1865), contains the grave of Father Michael Walsh, Father O'Flynn in the celebrated song.

POWERSCOURT ESTATE (381 C2) ★
COUNTY WICKLOW

Near the village of Enniskerry stands Powerscourt Estate, the site of Ireland's best-known gardens. An impressive drive leads to the shell of a Palladian mansion, which was sadly gutted by fire in 1974. Laid out in the Victorian era, the gardens feature ornate sculptures, fountains and terraces. About 6.5 kilometers (4 miles) away is the spectacular Powerscourt Waterfall; at 120 meters (400 feet), it is the highest in Ireland.

A LUCKY LUNCHEON

King George IV announced in 1821 that he would visit magnificent Powerscourt House, built on land granted by James I. In anticipation of the visit, a path from the house to the waterfall in the grounds was laid out. As the waterfall was not deemed dramatic enough for a king, an artificial lake with sluice gates was created at the top of the fall for greater effect. However, George IV delighted so much in the banquet at the mansion that insufficient time was left to admire the waterfall. Perhaps this was just as well, for when the sluice gates were opened, the platform intended for the king was destroyed by the great flood of water.

RATHMULLAN (381 B4)
COUNTY DONEGAL *pop. 600*

Rathmullan, a popular resort, is a picturesque village with a sandy beach backed by high hills. The town has been the stage for important events in Irish history. In 1587 Ulster chieftain Red Hugh O'Donnell, Earl of Tyrconnell, was captured in Rathmullan harbor after being lured on board a disguised English ship. Twenty years later, Rathmullan witnessed the Flight of the Earls, the exile of Ulster's nobility. A heritage center recounts these events.

ROSSLARE (381 C1)
COUNTY WEXFORD *pop. 800*

Rosslare is a popular vacation resort with 10 kilometers (6 miles) of fine beaches. It is also noted for its 18-hole championship golf course and other sporting facilities. The harbor, the terminus of car ferries from Fishguard in Wales and Le Havre and Cherbourg in France, is about 8 kilometers (5 miles) south.

Our Lady's Island, joined to the mainland by a causeway, has been the objective of pilgrims for centuries. A 12th-century Norman castle and ruined Augustinian priory are on the island. The Saltee Islands, off Kilmore Quay, together form a bird sanctuary.

SKERRIES (381 C2)
COUNTY DUBLIN *pop. 5,800*

Skerries is a highly popular resort with a fine sandy beach and dry climate. Golf, tennis, fishing and watersports abound. Three small islands – St. Patrick's, Colt and Shenick's – are worth exploring.

SLIGO (381 B3)
COUNTY SLIGO *pop. 17,200*

Surrounded by the Ox Mountains, Sligo is where William Butler Yeats spent many years of his life. The poet is buried in a churchyard at Drumcliff near the ruins of a monastery founded by St. Columba in 574 AD. Yeats' epitaph, a quotation from one of his best-known poems, reads: "Cast a cold Eye On Life, on Death. Horseman, pass by."

The Yeats Memorial Building, Hyde Bridge, hosts the annual Yeats International Summer School in August. The County Museum, in Stephen Street, includes Yeats memorabilia, while the County Art Gallery has paintings by the poet's father and brother.

REPUBLIC OF IRELAND

The area around Sligo Bay is also known for its interesting archeological remains, including the ruins of 13th-century Sligo Abbey. Other places of interest are Doorly Park's walking paths and racecourse, the town hall, the courthouse, ancient St. John's Church and Summerhill College.

Boat excursions can be made to Aghamore on Lough Gill, the Lake Isle of Innisfree and past the Dooney Rock to Dromahair, site of a feudal castle.

CARROWMORE, about 5 kilometers (3 miles) from Sligo, has one of the largest groups of megalithic remains in Western Europe, with dolmens, stone circles and about 60 tombs. The oldest dolmen is thought to date back to 4000 BC.

CREEVYKEEL COURT CAIRN, on the Sligo–Burdoran Road, a neolithic court-tomb dating from about 3000 BC, was excavated by a Harvard archeological expedition in 1935. Many of the finds are in the National Museum in Dublin.

LISSADELL HOUSE is a Georgian mansion overlooking Sligo Bay. William Butler Yeats was a frequent guest of the Gore-Booth family who resided in this house.

THOR BALLYLEE (381 B2)
GALWAY
This 14th-century Norman tower house was the residence of poet William Butler Yeats between 1917 and 1928.

The tower, which has been restored to appear as it was when Yeats lived there, houses an interpretative center with audiovisual presentations and displays of the poet's work. Visitors can climb up to the tower by "the narrow winding stair," a common image in Yeats' poetry.

TIPPERARY (381 B2)
COUNTY TIPPERARY pop. 5,000
Although Tipperary dates from the 12th century, it has few historic remains. The town lies in the Golden Vale of Tipperary, the subject of Jack Judge's song

from World War I. To the south is the Galtee mountain range. Hiking, climbing, fishing and hunting are popular pastimes in this region.

TRALEE (381 A1)
COUNTY KERRY pop. 16,500
Tralee is the starting point for trips to the remote Dingle Peninsula, a beautiful expanse of mountains with spectacular sea views. In late August the Festival of Kerry features a week of celebrations culminating in a beauty contest to select the "Rose of Tralee." Tralee is also home to Siamsa Tíre, the National Folk Theatre of Ireland.

TRIM (381 C2)
COUNTY MEATH pop. 3,500
Trim, an agricultural town in the Boyne valley, is one of the oldest ecclesiastical centers in Ireland. Of the original walls enclosing the town, only two gates remain. The 38-meter (125-foot), 13th-century Yellow Steeple, the last remnant of an Augustinian abbey, dominates the local skyline.

TRIM CASTLE, founded in the 12th century, is the largest Norman fortress in Ireland. The 20-meter (70-foot) walls and adjoining towers cover about 1 hectare (2½ acres).

WATERFORD (381 B1)
COUNTY WATERFORD pop. 38,500
World-renowned as the home of an exquisite glass industry, Waterford is also a large seaport with a fine harbor. Founded by Norsemen in the 10th century, it retains its anglicized Norse name.

Places of interest include the 18th-century Cathedral of the Holy Trinity, Christ Church Cathedral and the ruins of Blackfriars Abbey, a Dominican friary founded in 1226. The council chamber in the city hall has a striking Waterford glass chandelier, made in 1802; a copy can be found in Philadelphia's Independence Hall. The famous Waterford Glass Factory is sited about 2 kilometers (1 mile) south of the town.

Tramore, 11 kilometers (7 miles) from town, is a modern resort, while Dunmore East is a popular picnic spot with opportunities for watersports and deep-sea fishing. Waterford hosts the two-week International Light Opera Festival from mid-September to early October.

FRENCH CHURCH, dating from 1240, received its name when it was used by Huguenot refugees in the 18th century. Remains of this national monument include the 15th-century tower, chancel, belfry and east window.

REGINALD'S TOWER, built in 1003 by Vikings, is a circular 24-meter (80-foot) tower with walls 3 meters (10 feet) thick. Restored in 1819, it now serves as a municipal museum.

WATERVILLE (381 A1)
COUNTY KERRY *pop. 500*
Waterville is renowned for its championship golf course and for the excellent game fishing at nearby Lough Currane. Staigue Fort, south east, is a well-preserved *cashel*, (stone ring fort) dating from around 1000 BC.

DERRYNANE HOUSE, located 16 kilometers (10 miles) south near Caherdaniel, is a former home of Daniel O'Connell "The Liberator," first of the great 19th-century Irish leaders. The surrounding 130-hectare (320-acre) park encompasses and provides superb scenery.

WESTPORT (381 A3)
COUNTY MAYO *pop. 3,400*
A major salt-water fishing center on Clew Bay, Westport is an attractive wooded town. Excursions can be made to Achill Island, Ireland's largest; to the mountain of Croagh Patrick, site of a pilgrimage on the last Sunday in July; and to Clare Island, with precipitous cliffs.

WESTPORT HOUSE is a handsome Georgian mansion on Westport Quay, just over 2 kilometers (1 mile) from the town. Designed for the Marquess of Sligo by 18th-century architects, Richard Cassels and James Wyatt, the house boasts exquisite Georgian and Victorian furniture, antique silver, Waterford glass and superb family portraits.

WEXFORD (381 C1)
COUNTY WEXFORD *pop. 11,400*
Wexford is an ancient seaport with narrow, winding streets and a medieval atmosphere. It was fortified under the Normans; the Westgate Tower, the remains of the town wall and the bull-ring date from that period.

In Crescent Quay, overlooking the harbor, a bronze statue commemorates Commodore John Barry, local-born founder of the U.S. Navy. The world-renowned Wexford Opera Festival, held in late October/early November, features international operatic soloists.

IRISH NATIONAL HERITAGE PARK, at nearby Ferrycarrig, re-creates Ireland's ancient history up to Anglo-Norman times. The open-air site includes replicas of Stone Age settlements, ring forts and a Norman castle.

JOHNSTOWN CASTLE, 6.5 kilometers (4 miles) south west, is a 19th-century mansion incorporating the remains of a 15th-century castle. It now houses a research center of the Agriculture Institute and the Irish Agricultural Museum. The attractive grounds are open to the public.

SELSKAR ABBEY, near Westgate Tower, is now a ruin. In 1172, King Henry II did 40 days' penance at the abbey for the murder of Thomas à Becket.

WESTGATE, a 13th-century gate tower, is the setting for the Wexford Medieval Experience, an audiovisual display which recounts the town's early history.

WEXFORD WILDFOWL RESERVE is on the north shore of Wexford harbor. Among the birds that winter on the mudflats are Greenland white-fronted geese.

ITALY

IT IS IMPOSSIBLE TO DISLIKE THE
ITALIANS. THEY MAY CAUSE CHAOS,
BE THE MOST INCONSIDERATE
DRIVERS IN THE WORLD, LOUD,
UNPUNCTUAL AND INFURIATING, BUT THEY ARE
PASSIONATE, FRIENDLY AND SYMPATHETIC, THEY
LOVE FOOD AND DRINK, PEOPLE AND LIFE ITSELF.
THEY ALSO LOVE THEIR COUNTRY, AND WHO CAN
BLAME THEM? ITALY MAY NOT LIE PHYSICALLY AT
THE HEART OF EUROPE, BUT IT LIES AT THE HEART
OF ITS CULTURE AND RULED ONE OF THE LARGEST
EMPIRES EVER KNOWN.

FROM THE TOP OF ITS BOOT TO THE TIP OF ITS TOE,
ITALY OFFERS AN EMBARRASSMENT OF RICHES: IN
THE NORTH, THE ALPS AND THE ITALIAN LAKES,
GENOA IN THE WEST, AND THE CANALS OF VENICE
IN THE EAST. SOUTH ARE TUSCANY AND UMBRIA,
WITH THE GLORIOUS ART TREA-
SURES OF FLORENCE. ROME,
NAPLES AND CAPRI LEAD ON TO
RUGGED, UNSPOILED CALABRIA.

Left THE MAGNIFICENT DUOMO IN FLORENCE DOMINATES PIAZZA DEL DUOMO
Above left GONDOLIERS IN VENICE ARE A COLORFUL SIGHT
Above right GUARDS AT THE VATICAN CITY PROTECT A POPULATION OF 400

Things to Know

- **Area:** 301,225 square kilometers (116,303 square miles)
- **Population:** 57,500,000
- **Capital:** Roma (Rome)
- **Language:** Italian
- **Religion:** Roman Catholic.
- **Economy:** Tourism, industry, agriculture. Machinery, food, tobacco and textiles are main products; also leading mercury producer. Crops include wheat, rice, citrus fruits, grapes and olives; renowned for wine production.
- **Passport Requirements:** Required for U.S. citizens.
- **Visa Requirements:** Not required for stays up to three months, after which a three-month extension can be obtained.
- **Duty-Free Items:** 200 cigarettes or 50 cigars or 250 grams of tobacco; two liters of wine and one liter of spirits; fine perfume, up to half a liter; two still cameras with up to 10 rolls of film for each, one movie camera with 10 rolls of movie film, one video camera; souvenirs from other countries up to $45 in value. Also see *The European Union on p.5.*
- **Currency:** The currency unit is the Italian *lira* (LIT). Due to currency fluctuations, the exchange rate is subject to frequent change. There is no limit on the amount of foreign currency that can be brought into the country, but all such monies must be declared.
- **Bank Opening Hours:** 8:30am–1:30pm and 3–4pm Monday–Friday.
- **Store Opening Hours:** 8:30 or 9am–7:30 or 8pm Monday–Saturday, with a siesta between 1 and 4pm.
- **Museum Opening Hours:** State museums open 9am–2pm Tuesday–Saturday, 9am–1pm Sunday, closed Monday.
- **Special Regulations:** Numbered fiscal receipts (*ricevuta fiscale*) are issued for certain goods and services. They indicate the price charged and the total cost after adding Value Added Tax (V.A.T.), a tax on non-essential items. Tourists should be sure to obtain such receipts, as they are required by law.

History

Because of its vast shoreline and strategic location, Italy has long been the target of invasion. Phoenicians, Carthaginians and Greeks came and established colonies, and the mysterious Etruscans emerged as dominant in much of present-day Lazio and Tuscany. But by the end of the 6th century BC, the Romans had ousted the Etruscan kings and started on the path of world conquest

As the boundaries of the Roman Empire expanded, so did the ambitions and wealth of the ruling upper class. Even when the empire was at its zenith, however, the lower classes and slaves began to revolt against this luxury and decadence. As tensions escalated, a hero emerged to restore order – Julius Caesar. His successor, Octavius, took the title of emperor in 27 BC, and the empire flourished until the death of Aurelius in 180 AD, when decline set in.

In subsequent centuries Rome was ruled by foreign kings, invaded by barbarians and witness to the growth in power of the papacy. Independent states and sovereign kingdoms developed, and in time the power of the cities counterbalanced the increasing power of the pope. Influential families such as the Medicis of Florence brought scholars and artists to their cities and launched the artistic movement known as the Renaissance. At the same time, French, Austrian and Spanish armies were fighting for control of the peninsula. After years of conflict, citizens began to appeal for one unified government instead of several city-states, this movement being called "Risorgimento," or resurrection. Italy finally became one kingdom under Victor Emmanuel II in 1861.

Decades later, dissatisfaction with the economy and continued religious influence left the Italian people seeking another Caesar-like savior. They chose 39-year-old Benito Mussolini and the

Fascist Party. Mussolini's politics brought Italy into World War II and devastated both the economy and the countryside. Postwar Italy became a democratic republic and has been administered by more than 50 governments since. American aid and membership of the European Community resulted in economic recovery up until the late 1970s.

Inflation, unemployment, terrorism and government scandal then led to yet another troubled period. In April, 1993, the Italian people voted overwhelmingly for sweeping electoral reforms designed to weaken the influence of powerful party leaders. In March, 1994, the conservative "Freedom Alliance" won the general elections, and in May, media magnate Silvio Berlusconi was named prime minister. His coalition government was short-lived, however, Berlusconi himself resigning after accusations of bribery.

FOOD AND DRINK

Pasta, the national staple, comes in a variety of sizes and shapes, while risotto, or rice dishes, are also numerous. The classic Neapolitan pizza is made with tomato sauce, mozzarella cheese and anchovies. Prosciutto, a dark, spicy ham usually served on melon, is a favorite appetizer while *Antipasto*, the Italian *hors-d'oeuvre*, is often a meal in itself. Tempting desserts range from fresh fruit to ices, or *gelati*. Locally made wine is the national beverage, but the meal's end is properly celebrated by drinking one or more cups of aromatic espresso coffee.

SPORTS AND RECREATION

A number of outstanding mountain resorts make Italy a major destination for skiers, and the Alpine regions of the north are also excellent for climbing. The Italian Riviera in the north west, the Versilia, the Tyrrhenian coast, Sicily, Sardinia, and the Adriatic coast (including famous resorts like Rimini,

Riccione, Grado, Lignano and Jesolo Lido) have fine bathing facilities. The Acqua Santa and Olgiata golf courses near Rome are two of the best, with many facilities in addition to the links. Soccer is the national sport.

GETTING AROUND

Main and secondary roads are generally good in Italy; even mountain roads are well-engineered.

A comprehensive system of highways, or *autostrade*, reaches most parts of the country.

The wearing of seat belts, if the car is so equipped, is mandatory. Children under 3 cannot ride in the front or back unless using a seat fitted with a restraint system; children between 3 and twelve may only ride in the front if they are wearing a restraint system. Speed limits are 50 k.p.h. (30 m.p.h.) in town and 90 k.p.h. (55 m.p.h.) on out-of-town roads; on the highways 130 k.p.h. (80 m.p.h.). Visiting motorists must pay fines for motoring violations on the spot in Italian lira.

AUTOMOBILE CLUB
Automobile Club d'Italia
(Automobile Club of Italy), 8 Via Marsala, Rome, has branch offices in various cities throughout Italy. The symbol ▲ beside a city name indicates the presence of an AAA-affiliated automobile club branch. Not all auto clubs offer full travel services to AAA members.

ACCOMMODATIONS

Hotels in Italy are classified into five categories. Regional and provincial tourist offices publish a list of hotels and guest houses and their ratings annually.

Campeggiare in Italia lists campgrounds and youth hostels throughout Italy. For more information, contact Federcampeggio, PO Box 23, 50041 Calenzano

- **BEST BUYS:** Leather goods, gloves, Venetian glass, jewelry, prints and silk. Also silver, straw products and porcelain.
- **PUBLIC HOLIDAYS:** January 1; January 6; Easter Monday; World War II Liberation Day – April 25; Labor Day – May 1; Assumption Day – August 15; All Saints Day – November 1; Immaculate Conception – December 8; December 25–26.
- **USEFUL TELEPHONE NUMBERS:** Police (*Carabinieri*): 112
  Emergency numbers:
  Police: 113
  Fire: 113
  Ambulance: 113
  Car breakdown: 116
- **NATIONAL TOURIST OFFICES:** Italian Government Travel Office
  630 Fifth Avenue, Suite 1565
  Rockefeller Center
  New York
  NY 10111
  Tel: 212/245 4822
  Fax: 212/586 9249
  Italian Government Travel Office
  2400 Wilshire Boulevard
  Suite 550
  Los Angeles
  CA 90025
  Tel: 310/820 0098
  Fax: 310/820 6357
  Italian State Tourist Office
  1 Princes Street
  London
  W1 8AY
  Tel: 0171 408 1254
  Fax: 0171 493 6695
  Italian State Tourist Board
  (E.N.I.T.)
  Via Marghera 2
  00185 Rome
  Tel: 39 6 49 711
  Fax: 39 6 446 3379
- **AMERICAN EMBASSY:**
  Via Vittorio Veneto 119a
  Palazzo Margherita
  00187 Rome
  Tel: 39 6 46 741
  Fax: 39 6 488 2672

(tel: 055 882391). Some campgrounds might give a reduced rate with an international camping carnet.

TIPPING

If a gratuity charge is not included in the restaurant bill, leave a tip of 10 to 15 percent. Tip taxi-drivers about 15 percent of the fare, and gas-station attendants, chambermaids, doormen, theater ushers and hairdressers the equivalent of about 70¢ each. Bellhops should get the equivalent of about $1 per bag.

PRINCIPAL TOURING AREAS

Note: For descriptions of cities in **bold** type, see individual city listings.

CAMPANIA AND THE SOUTH

Campania begins in the mountainous southern interior and sweeps toward the coast in a series of fertile fields. The broad Bay of Naples is the historic and economic heart of the region, and shelters the islands of *Capri* and *Ischia*. Here is the city of **Napoli,** or **Naples**, with Vesuvius rising formidably above it.

On the other side of Sorrentine Peninsula are the unspoiled scenery and medieval relics of the **Amalfi** coast. Further south are Basilicata and Calabria and, along the eastern side, Puglia.

EMILIA-ROMAGNA

Across the River Po from Veneto and Lombardy is Emilia, a vast area which takes its name from the Via Emilia, the Roman road that was a principal north–south link for 2,000 years. The vigorous medieval communes of this region became splendid capitals of the Renaissance: **Ferrara, Módena, Piacenza** and **Parma. Bologna**, with its old red-brick buildings, instead recalls the Middle Ages.

Romagna is the territory of the ancient Byzantine province of **Ravenna**, the last capital of the Roman Empire of the

West. To the south is seaside **Rímini**, with its Malatestan Temple.

LAZIO, ABRUZZO AND MOLISE
Lazio is characterized by a central, rolling plain rimmed by blue, misty mountains. Probably more noticeable is the stamp of Roma, or Rome, announced before it is even reached by ancient ruins as well as the monuments of later centuries. Abruzzo, bordering the Adriatic, has as its capital the mountain town of L'Aquila, while the small region of Molise, to the south, is less visited.

LIGURIA
Liguria follows the western coast from the French frontier to the Gulf of Genoa. Génova, or Genoa, dominated the trade of the eastern Mediterranean for centuries and is still Italy's largest mercantile port. To the north and south are the two Italian rivieras, while inland are a number of excellent centers offering winter-sports.

LOMBARDIA
This attractive region originates at the foot of the Alps and unfolds into a broad plain studded with natural and man-made lakes. These clear, blue lakes, plied by steamers, reflect graceful towns. It is also home to such fine old cities as **Milano (Milan)**, **Mantova (Mantua)**, **Pavia** and **Bergamo**, and to smaller towns such as **Como, Cremona** and **Bréscia**.

PIEDMONT AND VALLE D'AOSTA
The northern Piedmont region forms a giant geographical amphitheater that attracts those who come to ski, hike or relax at the resorts. Further south is an area rich in history, agriculture and industry, the latter centered on **Torino**, or **Turin**. Just north of Piedmont is the small, mountainous region of Valle d'Aosta, a delightful center famous for skiing and dairy farming.

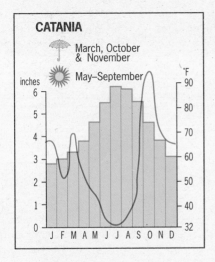

CATANIA
March, October & November
May–September

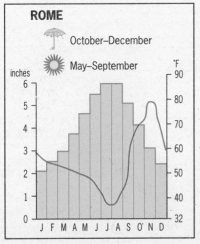

ROME
October–December
May–September

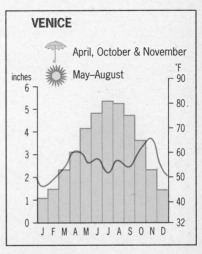

VENICE
April, October & November
May–August

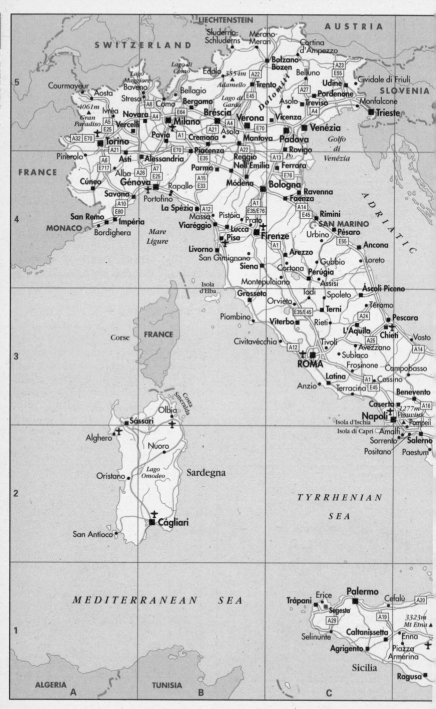

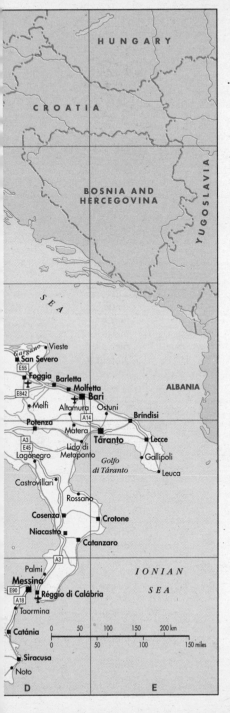

SICILIA AND SARDEGNA

Sicilia, or **Sicily**, the largest and one of the most beautiful islands in the Mediterranean, is an archeological storehouse for the remains of past civilizations. The Emerald Coast of **Sardegna**, or **Sardinia**, is the playground of the jet set, while other parts of the island retain native folklore and customs.

TOSCANA, MARCHE AND UMBRIA

Nature is friendliest in Toscana, offering gentle mountains and rich forests bathed in misty vapor and soft color. Set within this great garden is the flower of the Renaissance, **Firenze**, or **Florence**, the city that produced the period's representive figures. Toscana has older memories, too – for instance in medieval **Siena** and **Lucca** – and in such newer resorts as Viaréggio, and the busy port of Livorno.

The Marche and Umbria border on Toscana and, in a way, complete it, forming a continuation of the countryside. The hilly Marche side of the Apennines slopes to the sea, terminating in a long row of vacation towns. Gentle, rolling Umbria was the cradle of the Franciscan movement and the home of its founder, St. Francis of Assisi.

VENETO AND TRENTINO-ALTO ADIGE

Veneto embraces the upper basin of the Adriatic, forming a great semicircle; most of the region is a flourishing, fertile plain with such important cities as Verona, **Vicenza** and **Padova**, or **Padua**. And in the watery centre of the Adriatic semicircle is **Venézia**, or **Venice**, city of canals, doges, *palazzi* and *piazze*.

Trentino-Alto Adige lies between Veneto and the Venoste, Breonie and Aurine Alps. The high, rugged country includes the Dolomites, sheer vertical projections rising to staggering heights.

Situated in this area are the three resort towns of Bolzano, turn-of-the-century **Merano,** and historically interesting **Trento**.

USEFUL EXPRESSIONS IN ITALIAN

hello	ciao (on the telephone, **pronto**)	straight ahead	**sempre diritto**
good morning	**buongiorno**	vacant/occupied	**libero/occupato**
good evening	**buona sera**	airport	**aeroporto**
good night	**buona notte**	train	**il treno**
good-bye	**arrivederci, ciao, arrivederla** (formal)	platform	**il binario**
		bus stop	**la fermata**
please	**per favore, per piacere**	ticket	**il biglietto**
		gas station	**la stazione di rifornimento**
thank you	**grazie**	police station	**il posto di polizia**
yes/no	**sì/no**	post office	**l'ufficio postale**
excuse me	**mi scusi**	hotel	**l'albergo**
excuse me (in a crowd)	**permesso**	restaurant	**il ristorante**
		doctor	**il medico**
I'm sorry	**mi dispiace**	pharmacy	**la farmacia**
you're welcome	**prego**	church	**la chiesa**
How are you?	**Come stai/sta?**	museum	**il museo**
I'm fine	**Sto bene**		

Do you speak English?	**Parla inglese?**
I don't understand.	**Non capisco.**
What is the time?	**Che ore sono?**
How much is that?	**Quant'è?**
Where are the restrooms?	**Dove sono i gabinetti?**
I'd like ...	**Vorrei ...**
The check, please.	**Il conto, per favore.**
Is service included?	**É compreso il servizio?**
Can you help me, please?	**Per favore, mi aiuta?**
I want to go to...	**Vorrei andare a...**
Where are we?	**Dove siamo?**
Are we far from...?	**Siamo lontani da...?**
Do you take credit cards?	**Accetta carta di credito?**
Where is the nearest bank?	**Dov'è la banca più vicina?**
where	**dove**
when	**quando**
how	**come**
hot/cold	**caldo/freddo**
open/closed	**aperto/chiuso**
yesterday	**ieri**
today	**oggi**
tomorrow	**domani**
to the left	**a sinistra**
to the right	**a destra**

DAYS OF THE WEEK

Sunday	**domenica**
Monday	**lunedì**
Tuesday	**martedì**
Wednesday	**mercoledì**
Thursday	**giovedì**
Friday	**venerdì**
Saturday	**sabato**

NUMBERS

1	**uno (a)**
2	**due**
3	**tre**
4	**quattro**
5	**cinque**
6	**sei**
7	**sette**
8	**otto**
9	**nove**
10	**dieci**
20	**venti**
30	**trenta**
40	**quaranta**
50	**cinquanta**
60	**sessanta**
70	**settanta**
80	**ottanta**
90	**novanta**
100	**cento**
1,000	**mille**

ROMA *pop. 2,791,300*

ITALY

The Colosseo, or Colosseum, in Rome, proved an impressive blueprint for future stadia.

HISTORY

Legend tells us that Rome was founded by Romulus and Remus, twin sons of the god Mars who were nursed by a wolf. More reliable sources date the inception of the city from the 8th century BC, when a village was founded on the banks of the Tiber River by the Etruscans as a meeting-place and market. The settlement prospered, fortifications were built, and by 509 BC

ROMULUS AND REMUS

According to legend, the twins were the children of Rhea, a vestal virgin, and the god Mars. Abandoned on the Palatine hill, they were suckled by a wolf before being adopted by a shepherd. In adulthood, the brothers were told by Mars to found a settlement on the Palatine. Unable to agree on a name or on who should rule, they invoked the gods to settle the matter, but the signs were inconclusive; in the ensuing fight Romulus killed Remus.

Rome was a kingdom ruled by the infamous Tarquinius "the Proud." He was ousted in that year, and the Roman Republic was created.

Internal political struggles failed to halt the city's expansion and the republic became an empire. The republic foundered during the 1st century BC, and 13 years of civil war succeeded Julius Caesar's assassination. Caesar's adopted son, Octavius (Augustus Caesar), led one faction to victory around 30 BC, and took the title of Emperor.

The Roman legions swept outward, conquered all of Italy, spread across the Mediterranean lands and, by the end of the 2nd century AD, encompassed most of the known world. Meanwhile, art flourished, monumental buildings were erected and great public works undertaken. The Pantheon, today the only fully preserved Roman structure, dates from this time, as do the ruined Colosseo, parts of the Foro Romano and Trajan's victory column.

Beginning about the time of Emperor Marcus Aurelius' death in 180 AD, a

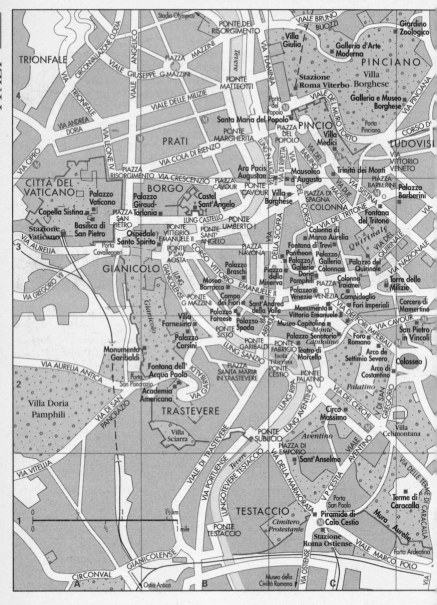

slow, steady decline plagued the empire. The attrition accelerated during the 4th century when the empire was finally split into two parts, eastern and western, and the death knell sounded when power moved from Rome to Constantinople. Goths, followed by Vandals, plundered the city; by 476 AD the Western Empire had ceased to exist.

With the establishment of Rome as the capital of Western Christianity, the city once again began an ascent to glory. This culminated in its role as one of the birthplaces of the Renaissance in the

kingdom of Italy was created in 1861 with Rome still in the hands of French troops, who supported the Pope. In 1870 Rome was liberated and took over from Florence the role of state capital.

During the 19th and early 20th centuries, both the church and state vied for ownership of Rome. In 1929 the Roman Question was resolved with the signing of the Lateran Treaty by Benito Mussolini and Cardinal Gaspari. Under the agreement, a Vatican city-state under church rule was created within Rome. Toward the end of World War II, Rome was declared an open city and as a result was saved from wholesale destruction.

Since the establishment of the Republic of Italy in 1946, the city has grown both in population and unplanned building, its tentacles spreading into the hinterland. The center, however, with its churches, ancient palaces and monuments, spacious parks, tree-lined boulevards, fountains, outdoor cafés and elegant shops, makes Rome one of the world's most attractive cities. Cultural diversity also contributes to Rome's popularity with visitors. During the social season, from November to May, there is a wide range of offerings in opera, concerts and theater. Special events in Rome include the Good Friday Procession, the Flower Festival in mid-June and the Festa de Noiantri in Trastevere in July.

THE FOUNTAINS OF ROME

Rome has more fountains than any other city in the world, many of them masterpieces of design and sculpture, such as Bernini's Fontana dei Quattro Fiumi in Piazza Navona and the ever-popular Fontana di Trevi.

Two other fountains to look for are Bernini's Fontana delle Api in Piazza Barberini, which includes three bees (*api*), Barberini family emblems and the Fontana della Barcaccia, in Piazza di Spagna, in the form of a half-sunken boat.

15th century, a "rebirth" of painting, sculpture and architecture that has provided inspiration and beauty for artist and admirer alike.

By the 19th century, Rome had become a provincial backwater, but was soon to regain prominence. The unified

ITALY

GETTING THERE
BY CAR

Ancient history records that all roads lead to Rome. A glance at any map assures today's traveler that things have not changed – roads radiate from Rome like spokes from a hub.

From the north west, the *autostrada* from Civitavecchia (A12) angles down the coast, connecting with Via Aurelia (SS1) and entering the city from the west. Continuing clockwise, the Vie Cassia (SS2), Flamina (SS3), Autostrada del Sole (A1) and Via Salaria (SS4) lead into the northern outskirts.

Via Tiburtina (SS5), Autostrada L'Aquila (A24) and Via Casilina (SS6) are the eastern approaches to Rome, while the Autostrada del Sole (A1) and Via Appia Nuova (SS7) wend their way into the southeastern section of the city.

From the south and south west, respectively, the Coast Road to Naples (SS148) and Via del Mare (SS 8) complete the main approach routes to Rome. All these routes join the Gran Raccordo Anulare (Circular Road) 12 kilometers (7 miles) from the city center, allowing motorists to bypass the center and enter from the most convenient direction.

Note: Most *autostrade* are toll roads.

BY PLANE, TRAIN AND BUS

The Leonardo da Vinci Airport, at Fiumicino, serves Rome. Train service to and from the airport is available at the Roma-Ostiense railway station at Piazzale dei Partigiani. The trip includes shuttle-bus service from Roma-Ostiense railway station to Termini railway station (Piazza dei Cinquecento) and vice versa.

The most important train station in Rome is the Stazione Termini. Ticket offices are to the right of the entrance; the *albergo diurno* (offering such travel amenities as baths, barber service, hair-dressing, pressing and cleaning) and the subway station are in the basement. Trolleys are available for carrying luggage.

C.I.T. Bus Terminal, Piazza della Republica 64, serves deluxe buses from Naples, Florence, Venice and Milan.

GETTING AROUND
STREET SYSTEM

For the uninitiated, driving on Rome's narrow, winding streets can be a night-mare. Numerous areas in the center of the city have been restricted to bus and taxi traffic or have been pedestrianized. There are many one-way streets. If you must drive, be alert at all times and let the passengers do the sightseeing. The best tip is to stick to the main avenues. Avoid the rush hours – 7:30–9am, 12:30–2:30pm and 4:30– 8:30pm. A detailed street map, available at tourist centers, is essential. Also check driving restrictions for foreign motorists.

PARKING

On-street parking, except during the Italian holiday month of August, is scant. A wise policy is not to depend on it, and take public transit instead.

CAR RENTAL

Vehicles can be rented in the Rome area with or without drivers; car-rental agencies are listed in the telephone directory under the heading *Autonoleggio*.

TAXIS

A good way to enjoy sightseeing is to take a taxi. Cab stands are at most busy intersections and at piazzas; taxis do not cruise. For assistance, telephone Radio-taxi (check telephone numbers in the Rome telephone directory). It is best to use only metered taxis. Additional charges are made for luggage, for service during late-night and early-morning hours and for trips to or from the airport.

PUBLIC TRANSPORTATION

Public transportation in Rome is fast and inexpensive. Among the most important lines are the 64, running through the center of the city from the Stazione Termini to the Basilica di San Pietro; the 87, through Piazza di Spagna from Piazza Cavour to St. John Lateran; and the 30, which passes many important points in its circuit around the city. Large parcels are charged the same as passengers;

check for exact size limitations. Try to avoid the rush hours.

There are two underground, or subway, lines: the "A" line, Ottaviano–Anagnina, with stops at Anagnina, Cinecitta, Subaugusta, Giulio Agricola, Lucio Sestio, Numidio Quadrato, Porta Furba, Arco de Travertino, Colli Albani, Furio Camillo, Ponte Lungo, Re di Roma, S. Giovanni, Manzoni, Vittorio E., Termini, Repubblica, Barberini, Spagna and Flaminio; and the "B" line, Rebibbia–Eur, with stops at Rebibbia, P. Mammolo, S. M. Soccorso, Pietralata, M. Tiburtini, Quintiliani, Tiburtina FS (railroad station), Bologna, Policlinico, C. Pretorio, Termini FS (railroad station), Cavour, Colosseo, Circo Massimo, Piramide, Garbatella, Basilica St. Paolo, Marconi, Magliana, Eur Palasport, Eur Fermi and Laurentina.

WHAT TO DO
SIGHTSEEING
The best way to see Rome properly is on foot, as many of the smaller streets and monuments are inaccessible to vehicular traffic. Always remember to cross the road on the striped sections.

CARRIAGE TOURS
Every visitor should take a horse-drawn carriage at least to the Villa Borghese, the Gianicolo and the Via Appia. Fares can be expensive; extra charges are made for night rides and luggage.

SPORTS AND RECREATION
Soccer, one of the great international sports, pervades Rome. Home teams Roma and Lazio play on alternate Sunday afternoons at the Stadio Olimpico from September to May. Basketball, also played at the professional level, is enjoyed at the Palazzo and Palazzetto dello Sport, EUR.

Horse racing is a Roman preoccupation. Flat racing and steeplechasing are held at the Ippodromo della Capanelle, trotting at the Ippodromo di Tordi Valle. An annual May event is the Rome International Horse Show.

Rome has a generous share of swimming pools. The Piscine delle Rosa in EUR is an outdoor pool open in summer. Romans also enjoy the beaches at Ostia, Fregene (both very dirty and crowded), Santa Marinella and San Severo (further north and slightly more salubrious).

WHERE TO SHOP
The elegant shops of Rome will afford unlimited pleasure, but, as always, it pays to comparison shop. The main shopping area is formed by the Via Frattina, Piazza di Spagna, Via Condotti and the Via Sistina. The Via Condotti, opposite the Piazza di Spagna, is comparable to Fifth Avenue in New York City. There are also elegant specialty shops along the Via Veneto. For something different, you might enjoy the Roman flea market held on Sunday mornings at Porta Portese. Some of the best buys in Rome are sportswear, silks, leather goods (particularly shoes, handbags and gloves), silverware, table linens and jewelry. Most shops are open from 8:30 or 9am to 1pm and from 3:30 or 4pm to 7:30 or 8pm. Many are closed on Monday mornings.

WHERE TO STAY – WHERE TO EAT
With hotels of all classes available in Rome, there are accommodations to suit every pocket. Careful consideration should be given to the location of your hotel and to individual preferences.

Many fashionable hotels are in the area bounded by Via Veneto, Piazza Barberini and Trinità dei Monti (near the Spanish Steps). The central railroad station offers a variety of affordable hotels. For those wishing to avoid the traffic in the city center, hotels near the Via Aurelia (south of the Vatican), or north, in the vicinity of the Villa Borghese near the Via Flaminia or Salaria, are recommended.

Shoppers will probably opt to stay between Piazza di Spagna and Via del Corso or on more moderately priced Via Cola di Rienzo, across the Tiber River (Tevere). Hotels between Via del Corso and the Tiber or near Via Fori Imperiali are

ITALY

convenient for those wishing to explore the narrow streets, open-air markets and famous landmarks of the historic center.

Excellent food is as inherent to Rome as its ancient monuments. *Ristoranti*, or *trattorie* are numerous, and vary from the most elegant to the most informal and from the native to the international.

Traditionally, an Italian meal consists of pasta, followed by a meat or fish course and dessert (fresh fruit), accompanied by red or white wine. Reservations are advised at all restaurants. The many cafés in the city offer coffee, aperitifs and a variety of snacks for those unaccustomed to late Roman dining hours. It is considered improper in Rome to leave a tip of less than the equivalent of 40¢, even though a 10 to 15 per cent service charge is likely to be added to your bill.

ENTERTAINMENT
NIGHTLIFE
As in any great city, nightlife in Rome can be as varied as the visitor. Movie theaters are numerous and offer films of all kinds in both Italian and English.

Nightclubs are expensive but offer entertainment ranging from sipping a drink in an elegant atmosphere to dancing or quaffing beer with gregarious students. Most clubs close during stretches of summer, particularly August. **Note**: The mention of any area or establishment in the preceding sections is for information only and does not imply endorsement by AAA.

THEATER AND CONCERTS
The concert season in Rome runs from October to June. Noted soloists can be heard at the Accademia di Santa Cecilia at Via della Conciliazione 4 or Via dei Greci 18. The Accademia Filarmonica perform at the Teatro Olimpico.

Opera is a festive occasion in Rome. The Teatro dell' Opera features productions from late November until June, and the Terme di Caracalla stages open-air opera from July through August.

Theatergoing in Rome focuses upon revivals of classics, especially Italian versions of Shakespeare. Smaller establishments present music-hall productions, political satires and parodies. The Sistina Theater features musical revues; the Greek Theater at Ostia Antica is the site of classic outdoor theater.

ESPECIALLY FOR CHILDREN
Rome is a fine vacation spot for children of all ages. The list below is a sample of suitable attractions.

Having learned the origin of Rome, youngsters can appreciate the she-wolf caged on the Capitoline Hill steps; the animal maintains a 3,000-year-old tradition. The Foro Romano, the Colosseo, with its memories of bloodthirsty games, and the frescoed catacombs will all stimulate young imaginations. The Museo della Civiltà Romana, with its scale model of historic Rome, and the riches of the Vatican leave lasting impressions. Children will also enjoy the Pincio's puppet show, which easily transcends language barriers. The zoo in the Villa Borghese is another possibility.

For play opportunities, try the myriad fountains of Rome or the Luna Amusement Park at EUR. Horse-drawn carriage rides are appealing to all ages.

PLACES OF INTEREST

ACCADEMIA AMERICANA (412 B2), above the Paolina Fountain on the Gianicolo, is a 20th-century palace built to resemble a Roman *palazzo*. It is the home and studio of many American musicians, painters, scholars, sculptors and writers, and contains a library and museum.

ARA PACIS AUGUSTAE (412 B4), near Via di Ripetta, was constructed by order of the Senate in 13–9 BC as a tribute to the peace that reigned throughout the empire at that time. There are superb bas-reliefs.

ARCO DI COSTANTINO (412 C2), at the end of Piazzale del Colosseo between the Caelian and Palatine hills, commemo-

ITALY

rates Constantine's victory over Maxentius in 312 AD. It is a triple arch and many of its reliefs were made from fragments of other monuments.

ARCO DI SETTIMIO SEVERO (412 C2), in the Foro Romano, was erected as a tribute to Emperor Septimius Severus and his sons, Caracalla and Publius Septimius Geta, for their outstanding battle achievements. Later, Caracalla murdered his brother and wrote a new inscription deleting Geta's name, but traces of the old inscription are still visible.

CAMPIDOGLIO (412 C3), the sacred hill of ancient Rome, holds the imposing Piazza del Campidoglio, designed by Michelangelo. The piazza is surrounded by the Palazzo Senatorio and, together forming the Museo Capitolino with wonderful classical sculpture, Palazzo dei Conservatori and Palazzo Nuovo. In the center of the piazza is a copy of the equestrian statue of Marcus Aurelius.

CARCERE DI MAMERTINO (San Pietro in Carcere) (412 C2) is beneath the church of San Giuseppe dei Falegnami. It served as a dungeon for captives awaiting execution; St. Peter was imprisoned here.

CASTEL SANT' ANGELO (412 B3) ★, Lungotevere Castello, is a huge edifice with thick walls and a tower. Erected by Emperor Hadrian as a mausoleum and later used as a prison, barracks and papal fortress, it is now a museum with military relics and works of art.

CATACOMBS, the subterranean cemeteries surrounding Rome, were used by early Christians for meetings and worship. In 313, Constantine ended Christian persecution, and major tombs were transferred to nearby churches.
Priscilla Catacombs, on Via Salaria, are noted for their 2nd-century frescoes; the *Virgin and Child with Isiah* is the oldest known painting of the Virgin Mary.
San Callisto, Rome's largest system of catacombs, was the papal burial place in the 3rd century. The tomb of St. Cecilia, with frescoes from the 7th and 8th centuries, is particularly imposing. Like the San Sebastiano catacombs, these lie beside Via Appia Antica.
San Sebastiano has frescoes and stuccoed tombs, some pre-Christian. The Basilica of St. Sebastian is above. The bodies of apostles Peter and Paul were temporarily housed here in the 3rd century.

CIMITERO PROTESTANTE (412 C1), Via Caio Cestio, is a peaceful, shady spot set within a grove of cypress trees. It shelters the grave of John Keats and the ashes of Percy Bysshe Shelley, along with the remains of other expatriates.

CIRCO MASSIMO (Circus Maximus) (412 C2), on Via del Circo Massimo, was the largest Roman circus, holding 30,000. Begun around 326 BC, it was much modified during its existence. Used first for chariot races, later as the site of Christian slaughter and games, it was destroyed by fire; a grassy hollow is all that remains.

COLONNA DI MARCO AURELIO (412 C3), in Piazza Colonna, consists of 27 drums of sculptured marble. Grand bas-reliefs portray Marcus Aurelius' 2nd-century victories over the Germans; a statue of St. Paul surmounts the column and replaces an earlier one of Aurelius.

COLONNA TRAIANEI (Trajan's Column) (412 C3), in the Forum of Trajan, one of the Fori Imperiali, is among the city's most striking monuments. It was erected in 113 AD and dedicated to the emperor

ITALY

for his victory over the Dacians (a tribe of present-day Romania); a frieze of bas-reliefs tells the story.

COLOSSEO (Colosseum) (412 D2) ★, begun about 72 AD, is the best-known and best-preserved structure remaining from ancient Rome. It was capable of holding 87,000 to view gladiatorial contests, hunts and naval battles (almost certainly not Christian martyrdoms). Many of the materials of this magnificent edifice were later used in the construction of various churches and palaces.

DOMUS AUREA (Golden House) (412 D2), near the Colosseo, was Nero's palace built after the burning of Rome in 64 AD. Little remains today and Trajan's baths (unexcavated) cover much of the site.

FONTANA DI TREVI (412 C3) ★ is one of the most impressive of Rome's many fountains. The waters play about a sculpture of Neptune, the sea god, riding in a winged chariot drawn by horses led by marble tritons. Traditionally, visitors throw a coin in the fountain if they wish to return to Rome.

FORO ROMANO (412 C2) ★, center of public life in Rome until the 2nd century AD, is crowded with the jumbled ruins of basilicas, temples and other buildings, including the Arch of Septimius Severus, built in 203 AD; the temples of Saturn (a Roman god), Castor and Pollux (Helen of Troy's twin brothers), Julius Caesar (erected on the spot where Caesar was cremated), Vesta (the vestal virgins) and Emperor Antoninus and Empress Faustina; the Arch of Titus; and the well-preserved Curia, where the senate met.

GALLERIA E MUSEO BORGHESE (412 D4) ★, in the Casino of the Villa Borghese (see p.421), houses the paintings and sculptures collected by the Borghese family and now owned by the state. Sculptures by Bernini and Canova, and paintings by Titian, Raphael and Antonello da Messina are highlighted.

GALLERIA COLONNA (412 C3), 17 Via della Pilotta in the Palazzo Colonna, comprises a great private collection of largely late-Renaissance and baroque paintings, with works by Botticelli, Rubens, Tintoretto and Van Dyck.

GALLERIA D'ARTE MODERNA (412 C4), 131 Viale delle Belle Arti, contains a collection of Italian and foreign art from the 19th century to the present. The 20th-century Italian wing has works by Marino Marini, Giacomo Manzù and the Futurists Boccioni and de Chirico.

GIANICOLO (Janiculum) (412 B3) Rome's highest hill (though not one of the original seven), offers a spectacular view of the city. It also includes a small park containing the lovely Paolina Fountain. Monumento di Garibaldi, on the summit, is an imposing creation by Gallori.

ISOLA TIBERINA (412 C2), near the Teatro di Marcello, is a boat-shaped island. To enhance this illusion, the Romans created a stone bow at one end and erected an obelisk to serve as a mast. The island can be reached via the Ponte Fabricio, the oldest bridge in Rome (62 BC).

MAUSOLEO D'AUGUSTO (412 C4), in the Piazza Augusto Imperatore, a circular structure like the Castel Sant' Angelo, for which it was a model, contains the crypts of emperors Augustus, Claudius, Nerva and Tiberius, and other members of this royal family. It has been used as a fortress, bull ring and concert hall.

MONUMENTO VITTORIO EMANUELE II (412 C3), in Piazza Venezia, is a huge Bréscian marble work by Giuseppe Sacconi (1911). Dedicated to Italian unity, it contains the tomb of the Unknown Soldier.

MURA AURELIE (412 E3), a wall begun by Emperor Aurelian in 271 AD, encircled the seven hills of Rome: Aventine, Caelian, Capitoline, Esquiline, Palatine, Quirinal and Viminal. Extensive sections remain well preserved.

MUSEO BARRACCO (412 B3), near Campo dei Fiori, houses ancient sculpture, including Assyrian, Babylonian, Egyptian, Etruscan, Greek and Roman art.

MUSEO CAPITOLINO (412 C2), on the Piazza del Campidoglio, is a most Roman museum, with many masterpieces of classical sculpture in both sections (see *Campidoglio*, p.417). Look out for the *Dying Gaul*, *Capitoline Venus* (in Palazzo Nuovo), the *Spinario* and *Capitoline Wolf* (Palazzo dei Conservatori).

MUSEO DELLA CIVILTÀ ROMANA, Piazzale Giovanni Agnelli, EUR documents daily life in Rome from its beginnings through the empire. Outstanding is an excellent model of the city in the 4th century, when it was at its height.

MUSEO NAZIONALE ROMANO (412 D3), in a monastery in the Terme di Diocleziano, displays some of the world's finest antique sculptures and mosaics.

OSTIA ANTICA, former Roman port, is a whole excavated city; it is the best preserved Roman town after Pompeii. Ostia is 30 minutes from Rome by train or car. The setting among pines is delightful, and there is much to see: baths, an amphitheater; ancient shipping offices; and even a Roman bar.

PALATINO (412 C2) was the first of Rome's seven hills to be inhabited. It is a peaceful spot, dotted with fragmentary ruins, including imperial palaces Domus Augustana, Domus Tiberiana (within the Farnese Gardens) and Domus Severiana, and the Stadium built by Domitian.

PALAZZO BARBERINI (412 D3), Via delle Quattro Fontane, is an impressive 17th-century structure by Maderno, Borromini and Bernini. Galleria Nazionale d'Arte Antica contains a magnificent collection of paintings from the early Renaissance to late baroque. There are works by Raphael, Titian and Tintoretto among many other great names.

PALAZZO FARNESE (412 C3), on Piazza Farnese, is one of the prettiest palaces in Rome. It was begun by Antonio da Sangallo the Younger in 1514 and completed by Michelangelo in 1546. The palace now houses the French Embassy and is not regularly open to the public.

PALAZZO DEL QUIRINALE (412 C3), on Via del Quirinale, was a former palace of kings and popes; it is now the residence of Italy's president. The palace is closed to the public, but a changing of the guard ceremony, complete with a brass band, takes place outside daily at 6pm.

PALAZZO VENEZIA (412 C3), abutting the Piazza Venezia, is a 15th-century palace that was once a papal residence and later the home of Benito Mussolini. A small museum houses an exceptionally fine collection of Renaissance sculptures.

PALAZZO-GALLERIA DORIA PAMPHILI (412 C3) is a huge palace, part of which is open to the public; it contains four galleries crammed with paintings. The collection's prize exhibit is the portrait by Velasquez of Pope Innocent X.

PANTHEON (412 C3) ★, Piazza della Rotonda, is the city's best-preserved monument of ancient Rome. First built by Marcus Agrippa (son-in-law of Augustus) as a temple dedicated to the seven planetary gods, it was replaced in its present form by Hadrian around 125 AD. In 609 it was consecrated and became the Church of Santa Maria dei Martiri. The exterior is brick; the interior, green and white marble. Sunlight streams in through a 9-meter (30-foot) opening at the top of the impressive concrete dome, an extraordinary achievement of the Roman engineers. The church floor slopes toward the center where drains catch the rainwater.

Bronze tiles that once covered the interior are gone; some were melted down to be used in making the columns of Bernini's baldachino in the Basilica di San Pietro.

ITALY

PIAZZA CAMPO DEI FIORI (412 B3) is one of Rome's most enjoyable squares, scene of a picturesque daily food and flower market, and somewhere to relax while observing everyday Roman life.

PIAZZA NAVONA (412 B3), off Corso del Rinascimento, occupies the site of the great hippodrome built by Emperor Domitian. A typical 17th-century Roman square, it is the meeting-place of the city. In the center Bernini's famous Fountain of the Rivers fronts Borromini's Church of St. Agnes in Agony.

PIAZZA DELLA MINERVA (412 C3), near the Pantheon, has perhaps Bernini's most charming public work, a marble elephant toting an obelisk taken from a temple of Isis. The Church of Santa Maria Sopra Minerva is Rome's only Gothic church, built in 1280 over an earlier church, itself on the ruins of a temple to Minerva.

PIAZZA MATTEI, along the Via dei Falegnami, contains the delightful Fountain of the Tortoises, a piece sculpted by Taddeo Landini in the 16th century with tortoises added by Bernini.

PIAZZA DELLA REPUBBLICA (412 D3), off the Via Nazionale, has seen better days, but is distinguished by the Fountain of the Naiads (1901). The Baths of Diocletian are to be found within the Church of Santa Maria degli Angeli.

PIAZZA DI SANTA MARIA IN TRASTEVERE (412 B2) is the heart of one of the oldest sections in Rome. It fronts the first church in Rome, a basilica based on a chapel founded in the 3rd century BC.

PIAZZA DI SPAGNA (412 C3) is one of Rome's most popular spots, best known for the elegant "Spanish Steps." At the top is the Chiesa di Trinità dei Monti.

PIRAMIDE DI CAIO CESTIO (412 C1), in the Protestant Cemetery, was erected in 12 BC and is 27 meters (88 feet) tall. It is the tomb of the unremarkable Caius Cestius.

SANT' ANDREA DELLA VALLE (412 B3), on Corso Vittorio Emanuele II, is a beautiful 17th-century church with the second-largest dome in Rome. The first act of Puccini's *Tosca* is set in the church.

SAN CLEMENTE (412 D2), on Via di San Giovanni in Laterano, has the best-preserved medieval interior in Rome. At its lowest level are a 1st-century Roman palace and a 3rd-century Mithraic temple.

SAN GIOVANNI IN LATERANO (412 D2), on the Piazza di Porta San Giovanni, is the Cathedral of Rome. The impressive façade is adorned with 16 huge statues of Christ, the apostles and the saints; the interior contains many relics and artworks. The Lateran Palace adjoins the cathedral and the Baptistery is the earliest anywhere. Opposite the palace stands the Scala Santa, the staircase believed to have come from Pontius Pilate's house in Jerusalem.

SAN LORENZO FUORI LE MURA (412 E3), is located off Via Tiburtina, and was formed by two churches built end to end: San Lorenzo, erected by Constantine, and Madonna Della Vergine, built by Pope Sixtus III. There is a 13th-century papal choir of marble.

SANTA MARIA DEGLI ANGELI (412 D3), on Piazza della Repubblica, was transformed into a church by Michelangelo from the central hall of the Terme di Diocleziano.

SANTA MARIA MAGGIORE (412 D3) ★, Piazza di Santa Maria Maggiore, dates from the 5th century, but has been twice restored. Inside are 40 ancient columns in the nave, 5th-century and 13th-century mosaics, and a ceiling gilded by Giuliano da Sangallo with the first gold brought from the New World by Christopher Columbus. Mass has been celebrated here every day since the 5th century.

SANTA MARIA DEL POPOLO (412 C4) was supposedly originally built on the site of Nero's tomb in 1099 as a kind of exorcism. The present church is noteworthy for two dramatic masterpieces by Caravaggio, Pinturrichio's frescoes behind the altar and Raphael's Cappella Chigi.

SAN PAOLO FUORI LE MURA, near Porta San Paolo, was originally constructed over the tomb of St. Paul. It is an authentic reproduction of the original, destroyed by fire in 1823. This church, San Giovanni in Laterano, Santa Maria Maggiore and the Basilica di San Pietro constitute the four patriarchal basilicas.

SAN PIETRO IN VINCOLI (412 D2), Piazza di San Pietro in Vincoli, was created in 432 to house the chains that bound St. Peter after his arrest in Rome. The relics themselves are visible under the main altar, but the church's main attraction is the statue of Moses by Michelangelo. It was originally intended for a tomb for Pope Julius II, never completed.

SANTO STEFANO ROTONDO (412 D2), in Via di Santo Stefano Rotondo, dating from the 5th century, was once one of Christendom's most important churches. The granite and marble interior is decorated with medieval frescoes showing horrific scenes of torture and butchery. Near the entrance is the alleged throne of Gregory the Great.

TEATRO DI MARCELLO (412 C2), near Via del Teatro di Marcello, was begun by order of Julius Caesar and completed by Caesar Augustus. It went out of use in the 3rd century, when bloodthirsty entertainment at the Colosseum was more popular than dramas performed here.

TERME DI CARACALLA (412 D1), along Via delle Terme di Caracalla, were luxurious edifices with a stadium, extensive galleries, libraries, and facilities for 2,000 bathers. Percy Bysshe Shelley composed part of his *Prometheus Unbound* here.

TERME DI DIOCLEZIANO (412 D3), on the Piazza della Repubblica, were the largest

baths in Rome, with a capacity of 3,000. What remains is incorporated in the church of Santa Maria degli Angeli and the Museo Nazionale Romano.

TORRE DELLE MILIZIE (412 C3), on Via 4 Novembre, is a 13th-century tower on a Byzantine base next to the 2nd-century ruin of Trajan's Market. It was anachronistically claimed to be the tower where Nero fiddled while Rome burned.

VATICAN CITY – *see p.445*.

VIA APPIA ANTICA (412 D1), the ancient Roman highway, is flanked by cypress trees, monuments, tombs, marbles and statues reflecting past glories. The road, still partially paved with Roman cobbles, starts from Porta San Sebastiano.

VILLA ADRIANA – *see Tivoli on p.443*.

VILLA BORGHESE (412 C4) ★, one of the finest parks in the city, faces Porta Pinciana at the top of Via Veneto. No private automobile traffic is permitted; Rome's largest underground garage is near the entrance. The park features temples, statues, fountains, a zoo and the Galleria Borghese (see p.418). The nearby Pincio, an exquisite botanical garden, was created by the early 19th-century architect Giuseppe Valadier.

VILLA DORIA PAMPHILI (412 A2) is on the Gianicolo hill off the Via Aurelia Antica. Rome's largest park, it covers hundreds of hectares with lawns, woods, fountains and lakes, and is a good place to escape the crowds.

VILLA D'ESTE – *see Tivoli on p.443*.

VILLA GIULIA (412 C4) ★, Viale Delle Belle Arti, near the Galleria Borghese, houses the Museo Nazionale Etrusco, the world's largest collection of Etruscan art and artifacts. Its best-known exhibit is the *Sarcophagus of the Married Couple*, a touching sculptural portrait of connubial happiness. The villa itself is a delightful Renaissance country house.

PLACES OF INTEREST

ITALY

AMALFI (408 D2)
CAMPANIA *pop. 5,800*
At one time Amalfi ruled commerce and shipping on the Mediterranean. It became the first independent Italian maritime republic and reached its zenith in the 11th century.

During the 1230s, however, Genoa and Pisa tumbled Amalfi from its position of power. The sea eventually took its harbor, and the city evolved into the pleasant holiday center of today.

THE AMALFI COAST DRIVE

The southern part of the Sorrentine Peninsula is one of the most beautiful coastlines in Europe, and to drive the precipitous Corniche Road that winds along it is an unforgettable experience. The road runs from Sorrento via Positano and Amalfi to Salerno, giving glimpses of small resorts and tiny fishing hamlets *en route.*

DUOMO DI SANT' ANDREA (Cathedral of St. Andrew) Piazza del Duomo, dates from the 11th century. The body of St. Andrew reposes in the crypt. The adjoining cloisters date from 1103.

GROTTA DELLO SMERALDO (Emerald Grotto) is 12 kilometers (7 miles) west. Reflected light turns the grotto's clear water and stalactites a rich green.

▲ ANCONA (408 C4)
MARCHE *pop. 103,200*
The Adriatic seaport of Ancona was founded in the 4th century BC by Greeks from Syracuse and colonized by Rome a century later. Like many Italian cities, it was an independent republic during the Middle Ages, but from 1532 to 1860 it formed part of the papal states.

Ancona suffered severe damage during World War II and in a later earthquake, although some of its ancient monuments survived or were restored. Today this busy commercial and industrial city is noted as a resort and for the manufacture of accordions and guitars.

ARCO DI TRAIANO (Arch of Trajan) was erected in 115 AD to honor the emperor who developed the port.

DUOMO DI SAN CIRIACO (Cathedral of St. Cyriacus) dominates the city and harbor. The sturdy Romanesque structure incorporates the Byzantine Greek-cross floor plan; two lions of Verona marble guard its Gothic entrance.

MUSEO NAZIONALE DELLE MARCHE, in the 16th-century Palazzo Ferretti, provides a comprehensive survey of the archeology of the Marche region.

▲ AOSTA (408 A5)
VALLE D'AOSTA *pop. 36,100*
A leading holiday resort as well as the capital of the region, Aosta was founded about 25 BC by the Romans. The remnants of a theater, amphitheater, forum and impressive double gateway are among the monuments within the Roman walls that still partially enclose the old city. The 1st-century Arco di Augusto (Arch of Augustus) can be found on Via Sant' Anselmo near the old Roman bridge.

Dwarfed by the surrounding Alps, Aosta is the Italian terminus of three auto routes to France and Switzerland. A cable car runs from Aosta to the winter-sports area at Pila. To the south is the Gran Paradiso National Park.

COLLEGIATA DI SANT' ORSO (Collegiate Church of St. Orso) ranges in age from the 8th century (the crypt), to the 12th century (the nave) and the 15th century (the choir stalls). The carved capitals of the Romanesque cloister depict biblical events and an old folk fable.

▲ L'AQUILA (408 C3)
ABRUZZO pop. 67,800

Against the hulking backdrop of the Gran Sasso, L'Aquila, capital of the Abruzzo, rises behind its ramparts. Today it is a major resort, popular in both winter and summer. Of note is the Fontana delle 99 Cannelle (Fountain of the 99 Spouts). This recalls a local legend claiming that the town was created by Emperor Frederick II by combining the populations of 99 villages. To perpetuate the legend, the clock tower of the Palazzo di Giustizia sounds 99 strokes every evening.

BASILICA DI SAN BERNARDINO DA SIENA crowns a small piazza stairway on Via San Bernardino. The Renaissance façade dates from 1527, the rest of the structure from the mid-1400s.

BASILICA DI SANTA MARIA DI COLLE-MAGGIO is at the end of the Piazza Collemaggio. The Romanesque structure was begun in the late 13th century; the façade, noted for its rose windows, was added in the 14th century.

CASTELLO, a 16th-century Spanish fortress, dominates the town. It houses the National Museum of the Abruzzo.

▲ AREZZO (408 C4)
TOSCANA pop. 91,900

The familiar "do-re-mi-fa-so" originated in Arezzo as part of the first system of musical notation, invented by Guido d'Arezzo in the 11th century. The poet Petrarch was born in this village, as was Giorgio Vasari, a painter, sculptor and architect who chronicled the lives of various Renaissance artists.

On the first Sunday in September, Giostra del Saraceno, a tournament in which mounted lancers charge a dummy, is held in Arezzo's Piazza Grande. This spectacle involves thousands of citizens all clad in 13th-century garb.

CHIESA DI SAN FRANCESCO, a 14th-century Gothic structure, houses celebrated frescoes by Piero della Francesca. A 15th-century stained-glass window in the façade is by Guillaume de Marcillat.

DUOMO, begun in 1277, stands above the main square, Piazza Grande. It contains *Mary Magdalen*, another fresco by Piero della Francesca, and the massive 16th-century tomb of Bishop Guido Tarlati.

MUSEO ARCHEOLOGICO (Archeological Museum), Via Magaritone 10, is next to the Roman amphitheater. It contains fine collections of locally produced 1st-century BC vases and Etruscan figures.

SANTA MARIA DELLA PIEVE, a parish church on the Piazza Grande, was built in the early 14th century. The delicate arcades of its Romanesque façade reveal the Pisan influence.

▲ ÁSCOLI PICENO (408 C3)
MARCHE pop. 56,000

The Picini tribe founded the town, which was destroyed by the Romans in the 1st century BC and rebuilt in a chessboard pattern. Medieval Ascoli Piceno is best seen from the Roman Ponte Solesta, which arches 24 meters (80 feet) above the Tronto River.

PIAZZA DEL POPOLO (People's Square) is the heart of the old city. The flagstone piazza is bordered by the 13th-century Palazzo del Popolo, which has a Renaissance courtyard; the Chiesa di San Francesco (Church of St. Francis), begun in the 13th century; and the 16th-century Loggia dei Mercanti (Merchants'

Loggia). On the first Sunday in August the square is the focus of the Tournament of the Quintana festival.

ASOLO (408 B6)
VENETO *pop. 3,500*

The actress Eleonore Duse was born and is buried in this medieval town, and the poet Robert Browning was a resident. The Museo Civico contains memorabilia of both. The Castello was also home to Caterina Cornaro, 15th-century queen of Cyprus, who was given Asolo in return for surrendering Cyprus to the Venetians.

ASSISI (408 C4) ★
UMBRIA *pop. 25,000*

A gentle landscape outside its walls and a history of gentle saints within characterize serene Assisi, birthplace of St. Francis and St. Clare.

Assisi has changed little since the days of St. Francis, but tourism has brought inevitable crowds and commercialism. Nevertheless, it is one of the most charming towns in Umbria. The Rocca Maggiore, a 14th-century castle, offers a sweeping view, and on the town's main square is the 1st-century Temple of Minerva and the medieval town hall.

BASILICA DI SAN FRANCESCO, consecrated in 1253, consists of two churches surmounting a crypt. In the upper basilica are the noted Giotto frescoes, 28 scenes from the life of St. Francis and Giovanni Cimabue's painting of the Crucifixion. The lower basilica contains frescoes by Simone Martini on the life of St. Martin. The tomb of St. Francis is in the crypt.

CHIESA DI SANTA CHIARA (Church of St. Clare), completed in 1265, is dedicated to the founder of the Poor Clares. The saint reposes open to view in the crypt.

DUOMO DI SAN RUFINO (Cathedral of St. Rufinus) is a Romanesque building noted for its belltower and façade. The interior houses the font where St. Francis and St. Clare were baptized.

▲ ASTI (408 A4)
PIEMONTE *pop. 74,500*

Asti, in the Tárano wine-producing region, lends its name to the popular sparkling wine Asti Spumante. Settled by the Romans, the city was a bishopric in the 10th century and a prosperous commune in the Middle Ages.

Traces of Asti's past can be seen in the city's many towers, which include those of a 14th-century Gothic cathedral. The Collegiate Church of San Secundo was built in the 13th and 14th centuries; it has a Romanesque tower and Gothic decorations. On the third Sunday in September, Asti holds its Palio, a bareback horse race said to be the oldest in Italy, originating in 1275.

▲ BARI (408 D3)
PUGLIA *pop. 354,000*

A major seaport, modern industrial Bari, Puglia's capital, spreads gridlike around its medieval core. The Castello (castle), first built by the Normans in 1131, is among the many interesting buildings in the old quarter. Alberobello and Fasano, about 55 kilometers (34 miles) south east, contain a number of *trulli*, the low, cone-roofed dwellings of unknown origin for which the region is noted.

BASILICA DI SAN NICOLA (Basilica of St. Nicholas), built 1097–1197 on the site of a Byzantine governor's residence, incorporates two towers from the earlier

---

ST. FRANCIS OF ASSISI

St. Francis was born in 1182. Like many 12th-century males he spent his youth womanizing and wining, until a nearly fatal illness converted him to a life of poverty, penitence and prayer. In 1210 he founded the mendicant Franciscan Order. St. Clare, a devoted follower of Francis, established the Order of Poor Clares in 1212 and retired to the nearby Convento di San Damiano.

---

structure. Noteworthy are the magnificent bishop's throne and the relics of St. Nicholas, the original Santa Claus.

CATTEDRALE DI SAN SABINO, built in 1170, also employs elements of earlier Byzantine edifices.

BARLETTA (408 D3)
PUGLIA *pop. 89,000*
Barletta, a large agricultural and commercial center on the Adriatic, has a 12th–14th-century Duomo (cathedral) and two good beaches.

CASTEL DEL MONTE, about 26 kilometers (16 miles) south, is a commanding octagonal castle with a tower at each angle; it was built by Emperor Frederick II.

CASTELLO, in Barletta, is another of Frederick II's castles, built on the foundations of a Norman fortress and with 16th-century Spanish bastions.

COLOSSO, a bronze Roman statue measuring 5 meters (16 feet), believed to represent a Byzantine emperor, is the largest known bronze statue in existence.

BAVENO (408 B5)
PIEMONTE *pop. 4,400*
Baveno is a quiet resort on Lake Maggiore. Excursions can be made to unspoiled Isola Superiore; Isola Bella, known for its Palazzo Borromeo; and Isola Madre.

▲ BERGAMO (408 B5)
LOMBARDIA *pop. 118,000*
Bergamo is one of the most beautifully situated cities in Lombardia. On the plain is the modern Città Bassa (Lower Town), but 120 meters (400 feet) above, guarded by its ancient Venetian walls, is the Città Alta (Upper Town).

After rising and falling with Rome and serving as the seat of a Lombard duchy, the city became Venetian territory in 1428, which it remained for over 350 years. In the 16th century there developed here the Commedia dell' Arte form

of theater; Bergamo also fostered the Bergamasque School of painting.

CITTÀ ALTA has at its heart the Piazzia Vecchia, with its fountain and fine bordering buildings. Palazzo della Ragione, built in 1199 and reconstructed in the 16th century, is one of the oldest such palaces in the country.

Battistero (Baptistery), an octagonal structure dating from the 14th century, was once part of Santa Maria Maggiore.

Cappella Colleoni (Colleoni Chapel), the mausoleum of the *condottiere* (mercenary soldier) Bartolomeo Colleoni, was completed in 1476. Richly sculptured marble marks the façade. Inside are delicately carved bas-reliefs; the ceiling frescoes were added by Giovanni Battista Tiepolo in the 18th century.

Santa Maria Maggiore was begun in 1137. While the outside is unimposing, the interior was lavishly decorated in the 16th and 17th centuries.

CITTÀ BASSA

Accademia Carrara (Carrara Academy), features the Bergamasque and Venetian schools of painting from the 16th to the 18th centuries.

▲ BOLOGNA (408 B4) ★
EMILIA-ROMAGNA *pop. 412,000*
One of Italy's oldest cities, Bologna was first recorded as the Etruscan village of Felsina. The Romans, who renamed it Bononia, ultimately lost it to the northern hordes. During the ensuing dark centuries, Bologna's university was one of the few lights of learning in Europe.

Today, Bologna is a major commercial and manufacturing center. Distinctive reminders of its medieval heyday are the red-brick houses and low arcades lining the narrow streets. The Via Zamboni is noted for its lovely private *palazzi*.

BASILICA DI SAN PETRONIO (Basilica of St. Petronius), honoring the city's patron saint, was begun in 1390 on a grandiose scale but was never completed. The transeptless nave is huge: its interior

ITALY

measures 58 by 131 meters (190 by 430 feet). The initial style was Gothic, but the architectural expressions of the succeeding periods are evident.

CHIESA DI SANTO STEFANO consists of several distinct sanctuaries. Of particular interest are the Church of St. Vitalis and Agricola, built from the 8th to the 11th centuries, and the Church of the Holy Sepulcher, dating from the 12th century. The basin in which Pontius Pilate reputedly washed his hands of the Crucifixion (actually 8th century) is in a courtyard behind the latter.

CIVICO MUSEO BIBLIOGRAFICO MUSICALE (Musical Bibliographical Museum), Piazza Rossini, contains collections of rare books, antique musical scores and autographs of well-known composers.

FONTANA DEL NETTUNO (Neptune's Fountain; 1566), by Giambologna, occupies the piazza of the same name.

GALLERIA COMUNALE D'ARTE MODERNA (Modern Art Gallery) exhibits modern paintings and sculpture.

MUSEO CIVICO ARCHEOLOGICO (Municipal Archeological Museum), Via Archiginnasio 2, faces the east side of San Petronio and contains Egyptian, Etruscan and Roman antiquities.

PALAZZO DEL PODESTÀ (Governor's Palace) is across the Piazza Maggiore from San Petronio. The Renaissance façade has some fine stonework.

PINACOTECA NAZIONALE (National Picture Gallery), at Via delle Belle Arti and Via Zamboni, houses one of Europe's finest collections, with special emphasis on the work of the Bolognese School from the 14th to 17th centuries, and the Caracci and their followers.

QUADRERIA DEL CONSERVATORIO (Conservatory Picture Gallery) displays paintings by Gainsborough and Crespi.

TORRE ASINELLI AND TORRE GARISENDA, both leaning, are in the Piazza di Porta Ravegnana. The former, 96 meters (315 feet) high, rewards a 426-step climb with a good view; the latter is 50 meters (165 feet) high.

UNIVERSITÀ, at Via Zamboni and Via Trombetti, is the oldest university in Europe (founded 11th century).

▲ BRÉSCIA (408 B5)
LOMBARDIA *pop. 197,000*
The demand for fine armor and swords made Bréscia one of the wealthiest cities in Italy during the Middle Ages. Still a busy industrial and agricultural center, Lombardia's second city has a pleasant location, but some of it is unappealing with unattractive Fascist architecture.

The Museum of the Roman Age and the Museum of Christian Art are part of a cluster of museums on the Via dei Musei that house antiquities and a variety of ecclesiastical displays.

LOGGIA, the 16th-century town hall, is an unusual building with an open portico and marble decorations. On the same piazza are two late 15th-century palaces.

PINACOTECA (Picture Gallery), on the Via Martinengo da Barco, displays mainly local paintings.

ROTONDA, in the Piazza del Duomo, is the *duomo vecchio* (old cathedral). Outwardly dwarfed by the marble *duomo nuovo*, or new cathedral, the round Romanesque structure houses a fine rose marble bishop's sarcophagus. Additional sarcophagi are in the 11th-century crypt.

▲ BRINDISI (408 E3)
PUGLIA *pop. 93,200*
In medieval times Brindisi was an embarkation point for the Holy Land; nowadays, it is a main ferry port for Greece. A 20-meter (65-foot), 1st-century BC marble column close to the harbor marks the end of the Appian Way.

CAPRI (408 C2)
CAMPANIA *pop. 12,700*

The isle of Capri has drawn visitors from Roman emperors to modern tourists. It has an excellent year-round climate and a wide variety of landscapes.

The island can be reached from Naples by steamer or hydrofoil. Crossing time is about 1½ hours by steamer and 40 minutes by hydrofoil.

ANACAPRI is the name given to the town and to the whole western part of the island. Both are dominated by 580-meter (1,903-foot) Monte Solaro, the highest point on Capri; the summit commands a panorama extending from the Bay of Naples to the mountains of Calabria.

CAPRI TOWN is reached by funicular from the Marina Grande clock. It has a 17th-century Duomo and the Giardino di Augusto, founded by Emperor Augustus, provides wonderful views.

GROTTA AZZURRA (Blue Grotto), 4 kilometers (2½ miles) from Anacapri on the northern coast, is the best known of the island's grottoes. It measures nearly 30 meters (100 feet) high, 55 meters (180 feet) long and 15 meters (50 feet) wide. Light refracted from the deep water creates the ever-changing shades of blue, best seen in the morning.

VILLA IOVIS (Jove's Villa), Via Tiberio, the remains of Emperor Tiberius' most lavish villa, tops Monte Tiberio. From the promenade there are panoramic views of the surrounding countryside. It takes almost an hour to walk to the villa.

▲ CASERTA (408 D3)
CAMPANIA *pop. 69,300*

Caserta was the 18th-century showplace of the Kingdom of Naples. During World War II it was the headquarters of Allied Forces in the Mediterranean.

LA REGGIA (Royal Palace) was intended to be the Versailles of the Bourbon kings of Naples and Sicily. Built 1752–74, the 1,200-room palace has four courts and 34 staircases. The royal apartments are richly decorated, and the palace borders a 100-hectare (247-acre) landscaped park.

CASSINO (408 C3)
LATIUM *pop. 34,500*

Cassino's monastery of Montecassino, founded by St. Benedict in 529 AD as headquarters of the Benedictine movement, featured prominently in the battle for liberation of the area by the Allies in World War II. The Germans held Cassino against repeated attacks between October 1943 and May 1944. Eventually, a fierce assault by Polish troops (1,000 of whom died) forced the Germans to abandon the ruined monastery. It has been faithfully reconstructed, but lacks atmosphere.

▲ CATANZARO (408 D2)
CALABRIA *pop. 103,800*

Busy Catanzaro, Calabria's capital, is on a high cliff within sight of the Ionian Sea. Behind it rises the Sila Massif, a plateau that reaches 2,533 meters (8,310 feet). Excursions can be made southward along the Ionian coast and around the "toe" of Italy to Reggio Calabria, the former capital of the province, or northward over the Sila to Cosenza.

CIVIDALE DEL FRIULI (408 C5)
FRIULI-VENEZIA GIULIA *pop. 9,000*

Founded by Julius Caesar, Cividale del Friuli is one of the few places in Italy to still see the legacy of the Lombards, a Teutonic tribe that swept into Italy after the fall of the Roman Empire. The Tempietto Lombardo, particularly its carved stucco arch, is the finest example of Lombard art, but the 15th-century Duomo contains other examples, notably the 8th-century Altar of Ratchis. Lombard artifacts are displayed in the Museo Archeologico.

▲ COMO (408 B5)
LOMBARDIA *pop. 88,800*

Como is at the extreme southern end of Lake Como, its green banks providing

ITALY

an attractive contrast to the distant snow-capped mountain range.

DUOMO is a splendid Gothic-Renaissance marble cathedral. The façade was decorated by the Rodari brothers; fine tapestries hang inside.

CORTONA (408 C4)
TUSCANY *pop. 3,200*

Cortona sits on Monte Egidio, and the views from its ramparts are among the best in Tuscany. In addition to its crumbling Duomo, churches include 13th-century Sant'Agostino; 14th-century San Nicolò, with an altarpiece by Luca Signorelli, who was born here; and the Renaissance Santa Mariadel Calcinaio. There is fine Renaissance art in the Museo Diocesano and an Etruscan museum in the Palazzo Casali.

▲ CREMONA (408 B5)
LOMBARDIA *pop. 75,100*

This quiet, agricultural town, noted for its medieval appearance, was where Antonio Stradivari and other noted violin-makers perfected their art during the 17th and 18th centuries. Claudio Monteverdi, whose *Orfeo* is considered to have laid the groundwork for modern opera, was born in Cremona.

MUSEO CIVICO (Civic Museum), Via Ugolani, is in the late-Renaissance Palazzo Affaitati. The museum houses Roman remains, violins and paintings by the 16th-century Cremona school.

MUSEO STRADIVARIANO (Stradivarius Museum), Via Palestro 17, exhibits plans, models, molds and tools belonging to violin-maker Antonio Stradivari.

PIAZZA DEL COMUNE (Town Square) is an impressive plaza bordered by some of Cremona's primary attractions. The Duomo, begun in the 12th century, has Romanesque, Gothic and Renaissance features. The 13th-century Torrazzo, at 115 meters (370 feet) high, is one of the tallest towers in Italy. The octagonal

Battistero (Baptistery), the Loggia dei Militi (Soldier's Loggia) and the Palazzo Comunale (Town Hall), containing violins by Stradivari and the Amati family, are also on the square.

ELBA (408 B3)
TOSCANA

Largest island of the Tuscan archipelago in the Tyrrhenian Sea, mountainous Elba can be reached by ferry from Piombino and Livorno. The island's highest point is 1,019 meters (3,343 feet) Monte Capanne, and its largest beach is Marina di Campo on the south coast. However, Elba is best known as the island where Napoléon Bonaparte spent 10 months of exile 1814–15.

PORTOFERRAIO is the chief town of Elba. Places to see are Misericordia Church, with its bronze reproduction of Napoléon Bonaparte's death mask; the Palazzina dei Mulini, with the emperor's suite of rooms; and his summer house, San Martino Villa.

FAENZA (408 C4)
EMILIA-ROMAGNA *pop. 54,000*

Faenza, on the banks of the Lamone River, is best known for its faience, or majolica. Faience masterpieces are on display at the Museo Internazionale delle Ceramiche, which details the history of fired pottery with the emphasis on faience-ware.

In the Piazza della Libertà is the early Renaissance cathedral, with its unfinished façade, and two medieval palaces.

▲ FERRARA (408 C4)
EMILIA-ROMAGNA *pop. 140,600*

An agricultural and industrial center on a broad plain, Ferrara still preserves a Renaissance atmosphere, recalling the time (1264–1598) when it was the seat of the powerful Este family.

Great patrons of the arts, the Este imported Roger van der Weyden, Paolo Veronese and Pisanello to Ferrara, who formed the stylistic basis for the Ferrara School of painting.

CASTELLO ESTENSE is the moat-girt 14th-century castle of the Este family. The grim dungeons once held Parisina, wife of Duke Nicolò III, and her lover before they were executed.

DUOMO, the 12th-century cathedral, has a marble façade with a carved portal depicting the Last Judgement. Unusual 12th-century bas-reliefs, statues by Jacopo della Quercia and works by Cosimo Tura are in the museum.

PALAZZO DEI DIAMANTI is faced with blocks of marble faceted like diamonds. One of the best collections of Ferraran paintings is in the Pinacoteca Nazionale.

PALAZZO DI LUDOVICO IL MORO (Palace of Ludovico the Moor) houses an archeological museum with Etruscan and Greek items.

PALAZZO SCHIFANOLA, built in the 15th century, was the pleasure resort of the Este. The frescoes in the Sala dei Mesi (Hall of Months) depict arcadian scenes.

▲ FIRENZE (408 B4) ★
TOSCANA *pop. 408,400*
Firenze, or Florence, was founded by Julius Caesar in 59 BC. In the 6th century it was conquered by the Lombards, who ruled the city for 200 years before it came under the control of the Holy Roman Empire. In 1115, Florence became an independent city-state.

The first period of Florentine art, with Romanesque church architecture, began between the 11th and 12th centuries. Then came the split of the townspeople (between the Guelphs, or the papal party, and the Ghibellines, the imperial party) that was to last for centuries.

In 1252, the gold florin was first minted in Florence. This was the first coin to be used extensively for trading and banking, and formed the standard medium of exchange until the 16th century.

The early 15th century brought the beginning of the Renaissance. The powerful Medici family, bankers who became rulers, were enthusiastic patrons of the arts. Brunelleschi in architecture, Donatello in sculpture and Masaccio in painting all broke new ground in early 15th-century Florence. In the High Renaissance of the early 16th century, four of the greatest names in Italian art – Botticelli, Leonardo da Vinci, Raphael and Michelangelo – once worked here.

Few visitors leave Florence untouched by its beauty. One can stroll for hours just enjoying the scenery, window-shopping, pausing among the sellers of second-hand books and scrutinizing the open-air stalls that decorate the streets.

Events in Florence include Scoppio del Carro on Easter Sunday, the Florence May Music Festival during May and June, and the football games in 16th-century costume in late June to celebrate the feast day of St. John the Baptist, Florence's patron saint.

Some 8 kilometers (5 miles) north is Fiesole, where the views of Florence are astounding. The 11th-century cathedral has carvings by Mino da Fiesole and the Teatro Romano, where classical plays are still performed, dates from 80 BC.

BATTISTERO (Baptistery) (430 C2), decorated in Romanesque style, was originally built in the 5th century. The 14th-century bronze doors are world-renowned, especially the East Doors, Lorenzo Ghiberti's "Gates of Paradise."

What you see here is a replica, the originals having been moved to the Museo dell'Opera del Duomo.

CHIESA DI SANTA CROCE (430 E1), built in the 14th century but with a 19th-century façade, contains fine monuments and the tombs of Michelangelo, Niccolo Machiavelli, Galileo and many others; it also has frescoes by Giotto and father and son Taddeo and Agnolo Gaddi.

CHIESA DI SAN LORENZO (430 C4) is one of the best expressions of Renaissance religious architecture. The interior by Filippo Brunelleschi is fine, but the main attraction is the Medici Chapel behind

ITALY

the church and the tombs there, sculpted by Michelangelo. He also designed the extraordinary Biblioteca Laurenziana.

CHIESA DI SANTA MARIA DEL CARMINE (430 A1) is a must for the frescoes in its Brancacci Chapel. This cycle of paint-

ings by Masaccio, depicting biblical scenes, was completed by Filippino Lippi after Masaccio's early death.

CHIESA DI SANTA MARIA NOVELLA (430 B3), which was begun in 1278, has some of Florence's greatest Renaissance paint-

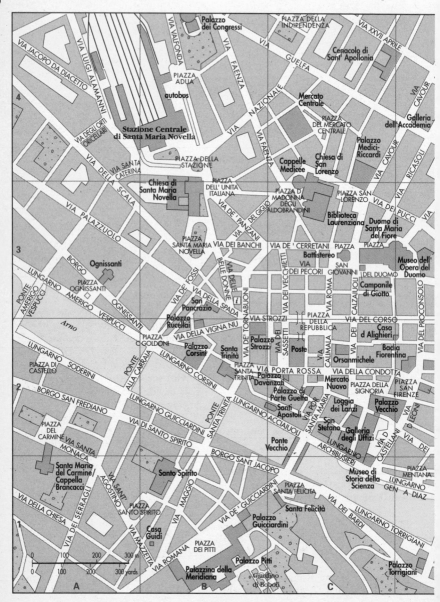

ings: Masaccio's innovative *Trinity*; Orcagna's altarpiece; and Ghirlandaio's charming versions of the lives of the Virgin and John the Baptist. Also worth seeing are the Cappella Strozzi, frescoed by Filippino Lippi, and the Cloisters with Uccello's *Noah's Flood*.

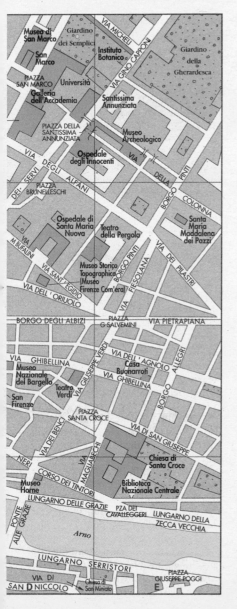

CHIESA DI SAN MINIATO, is Florence's best Romanesque church. The marble façade and the superb interior, with its unusual raised choir, are 11th century. The highlight is the Cardinal of Portugal's chapel.

DUOMO DI SANTA MARIA DEL FIORE (430 C3), in the Gothic style, features Brunelleschi's vast dome, a miracle of early engineering. The 14th-century Campanile (bell-tower), to a design by Giotto, is 80 meters (265 feet) high and can be climbed.

GALLERIA DELL'ACCADEMIA (430 D4), Via Ricasoli 60, is visited for its collection of Michelangelo sculptures, including the original *David*. There is also a *Pietà*, an incomplete *St. Matthew* and *Four Slaves*, struggling to escape the stone.

GALLERIA DEGLI UFFIZI (430 C2), Piazzale degli Uffizi, houses one of the richest collections of masterpieces in the world. The gallery is in the Uffizi Palace, built in the 1560s as government offices.

Highlights include the *Annunciation* of Simone Martini; the Botticelli Room, which contains the *Birth of Venus* and *Primavera* by that artist; Leonardo da Vinci's *Annunciation*; Michelangelo's *Doni Tondo;* and Titian's *Venus of Urbino*.

MUSEO NAZIONALE DEL BARGELLO (430 D2), Via del Proconsolo 4, is a magnificent collection of Renaissance sculpture. There are works by Brunelleschi, Cellini, Donatello, Giotto, Giambologna, Michelangelo and Luca Della Robbia.

MUSEO DI SAN MARCO (430 D4), Piazza San Marco 2, housed in the Monastery of St. Mark, is a repository of works by Fra Angelico, who was a monk here (1436–7). Besides his frescoes *in situ* – including the wonderful *Annunciation* – there are works from other Florentine churches.

MUSEO DI STORIA DELLA SCIENZA (430 C2), Piazza dei Giudici 1, explores technology in the Renaissance period, and the links between art and science.

PALAZZO MEDICI-RICCARDI (430 C4), Via Cavour 1, was built for Cosimo the Elder by Michelozzo in 1444.

The chapel is the only surviving feature of the original design, with Gozzoli's *Journey of the Magi* fresco.

MICHELANGELO'S *DAVID*

The original of the world's most reproduced piece of sculpture, on display in the Galleria dell' Accademia, is not seen as its creator intended – as a piece of public sculpture. For this, you should view the replica outside the Palazzo Vecchio. In the gallery, David's head, hands and arms clearly are out of proportion; the deliberate distortions give a monumental effect.

PALAZZO PITTI (430 B1), in 15th-century Renaissance style, houses six museums, of which the Galleria Palatine is the most important. Its noted collection of 11 Raphaels includes the *Madonna of the Chair* and the *Grand Duke's Madonna*, as well as works by Filippo Lippi, Titian, Fra Bartolommeo, Andrea del Sarto, Rubens, Tintoretto and Van Dyck.

PIAZZA DELLA SIGNORIA (430 C2) is dominated by the Palazzo Vecchio, built in the 14th century to house the *signoria*, Florence's ruling council. The nearby Loggia della Signoria (or dei Lanzi) houses two famous sculptures: Cellini's *Perseus* and Giambologna's *Rape of the Sabine*.

PONTE VECCHIO (Old Bridge) (430 C2) dates from the 10th century. It is lined with jewelers' and silversmiths' shops.

FLORENCE – *see Firenze on p.429.*

GARGANO (408 D3)
PUGLIA
The wild, rocky peninsula of Gargano has religious sites at Monte Sant' Angelo, San Marco and elsewhere; salt lakes at Lesina and Varano; and evidence of prehistoric man at Peschici. The whole peninsula is covered by the mainly beech Umbra Forest.

MONTE SANT' ANGELO is perched on top of a limestone cliff. The unusual Sanctuary of St. Michael occupies the spot where the saint is said to have miraculously appeared to shepherds in a cave.

GENOA – *see Génova below.*

▲ **GÉNOVA** (408 B4)
LIGURIA *pop. 701,000*
Italy's leading seaport and chief commercial center, Génova, or Genoa, is laid out along the seashore like an amphitheater. Medieval churches, 16th- century palaces and modern commercial streets justify the city's nickname of "La Superba" (The Proud).

GALLERIA DI PALAZZO BIANCO, 11 Via Garibaldi, is Genoa's most important art gallery, with impressive works by Flemish, Dutch and local masters.

GALLERIA DI PALAZZO ROSSO, 18 Via Garibaldi, displays tapestries, furniture and major works of art, including portraits by Anthony Van Dyck.

MUSEO DEL TESORO DI SAN LORENZO, in the Cathedral of San Lorenzo, is a treasury of relics, including the Sacro Catino, believed to be the Holy Grail.

PALAZZO DUCALE (Ducal Palace), mainly dating from the 17th and 18th centuries, was the palace of the Genoese Doges.

SANT' AGOSTINO, in Piazzo Sarzano, was built 1260–82. Badly damaged during World War II, it is now restored. Next to the church is the original triangular cloister, containing a sculpture museum.

SAN DONATO is a small Romanesque church housing a beautiful 16th-century triptych with the *Adoration of the Magi* by Jan van Cleve.

GUBBIO (408 C4)
UMBRIA

Medieval Gubbio is renowned for its ancient festivals. The Feast of the Candles, in which three teams race uphill to the Abbey of St. Ubaldo carrying huge candle-shaped pillars, takes place on May 15; the Joust of the Balestrieri is held on the last Sunday in May.

PALAZZO DEI CONSOLI, a massive Gothic building, dominates the town. In the museum housed here are the Tavole Eugubine (Gubbio Tablets), ancient bronze plaques bearing inscriptions in the old Umbrian language and in Latin.

HERCULANEUM – *see Napoli on p.435.*

ISCHIA (408 C3)
CAMPANIA *pop. 44,000*

A volcanic island in the Bay of Naples, Ischia is rich in therapeutic mineral waters. It can be reached by steamer from Naples in 1½ hours and by hydrofoil in 45 minutes.

▲ LECCE (408 E2)
PUGLIA *pop. 102,300*

Lecce is remarkable for its many beautiful baroque buildings, notably the Cathedral and the Basilica di Santa Croce. There are also the remains of a Roman theater and an amphitheater.

LORETO (408 C4)
MARCHE *pop. 10,600*

SANTUARIO DELLA SANTA CASA is said to have been the Nazareth home of the Virgin Mary. In the 13th century, angels reputedly carried the house to its present site, where it is a major pilgrimage site. The 15th-century façade of the church built around the house is particularly fine. Bronze doors depict the expulsion of Adam and Eve; the sacristies have remarkable frescoes of angels.

▲ LUCCA (408 B4)
TOSCANA *pop. 86,400*

Lucca is one of Tuscany's finest cities, boasting a cathedral, many historic buildings and massive Renaissance walls with three gates intact. The Roman street grid survives within the ramparts.

CHIESA DI SAN MICHELE, is 12th century and has a glorious façade with three columned galleries. Inside are paintings by Filippo Lippi and Luca Della Robbia.

DUOMO, a cathedral built from the 10th to 15th centuries, also has a tiered façade. It contains what is supposed to be a true effigy of Christ.

▲ MANTOVA (408 B5)
LOMBARDIA *pop. 54,200*

Mantova, or Mantua, was the seat of Italy's Gonzaga family and their court from the 14th to 18th centuries. They built the immense Palazzo Ducale, still containing some of their art collection.

CASTELLO DI SAN GIORGIO, facing the Ducal Palace, is a 14th-century Gonzaga fortress known for the Camera degli Sposi, a matrimonial room containing superb frescoes by Mantegna.

PALAZZO TE is another Gonzaga palace, built in 1527 for the mistress of Duke Federico II. It contains the frescoed Room of the Giants.

MANTUA – *see Mantova above.*

▲ MATERA (408 D2)
BASILICATA *pop. 57,100*

Much of Matera's old quarter is built into the rock that forms the base of the hill supporting the 13th-century town cathedral. Views from the Strada Panoramica dei Sassi include the caves and stone stairways of the old quarter and the desolate gorge below.

MELFI (408 D3)
BASILICATA *pop. 13,900*

The Normans captured Melfi in 1041 and made it their first southern Italian capital. In 1059 Robert Guiscard was recognized by Pope Nicholas II as Duke of Apulia and Calabria in the eight-towered castle at the top of the town; today there is a museum of antiquities here. The 12th-century cathedral was rebuilt after an earthquake which its campanile survived.

MERANO (408 B5)
TRENTINO-ALTO ADIGE *pop. 33,800*
Merano is a major health and vacation resort at the foot of the Val Venosta. It has a mild climate and its medicinal waters have been lauded since the 4th century BC.

MILAN – *see Milano below*.

▲ MILANO (408 B5)
LOMBARDIA *pop. 1,423,100*
Italy's leading commercial and industrial center, Milano, or Milan, is in the center of the Po Valley. Thoroughly modern in appearance, the city is also a storehouse of artistic treasures, its greatest being Leonardo da Vinci's *Last Supper*.

Milan was one of the most important cities in Christendom in the 4th century, and was again prominent under Charlemagne. But its economic and cultural heyday was in the Middle Ages, under the Visconti and Sforza families.

CASTELLO SFORZESCO, Piazza Castello, a 15th-century castle, houses the unfinished *Pietà Rondanini* by Michelangelo, and medieval and Renaissance collections in the Museo d'Arte Antica.

The Pinacoteca, the art library and the Trivulziana Library Museum of Old Musical Instruments are also of worthy of a visit.

DUOMO the largest Gothic cathedral in Italy, its spire topped by the golden *Madonnina* 108 meters (355 feet) above the ground. The roof and treasury can be visited by the public. A museum in the nearby Palazzo Reale houses statues, sketches and relics.

MUSEO POLDI PEZZOLI, 12 Via Manzoni, is a small palace with paintings, jewelry, arms and a collection of clocks.

PINACOTECA AMBROSIANA, 2 Piazza Pio XI, contains art exhibits dating from the 14th century. Of particular interest are wonderful works by such masters as Botticelli, Raphael, Titian, Caravaggio and Leonardo da Vinci.

PINACOTECA DI BRERA, 28 Via Brera, one of Italy's most important art galleries, contains such noted art pieces as Andrea Mantegna's *Dead Christ* and a magnificent *Pietà* by Giovanni Bellini.

SANTA MARIA DELLE GRAZIE, a 15th-century Renaissance church, houses frescoes by Gaudenzio Ferrari and, most notably, the *Last Supper* by Leonardo da Vinci on the refectory wall.

TEATRO ALLA SCALA is the best-known opera house in the world. It was built in 1776 and has acoustics considered by many to be perfect.

In the foyer are statues of Bellini, Donizetti, Rossini and Verdi. Museo Teatrale alla Scala is next to the theater.

SHOPPING IN MILAN
Milan is Italy's capital of design and high fashion, and is *the* place to shop for quality clothes, accessories and luxury goods.
The "Quadrilatero d'Oro" (Golden Quadrilateral), the area defined by Via Monte Napoleone, Via della Spiga, Via Borgo Spesso and Via Sant'Andrea, contains the top designer shops. For shopping – or simply strolling – in elegant surroundings, visit the 19th-century Galleria Vittorio Emanuele.

▲ MÓDENA (408 B4)
EMILIA-ROMAGNA *pop. 177,800*
Formerly the capital of the great Duchy of Este, Módena retains much evidence of that 600-year rule.

DUOMO is a Romanesque masterpiece dedicated to St. Geminian, Módena's patron saint. The sculptured decoration, particularly the bas-relief doorways and rood screen, is credited to Viligelmo.

MONTEPULCIANO (408 C4)
TOSCANA *pop. 14,400*
Montepulciano has preserved many of the Renaissance and Gothic buildings that still frame the old town's Piazza Grand, or stand along its narrow streets. Duomo, the cathedral, was built in 1570 and has an unfinished façade. Inside are statues and monuments by Michelozzo. Palazzo Comunale, the town hall, is a large 14th-century building whose tower reveals an excellent view. The Church of San Biagio, outside the town's walls, is one of Italy's most important Renaissance churches.

NAPLES – *see Napoli below.*

▲ NAPOLI (408 C3) ★
CAMPANIA *pop. 1,206,000*
Napoli, or Naples lies on the enchanting Bay of Naples, over which rises the cone of Mount Vesuvius. The city is the commercial, cultural and artistic center of southern Italy, and an important port on the Mediterranean.

CERTOSA DI SAN MARTINO, a former Carthusian monastery in the Neapolitan baroque style, is now a museum.

DUOMO SAN GENNARO contains the treasure of the patron saint of Naples and fragments of a 4th-century basilica founded by Emperor Constantine.

ERCOLANO (Herculaneum), lying 7 kilometers (4 miles) south east, was buried by mud from the 79 AD eruption of Vesuvius. Though smaller than Pompeii, it is better preserved, some buildings standing two stories high. Of note are the houses of Deer, Telephus and Samnite, and the temples of Diana, Mercury and Venus.

MOUNT VESUVIUS is 1,277 meters (4,190 feet) high and still active. Eruptions have occurred since 79 AD (when the cities of Pompeii and Herculaneum were destroyed), the last time being in 1944. Visitors can climb to the rim of the crater.

MUSEU NAZIONALE ARCHEOLOGICO contains the best finds from Pompeii and Herculaneum. There are wall paintings and mosaics from these and other Campanian sites on the upper floor. The *Battle of Issus* mosaic is particularly fine.

PALAZZO REALE DI CAPODIMONTE, to the north of the city, is a former royal palace. It houses a picture gallery with an excellent collection of native and foreign works, largely Renaissance.

POMPEII (408 D3) is at the foot of Mount Vesuvius, whose eruption buried it in volcanic ash in 79 AD. Excavations have revealed life in this ancient city as it was nearly 2,000 years ago. Look for the Antiquarium, Forum, Stabian Baths, Casa dei Vettii and Villa of the Mysteries. The ornamental mural designs representing four different periods retain brilliant colors.

THE GENUINE PIZZA
Pizzas originated in Naples in the 18th century, and only one cooked in a wood-fired brick oven can claim to be genuine. Traditional toppings include tomatoes, mozzarella and fresh basil, in the colors of the Italian flag and devised in honor of Queen Margherita.

TEATRO SAN CARLO, on Via Vittorio Emanuele III, was built in 1737 and is one of Europe's grandest opera houses.

ORVIETO (408 C3)
UMBRIA *pop. 21,500*
This hill town has preserved its medieval appearance; Orvieto wine is produced here.

DUOMO, started in the 13th century, is perhaps Italy's finest Gothic cathedral. Its façade is adorned with mosaics,

ITALY

carved stonework and statuary; inside is Luca Signorelli's *Last Judgement*.

POZZO DI SAN PATRIZIO (St. Patrick's Well) was dug in 1537 by order of Pope Clement VII de Medici to supply the town with water in case of siege.

▲ PADOVA (408 C5)
VENETO *pop. 228,100*
According to legend Padova, or Padua, was founded by Antenore, a Trojan prince; under the Romans, it became one of the empire's richest cities. Destroyed by the Lombards in 602 AD, it flourished again as a Venetian territory during the Middle Ages. Today it is a busy, sprawling city, much rebuilt after World War II bomb damage.

BASILICA DI SANT' ANTONIO is a fine 13th-century Roman-Gothic building with Byzantine cupolas. Relics of St. Anthony, whose tomb is present, are in the treasury chapel; bronze bas-reliefs by Donatello embellish the high altar.

CAPPELLA DEGLI SCROVEGNI, is located on Corso Garibaldi. It houses one of Italy's greatest fresco cycles, Giotto's 38 scenes from the lives of Christ and the Virgin Mary.

GATTAMELATA, in the Piazza del Santo, is a magnificent bronze statue (1453) by Donatello of Erasmo da Narni, the great Venetian *condottiere*.

MUSEO CIVICO (Civic Museum), Piazza Eremitani, is housed in the cloisters of the restored Monastery of Eremitani.

On display is an interesting and varied collection of archeological items, sculptures, coins and paintings.

PALAZZO DELLA RAGIONE, near the Piazza delle Frutta, is the law court built in the 13th and 14th centuries. In the attic salon are 15th-century frescos and the Stone of Dishonor.

PADUA – *see Padova above.*

PAESTUM (408 D2)
CAMPANIA *pop. 900*
Paestum was once the ancient Greek city of Poseidonia. All that remains is a handful of well-preserved temples: the Temple of Neptune, the Basilica and the Temple of Ceres. The museum contains architectural fragments, sculpture and tomb paintings.

▲ PARMA (408 B4)
EMILIA-ROMAGNA *pop. 174,000*
Parma, one of Italy's most prosperous cities, is a busy commercial and agricultural center. It is notable for the numerous monuments and art collections that recall its past as capital of the Duchy of Farnese.

Correggio was born just east of Parma, and left notable frescoes in the Cathedral, the Church of San Giovanni Evangelista, and the Camera di San Paolo. Verdi was also born here, as was the conductor Arturo Toscanini.

BATTISTERO, a baptistery built of Verona red marble, was started in 1196 but not completed until 1307. Benedetto Antelami's Romanesque sculptures are some of Italy's most expressive.

DUOMO is a 12th-century Romanesque cathedral containing Correggio's great fresco *The Assumption*. The sculptured episcopal throne and *Deposition* bas-relief are by Benedetto Antelami.

PALAZZO DELLA PILOTTA houses the National Gallery, displaying paintings by Correggio and his pupil Parmigianini. Other artists represented are El Greco, Leonardo da Vinci, Holbein, Giovanni Battista Tiepolo and Van Dyck. Also within the palace are the Teatro Farnese (one of the most important 17th-century Italian theaters), the Palatine Library and the Bodoni Museum.

▲ PAVIA (408 B5)
LOMBARDIA *pop. 84,600*
Pavia, a former Lombard capital, had a stirring history before it came under the

aegis of the Visconti and Sforza families of Milan. It is now a fascinating collection of medieval streets and buildings.

CERTOSA DI PAVIA, a 1376 Carthusian monastery 10 kilometers (6 miles) from Pavia, is a masterpiece of Renaissance art. The façade of the monastery is decorated with marble slabs and delicate sculptures. Painted portraits of monks seem to watch visitors from the first chapel.

SAN MICHELE is a 12th-century church with a majestic façade. Medieval emperors were crowned here.

SAN PIETRO IN CIEL D'ORO, built in 1132, holds relics of St. Augustine and the tomb of the philosopher Boethius.

▲ PERÚGIA (408 C4)
UMBRIA *pop. 150,000*
Capital of its region, Perúgia held strategic importance for the Etruscans and Romans. It has early fortifications, including the remains of two Etruscan gates. Events include the Umbria Jazz Festival (July) and the Umbria Sacred Music Festival (September).

COLLEGIO DEL CAMBIO, Corso Vannucci 25, is the old 15th-century stock exchange building. Frescos by Il Perugino, teacher of Raphael, and his pupils adorn the council chamber.

DUOMO, Piazza Dante, was built in the Gothic style 1345–1490, but the interior is baroque.
The wrought-iron grilles are of interest, and a chapel is reputed to contain the Virgin Mary's wedding ring.

FONTANA MAGGIORE, Piazza 4 Novembre, is an ornate fountain dating from 1278. Sculptures are by Nicola Pisano and his son, Giovanni.

GALLERIA NAZIONALE DELL' UMBRIA, in the Palazzo dei Priori, exhibits Umbrian and Tuscan masterpieces.

PALAZZO DEI PRIORI (Sala dei Notari), Piazza 4 Novembre, is a grandiose palace dating from the 13th to 15th centuries. The great staircase leads to a marble pulpit from which the priors addressed the township.

SAN BERNARDINO, Via dei Priori, is a fine Renaissance-style church in multi-colored marble built in 1461. Scenes from the life of the saint and figures of angel musicians decorate the façade.

SAN PIETRO, on Corso Cavour, has been rebuilt several times since its construction in the 10th century.
It is a graceful church with an unusual bell-tower and the 16th-century stalls display carvings of the saints and Renaissance ornamentation.

▲ PÉSARO (408 C4)
MARCHE *pop. 90,600*
The beach resort of Pésaro is most famous for its Rossini Opera Festival and for ceramics. Pésaro was also the home of operatic composer Gioacchino Rossini, whose house is open to visitors. The principal building is the 16th-century Palazzo Ducale; the main art treasure is Bellini's *Coronation of the Virgin* in the Museo Civico.

▲ PIACENZA (408 B5)
EMILIA-ROMAGNA *pop. 103,000*
Piacenza is near the Po River at the end of the ancient Roman Via Emilia, which connects it with Milan. Founded in 218 BC by the Romans, it saw a long power struggle among leading families. Peace came during the Renaissance under the Farnese.
Visitors can still see the Farnese Palace, an impressive 16th-century structure that now houses the Museo Civico. Among the town's other attractions are the 12th-century Lombard-Romanesque cathedral with baroque frescoes by Barbieri Guercino, the 13th-century town hall in Lombard style, and the two splendid equestrian statues in Piazza dei Cavalli.

▲ PISA (408 B4) ★
TOSCANA *pop. 98,000*

Pisa is one of the finest towns in Italy, a veritable storehouse of famous buildings. Major sights form the Campo dei Miracoli (Field of Miracles); the Piazza dei Cavalieri is also interesting for its 16th- and 17th-century Pisan architecture. The Battle of the Bridge, a medieval parade and contest, is held on the last Sunday in June.

BATTISTERO (1278), a massive circular baptistery with an intriguing pulpit by Nicola Pisano, is known for its unusual echo-making qualities.

CAMPANILE, or Torre Pendente, the "Leaning Tower of Pisa," was begun in 1174 as a bell-tower for the cathedral. The white marble tower is 55 meters (180 feet) tall and has leaned since it was built. The tower became too dangerous and was closed to visitors in 1990; efforts are being made to stabilize it.

DUOMO, opposite the "Leaning Tower," is an enormous marble cathedral in Romanesque-Pisan style. The bronze door panels by Bonnano Pisano (about 1180), depict the life of Christ. The marvelous carved pulpit is the work of Giovanni Pisano.

MUSEO NAZIONALE, in the 15th-century Monastery of St. Matthew, contains medieval sculptures and painting.

MUSEO DELL' OPERA DEL DUOMO contains sculpture, paintings and church vestments from the cathedral and baptistery.

SANTA MARIA DELLA SPINA (St. Mary of the Thorn) is in Roman-Gothic style. The outer ornamentation illustrates the Pisan School of art.

▲ PISTOIA (408 B4)
TOSCANA *pop. 89,000*

This provincial capital has a superb medieval center, its many buildings including the Church of Sant' Andrea, with a fine sculptured pulpit; the Palazzo Pretorio; the Ospedale del Ceppo, known for its terracotta frieze by Giovanni della Robbia; and the Church of San Bartolomeo in Pantano.

The Cathedral of San Zeno is one of the most impressive buildings of all, combining Romanesque and baroque architecture. The Gothic Palazzo del Comune is also impressive; inside is the Museo Civico, displaying local paintings, sculptures and artifacts.

POMPEII – *see Napoli on p.435.*

PORTOFINO (408 B4)
LIGURIA *pop. 600*

Sheltered below Monte Portofino, attractive Portofino has become a popular (and expensive) gathering place for the rich and famous.

POSITANO (408 D2)
CAMPANIA *pop. 2,600*

Picture-postcard Positano, a relaxing place with no particular sights, has become a place to see and be seen.

RAPALLO (408 B4)
LIGURIA *pop. 29,700*

One of the best-known and most attractive resorts on the Italian Riviera, Rapallo is popular all year round.

Several medieval monuments are preserved, including the castle (used for exhibitions), and a convent, which is now a theater.

RAVELLO
CAMPANIA *pop. 2,400*

Picturesque Ravello, some 350 meters (1,150 feet) above Amalfi, affords a magnificent view of the Amalfi Coast.

The Villa Cimbrone, with its lush gardens, as well as the ancient cathedral, are both of interest.

VILLA RUFOLO, an 11th-century Saracenic-Romanesque structure that was at various times occupied by the Rufolo family and several popes, has a fountain-decked garden.

RAVENNA (408 C4) ★
EMILIA-ROMAGNA *pop. 136,700*
Briefly the capital of the Western Roman Empire, then capital of the Byzantine exarchate of Ravenna from the 6th to the 8th centuries, the city is famous for its glorious mosaics of the Byzantine era. Among its many attractions are the Basilica of St. Apollinare in Classe, 4 kilometers (2½ miles) from Ravenna, and the Archepiscopal Chapel in the Museum of the Archbishop's Palace.

BATTISTERO DEGLI ORTÓDOSSI, generally known as the Neonian Baptistery, was supposedly a Roman bathhouse before becoming a church in the 5th century.

MAUSOLEO DI GALLA PLACIDIA, Via Fiandrini, built in the 5th century, is noted for its rich mosaics.

SANT' APOLLINARE NUOVO, a 6th-century church, is known for its procession of mosaic saints and martyrs along the wall of the nave on the men's side of the building. On the women's side is a procession of 22 virgins led by the Magi.

SAN VITALE, an octagonal church built in 547, is spectacularly decorated with brightly colored mosaics of blue, green and gold, including those of the Byzantine Emperor Justinian, Empress Theodora and their court. Adjoining the monastery is the Museo Nazionale, housing an array of antiques.

▲ RÉGGIO DI CALÁBRIA (408 D1)
CALÁBRIA *pop. 178,500*
MUSEO NAZIONALE, Piazza de Nava, is Réggio's only worthwhile attraction. It contains terracotta sculptures, votive tablets and paintings by Antonello da Messina; its highlight is the Bronzi di Riaca, two 5th-century BC bronze figures recovered from the sea off Réggio.

▲ RÍMINI (408 C4)
EMILIA-ROMAGNA *pop. 130,000*
Rímini is a large, brash seaside resort well known for its excellent beach. The city also contains Roman ruins and Renaissance works of art. It was here that Julius Caesar defied the Roman senate by marching across the Rubicon and on to Rome.

ARCO D'AUGUSTO (Arch of Augustus), was built in 27 BC to commemorate the inaugural year of Augustus' reign.

PONTE DI TIBERIO (Bridge of Tiberius), also known as the Bridge of Augustus, spans the Marecchia River at the end of Corso d'Augusto. Made of Istrian travertine, the 63-meter (206-foot) bridge has five arches. Building it took from 14 to 21 AD and it remains in use today.

TEMPIO MALATESTIANO, a fine creation of the Renaissance, was erected by Sigismondo Malatesta, who ruled Rímini in the 15th century. The temple features admirable sculptures and bas-reliefs.

ROMA (ROME) – *see p.411.*

▲ SALERNO (408 D2)
CAMPANIA *pop. 152,400*
Salerno, a busy port with an interesting medieval core, was the scene of the 1943 Allied landing in World War II.

SAN GIMIGNANO (408 B4)
TOSCANA *pop. 7,000*
Perhaps more than any other Italian town, attractive, little San Gimignano has preserved its medieval appearance. Its former name was San Gimignano delle Belle Torri because of its 72 fortress-like towers, 14 of which are still standing today.

COLLEGIATA contains frescoes by early Renaissance artists including Benozzo Gozzoli and Taddeo di Bartolo. Best of all are those by Domenico Ghirlandaio in the Santa Fina chapel.

VIA SAN MATTEO is a charming, narrow medieval street lined with ancient houses. It leads to the fine Romanesque church of Sant' Agostino.

ITALY

SARDEGNA (408 B2)

Sardegna, or Sardinia, is enjoying increased popularity among travelers, who have discovered the island's distinct and colorful culture. Largely mountainous, Sardinia also offers attractive beaches, coves and grottoes, and sophisticated resorts on the Costa Smeralda.

The prehistoric inhabitants of Sardinia left relics of a unique and mysterious culture: tiny rock-cut tombs; "giants" tombs, characterized by huge, stone slabs; and *nuraghi*, curious stone fortresses and towers. Later came the Phoenicians, Carthaginians, Romans, Vandals, Byzantines and Arabs. The Spanish ruled Sardinia from 1479 to 1720, when the Piedmont dukes of Savoy gained control.

ALGHERO, founded in the 12th century, is a busy seaside town. Its Catalan heritage is reflected in many buildings, churches, fortifications and cultural events. There are prehistoric sites, grottoes and caves near by, notably Neptune's Grotto at Capo Caccia.

▲ CÁGLIARI is the large though pleasant capital and chief seaport of Sardinia. The city dates back to Phoenician times and there are the remains of a Roman amphitheater. The Duomo, on the Piazza Palazzo, was originally built in 1162, but was given a baroque interior in the 17th century and a mock-Romanesque façade in 1933.

The Museo Archeologico Nazionale houses both an archeological museum and a picture gallery. Particularly interesting are the bronze statuettes from the Nuraghic civilization.

COSTA SMERALDA, the extremely picturesque coast of northeastern Sardinia, was developed by the Aga Khan in the 1960s. A mecca for the jet set, it is ideal for watersports.

▲ NUORO stands at 550 meters (1,800 feet) near the foot of Mount Ortobene. Atop the mountain is a statue of Christ the Redeemer, the goal of a procession on the Feast of the Redeemer on August 29. Sardinia's foremost folk museum, the Museo della Vita e Tradizioni Popolari, is located here.

OLBIA is an ancient city, founded by the Carthaginians and once under Roman rule. Although this port, is a major gateway to Sardinia, there is little to see beyond the Romanesque Cathedral of San Simplicio, center for Olbia's main festival in mid-May.

▲ SÁSSARI, though a modern town, has a medieval center and some fine relics of the past. Among them is the Duomo, with its baroque façade. Look also for the ornate Fonte del Rosello, a late-Renaissance fountain, and the 18th-century Ducal Palace, now the town hall. The Museo Sanna, in the modern town, is an archeological museum.

SARDINIA – *see Sardegna above.*

SICILIA (408 C1) ★

Sicilia, or Sicily, one of the most beautiful islands in the Mediterranean, is also the largest. It was part of Magna Graecia, the Greek Mediterranean empire, from about 800 to 300 BC. After suffering the rule of Romans, Arabs, Normans, the French and the Spanish, Sicily gained a degree of autonomy in 1947, having its own Assembly in Palermo.

Sicily has vast stretches of beautiful scenery, from volcanic Mount Etna to sandy beaches (though parts of the coast have been spoiled by building activities). Some of the islands off Sicily still offer peaceful, unspoiled retreats.

Sicily has a rich archeological store: Greek temples and theaters, Roman mosaics, paleolithic cave art and rock-cut tombs of the Bronze Age period. The later architectural heritage is also rich, with Norman churches, Swabian castles and some superb baroque buildings.

▲ AGRIGENTO, founded by the Greeks as Akragas in 582 BC, has, in its Valley of

Temples, one of Europe's greatest archeological sites: the Greek Tempio della Concordia (Temple of Concord). The base and 34 columns are visible from a considerable distance. There are four other temples on the site. About a kilometer (½ mile) away is the Museo Archeologico Nazionale (Archeological Museum), containing a fine collection of finds from the area.

▲ CATÁNIA, Sicily's second city, stands at the southern foot of Mount Etna, which has destroyed it several times. Catánia's streets and attractive buildings date from the reconstruction following the earthquake of 1693. Castello Ursino (1287) now houses the Civic Museum. The Duomo, originally Norman, was remodeled in baroque style. The Church of San Nicolo is Sicily's largest.

Mount Etna is Europe's tallest and most active volcano; it experienced its tenth major eruption of the century in December 1991. It is possible to visit the summit during less active periods.

THE SICILIAN MAFIA

Sicily's history of foreign domination and the consequent distrust of and isolation from the state provided a fertile soil for a form of local – and lawless – authority. Before World War II Mussolini tried ruthlessly to eradicate the Mafia. It was the Allies who revived the organization, enlisting Mafia help in the invasion of Sicily and afterwards giving control of towns to men with Mafia connections. The present-day power of the Mafia is known only too well.

▲ ENNA, perched on a crag at 915 meters (3,000 feet), has a genial climate, even in summer. The Citadel, or Castello de Lombardia, is a medieval fortress with mighty ramparts and six towers, the tallest of which provides an excellent view. The 14th-century Duomo has an interesting 16th-century interior.

▲ MESSINA, at the northern end of the Straits of Messina, is the natural entrance to Sicily, and there are regular passenger- and car-ferry services from the Italian mainland. The city is completely modern, having been destroyed by an earthquake in 1908.

The reconstructed cathedral has an astronomical clock in the campanile, reputed to be one of the largest of its kind in the world. The Museo Nazionale contains two paintings by Michelangelo da Caravaggio and other notable works from the 13th to 16th centuries.

NOTO is one of the gems of Sicily, a town completely rebuilt in baroque style after a devastating earthquake in 1693.

▲ PALERMO is the capital, largest city and principal port of Sicily. Although poverty and neglect make parts of Palermo uninviting, the city's location and varied architecture compensate for this. Several splendid buildings date from the time of Roger, King of Sicily, who first united the Greek, Arabic and Norman influences of southern Italy under an enlightened rule in the 12th century.

Capella Palatina (Palatine Chapel), Palermo's jewel, is part of the Palace of the Normans, the Sicilian Parliament building. Built between 1130 and 1140, it has lavish Arab-Norman decoration.

Cattedrale was consecrated in 1185. Its 18th-century interior is dull, but contains Norman royal tombs and a rich treasury.

Chiesa Della Martorana, on Piazza Bellini, was founded in 1143. The original church, now fronted by a 17th-century façade, contains some particularly fine Byzantine mosaics.

Chiesa di San Giovanni Degli Eremiti (Church of St. John of the Hermits), entirely Arabic in appearance, was built in 1132. A peaceful garden with 13th-century cloisters adjoins the church.

Duomo in Monreale (Cathedral in Monreale) 8 kilometers (5 miles) south, is one of the world's outstanding Norman structures. Magnificent 12th-century mosaics depict Christ enthroned

ITALY

and biblical events. The decoration of the adjoining cloisters reinforces the Moorish style.

Museo Archeologico Nazionale, in a 16th-century monastery at Piazza Olivella, contains an important collection of Sicilian artifacts. The bas-reliefs from Selinunte are of special note.

PIAZZA ARMERINA, in the province of Enna, contains monuments of the Norman and Aragonese periods, as well as baroque churches and palaces. A baroque cathedral, built 1605–64, can be seen at the highest point in the city.

However, most visitors come for the Imperial Roman Villa at Casale, 5.5 kilometers (3½ miles) south west of the city. The ruins, which date from the 4th century AD, include columned courtyards, baths and personal apartments. Most spectacular, however, are the mosaics.

SEGESTA, an ancient town in western Sicily, is the site of a 5th-century BC temple and a Hellenistic theater.

SELINUNTE, south of Segesta, was a flourishing Greek city in the 5th century BC. Destroyed by Carthaginians in the 4th century BC, the city was later inhabited by Arabs and Byzantines. Earthquakes worked the final destruction. The site is divided into two sections: there are three temples near the entrance and four more on the acropolis to the west.

▲ SIRACUSA, or Syracuse, was the bulwark of Greek civiliszation in the 4th century BC and the rival of Athens, Carthage and Rome.

Old City. The island of Ortygia, on which the initial settlement was made in 734 BC, is the Città Vechia (Old City), its narrow streets lined with medieval and baroque buildings. The Duomo is a 7th-century cathedral incorporating in its structure the 5th-century BC Temple of Athena that preceded it. The Fonte Aretusa is a freshwater spring on a waterfront terrace. The Museo Regionale d'Arte Medioevale e Moderna (Regional Museum of Medieval and Modern Art), in the Palazzo Bellomo, contains a fine collection of medieval and modern art. **Parco Archeologico**, along the northern edge of the city, contains both Greek and Roman ruins. The Anfiteatro Romano is a Roman amphitheater dating from the 2nd century; the Catacombe di San Giovanni includes the crypt of San Marziano, which was part of the island's first cathedral; and the Latomia del Paradiso, the "Paradise Quarry" is noted for an echo in the grotto called the ear of Dionysius. The 15,000-seat Teatro Greco (Greek Theater) is the most complete in the Greek world. Classical drama is still presented here. One of Italy's best archeological collections is the purpose-built Museo Archeologico, east of the Parco.

TAORMINA is Sicily's most popular resort. Above the town is a Greek theater, remodeled by the Romans.

▲ SIENA (408 B4) ★
TOSCANA *pop. 57,700*
Siena is Tuscany's most fascinating city after Florence because of its medieval atmosphere and the number and richness of its artistic possessions. The city's heyday was in the 12th and 13th centuries, when it became a major city of Europe. Every 2 July and 16 August Siena holds its Palio, a 16th-century pageant and horse race.

DUOMO is a masterpiece of Gothic-Italian architecture of the 13th and 14th centuries. Off the left aisle is the Libreria Piccolomini, built during the late 15th century, which contains frescoes and portraits by Pinturicchio. Behind the cathedral stands the baptistery, with a 16th-century Gothic façade.

MUSEO DELL'OPERA DEL DUOMO houses paintings and sculptures, including the *Maestà* by Duccio di Buoninsegna.

PALAZZO PUBBLICO (Town Hall), on the Piazza del Campo, is an elegant Gothic structure. It houses the Museo Civico with frescoes by Martini, Lorenzetti and other pre-Renaissance artists. The Torre del Mangia, next to the palace, has great views from the top of its 503 steps.

PINACOTECA NAZIONALE, 29 Via San Pietro, has the city's largest collection of Sienese art.

SORRENTO (408 D2)
CAMPANIA *pop. 17,500*
Sorrento stands along the Amalfi Drive, on a natural terrace above the Bay of Naples. The beauty of this popular holiday resort has drawn visitors for centuries. The Correale Museum, in a former palace, contains local paintings, crafts and archeological finds.

THE PALIO
The most famous horse race in Italy is held twice a year, on July 2 and August 16. Siena's Palio has existed since the Middle Ages and is an expression of the rivalry between the city's 17 *contrade*, or districts, which command total allegiance from their inhabitants. Ten *contrade* are selected by lot to take part, and thereafter the competitiveness increases up to the day of the race, with parades and pageantry during the preceding days. The bareback race around the Campo lasts barely 90 seconds.

SPOLETO (408 C3)
UMBRIA *pop. 38,000*
Spoleto's history goes back more than 2,500 years, and much of its past has left visible traces. Most important are the ruins of the Roman theater and amphitheater; the Museo Archeologico, and the Ponte delle Torri, a 14th-century aqueduct.
From mid-June to mid-July the Festival dei Due Mondi (Festival of Two Worlds), which is organized by the composer Gian Carlo Menotti, takes place here.

DUOMO, Piazza del Duomo, was built in 1067 and restored in the 12th century. Its magnificent doorway features a Renaissance porch surrounded by mosaics. Inside are frescos by Filippo Lippi and Penturicchio.

SUBIACO (408 C3)
LAZIO *pop. 6,800*
In the late 5th century, St. Benedict retired to a cave here to write his *Rule*, the foundation on which much of western monasticism is based.
After his departure, 12 monasteries were founded nearby.

▲ TÁRANTO (408 E2)
PUGLIA *pop. 244,000*
A Spartan colony in the 8th century BC, Táranto is a maritime city and military port of considerable importance. The Città Vecchia (Old Town) is the site of an Aragonese castle, a cathedral and a fascinating fish market.

MUSEO NAZIONALE, Corso Umberto 1, second only in importance among southern Italian museums to the Archeological Museum in Naples, contains a wealth of material on the art and civilization of Magna Graecia.

TIVOLI (408 C3)
LAZIO *pop. 52,000*
Set on a hilltop Tivoli was most important in Roman times for its travertine marble, from which much of imperial Rome was built. It was also a popular retreat from the city.

VILLA ADRIANA (Hadrian's Villa), 7 kilometers (4 miles) south, is the ruin of the largest and richest of the Roman villas. Begun by Emperor Hadrian in 125 AD, it contained a vast wealth of art treasures, as well as picturesque grounds.

VILLA D'ESTE, originally a Benedictine monastery, is better known as the 16th-century residence of Cardinal Ippolito d'Este. The gardens are the principal attraction today.

ITALY

TODI (408 C3)
UMBRIA *pop. 6,200*
Todi's three sets of concentric town walls are Etruscan, Roman and medieval in date, and the central Piazza del Popolo is a medieval showpiece with its Romanesque Duomo and a harmonious col- lection of palaces.

Near the public gardens is the Church of Santa Maria della Consolazione, considered by some to be Italy's finest Renaissance church.

▲ TORINO (408 A5)
PIEMONTE *pop. 991,900*
Torino, or Turin, rose to importance after the Savoy dukes made it their capital in 1574. The Savoy rulers – who took the title of Kings of Piedmont in the 18th century – were to become the royal family of Italy after unification.

Today it is an attractive, modern city, despite being home to some of Italy's largest factories, including the Fiat Automobile Works.

DUOMO SAN GIOVANNI, a Renaissance cathedral, is noted for the Chapel of the Holy Shroud, housing the shroud which until recently was believed to have been used for Christ after the Crucifixion.

MUSEO DELL' AUTOMOBILE CARLO BIS-CARETTI DI RUFFIA, south of town at 40 Corso Unità d'Italia, is one of the most comprehensive automobile museums in the world.

PALAZZO DELL' ACCADEMIA DELLE SCIEN-ZE is just off the Piazza San Carlo. The huge 17th-century palace houses two excellent museums.
Galleria Sabauda is particularly well endowed with paintings by Flemish and Dutch masters. Of special note is the Collezione Gualino, an outstanding group of 15th- to 16th-century Florentine furniture, gold and silver articles, paintings and sculptures.
Museo Egizio is considered the most important Egyptian museum outside Egypt. A complete funerary chamber,

effigies of Rameses II and a host of everyday objects are displayed.

PALAZZO MADAMA, in the Piazza Castello, houses the Museo Civico dell' Arte, with its varied collection of Gothic items. In addition, there are furnished 18th-century rooms, a Venetian state barge used by the kings of Sicily, fabrics, leatherwork, bronzes and porcelain.

PALAZZO REALE, on Piazza Castello, was the residence of the Savoy princes until 1865. It has gaudily decorated state apartments and displays of arms and armor. The pleasant Giardino Reale (Royal Garden) lies behind the palace.

▲ TRENTO (408 B5)
TRENTINO-ALTO ADIGE *pop. 102,100*
Formerly part of the Austrian Tyrol, Trento presents a fascinating blend of the Germanic and Mediterranean worlds in its culture, languages and cuisine. It was the site from 1545 to 1563 of the Council of Trent, which sought to modernize the Catholic Church as part of the counter-Reformation. The 13th-century cathedral, where the council sometimes met, is of particular interest.

CASTELLO DEL BUON CONSIGLIO, Via Bernardo Clesio, was once the home of the city's bishop princes. Frescoed salons house the varied collections of the Museo Provinciale d'Arte, including bronzes, ceramics, Meissen figurines, and a fresco cycle.

▲ TREVISO (408 C5)
VENETO *pop. 83,900*
The ancient walled city of Treviso is now a busy provincial capital. In the old quarter are the Palazzo dei Trecento and the Loggia dei Cavalieri, both in Romanesque style, and the Duomo, with paintings by Titian. Much restoration followed World War II bomb damage.

CHIESA DI SAN NICOLO, a 14th-century Gothic church, has frescoes by Tomaso da Modena and some decorated tombs.

▲ TRIESTE (408 C5)
FRIULI-VENEZIA GIULIA *pop. 231,000*
Lively, modern Trieste goes back to Roman times (there is a 2nd-century theater), but its golden age was under the Austro-Hungarian Empire.

CATTEDRALE DI SAN GIUSTO was built in the 14th century. The church is a mixture of styles and contains Byzantine mosaics and medieval frescoes.

TURIN – *see Torino on p.444.*

▲ UDINE (408 C5)
FRIULI-VENEZIA GIULIA *pop. 98,300*
Erected upon a mound said to have been built by the army of Attila the Hun, Udine contains numerous elegant buildings, including the Loggia del Lionello and the Palazzo del Comune (town hall).

CASTELLO (Castle), overlooking the town from its hilltop, was built in the early 16th century. The Museo Civico houses paintings by various Italian masters.

DUOMO, built in the 13th century, has paintings by Tiepolo.

PIAZZA DELLA LIBERTÀ, in the center of town, has fine colonnades, statues and an attractive fountain.

URBINO (408 C4)
MARCHE *pop. 15,400*
Imposing walls and gates still enclose romantic Urbino, an old city balanced on two steep hills. Narrow, winding streets contain Renaissance buildings, a small university, old churches and a palace. In the 15th century Urbino possessed one of the most cultured courts in the whole of Italy under the Montefeltro dukes. The painter Raphael was born in Urbino, and his home on Via Rafaello is open for viewing. Also worth a visit is St. Bernardino's Church, just south of town.

PALAZZO DUCALE, built by Federico da Montefeltro, is a magnificent Renaissance palace. It houses the Galleria Nazionale delle Marche, most notable for two works by Piero della Francesca. Federico's study has *trompe-l'oeil* décor in inlaid wood.

VATICAN CITY (412 A3) ★
Vatican City (Città del Vaticano), the center of Roman Catholicism, is an independent sovereign state governed by the Pope and the College of Cardinals. The 43-hectare (106-acre) city was created in 1929 by the Lateran Treaty between the Holy See and the Italian government.

The Via della Conciliazione is the main approach to the Vatican. It leads to the Piazza San Pietro, created by Giovanni Lorenzo Bernini and considered one of the most celebrated squares in the world. Twin Doric colonnades topped with statues of saints and martyrs flank either side; a 26-meter (85-foot) high obelisk rises from the center. At the head of the square is the Basilica di San Pietro; to the right is the Palazzo Vaticano.

BASILICA DI SAN PIETRO (St. Peter's Basilica) ★ is the largest and most awe-inspiring church in Christendom. It was conceived in 1452 to be raised on the site of a church built by Constantine in the 4th century.

The enormous interior, which has standing room for 100,000, is richly adorned with art. Of special note are *La Pietà*, the great sculpture by Michelangelo; the 13th-century statue of St. Peter; and the 26-meter (85-foot) bronze baldachin, or canopy, by Bernini, over the high altar and presumed tomb of St. Peter. The dome, designed by Michelangelo and finished 24 years after his death by Giacome della Porta, can be reached by an elevator and provides an excellent vantage point.

CAPPELLA SISTINA (Sistine Chapel) ★ is lavishly decorated with fine frescoes by some of the greats of the Renaissance, including Botticelli, Ghirlandaio and di Cosimo. Christ's life is depicted on the right wall; on the left is the life of Moses.

Most magnificent of all are the famed chapel ceiling which took Michelangelo four years to complete and his terrifying *Last Judgement* behind the altar.

PALAZZO VATICANO (Vatican Palace), a complex of many buildings, covers 5.5 hectares (13½ acres) and contains about 1,400 rooms. To cover the museums adequately you will need at least a day. There are color-coded routes to follow.

Biblioteca Apostolica Vaticana is one of the world's richest libraries, containing manuscripts in the handwriting of Petrarch, Michelangelo and Luther among many others, beautifully illuminated and ancient papyri.

Capella di Nicolo V is worth a look for Fra Angelico's lovely frescoes.

Museo Gregoriano-Etrusco is one of Italy's best museums dedicated to the Etruscan civilization.

Museo Pio-Clementino contains the best of the Vatican's classical sculpture collection, including the *Laocoön*, the *Apollo Belvedere* and the athlete figure known as the *Apoxyomenos*.

Pinacoteca holds Rome's finest collection of paintings. It is particularly strong in the schools of Siena, Umbria and the Marches.

Stanze di Raffaello were decorated by Raphael (and his pupils) for Pope Julius II. The magnificent frescoes include the famous *School of Athens*.

PAPAL AUDIENCES

General audiences with His Holiness are usually held on Wednesday at 11am, either in St. Peter's Square or the Audiences Room, and in summer at Castel Gandolfo. To participate in a general audience, you must apply to the office of the Prefetto della Casa Pontificia at the Vatican. Americans should apply to the North American College, Via dell' Umilta 30. Catholics are asked to take a letter of introduction from their parish priest.

▲ **VENÉZIA** (408 C5) ★
VENETO *pop. 317,800*
See map on p.448.

Venézia, or Venice, is singular among the world's cities. It is built over a sprawling archipelago 4 kilometers (2½ miles) from the mainland, encompassing 118 islands separated by more than 150 canals.

Refugees fleeing the Barbarian hordes founded the first Venetian settlement in the 6th century. By the 13th century, the Republic of St. Mark dominated trade in the eastern Mediterranean and ruled an empire that extended from the Dalmatian coast to Crete, Cyprus and several Aegean islands. However, the advance of the Turks in the East, and the discovery of America and other trade routes in the West crippled the Venetian economy, and decline set in.

Despite these woes, Venice entered its artistic golden age from the 16th to the 18th centuries: many magnificent structures were erected, and painters Giovanni Bellini, Titian, Tintoretto and others gained world renown. Napoleon Bonaparte finally overthrew the old republic in 1797, and the new nation-state of Italy annexed the city and its dominions in 1866.

Visitors can drive into Venice via the Ponte della Libertà to the Piazzale Roma. There are some parking lots and garages in the area and visitors should use these, as any illegally parked cars will be towed away. Private boat, gondola and ferry connections to Venice proper are available; a porter might be necessary for transporting luggage.

Events in Venice include its opera season from December to June, a carnival in February, boat races in May, an international art exhibition from late June to mid-September, the Feast of the Redeemer in July, the Venice Film Festival from late August to early September, and the colorful Historical Regatta in early September. Trips can be made to the Lido, a fashionable seaside resort; the islands of Murano, known for blown glass; Burano, known for lace; and Torcello, with medieval monuments.

BASILICA DI SAN MARCO (448 D2), a Byzantine masterpiece, was begun as a tomb for St. Mark, whose body reputedly was stolen from Alexandria by two Venetians in the 9th century. Above the main doors are gilded copper facsimiles of the well-known *Four Horses*, possibly a 4th-century BC Greek work, or more likely, 3rd century AD Roman.

CANAL GRANDE (448 C2), the main thoroughfare, has more than 200 palaces.

COLLEZIONE GUGGENHEIM (448 C1) is a superb collection of modern art amassed by millionairess Peggy Guggenheim.

VENETIAN GLASS

Venice's glass industry has been based on the island of Murano since 1291, when it was moved out of Venice itself because of the fire risk. The glass-blowing furnaces still glow today and many workshops can be visited.

GALLERIA DELL' ACCADEMIA (448 C1), the city's most important art gallery. It presents a survey of Venetian painting, with fine works by giants such as Giovanni Bellini, Carpaccio, Andrea Mantegna, Giorgione and Titian.

PALAZZO DUCALE (Doge's Palace) (448 D2) is an imposing construction built in the 14th century in Venetian-Gothic style. It was the seat of government of the republic and the home of the doges. Tintoretto's *Paradise* adorns a wall of the grand council chamber and on the ceiling is painted Veronese's *Apotheosis of Venice*.

PIAZZA SAN MARCO (St. Mark's Square) (448 D2), the heart of Venice, is an immense square bordered on three sides by palatial arcades lined with outdoor cafés and shops. Gondolas (which have been painted black since the passage of a 1562 law to curtail ostentation) can be hired at the San Marco Station.

PONTE DI RIALTO (448 D2) is one of the three bridges that cross the Canal Grande (until 1854 it was the only crossing point). It is lined with luxury shops.

PONTE DEI SOSPIRI (Bridge of Sighs) (448 D2) connects the Palazzo Ducale with the prisons. Completed in 1600, the bridge was supposedly named after the sighs of condemned convicts.

SAN GIÓRGIO MAGGIORE (448 E1) is situated on a small island across the lagoon. It contains two of Tintoretto's masterpieces: *Last Supper* and *Descent of Manna*.

SANTA MARIA GLORIOSA DEI FRARI (448 B2) houses Titian's *Assumption* and Bellini's *Madonna and Child*.

SANTA MARIA DELLA SALUTE (448 C1), dedicated to the Virgin Mary after the plague of 1630, contains paintings by Titian.

SCUOLA GRANDE DI SAN ROCCO (448 B2), completed in 1560, is one of the great Venetian *scuole*, establishments set up to help the city's needy. Its glory is the decorations by Tintoretto.

VENICE – *see Venézia on p.446.*

▲ **VERONA** (408 B5)
VENETO *pop. 259,000*
Verona is known for its Roman, medieval and Renaissance buildings, and was immortalized in Shakespeare's *Two Gentlemen of Verona* and *Romeo and Juliet*. The buildings where Romeo and Juliet supposedly lived can be seen. During July and August, operas are presented at Verona's Roman amphitheater.

ARCHE SCALIGERE are the tombs of the Della Scala family, who ruled Verona in the 13th and 14th centuries.

ARENA, in Piazza Bra, seats 22,000 and is one of the largest of all Roman amphitheaters.

ITALY

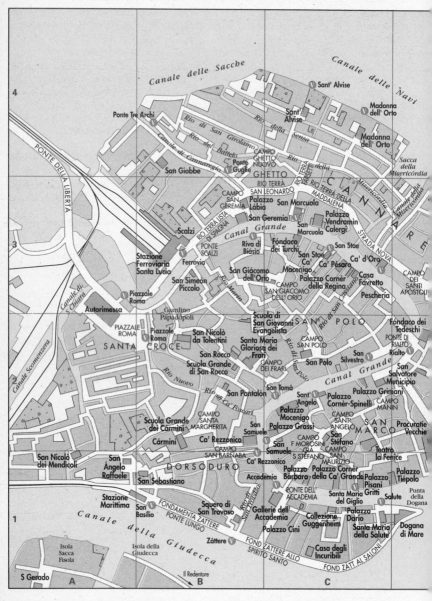

Canale delle Sacche

Canale delle Navi

4   Sant' Alvise

Ponte Tre Archi   Sant' Alvise   Madonna dell' Orto

Rio di San Girolamo

Canale di Cannaregio   Rio dei Batteto   Rio della Sensse   Madonna dell' Orto

Sacca della Misericórdia

Ponte Guglie   CAMPO GHETTO NUOVO

San Giobbe   GHETTO   RIO TERRÀ   Rio Terrà Farsetti

CAMPO SAN GEREMIA   Palazzo Lábia   San Leonardo   San Marcuola   RIO TERRÀ DELLA MADDALENA

CANN

Scalzi   San Geremia   Palazzo Vendramin Calergi

RE

3   Stazione Ferroviaria Santa Lucia   RIO TERRA LISTA DI SPAGNA   Canal Grande   San Marcuola   STRADA NOVA

Canale di S. Chiara   PONTE DEGLI SCALZI   Riva di Biásio   Fóndaco dei Turchi   San Stae   Ca' d'Oro   CAMPO DEI SANTI APOSTOLI

Ferrovia   San Stae   Ca'   Ca' Pésaro

San Simeón Piccolo   San Giácomo dell'Orio   Mocenigo   Casa Favretto

Piazzale Roma   CAMPO SAN GIACOMO DELL' ORIO   Palazzo Corner della Regina   Pescheria

Autorimessa   Rio di Martino   Scuola di San Giovanni Evangelista   SAN POLO   Rio di San Cristoforo   Fóndaco dei Tedeschi

Giardino Papadópoli   PONTE DI RIALTO

PIAZZALE ROMA   Piazzale Roma   San Nicolò da Tolentini   Santa Maria Gloriosa dei Frari   CAMPO SAN POLO   San Polo   San Silvestro   Rialto   San Salvatore

SANTA CROCE   San Rocco   Municipio

2   Canale Scomenzera   Scuola Grande di San Rocco   Rio Nuovo   CAMPO DEI FRARI   Rio di San Polo   Canal Grande

Rio di Ca' Foscari   San Tomà   Sant' Angelo   Palazzo Grimani

San Pantalòn   Palazzo Mocenigo   Palazzo Corner-Spinelli   CAMPO MANIN

Scuola Grande dei Cármini   CAMPO SANTA MARGHERITA   Palazzo Grassi   CAMPO SANT' ANGELO   Procuratíe Vecchie

Cármini   Ca' Rezzonico   San Samuele   San Stéfano   SAN MARCO

San F Morosini Gia   Teatro la Fenice

CAMPO SAN BARNABA   Ca' Rezzonico   San Samuele   S STEFANO   CAMPO SAN MAURIZIO

San Nicolò dei Mendicoli   San Ángelo Raffaele   DORSODURO   Accademia   Palazzo Bárbaro   Palazzo Corner della Ca' Grande   Palazzo Tiépolo

San Sebastiano   PONTE DELL' ACCADEMIA   Palazzo Pisani Gritti

1   Stazione Marittima   San Basilio   Squero di San Trovaso   Santa Maria del Giglio   Salute   Punta della Dogana

FONDAMENTA ZATTERE   PONTE LUNGO   Rio di San Trovaso   Gallerie dell' Accademia   Collezione Guggenheim   Palazzo Dario   Dogana di Mare

Canale della Giudecca   Záttere   Palazzo Cini   Santa Maria della Salute

Isola Sacca Fisola   Isola della Giudecca   FOND ZATTERE ALLO SPIRITO SANTO   Casa degli Incurabili   FOND ZATT AI SALONI

S Gerado   Il Redentore

A   B   C

BASILICA DI SAN ZENO MAGGIORE is perhaps northern Italy's finest Romanesque church. Its features include a huge rose window, 12th-century bronze door panels with biblical scenes, Mantegna's *Madonna and Saints*, and on the north side of the basilica beautiful cloisters.

CASTELVECCHIO, a 14th-century fortress-palace, houses the Museo Civico d'Arte, displaying works of the Veronese school.

CHIESA DI SANT' ANASTASIA, a Gothic church built 1290–1480, is noted for its double portal and fine works of art.

0 100 200 300 400 500 m
0 100 200 300 400 500 yards

Murano
Collona

San Michele

Cimitero
San
Michele

Isola di
San
Michele

Canale delle Fondamenta Nuove

FONDAMENTA NUOVE

Fondamenta
Nuove

Gesuiti
(Santa Maria
Assunta)

Rio dei Gesuiti

Ospedale Civile

Rio dei Mendicanti

Santa Maria
dei Miracoli

Santi Giovanni e
Paolo (San Zanipolo)

Tana
Celestia

Colleoni

CAMPO
SANTI GIOVANNI
E PAOLO

Rio di San Gristimo

CAMPO
SANTA MARIA
FORMOSA

San Francesco
della Vigna

Santa Maria
Formosa

Palazzo Querini
Stampalia
e Pinacoteca

Scuola di San Giorgio
degli Schiavoni

Rio della Pietà

CASTELLO

San Giorgio
dei Greci

Torre dell'
Orologio

Basilica di
San Marco

CAMPO
SAN
ZACCARIA

San Zaccaria

CAMPO
BANDIERA
E MORO

Arsenale

PIAZZA
SAN
MARCO

Palazzo
Ducale

Prigioni

Santa Maria
della Pietà

San Giovanni
in Bragora

San
Martino

Campanile

RIVA DEGLI SCHIAVONI

Museo
Storico
Navale

Procuratie
Nuove

Ponte
dei Sospiri

San Zaccaria

Riva degli
Schiavoni

Giardini
ex Reali

Arsenale

San Marco

San Biàgio

Bacino di
San Marco

Canale di San Marco

San Pietro
di Castello

San Giorgio

Isola di
San
Giorgio
Maggiore

San Giorgio
Maggiore

D   E

DUOMO was originally a Roman basilica. The present cathedral was begun in the 12th century and the Gothic nave dates from the 15th century. Titian's *Assumption of the Virgin* is in the first chapel on the left, and outside the cathedral is an Early Christian mosaic.

PIAZZA DELLE ERBE has been a commercial center for 2,000 years. Medieval buildings form the backdrop.

PIAZZA DEI SIGNORI is an impressive set of buildings begun in the 12th century. The Loggia del Consiglio, a fine Renaissance building, is on the square, where there is a monument to Dante.

TEATRO ROMANO is one of the best-preserved theaters in northern Italy. It was built during the reign of Augustus. Near by is an archeological museum.

▲ VICENZA (408 C5)
VENETO *pop. 109,300*
Vicenza is renowned for its beautiful 16th century buildings by Andrea Palladio.

BASILICA PALLADIANA, Piazza dei Signori, was Palladio's first public building. It is a massive structure with two stories of grand colonnades.

PALAZZO CHIERICATI, Piazza Matteotti, is crowned with many statues; it houses the Museo Civico, displaying archeological exhibits, and a picture gallery.

TEATRO OLIMPICO, Piazza Matteotti, is a charming 16th-century, classical Renaissance theater.

▲ VITERBO (408 C3)
LAZIO *pop. 60,200*
Viterbo, the main city of northern Lazio, was important as a papal residence from 1257 to 1281, when it rivaled Rome. The charm of Viterbo's Città Medioevale is still evident. During the Festival of Santa Rosa, September 3–4, a merry crowd follows a 30-meter (100-foot) high imitation belfry through the streets.

DUOMO is a simple Romanesque building of 1192 with a Gothic campanile.

PALAZZO DEI PAPI (Papal Palace) dates from 1266 and now serves as the seat of an archbishopric. Slender columns and delicate arches produce a lacy effect.

THINGS TO KNOW

- **AREA:** 62 square kilometers (24 square miles)
- **POPULATION:** 26,900
- **CAPITAL:** San Marino
- **LANGUAGE:** Italian
- **ECONOMY:** Agriculture, tourism, printing of postage stamps. Exports include grain, coins, wine and textiles.
- **ELECTRICITY:** 220 volts, continental two-round-pin plugs. Adaptor/transformer required for non-continental appliances.
- **PASSPORT REQUIREMENTS:** Required for U.S. citizens.
- **VISA REQUIREMENTS:** Not required for stays up to three months, after which a three-month extension can be obtained.
- **DUTY-FREE ITEMS:** *See Italy.*
- **CURRENCY:** Currency units are the Italian *lira* and the San Marino *lira* (LIT). Due to currency fluctuations, exchange rates are subject to frequent change.
- **BANK OPENING HOURS:** 8:30am–1:30pm and 3–4pm Monday–Friday. **STORE OPENING HOURS:** 8:30 or 9am–7:30 or 8pm Monday–Saturday, with a siesta between 1 and 4pm.
- **PUBLIC HOLIDAYS:** January 1; January 6; Easter Monday; World War II Liberation Day, April 25; Labor Day, May 1; Assumption Day, August 15; All Saints Day, November 1; Immaculate Conception, December 8; December 25–26.
- **USEFUL TELEPHONE NUMBERS:**
  Police 113
  Fire 113
  Ambulance 113
- **NATIONAL TOURIST OFFICE:**
  Consulate General of the Republic of San Marino
  186 Lehrer Avenue
  New York, NY 11003
  Tel: 516/242 2212
- **AMERICAN EMBASSY:**
  Via Vittorio Veneto 119a
  Palazzo Margherita
  00187 Rome
  Tel: 39 6 46 741
  Fax: 39 6 488 2672

SAN MARINO
(408 C4)

HISTORY

The country's history is thought to have begun around 300 AD, when the Dalmatian stonecutter Marinus came to Monte Titano to escape Christian persecutions of Emperor Diocletian. Later canonized, St. Marinus, or San Marino, bequeathed the mountain's slopes to the local community on the stipulation that liberty and the Christian religion be protected. Over the centuries, this little-known enclave maintained its freedom in isolation from the rest of the world. Indeed, the inhabitants once refused an offer of increased territory from Napoléon Bonaparte, believing only that small size and a modest economy would ensure their treasured independence.

Surrounded by Italy, San Marino is governed by the Grand and General Council, whose 60 members are elected every 5 years. Executive powers are held by the Congress of State. These officials are selected by and from the Grand Council for six-months. A small army is kept for ceremonial purposes. San Marino is linked to Italy by a customs union of 1862 and a treaty of friendship since 1897. Communist-led coalitions ruled from 1947 to 1957 and 1978 to 1986.

AUTOMOBILE CLUB
Federazione Auto Motoristica Sammarinese (Automobile Federation of San Marino), which has an office at 99 Via Gingno Serravalle, San Marino, is the club in San Marino affiliated with AAA. Not all auto clubs offer full travel services to AAA members.

GETTING AROUND

San Marino is easily reached by car. The main approach is Italian Highway 72 from Rimini, but there are two alternate secondary road approaches. Road 258 links Rimini and Sansepolcro, and a narrow, unclassified road connects Sansepolcro and Urbino. Insurance requirements and traffic regulations are the same as those for Italy.

ACCOMMODATIONS

Accommodations in San Marino range from modestly priced to expensive, depending on the appointments. A Continental breakfast is included in the price of most rooms; some of the most costly hotels include a full breakfast. Campers will find several campgrounds in San Marino; the local tourist office on Contrada Omagnano has specific information on campgrounds.

TIPPING

Restaurants and hotels in San Marino often add service charges to their bills, but check to make sure. If no charge has been added, tip 10 to 15 percent. For small services, the equivalent of 75¢ to $1.50 is appropriate.

LANGUAGE

For a list of useful words and phrases in Italian, please see p.410.

Guita Rock and Tower, a magnificent sight.

PLACES OF INTEREST

▲ SAN MARINO

pop. 4,500

Red-roofed stone houses and old ramparts add to the medieval character of San Marino, the nation's capital on the western slope of Monte Titano. A major road connects San Marino to Rimini, Italy, 24 kilometers (15 miles) north east. Although automobiles are prohibited within the town walls, a tour on foot can include the 19th-century Basilica di San Marino, where St. Marinus, the nation's patron saint, is buried, and the Palazzo dei Valloni, which houses the national library. A variety of shops, many of which stay open late into the night, line San Marino's narrow streets.

PALAZZO DEL GOVERNO is the 19th-century Gothic-style government headquarters facing the Piazza della Liberta. The building contains two portraits of St. Marinus, one of which was executed by Il Guercino.

ROCCHE'S three tower fortresses were strategically built on the three peaks of Monte Titano to guard against invasion. These carefully preserved citadels are connected by a path and offer a panorama of the countryside, the Italian city of Rimini and magnificent views across the Adriatic Sea; sometimes the Dalmatian Coast can be seen. The first tower, Guaita, and the second tower, Cesta, can be visited. Inside Cesta is the Ancient Weapons Museum.

SAN FRANCESCO, the Church of St. Francis, was erected in the 14th century on the site of an older church.

MALTA & GOZO

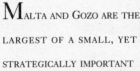

MALTA AND GOZO ARE THE LARGEST OF A SMALL, YET STRATEGICALLY IMPORTANT GROUP OF ISLANDS SITUATED IN THE SOUTHERN MEDITERRANEAN.

THE HARBORS AROUND MALTA'S COASTS HAVE SEEN THE ARRIVAL OF SEVERAL ILLUSTRIOUS NAMES IN WORLD HISTORY, STARTING WITH ST. PAUL. FLEEING FROM SULEIMAN THE MAGNIFICENT, THE KNIGHTS OF ST. JOHN LEFT RHODES FOR MALTA AND RULED IT FOR ALMOST 300 YEARS. GREEKS, ROMANS, NORMANS, ARABS, ITALIANS, FRENCH, AND BRITISH HAVE SINCE ALL INVADED, RULED, AND LEFT THEIR MARK.

MALTESE IS SPOKEN LIKE ARABIC, YET WRITTEN IN ROMAN SCRIPT. PLACE NAMES SEEM DRAWN FROM A FICTIONAL WORLD: XAGĦRA, MARSAXLOKK, BIRŻEBBUĠA. BUT THE LANDSCAPE IS REAL ENOUGH, WITH ROCKY COVES, BEACHES, BLUE SEAS AND LEMON TREES BLOWN BY THE HOT SIROCCO WIND FROM AFRICA.

Left MARSAXLOKK BAY HAS KEPT ITS CHARM DESPITE THE ARRIVAL OF TOURISTS
Above left COLORFUL FISHING BOATS ARE SEEN ALL OVER THE ISLAND
Above right THIS CHURCH IN MDINA SHOWS A TYPICAL RELIGIOUS DETAIL

THINGS TO KNOW

- **AREA:** 316 square kilometers (122 square miles)
- **POPULATION:** 362,000
- **CAPITAL:** Valletta
- **LANGUAGES:** Maltese and English.
- **PASSPORT REQUIREMENTS:** Required for U.S. citizens.
- **VISA REQUIREMENTS:** Not required for stays up to three months.
- **DUTY-FREE ITEMS:** 200 cigarettes or equivalent cigars and tobacco; one bottle spirits and one bottle wine; reasonable quantity perfume; personal goods.
- **CURRENCY:** The *Maltese lira* (LM), divided into 100 *cents* and each cent into 10 *mils*. Due to currency fluctuations, the exchange rate is subject to change.
- **BANK OPENING HOURS:** 8:30am–12:30pm Monday–Friday, 8:30–11:30am Saturday.
- **STORE OPENING HOURS:** 9am–1pm and 3:30–7pm Monday–Saturday.
- **PUBLIC HOLIDAYS:** January 1; St Paul's Shipwreck, February 10; St Joseph's Day, March 19; Good Friday; Freedom Day, March 31; Labor Day, May 1; Sette Giugno, June 7; Feast of Saints Peter and Paul, June 28; Assumption Day, August 15; Our Lady of Victories, September 8; Independence Day, September 21; Feast of the Immaculate Conception, December 8; Republic Day, December 13; December 25.
- **NATIONAL TOURIST OFFICES:**
  Maltese National Tourist Office
  Empire State Building
  350 5th Avenue, Suite 4412
  New York, NY 10118
  Tel: 212/695 9520
  Fax: 212/695 8229
  National Tourist Organization
  280 Republic Street
  Valletta
  Tel: 356 224444
  Fax: 356 220401
- **AMERICAN EMBASSY:**
  Development House, Third Floor
  St Anne Street
  Floriana
  Tel: 356 235960; Fax: 356 243229

HISTORY

The first settlers on this rocky archipelago were farmers who sailed from Sicily about 7,000 years ago. The prehistoric eras remain remarkably well preserved. The great megalithic temples of Malta, which contain some of the oldest free-standing statues in the world, were built from 4000 to 2000 BC. Temples and tombs housed a wealth of stone idols, carvings, pottery and implements, much of which is preserved in Valletta's Museum of Archeology.

The first identifiable race to colonize the islands were the Phoenicians in the early 7th century BC. The Carthaginians ruled from 515 to 218 BC, their domination being brought to a sudden end by Roman annexation. The Maltese acquired a degree of self-government under Roman rule, minting their own coinage and controlling domestic affairs. Maltese ruins from this era indicate a high degree of wealth and sophistication.

With the fall of the Roman Empire, Malta came under the control of Constantinople and then, in 870 AD, fell to the Arabs. Various European rulers held sway until 1530 when the Knights of St. John of Jerusalem were granted the islands by the Holy Roman Emperor. Having repulsed the Turks in the Great Siege, the Knights occupied and protected the islands until the Napoleonic Wars. This era ended in 1814 when Malta gained its last overseer – the British. The country achieved independence in 1964, becoming a member of the British Commonwealth. Ten years later Malta became a republic, and in 1979 British forces finally left.

FOOD AND DRINK

Although hotels and restaurants generally serve European or English food, the local specialties are well worth trying. Fish is abundant and includes tuna, grouper, swordfish and seabass. *Lampuki*, which shoal around Malta in the fall, are often prepared in a pie. Typical Maltese meat dishes are *bragioli*, similar to beef olives; rabbit stew; and *timpana*, a meat and macaroni pie. Interesting dishes are made from pumpkin dried on roof-tops, and the local grapes are pressed into fine wines. Maltese beer is popular too.

SPORTS AND RECREATION

Ideally located in the middle of the Mediterranean, Malta enjoys a hot, dry summer of clear skies, unpolluted blue waters and sea breezes. The winter season, from November to March, is mild. Opportunities for outdoor activities abound, including riding, shooting, fishing and watersports. Sailing regattas are held from May through to October. Many hotels have swimming pools and a few also have tennis courts. The Marsa Sports Club, within a 10-minute drive of Valletta, has facilities for tennis, golf, cricket, polo, racket ball and badminton; temporary membership can be arranged. Soccer is Malta's most popular spectator sport; horse racing and water polo offer great competition during their respective seasons.

More leisurely pursuits include touring Valletta's harbor in a cruiser or a *ðghajsa*, a traditional rowing boat; attending an open-air performance at the St. Anton Gardens; or participating in the colorful February Carnival, held just before Lent. The Maltese love evening celebrations, and fireworks displays take place during the fiesta season between June and September. Meanwhile, the fascinating tombs and temples of the islands are great to explore by day.

GETTING AROUND

Malta and Gozo are linked by a regular roll-on-roll-off ferry service. Car and passenger services connect Malta to Réggio di Calabria, Naples, Genoa and Livorno in mainland Italy, and to Catania and Palermo in Sicily. There is also a high-speed passenger-only catamaran service to Sicily. Malta's main seaport is at Grand Harbor, Valletta. Luqa Airport has frequent flights to and from major European cities. Taxis with controlled rates and inexpensive buses connect all towns to Valletta.

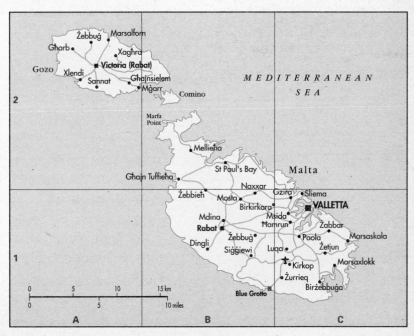

Main towns are linked by good roads, but minor roads on Malta are poorly surfaced. Sandy beaches, which are mostly on the north-west coast, can be reached via good roads. The south-west coast, predominately sheer cliffs, has very few roads, but there is one leading to the Blue Grotto. Located at Wied Iż Żurrieq, the Grotto consists of a group of sea caves featuring brilliant colors and underwater flora; visitors can take a bus from Valletta if they prefer not to drive there themselves.

Driving is on the left. The wearing of seat belts is mandatory, as are crash helmets for motorbikes. Speed limits are 40 k.p.h. (25 m.p.h.) in urban areas and 65 k.p.h. (40 m.p.h.) on highways. There are no on-the-spot fines.

ACCOMMODATIONS

Malta classifies its hotels using from one to five stars. There are also complexes, guest houses, apartments and villas.

Most accommodation is near the coast; all room rates include breakfast. There are no campgrounds in Malta.

SPECIAL EVENTS

Carnival Days are held in early February; dating back to 1535, they offer brass bands and a folk-dancing competition in Valletta's Freedom Square. More solemn is the Good Friday procession held each year in 19 Maltese towns and villages, when life-size statues and costumed participants enact scenes from the life and Passion of Christ. An International Trade Fair is held at Naxxar in the first two weeks of July.

TIPPING

A 15 percent V.A.T. levy charge is added to bills for meals consumed in restaurants. Tipping will always be appreciated.

AUTOMOBILE CLUB

MTC Touring Services, 47 Ta' Xbiex Seafront, Msida. The **Touring Club (Malta)** is at Philcyn House, Ursuline Sisters Street, G'Mangia. The symbol ▲ beside a city name indicates the presence of an AAA-affiliated automobile club branch. Not all auto clubs offer full travel services to AAA members.

USEFUL EXPRESSIONS IN MALTESE

good morning	bonju
good evening	bonswa
yes/no	iva/le
please	jekk joghgbok
thank you	grazzi
excuse me	skuzzi
how much...?	kemm...?

NUMBERS

1	wiehed
2	tnejn
3	tlieta
4	erbgħa
5	hamsa
6	sitta
7	sebgħa
8	tmienja
9	disgħa
10	għaxra

VALLETTA

October–February
inches   April–September   °F

PLACES OF INTEREST

▲ VALLETTA (455 C1) ★

MALTA *pop. 15,500*

Valletta, the capital of Malta, is most reminiscent of the Knights of St. John. The city was built by the French Grand Master of the Knights, Jean de la Valette, after the epic Turkish siege of 1565. Rising perpendicularly from the water's edge, Valette's city commands an excellent view over the historic Grand Harbour.

Manoel Theatre, one of the few remaining 18th-century European theaters, has been restored and is now the main venue for music, opera, dance and drama. The main season lasts from October through to May.

Auberge de Castile et Léon, built in the late 16th century, is the finest and best preserved of the original eight palaces of the Knights of St. John. Used as the British military headquarters until 1970, it now houses several government departments as well as the office of the prime minister.

Across the harbor from Valletta are Vittoriosa, Cospicua and Senglea, known collectively as the Three Cities. The knights settled in Vittoriosa before Valletta was built, and constructed churches, chapels, forts and inns. The cities bore the brunt of the Turkish siege, and more recently came under attack during World War II. More information on the history of Valletta and the surrounding area can be obtained at the Malta National Tourist Office information bureau in Freedom Square.

GHAR DALAM ★, 11 kilometers (7 miles) south, on the bus route to Birżebbuġa is a prehistoric cave dating from the late Stone Age. The cave has many fossilized remains of such extinct species as dwarf elephants and hippopotamuses, which roamed the island some 250,000 years ago, as well as later neolithic pottery. A small museum displays a fascinating collection of teeth, tusks and bones of animals that have been found here.

HYPOGEUM OF HAL SAFLIENI ★, 6 kilometers (4 miles) south in Paola, is a complex of underground chambers and corridors once used for multiple burials and rituals. The catacombs were built in three levels descending to a depth of nearly 12 meters (40 feet) below the surface. The remains of some 7,000 human bodies, along with their personal ornaments, were discovered on the lower level. The highest level is the oldest, dating to around 3000 BC. Statuettes, pottery and ornaments from the chambers can be seen in Valletta's Museum of Archeology (see below).

NATIONAL MUSEUM OF ARCHEOLOGY, Republic Street, is in the Auberge de Provence. It houses important collections pertaining to Maltese archeology and history.

Prehistoric relics from the Tarxien, Ħaġar Qim and Hypogeum sites are displayed on the ground floor, along with fascinating small-scale reconstructions of the temple complexes; the top floor contains Phoenician and Punic antiquities.

NATIONAL MUSEUM OF FINE ARTS, South Street is an 18th-century palace that houses paintings from medieval Italian to modern Maltese. The basement holds memorabilia of the Order of St. John, including portraits of dignitaries, sculpture, ceramics and silverware.

NATIONAL WAR MUSEUM, Fort St. Elmo, contains a replica of Malta's Gladiator aircraft, the *Faith*, which defended the island in World War II. Another highlight is the George Cross awarded to Malta by King George VI on April 15, 1942 for the bravery of her people during the war. Also on display is a large collection of uniforms, weapons and military vehicles.

PALACE OF THE GRAND MASTERS ★, Republic Street, was designed by Gerolamo Cassar and completed in 1574. Its features include luxuriously furnished state apartments with portraits of the Grand Masters and European monarchs, as well as the Tapestry Chamber, which is lined with Gobelin tapestries. The palace is now the presidential office and Malta's Parliament House.
Armory at the Palace, contains arms and armor of various periods with descriptions, including the suits of celebrated warriors and Turkish shields taken during the 1565 siege.

ST. JOHN'S CO-CATHEDRAL ★, St. John's Square, was built for the Knights in 1573–7 by Gerolamo Cassar. No expense was spared in the decoration of the walls and chapels. The crypt houses the tombs of the first 12 Grand Masters of St. John. In the oratory is Michelangelo Caravaggio's masterpiece, *The Beheading of St. John*.
A museum displays illuminated missals, sacred vestments and Flemish tapestries based upon cartoons by Peter Paul Rubens and Nicolas Poussin.

TARXIEN TEMPLES ★, lying 6 kilometers (4 miles) south in Paola, are probably the best-preserved examples of megalithic temples on Malta. Dating between 3500 and 2500 BC, this monument comprises three interconnecting main temples and the remains of an older temple. The chambers are decorated with carvings and contain elaborate altars for animal sacrifice. Some of the original remains have been removed to the National Museum of Archeology (*see p 457*).

UPPER BARRACCA GARDENS, near Castile Place, provide excellent panoramas of the Grand Harbour.

MDINA (455 B1) ★
MALTA *pop. 400*
Medieval Mdina, rising above the plains of central Malta, is justifiably known as "The Silent City." This former capital of Malta is tightly packed with palaces and mansions, many of which still belong to Maltese nobility. The battlements command a superb view of the island. Some of the buildings and walls originated in the Middle Ages, although the town's history goes back even further. The Cathedral of St. Paul is believed to occupy the site of the house of Publius, the Roman governor who was converted to Christianity by St. Paul and who became the first Bishop of Malta.
Other buildings of interest are the old Seminary, which houses the Cathedral Museum, the dungeons and the medieval Palazzo Falzon. Visitors may observe Mdina glass-blowers practicing their craft at the Ta'Qali Crafts Village about 2 kilometers (1¼ miles) from the city.

CATHEDRAL ★, destroyed by an earthquake in 1693, was rebuilt by Lorenzo Gafà in 1697–1702. The dynamic dome, seen from afar, is arguably the finest in Malta. The Cathedral Museum contains various art treasures, including paintings, prints, silverware and a fine collection of woodcuts by Albrecht Dürer.

NATIONAL MUSEUM OF NATURAL HISTORY ★, at Vilhena Palace, has seven sections displaying local and foreign collections of skeletons, fish, insects, birds, shells, fossils and geological items. The magisterial palace, built by Grand Master Vilhena in the 18th century, was used as a British troops hospital from 1860.

RABAT (455 B1) ★
MALTA *pop. 13,000*

Rabat's early prosperity is confirmed by the remains of a Roman villa. In those days, Rabat and Mdina were one city. The ditch protecting Mdina and making Rabat its suburb was dug by the Arabs. Today a bustling town, Rabat is visited for its churches, Roman remains and the extensive catacombs beneath its streets. The 4th-century Christian catacombs contain canopied graves and saddle-backed tombs cut in imitation of Greek sarcophagi. An unusual feature of the Maltese catacombs is the presence of rock *agape* tables where mourners partook of farewell meals.

Also of interest is Verdala Castle, a 16th-century summer residence of the Grand Master Verdalle. Today it is used by foreign VIPs and by the president as a summer residence. Rabat and adjacent Mdina are most lively on June 29, during the Feast of St. Peter and St. Paul, otherwise known as Imnarja.

BUSKETT GARDENS ★ have extensive vineyards and orchards of orange and lemon trees; they are open year round, but are at their best in spring. The Feast of St. Peter and St. Paul begins here.

MUSEUM OF ROMAN ANTIQUITIES displays evidence of the wealth of Malta during Roman rule between 218 BC and the 5th century AD. Among the highlights are some fine mosaics.

ST. AGATHA AND ST. PAUL'S CATACOMBS, on the south-west edge of Rabat, are typical of the underground Christian cemeteries that were common in the 4th and 5th centuries.

ST. PAUL'S GROTTO ★, a cave below the Chapel of St. Publius (adjoining the Church of St. Paul), is where St. Paul is said to have lived during his three-month stay on the island after a shipwreck in AD 60. A marble statue of St. Paul lies below dimly lit catacombs.

SLIEMA (455 C1)
MALTA *pop. 22,000*

This coastal resort, along with the neighboring St. Julian-St. George area, is Malta's largest town. Sliema encompasses some of the island's most frequented spots, including a 3-kilometer (2-mile) seafront promenade and an attractive hotel district sprinkled with shops and cafés. There are no sandy beaches, but smooth rocks and lidos on the north side afford good bathing. In St. Julian's Bay is the Dragonara Palace Casino, a 19th-century mansion whose elegant rooms form the setting for baccarat, boule, blackjack and roulette. Sliema has the largest concentration of hotels in Malta and the best choice of facilities. The Yacht Marina offers modern equipment for boating.

VICTORIA (455 A2) ★
GOZO *pop. 6,000*

Named after Queen Victoria in 1897 on the occasion of her Diamond Jubilee, the capital of Gozo is often referred to by its older name of Rabat. It is the geographical, political and spiritual center of the island.

On a hill dominating the town are the ruins of an ancient citadel known as Gran Castello. Inside the walls are a late 17th-century cathedral, the old Bishop's Palace, the Law Courts and several small museums. The Feast of St. George on July 18 and the Feast of the Assumption on August 15 are celebrated with an array of festivities.

ĠGANTIJA PREHISTORIC TEMPLE ★, about 3 kilometers (2 miles) east on the Xagħra plateau, is Gozo's finest example of a Copper Age temple. The two megalithic monuments are well preserved; many of the walls, measuring some 5 meters (16 feet) high, are still standing. The setting, affording a glorious panorama over Gozo, is worth a visit in itself.

THE NETHERLANDS

Nowhere in Europe do image and reality clash so much as in The Netherlands. For a land with an old-fashioned image of windmills, tulips, cheeses and clogs, it is one of the most liberal countries in Europe. While drugs are not legal, they are tolerated. This city of bicycles and canals boasts many art museums, with works by Van Gogh and many Rembrandt masterpieces, such as *The Nightwatch*.

A more modern nightwatch takes place in Amsterdam's infamous red-light district. If Holland surprises, so too will its people, in the main for their friendliness, easy-going nature, and a command of the English language which puts most native speakers to shame.

Left Tulips and windmills – symbols of the Dutch countryside
Above left Cycling is the ideal way to get around Amsterdam
Above right Why not try a pair of clogs for size?

Things to Know

- **Area:** 40,844 square kilometers (15,770 square miles).
- **Population:** 14,864,000
- **Capital:** Amsterdam
- **Language:** Dutch
- **Religion:** Roman Catholic, Protestant.
- **Economy:** Industry, commerce, horticulture. Light machinery, chemicals, textiles, food processing, ship building; petroleum products, natural gas; trade and finance, tourism. Farms, usually small, produce mostly cattle, flower bulbs and blossoms, fruits and vegetables.
- **Electricity:** 220 volts, continental two-round-pin plugs. Adaptor and/or transformer required for non-continental appliances.
- **Passport Requirements:** Required for U.S. citizens.
- **Visa Requirements:** Not required for stays up to 3 months.
- **Duty-Free Items:** 200 cigarettes or 50 cigars or 100 cigarillos or 250 grams of tobacco; I liter of spirits over 22 proof or 2 liters of spirits under 22 proof, 2 liters of non-sparkling wine; 8 liters non-sparkling Luxembourg wine; ¼ liter of eau de cologne; 50 grams of perfume; 500 grams of coffee; 100 grams of tea; two still cameras with 24 rolls of film; two movie cameras with 10 rolls of film, one video camera; personal goods worth up to 125 LNG. Also see *the European Union* on p.5.
- **Currency:** The currency unit is the *guilder* (NLG), divided into 100 *cents*. Due to currency fluctuations, the exchange rate is subject to frequent change. There is no limit on import or export of Dutch or foreign currency, but the export of Dutch silver coins is limited.
- **Bank Opening Hours:** 9am–4 or 5pm, Monday–Friday, sometimes to 8pm on late-night shopping evenings.
- **Store Opening Hours:** Food stores are generally open from 8:30 or 9am–5:30 or 6pm Monday to Friday; 8:30 or 9am–4 or 5pm Saturday. Many are closed for a half day each week, but the

History

The Netherlands' history as a nation began in 1384, when Burgundian Dukes Philip the Good and Charles the Bold obtained control of the divided lowland states and unified them. The marriage of a Burgundian daughter, Mary, to an Austrian Habsburg, Maximilian I, brought about Habsburg rule in 1477. Maximilian's son married a Spanish princess, and his grandson, Philip II, became heir to the throne of the Netherlands and Spain in 1555. Philip was ruthless in his support of Spain against a Protestant majority of the Netherlands, which resisted the coming of the Spanish Inquisition.

William the Silent, Prince of Orange and governor of the three Netherlands provinces, became leader in the struggle for independence. After an ill-fated truce, the Dutch and Spanish resumed fighting and it remained for William's grandson to see the successful end of the War for Dutch Independence in 1648.

A Golden Age began in the Netherlands under the rule of the House of Orange in the 17th century, with the growth of a merchant fleet that led the world.

The successors of William the Silent were forced from power in 1653 by supporters of powerful Dutch statesman Jan de Witt, whose task it became to combat England for command of the seas. Dutch land defenses became neglected and the Netherlands were invaded by the French. The House of Orange was recalled, now led by the brilliant military strategist William III, and peace was achieved with England and France.

The explosive force of the French Revolution brought revolutionaries to the Netherlands to found the Batavian Republic, soon to be taken over by Napoléon Bonaparte's empire. After Napoléon's defeat, the House of Orange returned to the Netherlands throne, and there was a short-lived attempt at union with Belgium. The people of the Netherlands were granted new rights in the late 19th century as a separate country under a constitutional monarchy, the form of government the Netherlands retains today.

Occupied by Germany during World War II, the Netherlands dropped its neutral status after the war and joined the North Atlantic Treaty Organization (N.A.T.O.). In 1958 the nation joined the European Community. From the late 1950s to the early 1970s the government was controlled by the People's Party, primarily Catholic but also including Protestants. In 1973, the Labor Party gained control. Although a succession of various coalitions have vied for political power since then, Dutch politics can generally be described as peaceful.

FOOD AND DRINK

Dutch food includes *erwtensoep*, a thick pea soup with bits of sausage or pork; *boerenkool met worst*, a combination of

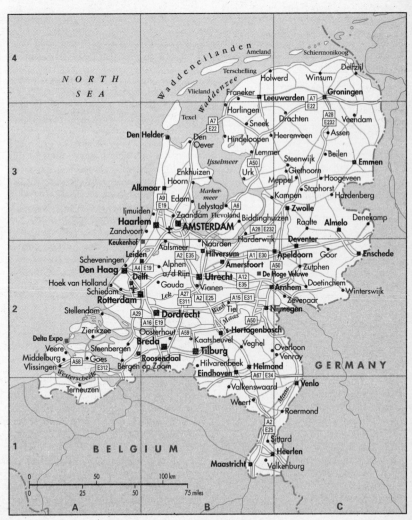

day varies with location. Most other stores and department stores open 9am–5:30pm Monday–Friday, 9am–4pm Saturday.

- BEST BUYS: Delft pottery, crystal, silver, pewter, wooden shoes, costumed dolls, fashions, antiques, flower bulbs. Diamonds from the diamond-cutting center of Amsterdam.
- PUBLIC HOLIDAYS: January 1; Good Friday; Easter Monday; Queen's Birthday Celebration, April 30; Liberation Day, May 5; Ascension Day; Whitmonday; December 25; Boxing Day, December 26.
- USEFUL TELEPHONE NUMBERS:
  Police: **0611**
  Fire: **0611**
  Ambulance: **0611**
- NATIONAL TOURIST OFFICES:
  Netherlands Board of Tourism
  21st Floor
  355 Lexington Avenue
  New York
  NY10017
  Tel: 212/370 7367
  Fax: 212/370 9507
  Netherlands Board of Tourism
  9841 Airport Boulevard
  10th Floor
  Los Angeles
  CA 90045
  Tel: 310/348 9333
  Fax: 310/348 9344
  Netherlands Board of Tourism
  PO Box 523
  London
  SW1F 6NI
  England
  Tel: 01891 200 277
  Fax: 0171 828 7941
  V.V.V. Tourist Office
  Amsterdam Centraal Station
  Stationsplein 10
  1012 AB Amsterdam
  Tel: 634 034066
  Fax: 20 625 2869
- AMERICAN EMBASSY:
  Lange Voorhout 102
  2514 EJ Den Haag
  Tel: 070 310 9209
  Fax: 070 361 4688

vegetables and sausage, and *Rijsttafel*, an exotic Indonesian meal consisting of 20 or 30 tempting varieties of spicy food served with rice. Dutch cheeses are among the world's finest. Dessert may be a selection of the light pancakes called *flensjes* or waffles. Dutch beer is excellent.

The Netherlands sponsors two schemes catering to the culinary desires of its visitors. Many restaurants offer a fixed-price tourist menu. Alternatively, for traditional Dutch fare, go to one of the restaurants displaying the *Nederlands Dis* sign of a red, white and blue soup tureen. Tourist offices supply brochures listing the establishments participating in these schemes.

For a more casual atmosphere, try the *bruine kroeger* (brown cafés), which offer delicious lager, or *jenever* (Dutch gin).

SPORTS AND RECREATION
Soccer is the most popular sport in the Netherlands. Auto and motorcycle races are held every year at Zandvoort. Watersports come naturally to the Dutch, who enjoy miles of uninterrupted coastline and lakeshores. Excellent golf courses are near Den Haag (The Hague), Amsterdam, Utrecht and Zandvoort, and information about walking routes and organized walking tours can be obtained at V.V.V. (tourist) offices.

GETTING AROUND
The direct cross-channel ferry service of roughly 200 kilometers (125 miles) makes England a close neighbor. Services operate from Harwich to the Hook of Holland (Hoek van Holland), Hull to Rotterdam (Europoort), and Sheerness to Vlissingen (Flushing). The trip takes 7–14 hours, depending on the point of departure. Ferries also serve many parts of the country, including Zeeland, Flanders, some islands of South Holland and the Wadden Islands (Waddeneilanden) which lie to the north of the mainland. The Netherlands also can be easily reached by driving through France and Belgium.

AUTOMOBILE CLUB
Koninklijke Nederlandse Toeristenbond (ANWB, Royal Dutch Touring Club), Wassenaarseweg 220, The Hague, has branch offices in various cities throughout the Netherlands. The symbol ▲ beside a city name indicates the presence of a AAA-affiliated automobile club branch. Not all auto clubs offer full travel services to AAA members.

The distance from Calais, France, to The Hague is about 320 kilometers (200 miles) – less than a day's drive.

Within the Netherlands, highways are marked by blue signs with white letters, secondary roads by white signs with black letters, and the country lanes by low signs called "toadstools."

The best way to see the countryside, however, is to use the minor roads, especially those along the canals. The wearing of seat belts, if the car is so equipped, is mandatory for the driver and front-seat passengers. Children can occupy the front seat only if wearing a seat belt that does not cross the chest (for ages 4–11) or sitting in an approved child safety seat (for under age 4).

Visiting motorists are required to pay fines for motoring violations on the spot with Dutch guilders.

Speed limits are 50 k.p.h. (30 m.p.h.) in town, 80 k.p.h. (50 m.p.h.) out of town and 120 k.p.h. (75 m.p.h.) on highways unless posted signs indicate otherwise.

Information on the Netherlands' principal touring areas can be obtained from local tourist information offices marked by a blue V.V.V. *i-Nederland* sign on a triangular field of white. These signs also are posted on roads approaching towns with a V.V.V. office.

The Netherlands is divided into zones for public transportation by bus, tram and subway; each transportation company charges the same price per zone. Visitors can buy a *Nationale Strippenkaart* (National Strip Card) for the zone-operated ticket system at railroad stations, transportation companies, post offices and some V.V.V. offices.

ACCOMMODATIONS
Reservations should be made far in advance in the Netherlands, particularly in Amsterdam. The Netherlands Reservation Center (N.R.C.), provides free hotel booking services. For further information or reservations, write to N.R.C., PO Box 404, 2260 AK Leidschendam, or tel: 070 320 2500.

Once in the Netherlands, local tourist offices can help you find accommodation for a small fee. Youth hostels in the Netherlands accommodate travelers of all ages, including families, who are members of a youth hostel organization in their own country or who possess an international youth hostel card.

There are approximately 900 campgrounds throughout the Netherlands. An international camping carnet is not required, but some sites may still request it.

TIPPING
Hotels and restaurants add a 15 percent gratuity charge to their bills, so it is not necessary to tip further.

PRINCIPAL TOURING AREAS
Note: For descriptions of cities in **bold type**, see individual city listings.

ZEELAND
The province of Zeeland is a favorite of watersports enthusiasts, as the Meuse and Rhine rivers flow into the North Sea, forming large estuaries that divide the area into islands and peninsulas.

The port city of Vlissingen, provincial capital **Middelburg** and ancient Zierikzee are of special interest.

ON YOUR BIKE

The bicycle is part of the Dutch way of life, and by using the dedicated network of cycle tracks (fietspaden) totaling some 10,000-kilometers (6,200 miles) it is one of the best ways of getting around.

If you were so inclined, you could tour the whole of the Netherlands on these well sign-posted routes – they even have their own crossings and traffic lights.

One particular breathtaking route is the road across the top of the Aasluitdijk, the dam across the Ijsselmeer. However, in high winds this 30-kilometer (19-mile) ride can be a little hair-raising, to say the least.

HOLLAND AND UTRECHT

Composed of the provinces of Noord-Holland, Zuid-Holland and Utrecht, this region is especially popular with travelers. It includes the Netherlands' main tourist destinations: **Amsterdam, Aalsmeer; Den Haag (The Hague)**, Utrecht and **Rotterdam**.

Outside the cities, it is a land of sand dunes, windmills and bulb fields and is noted for cheese and beer.

The provinces of Noord-Holland and Utrecht share the lush, hilly – and wealthy – district known as Gooiland. Located within the triangle formed by Amsterdam, Utrecht and **Amersfoort**, it is a convenient starting point for major excursion points.

The Golden Coast, a strip of white sand beaches extending from the Hoek van Holland (Hook of Holland) to **Texel Island,** is noted for its seaside resorts.

FLEVOLAND

The newest province in the Netherlands, Flevoland was reclaimed from the Zuider Zee and consists of three main polders: the North-east Polder, East Flevoland and South Flevoland.

This green province in the heart of the water region is just a short drive north east from **Amsterdam**.

IJSSEL VALLEY

Noted for its castles, the Ijssel Valley is a peaceful region of forests and orchards. Giethoorn, north of **Zwolle**, has no streets, and everyone travels by canal.

Staphorst, one of the country's most unusual cities, is renowned for its colorful costumes and steadfast customs.

NORTH

Friesland, Groningen and Drenthe provinces are in a major dairy area that has many lakes and canals, quaint market towns and marshes that are now national parks.

SOUTH EAST

The southeastern provinces are not particularly well traveled by tourists, although they do have much to offer.

North Brabant is a land of folklore, forests, moors and farmsteads. Its capital, **'S Hertogenbosch,** or **Den Bosch,** boasts the finely sculptured St. John's Cathedral and a baroque town hall. Nearby Tilburg has a safari and recreation park.

Industrial **Maastricht** is a convenient base for exploring Limburg, a province with rich architectural traditions.

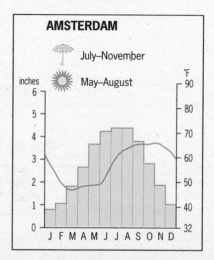

USEFUL EXPRESSIONS IN DUTCH

Note: You'll find that virtually everyone in the Netherlands speaks English fluently, particularly in Amsterdam. In fact, English is rapidly becoming the first language of Amsterdam. Signs are written in Dutch and English, and menus are printed in several languages, so confusion is rare.

hello	dag
good morning	goede morgen
good afternòon	goede middag
good evening	goede avond
good night	goedenacht
good-bye	tot ziens
please/thankyou	alstublieft/dank u
yes	ja
no	nee
excuse me	pardon
you're welcome	tot uw dienst
Do you speak English?	Spreekt u Engels?
I don't understand.	Ik begrijp het niet.
What is the time?	Hoe laat is het?
How much is that?	Was kost dit?
Do you take credit cards?	Accepteert u kredietkaarten
Where are the restrooms?	Waar zijn de toiletten?
I'd like ...	Ik wil graag ...
Can you help me, please?	Help mij, alstublieft?
where	waar
when	wanneer
how	hoe
old/new	oud/niew
open/closed	open/dicht
yesterday	gisteren
today	vandaag
tomorrow	morgen
no entry	verboden toegang
post office	postkantoor
pharmacy	apotheek
hospital	ziekenhuis
postcard	briefkaart
telephone booth	telefooncel
hotel	het hotel
gas station	het benzinestation
traffic lights	de verkeerslichten
trailer	de aanhangwagen
baker	de bakker
bookshop	de boekwinkel

department store	het warenhuis
liquor store	de slijterij
accident	het ongeluk
ambulance	de ziekenwagon
blister	de blaar
burn	de brandwond
cold	de verkoudheid
contact lenses	de contactlezen
dentist	de tandarts
earache	de oorpijn
fever	de koorts
first aid	eerst hulp
hayfever	de hooikoorts
headache	de hoofdpijn
hospital	het ziekenhuis
migraine	de migraine
painkiller	de pijnstiller
sore throat	de zere keel
temperature	de temperatuur
toothache	de kiespijn
doctor	de dokter

DAYS OF THE WEEK

Sunday	zondag
Monday	maandag
Tuesday	dinsdag
Wednesday	woensdag
Thursday	donderdag
Friday	vrijdag
Saturday	zaterdag

NUMBERS

1	een	21	eenentwintig
2	twee	22	tweëntwintig
3	drie	30	dertig
4	vier	40	veertig
5	vijf	50	vijftig
6	zes	60	zestig
7	zeven	70	zeventig
8	acht	80	tachtig
9	negen	90	negentig
10	tien	100	honderd
20	twintig	1,000	duizend

PLACES OF INTEREST

▲ AMSTERDAM ★

NOORD-HOLLAND *pop. 715,400*

Water is the distinguishing feature of this cosmopolitan city. Amsterdam consists of 70 islands that are separated by 80 kilometers (50 miles) of canals and connected by more than 1,000 bridges. Perhaps the best introduction to the city's charm is a canal cruise on one of the glass-topped boats that depart from the convenient downtown docks.

Amsterdam's historic inner city contains many places of interest, including the 19th-century Sint Nicolaas kerk, the medieval weigh-house and Centraal Station, erected in 1889.

Two of the city's outstanding parks are Vondelpark and Amsterdamse Bos. Also of interest are the University of Amsterdam, founded 1632, and the Free Reformed University, founded 1880.

Since the time of Rembrandt, Amsterdam has been an artistic center, and the city is celebrated for its museums – there are more than 40.

Other entertainment possibilities are the Muziektheater, which is the home of the National Ballet and National Opera Company and the Concertgebouw with its outstanding symphony orchestra. Most dramatic productions are given in Dutch, except the opera, which is sung in the original language. For the majority of theater, music, ballet and opera performances, seats can be reserved in advance at the Amsterdam Uit Buro and the V.V.V. tourist office.

Amsterdam also has several movie theaters where foreign movies are often shown, and there is plenty of nightlife which is frequently loud and lively.

Amsterdam is a shopper's city as well. Antique shops along the Spiegelgracht and the Rokin offer everything from porcelain to pewter, while the World Trade Center at Strawinskylaan 1 is a modern shopping and business complex with boutiques and eateries. Also popular are the many small shops along the canals which are well worth exploring.

Trips can be taken to the flower centers of Aalsmeer, 10 kilometers (6 miles) south west, and Haarlem 10 kilometers (6 miles) west. The drive south from Haarlem to Leiden or north to Den Helder takes in much of the country's bulb-growing area; the best time for this drive is from spring to fall. Cheese markets near Amsterdam are at Alkmaar, Edam and Gouda.

Nearby Marken and Volendam are picturesque fishing villages noted for the traditional costumes worn by their inhabitants.

AMSTELKRING MUSEUM (also known as Ons Lieve Heer Op Solder – "Our Lord in the Attic") (470 C3), Oudezijds Voorburgwal 40, is a 17th-century merchant's house with an unusual baroque church hidden in its attic. Houses of this kind were common during the 16th and 17th centuries when Catholic worship was forbidden. Ons Lieve Heer Op Solder is the best preserved of those that remain.

AMSTERDAM HISTORISCH MUSEUM (470 C3), Kalverstraat 92, includes numerous prints and drawings associated with the city's history. The museum is housed in the former Municipal Orphanage, which was founded in 1580.

ANNE FRANKHUIS (470 B3) ★, Prinsengracht 263, is the restored building where the author of *A Diary of a Young Girl* and her family hid from the Germans 1942–4, prior to their imprisonment in Nazi concentration camps. Only Anne Frank's father, Otto, survived. The rooms where the family hid have been left as they were in 1944, down to the pictures put on the wall by Anne.

ARTIS ZOO AND PLANETARIUM (470 E2), Plantage Kerklaan 40, houses more than 6,000 animals. Highlights include reptile, mammal and nocturnal animal houses. The Planetarium offers an exposition of the stars and a history of the universe.

BEGIJNHOF (470 C2), on a tiny side street between Kalverstraat 130 and 132, is a tree-shaded courtyard surrounded by houses. No. 34, known as Het Houten Huis, "the Wooden House," dates back to 1470 and is the oldest surviving building in the city. The Begijnhof was founded in 1346 for *Beguines*, or lay nuns.

DIAMOND-CUTTING WORKSHOPS are scattered throughout the city, and most are open to visitors.

The largest of these factories is Van Moppes Diamant, at Albert Cuypstraat 2–6; visitors are shown every phase of diamond cutting, shaping and polishing.

HEINEKEN BRAUWERIJ (Heineken Brewery Museum) (470 C1), Stadhouderskade 78, is a renovated brewery. On display are parts of the copper brewhouse and stables with horses, carts and carriages.

KONINKLIJK PALEIS (Royal Palace) (470 C3), on the Damplein, is the city residence of Queen Beatrix. Built by architect Jacob Van Campen 1648–62 as the town hall, the building was turned into a royal palace in 1808, when Louis Napoléon made it his residence. The royal apartments contain a wealth of Empire furniture and marble sculpture.

MUNTTOREN (470 C2), Muntplein, was built in 1618 over a medieval gate. Later that century, coins were minted at the site, hence the name Munttoren, which means Mint Tower.

MUSEUM WILLET-HOLTHUYSEN (470 C2), located at Herengracht 605, is a 17th-century patrician canal house containing exquisite collections of period furniture, porcelain and glass. The 18th-century garden is a delight.

NEDERLANDS SCHEEPVAART MUSEUM (470 E3) ★ (Maritime Museum), Kattenburgerplein 1, is housed in the former arsenal of the Amsterdam Admiralty. It presents the illustrious history of Dutch navigation and there is a replica of the 18th-century three-masted ship *The Amsterdam* moored outside.

NIEUWE KERK (470 C3), Dam Square, was built in 1468. Gutted by fire in 1645, the principal features of the interior date from the Golden Age. Since the early 19th century the church has been the coronation site of the House of Orange.

OUDE KERK (470 C3), Oudekerksplein 23, was consecrated in 1306 and is the city's oldest church. Especially noteworthy are the 16th- and 17th-century stained-glass windows.

REMBRANDTHUIS (470 C3), Jodenbreestraat 4–6, is where the great artist lived 1639–60. The house contains a collection of Rembrandt's etchings, drawings, period furniture and memorabilia.

RIJKSMUSEUM (470 B1) ★ (National Museum), Stadhouderskade 42, has world-famous collections featuring canvases by celebrated artists.

Among the museum's most famous works are Rembrandt's *Night Watch* and *The Jewish Bride*.

THE NETHERLANDS

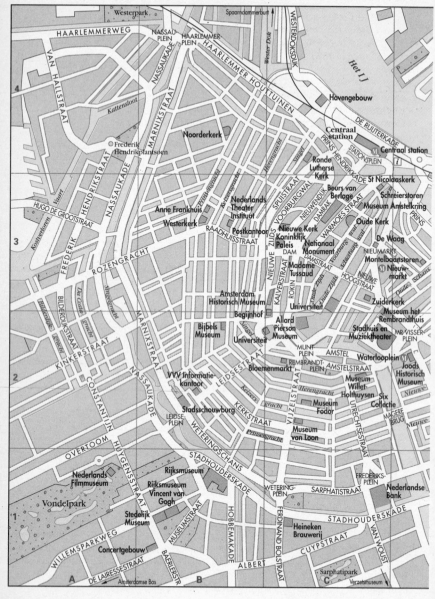

The Delft School is also well represented, with several fine paintings by Jan Vermeer in the collection.

RIJKSMUSEUM VINCENT VAN GOGH (470 B1) ★, Paulus Potterstraat 7, presents an outstanding collection of Vincent Van Gogh's art, consisting of some 200 oil paintings and 600 drawings.

The collection illustrates the artist's career, from his early studies of peasant life right up to the anguished paintings he produced just before he committed suicide in 1890.

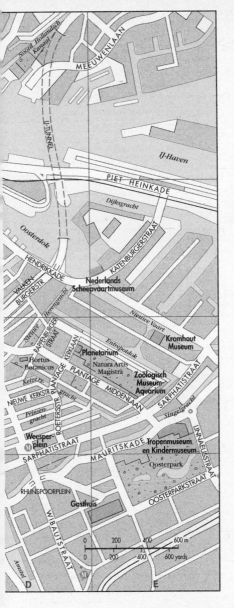

RED-LIGHT DISTRICT

Like every port city, Amsterdam has had commercialized sex available for many centuries. Prostitutes operating in the 17th century had to pay rent to the city bailiff. He therefore had a vested interest in ensuring that they did not stray from the area. If they did, he sent a drum and flute-playing guard to expose both client and prostitute, thus driving them back to their designated area. Although the red-light district is still here, it must be unique in that it is now a viable tourist attraction as well. You will be as safe as in any other large city, as long as you take precaution against theft, and do not take photographs. However, be prepared to be shocked!

AALSMEER (463 B2)
NOORD-HOLLAND *pop. 22,100*

Aalsmeer is a small town wholly devoted to fresh flowers. Blooms of every imaginable variety are cut early in the morning and taken to Aalsmeer's flower market, the largest in the world.

AALSMEER FLOWER MARKET, covering 45 hectares (111 acres), sells millions of blossoms every year. They are classified and set in lots for potential buyers, who place bids electronically. Sold before noon the flowers are packed and flown to European cities for resale the same day.

Visitors can view the market activities from a gallery; it is advisable to arrive before 8am to avoid the crowds.

▲ ALKMAAR (463 B3)
NOORD-HOLLAND *pop. 91,800*

Alkmaar is an old town famed for its cheese market. The Waagplein, a picturesque square surrounded by 17th-century buildings and canals, provides the stage for this colorful event. Huge rounds of Gouda and red-skinned Edam are heaped in impressive piles for buyers to inspect, sample and haggle for.

WESTERKERK (470 B3), corner of Westermarkt and Prinsengracht, was built 1620–31. On top of the church's elegant 86-meter (282-foot) tower is the imperial crown donated by Emperor Maximilian. Popularly known as "Langer Jan" (Long John), the tower is the tallest in the city.

To complete the sale, cheese porters wearing the dress of the ancient cheese-trade guild, haul the cheeses in barrows to the Waag (Weigh House) and then to the boat or truck of the buyer.

KAASMUSEUM (Cheese Museum), in the Waag, exhibits antique cheese- and butter-making implements, and gives an interesting account of the cheese-making process.

▲ AMERSFOORT (463 B2)
UTRECHT *pop. 104,400*

Principally a manufacturing town, Amersfoort nevertheless preserves much of its medieval aspect. Spanning the Eem River in the town's north is the Kopplepoort, a restored watergate dating from the 15th century. Visible at some distance from Amersfoort is the 100-meter (328-foot) Onze Lieve Vrouwe Toren. This imposing Gothic tower is all that remains of a 15th-century church.

Amersfoort is close to many natural beauty spots, including parts of the Den Treek-Henschofen, Randenbroek and Lockhorst estates. The estates are open to the public year-round.

MUSEUM FLEHITE, Westsingel 50, houses prehistoric items unearthed near Amersfoort, medieval objects and collections of Delftware and Chinese porcelain.

▲ APELDOORN (463 C2)
GELDERLAND *pop. 148,700*

The large town of Apeldoorn is located in the Veluwe region and encompasses thousands of acres of parks and estates.

Though not historically noteworthy, Apeldoorn does have several museums, old churches and castles. The Het Loo Palace, built for Prince William III, and the former residence of Queen Wilhelmina, is outstanding.

BERG EN BOS is probably the best known of Apeldoorn's scenic parks. In addition to 397 hectares (980 acres) of woods, meadows and floral displays, there is a natural habitat zoo with more than 250 monkeys roaming freely in the trees high above the heads of visitors.

HET LOO PALACE, Koninklijk Park, is restored to its 18th-century glory and now houses a museum illustrating 300 years of the domestic history of the House of Orange. Reproductions of the original formal gardens are superb.

▲ ARNHEM (463 B2)
GELDERLAND *pop. 132,900*

Arnhem, on the Rhine, is in an attractive region of castles, gardens and orchards. Heavily bombed during World War II, it has been rebuilt to include wide avenues and numerous parks.

AIRBORNE MUSEUM, Utrechtseweg 232, preserves the memory of the World War II Battle of Arnhem. The museum is housed in the Hotel Hartenstein, the British H.Q. at the time, and contains photographs, weapons and uniforms.

BURGERS' ZOO, Schelmseweg 85, is known for its spacious, natural-looking enclosures, including a chimpanzee and gorilla island, a wolf wood, a tropical house and free-flight aviaries.

NEDERLANDS OPENLUCHT MUSEUM, Schelmseweg 89, off Highway N 93, is a delightful open-air museum preserving the Dutch past with reconstructed farms, mills, schools and inns. Curiosities include a paper mill from the Veluwe region, a garden of medicinal plants and a brewery from Brabant.

▲ BREDA (463 B2)
NOORD-BRABANT *pop. 126,700*

An important event in the Dutch battle for independence took place in Breda in 1566, when a group of Dutch nobles issued the historic Compromise of Breda in protest against Spanish rule.

Bouvigne Castle, with its moat and scenic gardens, is on the outskirts of town and Zundert, 13 kilometers (8 miles) south, is notable as the birthplace of Vincent Van Gogh.

STEDELIJK EN BISSCHOPPELIJK MUSEUM (Municipal and Episcopal Museum), Grote Markt 19, displays ecclesiastical art and objects relating to the history of Breda, as well as coins and prints.

DELFT (463 A2)
ZUID-HOLLAND *pop. 90,000*

Delft is known as Prinsenstad – "City of Princes" – and indeed the Gothic and Renaissance houses lining the ancient streets and canals give it a unique charm. Delft is famous for its porcelain industry, and the city's potters still make the renowned blue china first produced in the 17th century. The painter Jan Vermeer was born in Delft in 1632.

HET PRINSENHOF, St. Agathaplein 1. Formerly a convent, the Prinsenhof became the headquarters of William the Silent during the Dutch Revolt against Spanish rule. William was assassinated here in 1584. The Prinsenhof is now a museum housing exhibits of tapestries, silver, ceramics and paintings.

NIEUWE KERK, Markt, was built in the 14th and 15th centuries. The church contains the ornate tomb of William the Silent and those of other descendants of the House of Orange. Scenic views are available from the top of the tower, which is over 107 meters (350 feet). The tower's magnificent bell carillon was created by the Hemony brothers in 1663.

OUDE KERK, Oude Delft, is a vast 13th-century Gothic church with a leaning tower. Vermeer is buried inside.

DE PORCELEYNE FLES (The Porcelain Jar), Rotterdamseweg 196, has been producing Delftware since 1653. The factory still uses traditional methods of production. Visitors can watch potters and artists at work and buy examples of their craft in the factory showroom.

▲ DORDRECHT (463 B2)
ZUID-HOLLAND *pop. 111,800*

On the Merwede River, Dordrecht is the oldest town in Holland and an active port and yachting centre. Its beautiful surroundings have been an inspiration to several artists.

DORDRECHT MUSEUM, Museumstraat 40, has a good collection of 17th-century paintings by artists born in Dordrecht.

GROTE KERK, Grotekerksplein, was built in Brabantine Gothic style in the 15th century after an earlier church was destroyed by fire. The church has impressive carved oak choir stalls dating from 1538 to 1541. Visitors can climb the 70-meter (230-foot) bell tower, which has a 49-bell carillon.

EDAM (463 B3)
NOORD-HOLLAND *pop. 25,000*

The seaport of Edam, famous for the cheese, has been producing it since the 16th century and the Kaaswaag "Cheese Weigh House," dating from 1778, is a reminder of those days. A cheese market is held in Edam on Wednesday mornings during the summer.

EDAMS MUSEUM, Damplein 8, in the 16th-century Captain's House, has an unusual floating cellar which was built by a retired ship's captain who longed for the feel of the sea. In the front room are portraits of some of the town's most unusual citizens.

GROTE KERK ST. NICOLAAS was founded at the end of the 15th century and has been completely restored. There are 30 stained-glass windows which were and are still created in the 17th century are worth seeing.

ENKHUIZEN (463 B3) ★
NOORD-HOLLAND *pop. 16,000*

Crisscrossed by canals, Enkhuizen is considered one of the country's prettiest towns. Many buildings from the 15th to 17th centuries have been preserved, including the birthplace of painter Paulus Potter and the 17th-century town hall and prison.

THE NETHERLANDS

ZUIDERZEEMUSEUM, Wierdijk 18, has two parts. The outdoor Buitenmuseum comprises 135 houses and workplaces surrounded by reconstructed streets and gardens. The Binnenmuseum indoors houses items from the Zuider Zee area, including ships, ship models, fishing implements and costumes.

▲ ENSCHEDE (463 C2)
OVERLJSSEL *pop. 147,000*
Enschede lies on the Twente Canal and has a respected technical university and textile school. It has two very good museums, one covering art and the other the local textile industry. The lovely town of Ootmarsum is nearby.

FRANEKER (463 B4)
FRIESLAND *pop. 20,800*
A picturesque old town, Franeker was known between the 16th and 19th centuries for its university.

Traces of Franeker's past can still be seen in the old city battlements and Gothic-Renaissance buildings.

PLANETARIUM EISE EISINGA, Eise Eisingastraat 3, is the 18th-century home of a local wool-comber, Eise Eisinga, who built a planetarium on his living-room ceiling in order to demonstrate the movements of the planets.

▲ GOUDA (463 B2)
ZUID-HOLLAND *pop. 67,400*
Situated on the Ijssel River, Gouda is famed for its cheese, waffles, candles, pottery and pipes. The major attraction is the cheese market, held once a week in the 17th-century weigh house.

Gouda is a good starting point for exploring the surrounding countryside. Excursions can be made to the Reeuwijk Lakes, excellent for watersports, and at nearby Oudewater, the witches' scales dating from 1595 are still in use.

HET CATHARINA GASTHUIS, Oosthaven 9. The Hospice of St. Catherine was founded as an almshouse in 1310, but the present building dates from 1665,

when it became a hospital. The patrician structure now houses a museum with exhibits such as an old apothecary shop, a hospital kitchen, period household rooms and antique toys.

ST. JANSKERK (St. John's Church), Markt, is a late Gothic cross-basilica church dating from the 16th century. The outstanding stained-glass windows were donated by, among others, Philip II of Spain and William of Orange.

▲ GRONINGEN (463 C4)
GRONINGEN *pop. 169,600*
Groningen is one of the leading business centers in the north of the Netherlands, and it also has a prestigious university, founded in 1614.

GRONINGEN MUSEUM, recently rehoused in Ubbo Emmiussingel, a new building opposite the rail station, has a remarkable display of Chinese ceramics which were salvaged in 1985 from the Dutch ship *Geldermalsen*, which sank in the South China Seas in 1572.

NOORDELIJK SCHEEPVAART MUSEUM, Brugstraat 24–26, occupies two 16th-century merchants' houses. It illustrates the maritime history of Northern Holland from earliest times and has models and paintings of old ships, navigation instruments, anchors, figureheads and ships' flags.

▲ DEN HAAG (463 A2) ★
ZUID-HOLLAND *pop. 445,300*
Seat of the government and official residence of Queen Beatrix, Den Haag, or The Hague, is a royal, aristocratic city with large squares, broad streets, imposing buildings and fine mansions. S'Gravenhage, as it is officially known to the Dutch, is the most cosmopolitan city in Holland, and is the home of the International Court of Justice.

The city tourist offices supply information on various tours and excursions, including canal cruises and a guided tour of the city's royal palaces.

In July, The Hague celebrates the North Sea Jazz Festival at the Nederlands Congresgebouw which draws top artists from around the world.

Around 3 kilometers (2 miles) from the city center is the delightful seaside resort of Scheveningen.

BINNENHOF is a group of buildings which takes its name from the inner courtyard of the castle built in 1250 by Count William II. Today it is home to the two chambers of the Netherlands' Houses of Parliament. The Ridderzaal, or Hall of Knights, is the site of the state opening of Parliament.

GEMEENTHEMUSEUM, Stadhouderslaan 41, exhibits 19th- and 20th-century paintings and sculptures, including a large collection of works by the modern Dutch artist Piet Mondriaan. There also are displays of musical instruments, costumes and Islamic and Dutch pottery.

MAURITSHUIS ROYAL, Korte Vijverberg 8, is a 17th-century patrician mansion that now houses a magnificent art gallery, considered one of the finest in Europe. Highlights of the collection include Rembrandt's *The Anatomy Lesson of Dr. Tulp*, and Jan Vermeer's *View of Delft*.

PANORAMA MESDAG, Zeestraat 65, features the *Panorama of Scheveningen*, one of the last surviving cycloramas of the 19th-century. Painted by H. W. Mesdag and his team, the immense circular painting depicts the popular seaside resort as it was in 1881.

VREDESPALEIS, Carnegieplein 2, was erected 1908–13 as a gift from Andrew Carnegie. It is the seat of the International Court of Justice, principal judicial organ of the United Nations.

▲ HAARLEM (463 B3) ★
NOORD-HOLLAND *pop. 150,000*
Historic Haarlem lies at the heart of the bulb-growing region of Holland, and is one of the most luxurious residential

QUEEN BEATRIX
Amid great controversy, Queen Beatrix was crowned on April 30, 1980. The festivities didn't quite go according to plan, however, when protesters objecting to the cost of the investiture and seeking to highlight the housing crisis, fought with police, which resulted in a full-scale riot.

One of the richest women in Europe (second only to Queen Elizabeth II of Britain), she has now won the respect and affection of the people. She works to promote Dutch interests at home and abroad, and defines her job: "The kingdom is something to be marketed, just like oranges."

This modern royal family live in Den Haag, in extensive parkland. Tour operators offer royal tours, taking in the lovely 17th-century Huis ten Bosch (House in the Woods).

areas in the country. Around the Grote Markt are majestic buildings dating from the 15th century. Haarlem's principal architectural treasures – the almshouses, private mansions and the Vleeshal (meat market) – date from the 17th century.

The bulb fields to the south of the city are worth visiting. Lisse, about 15 kilometers (9 miles) south, is noted for its Keukenhof Gardens, featuring a 28-hectare (70-acre) bulb exhibition.

DE HALLEN, Grote Markt, the city's former fish and meat markets (Vishal and Vleeshal) now house temporary art exhibitions. Built in 1603 by Lieven de Key, the elaborately decorated Vleeshal is considered an outstanding example of Dutch Renaissance architecture.

FRANS HALS MUSEUM, Groot Heiligland 62, is housed in the almshouse where the great Dutch painter Frans Hals spent the last years of his life. The museum contains an impressive collection of paintings by Hals and several other 17th- century masters.

TEYLERS MUSEUM, Spaarne 16, houses drawings and paintings of the Dutch, Italian and French schools from the Renaissance to the present and includes 25 drawings by Michelangelo. Founded in 1778, it is the oldest museum in the Netherlands.

THE HAGUE – see *Den Haag on p.474.*

▲ DEN HELDER (463 B3)
NOORD-HOLLAND *pop. 61,200*
Located at the northern tip of North Holland in the country's main bulb-growing area, Den Helder is a scenic tourist destination. It is also the Netherlands' main naval base and for three days in mid-summer, the Dutch Navy invites the public to see its fleet.

HELDERS MARINEMUSEUM HET TORENTJE, Hoofdgracht 14, illustrates the history of the Royal Dutch Navy from the early 17th century to the present. Displays feature seagoing vessels, airplanes, uniforms and weaponry.

▲ 'S HERTOGENBOSCH (463 B2)
NOORD-BRABANT *pop. 93,200*
'S Hertogenbosch, or Den Bosch, is the capital of North Brabant. Once a powerful fortress, it is now an industrial and commercial city. Places of interest include Gothic St. Janskathedraal, a large cattle market and the baroque town hall. The city's carnival celebration is among the most festive in the country.

DE EFTELING RECREATION PARK, 24 kilometers (15 miles) west of Den Bosch, is a family theme park, drawing more than a million visitors a year. The complex includes thrill and fantasy rides based on traditional fairytales and legends.

NOORDBRABANTS MUSEUM, Verwerstraat 41, occupies an 18th-century mansion, the former seat of the provincial governor. It contains archeological finds, paintings, silver and pewter, as well as old coins and medals.

ST. JANSKATHEDRAAL ★, Parade, is considered the finest Gothic cathedral in the Netherlands. The interior boasts ornately carved choir stalls from 1480 and a miracle-working 13th-century figure of the Madonna, "Our Sweet Lady of Den Bosch," in the Lady Chapel.

DE HOGE VELUWE (463 B2) ★
De Hoge Veluwe, Hoenderloo, is a national park which was formerly the estate of Anton and Hélène Kröller-Müller. It is the Netherlands' largest nature reserve and contains 5,500 hectares (13,600 acres) of sand dunes, woods and grassland. Deer, boar, wild sheep and other animals live in the park in their natural habitats. Also within the park are St. Hubertus hunting lodge, named for the patron saint of hunting and an art museum.

RIJKSMUSEUM KRÖLLER-MÜLLER, in the park, houses a permanent collection of paintings and sculptures, which was bequeathed to the nation, along with the park by Hélène Kröller-Müller. The museum houses an extensive Vincent Van Gogh collection, and a sculpture park surrounding the main gallery has works by August Rodin, Henry Moore and Barbara Hepworth arranged among the trees and shrubs.

HOORN (463 B3)
NOORD-HOLLAND *pop. 59,000*
Once a major seaport, Hoorn is a popular resort with two fine yacht harbors on Ijsselmeer. It is noted for its patrician mansions dating from the Golden Age. Other reminders of the town's past are the baroque Waag, dating from 1609, the Renaissance Oosterpoort, a watch house, and the Noorderkerk, a late-Gothic church built of timber in 1426 and reconstructed in stone 1441–1519.

In Schagen, 10 kilometers (6 miles) north west, the Old Dutch Market presents a colorful spectacle with crafts, costumes and folk-dancing.

▲ LEEUWARDEN (463 B4)
FRIESLAND *pop. 86,400*

Leeuwarden is the capital of Friesland, situated in a region of lakes and canals. The town has the largest cattle market in the Netherlands and a thriving dairy industry. Places of interest include Oldehove Tower, which has been leaning since 1532, and the Princessehof, a museum featuring Asian art. Also of interest are the late 16th-century Waag and the 15th-century Grote Kerk.

FRIES MUSEUM, Turfmarkt 24, houses relics relating to the history and culture of Friesland from prehistoric times.

▲ LEIDEN (463 B2)
ZUID-HOLLAND *pop. 113,000*

Leiden holds special significance for Americans. A small group of English Separatists, who later became known as the Pilgrims, migrated to this town from England in search of religious freedom. In 1620, after 10 years' residence, they left for Delfshaven, near Rotterdam, where they boarded the *Speedwell* for England on the first leg of their journey to the New World. However, the vessel was declared unseaworthy in England and the group joined others aboard the *Mayflower* for the two-month voyage across the Atlantic.

Leiden also is significant in the world of art, as it was the birthplace of Rembrandt in 1606. Many other Dutch painters, including Jan Steen, lived and worked in Leiden.

MOLENMUSEUM DE VALK (Windmill Museum), 2e Binnenvestgracht 1, housed in a restored 18th-century windmill, illustrates the use of wind power in Holland over the centuries.

RIJKSMUSEUM VAN OUDHEDEN (National Museum of Antiquities), Rapenburg 28, has world-renowned collections from Egypt, Greece and Rome. The mummy

and sarcophagi exhibit is outstanding, together with the reconstruction of a pharaoh's death chamber.

UNIVERSITY OF LEIDEN was founded in 1575 when The Prince of Orange offered it to the city residents as a reward for resisting a Spanish siege lasting 131 days. It is the oldest in the country.

▲ LELYSTAD (463 B3)
FLEVOLAND *pop. 57,600*

Founded in 1967, this ultra-modern town is the capital of the Netherlands' newest province, Flevoland, which is the creation of an ambitious land reclamation scheme initiated by the engineer Dr. Cornelius Lely.

FLEVOHOF is a 150-hectare (370-acre) complex recreating in microcosm a Dutch agricultural and horticultural community. It features two progressive working farms where visitors can experience "learning by doing" through sorting eggs, making butter and cheese, or even watching the birth of a calf.

RIJKSMUSEUM VOOR SCHEEPSARCHELOGIE (Museum of Ship Archeology), Vossemeerdijk 21, displays excavated wrecks and their contents from some of the 400 shipwrecks made accessible since 1932 by the reclamation of the Zuider Zee.

LISSE – *see Haarlem on p.475.*

▲ MAASTRICHT (463 B1) ★
LIMBURG *pop. 118,000*

Wedged between Belgium and Germany at the Netherlands' southernmost tip, Maastricht is the capital of Limburg and is an exciting city with an unusual mixture of languages and customs.

Dating from Roman times, Maastricht's history of French, Spanish and German occupation is reflected in its architecture.

In 1992 the city was well and truly put on the map by witnessing the signing of the historic Maastricht Treaty by the countries of the European Union.

BONNEFANTENMUSEUM is housed in a controversial new building at Avenue Cermamique 250. The museum contains interesting archeological artefacts discovered locally, some dating back to Roman times. The museum's art collection includes works by Brueghel, Rubens and Van Orley. One of the most fascinating exhibits is a scale model of Maastricht in 1748.

HELPOORT, St. Bernardusstraat 24, dates from 1229 and is the oldest surviving city gate in the Netherlands.

KAZEMETEN (Casemates), Waldeck Park, are a series of fortifications developed between 1575 and 1825. They comprise a system of dry trenches and bastions with bomb-proof shelters and mine galleries. Near the entrance is a bronze statue of d'Artagnan, the real-life musketeer immortalised by novelist Alexandre Dumas, who was killed during a siege of the town in 1673.

ONZE LIEVE VROUWEBASILIEK (Basilica of Our Lady), Vrouweplein, was built upon Roman foundations in around 1000 AD. The fortress-like west front was once part of the city's defenses.

ST. SERVAASBASILEK, the oldest church in Holland, was originally built in the 6th century over the grave of St. Servatius, the first bishop of Maastricht. The present Romanesque structure dates mainly from the 11th, 12th and 13th centuries. The Treasury contains a rich collection of religious artifacts including relics pertaining to St. Servatius himself.

▲ MIDDELBURG (463 A2)
ZEELAND *pop. 40,000*
Middelburg is on the island of Walcheren. The region has remained largely unchanged since the late 17th century, although it was badly damaged during World War II.

ABDIJKERKEN (Abbey Churches), Onderdentoren, consists of three churches that were originally part of a monastery founded in 1150. Following the expulsion of the monks in 1574 during the revolt against the Spanish, the abbey buildings became the seat of provincial government.

STADHUIS is an outstanding example of 15th-century Flemish Gothic architecture. The façade has 25 statues of the Counts and Countesses of Zeeland set between Gothic windows.

MUIDEN – *see Naarden below*.

NAARDEN (463 B2)
NOORD-HOLLAND *pop. 16,500*
The French, Spanish and Prussians subjected tiny Naarden to numerous raids, massacres and occupations since its origin in 1350, but the fortified town has remained surprisingly intact due to the construction of a double belt of walls and moats in the 17th century.

Naarden has been completely restored and has now been given status as a national monument.

MUIDERSLOT, about 8 kilometers (5 miles) north west from Naarden, is a moated castle built in 1250 to defend the mouth of the Vecht River.

The interior reflects the castle's heyday during the 17th century. Of special interest are the botanical gardens and the view of Ijsselmeer.

▲ NIJMEGEN (463 B2)
GELDERLAND *pop. 144,700*
Nijmegen, on the Rhine Delta, is one of the Netherlands' oldest cities. About 2,000 years ago the Romans realized the area's geographical potential and founded the city.

The remains of a palace built by Emperor Charlemagne can still be seen. Despite extensive damage during World War II, Nijmegen has managed to retain several of its old buildings.

The restored Weigh House and the 16th-century town hall are particularly interesting.

BEVRIJDINGSMUSEUM 1944 (Liberation Museum 1944), 10 kilometers (6 miles) south, gives a complete account of the airborne invasion Market Garden and Operation Veritable, which led to the liberation of the Netherlands during World War II.

OVERLOON (463 B2)
NOORD-BRABANT *pop. 8,000*
The site of one of the fiercest tank battles of World War II, Overloon was devastated by German and British-American shellfire.

Today the quiet community commemorates the episode with its National War and Resistance Museum, in a large wooded park, displaying tanks, torpedo boats, aircraft and weapons. The museum also contains a chapel honoring all who gave their lives for their countries.

▲ ROTTERDAM (463 A2) ★
ZUID-HOLLAND *pop. 589,700*
The bustling city of Rotterdam is the second largest city in Holland and symbolizes the heart, courage and industry of the Dutch people. The city was almost destroyed by German bombs in 1940 and the new city is noted for its modern, imaginative architecture. The port has regained its position as one of the world's largest with at least 150 shipping lines linking Rotterdam with foreign lands.

There is a fascinating array of shops in the center and Spido Harbor Tours offers boat tours of the harbor all year and cruises to the Europoort and the Delta Expo in summer.

Once a port town in its own right, Delfshaven in Rotterdam's western district was the point of departure for the *Speedwell*, in 1620.

Several buildings from that period, including the Dutch East India Company Warehouse and the house of the Grainsack Carriers, still stand.

BOYMANS-VAN BEUNINGEN MUSEUM, Museumpark 18-20, contains an outstanding collection of early and modern paintings. Among its treasures are works by the Dutch Masters, from Van Gogh to Rembrandt, and by modern artists such as Picasso and Salvador Dali.

DIERENPARK BLIJDORP (Blijdorp Zoo), Van Aerssenlaan 49, is one of the most modern zoos in Europe. Man-made rain forests harbor tropical birds; rare animals include European bison and pygmy hippopotami. The zoo specializes in breeding species threatened with extinction.

THE LOCALS

Remembering that there are exceptions to every rule, the Dutch are renowned for their tolerance and liberal attitudes. The expression *laissez faire* sums up the attitude of most citizens, because they strongly believe in the rights of individuals and oppose officialdom and interference. However, when this is exploited, the Dutch work by consensus, as was seen in the 1980s when parts of Amsterdam and Rotterdam were becoming unsafe for the average person to visit. Groups of local people formed community action groups, and with the help of the authorities, rejuvenated the run-down areas which had been the haunt of drug pushers and addicts.

EUROMAST, Parkhaven 20, is a 185-meter (607-foot) tower, with a revolving glass Space Cabin that affords a spectacular view of the city of Rotterdam.

MARITIEM MUSEUM PRINS HENDRIK, Leuvehaven 1, is devoted to the city's maritime history. The main building has a small display of model ships, maps and nautical instruments. An outdoor museum along the harbor displays a fleet of ships whose highlight is the warship *De Buffel*, a Royal Navy vessel which was in active service 1868–96.

MILLS OF KINDERDIJK, 20 kilometers (12 miles) east, is the best-known windmill area in the country; 19 of these picturesque structures were built around 1740 for draining excess water from the polders. The mills now only operate for the benefit of tourists.

OUDE KERK, Aelbrechtstolk 22 in Delfshaven, is the church where the Pilgrims met before sailing on their journey for the New World.

TOY-TOY MUSEUM, Groene Wetering 41, displays rare 19th- and 20th-century dolls originating from France, Germany and England. Exhibits also include mechanical toys dating from 1700.

SCHEVENINGEN – *see Den Haag on p.474.*

▲ SCHIEDAM (463 A2)
ZUID HOLLAND *pop. 71,100*
Schiedam is an old fishing port from the 13th century. The city was important for its fish and grain trade until it was overshadowed by nearby Rotterdam.

Schiedam still has several medieval buildings, including the 15th-century Church of St. John and the Mathenesse Castle ruins.

DELTA EXPO, 17 kilometers (11 miles) south west of Schiedam, is reached from the mainland by a good highway.

The Delta Expo illustrates in model form the fascinating history and development of the Delta Plan. This was a unique project, engineered in response to the disastrous flood of 1953, to build a series of dams that would protect the region from further disaster.

TEXEL ISLAND (463 B3)
NOORD-HOLLAND *pop. 12,800*
Texel is the largest of the Wadden Islands and is a popular seaside resort.

The island is one of Europe's most important bird-breeding grounds, and there are plenty of opportunities for outdoor activities.

The island's market town is Den Burg, although De Koog is considered the main resort.

ECOMARE, Ruyslaan 92, near De Koog, has a bird and sea lion sanctuary.

THE FRISIAN ISLANDS
The further north you travel, the smaller, wilder and more remote the five Frisian islands become.
Texel is the most southerly island and the only one where you will find cars in any number. It can be busy on summer weekends, as sunbathers and windsurfers pour out of the cities.
Vlieland attracts naturists and birdwatchers and has the largest nudist beach in Europe.
Terschelling is where many ships have been wrecked on the sandbanks. One of the most famous was the *Lutine*, whose bell was the only part to be recovered and is still rung at Lloyd's, the London insurance market, whenever a ship is lost at sea.

▲ UTRECHT (463 B2) ★
UTRECHT *pop. 232,700*
Utrecht is one of the oldest towns in the Netherlands. Founded around 695 AD by St. Willibrord, it was the site of the Treaty of Utrecht, which concluded the War of the Spanish Succession in 1713.

Among its many curiosities are high-gabled houses, canals and picturesque watergates.

Utrecht is also a good starting point for exploring the castles in the surrounding countryside, such as the 19th-century Castle de Haar at Haarzuilens and Castle Doorn, the former residence of Kaiser Wilhelm II.

CENTRAAL MUSEUM, Agnietenstraat 1, contains an exhibit on city history, highlighted by a Viking ship that dates back to the year 1200.

Other displays include paintings from the Utrecht school of art, sculpture, costumes and a 17th-century dollhouse.

DOMKERK, Domplein, is a Dutch Reformed cathedral built between 1254 and 1517.

A hurricane destroyed the nave in 1674, leaving only the Gothic choir and transepts. The peaceful 14th-century cloisters linking the cathedral and the university are worth visiting.

DOMTOREN, next to the church, is an unusual 112-meter (367-foot) tower affording an extensive view of the surrounding area.

NATIONAL MUSEUM VAN SPEELKLOK TOT PIEREMENT (National Museum from Musical Clock to the Barrel Organ), Buurkerkhof 10, is a delightful museum illustrating the history of mechanical musical instruments. It contains street organs, pianolas, funfair and dance organs in full working order.

NEDERLANDS SPOORWEGMUSEUM (Dutch Railway Museum), Maliebaanstation, covers the history of the railroads and trams in the Netherlands. Housed in a disused station built in 1874, the museum contains original locomotives and rolling stock.

RIETVELD-SCHRÖDERHUIS, Prins Hendriklaan 50a, is a striking, modern house with a unique interior design, that was built in 1924 for Mrs. Truus Schröder-Schräder by Gerrit Rietveld, who was one of the leading architects in the De Stijl movement.

It is now a designated world-heritage monument. Viewing is by appointment only (telephone 362310).

RIJKSMUEUM HET CATHARIJNECONVENT, Nieuwegracht 63, housed in a 16th-century Carmelite convent, portrays the history of Christianity in the Netherlands through an extensive collection of religious art.

VALKENBURG (463 B1)
LIMBURG pop. 18,000
Sited in the middle of the beautiful Guel Valley, Valkenburg is a resort best known for its Grottoes of Cauberg, which date from prehistoric times.

The ruins of a medieval castle, the stronghold of the lords of Valkenburg, dominate the town.

Other attractions include Thermae 2,000, a modern spa center, a fairytale park and Lourdesgrot, a replica of the shrine at Lourdes.

VEERE (463 A2)
ZEELAND pop. 4,900
Veere, 8 kilometers (5 miles) north of Middleburg, prospered as a trading port between the 15th and 18th centuries when it dominated the Dutch trade in Scottish wool. The elegant 16th-century Schotze Huizen (Scottish Houses), the homes of wealthy Scottish merchants, testify to the town's past splendor.

Also of interest are the 14th-century Grote Kerk and the Oude Stadhuis (Old Town Hall), a late-Gothic building housing the town's museum.

ZIERIKZEE (463 A2)
ZEELAND pop. 9,900
An important trading port in the Middle Ages, Zierikzee is today renowned as a popular yachting resort.

Of interest to visitors are the remains of the town's fortifications, including medieval Nobelport (Nobel Gate), and the attractive 17th-century merchants' houses lining the old canals. S'Gravensteen, a prison until 1923, now houses a maritime museum.

▲ ZWOLLE (463 C3)
OVERIJSSEL pop. 97,100
Zwolle, capital of Overijssel, is a charming city whose ramparts have been replaced by delightful parks and shaded retreats. Places of interest include the Church of Our Lady, with its 15th-century Pepperpot Tower, and the town hall, noted for its attractive Gothic marriage room.

PORTUGAL

The shadow of Spain has kept Portugal partly hidden, and those who find it delight in its culture, countryside, mountainous interior and ancient villages.

Portugal seems almost all shoreline, from the remote rural areas of the north to the sun-drenched sandy beaches of the Algarve. This long coastline has made Portugal a nation of fishermen, and seafarers. Many of the great maritime explorers were Portuguese, including Vasco da Gama. Successful navigators return, bringing their influences with them, and nowhere are these more evident than in the vibrant capital city of Lisbon, with its parks, churches and cobbled streets, mosaics and monuments, *FADO* music in back-street bars, and mix of crumbling grandeur and startling new buildings.

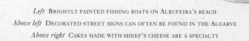

Left Brightly painted fishing boats on Albufeira's beach
Above left Decorated street signs can often be found in the Algarve
Above right Cakes made with sheep's cheese are a specialty

THINGS TO KNOW

- **AREA:** 94,250 square kilometers (36,390 square miles).
- **POPULATION:** 9,833,000
- **CAPITAL:** Lisboa (Lisbon).
- **LANGUAGES:** Portuguese, English and French.
- **ECONOMY:** Tourism, agriculture, production of wine, textiles, fish, cork, leather goods and olive oil.
- **PASSPORT REQUIREMENTS:** Required for U.S. citizens.
- **VISA REQUIREMENTS:** Not required for stays up to 60 days.
- **DUTY-FREE ITEMS:** 200 cigarettes, 100 cigarillos, 50 cigars or 250 grams tobacco (for non-European visitors 400 cigarettes, 200 cigarillos, 100 cigars, 500 grams tobacco); however if on the way to Portugal a stopover of more than 24 hours is made in any European country, the duty-free allowance is reduced; 2 liters of wine; 1 liter of spirits; 1/4 liter of eau de cologne; 50 grams perfume; 100 grams of tea or 40 grams of tea extract; personal goods to be used during the stay; and gifts and souvenirs to a value of 7,500$00 (to 3,750$00 for those under 15). See *The European Union* on p.5.
- **CURRENCY:** The currency unit is the *escudo* (ESC), divided into 100 *centavos*. Due to currency fluctuations, the exchange rate is subject to frequent change. In writing, the escudo is shown with a centrally placed dollar sign between the escudo and centavo amounts; for example, 3$20. There are no restrictions on the importation of local or foreign currency, but amounts exceeding the equivalent of 500,000 escudos must be declared upon arrival. Any amount of foreign currency may be exported provided it was declared on entry, but no more than 1,000,000 escudos may be exported. Note: Foreign visitors entering Portugal must have a minimum of ESC.10,000$00 and a further ESC.3,000$00 for each day of their intended stay in the country. These amounts can be in any currency.

HISTORY

Although Portugal traces its origin to prehistoric times, the country's role in the history of Western civilization began with Roman occupation in the 2nd century BC. In turn the Roman settlements were invaded by the Visigoths, who were later Christianized. Moslem rule came with the Moors, an Islamic people who ruled Portugal up until the 12th century. Portugal's first king, Afonso Henriques, drove the Moors from the city of Santarém in 1147 and, banding with passing Crusaders, took the capital, Lisbon, or Lisboa. About a century later, the last of the Moors were ousted.

In the early 15th century, Prince Henry the Navigator inspired a period of great explorations. During the late 16th century, Portugal fell under Spanish domination, but recovered its independence in 1640 and regained prosperity during the 18th century.

In the 19th century, the country was ravaged first by the Napoleonic Wars and later by civil strife. In 1908 King Carlos I was assassinated in Lisbon and Portugal became a republic. For much of the 20th century Portugal was subject to a military dictatorship. There was a brief socialist revolution in 1974 but free elections were held in 1976. In 1989 Portugal's parliament officially abolished the socialist economy and called for the denationalization of industry.

FOOD AND DRINK

Cooking in Portugal is considered a fine art, which makes the cuisine among the best in Europe. The Portuguese excel in preparing lobster, shrimp, prawn, crab, clam, mussel and oyster dishes. Also delicious are tuna, sardines and *bacalhau*, a salted dried cod. Other specialties are *caldo verde*, a soup made of potatoes and cabbage, and *gaspacho*, the tomato and cucumber soup of Alentojo.

Portuguese desserts are varied and typically very rich; *arroz doce* is probably the most common after-dinner choice The national drink is wine, produced all over the country. Port and Madeira are served before and after meals. Portuguese beer is also popular.

SPORTS AND RECREATION

Golf is inexpensive in the large cities and the better resorts; costs are reasonable even at the Estoril Country Club. Estoril also offers swimming, as do a lot of resorts all along the coast.

In the Serra da Estréla Mountains, in central Portugal, the ski season is from December through March.

The most popular spectator sport is soccer, and games are played in stadiums throughout the country every Sunday from September through June.

GETTING AROUND

Public transportation is generally inexpensive. Prices are comparatively low on the streetcar and subway systems. The best fares can be obtained by purchasing a series of 10 or 20 tickets at one time.

Airports at Faro and Porto have made the Algarve coast and the northern districts more easily accessible. Europabus is also a convenient method of travel.

Motorists will find that a well-maintained network of national highways, designated by the letters "EN" followed by a number, reaches virtually all corners of Portugal. A large section of the Auto-Estrada (superhighway) is open,

---

SPORT

In Portugal a bullfight is called a *tourada*. It is considered an art rather than a sport and differs from the Spanish *corrida*. As a result of a mishap which took place in the 18th century, the bull is never killed. The star of the show is the *cavaleiro* (horseman) who shows off his skills on horseback. When the bull is deemed exhausted a group of eight men known as *forcados* come on and perform a series of maneuvers to master the bull, including an attempt to seize its horns. Touradas are held in Lisbon on Thursdays and Sundays from Easter Sunday to October.

---

with more under construction. Tolls are charged on most sections. The driver and all passengers must wear seat belts, if available. Children under 12 must occupy rear seats unless wearing an appropriate restraint. Speed limits are 50 k.p.h. (30 m.p.h.) in town, 90 k.p.h. (55 m.p.h.) on out-of-town roads and 120 k.p.h. (75 m.p.h.) on highways. A visitor who has held a driver's license for under 1 year must not exceed 90 k.p.h. (55 m.p.h.).

All motorists are required to pay fines for violations on the spot in Portuguese escudos.

ACCOMMODATIONS

Hotels in Portugal are ranked from one to five stars. The government has encouraged construction of well-equipped hotels, particularly in the Algarve region. *Pousadas*, modern, state-owned roadside inns, are often in scenic areas and converted historic buildings. *Estalagens* are small, well-appointed inns, privately owned but supervised by the Ministry of Tourism. Lists of *pousadas* and *estalagens* can be obtained from tourist offices. These inns are usually very busy, especially in summer, so reserving well in advance is advised.

AUTOMOBILE CLUB
Automovel Club de Portugal
(ACP, Automobile Club of Portugal) has its headquarters at Rua Rosa Araújo 24, Lisbon. The symbol ▲ beside the city name indicates the presence of a AAA-affiliated automobile club branch. Not all auto clubs offer full travel services to AAA members.

- **BANK OPENING HOURS:** 8:30am–3pm Monday–Friday. Closed national holidays. A bank at Sacavém International Airport and one in downtown Lisbon are open daily 24 hours.
- **STORE OPENING HOURS:** 9am–1pm and 3–7pm Monday–Friday, 9am–1pm Saturday. Some large shopping complexes open daily 9am–Midnight (most are in Lisbon).
- **BEST BUYS:** Cork products, Madeira lace, hand-knit woolen sweaters, hand-sewn Arraiolos rugs, sterling silver jewelry, antiques, gold jewelry, embroidered material, leather goods, filigree jewelry, port and Madeira wine, pottery, folk crafts and ceramic tiles.
- **PUBLIC HOLIDAYS:** January 1; Shrove Tuesday; Good Friday; Liberty Day, April 25; Labor Day, May 1; Corpus Christi; National Day, June 10; Assumption, August 15; Proclamation of the Republic, October 5; All Saint's Day, November 1; Independence Day, December 1; Immaculate Conception, December 8; December 25.
- **USEFUL TELEPHONE NUMBERS:** Police 115; Fire 115; Ambulance 115.
- **NATIONAL TOURIST OFFICES:** Portuguese National Tourist Office 590 Fifth Avenue, Fourth Floor New York, NY 10036 Tel: 212/354 4403 Fax: 212/764 6137 Portuguese National Tourist Office 22–25a Sackville Street London W1X 1DE Tel: 0171 494 1441 Fax: 0171 494 1861
- **LOCAL TOURIST OFFICES:** Lisbon: Praça dos Restauradores (Palácio Foz). Tel: 01 3463643 Estoril: Arcadas do Parque. Tel: 01 4680113 Cascais: Avenida Dom Carlos 1. Tel: 01 486 8204
- **AMERICAN EMBASSY:** Av. das Forças Armadas 1600 Lisboa Portugal Tel: 01 726 6600

For those who enjoy guesthouses, *pensões* are readily available. The Portuguese Directorate for Tourism has developed what it calls *turismo de habitação*, which are either *solares*, spacious country manor houses, or *quintas*, country estates, restored to function as guesthouses. Most are located in Minho province, and some date as far back as the 15th century. More information on these can be obtained from the Portuguese National Tourist Office (see *Things to Know* box).

Youth hostel's minimum age is usually 7 years. Some hostels allow only male or only female guests. Campers will find good campgrounds near Portugal's major cities. Automovel Club de Portugal can book tent sites, recreational vehicle hookups, etc., for travelers. An international camping carnet is recommended.

TIPPING

Portuguese hotels and restaurants include a 10 percent service fee in bills, but service personnel expect another 5–10 percent; use your discretion.

PRINCIPAL TOURING AREAS

Note: For descriptions of cities in **bold type**, see individual city listings.

THE ALGARVE

Separated from the rest of Portugal by the Caldeirão and Monchique mountains, the Algarve is the southernmost province of Portugal. A number of resort complexes have sprung up but little has spoiled the white sand beaches for which the Algarve is known. Towns such as **Olhão** preserve traces of the past in their churches, palaces and white "sugar cube" houses.

The Algarve's prettiest area begins with the seaport of **Faro**. Popular neighboring cities are Silves and scenic **Portimão**. **Sagres**, which preserves mementoes of Prince Henry the Navigator, faces Africa on Portugal's southwestern tip.

PORTUGAL

MADEIRA AND THE AZORES

IIha da Madeira, or **Madeira Island**, is a paradise island bathed in sunshine off the north-west coast of Africa. The **IIhas dos Açores**, or **Azores**, with their hot-water springs and green pastures, consist of nine islands 1,280 kilometers (795 miles) west of Portugal. Mists, mountains and white-washed houses lend them an unusual beauty.

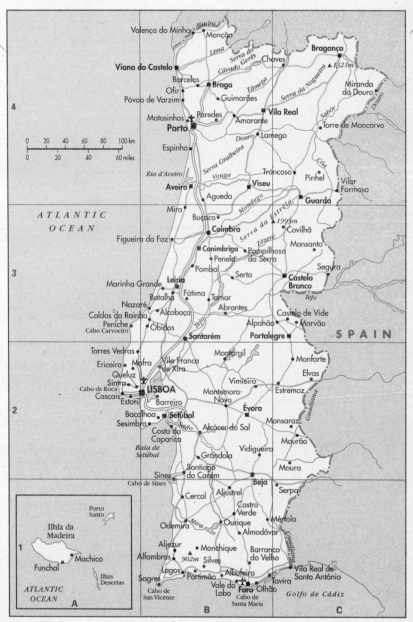

PORTUGAL

LISBON AND CENTRAL PORTUGAL

The colorful houses high on the steep, narrow streets of **Lisboa**, or **Lisbon**, give the capital a special charm. **Estoril**, with its fine beach, is only a short drive away, and beyond lies **Sintra**, or **Cintra**, known for its pretty setting and stately palaces.

Southeast of Lisbon is ancient **Setúbal**, which is an important port and fishing center. Nearby are the ruins of the Roman Troia City. On the coast north of Lisbon is the fishing village of **Nazaré**.

Near the center of the country, the Beira provinces comprise cool mountains, sunscorched plains and villages perched on the granite slopes of the Serra da Estréla Mountains.

NORTHERN PORTUGAL

Douro province, whose capital is **Porto**, or **Oporto**, is known for its port wine. Visitors can wander through bottle-lined, dark caves where the wine is made. This part of the country has streams and rivers, woods, lush greenness and a general impression of great prosperity.

In the north is the mountainous province of Mingo, where grapes and grain are important. **Braga**, the provincial capital, has a fine cathedral.

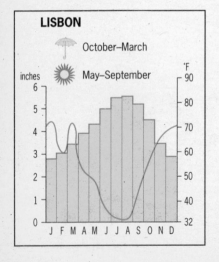

USEFUL EXPRESSIONS IN PORTUGUESE

hello	olá
good-bye	adeus
good morning	bom dia
good afternoon	boa tarde
good night	boa noite
please	por favor
thank you	obrigada (f), obrigado (m)
yes/no	sim/não
why/when	porquê/quando
how/what	como/que
Do you speak English?	fala inglês?
I do not understand.	nâo compreendo
you're welcome	de nada
excuse me	com licença
How much is ...?	Quanto é ...?
What time is it?	Que horas sâo?
today	hoje
tomorrow	amanhã
yesterday	ontem
where is ...?	onde é ...?
I would like ...	queria ...
restroom	casa de banho
old/new	velho/novo
cheap/expensive	barato/caro
open/closed	aberto/fechado

DAYS OF THE WEEK

Sunday	domingo
Monday	segunda-feira
Tuesday	terça-feira
Wednesday	quarta-feira
Thursday	quinta-feira
Friday	sexta-feira
Saturday	sábado

NUMBERS

1	uma (f); um (m)
2	daus (f); dois (m)
3	três
4	quatro
5	cinco
6	seis
7	sete
8	oito
9	nove
10	dez

PLACES OF INTEREST

★ HIGHLIGHTS ★

Batalha	(see p.492)
Coimbra	(see p.492)
Évora	(see p.493)
Lisboa –	(see p.489)
Castelo de São Jorge	
Mosteiro dos Jerónimos	
Museu Calouste	(see p.490)
Gulbenkian	
Madeira and Funchal	(see p.494)
Porto	(see p.495)
Sagres	(see p.497)
Sintra	(see p.497)
Tomar	(see p.497)

PORTUGAL

▲ LISBOA (487 B2) ★

ESTREMADURA *pop. 1,000,000*

Portugal's capital city, Lisboa, or Lisbon, has always reached out to the sea from its sheltered position by the Tajo River. Lisbon's seven hills provide a varied setting, and charm is everywhere in the tiled roofs and softly colored houses. The city can be reached by plane via Portela de Sacavém International Airport, 8 kilometers (5 miles) north.

The legendary founder of Lisbon was Ulysses, but the theory of Phoenician origin is probably more realistic. Occupiers in later years included the Romans, Visigoths and, beginning in the 8th century, the Moors.

On the morning of All Saints' Day in 1755, an earthquake struck Lisbon, killing about 40,000 people. The royal minister, the Marqués de Pombal, began rebuilding and his layout of a carefully planned street system is still in use.

Lisbon can be roughly divided into six districts. Baixa is the central business district. The two main streets, Rua Garrett – also called the Chiado – and Rua Augusta, are lined with fashionable stores. Among the attractions are Rossio Square and the National Theatre of Dona Maria II. East of Baixa is Eastern Lisbon, which has the ancient Castelo São Jorge and Sé (Cathedral).

The Bairro Alto area lies north of Baixa, and the ancient part of this section contains the Church of São Roque and the Chapel of São João Baptista. Alfama, the oldest part of the city, dates from the Moorish occupation in the 8th through the 12th centuries.

The museums in the Belém and Ajuda districts include the Coach Museum, Padrao dos Descobrimentos Mosteiro dos Jerónimos and Torre de Belém.

Visitors to Lisbon can take advantage of the Tourist Ticket, which offers unlimited use of all city buses, streetcars, subways and cable cars.

CASTELO DE SÃO JORGE (490 E2) ★ Largo do Chão da Feira and Largo do Menino de Deus, is in the Alfama district near the Tejo River. Constructed by the Visigoths in the 5th century, rebuilt by the Moors in the 9th century and modified during the reign of Afonso I, it has dominated Lisbon life for 1,500 years from the city's highest hill.

MOSTEIRO DOS JERÓNIMOS (490 A1) ★ Praça do Império, Belém, is a Hieronymite monastery built in the early 16th century by order of Manuel I with the riches of the trade with India. The monastery survived the 1755 earthquake.

IGREJA DE SANTA MARIA DE BELÉM (490 A1) houses a Cross of the Holy Order, a statue of Prince Henry the Navigator and the tomb of Vasco de Gama.

> **ATTRACTION SCHEDULES IN PORTUGAL**
>
> Museums in Portugal are generally open 10am–6pm Tuesday– Sunday, with some closing for lunch between 12:30 and 2pm. Palaces are usually open 10am–5pm Wednesday–Monday. Museums and palaces are closed on public holidays. Other attractions often follow this schedule.

MUSEU CALOUSTE GULBENKIAN (490 D3) ★ is in a modern building on Avenida de Berna near Praça de Espanha. The museum's displays date from Egyptian antiquity to the present and include paintings, sculptures, furniture, ceramics, tapestries, jewelry and paintings, including works by Rembrandt, Gainsborough, Manet and Renoir.

TRADITIONAL MUSIC

Fados form a distinctive part of Portugal's folklore. Showing influences of the early songs of the Troubadors and the sailors, the *fado* has a deeply melancholic air, relating to love, passions, destiny, with the singer, or f*adista*, accompanied by one or two guitarists. The old quarter of Lisbon is a good place in which to hear the traditional *fados*. They are also popular, in a slightly different style, in Coimbra, where they are often performed by the students.

MUSEU-ESCOLA DE ARTES DECORATIVAS (Museum-Academy of Decorative Arts) (490 E2), in an Alfama palace on Largo das Portas do Sol 2, is a study in 18th- and 19th-century Portuguese design. Precious furniture, silver and rugs combine in lavish displays.

MUSEU MILITAR (Military Museum) (490 E2), Largo dos Caminhos de Ferro, Santa Apolónia, contains a display of arms and armor from the 9th to 20th centuries.

MUSEU NACIONAL DE ARTE ANTIGA (National Museum of Ancient Art) (490 C1), facing the port at 9 Rua Janelas Verdes, is Portugal's most outstanding art gallery. Renowned for its collection of Portuguese pictures, the museum also has pottery, porcelain and silverware and superb foreign paintings.

MUSEU NACIONAL DOS COCHES (490 B1), in the 18th-century former riding school of Belém Palace on Praça Alfonso de Albuquerque, contains an outstanding collection of state coaches and carriages of the 17th-19th centuries.

PADRÃO DOS DESCOBRIMENTOS (490 A1), in Belém, is a monument to the discoveries of Prince Henry the Navigator. His statue stands at the prow of a stone ship overlooking the Tejos River. Behind him crowd other Portuguese explorers, joined by religious figures and representatives of all walks of life who took part in the discoveries. At the base of the monument is a compass and a mosaic map of the world as it was known to Prince Henry.

PRAÇA DO COMÉRCIO (490 E2), known as the Terreiro do Paço or "Black Horse Square" to the English, is one of the country's loveliest squares.

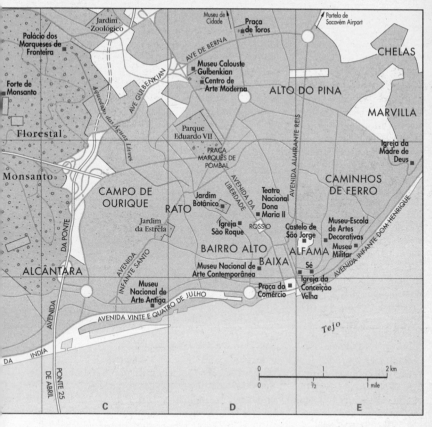

SÉ (490 E2), the Cathedral of Lisbon, towers over the Tejos River in the Alfama district. Tours are available except during Mass.

ALBUFEIRA (487 B1)
(FARO), ALGARVE *pop. 15,000*
From a small, picturesque fishing village, Albufeira has developed into a busy resort. It has still retained its charm, however, with cobbled streets leading uphill to the old village. There are good views down over the fine swimming beach and the attractive boating cove, where the fishermen work.

ALCOBAÇA (487 B3)
ESTREMADURA *pop. 5,400*
The Cistercian community that settled in Alcobaça in the 12th century exer-

cised a powerful influence throughout medieval Portugal.

MOSTEIRO DE SANTA MARIA DE ALCOBAÇA (Santa Maria Monastery) was founded by King Afonso I in 1178. Though restored several times, the monastery retains its noble Cistercian lines.

▲ AVEIRO (487 B4)
BEIRA LITORAL *pop. 30,000*
Aveiro's canals and lagoons are suggestive of Holland or Venice. In fact, Aveiro is often referred to as the "Venice of Portugal."

AZORES ISLANDS
ILHAS DOS AÇORES *pop. 250,000*
Still serene and unspoiled, the Ilhas dos Açores, or Azores, offer numerous

opportunities for relaxation. When discovered in the 15th century they were uninhabited; today a small population ensures their continuing tranquillity.

Covered with vegetation and groves of fruit trees, the nine islands extend for almost 800 kilometers (500 miles) in the Atlantic Ocean, 1,280 kilometers (800 miles) west of Portugal. The islands have international air links with Portugal, the U.S.A. and Canada. A regional airline connects all the islands except for Corvo, · which are also linked by small boats.

The island group has only a handful of beaches, but fishing and skin diving are popular alternatives to swimming. Any activity, however, is enjoyed in a lush and striking landscape and a climate that is warm and sunny from May to September.

On São Miguel, the largest island, Ponta Delgada houses over half of the Azores' inhabitants. This cosmopolitan capital city with its black-and-white mosaic sidewalks is a convenient excursion center.

Angra do Heroismo, capital of Terceira, is a pretty, flower-bedecked town with cobbled streets. Vila do Porto, capital of Santa Maria island, is noted for its old houses and 16th-century church.

BARCELOS (487 B4)
MINHO *pop. 4,000*
Barcelos is known for its brightly colored *O Galo de Barcelos*, or pottery roosters, which have become a ubiquitous Portuguese symbol.

BATALHA (487 B3) ★
BEIRA LITORAL *pop. 7,700*
In 1385, João I of Portugal defeated Juan I of Castile in a battle waged 15 kilometers (9 miles) south of Batalha at Aljubarrota. As a result the young king secured 200 years of independence from Spain. In gratitude João vowed to build a great church to the Virgin Mary which has grown into the present monastery.

MOSTEIRO DA BATALHA, the monastery João I dedicated to Santa Maria da Vitoria, was begun in Gothic design;

later rulers expanded and embellished the Gothic themes.

The chapter house, an architectural feat that gave rise to legends, was built without supporting shafts. It contains Portugal's Tomb of the Unknown Soldier and the tomb of Prince Henry the Navigator.

▲ BRAGA (487 B4)
MINHO *pop. 64,100*
Braga is the capital of the province of Minho. It has been a religious center since the 5th century. Pilgrimages are made to Braga each year. Among the town's architectural highlights is the 11th-century Manueline cathedral, with beautiful chapels, tombs, statues and religious treasures.

PARQUE NACIONAL DA PENEDA-GERÊS (National Park of Peneda-Gerês) is an extensive park between the provinces of Minho and Tras-os-Montes.

BRAGANÇA (487 C4)
TRAS-OS-MONTES *pop. 14,700*
The ancient town of Bragança has a magnificent medieval fortress encircled by formidable walls. Evidence of the town's Moorish background is the architecture of its 12th-century five-sided town hall.

CASCAIS (487 A2)
ESTREMADURA *pop. 29,900*
Cascais is a fashionable Atlantic resort that retains the simple charm of a fishing village while having one of the country's finest beaches, Praia do Guincho.

▲ COIMBRA (487 B3) ★
BEIRA LITORAL *pop. 79,800*
Coimbra, on the banks of the Mondego River, was once the capital of Portugal. It was a powerful city under the Romans, and in the 16th century was the artistic and intellectual center of the country. Today much of the city's life revolves around the university, founded in 1290.

CONIMBRIGA, 14 kilometers (9 miles) south, is an unoccupied Roman city where visitors can see ruins uncovered by recent excavations. The city is known for its well-preserved mosaics.

MOSTEIRO DE SANTA CRUZ (Monastery of the Holy Cross), built in the 16th century, contains the tombs of the first two Portuguese kings.

MUSEU DE MACHADO DE CASTRO is in a former palace, which was restored in 1592. The museum contains paintings, sculptures and ceramics from the 13th and 14th centuries.

PORTUGAL DOS PEQUENITOS (Portugal in Miniature) is a children's attraction with tiny castles, cathedrals and cottages.

SÉ VELHA (Old Cathedral) is the 12th-century Romanesque cathedral.

ELVAS (487 C2)
ALTO ALENTEJO *pop. 14,000*
Elvas is enclosed by impressive 17th century ramparts. A remarkable four-tiered Amoreira Aqueduct, constructed 1498–1622, crosses the plain to bring water to Elvas.

ESTORIL (487 A2)
ESTREMADURA *pop. 25,200*
Estoril, connected to Lisbon by an excellent electric train system, is Portugal's largest and most fashionable seaside resort.

▲ ÉVORA (487 B2) ★
ALTO ALENTEJO *pop. 35,100*
From 1165 to 1580, when Portugal was at the height of its power and prestige, Evora was the preferred seat of the country's kings.

Decline began, however, when Spain conquered Portugal in 1580; Évora never recovered its former eminence. Today it is a major tourist attraction, and cultural center, given world heritage status by U.N.E.S.C.O.

Surrounded by walls that date mostly from the 14th and 17th centuries, Évora's older sections are primarily

Moorish, characterized by hanging gardens, patios and alleys with arches.

ERMIDA DE SÃO BRÁS is a Gothic-Mudejar hermitage south of the city walls near the station. Multiple turrets surmounted by spires decorate this fortress-like building which was founded around 1485.

IGREJA DE SÃO FRANCISCO, Rua da República, is near the town center. The church is typical of the local Gothic-Manueline style of 1480–1510, with a baroque altar and a nave topped with arches of various designs. In the macabre Chapel of Bones, the skulls and bones of 5,000 monks cover the walls and pillars.

MUSEU REGIONAL (Regional Museum), Largo Marqués de Marialva, is in the old bishop's palace next to the cathedral.

SÉ, in the town center on Largo Marqués de Marialva, is Évora's cathedral. Begun in 1186, the Gothic church has a neo-classical main chapel and Renaissance choir stalls. The treasury in the chapter house has a fine collection of gold and silver-work, paintings, sculptures and vestments.

TEMPLO ROMANO (Roman Temple), Largo Bonde de Vila-Flor, faces a garden near the cathedral. Probably dedicated to Diana in the second century, this Corinthian temple of Estremoz marble was used as a fortress in medieval times and excavated during the 19th century.

▲ FARO (487 B1)
ALGARVE *pop. 28,600*
Capital of the Algarve province, the sea-port of Faro occupies an enviable setting midway along the southern coast.

The town has a number of temples and monuments. The most important are the ancient cathedral; the Church of Our Lady of Carmo, with the Chapel of the Bones; the Chapel and Museum of St Antonio; and the Convent of Our Lady of Assunçao, with its noteworthy cloister. Faro also has a local museum.

FÁTIMA

The shrine at Fátima is a famous pilgrimage center, visited by many pilgrims on the 13th of each month. May and October are the major dates, with torchlit processions, night vigils and Masses. The story goes back to May 13, 1917, when three young shepherds claimed to have had a vision of the Virgin Mary. Her message was supposedly repeated on the same date on each following month until October 13 when mysterious happenings were witnessed by a large crowd. In 1930 belief in Our Lady of Fátima was authorised by the Bishop of Leiria.

FÁTIMA (487 B3)
RIBATEJO *pop. 7,300*
The Sanctuary here is one of Europe's most revered shrines, second only to Lourdes in France.

▲ FIGUEIRA DA FOZ (487 B3)
BEIRA LITORAL *pop. 13,400*
Figueira da Foz is another attractive beach area. Shops, cafés, and a casino and tennis courts add to the popularity of this seaside resort.

FUNCHAL – *see Madeira opposite.*

GUARDA (487 C4)
BEIRA ALTA *pop. 15,000*
Fortified in the late 12th century by Sancho I, Guarda, known as the "City of Health," is on the northeastern slope of the Estrela Mountains and is one of the oldest and highest towns in Portugal.

GUIMARÃES (487 B4)
MINGO *pop. 25,000*
Founded by the Celts in 500 BC, Guimarães was the birthplace of the first king of Portugal and was the first capital. The town is surrounded by Moorish fortifications and ancient architecture.

LAGOS (487 B1)
ALGARVE *pop. 10,500*
Popular as a vacation resort today, Lagos was the starting point for Henry the Navigator's 15th-century expeditions to Africa. Places of interest include the old slave market in the Praça da República (Republic Square).
Ponta da Piedade, a rugged promontory with some of the most striking rock formations in the Algarve, is just 3 kilometers (2 miles) south.

LAMEGO (487 B4)
BEIRA ALTA *pop. 10,000*
Surrounded by orchards and vineyards, the Lamego region produces sparkling wines. Lamego is famed for the shrine of Nossa Senhora dos Remédios which attracts pilgrims from all parts of the country. The main pilgrimage takes place on September 8 each year.

MADEIRA (487 A1) ★
ILHA DA MADEIRA *pop. 300,000*
Off the coast of Morocco is Portugal's other world, Ilha da Madeira, or Madeira Island. It is the largest island in the Madeira Archipelago, with an area of 740 square kilometers (286 square miles). It lies some 900 kilometers (560 miles) southwest of Lisbon. Entirely volcanic in origin, Madeira's peaks stretch out of the sea from their "valleys" in the ocean depths. The volcanic soil combines with the mild climate to bring forth an abundance of colorful vegetation.

Although reportedly known to other nations in earlier times, the Madeira archipelago was rediscovered in the early part of the 15th century by Portugal, and colonization began. Today the Madeira Islands are an integral part of Portugal.

Madeira Island is an elongated stretch of land reaching east and west. Along the center runs a mountain chain, a spectacular contrast to the fertile lands along the coasts where sugarcane, bananas and grapes flourish. Terraces of farmland extend into the hills, adding tiers of green beauty to the landscape. Although there are no real beaches, hotels usually have large man-made pools. It is its ideal climate that brings Madeira fame as a year-round resort.

Madeira exports a superb embroidery which carries the island's name, as does the wine, which many feel ranks among the world's best. Wicker baskets and furniture also show fine craftsmanship.

Ilha do Pôrto Santo is the only other inhabited island in the archipelago.

⚑ FUNCHAL has a population of about 120,000. Madeira Island's capital, it has a wide selection of resort hotels; watersports, golf and tennis are popular.

A Madeiran way to tour the city attractions is by bullock-pulled sled; the descent by wicker toboggan at the nearby town of Monte is another popular and exciting ride.

Igreja de Santa Maria Maior, a striking white stucco church, has a contrasting black lava scroll design in baroque style.

Mercado dos Lavradores (Lavradores Market) has vendors in colorful costumes selling flowers, fruit, vegetables, fish and other wares.

Sé (Cathedral), constructed by the Knights of the Order of Christ, is done in white stucco with contrasting black basalt and red tufa rock.

MARVÃO (487 C3)
ALTO ALENTEJO *pop. 300*

Marvão, on a precipitous hill near the Spanish border, has steep streets, fine wrought-iron balconies and the ruins of a 13th-century castle.

The town is surrounded by a high stone wall, indicating Marvão's great military importance during the Middle Ages. The views are astonishing. Cars should be parked in the parking lot at the entrance to town.

NAZARÉ (487 B3)
ESTREMADURA *pop. 10,500*

The picturesque seaside village of Nazaré is known for its clothes, customs and traditions. The fishermen dress in brilliant checked shirts and pants; the women in long dresses. In addition to

the fishermen's quarter, the Sítio – a village set on a very high cliff and reached by a funicular – is worth visiting, especially for the breath-taking views.

OLHÃO (487 B1)
ALGARVE *pop. 34,600*

Olhão resembles a North African town more than a European one. The narrow streets are bordered by high blank walls and cubical white houses, making it one of the most unusual towns in Europe. Olhão's distinctions have attracted many artists.

OPORTO – *see Porto below.*

PORTIMÃO (487 B1)
ALGARVE *pop. 27,000*

Portimão has a bustling harbor lined with fishing boats.

PRAIA DA ROCHA, a seaside resort 3 kilometers (2 miles) north, has a mild climate, picturesque beaches of white and yellow sand, and unusual rock formations sometimes suggestive of animals. Boat excursions can be made to Lagos see p.494.

THE BLOSSOMS OF THE ALGARVE

In January and February the Algarve is transformed into a fairyland of white and pale pink almond blossoms. According to legend, the almond trees were planted by a Moorish chieftain, long ago, to please his wife who yearned for the snows of her native Scandinavia. One fine day the princess awoke and was delighted to find the area covered in blossoms, resembling snow.

⚑ PORTO (487 B4) ★
DOURO LITORAL *pop. 335,900*

Porto, or Oporto, is Portugal's second largest city, occupying an imposing position on the right bank of the Douro River. Three magnificent bridges span

PORTUGAL

the river and from the riverbank rise steep streets with tiers of pastel-colored houses and white churches lined with bright blue tiles.

In Roman times, Oporto was two distinct cities, Oporto and Cale, whose combined names gave the nation of Portugal its name. Also deriving its name from this ancient source is the port wine for which Oporto is known. From vineyards far up the Douro Valley, grapes are brought to the suburb of Vila Nova de Gaia for blending and ageing. Visitors are welcome at the big, dark warehouses where vats and barrels wait out the years as the wines mature.

A little more than 20 kilometers (12 miles) north west of Oporto are the beach resorts of Póvoa de Varzim and Vila do Conde. Both have fascinating pasts as old fishing villages, and many unusual local customs remain.

IGREJA DOS CLÉRIGOS, the 18th-century Church of the Clergy, is an example of restrained baroque design. Its tower, Torre dos Clérigos, has massive yet seemingly delicate stone carvings. From its summit there is an excellent view.

IGREJA SÃO FRANCISCO (Saint Francis Church), on Largo de São Francisco, is a 14th-century Gothic church. It retains its original rose window and a wealth of 17- and 18th-century gilded woodcarvings.

MUSEU SOARES DOS REIS, 56 Rua de D Manuel II, is a National Museum. Once the 18th-century Carrancas Palace, the museum offers displays including wrought gold and silver, ceramics, religious articles, paintings and sculptures.

SÉ, the cathedral, was formerly a fortress-church. Representing the original Romanesque design of the cathedral are its twin towers and wonderful 13th-century rose window. The Gothic cloister was a 14th-century addition, while architects of the 17th and 18th centuries made numerous alterations. The Chapel of the Holy Sacrament has a superb altar.

PORT

One of Portugal's best-known drinks is undoubtedly the sweet, fortified wine known as port, derived from vines cultivated in the Upper Douro. These days the cut grapes are mostly crushed mechanically, followed by the fermenting process. Later a fortifying brandy is added. The wine is then placed in casks and stored in cellars where it continues to mature. The resulting wine is then shipped all over the world from Porto, hence the name.
The Ponte de Dom Luis bridge over the Douro River connects Porto with the Vila de Gaia, where the wine can be sampled.

QUELUZ (487 A2)
ESTREMADURA *pop. 47,900*
QUELUZ PALACE, built in the 18th century, was the sumptuous residence of Queen Maria I. Features include the rose stucco façade; the guard's room and the throne room, famed for its mirrored doors and Venetian chandeliers. The gardens have lavish flower displays, clipped hedges, lakes, fountains and statues.

SAGRES (487 B1) ★
ALGARVE *pop. 2,000*
In the windy coastal town of Sagres, Henry the Navigator lived and mapped out the routes taken by the first Portuguese explorers.

FORTALEZA is Prince Henry's former residence and where he founded his Navigation School. A 30-minute movie chronicles major events of the Great Discoveries era; an English version is presented daily.

▲ SETÚBAL (487 B2)
ESTREMADURA *pop. 97,800*
The Setúbal area dates from Roman times: At low tide the foundations of Roman villas are still visible through the

sand, and from time to time Roman coins or pottery are found.

IGREJA DE SANTA MARIA DA GRAÇA, a 16th-century church, features highly ornate gold and polychrome decorations.

SINTRA (487 A2) ★
ESTREMADURA *pop. 21,000*

Abundant vegetation gives a lush beauty to the hillside setting of ancient Sintra, or Cintra. In sharp contrast, manmade fortresses crown the stern, bare stone peak of Serra de Sintra high above the town.

CASTELO DOS MOUROS (Castle of the Moors), begun in the 7th century, looks down from nearby mountain heights. It was captured from the Moors in 1147, marking the return of Christianity, but is now partially ruined.

MONSERRATE, near Sintra, is a castle with an outstanding botanical garden.

PALÁCIO DA PENA (Pena Palace), like the Castelo dos Mouros, towers over the town from a spectacular height. It is a fascinating 19th-century creation built by Fernando II on the site of an old monastery. A large and lovely park surrounds the castle.

PALÁCIO NACIONAL DE SINTRA (Sintra National Palace), in the center of town, is a royal palace with a special dignity. Its two huge cone-shaped chimneys are the most prominent landmarks in Sintra. Palace interiors are lavishly decorated and include a fine representation of *azulejos*, or brightly colored tiles.

TOMAR (487 B3) ★
RIBATEJO *pop. 15,000*

Tomar is one of the prettiest towns in Portugal; its narrow, winding streets open unexpectedly onto wide squares. Built long before the era of the automobile, local thoroughfares are seldom wider than a single lane.

Among Tomar's attractions are many beautiful churches, including the Convent of Christ, which contains a magnificent series of cloisters. The 12th-century convent was built by the Knights Templar, a powerful religious-military order. In the Jewish quarter a synagogue houses the Portuguese-Hebrew Museum.

The Festa dos Tabuleiros, or Trays Festival, is held every two years in July. It features a religious procession in which hundreds of girls parade through the old part of town balancing elaborately decorated towers on their heads.

VALE DO LOBO (487 B1)
FARO (ALGARVE)

Located some 14 kilometers (9 miles) west of Faro, this well-planned development consists of villas and apartments, swimming pools, bars and restaurants, attractively set among pine trees. The resort offers highest quality facilities for golf, tennis and other sports.

VIANA DO CASTELO (487 B4)
MINHO *pop. 16,000*

On the left bank of the Lima River, Viana do Castelo has been celebrated for its beauty since Roman times. Radiating from the square are narrow, paved streets with old granite houses, wrought-iron balconies and lively Renaissance mansions. The Romanesque-Gothic church, Igreja Matriz, is noted for its wooden sculptures.

Cod fishing first brought prosperity in the 16th century. Viana do Castelo is now as well known for its crafts and folk costumes as for its beaches.

▲ VILA REAL (487 B4)
TRÁS-OS-MONTES *pop. 13,900*

Vila Real, overlooking the Corgo and Cabril gorges, is an ancient town in a fertile wine region. The cathedral and other churches are important.

VILA REAL, the residence of the Counts of Vila Real, is one of Europe's great country houses, with beautiful furnishings and many works of art. Next to the palace is a baroque chapel built in 1750.

DENMARK

Mainland Denmark (Jutland/Jylland) juts up into the North Sea. It is low-lying and fertile with extensive pasture for livestock, and has a long coastline for fishing. A bridge links Jutland with Funen (Fyn), Denmark's second region, the third being Zealand (Sjælland), on which stands Copenhagen (København).

The people are easy going, and have an excellent system of education, health and social welfare which causes them to turn their back a little on the European Union, wondering if they have more to lose than to gain.

Copenhagen has been the capital since the 15th century, when it was also the capital of Norway and Sweden. It is the largest and liveliest of the region's cities, its Tivoli Gardens a magnet for locals and visitors alike for the last 150 years.

Left København, Denmark's capital, has a very attractive and colorful old harbor, known as Nyhavn
Above The Little Mermaid on København's waterfront is a sailor's dream

Things to Know

- **Area:** 42,302 square kilometers (16,633 square miles)
- **Population:** 5,134,000
- **Capital:** København (Copenhagen)
- **Language:** Danish
- **Economy:** Industry, agriculture, meat and dairy products. Fishing and tourism are also important.
- **Passport Requirements:** Required for U.S. citizens.
- **Visa Requirements:** Not required for stays up to three months total in the Scandinavian countries (Denmark, Finland, Iceland, Norway, Sweden).
- **Duty-Free Items:** See *The European Union*, on p.5.
- **Currency:** The currency unit is the Danish *krone* (DKR), divided into 100 *øre*. Due to currency fluctuations, the exchange rate is subject to frequent change. There is no limit on the import or export of foreign or Danish currency.
- **Bank Opening Hours:** 9:30am–4pm Monday–Wednesday and Friday, 9:30–6pm Thursday (in Copenhagen).
- **Public Holidays:** January 1; Maundy Thursday; Good Friday; Easter Sunday and Monday; Great Prayer Day, fourth Friday after Easter; Ascension Day; Whitsunday and Whitmonday; Constitution Day (half day), June 5; December 25–26.
- **National Tourist Offices:**
  Danish Tourist Board
  655 Third Avenue, 18th floor
  New York, NY 10017
  Tel: 212/ 949 2333
  Fax: 212/286 0896
  Turistrådet
  Vesterbrogade No.6D
  1620 Copenhagen Ø
  Tel: 33 11 14 15
  Fax: 33 93 14 16
- **American Embassy:**
  Dag Hammarskjöldsalle 24
  DK-2100 Copenhagen Ø
  Denmark
  Tel: 31 42 31 44
  Fax: 35 43 02 23

History

Danish ships led the way when the Viking conquest of Western Europe and the British Isles began between the 8th to 10th centuries. During this period the sailing and shipbuilding fame of the Norsemen spread throughout the Continent. The Kalmar Union of Denmark, Sweden and Norway was created in 1397 under Queen Margrethe I and lasted right up until the death of Christopher III in 1448.

Seventeenth-century Denmark witnessed the establishment of a monarchy under Christian V and several defeats by then independent Sweden. In the 19th century, Norway was lost, and German duchies were surrendered in battles with Prussia. The country has been a constitutional monarchy since a new constitution in 1848 ended the absolute power of the crown.

Food and Drink

One meal a day, normally *frokost* (lunch), consists of *smørrebrød* – open sandwiches, that consist of fish, herring, meat, paté, cheese and/or salads of different kinds on brown bread and butter. The "hot" meal of the day, *aftensmad* or *middag* (dinner) could be a fish or a meat course followed by dessert. A typical dish would be *flaekesteg med rødkål* (roast pork with red cabbage and sucker browned potatoes), or *stegt rødspaette med persillesovs* (fried plaice with parsley/white sauce flavored with parsley). The Danes are proud of their hams, cheeses and pastries. *Snaps* (Ålborg akvavit) is the national drink, and Danish beer has an international reputation.

Automobile Club
Forenede Danske Motorejere
(FDM, Federation of Danish Motorists); Firskovvej 32, Lyngby, has branches in cities throughout Denmark. The symbol ▲ beside a city name indicates the presence of a AAA-affiliated automobile club branch. All auto clubs offer full travel services to AAA members.

SPORTS AND RECREATION

Denmark has fine facilities for most land and water sports. Tennis and riding clubs are plentiful, and many cities have golf courses. Soccer is the favorite spectator sport. In this seafaring nation, all water sports are extremely popular on the bays, lakes and streams.

GETTING AROUND

Ferries are essential links between highway and railroad stops on the major islands. Reservations are necessary, especially in summer. On land, you can buy a number of bus and rail combination packages from Danish State Railways (D.S.B.) and other companies. Major cities sell special travel cards for use on buses and trains, which may include discounts on museum entrance fees. Bicycles, used throughout the country, can be rented from D.S.B. Local tourist offices also have information about bicycle rental. Car rental

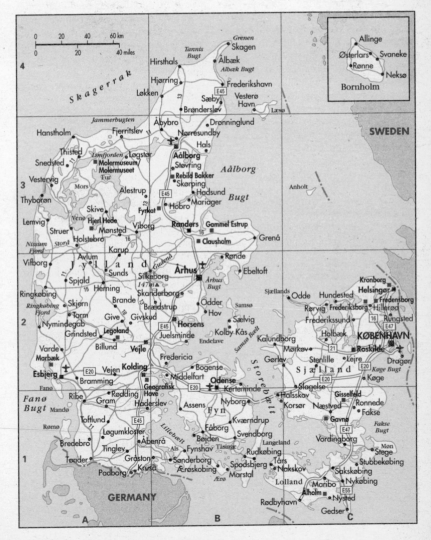

services operate from the major cities. Taking a motorboat or horse-cab tour is another good way to see Copenhagen.

If you are driving, you can reach Denmark by traveling north from Germany and entering at either Kruså or Padborg or by taking the car ferry from Puttgarden to Rødbyhavn. Ferries also operate directly from Harwich or Newcastle-upon-Tyne, England, to Esbjerg on the west coast of Jylland.

Roads in Denmark are generally very good and well marked. Main highways are marked with green and white signs bearing numbers with the prefix "E." Primary roads are designated by one- or two-digit numbers on yellow signs, and secondary roads are labeled with three-digit numbers on white signs.

Front- and rear-seat occupants must wear seat belts if the vehicle has them. A child under 7 years **must** use a suitable restraint system; it is recommended that a child under 3 years sit in a baby seat and not travel in front. All motorists must drive with low-beam headlights on during the day. Visiting motorists are required to pay fines for motoring violations on the spot. Speed limits are 50 k.p.h. (30 m.p.h.) in town, 80 k.p.h. (50 m.p.h.) on out-of-town roads and 100 k.p.h. (60 m.p.h.) on highways, unless otherwise posted.

ACCOMMODATIONS

Hotels are not classified in Denmark. Many establishments offer breakfast and include Value Added Taxes (V.A.T.) and service charges in their room rates. Several international hotel chains operate in Denmark and issue vouchers with discounts at certain periods. Mission hotels, are good value but do not serve alcohol. *Kroer* are small country inns, many of which are very old; they offer comfortable lodgings and good food for reasonable prices. The Danish National Tourist Board publishes a list of hotels, and local tourist offices can assist you in finding a place to stay.

Over 100 youth and family hostels also serve travelers in Denmark with accommodations of a high standard. The country has more than 500 campgrounds; some campgrounds have cottages that can be rented. The Federation of Danish Motorists (see *Automobile Club on p.500*) operates about 25 camping areas, which welcome members of other automobile clubs. An international camping carnet or Danish camping carnet, which can be purchased at all Danish campgrounds, is required.

TIPPING

Restaurants generally include a gratuity charge in the bill. Tips are included in taxi fares, but railroad porters and washroom attendants expect small tips.

PRINCIPAL TOURING AREAS

Note: For descriptions of cities in **bold type**, see individual city listings.

The government of Denmark has formulated a number of tours called the Green Roads. These tours avoid expressways and include all major points of interest, as well as many others.

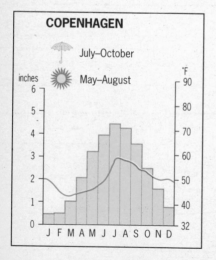

COPENHAGEN

July–October

May–August

THE MARGUERITE ROUTE

This is a tourist route for car drivers, devised by the Danish Council of Tourist Trade. It takes visitors along 3,540 kilometers (2,200 miles) of roads, often minor ones, past lovely scenery. The route is easy to follow as its sign – a white flower with a yellow center on a brown background – appears frequently at the roadside. Although it is one route, it has been divided into four sections: from Helsingør to Kruså, from Kruså to Dronninglund (and back via a different route) and from Dronninglund to Helsingør.

KØBENHAVN – ODENSE – RIBE –ESBJERG

Green Road North leads from **København**, or **Copenhagen**, on the eastern coast of the east island of Sjælland (Zealand), and proceeds south west through medieval **Roskilde** and Slagelse, the site of a Viking garrison, to the port of Korsør. From Korsør a ferry runs to Fyn Island and crosses a waterway known as Storebælt (the Big Belt). At **Nyborg**, the site of the oldest castle in Denmark, the road winds northward along the coast to Kerteminde, and then curves to **Odense**, capital of Fyn and home of the story-teller Hans Christian Andersen. The route then passes through Hindevad, on to Middelfart and the Lille Bælt Bridge to the Jylland (Jutland) Peninsula, the Danish mainland.

South of the fjord-head city of **Kolding**, the road passes by quaint Christiansfeld, then veers across the moors through Rødding to **Ribe**. A short distance up the west coast is the major port of **Esbjerg**.

Grand Southern Green Road leaves the Green Road North at **Nyborg**, and goes directly to Odense. Turning south, the route passes close to the beautiful Egeskov manor house at Kvaerndrup. The tour continues south through the chateau country of Fyn to **Svendborg**, then heads west through Ollerup to the 18th-century town of **Fåborg**. Next is Bøjden and a ferry to Fynshav, on the island of Als.

The route then cuts across the base of the peninsula via **Sønderborg**, Gråsten and Kollund to **Tønder**, which commemorates medieval times in its museum and in the charm of its Main Street. It rejoins the Green Road West route in nearby Møgeltønder and continues to **Esbjerg**.

KRUSÅ–FREDERIKSHAVN

This tour runs the length of Jylland from the German border at Flensburg. From **Frederikshavn**, centre of a beach resort area, ships sail to Göteborg, Sweden, and Oslo, Norway.

Green Road East follows a path along the east coast of the peninsula. From Kruså it reaches the important fjord port of Åbenrå via a loop through Gråsten, the dowager Queen's summer residence, and **Sønderborg**. The road proceeds due north past Christiansfeld, **Kolding** and Vejle to the industrial port of Horsens.

From **Århus**, Denmark's second largest city, the route continues to **Randers** and Mariager, on Mariager Fjord. Here it turns inland along the fjord to Hobro, then runs north to Rebild. **Aålborg** is the next large city before the route bears north east to Sæby and **Frederikshavn**.

Green Road West leaves Kruså and travels through **Tønder** and Ribe – a side trip can be made to **Esbjerg** – to Varde. Here it turns north west to the beach resort of Nymindegab, then travels along the narrow strand between the Ringkøbing Fjord and the sea to Søndervig and **Ringkøbing**.

Leaving the dunelands, the route goes east to **Holstebro** and north to **Skive**, where it turns north west. It follows the northwest shore of the great Limfjorden, where the largest island, Mors, has interesting geological deposits and good oysters! The road veers east to Åbybro where it turns north.

A final arch through Løkken and the commercial center of Hjørring takes the tour to end at Skagen, on the peninsula's tip.

RØDBYHAVN–KØBENHAVN–HELSINGØR

Rødbyhavn, on Lolland Island near Rødby, is the main ferry port from Puttgarden on Fehmarn Island in Germany. From Helsingør, or Elsinore, a ferry crosses to Helsingborg, Sweden. The two tours described below begin at Rødbyhavn.

Green Road East starts on Lolland and leads from Rødbyhavn east to Nysted, noted for its antique automobile collection at Ålholm Castle. The tour route then turns north and proceeds by bridge to Nykøbing, on the island of Falster, and Stubbekøbing, where there is a ferry to Bogø Island and a bridge leading to the steep chalk cliffs on the island of Møn. The road crosses the eastern bulge of Sjælland through Praestø to Køge, where there are several fine manors. It curves along Køge Bay to København (Copenhagen). North of the capital city it follows the coast to Helsingør (Elsinore), passing resorts and historic sites. An extension proceeds west along the northern coast of Sjælland, through Hornbaek and other resorts, ending on the peninsula of Sjællands Odde.

Green Road West heads north across the island of Lolland from Rødbyhavn to Maribo and Knuthenborg Safari Park, then east through Sakskøbing. It crosses the Storstrøms bridge to Vordingborg, Sjælland, and continues north to the medieval town of Næstved.

From Næstved the route meanders through Gisselfeld Manor to Køge. Beyond Copenhagen it reaches Elsinore by way of Hillerød and Fredensborg.

USEFUL EXPRESSIONS IN DANISH

hello/good morning	godmorgen
good-bye	farvel
good afternoon	goddag
good evening	godaften
please/thankyou	vær så venlig/tak
yes/no	ja/nej
excuse me	undskyld
you're welcome	åh, jeg be'r
Does anyone here speak English?	Er der nogen her der taler engelsk?
I don't understand.	Jeg forstår ikke.
Where are the restrooms?	Hvor er toilettet?
Do you take credit cards?	Tager De kreditkort?
How much is that?	Hvor meget koster dat?
What time is it?	Hvad er klokken?
where/when	hvor/hvornår/
how	hvordan
yesterday	i går
today/tomorrow	i dag/i morgen
What does this mean?	Hvad betyder dette?
cheap/expensive	billig/dyr
open/closed	åben/lukket
vacant/occupied	fri/optaget
good/bad	god/darlig

DAYS OF THE WEEK

Sunday	søndag
Monday	mandag
Tuesday	tirsdag
Wednesday	onsdag
Thursday	torsdag
Friday	fredag
Saturday	lørdag

NUMBERS

1	en
2	to
3	tre
4	fire
5	fem
6	seks
7	syv
8	otte
9	ni
10	ti

PLACES OF INTEREST

★ HIGHLIGHTS ★	
Århus	(see p.507)
Fåborg	(see p.508)
Helsingør	(see p.509)
Hillerød	(see p.509)
Humlebſk	(see p.510)
København	(see p.505)
Odense	(see p.510)
Rungsted Karen	
Blixen Museum	(see p.512)
Skagen	(see p.512)
Svendborg	(see p.513)
Egeskov Castle	

COPENHAGEN – *see København below.*

▲ KØBENHAVN ★
SJÆLLAND *pop. 1,400,000*

Although Vikings and fishermen had known this site for years as Havn (Harbor), the founding of København, or Copenhagen, dates from 1167. As commerce flourished, the name was changed to Køpmannæhafn (Merchants' Harbor); in 1443 the city became capital of the Kingdom of Denmark.

Home to a quarter of Denmark's population, the capital city is a focus for commerce, culture and industry and has a cosmopolitan atmosphere.

Although Copenhagen's impressive theaters, museums and churches interest many, its best-loved attractions include the Tivoli Gardens, the Langelinie harbor with its Lille Havfrue (Little Mermaid) statue and the busy shopping promenade known as Strøget.

A canal tour is a relaxing way to get your bearings.

Kastrup, Copenhagen's International Airport, is 10 kilometers (6 miles) south.

Guided tours of the Tuborg and Carlsberg breweries as well as the Royal Copenhagen china factory are popular tourist trips.

The Copenhagen Card offers unlimited travel on buses and trains in Copenhagen and nearby, as well as free admission to more than 60 museums and other discounts.

AMALIENBORG (506 D3), Amaliegade, has been the royal palace since 1794. Guard changes are at noon when the Queen is at home. (Closed to the public).

FRIHEDSMUSEET (Resistance Museum) (506 A5), Churchillparken, has collections of objects relating to World War II.

KØBENHAVNS BYMUSEET (Copenhagen City Museum) (506 A1), 59 Vesterbrogade, describes the history of the city.

LILLE HAVFRUE (Little Mermaid) (506 E4), the well-known sculpture on the harbor promenade, is the symbol of the city.

NATIONALMUSEET (506 C2), Ny Vestergade 10, contains special collections that deal with Denmark from the ice age through the Viking period.

ORLOGSMUSEET (The Royal Naval Museum) (506 D2), 58A Overgaden Oven Vandet, details the history of the navy in a renovated naval hospital.

ROSENBORG SLOT (506 C3) 4A Øster Voldgade, a Renaissance building erected by Christian IV, contains the Danish crown jewels and other treasures.

RUNDETÅRN (Round Tower) (506 C3), Købmagergade 52A, was built in 1643 by Christian IV. It was erected to adjoin the Church of the Trinity and was used as an observatory.

STATENS MUSEUM FOR KUNST (Royal Museum of Fine Arts) (506 C4), Solvgade, houses the national collection of works by Danish artists from the 16th century as well as works by French and Dutch old masters.

TIVOLI (506 B2) is considered to be the heart of Copenhagen. This 8-hectare

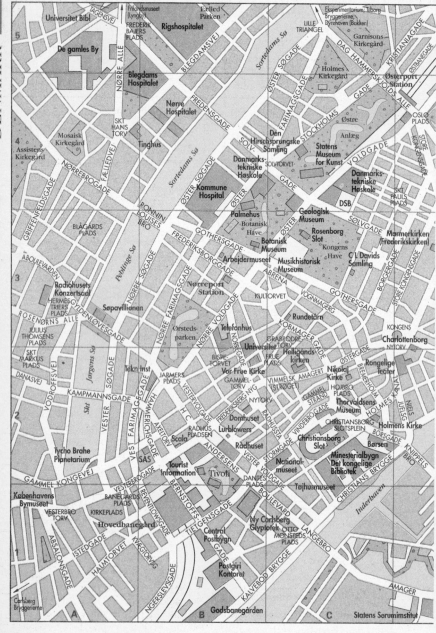

(20-acre) pleasure garden has been a celebrated amusement park since 1843.

In addition to rides, there are free concerts, puppet shows and ballet performances, illuminated gardens, fireworks, parades and supervised play grounds. A variety of restaurants and cafés add to the charm.

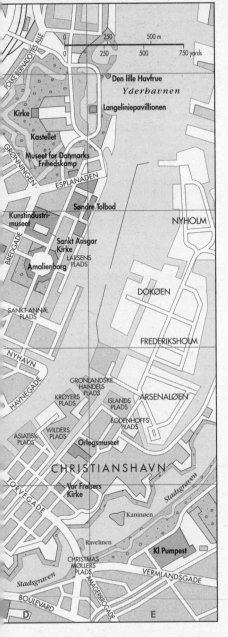

VOR FRELSERS KIRKE (Our Saviors' Church) (506 D1) Prinsessegade, is a baroque church with an external staircase around the spire.

▲ AÅLBORG (501 B3)

JYLLAND *pop. 155,000*

Aålborg is a highly industrialized transportation center, and is known for manufacturing *akvavit*, Denmark's national drink. Aålborg's modern architecture contrasts with such structures as the 15th-century Holy Ghost Monastery and the 16th-century Aålborghus Castle. The many entertainment spots and colorful cafés give hard-working Aålborg a light-hearted atmosphere.

NORDJYLLANDS KUNSTMUSEUM (North Jutland Art Museum), Kong Christians Alle 50, was designed mainly by Finnish architect Alvar Ålto. Collections include Danish art of the 20th century as well as works by Picasso and Le Corbusier.

▲ ÅRHUS (501 B2) ★

JYLLAND *pop. 250,000*

Denmark's second largest city, Århus, is a popular resort. The city has been an episcopal center since the 10th century. Many very old structures can still be seen, including the early medieval Vor Frue Kirke (Church of Our Lady).

DEN GAMLE BY (The Old Town), Viborgvej/Eugen Warmingsvej, is an open-air museum with a fascinating collection of more than seventy 17th- and 18th-century houses moved here from all over Denmark.

DOMKIRKEN (Cathedral), Store Torv/Bispetorv, was begun in 1201. It has an intricately carved pulpit as well as some fine frescoes.

ÆRØSKØBING (501 B1)

ÆRO *pop. 1,200*

Ærøskøbing, on Ærø Island, has a museum displaying more than 400 model ships. Hammerichs Hus is a merchant's house with various items from South

TYCHO BRAHE PLANETARIUM, G1, Kongevej 10, was named for the renowned 16th-century Danish astronomer. Interesting star shows are given.

DENMARK

Jylland and nearby islands. The town itself has many 17th- and 18th-century houses lining cobbled streets.

BILLUND (501 A2)
JYLLAND *pop. 4,600*

LEGOLAND, near Billund airport and the factory where Lego toys are made, is a children's park erected from more than 35 million Lego bricks. Features include a miniature re-creation of a Danish town and of prominent buildings and sights from around the world.

There is a large collection of antique dolls and dolls-houses, and concerts, plays and movies are presented in the 200-seat children's theater.

BORNHOLM ISLAND (501 C4)
pop. 47,200

The easternmost Danish island in the Baltic Sea is 7 hours from Copenhagen by ferry. The island has been Danish since 1660. Four round churches that remain today were constructed as fortifications against earlier attacks by pagan islanders. The 12th-century round church at Østerlars is notable.

At the northern tip of the island on a steep seaside cliff are the ruins of 13th-century Hammershus Castle. White sand beaches, smokehouses for herring, pastel-painted homes and a countryside conducive to walking and cycling add to Bornholm's charm.

ELSINORE – *see Helsingør*.

▲ ESBJERG (501 A2)
JYLLAND *pop. 80,000*

Esbjerg, one of Denmark's most important fishing ports, is a vital import-export and industrial center. After the port was built late in the 19th century, the city grew quickly from a tiny village. Today the lively fish auction halls, said to be the largest in Northern Europe, can be visited on weekdays during the summer and there is an interesting fisheries museum. Esbjerg is a point of departure for passenger ships bound for Great Britain and for Denmark's Faroe Islands,

more than 1,000 kilometers (620 miles) north west in the Atlantic.

FANØ is a few miles south east of Esbjerg and is easily reached by ferry. The island's sandy beach runs for 16 kilometers (10 miles), and is popular. Relatively peaceful, Fanø is a good place to camp.

FÅBORG (501 B1) ★
FYN *pop. 18,000*

Fåborg, an 18th-century market town, is well preserved: streets and some houses date from the late 18th century. Of interest are the Clock Tower, Art Museum of the Funen Painters, and the western town gate.

MARKETS, FAIRS AND FESTIVALS

Market days are a regular weekly feature all over Denmark, with the market square or pedestrianized street filled with decorated stalls piled high with local produce. Many towns hold junk fairs and flea markets – there's a junk market in Esbjerg on the first Saturday of each month. Agricultural fairs are very popular at Roskilde and Åbenrå (both in June) when cattle, horses and sheep are for sale. In addition, there are Norse fairs, Viking markets and Tilting festivals. Many coastal towns have Harbor or Herring festivals, and everywhere there is music to suit all tastes, often performed in fine settings such as castles, and in parks. Midsummer Day is celebrated with bonfires – for more information contact the relevant local tourist office.

FAERØERNE
pop. 41,600

More than 1,000 kilometers (620 miles) from Denmark's west coast lie the Faerøerne, or Faroe Islands, a triangle of 18 windswept islands – 17 of them are inhabited. The best time for a visit is from mid-May through September. Torshavn, the capital, is on Streymoy.

Seabirds by the thousands flock to the craggy seaside cliffs, especially near Vestmanna on Streymoy. Ancient structures can still be seen in villages clustered around old churches. Modern towns reflect the Faroes' dependence on the fishing industry. A network of buses, ships and ferries connects towns and villages; rental cars are available.

A visit to the Faroe Islands requires planning because ferries, from Esbjerg and Hantsholm, and flights, from Copenhagen, do not operate every day.

FAROE ISLANDS – *see Faerøerne on p.508.*

FREDERICIA (501 B2)
JYLLAND *pop. 36,000*
Fredericia is a fortified town built by King Frederik III in 1649 to defend the Jylland Peninsula. The ramparts are among the best preserved in Europe.

▲ FREDERIKSHAVN (501 B4)
JYLLAND *pop. 28,000*
Frederikshavn's fine natural harbor has made it the main gateway to Denmark from Norway and Sweden, and a busy fishing port. The town was fortified in the 17th century to assure safe commerce with Norway. The coast near Frederikshavn has popular beaches.

FREDERIKSSUND (501 C2)
SJÆLLAND *pop. 13,800*
Frederikssund is noted for its annual 16-day Viking Festival, held late June through early July.

JÆGERPRIS SLOT became a royal summer residence in 1848 for King Frederik VII and Countess Danner, his wife. The rooms remain richly furnished.

HELSINGØR (501 C2) ★
SJÆLLAND *pop. 57,000*
Immortalized by Shakespeare, who chose its castle for the setting of *Hamlet*, Helsingør, or Elsinore, has a story apart

from that of the "melancholy Dane." It is a seaport, resort, ship-building and commercial center, with ferry routes to nearby Sweden.

Today, Elsinore's old half-timbered houses suggest former times, but the city is located in a popular beach area where such modern resorts as Hornblk share the white-sand coast with villages, fishing harbors and woods.

KARMELITERKLOSTRET OG SANKT MARIL' KIRKE (Carmelite Cloister and St. Mary's Church) is a well-preserved 15th-century church and abbey.

KRONBORG still seems to be haunted by the tragic story of Hamlet. The castle's Renaissance grace and great size, especially the ramparts, are as impressive today as in Shakespeare's time.

MARIENLYST is a Louis XVI palace that dates from the late 16th century.

▲ HILLERØD (501 C2) ★
SJLLLAND *pop. 34,400*
FREDERIKSBORG, a large castle that uses a lake as its moat, was completed in the early 17th century by Christian IV and kings were crowned in the sumptuous chapel. The castle is now a National-Historical Museum with a wealth of antiques and paintings that illustrate the history of Denmark.

▲ HOLBÆK (501 C2)
SJLLLAND *pop. 21,500*
Founded in 1270, Holbæk is a port and trade center and a good base for trips to Odsherred, the sunny land surrounding the town and stretching some 70 kilometers (44 miles) to the west.

▲ HOLSTEBRO (501 A3)
JYLLAND *pop. 38,000*
Holstebro, on the Storå River, dates from the 13th century. The Museum of Art contains modern Danish art and works by Matisse and Picasso. An unusual church in the town was built around an inner courtyard.

HUMLEBÆK (501 C2) ★

LOUISIANAMUSEET, Humlebæk, has a fine collection of contemporary art that includes the work of Henry Moore, Max Ernst and Alberto Giacometti both indoors and in a landscaped garden.

KØGE (501 C2)

SJÆLLAND *pop. 35,000*

Picturesque Køge is noted for its half-timbered houses, especially the one at 20 Kirkstræde, which was built in 1527 and is Denmark's oldest date-marked house. In the surrounding area are a number of fine castles.

DIGGING UP THE PAST

In a land where the Iron Age, Bronze Age and Stone Age are gradually yielding their treasures, it is not surprising that the Danes are so keen at re-creating the past. Apart from excellent museum collections, such as finds from the Stone Age at Aålborg Historical Museum, from the Iron Age at Silkeborg and from the Bronze Age at the National Museum in Copenhagen, other centers have re-created realistic dwellings.
The Historical-Archeological Center at Lejre has reconstructed an Iron Age Village and at Hollufgård near Odense, early prehistoric houses have been built.

▲ KOLDING (501 A2)

JYLLAND *pop. 43,700*

Amid some of the most spectacular scenery in Denmark, Kolding is on a fjord that cuts into the eastern shore of Jylland. South east of the town a garden (Geografiske Have) contains plants and flowers from around the world.

MARSTAL (501 B1)

ÆRØ *pop. 4,000*

The largest town on the old-world island of Aerø, Marstal is linked by ferry to Rudkøbing, on the neighboring island of Langeland. With its cobbled streets, it is a favorite port of call for sailing ships.

▲ NÆSTVED (501 C1)

SJÆLLAND *pop. 38,200*

A thriving industrial center, Næstved has kept its medieval charm in many half-timbered houses. On Wednesday mornings the brightly colored cavalry ride through town blowing trumpets.

NAKSKOV (501 B1)

LOLLAND *pop. 16,400*

Nakskov is a harbor town with a number of picturesque half-timbered houses. An excellent beach is nearby.

NYBORG (501 B1)

FYN *pop. 18,000*

An old fortress town, Nyborg is the terminus of train ferries that cross the 32-kilometer (20-mile) wide Store Bælt to Sjælland. In a park 2 kilometers (1½ miles) south is 16th-century Holcken-havn Castle.

NYBORG SLOT, dating from 1170, is one of the oldest royal castles in Scandinavia.

▲ NYKØBING (501 C1)

FALSTER *pop. 26,000*

Nykøbing, the main town on the island of Falster, is on Guldborg Sound. Historic Gråbrødrekirken was built in 1532.

NYSTED (501 C1)

LOLLAND *pop. 1,400*

ÅLHOLM SLOT, a large 12th-century castle, is noted for its museum of antique automobiles where 200 vehicles of the period 1886–1936 are displayed.

▲ ODENSE (501 B2) ★

FYN *pop. 170,000*

Odense, the third largest city in Denmark, is the capital and largest town on the island of Fyn (Funen). One of the oldest settlements in Scandinavia, it dates from the 9th century. Odense has two faces: the fairy-tale appearance of its streets and houses and the modern

DENMARK

visage of manufactures, commerce and shipping. Writer Hans Christian Andersen was born here in 1805. The house where he was born and his childhood home are both museums.

CARL NIELSEN MUSEET is a museum devoted to the life and work of Denmark's most famous composer, and of his wife, the sculptress Anne Marie.

FYNS OLDTID-HOLLUF-GÅRD (Funen Prehistory Museum), Hestehaven 201, is situated in a 16th-century manor house which is the new cultural center of Odense. It includes a collection ranging from prehistory through the Viking age.

MØNTERGÅRDEN (Museum of Cultural and Urban History), Overgade 48–50, is a collection of 16th-and 17th-century buildings, suitably furnished.

SANKT HANS KIRKE (St. Hans Church), Nørregade 42, dates from the 13th century and has Denmark's only open-air pulpit. Adjoining it is 18th-century Odense Castle.

SANKT KNUDS KIRKE (St. Canute's Church) is 13th-century Gothic. It contains the tomb of King Canute the Holy, who was martyred in the 11th century.

⚠ RANDERS (501 B3)
JYLLAND *pop. 60,000*
Randers, an old town ringed by parks, is on the Nørre and Gudenå rivers, both of which lend themselves to canoeing and fishing. Interesting buildings and houses line the narrow streets; of special note is 15th-century St. Morten's Church.

GAMMEL ESTRUP is a castle east of Randers near Auning and is one of Denmark's most magnificent 15th-century manor houses.

The castle now houses the Jyllands Herragårdsmuseum (Jutland's Manor House Museum). Collections are of national interest and focus on folklore, painting, furniture, tapestries and china. **Dansk Landbrugesmuseum** (Danish Agricultural Museum) is housed in the farm buildings of the Gammel Estrup.

REBILD BAKKER, about 25 kilometer (16 miles) north, has the Danish-American Emigration Museum including a replica Abraham Lincoln log cabin.

RIBE (501 A1)
JYLLAND *pop. 8,000*
A medieval cathedral town founded about 860 AD, Ribe is Denmark's oldest community, with the largest number of Renaissance half-timbered houses anywhere in the country.

DOMKIRKE (Cathedral) was built during the 12th century. It combines late Romanesque and early Gothic styles.

HANS TAUSENS HUS, Torvet 17, is the oldest remaining bishop's palace in Denmark, now an archeology museum.

ST. CATHARINÆ CHURCH AND ABBEY was founded by the Dominicans (Black Friars) in 1228. Today it is among the best preserved of Denmark's abbeys.

RINGKØBING (501 A2)
JYLLAND *pop. 8,400*
Founded in 1250, Ringkøbing is a fjordside town surrounded by dunes. The

DENMARK

well-preserved town center boasts a town hall and a museum containing some remarkable prehistoric finds. A beach is 9 kilometers (6 miles) away.

SOMMERLAND WEST, 7 kilometers (4 miles) north of town at Hee, is a wildlife and bird sanctuary with a children's amusement park and a Viking village with demonstrations of weaving, baking, archery etc.

RØMØ (501 A1)
JYLLAND
Linked to the mainland by a causeway, Rømø is a popular seaside resort. The island's west coast supports a rich variety of bird species and has fine beaches.

NATIONALMUSEETS KOMMANDØRGÅRD at nearby Toftum portrays the lifestyle of Rømø's prosperous 18th-century commanders (whalers).

▲ ROSKILDE (501 C2)
SJÆLLAND *pop. 50,000*
Roskilde on the Roskilde Fjord, was the capital city of Denmark from the 10th century until 1443 and was the king's residence until the Reformation.

PALÆSAMLINGERNE (Palace Collections), Staendertorvet 3E, includes exhibits of furniture and paintings in the east wing of the former Bishop's Palace.

ROSKILDE DOMKIRKE is an 800-year-old cathedral containing centuries-old tombs of 38 Danish kings and queens.

ROSKILDE MUSEUM, 18 Sct. Ols Gade, is a museum of cultural history containing local costumes, embroidery and toys.

VIKINGESKIBSHALLEN (Viking Ship Hall), Strandengen, houses five ancient ships raised from Roskilde Fjord.

RUDKØBING (501 B1)
LANGELAND *pop. 7,000*
Rudkøbing is the largest town on Langeland Island with many timber framed and 18th-century houses. Tranekær Castle north of town, is not open, but the grounds are.

RUNGSTED (501 C2) ★
SJÆLLAND *pop. 6,100*
KAREN BLIXEN MUSEUM is the birthplace of the Danish author whose pen name was Isak Dinesen. Her most renowned work is *Out of Africa*. The house has elegant rooms that have been left untouched since Blixen's death in 1962.

▲ SILKEBORG (501 A2)
JYLLAND *pop. 34,180*
On the banks of Denmark's longest river and surrounded by beautiful countryside, Silkeborg is one of the country's leading holiday centers. About 25 kilometers (16 miles) south east is Skanderborg, which has a small museum and the remains of a medieval castle. On the way to Skanderborg are forests and a chain of scenic lakes.

JUTLAND AUTOMOBILE MUSEUM, about 25 kilometers (16 miles) north east at Gjern, maintains a collection of some 135 restored veteran and vintage cars from 1900 to 1942.

SILKEBORG MUSEUM, in the Hovedgården, exhibits stone implements, ancient jewelry and glass. The museum's most important exhibit is the well-preserved head of the 2,200-year-old Tollund Man.

SKAGEN (501 B4) ★
JYLLAND *pop. 12,000*
The fishing center of Skagen has flourished at the gateway between the Kattegat and the North Sea since the Middle Ages. During the 19th century the town became a cultural center, and interest in the arts continues as artists are drawn to the extended daylight of Denmark's northernmost town. The area is also a popular seaside resort.

SKAGEN FORTIDSMINDER is an open-air museum in several buildings, furnished

THE VIKINGS

Ships at Roskilde forts and burial grounds have provided a lot of clues about these warlike people who lived in Denmark about 1,000 years ago.
Among the most exciting finds are the four ring forts at Trelleborg, Aggersborg, Nonnebakken and Fyrkat. The ring at Fyrkat was used for about 20 years and consisted of a circular rampart, covered with wooden palisades, which was protected from the outside by a moat. Streets led to the houses, each inhabited by about 50 people, which were grouped around squares. Smaller buildings are likely to have been workshops and storerooms. Viking graves here have yielded pots and spindles, rings and keys, proving that Vikings were not always at war and had achieved a high degree of technical skill.
Viking finds are to be seen at the Hobro Museum and at the large burial site at Lindholm Hoje, near Aålborg.

to show the hard lives of fisherfolk and lifeboat men of the last two centuries.

SKAGEN MUSEUM, Brøndumvej, displays Danish paintings and sculpture created by local artists 1830–1930.

▲ SKIVE (501 A3)
JYLLAND pop. 19,400
Skive is an industrial town on the Skivefjord. A medieval church contains distinctive 16th-century frescoes, and the local museum displays both antiquities and a modern art collection.

HJERL HEDES FRILANDSMUSEUM, southwest of Skive is a large open-air museum showing the development of the Danish village from 1500–1900. Old buildings have been collected from all over Denmark and set up here.

▲ SØNDERBORG (501 B1)
JYLLAND pop. 30,000
Sønderborg is a busy commercial, industrial and educational center on the island of Als. Its castle, Sønderberg Slot, has an interesting chapel and museum.

STEGE (501 C1)
MØN pop. 4,000
Stege is a pleasant country town with some ancient buildings. On the eastern side of Møn Island are chalk cliffs carved by erosion into peculiar conical shapes.

▲ SVENDBORG (501 B1)
FYN pop. 37,500
The harbor town and yachting resort of Svendborg dates from the 12th century. A bridge connects Svendborg to the islands of Tåsinge and Langeland, and there is a frequent ferry service to the small nearby islands for swimming.

EGESKOV ★, 15 kilometre (9 miles) north at Kværndrup, is one of Denmark's most romantic castles. Built in a lake on a foundation of oak piles, the 16th-century mansion has round corner towers and conical roofs. Inside is a series of period furnished rooms and old workshops. There is also a floral park and a museum of antique cars and airplanes.

TØNDER (501 A1)
JYLLAND pop. 8,000
Tønder has been known for its lace industry since the 17th century. Displays of lace, along with locally made silver, can be seen in the Tønder Museum.

▲ VIBORG (501 A3)
JYLLAND pop. 29,400
Historic Viborg's setting is the lake area around the Dollerup Hills. Hans Tausen's religious movement, which began the Danish Reformation in the 16th century, originated in this town.

DOMKIRKE (Cathedral), built 1120–80 and said to be one of the largest granite churches in Europe, retains its original Romanesque crypt.

FINLAND

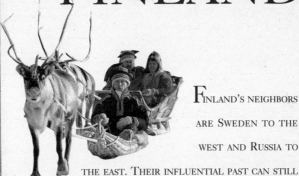

Finland's neighbors are Sweden to the west and Russia to the east. Their influential past can still be seen, not least in Swedish remaining alongside Finnish as an official language. Despite this, Finnish culture is unique.

Much of Finland's surface is water, with most of it in the Lakelands in the south. However, Lake Inari, covering 1,000 square kilometers (385 square miles), is in the extreme north. This is Lappland, land of the Midnight Sun and the Northern Lights.

The capital, Helsinki, is a sea-faring city, and built on a series of peninsulas linked by bridges over the inlets. Ferries journey to the nearby islands, and to Suomenlinna, Finland's Castle, first built in 1748 but now so large that it spreads across several islands, providing today's Finns with parks, walks and museums.

Left Finland's northern lakeland region is breathtakingly beautiful
Above A far superior way to get around – take a ride with a reindeer

THINGS TO KNOW

- **AREA:** 337,113 square kilometers (130,160 square miles).
- **POPULATION:** 4,977,000
- **CAPITAL:** Helsinki (Helsingfors)
- **LANGUAGE:** Finnish and Swedish.
- **ECONOMY:** Machinery and forest products. Tourism, shipbuilding, and textile industries also important.
- **PASSPORT REQUIREMENTS:** Required for U.S. citizens.
- **VISA REQUIREMENTS:** Not required for stays up to three months total in the Scandinavian countries.
- **DUTY-FREE ITEMS:** 200 cigarettes or 250 grams of other tobacco products; 2 liters of beer and 2 liters of wine or 1 liter of wine and 1 liter of spirits; cameras and a reasonable amount of film; televisions; bicycles and other sports goods.
- **CURRENCY:** The currency unit is the Finnish *markka* (F.I.M.), divided into 100 *penni*. Due to currency fluctuations, the exchange rate is subject to frequent change. Unlimited amounts of foreign currency may be imported. Imported Finnish currency over 10,000 FIM must be declared on arrival.
- **BANK OPENING HOURS:** 9am–4pm Monday–Friday.
- **PUBLIC HOLIDAYS:** January 1; January 6; Good Friday; Easter Monday; Labor Day, May 1; first Saturday after Ascension Day; Midsummer's Day, Saturday nearest June 24; All Saints' Day, first Saturday in November; Independence Day, December 6; December 25–26.
- **NATIONAL TOURIST OFFICES:** Scandinavian National Tourist Boards 655 Third Ave New York, NY 10017 Tel: 212/949 2333; Fax: 212/9835260 Finnish Tourist Board Head Office P.O. Box 625 00101, Helsinki, Finland Tel: 80 403011; Fax: 80 448841
- **AMERICAN EMBASSY:** Itäinen Puistotie 14 00140 Helsinki, Finland Tel: 90 171931; Fax: 80 174681

HISTORY

Two thousand years ago, the area that is now Finland was inhabited by nomadic Sami (Lapps). Beginning about 100 AD, people of Finno-Ugric stock settled in the area, and most of the Sami retreated to the north.

Three major groups established themselves: Finns, Tavastians and Karelians. It was not until the arrival of Swedish crusaders that Finland became unified. Although Sweden was largely responsible for the introduction of Christianity to the country, Russians preached Greek Orthodoxy in the east.

For 600 years from the 12th-century Peace of Nöteborg, most of Finland was ruled by Sweden. However, the country was allowed to develop its own social order and language.

The eastern frontier was frequently harassed by Russia. In 1809, Tsar Alexander I invaded. Finland was granted virtual autonomy as a grand duchy of Russia. Finland established its independence during the turmoil that followed World War I and the Russian Revolution. By the end of World War II Finland had had to cede territories in the north and the south east (Karelia) to the U.S.S.R. Rapid reconstruction and economic progress took place during the postwar years.

Modern Finland is a parliamentary democracy, with highest powers vested in a president and in a single chamber parliament. Finland was the first European nation to grant women political rights equal to those enjoyed by men.

FOOD AND DRINK

Fish is at the heart of Finnish cuisine, and an array of dishes is built around salmon, whitefish and Baltic herring. Crawfish, in season from late July to September, are enthusiastically consumed. Finnish cookery also includes a variety of meats and soups. Regional dishes include *kalakukko*, a pie of fish and pork, and *karjalan piirakka*, a rye pastry stuffed with rice or potato and eaten with egg butter. Reindeer meat is prepared in many different ways.

Finnish restaurants have been greatly influenced by Swedish, Russian and French cooking, and visitors find the result pleasing. Many still serve *voileipäpöytä*, the traditional Swedish *smörgåsbord*, for lunch. Distinctively Finnish beverages are vodka and liqueurs of *mesimarja* (arctic bramble), *lakka* (cloudberry) and *polar* (cranberry).

SPORTS AND RECREATION

Not surprisingly, water-related sports are those most enjoyed by Finns. Boating and fishing continue all year, and sea and lake water are warm enough for swimming in the summer. The water also attracts boating and canoeing enthusiasts. Less energetic visitors can take excursions on lake steamers. Northern Finland offers salmon, perch and other catches for summertime anglers. Larger towns offer tennis, riding and horse racing. International track events are held in Helsinki's Olympic Stadium.

In winter, Finland is a magnet for cross-country skiers. Evidence of this is the Finlandia Ski Race, which draws some 10,000 participants each winter. Other activities are ice fishing, ice skating and snowmobiling. Tours using reindeer-drawn sleighs are available in Lappland.

Sauna is a science in Finland. There is roughly one sauna for every five Finns, so visitors are never far from one of these warm, wood-lined rooms. When water is tossed onto stones topping a special stove, the resulting *löyly*, or steam, causes the room's occupants to perspire. This is traditionally followed by a cooling dip in a lake or the sea.

GETTING AROUND

A steamer network provides ferry and excursion services. Ferries are available between June and August. Major train routes are concentrated in the south; Finnrail passes are available for one to three weeks of unlimited travel at a discount. Finnair, the international and internal airline, connects all major cities and offers a 15-day unlimited travel pass. In Helsinki and elsewhere, buses and streetcars are inexpensive with the purchase of multiride tickets. Taxis and rental cars are plentiful, but not cheap.

Magnificent scenery rewards driving in Finland. The overland trip is accomplished by driving through Sweden or Norway to Lappland, although many prefer to take their cars by ship directly to Helsinki. Departures are from Stockholm, Sweden, daily; from Travemünde, Germany, on alternate days; and even weekly 4-day crossings from Purfleet, England.

The use of seat belts in vehicles so equipped is mandatory for driver and passengers. Motorists must drive with headlights on low beam at all times during the day when outside towns. Speed limits are 50 k.p.h. (30 m.p.h.) in town, between 60 k.p.h. (35 m.p.h.) and 100 k.p.h. (60 m.p.h.) on country roads, depending on road quality, and 120 k.p.h. (75 m.p.h.) on highways. Visiting motorists fined for parking violations must pay the fine with Finnish markkas or traveler's checks at a post office.

ACCOMMODATIONS

Although Finland does not classify its hotels, several chains offer high-quality lodging. Among these are Arctia Hotels, Best Western, Better Service, Cumulus, Finlandia Hotels, Finnish Travel Association, Fontana, Rantasipi, Rivoli, Scanhotels and SOKOS. Rantasipi operates a number of large first-class country hotels in scenic areas.

There are about 50 youth and family hostels, open all year. Most provide some meals. If meals are not offered, guests can normally use the kitchen. Guests of all ages are welcome.

Campers have a choice of about 340 sites of varying standards. Most of these campgrounds have chalets that can be rented. Although camping away from officially designated grounds is allowed, you must first obtain permission from the landowner. An international camping carnet is recommended.

TIPPING

Because a service charge is included in restaurant bills and taxi fares, tips are not necessary. Railroad porters, washroom attendants, doormen and coat checkers, however, do expect tips.

PRINCIPAL TOURING AREAS

Note: For descriptions of cities in **bold type**, see individual city listings.

THE LAKELAND AND FOREST LAND

Most of Finland's thousands of lakes are in an area stretching from the eastern border to within 96 kilometers (60 miles) of the western coast. Many of these are linked by waterways, which are popular for excursions. The eastern section of the lake region is dominated by Lake Saimaa, a vast series of interconnected lakes dotted with about 33,000 islands. This wet and wild expanse, amounting to 25 percent of the country's area, is broken by Kuopio and **Jyväskylä**, lake-based cities popular for water sports. **Tampere** is the lakeland's largest city.

The area north of the lakeland along the eastern border is remote and largely unspoiled and is a popular destination for canoeists and hikers.

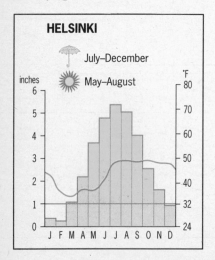

HELSINKI

July–December
May–August

> AUTOMOBILE CLUB
> **Autoliitto** (Automobile and Touring Club of Finland) has offices at Hämeentie 105, Helsinki. The symbol ▲ beside a city name indicates the presence of a AAA-affiliated automobile club branch. Not all auto clubs offer full travel services to AAA members.

THE NORTH

The rugged northern third of Finland is much more than snow and northern lights. Plants live a complete cycle during the three summer months, then are replaced by the blazing colors of *ruska*, the Lappland autumn. In the northeasternmost section dwell about 4,000 Sami, many of whom still herd reindeer, which graze freely for most of the year.

The provincial capital is **Rovaniemi**, only 10 kilometers (6 miles) from the Arctic Circle. Although the province is sparsely settled, its four cities are easily accessible through daily air and rail services.

THE SOUTHERN COAST

Finland's southern coast stretches from Pori, on the Baltic Sea, to the eastern border. Low red or gray granite rocks characterize the coast, but there are a few sandy beaches. Because there are almost no tides, the seashore resembles a lakeshore. Off the southwestern coast are the Åland-Ahvenanmaa (Åland Islands), an archipelago of more than 30,000 granite islands, islets and reefs that is Finland's warmest region.

The **Helsinki** metropolitan area to the south east is the most densely populated region, with about 750,000 inhabitants. The coast along the Gulf of Finland has several ports and former garrison towns that preserve traditional ways of life.

THE WESTERN COAST

Lying among the Gulf of Bothnia from **Kemi** to **Pori**, the western coast of Finland is lined with farms and long sandy beaches. This region has the country's sunniest and driest climate. Picturesque old wooden houses grace many of the towns, where local traditions are kept alive through annual festivals. Between **Vaasa** and **Kokkola** are islands with old fishing villages. **Turku-Åbo**, the old capital, is Finland's second city, and the heart of the Swedish-speaking area. Oulu is the region's main commercial and educational center.

USEFUL EXPRESSIONS IN FINNISH

Finnish has no relationship to the other Scandinavian languages, although a percentage of Finns speak Swedish. Pronunciation corresponds to the spelling, with the first syllable always stressed.

good morning	**hyvää huomenta**
good evening	**hyvää iltaa**
good night	**hyvää yötä**
good-bye	**hyvästi**
yes/no	**kyllä/ei**
please	**olkaa hyvä**
thankyou	**kiitos**
excuse me	**anteeksi**
you're welcome	**ei kestä**
Does anyone here speak English?	**Puhuuko kukaan englantia?**
I don't understand.	**En ymmärrä.**
Where are the restrooms?	**Missä on wc?**
Do you take credit cards?	**Voinko maksaa luottokortilla?**
How much is that?	**Mitä se maksaa?**
What time is it?	**Paljonko kello on?**
when	**milloin**
where	**missä**
how	**kuinka**
how long	**miten kauan**
how far	**miten kaukana**
yesterday	**eilen**
today	**tänään**
tomorrow	**huomenna**
good/bad	**hyvä/huono**
cheap/expensive	**halpa/kallis**
open/closed	**avoin/suljettu**
old/new	**vanha/uusi**
hot/cold	**kuuma/kylmä**
big/small	**suuri/pieni**
left/right	**vasen/oikea**
early/late	**aikainen/myöhäinen**

DAYS OF THE WEEK

Sunday	**sunnuntai**
Monday	**maanantai**
Tuesday	**tiistai**
Wednesday	**keskiviiko**
Thursday	**torstai**
Friday	**perjantai**
Saturday	**lauantai**

PLACES OF INTEREST

▲ HELSINKI (517 A1) ★

UUSIMAA *pop.500,000*

The capital and leading seaport of Finland is bounded on the north by fields and forests and on the south by the Gulf of Finland. The commercial, industrial and political heart of Finland, it is also a historical city.

Helsinki (Helsingfors) was founded by King Gustav Vasa in 1550 as a trading center, but the city did not begin to flourish until the Suomenlimma fortress was built in the 18th century. With this protection from invasion, Helsinki gained importance in international shipping and trading.

Few early buildings remain, mainly because most were built of wood and succumbed to fires and invasions.

The great, wide thoroughfare, Mannerheimintie, was named after Finland's leader during World War II, General Mannerheim. Near the south end is Esplanadi, an old-fashioned tree-lined promenade, leading to South Harbor. Mannerheimintie is a great shopping street with many fine buildings and statues.

Major Finnish academic institutions as well as the country's finest museums, theaters and orchestras have their headquarters in Helsinki. The Helsinki Festival, held in late summer, provides a showcase for some of Finland's finest music, dance and arts programs.

A remarkable feature of Helsinki is its wealth of greenery and uncluttered space. The central city abounds in parks, and plans for future development ensure that at least 30 percent of the total metropolitan area will remain free of construction.

The Helsinki Card offers unlimited travel on buses, trams, trains and the metro in the metropolitan area. The card also gives discounts for car and bicycle rentals, guided walking tours and several restaurants, as well as free admission to various museums and sights. It is valid for 1–3 days and can be purchased from the Helsinki City Tourist Office, Pohjoisesplanadi 19; the Hotel Booking Center in the Railway Station; Stockmann's department store; and all major hotels.

FINLANDIATALO ★, Mannerheimintie, is close to both the National and City museums. The concert hall, designed by Alvar Aalto, houses both Helsinki's symphony orchestras as well as many visiting orchestras and artistes. It has a fine view over a beautiful lake. A little further on is the new National Opera House (opened 1994) a lovely white and glass building with superb acoustics, also overlooking the lake.

KANSALLIS MUSEO, Mannerheimintie 34, is Finland's national museum. The prehistory section contains reminders of Stone, Iron and Bronze Age inhabitants of Finland as well as other parts of Europe. The modern history section displays clothing, household items and artwork from the medieval period to the present. A third section includes Amerindian objects and a wealth of material relating to Finnish folk culture.

KAUPPATORI ★ (Market Square) is the site of Helsinki's principal year-round market, close to South Harbor. Fresh produce and flowers are sold in the outdoor stalls, and dairy products and meat in the covered hall; freshly caught fish are sold from boats alongside the quay.

THE RAILWAY STATION ★ is a striking pinkish, granite building, with a green clocktower, all designed by Saarinen. Today it also houses a metro stop and underground shopping mall. On the north of station square is the National Theater, with a statue of Finland's national writer, Aleksis Kivi, in front.

SENAATINTORI ★ (Senate Square) is the site of several important buildings. On the north side is the great white stone cathedral Tuomiokirkko; on the west, Helsinki's university; and on the east, the Government Palace. Most of the imposing structures were designed by architect Carl L.Engel. The university has botanical gardens and museums of zoology, mineralogy, medicine, agriculture and paleontology.

SUOMENLINNA, nicknamed the "Gibraltar of the North," is the great island/fortress at the entrance to Helsinki's harbor. Suomenlinna now has parks, seaside walks, pavilions, restaurants and an open-air theater. Two military museums operate in sections of the former fortress.

USPENSKIN KATEDRAALI ★ is a large Greek Orthodox cathedral that towers above Katajanokka Hill and the island it occupies.

VALTION TAIDEMUSEO (Finnish National Gallery), Kaiuokatu 2–4, is the principal art gallery. The neo-Renaissance building contains four parts: Ateneum (Museum of Finnish Art), Museum of Foreign Art, Museum of Contemporary Art and the Central Art Archive.

ÅLAND ISLANDS (517 A1)
pop. 24,500

The 6,500 granite islands, islets and reefs that make up the Province of Åland lie in the southern Gulf of Bothnia midway between Finland and Sweden. The archipelago, totaling some 30,000 isles, covers about 6,084 square kilometers (2,350 square miles), but less than a fifth of this is above water. It is not surprising that Nordic seafarers settled in these islands early in the Middle Ages. Runic inscriptions and other archeological finds have provided clues about these early residents.

Today Åland, with its strong Swedish heritage, is nominally part of Finland, but virtually autonomous. The citizenry fly their own flag, elect their own parliament and formulate most of their own political and economic policies.

Long populated by fishermen and farmers, Åland attracts summer vacationers who come to fish, swim and hike.

Mariehamn is the provincial capital and principal port, with frequent ferry services to Finland and Sweden. Most of Åland's hotels and many of its man-made attractions are in this town. Interesting cave formations are near Getabergen, while the fortress of Kastelholm and the Borgboda Viking fort are in the Sund district.

ÅLAND MUSEO, Öhbergsvägen 1, Mariehamn, is the province's museum of local history. Collections include Stone Age artifacts and later items.

BOMARSUND, Sund, is the site of a fortress begun by the Russians in 1830. A Franco-British naval force captured and razed the fortress in 1854. Scattered but impressive ramparts remain.

KASTELHOLMS SLOTT (Kastelholm Ruins), Sund, was built by the Swedes in the 14th century to strengthen their position in the Baltic.

FINLAND

POMMERN, a four-masted barque in Mariehamn's harbor, is now a museum. It was the last of the stately vessels that carried cargoes of grain from Australia to England until the 1930s.

ESPOO (517 A1) ★
UUSIMAA *pop. 176,000*
Coastal Espoo in southern Finland was first settled more than 5,000 years ago. Espoo emerged as an independent country parish in the 13th century. Much later it was absorbed as a suburb of Helsinki but in 1972, Espoo obtained its town charter and has become the second largest city in the country.

Interesting for its natural features and recreational opportunities, Espoo also has manmade attractions. Among the oldest structures is the stone parish church, dating from the 15th century. Espoo Manor, now privately owned, was founded by the Swedish King Gustav Vasa in the 16th century. The University of Technology at Otaniemi has ultra-modern buildings designed by the well-known architect Alvar Aalto.

The city's best-known attraction is the garden city of Tapiola. This innovative community has become a prototype for planned towns around the world. Houses, businesses, recreational and other facilities for more than 16,000 residents exist in a carefully planned, beautiful setting.

GALLEN-KALLELA MUSEO, Leppävaara, Tarvaspää, was the studio/home of Finnish artist Akseli Gallen-Kallela until his death in 1931. Built by the artist 1911–13, the turreted, graystone and concrete structure contains more than 100 of his oils, graphics and drawings.

HVITTRÄSK ★, Kirkonummi, built around 1900 as a studio/home by the architects Eliel Saarinen, Armas Lindgren and Herman Gesellius, is a superb group of stone and timber buildings, blending into the countryside. There are arts exhibits and Saarinen's house, containing original furnishings.

HÄMEENLINNA (517 A1) ★
HÄME *pop. 43,000*
Hämeenlinna is surrounded by forested cliffs and long, narrow ridges of coarse gravel in the Lake Vanajavesi basin. Originally a garrison town, Finland's oldest inland settlement is now an educational center. On the lake is Aulangon Puisto, a recreational playground, and the southern terminus of the Silver Line watercoach.

AULANGON PUISTO ★ (Aulanko Forest Park) is north of town on the former Karlberg Estate. Once barren and stony, this national park now supports both

A LAND OF FESTIVALS
Finland must have more festivals per head than any country, not invented festivals, aimed at tourists, but real festivals. These are often rooted in the strong Labor movement which bred the Valkeakoski Festival of Workers' Music, with many marching bands, and the old fire brigades which got together for music and dance. The biggest, Kaustinen Folk Music Festival, attracts an audience of 92,000, not just to listen, but to learn and play, and there are rock festivals, as at Ruissalo, and Pori for jazz. The first classical festival, Savonlinna Opera Festival, began in 1912, its castle setting the most dramatic anywhere. Close to the border with Russia is the Kuhmo Chamber Music Festival, played against the silence of forest and hill. The Korsholm Festival, based at Vaasa, is now linked to Umeå Festival on the Swedish side of the Gulf of Bothnia.

vegetation and animal life. Aulanko has a big, modern hotel, a golf course, tennis courts, saunas, beaches, ski trails, campsites, youth hostels and a sightseeing tower and fairy-tale castle.

HÄMEEN LINNA ★ (Häme Castle) is in the center of town. It was built more than 700 years ago by Birger Jarl, the ruler of Sweden 1248–66, on what was then the shore of Lake Vanajavesi.

IITTALA GLASS WORKS, 5 kilometers (3 miles) north east, demonstrates the art of glass-blowing and sells some of Finland's best glassware.

SIBELIUS' BIRTHPLACE ★, Hallituskatu 11, contains the piano, harmonium, violin and numerous manuscripts of Finland's great composer Jean Sibelius, born 1865 There are also pictures of the young composer with his two siblings playing trios, and other memorabilia.

HANKO (517 A1) ★
UUSIMAA *pop. 10,700*
Hanko, which has the only free port in Finland, is at the southernmost tip of the country. The city is described in old documents as the most pleasant and secure harbor in which a ship could dock. In the late 1800s Hanko became a major embarkation point for Finnish immigrants to the United States and Canada. Now it is a resort, popular for Baltic Sea air, beaches and high cliffs.

GÄDDTARMEN, Tullholmarna Island, bears evidence of the region's history: In this natural harbor are rock inscriptions dating from as early as 1400; about 400 of them have been restored.

IMATRA (517 B1)
KYMI *pop. 33,000*
Imatra has been a tourist center since the 19th century, when the rapids of the Vuoksi River drew such visitors as Catherine the Great, Alexandre Dumas and Richard Wagner. Although the rapids are now controlled by Finland's largest hydroelectric plant, the waters are allowed to follow their old course through the center of town in the summer. During the week-long International Big Band Music Festival in July, various performances, and concerts take place.

A major landmark in Imatra is the Church of the Three Crosses, designed by Alvar Aalto, the church features a high belfry representing a down shot arrow. It has three huge crosses and 103 windows, only two of which are the same.

JAKOBSTAD (517 A2)
VAASA *pop. 20,000*
Jakobstad is known for its tobacco industry, which has been the town's mainstay since 1762. The Rettig (Strengberg) cigarette factory, is the world's second oldest such factory in operation.

NANOQ (Arctic Museum), at Fäboda, is 6 kilometers (4 miles) west. The only Arctic museum in Finland, Nanoq displays artifacts of Arctic cultures, hunting equipment dating from the 17th century and items from Arctic expeditions.

JÄRVENPÄÄ (517 B1) ★
UUSIMAA *pop. 33,500*
Finnish composer Jean Sibelius spent most of his life in Järvenpää. Sibelius channeled his love of nature, mythology and northern Finland's landscapes into compositions that greatly contributed to the symphonic repertoire.

AINOLA, was the home of Sibelius and his wife Aino for 53 years – they are buried under a huge, plain gravestone in the quiet garden. Inside, the composer's piano stands in the drawing room, along with other exhibits.

▲ JYVÄSKYLÄ (517 B2)
KESKI-SUOMI *pop. 71,000*
Jyväskylä was founded in 1837 and led a peaceful academic existence until 1934, when manufacturing took precedence. Industry is balanced by several museums and the Jyväskylä Arts Festival, in early June, which includes musical events and art exhibitions.

ALVAR AALTO MUSEO, 7 Alvar Aalto Katu, displays the sketches, drawing, designs and furniture of Alvar Aalto, a popular Finnish artist, architect and designer.

FINLAND

▲ KEMI (517 A3)
LAPPI *pop. 26,000*
The southernmost community in Lappland, Kemi is an excellent point from which to view the Aurora Borealis in early and mid-winter.

THE SAMPO, Ajos Harbor, offers two-to six-hour cruises aboard a fully operational, 3,500-ton ice-breaker.

KOTKA (517 B1)
KYMI *pop. 57,000*
This fortress ruins of Kukouri attest to Kotka Delta's role in history. The late 18th-century bastion and the Russian garrison town preceding the present town were virtually eliminated by a British fleet in 1855. Modern Kotka did not appear until later that century. The deep natural harbors rendered the spot ideal for an expanding timber industry.

Kotka has spacious parks and interesting architecture. Notable buildings include the Työvaentalo, or Workers' House, designed by Eliel Saarinen, and a cellulose factory by Alvar Aalto.

The city's oldest structure is the Greek Orthodox Church of St. Nicholas, built in 1795 for use by personnel of a Russian naval base. A small museum on the islet of Varissaari houses reminders of a 1790 naval battle in which Finnish-Swedish forces defeated the Russians.

Surviving from the early 19th century is the Imperial Tsar's Fishing Lodge at Langinkoski. A maritime festival is held during August each year.

In summer local residents as well as outsiders head for Kaunissaari, 20 kilometers (12 miles) southwest of Kotka in the Gulf of Finland. The island has pine forests and sandy beaches. A fishing village offers indoor lodging for those who are not camping.

▲ LAHTI (517 B1)
HÄME *pop. 95,000*
Lahti was founded in 1905 on the site of a former trading post on Lake Vesijärvi on the extensive Salpausselkä ridge system, the setting for major world skiing championships. Lahti Sports Center has some of Finland's best winter sports facilities, with a superb view from the top of the highest ski-jump, and first-class cross-country and downhill skiing in several centers, plus annual winter games in March. One of Finland's most modern cities, Lahti has innovative architecture that creates impressions of light and space in an urban area; visitors might never suspect it is home to several large manufacturing concerns.

In addition to its sports facilities, Lahti offers refreshing lake scenery and water activities. The city has a number of museums, including a historical, a ski and an art museum. The last church designed by Alvar Aalto, the Ristinkirkko, is in the middle of the city. Nearby in Hollola is a medieval church and the Pyhäniemi Art Manor.

Local events include the annual Midnight Sun Song Festival and the Poster Biennial and Writers Festival held in June.

LAPPEENRANTA (517 B1)
KYMI *pop. 55,000*
Founded in the mid-17th century, Lappeenranta first functioned as a Swedish garrison on the Russian border. After mineral springs were discovered in 1824, the town gained repute as a summer vacation spot. Today, Lappeenranta is South Karelia's main town, and better known for its position on the Saimaa Canal, at the end of an extensive network of lakes. The town's old fortress contains a local history museum, an art museum and the oldest Orthodox church in Finland.

MARIEHAMN – *see Åland Islands on p.521.*

MIKKELI (517 B1)
MIKKELI *pop. 32,000*
At the intersection of several major roads is Mikkeli, capital of Mikkeli Province and center of trade in the South Savo. On the shore of Lake Saimaa, the town becomes a lively resort in summer; in winter it is popular for skiing.

Mikkeli, founded in 1838, was the site of Field Marshal von Mannerheim's headquarters during the fighting with the U.S.S.R. in World War II and now has a museum which chronicles this phrase of Finnish history.

▲ OULU (517 B3)
OULU *pop. 103,000*
An old trading and shipping post at the mouth of the Oulujoki River, Oulu has been important since medieval times, and because of its early commercial activities, the town was once fortified.

Today Oulu is the sixth largest town in Finland and operates one of the most modern paper factories in the world, a medical center and Technopolis – a village of high technology. A university and several other schools contribute to Oulu's reputation. The city offers many opportunities for boating, swimming and other watersports.

Turkansaari, on an island in the Oulujoki, is an open-air museum, with typical folk buildings, open in summer.

THE SAUNA

The world's best saunas are in Finland, where they have been known for 2,000 years. The country has well over half a million saunas, not counting those in private houses, lakeside summer cabins, or communal saunas in many apartment blocks, in which each family has its own time. The family sauna is an important point in family life, and a social ritual with guests. Finnish saunas are hot, up to 100°C (212°F), (invariably too much for foreigners) and are generally followed by a dip in a plunge pool, along with a beer or soft drink to replace the liquid. Except for families, saunas are usually single sex. Best of all is the lakeside summer house with a wood-fired sauna built over the lake, the after-sauna plunge a simple dive into the water below.

▲ PORI (517 A1)
TURKU-PORI *pop. 77,000*
On the lower course of the Kokemäenjoki River, Pori was established in 1558. Founded at the point where the river flows into the sea, the center of town is now 20 kilometers (12 miles) from the coast. Most of the city occupies the left bank of the river and is connected to its smaller part by a majestic old bridge. After a major fire in 1852 the town was modernized, but unusual architectural sights, including the Venetian-style town hall, remain.

The old town has one attraction of very contemporary interest – the Pori International Jazz Festival, held each year during the second weekend of July, takes place in Kirjurinluoto Park on Kirjurinluoto Island.

▲ PORVOO-BORGÅ (517 B1) ★
(BORGÅ) UUSIMAA *pop. 20,000*
Picturesque Porvoo is a national center for artists and writers; book manufacturing is the major industry. Quaint 18th-century buildings with colorful roofs and an early 15th-century Gothic cathedral are reminders of the town's past. Other interesting sites are the 1764 Old Town Hall, a historical museum and the Edelfelt-Vallgren Art Museum.

J. L. RUNEBERG'S HOME, 3 Aleksanterinkatu, was the home of the Finnish national poet, Johan Ludvig Runeberg, born in 1804; the house is restored to its original appearance.

▲ RAUMA (517 A1) ★
TURKU-PORI *pop. 38,500*
The brightly painted wooden buildings in Rauma's old town date from the 18th century, but the town was founded 500 years earlier at a trade route junction. Two local characteristics originated in the 17th century: the fine lace made in the town and the unique Rauma language, a mixture of Latin, Old Flemish, Estonian, Swedish and English. It now thrives as a center of word-processing and metal industries.

FINLAND

FINLAND

In addition to the old town, attractions include the Rauma Museum; the Church of the Holy Cross, a 15th-century Franciscan monastery church; and Marela House, a 19th-century ship-owner's home. Lace making can be seen daily at Priia House in the summer.

RAUMA ART MUSEUM, 37 Kuninkaakatu, displays 19th- and 20th-century Finnish art in an 18th-century burgher's house.

ROVANIEMI (517 B3) ★
LAPPI *pop. 34,000*
The capital of Finnish Lappland, this Arctic town at the confluence of two rivers has become the north's principal city. Fur trading and reindeer herding, once common activities, were largely supplanted by lumber operations near the end of the 19th century.

Lappla House is home to the Arctic Center and the Lappland Provincial Museum. The Lappland Forestry Museum and the Ethnographic Museum are on the outskirts of town. But the best feel of the past comes from the Pöykkölä Museum, 19th-century farm buildings near the river 3 kilometers (2 miles) south. Rovaniemi's biggest attractions are the natural kind. Snowmobile, reindeer and husky safaris are available in winter; riverboat trips and rafting in summer.

SAVONLINNA (517 B2)
MIKKELI *pop. 28,500*
The frontier town of Savonlinna, sacked and destroyed many times during its turbulent history, is now a popular resort. The medieval fortress has become a monument, and festivals have replaced sieges.

The best time to visit is in July during Savonlinna Music Summer, which includes concerts and an outdoor opera.

OLAVINLINNA is the best preserved medieval fortress in Finland. The castle was built by Erik Axelsson Tort in the 15th century to protect Savonlinna from Russia. Completely restored, the fortress is now a national monument.

▲ TAMPERE (517 A1) ★
HÄME *pop. 175,000*
The northernmost point of a triangle it forms with Turku and Helsinki, Tampere is the largest Finnish inland city, situated on an isthmus between two large lakes. The city is a major center for lake traffic and cruises. Although highly industrialized, beautiful Tampere has benefited from astute city planning. Old factory areas such as Finlaysons (founded by a Scot, James Finlayson) became almost towns within a town. Finlayson's hospital, factory, school and church still stand and should not be missed. Neither should nearby Finlayson Palatsi. The bustle of business and manufacture is balanced by the serenity of leafy parks and rows of old wooden houses. Numerous museums cover local history, art, natural science, dolls and sports. Architect Lars Sonck designed Tampere Cathedral in 1907, in National Romantic style. The Kalevala Church is an amazing modern building, rising like a sail, with a soaring interior and a vast organ.

Annual events include the Tampere Film Festival held in February and March; the Tampere International Theater Festival in August; and the Tampere Jazz Happening in November. Pispala Schottis, an international folk dance festival, takes place in early June every other even year.

TAMPERE HALL ★ is a spectacular blue-white building, with a lobby fountain. The main hall holds 2,000, bigger than Helsinki's Finlandiatalo.

▲ TURKU (ÅBO) (517 A1) ★
TURKU-PORI *pop. 158,000*
Turku, as Åbo, was the capital of Finland during Swedish times. It was the commercial center of what was then called Osterland (Eastern Land), as it once was in relation to Sweden, long before the name Finland came into use. It is still a trade center, as well as the site of Finland's greatest historical treasures.

Despite devastating fires over the centuries, the last in 1827, much of old

Turku remains, including the medieval castle and cathedral.

LUOSTARINMÄKI HANDWERKMUSEUM (Handicrafts Museum) features more than 30 workshops that represent different trades and their history from the 18th and 19th centuries.

THE ORTHODOX CATHEDRAL, serving a Russian community during Grand Duchy days, is now attached to Constantinople, with a congregation of 2,000. It has all the rich beauty of an Orthodox Cathedral including many fine paintings.

RUISSALO ISLAND, reached swiftly by boat or bridge, has the best beaches, and is an odd mix of art and rock music. The 19th-century "Villa Roma" holds a summer exhibition of top-class painting, glass and textiles and, also in summer, the island hosts Ruisrock, the world's oldest rock festival.

SIBELIUS MUSEO, 17 Piispankatu, displays musical instruments and the manuscripts of Jean Sibelius.

TUOMIOKIRKKO (Cathedral), downtown by the Aura River, was consecrated in 1290 and guided the religious life of Finland for centuries. The cathedral is one of northern Europe's most outstanding historical monuments.

TURUN LINNA (Turku Castle) is to the west of town near Kanavaniemi Harbor. It dates from the late 13th century, with parts built in the 14th and 16th centuries. The castle was restored 1946–61.

WÄINO AALTONEN MUSEUM, Östra Strandgatan, holds many works by this famous artist, including the huge statues of *Peace* and *Faith*.

⚠ VAASA (517 A2) ★
VAASA pop. 54,000
Busy Vaasa or Vasa, on the Gulf of Bothnia, is characterized by seashore parks, broad boulevards and long green esplanades. Founded in 1606, the city was almost destroyed by fire in 1852, but was reconstructed and modernized. Now it is an important seaport and manufacturing and arts center. The Korsholm Music Festival takes place in late June and early July.

BRAGEGÅRDEN MUSEO, Hietalahti, is an open-air museum with exhibits relating to daily Finnish life. Displays highlight the seal-hunting tradition.

OSTROBOTHNIA MUSEO, 3 Museokatu, displays feature centuries of Vaasa and regional culture. The 19th- and 20th-century Finnish art collection is supplemented by 16th- and 17th-century Italian, Dutch, Flemish and German works of art.

THE KALEVALA

This marvelous collection of poetry and prose is often described as "Finland's national poem," or "Finland's epic poem," and played its part in raising the Finns' sense of their own nationality. In the Grand Duchy days, the writer Elias Lönnrot embarked on a great journey to record Finland's traditional stories and poems, before they were lost, traveling into Karelia and other parts where the oral tradition was strong. Then, welding together this collection, he produced *The Kalevala*, a mixture of heroic deed, violence, grief and passion, with something of the style of a Norse saga. Its impact was startling, and became even stronger when the painter Askeli Gallen-Kallela produced a series of some 100 great paintings of vivid Kalevala scenes, which decorated the Finnish Pavilion at the Paris Exhibition in 1900. It almost seemed to be Finland's introduction to the wider world.

ICELAND

ICELAND WAS BORN OUT OF VOLCANIC ACTION, LEAVING A LANDSCAPE THAT WAS AN APT SETTING FOR JULES VERNE'S *JOURNEY TO THE CENTRE OF THE EARTH*. IT IS A LAND OF PEAKS, GEYSERS, GLACIERS, LAKES AND ASTONISHING SCENERY THAT WOULD TAKE YOUR BREATH AWAY IF THE COLD HAD NOT ALREADY DONE SO.

IN FACT IT IS NOT AS COLD AS MIGHT BE EXPECTED, ALTHOUGH THE WINTER GLOOM IS RELIEVED ONLY IN THE DAY FOR A FEW HOURS AND AT NIGHT BY THE EERIE GLOW OF THE NORTHERN LIGHTS. IN SUMMER THE SUN SCARCELY SETS, MAKING THIS STRANGE LAND EVEN STRANGER AT THE SUN-LIT MIDNIGHT HOUR.

LESS THAN ONE PERCENT OF THE LAND IS CULTIVATED, THE PEOPLE TURNING INSTEAD TO THE SEA TO PROVIDE A LIVELIHOOD. IN REYKJAVÍK, THE CAPITAL, IT IS ICELANDIC CULTURE YOU FIND, WITH MUSEUMS DEVOTED TO NAMES LITTLE-KNOWN ELSEWHERE: JÓNSSON AND SVEINSSON.

Left THINGVELLIR CHURCH AND FARMHOUSE IS WHERE THE DECLARATION OF THE ICELANDIC REPUBLIC WAS MADE IN 1944
Above left THERE ARE SIGNS OF VOLCANIC ACTIVITY EVERYWHERE IN ICELAND
Above right LIEF ERIKSSON, THE ICELANDIC NAVIGATOR, IN VIKING COSTUME

Things to Know

- **Area:** 103,000 square kilometers (39,756 square miles)
- **Population:** 266,786
- **Capital:** Reykjavík
- **Language:** Icelandic
- **Economy:** Agricultural, with cattle and sheep ranching. Fish-processing industries account for majority of exports.
- **Passport Requirements:** Required for U.S. citizens.
- **Visa Requirements:** Not required for stays up to three months total in the Scandinavian countries.
- **Duty-Free Items:** 200 cigarettes or 250 grams of tobacco; 1 liter of spirits up to 47 percent alcohol; 1 liter of wine up to 21 percent alcohol; reasonable amounts of clothing, and camping equipment, etc.
- **Currency:** The currency unit is the Icelandic *krona* (IKR), divided into 100 *eyrir*. Due to currency fluctuations, the exchange rate is subject to change. There is no limit on the import of foreign or Icelandic currency.
- **Bank Opening Hours:** 9:15am–4pm Monday–Wednesday and Friday; 9:15am–4pm and 5–6pm Thursday.
- **Best Buys:** Wool, whalebone carvings, sealskin articles, ceramics, silverwork, sheepskin and ponyskin rugs.
- **Public Holidays:** January 1; Maundy Thursday; Good Friday; Easter Monday; First Day of Summer; Labor Day, May 1; Ascension Day; Whitmonday; National Day, June 17; Bank Holiday, first Monday in August; December 25; Boxing Day, December 26.
- **National Tourist Offices:** Icelandic National Tourist Board 655 Third Ave New York. NY 10017 Tel: 212/949 2333; Fax: 212/983 5260 Icelandic Tourist Information: Gimli Laekjargata 3 101 Reykjavik Tel: 552 7488; Fax: 562 4749
- **American Embassy:** Laufásvegur 21 101 Reykjavík, Iceland Tel: 562 9100; Fax: 562 9110

History

Living evidence of geological movement, 20-million-year-old Iceland widens almost an inch a year. Though the island was inhabited briefly during the 8th century by Irish hermits, permanent settlement began in 874 AD when a Norwegian, Ingólfur Arnarson, arrived. In 930 AD the homesteaders formed a legislature, the Althing.

The Icelanders embarked upon further exploration; Eiríkur Thorvaldsson, dubbed the Red, colonized Greenland from about 986 AD. Eiríkur's son, Leifur the Lucky, reached North America about 1000 and established a colony called Vinland the Good. Also in 1000, Christianity was adopted.

From the 10th to the 14th centuries a literary form, the Icelandic Saga, was developed in the native language and was used to spin stories of the gods, record historical events and glorify heroes. During this period Iceland became governed first by Norway in 1262 and then joined to Denmark in 1380. In 1800 the last vestige of the democratic commonwealth, the Althing, was formally abolished.

A 19th-century independence movement led, in 1874, to the restoration of the Althing as a legislative power. Iceland was declared a republic on 17 June 1944. Today it is governed by the 60-member Althing, with a premier and a president who is head of state. In 1980, Vigdís Finnbogadóttir was the first woman elected as president.

Automobile Club
Félag Islenzkra Bifreidaeigenda
(Icelandic Automobile Association), which has offices at Borgartún 33, Reykjavík, is the Icelandic club affiliated with AAA. Not all auto clubs offer full travel services to AAA members.

FOOD

Although international cuisine is readily available, visitors should sample the local fare. Seafood and lamb are staples and are utilized in such dishes as *hangikjöt*, smoked mutton; *saltfiskur*, salt cod; *humar*, a small lobster delicacy; and *hardfiskur*, dried fish. A tasty treat, at least according to Icelanders, is *svid*, sheep's head. Other Icelandic favorites are *blódmör*, blood sausage; *lifrarpylsa*, liver sausage; and *skyr*, the local yoghurt. Snacks that go well with *schnapps* are herring, pickled whale blubber and *hákarl*, dried shark. The traditional Christmas feast is *rjúpa*.

SPORTS AND RECREATION

Sports enthusiasts pursue skiing at Akureyri, Isafjördur and Siglufjördur, where the season is from mid-February to May; summer skiing is in the Kerlingarfjöll region and near Langjökull Glacier. The volcanoes challenge the most experienced climber. Golf is popular; the 10 courses in the country include those at Reykjavík and Akureyri. Spectators can watch the intricate contest of skill and balance shown in *glima*, traditional Icelandic wrestling.

Rich in wildlife, Iceland has well-stocked lakes and rivers to attract fishing enthusiasts; permits must be obtained from the landowner. Hunting is governed by strict regulations but birdwatching is encouraged, and many come for this purpose, often allied to scenic photography. Pony trekking is widely available and is a good way to enjoy the invigorating air and see the countryside.

GETTING AROUND

Iceland has no railroads and relatively few paved roads. Nevertheless, public transportation is one of the best bargains. Bus routes crisscross nearly all inhabited regions; several discount passes are available. The Omnibus Passport, which can only be purchased in Iceland, allows 1–4 weeks of unlimited travel on any scheduled route. The Full-Circle Passport allows unlimited travel around the main island ring road.

Because of road conditions and natural obstructions such as glaciers and lava fields, air travel is often considerably more convenient. Icelandair provides most flights to and within the country

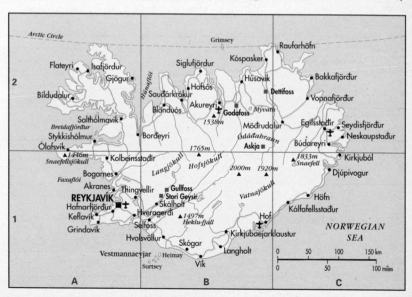

ICELAND

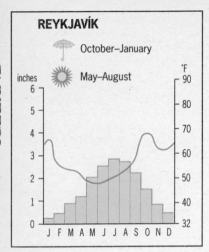

REYKJAVÍK

☂ October–January

☀ May–August

inches: 6, 5, 4, 3, 2, 1, 0

°F: 90, 80, 70, 60, 50, 40, 32

J F M A M J J A S O N D

and also offers discounts for multi-flights within Iceland. State Shipping Department steamers ply the waters between all ports, and various ferry companies have services across the fjords. Taxis and rental cars are available.

The Touring Club of Iceland operates huts equipped with beds and cooking facilities in uninhabited areas, where travelers may stay. Refuge huts are equipped with fuel, beds and rations to be used *only* during an emergency. The best way to travel through the interior is by four-wheel-drive vehicle, accompanied by an experienced guide.

ACCOMMODATIONS

Accommodations in Iceland are small, simple and plentiful. Camping gear can be rented in Reykjavík. Edda Hotels are good value, often converted for the holidays from school accommodations, with a wide range of rooms, good food, and often swimming pools. Youth hostels operate in Reykjavík and elsewhere and are open to all. Farmhouses are also popular vacation accommodations.

TIPPING

Service fees are included in most bills in Iceland, so tipping is not expected and may even be resented.

USEFUL EXPRESSIONS IN ICELANDIC

hello	góðan daginn
good bye	bless
please	gjörðu svo vel
thankyou	takk fyrir
yes/no	já/nei
Does anyone here speak English?	Er einhver hér sem talar ensku?
I don't understand.	Ég skil ekki.
Where are the restrooms?	Hvar er snyrtingin?
Do you take credit cards?	Takið pér kredit kort?
How much is that?	Hvað kostar petta?
I'd like...	Mig myndi langa...
What time is it?	Hvað er klukkan?
left	vinstri
right	hœgri
passport	vegabréf
telephone	sími
church	kirkja
bridge	brú
doctor	læknir
hospital	spítali
information office	upplýsingaskrifstofa
museum	safn
pharmacy	apótek
police station	lögreglustöð
post office	pósthús
store	búð
supermarket	stórmarkaður
bus	straetisvagn
gas	bensín
early/late	snemma/seint
easy	auðvelt
difficult	erfitt
free (vacant)	laust
occupied	uppteki
open/closed	opið/loka
good/bad	gott/slœmt
cheap/expensive	ódýrt/dýrt

DAYS OF THE WEEK

Sunday	Sunnudagur
Monday	Mánudagur
Tuesday	Thriðjudagur
Wednesday	Miðvikudagur
Thursday	Fimmtudagur
Friday	Föstudagur
Saturday	Laugardagur

PLACES OF INTEREST

▲ Reykjavík (531 A1) ★
pop. 97,000

Reykjavík ("Bay of Smokes") was so named in 874 AD when Iceland's first Norse colonist, Ingólfur Arnarson, sighted the numerous hot springs on the Seltjarnarnes Peninsula. Today this remarkably pollution-free city on Faxa Bay is a major seaport, the capital of Iceland and the home of 40 percent of the country's population. Winter weather is similar to New York City's, which is hundreds of miles further south.

Reykjavík's predominantly 20th-century architecture presents a clean and attractive appearance. There are few chimneys; heat is almost exclusively supplied by steam piped from nearby hot springs. It also gives Reykjavík several magnificently hot, outdoor swimming pools, which can be used throughout the year. The sunsets in this smokeless city can be spectacular.

Reykjavík has 80 eating-places, serving international and local cuisine. Nightlife centers on the hotels and restaurants. Liquor tends to be expensive.

For its small population, Iceland is remarkably rich in arts and culture, with at least three fine art galleries in Reykjavík, in addition to the National Gallery. There are two theaters: the National, which is open only in winter, and the City Theatre.

Places of interest include the National Library and Archives, National Art Gallery and Museum of Natural History. The Danish baroque Parliament Building and the small Lutheran cathedral face the Austurvollur, the main square. The botanical gardens in Laugardalur are open in the summer. Shoppers seek out Austurstræti.

ÁRBAEJARSAFN is a folk museum on Reykjavík's eastern outskirts. Its center is the Árbaer farmhouse, surrounded by other late 19th-century structures, including a sod and stone church.

ASMUNDUR SVEINSSON GALLERY contains a collection of original sculpture by Sveinsson, a well-known Icelandic artist.

BLUE LAGOON ★, 48 kilometers (30 miles) southwest of Reykjavík, near the fishing village of Grindavik, is a pool of mineral rich geothermal salty water. The Lagoon's amazing blue color and its warmth attract more than 100,000 visitors each year, to splash and soak. More recently, the water has been found to be useful in helping certain skin diseases and Blue Lagoon has a special skin clinic.

GULLFOSS ★ (Golden Falls) is 123 kilometers (76 miles) east. The waters of the Hvítá cascade 27.5 meters (90 feet) through a rocky gorge.

HEKLU-FJALL (Mount Hekla), 120 kilometers (75 miles) east, is a famous volcano. In times past it was regarded as the entrance to Hell but is now a major tourist attraction. Accessible by a long but fairly easy climb, the summit offers a spectacular view.

HVERAGERDI ★, 40 kilometers (25 miles) south is the headquarters of the horticulture industry. The greenhouses are heated by steam from local hot springs. The complex also has an excellent hotel – an unusual and pleasant place to stay.

KJARVALSSTAOIR, in Miklatún Park, exhibits some of the works of the painter Johannes Kjarval.

SKÁLHOLT ★, 29 kilometers (18 miles) east of Stori Geysir, has had a Christian Church for nine centuries, and the present handsome white church is the eleventh on this site.

LISTASAFN EINARS JÓNSSONAR (Art Museum of Einar Jónsson) displays works by Iceland's most prominent sculptor.

STORI GEYSIR ★, 118 kilometers (73 miles) east has given its name to similar hot springs all over the world. Although its performance today is somewhat erratic, it gained international fame centuries ago by regularly projecting a column of boiling water nearly 60 meters (200 feet).

The geyser is in a scenic area where numerous smaller hissing springs and rumbling craters constantly expel hot steam, water and mud.

THINGVELLIR ★, 50 kilometers (31 miles) east is regarded as a sacred place by Icelanders; in 930 AD the world's oldest extant legislative body, the Althing, first convened at this site.

Of special note are the speaker's rock and a few remains of the sod and brick shelters that the deputies raised and used as dwelling places during their two-week assemblies.

With some of the most outstanding scenery in the country, this national park ranks among Iceland's most popular tourist destinations.

THJÖDMINJASAFNID (National Museum of Iceland), Suourgata, displays a collection of medieval art objects. Noteworthy exhibits include silverwork, national costumes and Viking artifacts.

SNÆFELLSNES PENINSULA ★, 240 kilometers (150 miles) north of Reykjavík, has the cone-shaped Snæfellsjökull 1,446 meters (4,743 feet), an ice-covered extinct volcano, Jules Verne's starting point for *Journey to the Centre of the Earth*. To the north, Stykkisholmur (a peninsula) points into Breidafjordur, which offers spectacular boat tours through the offshore islands.

A car-ferry also runs across the bay to Brjánslækur on the northern side, saving a 240-kilometer (150-mile) drive.

ÓLAFSVIK, along the peninsula's northern coast, below Snæfellsjökull, held Iceland's first trading license from 1687.

Today, its main industry is fishing, and it offers a lively harbor, Gamla Pakkhúsid (Old Packing House), an 1844 trading house, and a beautiful, modern church.

THE ICELAND HORSE

These sturdy, sure-footed little beasts are pure descendants of the animals brought from Norway as long ago as the 9th century. No horses have been imported into Iceland for over 800 years – it is now illegal to do so – and this means that these small horses, little bigger than ponies, but strong enough to carry a big man, have changed little over the years, though they have adapted well to a harsh terrain. Nothing could be more sure-footed than these strong horses, who served until World War II as the main means of transport, and are still used in the September *réttir*, the sheep round-up. Horse-riding and trekking is popular with Icelanders, as are the many riding tours with visitors.

AKUREYRI (531 B2)
pop. 14,100

Akureyri, the chief city of northern Iceland, is at the mouth of the scenic Eyjafjördur. Until recent times a small trading post, Akureyri has evolved into an attractive, modern town and thriving commercial center. Of special interest are the botanical gardens and the modern Lutheran church.

Akureyri is a major winter sports resort. The slopes of Mount Hlídarfjall provide skiing well into May; ice skating, hiking and fishing are also popular.

Roads connecting Akureyi with Reykjavík are mostly asphalted or paved. The 430-kilometer (267-mile) trip takes about eight hours and there are daily flights from the capital. Transportation routes near Akureyri are quite primitive and sometimes dangerous; consequently, travelers should join an escorted tour or seek local advice before setting out for this area.

ASKJA, 230 kilometers (143 miles) southeast, is a large volcanic caldera. It attracted world attention in 1875 when it was the site of a tremendous explosion. Several minor eruptions have occurred since, the last in 1961. The summit offers a spectacular view of the Vatnajökull, Europe's largest glacier. Covering more than 8,340 square kilometers (3,240 square miles), Vatnajökull is also a center of volcanic activity.

DETTIFOSS ★, 134 kilometers (83 miles) east is Iceland's highest waterfall. Here the swift waters of the Jökulsa á Fjöllum cascade nearly 44 meters (145 feet) through rocky surroundings.

GODAFOSS ★ is 49 kilometers (30 miles) east on the Skjálfandi River. The "Falls of the Gods" received its name in 1000 AD when Thorgeir, president of the Althing, discarded his pagan gods for Christianity.

MÝVATN is a spectacular lake 104 kilometers (65 miles) east. The extensive lava fields are evidence that the area was once a center of volcanic activity. No major eruption has occurred since 1729, although a brief one in 1975 created a lava flow into uninhabited wilderness. The shallow lake – only 4 meters (13 feet) deep – is studded with immense lava blocks in strange shapes. Among the more notable are Dimmuborgir (the Black Castles), a series of rocks, caves and canyons on the eastern shore.

HEIMAY – *see Vestmannaeyjar below.*

SURTSEY – *see Vestmannaeyjar below.*

▲ VESTMANNAEYJAR (531 B1)
pop. 4,800
Off Iceland's southern coast, the 15 Westmann Islands, or Vestmannaeyjar, are of volcanic origin. According to legend, their name was derived from some Irish slaves – called West Men because of their British homeland west of Scandinavia – who fled to this Atlantic landfall to escape their Viking masters in the 9th century.

Though sparsely covered with vegetation, most of the islands are surrounded by cliffs that teem with a variety of birdlife. Opportunities for birdwatching are excellent. Egg climbing can be witnessed, although this dangerous practice of scaling cliffs to gather eggs has become increasingly rare. Strict regulations govern the hunting and filming of nesting birds.

A three-day festival is held in the islands in the first week in August to celebrate Iceland's independence.

HEIMAY, the largest and only inhabited island, was Iceland's chief fishing center until January 1973, when a volcanic eruption split the earth near the port of Vestmannaeyjar. The island's 5,000 inhabitants were evacuated and 300 of the 1,400 houses were buried under ash.

Since that time, there have been no further eruptions, and most inhabitants have returned, but island topography and the town have both changed.

SURTSEY, newest of the Westmann Islands, was created in November 1963, when a volcanic eruption shook the North Atlantic. The island is still an active volcano beneath a cooling crust.

Boat trips can be made around Surtsey, but special permission must be obtained to land.

WESTMANN ISLANDS –
see Vestmannaeyjar above.

NORWAY

Norway has more coastline (over 2,000 kilometers – 1,200 miles) for its size than any other country in the world. A third of Norway is inside the Arctic Circle, the land of the Lapps and reindeer, but the rest has forest and fjords slicing into the craggy mountains. The Jotunheimen range, the Home of the Giants, is aptly named as here is the highest point in Scandinavia, Glittertinden.

Norway has one of the lowest population densities on earth. Almost 500,000 live in the capital, Oslo, a city with a modern, clean feel, yet containing many old buildings. At the head of a fjord, ferries leave Oslo for the islands off-shore, for swimming and sun-bathing – in summer the sun does not set until almost midnight.

Left Cruise ships venture inland as far as Geirangerfjord
Above left Wooden houses line the waterfront at Bergen
Above Fishing is one of main industries in Norway

THINGS TO KNOW

- **AREA:** 324,219 square kilometers (125,181 square miles)
- **POPULATION:** 4,160,000
- **CAPITAL:** Oslo
- **LANGUAGE:** Norwegian
- **ECONOMY:** Oil processing, paper and food manufacturing. Fishing, shipbuilding and hydroelectric power production are also important. Small farming.
- **PASSPORT REQUIREMENTS:** Required for U.S. citizens.
- **VISA REQUIREMENTS:** Not required for stays up to three months total in the Scandinavian countries (Denmark, Finland, Iceland, Norway and Sweden).
- **DUTY-FREE ITEMS:** 200 cigarettes or 50 cigars or 250 grams of tobacco; 1 liter of spirits or wine; cameras and a reasonable amount of film; personal goods that have been used. Visitors must be at least 20 years old to import or export alcohol. **Note:** Norway has revised its tax-free shopping system. Instead of being reimbursed by mail for Value Added Tax (V.A.T.) paid in Norway, tourists are now repaid in cash as they leave the country. When buying items with a total value exceeding 300 NOK at Norwegian stores that display the "Tax Free for Tourists" sign, visitors are issued a check for the amount they are due. Provided the items have not been used, the money is returned to them at refund offices at all international airports, border stations and ships on presentation of a passport.
- **CURRENCY:** The currency unit, the Norwegian *krone* (NOK), is divided into 100 *øre*. Due to currency fluctuations, the exchange rate is subject to frequent change. There are no restrictions on the import of foreign or Norwegian currency, but it is recommended that any large amount be declared on arrival in case it needs to be exported later. No more than 5,000 NOK may be exported.
- **BANK OPENING HOURS:** 8:15am–3pm Monday–Friday (or 3:30pm in winter); some banks are open until 5pm on Thursday.

HISTORY

Norwegian heritage recalls a people who reacted to the difficulties of the land with genius and daring. With only a small percentage of the land tillable, the Vikings found their fortune at sea, raiding throughout Europe in the years 800 to 1100 AD. As fearless as their warlike gods, tall, blond, blue-eyed Vikings in leather and metal helmets brandished battle-axes as they crossed the seas in their distinctive longships to conquer.

In their path the Vikings left awakened trade and evidence of their culture. The Scandinavian story form, the Saga, handed down Viking adventures and was incorporated into the literature of many parts of the world. Returning to Norway with new wealth and cultural impulses, the Viking people moved toward unification under one powerful leader who could subdue their many chiefs.

The martyrdom of King Olav II (St. Olav) in 1030 AD marked the establishment of Christianity throughout Norway. For more than 400 years the country was united with Denmark and later with Sweden. Norway has been a constitutional monarchy since a constitution was established in 1814. After a peaceful separation from Sweden in 1905, the Norwegian parliament, the *Storting*, elected Danish Prince Charles to be king.

King Harald V is the present king of Norway. The royal family are a treasured part of Norwegian life. On Constitution Day in Oslo thousands of school children parade up the grand avenue Karl Jogansgate to the Palace Gardens. Embracing the active Norwegian lifestyle, the royal family sails, skis and personally congratulates such champions as the skiers at mammoth Holmenkollen Ski Jump in Oslo.

FOOD AND DRINK

Norwegians prepare salmon and trout for the table with recipes evolved over

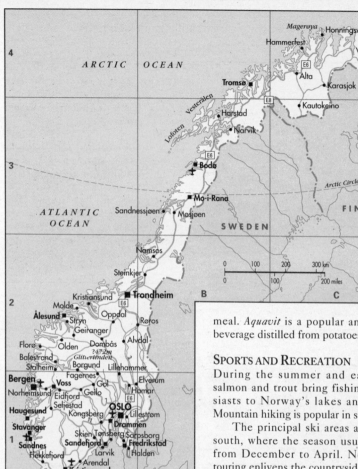

meal. *Aquavit* is a popular and potent beverage distilled from potatoes.

SPORTS AND RECREATION

During the summer and early fall, salmon and trout bring fishing enthusiasts to Norway's lakes and rivers. Mountain hiking is popular in summer.

The principal ski areas are in the south, where the season usually lasts from December to April. Nordic ski touring enlivens the countryside, and ski jumping attracts competitors and spectators. Even summer skiing is possible, both at Stryn, Galdhøpiggen and also further north.

GETTING AROUND

Boats and steamers play an important part in Norway's transportation picture, and scenic cruises, available from the larger cities, are a popular way to see the whole country.

Ferry services are available from other countries. Internal ferry services are less important now than in the past because of the system of improved and modern roads, but the ferries remain useful for short trips.

the centuries. Perhaps the crowning achievement is smoked salmon, which is often a highlight of the Norwegian *koldtbord*, an abundant buffet found at many hotels. A smaller version of the *koldtbord* is the *smørbrød*, the Norwegian open-faced sandwich. Tempting appetites are such distinctive foods as reindeer steaks, *fårikål* (mutton and cabbage stew), *kjøttkaker* (meat cakes) and goat's-milk cheeses. Fresh from the dew of their mountain home, *multer* (cloudberries) bring their unique flavor to top off a

- STORE OPENING HOURS: 9am–4 or 5pm
  Monday–Wednesday and Friday,
  9am–6, 7 or 8pm Thursday, 9am–1, 2 or
  3pm Saturday; store hours may be
  shortened in mid-summer.
- BEST BUYS: Silver and enamelware,
  ceramics, woodcarvings and
  furniture; sweaters, glass, ski
  clothes and equipment.
- PUBLIC HOLIDAYS: January 1; Maundy
  Thursday; Good Friday; Easter
  Monday; May Day, May 1; Ascension
  Day; National Day, May 17;
  Whitmonday; December 25; Boxing
  Day, December 26.
- NATIONAL TOURIST OFFICES:
  Scandinavian National Tourist Board
  655 Third Avenue.
  New York
  NY 10017
  Tel: 212/949 2333
  Fax: 212/983 5260
  Norwegian Tourist Board
  PO Box 2893 Solli
  Drammensveien 40
  N-0230 Oslo
  Tel: 022 92-52-00
  Fax: 022 56-05-05
- AMERICAN EMBASSY:
  Drammensveien 18
  N-0255 Oslo 2
  Norway
  Tel: 022 44-85-50; Fax: 022 44-33-63

AUTOMOBILE CLUB
Kongelig Norsk Automobilklub
(K.N.A., Royal Norwegian
Automobile Club), Drammensveien
20-C, Oslo, and **Norges
Automobil-Forbund**
(Norway Automobile Association),
Storgaten 2, Oslo, have branch
offices in various cities
throughout Norway.
The symbol ▲ beside a city name
indicates the presence of a AAA-
affiliated automobile club branch.
Not all auto clubs offer full travel
services to AAA members.

Norway's internal air network has around 100 airports, some small. Railroads generally parallel the main roads; the Oslo–Bergen Railway offers tourist trains with special commentaries in English. Larger cities sell tourist cards good for unlimited trips on buses and streetcars on a specified number of days.

The two-lane national highways, or *motorveig*, are hard surfaced and concentrated in the south and along the coast; secondary roads are gravel surfaced. Motorists entering Bergen and Oslo must pay city tolls. Low speeds are recommended for the narrow roads of western Norway. During the winter months some roads are not suitable for driving. Road information is available from the Oslo Tourist Office, telephone 22 33-43-86, or the Norges Automobil-Forbund Information Center in Oslo, telephone 22 34-16-00.

Speed limits are 50 k.p.h. (30 m.p.h.) in town and 80–90 k.p.h. (50–55 m.p.h.) on out-of-town roads, including highways. Motorists must drive with low-beam headlights on during the day, and all vehicles must be equipped with replacement bulbs. Seat belt use is mandatory for drivers and passengers; children under 7 years must use a suitable seat restraint. Visiting motorists are required to pay fines for motoring violations on the spot with Norwegian krone.

ACCOMMODATIONS

Although Norway does not rate its hotels, it strictly guards the use of the word "hotel" by specifying what services must be offered at hotels and various other kinds of lodgings. Establishments that cater mainly to international tourists are the *turisthotell* or *høyfjellshotell* (mountain hotels); *pensionater, hospitser* or *fjellstuer* (mountain lodges); and *turiststasjoner* (tourist stations). *Gards* (farms that accept guests) are normally very well run and offer excellent opportunities to meet Norwegians.

Most hotel chains offer discount cards on the normal rates. The major discount programs are the Fjord Pass, Best Western Hotel Check and Bonus Pass. The Scandinavian National Tourist Boards can provide information about special rates.

Norway's 1,400 campgrounds are classified with one to three stars. While an international camping carnet is not required, some sites might still ask for it. Many sites have cottages for rent. In the Lofoten area, fishing cottages are frequently available for rent during the summer. Youth hostels welcome visitors of all ages and often have family rooms.

TIPPING

Restaurants include a service fee in the bill, but you can add 5 to 10 percent if service is excellent. Tip porters 5 krone per bag and chambermaids and other service personnel about 5 krone each.

PRINCIPAL TOURING AREAS

Note: For descriptions of cities in **bold** type, see individual city listings.

MOUNTAINS AND VALLEYS OF THE SOUTH

Bustling **Oslo**, encircled by hills and overlooking a region of lakes and forests, is a scenic beginning for a tour of the southern mountains and valleys. Many roads lead from Oslo to such resorts as **Arendal** and the village of Fevik; also worth visiting are **Larvik** and Sandefjord.

North east of Oslo is Norway's largest lake, 99-kilometer (62-mile) Mjøsa, leading toward the north west into the legend-rich Gudbrandsdal. Smaller lakes are scattered over the valley, and the climate is relatively mild. On old family farms, customs and speech remain almost unchanged by modern life.

Gudbrandsdal is part of the legend of tall-tale-teller Peer Gynt, as are the Jotunheim Mountains to the west. Their

name means "Home of the Giants," and a view of these awe-inspiring peaks proves the aptness of the name. The Oslo–Bergen Railway offers a view of the Jotunheim panorama; mountain roads pass the same view. Hikers find challenging terrain in the Jotunheim.

THE SOUTHERN FJORD COUNTRY

A trip to Norway should include fjord exploration. The fjords are loveliest when the orchards blossom in May and June, the peak tourist season, but Gulf Stream waters and winds make fjord vacations practical all year.

In the south-west corner of fjord country, green farmland hugs the edge of steep cliffs. **Stavanger**'s wooden buildings and narrow, winding streets reflect its medieval origin. Today this major seaport, the focal point of the oil industry, adds modern ways of living to its tradition.

A short distance north around the coast, beautiful Hardangerfjord justifies its reputation as the inspiration of many artists. Sharing the view of Hardangerfjord are such picturesque villages as Øystese, Ulvik, Lofthus, Kinsarvik and Eidfjord. Near Eidfjord can be seen Voringsfossen – Norway's most famous waterfall.

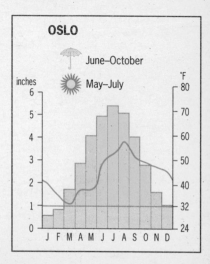

NORWAY

North of Hardangerfjord is **Bergen**, Norway's second largest city, also a busy port and cultural center. A first glimpse of Bergen is not easily forgotten. It is set among seven mountains, and within the town, brightly painted houses seem to be stacked on top of one another up the steep slopes.

The longest fjord is Sognefjord. Deep in its many branches are fascinating towns like Gudvangen, Stalheim and Laerdal. Farther north is Nordfjord, which gets waters from an inland glacier. There are many tourist resorts in the fjord region.

The Trondheimsfjord area is filled with natural beauty and historical sites that are reminders of medieval days of religious and political leadership in the area. The royal town of **Trondheim**, Norway's third largest city, stands just at the entrance of the long, narrow area that leads to Norway's northland.

THE NORTH
Whether traveling by car or steamer, a trip to the roof of Europe is an unforgettable experience. This land beyond the Arctic Circle, where the sun shines 24 hours a day from May to August, is one of weird rock formations and endless moors. It is also the land of the Sami (Lapps), who follow the reindeer herds to the coast each spring. In the fall they return to the inland plateau, to which Alta, a cluster of hamlets, is the gateway.

Hammerfest, in Norway's northern reaches, inspires with the hardiness of people living on the fringes of the Earth. From Hammerfest you can continue into the Arctic on the island of Magerøya.

USEFUL EXPRESSIONS IN NORWEGIAN

hello/good morning	god morgen	old/new	gammel/ny
good-bye	adjø	church	kirke
good afternoon	god dag	museum	museum, museet
good evening	god kveld	town hall	rådhuset
please/thankyou	vennligst/takk	post office	postkontoret
yes/no	ja/nei	station	jernbanestasjonen
excuse me	unnksyld	bank	bank
you're welcome	ingen årsak	credit card	kredittkort
Does anyone here speak English?	Er det noen her som snakker engelsk?	doctor	lege
		right/left	til høyre/til venstre
I don't understand.	Jeg forsår ikke.	straight ahead	rett fram
Where are the restrooms?	Hvor er toalettet?	breakdown	motorstopp
		gas station	bensinstasjon
How much is that?	Hvor mye koster det?	street	gate
		square	plass
What time is it?	Hvor mange er klokken?	tower	tårn

DAYS OF THE WEEK

where/when/how	hvor/når/hvordan	Sunday	søndag
yesterday/today/	i går/i dag/	Monday	mandag
tomorrow	i morgen	Tuesday	tirsdag
What does this mean?	Hva betyr dette?	Wednesday	onsdag
		Thursday	torsdag
cheap/expensive	billig/dyr	Friday	fredag
open/closed	åpen/lukket	Saturday	lørdag

PLACES OF INTEREST

▲ OSLO ★

OSLO *pop. 460,000*

Oslo, Norway's capital, is at the head of Oslofjord, encircled by wooded hills and snowcapped peaks. It is the country's leading industrial and cultural center and chief port.

Visitors to Oslo will find a full range of activities among the many art galleries, museums, nightclubs, restaurants, movies (in English) and theaters. The National Theater has productions of Norwegian classics, while more experimental theater productions take place at the Central Theater and the Open Theater.

The purchase of an *Oslo Kort* (Oslo Card) entitles visitors to free travel on streetcars, buses, and railroads (NSB) as well as many other discounts. Cards, valid for 1–3 days, are sold at many outlets.

AKERSHUS SLOTT (543 B1) ★, located at Festningsplassen, is a large fortress overlooking the harbor, and one of Norway's principal medieval monuments. Constructed in the 14th century, it served as the royal residence from 1319 to 1380.

NORWAY

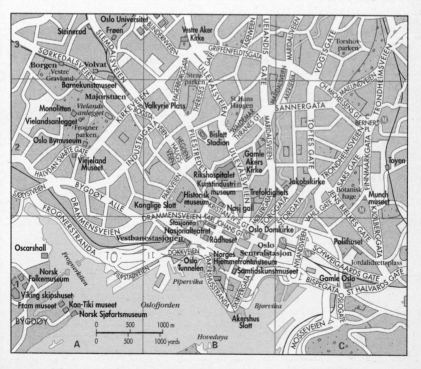

NORWAY

BARNEKUNSTMUSEET (International Museum for Children's Art) (543 A3), Lille Frøensvei 4, displays children's art from more than 150 countries. There are various activities available for children.

DOMKIRKE (Oslo Cathedral) (543 B1), Stortorvet 1, was built 1694–9 and restored in the 19th century; the altarpiece and pulpit date from 1690.

FRAMMUSEET (543 A1), Bygdøynes, houses the beautifully kept ship *Fram*. She was built for Fridtjof Nansen's expedition of 1893–6 to the Arctic, and also carried Roald Amundsen on his voyage to Antarctica, where he reached the South Pole in 1911.

FROGNERPARKEN (Frogner Park – not to be confused with Frognerseteren) (543 A2) is the site of the renowned Vigeland sculptures. The Norwegian sculptor Gustav Vigeland created a world of human beings and animals in stone, plaster and bronze.

HISTORISKMUSEET (543 B2), University of Oslo, Frederiksgt 2, has three museums, including the Ethnographic Museum and the Myntkabinettet, a collection of coins and medals.

The Oldsalssamling, the university's antique collection, includes weapons, ornaments and household items from the Stone Age to the present.

HOLMENKOLLEN ★ is just behind the city. The site of international skiing events, it features an excellent ski jump. A major international event is held in March each year.

Skimuseet (Ski Museum), Kongevei 5, presents the 2,500-year history of this Norwegian sport.

KONGLIGE SLOTT (Royal Palace) (543 B2) can be found at Drammensvei 1 in Oslo's central park. Although the interior of the palace is closed to the public, the colorful changing of the guard can be seen daily at 1:30pm.

KON-TIKIMUSEET (543 A1), Bygdøynesvei 36, contains the raft that Thor Heyerdahl used to substantiate his claim that prehistoric South Americans settled the Polynesian islands.

The museum also has *Ra II*, Heyerdahl's second craft, a reed boat which he built in Egypt, to test the theory that this sort of boat could have reached the Americas before Columbus.

KUNSTINDUSTRIMUSEET (Museum of Applied Arts) (543 B2), St. Olavsgt 1, has exhibits from Norway and other countries dating from the late 13th century to the present. The 12th-century Baldishol Tapestry is one of only five remaining Romanesque tapestries in the world.

MUNCHMUSEET (543 C2) ★, Tøyengt 53, houses the city's art collection left by the painter Edvard Munch. It contains 1,100 of his paintings, 18,000 graphic plates, drawings, prints and sculptures, as well as his books, letters and private papers.

NASJONALGALLERIET (National Gallery) (543 B2), at Universitetsgt 13, emphasizes Norwegian painting, sculpture, drawing and engraving but also includes works by Van Gogh, Matisse and Cezanne. Two rooms are devoted to Munch.

NORGES HJEMMEFRONTMUSEET (Norwegian Resistance Museum) (543 B1), Akershus, depicts the German occupation of Norway during World War II.

NORSK FOLKEMUSEET (Norwegian Folk Museum) (543 A1) at Museumsvei 10, Bygdøy, is in an attractive park. The open-air section boasts 170 wooden buildings from throughout the country. Highlights are a 12th- to 13th-century stave church and the Old Town.

NORSK SJØFARTSMUSEET (Norwegian Maritime Museum) (543 A1), Bygdøynesvei 37, exhibits Norwegian maritime traditions through the ages. *Gjøa*, the vessel Amundsen used to navigate the Northwest passage, is on display.

RÅDHUSET (Oslo City Hall) (543 B2) ★, Rådhusplassen, is an impressive contemporary building with two square towers. Norway's leading artists contributed to the decoration in the 1930s and 1940s.

VIKINGSKIPSHUSET (Viking Ship Museum) (543 A1), Huk Aveny 38, Bygdøy, houses three Viking ships, found along the Oslofjord.

▲ ÅLESUND (539 A2) ★
MØRE OG ROMSDAL *pop. 40,500*
Stretching into the Borgundfjord, Ålesund abounds with natural beauty. The Sunnmørsalpene, or Sunnmøre Alps, provide a backdrop to one of Norway's most attractive towns. The town is best known for its art-nouveau architecture, having been rebuilt after a fire in 1904.

Ålesund's major attraction is the scenic wonder of its fjords and peaks, including Mount Aksla in the center of the town, with some 418 steps to the top.

The surrounding area has fine fishing, caves, cliffs, white beaches and little harbors. The best island is Runde, with 200 bird species recorded on its cliffs.

ÅLESUND MUSEET, Rasmus Ronnebergsgt 16, contains collections that illustrate the history of the fishing industry and the surrounding area.

▲ ARENDAL (539 A1)
AUST-AGDER *pop. 12,000*
On the southern coast of the Nidelven, Arendal is an inviting excursion center with a mixture of ancient and modern streets and buildings. Trinity Church's soaring spire and the 19th-century town hall, housing a portrait gallery, are highlights of Arendal's diverse architecture.

MERDØGÅRD MUSEET, on Merdø island, was an 18th-century sea captain's home. Exhibits depict the windjammer era.

▲ BERGEN (539 A1) ★
BERGEN *pop. 210,000*
Bergen was founded in 1070 by King Olav Kyrre and became the capital of Norway in the 13th century. The city has long been an important shipping and commercial center.

Although periodically ravaged by fire, many fine examples of medieval and Renaissance architecture remain. The broad avenues and open spaces are testimonials to the city planners, who used the thoroughfares as a tool to prevent the rapid spread of flames.

The chief event during the tourist season and the cultural event of the year is the Bergen International Festival, which takes place in late May and early June. This festival of music, drama, folklore, opera and ballet coincides with Fjord Blossom Time, when the country is radiant with the colors of spring.

In addition to those listed below, points of interest in and around Bergen include the Bergen Art Gallery; Bergen

---

NATIONAL DAY
You can hardly get around a Norwegian community on May 17 in any other way than on foot. No matter how small the village, it is certain to have its own parade, and in Oslo the streets are packed with people walking toward the Palace. They are a brilliant sight, many in the unique and beautiful national dress or *bunad*, which varies from region to region, a dress from the past that, in Norway, is not just worn as a costume or by dancers, but as formal dress wear. For every parade, the colors are the Norwegian flag's red, blue, and white, carried by children, with parents carrying children too small to walk, all singing patriotic songs.

In Oslo, so many file past the Royal Family, that it takes hours but, whether it be Oslo in the May sun, northern Norway in the snow, or anywhere else in the world, on May 17, Norwegians will celebrate Norway.

NORWAY

Fisheries, Theatrical and Natural History museums; Rosenkrantz Tower, built in 1563; and Bergen Cathedral.

BERGENHUS is a 12th-century fortress that guards Bergen's harbor. It contains several interesting medieval monuments, including the 16th-century Rosenkrantz Tower.

Haakonshallen (Haakon's Hall) is Norway's most venerated secular building. Erected by King Haakon IV Haakonsson as a wedding and coronation palace, this restored 13th-century structure is used on formal occasions.

BRYGGEN ★, the Hanseatic Wharf, now on the U.N.E.S.C.O. list of World Heritage sites, is a wide quay facing the harbor. In the gabled wooden houses, Bergen's German merchants conducted business during the Hanseatic period. This all-male enclave maintained strict laws and never mingled with the community. Most of the buildings were destroyed by the fire of 1702, but have since been reconstructed. Some of the workshops are open.

Bryggens Museet has the earliest archeological remains from Bergen's medieval past. There are also sensitive re-creations of medieval rooms, from days when Bergen was a small seafaring town.

Hanseatisk Museet (Hanseatic Museum) is one of the oldest timber buildings on the Bryggen. Furnished in 16th-century style, it depicts the cold daily life of the merchants and their young apprentices (no heating was allowed for fear of fire). Dining and work rooms and the youngsters' tiny box beds remain.

Schötsuene, Øvregt 50, were the merchants' assembly rooms, well-warmed for social life. The long central table has both Bible and cane, for this was also the apprentices' school.

FISKETORGET (Fish Market) has an array of busy, crowded stalls selling fish, flowers, fruits and vegetables. Bergen shoppers stop regularly to select and carry home their fresh purchases.

FLØYEN is one of the seven hills surrounding Bergen. The 319-meter (1,050-foot) peak, reached by funicular, affords a superb view as well as miles of lakes, trees and trails.

GAMLE BERGEN (Old Bergen), Elsero, is a lovely open-air museum facing Sandviken harbor. It has more than 35 old wooden houses with interiors patterned after dwellings and shops from the 18th to the 20th centuries.

MARIAKIRKEN (St. Mary's Church), built before 1150, is Bergen's oldest building and one of the finest churches in Norway.

STENERSEN'S COLLECTION, Rasmus Meyers Allé 3, includes works by Edvard Munch, as well as a select collection of Norwegian paintings and furniture.

TROLDHAUGEN (Hill of Trolls) is at Hop, 8 kilometers (5 miles) south overlooking the lake Nordåsvann. In beautiful grounds, this was the summer home of the composer Edvard Grieg for the last 22 years of his life. He and his wife are buried here. The house is furnished as it was in Grieg's time, with his grand piano in the drawing room. Grieg's *hytte* (small cabin), where he worked, overlooks the lake. There is also a concert hall.

UNIVERSITET (University of Bergen) opened its doors in 1948. On the grounds are the city's botanical gardens and several fine museums, including the Museum of Natural History.

Bergens Sjøfartsmuseet (Maritime Museum), Sydneshaugen, has displays pertaining to shipping history from the Viking period through modern times.

Historisk Museum (Historical Museum), Sydneshaugen, has collections of items from prehistory to the present, including rare pieces of medieval religious art.

▲ BODØ (539 B3)
NORDLAND *pop. 37,000*
Bodø is just north of the Arctic Circle in the land of the midnight sun, where

---

LEAVING FOR A BETTER LIFE

In 1825, the Norwegian sloop, *Restauration*, took 52 passengers and crew from Stavanger to North America. By the end of the century, 750,000 Norwegians had left the country. The first group had religious motives and aimed to found a classless society. Later, poverty and lack of opportunity drove people out. The American Homestead Law of 1862, which granted land to immigrants, turned the early trickle into a flood, and many who had been farm laborers in Norway became *odelbonde* farm owners. Many settled in Illinois, where the icy winters were something they could deal with, as well as heading for Iowa. Where they settled, Norwegian schools, language, and other customs remained for many generations and today you have only to read Garrison Keillor's *Lake Wobegon Days* to realize that, in some places, the traditions live on.

---

there is constant daylight from late April to mid-August. The town is set against a backdrop of high mountains that provide splendid views of the surrounding countryside.

In addition to the nearby mountains, Bodø's attractions include the town's modern cathedral, distinguished by the beauty of its architecture and stained glass; the Nordland Museum, with displays of local arts and crafts; and the 13th-century Bodin Church, 3 kilometers (2 miles) outside town, which contains a magnificently carved altarpiece from 1670.

BORGUND (539 A2)
SOGN OG FJORDANE *pop. 1,200*
Borgund is known for its fine stave church and its fish ladder. At the ladder, about 2.5 kilometers (1½ miles) east on

E68, salmon fight their way upstream to their spawning grounds.

BORGUND STAVKIRKE, built in 1150, is one of the oldest Christian buildings in Scandinavia. Distinguished by its superimposed roofs and conical turret, it also incorporates several pagan elements.

SUNNMØRE MUSEET is an open-air museum with 30 old timber dwellings, a medieval church and an excavated Viking town. It also has a collection of boats, some of them over 600 years old.

URNES STAVKIRKE, built 1130–50, is thought to be the oldest stave church in Norway; parts of an even older church were used in its construction.

▲ FAGERNES (539 A1)
OPPLAND *pop. 1,800*
Fagernes is one of Norway's foremost mountain resorts, partially encircling an extension of the lovely Strandefjord.

VALDRES FOLKEMUSEET, just outside the town is a collection of about 70 wooden buildings dating 1200–1850. Folk dancing programs, accompanied by Hardanger fiddles and other instruments unique to Norway, are given to celebrate the region's rich musical tradition.

▲ FREDRIKSTAD (539 A1)
ØSTFOLD *pop. 27,200*
Fredrikstad is on the eastern shore of the Oslofjord at the mouth of the Glomma River. The 17th-century Old Town is fortified with moat, ramparts, drawbridge and sortie gates.

GEILO (539 A1)
BUSKERUD *pop. 2,000*
One of the largest winter sports resorts in Scandinavia, Geilo maintains 20 ski slopes for beginners and experts.

GEIRANGER (539 A2)
MØRE OG ROMSDAL *pop. 4,800*
At the head of the Geirangerfjord is the charming village of Geiranger. North, on

the way to Valldal, are the beautiful waterfalls De Syv Søstre, or The Seven Sisters, and Brudesløret, or Bridal Veil.

▲ HALDEN (539 A1)
ØSTFOLD *pop. 26,100*

Halden is a border town that withstood numerous Swedish attacks during the 17th and 18th centuries. The Fredriksten Fort still dominates the settlement and is a major tourist attraction. Inside are restaurants, cafés and museums; the ramparts afford views of the Swedish borderlands.

HAMMERFEST (539 C4)
FINNMARK *pop. 9,500*

Hammerfest is the world's northernmost town, long making its living from fishing, and now Norway's main trawler port. In 1891, it was the first European town to have electric street lighting! The unusual new church, built in 1961, has a shape inspired by traditional wooden fish drying racks.

▲ HAUGESUND (539 A1)
ROGALAND *pop. 28,000*

Once a major fishing center, Haugesund now derives its income from the oil industry. The town gained historical fame when Harald Fairhair united Norway during a series of battles 872–930 AD. Haugesund hosts the Norwegian Film Festival.

HONNINGSVÅG (539 C4)
FINNMARK *pop. 3,400*

Honningsvåg is the northernmost village in Norway. Reached by ferry from Repvag or by steamer from Tromsø, it sits on a green mountainside behind a fine harbor. Bus excursions to the North Cape provide spectacular sights of the midnight sun over the Arctic Ocean.

▲ KONGSBERG (539 A1)
BUDKERUD *pop. 20,000*

Formerly a silver-mining center on the Lågen River, Kongsberg maintains a miniature train that carries tourists through the mining tunnels. Other sites include Lågendal Museet, the Arsenal, the Royal Mint and the Norwegian Mining Museum. Kongsberg Church is Norway's largest.

▲ KRISTIANSAND (539 A1) ★
VEST-AGDER *pop. 66,300*

On a peninsula at the estuary of the Otra River, Kristiansand is Norway's second largest port and the capital of the South Coast area. Built by King Christian IV of Denmark in 1641, it is now an important center of nickel refining. Kristiansand Folk Museet and Ravnedal Municipal Park are of interest.

KRISTIANSAND DOMKIRKE ★, Kirkegt, is a 17th-century Gothic cathedral, rebuilt in 1895. It contains an attractive altarpiece

---

HURTIGRUTEN – THE COASTAL STEAMER

Every evening at 10pm, the big ship sails out of Bergen's fjord harbor, the start of a 2,300-kilometer (1,250-nautical-mile) trip north, across the Arctic Circle, around North Cape, to Kirkenes on the Russian border, with some 40 stops on the way there and back. At one time, this was the only way to travel in northern Norway, when winter closed mountain roads. *Hurtigruten* reached its centenary in 1994. Today, it is a favorite 12-day tour for visitors, though Norwegians still hop on and off, using the boat as a bus between the ports, and steamers carry much cargo. Passengers get off to explore places such as Trondheim, Hammerfest, and Trollfjord, so narrow no big cruise ship could fit. Then there is the North Cape, the highlight of the voyage. There is a lot of fun on board, the most festive occasion coming at the crossing of the Arctic Circle, with Santa Claus on deck and certificates for everyone.

by Eilif Petersen as well as statues of the Four Evangelists.

KRISTIANSAND DYREPARK ★, is a 45-hectare (111-acre) park containing a storybook miniature village, water park, fairgrounds and an animal reserve.

KRISTIANSAND KANON MUSEUM displays one of the largest guns in the world. Its range extends over some 56 kilometers (35 miles).

KRISTIANSAND KUNSTFORENING, on Markensgt, exhibits Norwegian paintings and highlights works by South Coast artists.

ODDERRØY, an island in the harbor connected to the mainland by a bridge, bears the remains of several ancient fortresses, including Christiansholm, created by Frederik III in 1674.

VEST-AGDER FYLKES MUSEET, Kongsgård, is an open-air museum with some 30 dwellings. Dating from 1600, they display collections of folk furniture, textiles, and antique church relics.

▲ KRISTIANSUND (539 B2)
MØRE OG ROMSDAL *pop. 17,900*
Kristiansund is built on three islands connected by bridges and ferry boats. This busy fishing port is the home of a trawling fleet. The marketplace, broad streets and brightly painted houses give Kristiansund a charming appearance. *Sunbåten*, the harbor boat, tours Kristiansund's three islands.

DEN GAMLE BYEN (The Old Town), has an old Customs House, the town's first hospital and school, and old warehouses.

LARVIK (539 A1)
VESTFOLD *pop. 9,000*
A delightful seaside resort on the North Sea at the mouth of the Lågen River, Larvik is a center for bathing, boating and salmon fishing. Nearby Lade Farris is known for its natural mineral springs.

LARVIK KIRKE, on Kirkestredet, is a 17th-century church with an attractive interior noted for its numerous paintings, including one by Lucas Cranach.

LILLEHAMMER (539 A1) ★
OPPLAND *pop. 22,800*
Norway's best known resort, Lillehammer is at the northern edge of Mjøsa, the country's largest lake.

A favorite spot for people who love the outdoors, Lillehammer offers a full spectrum of sporting opportunities. Popular summer diversions are angling, horseback riding, swimming, boating and waterskiing. The *Skibladner*, Norway's only remaining paddle steamer, offers cruises on Mjøsa in summer. In winter, eight lifts transport skiers to nearby slopes. Lillehammer hosted the 1994 Winter Olympic Games.

AULESTAD, 19 kilometers (12 miles) north, was home to the great Norwegian poet, dramatist and novelist Bjørnstjerne Bjørnson, who wrote the Norwegian national anthem. It is now a museum.

HELLERISTRINGER (Rock Sculptures) are at Drotten, 10 kilometers (6 miles) north. These 4,000-year-old monuments are embellished with animal motifs.

MAIHAUGEN constitutes one of the largest open-air museums in Europe. The 100 old wooden buildings from the Gudbrandsdal contain some 30,000 utensils and articles of furniture.

LOFOTEN ISLANDS (539 B3)
NORDLAND *pop. 27,000*
A wall of mountains interrupted by narrow fjords and navigable sounds makes up the Lofoten Islands (Lofoten Vesterålen). Fishermen congregate from January to March for the cod migration, swimmers enjoy waters warmed by the Gulf Stream in the summer and mountaineers find a variety of challenging climbs all year. The Røst group, a cluster of about 365 islands, makes up one of the largest bird sanctuaries in Europe.

NORWAY

▲ MOLDE (539 A2)
MØRE OG ROMSDAL *pop. 21,500*

Molde is Norway's city of roses. In this town overshadowed by the Romsdal Mountains are several attractive parks and gardens. On the Romsdalsfjord, Molde offers opportunities for boating, fishing and mountain climbing.

Boat tours travel to the island resort of Hjertøya, to the picturesque fishing villages Bud and Bjørnsund on the Atlantic coast and to the holy island of Veøy, with its medieval stone church.

Other attractions include the orchard town of Andalsnes, a noted fishing resort to the south west. Rødven is known for its 14th-century stave church, and Mardalsfoss, a 300-meter (985-foot) waterfall at Eikesdalen that is one of Europe's highest. A scenic tour can be made to Geiranger *(see p.547)* by way of the *Trollstigveien*, or Path of Trolls, which zigzags up steep mountain slopes.

NARVIK (539 B3)
NORDLAND *pop. 18,000*

Narvik is a busy port primarily concerned with exporting iron ore. The town experienced considerable damage during World War II but has been rebuilt. It is now a popular tourist destination because of its mountain setting and views of the midnight sun.

RØROS (539 B2) ★
SØR-TRØNDELAG *pop. 3,300*

Røros, with its many unpainted timber houses, looks much as it did when the first copper mines opened in 1644. Slag heaps, a smelter and poor mining houses make the 1,000-or-so buildings authentic enough to gain a place on the U.N.E.S.C.O. list of World Heritage Sites. The stone church with its white steeple is very fine. Røros Museum, in the Smelting Works, has mining displays, and underground tours go 50 meters (160 feet) below Olav's Gruva (mine), some 14 kilometers (9 miles) west, with all its machinery. Røros is also a winter sports center and other points of interest include Korthaugen Fortress, erected in 1711.

▲ SKIEN (539 A1)
TELEMARK *pop. 46,700*

Industrialized Skien, on the north bank of the Skienselv, was the birthplace of dramatist Henrik Ibsen in 1828. The farm where he grew up is just north of town and is preserved as a monument.

▲ STAVANGER (539 A1) ★
ROGALAND *pop. 100,000*

When Harald Fairhair won the Battle of Hafrsfjord near Stavanger in 872 AD, he united Norway for the first time. The old city, the country's fourth largest, has become a major port and oil production center. Modern Stavanger is a charming blend of fishing village and modern city, sprinkled with parks, gardens and lakes.

Points of interest include the Stavanger Museum, with historical and zoological exhibits, and the Kongsgård, a former royal manor that is now a school. Market Square is lined with fish, fruit and vegetable stalls and is especially active before noon.

CANNING MUSEUM Until World War II Stavanger prospered on sardines, with 70 canning factories. Once a working factory, the museum has curing ovens and guides who demonstrate a life of threading, smoking and packing sardines.

GAMLE STAVANGER (Old Stavanger) is preserved from the late 17th and 18th centuries, with more than 150 wooden houses, cobbled streets and old-fashioned street lamps. This is no museum. People live here and take pride in keeping their homes in character.

MARITIME MUSEUM, close to the harbor deals with the town's maritime history, from sailing ships to oil platforms. Its old shop has goods that would have been sold in the 1930s, and the owner's office and comfortable apartment remain as they were then.

STAVANGER DOMKIRKE, a 12th-century cathedral at Haakon VII's Gate, is one of Norway's most attractive churches.

Rebuilt about 1300 with a Gothic chancel, this Anglo-Norman structure has a pulpit with some interesting wood-carvings dating from 1658.

VISTEHOLA is a 6,000-year-old cave at Randaberg, 10 kilometers (6 miles) from Stavanger. It is believed to be the oldest homestead in Scandinavia. Excavations have uncovered ancient animal skeletons and tools made of horn and bone.

▲ TØNSBERG (539 A1)
VESTFOLD *pop. 33,000*
Tønsberg is the oldest town in Scandinavia, founded before 871 AD. This ancient fortress city on the coast south of Oslo is now an important shipping center.

▲ TROMSØ (539 B4) ★
TRØMS *pop. 53,000*
Tromsø is the largest town in northern Norway, has the world's most northerly university, and a lively student life. The study of the northern lights, observed especially in December and January, is made by the Rockefeller-sponsored Auroral Observatory. Expeditions can be arranged to the Arctic island of Spitzbergen.

ISHAVSKATEDRALEN (Arctic Cathedral) is coated in aluminum and said to symbolize Norwegian nature, culture and faith.
   The cathedral is a perfect example of modern architecture and contains one of the largest stained-glass windows throughout Europe.
   In the center of the town is the original **Domkirke** (Cathedral), one of Norway's biggest wooden churches.

NORDLYSPLANETARIET (Northern Lights Planetarium) presents *Arctic Lights*, a representation of the aurora borealis, or northern lights.

POLARMUSEET celebrates the Arctic in vivid pictures along with memorabilia of explorers and other aspects of Arctic life, including a Sami exhibit.

▲ TRONDHEIM (539 A2) ★
SØR-TRØNDELAG *pop. 140,000*
Founded in 997 AD, Trondheim is the principal city in north-central Norway. Trondheim is known as the Royal Town because Norwegian kings are crowned in the cathedral. Excellent sailing, fishing and skiing are nearby.

ERKEBISPEGÅRDEN, bordering Bispegt, was formerly the Archbishop's Palace, built in the 12th century.

KRISTIANSTEN FESTNING, off Brubakken, is the town fortress built by General Caspar de Cicignon 1676–82.

NIDAROS DOMKIRKE (Nidaros Cathedral), next to Erkebispegården, is Norway's national shrine. One of Europe's finest Gothic buildings, it was built in the early 11th century and is noted for its interesting sculptures. In ancient times, the Cathedral was used for Royal Coronations, and since 1988 it has housed the Crown Jewels, a beautiful regalia, on display in summer.

RINGVE MUSIKHISTORISK MUSEET (Ringve Museum of Musical History), Ringve Mansion at Lade, contains instruments of the type played by Beethoven and Mozart demonstrated by guides who play them. Oriental countries are represented by exotic instruments of fine mosaic and ivory.

▲ VOSS (539 A1)
HORDALAND *pop. 14,100*
Voss is a center for traditional Norwegian culture, the place to see the old dances performed in authentic dress. Voss has also produced a remarkable number of Hardanger fiddle-players as well as other musicians and artists. As a resort it has fine facilities for skiing and summer watersports.

VANGSKYRKJA (church) was built by King Magnus the Lawmaker in 1277. The octagonal steeple is unique, and inside the church are rich decorations.

NORWAY

SWEDEN

The biggest of the Scandinavian countries, Sweden's past and present dominance is sometimes resented by its neighbors. Often at war in the past, Sweden remained neutral throughout the two world wars and has retained a cool and prosperous presence.

Sweden is scenically prosperous too, covering 1,600 kilometers (1,000 miles) by 500 kilometers (310 miles). In the north it shares Mountains with Norway, while farther south is lake land, including huge Lake Vänern. There are about 100,000 lakes scattered throughout Sweden, and with forest covering 60 percent of the country there would seem to be little room for anything else but wood and water.

Stockholm is Sweden's capital, sprawled over islands and around inlets, with an Old Town of 16th- and 17th-century buildings.

Left GAMLA STAN, STOCKHOLM'S OLD TOWN, IS FULL OF WATERFRONTS AND NARROW LANES, THE MOST BEAUTIFUL OF SCANDINAVIA'S CAPITALS
Above ORUST HAS LOTS OF PRETTY FISHING VILLAGES LIKE HÄLLVIKSSTRAND

THINGS TO KNOW

- **AREA:** 449,963 square kilometers (173,731 square miles).
- **POPULATION:** 8,692,000
- **CAPITAL:** Stockholm
- **LANGUAGE:** Swedish
- **ECONOMY:** Industry, trade, forestry. Machinery, iron, steel, wood and paper products; iron ore (especially Lappland); farmland produces cattle, grains, potatoes, sugar beets.
- **PASSPORT REQUIREMENTS:** Required for U.S. citizens.
- **VISA REQUIREMENTS:** Not required for stays up to three months total in the Scandinavian countries (Denmark, Finland, Iceland, Norway and Sweden)
- **DUTY-FREE ITEMS:** 400 cigarettes or 200 cigarillos or 500 grams of tobacco; 1 liter of wine and 1 liter of spirits (or 2 liters of wine); 2 liters of beers; perfume for personal use; cameras and a reasonable amount of film; one video camera.
- **CURRENCY:** The currency unit, the Swedish *krona* (SKR), is divided into 100 *öre*. Due to currency fluctuations, the exchange rate is subject to frequent change. No limit on import or export of foreign currency.
- **BANK OPENING HOURS:** 9:30am–3pm Monday–Friday; many banks remain open until 5:30 or 6pm on Monday or Thursday. In small towns and rural areas bank hours are 10am–2pm Monday–Friday.
- **STORE OPENING HOURS:** 9am–6pm Monday–Friday; on Saturday stores open at 9am and close between 1 and 4pm. In some larger towns, department stores remain open until 8pm; some also open Sunday.
- **BEST BUYS:** Glassware, ceramics and pottery; furniture and carved wood; stainless steel, silver and other metal items; textiles, rugs and wall hangings; and reindeer souvenirs from Lappland.
- Note: Sweden has a system for cash refunds of Value Added Tax (V.A.T.). Visitors who show a passport when making a purchase in a shop displaying the "Tax Free for Tourists" sign will

HISTORY

The settlement of Sweden began about 12000 BC when hunter/gatherers crossed a land bridge from continental Europe. By 1500 BC the population was trading with the Danube Basin and the Mediterranean. From the 9th to the 11th centuries AD Swedish Vikings controlled trade across the Baltic and ranged as far south as Constantinople.

By the end of the 11th century Christianity had replaced paganism and helped to unify the country under a single ruler. The first Swedish parliament, the bicameral *Riksdag*, was established in the year 1435.

In the early 1600s Sweden became a great northern European power seeking control over the Baltic Sea and the western trade routes of the Russian empire. Impoverished by wars in the 18th and early 19th century, Sweden adopted policies of non-alignment and neutrality that continue unbroken.

Nineteenth-century Sweden was a poor country whose population more than doubled despite much emigration. Many democratic reforms were enacted, however, including compulsory free education, equal rights of inheritance for men and women, religious freedom and parliamentary reforms. In the last half of the century Sweden's industrialization began, based upon iron ores and forests.

In the 20th century Sweden has experienced almost continuous economic growth and increased prosperity. In 1932 the Social Democratic Party gained control of the government, a control that it has maintained with only two short breaks since.

Somewhat delayed by World War II, in which Sweden remained neutral, social welfare laws were enacted establishing pensions, health insurance, a tax reorganisation which redistributed wealth, and educational reforms and expansions.

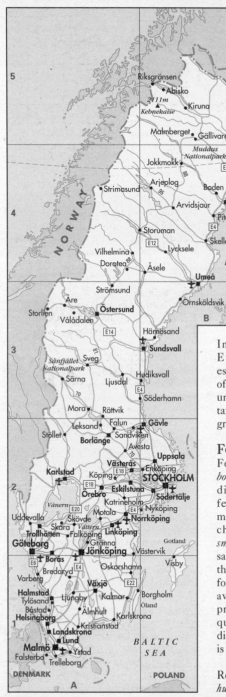

In 1994 Sweden voted to join the European Union. Sweden has not escaped the general economic problems of the 1990s, however, and the previous unquestioned support for relatively high taxation and generous social welfare programs may be changing.

FOOD AND DRINK

Food in Sweden often means a *smörgåsbord*. This wide selection of hot and cold dishes served buffet style usually features pickled or smoked herring, meats, sausages, fish delicacies and cheese. Another Swedish treat is *smörgås*. The *smörgås* is an open faced sandwich and may be covered with anything from lobster to cold turkey. Other foods popular with Swedes are crayfish, available in early fall, seafood, dairy products and pastries. Common thirst quenchers are *aquavit*, a potent drink distilled from potatoes, and beer, which is usually very mild.

Restaurants all over the country serve *husmanskost*, literally "home cooking,"

receive a check for the V.A.T. amount. Checks can be cashed at airports, on certain ferries and at ferry ports on departure.

- **PUBLIC HOLIDAYS:** January 1; Epiphany, January 6; Good Friday; Easter Monday; Labor Day, May 1; Ascension Day; Whitmonday; Midsummer's Day; All Saints' Day; December 25; Boxing Day, December 26.
- **NATIONAL TOURIST OFFICES:** Scandinavian National Tourist Boards 655 Third Ave. New York, NY 10017 Tel: 212/949 2333 Fax: 212/697 0835 Swedish Travel and Tourism Council 73 Welbeck Street London W1M 8AN Tel: 0171 487 3135 Fax: 0171 935 5853 Sweden House Corner Hamngatan/Kungsträdgården Box 7542 S-10393 Stockholm Tel: 08 789-24-00 Fax: 08 789-24-50
- **AMERICAN EMBASSY:** Strandvägen 101 11589 Stockholm Sweden Tel: 08 783-53-00 Fax: 08 661-19-64

AUTOMOBILE CLUBS
Motormännens Riksförbund (Swedish Automobile Association), 32 Sturegatan, Stockholm, and the **Svenska Turistföreningen** (S.T.F., Swedish Touring Club), Kungsgaten 2, Stockholm, also have offices in Malmö and Göteborg. The symbol ▲ beside a city name indicates the presence of a AAA-affiliated automobile club branch. Not all auto clubs offer full travel services to AAA members.

---

based on traditional Swedish recipes. Each province has its specialty, which is often served as the dish of the day.

SPORTS AND RECREATION

Avid sports enthusiasts, Swedes have excellent recreational facilities. Lakes and mountains throughout Sweden attract visitors all year for camping, hiking, fishing, boating and swimming. Skiing attracts Swedes and visitors alike in this land ideally suited for miles of cross-country ski trails. The north harbors numerous resorts – Abisko, Åre, Storlien, Riksgränsen and Vålådalen – that offer skiing, skating, ice hockey, tobogganing and curling. Some of Sweden's favorite seaside resorts are Båstad, Falsterbo, Saltsjöbaden, Tylösand and Visby. Sweden has many golf courses and good facilities for tennis also. With more than 96,000 fish-filled lakes, Sweden is a fisherman's paradise. Facilities are available at most resorts. Karlstad is especially popular for fishing.

GETTING AROUND

Sweden can be reached by ferry from Harwich and Newcastle, England; Fredrikshavn, Denmark; and Kiel, Germany, to Göteborg (Gothenburg). There also are ferries from Elsinore and Grenå, Denmark, to Helsingborg; and Travemünde, Germany, to Trelleborg. There are also connections from Finland, Estonia, Poland and Norway.

All Sweden's roads are toll free, including the *motortrafikled*, or highway, and *motorväg*, or superhighway. Road surfaces in the south are generally good, but those in central and northern areas are often just loose gravel. If the vehicle has seat belts, wearing them is compulsory; a child of 7 years or under may not occupy a front seat unless using a suitable restraint system. Low beams should be used at all times during the day. Speed limits are 50 k.p.h. (30 m.p.h.) in town, 70–90 k.p.h. (40–55 m.p.h.) on out-of-town roads and 90–110 k.p.h. (55–65 m.p.h.) on *motorväg*. There are no on-the-spot fines.

ACCOMMODATIONS

A wide variety of accommodations are found in Sweden. Though there is no official rating system, Swedish hotels have a particularly good reputation. The Swedish Tourist Board publishes an annual hotel guide, as well as a guide covering less expensive alternatives. Many hotels offer discounted rates in summer and at weekends; summer chalets are slightly less expensive. A number of farms also offer bed and breakfast. Budget-priced accommodations are available in simple rooms that do not include breakfast; a *rum*, or room, sign identifies this type of lodging. Most *turistbyrå*, local tourist offices, will book a *rum* or lodging at a farm. The best deals are found at Sweden's 750 officially approved campgrounds, open in April or May through August; some are even open in winter. An international camping carnet is required.

TIPPING

A service charge of 15 percent is usually included in hotel bills, so there is no need to tip further unless for special attention. The same is true in restaurants, where an 18 percent V.A.T. and service charge are included in the price. Tip taxi drivers and hairdressers by rounding up to the next 10.

PRINCIPAL TOURING AREAS

Note: For descriptions of cities in **bold type**, see individual city listings.

THE WEST COAST AND LAKELANDS

Sweden's lake district is popular with vacationers all year. The huge lakes Vänern and Vättern, and thousands of smaller waterways, make Götaland excellent for water sports. A boat trip yields spectacular scenery. **Göteborg** is a good center for exploring.

THE SOUTHLAND

Skåne is chateau country; there are more than 200 castles in Sweden's southern-most province. Skåne also offers white sand beaches, fertile farmland and medieval churches.

Filled with reminders from bygone eras are the nature havens of Öland and Götland, large islands off Sweden's south-east coast. From the bridge that links Öland with the mainland at **Kalmar**, it is a short drive to Öland's capital, **Borgholm**. **Visby**, on Götland, is served by air and ferry connections.

NORRLAND

Northern Sweden is like a giant park. Vast lakes and swift streams lure anglers, high mountains beckon skiers, and lovely scenery attracts campers and hikers. **Åre**, Storlien, Vålådalen are popular all year, but especially in the ski season.

In the far north, Lappland's inhabitants still live much as they did centuries ago. Some Sami depend upon reindeer for survival, and a few still dwell in tents. The resorts of **Abisko** and Riksgränsen are popular with skiers.

STOCKHOLM AND AROUND

Stockholm is a good starting point for exploring. The nation's capital is a cultural center offering opera, concerts, museums and art galleries and is within

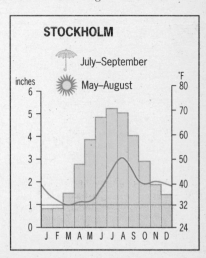

driving distance of most of Svealand's attractions. Sweden's most outstanding university can be found at **Uppsala**.

DALARNA – FOLKLORE COUNTRY

Dalarna, in Svealand, is renowned for its culture and folklore. The inhabitants still adhere to ancient customs and wear regional costumes on festive occasions. Festivals are numerous, and most villages have midsummer celebrations. The resorts of **Rättvik**, Leksand, **Mora** and Tällberg are surrounded by lakes, birch meadows and green hills.

USEFUL EXPRESSIONS IN SWEDISH

hello/good morning	god morgon	doctor	läkare, doktor
good-bye	adjö	restrooms	toaletten
good afternoon	god dag	right	till höger
good evening	god kväll	left	till vänster
good night	god natt	straight ahead	rakt fram
please	var så god	breakdown	motorstopp
thankyou	tack	gas station	bensinstation
yes/no	ja/nej	street	gatan
excuse me	ursäkta mig	square	platsen
you're welcome	ingen orsak	tower	torn
Does anyone here speak English?	Finns det någon här som talar engelska?	castle	slott
		bridge	bro
I don't understand.	Jag förstår inte.	**DAYS OF THE WEEK**	
Where are the restrooms?	Var är toaletten?	Sunday	söndag
		Monday	måndag
Do you take credit cards?	Kan jag beta la med kredikort?	Tuesday	tisdag
		Wednesday	onsdag
How much is that?	Hur mycket kostar det?	Thursday	torsdag
		Friday	fredag
I'd like...	jag skulle vilja ha	Saturday	lördag
What time is it?	Hur mycket är klockan?		

where/when/how	var/när/hur	**NUMBERS**		
yesterday/today/ tomorrow	igår/idag/ i morgen	1	en, ett	70 sjuttio
		2	två	80 åttio
What does this mean?	Vad betyder det här?	3	tre	90 nittio
		4	fyra	100 hundra
cheap/expensive	billig/dyr	5	fem	1,000 tusen
open/closed	öppen/stängd	6	sex	
vacant/occupied	ledig/upptagen	7	sju	
good/bad	bra/dålig	8	åtta	
old/new	gammal/ny	9	nio, nie	
church	kyrkan	10	tio, tie	
museum	museet	20	tjugo	
town hall	rådhuset	21	tjugo en	
post office	postkontoret	22	tjugo två	
newspaper	tidning	30	trettio	
station	järnvägsstationen	40	fyrtio	
bank	bank	50	femtio	
		60	sextio	

PLACES OF INTEREST

SWEDEN

▲ STOCKHOLM ★

STOCKHOLMS LÄN *pop. 684,500*
See map on p.560.

Spread over several peninsulas and 13 islands in Lake Mälaren and the Baltic Sea, Stockholm is Sweden's capital and largest city. Canals and bridges lace the "City on the Water" founded in the 13th century. Once occupied by the Danes, it has been Sweden's since 1523.

The city underwent a renaissance in the 18th century, when cultural enrichment followed architectural and governmental expansion. Stockholm's great literary and scientific academies were founded in this period.

A tour of Stockholm should begin with Gamla Stan, the Old Town of Stadsholmen, an island in the center of the city. This area retains its medieval charm and has many government buildings. As most streets are narrow – Mårten Trotzigs Gränd is little more than 1 meter (3 feet) wide – the best way to see Gamla Stan is on foot. Stockholm's nightlife is based in the nightclubs and bars here; by day boutiques and antique shops flourish. Stora Nygt is the principal thoroughfare in this area.

From Stortorget, a large square by the Royal Palace, most attractions of Gamla Stan are within easy reach. Skeppsbron is a quay on the eastern shore that is lined with 17th- and 18th-century trading houses. Other points of interest are Storkyrkan, a 13th-century cathedral, and Tyska Kyrkan, the German Church of St. Gertrude.

Together with Stadsholmen, the islands of Riddarholmen, Helgeandsholmen and Stromsborg make up the "Town Between the Bridges." Helgeandsholmen, or "Island of the Holy Ghost," is the seat of parliament. Riddarholmen, the Island of Knights, is the location of Riddarholmskyrkan, the royal memorial church since the 17th century.

Across North Bridge from Stadsholmen is Normalm, Stockholm's commercial center. The 18th-century Foreign Office and the Royal Opera are next to Gustav Adolfs Torg.

Stockholm's principal shopping area is the Sergelstorget area, a completely

---

THE ART GALLERY UNDERGROUND

Stockholm's *Tunnelbanan* (underground) must be the most beautiful in the world. Its stations are full of art of all sorts. The idea originated in the 1940s, but it was not until 1957 that T-Centralen, the hub of the network, could display the first three by Egon Möller-Nielsen, decorations on track walls made of white clinker and ceramic figures, with glass prisms in patterns and colors. Gradually ticket halls, platforms, ceilings, and even the track walls were covered with wonderful murals gathered in from some 70 artists. People argue about which is the best, but the Akalla train (route 11) is hard to beat – its entrance is like going down into a strange, deep cavern.

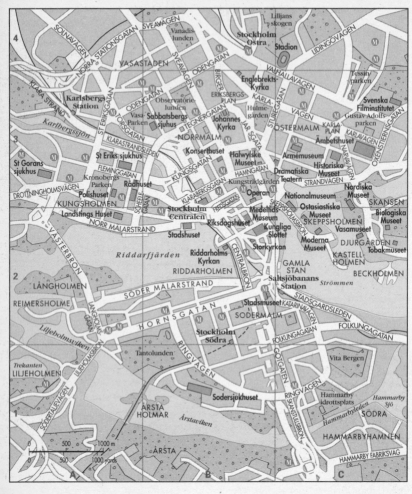

rebuilt section in Central Norrmalm. Several large department stores and Sergelgatan shopping mall are here.

Humlegården, or Hop Garden, the site of the Royal Library, lies to the west of Normalm, as does Nybroplan, home to the Royal Dramatic Theater. East of Nybroplan are the Army Museum, the National Museum of History, the Royal Numismatic Collection and, farther east, the Maritime Museum and Technical Museum. The Ethnographic Museum has displays from the Orient and is near Kaknastornet, a 116-meter (380-foot) tower with a panoramic view of the city.

South of Östermalm is Djurgården, or Deer Park, once a Royal hunting park. Oak trees, some of them 1,000 years old, grow on the island, which is Stockholm's largest park area. Lundsgröna, also on the island, is a popular amusement park.

Skeppsholmen and Kastellholmen are islands east of Stadsholmen. The two islands once comprised a naval base. Several old military buildings now house the Museum of Modern Art and Asiatic Antiquities.

Tourists in Stockholm can purchase the special ticket *Stockholmskortet*, "The Key to Stockholm," which entitles the traveler to free transportation on buses, subways and suburban railways, as well as sightseeing trips and free admission to 50 of Stockholm's main attractions, including the Royal Palace, the *Vasa* Museum and Gripsholm Castle. Valid from 12–36 hours, the card is available at the tourist center in Kungsträdgården, and at the Hotellcentraler at the Central Railroad Station.

DROTTNINGHOLM ★ is on Lovon, an island west of Stockholm. Surrounded by formal gardens, the 17th-century French-style palace contains portraits of European monarchs. Gustavus III established the Drottningholm Court Theater in the 18th century. After his assassination it lay closed and forgotten until the 1920s, when it was discovered with its 18th-century stage equipment, seating and character intact.

GAMLA STAN (560 B2), the Old Town, is a maze of narrow streets and old buildings, ideal for browsing and shopping.

GRIPSHOLM SLOTT ★ lies 60 kilometers (37 miles) west on an island in Mälaren and is considered to be the "Swedish Pantheon." Dating from 1383 and rebuilt in 1537, the castle served as a refuge for the country's kings. Highlights include a silk and velvet-lined throne, Swedish and Foreign Portrait Galleries and 18th-century theater. Extensive gardens and a deer park surround the castle.

HAGA PARK MUSEUM AND GUSTAV IIIs PAVILJONG, Haga was Gustav III's retreat, a graceful pavilion, with beautiful interiors.

HISTORISKA MUSEUM (560 C3) ★ , Narvaväg 13–17, opened an addition to its prehistoric antiquities in 1994.

The Gold Room, in a vault some 7 meters (23 feet) below ground, houses rare gold from as early as the 5th century, a fine addition to a fine collection of Sweden's past.

KAKNÄSTÅRNET ★ , north of Djurgården. The television/radio tower at some 150 meters (500 feet) is Stockholm's tallest building. The best view in and of the city, with a restaurant at the top.

KUNGLIGA SLOTTET (560 B2) ★ , the Royal Palace in Gamla Stan, was built in 1697–1754. Art collections, tapestries and marble statuary occupy the 608 rooms. The king's silver throne is in the Hall of State, and the Swedish Crown Jewels are in the Treasury. A summer highlight is the daily Changing of the Guard.

NORDISKA MUSEET (Nordic Museum) (560 C3), on Djurgården, depicts folk art and daily life in Scandinavia since 1500. It also houses the Royal Armory.

ROSENDALS SLOTT, on Djurgården, was built in the 1820s as a royal summer residence. The original interiors are well preserved.

SKANSEN ★ , on Djurgården, is one of the world's oldest open-air museums. About 150 buildings date from several periods; the grounds comprize a zoo, parks and gardens.

STRINDBERGMUSEET, Drottninggatan 85, is the house where the dramatist August Strindberg lived from 1908 until his death in 1912. Exhibits chronicle his life.

ULRIKSDAL CASTLE ★ , Solna, was used by King Gustav VI Adolf and Queen Louise (the parents of the present King) from 1923–73. Their apartments are preserved, along with earlier rooms, all with beautiful antiques. The park has a splendid 17th-century conservatory.

VASAMUSEET (560 C2) ★ , Djurgården, houses the restored 17th-century warship *Vasa*. At the time the world's largest warship, the 70-meter (226-foot) *Vasa* sank in the Stockholm harbor on her maiden voyage in 1628. She was recovered in 1961 and has now been carefully restored to her original condition.

SWEDEN

ABISKO (555 B5) ★
LAPPLAND

Abisko is a well-known resort on Lake Torneträsk, a narrow body of water that extends almost to the Norwegian border. Abisko's location at the entrance to Abisko National Park and at the start of the 394-kilometer (245-mile) Royal Trail (Kungsleden), makes it a popular destination for hikers, campers, skiers and summer boat trips and watersports.

BJÖRKLIDEN, some 7 kilometers (5 miles) north of Abisko, has the highest-altitude mountain station in Sweden, at some 1,200 meters (4,000 feet). Here, they ski all year, and sunbathe in summer, when the lower snow-free slopes are covered with rare and beautiful plants.

ÅRE (555 A3)
JÄMTLAND *pop. 9,900*

The Jämtland village of Åre, one of Sweden's top ski resorts, lies at the foot of 1,350-meter (4,429-foot) Mount Åre in a lush valley of the same name.

BORGHOLM (555 A1) ★
ÖLAND *pop. 11,600*

Borgholm plays a dual role as the chief city of Öland Island and as a popular summer resort. Its temperate climate and excellent bathing facilities attract visitors. Places of interest include Solliden, a summer residence of the Swedish royal family. Built in 1906, it has Italian gardens and is open daily.

Windmills, a variety of plant life and many species of visiting birds characterize Öland Island. There are 16 primitive forts, including the ruins of one at Gråborg that has walls 8 meters (26 feet) high and dates from 500 AD. Several Viking burial grounds are on the island, and there are Stone Age tombs at Resmo and Bronze Age burial mounds at Mysinge Hog. The Trollskogen, or Enchanted Forest, is a thick pine grove that is threaded by pleasant hiking trails.

BORGHOLM SLOTTET, overlooking Borgholm, originated as a medieval stronghold and was rebuilt as a Renaissance palace in the 16th century. Though ravaged by fire in 1806, Borgholm remains the biggest and most imposing ruined fortress in Sweden.

EKETORP is a re-created fortified village of the type built by the early people whose graves remain nearby. With huts and buildings, it shows the lifestyle this bustling community would have enjoyed from 300 to 1300 AD.

▲ ESKILSTUNA (555 A2)
SÖDERMANLAND *pop. 89,500*

Industrial Eskilstuna is noted for its modern architecture and scenic location. Places of interest include Stora Sunby Slottet, the only Norman fortress in Sweden, and People's Park, which has the country's second largest zoo.

The Rademacher Smithy has well-preserved forges; the quality of Eskilstuna knives, scissors, and measuring tools is widely respected.

FALKÖPING (555 A2)
VÄSTERGÖTLAND *pop. 31,900*

Falköping is an excursion center for Västergötland. Contrasting with the region's modern farms are remarkable runic stones, old churches and graves dating from the Stone Age.

▲ FALUN (555 A2) ★
DALARNA *pop. 54,600*

Falun, capital of Dalarna, is noted for its copper mine. Established in the 13th century by the Stora Kopparbergs Bergslag Co., the mine helped Sweden to attain military superiority in northern Europe in the 16th and 17th centuries by providing copper for cannonballs. Visitors can descend the 50-meter (160-foot) elevator shaft and take a guided tour.

CARL LARSSON'S HOME at Sundborn, some 10 kilometers (6 miles) from Falun, commemorates a famous Dalarna painter, who specialized in domestic scenes. Here you can see the interiors he used as his inspiration much as they were in the 19th century. There are also tours of Sundborn Kyrka and the parsonage which have Larsson collections.

▲ GÖTEBORG (555 A2) ★
GÖTEBORGS OCH BOHUSLÄN
pop. 483,400

Göteborg, or Gothenburg, is Sweden's second largest city. Situated on the Göta River its busy harbor, one of the principal sights, can be explored by boat.

Tree-lined streets and parks add to Gothenburg's charm. Slottsskogen, a forested area, has a deer park, open-air museum, biological museum and playgrounds. The green Allé extends more than a mile beyond the city moat.

Gothenburg was founded in 1621 by the warrior king, Gustav II Adolf. His statue stands in the square that bears his name, Gustav Adolf Torg. The Old Town surrounding the square is a delightful section with Dutch-built canals and old buildings. Points of interest include the garrison overlooking the harbor, the town hall, cathedral, Kristine Kyrka, and warehouses of the Swedish East India Company.

Good theaters, concert halls, museums, restaurants and shops dot the city. The Götaplatsen, a square, is the cultural heart of the city, with the City Theater, Concert Hall and Art Gallery. Gothenburg's main thoroughfare for shopping is Kungsportsavenyen, known simply as Avenyn.

Visitors can fish, boat, sail and play tennis and golf in Gothenburg. Excursions depart for the numerous offshore islands, including the resort of Marstrand, noted for its medieval fortress and annual regatta. Comfortable steamers ply wide lakes past areas noted for their scenic beauty.

Gothenburg offers tourists *Göteborgskortet*, a special discount card that gives free travel on buses and trams, free parking and sightseeing tours, a free boat tour to Denmark and admission to museums, nightspots and other attractions. It includes discounts at car rental agencies, hotels and restaurants. Valid from 12–36 hours, *Göteborgskortet* can be purchased at the tourist information office at Kungsportsplatsen 2.

KONST MUSEET, on Götaplatsen, has collections of works by old masters, French Impressionists and modern artists, with particular emphasis on Scandinavian artists of the Nordic Light period at the turn-of-the-century, who gathered at Skagen in northern Denmark.

KRONHUSET, Kronhusgt 1, dates from 1650 and is the city's oldest building. Once an arsenal, it is now an historical museum and has exhibits on the development of the area since ancient times. Beside Kronhuset, two large buildings were once artillery workshops, and are now Kronhusbodarna, shops and workshops which demonstrate and sell craftware and delicious old-fashioned cakes and spice buns.

LISEBERG is one of Sweden's biggest and best outdoor amusement parks, dating back to 1923 and the Gothenburg Exhibition.

THE GÖTA CANAL

Every Swede's dream is to travel the Göta Canal, four to five days on one of the elegant old 19th-century canal boats that glide slowly along a waterway linking Gothenburg and Stockholm.

The original purpose of this engineering miracle through several lakes including Lake Mälaren and the Great Lakes, Vänern and Vättern, was to carry timber, iron and other products to the growing industries along its banks.

Today the boats take Swedish and foreign passengers on a peaceful, relaxing trip with time to stop at an interesting church or enjoy a meal at one of the many *Herrgård* (manor houses) dotted throughout these long-inhabited areas.

TRÄDGÅRDSFÖRENINGEN has beautiful formal gardens, with fine statues by Scandinavian sculptors, an elegant Palm House dating from 1878, as well as Water, Camellia, and Mediterranean Houses.

GRÄNNA (555 A2)
SMÅLAND *pop. 3,800*
Gränna is a popular vacation center in the orchard district on the eastern shores of Lake Vättern. In late May or early June, the Hot Air Balloon Rally draws participants from around the world.

▲ HALMSTAD (555 A1)
HALLAND *pop. 81,000*
Capital of fertile Halland, Halmstad was a meeting place for Danish and Swedish leaders when the two countries were united. Older sections of the city still maintain a distinctly Danish air. The 16th-century Halmstad Slottet now serves as the governor's residence. Norreport, or North Gate, is a fortification dating from 1605. Hallandsgården, an open-air museum, and 14th-century Halmstad Kyrka are both worth visiting.

▲ HELSINGBORG (555 A1)
SKÅNE *pop. 110,800*
Helsingborg, on the Oresund, is a picturesque seaport founded in 1085. The Kärnan, an 11th-century tower-fortress, provides a view of the channel and the Danish coast beyond. Kulla-Gunnarstorp is an old chateau, and Krapperup was the castle residence of the Gyllenstierna family, the Guildensterns of *Hamlet*.

▲ JÖNKÖPING (555 A2)
SMÅLAND *pop. 112,800*
Jönköping is on the southern edge of Lake Vättern. A match museum is on the site of a 19th-century factory where the first safety match was made and struck.

The Christine Kyrka dates from 1673; the town hall, built in the 17th century, contains the Museum of the Småland Archeological Society, which displays religious art treasures. Habo Kyrka, a gabled wooden church built in 1680, has an attractive painted interior.

STADSPARKEN is an extensive nature reserve rivalling Skansen Park in Stockholm.

KALMAR (555 A1)
SMÅLAND *pop. 56,800*
The site of the Union of Kalmar, an agreement uniting Sweden, Denmark and Norway in 1397, Kalmar is the ancient key to Sweden. In medieval times, whoever controlled this fortress ruled Sweden. Today it is one of the country's most popular tourist resorts.

The older sections of the city occupy an island and contain remnants of the ancient city walls, several parks and a 17th-century cathedral. The cathedral is in Kvarnholmen, the oldest part of town. Excursions can be made to nearby Öland Island (*see Borgholm on p.562*) and to the internationally known glassworks at Strömsbergshyttan, Orrefors and Kosta.

KALMAR SLOTT, one of Sweden's outstanding Renaissance castles, was begun in the 12th century. Kalmar has lavish courts, a rococo chapel, a dark dungeon, medieval battlements, round towers and a surrounding moat. The museum's most important exhibit is the remains of the *Kronan*, a warship sunk here in 1676 by a Danish-Dutch fleet. Discovered in 1980, divers still bring up new treasures showing life on a 17th-century vessel.

KARLSKRONA (555 A1)
BLEKINGE *pop. 59,300*
Karlskrona, Sweden's principal naval base, occupies a series of islands. Impressive buildings line its wide streets, and include Varvsmuseet, or Shipyard Museum, formerly a sailor's barracks, and Holy Trinity Church. There is also an evocative emigrants' monument, *Karl-Oskar och Kristina*, in memory of the many who left Sweden.

KIRUNA (555 B5)
LAPPLAND *pop. 26,200*
In terms of land area, Kiruna is one of the largest cities in the world. Its city limits encompass 5,000 square kilo-

meters (1,931 square miles) of the richest iron ore region in the world; two huge mines, Kirunavaara and Luossavaara; and countless reindeer herds. About 160 kilometers (100 miles) north of the Arctic Circle, Kiruna is in the Land of the Midnight Sun, where constant daylight reigns from the end of May to mid-July. The city proper is a small mining and market center.

Despite its northern location, Kiruna has a mild climate suitable for boating, hiking, fishing, skiing and climbing in season. Of special interest is Kiruna Kyrka, built like a Lapp hut. Excursions can be made into the countryside, where the nomadic Lapps still live much as they did centuries ago.

▲ LINKÖPING (555 A2)
ÖSTERGÖTLAND pop. 126,300

Inhabited since the Bronze Age, Linköping is the capital of Östergötland province. It is one of Sweden's foremost literary and religious centers, as well as home to Saab and Svenska industries.

The Romanesque and Gothic cathedral, built in the 13th century, dominates the city. Places of interest are the Provincial and City Museum, which displays modern architectural techniques; the Church of St. Lars, which has several paintings by the Swedish peasant artist Pehr Hoerberg; and the 1734 Lutheran bishop's palace.

LUND (555 A1) ★
SKÅNE pop. 92,000

Historic Lund was founded in 1035 by King Knut (Canute) of Denmark and England. In 1103, it became the seat of the archbishop of all Scandinavia. Soon after, the city flourished as a major religious center and, briefly, as the capital of Denmark. Sweden permanently incorporated the city in 1658.

Today Lund is a growing industrial city and the cultural and intellectual center of southern Sweden. On April 30th, Walpurgis Eve, students stage a colorful procession and engage in boisterous merrymaking.

City attractions include the Museum of Cultural History. The castle of Trollenäs, near Eslövis, is easily reached from Lund, as is the village of Dalby.

DOMKYRKAN, a 12th-century Romanesque structure, is considered one of the most beautiful cathedrals in Sweden. Its huge clock, dating from 1380, records the position of the stars and accompanies moving wooden figures with a Bach hymn every day at noon and 3pm.

▲ MALMÖ (555 A1) ★
SKÅNE pop. 236,600

The major port and industrial center of Malmö has preserved many of its old buildings. The town hall dates from the 16th century; the governor's residence dates from the 18th century. Gothic St. Peter's Church has superb ceiling paintings and an intricate, working clock. The Malmö Museum is on Malmöhus Slottet.

ALLEMANSRÄTT

Allemansrätt (Everyone's Right) is an ancient right in Sweden (and other Nordic countries). It means that you can walk, ski or ride anywhere and not be turned back by a landowner, and can pick any wild berries, mushrooms and flowers that are not protected species. You can swim, sail, moor a boat and go ashore anywhere except close to a house or on land in a prohibited (usually military) area.

The other side of all this liberty is that everyone must be sensible. It is not O.K. to walk over a garden, nor to disturb or destroy anything, fires must be controlled and camping close to a house is not welcomed. A single, discreet tent for one night is fine, but people using groups of tents, or staying for a long time should ask first. Driving off-road is not acceptable, but is a small price to pay for this generous *Allemansrätt*.

Tourists can buy *Malmökortet*, a card that entitles the bearer to free bus rides and parking in the city, as well as discounts on rail travel and sightseeing tours. The card also provides free admission to museums, nightspots and other attractions. Valid from 12–36 hours, it can be bought at the Malmö Tourist Office at Skeppsbron 2 and hotels in Malmö.

Skåne is Sweden's chateau country and can easily be explored from Malmö. Many of the 250 *Herrgård* (manor houses) and castles, are open to the public, as hotels, or for concerts, or as museums.

MORA (555 A3)
DALARNA *pop. 20,900*
Mora, on Lake Siljan, has memorials to early 20th-century artist Anders Zorn

---

THE SWEDISH SKÅL

The Swedes, other Scandinavians tell you, are very formal indeed, and their attitude to the drinking toast, the *skål*, sums it up. At a dinner party it is not acceptable. to pick up your glass as it is filled to take a gulp. Swedes expect to wait until the host (usually) or hostess raises his or her glass and says: *Välkommen och skål* (Welcome and skål). Then comes the difficult bit because the idea is to catch everyone's eye in turn, and to *skål* before the first sip. Later, various guests will propose toasts and everyone goes through the communal *skål* again. One person may also later raise a glass to another, and make a more private *skål*.
One thing not to forget is that no one should *skål* the hostess for the first hour. This is because she is supposed to be organizing the next course! Remember that this is informality! – a formal occasion is even stricter about where and when to *skål*!

---

and King Gustav Vasa. The house where Zorn was born still stands; the Zorn Museum contains some of his works.

The Vasaloppet is a skiing event held annually to honor King Gustav Vasa. In 1521, the town's inhabitants rejected the future king's leadership but, after changing their minds, sent two skiers to halt his flight to Norway. Now skiers from all over the world come to Mora, usually on the first Sunday in March, to race across the 85-kilometer (53-mile) route traversed by those messengers nearly 500 years ago.

▲ NORRKÖPING (555 A2)
ÖSTERGÖTLAND *pop. 120,700*
Sweden's foremost textile-manufacturing city, Norrköping has several attractive parks by the Motala River. Gamla Torget, or old square, has some quaint old houses, but the city is noted principally as an excursion center.

OSTERSUND (555 A3)
JAMTLAND *pop. 59,000*
A commercial and industrial center, Östersund is on a hill overlooking the island of Frösön in Lake Storsjön. The Jämtli is an open air museum that has displays of cultural and historical interest.

RÄTTVIK (555 A3) ★
DALARNA *pop. 11,400*
One of Sweden's resorts, Rättvik, is on Lake Siljan. The town has a 14th-century church and is the site of events. Curling competitions are held in February, and handicrafts exhibited in July. Folk and dance festivals are presented.

Excursions can be made to the Vidalbick Observation Tower at Lerdalshöjden, and to Nittsjö pottery works.

SKARA (555 A2)
VÄSTERGÖTLAND *pop. 13,700*
Important as a religious center in the Middle Ages, Skara has preserved its 14th-century cathedral, a Gothic masterpiece. The Västergötland Museum and the open-air museum together present a picture of regional history.

▲ UMEÅ (555 B3)
VÄSTERBOTTEN *pop. 94,900*
A thriving industrial and commercial port
on the Umeälv River, the university town
of Umea is known for its wooden goods.
North east are the restored buildings of
the Gammlia Open Air Museum. There
is a skiing museum in Lars Fägrares
Gård. Umeå also has Västerbotten
county's main Sami Museum.

▲ UPPSALA (555 B2) ★
UPPLAND *pop. 174,500*
The name Uppsala has long been
synonymous with learning: one of
Europe's outstanding educational centers, the University of Uppsala, was
founded in 1477.

GAMLA UPPSALA (Old Uppsala) is 4 kilometers (2½ miles) to the north and is the
former Swedish Viking capital. The
Tingshögen served as the court mound
where medieval laws were made and
administered. Viking kings were also
chosen at this site, and three are buried
nearby in mounds known as the
"Pyramids of Scandinavia."

LINNETRÄDGÅRDEN contains the townhouse, the grounds and the botanical
gardens of Carolus Linnaeus, the father
of modern botany. Many of his possessions are on exhibit. Hammerby, just
south east of Uppsala center, was the
great botanist's summer home, a charming 18th-century building, half manor/
half farm. The small botanic garden
delights gardeners.

UPPSALA UNIVERSITET has educated
many prominent persons, including
Carolus Linnaeus. A good time to visit
the university is April 30, Walpurgis
Eve, when Uppsala is host to Sweden's
traditional student festival. The library,
Carolina Rediviva, has an outstanding
collection. Its greatest treasure is the
Codex Argentus, the "Silver Bible."
Dating from 500 AD, this is the earliest
work extant in ancient Gothic, an
Eastern Germanic language.

▲ VÄSTERÅS (555 A2)
VÄSTMANLAND *pop. 120,800*
An old town on Lake Mälaven, Västerås
became industrialized early in the 20th
century and now mainly manufactures
electrical goods. Elements of the past
persist, however, in the 13th-century
cathedral, which contains Belgian and
German 15th- and 16th-century decorations, and the 13th-century castle, which
has a museum of local history.

▲ VÄXJÖ (555 A1) ★
SMÅLAND *pop. 70,700*
Växjö is an ancient religious settlement
that has evolved into an important
industrial and educational center. The
restored cathedral dates from the 12th
century, and the Utvandrarnas Hus, or
Emigrant's House, documents the 19th-
century exodus of thousands of citizens
to the United States. The Småland
Museum includes an exhibit on the local
glass-blowing trade. Växjö lies at the
eastern limit of Småland's "Kingdom of
Glass," the area between here and
Kalmar, which has 16 of Sweden's most
famous glassworks. They show glass-
blowing and have museums and shops.

VISBY (555 B1)
GOTLAND *pop. 21,300*
Visby, on Gotland Island, is one of
Sweden's outstanding tourist attractions.
Dating from about 2000 BC, Visby
reached prominence in medieval times
when it joined the Hanseatic League, a
confederation of merchants in northern
Europe. By the 13th century, the city
was a powerful commercial center, minted its own coins and had a code of law.

The principal attractions in Visby are
its medieval fortifications. The city is
surrounded on three sides by a 13th-
century stone wall 3 kilometers (2 miles)
long. This has 38 towers, including the
12th-century Kruttornet which overlooks
the harbor. Various ruined medieval
churches also remain, and the Church of
St. Maria, which served the German
merchant community in the city's heyday, is still in use for worship.

SPAIN

THE SPANIARDS ARE A JUSTIFIABLY PROUD PEOPLE, OCCUPIERS OF A COUNTRY WHICH HAS ABSORBED MANY INFLUENCES, YET HAS ALWAYS RETAINED A STRONG SENSE OF ITS OWN IDENTITY. FRINGED BY GOLDEN BEACHES, IT HAS AN INTERIOR WITH MOUNTAIN RANGES AS GRAND AS THEIR NAMES ARE DRAMATIC.

A VISIT SHOULD NOT BE CONFINED TO THE COAST AND THE CAPITAL, MADRID. SEVILLE HAS THE ALCÁZAR PALACE, BUILT BY THE MOORS IN 1181, WHILE THE MOSQUE IN CÓRDOBA DATES BACK TO THE 8TH CENTURY. GRANADA HAS THE INCOMPARABLE ALHAMBRA PALACE, AND NEARBY THE MOUNTAINS OF THE SIERRA NEVADA. BARCELONA AND MADRID ALSO VIE FOR ATTENTION. BARCELONA, FOUNDED IN THE 3RD CENTURY BC, IS THE CENTER OF CATALAN CULTURE AND HOSTED THE 1992 OLYMPIC GAMES. MADRID IS A CITY OF BOULEVARDS AND PLAZAS, AND IS HOME TO THE PRADO MUSEUM.

Left GAUDI'S CASA BATLLÓ, IN BARCELONA, HAS AN AMAZING ROOFLINE
Above left A TYPICAL ICON, AT THE IGLESIA SAN SEBASTIAN IN ESTELPA
Above right THIS BULL IS ADVERTIZING SHERRY, SPAIN'S FAMOUS EXPORT

Things to Know

- **Area:** 504,781 square kilometers (194,896 square miles)
- **Population:** 40,358,400
- **Capital:** Madrid
- **Languages:** Spanish, Basque, Catalan and Galician.
- **Economy:** Industry, mining, tourism, agriculture, forestry. Machinery, chemicals, steel, textiles, shoes, shipbuilding; coal and iron; potatoes, cattle, wine. Tourism is important.
- **Passport Requirements:** Required for U.S. citizens.
- **Visa Requirements:** Not required for stays up to 90 days
- **Duty Free Items:** 200 cigarettes, 50 cigars or 250 grams of tobacco (for non-European visitors: 400 cigarettes, 200 cigarillos, 100 cigars) however, if on the way to Spain a stopover of more than 24 hours is made in any European country, the duty free allowance of cigarettes, tobacco and distilled liquor is reduced; 2 liters of wine and 1 liter of alcohol over 22 proof or 2 liters up to 22 proof; 50 grams of perfume; ¼ liter of toilet water; one still camera with 10 rolls of film; and one video camera; personal jewelry; portable tape recorder; sports equipment. See also *The European Union* on p.5.
- **Currency:** The unit of currency is the Spanish *peseta* (P.T.S.). Due to currency fluctuations, the exchange rate is subject to frequent change. There is no limit on the import of foreign currency, but the amount exported cannot exceed the amount imported. There is no limit on the import of pesetas, but amounts exceeding 1,000,000 pesetas must be declared on entry. No more than 1,000,000 pesetas may be exported.
- **Bank Opening Hours:** 8:30am–2pm Monday–Friday, closed Saturday June–September; 8:30am–2:30pm Monday–Thursday, 8:30am–2pm Friday, 8:30am–1pm Saturday for the rest of the year.
- **Store Opening Hours:** 9:30am–1:30pm and 3:30 or 4:30–8:30pm Monday–Friday, 9am–1pm Saturday.

History

The Moorish reign, which began in the 8th century, left a pronounced mark on Spain. The Moors built cities, libraries and universities that were the intellectual showpieces of Europe.

By the late 13th century the Moslem government had been overthrown by Christian forces. The 1469 marriage of Ferdinand II of Aragon and Isabella of Castile, the "Catholic Kings," united the Christian kingdoms. Granada, the last Moslem kingdom, was captured in 1492 – the same year the "Catholic Kings" sponsored Christopher Columbus' departure for the New World.

The riches that the New World brought made Spain the greatest European power of the next century. However, decline followed and Spain suffered from costly wars and poor government.

In 1808 France's Napoléon Bonaparte gained control of Spain and appointed his brother Joseph king but, with British and Portuguese help, France was expelled in the subsequent War of Independence of 1808–13. An internal struggle for the throne followed, and the ensuing Carlist Wars ended with the return of the Bourbons in 1876.

By the 1930s, Spanish life and politics were deeply polarized. The February 1936 election of a coalition led by the left touched off a military coup organized by conservatives and the army. From this developed the Spanish Civil War, of 1936–9. The Nationalists, the rebels, were commanded by General Franco and had help from Fascist Italy and Nazi Germany. The Republicans accepted aid from the Soviet Union as well as volunteers from other countries. The Nationalists won the bitter struggle.

Franco was now the leader of a nation impoverished and embittered by a long, costly war. Franco remained neutral during World War II, but did send some military assistance to Hitler. After Franco's death in 1975, Spain became a monarchy again and King Juan Carlos I was sworn in.

Democratic governments since then have maintained Spain's membership of NATO and brought Spain into the European Union.

FOOD AND DRINK
Spanish cuisine might be a surprise. With menus as varied as those in France and Italy, meals are usually substantial and as inexpensive as anywhere in Western Europe.

There are several regional specialties: the north is noted for sauces, the Castilian Plateau for roasts and the south east for rice dishes. A national fondness for seafood means shrimp, clam, crawfish and crab are available everywhere.

Gazpacho, a cold soup of tomato, seasoned with garlic, has become internationally celebrated. *Paella*, especially good in Valencia, is a casserole of rice, saffron, peas and pimiento, with seafood and chicken added.
Tortilla Española, an omelette as only the Spanish make it, is a combination of eggs, potatoes and onions. Fruit-flavored *Sangriá* and other wines are commonly served; beer is also popular. Sherry (*jerez*) is available in a wide range of flavors and degrees of sweetness.

Lunch is served from 1:30pm onwards, but 3pm is the most popular time. Dinner in a restaurant hardly ever begins before 9:30pm, except in the state-owned *paradores*, where it is served from 8:30 to 11pm.
Hosterias, state-operated restaurants, serve regional specialties. *Tapas*, substantial snacks often of seafood or meat, are available at most cafés.

SPORTS AND RECREATION
A *corrida*, or bullfight, is neither a fight nor a sport. It is rather an artistic pageant and drama. Bullfighting was first known

on the island of Crete 4,000 years ago. Since the 18th century bullfighting in Spain has been a profession, but only recently has the pay compensated for the risks. The season is from Easter through October. Bullfights are held in Madrid on Sundays, holidays and many Saturdays. The summer festivals of smaller towns offer other chances to see this spectacle.

Bullfights are an integral part of Spain's heritage. Some people find these spectacles inhumane, so the option to attend should be a strictly personal decision. If you don't wish to attend a bullfight, but would like to enjoy some of the color and excitement of the event, the *apartado* is an alternative. During the *apartado* the animals are selected by emissaries of the matadors. This ritual enables spectators to view the proceedings from the lower tiers of the ring without having to witness the outcome of the fight.

Spaniards are enthusiastic about soccer, and on Sundays from October to May stadiums all over the country overflow with shouting fans. Madrid's racetrack, the Zarzuela, has horse racing in the spring and fall; Seville's Pineda course, from April through September.

There are numerous golf courses in Spain, many of outstanding quality. Tennis and swimming are available in all the large cities and resorts, and Spain has many opportunities for sailing and other watersports. Hunting and fishing opportunities are among the best in Europe. Some 607,000 hectares (1½ million acres) have been set aside as national and game preserves. Climbing and hunting are excellent in the Picos de Europa Mountains near Santander. Best skiing is in the Pyrenées, the most known Baquiera-Beret, Formigal, Candanchu, Cerler and Sierra Nevada.

GETTING AROUND
Travelers in Spain have their choice of transportation. The government-owned rail network RENFE, which covers the

These times may vary according to the season.

- **BEST BUYS:** Jewelry, woodcarvings, Toledo ware. Talavera porcelains, *mantillas*, linens, gloves, lace, leather goods, perfume, all types of pottery and glassware.
- **PUBLIC HOLIDAYS:** January 1; Epiphany, January 6; St. Joseph's Day, March 19; Maundy Thursday; Good Friday; Easter Monday; May 1; Ascension Day; Corpus Christi; St. James, July 25; Assumption Day, August 15; *Día de la Hispanidad*, October 12; All Saints' Day, November 1; Constitution Day, December 6; Immaculate Conception, December 8; December 25.

Many attractions and places of interest are closed on major religious holidays.

- **USEFUL TELEPHONE NUMBERS:**
Police: 091
Ambulance: 329 7766 Fire: 080
- **NATIONAL TOURIST OFFICES:**
National Tourist Office of Spain
665 Fifth Avenue
New York, NY 10022
Tel: 212/759 8822
Fax: 212/980 1053
Spanish Tourist Office
8383 Wilshire Boulevard, Suite 960
Beverley Hills
CA 90211
Los Angeles
Tel: 213/658 7192
Fax: 213/658 1061
Tourist Office of Spain
1221 Brickell Avenue
Miami, Florida 33131
Tel: 305/358 1992
Fax: 305/358 8223
Spanish TouristOffice
57–58 St. James's Street
London SW1A 1LD
Tel: 0171 499 1169/0901
Fax: 0171 629 4257
- **AMERICAN EMBASSY:**
Serrano 75
Madrid
Tel: 341 577 4000 (3491 outside Madrid)
Fax: 341 577 5735

AUTOMOBILE CLUB
Real Automóvil Club de España
(Royal Automobile Club of Spain), 10 José Abascal, Madrid, has branch offices in various cities throughout Spain. The symbol ▲ beside a city name indicates the presence of an AAA-affiliated automobile club branch. Not all auto clubs offer full travel services to AAA members.

---

entire country, is efficient and inexpensive. Several bus lines have moderately priced package tours and the airline Iberia links the major cities.

The best roads in Spain are the *autopistas*, limited-access dual highways, which are designated by the letter "A" followed by a number. Aside from a few toll-free stretches around Barcelona and Madrid, tolls are charged.

The other dependable thoroughfares are the *nacional* roads that are designated with an "N." Generally in good condition, these two-lane highways are wide, have hard shoulders and are constantly being improved. Roads other than these are designated "C" for *comarcal*, or regional, are usually narrow and not quite as well-maintained.

Speed limits are 50 k.p.h. (30 m.p.h.) in town, 90–100 k.p.h. (55–60 m.p.h.) on out-of-town roads and 120 k.p.h. (75 m.p.h.) on the *autopista*.

Seat belt use is mandatory for all passengers while traveling outside urban areas and on such roads as the M30 in Madrid. A child under 12 may not occupy a front seat unless using a suitable restraint system.

Visiting motorists are required to pay fines for violations on the spot with Spanish pesetas. An International Driving Permit is required. Insurance cover should include a Bail Bond.

ACCOMMODATIONS

Hotels in Spain are graded from one to five-star with five stars being the highest rating. Classifications are posted on signs outside each establishment. As pilgrims to Santiago de Compostela during the Middle Ages found the road lined with priories and hospices, today's visitors to Spain can find accommodations and refreshments through the nationwide network of *paradores*. Some of these state-operated hotels are housed in beautifully restored castles, palaces and convents. Privately-owned country inns and hotels are usually simple, but serve three meals a day. Spas and health resorts normally have accommodations for travelers. Youth hostels give priority to those under 26.

Of Spain's 700 campgrounds, over 100 are on the Costa Brava. They are ranked in four categories. For information contact Federación Española de Empresarios de Campings y C.V., San Bernardo 97–99, Edificio Colomina, E-28015 Madrid; or the National Tourist Office of Spain. An international camping carnet is advised but not compulsory, however, some campgrounds may give a reduced rate if you have one.

TIPPING

Hotels and restaurants in Spain add a 15 percent service charge to their bills, but service personnel expect an additional 5–10 percent. Tip taxi drivers 5 percent of the fare, porters 50 pesetas and housekeepers about 65 pesetas per day.

PRINCIPAL TOURING AREAS

Note: For descriptions of cities in bold type, see individual city listings.

ANDALUSIA

The region stretching from the Portuguese border almost to Cartagena and inland past Córdoba was the seat of Moorish power, and later the launching site for voyages in the Age of Discovery.

From Portugal to the Strait of Gibraltar is a land of sandy beaches, sunny skies, pine forests and olive groves: the Costa de la Luz. From the strait to Almería lies the Costa del Sol, site of the long, narrow, flower-bedecked streets of ancient Cádiz. The beaches in the provinces of Cádiz and Málaga are low and sandy; those close to Granada are more rugged. The country's major resorts are west of Málaga and include Torremolinos, Marbella, and Fuengirola. A cliff-hugging highway runs east from Málaga through the banana groves surrounding Almuñécar to the rugged mountains at Almería. Mostly ignored by the tourist crowds, this coast abounds with lush gardens and terraced fields, solitary coves and clean beaches.

From the coast, the land rises to the southern edge of Spain's vast and arid central plateau. Here is Granada, once the heart of Moorish Spain and retaining the sumptuous architecture epitomized by the famed Alhambra. Sevilla, or Seville, has a centuries-old blend of architectural styles. Córdoba, the cathedral city of Jaén and the old bridge of Ronda are all historic sites with much to offer the visitor.

MURCIA AND VALENCIA

Extending along the eastern coast roughly from Cartagena to Castellón de la Plana is the historic "Levante," where the Phoenicians landed long ago to trade for minerals dug by Iberians and Celts.

From Cartagena to just south of Valencia, the Costa Blanca offers an interesting mixture of beaches, mountains and farmland. The land near Cartagena is fairly flat, rising to the rugged mountains near Alicante.

Inland is Murcia. Arabic words strongly color the local dialect, and the architecture hints of the town's 8th-century Moorish origin. Alicante harks back to the Carthaginian colony of the 3rd century BC through the Oriental flavor of the palm trees that line its waterfront.

SPAIN

The Costa del Azahar, stretching from **Valencia** to Castellón de la Plana, takes its name from the orange blossoms that scent the air. A continuous mountain chain stands guard close to the waters of this area. The great seaport of Valencia contains many fine old buildings and claims possession of the Holy Grail.

CATALONIA

Catalonia, most commercial of Spain's regions, borders France; much of its cuisine compares favorably with that of its neighbor. The celebrated Monastery of **Montserrat** is a highlight, with its spectacular mountian setting and **Girona** is noted for its baroque cathedral; however,

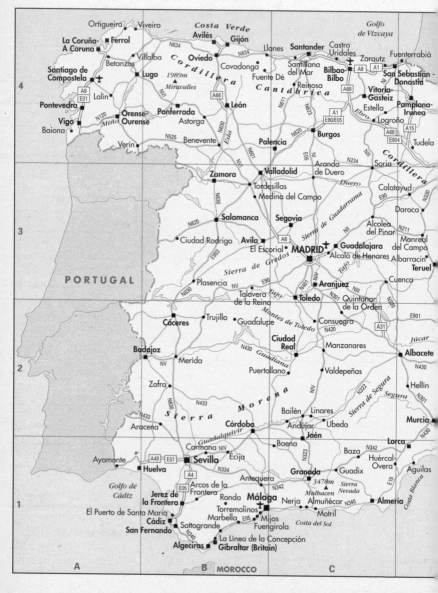

sophisticated **Barcelona**, second largest city in Spain, is the east's greatest pride.

The Costa Brava, or "wild coast," has long been a big tourist attraction with its beautiful inlets and hidden caves. Some of the best opportunities for fun in the sun occur in the resort towns of Bagur,

Blanes, Lloret de Mar, Palamós, Rosas and San Feliú de Guixols.

ARAGON AND NAVARRE

Inland from Catalonia is Aragon and to its west, Navarre. Once an independent kingdom, Aragon was united with Spain in the 15th century. Dominated by its capital **Zaragoza**, this hot, mountainous and largely infertile region stretches from the Pyrenées nearly to **Valencia**.

Dominated by the Pyrenées, Navarre was a Christian stronghold during the Moorish occupation of Spain. The major city is **Pamplona**, the site of the colorful Fiesta de San Fermin, during which bulls run through the city's streets.

THE BASQUE PROVINCES

The Basque region, stretching along the coast from Navarre to just past **Bilbao**, or Bilbo in Basque, is the seat of an ancient culture. The inhabitants of this area are thought to be descendants of the original settlers of the Iberian Peninsula.

Administrative headquarters of the region during the Spanish Civil War, **Bilbao** is an industrial center and excellent departure point for excursions into the adjoining countryside. South east is **Vitoria**, or Gasteiz in Basque, thought by some to resemble an English country village. Small mountain communities that have changed little since Christopher Columbus' voyages to America dot the countryside. **San Sebastián**, or Donostia in Basque, is on the coast 19 kilometers (12 miles) from France. The Cornisa Cantabrica, as Spain's northern coast is known, is characterized in this area by steep forested cliffs and sandy beaches.

CASTILE

Reaching west from the Basque Provinces past Santander and extending south to Andalusia are the Castilian regions, historically divided between **Segovia** and **Madrid** into Old Castile and New Castile. Isolated from outside influences, much of the region has changed little

SPAIN

since the time of Cervantes. Though sun-baked in summer, the area can be bitterly cold in winter. The most popular time to visit is during the spring fiesta season.

In Old Castile are **Burgos**, with its most Spanish of Spanish Gothic cathedrals, and **Valladolid**, home of Cervantes. Visitors can also see **Segovia**, where a Roman aqueduct still carries water, and Logroño, center of a fertile wine-producing region. The cathedrals of Palencia and walls of **Avila** are other highlights of the region.

New Castile is the site of modern **Madrid**, whose principal attraction is the Prado Museum. El Greco's **Toledo**, whose ancient buildings reflect Moorish and Roman influences, is worth an extended visit.

EXTREMADURA AND LEÓN

Between New Castile and the Portuguese border lies Extremadura, a region of lush lowlands and plains dotted with castles. Andalusia is to the south.

Built in the lowlands by the Moors, **Badajoz** reflects the occupation by both Moors and Christians. Although its founding pre-dates the birth of Christ, the palaces, towers and narrow winding streets of **Cáceres** suggest the city's medieval heritage. South is Merída, once the capital of the Roman province of Lusitania, now the site of one of Spain's finest archeological museums and many Roman ruins.

The León region lies inland, north of Extremadura and west of Old Castile. This area contains the many medieval buildings of León and the Romanesque architecture of Zamora. The ancient university, twin cathedrals and unusual Casa de las Conchas of **Salamanca** are also interesting.

GALICIA AND ASTURIAS

Rugged and little-known Galicia and Asturias in northwestern Spain have a wealth of beautiful scenery. Summers on the beaches are cool and pleasant, and there is excellent river fishing.

Galicia, known as the "Ireland of Iberia," is a green and charming region in the country's far northwestern corner. It preserves its Celtic background in culture and such old cities as Ferrol, now the country's main shipbuilding center, as well as **La Coruña**, noted for its Tower of Hercules.

The region's chief attraction is beautiful **Santiago de Compostela**, which, with Jerusalem and Rome, was one of the "sainted cities" of the Middle Ages. The town is at its most colorful during the Feast of St. James in July, but the best time to tour the rest of the area is in May, June, September and October.

Asturias, between Galicia and the tip of Old Castile, still has evidence of the Celtic settlements that pre-dated the Roman occupation. Asturians, who boast of playing the bagpipe centuries before the Scots, relive their ancient origins in colorful costumes and dances on fiesta days. The battlefield of Covadonga, where the struggle of the Christian Reconquest began, is a landmark for Spanish nationalism.

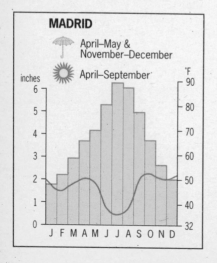

MADRID

April–May & November–December

April–September

inches		°F
6		90
5		80
4		70
3		60
2		50
1		40
0		32

J F M A M J J A S O N D

ISLAS BALEARES AND CANARIAS

The beaches, resorts and scenery of the **Islas Baleares**, or Balearic Islands, in the Mediterranean and the **Islas Canarias**, or Canary Islands, in the Atlantic have long made Spain popular with vacationers.

Off the east coast of Spain, the popular Balearic Islands of **Mallorca, Menorca, Ibiza**, and Formentera and Cabrera, have something for everyone, including unspoiled beaches, picturesque towns, and a mild climate.

Mountainous Mallorca, lively Ibiza, and the more tranquil Menorca are the leading resort areas.

Equally interesting are the volcanic Canaries, rising steeply from the Atlantic off the north-west African coast. There are seven islands in the group; their scenery ranges from lush jungles to stark desert. The cities of **Las Palmas**, on Gran Canaria, and **Santa Cruz**, on Tenerife, are the most frequented vacation spots.

USEFUL EXPRESSIONS IN SPANISH

PRONUNCIATION TIPS

a – as in tar
e – as in let
i – as in marine
o – as in Tom
u – as in rule
b and **v** – similar, like a soft 'b'
c – like 'th' in thin before 'e' or 'i'; otherwise as in cat
g – like 'ch' in loch before 'e' or 'i'; otherwise as in get
j – like 'ch' in loch
ll – like 'lli' in million
ñ – like 'ni' in onion
r – strong and rolled, rr more so
z – like 'th' in thin

hello	hola
good morning	buenos días
good evening	buenas tardes
good night	buenas noches
good-bye	adiós
please/thank you	por favor/gracias
yes/no	sí/no
excuse me	perdón
you're welcome	de nada
I am sorry, I don't speak Spanish	lo siento, pero no hablo español
Does anyone here speak English?	¿Hay alguien aqui que hable inglés?
I do not understand.	No comprendo.
What is the time?	¿Qué hora es?
How much is that?	¿Cuánto cuesta esto?

Where are the restrooms?	¿Dónde están los servicios?
I'd like ...	Quisiera ...
Can you help me, please?	¿Puede usted ayúdeme, por favor?
where/when/how	dónde/cuándo/cómo
open/closed	abierto/cerrado
big/smal	grande/pequeño
Do you take credit cards?	¿Acepta usted tarjetas de crédito?
yesterday/today/ tomorrow	ayer/hoy/ mañana
to the left	a la izquierda
to the right	a la derecha
vacant/occupied	libre/ocupado

DAYS OF THE WEEK

Sunday	domingo
Monday	lunes
Tuesday	martes
Wednesday	miercoles
Thursday	jueves
Friday	viernes
Saturday	sábado

NUMBERS

1	uno	9	nueve
2	dos	10	diez
3	tres	20	veinte
4	cuatro	30	treinta
5	cinco	40	cuarenta
6	seis	50	cincuenta
7	siete	100	cien
8	ocho	1,000	mil

PLACES OF INTEREST

SPAIN

▲ **MADRID** ★ (See map on p.580)
MADRID *pop. 3,108,500*

Although the rest of Spain is rich in ancient history, modern Madrid effectively manages to hide its past. The colorful capital was once a Moorish Fortress, but had become a relatively unknown village before Philip II formally establiŝhed it as the seat of government in 1561.

The older section has narrow streets and picturesque 17th-century buildings. The royal Casa de la Panadería, built in 1672, is one of the oldest edifices on the historic Plaza Mayor.

Many visitors begin their sightseeing at the Puerta del Sol. It is a starting point for the major thoroughfare of the Calle de Alcalá. This street, which contains the Museo d'Academia Real de Bellas Artes des San Fernando, an art and music academy housing works by Murillo and Goya, intersects the Paseo del Prado, which is known for the Prado Museum. Dominating the Calle de Bailén at the west end of town is the Palacio Real, a must on every sightseeing list.

A cultural as well as geographic center, Madrid is noted for the arts. The National Orchestra presents regular concerts at the Royal Theater. Devotees can easily spend at least a day in the nearby Prado, and there are more than 20 other museums in the city. Operettas, top dance groups and musical revues can be seen at the Teatro de la Zarzuela; the Teatro Español produces the best of Spanish classical theater. Nightclubs feature flamenco music and dance.

The bullfighting season in Madrid lasts from Easter to October. Golf is played at 10 courses. Soccer is a favorite diversion; horse racing can be seen at Hippodrome de la Zarzuela (racecourse).

Madrid is an ideal place for shopping: The best shops are on La Gran Vía, Alcalá, Carrera San Jerónimo, Serrano, Sevilla and Peligros. Jewelry, pottery, linens, leather goods, and lace mantillas are possible items. El Rastro, on Ribera de Curtidores, is a former thieves' market offering thousands of second-hand bargains. The market is best on Sunday morning, but bargaining is essential. Try Calle del Prado for antiques.

BIBLIOTECA NACIONAL (National Library) (580 D3), entered from Paseo de Recoletos. contains more than one million volumes, in addition to many early manuscripts.

TAPAS

The popularity of *tapas* bars has spread both within and outside Spain. *Tapar* means to cover, in a general sense, and so *tapas* relates to the time when drinks were covered by a small plate with a snack on top. These days *tapas* are served separately and include a great variety of small dishes, ranging from olives, Spanish ham or omelette slices, to tasty meat or seafood snacks. Madrid is renowned for its lively bars, a number of which are located around the old Plaza Mayor. A round of the *tapas* bars, each with its own character, is a most enjoyable way of spending an evening, either pre- or in lieu of dinner.

CATEDRAL DE SAN ISIDRO (580 C1), on Calle de Toledo near Plaza Mayor, was built 1622–64 by the Jesuits.

MUSEO CERRALBO (580 B3), 17 Ventura Rodríguez, was bequeathed to the state by the Marquis Cerralbo.

Included are paintings by El Greco, José Ribera, Titian and Van Dyck. A collection of arms, china and tapestries is also shown.

MUSEO D'ACADEMIA REAL DE BELLES ARTES DE SAN FERNANDO (580 C2), 13 Alcalá, is in the renovated Palace of Juan de Goyeneche, which dates from 1710. The more than 1,700 paintings and sculptures include works by El Greco, Murillo, Goya and Velázquez.

MUSEO DEL PRADO (580 D2) ★, Paseo del Prado, houses in an 18th-century building one of the most complete and valuable collections of paintings in the world. Its masterpieces include works by Velázquez, Ribera, Murillo, Goya, El Greco, Rubens, Titian, Fra Angelico, Raphael, Correggio, Tintoretto, Van Dyck and other masters. The museum contains classical sculptures as well as coin, enamel, gold and silver collections.

PALACIO DE VILLA HERMOSA, Paseo del Prado 8. Prepared as an extension to the Prado Museum, this former palace houses the private collection of Baron Thyssen-Bornemisza.

PALACIO REAL (Royal Palace) (580 B2), in the Plaza de Oriente, is beautifully decorated and richly furnished. The palace was erected in the 18th century on the site of a 9th-century fortress. There is a grand marble staircase, a scarlet and gold throne room, with an intricate ceiling and 800 valuable tapestries.

EL PARDO is 14 kilometers (9 miles) north west off Highway N4. This extensive, thickly wooded natural park surrounding the village of El Pardo harbors an abundance of large and small game.

Nearby Pardo Palace was built by Carlos V around a royal shooting lodge.

PARQUE DEL RETIRO (580 D2), a 130-hectare (320-acre) park, includes a lake, fountains, and a series of shady walks, carriage drives and bridle paths.

PLAZA COLON (580 D3), including the civic center, has daily tours.

PLAZA MONUMENTAL, Patio de Caballos, is the larger of the city's two bullrings. Bullfights are staged on Sunday and some Thursdays from Easter through October. The Bullfighting Museum on the Plaza de Toros de Ventas contains paintings, engravings and models depicting the history of the *corrida*.

ALCALÁ DE HENARES (574 C3)
MADRID *pop. 142,900*
Alcalá de Henares enjoys a distinguished reputation as the birthplace of Miguel de Cervantes, creator of *Don Quixote*; of Catherine of Aragon, first wife of King Henry VIII of England; and of Ferdinand I, King of Aragon 1412–16. In addition, the University of Madrid, although later transferred to the capital, originated in the Colegio Mayor de San Ildefonso, founded in the late 15th century. The old university buildings have been restored and are still in scholastic use. Of particular interest are the exquisite façade of the Colegio, the Magistral Church and the Archbishop's Palace.

Miguel de Cervantes Saavedra was born in Alcalá de Henares in 1547. He reached fame with his masterpiece *Don Quixote* published in two parts, in 1605 and 1615. Memories of Cervantes survive in the house of his birth and in the baptistry of the Church of Santa María la Mayor, which has his birth certificate.

▲ ALICANTE (574 D2)
ALICANTE *pop. 261,000*
The Carthaginians founded Alicante in 325 BC. The Romans captured the city in 210 BC, and the Moors occupied it 718–1246 AD. Considered the tourist

capital of the Costa Blanca, Alicante is noted for a variety of historical monuments and its mild climate; it is also the commercial port for Madrid. In June the parades from a colorful festival dedicated to San Juan fill the city's streets.

Old and new Alicante meet near the city center. In the newest districts, modern hotels, restaurants and shops line such streets as the Rambla and attractive multi-colored Explanada de España. A number of interesting buildings fill the town's old quarter, including the baroque town hall, the Renaissance cathedral and the 15th- and 16th-century church, Santa María.

SPAIN

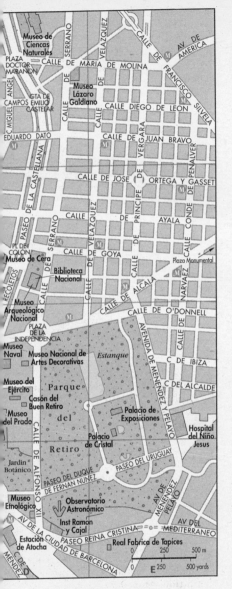

beneath towering mountains. The town is dominated by the impressive Alcazába and the ruins of the old Castillo de San Cristobal, which stands on an adjoining hill. Paseo de Almería is the city's main shopping thoroughfare.

ALCAZÁBA overlooks the city. Built in the 8th century, this Moorish fortress is Almería's most important monument. Of the battlements that surrounded it, only the 15th-century Torre de Homenaje, or Tower of Homage, remains.

CATEDRAL, Plaza de la Catedral, was built 1524–43. Although it has a Renaissance façade, the cathedral is principally Gothic in style. It contains paintings by Cano and Murillo.

▲ AVILA (574 B3)
AVILA pop. 41,700
Surrounded on three sides by mountains, historic Avila maintains its medieval appearance. For centuries this former Roman outpost was the object of a Moorish-Christian struggle, until the construction of its walls in 1090 brought it permanently under Christian control. The completely walled city honors St. Teresa with a church and convent. Other sights are the cathedral and the Church of San Pedro. Nearby are scenic Sierra de Gredos and El Arenal.

CATEDRAL, Plaza de la Catedral, is a church and fortress forming part of the

Alicante lends itself to sports and leisure activities, with tennis courts, a bullring, yachting club and good beaches.

▲ ALMERÍA (574 C1)
ALMERÍA pop. 41,000
Roman harbor, Moorish stronghold and Spanish port, Almería overlooks the sea

SAINT TERESA OF AVILA
Avila is the birthplace of Saint Teresa, who was known for her visions and mystical writings. She became a Carmelite nun when she was 18 and spent some 30 years in the Convent of the Incarnation in Avila, becoming prioress in her later years. In the chapel on the site of her birthplace are writings and relics. Saint Teresa was canonized in 1622.

town's ancient ramparts. Begun in the 12th century, the Romanesque and Gothic structure has an unusual red and yellow stone interior.

REAL MONASTERIO DE SANTO TOMAS, Plaza de Granada, houses the alabaster tomb of Prince John, the only son of Ferdinand and Isabella. Beneath the chapel in the Cloister of Reyes is an unusual museum of Far Eastern art.

THE WALLS, begun in 1090, are the best preserved in Spain. They average 10 meters (33 feet) in height and have a perimeter of 2,535 meters (8,287 feet). Forming a hexagon around the town, they are strengthened by 88 bastions and towers and crowned by embrasures. The sentry path is open.

▲ BADAJOZ (574 B2)
BADAJOZ *pop. 114,400*
Badajoz was founded in the 11th century by the Moors. On the Guadiana River near the border of Portugal, it has continued to be a frontier outpost; even the churches and houses present a fortified appearance. The old quarter is surrounded by medieval walls and can be entered through the 16th-century Puerta de las Palmas, which faces the Puente de las Palmas, an impressive bridge. Inside are narrow streets, broad plazas and parks.

ALCAZÁBA overlooks the city. Badajoz's Moorish rulers established themselves on the summit of Orinaca in the 11th century. Attractions include gardens, the ruins of a medieval castle and the Museo Arqueológico's Roman statues.

BALEARIC ISLANDS – *see p.598.*

▲ BARCELONA (574 E3) ★
BARCELONA *pop. 1,712,350*
A leading Mediterranean seaport, Barcelona is the country's second largest city and its greatest industrial center. Tree-lined boulevards, gardens, fountains, well-designed public buildings and stores lend an air of elegance.

Among the most colorful times to visit are the Eves of St. John and St. Peter's Day, June 23 and 28 respectively, and the Eve of Virgen del Carmen, July 15, when a carnival atmosphere prevails.

Barcelona is the capital of historic Catalonia. It was founded in the 3rd century BC by Hamilcar Barca of Carthage and later ruled by Romans, Visigoths, Moors and Franks. After Catalonia united with Aragon in the Middle Ages, Barcelona became a commercial center.

A feature of Barcelona is the tree-lined Las Rambla, a series of avenues which runs from the Monument a Colom (Columbus Monument) in the harbor to the Plaça de Catalunya. The old Gothic Quarter, Barri Gotic, is a fascinating maze of narrow streets and dark alleys.

CATEDRAL (583 C3), Plaça de la Seu, exemplifies Mediterranean Gothic architecture. Built 1298–1450, this large church has two bell towers and interesting woodcarvings. The Pietà of Archdeacon Desplá is the cathedral's principal treasure.

IGLESIA DE SANT PAU DEL CAMP (583 B2), 101 Calle de San Pablo, is dedicated to St. Paul. One of Barcelona's oldest churches, the early Romanesque structure dates from the 10th century.

IGLESIA MAYOR DE SANTA ANA (583 B2), 3 Calle Rivadeneyra, was built in Romanesque style in the 12th century. Beautiful Gothic arches adorn its 16th-century cloisters.

MONTJUIC (583 B1), a mountain on the south side of Barcelona, overlooks the city as a scenic public park. Still retaining buildings from the 1929 International Exhibition. Montjuic also boasts the Palau Nacional and the Barcelona Fountains, a spectacle of light and water.

MUSEU D'HISTÒRIA DE LA CIUTAT (583 C2), Plaça del Rei, is Barcelona's local history museum. Housed in a 15th-century building, excavations reveal the ancient Roman city.

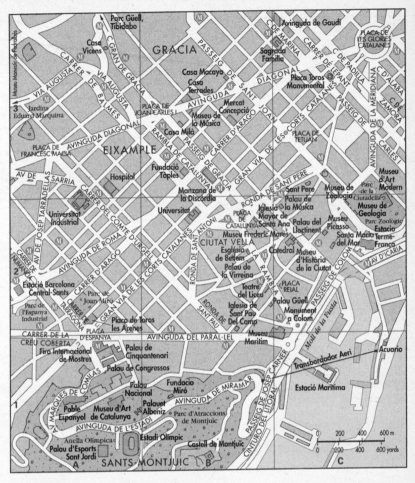

MUSEU PICASSO (583 C2), 15 Calle de Montcada, contains many drawings, paintings and engravings by Spain's most famous modern artist. The museum is housed in the Gothic palaces of Berenguer d'Aguilar and Castellet.

PALAU DE LA VIRREINA (583 B2), 99 Rambla, is an outstanding baroque palace dating from 1776. The palace acts as an exhibition hall, with various exhibitions throughout the year.

PARC GÜELL, at the north end of the Gracia quarter, was commissioned from architect Antonio Gaudí at the turn of

the 20th century and originally planned as a garden city. Lack of money forced the city to abandon the project for many years until it was eventually converted into a public park.

PARC DE LA CIUTADELLA (583 C2), a park laid out in the early 18th century, contains multiple attractions. Museums, monuments and statues, a lovely waterfall, Spain's largest zoo and an attractive baroque church are within its walls.

PLAÇA DE CATALUNYA (583 B2) is the largest and busiest square. Embellished with attractive gardens and impressive

SPAIN

groups of sculptures, it is a good starting point for a walking tour of the city.

POBLE ESPANYOL (Spanish Village) was built for the 1929 World's Fair, held at Montjuic. Working craftsmen, whose wares can be purchased, populate the streets, squares and houses.

TEMPLO EXPIATORIO DE LA SAGRADA FAMILIA (583 C3), at Calle Mallorca and Calle Provenza, is Barcelona's best known and controversial monument. Architect Antonio Gaudí planned three façades in 1891 for his new Barcelona Cathedral, but the innovative Templo Expiatorio, dedicated to the birth of Christ, was the only one completed.

TIBIDABO, just outside the city, is a high mountain affording a view of Barcelona, surrounding villages and the sea. It is the site of an amusement park and a funicular railroad.

TORRE DE COLLSEROL is a modern communications tower built for the 1992 Summer Olympics. A viewing gallery on the 10th level is accessible by a glass elevator departing from within Tibidabo.

BETANZOS (574 A4)
LA CORUÑA *pop. 11,400*
Medieval Betanzos lies in a picturesque region at the confluence of the Mendo and Mandeo Rivers. The narrow old streets are lined with churches; among the most interesting are the Santa María del Azogue and the 14th-century Church of San Francisco.

BILBAO (574 C4)
VIZCAYA *pop. 369,000*
A major industrial center, Bilbao, or Bilbo in Basque, is also a strategic port in the Basque country. Most of the city's attractions are concentrated in the old town along the Nervion River. Along the Siete Calles, or Seven Streets, are Bilbao's older buildings, including the interesting churches of San Antonio, Santos Juanes and San Nicolás.

MUSEO DE BELLAS ARTES consists of two buildings connected by a corridor. The newer building contains more contemporary works. The museum specializes in Spanish and Basque art. Of special note are the works by El Greco, Goya and José Ribera. Renaissance Dutch and Italian artists are also represented.

▲ BURGOS (574 C4)
BURGOS *pop. 156,400*
Burgos is synonymous with the name El Cid. Born just 10 kilometers (6 miles) away in the village of Vivar, this Spanish national hero, whose name means "the lord" in Arabic, spent much of his life in Burgos. From Burgos he embarked on his 11th-century campaign which resulted in remarkable victories over the Moors.

Founded in 884 AD, Burgos was the capital of Castile until the 16th century, when its political prestige was lost to the newly declared capital, Madrid.

A wealth of medieval architecture characterizes Burgos, and the city is principally visited by travelers interested in its Romanesque fortifications, Gothic churches and Renaissance mansions. The oldest quarter is on the slopes of Cerro de San Miguel, site of castle ruins.

CARTUJA DE MIRAFLORES, Paseo de la Quinta, is 4 kilometers (2½ miles) east. Founded by Juan II of Castile in the 15th century, this Carthusian monastery resembles a medieval fortress. The monks are known for the rosaries they make from thousands of rose petals.

CATEDRAL, Plaza de Santa María, dominates the Burgos skyline. One of Spain's most outstanding Gothic structures, this magnificent church, begun in 1221 was completed in the mid-13th century.

The cathedral art includes a painting of Mary Magdalene by Leonardo da Vinci and numerous gold, ivory and silver items. Also present is the tomb of the 11th-century Spanish hero, El Cid.

CONVENTO DE LAS HUELGAS, Paseo de la Isla, is 1 kilometer (½ mile) west of town.

Alfonso VIII, who converted this former summer palace to a Cistercian convent in 1180, is buried at this site.

MONASTERIO DE SAN PEDRO DE CARDEÑA, 11km (7 miles) south east, is a 17th-century monastery with Romanesque traces. El Cid came in exile to this stern abbey and his remains rested in the monastery from 1099 to 1919.

MUSEO ARQUEOLÓGICO, Calle Miranda, is in an exceptional Renaissance house, an example of the best domestic architecture of 16th-century Spain. There is a lovely Renaissance courtyard; inside are displays of archeological finds.

▲ CÁCERES (574 B2)
CÁCERES *pop. 71,800*
Roman settlement, Moorish metropolis and Spanish fortress'. Cáceres is one of the best-preserved feudal towns in Europe. The old quarter is surrounded by medieval fortifications with towers and gates. Inside, along narrow streets and broad plazas, are buildings from the 15th to 18th centuries.

Places of interest in the old town include the churches San Mateo, San Francisco Javier and Santa María. Among the outstanding palaces are Golfines de Abajo, Episcopal and Golfines de Arriba. There are two especially beautiful mansions, the Casa de las Cigüeñas and the Casa de las Veletas.

▲ CÁDIZ (574 B1)
CÁDIZ *pop. 153,000*
Phoenicians from Tyre founded Cádiz about 1100 BC. Carthaginians captured the colony 600 years later and were followed by Romans, Visigoths and Moors. In 1262 the city became a part of Christian Spain. After the discovery of America, it was the headquarters of the Spanish treasure fleet and became the wealthiest port in Western Europe.

On a peninsula extending into the Atlantic, Cádiz exudes a maritime atmosphere. The old city, where numerous flat-roofed white houses have

Moorish watchtowers, is the site of most attractions, including such churches as San Felipe Neri, with a painting by Murillo, and Santa Cueva, with wall paintings by Goya. Among other points of interest are the Catedral Vieja, or Old Cathedral, dating from the 13th century, and the old fortress and lighthouse at San Sebastián west of town.

Cádiz is the cultural and recreational center of the Costa de la Luz. The city has one theater, a 14,000-seat bullring and some long sandy beaches, including La Victoria, Cortadura and La Caleta. It is a good headquarters for exploring the Costa de la Luz, a major resort area, and the "white towns" inland.

CATEDRAL, built 1772–1838, is of Andalusian baroque architectural style. It contains a magnificent collection of sculptures and art objects.

HOSPITAL DE MUJERES, the former Women's Hospital, is a fine baroque building. The church houses El Greco's *Ecstasy of St. Francis.*

MUSEO DE PINTURA has one of Spain's richest art exhibits, including works by Francisco de Zurbarán.

CANARY ISLANDS – *see p.600.*

CARTAGENA (574 D1)
MURCIA *pop. 172,700*
Hasdrubal of Carthage founded Nova Cartago in 223 BC; 18 years later the Romans seized it and the surrounding gold and silver mines and transformed the city into a prosperous port. The city later endured occupations of Goths and Moors until the Christian Reconquest. Today it is Spain's chief naval base.

CONSUEGRA (574 C2)
TOLEDO *pop. 10,000*
Deep in the heart of La Mancha, Consuegra offers windmills with the added bonus of an old ruined castle standing on the hilltop. The village has an attractive square surrounded by

SPAIN

buildings of note and is the burial place of Diego, son of El Cid.

▲ CÓRDOBA (574 B2) ★
CÓRDOBA *pop. 300,000*
In the 10th century, Córdoba was one of the great cities of the world. Its caliphs exercised political and religious authority over an empire that included much

---

THE WINDMILL ROUTE OF LA MANCHA

To capture the flavor of Don Quixote-land, with its vast, flat plains and windmills, head for Consuegra, south east of Toledo, and join the N420 east. You will pass a host of typical Manchegan villages, such as Puerto Lápice, Alcázar de San Juan, Campo de Criptana, El Toboso (legendary House of the Lady Dulcinea) and Mota del Cuervo, complete with windmills galore!

---

of Spain and North Africa; its schools and libraries attracted scholars and artists. This former Moorish metropolis and its art treasures are among Spain's principal tourist attractions. The climate is usually temperate, although July and August can be torrid.

Probably of Carthaginian origin, Córdoba became a Roman colony in 152 BC. After periods of Vandal and Visigothic control, the Moors occupied the city in 711 AD. Forty-five years later, the city was made the capital of Moorish Spain by Abd-al-Rahman I.

The 10th century was Córdoba's Golden Age. Renowned for its great library, university and mosque, the city was the home of outstanding scientists, mathematicians, astronomers, geographers, theologians and philosophers. The arts flourished as silversmiths, leathermakers and architects augmented the capital's splendor. But decline set in following a period of political turmoil in the 11th century, and Córdoba never recovered its prestige.

Most places of interest are in the old city surrounding the Mezquita. A good way to see this area of narrow streets and whitewashed houses is on foot. Stroll down the quaint alleys called *callejas*: Flores, Rincones de Oro, Los Arquillos, Los Siete Infantes de Lara, La Luna and Junio Galión are the most interesting. Judería is the former Jewish quarter.

The city is also noted for its plazas; Corredera, the best known, is surrounded by 17th-century arcades. Potro has a 16th-century fountain and an inn that dates from the time of Cervantes. Many others face churches. Neo-classical Santa Victoria and 16th-century San Salvador flank Plaza del Salvador. A Capuchin convent fronts Los Dolores. The Convento de la Merced looks upon Colón, and 18th-century La Magdalena faces the plaza of the same name.

Other attractions include old fortifications and churches. The ruined Alcázar citadel dates from Moorish times. The Sevilla, Portilla and Almodovar gates are the only remains of Córdoba's medieval walls. Several churches reflect a range of architectural styles and periods. The 14th-century synagogue, the only remaining Jewish house of worship in Andalusia, contains fine stucco work.

MEZQUITA, in the Arab city facing the Roman bridge, is a former mosque that is now a cathedral. Built in the 8th century on the site of a Roman temple and Visigothic church, the Zeca, or House of Purification, grew in splendor until the 10th century when it was one of Islam's most outstanding religious structures. In the 13th century it was consecrated to the Assumption of Mary. Despite subsequent additions, it still looks much as it did in its heyday in the Moorish times.
The building's most outstanding attraction is the Mihrab, an octagonal prayer niche topped with a dome carved from a single block of white marble. It is especially noted for its mosaics. The 16th-century Capilla Mayor and most of the other Christian chapels contain interesting art objects.

MUSEO MUNICIPAL TAURINO Y DE ARTE CÓRDOBES, Plaza Bulas, is in the Casa de las Bulas in the Barrio de la Judería. Its displays include traditional Córdoban arts, leatherwork and silverwork. The bullfighting section has memorabilia of the four native Córdoban matadors known as the "Caliphs," as well as posters, trophies and uniforms.

MUSEO PROVINCIAL DE BELLAS ARTES, Plaza del Potro in the city center, has paintings by such noted Spanish and foreign masters as Murillo, Zurbarán, Goya, Raphael, Titian and Rubens.

PUENTE ROMANO spans the Guadalquivir River in front of the Mezquita. Built during the time of Julius Caesar, the bridge has been restored several times and is still in use. It has a Renaissance gateway.

RUINAS DE MEDINA AZAHARA are 10 kilometers (6 miles) west off Highway C431. In the sumptuous retreat built by Córdoban caliphs in the 10th century, Abd-al-Rahman III and his successors held court. Attractions include the Royal or Viziers' Hall, mosque and a museum with outstanding art.

▲ LA CORUÑA (574 A4)
CORUÑA *pop. 245,000*
An important cultural center and largest town and port in Galicia, La Coruña has a rich historical background. Wide streets and modern buildings distinguish the city, although the old town districts still preserve traces of the past. The 12th-century, Romanesque Church of Santiago is the oldest church. A week in mid-August is devoted to La Semana Grande, a festival known for its regattas, sporting events and pageants.

TORRE DE HERCULES (Tower of Hercules) is a 57-meter (185-foot) Roman lighthouse. Although the lighthouse is said to have been built by a Celtic chieftain in the 2nd century, some historians believe that the structure existed many centuries before Christ.

▲ CUENCA (574 C3)
CUENCA *pop. 42,800*
The town of Cuenca lies on a spectacular rocky spur of land between the Júcar River and its tributary, the Huécar. Over the centuries, these rivers have carved deep ravines, creating a stark, wild landscape. In the Barrio del Castillo, the castle district and old quarter, houses known as *Casas Colgadas*, or "Hanging Houses," cling to the sides and edges of these steep slopes.

The government has restored three of Cuenca's hanging houses and declared them national monuments.

CATEDRAL, Plaza Mayor, is a national monument dating from the 12th century. The church was begun in Norman Gothic style and finished with Anglo-Norman elements; its wrought-iron grilles and tapestries are noteworthy.

THE CUENCA MUSEUM, in La Casa del Curato across from the hanging house, displays archeological finds. The Roman period rooms are especially outstanding.

THE DIOCESAN MUSEUM OF SACRED ART, ground floor of the Episcopal Palace, houses an impressive collection of religious and modern art and valuable objects from the cathedral and other churches within the Diocese of Cuenca. Among the treasures are paintings by El Greco, a 14th-century Byzantine diptych, Cuenca tapestries and carpets, and a collection of monstrances from the 15th to 18th centuries.

MUSEO DE ARTE ABSTRACTO ESPAÑOL, in a hanging house on Calle Canonigos, has a curious Gothic interior and a lovely mudéjar ceiling. Its unusual art collection includes works by some of Spain's most important abstract artists.

EL ESCORIAL (574 C3) ★
MADRID *pop. 6,200*
SAN LORENZO DEL ESCORIAL is the magnificent monastery and summer palace inspired and built by King Philip II in

the foothills of the Guadarrama Mountains. Constructed with uncemented granite blocks and completed in 1584, the complex includes a monumental, austere domed church surrounded by chapels, each decorated by such masters as Benvenuto Cellini.

The Royal Pantheon of black marble and bronze, contains the tombs of Spanish kings and queens; in the chapter halls is an art collection that includes works by El Greco, Hieronymus Bosch, Titian, Tintoretto and others. The library houses a rare collection of 2,700 manuscripts and 40,000 books. The rooms of Maderas Finas, or Fine Woods, are royal apartments from the 17th century, decorated with inlaid woods.

VALLE DE LOS CAIDOS (Valley of the Fallen) commemorates the Spanish Civil War with a 148-meter (485-foot) cross towering above a green valley. Below the cross, a crypt and chapel are carved into the granite mountainside.

GIRONA (574 E4)
GIRONA *pop. 70,900*
Colorful Girona is crossed by the Onyar River and an international railroad line. Originally an Iberian stronghold in the 4th century, Girona has since passed through several hands.

During medieval times the Jewish community settled in El Cail, an area with steep, narrow streets.

BANYS ARABS (Arabian Baths) are in a Romanesque building and are based on the Roman public baths.

CATEDRAL, dating from the 11th–17th centuries, is a mixture of architectural styles. The cloister and part of the tower remain from the original Romanesque building. Housed in the cathedral, the Capitular Museo contains an 11th-century tapestry, the Tapestry of the Creation.

L'ESGLESIA DE SANT FELIU, built in the 14th–17th centuries, is known for its octagonal bell tower decorated in the Gothic style. Notable treasures include eight pagan and Christian sarcophagi.

MONESTIR DE SANT PERE DE GALLIGANTS, a monastery that dates from the 11th–12th centuries, houses a noteworthy archeological museum. The cloister is an excellent example of Catalonian Roman esque architecture.

GRANADA (574 C1) ★
GRANADA *pop. 254,000*
It is still possible to fall under the spell of Granada. Indeed, this magnificent city, so rich in relics of its past, is one of Spain's outstanding tourist attractions. Splendid Moorish palaces and fortifications contrast sharply with churches of more recent origin. The Alhambra, the Moorish citadel overlooking the city, is among the world's most highly regarded architectural creations.

Granada rose to fame in 1238 when the Moors transferred the seat of their diminishing dominions to this Andalusian city. It then became a cultural capital, boasting world-renowned artists, architects and scholars.

Much of Granada's Moslem past can be seen in the Albaicín, the old quarter facing the Alhambra across the Darro. This section of the city contains private dwellings, narrow streets and plazas, remains of Moorish fortifications and the Arab baths. Santa Isabel la Real, a former mosque, is now a church with a Gothic portal. The 13th-century tower of Gothic San Juan de los Reyes is a former minaret, and the church courtyard of 16th-century El Salvador was once part of a mosque.

Although not as old as the Albaicín, Granada's other districts contain their own distinctive reminders of the past, many reflecting Christian interests. Attractions in the Antequeruela, the area south west of the Alhambra, include interesting churches, most notably Nuestra Señora de las Angustias, in addition to the 16th-century morisco-style Casa de los Tiros.

Among Granada's annual celebrations are colorful religious processions during Corpus Christi, Holy Week and other feasts. But the chief attraction is the International Festival of Music and Dance. Held in late June and early July, it features concerts and ballets.

ALHAMBRA is Spain's outstanding symbol of Moorish heritage and, as a result, one of the country's most visited tourist attractions. The 13th-century ruler al-Ahmer began construction of the first palace on this plateau overlooking Granada in 1238. During the next 100 years, others added more and soon this magnificent complex became a world-renowned center of Moslem art, culture and politics. Although the name properly belongs only to the palace, it is usually applied to the entire fortified complex.

ALAMEDA DE LA ALHAMBRA is an attractive park that encompasses the southern portions of the Alhambra. At this site the Moors planted orange and myrtle trees; the Duke of Wellington added a grove of English elms in 1812.

ALCAZÁBA is the oldest part of the Alhambra. The Moorish caliphs built this citadel in the 11th century on the Alhambra's precipitous western end. Only the massive outer walls, towers and ramparts remain.

GENERALIFE is the former summer retreat of Moorish kings. Although physically distinct from the rest of the Alhambra, this 14th-century palace is usually visited along with the rest of the Moorish complex. It is noted for its maze of terraces, grottoes, flowing fountains and pools.

PALACIO ARABE, variously referred to as the Moorish palace, Alhambra or Alcázar, is Granada's most outstanding Moorish structure. The interior of this splendid 14th-century palace is a seemingly endless procession of intricately carved ceilings, arches, columns and fountains, beautiful sculptures and brightly tiled floors and walls.

Visitors enter the Palacio Arabe through the Patio de los Arrayanes, or Courtyard of Myrtles, which contains an impressive marble colonnade and pool. The chief attraction is the Patio de los Leones, or Courtyard of the Lions. Surrounded by many white marble columns and paved with colored tiles, it contains the Fountain of the Lions.

Other points of interest in the palace include the Sala de Abencerrajes, with its lofty, brightly colored, domed ceiling; the Mirador de Lindaraja, or Daraxa, decorated with paneled ceiling and arabesques; and the Sala de las Dos Hermanas or Hall of the Two Sisters, a domed room with a fountain. The beautiful Sala de los Embajadores, the largest room, was the sultans' reception room.

PALACIO DE CARLOS V is next to the Palacio Arabe. Begun in 1526, this Renaissance palace was never finished. It houses a museum depicting the artistic history of Granada and the National Museum of Hispanic-Moorish Art.

CAPILLA REAL (Royal Chapel) is attached to the south side of the cathedral. Erected 1506–17 as a mausoleum for Ferdinand V and Isabella I, this Gothic church has housed their remains since 1521. Of special note are the crown and scepter of Isabella, the plateresque doorway and 16th-century grille.

LA CARTUJA, 1.5 kilometers (1 mile) on the Calle Real de la Cartuja. Begun in 1516, the Carthusian monastery was called the Christian Alhambra because of its beautiful stucco work. Only the cloisters, church and sacristy remain. All three contain interesting paintings.

CATEDRAL, city center in the Moslem town, is dedicated to Santa María de la Encarnación. Diego de Siloé began this memorial to the Reconquest in 1528; it was finished in 1703. The Renaissance exterior is embellished with jasper and

SPAIN

colored marble and is topped with an impressive dome.

▲ HUELVA (574 A1)
HUELVA *pop. 150,000*

After the King of Portugal rejected Christopher Columbus' scheme for a western voyage in 1484, Columbus came for help to this city at the confluence of the Odiel and Tinto rivers. The discoverer is commemorated by an annual festival early in August.

In spite of origins linked to the Phoenicians, Huelva exhibits a modern appearance. The city center, La Placeta, bustles with stores and cafés. Notable among the old churches are the 1605 La Merced; San Pedro, with traces of a former mosque; and Concepción, with two paintings by Zurbarán.

Visitors can sample the region's distinctive cuisine. Such fish dishes as *choco con habas*, squid with broad beans, are among the specialties.

The Convento de la Virgen de la Cinta, 2 kilometers (1¼ miles) south east, contains a series of faience tiles depicting the discovery of America. From Palos de la Frontera, 10 kilometers (6 miles) south east of Huelva, Columbus set sail after recruiting a crew in front of the 15th-century Iglesia de San Jorge.

DONANA NATIONAL PARK, 32 kilometers (20 miles) east, is one of the most important and extensive national parks in the whole of Europe. A guided tour is recommended.

JEREZ DE LA FRONTERA (574 B1)
CÁDIZ *pop. 183,000*

Sherry takes it name from Jerez de la Frontera, known for wines of all kinds. Jerez is surrounded by vineyards and has wine cellars open to thirsty visitors.

Dating from before Roman times, Jerez also offers an old quarter of white-washed houses.

Attractions include remains of the old Arab walls, the 11th-century Alcázar as well as two churches, Gothic San Marcos and baroque Colegiata.

▲ MÁLAGA (574 B1)
MÁLAGA *pop. 512,000*

Capital of the Costa del Sol, the cosmopolitan resort area of Spain's southern coast, Málaga is popular with tourists all year. The Phoenicians founded a port here in the 12th century BC. Romans, Visigoths and Moors followed, and in 1487 the city became a part of Christian Spain.

The birthplace of Pablo Picasso is in the Plaza de la Merced. Several old churches include Gothic Sagrario, with

---

SHERRY

Jerez de la Frontera is famous for *jerez* (sherry) which has been produced here since the 18th century.

The four main types are the extra dry *fino*, more full-bodied *amontillado*, golden *oloroso* and sweet *dulce*. Wine tasting rounds of the *bodegas* are always enjoyable. A wine harvest festival, held here in early September, includes *flamenco* among its joyous celebrations.

---

interesting 16th-century altar decorations; 15th-century Santiago, with a mudéjar tower; and medieval Victoria, which contains a tomb with some macabre decorations.

ALCAZÁBA, on the Calle de la Alcazábiella, was the palace of Málaga's Arab kings. Reconstructed, it houses the Museo Arqueológico and its gardens.

MUSEO DE BELLAS ARTES, San Agustino 6, is an ancient palace and now contains works of art ranging from Roman mosaics to pieces by Picasso.

MARBELLA (574 B1)
MÁLAGA *pop. 66,000*

Marbella is still considered the center of the Costa del Sol, even though its old jetset image has seen better days. The fortifications above the old town offer a pleasant stroll, and pretty restaurants can be found around Plaza de los Naranjos (Square of Orange Trees).

MONTSERRAT (574 E3) ★
BARCELONA *pop. 500*

This town is known as the site of the revered Monastery of Montserrat. The countless legends were undoubtedly inspired by the appearance of the jagged mountain, which rises about 1,200 meters (3,940 feet) from the Llobregat River and is outlined with monoliths resembling immense stone figures.

Montserrat also offers a museum with works by El Greco and Caravaggio.

MONASTERIO, founded in 880 AD, is the home of many Benedictine monks. The principal treasure, the Black Virgin of Montserrat, is the object of thousands of pilgrimages annually.

▲ ORENSE (574 A4)
ORENSE *pop. 96,100*

Little remains of ancient Orense; it was destroyed by the Moors during the 8th century, but the hot springs that gave Orense its name first attracted the Romans.

One of the oldest surviving buildings in the city is the 12th-century cathedral, whose Portico of Paradise and rich decorations are typical of that period. Yet another notable structure is the seven-arch bridge across the Miño River. One of Spain's most impressive spans, it was built by Bishop Lorenzo in 1230.

▲ OVIEDO (574 B4)   •
OVIEDO *pop. 182,000*

Ancient Oviedo was once capital of the kingdom of Asturias, later to become Oviedo Province. Founded in the 8th century around a monastery, the town retains many splendid buildings dating from the 8th–12th centuries. Two museums display archeological finds that pre-date the Roman occupation.

CATEDRAL, a 14th-century Gothic structure, has an 80-meter (265-foot) tower decorated with filigree. The building

also has fine carved portals and beautiful stained-glass windows.

PAMPLONA (574 D4)
NAVARRA *pop. 183,100*

Ernest Hemingway made Pamplona the setting for his *The Sun Also Rises,* and the Fiesta de San Fermín the writer described is perhaps this old city's most outstanding tourist attraction. Each day during one week in July, the bulls run through the streets from corral to *corrida,* preceded by young men running pell mell. Other activities include bullfights and general merrymaking.

LA ESCOLONÍA

The monastery of Montserrat is renowned for both its library and music. The music school, with its boys' choir *La Escolonía,* dates back to the 13th century and is the oldest in Europe. The boys sing like angels and to hear a performance (given daily) can be a very moving experience.

CATEDRAL is Pamplona's most outstanding monument. Although founded in 1120, this French Gothic church dates mainly from the 14th and 15th centuries.

SAN SATURNINO, is the town's oldest, and finest Romanesque building.

RONDA (574 B1)
MÁLAGA *pop. 32,000*

Ronda is a picturesque town flanking the deep gorge of the Guadalevín River from atop a rocky plateau. Its spectacular setting and famous bridge, the Puente Nuevo, linking the old town with the new, makes this a great attraction. The old town is on the south side of the ravine; its attractions include Roman ruins, the old Arab Quarter and Santa María la Mayor, a cathedral that combines Gothic and Renaissance influences. North of the river, the "new" town is the site of 15th-century residences and the 18th-century bullring.

SPAIN

▲ **SALAMANCA** (574 B3)
SALAMANCA *pop. 167,100*

Salamanca has had a long and colorful history marked by Roman settlement and struggles between Christians and Moors. The great days of this city on the Tormes River, however, began in the 13th century with the founding of the university, which became a leading European learning center. The majestic old cathedral towering above the city is the principal landmark; the Palacio Monterrey, on the Plaza Agustinas, is a 16th-century seignorial mansion.

A good time to visit Salamanca is during fiesta time in mid-September, when fairs, bullfights, parades, folklore, livestock exhibitions and an international horse show enliven the city.

CATEDRAL NUEVA, Plaza de Anaya, was begun in 1513 and finished two centuries later, resulting in an unusual combination of architectural styles. Its principal feature is the façade with bas-reliefs of the Nativity and Adoration.

CATEDRAL VIEJA, surrounded on three sides by the new cathedral, is a 12th-century church with magnificent chapels and tombs. The Patio Chico, or small patio, offers a view of the remarkable Romanesque apses and the Torre del Gallo, or Cock Tower. The most outstanding feature is the dome, with scenes from the Apocalypse.

PLAZA MAYOR, the heart of the city in both location and spirit, is one of the most beautiful portico squares in Spain. Surrounded by 18th-century baroque buildings, it was originally constructed for use as a bullring.

UNIVERSIDAD, near the Plaza Mayor, was founded in 1215 and is the oldest in Spain. Its façade is an excellent example of the Spanish plateresque style. The church and library are especially interesting, as are the lower courtyard and a lecture hall housing the ceiling fresco *Sky of Salamanca*.

▲ **SAN SEBASTIÁN** (574 C4)
GUIPÚZCOA *pop. 175,100*

The white buildings of San Sebastián, or Donostia in Basque, provide a pleasant contrast to the green fields and mountains surrounding this leading summer resort. The city's harbor bustles with fishing boats and La Concha, a large sandy beach, offers sporting activities.

San Sebastián is divided into two areas. The old quarter has interesting buildings, including two churches, 16th-century San Vicente and 18th-century Santa María. The newer district faces La Concha and its promenade. The Avenida de la Libertad, with nightclubs and stores, is the main thoroughfare.

San Sebastián is host to several festivals from July to September: The two week *Festivales de España* features musical events; Basque Week celebrates local traditions, arts and crafts; and the motion picture festival presents movies of international renown. Accommodations are almost impossible to obtain in summer, when the city becomes the seat of the Spanish government.

MUSEO MUNICIPAL DE SAN TELMO, a former monastery dating from the 16th century, contains murals by José María Sert, a noted Catalan artist.

SANTIAGO DE COMPOSTELA
(574 A4) ★
LA CORUÑA *pop. 93,700*

The discovery of the tomb of St. James the Elder, who was beheaded in Palestine and his body brought to Spain, marked the beginning of Santiago de Compostela. The cathedral erected over the tomb became the nucleus around which the town was built. During the Middle Ages, it rivaled Rome and Jerusalem as the goal of pilgrims. Modern Santiago furthers its religious traditions as the site of Holy Year celebrations held when the Festival of St. James, 25 July, falls on a Sunday; the next festival will be held in 1999.

CATEDRAL, is one of the most magnificent in Spain. In 12th-century Romanesque style with an overlay of baroque carving, the edifice also combines delicate Gothic with elegant plateresque.

The Apostle St. James the Elder is said to be buried under the high altar, which is decorated with baroque gold and silver.

MUSEO, in the cloister by the cathedral, contains archeological remains, valuable liturgical ornaments and fine tapestries.

CONVENTO DE SAN FRANCISCO is believed to have been founded by St. Francis of Assisi when he came here on a pilgrimage in 1214.

MONASTERIO DE SAN MARTIN PINARIO was founded by monks who served in the cathedral. It was one of the most important in Galicia, with a resplendent baroque high altar.

SANTA MARIA LA REAL DEL SAR, on the city outskirts, is of Romanesque architecture with an enchanting cloister surrounded by pillars with richly carved capitals. The walls and columns of this beautiful church lean at a peculiar angle,

---

THE INCENSE OF SANTIAGO DE COMPOSTELA

The spectacle of the *Botafumeiro* ritual, which happens on feast days and special occasions in the cathedral of Santiago de Compostela, should not be missed if possible.

This huge incense burner is brought out and hung from the transept dome. It then swings to the eaves with eight men clinging madly on to it by a rope.

The tradition goes back to the times when the presence of vast numbers of pilgrims who came to worship at the shrine necessitated strong fumigation!

---

but no one has been able to decide whether this is the result of faulty foundations or the intent of the builders.

SANTILLANA DEL MAR (574 C4)
SANTANDER *pop. 3,900*

Santillana del Mar grew up around the 6th-century Monastery of Santa Juliana and was recently declared a national monument. Besides the adjacent Caves of Altamira, the town is noted for a 12th-century Romanesque Collegiate Church and numerous residences bearing coats of arms and emblems.

A short distance away are the Cuevas de Altamira (Altamira Caves) which contain paintings of bison, horses, deer and other animals, dating back to 14,000–9000 BC. A limited number of visitors are allowed in.

▲ SEGOVIA (574 C3) ★
SEGOVIA *pop. 53,200,*

On the Eresma and Clamores rivers in the central Guadarrama mountains, 2,000-year-old Segovia has been inhabited since before the Roman Conquest. Isabella I was proclaimed queen in Segovia in 1474, and much of the town appears to have changed little in succeeding centuries. A walk on the ramparts dividing the upper and lower towns affords a good view of twisting streets leading to picturesque plazas and interesting churches.

The 16th-century Carmelite convent houses the tomb of St. John of the Cross. The Chapter House has Gobelin tapestries and a fine coffered ceiling. North west near the village of Santa María la Real de Nieva is 15th-century Coca Castle, one of Spain's finest and best-preserved castles.

La Granja de San Ildefonso, 12 kilometers (7 miles) south east, is an elaborate palace and estate with gardens similar to those at Versailles in France.

ACUEDUCTO ROMANO, town center, was built in the 1st century AD and is one of the world's best-preserved Roman remains. The perfectly fitting granite blocks form 118 arches reaching a height of 29 meters (95 feet) in the Plaza del Azoguejo. It still carries water to part of the city.

SPAIN

ALCÁZAR, Plaza del Álcázar, is a remarkable 13th-century palace serving as Segovia's principal landmark. Enhanced by magnificent chambers added in a 15th-century renovation, it was gutted by fire in 1862 and later rebuilt. The throne, gallery, and pineapple rooms feature period furniture and motifs.

CATEDRAL, Plaza Catedral, has earned the nickname "Lady of Cathedrals" for its graceful elegance. The 16th-century church is an excellent example of Spanish Gothic; its museum contains masterpieces by Van Dyck, Morales and Benvenuto Cellini.

▲ SEVILLA (574 B1) ★
SEVILLA *pop. 659,000*
Sevilla, or Seville, ranks as one of the globe's great tourist centers. Don Juan romanced and Figaro barbered in Seville; today, gypsies still sing age-old ballads, flamenco dancers whirl, and matadors tease rushing bulls.

Founded by ancient Iberians, Seville later flourished under Romans, Vandals, Visigoths and Moors. In 1503, after the Reconquest, the Spanish Crown established the Casa de Contratación, or House of Trade, and for 200 years this port on the Guadalquivir River dominated Spain's New World trade.

Among Seville's greatest charms are its neighborhoods, or *barrios*, which can best be seen on foot. Macarena, in the north, has remains of Roman walls and an Arab gate. San Bernardo, also in the north, includes the Alameda de Hércules, a parkway with two Roman columns, and the Calle de la Feria, an area with a Thursday morning flea market. Santa Clara and San Vicente are west of San Bernardo and feature aristocratic homes and medieval convents.

The best-known of Seville's districts is the Barrio de Santa Cruz, a labyrinth of alleys and balconied houses with charming streets and plazas. Calle de las Sierpes is a favorite street for strollers.

The 18th-century Fábrica de Tabacos, a former tobacco factory that houses a university, is in the Calle de San Fernando. The 18th-century baroque Palacio de San Telmo is near the bridge of the same name and the 16th-century plateresque Ayuntamiento, or Town Hall, is in the Plaza Nueva.

Seville is a city of churches, which, in addition to the renowned cathedral, include 13th-century Santa Ana in the waterfront district of Triana, 14th-century San Esteban in the city's east and baroque La Magdalena in the west.

Other ecclesiastical attractions are the city's convents and monasteries: 17th-century Santa Paula is in the north east; mudéjar San Clemente is in Santa Clara, as is Santa Clara and its Torre de Don Fadrique. West of the cathedral is the 17th-century Hospital de la Caridad, or Charity Hospital; it contains an interesting collection of art objects.

The most outstanding of the city's annual festivities is Holy Week. Since the 16th century, religious *cofradías*, or confraternities, have staged elaborate processions through the streets. Today 53 such groups present more than 100 *pasos* depicting the Passion of Christ and Our Lady of Sorrows every evening from Palm Sunday to Maundy Thursday and the morning of Good Friday. Nearly all of Seville's celebrations, including such religious holidays as Corpus Christi and Epiphany, attract large crowds, so reservations for accommodations are advisable.

Following Easter, Seville celebrates its *feria*. Originally a 19th-century livestock show, the fair features animal exhibitions and other entertainments in a tent city in the Los Remedios district. A typical fair day begins with a noon parade noted for impressive horsemanship, which is followed by music, dancing and revelry on the *prado*. After a siesta, matadors perform in the Plaza de Toros, and merrymaking begins anew.

Seville also boasts other annual events. Religious processions highlight Corpus Christi and Epiphany. For Immaculate Conception, city buildings are illuminated, and in late September the Michaelmas fair features bullfights.

ALCÁZAR is near the cathedral in the Plaza del Triunfo. Seville's Moorish sovereigns began construction of a fortress palace in 1181. From that period, however, only the impressive Patio del Yeso remains. Under the stewardship of 14th-century Pedro the Cruel and later monarchs, Moorish architects built lavish courts, apartments and gardens.

ARCHIVO DE INDIAS, Plaza del Triunfo, is in the Renaissance Casa Lonja, the former merchants' exchange. Noted for its red marble staircase, the building houses the Archives of the Indies, and a collection of books, maps, manuscripts and documents depicting the history of Spain's vanished New World empire.

FLAMENCO

While good *flamenco* may be seen in Madrid, Málaga or countless places, it has close associations with Sevilla, and to see a good *tablao*, or performance, can be unforgettable. The gypsy and Arab origins of flamenco are from Andalusia, with the *cante jondo*, literally "deep song," considered the heart and soul of flamenco, relating to passions, deep emotions, unhappiness in love and other such human feelings! A good performance has terrific atmosphere and plenty of high drama.

CASA DE PILATOS (Pilate's House), Calle de Aguilas, is a 16th-century mudéjar palace, built as a reproduction of Pontius Pilate's Praetorium in Jerusalem.

CATEDRAL, Avénida de la Constitución, is the largest cathedral in Spain and third largest in Christendom. Begun in 1402, the Gothic church is dedicated to Santa María de la Sede. Priceless paintings, 15th century choir stalls and chapels enclosed by exquisite iron screens decorate the interior. In the south transept is the tomb of Christopher Columbus.

During the festivals of Corpus Christi and the Immaculate Conception, altar boys stage a ceremony that includes a dance with castanets.

TORRE DE LA GIRALDA, in the northwest corner of the cathedral, dominates Seville's skyline. Built in 1184 as a minaret, the 92-meter (300-foot) tower now houses the church's 25 bells.

HOSPITAL DE LOS VENERABLES SACERDOTES, in the Barrio de Santa Cruz, opened in 1675 as the Paupers' House of the Venerable Priests. It now contains a museum and a baroque church.

ITALICA is an ancient Roman city 8 kilometers (5 miles) north on Highway N630 at Santiponce. The remains of an amphitheater, villas, theater and streets can still be seen in this settlement, which was the birthplace of the Emperors Trajan and Hadrian.

MUSEO DE BELLAS ARTES, Plaza del Museo 9, is one of the oldest museums in Spain. Its painting collection, dating from the 16th–20th centuries, includes works by El Greco, Goya and Velázquez.

SEVILLE – *see Sevilla on p.594.*

TARRAGONA (574 E3)
TARRAGONA *pop. 111,900*
Tarragona was once the capital of the Iberian Cerretani; there are still traces of the walls that encircled the town. The Paleo-Christian Museum 1.6 kilometers (1 mile) from the city has examples of burials from the 3rd–6th centuries.

ARCO DE BARA, 20 kilometers (12 miles) north on Highway N340, was built in the 2nd century by Romans. The two stone pillars of the arch are carved to form false Corinthian columns.

CATEDRAL, in the city center, is a skilful blend of Romanesque and Gothic architecture. The façade of the 12th-century building features a rose window and magnificent sculptures; the decorations on the main altar are superb.

PUENTE DEL DIABLO (Devil's Bridge) is a Roman aqueduct 4 kilometers (2½ miles) from Tarragona on Highway N240. The well-preserved, double-arched structure is one of the most impressive Roman remains in Spain.

▲ TOLEDO (574 C3) ★
TOLEDO pop. 60,200

As El Greco painted it, Toledo was a divine city illuminating medieval Spain; as the Romans and Moors saw it, the town was an excellent site for a walled fortress. But today's visitor remembers the city for its rich heritage, so well-preserved that the urban area has been named a national monument. Capital of the province of the same name, Toledo lies on the central Spanish plain. The Tagus River hugs the town on three sides, much like a castle moat.

An excursion into the almost inexhaustible architectural treasury that is Toledo might begin from either of two bridges spanning the Tagus, each at the foot of the medieval town. The outer walls, of Arab, Visigothic and Christian origins, contain well-preserved gateways. From the picturesque Zocodover Square in the center of town, the main street, Comercio, leads to the celebrated cathedral. Other sights in the environs are mosques, mudéjar synagogues, Christian churches and several museums, parks and paseos. The 15th-century Castillo de Guadamur, 14 kilometers (9 miles) south west, is one of Spain's finest and best-preserved castles.

The craftsmen of Toledo are nearly as well-known as its sights. Artisans still produce damascened work in the style inherited from the Moors, as well as traditional bullfighters' swords and modern military swords.

EL ALCÁZAR, Cuesta del Alcázar, overlooks the city. Built in its present form by Charles V, the fortress stands on the site of a 3rd-century Roman palace. This plateresque citadel was nearly destroyed during the Civil War. It has since been restored and is now a national monument.

CASA Y MUSEO DEL GRECO is in the Judería. El Greco lived in this vicinity, and this well-preserved mansion houses many of his personal effects. The museum has a collection of his paintings.

CATEDRAL, begun in 1226, was completed in the late 1400s. The Spanish Gothic church is celebrated for its mudéjar decorations and more than 750 stained-glass windows. Also renowned are the Treasury and Sacristy, with works by Van Dyck, El Greco, Velázquez and Goya.

HOSPITAL DE TAVERA, north on the road to Madrid, is a restored 16th-century hospital with a pharmacy, church and exquisite patio. Adjoining the main building is the Palace of the Dukes of Lerma; the art collection contains the last picture painted by El Greco.

MEZQUITA DEL CRISTO DE LA LUZ is opposite the Puerta del Sol. Built as a mosque in the 10th century and converted to Christian use after the Reconquest, this Moorish structure contains some 12th-century Christian frescoes.

SANTO TOMÉ, Calle Santo Tomé, is a 14th-century mudéjar church with a notable spire. El Greco's most renowned work, *The Burial of Count Orgaz*, can be seen in one of the chapels.

SINAGOGA DE SANTA MARIA LA BLANCA, Judería near the Calle de los Reyes Católicos, is Spain's oldest synagogue.

TORREMOLINOS (574 B1)
MÁLAGA pop. 25,000

The first resort to give a name to the Costa del Sol, Torremolinos has long been a favorite with visitors seeking sun and sand. After sunbathing, sightseeing and shopping, there is the lively nightlife of Torremolinos' bars and discos.

▲ VALENCIA (574 D2)
VALENCIA *pop. 753,000*

A sunny garden city surrounded by orange groves, Valencia lies on the Turia River. Excellent communications link the third largest city in Spain to Barcelona and Madrid. Like its two sisters, Valencia's turbulent history has included past occupation by the Romans, Moors and French.

Valencia's many churches include the cathedral; the convent of Santo Domingo, with its outstanding Gothic cloister; and the Renaissance Colegio del Patriarca, with a collection of fine tapestries and paintings. Civic buildings include the Lonja de Mercado, the 18th-century Palacio de Justicia and the Casa de las Rocas, which houses *rocas* or chariots. The picturesque flower market and botanical gardens are worth a visit, as are the museums, including the National Ceramics Museum.

Valencia is most memorable during its colorful holidays. The noisiest and happiest is Las Fallas, which celebrates the coming of spring. The Festival of St. James in July is also important.

CATEDRAL, on Plaza de la Virgen, is a 13th-century structure combining Romanesque and Gothic elements.

Most outstanding are the "Palau" door, a masterpiece of gold and silver called the "Custodia," and the Chapel of the Holy Grail, which is said to house the original relic.

▲ VALLADOLID (574 B3)
VALLADOLID *pop. 328,000*

Valladolid, Spain's former capital, was the residence of the kings of Castile in the 15th century before Philip II made Madrid his capital. A university city of modern appearance, it is in the heart of Old Castile. Here Philip II was born, Cervantes lived, Ferdinand V and Isabella I married and Christopher Columbus died.

MUSEO NACIONAL DE ESCULTURA (National Museum of Sculpture), on Cadenas San Gregorio, contains the best and most representative pieces of Spanish polychrome woodwork.

VITORIA (574 C4)
ALAVA *pop. 199,400*

Historic Vitoria, or Gasteiz in Basque, was founded by the Visigoths in 581 AD. The city was fortified by Sancho the Wise of Navarre in 1181.

Vitoria is divided into two districts. There are Gothic mansions, complete with heraldic escutcheons over the doors, which line narrow streets in the old district; while in the newer area is picturesque La Florida park.

CATEDRAL DE SANTA MARIA was founded in 1180 and reconstructed in the 14th century. It has a 17th-century tower and paintings by Van Dyck and Rubens.

SAN MIGUEL is a 14th-century Gothic church. Of particular interest are the beautiful altar and the jasper Virgen Blanca de Vitoria, the White Virgin of Vitoria.

▲ ZARAGOZA (574 D3)
ZARAGOZA *pop. 600,500*

Although it pre-dates Roman occupation, Zaragoza is best known for its association with the artist, Francisco José de Goya, born in this province at Fuendetodos. Many of his paintings, as well as works by other renowned artists, are displayed in the city.

BASILICA DE NUESTRA SEÑORA DEL PILAR is a baroque structure with cupolas and blue tiles. There are splendid frescoes by Francisco José de Goya and Francisco Bayeu in the choir; a treasury contains gold plate and jewels.

CASTILLO DE ALJAFERIA is an 11th-century Moorish castle whose original walls and oratory, or chapel, still stand.

MUSEO PROVINCIAL DE BELLAS ARTES exhibits a collection of paintings by Goya and El Greco's *St Francis*.

SPAIN

ISLAS BALEARES

(574 E2)

Carthaginians, Romans, Vandals and Arabs have over the centuries invaded the Islas Baleares, or Balearic Islands. In modern times the 16 islands are besieged by invaders of a different sort – tourists. As a result, cosmopolitan resorts offer visitors sandy beaches, lively nightlife and sports.

The beaches of the Balearic Islands are the principal attractions, and the four major islands – Formentera, Ibiza, Mallorca and Menorca – have countless sand-rimmed coves. If you're looking for uncrowded beaches, head for the smaller isles, such as Formentera, or the more remote parts of Ibiza and Menorca.

The interiors of the islands also are worth visiting. In quaint hill villages and valleys, old customs prevail, including traditional folk dancing. Local craftspeople produce hand-made shoes, gloves and other leather goods, embroideries, wood carvings, glassware, ceramics, wrought-iron items and raffia. There is a steamer service from Barcelona and Valencia to Mallorca, Menorca and Ibiza, which are also accessible by air. Various watercraft serve the other islands from Palma de Mallorca.

IBIZA (574 E2)
ISLAS BALEARES pop. 50,000

The gleaming white sand beaches of Ibiza make this island second only to Mallorca in popularity with tourists. Among Ibiza's most popular resorts are San Antonio on the west coast, Santa Eulalia, north east of Ibiza town and Portinatx which lies on the north coast.

IBIZA on the island of the same name, was founded by the Carthaginians more than 2,600 years ago, but most of its antiquities are of more recent origin. The old town, "Dalt Villa," is most attractive, with walls dating from the 15th and 16th centuries.

MALLORCA (574 E1)
ISLAS BALEARES pop. 613,800

Largest of the Balearic Islands, Mallórca is the most frequently visited. Its shores are rimmed with fine sandy beaches, the interior has exceptional mountain scenery, and its capital Palma, is a resort of world renown. The island's south west is favored by tourists. The beaches around Palma have spawned increased resort development, and there are hundreds of clubs, hotels and restaurants.

Although less visited than the southwest, the rest of Mallorca is just as interesting. In the interior are quaint hill villages. Along the south and east coasts are such fine beaches as Cala d'Or, a lovely cove where pine trees grow to the water's edge. On the north coast are the popular seaside resorts of Puerto Alcúdia and Puerto Pollensa and Formentor, a stunning area of pine woods.

The west coast provides some of Mallorca's most spectacular scenery. From the rugged cliffs and caves of Cala San Vicente in the north to the great stone mass of the Dragonera islet in the south, the mountains climb to heights of more than 900 meters (2,950 feet).

ALCÚDIA, an ancient town with a Roman theater and a medieval city gate, Alcúdia was the last stronghold of the Moors when Jaime the Conqueror landed in the western part of the island. It is at the northern end of the Bay of Alcúdia.

ARTÁ, a pleasant hillside town, has a small archeological museum and is next to several prehistoric settlements where some megalithic remains can be seen. The excellent beach of Cala Ratjada is 10 kilometers (6 miles) west.
Cuevas De Arta are 9 kilometers (6 miles) east. These impressive caves descend more than 390 meters (1,280 feet) and contain some of Mallorca's largest subterranean rock formations.

DEYÁ, Deyá has long been the haunt of writers and artists. One of its most famous guests was the poet Robert

Graves, who made it his permanent home and was buried here in 1985. It continues to attract art lovers as well as the rich and famous.

MANACOR is noted for the production of Mallorca pearls. The factory where the artificial pearls are made and the town's archeological museum can be visited.

Cueva De Los Hams (Cave of the Fishhooks) is 11 kilometers (7 miles) east. The cave follows the course of a former underground river and owes its name to the strange limestone formations.

Cuevas Del Drach (Limestone Caverns) are 13 kilometers (8 miles) east near Porto Cristo. They extend more than 1.6 kilometres (1 mile) and contain one of Europe's largest underground lakes.

▲ PALMA (574 E1) (pop. 297,000), once a great maritime power, is now a cosmopolitan resort and the chief city of the Balearic Islands. It enjoys a magnificent seaside setting on the Bahía de Palma and attracts vacationers to its beaches, shopping stalls and nightclubs. Because it is within driving distance of all of Mallorca's points of interest, it is a convenient center for exploring the island.

A tour of Palma should include the old city, an area of narrow streets, many open to pedestrian traffic only. Attractions include the Arco de la Almudaina, a Moorish arch; Baños Arabes, the 11th-century Arab baths; such churches as Gothic San Francisco and baroque Montesión; and several other old buildings. This area is also Palma's principal shopping district.

The newest districts encompass elegant stores, luxurious hotels, lively nightclubs with colorful cabarets, fine restaurants and multilingual movie houses. During the summer season there are bullfights in the 18,000-seat coliseum, Coliseo Balear, as well as horse racing and *jai alai* (pelota) events.

And, of course, there are beaches. To the east, the sands of the Ribera de Levante extend 13 kilometers (8 miles) from Ciudad Jardín to El Arenal. To the west is the Ribera de Poniente and beyond are Santa Ponsa and Cala Fornells; the latter, one of Mallorca's less crowded beaches, is 20 kilometers (12 miles) from Palma.

La Almudaina, the former residence of Arab governors and later of Mallorcan kings, is the official reception hall of the king of Spain. Little remains of the Arab influence; the building was reconstructed in the 16th century. The two courtyards are of special interest.

Ayuntamiento, Plaza de Cort, is Palma's 16th-century town hall. Its style a blend of Italian Renaissance and baroque, the building contains a library and a display of paintings.

Castillo De Bellver is on a pine-clad hill west of town. Construction of this fortress began in the 13th century. Since then it has served primarily as a military stronghold and prison.

Catedral, known as La Seu, facing the bay, dominates Palma's skyline. Begun in 1230, this large Gothic church has numerous carvings, frescoes, paintings and other art objects. It also contains the tombs of Mallorcan kings and a museum with displays of religious ornaments and jewelry.

MENORCA (574 E2)
ISLAS BALEARES *pop. 64,000*

Pretty Menorca, north east of Mallorca and second largest of the Balearic Islands, is noted for its beaches. These fine sandy expanses range from crowded, popular Cala Santa Galdana to almost-deserted Cala Mezquida. Indeed, the entire north and south coast of the island is lined with rugged coves and quiet bathing spots.

Menorca's places of interest include 350-meter (1,148-foot) Monte Toro; the archeological site of Naveta de Tudons, which has some megalithic monuments; and the Old World port of Ciudadela, with its interesting cathedral.

The capital, Mahon, has an archeological museum with a variety of exhibits. Menorca is also known for its *caldereta de lagosta*, a lobster specialty and a favorite of King Juan Carlos I, and *mahonesa*, a local creation better known as mayonnaise.

ISLAS CANARIAS

(574 E1)

SPAIN

Off the Atlantic coast of Africa, the Islas Canarias, or Canary Islands, have been a favorite vacation spot throughout the 20th century. The scenery varies from lush tropical jungles to stark, arid deserts. There are beaches of white sand, black sand and shingle. More than 900 varieties of flowering plant grow, and the 220 species of bird include the native canary.

During the ancient and medieval periods, the Guanches inhabited the Canary Islands, but during the Spanish conquest of 1401–96, the aboriginal population decreased. Nevertheless, evidence of their ultimate absorption into the population is suggested by many of the islanders' family names.

Of the seven major islands, Gran Canaria, La Palma, Tenerife, Lanzarote and Fuerteventura are the most tourist-oriented, offering modern facilities and beaches. Those seeking solitude should head for El Hierro, Fuerteventura, volcanic Lanzarote, or La Gomera. Of special interest to shoppers is the islands' status as free ports.

LA GOMERA (574 D1)
ISLAS CANARIAS *pop. 17,500*
Columbus stopped in La Gomera on his way to the New World in 1492. His visit is commemorated in the Torre del Conde, an old fortress. La Gomera's fame, however, stems more from the island's steep seaside cliffs, mountainous interior and unique whistling language, which allows islanders to communicate from mountain to mountain and is said to be more reliable than the local telephone service.

Since tourist development began only recently on Gomera, the island is less crowded than the other Canaries. Places of interest include Hermigua, Alto de Garajonay, Playa Santiago, and El Bosque del Cedro.

At the capital, San Sebastián, is La Iglesia de la Asunción where Columbus heard mass before sailing to America. Vallehermoso, a fruit-growing region, is bordered by Los Organos, a series of cliffs lining the island's north coast. Tours of Garajonay National Park are available. El Bosque del Cedro is a cedar forest and Playa Santiago has a beach.

GRAN CANARIA (574 E1)
ISLAS CANARIAS *pop. 700,000*
Gran Canaria, the Canary Islands' most populous and third largest island, is a mixture of several continents. From 1,979-meter (6,496-foot) Roque Nublo in the interior to the coasts, plants of Europe, Africa and the Americas thrive, including palm, pine, grape, coffee, sugarcane, banana, almond and tomato. The best beaches on the island are in the south, an area of considerable development.

Of interest are the southern resorts of San Agustín, Playa de Inglés and Maspalomas, all with fine beaches; the interior towns of Tejeda and San Bartolomé de Tirajana, which are surrounded by rugged rocky peaks; and the southwestern village of Mogán and its nearby seaside cliffs.

▲ LAS PALMAS (574 E1) (*pop. 342,000*) is a cosmopolitan resort, port and metropolis on Gran Canaria, enjoys a setting between mountains and the sea. The city boasts numerous shops offering a variety of items at bargain prices. Nearby are fine beaches, including Las Canteras, a wide, sandy expanse protected from currents by a natural volcanic reef offshore. Puerto de la Luz is 5 kilometers (3 miles) north, and the airport is 26 kilometers (16 miles) south.

Casa de Colón is the former governor's palace. Christopher Columbus stayed here before embarking on his first voyage to the New World.

The attractive building now houses a museum of arts and crafts of the Colombian period.

Islas Canarias (Santa Cruz)

Lanzarote (574 E1)

ISLAS CANARIAS *pop. 80,000*

As recently as the 19th century, Lanzarote's numerous volcanoes spewed rivers of molten lava. Even today, fissures in the desert-like slopes of Montaña del Fuego, the Mountain of Fire, are hot enough to fry eggs. With more than 300 volcanic cones, Lanzarote is one of the most beautiful islands in the Canaries. Red, black and white sand beaches, many remarkably uncrowded, line its shores. Despite a dry climate, the island abounds with vineyards and fruit plantations. Arrecife, the chief town, has two fortresses: San Gabriel and San José.

La Palma (574 D1)

ISLAS CANARIAS *pop. 82,000*

Emerald-tinted forests and aquamarine waters combine to make La Palma a gem of the Canaries. La Caldera de Taburiente, a giant volcanic crater, dominates the island's interior. A national park surrounding the crater is filled with immense pine groves. The 2,398-meter (7,871-foot) Roque de los Muchachos and the more accessible La Cumbrecita lookout point afford excellent views.

SANTA CRUZ (574 D1) *(pop. 18,000),* on the island of La Palma, surveys the sea from the slopes of a volcanic crater, a location that curves impressively like an amphitheater. The modern buildings lining the attractive avenues are counterbalanced by old mansions with wooden balconies.

Tenerife (574 E1)

ISLAS CANARIAS *pop. 428,000*

Largest of the Canary Islands, Tenerife is also one of the most beautiful. Its scenery varies from the fertile valleys of Orotava and Güimar to the lava fields of Las Cañadas.

The north east has attracted most tourists up to now, but development in the south has also begun.

Places of interest include the popular year-round swimming resorts of Puerto de la Cruz, Playa de las Americas and Los Cristianos. Among the most notable beaches are Playa de Medano, 90 kilometers (56 miles) from Santa Cruz, and Los Realejos.

LAS CAÑADAS DEL TEIDE, a national park in the center of the island, is 2,000 meters (6,562 feet) above sea level.

Spread over an 80-square-kilometer (31-square-mile) volcanic crater are moonlike rock formations and extensive lava fields.

To the north rises the 3,717-meter (12,198-foot) Pico de Teide. This spectacular volcanic cone is accessible by cable car daily, weather permitting.

LA OROTAVA *(pop. 31,400)* is best visited during June, situated in the beautiful Orotava Valley on Tenerife.

Set among lush banana plantations and pine groves overshadowed by snow-capped Teide, the town is the scene of the most colorful festival in the Canaries. For Corpus Christi, the inhabitants carpet streets and plazas with flowers and there then follows a religious procession. Four days later, during the Romeria de San Isidro, they dress in colorful costumes for a parade.

PUERTO DE LA CRUZ *(pop. 39,200)* is where most tourists visiting Tenerife head for.

Hotels, restaurants and nightclubs abound in the city's modern surroundings. Along the Avenida de Colón are natural pools of water and a spectacular lido built into the sea.

The black volcanic sand beaches of the north coast are nearby.

▲ SANTA CRUZ (574 E1) *(pop. 190,800).* During the Napoleonic Wars, the British Admiral Lord Nelson lost a battle while attempting to take this city; his captured flags are still treasured relics in the Museo Militar.

This bustling metropolis on Tenerife is more known, however, for its harbor, colorful parks and plazas and crowded shopping stalls.

ANDORRA

Things to Know

- **Area:** 467 square kilometers (180 square miles)
- **Population:** 60,000
- **Capital:** Andorra la Vella
- **Languages:** Catalan is the official language; French and Spanish also spoken.
- **Passport Requirements:** Advised for U.S. visitors. Spanish and French borders require a valid passport.
- **Visa Requirements:** Not required for stays up to three months.
- **Duty-Free Items:** No restrictions on goods brought into or taken out of Andorra; however, visitors entering or leaving Spain or France must comply with these countries' regulations.
- **Currency:** The currency units are the Spanish *peseta* (PTS) and the French *franc* (FF). Due to currency fluctuations, the exchange rate is subject to frequent change. No limit on currency brought into or taken out of Andorra.
- **Bank Opening Hours:** 9am–1pm, 3–5pm Monday–Friday, 9am–12 noon Saturday
- **Best Buys:** Cameras, electronic equipment, watches, porcelain, crystal, perfume, costumed dolls, woodcarvings, flags, leather jackets, jewelry, sports items. As a duty-free zone, Andorra offers low prices on all goods.
- **Public Holidays:** January 1; King's Day, January 6; March 19; Good Friday; May 1; Whitmonday; Assumption Day, August 15; Andorran National Feast Day, September 8; December 25; Boxing Day, December 26. Villages celebrate local holidays and saints' days.
- **National Tourist Offices:** There are no Tourist Offices for Andorra in the United States. The best place to obtain information would be the Spanish Tourist Office. (See p.572.) Andorra Delegation in Britain 63 Westover Road London SW18 2RF Tel: 0181 874 4806
- **American Embassy** The are no Embassies or Consulates in Andorra. (See p.572.)

History

Until May 1993, Andorra was a co-principality, owing tribute in a feudal style to two overlords (the President of France and the Spanish Bishop of Seu d'Urgell), but it now enjoys virtual autonomy. The government is now largely in the hands of a 28-member Council General which initiates legislation and elects a head called the Sindic General.

Food

Andorra's heritage has created a cuisine that combines the best of French and Spanish cooking. *Gazpacho, vichyssoise, paella* and *flan* (custard) are local favorites.

Getting Around

Although highways in Andorra are still under development, motoring should present no problems. The N22 from France (becoming the CG2 in Andorra) is occasionally closed by snow for short periods in winter. The CG3 is an internal (touring) route from Andorra la Vella through La Massana, Ordino, El Serrat and the mountains of the north west. All side roads radiating from the main roads are prefixed with a "V."

A child under 10 cannot travel in the front seat. Speed limits are 40 k.p.h. (25 m.p.h.) in town and 90 k.p.h. (55 m.p.h.) on out-of-town roads. Visiting motorists are required to pay fines for violations on the spot with Andorran currency.

Accommodations

Breakfast is included in the price of some hotel rooms. Andorra's campgrounds are open year-round.

Automobile Club
The Automobil Club d'Andorra (Automobile Club of Andorra) is at rue Babot Camp 4, Andorra la Vella. Not all auto clubs offer full travel services to AAA members.

PLACES OF INTEREST

▲ ANDORRA LA VELLA
pop. 16,000, elev. 1,029m. (3,376 ft.)
The village capital of Andorra, Andorra la Vella, is in a high valley encircled by towering peaks. Despite its altitude, the town has a moderate climate. Winters are cold, but the sun always seems to shine. Hotels and restaurants are both inviting and inexpensive. Because of Andorra's lack of taxes, shops in the village offer some of Europe's best goods at very competitive prices. The annual three-day village festival begins the first Saturday in August.

CASA DE LA VALL (the House of the Valley), a 16th-century stucco building, is the meeting place of Andorra's government and Council General.

CANILLO
pop. 500, elev. 1,559m. (5,118ft.)
A scenic village near the waterfall of Les Moles, Canillo has maintained much of its medieval appearance. Slate-roofed houses, a 12th-century chapel, old mills and an unusual seven-armed Gothic cross are among the points of interest. A three-day fiesta begins the third Saturday in July.

ENCAMP
pop. 6,400, elev. 1,265m. (4,153ft.)
At Encamp the belfries of granite churches contrast with the modern transmitter of Radio Andorra. More romantic, are the views of the mountains and the racing Valira River. The most dramatic panoramas can be seen from the cable lift to Engolasters Lake. Also nearby is the village of Les Bons, known for its Romanesque chapel. A village fiesta is held August 15–17.

NOTRE DAME DE MERITXELL, north of town, is the site of an annual pilgrimage in September. According to legend, the wooden image of the Virgin Mary was discovered in mid-winter under a blooming rose bush.

LA MASSANA
pop. 1,700, elev. 1,240m. (4,068ft.)
La Massana is known for its Romanesque art and nearby bridge spanning the gorge of Sant Antoni de la Grella. From June to September the village has numerous fiestas, concerts and other events.

LES ESCALDES
pop. 12,300, elev. 1,054m. (3,458ft.)
Les Escaldes is known for its thermal springs, which are pumped into hotels for the therapeutic benefit of visitors. The waters are available to the public from a fountain in the village square. An annual festival takes place in July.

ORDINO
pop. 500, elev. 1,304m. (4,281ft.)
Ordino has old churches and well-preserved Spanish-style homes. The village church dates from the 16th century. Casa Rosell has a dovecote and private chapel. Nearby, the peak of Casamanya soars to more than 2,000 meters (6,560 feet), offering magnificent views.

Classical music festivals take place regularly in Ordino. The annual fiesta is held the third week in September.

CASA PLANDOLIT dates back to the early 1600s. The house features wine and meat cellars, a music room, a bakery, a family chapel and wrought-iron balconies, and has fine gardens. Historical documents, paintings and period furnishings are displayed.

SANT JULIÁ DE LÓRIA
elev. 939m. (3,081ft.)
Its geographical position near Spain's northern plains made Sant Juliá de Lória a commercial center as early as the Middle Ages. The town is known for its exceptionally beautiful woodlands which are laced with roads and footpaths. Sant Juliá de Lória also merits attention for its fiestas, fairs and remnants of Romanesque art. A major three-day festival begins the last Sunday in July.

THINGS TO KNOW

- **AREA:** 6 square kilometers (2.3 square miles)
- **POPULATION:** 32,000
- **CAPITAL:** Gibraltar
- **LANGUAGES:** English and Spanish
- **ECONOMY:** Port commerce, tourism, financial services.
- **PASSPORT REQUIREMENTS:** Required for U.S. citizens
- **VISA REQUIREMENTS:** Not required
- **CURRENCY:** The currency unit, the Gibraltar pound (GP), is divided into 100 pence (p). Due to currency fluctuations, the exchange rate is subject to frequent change. No restrictions on import of currency, but only currency declared on arrival may be exported. United Kingdom and Gibraltar government notes and coins are legal tender.
- **BANK OPENING HOURS:** 9am–3:30pm Monday–Thursday, 9am–3:30pm and 4:30–6pm Friday.
- **SHOP OPENING HOURS:** 9am–7pm Monday–Friday; 9am–1pm Saturday.
- **BEST BUYS:** Perfume, cameras, crystal, cigars, cigarettes, electrical goods, jewelry, watches, ceramics and luxury items from other European countries.
- **PUBLIC HOLIDAYS:** January 1; Commonwealth Day; Good Friday; Easter Monday; May Day, first Monday in May; Spring Bank Holiday, last Monday in May; the Queen's Birthday, June 8; Late Summer Bank Holiday, last Monday in August; December 25–26.
- **NATIONAL TOURIST OFFICES:** Gibraltar Information Bureau 710 The Madison Offices 1155 15th Street NW Washington DC 20005, U.S.A. Tel: 202/452 1108; Fax: 202/872 8543 Gibraltar Information Bureau Arundel Great Court 179 The Strand London, England WC2R 1EH Tel: 0171 836 0777
- **AMERICAN EMBASSY:** 24 Grosvenor Square London W1A 1AE Tel: 0171 499 9000

GIBRALTAR

HISTORY

One of the fabled Pillars of Hercules, the Rock marked the limits of civilization in ancient times. In 711 AD Tarik-ibn-Zeyad led the Moorish assault on the promontory and named it for himself. The name Gibel-Tarik or Mount Tarik, was corrupted over the centuries into the modern name of Gibraltar. Although the Moors were able to maintain occupancy for the next 600 years, they were driven out of Spain.

Under the captaincy of Queen Isabella, Spain finally gained control of the Moorish stronghold in 1462, only to lose it to the British in 1704 during the War of the Spanish Succession. Since that time, this crown colony has withstood 14 sieges and has served as a strategic naval base. More recently the status of Gibraltar has been disputed diplomatically by Britain and Spain. The people have voted to remain British-ruled, however, and Gibraltar now welcomes travelers of all nationalities.

SPORTS AND RECREATION

In Mediterranean waters, swimming is enjoyable at Catalan Bay or the modern resorts of Eastern Beach and Sandy Bay. On the western side, favorites are Camp Bay and Little Bay.

Gibraltar is also a favored spot for yachtsmen and sea-anglers, with excellent marinas.

GETTING AROUND

Gibraltar can be entered from Spain via the La Línea customs post. A ferry runs from Tangier, Morocco, to Gibraltar. Round-trip excursions between Gibraltar and Morocco are offered in summer.

Seat belts are not mandatory, although a child should not occupy a front seat.

Speed limits are 30 k.p.h. (20 m.p.h.) in the city and 50 k.p.h. (30 m.p.h.) outside the city. Visiting motorists are required to pay fines for parking violations on the spot in Gibraltar pounds.

PLACES OF INTEREST

Set beneath the northwestern corner of the Rock, Gibraltar Town melds the blue-helmeted policemen and red mailboxes of Britain with oriental bazaars and international restaurants. The town has been fortified over the centuries, and much of the old garrison still stands. Points of interest include the casino; the Gibraltar Museum, with anthropological, coin and stamp collections; and the busy harbor.

The development of a port has attracted more ships to Gibraltar and is responsible for the town's transformation into an attractive tourist resort. Swimming, snorkeling, fishing, rowing, yachting, tennis and cricket are all very popular. Nightlife comprises of several movie theaters and nightclubs, and the Main Street is the principal shopping thoroughfare.

ALAMEDA GARDENS, at the south end of town off Europa Road, is a park with subtropical vegetation, scenic walks and a fine view of the sea. Opened in 1816, the gardens contain a wide array of flowers, trees and shrubs, as well as an open-air theater.

APES' DEN, halfway up the Rock, is the best spot for viewing the Barbary apes, the only wild monkeys found on the European continent. Residents of the Rock for centuries, they are free to roam as they choose but tend to frequent the upper cliffs. The Den is one of their favorite spots. Legend has it that British rule will end when the apes are gone from the Rock.

EUROPA POINT, south of Europa Road, marks the end of the Continent. On this promontory, lights at the Shrine of our Lady of Europe guided sailors in medieval times. Today sailors are aided by a 20-meter (60-foot) lighthouse, opened on August 1, 1841. It can be seen at a distance of 27 kilometers (17 miles) while looking out from the point the coast of Africa is visible on a clear day.

THE GALLERIES are north east at the end of Queens Road. During the French and Spanish Great Siege of 1779–83, military miners dug these tunnels 115 meters (370 feet) into the Rock, where they mounted four cannons in small windows called notches. More guns were added up to and including World War II. Today there are some 48 kilometers (30 miles) of tunnels, and many can be explored. Full-size figures depict scenes during the Great Siege.

MOORISH BATH, under the Gibraltar Museum, is an outstanding example of Moroccan architecture. The 14th-century structure with its 16-sided vaulted roof incorporates hot and cold baths and a steam room.

ROCK OF GIBRALTAR is the crown colony's chief attraction. Views of Europe, Africa and the Mediterranean can be had via a six-minute cable car ride to the summit. A large sundial can be seen below the north face. The fare includes the cable car round trip, a stop at the Apes' Den, and entry to the nature reserve and St. Michael's Cave. The ride begins at the boarding station in the Grand Parade at the southern end of Main Street.

ST MICHAEL'S CAVE, is south east of town on a side road off Queens Road. Not fully explored until 1936–8, this immense cavern is 250 meters (820 feet) above sea level. The cave is steeped in legend: At one time it was believed that Gibraltar was linked to Africa by a subterranean passage at this site. Concerts are frequently held in the upper hall, where colored lights illuminate stalagmites and stalactites. The Cave's origins go back to the warm glacial period, some 250,000 years ago.

Birdwatchers should note that in spring and fall, Gibraltar becomes a staging post for hundreds of thousands of birds who are in the process of migrating between Europe and Africa.

SWITZERLAND

Switzerland is united by its divisions. One of the most prosperous economies in Europe is produced by a nation divided first of all into four different languages – German, French, Italian and Romansch – as well as two religious groups, Protestants and Catholics.

There is little division in the scenery, however, with most of the country given to the various Alpine mountain ranges which dominate the southern and central regions. Between the Alps and the Jura lies the Swiss Plateau, where most of the people live. It runs between two huge lakes: Lake Constance (Bodensee) in the north east and Lake Geneva (Lac Léman) in the south west.

Left There are fantastic views to be had from the pretty mountain-top chalets in the Bernese Oberland

Above The Alphorn is a surviving tradition in Appenzell

THINGS TO KNOW

- **AREA:** 41,287 square kilometers (15,941 square miles)
- **POPULATION:** 6,675,000
- **CAPITAL:** Bern
- **LANGUAGES:** French, German, Italian and Romansch
  RELIGION: Switzerland is essentially divided between Roman Catholics and Protestants. However, other dominations are represented in the larger cities.
- **ECONOMY:** Lack of raw materials and minerals demands a processing industry. Chief exports are machinery, chemicals and watches. Rich in forests and waterpower. There is also a small amount of farming, mainly producing cheese and dairy produce. Tourism is also extremely important, particularly with the skiing industry.
- **ELECTRICITY:** Standard current is 220-volts AC; 50-cycles – supplied from sockets designed for three-pin round plugs.
- **PASSPORT REQUIREMENTS:** A valid passport is required for U.S. citizens.
- **VISA REQUIREMENTS:** Not required provided visitors do not become employed at any time.
- **DUTY-FREE ITEMS:** 400 cigarettes or 100 cigars or 500 grams tobacco; 2 liters of wine and 1 liter of liquor; two still cameras or one movie camera and one still camera; reasonable amount of film for personal use only; one video camera and normal accessories. Half of these quantities are allowed for visitors entering from another European country, except for wines and spirits.
- **CURRENCY:** The unit of currency is the Swiss *franc* (SF), divided into 100 *centimes*. Due to currency fluctuations, the exchange rate is subject to change. There are no import or export restrictions for Swiss or foreign currency.
- **BANK OPENING HOURS:** 8:15am or 8:30am–4:30pm Monday–Friday; exchange of currency daily until 10pm at large railroad stations and airports.

HISTORY

Today a land of peaceful prosperity, Switzerland has been the scene of many invasions. In ancient times, the Helvetians and other Celtic tribes crossed the Rhine River and established settlements along the lakes of this mountainous land. Inevitably the Romans conquered; their era lasted 400 years. During the Roman Empire's decline, the Burgundians and Franks invaded. It was during the Frankish period that Christianity was introduced. The Habsburgs entered the picture in 1273 when Rudolf of Habsburg became German Emperor. He soon reigned over all of central Europe and the Alpine lands, but the Habsburg rule was an

unpopular one, and the cities and cantons that made up present-day Switzerland began to yearn for freedom.

When Rudolf died, the three forest cantons of Uri, Unterwalden and Schwyz (which gave Switzerland its name) united and freed themselves from Habsburg domination, forming the nucleus of the Swiss Confederation. Independence was recognised in 1648, while other towns and villages were struggling to free themselves. These years of bitter wars and invasions by greedy neighbours left the Swiss with a strong sense of independence. They felt the establishment and maintenance of neutrality, which still prevails, was necessary for their country's survival. Switzerland remains ready to defend itself with a citizen army comprising every able-bodied male, each of whom keeps his gun at home.

Switzerland is a confederation of 26 cantons. National authority rests in a bicameral parliament and a federal council with seven members and a presidency which rotates between them for one-year terms. Each canton is in fact a sovereign state with its own government and control over its internal affairs.

FOOD AND DRINK

As Switzerland is so multi-cultural, each region has its own specialty. However, *fondue* and *râclette* originated in

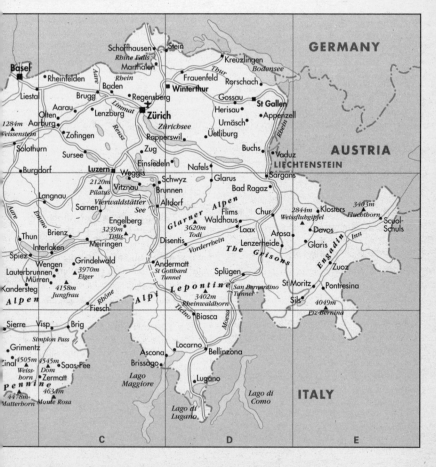

- **STORE OPENING HOURS:** 8am–noon and 2–6:30pm Monday–Friday; (open during lunch in large cities); 8am–4 or 5pm Saturday; some close Monday mornings.
- **BEST BUYS:** Watches, clocks, typewriters, chocolate, cheese, toys, music boxes, handkerchiefs, handicrafts and embroideries.
  Note: It is against U.S. customs regulations to bring liqueur-filled confections into the United States.
- **PUBLIC HOLIDAYS:** New Year's Day; January 2; Epiphany; Good Friday; Easter Monday; Ascension Day; Whit Monday and December 25–26. Some cantons may celebrate additional holidays such as May 1, Corpus Christi, All Saints' and National Day (August 1) among others.
- **USEFUL TELEPHONE NUMBERS:**
  Police: 117
  Fire: 118
  Ambulance: 144
- **NATIONAL TOURIST OFFICES:**
  Swiss National Tourist Office
  608 Fifth Ave
  New York
  NY 10020
  Tel: 212/757 5944
  Swiss National Tourist Office
  222 Fepulveda Building
  Suite 1570
  El Segundo
  Los Angeles
  CA 90245
  Tel: 310/335 5980
  Swiss National Tourist Office
  Swiss Centre
  1 New Coventry Street
  London W1V
  Tel: 0171 734 1921
  Schweizerische Verkehrszentrale
  (Swiss National Tourist Office)
  Bellariastrasse 38
  CH-8023 Zürich
  Tel: 01 2023737
- **AMERICAN EMBASSY:**
  Jubiläumsstrasse 93
  CH-3005 Bern
  Switzerland
  Tel: 03 437011

Switzerland and must not be missed. For dessert try *leckerli* or some chocolate for which Switzerland is famous.

Among the most popular wines are *Dôle*, *Nostrano* and *Maienfelder* (red); *Dézalay*, *Yvorne* and *Fendant* (white). The fruit brandies, *Schnapps*, are also very popular.

SPORTS AND RECREATION

Mountaineering and skiing head the list of sporting activities in Switzerland. Guides for mountain climbing trips can be engaged by the day, week or month; the mountaineering school at Rosenlaui, near Meiringen, is good for information. Prominent ski resorts are Davos, St. Moritz, Verbier and Engelberg. Generally the ski season continues from December to late-March or at resorts above 1,524 meters (5,000 feet) this extends to mid-May. Skiing is also possible all year round on glaciers at higher elevations.

In summer, the efficiently waymarked footpath network attracts casual ramblers and mountain hikers. The many lakes offer endless opportunities for watersports of all kinds and there are plenty of lidos and swimming pools.

GETTING AROUND

Switzerland's four international airports at Basel, Bern, Geneva and Zürich link the country with around 110 foreign cities. Both Geneva and Zürich airports have stations on the railroad network, making onward travel particularly easy. A fly-rail baggage system enables bag-

---

AUTOMOBILE CLUB
The **Touring Club Suisse** (TCS, Swiss Touring Club), rue Pierre-Fatio 9, Genève, has offices in cities throughout Switzerland. The symbol ▲ beside a city name indicates the presence of a AAA-affiliated automobile club branch. Not all clubs offer full travel services to AAA members.

gage to be checked in at the airport abroad to a range of rail destinations within Switzerland (and vice-versa).

All Swiss trains are electric, reasonably fast, reliable and connected to most parts of the country. Numerous tunnels, rack and pinion railroads and cable cars have overcome the obstacles posed by some of Europe's highest mountains. Numerous concessions minimize the cost of rail travel for the visitor, particularly the Swiss Pass.

The Swiss Pass is also valid on steamer services and alpine postbuses. Steamer services operate on the larger lakes while the bright yellow postbuses carry both mail and passengers to areas not accessible by rail. Public transportation in cities is well developed, with trams as well as buses in the larger cities.

The road system in Switzerland is generally excellent. Mountain roads incur problems such as hairpin bends and postbuses demanding their right of way. Although on the whole, the challenge of the Alpine passes has been removed through the building of great tunnels.

Drivers and all passengers over seven years old must wear seat belts where equipped, and children under 12 must travel in the rear seats. Speed limits are 50 k.p.h. (30 m.p.h.) in built-up areas (indicated by the place sign), 80 k.p.h. (50 m.p.h.) on other roads, 120 k.p.h. (75 m.p.h.) on highways. An annual highway tax of Sfr. 40 (the *Vignette*) is payable for vehicles entering the country. Motoring fines may have to be paid on the spot.

ACCOMMODATIONS

Standards of lodging in Switzerland are among the highest in the world. The Swiss Hotel Association rates hotels from one to five stars, (five being the highest). The Swiss National Tourist Office can provide you with a list of accommodations. In many areas there is also a choice of chalets, apartments and youth hostels.

Campers have their choice of about 450 campgrounds, many in scenic areas near resorts and along major roads.

TIPPING

Restaurants, hotels and taxi fares all include a 15 percent gratuity in their bills, so extra tipping is your own choice.

LANGUAGE

Useful terms are to be found in all three main languages, German, French and Italian, in the relevent country chapters.

PRINCIPAL TOURING AREAS

Note: For descriptions of cities in **bold type**, see individual city listings.

THE BERNESE OBERLAND AND CENTRAL SWITZERLAND

The Bernese Oberland, "Aristocrat of Alpine Scenery", contains nine valleys and several lakes. Bathe in Lake Brienz, in view of fig trees and vineyards, and 3 hours later ski on eternal snow and ice. The lakes at **Brienz** and **Thun** are popular for rowing and swimming, and **Interlaken** is a good base for exploring the mountains.

South east of Interlaken is **Grindelwald**; in no other place in the Alps do the glaciers so closely approach the lush vegetation of the countryside. To the south is the great wall of rock formed by the world-renamed trio of *Jungfrau*, *Eiger* and *Mönch* (Maiden, Ogre, and Monk).

North west lies the ancient city of **Bern**, capital of the Swiss Federation. Bordering a lake is bustling **Luzern**, or **Lucerne**, a main excursion center for resorts such as **Engelberg** and Andermatt. Boat trips leave Lucerne regularly for a number of historic villages nearby.

EASTERN SWITZERLAND

Bordering on Liechtenstein, Germany and Austria, this part of Switzerland consists of two distinct regions.

In the south east is Graubünden, or Grisons, with some of the highest valleys in the country. The canton has many world famous resorts such as **St. Moritz**, **Davos** and **Pontresina.**

Well-maintained roads wind through breathtaking scenery in this part of Switzerland. Also of interest are **Arosa**, with its lakes, and the capital city of **Chur**, surrounded by wooded mountains.

Northeastern Switzerland includes the canton of **Appenzell**, rolling countryside famous for its fruit and pastoral products. The abbey town of **St. Gallen** is known for the delicate hand embroidery it produces. From the summit of the Säntis mountain 2,005 meters (6,578 feet) there is one of the finest panoramas to be had in the whole country.

West is **Winterthur**, guarded by castles that overlook this ancient city from surrounding hills.

SOUTHERN SWITZERLAND

Ticino, the southernmost canton, has an Italian character and atmosphere. This sunny, luxuriant territory boasts an almost Mediterranean climate and Italian-speaking people; while at the same time, still remains totally Swiss .

The Sottoceneri region is one of contrasts between **Lugano**, a bustling city with a lake and beaches, and the charming villages tucked in the surrounding valleys. **Bellinzona**, capital of the canton, and the northern valley compose a second area. Forming a third is lakeside **Locarno** and its neighboring valleys. There is an excellent beach 4 kilometers (2½ miles) from Locarno in **Ascona**.

SOUTH-WEST SWITZERLAND

This region is divided into two distinct areas – to the west the area around Lake Geneva and to the east the Valais and the Upper Rhône River Valley.

The beauty of Lake Geneva (Lac Léman) has often been celebrated in the arts. Paddle steamers shuttle across the

lake, serving French and Swiss ports. Neighboring **Vevey** and **Montreux** have long been popular resorts, and villages surrounded by vineyards rise 305 meters (1,000 feet) from the lakeside. To the south is the Mont Blanc mountain range, extending into the heart of Europe.

The Valais region begins at the east end of Lake Geneva (Lac Léman). From the long, deep valley of the Rhine, numerous valleys branch off, leading to some picturesque and spectacular scenery.

ZÜRICH AND THE NORTH

German-speaking **Zürich**, with its fine stores, luxury hotels and restaurants, is a lively metropolis and the largest city in Switzerland. Gardens and villas extend from the lake in the center of the city to the tops of the encircling hill.

The verdant countryside of northern Switzerland has its own fascination, with many charming villages and small historic towns. The Rhine runs westward from Lake Constance (Bodensee) forming the border with Germany for much of its course and crashing over famous falls near the old town of **Schaffhausen**. **Basel**, the country's second largest city, has a historic core as well as modern industries and commerce.

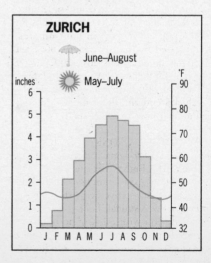

PLACES OF INTEREST

▲ BERN (609 B2) ★

BERN *pop. 134,000*

Bern has been capital of the Swiss confederation since 1848. According to legend, this city on the banks of the Aare River received its name when Berthold V, Duke of Zähringen, told his followers that the city would be named after the first animal he killed. Thus the "Bear of Bern" became its trademark.

Turreted buildings, beautiful fountains and miles of arcaded sidewalks decorate the old town like illustrations in a fairy tale, while the figures in the Clock Tower re-enact the world's oldest horological play. Other highlights of the old town are the 15th-century Town Hall and the Gothic cathedral. Some of the finest viewpoints over the city and its surroundings are from immaculately maintained parks like the *Rosengarten* (Rose Garden), and the Grosse Schanze.

The opera and theater seasons are late September through to June. Opera and ballet are presented at the Stadttheatre, and concerts at a number of other halls.

Bern is the principal starting point for trips to the Bernese Oberland; daily tours of varying duration are offered. Lakeside roads in this region afford incomparable views, and other well-maintained roads lead upward to funicular railroad stations.

BÄRENGRABEN off Nydeggbrücke on the east bank of the Aare, is the city's bear pit. The inhabitants, who amuse visitors for the price of a carrot, have been an attraction since the late 15th century.

BERNISCHES HISTORISCHES MUSEUM (Bernese Historical Museum), housed in a mock-Gothic building, highlighting the history of the city and canton of Bern.

BUNDESHAUS (Federal Palace), where extensive views of the Bernese Alps can be enjoyed on the terrace of the domed Florentine Renaissance-style building.

KUNSTMUSEUM (Fine Arts Museum) is one of the best collections of both Swiss and international painting. Paul Klee was a native of Bern, and there is an extensive collection of his unique works.

MÜNSTER is considered the most beautiful ecclesiastical building in Switzerland. Begun in 1421, it took 150 years to complete. Of note are the stained-glass windows and the superbly carved main portal depicting the Last Judgement.

SCHWEIZERISCHES ALPINES MUSEUM (Swiss Alpine Museum) contains fascinating exhibits on the natural history of the Alps and the story of mountaineering.

ZEITGLOCKENTURM (Clock Tower) is the oldest structure in Bern, dating from the 12th century. Built by Kaspar Brunner, it features an astronomical clock and a delightful figure-play.

APPENZELL (609 D3)

APPENZELL INNER-RHODEN

pop. 5,300, elev. 780m. (2,559ft.)

In a countryside rich with meadows, the picturesque little capital of Appenzell retains many of its old customs. On the last Sunday of April, residents attend the Landsgemeinde, an open-air meeting at which citizens vote directly on the laws by which they are governed. Colorful processions to and from the mountains take place as farmers move their cattle to

SWITZERLAND

the Alpine pastures for eight to 12 weeks in the summer. The areas mountains are accessible by cable cars and hiking trails.

AROSA (609 D2)
GRAUBÜNDEN *pop. 2,900, elev. 1,875m. (6,152ft.)*
Arosa is world known as a winter sports resort. One of the largest ski schools in the country, four practice slopes, ice hockey rinks, skating rinks, toboggan runs and curling facilities attract hundreds of cold-weather athletes.

ASCONA (609 D1)
TICINO *pop. 4,800*
Ascona lies on a protected bay at the northern end of the mainly Italian Lake Maggiore. The town began as a fishing village, but its mild, sunny climate slowly transformed it into a favorite vacation spot. Narrow streets and alleys are lined with antique and arts-and-crafts shops.

▲ BADEN (609 C3)
AARGAU *pop. 14,200*
Baden is Switzerland's oldest spa and health resort. The Old Town is medieval, though much of it was rebuilt in the 18th century following an attack by an army from Bern. Dominated by the ruins of Stein Castle, Baden is picturesquely sited on the Limmat River.

LANDVOGTEISCHLOSS (Bailiffs' Castle) dates from the 15th century. The museum in the keep contains arms, period furniture and local costumes; the upper floor gives fine views of the Old Town.

SCHWEIZER KINDERMUSEUM (Swiss Children's Museum), Oelrainstrasse 29, promotes and conducts research into children's culture. Exhibits portray the world of children over the past 200 years.

▲ BASEL (609 B3) ★
BASEL-STADT *pop. 175,000*
As Switzerland's second largest city, Basel has both economic and historic importance. Sprawling on both banks of a wide curve of the Rhine, it is the meeting place of three countries: Switzerland, France and Germany. The Vosges and Jura mountains in France and the Black Forest in Germany are close by.

Basel was the home of the German painter Hans Holbein the Younger and the Dutch humanist Erasmus, who paved the way for the Reformation. The University of Basel, built in 1460, is the oldest in Switzerland. While it is proud of its history, Basel is also a progressive city. It is a large inland port, a center of international banking, and the site of many highly developed pharmaceutical and chemical industries.

The rumbustious three-day Fasnacht Carnival in February or March and the Swiss Industries Fair in the spring are of special interest. As is the fall fair, celebrating the city's accomplishments.

HISTORISCHES MUSEUM (History Museum), Barfüsserplate, is housed in a 14th-century Franciscan church. Its collection of religious and art pieces tell the story of Basel and its surroundings from the Middle Ages onwards.

KUNSTMUSEUM (Fine Arts Museum), St. Albangraben 16, is the city's pride and joy, one of Europe's great art galleries. It has 15th- and 16th-century masterpieces by Konrad Witz, Nikolaus Manuel and the Holbeins, as well as modern art by Picasso, Braque, Léger and Arp.

MÜNSTER (Cathedral), Münsterplatz, was consecrated in the 11th century, subsequently destroyed and completely restored in the last century. Its twin towers and patterned roof tiles, is one of the city's great landmarks.

RATHAUS (Town Hall), a red sandstone 16th-century town hall dominating the market square, is enhanced by frescoes and carvings on its walls and ceilings.

ZOOLOGISCHER GARTEN, is perhaps the finest in the country, laid out in a spacious park near the city center. Children will be delighted by the children's zoo.

▲ BELLINZONA (609 D1)

TICINO *pop. 25,000*

Bellinzona, capital of the Ticino canton is the gateway to all of Italian Switzerland, and consequently has a distinct Italian atmosphere. Its strategic importance is emphasized by the three castles which guard it. The Castello Grande, Montebello, and di Sasso Corbaro are splendid examples of fortification design; the last two contain museums.

▲ BIEL-BIENNE (609 B3)

BERN *pop. 52,000*

Known for its watchmaking, Biel-Bienne is an important industrial and commercial center. The Old Quarter still bears the stamp of its historic past with many fine, old buildings and medieval fountains.

BRIENZ (609 C2)

BERN *pop. 3,000*

On the northern end of Lake Brienz, this quaint village, well known for the local craft of woodcarving lies at the foot of the Brienzer Rothorn (2,350 meters /7,710 feet). Preserved wooden houses and narrow alleyways are complemented by a promenade alongside the lake.

BALLENBERG (Swiss Open Air Museum) is a 63-hectare (155-acre) living-history museum with 70 original farmhouses dating from the 16th century. All structures, furnished in period, were dismantled and moved from various parts of the country and rebuilt here. Costumed workers demonstrate the arts and crafts of the times.

BRIENZER ROTHORN BAHN This rack railroad, almost climbing to the top of the Brienzer Rothorn is still worked by steam engines built as long ago as the 1890s. It is one of the most spectacular rides in the Swiss Alps.

▲ LA CHAUX-DE-FONDS (609 B3)

NEUCHÂTEL *pop. 37,000, elev. 992m. (3,255ft.)*

La Chaux-de-Fonds is the center of the country's watchmaking industry. The Horological Museum, built underground in the middle of a park, is the definitive museum of humankind's attempts to record the passage of time.

▲ CHUR (609 D2)

GRAUBÜNDEN *pop. 32,000*

As the guardian of Alpine routes since 15 BC, Chur is probably the country's oldest settlement. Although mountains surround this ancient city, there are direct connections to most of the ski resorts in the region.

A train excursion running south east from Chur to the Engadine Valley of the Rhaetian Alps, passes the picturesque village of Filisur. Near Filisur is Greifenstein Castle and "La Chanzla", a huge rock with a 10-meter (33-foot) painting of the Devil.

KUNSTMUSEUM (Art Gallery) Postplatz, has pictures by Graubünden artists, whom the canton seems to have produced in unusual quantity.

RHÄTISCHES MUSEUM is devoted to the art and folklore of Graubünden, with paintings and sculptures from the 18th century to the present as well as a noteworthy collection of prehistoric artifacts.

CRANS MONTANA (609 B1)

VALAIS *pop. 700, elev. 1,470m. (4,822ft.)*
Overlooking the Rhône Valley, with a panorama of the Alps from Mont Blanc to the Matterhorn, skiing is available year-round on the Plaine Morte glacier. The town is host to many golf tournaments as the golf course here is one of Europe's best.

DAVOS (609 E2) ★

GRAUBÜNDEN *pop. 12,000, elev. 1,560m. (5,120ft.)*
The countryside surrounding Davos, one of the highest towns in Europe, is ideal for both downhill and cross-country skiing. Davos-Dorf and Davos-Platz form one of the oldest and best-known Alpine health resorts with 322 kilometers (200 miles) of trails, but it is equally

known as a winter sports center. It has Europe's largest ice-skating rink and two ski schools. The Parsennbahn funicular railroad takes skiers up to Weissfluhjoch, a departure point for several ski runs. The town is also a focal point of scientific research, and a center of the arts.

KIRCHNER MUSEUM contains the world's largest collection of the works, and other materials, of German expressionist painter Ernst Ludwig Kirchner.

▲ DELÉMONT (609 B3)
JURA *pop. 12,000*
Delémont, the capital of the Jura canton, is a renowned watchmaking center. Although the town has a modern appearance, it retains some of its 16th-century character, especially around the town hall and the Church of St. Marcellus.

EINSIEDELN (609 D3)
SCHWYZ *pop. 10,500, elev. 910m. (2,986ft.)*
Einsiedeln is the site of Switzerland's most famous monastery, one of Europe's most important places of Pilgrimage. Inside the Holy Chapel, built over the site of the hut where a saintly hermit called Meinrad lived in the 9th century, is a Black Madonna. This tiny wooden statuette holding the Infant Christ is an object of great veneration.

ENGELBERG (609 C2)
OBWALDEN *pop. 2,800, elev. 1,050m. (3,445ft.)*
At the foot of Mount Titlis, this vacation resort is especially popular for winter sports; skiing can be enjoyed December through June thanks to the Titlis glacier. In summer regularly scheduled events of music, theater and colorful folk entertainment attract visitors and residents alike. The Benedictine Abbey has one of the largest pipe organs in Switzerland.

FLIMS WALDHAUS (609 D2)
GRAUBÜNDEN *pop. 1,200, elev. 1,140m. (3,740ft.)*
On a sunny terrace above the Rhein Valley, sheltered from cold winds and snow-blocked roads, Flims' winter facilities are skiing, ice skating, curling and tobogganing. In the summer, visitors flock to Lake Cauma and enjoy tennis, riding, mountaineering and hiking in the pine woods.

▲ FRIBOURG (609 B2)
FRIBOURG *pop. 33,000*
The capital of its bilingual (French and German) canton, Fribourg is a historic city on the Saane River. The old town has a graceful medieval atmosphere; the modern quarter bustles with fine homes and schools. Chocolate is manufactured in this city, home to Switzerland's only bilingual Catholic University.

CATHÉDRALE ST.-NICOLAS begun in 1283, took five centuries to complete. Of note are the tower and the frescoed tympanum; a monumental pipe organ and fine sculptures grace the interior.

MUSÉE D'ART ET D'HISTOIRE, rue de Morat 12, displays a representative sample of Fribourg art and artistic crafts from the Middle Ages to the late 18th century. Late Gothic sculptures and paintings, and works by the contemporary artist Jean Tingueley are also displayed.

GENEVA – *see Genève below.*

▲ GENÈVE (609 A1) ★
GENÈVE *pop. 170,000*
(*see map on p.617.*)
Genève, or Geneva, has all the advantages of a big city plus its magnificent lakeside and mountain setting. Whether the view is of the red roofs and green gardens as seen from the carillon tower in the cathedral or from the deck of a steamer as it crosses Lake Geneva (Lac Léman), Genève is equally beautiful.
　　Genève has earned its place in world history through the efforts of great reformers and thinkers. They include Calvin (1509–64) who made the city the "Protestant Rome," Jean-Jacques Rousseau (1712–78) who prepared the way for the French Revolution, and

Henri Dunant (1828–1910) who persuaded governments to sign the Geneva Convention, limiting the effects of war and leading to the foundation of the International Red Cross.

The modern city faces the lake, and the old town, the Vieille Ville, huddles around the cathedral, embracing a maze of antique shops and bistros. In summer, Genève assumes an international atmosphere as visitors stroll along the quays and spend time in the cafés. Much of the activity centers on the Quai du Mont-Blanc, departure point for the paddle steamers that go across Lake Geneva (Lac Léman).

In August, the city holds its four-day Fête de Genève, replete with fireworks, singing, street dancing and parades.

Genève's Escalade in mid-December includes riders in period costumes, country markets, folk music and parades.

Year-round concert schedules include the Orchestre de la Suisse Romande's at the Victoria Hall during winter, and the grand opera from October to May, at the Grand Théâtre, near the Conservatoire.

Genève is the European headquarters of the United Nations, including the international headquarters of the World Health Organization.

CATHÉDRALE DE ST.-PIERRE (617 B2), rue St.-Pierre, dates from the 12th century, but was partly rebuilt in the 16th century. John Calvin's Chair commemorates the celebrated theologian who preached during the mid-16th century.

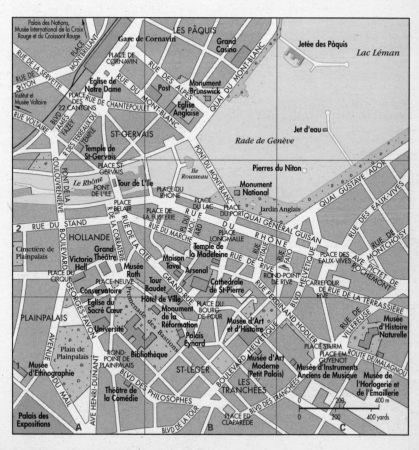

SWITZERLAND

Of particular note are the flamboyant Chapel of the Maccabees, with its fine stained glass, and the North Tower, offering a view of the Alps and Lake Geneva (Lac Léman).

HÔTEL DE VILLE (617 B1), Grande-Rue, is the town hall. The Geneva Convention, founding the International Red Cross, was signed in 1864 in a room later named in memory of a successful arbitration between America and Britain in 1871.

JET D'EAU (617 C3), a towering spray of lake water that reaches a height of 119 meters (390 feet), is Genève's landmark seen for miles, but only in the summer.

MAISON TAVEL (617 B2), 6 rue du Puits St.-Pierre, is a museum in Genève's oldest house dating from the 12th century. It depicts the history of the city from the 14th to 19th centuries. In the attic, visitors can see a relief map that represents Genève during the 1850s.

MUSÉE D'ART ET D'HISTOIRE (Museum of Art and History) (617 B1), 2 rue Charles-Galland, is one of Switzerland's great museums, an immense building housing coins, paintings, sculpture, clocks and watches, and archeological exhibits.

MUSÉE DE L'HORLOGERIE ET DE L'ÉMAILLERIE (Watch and Clock Museum) (617 C1), 15 route de Malagnou, exhibits clocks, watches and music boxes dating from the 16th century onwards.

MUSÉE D'HISTOIRE NATURELLE (Natural History Museum) (617 C1), 1 route de Malagnou, is one of the most important in Europe. Dinosaurs in their natural habitats are particularly fascinating. A science library has over 150,000 reference documents.

MUSÉE D'INSTRUMENTS ANCIENS DE MUSIQUE (Museum of Ancient Musical Instruments) (617 C1), 23 rue Francois Lefort, displays a varied collection of 16th- to 19th-century instruments.

GRINDELWALD (609 C2)
BERN *pop. 3,800, elev. 1,057m. (3,468ft.)*
Grindelwald, spread out over a sunny plateau, is one of the most popular year-round resorts in Switzerland. To the south are some of the great peaks of the Bernese Oberland, the Jungfrau and the Eiger, and the Grindelwald Glacier reaches almost to the village. All the popular winter sports facilities are usually available from December to March. Grindelwald also has an excellent climbing and mountaineering school.

GRUYÈRES (609 B2)
FRIBOURG *pop. 1,300, elev. 830m. (2,723ft.)*
Despite its seemingly precarious location, Gruyères is safe behind its medieval ramparts. A 12th-century castle dominates this town that owes its international reputation to the cheese that bears its name.

CHEESE RITES
Swiss cheese is famous, its flavor enhanced by the flower-rich pastures grazed by the country's cows. More than one hundred varieties are produced, though about three-quarters of the nation's appetite for cheese is satisfied by four big names – Gruyère, Emmenthal, Tilsit and Appenzeller.

GSTAAD (609 B2)
BERN *pop. 2,000, elev. 1,056m. (3,465ft.)*
Forests, mountains and glaciers surround fashionable Gstaad, which boasts 16th-century houses in the old part of town. As one of the leading winter and summer resorts in Switzerland, it has many community sports facilities. For those interested in viewing Alpine scenery, gondola rides are available in summer.

INTERLAKEN (609 C2)
BERN *pop. 13,000*
A Swiss health and pleasure resort, Interlaken combines the offerings of an international vacation spot with the

charm of a rustic village. The town lies between the lakes of Thun and Brienz, with a famous view of the Jungfrau rising at the end of the valley.

Interlaken was founded in 1133 by Augustinian monks and evolved into a popular resort during the 17th century. It is essentially an excursion center and gateway to the Bernese Oberland, as well as an important rail connection point to the Jungfraujoch, which, at an elevation of 3,453 meters (11,330 feet) is Europe's highest railroad station.

IN THE ARMY

Though every able-bodied Swiss male is still a citizen soldier, and the army, once mobilized, is one of the largest in Europe, the forces no longer enjoy the prestige they earned while manning the frontiers during the long years of the Second World War, effectively deterring any attack which the Axis powers might have been tempted to make.
The result of a recent referendum showed that a majority of young adults were in favor of abolishing the army altogether.

KANDERSTEG (609 B2)
BERN *pop. 1,000, elev. 1,200m. (3,937ft.)*
Surrounded by the spectacular scenery of the Bernese Oberland, Kandersteg is an old village built among the meadows of the valley floor. One of the finest walks in Switzerland leads along an ancient pack-horse route to the Gemmi Pass. A chairlift takes visitors most of the way up to the Oeschinensee, a beautiful small lake set amongst the rock wall of the Oberland.

▲ LAUSANNE (609 A2) ★
VAUD *pop. 118,000*
Lausanne, the capital of the French-speaking canton of Vaud, has many distinctions. Built on several hills, the town rises nearly 244 meters (800 feet) and is the second largest city on Lake

Geneva (Lac Léman). The home of the Swiss High Courts of Justice, the site of a great university and thriving cultural center, its exuberance has attracted foreigners since the 18th century.

Lausanne's concert and theater season runs from September to April. Plays in French are presented at Le Théâtre Municipal, where the International Festival of Lausanne takes place in May and June. Opera, ballet, concerts and performances by guest artists are held at the Théâtre du Beaulieu.

Lausanne is host to many scientific congresses and the National Autumn Agricultural, Industrial and Trade Fair. The city is also the headquarters of the International Olympic Committee.

CATHÉDRALE (the Cathedral of Notre Dame) is one of the finest Gothic churches in Switzerland. Its many fascinating features include an elaborately carved south door, 13th-century stalls, and a rose window. It is one of the few places left in the world to keep a night watch; a custodian calls out the hours throughout the night.

MUSÉE DE L'ÉLYSÉE (Élysée Museum), 18 avenue de l'Élysée, houses in an 18th-century mansion four floors of exhibits dedicated to the history of photography.

MUSÉE OLYMPIQUE (Olympic Museum), chronicles the history of the modern Olympic Games with photographs, medals, flags and other memorabilia. The International Olympic Committee was founded in Lausanne in 1915.

PALAIS DE RUMINE close to the cathedral, houses Lausanne University and several museums that deal with the fine arts, natural history, and botany.

LAUTERBRUNNEN (609 C2)
BERN *pop. 3,400, elev. 797m. (2,615ft.)*
A favorite center for mountain climbing, Lauterbrunnen is also a busy tourist center known for its spectacular waterfalls and mountain torrents. It is the starting-

SWITZERLAND

point of the railroad to the Jungfrau, where the highest station in Europe commands one of the most magnificent views in the world. Nearby, Trümmelbach Falls descend in five cascades through a narrow gorge below the Jungfrau; Staubbach Falls, also nearby, drops nearly 305 meters (1,000 feet).

LENZBURG (609 C3)
AARGAU *pop. 13,800*
The small industrial town of Lenzburg lies on the Aare River in a region peppered with castles. Nearby is Hallwil and Lenzburg Castle, both dating from the 11th century.

▲ LOCARNO (609 D1)
TICINO *pop. 14,100*
On the north shore of Lake Maggiore, Locarno has a mild climate, and rich vegetation. Ernest Hemingway immortalized Locarno in his novel *A Farewell to Arms*, and during the International Film Festival in August it is especially festive.

Lake excursions can be made to Ascona, Brissago, and across the Italian border to Stresa and the Borromean isles.

CASTELLO VISCONTI, Piazza Castello, is a medieval castle that features Roman relics as well as temporary exhibits. The archeological museum is of interest.

SAN VITTORE, Via della Collegiata, one of several fascinating churches in Locarno is a fine example of 12th-century Romanesque architecture.

LUCERNE – *See Luzern opposite*.

▲ LUGANO (609 D1)
TICINO *pop. 29,000*
Lugano, the largest town in the canton of Ticino, is on the shore of Lake Lugano. The old town is thoroughly Italian in character, but the hotels and villas beyond give it an international air. A March to October bill of concerts, includes free jazz festivals in July and late August. A huge fireworks display takes place on Lake Lugano in late July.

The Festival of the Grape Harvest, with folk music performances, is held from late September to early October.

Excursions to Monte Bré (925 meters/3,035 feet) and Monte San Salvatore (911 meters/2,990 feet), can be made, and a regular steamer service connects many places on Lake Lugano.

CHIESA DE SANTA MARIA DEGLI ANGIOLI a former convent constructed in 1499, has frescoes by Bernardino Luini, including the *Crucifixion*.

LA VILLA FAVORITA is a stately 17th-century mansion housing the Thyssen Collection, one of the finest private collections in Europe.

▲ LUZERN (609 C3) ★
LUZERN *pop. 60,000*
Luzern, or Lucerne, is the capital of its canton and considered one of the most beautiful cities in the country. On the shores of Lake Lucerne, the city's medieval heritage is evident in the walls and towers, the fine old churches and houses and above all in the unusual covered bridges that span the Reuss.

In 1992, Lucerne suffered a great loss, when its 14th-century Kapellbrücke, or Chapel Bridge, was destroyed by fire. Built in 1333, it was Europe's oldest covered bridge and connected the two parts of the Old Town. It has subsequently been fully restored.

During the International Music Festival, August to September, it is nearly impossible to find rooms unless reservations have been made in advance. Opera is presented from September to April in the Stadttheater, where plays and comedies are in German. An open-air market takes place Tuesday and Saturday along both river banks.

The classic excursion from Lucerne is to Mount Pilatus, a 2,120-meter (7,000-foot) pyramidal crag to which legend says Pontius Pilate was wafted by the Devil after the Crucifixion. It is reached by the world's steepest cogwheel mountain railroad from Alpnachstad.

HISTORISCHES MUSEUM (History Museum), Pfistergasse 24, is housed in a 16th-century arsenal. Exhibits include antique armor, uniforms, costumes, coins and the medieval Gothic fountain that originally stood in the wine market.

MUSEGGMAUER, the largest complex of medieval fortifications remaining in Switzerland, consists of nine towers and a substantial section of the city wall. Part of the wall and the Schirmer, Mannli and Zyt towers are open to the public May through to October.

VERKEHRSHAUS (Transport Museum) exhibits railroads, automobiles, planes, ships, space vehicles and a planetarium to name a few. This is one of the largest, most modern, and most fascinating transportation museums in Europe.

MEIRINGEN (609 C2)
BERN *pop. 2,800*
The principal town of the Hasli Valley, Meiringen is a popular Alpine resort, and ideally situated for touring the eastern parts of the Bernese Oberland.

AARE GORGE is a deep, narrow gorge through which passes the Aare River. A specially constructed footpath leads through this astonishing phenomenon.

MONTREUX (609 B2) ★
VAUD *pop. 20,400*
Montreux is a year-round health and pleasure resort at the east end of Lake Geneva (Lac Léman). The cosmopolitan town owes its fame to its mild climate and superb location, protected from the north by wooded and vine-clad slopes; it is at its liveliest during the summer. As a center of intellectual and artistic life, Montreux presents an extensive program of concerts, plays and variety shows, whose high point is reached during the Montreux Jazz Festival in July and the Music Festival in September.

The 2,042-meter (6,700-foot) Rochers-de-Naye offers a great view of the Alps and Lake Geneva (Lac Léman).

CHÂTEAU DE CHILLON is an imposing 13th-century fortress and former prison. The castle was built on a jagged rock rising out of the lake and was immortalized by Lord Byron in *The Prisoner of Chillon.* It is one of the best-preserved and most popular medieval castles in Europe.

MORGES (609 A2)
VAUD *pop. 13,000*
Morges, an elegant little harbor town on Lake Geneva (Lac Léman), was once one of the lake's most important commercial ports. It lies at the center of the wine-growing district of La Côte and from April to May holds a tulip festival.

MUSÉE MILITAIRE (Military Museum) is housed in the huge, four-towered castle. It contains collections of uniforms, weapons, flags and lead soldiers.

MÜRREN (609 C2)
BERN *pop. 350, elev. 1,096m. (3,597ft.)*
The highest village of the Bernese Oberland, Mürren is perched on a high rocky shelf. Looking down on the Lauterbrunnen Valley, it can only be reached by mountain railroad from Lauterbrunnen and by cablecar from Stechelberg. Another cablecar takes visitors to the revolving restaurant at the summit of the Schilthorn, some 3,048 meters (10,000 feet) high.

MURTEN (609 B2)
FRIBOURG *pop. 4,700*
On the eastern shore of the Murtensee, Murten has retained its medieval ramparts and walks along the top of the walls give views over the town's rooftops to the lake below. The ramparts boast 12 fortified towers, two main gates, and one of Switzerland's oldest clocks.

▲ NEUCHÂTEL (609 B2)
NEUCHÂTEL *pop. 32,000*
Neuchâtel, capital city of the canton of the same name, spreads for 5 kilometers (3 miles) along the shore of its lake at the foot of Chaumont. Set among vineyards, this picturesque town is also

noted for banking, watchmaking and the Institute for Horological Research.

MUSÉE CANTONAL D'ARCHÉOLOGIE (Canton Museum of Archeology), has many exhibits found in local caves dating back 50,000 years.

MUSÉE D'ART ET D'HISTOIRE (Art and History Museum), contains a large collection of works by French Impressionist painters, and a good selection of Swiss art. There are also exhibits of pottery, clocks, coins and automated figures.

NYON (609 A2)
VAUD *pop. 14,500*
The old port of Nyon dominates a hillside overlooking Lake Geneva (Lac Léman). The Old Town has remnants of medieval buildings, gardens and walks.

PONTRESINA (609 E2)
GRAUBÜNDEN *pop. 1,800, elev. 1,775m. (5,823ft.)*
One of the great mountain centers of the Alps and a much-frequented year-round resort, Pontresina is a starting point for glacier climbs and walking excursions to the Bernina group and the upper Engadine. The village offers innumerable opportunities for skiing tours in the surrounding mountains, intense sunshine and a healthful climate.

▲ RAPPERSWIL (609 D3)
ST. GALLEN *pop. 8,000*
Rapperswil is built on a little peninsula jutting into Lake Zürich. It has charming streets and a massive 13th-century castle. For years Rapperswil was virtually the capital of a Poland which had been absorbed by Russia, Prussia and Austria, and the castle contains a museum devoted to Polish exiles in Switzerland.

▲ ST. GALLEN (609 D3)
ST. GALLEN *pop. 72,000*
St. Gallen began as a Benedictine monastery in 612 AD, founded by the Irish hermit monk Gallus. A natural gateway to Switzerland from Germany or Austria,

HIGH-ALTITUDE HEALTH
Temples throbbing, gasping for breath and nauseated, you barely notice the sparkling snow, or the spectacular view below.
You might be suffering from Acute Mountain Sickness (A.M.S.). Usually striking at around 2,500 meters (8,000 feet), A.M.S. is your body's way of coping with the reduced oxygen of high altitudes. Among the symptoms are headaches, shortness of breath, loss of appetite, insomnia and lethargy. Some people complain of temporary weight gain or swelling of face, hands and feet.
If your A.M.S. is severe, stop ascending; you will recover in a few days. A quick descent will end the suffering immediately. You can reduce the impact of high altitude by being in top condition. If you smoke or suffer from heart or lung ailments, consult your physician. Alcohol and certain drugs will intensify the symptoms. A gradual ascent with a few days' acclimatization is best, if you have time. On the way up, eat light, nutritious meals and drink lots of water. A spicy, high-carbohydrate diet may ease the effects of low oxygen and encourage you to drink more. But beware of those crystal-clear mountain streams where parasites might lurk. Boil such water for at least 10 minutes.
Other high-altitude problems are sunburn and hypothermia. Dress in layers to protect yourself from the intense sun and fluctuations in temperature. Finally, after you unwind in the sauna or whirlpool bath at your hotel, remember to stand up carefully, for the heat relaxes your blood vessels and lowers your blood pressure.

St. Gallen is a main industrial center known for a 600-year textile industry.

INDUSTRIE UND GEWERBEMUSEUM (Textile Museum), Vadianstrasse 2, is known for its needlework collection, one of the most complete in Europe. The lacework and embroidery exhibit spans a total of five centuries.

STIFTSBIBLIOTHEK (Abbey Library) contains more than 100,000 books and manuscripts dating from the Middle Ages. The superb rococo rooms have delicate woodwork and painted ceilings.

ST.-MAURICE (609 B1)
VALAIS *pop. 3,800*
The ancient town of St.-Maurice stands among mountains on the west bank of the Rhône. Its restored 6th-century abbey church is one of the oldest in Switzerland. The Treasury is one of Europe's richest with many precious objects dating from the earliest days of Christianity.

ST. MORITZ (609 E2) ★
GRAUBÜNDEN *pop. 5,700, elev. 1,856m. (6,089ft.)*
The mineral spa of St. Moritz is one of the most acclaimed resorts in Europe. In the upper Engadine Valley on the shores of Lake St. Moritz, the town is ringed by high mountains. Winter sports include bobsledding on the Cresta Run, ski jumping, sledding, curling and skating. There is also a comprehensive range of summer recreation facilities. St. Moritz has an excellent museum devoted to explaining life in the Engadine, one of the country's most fascinating regions whose villages are unrivaled for their wonderful traditional architecture.

▲ SCHAFFHAUSEN (609 C3)
SCHAFFHAUSEN *pop. 34,000*
Capital of the northernmost canton of Switzerland, Schaffhausen is on the Rhine River. It is an idyllic medieval town; frescoed houses line the winding streets of some of the older sections.

The fortress Munot and Ritter house, with frescoes by Tobias Stimmer, are particularly noteworthy.

At nearby Neuhausen, the mighty 152-meter (500-feet) wide Rhine River plunges over its 23-meter (75-feet) high falls, the most powerful in Europe.

ROMANSCH LANGUAGE
About 40,000 Swiss, nearly all of them in the canton of Graubunden, speak Romansch as their first language. Romansch is a direct descendant of the Latin brought by Roman legions to these Alpine valleys 2,000 years ago, and although superficially similar to Italian, it is a quite distinct language in its own right. Its survival is all the more remarkable because of its division into many, very different, dialects.

▲ SCHWYZ (609 C2)
SCHWYZ *pop. 12,300*
Quiet little Schwyz is one of the oldest towns in the country and is famed as one of the three cantons to form the nucleus of the present Swiss Confederation. The Swiss declaration of independence, the Oath of Eternal Alliance, is preserved in the archives building along with paintings and other records of the period.

▲ SION (609 B1)
VALAIS *pop. 25,000*
Flanked by two vast rocks – the Tourbillon and Valère – Sion presents a striking appearance. The Tourbillon is crowned by castle ruins, while the fortified church on the Valère, which houses an old but working pipe organ, is one of Switzerland's finest sights.

The capital of the Valais canton has many fine medieval buildings. The orange-colored Town Hall, dating from the 17th century, is particularly striking. Archeological excavations have revealed that Neolithic people lived in this area 5,000 years ago.

SWITZERLAND

▲ SOLOTHURN (609 B3)
SOLOTHURN *pop. 15,800*
At the foot of the Jura Mountains on the banks of the Aare River, Solothurn is the site of one of the oldest Roman settlements north of the Alps.

The Old Town has some of the finest baroque buildings in Switzerland including the Jesuiten-Kirche (Church of the Jesuits) and St. Urtsen Kathedrale (Cathedral of St. Ursus). Parts of the town's fortifications are still intact, including the Krummturm (Twisted Tower). Among Solothurn's several museums is the Naturmuseum (Natural History Museum) great for children, the Kunstmuseum (Fine Art Museum) with good Swiss paintings of various periods, and the Zeughaus (Arsenal), with a huge collection of weapons.

SPIEZ (609 B2)
BERN *pop. 11,000*
Prettily located on the shores of Lake Thun, Spiez is a resort that has preserved much of its medieval charm.

Reached by chairlift, the nearby Weissenstein 1,275 meters (4,183 feet) has one of the finest panoramic views in Switzerland, extending from the Säntis in the east to Mont Blanc in the west.

THUN (609 B2)
BERN *pop. 39,000*
One of the most enchanting old towns in Switzerland, Thun overlooks Lake Thun and has a full view of the 3,610-meter (11,845-feet) Blümlisalp and other summits of the Bernese Oberland.

THUN CASTLE is reached by an unusual covered staircase. The Historical Museum, in one of the castle's four round towers, displays tapestries.

VERBIER (609 B1)
VALAIS *pop. 1,500, elev. 1,524m. (5,000ft.)*
First used by skiers in 1925, Verbier is a fashionable resort on the high Verbier Plateau. Positioned in the heart of one of the world's largest skiing areas, known as the Four Valleys, it boasts excellent ski runs and facilities. Summer activities include swimming, paragliding, hang-gliding, mountain-bicycling and golf.

VEVEY (609 B2)
VAUD *pop. 15,000*
Vevey is a "Swiss Riviera" resort with more than 8 kilometers (5 miles) of promenades along the shore of Lake Geneva (Lac Léman). It is at the center of the splendid terraced vineyards of the lake's north shore, and every 25 years the town is the scene of what is perhaps the most spectacular of European folk festivals, the *Fête des Vignerons* (Wine-growers' Festival).

Vevey's other mainstay is chocolate, and the Nestlé corporation has its headquarters here.

WENGEN (609 C2)
BERN *pop. 1,000, elev. 1,274m. (4,180ft.)*
On a sheltered terrace at the foot of the Jungfrau, Wengen is superbly positioned as one of the most elegant resorts on the Bernese Oberland. Private cars are not permitted, but Wengen is nevertheless one of the most accessible places in the Alps, linked by mountain railroad to Lauterbrunnen via the Kleine Scheidegg as well as to Jungfraujoch. Wengen is also at the center of a magnificent network of waymarked footpaths.

▲ WINTERTHUR (609 D3)
ZÜRICH *pop. 87,000*
Winterthur was founded in the 11th century by the counts of Kyburg, who granted it a charter with special privileges. The Reinhart Gallery has a superb collection of Swiss and European art.

SCHLOSS KYBURG, 6 kilometers (4 miles) south, was the ancestral home of the counts of Kyburg and ultimately of the Habsburgs. Displays in the 10th-century castle highlight antique furniture and arms.

ZERMATT (609 C1) ★
VALAIS *pop. 3,100, elev. 1,620m. (5,315ft.)*
Zermatt, known as a mountaineering center, gained recognition during the

period of the heroic attempts to conquer the 4,477-meter (14,690-foot) Matterhorn. This pyramidal mountain mass on the Swiss-Italian border forms an incomparable backdrop to the village.

ALPINES MUSEUM contains equipment and documents of the first successful ascent of the Matterhorn in 1865. A scale model of the massive mountain and reconstructions of old Zermatt add to an understanding of the town.

GORNERGRAT RACK-RAILWAY is the highest open-air railroad in Europe. It provides a magnificent view of the Matterhorn and its glistening glaciers.

▲ ZUG (609 C3)
ZUG *pop. 21,600*
A picturesque old town in a fine position on the lake of the same name, this little cantonal capital retains its early defense towers and a distinctly medieval flavor.

▲ ZÜRICH (609 C3) ★
ZÜRICH *pop. 344,000*
Switzerland's largest city is a world industrial leader whose air of prosperity blends with natural beauty and historical interest. Gardens slope down to the Lake of Zürich (Zürichsee), mingling green with blue and setting off the white-capped mountains.

The University of Zürich is where Albert Einstein studied, and has a zoological museum, while Carl Jung taught at the Polytechnic Institute.

During the International June Festival Weeks, the city echoes with orchestral music, opera, ballet and drama. For full year round schedules of opera, concerts, theater and ballet see the *Zürich Weekly Bulletin.*

Most stores radiate from the busy, centrally located Bahnhofstrasse, one of Europe's foremost avenues for luxury shopping. Fine jewelry, Swiss watches, high-fashion clothing and other luxury items abound in the exclusive stores.

Excursions can be made to the Zürichberg 686 meters (2,250 feet), or to the Uetliberg 873 meters (2,865 feet), with magnificent views and picnic grounds. Of the steamer excursions on the Lake of Zürich, the 4-hour trip to Rapperswil is one of the best.

GROSSMÜNSTER, has twin Romanesque towers that dominate the Zürich landscape, and an enormous statue of the Emperor Charlemagne surmounts the south tower.

KUNSTHAUS (Fine Arts Museum), 1 Heimplatz, has a fine collection of Swiss, French and German paintings from the 13th century to the present, as well as the largest collection of Edward Munch paintings outside Scandinavia.

LINDENHOF, above the Limmat River, is a favorite walking destination and yields a view of Zürich's old quarter. The hill once supported a Roman settlement.

ST. PETERSKIRCHE, the parish church of Zürich, has a massive late-Gothic steeple surmounted by Europes largest clockface, 9 meters (30 feet).

SCHWEIZERISCHES LANDESMUSEUM (Swiss National Museum), facing the railroad station, houses an extraordinarily rich collection of artifacts illustrating all aspects of the country's history from prehistoric times onward.

HOLD THE FRONT PAGE
Zürich is the home of one of the world's great newspapers, the *Neue Zürcher Zeiting* (*New Zürich News* or *N.Z.Z.*). Tabloid in format and sober in appearance and style, the *N.Z.Z.* monitors the doings of Zürich and its canton with the same thoroughness that it devotes to world finance, politics and culture. Learned articles on trends in academic philosophy may be interestingly juxtaposed with headlines like "Village barn burns; forty pigs die."

THINGS TO KNOW

- **AREA:** 160 square kilometers (62 square miles)
- **POPULATION:** 29,000
- **CAPITAL:** Vaduz
- **LANGUAGE:** German
- **ECONOMY:** Banking, agriculture. Tourism and the publication and sale of postage stamps also important.
- **PASSPORT REQUIREMENTS:** Required for U.S. citizens.
- **VISA REQUIREMENTS:** Not required provided visitors do not become employed.
- **DUTY-FREE ITEMS:** 400 cigarettes or 100 cigars or 500 grams tobacco; 2 liters of alcohol under 15 proof; 1 liter of alcohol over 15 proof; two still cameras; two movie cameras; one video camera with accessories; and personal goods to the value of 100 SF.
- **CURRENCY:** The unit of currency is the Swiss *franc* (SF), divided into 100 *centimes*. Due to currency fluctuations, the exchange rate is subject to frequent change. There are no restrictions on the import or export of currency.
- **BANK OPENING HOURS:** 8am–noon and 1:30–4:30pm Monday–Friday.
- **PUBLIC HOLIDAYS:** January 1 and January 2; Epiphany, January 6; Shrove Tuesday; Feast of St Joseph, March 19; Good Friday; Easter Monday; Labor Day, May 1; Ascension Day; Whitmonday; Corpus Christi; Feast of the Assumption, August 15; Nativity of our Lady; Immaculate Conception, September 8; All Saints Day, November 1; December 25; Boxing Day, December 26 or closest weekday.
- **NATIONAL TOURIST OFFICES:** Swiss National Tourist Office 608 Fifth Ave New York, NY 10020 Tel: 212/757 5944; Fax: 212/262 6116 Liechtensteininche Fremdenverkehrs-zenprale (Liechtenstein Tourist Board) Seaedtle 37 9490 Vaduz, Liechtenstein Tel: 75 232 1443; Fax: 75 232 0806
- **AMERICAN EMBASSY:** See Switzerland p.610.

LIECHTENSTEIN

HISTORY

The principality of Liechtenstein was founded in 1719. Independence was achieved in 1866, and the House of Liechtenstein has ruled ever since. United economically with Switzerland since 1923, the country is the world's only German-speaking monarchy. Elections in 1986 were the first in which women could vote.

GETTING AROUND

Liechtenstein attracts many tourists with its breathtaking scenery and imposing castles. The capital is Vaduz.

There are no border formalities for visitors entering Liechtenstein from Switzerland. Visitors entering from Austria are subject to normal procedures.

The nearest airport is at Zürich, a 130-kilometer (80-mile) drive from Vaduz. Good bus connections to Liechtenstein are available from railroad stations at Sargans and Buchs in Switzerland and Feldkirch in Austria. There is also a good internal bus service but only one rail station, at Nendeln.

Liechtenstein's roads are well maintained. The valley towns are linked by a route that parallels the Rhine, and modern roads climb to the Alpine resorts. Insurance requirements and traffic regulations are as those for Switzerland.

ACCOMMODATIONS

Hotels in Liechtenstein that belong to the Swiss Hotel Association are classified using one to four stars. Breakfast is usually included in the price. You can also find accommodations in chalets and inns. Camping is available in Triesen, and Bendern.

TIPPING

A service fee of 15 percent is included in most hotel and restaurant bills and taxi fares, so tipping is usually not necessary.

PLACES OF INTEREST

▲ VADUZ
VADUZ *pop. 4,900*

Medieval Vaduz is one of the smallest capitals in the world. Its one main thoroughfare runs along the edge of the Rhine River, and a few residential streets climb the precipitous hills to the prince's castle, originally built in the 12th century (not open to visitors). Scattered over the area are vineyards whose fruit, under skilled hands, becomes fine wine.

Home to one-sixth of Liechtenstein's population, Vaduz is a major administrative center, where small-scale factories often border open meadows.

ENGLANDERBAU (English Building), Städtle 37, houses the Liechtenstein State Art Collection. Temporary exhibitions are given of world-renowned works from the Prince of Liechtenstein's private collection, one of the oldest and most comprehensive in Europe.

LIECHTENSTEINISCHES LANDESMUSEUM (National Museum), Städtle 43, has archeological finds, carvings, coins, weapons and other objects which bring the history of this tiny state to life.

POSTMUSEUM (Postage Stamp Museum), Städtle 37, portrays philatelic history. Founded in 1930, the museum has a large collection of Liechtenstein stamps dating back to 1912. Temporary and permanent exhibits showcase stamps from around the world. There are also original sketches, designs and other material related to the production of stamps.

WILDSCHLOSS, or Ruine Schalun, is a 13th-century castle said to be the former seat of robber barons. It is a half-hour's scenic walk from Vaduz.

TRIESENBERG
TRIESENBERG *pop 2,400*

TRIESENBERG LOCAL MUSEUM exhibits historical items from the 13th-century Walser community that first settled in this area. Among the museum's highlights are a display of wood engravings by prominent local artist Rudolf Schadler and a slide show on the Alpine areas of Liechtenstein.

Das Rote Haus in Vaduz, a typical example of the many beautiful villages in Liechtenstein

Within Great Britain and Ireland
Miles 147 Average time (excluding stops): 2.47

On the Continent
Kilometers 583 Average time (excluding stops): 5.44

Miles in
Great Britain
and Ireland

Kilometers
on the
Continent

EUROPEAN
DRIVING DISTANCES

Useful Phrases At The Restaurant

DUTCH

water	water
coffee	koffie
tea	thee
milk	melk
beer	bier
wine	wijn
cider	appelwijn
bread	brood
eggs	eiren
soup	soep
fish	vis
lobster	kreeftesla
beef	rundvlees
pork	varkenvlees
ham	ham
chicken	kip
rice	rijst
potatoes	aardappelen
cabbage	kool
green peas	doperwten
vegetables	groenten
salad	salade
tomatoes	tomaten
mushrooms	champignons
cheese	kaas
fruit	fruit
pastries	gebak
ice-cream	ijs
cookies	beschult
orange	sinaasappel
apple	appel
banana	banaan
sugar	suiker
cream	room
salt	zout
pepper	peper
garlic	knoflook
butter	boter
knife	mes
fork	vork
spoon	lepel
glass	glas
cup	kopje
plate	bord
napkin	servet
rare	half rauw
medium	gaar
well-done	gebakken

Can I see the menu?
Geeft u mij het menu?
How much is the meal?
Hoeveel kost de maaltijd?
Is service included?
Is de bediening inbegrepen?
The bill, please.
De rekening, alstublieft.

FRENCH

water	eau
coffee	café
tea	the
milk	lait
beer	bier
wine	vin
bread	pain
eggs	oeuf
fish	poisson
meat	viande
beef	boeuf
pork	porc
lamb	agneau
ham	jambon
chicken	poulet
rice	riz
potatoes	pommes de terre
vegetables	legumes
salad	salade
tomatoes	tomates
lettuce	laitue
mushrooms	champignons
cheese	fromage
fruit	fruit
pastries	patisseries
ice-cream	glace
orange	orange
apple	pomme
banana	banane
sugar	sucre
cream	crème
salt	sel
pepper	poivre
garlic	ail
butter	beurre
knife	couteau
fork	forchette
spoon	cuillère
glass	verre
cup	tasse
plate	assiette
napkin	serviette
roasted	rôti
fried	frit
rare	saignant
medium	a point
well-done	bien cuit

Can I see the menu?
Est-ce que je peux voir le menu?
How much is the meal?
Quel est le prix du repas?
Is service included?
Le service est-il compris?
The bill, please.
L'addition, s'il-vous plaît.

GERMAN

water	Wasser
coffee	Kaffee
tea	Tee
milk	Milch
beer	Bier
wine	Wein
bread	Brot
eggs	Eier
fish	Fisch
beef	Rindfleisch
beefsteak	Beefsteak
pork	Schweinefleisch
ham	Schinken
chicken	Huhn
rice	Reis
potatoes	Kartoffeln
vegetables	Gemüse
green peas	Grune Erbsen
salad	Salat
tomatoes	Tomaten
mushrooms	Pilz
cheese	Käse
fruit	Frucht
pastries	Gebäck
ice-cream	Eis
cookies	Kekse
orange	Orange
apple	Apfel
banana	Banane
pear	Birne
cherries	Kirschen
strawberries	Erdbeeren
sugar	Zucker
cream	Sahne
salt	Salz
pepper	Pfeffer
garlic	Knoblauch
butter	Butter
knife	Messer
fork	Gabel
spoon	Löffel
glass	Glas
cup	Tasse
plate	Teller
napkin	Serviette
rare	Blutig
medium	Halbengleich
well-done	Durch

Can I see the menu?
Ziegen Sie mir die Speisekarte?
How much is the meal?
Was kostet die Mahlzeit?
Is service included?
Ist die Bedienung inbegriffen?
The bill, please.
Die Rechnung, bitte.

USEFUL PHRASES AT THE RESTAURANT

ITALIAN		SPANISH		SWEDISH	
water	acqua	water	agua	water	vatten
coffee	caffè	coffee	café	coffee	kaffe
tea	te	tea	te	tea	te
milk	latte	milk	leche	milk	mjolk
beer	birra	beer	cerveza	beer	ol
wine	vino	wine	vino	wine	vin
bread	pane	bread	pan	bread	brod
soup	zuppa	soup	sopa	soup	soppa
egg	uova	eggs	huevos	egg	agg
omelette	frittata	omelette	tortilla	fish	fisk
fish	pesce	fish	pescado	lobster	hummer
beef	manzo	lobster	langosta	beef	oxkott
beefsteak	bistecca	beef	vaca	beefsteak	biffstek
pork	maiale	beefsteak	bistec	pork	flask
ham	prosciutto	pork	cerdo	ham	skinka
lamb	agnello	ham	jamón	mutton	farkott
chicken	pollo	lamb	cordero	chicken	kyckling
rice	riso	chicken	pollo	rice	ris
potatoes	patate	rice	arroz	potatoes	potatis
vegetables	verdura	potatoes	patatas	vegetables	gronsaker
salad	insalata	vegetables	legumbres	cabbage	kal
tomatoes	pomodori	salad	ensalada	salad	sallad
lettuce	lattuga	tomatoes	tomates	tomatoes	tomater
mushrooms	funghi	lettuce	lechuga	green peas	grona arter
cheese	formaggio	mushrooms	hongos	mushroom	svamp
fruit	frutta	cheese	queso	cheese	ost
pastries	pasticceria	fruit	frutas	fruit	frukt
ice-cream	gelato	pastries	pasteleria	pastries	kakor
orange	arancia	ice-cream	helado	ice-cream	glass
apple	mela	orange	naranja	orange	apelsinsaft
banana	banana	apple	manzana	apple	apple
sugar	zucchero	banana	banana	banana	banan
cream	panna	sugar	azucar	sugar	socker
salt	sale	salt	sal	salt	salt
pepper	pepe	pepper	pimienta	pepper	peppar
garlic	aglio	garlic	ajo	garlic	vitlok
butter	burro	butter	mantequilla	butter	smor
knife	coltello	knife	cuchillo	knife	kniv
fork	forchetta	fork	tenedor	fork	gaffel
spoon	cucchiaio	spoon	cuchera	spoon	sked
glass	bicchiere	glass	vaso	glass	glas
cup	tazza	cup	taza	cup	kopp
plate	piatto	plate	plato	plate	tallrik
napkin	tovaglio	napkin	servilleta	napkin	servett
rare	al sangue	rare	poco pasado	rare	latt stek kott
medium	cotta a puntino	medium	a punto	medium	lagom
well-done	ben cotta	well-done	bien pasado	well-done	val kokat

Can I see the menu?
Mi faccia vedere la lista delle
vivande, per favore.
How much is the meal?
Qual e il prezzo del pasto?
Is service included?
Il servizio e compreso?
The bill, please.
Il conto, per favore.

Can I see the menu?
Muestreme el menu,
por favor?
How much is the meal?
Cuanto cuesta el cubierto?
Is service included?
Esta incluido el servicio?
The bill, please.
La cuenta, por favor.

Show me the menu?
Var god och visa mig
matsedeln?
How much is the meal?
Hur mycket kostar maltiden?
Is service included?
Ar det inklusive betjaning?
The bill, please.
Notan, var vanlig.

USEFUL PHRASES AT THE RESTAURANT

PORTUGUESE

water	agua
coffee	café
tea	cha
milk	leite
beer	cerveja
wine	vinho
bread	pao
egg	ovo
fish	peixe
beef	vaca
beefsteak	bife
pork	porco
ham	presunto
lamb	carneiro
chicken	frango
rice	arroz
potatoes	batatas
vegetables	legumes
salad	salada
tomatoes	tomates
lettuce	alface
mushrooms	cogumelos
cheeses	queijos
fruits	frutas
pastries	pastelaria
ice-cream	gelados
cookies	biscoitos
orange	laranja
apple	maca
banana	banana
sugar	acucar
cream	natas
salt	sal
pepper	pimenta
butter	manteiga
knife	faca
fork	garfo
spoon	colher
glass	copo
cup	chavena
plate	prato
napkin	guardanapo
rare	em sangue
medium	passado
well-done	bem passado

Can I see the menu?
Mostre-me a ementa?
How much is the meal?
Qual e o preco da refeicao?
Is service included?
A gorgeta esta incluida?
The bill, please.
A conta, paz favor.

HELPFUL PHRASES ON THE ROAD

DUTCH

I want to go to ...
Ik wil naar ...
May I park here?
Mag ik hier stoppen?
Go straight ahead.
Rijdt u rechtdoor.
To the right.
Rechts
To the left.
Links
How far is ...
Hoe ver hier vandaan is ...

a garage?	een garage?
a gas station?	een benzine station?
a doctor?	een doktor?
a police station?	een politie-bureau?
a phone box?	een telefooncel?
a post office?	een postkantoor?

FRENCH

I want to go to ...
Je voudrais aller à ...
May I park here?
Puis-je stationner ici?
Go straight ahead.
Roulez tout droit.
to the right.
à droite
to the left.
à gauche
How far is ...
A quelle distance se trouve ...

a garage?	un garage?
a gas station?	une poste a essence?
a doctor/hospital?	un médcin/hôpital
a police station?	une poste de police?
a phone box?	une cabine?
a post office?	la poste?

GERMAN

I want to go to ...
Ich möchte nach ... gehen.
May I park here?
Kann ich hier anhalten?
Go straight ahead.
Fahren Sie gerade aus.
To the right.
Nach rechts
To the left.
Nach links
How far is ...
Wie weit ist es ...

a garage?	zu einer Garage?
a gas station?	zu einer Tankstelle?
a doctor?	zu einem Arzt?
a police station?	zur Polizei?
a phone box?	zu einer Telefon?
a post office?	zur Post?

ITALIAN

I want to go to ...
Vorrei andare a ...
May I park here?
Posso fermarmi qui?
Go straight ahead.
Vada sempre diritto.
To the right.
A destra
To the left.
A sinistra
How far is ...
A che distanza se trova ...

a garage?	un garage?
a gas station?	un distributore de benzina?
a doctor?	un medico?
a police station?	un posto di polizia?
a phone box?	una cabina?
a post office?	l'ufficio postale?

SPANISH

I want to go to ...
Quiero ir a ...
May I park here?
Puedo detenerme aqui?
Go straight ahead.
Siga el camino recto.
to the right.
a la derecha
to the left.
a la izquierda
How far is ...
A que distancia esta ...

a garage?	un garage?
a gas station?	una estacion de gasolina?
a doctor?	un medico?
a police station?	una comisaria de policia?
a phone box?	una cabina?
a post office?	la oficina de correos?

INDEX

INDEX

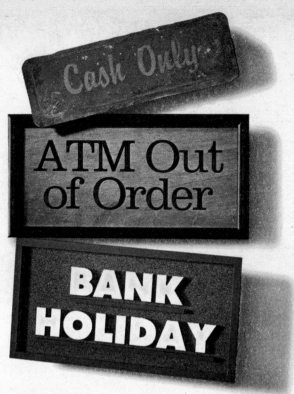

To avoid these common road hazards, begin your trip at AAA/CAA.

Get NO-FEE American Express® Travelers Cheques.

As a AAA/CAA member, you've trusted us to help you plan for all types of road and weather conditions. But what about the financial conditions? Will there be an ATM? When will the banks reopen? That's why AAA/CAA recommends you bring American Express Travelers Cheques. They're accepted virtually as cash in most places around the world. And they're quickly refundable, if lost or stolen. Pick them up at AAA/CAA when planning your trip, and you won't pay a fee. So, start your next vacation on the road to perfection with a trip to AAA/CAA for American Express Travelers Cheques, today.

Travel with someone you trust℠

AMERICAN EXPRESS

Travelers Cheques

KEEP ON ROLLIN'. *JOIN AAA.*

When you're ready to enjoy the good times, AAA keeps the fun rollin' with special discounts on family entertainment and travel. Or, when your car breaks down, AAA can get your wheels rollin' again. And, when you're planning a trip, AAA can get the ball rollin'.

◆ **Roll to security.** *Join AAA.*
  Relax and enjoy your time together with the peace of mind that your family is protected by AAA membership.

◆ **Roll to convenience.** *Join AAA.*
  Save time with the convenience of one-stop shopping at AAA's full-service travel agencies. The more time you save at AAA, the more time you'll have to enjoy your travels.

◆ **Roll to savings.** *Join AAA.*
  Save money on car rental, hotels, attraction tickets, emergency road service, and more.

Ready to roll? *Join AAA.* Call this toll-free number to become a AAA member now:

1-800-JOIN AAA (1-800-564-6222)

Travel With Someone You Trust^{SM}